LITERATURE CONNECTIONS
TO AMERICAN HISTORY, K–6

LITERATURE CONNECTIONS TO AMERICAN HISTORY, K–6

RESOURCES TO ENHANCE AND ENTICE

LYNDA G. ADAMSON

1998
Libraries Unlimited, Inc.
Englewood, Colorado

For Frank

LIBRARIES UNLIMITED, INC.
P.O. Box 6633
Englewood, CO 80155-6633
1-800-237-6124
www.lu.com

Production Editor: Stephen Haenel
Bibliography Copy Editor: Aviva Rothschild
Bibliography Proofreader: Ann Marie Damian
Layout and Design: Michael Florman

Library of Congress Cataloging-in-Publication Data

Adamson, Lynda G.
    Literature connections to American history, K-6 : resources to enhance and entice / Lynda G. Adamson.
        x, 542p. 19x26 cm.
        Includes bibliographical references and indexes.
        ISBN 1-56308-502-X
        1. United States--History--Juvenile literature--Bibliography.
2. United States--History--Juvenile fiction--Bibliography.
3. United States--History--CD-ROM catalogs. 4. United States--History--Juvenile films--Catalogs. I. Title.
E178.3.A27 1997
973--dc21   97-14283
                                                                    CIP

CONTENTS

Preface vii
Introduction ix

North America Before 1600 1
    Kindergarten Through Second Grade 1
    Grade Three 1
    Grade Four 2
    Grade Five 3
    Grade Six 4
The American Colonies, 1600-1774 6
    Kindergarten Through Second Grade 6
    Grade Three 7
    Grade Four 8
    Grade Five 10
    Grade Six 12
The American Revolution, 1775-1783 16
    Kindergarten Through Second Grade 16
    Grade Three 17
    Grade Four 18
    Grade Five 19
    Grade Six 21
The Early United States, 1784-1814 23
    Kindergarten Through Second Grade 23
    Grade Three 24
    Grade Four 25
    Grade Five 26
    Grade Six 28
The Settling of the West, Native Americans, and
    Sea Journeys, 1775-1916 31
    Kindergarten Through Second Grade 31
    Grade Three 32
    Grade Four 34
    Grade Five 38
    Grade Six 43
Immigrants and Multicultural Heritages, 1814 to the Present 49
    Kindergarten Through Second Grade 49
    Grade Three 49
    Grade Four 50
    Grade Five 51
    Grade Six 53

Slavery, Abolitionism, and Women's Rights, 1814-1865 55
    Kindergarten Through Second Grade 55
    Grade Three 56
    Grade Four 57
    Grade Five 59
    Grade Six 62

The Civil War, 1861-1865 66
    Kindergarten Through Second Grade 66
    Grade Three 66
    Grade Four 67
    Grade Five 69
    Grade Six 71

Reconstruction, the Progressive Era, and the Early Twentieth Century, 1866-1916 74
    Kindergarten Through Second Grade 74
    Grade Three 75
    Grade Four 77
    Grade Five 80
    Grade Six 84

World War I and the Depression, 1917-1941 89
    Kindergarten Through Second Grade 89
    Grade Three 90
    Grade Four 92
    Grade Five 94
    Grade Six 98

World War II, 1941-1945 104
    Kindergarten Through Second Grade 104
    Grade Three 105
    Grade Four 106
    Grade Five 108
    Grade Six 111

The Mid-Twentieth Century, 1946-1975 114
    Kindergarten Through Second Grade 114
    Grade Three 115
    Grade Four 116
    Grade Five 119
    Grade Six 123

Since 1975 128
    Kindergarten Through Second Grade 128
    Grade Three 128
    Grade Four 129
    Grade Five 131
    Grade Six 134

Books: An Annotated Bibliography 137
CD-ROMs: An Annotated Bibliography 467
Videotapes: An Annotated Bibliography 471

Author/Illustrator Index 493
Title Index 505
Subject Index 529

PREFACE

Studies show that people must respond emotionally to something in order to remember it. If young readers travel with Fawn in Whelan's *Night of the Full Moon* as U.S. federal troops remove her, her family, and her Potawatomi tribe from their ancestral home, or if they look at the torn and dirty books "discarded" from the white school that Cassie's teacher must issue to Cassie and her classmates in Taylor's *Roll of Thunder, Hear My Cry,* they will wonder why some laws can favor one group over another. By becoming angry at the helpless situations in which Fawn and Cassie find themselves, these readers remember the time and place of the incidents. Their responses might lead them to read further in additional sources about the government's treatment of other groups such as immigrants. They might want to know who entered the United States through Ellis Island and what fears they had when they arrived, often unable to speak English or sick from a long sea journey in steerage class. These vicarious experiences could even help readers empathize more readily with the difficulties of contemporary refugees or the hostility of people whose families have lived in America for many decades.

If a young reader becomes interested in a topic, a character, or a time period and asks for books or multimedia about them, the adult consulted needs timely retrieval capabilities. I have attempted to fulfill that need. This resource connects historical fiction, biography, history trade books, CD-ROMs, and videotapes for individual grade levels within specific time periods and geographic areas. The books, CD-ROMs, and videotapes included have received at least one favorable review, are well written, or fit a category for which few resources are available. Some of the books and videotapes are award winners, and I have listed awards won at the end of the annotations. Some of the books are out-of-print but are still available in many libraries. Reprints of them, especially award winners, regularly become available in paper or under the imprint of another publisher.

When I first began this project, it was to link "good reads" in historical fiction, biography, and history trade books. That focus has continued throughout the creation of this annotated bibliography. I did not anticipate finding as many entries as appear in this resource, but the writing in both biography and history trade books has improved. For that reason, I have listed biographies about the same person by several different authors. I have not made a choice as to which is the "best," because each has a different focus. Authors of biography as literature try to make their subjects come alive, and the authors here have achieved this goal. The annotations in the final section attempt to include different facts about the biographical subjects instead of always identifying a sometimes elusive nuance of difference among the authors' writing styles and themes.

History trade books differ from history textbooks because their authors rarely use passive voice, and they rely heavily on diaries, letters, documents, or other references that tell about the people who lived during the time. Thus, young readers might more often respond to these books than to history textbooks that seem to be filled with dull dates and incident inventories. Some of the history trade books included have more illustrations than text, but they can be valuable for enticing slow or unwilling readers to look for other books. These information books bridge the gap between nonillustrated books and videotapes.

The multimedia category covers CD-ROMs and videotapes. Because videotapes are more accessible for the classroom, or even for home use, I have omitted laser discs and filmstrips. But with computer use increasing in homes and schools, I have included favorably reviewed CD-ROMs or those on specific topics that will help readers find further information. Some of the more recent CD-ROMs have stunning pictures, film clips, and other attractions that may lead a viewer to books.

Because readers become interested in a variety of topics for many different reasons, the books in the historical fiction category listed in a specific grade level may or may not contain the names of those persons in the biographies, cover the variety of time periods in the history trade titles, or fulfill the traditional definition of "historical fiction." A specific correspondence of titles seems unnecessary. Andrew Jackson may not be named in *Night of the Full Moon,* but his decisions as President permeate the book. The same reader might want more information about other people who believed that white settlers, not Native Americans, should inhabit and control the fertile lands of the West. The book lists, along with the annotations, will reveal other resources on these subjects. Additionally, I have broadened the definition of historical fiction to include books outside the readers' memory rather than just those books whose authors are writing about time periods prior to two or more generations. Children and young adults today do not know the significance of America's role in the Persian Gulf War, and many do not understand that Bosnia is an area of the world in which people have recently repeated crimes as heinous as the Holocaust. Thus, I have included some books that might loosely be termed "historical fiction" or "contemporary realistic fiction" because they will give readers an insight into a time separate from their own.

While doing the research for this reference, I realized that it should include as many good books or videotapes published since 1990 as possible, plus some highly regarded works from prior years. I hope that adults will find most of the recommended books on library shelves or can order them from a publisher. I have tried to include a wide range of titles so that the researcher will have choices if the first title selected from the resource is not readily available. My goal is for young readers to have emotional responses to the people who have made history so that they, as future world decision-makers, can better understand themselves and the times in which they live.

Many publishers have made this resource easier to create by sending me recent books. Their generosity saved me many hours of searching. I would like to list their names, but I fear omitting even one of them. During this intensive period of work, two individuals have helped make this book possible. Elena Rodriguez at Gunston Middle School in Arlington, Virginia, allowed me to raid her library shelves for many days. Without her excellent collection, I would not have been able to easily locate many of the books that I included. The other indispensable helper was my husband, who edited the text. Additionally, G. Kim Dority and Stephen Haenel as well as other members of the editorial staff at Libraries Unlimited have offered excellent advice and aid in an effort to make this resource available.

INTRODUCTION

This resource divides naturally into two main parts. The first part lists authors and titles in the categories of historical fiction, biography, collective biography, history trade book, CD-ROM, and videotape within specific time periods according to grade levels. The second part contains annotated bibliographies of titles listed in the first part: books, CD-ROMs, and videotapes. The books, videotapes, and CD-ROMs merit inclusion because they have received favorable reviews, are well written, or are one of the few titles available on a particular subject, so the annotations are descriptive rather than evaluative.

The first part is divided into chapters based on chronological time periods. In each chapter, works appropriate for a particular grade level appear under that grade-level heading in their specific category of historical fiction, biography (including collective biography), history, and multimedia (CD-ROMs and videotapes). Books are alphabetized according to author's last name so the researcher can easily locate the annotation in the second part of the resource. CD-ROMs and videotapes are alphabetized in the second section according to their titles.

Some titles in the first part appear several different times. When a title about expansion into the West is suitable for grades four through six, the title appears under each grade level of four, five, and six in the chapter titled "The Settling of the West, Native Americans, and Sea Journeys, 1775-1916." Other titles appear in different chapters because their settings, either fiction or fact, occur in more than one place or involve more than one time period. For example, people with long lives such as Benjamin Franklin span several time periods. Benjamin Franklin functioned as a contributing citizen in the colonies, during the American Revolution, and during the infancy of the United States—three distinct and important periods in the formation of the nation.

I have based grade-level choices on recommended grade levels in review sources or publisher catalogs. In some cases, when the grade levels seemed unusually low or high, I have adjusted them after evaluating the text and the subject matter. For example, few fourth graders would probably be interested in a biography focusing on Abigail Adams's letters. However, a high school student who is curious about the seeds of women's rights could be very interested that Abigail wrote to her husband, John, suggesting that he remember women as he helped form the basic laws of the new nation. Those books and resources treating subjects with greater complexity appear in *Literature Connections to American History: Resources to Enhance and Entice, 7–12*. A younger reader would probably prefer the interaction of Abigail Adams with her children, including the future President John Quincy, rather than philosophical discussions between her and her husband.

The chapter divisions correspond as nearly as possible to general time periods in the history of America. In the late eighteenth, the nineteenth, and the early twentieth centuries, three distinct groups were functioning within the area that has become the continental United States. Pioneers began traveling to the frontier, which kept moving west as they displaced more and more Native Americans. Immigrants began coming from Asia and Europe around 1815 and moved to any area in which they thought they could succeed. The third group remained within the borders of the United States and divided into two hostile factions—those who felt that slaves should be freed and women should have equal rights (abolitionists and suffragists) and those who wanted to maintain the status quo of Anglo white male supremacy. Therefore, I have divided these groups into three parallel but separate chapters even though their concerns may have overlapped. Those settling the West might have a connection to the Civil War, but most often they were more anxious about encounters with Native Americans. Immigrants had other difficulties in facing a new culture while retaining their own traditions, and their problems have continued to the present.

The annotations include such information as author, title, publisher, price, ISBN, paper imprint, and grade levels. The book prices are accurate at printing, based on publishers' catalogs and such library buying sources as *Books in Print* and the distributor Baker and Taylor. I have made a similar attempt to include sources for books and their paper imprints, if available. The range of grade levels appears at the end of each bibliographic entry.

For easiest access to this resource, researchers should find the time period of interest in the table of contents. Grade levels under the chapter listings will tell where to locate the book and multimedia categories. In the grade-level listings, researchers should select titles. They then should refer to the appropriate section of the second part of the book. If an appropriate grade-level resource is not available, the researcher may be able to choose an appropriate title from the next highest or lowest grade-level categories. A final resource is the index, which lists all references to a particular subject.

NORTH AMERICA BEFORE 1600

KINDERGARTEN THROUGH SECOND GRADE

Historical Fiction ——————————————————————————
James. *The Mud Family*

Biography ————————————————————————————————
Accorsi. *My Name Is Pocahontas*

Fradin. *Hiawatha: Messenger of Peace*

History ——————————————————————————————————
Dewey. *Stories on Stone: Rock Art, Images from the Ancient Ones*

Maestro. *The Discovery of the Americas*

Medearis. *Our People*

Multimedia ——————————————————————————————

Video
Columbus Day

The Discovery of the Americas

GRADE THREE

Historical Fiction ——————————————————————————
Anderson. *Spanish Pioneers of the Southwest*
Anderson. *A Williamsburg Household*

Gates. *Journey to Center Place*
James. *The Mud Family*
Steele. *The Magic Amulet*

Wisniewski. *The Wave of the Sea-Wolf*

Biography ————————————————————————————————
Bonvillain. *Hiawatha: Founder of the Iroquois Confederacy*

Fradin. *Hiawatha: Messenger of Peace*

History ——————————————————————————————————
Brenner. *If You Were There in 1492*
Burns. *Mail*
Climo. *City! New York*
Climo. *City! San Francisco*
Coote. *The Sailor Through History*
Dewey. *Stories on Stone: Rock Art, Images from the Ancient Ones*

La Pierre. *Native American Rock Art*
Maestro. *The Discovery of the Americas*
Maestro. *The Story of Money*
Medearis. *Our People*
Morley. *Exploring North America*
San Souci. *N. C. Wyeth's Pilgrims*

Sherrow. *The Aztec Indians*
Sherrow. *The Iroquois Indians*
Sneve. *The Iroquois*
Trimble. *The Village of Blue Stone*
Wade. *St. Augustine: America's Oldest City*
Wilson. *Visual Timeline of Transportation*

1

Multimedia

Video

Columbus Day   *The Discovery of the Americas*

GRADE FOUR

Historical Fiction

Anderson. *Spanish Pioneers of the Southwest*
Anderson. *A Williamsburg Household*
Bird. *The Rainmakers*

Dorris. *Sees Behind Trees*
Gates. *Journey to Center Place*
Kittleman. *Canyons Beyond the Sky*

Steele. *The Magic Amulet*
Wisniewski. *The Wave of the Sea-Wolf*

Biography

Bonvillain. *Hiawatha: Founder of the Iroquois Confederacy*

Fradin. *Hiawatha: Messenger of Peace*

Wheeler. *Forest Diplomat: The Story of Hiawatha*

Collective Biography

Maestro. *Exploration and Conquest:1500-1620*

History

Arnold. *The Ancient Cliff Dwellers of Mesa Verde*
Arnold. *Stories in Stone: Rock Art Pictures by Early Americans*
Avakian. *A Historical Album of Massachusetts*
Avakian. *A Historical Album of New York*
Berrill. *Mummies, Masks, & Mourners*
Beyer. *The Totem Pole Indians of the Northwest*
Bosco. *Roanoke: The Story of the Lost Colony*
Brenner. *If You Were There in 1492*
Burns. *Mail*
Burns. *Money*
Childress. *Prehistoric People of North America*
Chrisp. *The Spanish Conquests in the New World*
Chrisp. *Voyages to the New World*
Climo. *City! New York*

Climo. *City! San Francisco*
Cocke. *A Historical Album of Virginia*
Cocke. *A Historical Album of Washington*
Coote. *The Sailor Through History*
Corbishley. *Secret Cities*
Cordoba. *Pre-Columbian Peoples of North America*
Deem. *How to Make a Mummy Talk*
Dewey. *Stories on Stone: Rock Art, Images from the Ancient Ones*
La Pierre. *Native American Rock Art*
Maestro. *The Discovery of the Americas*
Maestro. *The Story of Money*
Morley. *Exploring North America*
Ryan. *Explorers and Mapmakers*
San Souci. *N. C. Wyeth's Pilgrims*

Sattler. *Hominids: A Look Back at Our Ancestors*
Sherrow. *The Aztec Indians*
Sherrow. *The Iroquois Indians*
Sneve. *The Iroquois*
Stones and Bones: How Archaeologists Trace Human Origins
Topper. *A Historical Album of New Jersey*
Trimble. *The Village of Blue Stone*
Ventura. *1492: The Year of the New World*
Wade. *St. Augustine: America's Oldest City*
Warren. *Cities in the Sand: The Ancient Civilizations of the Southwest*
Wills. *A Historical Album of California*
Wills. *A Historical Album of Florida*
Wills. *A Historical Album of Illinois*
Wilson. *Visual Timeline of Transportation*

Multimedia

CD-ROM

SkyTrip America   *Total History*

Video

Columbus Day
    The Discovery of the Americas

Estevanico and the Seven
    Cities of Gold
The Iroquois

Native Americans: The
    History of a People
The Pilgrims at Plymouth

GRADE FIVE

Historical Fiction

Anderson. *Spanish Pioneers
    of the Southwest*
Anderson. *A Williamsburg
    Household*
Baker. *Walk the World's Rim*
Bird. *The Rainmakers*

Bruchac. *Children of the
    Longhouse*
Dorris. *Sees Behind Trees*
Garland. *Cabin 102*
Gates. *Journey to Center
    Place*

Hooks. *The Legend of the
    White Doe*
Kittleman. *Canyons Beyond
    the Sky*
Steele. *The Magic Amulet*
Wisniewski. *The Wave of the
    Sea-Wolf*

Biography

Bonvillain. *Hiawatha:
    Founder of the Iroquois
    Confederacy*

McClard. *Hiawatha and the
    Iroquois League*

Collective Biography

Maestro. *Exploration and
    Conquest: 1500-1620*

History

Arnold. *The Ancient Cliff
    Dwellers of Mesa Verde*
Arnold. *Stories in Stone:
    Rock Art Pictures by Early
    Americans*
Avakian. *A Historical Album
    of Massachusetts*
Avakian. *A Historical Album
    of New York*
Barboza. *Door of No Return:
    The Legend of Gorée Island*
Berrill. *Mummies, Masks, &
    Mourners*
Beyer. *The Totem Pole
    Indians of the Northwest*
Bosco. *Roanoke: The Story of
    the Lost Colony*
Brenner. *If You Were There in
    1492*
Brown. *Discovery and
    Settlement: 1490-1700*
Burns. *Mail*
Burns. *Money*
Capek. *Murals: Cave,
    Cathedral, to Street*
Childress. *Prehistoric People
    of North America*
Chrisp. *The Spanish
    Conquests in the New
    World*
Chrisp. *Voyages to the New
    World*

Climo. *City! New York*
Climo. *City! San Francisco*
Cocke. *A Historical Album of
    Virginia*
Cocke. *A Historical Album of
    Washington*
Colman. *Toilets, Bathtubs,
    Sinks, and Sewers*
Coote. *The Sailor Through
    History*
Corbishley. *Secret Cities*
Cordoba. *Pre-Columbian
    Peoples of North America*
Deem. *How to Make a
    Mummy Talk*
Jacobs. *The Tainos: The
    People Who Welcomed
    Columbus*
Karl. *America Alive: A
    History*
Katz. *Breaking the Chains:
    African-American Slave
    Resistance*
La Pierre. *Native American
    Rock Art*
Maestro. *The Discovery of the
    Americas*
Maestro. *The Story of Money*
Marrin. *Empires Lost and
    Won: The Spanish
    Heritage in the Southwest*

Medearis. *Come This Far to
    Freedom*
Monroe. *First Houses: Native
    American Homes and
    Sacred Structures*
Morley. *Exploring North
    America*
Platt. *The Smithsonian Visual
    Timeline of Inventions*
Ryan. *Explorers and
    Mapmakers*
San Souci. *N. C. Wyeth's
    Pilgrims*
Sattler. *The Earliest
    Americans*
Sattler. *Hominids: A Look
    Back at Our Ancestors*
Schouweiler. *The Lost Colony
    of Roanoke*
Sherrow. *The Aztec Indians*
Sherrow. *The Iroquois Indians*
Sneve. *The Iroquois*
*Stones and Bones: How
    Archaeologists Trace
    Human Origins*
Topper. *A Historical Album
    of New Jersey*
Trimble. *The Village of Blue
    Stone*
Ventura. *1492: The Year of
    the New World*

Wade. *St. Augustine: America's Oldest City*

Warren. *Cities in the Sand: The Ancient Civilizations of the Southwest*

Whitman. *Get Up and Go: American Road Travel*

Williams. *The Age of Discovery*

Wills. *A Historical Album of California*

Wills. *A Historical Album of Florida*

Wills. *A Historical Album of Illinois*

Wilson. *Visual Timeline of Transportation*

Multimedia

CD-ROM

American History Explorer

SkyTrip America

Total History

Video

Colonization and Settlement (1585-1763)
The Discovery of the Americas
Estevanico and the Seven Cities of Gold

The Iroquois
Native Americans: The History of a People
The Pilgrims at Plymouth

Three Worlds Meet (Origins-1620)

GRADE SIX

Historical Fiction

Anderson. *Spanish Pioneers of the Southwest*

Anderson. *A Williamsburg Household*

Baker. *Walk the World's Rim*

Bird. *The Rainmakers*

Bruchac. *Children of the Longhouse*

Dorris. *Sees Behind Trees*

Garland. *Cabin 102*

Garland. *Indio*

Gates. *Journey to Center Place*

Hooks. *The Legend of the White Doe*

Kittleman. *Canyons Beyond the Sky*

Spinka. *White Hare's Horses*

Steele. *The Magic Amulet*

Wisniewski. *The Wave of the Sea-Wolf*

Biography

McClard. *Hiawatha and the Iroquois League*

Collective Biography

Anderson. *Explorers Who Found New Worlds*

Maestro. *Exploration and Conquest: 1500-1620*

History

Arnold. *The Ancient Cliff Dwellers of Mesa Verde*

Arnold. *Stories in Stone: Rock Art Pictures by Early Americans*

Avakian. *A Historical Album of Massachusetts*

Avakian. *A Historical Album of New York*

Ayer. *The Anasazi*

Barboza. *Door of No Return: The Legend of Gorée Island*

Berrill. *Mummies, Masks, & Mourners*

Beyer. *The Totem Pole Indians of the Northwest*

Bosco. *Roanoke: The Story of the Lost Colony*

Brown. *Discovery and Settlement: 1490-1700*

Burns. *Money*

Capek. *Murals: Cave, Cathedral, to Street*

Childress. *Prehistoric People of North America*

Chrisp. *The Spanish Conquests in the New World*

Chrisp. *Voyages to the New World*

Climo. *City! New York*

Climo. *City! San Francisco*

Cocke. *A Historical Album of Virginia*

Cocke. *A Historical Album of Washington*

Colman. *Toilets, Bathtubs, Sinks, and Sewers*

Corbishley. *Secret Cities*

Cordoba. *Pre-Columbian Peoples of North America*

Cush. *Disasters That Shook the World*

Deem. *How to Make a Mummy Talk*

Hakim. *The First Americans*

Hakim. *Making Thirteen Colonies*

Jacobs. *The Tainos: The People Who Welcomed Columbus*

Karl. *America Alive: A History*

Katz. *Breaking the Chains: African-American Slave Resistance*

La Pierre. *Native American Rock Art*

Marrin. *Empires Lost and Won: The Spanish Heritage in the Southwest*

Medearis. *Come This Far to Freedom*

Monroe. *First Houses: Native American Homes and Sacred Structures*

Morley. *Exploring North America*

Platt. *The Smithsonian Visual Timeline of Inventions*

Ryan. *Explorers and Mapmakers*

San Souci. *N. C. Wyeth's Pilgrims*

Sattler. *The Earliest Americans*

Sattler. *Hominids: A Look Back at Our Ancestors*

Schouweiler. *The Lost Colony of Roanoke*

Sherrow. *The Aztec Indians*

Sherrow. *The Iroquois Indians*

Sneve. *The Iroquois*

Stones and Bones: How Archaeologists Trace Human Origins

Topper. *A Historical Album of New Jersey*

Trimble. *The Village of Blue Stone*

Ventura. *1492: The Year of the New World*

Warburton. *The Beginning of Writing*

Warren. *Cities in the Sand: The Ancient Civilizations of the Southwest*

Whitman. *Get Up and Go: American Road Travel*

Williams. *The Age of Discovery*

Wills. *A Historical Album of California*

Wills. *A Historical Album of Florida*

Wills. *A Historical Album of Illinois*

Wood. *Ancient America*

Multimedia

CD-ROM

American History Explorer

SkyTrip America

Total History

Video

Balancing the Budget
Colonization and Settlement (1585-1763)
The Discovery of the Americas

Estevanico and the Seven Cities of Gold
The Iroquois
Native Americans: The History of a People

Pilgrims at Plymouth, The
Three Worlds Meet (Origins-1620)

THE AMERICAN COLONIES, 1600-1774

Historical Fiction

Anderson. *Christmas on the Prairie*
Benchley. *Sam the Minuteman*
Bulla. *A Lion to Guard Us*
Bulla. *Pocahontas and the Strangers*
Dalgliesh. *The Thanksgiving Story*
Littlesugar. *The Spinner's Daughter*
Lobel. *On the Day Peter Stuyvesant Sailed into Town*

Monjo. *The House on Stink Alley: A Story About the Pilgrims in Holland*
Monjo. *King George's Head Was Made of Lead*
Monjo. *Poor Richard in France*
Sanders. *Here Comes the Mystery Man*
Sewall. *People of the Breaking Day*
Sewall. *The Pilgrims of Plimoth*
Turner. *Katie's Trunk*

Van Leeuwen. *Across the Wide Dark Sea: The Mayflower Journey*
Waters. *The Mayflower*
Waters. *Samuel Eaton's Day: A Day in the Life of a Pilgrim Boy*
Waters. *Sarah Morton's Day: A Day in the Life of a Pilgrim Girl*
Waters. *Tapenum's Day: A Wampanoag Indian Boy in Pilgrim Times*

Biography

Adler. *Benjamin Franklin: Printer, Inventor, Statesman*
Adler. *A Picture Book of Benjamin Franklin*
Adler. *A Picture Book of George Washington*
Adler. *A Picture Book of Patrick Henry*
Adler. *Remember Betsy Floss: And Other Colonial Riddles*
Aliki. *The Many Lives of Benjamin Franklin.*

Benjamin. *Young Pocahontas: Indian Princess*
Brown. *Sybil Rides for Independence*
Fradin. *Washington's Birthday*
Fritz. *George Washington's Mother*
Fritz. *What's the Big Idea, Ben Franklin?*
Fritz. *Why Don't You Get a Horse, Sam Adams?*
Fritz. *Will You Sign Here, John Hancock?*

Gleiter. *Pocahontas*
Graves. *John Smith*
Greene. *Benjamin Franklin*
Greene. *George Washington*
Greene. *Phillis Wheatley: First African American Poet*
Pinkney. *Dear Benjamin Banneker*
Quackenbush. *Benjamin Franklin and His Friends*
Scarf. *Meet Benjamin Franklin*

Collective Biography

Marzollo. *My First Book of Biographies.*

History

Anderson. *The First Thanksgiving Feast*
Appelbaum. *Giants in the Land*
Bowen. *Stranded at Plimoth Plantation 1626*

George. *The First Thanksgiving*
Gibbons. *The Great St. Lawrence Seaway*
Hayward. *The First Thanksgiving*

Medearis. *Our People*
Stamper. *New Friends in a New Land: A Thanksgiving Story*

Multimedia

Video

American Independence
Early Settlers
The First Thanksgiving
Pocahontas

Squanto and the First
 Thanksgiving
Thanksgiving

William Bradford: The First
 Thanksgiving

GRADE THREE

Historical Fiction

Anderson. *Christmas on the
 Prairie*
Benchley. *Sam the Minuteman*
Bulla. *A Lion to Guard Us*
Bulla. *Pocahontas and the
 Strangers*
Bulla. *Squanto, Friend of the
 Pilgrims*
Dalgliesh. *The Thanksgiving
 Story*
Edmonds. *The Matchlock Gun*
Fleischman. *The 13th Floor:
 A Ghost Story*
Littlesugar. *The Spinner's
 Daughter*
Lobel. *On the Day Peter
 Stuyvesant Sailed into Town*

Monjo. *The House on Stink
 Alley: A Story About the
 Pilgrims in Holland*
Monjo. *King George's Head
 Was Made of Lead*
Monjo. *Poor Richard in
 France*
Sanders. *Here Comes the
 Mystery Man*
Sewall. *People of the
 Breaking Day*
Sewall. *The Pilgrims of
 Plimoth*
Sewall. *Thunder from the
 Clear Sky*
Tripp. *Meet Felicity: An
 American Girl*

Turner. *Katie's Trunk*
Van Leeuwen. *Across the
 Wide Dark Sea: The
 Mayflower Journey*
Waters. *The Mayflower*
Waters. *Samuel Eaton's Day:
 A Day in the Life of a
 Pilgrim Boy*
Waters. *Sarah Morton's Day:
 A Day in the Life of a
 Pilgrim Girl*
Waters. *Tapenum's Day: A
 Wampanoag Indian Boy in
 Pilgrim Times*
West. *Voyage of the Half
 Moon*

Biography

Adler. *Benjamin Franklin:
 Printer, Inventor,
 Statesman*
Adler. *George Washington:
 Father of Our Country*
Adler. *A Picture Book of
 Benjamin Franklin*
Adler. *A Picture Book of
 George Washington*
Adler. *A Picture Book of
 Patrick Henry*
Adler. *Remember Betsy
 Floss: And Other Colonial
 Riddles*
Aliki. *The Many Lives of
 Benjamin Franklin*
Avi. *Finding Providence: The
 Story of Roger Williams*

Benjamin. *Young
 Pocahontas: Indian
 Princess*
Brown. *Sybil Rides for
 Independence*
D'Aulaire. *Benjamin Franklin*
Fradin. *Washington's Birthday*
Fritz. *George Washington's
 Mother*
Fritz. *What's the Big Idea,
 Ben Franklin?*
Fritz. *Why Don't You Get a
 Horse, Sam Adams?*
Fritz. *Will You Sign Here,
 John Hancock?*
Giblin. *George Washington*
Gleiter. *Pocahontas*
Gourse. *Pocahontas: Young
 Peacemaker*
Graves. *John Smith*

Greene. *Benjamin Franklin*
Greene. *George Washington*
Greene. *Phillis Wheatley:
 First African American
 Poet*
Lawson. *Ben and Me*
Parker. *Benjamin Franklin
 and Electricity*
Pinkney. *Dear Benjamin
 Banneker*
Quackenbush. *Benjamin
 Franklin and His Friends*
Scarf. *Meet Benjamin
 Franklin*
Sherrow. *Phillis Wheatley:
 Poet*
Swanson. *David Bushnell*
Yates. *Amos Fortune, Free
 Man*

Collective Biography

King. *First Facts About
 American Heroes*

Marzollo. *My First Book of
 Biographies*

History

Anderson. *The First Thanksgiving Feast*

Appelbaum. *Giants in the Land*

Bowen. *Stranded at Plimoth Plantation 1626*

Burns. *Mail*

Climo. *City! New York*

Climo. *City! San Francisco*

Coote. *The Sailor Through History*

English. *Transportation: Automobiles to Zeppelins*

George. *The First Thanksgiving*

Gibbons. *The Great St. Lawrence Seaway*

Guiberson. *Lighthouses: Watchers at Sea*

Hayward. *The First Thanksgiving*

Hopkins. *Hand in Hand: An American History Through Poetry*

Kalman. *Colonial Crafts*

Kalman. *Colonial Life*

Kalman. *A Colonial Town: Williamsburg*

Kalman. *Early Artisans*

Kalman. *Early Christmas*

Kalman. *Early Health and Medicine*

Kalman. *Early Loggers and the Sawmill*

Kalman. *18th Century Clothing*

Kalman. *Home Crafts*

Kalman. *Old-Time Toys*

Kent. *African-Americans in the Thirteen Colonies*

Kent. *Salem, Massachusetts*

Kent. *Williamsburg*

Krensky. *Witch Hunt: It Happened in Salem Village*

Landau. *The Abenaki*

Landau. *The Ottawa*

Lincoln. *The Pirate's Handbook*

Maestro. *The Story of Money*

Medearis. *Our People*

Reef. *Mount Vernon*

Roop. *Pilgrim Voices: Our First Year in the New World*

Stamper. *New Friends in a New Land: A Thanksgiving Story*

Steen. *Colonial Williamsburg*

Wilson. *Visual Timeline of Transportation*

Multimedia

Video

American Independence
Early Settlers
The First Thanksgiving
The Life and Times of George Washington

Pilgrim Journey
Pocahontas
Squanto and the First Thanksgiving

Thanksgiving
William Bradford: The First Thanksgiving

GRADE FOUR

Historical Fiction

Anderson. *Christmas on the Prairie*

Benchley. *Sam the Minuteman*

Bulla. *A Lion to Guard Us*

Bulla. *Pocahontas and the Strangers*

Bulla. *Squanto, Friend of the Pilgrims*

Clifford. *When the Great Canoes Came*

De Angeli. *Skippack School*

Edmonds. *The Matchlock Gun*

Field. *Calico Bush*

Fleischman. *The 13th Floor: A Ghost Story*

Hildick. *Hester Bidgood: Invetigatrix of Evill Deedes*

Holmes. *Cross of Gold*

Holmes. *Thunder Foot 1730*

Holmes. *Two Chimneys*

Monjo. *The House on Stink Alley: A Story About the Pilgrims in Holland*

Monjo. *King George's Head Was Made of Lead*

Monjo. *Poor Richard in France*

Morris. *The Dangerous Voyage*

Sanders. *Here Comes the Mystery Man*

Sewall. *People of the Breaking Day*

Sewall. *The Pilgrims of Plimoth*

Sewall. *Thunder from the Clear Sky*

Speare. *The Sign of the Beaver*

Tripp. *Meet Felicity: An American Girl*

Waters. *Samuel Eaton's Day: A Day in the Life of a Pilgrim Boy*

Waters. *Tapenum's Day: A Wampanoag Indian Boy in Pilgrim Times*

West. *Voyage of the Half Moon*

Biography

Adler. *Benjamin Franklin: Printer, Inventor, Statesman*

Adler. *George Washington: Father of Our Country*

Adler. *A Picture Book of Benjamin Franklin*

Adler. *A Picture Book of George Washington*

Adler. *Remember Betsy Floss: And Other Colonial Riddles*
Avi. *Finding Providence: The Story of Roger Williams*
Brill. *John Adams*
Brown. *Sybil Rides for Independence*
D'Aulaire. *Benjamin Franklin*
D'Aulaire. *George Washington*
de Varona. *Bernardo de Gálvez*
Fradin. *Washington's Birthday*
Fritz. *George Washington's Mother*
Fritz. *What's the Big Idea, Ben Franklin?*
Fritz. *Why Don't You Get a Horse, Sam Adams?*
Fritz. *Will You Sign Here, John Hancock?*
Giblin. *George Washington*
Gleiter. *Junípero Serra*
Gourse. *Pocahontas: Young Peacemaker*
Graves. *John Smith*
Lawson. *Ben and Me*
Osborne. *George Washington: Leader of a New Nation*
Osborne. *The Many Lives of Benjamin Franklin*
Parker. *Benjamin Franklin and Electricity*
Pinkney. *Dear Benjamin Banneker*
Quackenbush. *Benjamin Franklin and His Friends*
Scarf. *Meet Benjamin Franklin*
Sherrow. *Phillis Wheatley: Poet*
Swanson. *David Bushnell*
Wheeler. *Forest Warrior: The Story of Pontiac*
Yates. *Amos Fortune, Free Man*

Collective Biography

Altman. *Extraordinary Black Americans*
Clements. *The Picture History of Great Inventors*
Fleming. *Women of the Lights*
Jacobs. *Great Lives: World Religions*
King. *First Facts About American Heroes*
Provensen. *My Fellow Americans*

History

Appelbaum. *Giants in the Land*
Avakian. *A Historical Album of Massachusetts*
Avakian. *A Historical Album of New York*
Beyer. *The Totem Pole Indians of the Northwest*
Bowen. *Stranded at Plimoth Plantation 1626*
Burns. *Mail*
Burns. *Money*
Carter. *The Colonial Wars: Clashes in the Wilderness*
Climo. *City! New York*
Climo. *City! San Francisco*
Cocke. *A Historical Album of Virginia*
Coote. *The Sailor Through History*
Corbishley. *Secret Cities*
Egger-Bovet. *Book of the American Revolution*
English. *Transportation: Automobiles to Zeppelins*
George. *The First Thanksgiving*
Gibbons. *The Great St. Lawrence Seaway*
Giblin. *Be Seated: A Book About Chairs*
Goor. *Williamsburg: Cradle of the Revolution*
Guiberson. *Lighthouses: Watchers at Sea*
Hopkins. *Hand in Hand: An American History Through Poetry*
Howarth. *Colonial People*
Howarth. *Colonial Places*
Kalman. *Colonial Crafts*
Kalman. *Colonial Life*
Kalman. *A Colonial Town: Williamsburg*
Kalman. *Early Artisans*
Kalman. *Early Christmas*
Kalman. *Early Health and Medicine*
Kalman. *Early Loggers and the Sawmill*
Kalman. *18th Century Clothing*
Kalman. *Home Crafts*
Kalman. *Old-Time Toys*
Kent. *African-Americans in the Thirteen Colonies*
Kent. *Salem, Massachusetts*
Kent. *Williamsburg*
Krensky. *Witch Hunt: It Happened in Salem Village*
Landau. *The Abenaki*
Landau. *The Ottawa*
Lemke. *Missions of the Southern Coast [California]*
Lincoln. *The Pirate's Handbook*
Lizon. *Colonial Holidays and Entertainment*
MacMillan. *Missions of the Los Angeles Area*
Maestro. *The Story of Money*
McNeese. *America's Early Canals*
McNeese. *Early River Travel*
Moss. *Forts and Castles*
Oleksy. *The Boston Tea Party*
Phelan. *The Story of the Boston Massacre*
Reef. *Mount Vernon*
Roach. *In the Days of the Salem Witchcraft Trials*
Roop. *Pilgrim Voices: Our First Year in the New World*
Ross. *Witches*
Rowland-Warne. *Costume*
St. George. *Mason and Dixon's Line of Fire*
Stamper. *New Friends in a New Land: A Thanksgiving Story*
Steen. *Colonial Williamsburg*
Sullivan. *Children of Promise: African-American Literature and Art*
Topper. *A Historical Album of New Jersey*
Van Der Linde. *Devil in Salem Village*

White. *Missions of the San Francisco Bay Area*

Wills. *A Historical Album of Connecticut*

Wills. *A Historical Album of Illinois*

Wilson. *Visual Timeline of Transportation*

Multimedia

CD-ROM

Her Heritage: A Biographical Encyclopedia of American History

SkyTrip America

Total History

Video

American Independence
Candlemaking
Early Settlers
Great Black Innovators
Jamestown
The Life and Times of George Washington
The Loom

Making It Happen: Masters of Invention
Mission Life
Missions of California: Mission Santa Barbara
Native Americans: The History of a People
Patrick Henry's Fight for Individual Rights

Pilgrim Journey
Samuel Adams
Spinning Wheel
Squanto and the First Thanksgiving
Thanksgiving
William Bradford: The First Thanksgiving

GRADE FIVE

Historical Fiction

Anderson. *Christmas on the Prairie*
Avi. *Encounter at Easton*
Avi. *Night Journeys*
Bulla. *A Lion to Guard Us*
Bulla. *Pocahontas and the Strangers*
Bulla. *Squanto, Friend of the Pilgrims*
Clapp. *Witches' Children*
Clifford. *When the Great Canoes Came*
De Angeli. *Skippack School*
Duey. *Sarah Anne Hartford: Massachusetts, 1651*
Edmonds. *The Matchlock Gun*
Field. *Calico Bush*
Fleischman. *The 13th Floor: A Ghost Story*
Forbes. *Johnny Tremain*
Hildick. *Hester Bidgood: Invetigatrix of Evill Deedes*

Holmes. *Cross of Gold*
Holmes. *Thunder Foot 1730*
Holmes. *Two Chimneys*
Krensky. *The Printer's Apprentice*
Lasky. *Beyond the Burning Time*
Lasky. *A Journey to the New World: Diary, 1620*
Martinello. *With Domingo Leal in San Antonio 1734*
Monjo. *The House on Stink Alley: A Story About the Pilgrims in Holland*
Monjo. *King George's Head Was Made of Lead*
Monjo. *Poor Richard in France*
Morris. *The Dangerous Voyage*
Rawls. *Never Turn Back: Father Serra's Mission*

Richter. *The Light in the Forest*
Sewall. *People of the Breaking Day*
Sewall. *The Pilgrims of Plimoth*
Sewall. *Thunder from the Clear Sky*
Speare. *The Sign of the Beaver*
Speare. *The Witch of Blackbird Pond*
Steele. *Wayah of the Real People*
Tripp. *Meet Felicity: An American Girl*
Waters. *Samuel Eaton's Day: A Day in the Life of a Pilgrim Boy*
West. *Voyage of the Half Moon*
Wisler. *This New Land*

Biography

Adler. *George Washington: Father of Our Country*
Adler. *Remember Betsy Floss: And Other Colonial Riddles*
Brill. *John Adams*

Brown. *Sybil Rides for Independence*
Bruns. *George Washington*
Conle. *Benjamin Banneker: Scientist and Mathematician*

Cwiklik. *King Philip and the War with the Colonists*
D'Aulaire. *Benjamin Franklin*
D'Aulaire. *George Washington*
de Varona. *Bernardo de Gálvez*

Diamond. *Paul Cuffe: Merchant and Abolitionist*
Diamond. *Prince Hall: Social Reformer*
Dolan. *Junípero Serra*
Dwyer. *John Adams*
Feldman. *Benjamin Franklin: Scientist and Inventor*
Fritz. *What's the Big Idea, Ben Franklin?*
Fritz. *Why Don't You Get a Horse, Sam Adams?*
Fritz. *Will You Sign Here, John Hancock?*
Giblin. *George Washington*
Gleiter. *Junípero Serra*
Gourse. *Pocahontas: Young Peacemaker*
Graves. *John Smith*

Hilton. *The World of Young George Washington*
Hilton. *The World of Young Tom Jefferson*
IlgenFritz. *Anne Hutchinson*
LaFarelle. *Bernardo de Gálvez: Hero of the American Revolution*
Lawson. *Ben and Me*
Lindop. *George Washington, Thomas Jefferson, and Andrew Jackson*
Looby. *Benjamin Franklin*
Nichols. *A Matter of Conscience: Anne Hutchinson*
Osborne. *George Washington: Leader of a New Nation*

Osborne. *The Many Lives of Benjamin Franklin.*
Parker. *Benjamin Franklin and Electricity*
Pinkney. *Dear Benjamin Banneker*
Potter. *Benjamin Franklin*
Richmond. *Phillis Wheatley*
Roman. *King Philip: Wampanoag Rebel*
Sherrow. *Phillis Wheatley: Poet*
Shuter. *Charles Ball and American Slavery 1790's*
Swanson. *David Bushnell*
Yates. *Amos Fortune, Free Man*

Collective Biography

Altman. *Extraordinary Black Americans*
Clements. *The Picture History of Great Inventors*
Faber. *Great Lives: American Government*

Fleming. *Women of the Lights*
Jacobs. *Great Lives*: *World Religions*
Katz. *Proudly Red and Black: Stories of African and Native Americans*

King. *First Facts About American Heroes*
Provensen. *My Fellow Americans*

History

Appelbaum. *Giants in the Land*
Avakian. *A Historical Album of Massachusetts*
Avakian. *A Historical Album of New York*
Barboza. *Door of No Return: The Legend of Gorée Island*
Beyer. *The Totem Pole Indians of the Northwest*
Bowen. *Stranded at Plimoth Plantation 1626*
Brown. *Discovery and Settlement: 1490-1700*
Burns. *Mail*
Burns. *Money*
Carter. *The Colonial Wars: Clashes in the Wilderness*
Climo. *City! New York*
Climo. *City! San Francisco*
Cocke. *A Historical Album of Virginia*
Colman. *Strike: The Bitter Struggle of American Workers*
Colman. *Toilets, Bathtubs, Sinks, and Sewers*
Coote. *The Sailor Through History*
Corbishley. *Secret Cities*
Davies. *Transport: On Land, Road and Rail*

Earle. *Home Life in Colonial Days*
Egger-Bovet. *Book of the American Revolution*
English. *Transportation: Automobiles to Zeppelins*
Fradin. *The Connecticut Colony*
Fradin. *The Delaware Colony*
Fradin. *The Georgia Colony*
Fradin. *The Maryland Colony*
Fradin. *The Massachusetts Colony*
Fradin. *The New Hampshire Colony*
Fradin. *The New Jersey Colony*
Fradin. *The New York Colony*
Fradin. *The North Carolina Colony*
Fradin. *The Pennsylvania Colony*
Fradin. *The Rhode Island Colony*
Fradin. *The South Carolina Colony*
Fradin. *The Virginia Colony*
George. *The First Thanksgiving*
Gibbons. *The Great St. Lawrence Seaway*

Giblin. *Be Seated: A Book About Chairs*
Goor. *Williamsburg: Cradle of the Revolution*
Guiberson. *Lighthouses: Watchers at Sea*
Hirsch. *Taxation: Paying for Government*
Hopkins. *Hand in Hand: An American History Through Poetry*
Howarth. *Colonial People*
Howarth. *Colonial Places*
Kalman. *Colonial Crafts*
Kalman. *Colonial Life*
Kalman. *A Colonial Town: Williamsburg*
Kalman. *Early Artisans*
Kalman. *Early Christmas*
Kalman. *Early Health and Medicine*
Kalman. *Early Loggers and the Sawmill*
Kalman. *18th Century Clothing*
Kalman. *Home Crafts*
Kalman. *Old-Time Toys*
Karl. *America Alive: A History*
Katz. *Breaking the Chains: African-American Slave Resistance*

Kent. *African-Americans in the Thirteen Colonies*
Kent. *Salem, Massachusetts*
Krensky. *Witch Hunt: It Happened in Salem Village*
Landau. *The Abenaki*
Landau. *The Ottawa*
Lemke. *Missions of the Southern Coast [California]*
Lincoln. *The Pirate's Handbook*
Lizon. *Colonial Holidays and Entertainment*
MacMillan. *Missions of the Los Angeles Area*
Maestro. *The Story of Money*
Marrin. *Empires Lost and Won: The Spanish Heritage in the Southwest*
Marrin. *The Sea Rovers: Pirates, Privateers, and Buccaneers*
Marrin. *Struggle for a Continent: The French and Indian Wars: 1690-1760*
McNeese. *America's Early Canals*
McNeese. *Early River Travel*

Medearis. *Come This Far to Freedom*
Meltzer. *The Black Americans*
Monroe. *First Houses: Native American Homes and Sacred Structures*
Morley. *Clothes: For Work, Play and Display*
Moss. *Forts and Castles*
Oleksy. *The Boston Tea Party*
Phelan. *The Story of the Boston Massacre*
Platt. *Pirate*
Platt. *The Smithsonian Visual Timeline of Inventions*
Reef. *Mount Vernon*
Roach. *In the Days of the Salem Witchcraft Trials*
Roop. *Pilgrim Voices: Our First Year in the New World*
Ross. *Witches*
Rowland-Warne. *Costume*
St. George. *Mason and Dixon's Line of Fire*
Stamper. *New Friends in a New Land: A Thanksgiving Story*
Steen. *Colonial Williamsburg*
Steins. *A Nation Is Born: 1700-1820*

Stevens. *Colonial American Craftspeople*
Sullivan. *Children of Promise: African-American Literature and Art*
Sullivan. *Slave Ship: The Story of the Henrietta Marie*
Topper. *A Historical Album of New Jersey*
Van Der Linde. *Devil in Salem Village*
Warner. *Colonial American Homelife*
White. *Missions of the San Francisco Bay Area*
Whitman. *Get Up and Go: American Road Travel*
Williams. *The Age of Discovery*
Wills. *A Historical Album of Connecticut*
Wills. *A Historical Album of Illinois*
Wilson. *Visual Timeline of Transportation*
Zeinert. *The Salem Witchcraft Trials*

Multimedia

CD-ROM

American History Explorer
Eyewitness Encyclopedia of Science

Her Heritage: A Biographical Encyclopedia of American History

SkyTrip America
Total History

Video

American Independence
Candlemaking
Causes of Revolt
Colonization and Settlement (1585-1763)
Countdown to Independence: Causes of the American Revolution
The Early Colonists
Early Settlers
Great Black Innovators

Jamestown
Jamestown: The Beginning
The Life and Times of George Washington
The Loom
Making It Happen: Masters of Invention
Mission Life
Missions of California: Mission Santa Barbara

Native Americans: The History of a People
Patrick Henry's Fight for Individual Rights
Pilgrim Journey
Samuel Adams
Seeds of Liberty: The Causes of the American Revolution
Spinning Wheel

GRADE SIX

Historical Fiction

Anderson. *Christmas on the Prairie*
Avi. *Encounter at Easton*
Avi. *Night Journeys*

Bulla. *Pocahontas and the Strangers*
Bulla. *Squanto, Friend of the Pilgrims*
Clapp. *Witches' Children*

Clifford. *When the Great Canoes Came*
De Angeli. *Skippack School*
Duey. *Sarah Anne Hartford: Massachusetts, 1651*

Durrant. *Echohawk*
Edmonds. *The Matchlock Gun*
Field. *Calico Bush*
Fleischman. *Graven Images*
Fleischman. *The 13th Floor:
A Ghost Story*
Forbes. *Johnny Tremain*
Hildick. *Hester Bidgood:
Invetigatrix of Evill Deedes*
Holmes. *Cross of Gold*
Holmes. *Thunder Foot 1730*
Koller. *The Primrose Way*
Krensky. *The Printer's
Apprentice*

Lasky. *Beyond the Burning
Time*
Lasky. *A Journey to the New
World: Diary, 1620*
Martinello. *With Domingo
Leal in San Antonio 1734*
Monjo. *Poor Richard in
France*
Morris. *The Dangerous
Voyage*
O'Dell. *The Serpent Never
Sleeps: A Novel of
Jamestown and Pocahontas*

Rawls. *Never Turn Back:
Father Serra's Mission*
Richter. *The Light in the
Forest*
Speare. *The Sign of the Beaver*
Speare. *The Witch of
Blackbird Pond*
Steele. *Wayah of the Real
People*
Waters. *Samuel Eaton's Day:
A Day in the Life of a
Pilgrim Boy*
Wisler. *This New Land*

Biography

Adler. *Remember Betsy
Floss: And Other Colonial
Riddles*
Brill. *John Adams*
Bruns. *George Washington*
Conle. *Benjamin Banneker:
Scientist and
Mathematician*
Cwiklik. *King Philip and the
War with the Colonists*
D'Aulaire. *Benjamin Franklin*
D'Aulaire. *George
Washington*
de Varona. *Bernardo de
Gálvez*
Diamond. *Paul Cuffe:
Merchant and Abolitionist*
Diamond. *Prince Hall: Social
Reformer*
Dolan. *Junípero Serra*
Dwyer. *John Adams*
Farley. *Samuel Adams:
Grandfather of His Country*
Farley. *Thomas Paine:
Revolutionary Author*

Feldman. *Benjamin Franklin:
Scientist and Inventor*
Ford. *Paul Revere: Rider for
the Revolution*
Fritz. *The Double Life of
Pocahontas*
Fritz. *What's the Big Idea,
Ben Franklin?*
Fritz. *Why Don't You Get a
Horse, Sam Adams?*
Fritz. *Will You Sign Here,
John Hancock?*
Gleiter. *Junípero Serra*
Gourse. *Pocahontas: Young
Peacemaker*
Graves. *John Smith*
Hilton. *The World of Young
George Washington*
Hilton. *The World of Young
Tom Jefferson*
IlgenFritz. *Anne Hutchinson*
LaFarelle. *Bernardo de
Gálvez: Hero of the
American Revolution*
Lawson. *Ben and Me*

Lindop. *George Washington,
Thomas Jefferson, and
Andrew Jackson*
Looby. *Benjamin Franklin*
Nichols. *A Matter of
Conscience: The Trial of
Anne Hutchinson*
Osborne. *George
Washington: Leader of a
New Nation*
Osborne. *The Many Lives of
Benjamin Franklin*
Parker. *Benjamin Franklin
and Electricity*
Potter. *Benjamin Franklin*
Richmond. *Phillis Wheatley*
Roman. *King Philip:
Wampanoag Rebel*
Sherrow. *Phillis Wheatley:
Poet*
Shuter. *Charles Ball and
American Slavery 1790's*
Stewart. *Benjamin Franklin*
Swanson. *David Bushnell*
Yates. *Amos Fortune, Free
Man*

Collective Biography

Altman. *Extraordinary Black
Americans*
Clements. *The Picture
History of Great Inventors*
Faber. *Great Lives: American
Government*

Fleming. *Women of the Lights*
Jacobs. *Great Lives: World
Religions*
Katz. *Proudly Red and Black:
Stories of African and
Native Americans*

King. *First Facts About
American Heroes*
Myers. *Now Is Your Time*
Provensen. *My Fellow
Americans*
Rennert. *Female Writers*

History

Appelbaum. *Giants in the
Land*
Avakian. *A Historical Album
of Massachusetts*
Avakian. *A Historical Album
of New York*
Barboza. *Door of No Return:
The Legend of Gorée Island*

Beyer. *The Totem Pole
Indians of the Northwest*
Bowen. *Stranded at Plimoth
Plantation 1626*
Brown. *Discovery and
Settlement: 1490-1700*
Burns. *Money*
Carter. *The Colonial Wars:
Clashes in the Wilderness*

Climo. *City! New York*
Climo. *City! San Francisco*
Cocke. *A Historical Album of
Virginia*
Colman. *Strike: The Bitter
Struggle of American
Workers*
Colman. *Toilets, Bathtubs,
Sinks, and Sewers*

Corbishley. *Secret Cities*
Davies. *Transport: On Land, Road and Rail*
Earle. *Home Life in Colonial Days*
Egger-Bovet. *Book of the American Revolution*
English. *Transportation: Automobiles to Zeppelins*
Fradin. *The Connecticut Colony*
Fradin. *The Delaware Colony*
Fradin. *The Georgia Colony*
Fradin. *The Maryland Colony*
Fradin. *The Massachusetts Colony*
Fradin. *The New Hampshire Colony*
Fradin. *The New Jersey Colony*
Fradin. *The New York Colony*
Fradin. *The North Carolina Colony*
Fradin. *The Pennsylvania Colony*
Fradin. *The Rhode Island Colony*
Fradin. *The South Carolina Colony*
Fradin. *The Virginia Colony*
Gibbons. *The Great St. Lawrence Seaway*
Giblin. *Be Seated: A Book About Chairs*
Goor. *Williamsburg: Cradle of the Revolution*
Guiberson. *Lighthouses: Watchers at Sea*
Hakim. *From Colonies to Country*
Hakim. *Making Thirteen Colonies*
Hakim. *The New Nation*
Hirsch. *Taxation: Paying for Government*
Hopkins. *Hand in Hand: An American History Through Poetry*
Howarth. *Colonial People*
Howarth. *Colonial Places*
Kalman. *Colonial Crafts*

Kalman. *A Colonial Town: Williamsburg*
Kalman. *Early Artisans*
Kalman. *Early Christmas*
Kalman. *Early Health and Medicine*
Kalman. *Early Loggers and the Sawmill*
Kalman. *18th Century Clothing*
Kalman. *Home Crafts*
Kalman. *Old-Time Toys*
Karl. *America Alive: A History*
Katz. *Breaking the Chains: African-American Slave Resistance*
Kent. *Salem, Massachusetts*
Landau. *The Abenaki*
Landau. *The Ottawa*
Lemke. *Missions of the Southern Coast [California]*
Lincoln. *The Pirate's Handbook*
Lizon. *Colonial Holidays and Entertainment*
MacMillan. *Missions of the Los Angeles Area*
Markham. *Inventions that Changed Modern Life*
Marrin. *Empires Lost and Won: The Spanish Heritage in the Southwest*
Marrin. *The Sea Rovers: Pirates, Privateers, and Buccaneers*
Marrin. *Struggle for a Continent: The French and Indian Wars: 1690-1760*
McNeese. *America's Early Canals*
McNeese. *Early River Travel*
Medearis. *Come This Far to Freedom*
Meltzer. *The Black Americans*
Monroe. *First Houses: Native American Homes and Sacred Structures*
Morley. *Clothes: For Work, Play and Display*
Moss. *Forts and Castles*

Phelan. *The Story of the Boston Massacre*
Platt. *Pirate*
Platt. *The Smithsonian Visual Timeline of Inventions*
Reef. *Mount Vernon*
Roach. *In the Days of the Salem Witchcraft Trials*
Roop. *Pilgrim Voices: Our First Year in the New World*
Ross. *Witches*
Rowland-Warne. *Costume*
St. George. *Mason and Dixon's Line of Fire*
Steen. *Colonial Williamsburg*
Stein. *Witches*
Steins. *A Nation Is Born: 1700-1820*
Stevens. *Colonial American Craftspeople*
Sullivan. *Children of Promise: African-American Literature and Art*
Sullivan. *Slave Ship: The Story of the Henrietta Marie*
Time-Life. *African Americans: Voices of Triumph: Leadership*
Topper. *A Historical Album of New Jersey*
Van Der Linde. *Devil in Salem Village*
Warner. *Colonial American Homelife*
Wheeler. *Events that Changed American History*
White. *Missions of the San Francisco Bay Area*
Whitman. *Get Up and Go: American Road Travel*
Williams. *The Age of Discovery*
Williams. *Forts and Castles*
Wills. *A Historical Album of Connecticut*
Wills. *A Historical Album of Illinois*
Zeinert. *The Salem Witchcraft Trials*

Multimedia

CD-ROM

American History Explorer
Eyewitness Encyclopedia of Science

Her Heritage: A Biographical Encyclopedia of American History
SkyTrip America

Stowaway! Stephen Biesty's Incredible Cross-Sections
Total History
The Way Things Work

Video

American Independence
Candlemaking
Causes of Revolt
Colonization and Settlement (1585-1763)
Countdown to Independence: Causes of the American Revolution
The Early Colonists
Early Settlers
Great Black Innovators
Jamestown

Jamestown: The Beginning
The Life and Times of George Washington
The Life of George Washington
The Loom
Making It Happen: Masters of Invention
Mission Life
Missions of California: Mission Santa Barbara

Native Americans: The History of a People
Patrick Henry's Fight for Individual Rights
Pilgrim Journey
The Pilgrims' Story
Samuel Adams
Seeds of Liberty: The Causes of the American Revolution
Spinning Wheel

THE AMERICAN REVOLUTION, 1775-1783

KINDERGARTEN THROUGH SECOND GRADE

Historical Fiction

Gauche. *This Time, Tempe Wick?*

Hoobler. *The Sign Painter's Secret: The Story of a Revolutionary Girl*

Rappaport. *The Boston Coffee Party*

Biography

Adler. *Benjamin Franklin: Printer, Inventor, Statesman*

Adler. *A Picture Book of Benjamin Franklin*

Adler. *A Picture Book of George Washington*

Adler. *A Picture Book of Patrick Henry*

Adler. *A Picture Book of Paul Revere*

Adler. *Remember Betsy Floss: And Other Colonial Riddles*

Aliki. *The Many Lives of Benjamin Franklin*

Fradin. *Washington's Birthday*

Fritz. *And Then What Happened, Paul Revere?*

Fritz. *Shh! We're Writing the Constitution*

Fritz. *What's the Big Idea, Ben Franklin?*

Fritz. *Why Don't You Get a Horse, Sam Adams?*

Fritz. *Will You Sign Here, John Hancock?*

Gleiter. *Paul Revere*

Greene. *Benjamin Franklin*

Greene. *George Washington*

McGovern. *The Secret Soldier: The Story of Deborah Sampson*

Peterson. *Abigail Adams: "Dear Partner"*

Pinkney. *Dear Benjamin Banneker*

Quackenbush. *Benjamin Franklin and His Friends*

Quackenbush. *James Madison and Dolley Madison and Their Times*

Quackenbush. *Pass the Quill, I'll Write a Draft: A Story of Thomas Jefferson*

Sabin. *Young Abigail Adams*

Scarf. *Meet Benjamin Franklin*

Wallner. *Betsy Ross*

Collective Biography

Marzollo. *My First Book of Biographies*

History

Fisher. *Stars and Stripes: Our National Flag*

Fradin. *The Flag of the United States*

Medearis. *Our People*

Richards. *Monticello*

Spencer. *A Flag for Our Country*

Multimedia

Video

American Independence
Independence Day

Old Glory
United States Flag

GRADE THREE

Historical Fiction

Banim. *Drums at Saratoga*
Banim. *A Spy in the King's Colony*
Berleth. *Samuel's Choice*

Dalgliesh. *Adam and the Golden Cock.*
Duey. *Mary Alice Peale*
Gauch. *This Time, Tempe Wick?*

Hoobler. *The Sign Painter's Secret: The Story of a Revolutionary Girl*
Rappaport. *The Boston Coffee Party*

Biography

Adler. *Benjamin Franklin: Printer, Inventor, Statesman*
Adler. *George Washington: Father of Our Country*
Adler. *A Picture Book of Benjamin Franklin*
Adler. *A Picture Book of George Washington*
Adler. *A Picture Book of Patrick Henry*
Adler. *A Picture Book of Paul Revere*
Adler. *A Picture Book of Thomas Jefferson*
Adler. *Remember Betsy Floss: And Other Colonial Riddles*
Aliki. *The Many Lives of Benjamin Franklin*
D'Aulaire. *Benjamin Franklin*

Fradin. *Washington's Birthday*
Fritz. *And Then What Happened, Paul Revere?*
Fritz. *What's the Big Idea, Ben Franklin?*
Fritz. *Why Don't You Get a Horse, Sam Adams?*
Fritz. *Will You Sign Here, John Hancock?*
Giblin. *George Washington*
Giblin. *Thomas Jefferson: A Picture Book Biography*
Gleiter. *Paul Revere*
Greene. *Benjamin Franklin*
Greene. *George Washington*
Lawson. *Ben and Me*
Lawson. *Mr. Revere and I*
McGovern. *The Secret Soldier: The Story of Deborah Sampson*

Parker. *Benjamin Franklin and Electricity*
Peterson. *Abigail Adams: "Dear Partner"*
Pinkney. *Dear Benjamin Banneker*
Quackenbush. *Benjamin Franklin and His Friends*
Quackenbush. *James Madison and Dolley Madison and Their Times*
Quackenbush. *Pass the Quill, I'll Write a Draft: A Story of Thomas Jefferson*
Sabin. *Young Abigail Adams*
Scarf. *Meet Benjamin Franklin*
Wade. *Benedict Arnold*
Wallner. *Betsy Ross*

Collective Biography

King. *First Facts About American Heroes*

Marzollo. *My First Book of Biographies*

History

Brenner. *If You Were There in 1776*
Burns. *Mail*
English. *Transportation: Automobiles to Zeppelins*
Fisher. *Stars and Stripes: Our National Flag*
Fradin. *The Flag of the United States*
Hopkins. *Hand in Hand: An American History Through Poetry*

Johnson. *The Battle of Lexington and Concord*
Johnson. *Our National Symbols*
Landau. *The Abenaki*
Landau. *The Ottawa*
Maestro. *The Story of Money*
Maestro. *The Voice of the People*
Medearis. *Our People*
Paananen. *The Military: Defending the Nation*
Reef. *Mount Vernon*

Richards. *Monticello*
Rubel. *America's War of Independence*
Shuker-Haines. *Rights and Responsibilities: Using Your Freedom*
Spencer. *A Flag for Our Country*
Steen. *Independence Hall*
Stein. *The Declaration of Independence*
Stein. *Valley Forge*

Multimedia

Video

American Independence
Independence Day

The Life and Times of George Washington
Old Glory

United States Flag
Valley Forge: Young Spy

GRADE FOUR

Historical Fiction

Avi. *The Fighting Ground*
Banim. *Drums at Saratoga*
Banim. *A Spy in the King's Colony*
Berleth. *Samuel's Choice*
Collier. *War Comes to Willy Freeman*
Dalgliesh. *Adam and the Golden Cock.*

Duey. *Mary Alice Peale*
Gauche. *This Time, Tempe Wick?*
Hoobler. *The Sign Painter's Secret: The Story of a Revolutionary Girl*
Jensen. *The Riddle of Penncroft Farm*

Keehn. *Moon of Two Dark Horses*
Monjo. *A Namesake for Nathan*
Moore. *Distant Thunder*
Reit. *Guns for General Washington*
Woodruff. *George Washington's Socks*

Biography

Adler. *Benjamin Franklin: Printer, Inventor, Statesman*
Adler. *George Washington: Father of Our Country*
Adler. *A Picture Book of Benjamin Franklin*
Adler. *A Picture Book of George Washington*
Adler. *A Picture Book of Thomas Jefferson*
Adler. *Remember Betsy Floss: And Other Colonial Riddles*
Brill. *John Adams*
Clinton. *James Madison: Fourth President*
D'Aulaire. *Benjamin Franklin*
D'Aulaire. *George Washington*
Fradin. *Washington's Birthday*
Fritz. *And Then What Happened, Paul Revere?*

Fritz. *What's the Big Idea, Ben Franklin?*
Fritz. *Why Don't You Get a Horse, Sam Adams?*
Fritz. *Will You Sign Here, John Hancock?*
Genet. *Father Junípero Serra: Founder of California Missions*
Giblin. *George Washington*
Giblin. *Thomas Jefferson: A Picture Book Biography*
Lawson. *Ben and Me*
Lawson. *Mr. Revere and I*
Marsh. *Martha Washington*
McGovern. *The Secret Soldier: The Story of Deborah Sampson*
Osborne. *George Washington: Leader of a New Nation*
Osborne. *The Many Lives of Benjamin Franklin*

Parker. *Benjamin Franklin and Electricity*
Peterson. *Abigail Adams: "Dear Partner"*
Pinkney. *Dear Benjamin Banneker*
Quackenbush. *Benjamin Franklin and His Friends*
Quackenbush. *James Madison and Dolley Madison and Their Times*
Quackenbush. *Pass the Quill, I'll Write a Draft: A Story of Thomas Jefferson*
Sabin. *Young Abigail Adams*
Scarf. *Meet Benjamin Franklin*
Wade. *Benedict Arnold*
Wallner. *Betsy Ross*

Collective Biography

Altman. *Extraordinary Black Americans*
King. *First Facts About American Heroes*

Provensen. *My Fellow Americans*
Reef. *Black Fighting Men: A Proud History*

History

Beyer. *The Totem Pole Indians of the Northwest*
Bolick. *Mail Call!*
Brenner. *If You Were There in 1776*
Burns. *Mail*
Burns. *Money*
English. *Transportation: Automobiles to Zeppelins*
Fisher. *Stars and Stripes: Our National Flag*
Fradin. *The Flag of the United States*
Hoig. *It's the Fourth of July*

Hopkins. *Hand in Hand: An American History Through Poetry*
Johnson. *The Battle of Lexington and Concord*
Johnson. *Our National Symbols*
Kent. *The American Revolution*
Kirby. *Glorious Days, Dreadful Days: The Battle of Bunker Hill*
Landau. *The Abenaki*
Landau. *The Ottawa*

Maestro. *The Story of Money*
Maestro. *The Voice of the People*
McNeese. *America's Early Canals*
Nordstrom. *Concord and Lexington*
Paananen. *The Military: Defending the Nation*
Reef. *Mount Vernon*
Richards. *Monticello*
Rowland-Warne. *Costume*
Rubel. *America's War of Independence*

Shuker-Haines. *Rights and Responsibilities: Using Your Freedom*

Spencer. *A Flag for Our Country*

Steen. *Independence Hall*

Stein. *The Declaration of Independence*

Stein. *Valley Forge*

Multimedia

CD-ROM

Her Heritage: A Biographical Encyclopedia of American History

SkyTrip America Total History

Video

American Independence

Independence Day

The Life and Times of George Washington

Old Glory

Patrick Henry's Fight for Individual Rights

Samuel Adams

United States Flag

Valley Forge: Young Spy

GRADE FIVE

Historical Fiction

Avi. *Captain Grey*

Avi. *The Fighting Ground*

Banim. *Drums at Saratoga*

Banim. *A Spy in the King's Colony*

Berleth. *Samuel's Choice*

Caudill. *Tree of Freedom*

Collier. *War Comes to Willy Freeman*

Dalgliesh. *Adam and the Golden Cock*

Duey. *Mary Alice Peale*

Fritz. *Early Thunder*

Gregory. *The Winter of Red Snow: Diary, 1777-1778*

Hoobler. *The Sign Painter's Secret: The Story of a Revolutionary Girl*

Jensen. *The Riddle of Penncroft Farm*

Keehn. *Moon of Two Dark Horses*

Monjo. *A Namesake for Nathan*

Moore. *Distant Thunder*

Reit. *Guns for General Washington*

Woodruff. *George Washington's Socks*

Biography

Adler. *George Washington: Father of our Country*

Adler. *Remember Betsy Floss: And Other Colonial Riddles*

Brill. *John Adams*

Bruns. *George Washington*

Bruns. *Thomas Jefferson*

Clinton. *James Madison: Fourth President*

Conle. *Benjamin Banneker: Scientist and Mathematician*

D'Aulaire. *Benjamin Franklin*

D'Aulaire. *George Washington*

Diamond. *Paul Cuffe: Merchant and Abolitionist*

Diamond. *Prince Hall: Social Reformer*

Dwyer. *John Adams*

Feldman. *Benjamin Franklin: Scientist and Inventor*

Fritz. *And Then What Happened, Paul Revere?*

Fritz. *Traitor: The Case of Benedict Arnold*

Fritz. *What's the Big Idea, Ben Franklin?*

Fritz. *Why Don't You Get a Horse, Sam Adams?*

Fritz. *Will You Sign Here, John Hancock?*

Genet. *Father Junípero Serra: Founder of California Missions*

Giblin. *George Washington*

Giblin. *Thomas Jefferson: A Picture Book Biography*

Lawson. *Ben and Me*

Lawson. *Mr. Revere and I*

Leavell. *James Madison*

Lindop. *George Washington, Thomas Jefferson, and Andrew Jackson*

Looby. *Benjamin Franklin*

Marsh. *Martha Washington*

McGovern. *The Secret Soldier: The Story of Deborah Sampson*

Nardo. *Thomas Jefferson*

O'Brien. *Alexander Hamilton*

Osborne. *Abigail Adams: Women's Rights Advocate*

Osborne. *George Washington: Leader of a New Nation*

Osborne. *The Many Lives of Benjamin Franklin*

Parker. *Benjamin Franklin and Electricity*

Patterson. *Thomas Jefferson*

Peterson. *Abigail Adams: "Dear Partner"*

Pinkney. *Dear Benjamin Banneker*

Potter. *Benjamin Franklin*

Sabin. *Young Abigail Adams*

Sandak. *The Jeffersons*

Sandak. *The John Adamses*

Sandak. *The Washingtons*

Stefoff. *James Monroe: 5th President of the United States*

Stefoff. *John Adams: 2nd President of the United States*

Stefoff. *Thomas Jefferson: 3rd President of the United States*

Vail. *Thomas Paine*

Wade. *Benedict Arnold*

Zeinert. *The Memoirs of Andrew Sherburne*

Collective Biography

Altman. *Extraordinary Black Americans*

Clements. *The Picture History of Great Inventors*

Cohen. *The Ghosts of War*

Faber. *Great Lives: American Government*

Fleming. *Women of the Lights*

Jacobs. *Great Lives: World Religions*

Katz. *Proudly Red and Black: Stories of African and Native Americans*

King. *First Facts About American Heroes*

Provensen. *My Fellow Americans*

Reef. *Black Fighting Men: A Proud History*

Wilkinson. *Generals Who Changed the World*

History

Beyer. *The Totem Pole Indians of the Northwest*

Bolick. *Mail Call!*

Brenner. *If You Were There in 1776*

Burns. *Mail*

Burns. *Money*

Davies. *Transport: On Land, Road and Rail*

English. *Transportation: Automobiles to Zeppelins*

Hirsch. *Taxation: Paying for Government*

Hoig. *It's the Fourth of July*

Hopkins. *Hand in Hand: An American History Through Poetry*

Johnson. *The Battle of Lexington and Concord*

Johnson. *Our National Symbols*

Karl. *America Alive: A History*

Kent. *The American Revolution*

Kirby. *Glorious Days, Dreadful Days: The Battle of Bunker Hill*

Landau. *The Abenaki*

Landau. *The Ottawa*

Maestro. *The Story of Money*

Maestro. *The Voice of the People*

McNeese. *America's Early Canals*

Medearis. *Come This Far to Freedom*

Meltzer. *The Black Americans*

Morley. *Clothes: For Work, Play and Display*

Nordstrom. *Concord and Lexington*

Paananen. *The Military: Defending the Nation*

Platt. *The Smithsonian Visual Timeline of Inventions*

Reef. *Mount Vernon*

Richards. *Monticello*

Rowland-Warne. *Costume*

Rubel. *America's War of Independence*

Shuker-Haines. *Rights and Responsibilities: Using Your Freedom*

Spencer. *A Flag for Our Country*

Steen. *Independence Hall*

Stein. *The Declaration of Independence*

Stein. *Valley Forge*

Steins. *A Nation Is Born: 1700-1820*

Warner. *The U.S. Marine Corps*

Williams. *The Age of Discovery*

Multimedia

CD-ROM

American History Explorer

Her Heritage: A Biographical Encyclopedia of American History

SkyTrip America

Total History

Video

American Independence

The American Revolution

Causes of Revolt

Countdown to Independence: Causes of the American Revolution

The Life and Times of George Washington

A New Nation (1776-1815)

Old Glory

Patrick Henry's Fight for Individual Rights

Samuel Adams

Seeds of Liberty: The Causes of the American Revolution

United States Flag

Valley Forge: Young Spy

GRADE SIX

Historical Fiction

Avi. *The Fighting Ground*
Avi. *Captain Grey*
Berleth. *Samuel's Choice*
Caudill. *Tree of Freedom*
Collier. *War Comes to Willy Freeman*
DeFord. *An Enemy Among Them*
Duey. *Mary Alice Peale*
Fritz. *Early Thunder*
Gregory. *The Winter of Red Snow: Diary, 1777-1778*
Jensen. *The Riddle of Penncroft Farm*
Keehn. *Moon of Two Dark Horses*
Monjo. *A Namesake for Nathan*
Moore. *Distant Thunder*
Reit. *Guns for General Washington*
Woodruff. *George Washington's Socks*

Biography

Adler. *Remember Betsy Floss: And Other Colonial Riddles*
Beller. *Woman of Independence: The Life of Abigail Adams*
Brill. *John Adams*
Bruns. *George Washington*
Bruns. *Thomas Jefferson*
Clinton. *James Madison: Fourth President*
Conle. *Benjamin Banneker: Scientist and Mathematician*
D'Aulaire. *Benjamin Franklin*
D'Aulaire. *George Washington*
Diamond. *Paul Cuffe: Merchant and Abolitionist*
Diamond. *Prince Hall: Social Reformer*
Dwyer. *John Adams*
Farley. *Samuel Adams: Grandfather of His Country*
Farley. *Thomas Paine: Revolutionary Author*
Feldman. *Benjamin Franklin: Scientist and Inventor*
Ford. *Paul Revere: Rider for the Revolution*
Fritz. *And Then What Happened, Paul Revere?*
Fritz. *Traitor: The Case of Benedict Arnold*
Fritz. *What's the Big Idea, Ben Franklin?*
Fritz. *Why Don't You Get a Horse, Sam Adams?*
Fritz. *Will You Sign Here, John Hancock?*
Genet. *Father Junípero Serra: Founder of California Missions*
Latham. *Carry On, Mr. Bowditch*
Lawson. *Ben and Me*
Lawson. *Mr. Revere and I*
Leavell. *James Madison*
Lindop. *George Washington, Thomas Jefferson, and Andrew Jackson*
Looby. *Benjamin Franklin*
Marsh. *Martha Washington*
Nardo. *Thomas Jefferson*
O'Brien. *Alexander Hamilton*
Osborne. *Abigail Adams: Women's Rights Advocate*
Osborne. *George Washington: Leader of a New Nation*
Osborne. *The Many Lives of Benjamin Franklin*
Parker. *Benjamin Franklin and Electricity*
Patterson. *Thomas Jefferson*
Peterson. *Abigail Adams: "Dear Partner"*
Potter. *Benjamin Franklin*
Sandak. *The Jeffersons*
Sandak. *The John Adamses*
Sandak. *The Washingtons*
Stefoff. *James Monroe: 5th President of the United States*
Stefoff. *John Adams: 2nd President of the United States*
Stefoff. *Thomas Jefferson: 3rd President of the United States*
Stewart. *Benjamin Franklin*
Vail. *Thomas Paine*
Wade. *Benedict Arnold*
Zeinert. *The Memoirs of Andrew Sherburne*

Collective Biography

Altman. *Extraordinary Black Americans*
Clements. *The Picture History of Great Inventors*
Cohen. *The Ghosts of War*
Faber. *Great Lives: American Government*
Fleming. *Women of the Lights*
Jacobs. *Great Lives: World Religions*
Katz. *Proudly Red and Black: Stories of African and Native Americans*
King. *First Facts About American Heroes*
Myers. *Now Is Your Time*
Provensen. *My Fellow Americans*
Reef. *Black Fighting Men: A Proud History*
Rennert. *Female Writers*
Rennert. *Pioneers of Discovery*
Sheafer. *Women in America's Wars*
Wilkinson. *Generals Who Changed the World*

History

Beyer. *The Totem Pole Indians of the Northwest*
Bolick. *Mail Call!*
Brenner. *If You Were There in 1776*
Burns. *Money*
Davies. *Transport: On Land, Road and Rail*
Dolan. *The American Revolution*
English. *Transportation: Automobiles to Zeppelins*
Hakim. *From Colonies to Country*
Hakim. *The New Nation*
Hirsch. *Taxation: Paying for Government*
Hoig. *It's the Fourth of July*
Hopkins. *Hand in Hand: An American History Through Poetry*
Jaffe. *Who Were the Founding Fathers?*
Johnson. *The Battle of Lexington and Concord*

Karl. *America Alive: A History*
Kent. *The American Revolution*
Kirby. *Glorious Days, Dreadful Days: The Battle of Bunker Hill*
Landau. *The Abenaki*
Landau. *The Ottawa*
Maestro. *The Voice of the People*
McNeese. *America's Early Canals*
Medearis. *Come This Far to Freedom*
Meltzer. *The Black Americans*
Morley. *Clothes: For Work, Play and Display*
Murphy. *Young Patriot: The American Revolution as Experienced by One Boy*
Nordstrom. *Concord and Lexington*
Paananen. *The Military: Defending the Nation*

Platt. *The Smithsonian Visual Timeline of Inventions*
Reef. *Mount Vernon*
Rowland-Warne. *Costume*
Rubel. *America's War of Independence*
Shuker-Haines. *Rights and Responsibilities: Using Your Freedom*
Steen. *Independence Hall*
Stein. *The Declaration of Independence*
Stein. *Valley Forge*
Steins. *A Nation Is Born: 1700-1820*
Warner. *The U.S. Marine Corps*
Wheeler. *Events That Changed American History*
Williams. *The Age of Discovery*

Multimedia

CD-ROM

American History Explorer

Her Heritage: A Biographical Encyclopedia of American History

SkyTrip America
Total History

Video

American Independence
The American Revolution
Causes of Revolt
Countdown to Independence: Causes of the American Revolution

The Life and Times of George Washington
The Life of George Washington
A New Nation (1776-1815)
Patrick Henry's Fight for Individual Rights

Samuel Adams
Seeds of Liberty: The Causes of the American Revolution
United States Flag
Valley Forge: Young Spy

THE EARLY UNITED STATES, 1784-1814

KINDERGARTEN THROUGH SECOND GRADE

Historical Fiction

Greeson. *An American Army of Two*
Hopkinson. *Birdie's Lighthouse*
MacLachlan. *Three Names*
Manson. *A Dog Came, Too*

Martin. *Grandmother Bryant's Pocket*
McClung. *America's First Elephant*
McLerran. *The Year of the Ranch*

Minahan. *Abigail's Drum*
Monjo. *Grand Papa and Ellen Aroon*
Morrow. *Help for Mr. Peale*
Shub. *Cutlass in the Snow*

Biography

Adler. *Benjamin Franklin: Printer, Inventor, Statesman*
Adler. *A Picture Book of Benjamin Franklin*
Adler. *A Picture Book of George Washington*
Aliki. *The Many Lives of Benjamin Franklin*
Fradin. *Washington's Birthday*

Fritz. *What's the Big Idea, Ben Franklin?*
Greene. *Benjamin Franklin*
Greene. *George Washington*
Harness. *Young John Quincy*
Peterson. *Abigail Adams: "Dear Partner"*
Pinkney. *Dear Benjamin Banneker*
Quackenbush. *Benjamin Franklin and His Friends*

Quackenbush. *James Madison and Dolley Madison and Their Times*
Quackenbush. *Pass the Quill, I'll Write a Draft: A Story of Thomas Jefferson*
Sabin. *Young Abigail Adams*
Scarf. *Meet Benjamin Franklin*

Collective Biography

Marzollo. *My First Book of Biographies*

History

Fradin. *The Flag of the United States*
Goldish. *Our Supreme Court*
Medearis. *Our People*

Richards. *Monticello*
Steins. *Our Elections*

Wallner. *The First Air Voyage in the United States: Jean-Pierre Blanchard*

Multimedia

Video

American Independence
Equal Rights for All
President's Day

U.S. Songs and Poems
United States Constitution
Washington, D.C.

GRADE THREE

Historical Fiction

Beckman. *From the Ashes*
Brown. *George Washington's Ghost*
Greeson. *An American Army of Two*
MacLachlan. *Three Names*

Manson. *A Dog Came, Too*
Martin. *Grandmother Bryant's Pocket*
McLerran. *The Year of the Ranch*
Minahan. *Abigail's Drum*

Monjo. *Grand Papa and Ellen Aroon*
Morrow. *Help for Mr. Peale*
Shub. *Cutlass in the Snow*

Biography

Adler. *Benjamin Franklin: Printer, Inventor, Statesman*
Adler. *George Washington: Father of Our Country*
Adler. *A Picture Book of Benjamin Franklin*
Adler. *A Picture Book of George Washington*
Adler. *A Picture Book of Thomas Jefferson*
Aliki. *The Many Lives of Benjamin Franklin*
Anderson. *Martha Washington: First Lady of the Land*
D'Aulaire. *Benjamin Franklin*
Davidson. *Dolly Madison: Famous First Lady*

Fradin. *Washington's Birthday*
Fritz. *What's the Big Idea, Ben Franklin?*
Giblin. *George Washington*
Giblin. *Thomas Jefferson: A Picture Book Biography*
Greene. *Benjamin Franklin*
Greene. *George Washington*
Harness. *Young John Quincy*
Hopkinson. *Birdie's Lighthouse*
Landau. *Robert Fulton*
Latham. *Eli Whitney*
Lawson. *Ben and Me*
Parker. *Benjamin Franklin and Electricity*
Patterson. *Francis Scott Key: Poet and Patriot*

Peterson. *Abigail Adams: "Dear Partner"*
Pinkney. *Dear Benjamin Banneker*
Quackenbush. *Benjamin Franklin and His Friends*
Quackenbush. *James Madison and Dolley Madison and Their Times*
Quackenbush. *Pass the Quill, I'll Write a Draft: A Story of Thomas Jefferson*
Sabin. *Young Abigail Adams*
Scarf. *Meet Benjamin Franklin*
Wade. *Benedict Arnold*
Whitcraft. *Francis Scott Key*

Collective Biography

King. *First Facts About American Heroes*

Marzollo. *My First Book of Biographies*

Provensen. *The Buck Stops Here: The Presidents*

History

Bowler. *Trains*
Burns. *Mail*
Caulkins. *Pets of the Presidents*
Climo. *City! Washington, DC*
English. *Transportation: Automobiles to Zeppelins*
Fradin. *The Flag of the United States*
Goldish. *Our Supreme Court*
Guiberson. *Lighthouses: Watchers at Sea*
Guzzetti. *The White House*
Hoig. *Capital for the Nation*
Johnson. *Our National Symbols*
Kalman. *A Child's Day*
Kalman. *Children's Clothing of the 1800s*
Kalman. *Customs and Traditions*

Kalman. *Early Artisans*
Kalman. *Early Christmas*
Kalman. *Early Health and Medicine*
Kalman. *Early Schools*
Kalman. *Early Stores and Markets*
Kalman. *Early Travel*
Kalman. *Early Village Life*
Kalman. *Games from Long Ago*
Kalman. *Home Crafts*
Kalman. *19th Century Clothing*
Kalman. *Old-Time Toys*
Kalman. *A One-Room School*
Maestro. *The Story of Money*
Medearis. *Our People*
Morley. *Exploring North America*
Reef. *Mount Vernon*
Richards. *Monticello*

Sherrow. *The Big Book of U.S. Presidents*
Shuker-Haines. *Rights and Responsibilities: Using Your Freedom*
St. Pierre. *Our National Anthem*
Steen. *Independence Hall*
Stein. *The Story of the Powers of the Supreme Court*
Steins. *Our Elections*
Stern. *The Congress: America's Lawmakers*
Wallner. *The First Air Voyage in the United States: Jean-Pierre Blanchard*
Weber. *Our Congress*
Wilson. *Visual Timeline of Transportation*

Multimedia ————————————————————————————

CD-ROM

Inside the White House

Video

American Independence
Equal Rights for All
The Life and Times of George
Washington

President's Day
U.S. Songs and Poems
United States Constitution
Washington, D.C.

GRADE FOUR

Historical Fiction ————————————————————————————

Beckman. *From the Ashes*
Brown. *George Washington's*
Ghost
Collier. *Jump Ship to Freedom*
Collier. *Who Is Carrie?*
Fritz. *The Cabin Faced West*
Greeson. *An American Army*
of Two

Manson. *A Dog Came, Too*
Martin. *Grandmother*
Bryant's Pocket
McLerran. *The Year of the*
Ranch
Minahan. *Abigail's Drum*
Monjo. *Grand Papa and*
Ellen Aroon

Robinet. *Washington City Is*
Burning
Shub. *Cutlass in the Snow*
West. *Mr. Peale's Bones*
Whelan. *Once on This Island*

Biography ————————————————————————————

Adler. *Benjamin Franklin:*
Printer, Inventor,
Statesman
Adler. *George Washington:*
Father of our Country
Adler. *A Picture Book of*
Benjamin Franklin
Adler. *A Picture Book of*
George Washington
Adler. *A Picture Book of*
Thomas Jefferson
Alter. *Eli Whitney*
Anderson. *Martha*
Washington: First Lady of
the Land
Brill. *John Adams*
Clinton. *James Madison:*
Fourth President
D'Aulaire. *Benjamin Franklin*
D'Aulaire. *George*
Washington
Davidson. *Dolly Madison:*
Famous First Lady

Fitz-Gerald. *James Monroe:*
Fifth President
Fitz-Gerald. *William Henry*
Harrison: Ninth President
Fradin. *Washington's Birthday*
Fritz. *What's the Big Idea,*
Ben Franklin?
Giblin. *George Washington*
Giblin. *Thomas Jefferson: A*
Picture Book Biography
Hargrove. *Thomas Jefferson:*
Third President
Harness. *Young John Quincy*
Landau. *Robert Fulton*
Latham. *Eli Whitney*
Lawson. *Ben and Me*
Marsh. *Martha Washington*
Osborne. *George*
Washington: Leader of a
New Nation
Osborne. *The Many Lives of*
Benjamin Franklin

Parker. *Benjamin Franklin*
and Electricity
Patterson. *Francis Scott Key:*
Poet and Patriot
Peterson. *Abigail Adams:*
"Dear Partner"
Pinkney. *Dear Benjamin*
Banneker
Quackenbush. *Benjamin*
Franklin and His Friends
Quackenbush. *James*
Madison and Dolley
Madison and Their Times
Quackenbush. *Pass the Quill,*
I'll Write a Draft: A Story
of Thomas Jefferson
Quiri. *Dolley Madison*
Sabin. *Young Abigail Adams*
Scarf. *Meet Benjamin*
Franklin
Wade. *Benedict Arnold*
Whitcraft. *Francis Scott Key*

Collective Biography

Altman. *Extraordinary Black*
Americans
Clements. *The Picture*
History of Great Inventors
Fleming. *Women of the Lights*

King. *First Facts About*
American Heroes
Pascoe. *First Facts About the*
Presidents
Provensen. *The Buck Stops*
Here: The Presidents

Provensen. *My Fellow*
Americans
Rubel. *The Scholastic*
Encyclopedia of the
Presidents

History

Blue. *The White House Kids*
Bowler. *Trains*
Burns. *Mail*
Burns. *Money*
Caulkins. *Pets of the Presidents*
Climo. *City! Washington, DC*
English. *Transportation: Automobiles to Zeppelins*
Fradin. *The Flag of the United States*
Giblin. *Be Seated: A Book About Chairs*
Goldish. *Our Supreme Court*
Guiberson. *Lighthouses: Watchers at Sea*
Guzzetti. *The White House*
Hoig. *Capital for the Nation*
Johnson. *Our National Symbols*
Kalman. *A Child's Day*
Kalman. *Children's Clothing of the 1800s*
Kalman. *Customs and Traditions*

Kalman. *Early Artisans*
Kalman. *Early Christmas*
Kalman. *Early Health and Medicine*
Kalman. *Early Pleasures and Pastimes*
Kalman. *Early Schools*
Kalman. *Early Stores and Markets*
Kalman. *Early Travel*
Kalman. *Early Village Life*
Kalman. *Games from Long Ago*
Kalman. *Home Crafts*
Kalman. *19th Century Clothing*
Kalman. *Old-Time Toys*
Kalman. *A One-Room School*
Kroll. *By the Dawn's Early Light: The Star-Spangled Banner*
Kurtz. *U.S. Army*
Maestro. *The Story of Money*
McNeese. *America's Early Canals*

McNeese. *Early River Travel*
Morley. *Exploring North America*
Reef. *Mount Vernon*
Reef. *The Supreme Court*
Richards. *Monticello*
Rowland-Warne. *Costume*
Sandler. *Presidents*
Sherrow. *The Big Book of U.S. Presidents*
Shuker-Haines. *Rights and Responsibilities: Using Your Freedom*
St. Pierre. *Our National Anthem*
Steen. *Independence Hall*
Stein. *The Story of the Powers of the Supreme Court*
Steins. *Our Elections*
Stern. *The Congress: America's Lawmakers*
Weber. *Our Congress*
Wilson. *Visual Timeline of Transportation*

Multimedia

CD-ROM

American History Explorer

Her Heritage: A Biographical Encyclopedia of American History

Inside the White House
SkyTrip America
Total History

Video

American Independence
Equal Rights for All
The Life and Times of George Washington

Making It Happen: Masters of Invention
Patrick Henry's Fight for Individual Rights
President's Day

Samuel Adams
U.S. Songs and Poems
United States Constitution
Washington, D.C.

GRADE FIVE

Historical Fiction

Beckman. *From the Ashes*
Brown. *George Washington's Ghost*
Collier. *Jump Ship to Freedom*
Collier. *Who Is Carrie?*
Curry. *Moon Window*

Fritz. *The Cabin Faced West*
Hansen. *The Captive*
Manson. *A Dog Came, Too*
Minahan. *Abigail's Drum*
Monjo. *Grand Papa and Ellen Aroon*

Robinet. *Washington City Is Burning*
West. *Mr. Peale's Bones*
Whelan. *Once on This Island*
Wood. *Becoming Rosemary*

Biography

Adler. *George Washington: Father of Our Country*
Alter. *Eli Whitney*
Anderson. *Martha Washington: First Lady of the Land*
Brill. *John Adams*

Bruns. *George Washington*
Bruns. *Thomas Jefferson*
Clinton. *James Madison: Fourth President*
Coelho. *John Quincy Adams*

Conle. *Benjamin Banneker: Scientist and Mathematician*
D'Aulaire. *Benjamin Franklin*
D'Aulaire. *George Washington*

Davidson. *Dolly Madison: Famous First Lady*

Diamond. *Paul Cuffe: Merchant and Abolitionist*

Diamond. *Prince Hall: Social Reformer*

Dwyer. *John Adams*

Edwards. *Denmark Vesey: Slave Revolt Leader*

Feldman. *Benjamin Franklin: Scientist and Inventor*

Fitz-Gerald. *James Monroe: Fifth President*

Fitz-Gerald. *William Henry Harrison: Ninth President*

Fritz. *The Great Little Madison*

Fritz. *What's the Big Idea, Ben Franklin?*

Giblin. *George Washington*

Giblin. *Thomas Jefferson: A Picture Book Biography*

Hargrove. *Thomas Jefferson: Third President*

Klots. *Richard Allen: Religious Leader and Social Activist*

Landau. *Robert Fulton*

Latham. *Eli Whitney*

Lawson. *Ben and Me*

Leavell. *James Madison*

Lindop. *George Washington, Thomas Jefferson, and Andrew Jackson*

Looby. *Benjamin Franklin*

Marsh. *Martha Washington*

Nardo. *Thomas Jefferson*

O'Brien. *Alexander Hamilton*

Osborne. *Abigail Adams: Women's Rights Advocate*

Osborne. *George Washington: Leader of a New Nation*

Osborne. *The Many Lives of Benjamin Franklin*

Parker. *Benjamin Franklin and Electricity*

Patterson. *Francis Scott Key: Poet and Patriot*

Patterson. *Thomas Jefferson*

Peterson. *Abigail Adams: "Dear Partner"*

Pinkney. *Dear Benjamin Banneker*

Polikoff. *James Madison: 4th President*

Potter. *Benjamin Franklin*

Quiri. *Dolley Madison*

Sabin. *Young Abigail Adams*

Sandak. *The Jeffersons*

Sandak. *The John Adamses*

Sandak. *The Madisons*

Sandak. *The Washingtons*

Stefoff. *James Monroe: 5th President*

Stefoff. *John Adams: 2nd President*

Stefoff. *Thomas Jefferson: 3rd President*

Vail. *Thomas Paine*

Wade. *Benedict Arnold*

Wilson. *The Ingenious Mr. Peale*

Whitcraft. *Francis Scott Key*

Collective Biography

Allen. *As Long as the Rivers Flow: The Stories of Nine Native Americans*

Altman. *Extraordinary Black Americans*

Clements. *The Picture History of Great Inventors*

Cohen. *The Ghosts of War*

Faber. *Great Lives: American Government*

Fleming. *Women of the Lights*

Katz. *Proudly Red and Black: Stories of African and Native Americans*

King. *First Facts About American Heroes*

Pascoe. *First Facts About the Presidents*

Provensen. *The Buck Stops Here: The Presidents*

Provensen. *My Fellow Americans*

Rubel. *The Scholastic Encyclopedia of the Presidents*

History

Blue. *The White House Kids*

Bowler. *Trains*

Burns. *Mail*

Burns. *Money*

Caulkins. *Pets of the Presidents*

Climo. *City! Washington, DC*

Colman. *Toilets, Bathtubs, Sinks, and Sewers*

Davies. *Transport: On Land, Road and Rail*

Emert. *Top Lawyers and Their Famous Cases*

English. *Transportation: Automobiles to Zeppelins*

Giblin. *Be Seated: A Book About Chairs*

Goldish. *Our Supreme Court*

Guiberson. *Lighthouses: Watchers at Sea*

Guzzetti. *The White House*

Hirsch. *Taxation: Paying for Government*

Hoig. *Capital for the Nation*

Johnson. *Our National Symbols*

Kalman. *A Child's Day*

Kalman. *Children's Clothing of the 1800s*

Kalman. *Customs and Traditions*

Kalman. *Early Artisans*

Kalman. *Early Christmas*

Kalman. *Early Health and Medicine*

Kalman. *Early Pleasures and Pastimes*

Kalman. *Early Schools*

Kalman. *Early Stores and Markets*

Kalman. *Early Travel*

Kalman. *Early Village Life*

Kalman. *Games from Long Ago*

Kalman. *Home Crafts*

Kalman. *19th Century Clothing*

Kalman. *Old-Time Toys*

Kalman. *A One-Room School*

Karl. *America Alive: A History*

Kroll. *By the Dawn's Early Light: The Star-Spangled Banner*

Kurtz. *U.S. Army*

Lucas. *Civil Rights: The Long Struggle*

Maestro. *The Story of Money*

Marrin. *1812: The War Nobody Won*

McNeese. *America's Early Canals*

McNeese. *Early River Travel*

Medearis. *Come This Far to Freedom*

Meltzer. *The Black Americans*

Morley. *Clothes: For Work, Play and Display*

Morley. *Exploring North America*
Platt. *The Smithsonian Visual Timeline of Inventions*
Reef. *Mount Vernon*
Reef. *The Supreme Court*
Richards. *Monticello*
Rowland-Warne. *Costume*
Sandler. *Presidents*
Sherrow. *The Big Book of U.S. Presidents*

Shuker-Haines. *Rights and Responsibilities: Using Your Freedom*
Smith-Baranzini. *USKids History: The New American Nation*
St. Pierre. *Our National Anthem*
Steen. *Independence Hall*
Stein. *The Story of the Powers of the Supreme Court*

Steins. *A Nation Is Born: 1700-1820*
Steins. *Our Elections*
Stern. *The Congress: America's Lawmakers*
Warner. *The U.S. Marine Corps*
Weber. *Our Congress*
Whitman. *Get Up and Go: American Road Travel*
Wilson. *Visual Timeline of Transportation*

Multimedia

CD-ROM

American History Explorer
Eyewitness Encyclopedia of Science

Her Heritage: A Biographical Encyclopedia of American History
Inside the White House

Portraits of American Presidents
SkyTrip America
Total History

Video

American Independence
Equal Rights for All
Fort McHenry: Preserving the Spirit of Liberty
The Life and Times of George Washington
Making It Happen: Masters of Invention

A New Nation (1776-1815)
Our Federal Government: The Legislative Branch
Our Federal Government: The Presidency
Our Federal Government: The Supreme Court

Patrick Henry's Fight for Individual Rights
Samuel Adams
U.S. Songs and Poems
United States Constitution
Washington, D.C.

GRADE SIX

Historical Fiction

Beckman. *From the Ashes*
Brady. *Reluctant Hero*
Collier. *The Clock*
Collier. *Jump Ship to Freedom*
Collier. *Who Is Carrie?*
Curry. *Moon Window*

Fleischman. *Coming-and-Going Men*
Fleischman. *Path of the Pale Horse*
Fritz. *The Cabin Faced West*
Hansen. *The Captive*

Lawson. *If Pigs Could Fly*
Robinet. *Washington City Is Burning*
West. *Mr. Peale's Bones*
Whelan. *Once on This Island*
Wood. *Becoming Rosemary*

Biography

Adler. *Remember Betsy Floss: And Other Colonial Riddles*
Beller. *Woman of Independence: The Life of Abigail Adams*
Brill. *John Adams*
Bruns. *George Washington*
Bruns. *Thomas Jefferson*
Clinton. *James Madison: Fourth President*
Conle. *Benjamin Banneker: Scientist and Mathematician*
D'Aulaire. *Benjamin Franklin*
D'Aulaire. *George Washington*

Diamond. *Paul Cuffe: Merchant and Abolitionist*
Diamond. *Prince Hall: Social Reformer*
Dwyer. *John Adams*
Farley. *Samuel Adams: Grandfather of his Country*
Farley. *Thomas Paine: Revolutionary Author*
Feldman. *Benjamin Franklin: Scientist and Inventor*
Fritz. *And Then What Happened, Paul Revere?*
Fritz. *Traitor: The Case of Benedict Arnold*
Fritz. *What's the Big Idea, Ben Franklin?*

Fritz. *Why Don't You Get a Horse, Sam Adams?*
Fritz. *Will You Sign Here, John Hancock?*
Latham. *Carry On, Mr. Bowditch*
Lawson. *Ben and Me*
Lawson. *Mr. Revere and I*
Leavell. *James Madison*
Lindop. *George Washington, Thomas Jefferson, and Andrew Jackson*
Looby. *Benjamin Franklin*
Marsh. *Martha Washington*
Nardo. *Thomas Jefferson*
O'Brien. *Alexander Hamilton*

Osborne. *Abigail Adams:
Women's Rights Advocate*
Osborne. *George
Washington: Leader of a
New Nation*
Osborne. *The Many Lives of
Benjamin Franklin*
Parker. *Benjamin Franklin
and Electricity*

Patterson. *Thomas Jefferson*
Peterson. *Abigail Adams:
"Dear Partner"*
Potter. *Benjamin Franklin*
Sandak. *The Jeffersons*
Sandak. *The John Adamses*
Sandak. *The Washingtons*
Stefoff. *James Monroe: 5th
President*

Stefoff. *John Adams: 2nd
President*
Stefoff. *Thomas Jefferson:
3rd President*
Stewart. *Benjamin Franklin*
Vail. *Thomas Paine*
Wade. *Benedict Arnold*
Zeinert. *The Memoirs of
Andrew Sherburne*

Collective Biography

Allen. *As Long as the Rivers
Flow: The Stories of Nine
Native Americans*
Altman. *Extraordinary Black
Americans*
Beard. *The Presidents in
American History*
Blassingame. *The Look-It-Up
Book of Presidents*
Clements. *The Picture
History of Great Inventors*
Cohen. *The Ghosts of War*

Faber. *Great Lives: American
Government*
Fleming. *Women of the Lights*
Glenn. *Discover America's
Favorite Architects*
Katz. *Proudly Red and Black:
Stories of African and
Native Americans*
King. *First Facts About
American Heroes*
Myers. *Now Is Your Time*

Pascoe. *First Facts About the
Presidents*
Provensen. *The Buck Stops
Here: The Presidents*
Provensen. *My Fellow
Americans*
Rennert. *Pioneers of
Discovery*
Rubel. *The Scholastic
Encyclopedia of the
Presidents*

History

Blue. *The White House Kids*
Bowler. *Trains*
Burns. *Money*
Caulkins. *Pets of the
Presidents*
Climo. *City! Washington, DC*
Colman. *Toilets, Bathtubs,
Sinks, and Sewers*
Davies. *Transport: On Land,
Road and Rail*
Emert. *Top Lawyers and their
Famous Cases*
English. *Transportation:
Automobiles to Zeppelins*
Giblin. *Be Seated: A Book
About Chairs*
Goldish. *Our Supreme Court*
Guiberson. *Lighthouses:
Watchers at Sea*
Guzzetti. *The White House*
Hakim. *From Colonies to
Country*
Hakim. *The New Nation*
Hirsch. *Taxation: Paying for
Government*
Hoig. *Capital for the Nation*
Jaffe. *Who Were the
Founding Fathers?*
Kalman. *Customs and
Traditions*
Kalman. *Early Artisans*
Kalman. *Early Christmas*
Kalman. *Early Health and
Medicine*
Kalman. *Early Schools*

Kalman. *Early Stores and
Markets*
Kalman. *Early Travel*
Kalman. *Early Village Life*
Kalman. *Games from Long
Ago*
Kalman. *Home Crafts*
Kalman. *19th Century
Clothing*
Kalman. *Old-Time Toys*
Kalman. *A One-Room School*
Karl. *America Alive: A
History*
Kroll. *By the Dawn's Early
Light: The Star-Spangled
Banner*
Kurtz. *U.S. Army*
Lucas. *Civil Rights: The Long
Struggle*
Markham. *Inventions That
Changed Modern Life*
Marrin. *1812: The War
Nobody Won*
McNeese. *America's Early
Canals*
McNeese. *Early River Travel*
Medearis. *Come This Far to
Freedom*
Meltzer. *The Black Americans*
Morley. *Clothes: For Work,
Play and Display*
Morley. *Exploring North
America*

Patrick. *The Young Oxford
Companion to the Supreme
Court*
Platt. *The Smithsonian Visual
Timeline of Inventions*
Reef. *Mount Vernon*
Reef. *The Supreme Court*
Rowland-Warne. *Costume*
Sandler. *Presidents*
Shuker-Haines. *Rights and
Responsibilities: Using
Your Freedom*
Smith-Baranzini. *USKids
History: The New
American Nation*
St. George. *The White House:
Cornerstone of a Nation*
St. Pierre. *Our National
Anthem*
Steen. *Independence Hall*
Stein. *The Story of the
Powers of the Supreme
Court*
Steins. *A Nation Is Born:
1700-1820*
Steins. *Our Elections*
Stern. *The Congress:
America's Lawmakers*
Warner. *The U.S. Marine
Corps*
Weber. *Our Congress*
Wheeler. *Events That
Changed American History*
Whitman. *Get Up and Go:
American Road Travel*

Multimedia

CD-ROM

American History Explorer
Campaigns, Candidates and
the Presidency
Eyewitness Encyclopedia of
Science

Her Heritage: A Biographical
Encyclopedia of American
History
Inside the White House

Portraits of American
Presidents
SkyTrip America
Total History
The Way Things Work

Video

American Independence
Choosing a President
Equal Rights for All
Fort McHenry: Preserving
the Spirit of Liberty
The Life and Times of George
Washington
The Life of George
Washington

Making It Happen: Masters
of Invention
A New Nation (1776-1815)
Our Federal Government:
The Legislative Branch
Our Federal Government:
The Presidency
Our Federal Government:
The Supreme Court

Patrick Henry's Fight for
Individual Rights
Reading Terminal Market
Samuel Adams
U.S. Songs and Poems
United States Constitution
Washington, D.C.

THE SETTLING OF THE WEST, NATIVE AMERICANS, AND SEA JOURNEYS, 1775-1916

KINDERGARTEN THROUGH SECOND GRADE

Historical Fiction

Brenner. *Wagon Wheels*
Bunting. *Dandelions*
Bunting. *Train to Somewhere*
Byars. *The Golly Sisters Go West*
Byars. *The Golly Sisters Ride Again*
Byars. *Hooray for the Golly Sisters*
Coerr. *Buffalo Bill and the Pony Express*
Coerr. *The Josefina Story Quilt*
Cross. *Great-Grandma Tells of Threshing Day*
Gerrard. *Rosie and the Rustlers*
Gerrard. *Wagons West!*
Hancock. *Old Blue*
Harvey. *Cassie's Journey: Going West in the 1860s*
Harvey. *My Prairie Christmas*
Harvey. *My Prairie Year*
Hoobler. *Treasure in the Stream: The Story of a Gold Rush Girl*

Howard. *The Cellar*
Howard. *The Chickenhouse House*
Howard. *The Log Cabin Quilt*
Johnson. *Rosamund*
Kinsey-Warnock. *Wilderness Cat*
Kirkpatrick. *Plowie: A Story from the Prairie*
Krupinski. *Bluewater Journal: The Voyage of the Sea Tiger*
Kudlinski. *Earthquake!: A Story of Old San Francisco*
Kudlinski. *Shannon: A Chinatown Adventure, San Francisco, 1880*
Leeuwen. *A Fourth of July on the Plains*
Lemieux. *Full Worm Moon*
Levinson. *Snowshoe Thompson*
Leviton. *Nine for California*
Lydon. *A Birthday for Blue*
Roop. *The Buffalo Jump*
Sanders. *Aurora Means Dawn*

Stanley. *Saving Sweetness*
Sullivan. *Grandpa Was a Cowboy*
Turner. *Dakota Dugout*
Waters. *The Mysterious Horseman: An Adventure in Prairietown, 1836*
Whelan. *Next Spring an Oriole*
Wilder. *Christmas in the Big Woods*
Wilder. *Dance at Grandpa's*
Wilder. *The Deer in the Wood*
Wilder. *Going to Town*
Wilder. *Summertime in the Big Woods*
Wilder. *Winter Days in the Big Woods*
Williams. *Grandma Essie's Covered Wagon*
Wright. *Wagon Train: A Family Goes West in 1865*

Biography

Adler. *A Picture Book of Davy Crockett*
Adler. *A Picture Book of Sitting Bull*
Aliki. *The Story of Johnny Appleseed*
Blair. *Laura Ingalls Wilder*
Blassingame. *Jim Beckwourth: Black Trapper and Indian Chief*
Bruchac. *A Boy Called Slow: The True Story of Sitting Bull*
Christian. *Who'd Believe John Colter?*
Gleiter. *Annie Oakley*
Gleiter. *Kit Carson*
Gleiter. *Sacagawea*

Greene. *Black Elk: A Man with a Vision*
Greene. *Daniel Boone: Man of the Forests*
Greene. *John Chapman: The Man Who Was Johnny Appleseed*
Greene. *John Muir: Man of the Wild Places*
Greene. *Laura Ingalls Wilder*
Jakes. *Susanna of the Alamo*
Kellogg. *Johnny Appleseed*
Kroll. *Lewis and Clark*
Kunstler. *Davy Crockett*
Latham. *Sam Houston: Hero of Texas*
Lattimore. *Frida María: A Story of the Old Southwest*

Miller. *Buffalo Soldiers: The Story of Emanuel Stance*
Miller. *The Story of Nat Love*
Petersen. *Ishi: The Last of His People*
Pinkney. *Bill Pickett: Rodeo-Ridin' Cowboy*
Raphael. *Sacajawea: The Journey West*
Russell. *Along the Santa Fe Trail: Marion Russell's Own Story*
Wilkie. *Daniel Boone: Taming the Wilds*
Winter. *Cowboy Charlie: The Story of Charles M. Russell*

Collective Biography

Marzollo. *My First Book of Biographies*

History

Cobb. *The Quilt-Block History of Pioneer Days*
Duvall. *The Cayuga*
Duvall. *The Chumash*
Duvall. *The Mohawk*
Duvall. *The Oneida*
Duvall. *The Onondaga*
Duvall. *The Penobscot*

Duvall. *The Seneca*
Duvall. *The Tuscarora*
Harness. *The Amazing Impossible Erie Canal*
Harness. *They're Off: The Story of the Pony Express*

Krensky. *Striking It Rich: The Story of the California Gold Rush*
Lepthien. *The Mandans*
Medearis. *Our People*
Rounds. *Sod Houses on the Great Plains*
Sneve. *The Cheyennes*

Multimedia

Video

Song of Sacajawea
Native American Life

United States Expansion

GRADE THREE

Historical Fiction

Antle. *Beautiful Land: A Story of the Oklahoma Land Rush*
Armstrong. *Black-Eyed Susan*
Bader. *Golden Quest*
Berleth. *Mary Patten's Voyage*
Brenner. *Wagon Wheels*
Bunting. *Dandelions*
Bunting. *Train to Somewhere*
Byars. *The Golly Sisters Go West*
Byars. *The Golly Sisters Ride Again*
Byars. *Hooray for the Golly Sisters*
Coerr. *Buffalo Bill and the Pony Express*
Coerr. *The Josefina Story Quilt*
Cross. *Great-Grandma Tells of Threshing Day*
Fleischman. *Humbug Mountain*
Gerrard. *Rosie and the Rustlers*
Gerrard. *Wagons West!*
Goldin. *Red Means Good Fortune: A Story of San Francisco's Chinatown*
Gregory. *Earthquake at Dawn*
Gregory. *The Legend of Jimmy Spoon*
Hancock. *Old Blue*

Harvey. *Cassie's Journey: Going West in the 1860s*
Harvey. *My Prairie Christmas*
Harvey. *My Prairie Year*
Henry. *A Clearing in the Forest*
Hilts. *Timmy O'Dowd and the Big Ditch*
Hoobler. *Treasure in the Stream: The Story of a Gold Rush Girl*
Howard. *The Cellar*
Howard. *The Chickenhouse House*
Johnson. *Rosamund*
Kinsey-Warnock. *Wilderness Cat*
Kirkpatrick. *Plowie: A Story from the Prairie*
Krupinski. *Bluewater Journal: The Voyage of the Sea Tiger*
Kudlinski. *Earthquake!: A Story of Old San Francisco*
Kudlinski. *Facing West: A Story of the Oregon Trail*
Kudlinski. *Lone Star: A Story of the Texas Rangers*
Kudlinski. *Shannon: A Chinatown Adventure, San Francisco, 1880*
Lawlor. *Addie Across the Prairie*

Lawlor. *Addie's Dakota Winter*
Lawlor. *Addie's Long Summer*
Lawlor. *George on His Own*
Leeuwen. *A Fourth of July on the Plains*
Lemieux. *Full Worm Moon*
Levinson. *Snowshoe Thompson*
Levitin. *Nine for California*
Love. *Bess's Log Cabin Quilt*
Lydon. *A Birthday for Blue*
MacBride. *In the Land of the Big Red Apple*
MacBride. *Little Farm in the Ozarks*
MacBride. *Little House on Rocky Ridge*
MacBride. *Little Town in the Ozarks*
MacLachlan. *Sarah, Plain and Tall*
MacLachlan. *Skylark*
Rawls. *Dame Shirley and the Gold Rush*
Roop. *The Buffalo Jump*
Sanders. *Aurora Means Dawn*
Shura. *Kate's Book*
Stanley. *Saving Sweetness*
Steele. *The Buffalo Knife*
Steele. *Flaming Arrows*
Steele. *The Lone Hunt*
Steele. *Tomahawk Border*
Steele. *Trail Through Danger*

Steele. *Wilderness Journey*
Steele. *Winter Danger*
Stevens. *Trouble for Lucy*
Sullivan. *Grandpa Was a Cowboy*
Turner. *Dakota Dugout*
Waters. *The Mysterious Horseman: An Adventure in Prairietown, 1836*
Whelan. *Hannah*
Whelan. *The Indian School*

Whelan. *Next Spring an Oriole*
Whelan. *Night of the Full Moon*
Wilder. *By the Shores of Silver Lake*
Wilder. *Farmer Boy*
Wilder. *The First Four Years*
Wilder. *Little House in the Big Woods*
Wilder. *Little House on the Prairie*

Wilder. *Little Town on the Prairie*
Wilder. *On the Banks of Plum Creek*
Wilder. *The Long Winter*
Wilkes. *Little House in Brookfield*
Woodruff. *Dear Levi: Letters from the Overland Trail*
Wright. *Wagon Train: A Family Goes West in 1865*

Biography

Adler. *A Picture Book of Davy Crockett*
Adler. *A Picture Book of Sitting Bull*
Aliki. *The Story of Johnny Appleseed*
Anderson. *John James Audubon: Wildlife Artist*
Blair. *Laura Ingalls Wilder*
Blassingame. *Jim Beckwourth: Black Trapper and Indian Chief*
Bruchac. *A Boy Called Slow: The True Story of Sitting Bull*
Christian. *Who'd Believe John Colter?*
Doss. *Plenty Coups*
Fleischman. *Townsend's Warbler*
Fraser. *In Search of the Grand Canyon: John Wesley Powell*
Gleiter. *Annie Oakley*
Gleiter. *Kit Carson*
Gleiter. *Sacagawea*
Graves. *Annie Oakey: The Shooting Star*
Greene. *Black Elk: A Man with a Vision*
Greene. *Daniel Boone: Man of the Forests*

Greene. *John Chapman: The Man Who Was Johnny Appleseed*
Greene. *John Muir: Man of the Wild Places*
Greene. *Laura Ingalls Wilder*
Hilts. *Quanah Parker*
Jakes. *Susanna of the Alamo*
Jeffery. *Geronimo*
Jeffredo-Warden. *Ishi*
Kellogg. *Johnny Appleseed*
Kent. *Geronimo*
Kent. *Tecumseh*
Knight. *The Way West: Journal of a Pioneer Woman*
Kroll. *Lewis and Clark*
Kunstler. *Davy Crockett*
Kvasnicka. *Hole-in-the-Day*
Lasky. *Searching for Laura Ingalls: A Reader's Journey*
Latham. *David Farragut*
Latham. *Sam Houston: Hero of Texas*
Lattimore. *Frida María: A Story of the Old Southwest*
Lawlor. *The Real Johnny Appleseed*
Low. *John Ross*
Luce. *Jim Bridger: Man of the Mountains*

Miller. *Buffalo Soldiers: The Story of Emanuel Stance*
Miller. *The Story of Nat Love*
Morrow. *Sarah Winnemucca*
Moseley. *Davy Crockett: Hero of the Wild Frontier*
Petersen. *Ishi: The Last of His People*
Pinkney. *Bill Pickett: Rodeo-Ridin' Cowboy*
Plain. *George Catlin*
Raphael. *Daniel Boone: Frontier Hero*
Raphael. *Sacajawea: The Journey West*
Rowland. *The Story of Sacajawea: Guide to Lewis and Clark*
Russell. *Along the Santa Fe Trail: Marion Russell's Own Story*
Stine. *The Story of Laura Ingalls Wilder*
Talmadge. *John Muir: At Home in the Wild*
Viola. *Osceola*
Viola. *Sitting Bull*
Wilkie. *Daniel Boone: Taming the Wilds*
Winter. *Cowboy Charlie: The Story of Charles M. Russell*

Collective Biography

Duncan. *People of the West*

King. *First Facts About American Heroes*

Marzollo. *My First Book of Biographies*

History

Baldwin. *New England Whaler*
Bowler. *Trains*
Burby. *The Pueblo Indians*
Burns. *Mail*
Carlson. *Westward Ho!: An Activity Guide to the Wild West*
Carrick. *Whaling Days*
Claro. *The Apache Indians*

Claro. *The Cherokee Indians*
Climo. *City! San Francisco*
Cobb. *The Quilt-Block History of Pioneer Days*
Coote. *The Sailor Through History*
Duncan. *The West: An Illustrated History for Children*
Duvall. *The Cayuga*

Duvall. *The Chumash*
Duvall. *The Mohawk*
Duvall. *The Oneida*
Duvall. *The Onondaga*
Duvall. *The Penobscot*
Duvall. *The Seneca*
Duvall. *The Tuscarora*
English. *Transportation: Automobiles to Zeppelins*
Fraser. *Sanctuary*

Harness. *The Amazing Impossible Erie Canal*
Harness. *They're Off: The Story of the Pony Express*
Humble. *Ships*
Jackson. *The Winter Solstice*
Kalman. *Children's Clothing of the 1800s*
Kalman. *Customs and Traditions*
Kalman. *Early Artisans*
Kalman. *Early Christmas*
Kalman. *The Early Family Home*
Kalman. *Early Farm Life*
Kalman. *Early Health and Medicine*
Kalman. *Early Loggers and the Sawmill*
Kalman. *Early Schools*
Kalman. *Early Settler Storybook*
Kalman. *Early Stores and Markets*
Kalman. *Early Travel*
Kalman. *Early Village Life*
Kalman. *Food for the Settler*

Kalman. *Fort Life*
Kalman. *Games from Long Ago*
Kalman. *The Grist Mill*
Kalman. *Home Crafts*
Kalman. *The Kitchen*
Kalman. *19th Century Clothing*
Kalman. *Old-Time Toys*
Kalman. *A One-Room School*
Kalman. *Settler Sayings*
Kalman. *Tools and Gadgets*
Ketchum. *The Gold Rush*
Koslow. *The Seminole Indians*
Krensky. *Striking It Rich: The Story of the California Gold Rush*
Kroll. *Pony Express!*
Landau. *The Hopi*
Lepthien. *The Mandans*
Lincoln. *The Pirate's Handbook*
Maestro. *The Story of Money*
McDaniel. *The Powhatan Indians*
Medearis. *Our People*

Mooney. *The Comanche Indians*
Murdoch. *Cowboy*
O'Neill. *Wounded Knee*
Patent. *West by Covered Wagon*
Roessel. *Songs from the Loom: A Navajo Girl Learns to Weave*
Roop. *Off the Map: The Journals of Lewis and Clark*
Rounds. *Sod Houses on the Great Plains*
Silverstein. *The Alamo*
Sneve. *The Cherokees*
Sneve. *The Cheyennes*
Sneve. *The Hopis*
Sneve. *The Navajos*
Sneve. *The Nez Perce*
Sneve. *The Seminoles*
Sneve. *The Sioux*
Wilson. *Visual Timeline of Transportation*
Wood. *The Crow Indians*
Wood. *The Navajo Indians*

Multimedia

Video

Bright Eyes: Susette La Flesche Tibbles
Dr. Susan La Flesche Picotte
Family Life: Multiculturalism
Indians of the Northwest
Indians of the Plains

Indians of the Southeast
Indians of the Southwest
Native American Life
Sacajawea
Silent Communications: Trail Signs/Sign Language

Song of Sacajawea
United States Expansion
Westward Wagons

GRADE FOUR

Historical Fiction

Antle. *Beautiful Land: A Story of the Oklahoma Land Rush*
Armstrong. *Black-Eyed Susan*
Auch. *Journey to Nowhere*
Bader. *Golden Quest*
Beatty. *Hail Columbia*
Beatty. *Just Some Weeds from the Wilderness*
Beatty. *Lacy Makes a Match*
Beatty. *O the Red Rose Tree*
Beatty. *Red Rock over the River*
Beatty. *Something to Shout About*
Beatty. *That's One Ornery Orphan*

Berleth. *Mary Patten's Voyage*
Brink. *Caddie Woodlawn*
Bunting. *Dandelions*
Bunting. *Train to Somewhere*
Byars. *The Golly Sisters Ride Again*
Cross. *Great-Grandma Tells of Threshing Day*
Fleischman. *The Ghost in the Noonday Sun*
Fleischman. *Humbug Mountain*
Fleischman. *Jim Ugly*
Fleischman. *Mr. Mysterious & Co.*
Gipson. *Old Yeller*

Goldin. *Red Means Good Fortune*
Gregory. *Earthquake at Dawn*
Gregory. *The Legend of Jimmy Spoon*
Gregory. *The Stowaway: A Tale of California Pirates*
Hahn. *The Gentleman Outlaw and Me—Eli: A Story of the Old West*
Harvey. *Cassie's Journey: Going West in the 1860s*
Henry. *A Clearing in the Forest*
Hilts. *Timmy O'Dowd and the Big Ditch*
Holland. *The Journey Home*

Holmes. *Year of the Sevens 1777*
Hoobler. *Treasure in the Stream*
Howard. *The Cellar*
Howard. *The Chickenhouse House*
Karr. *Go West, Young Women!*
Keehn. *I Am Regina*
Kudlinski. *Earthquake!*
Kudlinski. *Facing West: A Story of the Oregon Trail*
Kudlinski. *Lone Star: A Story of the Texas Rangers*
Kudlinski. *Shannon: A Chinatown Adventure, San Francisco, 1880*
Lawlor. *Addie Across the Prairie*
Lawlor. *Addie's Dakota Winter*
Lawlor. *Addie's Long Summer*
Lawlor. *George on His Own*
Lawlor. *Gold in the Hills*
Leland. *Sallie Fox: The Story of a Pioneer Girl*
Love. *Bess's Log Cabin Quilt*
MacBride. *In the Land of the Big Red Apple*
MacBride. *Little Farm in the Ozarks*
MacBride. *Little House on Rocky Ridge*

MacBride. *Little Town in the Ozarks*
MacLachlan. *Sarah, Plain and Tall*
MacLachlan. *Skylark*
Paulsen. *Call Me Francis Tucker*
Rawls. *Dame Shirley and the Gold Rush*
Rockwood. *Groundhog's Horse*
Roop. *The Buffalo Jump*
Sanders. *Aurora Means Dawn*
Scott. *The Covered Wagon and Other Adventures*
Shaw. *Changes for Kirsten*
Shura. *Kate's Book*
Shura. *Kate's House*
Steele. *Flaming Arrows*
Steele. *The Buffalo Knife*
Steele. *The Lone Hunt*
Steele. *The Man with the Silver Eyes*
Steele. *Tomahawk Border*
Steele. *Trail Through Danger*
Steele. *Wilderness Journey*
Steele. *Winter Danger*
Stevens. *Trouble for Lucy*
Stewart. *On the Long Trail Home*
Sullivan. *Grandpa Was a Cowboy*
Toht. *Sodbuster*
Tunbo. *Stay Put, Robbie McAmis*

Turner. *Grasshopper Summer*
Van Leeuwen. *Bound for Oregon*
Waters. *The Mysterious Horseman*
Weitzman. *Thrashin' Time*
Whelan. *Hannah*
Whelan. *The Indian School*
Whelan. *Next Spring an Oriole*
Whelan. *Night of the Full Moon*
Wilder. *By the Shores of Silver Lake*
Wilder. *Farmer Boy*
Wilder. *The First Four Years*
Wilder. *Little House in the Big Woods*
Wilder. *Little House on the Prairie*
Wilder. *Little Town on the Prairie*
Wilder. *The Long Winter*
Wilder. *On the Banks of Plum Creek*
Wilder. *On the Way Home*
Wilkes. *Little House in Brookfield*
Wisler. *Jericho's Journey*
Woodruff. *Dear Levi: Letters from the Overland Trail*
Wright. *Wagon Train: A Family Goes West in 1865*

Biography

Anderson. *Charles Eastman*
Anderson. *John James Audubon: Wildlife Artist*
Anderson. *Laura Ingalls Wilder*
Blair. *Laura Ingalls Wilder*
Blassingame. *Jim Beckwourth: Black Trapper and Indian Chief*
Brown. *Sacagawea*
Brown. *Susette La Flesche*
Bruchac. *A Boy Called Slow: The True Story of Sitting Bull*
Chrisman. *David Farragut*
Christian. *Who'd Believe John Colter?*
Collins. *Pioneer Plowmaker: John Deere*
Connell. *These Lands Are Ours: Tecumseh's Fight*
Conrad. *Prairie Visions: Solomon Butcher*
Doss. *Plenty Coups*

Fleischman. *Townsend's Warbler*
Foster. *David Farragut*
Fraser. *In Search of the Grand Canyon: John Wesley Powell*
Fritz. *Make Way for Sam Houston*
Graves. *Annie Oakey: The Shooting Star*
Green. *Allan Pinkerton*
Green. *Bat Masterson*
Green. *Belle Star*
Green. *Billy the Kid*
Green. *Butch Cassidy*
Green. *The Dalton Gang*
Green. *Doc Holliday*
Green. *Jesse James*
Green. *Judge Roy Bean*
Green. *Wild Bill Hickock*
Green. *Wyatt Earp*
Greene. *Black Elk: A Man with a Vision*

Greene. *Daniel Boone: Man of the Forests*
Hilts. *Quanah Parker*
Jakes. *Susanna of the Alamo*
Jeffery. *Geronimo*
Jeffredo-Warden. *Ishi*
Jumper. *Osceola: Patriot and Warrior*
Kellogg. *Johnny Appleseed*
Kent. *Geronimo*
Kent. *Tecumseh*
Klausner. *Sequoyah's Gift*
Knight. *The Way West: Journal of a Pioneer Woman*
Kroll. *Lewis and Clark*
Kunstler. *Davy Crockett*
Kvasnicka. *Hole-in-the-Day*
Lasky. *Searching for Laura Ingalls: A Reader's Journey*
Latham. *David Farragut*
Latham. *Sam Houston: Hero of Texas*

Lattimore. *Frida María: A Story of the Old Southwest*

Lawlor. *Daniel Boone*

Lawlor. *The Real Johnny Appleseed*

Low. *John Ross*

Luce. *Jim Bridger: Man of the Mountains*

Miller. *Buffalo Soldiers: The Story of Emanuel Stance*

Morrow. *Sarah Winnemucca*

Moseley. *Davy Crockett: Hero of the Wild Frontier*

Naden. *John Muir: Saving the Wilderness*

Petersen. *Ishi: The Last of His People*

Plain. *George Catlin*

Quiri. *Dolley Madison*

Raphael. *Daniel Boone: Frontier Hero*

Roop. *Capturing Nature: John James Audubon*

Rowland. *The Story of Sacajawea: Guide to Lewis and Clark*

Sanford. *Bill Pickett: African-American Rodeo Star*

Sanford. *Brigham Young: Pioneer and Mormon Leader*

Sanford. *Buffalo Bill Cody: Showman of the Wild West*

Sanford. *Calamity Jane: A Frontier Original*

Sanford. *Daniel Boone: Wilderness Pioneer*

Sanford. *Davy Crockett: Defender of the Alamo*

Sanford. *John C. Frémont: Soldier and Pathfinder*

Sanford. *Kit Carson: Frontier Scout*

Sanford. *Sam Houston: Texas Hero*

Sanford. *Zebulon Pike: Explorer of the Southwest*

Stanley. *The True Adventure of Daniel Hall*

Stevenson. *Sitting Bull: Dakota Boy*

Stine. *The Story of Laura Ingalls Wilder*

Talmadge. *John Muir: At Home in the Wild*

Viola. *Osceola*

Viola. *Sitting Bull*

Wadsworth. *John Muir: Wilderness Protector*

Weidt. *Mr. Blue Jeans: Levi Strauss*

Weitzman. *The Mountain Man and the President*

Wheeler. *The Story of Sequoyah*

Wilkie. *Daniel Boone: Taming the Wilds*

Winter. *Cowboy Charlie: The Story of Charles M. Russell*

Collective Biography

Alter. *Women of the Old West*

Duncan. *People of the West*

Jacobs. *Great Lives*: *World Religions*

King. *First Facts About American Heroes*

Provensen. *My Fellow Americans*

Reef. *Black Fighting Men: A Proud History*

History

Abbink. *Missions of the Monterey Bay Area*

Alter. *Growing Up in the Old West*

Baldwin. *New England Whaler*

Behrens, June. *Missions of the Central Coast*

Bial. *Frontier Home*

Bowler. *Trains*

Blumberg. *The Incredible Journey of Lewis and Clark*

Burby. *The Pueblo Indians*

Burns. *Mail*

Burns. *Money*

Carlson. *A Historical Album of Minnesota*

Carlson. *Westward Ho!: An Activity Guide to the Wild West*

Carrick. *Whaling Days*

Carter. *Last Stand at the Alamo*

Carter. *The Mexican War: Manifest Destiny*

Carter. *The Spanish-American War: Imperial Ambitions*

Chrisp. *The Whalers*

Claro. *The Apache Indians*

Claro. *The Cherokee Indians*

Climo. *City! San Francisco*

Cobb. *The Quilt-Block History of Pioneer Days*

Cocke. *A Historical Album of Washington*

Cohen. *The Alaska Purchase*

Coote. *The Sailor Through History*

Cory. *Pueblo Indian*

Deem. *How to Make a Mummy Talk*

Di Certo. *The Pony Express: Hoofbeats in the Wilderness*

Doubleday. *Salt Lake City*

Duggleby. *Impossible Quests*

Duncan. *The West: An Illustrated History for Children*

Duvall. *The Cayuga*

Duvall. *The Chumash*

Duvall. *The Mohawk*

Duvall. *The Oneida*

Duvall. *The Onondaga*

Duvall. *The Penobscot*

Duvall. *The Seneca*

Duvall. *The Tuscarora*

English. *Transportation: Automobiles to Zeppelins*

Fraser. *Sanctuary*

Fraser. *Ten Mile Day: The Transcontinental Railroad*

Freedman. *An Indian Winter*

Fry. *The Orphan Train*

Giblin. *Be Seated: A Book About Chairs*

Gourley. *Hunting Neptune's Giants: American Whaling*

Hahn. *The Blackfoot*

Harness. *The Amazing Impossible Erie Canal*

Harness. *They're Off: The Story of the Pony Express*

Hicks. *The Sioux*

Humble. *Ships*

Jackson. *The Winter Solstice*

Kalman. *Children's Clothing of the 1800s*

Kalman. *Customs and Traditions*

Kalman. *Early Artisans*

Kalman. *Early Christmas*

Kalman. *The Early Family Home*

Kalman. *Early Farm Life*

Kalman. *Early Health and Medicine*
Kalman. *Early Loggers and the Sawmill*
Kalman. *Early Pleasures and Pastimes*
Kalman. *Early Schools*
Kalman. *Early Settler Storybook*
Kalman. *Early Stores and Markets*
Kalman. *Early Travel*
Kalman. *Early Village Life*
Kalman. *Food for the Settler*
Kalman. *Fort Life*
Kalman. *Games from Long Ago*
Kalman. *The Grist Mill*
Kalman. *Home Crafts*
Kalman. *The Kitchen*
Kalman. *19th Century Clothing*
Kalman. *Old-Time Toys*
Kalman. *A One-Room School*
Kalman. *Settler Sayings*
Kalman. *Tools and Gadgets*
Kerr. *Keeping Clean*
Ketchum. *The Gold Rush*
Klausmeier. *Cowboy*
Koslow. *The Seminole Indians*
Krensky. *Striking It Rich: The Story of the California Gold Rush*
Kroll. *Pony Express!*
Kurtz. *U.S. Army*
Lampton. *Epidemic*
Landau. *The Hopi*
Lavender. *The Santa Fe Trail*
Lavender. *Snowbound: The Tragic Story of the Donner Party*
Lee. *San Antonio*
Lemke. *Missions of the Southern Coast [California]*
Lepthien. *The Mandans*
Lincoln. *The Pirate's Handbook*
Lodge. *The Cheyenne*
Lodge. *The Comanche*
MacMillan. *Missions of the Los Angeles Area*

Maestro. *The Story of Money*
McDaniel. *The Powhatan Indians*
McGrath. *The Lewis and Clark Expedition*
McNeese. *America's Early Canals*
McNeese. *America's First Railroads*
McNeese. *Clippers and Whaling Ships*
McNeese. *Conestogas and Stagecoaches*
McNeese. *Early River Travel*
McNeese. *From Trails to Turnpikes*
McNeese. *West by Steamboat*
Meltzer. *Gold*
Miller. *Buffalo Gals*
Mooney. *The Comanche Indians*
Murdoch. *Cowboy*
Murdoch. *North American Indian*
Nelson. *Bull Whackers to Whistle Punks: Logging in the Old West*
Nirgiotis. *Erie Canal: Gateway to the West*
O'Neill. *Wounded Knee*
Patent. *West by Covered Wagon*
Pollard. *The Nineteenth Century*
Roessel. *Songs from the Loom: A Navajo Girl Learns to Weave*
Roop. *Off the Map: The Journals of Lewis and Clark*
Ross. *Bandits & Outlaws*
Rowland-Warne. *Costume*
Ryan. *Explorers and Mapmakers*
Savage. *Cowboys and Cow Towns of the Wild West*
Savage. *Gold Miners of the Wild West*
Savage. *Gunfighters of the Wild West*

Savage. *Pioneering Women of the Wild West*
Savage. *Pony Express Riders of the Wild West*
Savage. *Scouts of the Wild West*
Sherrow. *The Nez Perces*
Silverstein. *The Alamo*
Sita. *The Rattle and the Drum*
Smith. *A Historical Album of Kentucky*
Smith-Baranzini. *Book of the American Indians*
Sneve. *The Cherokees*
Sneve. *The Cheyennes*
Sneve. *The Hopis*
Sneve. *The Navajos*
Sneve. *The Nez Perce*
Sneve. *The Seminoles*
Sneve. *The Sioux*
Swanson. *Buffalo Sunrise: The Story of a North American Giant*
Ventura. *Food: Its Evolution Through the Ages*
White. *Missions of the San Francisco Bay Area*
Wills. *The Battle of Little Bighorn*
Wills. *A Historical Album of Alabama*
Wills. *A Historical Album of California*
Wills. *A Historical Album of Connecticut*
Wills. *A Historical Album of Florida*
Wills. *A Historical Album of Illinois*
Wills. *A Historical Album of Nebraska*
Wills. *A Historical Album of Oregon*
Wills. *A Historical Album of Texas*
Wilson. *Visual Timeline of Transportation*
Wood. *The Crow Indians*
Wood. *The Navajo Indians*
Yancey. *Desperadoes and Dynamite: Train Robbery*

Multimedia

CD-ROM

Her Heritage: A Biographical Encyclopedia of American History

SkyTrip America
Total History

Video

The Apache
Birth of a Community: Jews and the Gold Rush
Bright Eyes: Susette La Flesche Tibbles
Candlemaking
The Cherokee
The Cheyenne
The Chinook
The Creek
The Crow
Dr. Susan La Flesche Picotte
Family Life: Multiculturalism
Heritage of the Black West
A History of Native Americans
The Huron
Indians of California
Indians of the Northwest
Indians of the Plains
Indians of the Southeast
Indians of the Southwest

Kentucky Rifle
The Lenape
The Loom
Men of the Frontier
The Menominee
Mining Made the West
Mississippi Steamboats
Mountain Men
The Narragansett
Native American Life
Native Americans: The History of a People
Native Americans: People of the Desert
Native Americans: People of the Forest
Native Americans: People of the Plains
The Navajo
Placer Gold
Pony Express

The Potawatomi
Prairie Cabin: A Norwegian Pioneer Woman's Story
Pueblo
Railroads on the Frontier
Rancho Life
Sacajawea
The Seminole
Settlers of the West
Silent Communications: Trail Signs/Sign Language
Song of Sacajawea
Spinning Wheel
Stagecoach West
This World Is Not Our Home
United States Expansion
Westward Wagons
Women of the West
The Yankton Sioux

GRADE FIVE

Historical Fiction

Antle. *Beautiful Land: A Story of the Oklahoma Land Rush*
Armstrong. *Black-Eyed Susan*
Auch. *Journey to Nowhere*
Bader. *Golden Quest*
Beatty. *Behave Yourself, Bethany Brant*
Beatty. *Bonanza Girl*
Beatty. *By Crumbs, It's Mine!*
Beatty. *The Coach That Never Came*
Beatty. *Hail Columbia*
Beatty. *How Many Miles to Sundown?*
Beatty. *Jonathan Down Under*
Beatty. *Just Some Weeds from the Wilderness*
Beatty. *Lacy Makes a Match*
Beatty. *A Long Way to Whiskey Creek*
Beatty. *Melinda Takes a Hand.*
Beatty. *The Nickel-Plated Beauty*
Beatty. *O the Red Rose Tree*
Beatty. *Red Rock over the River*
Beatty. *Sarah and Me and the Lady from the Sea*

Beatty. *Something to Shout About*
Beatty. *That's One Ornery Orphan*
Berleth. *Mary Patten's Voyage*
Brink. *Caddie Woodlawn*
Conrad. *Prairie Songs*
Cross. *Great-Grandma Tells of Threshing Day*
Cushman. *The Ballad of Lucy Whipple*
DeFelice. *Weasel*
Donahue. *The Valley in Between*
Duey. *Anisett Lundberg: California, 1851*
Fleischman. *The Ghost in the Noonday Sun*
Fleischman. *Jim Ugly*
Fleischman. *Humbug Mountain*
Fleischman. *Mr. Mysterious & Co.*
Gipson. *Old Yeller*
Goldin. *Red Means Good Fortune*
Gregory. *Earthquake at Dawn*
Gregory. *Jenny of the Tetons*
Gregory. *Jimmy Spoon and the Pony Express*

Gregory. *The Legend of Jimmy Spoon*
Gregory. *The Stowaway: A Tale of California Pirates*
Hahn. *The Gentleman Outlaw and Me—Eli: A Story of the Old West*
Henry. *A Clearing in the Forest*
Hilts. *Timmy O'Dowd and the Big Ditch*
Holland. *The Journey Home*
Holmes. *Year of the Sevens 1777*
Hoobler. *Treasure in the Stream*
Karr. *Go West, Young Women!*
Karr. *Phoebe's Folly*
Keehn. *I Am Regina*
Kherdian. *Bridger: The Story of a Mountain Man*
Kudlinski. *Earthquake!: A Story of Old San Francisco*
Kudlinski. *Facing West: A Story of the Oregon Trail*
Kudlinski. *Lone Star: A Story of the Texas Rangers*
Kudlinski. *Shannon: A Chinatown Adventure, San Francisco, 1880*

Lawlor. *Addie Across the Prairie*

Lawlor. *Addie's Dakota Winter*

Lawlor. *Addie's Long Summer*

Lawlor. *George on His Own*

Lawlor. *Gold in the Hills*

Leland. *Sallie Fox: The Story of a Pioneer Girl*

Lenski. *Indian Captive: The Story of Mary Jemison*

Love. *Bess's Log Cabin Quilt*

Lyon. *Here and Then*

MacBride. *In the Land of the Big Red Apple*

MacBride. *Little House on Rocky Ridge*

MacBride. *Little Town in the Ozarks*

MacBride. *Little Farm in the Ozarks*

MacLachlan. *Sarah, Plain and Tall*

MacLachlan. *Skylark*

Mazzio. *Leaving Eldorado*

McClung. *The True Adventures of Grizzly Adams*

Moeri. *Save Queen of Sheba*

Morrow. *On to Oregon!*

Myers. *The Righteous Revenge of Artemis Bonner*

Nixon. *Caught in the Act: The Orphan Quartet Two*

O'Dell. *Island of the Blue Dolphins*

O'Dell. *Sing Down the Moon*

O'Dell. *Zia*

Paulsen. *Call Me Francis Tucker*

Paulsen. *Tucket's Ride*

Rawls. *Dame Shirley and the Gold Rush*

Rockwood. *Groundhog's Horse*

Sanders. *Aurora Means Dawn*

Scott. *The Covered Wagon and Other Adventures*

Shaw. *Changes for Kirsten*

Shura. *Kate's Book*

Shura. *Kate's House*

Steele. *The Buffalo Knife*

Steele. *Flaming Arrows*

Steele. *The Lone Hunt*

Steele. *The Man with the Silver Eyes*

Steele. *Tomahawk Border*

Steele. *Trail Through Danger*

Steele. *Wilderness Journey*

Steele. *Winter Danger*

Stevens. *Trouble for Lucy*

Stewart. *On the Long Trail Home*

Taylor. *Walking Up a Rainbow*

Toht. *Sodbuster*

Tunbo. *Stay Put, Robbie McAmis*

Turner. *Grasshopper Summer*

Van Leeuwen. *Bound for Oregon*

Weitzman. *Thrashin' Time*

Whelan. *Hannah*

Whelan. *The Indian School*

Whelan. *Night of the Full Moon*

Wilder. *By the Shores of Silver Lake*

Wilder. *Farmer Boy*

Wilder. *The First Four Years*

Wilder. *Little House in the Big Woods*

Wilder. *Little House on the Prairie*

Wilder. *Little Town on the Prairie*

Wilder. *The Long Winter*

Wilder. *On the Banks of Plum Creek*

Wilder. *On the Way Home*

Wilder. *These Happy Golden Years*

Wilkes. *Little House in Brookfield*

Wilson. *Earthquake!*

Wisler. *Jericho's Journey*

Woodruff. *Dear Levi: Letters from the Overland Trail*

Biography

Anderson. *Charles Eastman*

Anderson. *John James Audubon: Wildlife Artist*

Anderson. *Laura Ingalls Wilder*

Badt. *Charles Eastman: Sioux Physician and Author*

Bernotas. *Sitting Bull: Chief of the Sioux*

Black. *Sitting Bull and the Battle of the Little Bighorn*

Bland. *Osceola: Seminole Rebel*

Bland. *Pontiac: Ottawa Rebel*

Blassingame. *Jim Beckwourth: Black Trapper and Indian Chief*

Bolton. *Joseph Brant: Mohawk Chief*

Bonvillain. *Black Hawk: Sac Rebel*

Brown. *Sacagawea*

Brown. *Susette La Flesche*

Bruchac. *A Boy Called Slow: The True Story of Sitting Bull*

Carlson. *Harriet Tubman: Call to Freedom*

Cavan. *Daniel Boone and the Opening of the Ohio Country*

Chrisman. *David Farragut*

Christian. *Who'd Believe John Colter?*

Collins. *Pioneer Plowmaker: John Deere*

Connell. *These Lands Are Ours: Tecumseh's Fight*

Conrad. *Prairie Visions: Solomon Butcher*

Cox. *Mark Twain*

Cwiklik. *Sequoyah and the Cherokee Alphabet*

Cwiklik. *Tecumseh: Shawnee Rebel*

Dolan. *James Beckwourth: Frontiersman*

Doss. *Plenty Coups*

Faber. *Calamity Jane: Her Life and Her Legend*

Ferris. *Native American Doctor: The Story of Susan La Flesche Picotte*

Fitz-Gerald. *Meriwether Lewis and William Clark*

Fleischman. *Townsend's Warbler*

Force. *John Muir*

Foster. *David Farragut*

Fox. *Chief Joseph of the Nez Perce Indians*

Fraser. *In Search of the Grand Canyon: John Wesley Powell*

Fritz. *Make Way for Sam Houston*

Gaines. *John Wesley Powell and the Great Surveys of the American West*

Graves. *Annie Oakey: The Shooting Star*

Green. *Allan Pinkerton*

Green. *Bat Masterson*

Green. *Belle Star*

Green. *Billy the Kid*

Green. *Butch Cassidy*

Green. *The Dalton Gang*
Green. *Doc Holliday*
Green. *Jesse James*
Green. *Judge Roy Bean*
Green. *Wild Bill Hickock*
Green. *Wyatt Earp*
Guttmacher. *Crazy Horse: Sioux War Chief*
Harris. *John Charles Frémont and the Great Western Reconnaissance*
Henry. *Everyone Wears His Name: A Biography of Levi Strauss*
Hilts. *Quanah Parker*
Holler. *Pocahontas: Powhatan Peacemaker*
Jeffery. *Geronimo*
Jeffredo-Warden. *Ishi*
Jumper. *Osceola: Patriot and Warrior*
Kent. *Geronimo*
Kent. *Tecumseh*
Klausner. *Sequoyah's Gift*
Knight. *The Way West: Journal of a Pioneer Woman*
Kroll. *Lewis and Clark*
Kunstler. *Davy Crockett*
Kvasnicka. *Hole-in-the-Day*
Lasky. *Searching for Laura Ingalls: A Reader's Journey*
Latham. *David Farragut*
Latham. *Sam Houston: Hero of Texas*
Lawlor. *Daniel Boone*
Lawlor. *The Real Johnny Appleseed*
Ledbetter. *John Muir*
Low. *John Ross*
Luce. *Jim Bridger: Man of the Mountains*
McClung. *The True Adventures of Grizzly Adams*
Morrow. *Sarah Winnemucca*
Moseley. *Davy Crockett: Hero of the Wild Frontier*
Naden. *John Muir: Saving the Wilderness*
O'Rear. *Charles Goodnight: Pioneer Cowman*
Plain. *George Catlin*

Petersen. *Ishi: The Last of His People*
Quiri. *Dolley Madison*
Raphael. *Daniel Boone: Frontier Hero*
Rappaport. *The Flight of the Red Bird*
Roop. *Capturing Nature: John James Audubon*
Rowland. *The Story of Sacajawea: Guide to Lewis and Clark*
St. George. *To See with the Heart: The Life of Sitting Bull*
Sanford. *Bill Pickett: African-American Rodeo Star*
Sanford. *Brigham Young: Pioneer and Morman Leader*
Sanford. *Buffalo Bill Cody: Showman of the Wild West*
Sanford. *Calamity Jane: A Frontier Original*
Sanford. *Chief Joseph: Nez Percé Warrior*
Sanford. *Crazy Horse: Sioux Warrior*
Sanford. *Daniel Boone: Wilderness Pioneer*
Sanford. *Davy Crockett: Defender of the Alamo*
Sanford. *Geronimo: Apache Warrior*
Sanford. *John C. Frémont: Soldier and Pathfinder*
Sanford. *Kit Carson: Frontier Scout*
Sanford. *Osceola: Seminole Warrior*
Sanford. *Quanah Parker: Comanche Warrior*
Sanford. *Red Cloud: Sioux Warrior*
Sanford. *Sam Houston: Texas Hero*
Sanford. *Sitting Bull: Sioux Warrior*
Sanford. *Zebulon Pike: Explorer of the Southwest*
Schwarz. *Cochise, Apache Chief*

Schwarz. *Geronimo: Apache Warrior*
Scordato. *Sarah Winnemucca*
Scott. *Chief Joseph and the Nez Percés*
Shorto. *Geronimo and the Struggle for Apache Freedom*
Shorto. *Tecumseh and the Dream of an American Indian Nation*
Shumate. *Chief Gall: Sioux War Chief*
Shumate. *Sequoyah: Inventor of the Cherokee Alphabet*
Shuter. *Parkman and the Plains Indians*
Shuter. *Sarah Royce and the American West*
Sinnott. *Zebulon Pike*
Sonneborn. *Will Rogers: Cherokee Entertainer*
Stallones. *Zebulon Pike and the Explorers of the American Southwest*
Stanley. *The True Adventure of Daniel Hall*
Stevenson. *Sitting Bull: Dakota Boy*
Stine. *The Story of Laura Ingalls Wilder*
Sufrin. *George Catlin: Painter of the Indian West*
Talmadge. *John Muir: At Home in the Wild*
Taylor. *Chief Joseph: Nez Perce Leader*
Twist. *Lewis and Clark: Exploring the Northwest*
Viola. *Osceola*
Viola. *Sitting Bull*
Wadsworth. *John Muir: Wilderness Protector*
Weidt. *Mr. Blue Jeans: Levi Strauss*
Weitzman. *The Mountain Man and the President*
Wilson. *Quanah Parker: Comanche Chief*
Wormser. *Pinkerton: America's First Private Eye*

Collective Biography

Allen. *As Long as the Rivers Flow: The Stories of Nine Native Americans*

Allen. *Jedediah Smith and the Mountain Men of the American West*
Alter. *Women of the Old West*
Duncan. *People of the West*

Hazell. *Heroines: Great Women Through the Ages*
Jacobs. *Great Lives: World Religions*

Katz. *Black Women of the Old West*

Katz. *Proudly Red and Black: Stories of African and Native Americans*

King. *First Facts About American Heroes*

Mayberry. *Business Leaders Who Built Financial Empires*

Provensen. *My Fellow Americans*

Reef. *Black Fighting Men: A Proud History*

Walker. *Spiritual Leaders*

History

Abbink. *Missions of the Monterey Bay Area*

Alter. *Growing Up in the Old West*

Ashabranner. *A Strange and Distant Shore: Indians of the Great Plains in Exile*

Baldwin. *New England Whaler*

Behrens. *Missions of the Central Coast*

Bentley. *Brides, Midwives, and Widows*

Bentley. *Explorers, Trappers, and Guides*

Bial. *Frontier Home*

Blake. *The Gold Rush of 1849*

Blakely. *Native Americans and the U.S. Government*

Blumberg. *The Incredible Journey of Lewis and Clark*

Bonvillain. *The Haidas: People of the Northwest Coast*

Bowler. *Trains*

Burby. *The Pueblo Indians*

Burns. *Mail*

Burns. *Money*

Carlson. *A Historical Album of Minnesota*

Carlson. *Westward Ho!: An Activity Guide to the Wild West*

Carrick. *Whaling Days*

Carter. *Last Stand at the Alamo*

Carter. *The Mexican War: Manifest Destiny*

Carter. *The Spanish-American War: Imperial Ambitions*

Chrisp. *The Whalers*

Chu. *Going Home to Nicodemus*

Claro. *The Apache Indians*

Claro. *The Cherokee Indians*

Climo. *City! San Francisco*

Cobb. *The Quilt-Block History of Pioneer Days*

Cocke. *A Historical Album of Washington*

Cohen. *The Alaska Purchase*

Coote. *The Sailor Through History*

Cory. *Pueblo Indian*

Deem. *How to Make a Mummy Talk*

Di Certo. *The Pony Express: Hoofbeats in the Wilderness*

Diamond. *Smallpox and the American Indian*

Doubleday. *Salt Lake City*

Duggleby. *Impossible Quests*

Duncan. *The West: An Illustrated History for Children*

Elish. *The Transcontinental Railroad*

English. *Transportation: Automobiles to Zeppelins*

Ferrell. *The Battle of the Little Bighorn in American History*

Fisher. *The Oregon Trail*

Fisher. *Tracks Across America: The Story of the American Railroad, 1825-1900*

Fleischner. *The Apaches: People of the Southwest*

Fraser. *Sanctuary*

Fraser. *Ten Mile Day: The Transcontinental Railroad*

Freedman. *An Indian Winter*

Freedman. *Buffalo Hunt*

Fry. *The Orphan Train*

Giblin. *Be Seated: A Book About Chairs*

Giblin. *When Plague Strikes*

Gintzler. *Cowboys*

Gintzler. *Homesteaders*

Gintzler. *Prospectors*

Gourley. *Hunting Neptune's Giants: American Whaling*

Granfield. *Cowboy: An Album*

Green. *Women in American Indian Society*

Greenwood. *A Pioneer Sampler: A Pioneer Family in 1840*

Hahn. *The Blackfoot*

Harness. *The Amazing Impossible Erie Canal*

Harness. *They're Off: The Story of the Pony Express*

Harvey. *Farmers and Ranchers*

Herda. *Outlaws of the American West*

Hevly. *Preachers and Teachers*

Hicks. *The Sioux*

Hilton. *Miners, Merchants, and Maids*

Hirsch. *Taxation: Paying for Government*

Humble. *Ships*

Jacobs. *War with Mexico*

Kalman. *Children's Clothing of the 1800s*

Kalman. *Customs and Traditions*

Kalman. *Early Artisans*

Kalman. *Early Christmas*

Kalman. *The Early Family Home*

Kalman. *Early Farm Life*

Kalman. *Early Health and Medicine*

Kalman. *Early Loggers and the Sawmill*

Kalman. *Early Pleasures and Pastimes*

Kalman. *Early Schools*

Kalman. *Early Settler Storybook*

Kalman. *Early Stores and Markets*

Kalman. *Early Travel*

Kalman. *Early Village Life*

Kalman. *Food for the Settler*

Kalman. *Fort Life*

Kalman. *Games from Long Ago*

Kalman. *The Grist Mill*

Kalman. *Home Crafts*

Kalman. *The Kitchen*

Kalman. *19th Century Clothing*

Kalman. *Old-Time Toys*

Kalman. *A One-Room School*

Kalman. *Settler Sayings*

Kalman. *Tools and Gadgets*

Karl. *America Alive: A History*

Kerr. *Keeping Clean*

Ketchum. *The Gold Rush*

Klausmeier. *Cowboy*

Koslow. *The Seminole Indians*

Kroll. *Pony Express!*

Kurtz. *U.S. Army*

Lampton. *Epidemic*

Landau. *Cowboys*

Landau. *The Hopi*

Lavender. *The Santa Fe Trail*

Lavender. *Snowbound: The Tragic Story of the Donner Party*

Lee. *San Antonio*
Lemke. *Missions of the Southern Coast [California]*
Lincoln. *The Pirate's Handbook*
Lodge. *The Cheyenne*
Lodge. *The Comanche*
Lucas. *The Cherokees: People of the Southeast*
MacMillan. *Missions of the Los Angeles Area*
Maestro. *The Story of Money*
Marrin. *Empires Lost and Won: The Spanish Heritage in the Southwest*
McDaniel. *The Powhatan Indians*
McGrath. *The Lewis and Clark Expedition*
McNeese. *America's Early Canals*
McNeese. *America's First Railroads*
McNeese. *Clippers and Whaling Ships*
McNeese. *Conestogas and Stagecoaches*
McNeese. *Early River Travel*
McNeese. *From Trails to Turnpikes*
McNeese. *West by Steamboat*
Medearis. *Come This Far to Freedom*
Meltzer. *Gold*
Miller. *Buffalo Gals*
Mooney. *The Comanche Indians*
Morley. *Clothes: For Work, Play and Display*
Murdoch. *Cowboy*
Murdoch. *North American Indian*
Murphy. *Across America on an Emigrant Train*

Murphy. *Across the Plains in the Donner Party*
Nelson. *Bull Whackers to Whistle Punks: Logging in the Old West*
Nirgiotis. *Erie Canal: Gateway to the West*
O'Neill. *Wounded Knee*
Patent. *West by Covered Wagon*
Platt. *Pirate*
Platt. *The Smithsonian Visual Timeline of Inventions*
Pollard. *The Nineteenth Century*
Ritchie. *Frontier Life*
Roessel. *Songs from the Loom: A Navajo Girl Learns to Weave*
Roop. *Off the Map: The Journals of Lewis and Clark*
Ross. *Bandits & Outlaws*
Rowland-Warne. *Costume*
Ryan. *Explorers and Mapmakers*
Savage. *Cowboys and Cow Towns of the Wild West*
Savage. *Gold Miners of the Wild West*
Savage. *Gunfighters of the Wild West*
Savage. *Pioneering Women of the Wild West*
Savage. *Pony Express Riders of the Wild West*
Savage. *Scouts of the Wild West*
Sherrow. *The Nez Perces*
Silverstein. *The Alamo*
Sita. *The Rattle and the Drum*
Smith. *A Historical Album of Kentucky*
Smith-Baranzini. *Book of the American Indians*
Sneve. *The Cherokees*
Sneve. *The Hopis*
Sneve. *The Navajos*

Sneve. *The Nez Perce*
Sneve. *The Seminoles*
Sneve. *The Sioux*
Steedman. *A Frontier Fort on the Oregon Trail*
Steele, Philip. *Bighorn*
Stewart. *Where Lies Butch Cassidy?*
Swanson. *Buffalo Sunrise: The Story of a North American Giant*
Van Steenwyk. *The California Gold Rush*
Ventura. *Food: Its Evolution Through the Ages*
White. *Missions of the San Francisco Bay Area*
Whitman. *Get Up and Go: American Road Travel*
Wills. *The Battle of Little Bighorn*
Wills. *A Historical Album of Alabama*
Wills. *A Historical Album of California*
Wills. *A Historical Album of Connecticut*
Wills. *A Historical Album of Florida*
Wills. *A Historical Album of Illinois*
Wills. *A Historical Album of Nebraska*
Wills. *A Historical Album of Oregon*
Wills. *A Historical Album of Texas*
Wilson. *Visual Timeline of Transportation*
Winslow. *Loggers and Railroad Workers*
Wood. *The Crow Indians*
Wood. *The Navajo Indians*
Yancey. *Desperadoes and Dynamite: Train Robbery*

Multimedia

CD-ROM

Eyewitness Encyclopedia of Science

Her Heritage: A Biographical Encyclopedia of American History

SkyTrip America
Total History

Video

Across the Plains
The Apache
Birth of a Community: Jews and the Gold Rush
The Black West
Bright Eyes: Susette La Flesche Tibbles

Candlemaking
The Cherokee
The Cheyenne
The Chinook
The Creek
The Crow
Dr. Susan La Flesche Picotte

Family Life: Multiculturalism
Heritage of the Black West
A History of Native Americans
Homesteading: 70 Years on the Great Plains, 1862-1932
The Huron

Indians of California
Indians of the Northwest
Indians of the Plains
Indians of the Southeast
Indians of the Southwest
Kentucky Rifle
The Lenape
The Lewis and Clark Trail
The Loom
Men of the Frontier
The Menominee
Mining Made the West
Mississippi Steamboats
Mountain Men
The Narragansett
Native American Life
Native Americans: The
  History of a People

Native Americans: People of
  the Desert
Native Americans: People of
  the Forest
Native Americans: People of
  the Northwest Coast
Native Americans: People of
  the Plains
The Navajo
The Oregon Trail
Placer Gold
Pony Express
The Potawatomi
Prairie Cabin: A Norwegian
  Pioneer Woman's Story
Pueblo
Railroads on the Frontier
Rancho Life

Sacajawea
The Seminole
Settlers of the West
Silent Communications: Trail
  Signs/Sign Language
Song of Sacajawea
Spinning Wheel
Stagecoach West
This World Is Not Our Home
Through the Rockies
United States Expansion
Westward Wagons
Women of the West
Woodland Tribal Arts: Native
  American Arts
The Yankton Sioux

GRADE SIX

Historical Fiction

Antle. *Beautiful Land: A
  Story of the Oklahoma
  Land Rush*
Auch. *Journey to Nowhere*
Beatty. *Behave Yourself,
  Bethany Brant*
Beatty. *Bonanza Girl*
Beatty. *By Crumbs, It's Mine!*
Beatty. *The Coach That
  Never Came*
Beatty. *Hail Columbia*
Beatty. *How Many Miles to
  Sundown?*
Beatty. *Jonathan Down Under*
Beatty. *Just Some Weeds
  from the Wilderness*
Beatty. *Lacy Makes a Match*
Beatty. *A Long Way to
  Whiskey Creek*
Beatty. *Melinda Takes a
  Hand.*
Beatty. *The Nickel-Plated
  Beauty*
Beatty. *O the Red Rose Tree*
Beatty. *Red Rock over the
  River*
Beatty. *Sarah and Me and the
  Lady from the Sea*
Beatty. *Something to Shout
  About*
Beatty. *That's One Ornery
  Orphan*
Berleth. *Mary Patten's
  Voyage*

Brenner. *On the Frontier with
  Mr. Audubon*
Brink. *Caddie Woodlawn*
Bunting. *Dandelions*
Conrad. *Prairie Songs*
Cross. *Great-Grandma Tells
  of Threshing Day*
Cushman. *The Ballad of Lucy
  Whipple*
DeFelice. *Weasel*
Donahue. *The Valley in
  Between*
Duey. *Anisett Lundberg:
  California, 1851*
Fleischman. *The Ghost in the
  Noonday Sun*
Fleischman. *Jim Ugly*
Fleischman. *Humbug
  Mountain*
Fleischman. *Mr. Mysterious
  & Co.*
Gipson. *Old Yeller*
Goldin. *Red Means Good
  Fortune*
Gregory. *Earthquake at Dawn*
Gregory. *Jimmy Spoon and
  the Pony Express*
Gregory. *Jenny of the Tetons*
Gregory. *The Legend of
  Jimmy Spoon*
Gregory. *The Stowaway: A
  Tale of California Pirates*
Hahn. *The Gentleman Outlaw
  and Me—Eli: A Story of
  the Old West*

Henry. *A Clearing in the
  Forest*
Highwater. *Eyes of Darkness*
Holland. *The Journey Home*
Holmes. *Year of the Sevens
  1777*
Hotze. *A Circle Unbroken*
Karr. *Go West, Young
  Women!*
Karr. *Phoebe's Folly*
Keehn. *I Am Regina*
Kherdian. *Bridger: The Story
  of a Mountain Man*
Kudlinski. *Earthquake!: A
  Story of Old San Francisco*
Kudlinski. *Facing West: A
  Story of the Oregon Trail*
Kudlinski. *Lone Star: A Story
  of the Texas Rangers*
Kudlinski. *Shannon: A
  Chinatown Adventure, San
  Francisco, 1880*
Lawlor. *Addie Across the
  Prairie*
Lawlor. *Addie's Dakota
  Winter*
Lawlor. *Addie's Long Summer*
Lawlor. *George on His Own*
Lawlor. *Gold in the Hills*
Leland. *Sallie Fox: The Story
  of a Pioneer Girl*
Lenski. *Indian Captive: The
  Story of Mary Jemison*
MacBride. *In the Land of the
  Big Red Apple*

MacBride. *Little Farm in the Ozarks*

MacBride. *Little House on Rocky Ridge*

MacBride. *Little Town in the Ozarks*

MacLachlan. *Sarah, Plain and Tall*

Mazzio. *Leaving Eldorado*

McCall. *Message from the Mountains*

McClung. *Hugh Glass, Mountain Man*

McClung. *The True Adventures of Grizzly Adams*

McGraw. *Moccasin Trail*

Meyer. *Where the Broken Heart Still Beats: Cynthia Ann Parker*

Moeri. *Save Queen of Sheba*

Morrow. *On to Oregon!*

Myers. *The Righteous Revenge of Artemis Bonner*

Nixon. *Caught in the Act: The Orphan Quartet Two*

O'Dell. *Island of the Blue Dolphins*

O'Dell. *Sing Down the Moon*

O'Dell. *Thunder Rolling in the Mountains*

O'Dell. *Zia*

Paulsen. *Call Me Francis Tucker*

Paulsen. *Mr. Tucket*

Paulsen. *Tucket's Ride*

Rawls. *Dame Shirley and the Gold Rush*

Rockwood. *Groundhog's Horse*

Sandoz. *The Horsecatcher*

Scott. *The Covered Wagon and Other Adventures*

Shaw. *Changes for Kirsten*

Shura. *Kate's Book*

Shura. *Kate's House*

Steele. *The Buffalo Knife*

Steele. *Flaming Arrows*

Steele. *The Lone Hunt*

Steele. *The Man with the Silver Eyes*

Steele. *Tomahawk Border*

Steele. *Trail Through Danger*

Steele. *Wilderness Journey*

Steele. *Winter Danger*

Stevens. *Trouble for Lucy*

Stewart. *On the Long Trail Home*

Taylor. *Walking Up a Rainbow*

Toht. *Sodbuster*

Tunbo. *Stay Put, Robbie McAmis*

Turner. *Grasshopper Summer*

Van Leeuwen. *Bound for Oregon*

Wangerin. *The Crying for a Vision*

Weitzman. *Thrashin' Time*

Whelan. *The Indian School*

Wilder. *By the Shores of Silver Lake*

Wilder. *Farmer Boy*

Wilder. *The First Four Years*

Wilder. *Little House in the Big Woods*

Wilder. *Little House on the Prairie*

Wilder. *Little Town on the Prairie*

Wilder. *The Long Winter*

Wilder. *On the Banks of Plum Creek*

Wilder. *On the Way Home*

Wilder. *These Happy Golden Years*

Wilkes. *Little House in Brookfield*

Wilson. *Earthquake!*

Wisler. *Jericho's Journey*

Wisler. *Piper's Ferry*

Woodruff. *Dear Levi: Letters from the Overland Trail*

Biography

Anderson. *Charles Eastman*

Anderson. *John James Audubon: Wildlife Artist*

Anderson. *Laura Ingalls Wilder*

Badt. *Charles Eastman: Sioux Physician and Author*

Bernotas. *Sitting Bull: Chief of the Sioux*

Black. *Sitting Bull and the Battle of the Little Bighorn*

Bland. *Osceola: Seminole Rebel*

Bland. *Pontiac: Ottawa Rebel*

Blassingame. *Jim Beckwourth: Black Trapper and Indian Chief*

Bodow. *Sitting Bull: Sioux Leader*

Bolton. *Joseph Brant: Mohawk Chief*

Bonvillain. *Black Hawk: Sac Rebel*

Brown. *Sacagawea*

Brown. *Susette La Flesche*

Carlson. *Harriet Tubman: Call to Freedom*

Cavan. *Daniel Boone and the Opening of the Ohio Country*

Chrisman. *David Farragut*

Collins. *Pioneer Plowmaker: John Deere*

Connell. *These Lands Are Ours: Tecumseh's Fight*

Conrad. *Prairie Visions: Solomon Butcher*

Cox. *Mark Twain*

Cwiklik. *Sequoyah and the Cherokee Alphabet*

Cwiklik. *Tecumseh: Shawnee Rebel*

Dolan. *James Beckwourth: Frontiersman*

Faber. *Calamity Jane: Her Life and Her Legend*

Ferris. *Native American Doctor: The Story of Susan La Fleshe Picotte*

Fitz-Gerald. *Meriwether Lewis and William Clark*

Force. *John Muir*

Foster. *David Farragut*

Fox. *Chief Joseph of the Nez Perce Indians*

Fraser. *In Search of the Grand Canyon: John Wesley Powell*

Fritz. *Make Way for Sam Houston*

Gaines. *John Wesley Powell and the Great Surveys of the American West*

Goldman. *Crazy Horse: War Chief of the Oglala Sioux*

Graves. *Annie Oakey: The Shooting Star*

Green. *Allan Pinkerton*

Green. *Bat Masterson*

Green. *Belle Star*

Green. *Billy the Kid*

Green. *Butch Cassidy*

Green. *Doc Holliday*

Green. *Jesse James*

Green. *Judge Roy Bean*

Green. *The Dalton Gang*

Green. *Wild Bill Hickock*

Green. *Wyatt Earp*

Guttmacher. *Crazy Horse: Sioux War Chief*

Harris. *John Charles Frémont and the Great Western Reconnaissance*

Henry. *Everyone Wears His Name: A Biography of Levi Strauss*

Hilts. *Quanah Parker*

Holler. *Pocahontas: Powhatan Peacemaker*

Jumper. *Osceola: Patriot and Warrior*

Kent. *Geronimo*

Klausner. *Sequoyah's Gift*

Lasky. *Searching for Laura Ingalls: A Reader's Journey*

Latham. *David Farragut*

Latham. *Sam Houston: Hero of Texas*

Lawlor. *Daniel Boone*

Lawlor. *The Real Johnny Appleseed*

Lazar. *Red Cloud: Sioux War Chief*

Ledbetter. *John Muir*

Luce. *Jim Bridger: Man of the Mountains*

Marrin. *Plains Warrior: Chief Quanah Parker and the Comanches*

McClung. *The True Adventures of Grizzly Adams*

Morrison. *Chief Sarah: Sarah Winnemucca's Fight for Indian Rights*

Moseley. *Davy Crockett: Hero of the Wild Frontier*

Naden. *John Muir: Saving the Wilderness*

O'Rear. *Charles Goodnight: Pioneer Cowman*

Petersen. *Meriwether Lewis and William Clark*

Plain. *George Catlin*

Press. *Mark Twain*

Quiri. *Dolley Madison*

Rappaport. *The Flight of the Red Bird*

Roop. *Capturing Nature: John James Audubon*

Rowland. *The Story of Sacajawea: Guide to Lewis and Clark*

St. George. *To See with the Heart: The Life of Sitting Bull*

Sanford. *Bill Pickett: African-American Rodeo Star*

Sanford. *Brigham Young: Pioneer and Morman Leader*

Sanford. *Buffalo Bill Cody: Showman of the Wild West*

Sanford. *Calamity Jane: A Frontier Original*

Sanford. *Chief Joseph: Nez Percé Warrior*

Sanford. *Crazy Horse: Sioux Warrior*

Sanford. *Daniel Boone: Wilderness Pioneer*

Sanford. *Davy Crockett: Defender of the Alamo*

Sanford. *Geronimo: Apache Warrior*

Sanford. *John C. Frémont: Soldier and Pathfinder*

Sanford. *Kit Carson: Frontier Scout*

Sanford. *Osceola: Seminole Warrior*

Sanford. *Quanah Parker: Comanche Warrior*

Sanford. *Red Cloud: Sioux Warrior*

Sanford. *Sam Houston: Texas Hero*

Sanford. *Sitting Bull: Sioux Warrior*

Sanford. *Zebulon Pike: Explorer of the Southwest*

Schwarz. *Cochise, Apache Chief*

Schwarz. *Geronimo: Apache Warrior*

Scordato. *Sarah Winnemucca*

Scott. *Chief Joseph and the Nez Percés*

Shorto. *Geronimo and the Struggle for Apache Freedom*

Shorto. *Tecumseh and the Dream of an American Indian Nation*

Shumate. *Chief Gall: Sioux War Chief*

Shumate. *Sequoyah: Inventor of the Cherokee Alphabet*

Shuter. *Parkman and the Plains Indians*

Shuter. *Sarah Royce and the American West*

Sinnott. *Zebulon Pike*

Sonneborn. *Will Rogers: Cherokee Entertainer*

Stallones. *Zebulon Pike and the Explorers of the American Southwest*

Stanley. *The True Adventure of Daniel Hall*

Stevenson. *Sitting Bull: Dakota Boy*

Stiles. *Jesse James*

Sufrin. *George Catlin: Painter of the Indian West*

Taylor. *Chief Joseph: Nez Perce Leader*

Wadsworth. *John Muir: Wilderness Protector*

Weidt. *Mr. Blue Jeans: Levi Strauss*

Weitzman. *The Mountain Man and the President*

Wilson. *Quanah Parker: Comanche Chief*

Wormser. *Pinkerton: America's First Private Eye*

Collective Biography

Aaseng. *You Are the General II: 1800-1899*

Allen. *As Long as the Rivers Flow: The Stories of Nine Native Americans*

Allen. *Jedediah Smith and the Mountain Men of the American West*

Alter. *Women of the Old West*

Anderson. *Explorers Who Found New Worlds*

Duncan. *People of the West*

Hazell. *Heroines: Great Women Through the Ages*

Italia. *Courageous Crimefighters*

Jacobs. *Great Lives: World Religions*

Katz. *Black Women of the Old West*

Katz. *Proudly Red and Black: Stories of African and Native Americans*

King. *First Facts About American Heroes*

Mayberry. *Business Leaders Who Built Financial Empires*

Provensen. *My Fellow Americans*

Reef. *Black Fighting Men: A Proud History*

Rennert. *Pioneers of Discovery*

Stefoff. *Pioneers*

Walker. *Spiritual Leaders*

History

Abbink. *Missions of the Monterey Bay Area*

Alter. *Growing Up in the Old West*

Andrews. *Indians of the Plains*

Ashabranner. *A Strange and Distant Shore: Indians of the Great Plains in Exile*

Baldwin. *New England Whaler*

Barr. *The American Frontier*

Bealer. *Only the Names Remain*

Behrens. *Missions of the Central Coast*

Bentley. *Brides, Midwives, and Widows*

Bentley. *Explorers, Trappers, and Guides*

Bial. *Frontier Home*

Blake. *The Gold Rush of 1849*

Blakely. *Native Americans and the U.S. Government*

Blumberg. *The Incredible Journey of Lewis and Clark*

Bonvillain. *The Haidas: People of the Northwest Coast*

Bowler. *Trains*

Brill. *The Trail of Tears*

Burby. *The Pueblo Indians*

Burns. *Money*

Carlson. *A Historical Album of Minnesota*

Carlson. *Westward Ho!: An Activity Guide to the Wild West*

Carrick. *Whaling Days*

Carter. *Last Stand at the Alamo*

Carter. *The Mexican War: Manifest Destiny*

Carter. *The Spanish-American War: Imperial Ambitions*

Chrisp. *The Whalers*

Chu. *Going Home to Nicodemus*

Claro. *The Apache Indians*

Claro. *The Cherokee Indians*

Climo. *City! San Francisco*

Cobb. *The Quilt-Block History of Pioneer Days*

Cocke. *A Historical Album of Washington*

Cohen. *The Alaska Purchase*

Cory. *Pueblo Indian*

Cush. *Disasters That Shook the World*

Deem. *How to Make a Mummy Talk*

Di Certo. *The Pony Express: Hoofbeats in the Wilderness*

Diamond. *Smallpox and the American Indian*

Doubleday. *Salt Lake City*

Duggleby. *Impossible Quests*

Duncan. *The West: An Illustrated History for Children*

Dunn. *The Relocation of the North American Indian*

Elish. *The Transcontinental Railroad*

English. *Transportation: Automobiles to Zeppelins*

Ferrell. *The Battle of the Little Bighorn in American History*

Fisher. *The Oregon Trail*

Fisher. *Tracks Across America: The Story of the American Railroad, 1825-1900*

Fleischner. *The Apaches: People of the Southwest*

Fraser. *Ten Mile Day: The Transcontinental Railroad*

Freedman. *Buffalo Hunt*

Freedman. *Cowboys of the Wild West*

Freedman. *An Indian Winter*

Fry. *The Orphan Train*

Giblin. *Be Seated: A Book About Chairs*

Giblin. *When Plague Strikes*

Gintzler. *Cowboys*

Gintzler. *Homesteaders*

Gintzler. *Prospectors*

Gourley. *Hunting Neptune's Giants: American Whaling*

Granfield. *Cowboy: An Album*

Green. *Women in American Indian Society*

Greenwood. *A Pioneer Sampler: A Pioneer Family in 1840*

Hahn. *The Blackfoot*

Harness. *The Amazing Impossible Erie Canal*

Harvey. *Farmers and Ranchers*

Herda. *Outlaws of the American West*

Hevly. *Preachers and Teachers*

Hicks. *The Sioux*

Hilton. *Miners, Merchants, and Maids*

Hirsch. *Taxation: Paying for Government*

Humble. *Ships*

Jacobs. *War with Mexico*

Kalman. *Customs and Traditions*

Kalman. *Early Artisans*

Kalman. *Early Christmas*

Kalman. *The Early Family Home*

Kalman. *Early Farm Life*

Kalman. *Early Health and Medicine*

Kalman. *Early Loggers and the Sawmill*

Kalman. *Early Schools*

Kalman. *Early Settler Storybook*

Kalman. *Early Stores and Markets*

Kalman. *Early Travel*

Kalman. *Early Village Life*

Kalman. *Food for the Settler*

Kalman. *Games from Long Ago*

Kalman. *The Grist Mill*

Kalman. *Home Crafts*

Kalman. *The Kitchen*

Kalman. *19th Century Clothing*

Kalman. *Old-Time Toys*

Kalman. *A One-Room School*

Kalman. *Settler Sayings*

Kalman. *Tools and Gadgets*

Karl. *America Alive: A History*

Kerr. *Keeping Clean*

Ketchum. *The Gold Rush*

Klausmeier. *Cowboy*

Koslow. *The Seminole Indians*

Kurtz. *U.S. Army*

Lampton. *Epidemic*

Landau. *Cowboys*

Landau. *The Hopi*

Lavender. *The Santa Fe Trail*

Lavender. *Snowbound: The Tragic Story of the Donner Party*

Lee. *San Antonio*

Lemke. *Missions of the Southern Coast [California]*

Lincoln. *The Pirate's Handbook*

Lodge. *The Cheyenne*

Lodge. *The Comanche*

Lucas. *The Cherokees: People of the Southeast*

MacMillan. *Missions of the Los Angeles Area*

Marrin. *Cowboys, Indians and Gunfighters*

Marrin. *Empires Lost and Won: The Spanish Heritage in the Southwest*

McDaniel. *The Powhatan Indians*

McGrath. *The Lewis and Clark Expedition*

McNeese. *America's Early Canals*

McNeese. *America's First Railroads*

McNeese. *Clippers and Whaling Ships*

McNeese. *Conestogas and Stagecoaches*

McNeese. *Early River Travel*

McNeese. *From Trails to Turnpikes*

McNeese. *West by Steamboat*

Medearis. *Come This Far to Freedom*

Meltzer. *Gold*

Miller. *Buffalo Gals*

Mooney. *The Comanche Indians*

Morley. *Clothes: For Work, Play and Display*

Morris. *The Harvey Girls: The Women Who Civilized the West*

Murdoch. *Cowboy*

Murdoch. *North American Indian*

Murphy. *Across America on an Emigrant Train*

Murphy. *Across the Plains in the Donner Party*

Nelson. *Bull Whackers to Whistle Punks: Logging in the Old West*

Nirgiotis. *Erie Canal: Gateway to the West*

O'Neill. *Wounded Knee*

Platt. *Pirate*

Platt. *The Smithsonian Visual Timeline of Inventions*

Pollard. *The Nineteenth Century*

Ritchie. *Frontier Life*

Roessel. *Songs from the Loom: A Navajo Girl Learns to Weave*

Roop. *Off the Map: The Journals of Lewis and Clark*

Ross. *Bandits & Outlaws*

Rowland-Warne. *Costume*

Ryan. *Explorers and Mapmakers*

Savage. *Cowboys and Cow Towns of the Wild West*

Savage. *Gold Miners of the Wild West*

Savage. *Gunfighters of the Wild West*

Savage. *Pioneering Women of the Wild West*

Savage. *Pony Express Riders of the Wild West*

Savage. *Scouts of the Wild West*

Sherrow. *The Nez Perces*

Silverstein. *The Alamo*

Sita. *The Rattle and the Drum*

Smith. *A Historical Album of Kentucky*

Smith-Baranzini. *Book of the American Indians*

Sneve. *The Cherokees*

Sneve. *The Hopis*

Sneve. *The Navajos*

Sneve. *The Nez Perce*

Sneve. *The Sioux*

Steedman. *A Frontier Fort on the Oregon Trail*

Steele. *Bighorn*

Stefoff. *Children of the Westward Trail*

Stewart. *Cowboys in the Old West*

Stewart. *Where Lies Butch Cassidy?*

Swanson. *Buffalo Sunrise: The Story of a North American Giant*

Van Der Linde. *The Pony Express*

Van Steenwyk. *The California Gold Rush*

Ventura. *Food: Its Evolution Through the Ages*

Warburton. *The Beginning of Writing*

Warburton. *Railroads: Bridging the Continents*

Wheeler. *Events That Changed American History*

White. *Missions of the San Francisco Bay Area*

Whitman. *Get Up and Go: American Road Travel*

Wills. *The Battle of Little Bighorn*

Wills. *A Historical Album of Alabama*

Wills. *A Historical Album of California*

Wills. *A Historical Album of Connecticut*

Wills. *A Historical Album of Florida*

Wills. *A Historical Album of Illinois*

Wills. *A Historical Album of Nebraska*

Wills. *A Historical Album of Oregon*

Wills. *A Historical Album of Texas*

Winslow. *Loggers and Railroad Workers*

Wood. *The Crow Indians*

Wood. *The Navajo Indians*

Yancey. *Desperadoes and Dynamite: Train Robbery*

Multimedia

CD-ROM

Eyewitness Encyclopedia of Science

Her Heritage: A Biographical Encyclopedia of American History

One Tribe

SkyTrip America

Total History

The Way Things Work

Video

America's Westword Expansion

Across the Plains

The Apache

Birth of a Community: Jews and the Gold Rush

The Black West

Candlemaking

The Cherokee

The Cheyenne

The Chinook

The Creek

The Crow

Expansionism

The Final Steps

Frontier Forts and the American Indian Wars in Texas

Heritage of the Black West
A History of Native Americans
Homesteading: 70 Years on
the Great Plains,
1862-1932
The Huron
Indians of California
Indians of the Northwest
Indians of the Plains
Indians of the Southeast
Indians of the Southwest
Kentucky Rifle
The Lenape
The Lewis and Clark Trail
The Loom
Men of the Frontier
The Menominee
Mining Made the West
Mississippi Steamboats
Mountain Men
The Narragansett

Native American Life
Native American Medicine
Native Americans: The
History of a People
Native Americans: People of
the Desert
Native Americans: People of
the Forest
Native Americans: People of
the Northwest Coast
Native Americans: People of
the Plains
The Navajo
The Oregon Trail
Placer Gold
Pony Express
The Potawatomi
Prairie Cabin: A Norwegian
Pioneer Woman's Story
Pueblo
Railroads on the Frontier

Rancho Life
Sacajawea
The Seminole
Settlers of the West
Song of Sacajawea
Spinning Wheel
Stagecoach West
This World Is Not Our Home
Through the Rockies
Totem Poles: The Stories
They Tell
United States Expansion
The Unsinkable Delta Queen
Westward Expansion: The
Pioneer Challenge
Westward Wagons
Women of the West
Woodland Tribal Arts: Native
American Arts
The Yankton Sioux

IMMIGRANTS AND MULTICULTURAL HERITAGES, 1814 TO THE PRESENT

KINDERGARTEN THROUGH SECOND GRADE

Historical Fiction

Bartone. *American Too*
Coerr. *Chang's Paper Pony*
Goldin. *Fire!*
Harvey. *Immigrant Girl: Becky of Eldridge Street*
Leighton. *An Ellis Island Christmas*
Levinson. *Soon, Annala*
Levinson. *Watch the Stars Come Out*
Levitin. *A Piece of Home*
McGugan. *Josepha: A Prairie Boy's Story*
Oberman. *The Always Prayer Shawl*
Pryor. *The Dream Jar*
Sandin. *The Long Way to a New Land*
Sandin. *The Long Way Westward*
Say. *El Chino*
Sorensen. *New Hope*
Winter. *Klara's New World*

Biography

Mohr. *All for the Better: A Story of El Barrio*

Collective Biography

Marzollo. *My First Book of Biographies*

History

Bresnick-Perry. *Leaving for America*
Jacobs. *Ellis Island: New Hope in a New Land*
Lee. *Tracing Our Italian Roots*
MacMillan. *Chinese New Year*
MacMillan. *Jewish Holidays in the Spring*
MacMillan. *Ramadan and Id Al-Fitr*
MacMillan. *Tet: Vietnamese New Year*
Maestro. *Coming to America: The Story of Immigration*

Multimedia

Video

Immigration to the United States
Independence Day
St. Patrick's Day
What Is an American?
The Year of the Dragon

GRADE THREE

Historical Fiction

Bader. *East Side Story*
Bartone. *American Too*
Coerr. *Chang's Paper Pony*
Goldin. *Fire!*
Harvey. *Immigrant Girl: Becky of Eldridge Street*
Herman. *The House on Walenska Street*
Leighton. *An Ellis Island Christmas*
Levinson. *Soon, Annala*
Levinson. *Watch the Stars Come Out*
Levitin. *A Piece of Home*
Lord. *In the Year of the Boar and Jackie Robinson*

49

McGugan. *Josepha: A Prairie Boy's Story*
Oberman. *The Always Prayer Shawl*
Pryor. *The Dream Jar*
Sandin. *The Long Way to a New Land*
Sandin. *The Long Way Westward*
Say. *El Chino*
Sorensen. *New Hope*
Surat. *Angel Child, Dragon Child*
Winter. *Klara's New World*

Biography

Cedeno. *Cesar Chavez: Labor Leader*
Collins. *Farmworker's Friend: Cesar Chavez*
Mohr. *All for the Better: A Story of El Barrio*

Collective Biography

King. *First Facts About American Heroes*
Marzollo. *My First Book of Biographies*

History

Bial. *Shaker Home*
Bresnick-Perry. *Leaving for America*
Doherty. *The Erie Canal*
Fisher. *Ellis Island: Gateway to The New World*
Hoyt-Goldsmith. *Day of the Dead: A Mexican-American Celebration*
Jacobs. *Ellis Island: New Hope in a New Land*
Kalman. *Customs and Traditions*
Kalman. *Early Christmas*
Leder. *A Russian Jewish Family*
Lee. *Tracing Our Italian Roots*
Levine. *If Your Name Was Changed at Ellis Island*
MacMillan. *Chinese New Year*
MacMillan. *Jewish Holidays in the Spring*
MacMillan. *Ramadan and Id Al-Fitr*
MacMillan. *Tet: Vietnamese New Year*
Maestro. *Coming to America: The Story of Immigration*
Moscinski. *Tracing Our Irish Roots*
San Souci. *N. C. Wyeth's Pilgrims*
Stein. *Ellis Island*
Turner. *Shaker Hearts*

Multimedia

Video

Immigration to the United States
Independence Day
St. Patrick's Day
What Is an American?
The Year of the Dragon

GRADE FOUR

Historical Fiction

Bader. *East Side Story*
Blos. *Brooklyn Doesn't Rhyme*
Goldin. *Fire!*
Harvey. *Immigrant Girl: Becky of Eldridge Street*
Herman. *The House on Walenska Street*
Leighton. *An Ellis Island Christmas*
Lord. *In the Year of the Boar and Jackie Robinson*
Lord. *The Luck of Z.A.P. and Zoe*
Lord. *Today's Special: Z.A.P. and Zoe*
Lord. *Z.A.P., Zoe, & the Musketeers*
McGugan. *Josepha: A Prairie Boy's Story*
Pellowski. *First Farm in the Valley: Anna's Story*
Say. *El Chino*
Sorensen. *New Hope*
Surat. *Angel Child, Dragon Child*
Uchida. *Samurai of Gold Hill*
Vogt. *A Race for Land*
Winter. *Klara's New World*

Biography

Cedeno. *Cesar Chavez: Labor Leader*
Codye. *Luis W. Alvarez*
Codye. *Vilma Martinez*
Collins. *Farmworker's Friend: Cesar Chavez*
Conord. *Cesar Chavez: Union Leader*
Mohr. *All for the Better: A Story of El Barrio*

Collective Biography

King. *First Facts About American Heroes*
Provensen. *My Fellow Americans*

History

Anderson. *Immigration*
Bial. *Amish Home*
Bial. *Shaker Home*
Bolick. *Shaker Inventions*
Bolick. *Shaker Villages*
Bratman. *Becoming a Citizen: Adopting a New Home*
Daley. *The Chinese Americans*
de Ruiz. *La Causa: The Migrant Farmworkers' Story*
Doherty. *The Erie Canal*
Evitts. *Early Immigration in the United States*
Fisher. *Ellis Island: Gateway to the New World*
Halliburton. *The West Indian-American Experience*
Hamanaka. *The Journey: Japanese Americans, Racism, and Renewal*
Hoobler. *The Japanese American Family Album*
Hoyt-Goldsmith. *Day of the Dead: A Mexican-American Celebration*
Jacobs. *Ellis Island: New Hope in a New Land*
Kalman. *Customs and Traditions*
Kalman. *Early Christmas*
Kroll. *Ellis Island*
Langley. *Religion*
Leder. *A Russian Jewish Family*
Lee. *Tracing Our Italian Roots*
Levine. *If Your Name Was Changed at Ellis Island*
MacMillan. *Chinese New Year*
MacMillan. *Jewish Holidays in the Spring*
MacMillan. *Ramadan and Id Al-Fitr*
MacMillan. *Tet: Vietnamese New Year*
Maestro. *Coming to America: The Story of Immigration*
Mayberry. *Eastern Europe*
Moscinski. *Tracing Our Irish Roots*
Reef. *Ellis Island*
San Souci. *N. C. Wyeth's Pilgrims*
Sandler. *Immigrants*
Stein. *Ellis Island*
Turner. *Shaker Hearts*

Multimedia

CD-ROM

Her Heritage: A Biographical Encyclopedia of American History
SkyTrip America
Total History

Video

The Amish
Arab Americans
Freedom in Diversity
German Americans
Greek Americans
The Immigration Experience
Immigration to the United States
Independence Day
Irish Americans
Italian Americans
Japanese Americans
Jewish Americans
Korean Americans
Polish Americans
Puerto Ricans
St. Patrick's Day
What Is an American?
The Year of the Dragon

GRADE FIVE

Historical Fiction

Angell. *One-Way to Ansonia*
Bader. *East Side Story*
Blos. *Brooklyn Doesn't Rhyme*
Conlon-McKenna. *Wildflower Girl*
Herman. *The House on Walenska Street*
Howard. *Sister*
Lasky. *The Night Journey*
Levitin. *Annie's Promise*
Lord. *In the Year of the Boar and Jackie Robinson*
Lord. *The Luck of Z.A.P. and Zoe*
Lord. *Today's Special: Z.A.P. and Zoe*
Lord. *Z.A.P., Zoe, & the Musketeers*
Marvin. *A Bride for Anna's Papa*
McGugan. *Josepha: A Prairie Boy's Story*
Morpurgo. *Twist of Gold*
Pellowski. *First Farm in the Valley: Anna's Story*
Say. *El Chino*
Sherman. *Independence Avenue*
Surat. *Angel Child, Dragon Child*
Uchida. *Samurai of Gold Hill*
Vogt. *A Race for Land*
Wallace. *Buffalo Gal*
Winter. *Klara's New World*
Yep. *Dragon's Gate*

Biography

Cedeno. *Cesar Chavez: Labor Leader*
Codye. *Luis W. Alvarez*
Codye. *Vilma Martinez*
Collins. *Farmworker's Friend: Cesar Chavez*
Conord. *Cesar Chavez: Union Leader*

de Ruiz. *To Fly with the Swallows: A Story of Old California*

Gonzales. *Cesar Chavez: Leader for Migrant Farm Workers*

Rodriguez. *Cesar Chavez*

Sonder. *The Tenement Writer: An Immigrant's Story*

Uchida. *The Invisible Thread*

Collective Biography

King. *First Facts About American Heroes*

Mayberry. *Business Leaders Who Built Financial Empires*

Pile. *Women Business Leaders*

Provensen. *My Fellow Americans*

History

Anderson. *Immigration*

Ashabranner. *An Ancient Heritage: The Arab-American Minority*

Ashabranner. *Dark Harvest: Migrant Farmworkers*

Bandon. *Asian Indian Americans*

Bandon. *Chinese Americans*

Bandon. *Dominican Americans*

Bandon. *Filipino Americans*

Bandon. *Korean Americans*

Bandon. *Mexican Americans*

Bandon. *Vietnamese Americans*

Bandon. *West Indian Americans*

Bial. *Amish Home*

Bial. *Shaker Home*

Bolick. *Shaker Inventions*

Bolick. *Shaker Villages*

Bratman. *Becoming a Citizen: Adopting a New Home*

Catalano. *The Mexican Americans*

Cavan. *The Irish-American Experience*

Daley. *The Chinese Americans*

de Ruiz. *La Causa: The Migrant Farmworkers' Story*

Di Franco. *The Italian Americans*

Doherty. *The Erie Canal*

Evitts. *Early Immigration in the United States*

Fisher. *Ellis Island: Gateway to the New World*

Freedman. *Kids at Work: Lewis Hine Against Child Labor*

Goldish. *Immigration: How Should It Be Controlled?*

Halliburton. *The West Indian-American Experience*

Hamanaka. *The Journey: Japanese Americans, Racism, and Renewal*

Hoobler. *The Chinese American Family Album*

Hoobler. *The Irish American Family Album*

Hoobler. *The Italian American Family Album*

Hoobler. *The Japanese American Family Album*

Hoyt-Goldsmith. *Day of the Dead: A Mexican-American Celebration*

Jacobs. *Ellis Island: New Hope in a New Land*

Johnson. *The Irish in America*

Kalman. *Customs and Traditions*

Kalman. *Early Christmas*

Kitano. *The Japanese Americans*

Kroll. *Ellis Island*

Langley. *Religion*

Lawlor. *I Was Dreaming to Come to America*

Leathers. *The Japanese in America*

Leder. *A Russian Jewish Family*

Lee. *Tracing Our Italian Roots*

Lehrer. *The Korean Americans*

Levine. *If Your Name Was Changed at Ellis Island*

MacMillan. *Chinese New Year*

MacMillan. *Jewish Holidays in the Spring*

MacMillan. *Ramadan and Id Al-Fitr*

MacMillan. *Tet: Vietnamese New Year*

Mayberry. *Eastern Europe*

Mendez. *Cubans in America*

Moscinski. *Tracing Our Irish Roots*

Pinchot. *The Mexicans in America*

Reef. *Ellis Island*

San Souci. *N. C. Wyeth's Pilgrims*

Sandler. *Immigrants*

Saxon-Ford. *The Czech Americans*

Seymour-Jones. *Refugees*

Sherrow. *The Triangle Factory Fire*

Sinnott. *Chinese Railroad Workers*

Sinnott. *Extraordinary Asian Pacific Americans*

Stanley. *Big Annie of Calumet*

Stein. *Ellis Island*

Takaki. *India in the West*

Takaki. *Spacious Dreams*

Takaki. *The Chinese in Nineteenth Century America*

Turner. *Shaker Hearts*

Multimedia

CD-ROM

Eyewitness Encyclopedia of Science

Her Heritage: A Biographical Encyclopedia of American History

SkyTrip America

Total History

Video

The Amish
Arab Americans
Charles Garry: Street Fighter
  in the Courtroom
Freedom In Diversity
From East to West: The
  Asian-American Experience
German Americans
Greek Americans

Immigration and Cultural
  Change
The Immigration Experience
Irish Americans
Italian Americans
Japanese Americans
Jewish Americans
Korean Americans

One World, Many Worlds:
  Hispanic Diversity in the
  United States
Polish Americans
Prejudice: Monster Within
Puerto Ricans
What Is an American?
The Year of the Dragon

> ### GRADE SIX

Historical Fiction

Angell. One-Way to Ansonia
Blos. Brooklyn Doesn't
  Rhyme
Conlon-McKenna.
  Wildflower Girl
Howard. Sister
Lasky. The Night Journey
Levitin. Annie's Promise
Levitin. Silver Days
Lord. In the Year of the Boar
  and Jackie Robinson

Lord. The Luck of Z.A.P. and
  Zoe
Lord. Today's Special: Z.A.P.
  and Zoe
Lord. Z.A.P., Zoe, & the
  Musketeers
Marvin. A Bride for Anna's
  Papa
Morpurgo. Twist of Gold
Pellowski. First Farm in the
  Valley: Anna's Story

Sherman. Independence
  Avenue
Surat. Angel Child, Dragon
  Child
Uchida. Samurai of Gold Hill
Vogt. A Race for Land
Wallace. Buffalo Gal
Winter. Klara's New World
Yep. Dragon's Gate

Biography

Bruns. John Wesley Powell
Codye. Luis W. Alvarez
Codye. Vilma Martinez
Collins. Farmworker's
  Friend: Cesar Chavez
Conord. Cesar Chavez:
  Union Leader

de Ruiz. To Fly with the
  Swallows: A Story of Old
  California
Gonzales. Cesar Chavez:
  Leader for Migrant Farm
  Workers

Holmes. Cesar Chavez: Farm
  Worker Activist
Rodriguez. Cesar Chavez
Sonder. The Tenement
  Writer: An Immigrant's
  Story
Uchida. The Invisible Thread

Collective Biography

Glenn. Discover America's
  Favorite Architects
King. First Facts About
  American Heroes

Mayberry. Business Leaders
  Who Built Financial
  Empires
Pile. Women Business Leaders

Provensen. My Fellow
  Americans

History

Anderson. Immigration
Ashabranner. An Ancient
  Heritage: The
  Arab-American Minority
Ashabranner. Dark Harvest:
  Migrant Farmworkers
Bandon. Asian Indian
  Americans
Bandon. Chinese Americans
Bandon. Dominican
  Americans
Bandon. Filipino Americans
Bandon. Korean Americans
Bandon. Mexican Americans
Bandon. Vietnamese
  Americans

Bandon. West Indian
  Americans
Bial. Amish Home
Bial. Shaker Home
Bolick. Shaker Inventions
Bolick. Shaker Villages
Bratman. Becoming a Citizen:
  Adopting a New Home
Catalano. The Mexican
  Americans
Cavan. The Irish-American
  Experience
Daley. The Chinese
  Americans

de Ruiz. La Causa: The
  Migrant Farmworkers'
  Story
Di Franco. The Italian
  Americans
Evitts. Early Immigration in
  the United States
Fisher. Ellis Island: Gateway
  to the New World
Freedman. Kids at Work:
  Lewis Hine Against Child
  Labor
Goldish. Immigration: How
  Should It Be Controlled?
Greenberg. Newcomers to
  America

Halliburton. *The West Indian-American Experience*

Hamanaka. *The Journey: Japanese Americans, Racism, and Renewal*

Hoobler. *The Chinese American Family Album*

Hoobler. *The Irish American Family Album*

Hoobler. *The Italian American Family Album*

Hoobler. *The Japanese American Family Album*

Hoobler. *The Jewish American Family Album*

Hoyt-Goldsmith. *Day of the Dead: A Mexican-American Celebration*

Johnson. *The Irish in America*

Kalman. *Customs and Traditions*

Kalman. *Early Christmas*

Kitano. *The Japanese Americans*

Koral. *An Album of War Refugees*

Kroll. *Ellis Island*

Kuropas. *Ukrainians in America*

Langley. *Religion*

Lawlor. *I Was Dreaming to Come to America*

Leathers. *The Japanese in America*

Leder. *A Russian Jewish Family*

Lehrer. *The Korean Americans*

Levine. *If Your Name Was Changed at Ellis Island*

Magocsi. *The Russian Americans*

Mayberry. *Eastern Europe*

Mendez. *Cubans in America*

Moscinski. *Tracing Our Irish Roots*

Muggamin. *The Jewish Americans*

Pinchot. *The Mexicans in America*

Reef. *Ellis Island*

San Souci. *N. C. Wyeth's Pilgrims*

Sandler. *Immigrants*

Saxon-Ford. *The Czech Americans*

Seymour-Jones. *Refugees*

Sherrow. *The Triangle Factory Fire*

Sinnott. *Chinese Railroad Workers*

Sinnott. *Extraordinary Asian Pacific Americans*

Stanley. *Big Annie of Calumet*

Takaki. *The Chinese in Nineteenth Century America*

Takaki. *Democracy and Race*

Takaki. *Ethnic Islands*

Takaki. *From the Land of Morning Calm*

Takaki. *India in the West*

Takaki. *Issei and Nisei*

Takaki. *Raising Cane*

Takaki. *Spacious Dreams*

Takaki. *Strangers at the Gates Again*

Turner. *Shaker Hearts*

Multimedia

CD-ROM

Eyewitness Encyclopedia of Science

Her Heritage: A Biographical Encyclopedia of American History

One Tribe

SkyTrip America

Total History

The Way Things Work

Video

American Fever

The Amish

Arab Americans

Charles Garry: Street Fighter in the Courtroom

Freedom in Diversity

From East to West: The Asian-American Experience

German Americans

Greek Americans

Immigration and Cultural Change

The Immigration Experience

Irish Americans

Italian Americans

Japanese Americans

Jewish Americans

Korean Americans

Latino Art and Culture in the United States

One World, Many Worlds: Hispanic Diversity in the United States

Polish Americans

Prejudice: Monster Within

Puerto Ricans

What Is an American?

The Year of the Dragon

SLAVERY, ABOLITIONISM, AND WOMEN'S RIGHTS, 1814-1865

KINDERGARTEN THROUGH SECOND GRADE

Historical Fiction

Ackerman. *Araminta's Paint Box*
Blumberg. *Bloomers!*
Brighton. *Dearest Grandmama*
Brill. *Allen Jay and the Underground Railroad*
Carrick. *Stay Away from Simon!*
Conway. *Where Is Papa Now?*
De Angeli. *Thee, Hannah!*
Edwards. *Barefoot: Escape on the Underground Railroad*

Hoobler. *Next Stop, Freedom: The Story of a Slave Girl*
Hooks. *The Ballad of Belle Dorcas*
Hooks. *Freedom's Fruit*
Hopkinson. *Sweet Clara and the Freedom Quilt*
Johnson. *Now Let Me Fly: The Story of a Slave Family*
Kroll. *Mary McLean and the St. Patrick's Day Parade*
McPhail. *Farm Boy's Year*
Monjo. *The Drinking Gourd*
Morrow. *Edward's Portrait*

Olson. *The Lighthouse Keeper's Daughter*
Roop. *Keep the Lights Burning, Abbie*
Smalls-Hector. *Irene Jennie and the Christmas Masquerade*
Turner. *Nettie's Trip South*
Turner. *Sewing Quilts*
Welch. *Danger at the Breaker*
Winter. *Follow the Drinking Gourd*
Wright. *Journey to Freedom*
Wright. *Jumping the Broom*

Biography

Adler. *A Picture Book of Abraham Lincoln*
Adler. *A Picture Book of Frederick Douglass*
Adler. *A Picture Book of Harriet Tubman*
Adler. *A Picture Book of Sojourner Truth*
Barrett. *Nat Turner and the Slave Revolt*
Benjamin. *Young Harriet Tubman*

Brenner. *Abe Lincoln's Hat*
Greene. *Abraham Lincoln: President of a Divided Country*
Greene. *Robert E. Lee*
Gross. *True Stories About Abraham Lincoln*
Kunhardt. *Honest Abe*
Lawrence. *Harriet and the Promised Land*
Livingston. *Abraham Lincoln*

McKissack. *Frederick Douglass: Leader Against Slavery*
Miller. *Frederick Douglass: The Last Day of Slavery*
Schroeder. *Minty: A Story of Young Harriet Tubman*
Thaxter. *Celia's Island Journey*

Collective Biography

Marzollo. *My First Book of Biographies*

History

Gibbons. *Beacons of Light: Lighthouses*

Goldish. *Our Supreme Court*
Medearis. *Our People*

Steins. *Our Elections*

Multimedia

Video

African American Life Equal Rights for All

Follow the Drinking Gourd Who Owns the Sun?

GRADE THREE

Historical Fiction

Ackerman. *Araminta's Paint Box*

Avi. *The Barn*

Blumberg. *Bloomers!*

Brighton. *Dearest Grandmama*

Brill. *Allen Jay and the Underground Railroad*

Carrick. *Stay Away from Simon!*

Coleman. *The Foot Warmer and the Crow*

Conway. *Where Is Papa Now?*

De Angeli. *Thee, Hannah!*

Edwards. *Barefoot: Escape on the Underground Railroad*

Hoobler. *Next Stop, Freedom: The Story of a Slave Girl*

Hooks. *The Ballad of Belle Dorcas*

Hooks. *Freedom's Fruit*

Hopkinson. *Sweet Clara and the Freedom Quilt*

Hurmence. *A Girl Called Boy*

Johnson. *Now Let Me Fly: The Story of a Slave Family*

Kroll. *Mary McLean and the St. Patrick's Day Parade*

McCully. *The Bobbin Girl*

McPhail. *Farm Boy's Year*

Monjo. *The Drinking Gourd*

Morrow. *Edward's Portrait*

Olson. *The Lighthouse Keeper's Daughter*

Roop. *Keep the Lights Burning, Abbie*

Rosen. *A School for Pompey Walker*

Smalls-Hector. *Irene Jennie and the Christmas Masquerade*

Turner. *Nettie's Trip South*

Turner. *Sewing Quilts*

Welch. *Danger at the Breaker*

Winter. *Follow the Drinking Gourd*

Wright. *Journey to Freedom: A Story of the Underground Railroad*

Wright. *Jumping the Broom*

Biography

Adler. *A Picture Book of Abraham Lincoln*

Adler. *A Picture Book of Frederick Douglass*

Adler. *A Picture Book of Harriet Tubman*

Adler. *A Picture Book of Robert E. Lee*

Adler. *A Picture Book of Sojourner Truth*

Anderson. *Mary Todd Lincoln: President's Wife*

Ash. *The Story of Harriet Beecher Stowe*

Banta. *Douglass: Voice of Liberty*

Barrett. *Nat Turner and the Slave Revolt*

Benjamin. *Young Harriet Tubman*

Bennett. *Abraham Lincoln: Healing a Divided Nation*

Bennett. *Frederick Douglass and the War Against Slavery*

Bland. *Harriet Beecher Stowe: Antislavery Author*

Bowen. *A World of Knowing: Thomas Hopkins Gallaudet*

Brenner. *Abe Lincoln's Hat*

Burleigh. *A Man Named Thoreau*

Burns. *Harriet Tubman*

Collins. *John Brown and the Fight Against Slavery*

Colver. *Abraham Lincoln: For the People*

D'Aulaire. *Abraham Lincoln*

Davidson. *Dolly Madison: Famous First Lady*

Ferris. *Go Free or Die*

Ferris. *Walking the Road to Freedom*

Fritz. *Stonewall*

Fritz. *You Want Women to Vote, Lizzie Stanton?*

Girard. *Young Frederick Douglass*

Graves. *Robert E. Lee*

Greene. *Abraham Lincoln: President of a Divided Country*

Gross. *True Stories About Abraham Lincoln*

Harness. *Young Abe Lincoln: 1809-1837*

Henry. *Elizabeth Blackwell: Girl Doctor*

Jacobs. *Lincoln*

Kent. *The Story of John Brown's Raid on Harpers Ferry*

Kerby. *Samuel Morse*

Kunhardt. *Honest Abe*

Latham. *Samuel F. B. Morse*

Lawrence. *Harriet and the Promised Land*

Levin. *Susan B. Anthony*

Livingston. *Abraham Lincoln*

Lyons. *Deep Blues: Bill Traylor, Self-Taught Artist*

Lyons. *Master of Mahogany: Tom Day*

Malone. *Dorothea L. Dix*

McKissack. *Frederick Douglass: Leader Against Slavery*

McKissack. *Sojourner Truth: A Voice for Freedom*

Miller. *Frederick Douglass: The Last Day of Slavery*

Murphy. *Into the Deep Forest with Henry David*

Parlin. *Jackson: Pioneer and President*

Patterson. *Frederick Douglass: Freedom Fighter*

Peterson. *Henry Clay: Leader in Congress*

Schomp. *Frederick Douglass*

Schroeder. *Minty: A Story of Young Harriet Tubman*

Swain. *The Road to Seneca Falls: Elizabeth Cady Stanton*

Thaxter. *Celia's Island Journey*

Weiner. *The Story of Frederick Douglass: Voice of Freedom*

Collective Biography

Cohen. *The Ghost of Elvis*
King. *First Facts About American Heroes*

Marzollo. *My First Book of Biographies*

Provensen. *The Buck Stops Here: The Presidents*

History

Ash. *The Story of the Women's Movement*
Bowler. *Trains*
Burns. *Mail*
Caulkins. *Pets of the Presidents*
Climo. *City! Washington, DC*
English. *Transportation: Automobiles to Zeppelins*
Gibbons. *Beacons of Light: Lighthouses*
Goldish. *Our Supreme Court*
Guiberson. *Lighthouses: Watchers at Sea*
Guzzetti. *The White House*
Harvey. *Women's Voting Rights*

Johnson. *Seminole Diary*
Kalman. *Children's Clothing of the 1800s*
Kalman. *A Child's Day*
Kalman. *Customs and Traditions*
Kalman. *Early Artisans*
Kalman. *Early Christmas*
Kalman. *Early Health and Medicine*
Kalman. *Early Schools*
Kalman. *Early Stores and Markets*
Kalman. *Early Travel*
Kalman. *Early Village Life*
Kalman. *19th Century Clothing*

Kalman. *Old-Time Toys*
Kalman. *A One-Room School*
Maestro. *The Story of Money*
Medearis. *Our People*
Pleasant. *Kirsten's Cookbook*
Sherrow. *The Big Book of U.S. Presidents*
Stein. *The Story of the Powers of the Supreme Court*
Steins. *Our Elections*
Stern. *The Congress: America's Lawmakers*
Weber. *Our Congress*
Wilson. *Visual Timeline of Transportation*

Multimedia

Video

African American Life
Equal Rights for All
Follow the Drinking Gourd

Who Owns the Sun?
The Sellin' of Jamie Thomas

Old Sturbridge Village: Growing Up in New England

GRADE FOUR

Historical Fiction

Ackerman. *Araminta's Paint Box*
Avi. *The Barn*
Avi. *The Man Who Was Poe*
Avi. *Something's Upstairs: A Tale of Ghosts*
Blumberg. *Bloomers!*
Brill. *Allen Jay and the Underground Railroad*
Carrick. *Stay Away from Simon!*
Coleman. *The Foot Warmer and the Crow*
Curry. *What the Dickens!*

De Angeli. *Thee, Hannah!*
Edwards. *Barefoot: Escape on the Underground Railroad*
Fritz. *Brady*
Guccione. *Come Morning*
Hermes. *On Winter's Wind*
Holmes. *See You in Heaven*
Hoobler. *Next Stop, Freedom: The Story of a Slave Girl*
Hooks. *Freedom's Fruit*
Hooks. *The Ballad of Belle Dorcas*
Hurmence. *A Girl Called Boy*

Johnson. *Now Let Me Fly: The Story of a Slave Family*
McCully. *The Bobbin Girl*
Roop. *Keep the Lights Burning, Abbie*
Rosen. *A School for Pompey Walker*
Rosenburg. *William Parker*
Smucker. *Runaway to Freedom*
Turner. *Nettie's Trip South*
Turner. *Running for our Lives*
Wisler. *Caleb's Choice*

Biography

Adler. *A Picture Book of Frederick Douglass*
Adler. *A Picture Book of Harriet Tubman*
Adler. *A Picture Book of Robert E. Lee*
Adler. *A Picture Book of Sojourner Truth*

Anderson. *Mary Todd Lincoln: President's Wife*
Ash. *The Story of Harriet Beecher Stowe*
Banta. *Douglass: Voice of Liberty*
Barrett. *Nat Turner and the Slave Revolt*

Bennett. *Abraham Lincoln: Healing a Divided Nation*
Bennett. *Frederick Douglass and the War Against Slavery*
Bland. *Harriet Beecher Stowe: Antislavery Author*

Bowen. *A World of Knowing: Thomas Hopkins Gallaudet*

Burleigh. *A Man Named Thoreau*

Burns. *Harriet Tubman*

Cannon. *Robert E. Lee*

Casey. *Millard Fillmore: Thirteenth President*

Clinton. *Benjamin Harrison: Twenty-Third President*

Collins. *John Brown and the Fight Against Slavery*

Colver. *Abraham Lincoln: For the People*

Connell. *They Shall Be Heard: Susan B. Anthony and Elizabeth Cady Stanton*

D'Aulaire. *Abraham Lincoln*

Davidson. *Dolly Madison: Famous First Lady*

Everett. *John Brown: One Man Against Slavery*

Ferris. *Go Free or Die*

Ferris. *Walking the Road to Freedom*

Fitz-Gerald. *James Monroe: Fifth President*

Fitz-Gerald. *William Henry Harrison: Ninth President*

Fritz. *Harriet Beecher Stowe and the Beecher Preachers*

Fritz. *Stonewall*

Fritz. *You Want Women to Vote, Lizzie Stanton?*

Girard. *Young Frederick Douglass*

Graves. *Robert E. Lee*

Greene. *Louisa May Alcott: Author, Nurse, Suffragette*

Gross. *True Stories About Abraham Lincoln*

Hargrove. *Abraham Lincoln: Sixteenth President*

Hargrove. *Martin Van Buren: Eighth President*

Harness. *Young Abe Lincoln: 1809-1837*

Henry. *Elizabeth Blackwell: Girl Doctor*

Jacobs. *Lincoln*

Kent. *Andrew Johnson: Seventeenth President*

Kent. *The Story of John Brown's Raid on Harpers Ferry*

Kent. *Zachary Taylor: Twelfth President*

Kerby. *Frederick Douglass*

Kerby. *Samuel Morse*

Latham. *Samuel F. B. Morse*

Levin. *Susan B. Anthony*

Lillegard. *James K. Polk: Eleventh President*

Lillegard. *John Tyler: Tenth President*

Lyons. *Deep Blues: Bill Traylor, Self-Taught Artist*

Lyons. *Master of Mahogany: Tom Day*

Macht. *Sojourner Truth: Crusader for Civil Rights*

Malone. *Dorothea L. Dix*

Marston. *Isaac Johnson: From Slave to Stonecutter*

McKissack. *Frederick Douglass: The Black Lion*

McKissack. *Frederick Douglass: Leader Against Slavery*

McKissack. *Sojourner Truth: A Voice for Freedom*

McPherson. *I Speak for the Women: A Story About Lucy Stone*

Miller. *Frederick Douglass: The Last Day of Slavery*

Murphy. *Into the Deep Forest with Henry David*

Osinski. *Andrew Jackson: Seventh President*

Parlin. *Jackson: Pioneer and President*

Patterson. *Frederick Douglass: Freedom Fighter*

Peterson. *Henry Clay: Leader in Congress*

Reef. *Henry David Thoreau: A Neighbor to Nature*

Rosen. *A Fire in Her Bones: Mary Lyon*

Sandburg. *Abe Lincoln Grows Up*

Schleichert. *The Life of Dorothea Dix*

Schleichert. *The Life of Elizabeth Blackwell*

Schomp. *Frederick Douglass*

Swain. *The Road to Seneca Falls: Elizabeth Cady Stanton*

Thaxter. *Celia's Island Journey*

Weiner. *The Story of Frederick Douglass: Voice of Freedom*

Wilson. *The Ingenious Mr. Peale*

Collective Biography

Altman. *Extraordinary Black Americans*

Clements. *The Picture History of Great Inventors*

Fleming. *Women of the Lights*

Jacobs. *Great Lives: Human Rights*

King. *First Facts About American Heroes*

Pascoe. *First Facts About the Presidents*

Provensen. *The Buck Stops Here: The Presidents*

Provensen. *My Fellow Americans*

Rappaport. *Escape from Slavery: Five Journeys to Freedom*

Rubel. *The Scholastic Encyclopedia of the Presidents*

History

Ash. *The Story of the Women's Movement*

Bial. *The Underground Railroad*

Blue. *The White House Kids*

Bolick. *Mail Call!*

Bowler. *Trains*

Brill. *Let Women Vote!*

Burns. *Mail*

Burns. *Money*

Caulkins. *Pets of the Presidents*

Climo. *City! Washington, DC*

Connell. *Tales from the Underground Railroad*

English. *Transportation: Automobiles to Zeppelins*

Gibbons. *Beacons of Light: Lighthouses*

Giblin. *Be Seated: A Book About Chairs*

Goldish. *Our Supreme Court*

Guiberson. *Lighthouses: Watchers at Sea*

Guzzetti. *The White House*

Johnson. *Seminole Diary*

Jones. *The President Has Been Shot*

Hamilton. *Many Thousand Gone: African Americans*

Harvey. *Women's Voting Rights*

Kalman. *Children's Clothing of the 1800s*

Kalman. *A Child's Day*

Kalman. *Customs and Traditions*

Kalman. *Early Artisans*

Kalman. *Early Christmas*

Kalman. *Early Health and Medicine*

Kalman. *Early Pleasures and Pastimes*

Kalman. *Early Schools*

Kalman. *Early Stores and Markets*

Kalman. *Early Travel*

Kalman. *Early Village Life*

Kalman. *19th Century Clothing*

Kalman. *Old-Time Toys*

Kalman. *A One-Room School*

Kurtz. *U.S. Army*

Lampton. *Epidemic*

Maestro. *The Story of Money*

McKissack. *Christmas in the Big House, Christmas in the Quarters*

McNeese. *America's Early Canals*

McNeese. *America's First Railroads*

Pleasant. *Kirsten's Cookbook*

Pollard. *The Nineteenth Century*

Reef. *The Supreme Court*

Rowland-Warne. *Costume*

Sandler. *Presidents*

Sherrow. *The Big Book of U.S. Presidents*

Stein. *The Story of the Powers of the Supreme Court*

Steins. *Our Elections*

Stern. *The Congress: America's Lawmakers*

Sullivan. *Children of Promise: African-American Literature and Art*

Toynton. *Growing Up in America: 1830-1860*

Ventura. *Clothing*

Ventura. *Food: Its Evolution Through the Ages*

Weber. *Our Congress*

Wilson. *Visual Timeline of Transportation*

Multimedia

CD-ROM

Her Heritage: A Biographical Encyclopedia of American History

SkyTrip America

Total History

Video

Abraham Lincoln

African American Life

African Americans

Black Is My Color: The African American Experience

Blind Tom

Equal Rights for All

Follow the Drinking Gourd

Old Sturbridge Village: Growing Up in New England

Presenting Mr. Frederick Douglass

The Sellin' of Jamie Thomas

The Steam Engine: G. Stephenson

Who Owns the Sun?

GRADE FIVE

Historical Fiction

Avi. *The Barn*

Avi. *Beyond the Western Sea, Book Two: Lord Kirkle's Money*

Avi. *The Man Who Was Poe*

Avi. *Something's Upstairs: A Tale of Ghosts*

Avi. *The True Confessions of Charlotte Doyle*

Beatty. *Jayhawker*

Blumberg. *Bloomers!*

Brill. *Allen Jay and the Underground Railroad*

Carrick. *Stay Away from Simon!*

Coleman. *The Foot Warmer and the Crow*

Curry. *What the Dickens!*

De Angeli. *Thee, Hannah!*

DeFelice. *The Apprenticeship of Lucas Whitaker*

Duff. *Radical Red*

Fox. *The Slave Dancer*

Fritz. *Brady*

Gaeddert. *Breaking Free*

Guccione. *Come Morning*

Hamilton. *The House of Dies Drear*

Hermes. *On Winter's Wind*

Holmes. *See You in Heaven*

Hoobler. *Next Stop, Freedom: The Story of a Slave Girl*

Hooks. *The Ballad of Belle Dorcas*

Hooks. *Freedom's Fruit*

Hurmence. *A Girl Called Boy*

McCully. *The Bobbin Girl*

Nixon. *A Family Apart*

Paterson. *Jip: His Story*

Rosen. *A School for Pompey Walker*

Rosenburg. *William Parker*

Ruby. *Steal Away Home*

Smucker. *Runaway to Freedom*

Stone. *Autumn of the Royal Tar*

Turner. *Nettie's Trip South*

Turner. *Running for Our Lives*

Wisler. *Caleb's Choice*

Biography

Anderson. *Mary Todd Lincoln: President's Wife*

Ash. *The Story of Harriet Beecher Stowe*

Bennett. *Abraham Lincoln: Healing a Divided Nation*

Bennett. *Stonewall Jackson: Lee's Greatest Lieutenant*

Bentley. *"Dear Friend": Thomas Garrett and William Still*

Bisson. *Nat Turner: Slave Revolt Leader*

Bland. *Harriet Beecher Stowe: Antislavery Author*

Borzendowski. *John Russwurm*

Bowen. *A World of Knowing: Thomas Hopkins Gallaudet*

Brown. *Elizabeth Blackwell: Physician*

Brown. *Franklin Pierce: 14th President of the United States*

Brown. *Robert E. Lee*

Bruns. *Abraham Lincoln*

Burke. *Louisa May Alcott*

Burleigh. *A Man Named Thoreau*

Burns. *Harriet Tubman*

Cannon. *Robert E. Lee*

Carlson. *Harriet Tubman: Call to Freedom*

Casey. *Millard Fillmore: Thirteenth President*

Clinton. *Benjamin Harrison: Twenty-Third President*

Coelho. *John Quincy Adams*

Collins. *John Brown and the Fight Against Slavery*

Collins. *Zachary Taylor: 12th President*

Colver. *Abraham Lincoln: For the People*

Connell. *They Shall Be Heard: Susan B. Anthony and Elizabeth Cady Stanton*

D'Aulaire. *Abraham Lincoln*

Davidson. *Dolly Madison: Famous First Lady*

Douglass. *Escape from Slavery: The Boyhood of Frederick Douglass*

Dubowski. *Andrew Johnson: Rebuilding the Union*

Durwood. *John C. Calhoun*

Edwards. *Denmark Vesey: Slave Revolt Leader*

Ellis. *Martin Van Buren: 8th President*

Everett. *John Brown: One Man Against Slavery*

Falkof. *John Tyler: 10th President*

Ferris. *Go Free or Die*

Ferris. *Walking the Road to Freedom*

Fitz-Gerald. *James Monroe: Fifth President*

Fitz-Gerald. *William Henry Harrison: Ninth President*

Fritz. *The Great Little Madison*

Fritz. *Harriet Beecher Stowe and the Beecher Preachers*

Fritz. *Stonewall*

Fritz. *You Want Women to Vote, Lizzie Stanton?*

Graves. *Robert E. Lee*

Greenblatt. *James K. Polk*

Greene. *Louisa May Alcott: Author, Nurse, Suffragette*

Hamilton. *Anthony Burns: The Defeat and Triumph of a Fugitive Slave*

Hargrove. *Abraham Lincoln: Sixteenth President*

Hargrove. *Martin Van Buren: Eighth President*

Harness. *Young Abe Lincoln: 1809-1837*

Henry. *Elizabeth Blackwell: Girl Doctor*

Hilto. *The World of Young Andrew Jackson*

Jacobs. *Lincoln*

Jakoubek. *Harriet Beecher Stowe*

Kent. *Andrew Johnson: Seventeenth President*

Kent. *The Story of John Brown's Raid on Harpers Ferry*

Kent. *Zachary Taylor: Twelfth President*

Kerby. *Frederick Douglass*

Klots. *Richard Allen: Religious Leader and Social Activist*

Krass. *Sojourner Truth: Antislavery Activist*

Latham. *Samuel F. B. Morse*

Law. *Milliard Fillmore: 13th President*

Leavell. *James Madison*

Lillegard. *James K. Polk: Eleventh President*

Lillegard. *John Tyler: Tenth President*

Lindop. *George Washington, Thomas Jefferson, and Andrew Jackson*

Lindop. *James K. Polk, Abraham Lincoln, Theodore Roosevelt*

Lyons. *Deep Blues: Bill Traylor, Self-Taught Artist*

Lyons. *Master of Mahogany: Tom Day*

Macht. *Sojourner Truth: Crusader for Civil Rights*

Malone. *Dorothea L. Dix*

Marston. *Isaac Johnson: From Slave to Stonecutter*

McKissack. *Frederick Douglass: The Black Lion*

McKissack. *Sojourner Truth: Ain't I a Woman?*

McPherson. *I Speak for the Women: A Story About Lucy Stone*

Morris. *The Lincoln Way*

Murphy. *Into the Deep Forest with Henry David*

Osinski. *Andrew Jackson: Seventh President*

Parlin. *Jackson: Pioneer and President*

Patterson. *Frederick Douglass: Freedom Fighter*

Peterson. *Henry Clay: Leader in Congress*

Reef. *Henry David Thoreau: A Neighbor to Nature*

Rosen. *A Fire in Her Bones: Mary Lyon*

Russell. *Frederick Douglass: Abolitionist Editor*

Ryan. *Louisa May Alcott: Her Girlhood Diary*

Sandak. *The Jacksons*

Sandak. *The Lincolns*

Sandburg. *Abe Lincoln Grows Up*

Schleichert. *The Life of Dorothea Dix*

Schleichert. *The Life of Elizabeth Blackwell*

Schomp. *Frederick Douglass*

Scott. *John Brown of Harper's Ferry*

Stefoff. *Abraham Lincoln: 16th President*

Stefoff. *Andrew Jackson: 7th President*

Stefoff. *William Henry Harrison: 9th President*

Stevens. *Chester Arthur: 21st President*

Swain. *The Road to Seneca Falls: Elizabeth Cady Stanton*
Trump. *Lincoln's Little Girl: A True Story*

Viola. *Andrew Jackson*
Weiner. *The Story of Frederick Douglass: Voice of Freedom*

Weisberg. *Susan B. Anthony*
Wilson. *The Ingenious Mr. Peale*

Collective Biography

Altman. *Extraordinary Black Americans*
Clements. *The Picture History of Great Inventors*
Faber. *Great Lives: American Government*
Fleming. *Women of the Lights*
Hazell. *Heroines: Great Women Through the Ages*
Jacobs. *Great Lives: Human Rights*

Katz. *Proudly Red and Black: Stories of African and Native Americans*
King. *First Facts About American Heroes*
McKissack. *Rebels Against Slavery: American Slave Revolts*
Pascoe. *First Facts About the Presidents*

Provensen. *The Buck Stops Here: The Presidents*
Provensen. *My Fellow Americans*
Rappaport. *Escape from Slavery: Five Journeys to Freedom*
Rubel. *The Scholastic Encyclopedia of the Presidents*

History

Ash. *The Story of the Women's Movement*
Barboza. *Door of No Return: The Legend of Gorée Island*
Barrett. *Harpers Ferry: John Brown's Raid*
Bial. *The Underground Railroad*
Blue. *The White House Kids*
Bolick. *Mail Call!*
Bowler. *Trains*
Brill. *Let Women Vote!*
Burns. *Mail*
Burns. *Money*
Caulkins. *Pets of the Presidents*
Climo. *City! Washington, DC*
Colman. *Strike: The Bitter Struggle of American Workers*
Colman. *Toilets, Bathtubs, Sinks, and Sewers*
Connell. *Tales from the Underground Railroad*
Davies. *Transport: On Land, Road and Rail*
Emert. *Top Lawyers and their Famous Cases*
English. *Transportation: Automobiles to Zeppelins*
Fisher. *Tracks Across America: The Story of the American Railroad, 1825-1900*
Giblin. *Be Seated: A Book About Chairs*
Goldish. *Our Supreme Court*
Guiberson. *Lighthouses: Watchers at Sea*
Guzzetti. *The White House*
Hamilton. *Many Thousand Gone: African Americans*

Harvey. *Women's Voting Rights*
Hirsch. *Taxation: Paying for Government*
Johnson. *Seminole Diary*
Jones. *The President Has Been Shot*
Kalman. *A Child's Day*
Kalman. *Children's Clothing of the 1800s*
Kalman. *Customs and Traditions*
Kalman. *Early Artisans*
Kalman. *Early Christmas*
Kalman. *Early Health and Medicine*
Kalman. *Early Pleasures and Pastimes*
Kalman. *Early Schools*
Kalman. *Early Stores and Markets*
Kalman. *Early Travel*
Kalman. *Early Village Life*
Kalman. *19th Century Clothing*
Kalman. *Old-Time Toys*
Kalman. *A One-Room School*
Karl. *America Alive: A History*
Katz. *Breaking the Chains: African-American Slave Resistance*
Kurtz. *U.S. Army*
Lampton. *Epidemic*
Lucas. *Civil Rights: The Long Struggle*
Maestro. *The Story of Money*
McKissack. *Christmas in the Big House, Christmas in the Quarters*
McNeese. *America's Early Canals*

McNeese. *America's First Railroads*
Medearis. *Come This Far to Freedom*
Meltzer. *The Black Americans*
Morley. *Clothes: For Work, Play and Display*
Platt. *The Smithsonian Visual Timeline of Inventions*
Pleasant. *Kirsten's Cookbook*
Pollard. *The Nineteenth Century*
Reef. *The Supreme Court*
Rowland-Warne. *Costume*
Sandler. *Presidents*
Sherrow. *The Big Book of U.S. Presidents*
Stein. *The Story of the Powers of the Supreme Court*
Steins. *Our Elections*
Stepto. *Our Song, Our Toil: The Story of American Slavery as Told by Slaves*
Stern. *The Congress: America's Lawmakers*
Sullivan. *Children of Promise: African-American Literature and Art*
Taylor. *Black Abolitionists and Freedom Fighters*
Toynton. *Growing Up in America: 1830-1860*
Ventura. *Clothing*
Ventura. *Food: Its Evolution Through the Ages*
Weber. *Our Congress*
Whitman. *Get Up and Go: American Road Travel*
Wilson. *Visual Timeline of Transportation*

Multimedia

CD-ROM

American History Explorer
Eyewitness Encyclopedia of
Science

Her Heritage: A Biographical
Encyclopedia of American
History

Portraits of American
Presidents
SkyTrip America
Total History

Video

Abraham Lincoln
African American Life
African Americans
Black Is My Color: The
African American
Experience
Blind Tom
Causes of the Civil War
Democracy and Reform

Equal Rights for All
Follow the Drinking Gourd
The Life and Times of
Abraham Lincoln
Lincoln: A Photobiography
Old Sturbridge Village:
Growing Up in New
England

Presenting Mr. Frederick
Douglass
The Sellin' of Jamie Thomas
Slavery and Freedom
The Steam Engine: G.
Stephenson
Susan B. Anthony Story
Who Owns the Sun?

GRADE SIX

Historical Fiction

Avi. *The Barn*
Avi. *The Man Who Was Poe*
Avi. *Something's Upstairs: A*
Tale of Ghosts
Avi. *The True Confessions of*
Charlotte Doyle
Beatty. *Jayhawker*
Blos. *Brothers of the Heart*
Carrick. *Stay Away from*
Simon!
Coleman. *The Foot Warmer*
and the Crow
Curry. *What the Dickens!*

DeFelice. *The Apprenticeship*
of Lucas Whitaker
Duff. *Radical Red*
Fleischman. *The Borning*
Room
Fox. *The Slave Dancer*
Fritz. *Brady*
Gaeddert. *Breaking Free*
Guccione. *Come Morning*
Hamilton. *The House of Dies*
Drear
Hermes. *On Winter's Wind*
Hurmence. *A Girl Called Boy*
Nixon. *A Family Apart*

Paterson. *Jip: His Story*
Paterson. *Lyddie*
Rosen. *A School for Pompey*
Walker
Rosenburg. *William Parker*
Ruby. *Steal Away Home*
Smucker. *Runaway to*
Freedom
Stone. *Autumn of the Royal*
Tar
Turner. *Running for our Lives*
Walter. *Second Daughter*
Wisler. *Caleb's Choice*

Biography

Adler. *A Picture Book of*
Frederick Douglass
Anderson. *Mary Todd*
Lincoln: President's Wife
Ash. *The Story of Harriet*
Beecher Stowe
Banta. *Douglass: Voice of*
Liberty
Bennett. *Abraham Lincoln:*
Healing a Divided Nation
Bennett. *Frederick Douglass*
and the War Against
Slavery
Bennett. *Stonewall Jackson:*
Lee's Greatest Lieutenant
Bentley. *"Dear Friend":*
Thomas Garrett and
William Still
Bisson. *Nat Turner: Slave*
Revolt Leader

Bland. *Harriet Beecher*
Stowe: Antislavery Author
Borzendowski. *John*
Russwurm
Bowen. *A World of Knowing:*
Thomas Hopkins Gallaudet
Brown. *Elizabeth Blackwell:*
Physician
Brown. *Franklin Pierce: 14th*
President
Brown. *Robert E. Lee*
Bruns. *Abraham Lincoln*
Burke. *Louisa May Alcott*
Burleigh. *A Man Named*
Thoreau
Burns. *Harriet Tubman*
Cannon. *Robert E. Lee*
Carlson. *Harriet Tubman:*
Call to Freedom
Casey. *Millard Fillmore:*
Thirteenth President

Claflin. *Sojourner Truth and*
the Struggle for Freedom
Clinton. *Benjamin Harrison:*
Twenty-Third President
Coelho. *John Quincy Adams*
Collins. *John Brown and the*
Fight Against Slavery
Collins. *Zachary Taylor: 12th*
President
Colver. *Abraham Lincoln:*
For the People
Connell. *They Shall Be*
Heard: Susan B. Anthony
and Elizabeth Cady Stanton
Cullen-DuPont. *Elizabeth*
Cady Stanton and
Women's Liberty
D'Aulaire. *Abraham Lincoln*
Davidson. *Dolly Madison:*
Famous First Lady

Douglass. *Escape from Slavery: The Boyhood of Frederick Douglass*

Dubowski. *Andrew Johnson: Rebuilding the Union*

Durwood. *John C. Calhoun*

Edwards. *Denmark Vesey: Slave Revolt Leader*

Ellis. *Martin Van Buren: 8th President*

Everett. *John Brown: One Man Against Slavery*

Falkof. *John Tyler: 10th President*

Ferris. *Go Free or Die*

Ferris. *Walking the Road to Freedom*

Fitz-Gerald. *James Monroe: Fifth President*

Fitz-Gerald. *William Henry Harrison: Ninth President*

Freedman. *Lincoln: A Photobiography*

Fritz. *The Great Little Madison*

Fritz. *Harriet Beecher Stowe and the Beecher Preachers*

Fritz. *Stonewall*

Fritz. *You Want Women to Vote, Lizzie Stanton?*

Gehre. *Susan B. Anthony*

Girard. *Young Frederick Douglass*

Graham. *John Brown: A Cry for Freedom*

Graves. *Robert E. Lee*

Greenblatt. *James K. Polk*

Greene. *Louisa May Alcott: Author, Nurse, Suffragette*

Hamilton. *Anthony Burns: The Defeat and Triumph of a Fugitive Slave*

Hargrove. *Abraham Lincoln: Sixteenth President*

Hargrove. *Martin Van Buren: Eighth President*

Harness. *Young Abe Lincoln: 1809-1837*

Henry. *Elizabeth Blackwell: Girl Doctor*

Hilto. *The World of Young Andrew Jackson*

Jacobs. *Lincoln*

Jakoubek. *Harriet Beecher Stowe*

Johnston. *Harriet: The Life and World of Harriet Beecher Stowe*

Kendall. *Susan B. Anthony*

Kent. *Andrew Johnson: Seventeenth President*

Kent. *The Story of John Brown's Raid on Harpers Ferry*

Kent. *Zachary Taylor: Twelfth President*

Kerby. *Frederick Douglass*

Kerby. *Robert E. Lee*

Kerby. *Samuel Morse*

Klots. *Richard Allen: Religious Leader and Social Activist*

Krass. *Sojourner Truth: Antislavery Activist*

Latham. *Samuel F. B. Morse*

Law. *Milliard Fillmore: 13th President*

Leavell. *James Madison*

Levin. *Susan B. Anthony*

Lillegard. *James K. Polk: Eleventh President*

Lillegard. *John Tyler: Tenth President*

Lindop. *George Washington, Thomas Jefferson, and Andrew Jackson*

Lindop. *James K. Polk, Abraham Lincoln, Theodore Roosevelt*

Lyons. *Deep Blues: Bill Traylor, Self-Taught Artist*

Macht. *Sojourner Truth: Crusader for Civil Rights*

Malone. *Dorothea L. Dix*

Marrin. *Virginia's General: Robert E. Lee*

Marston. *Isaac Johnson: From Slave to Stonecutter*

McClard. *Harriet Tubman: Slavery and the Underground Railroad*

McKissack. *Frederick Douglass: The Black Lion*

McKissack. *Sojourner Truth: Ain't I a Woman?*

McPherson. *I Speak for the Women: A Story About Lucy Stone*

Morris. *The Lincoln Way*

Murphy. *Into the Deep Forest with Henry David*

Osinski. *Andrew Jackson: Seventh President*

Parlin. *Jackson: Pioneer and President*

Patterson. *Frederick Douglass: Freedom Fighter*

Peterson. *Henry Clay: Leader in Congress*

Pflueger. *Stonewall Jackson*

Potter. *John Brown: Militant Abolitionist*

Randolph. *Woodrow Wilson: President*

Reef. *Henry David Thoreau: A Neighbor to Nature*

Rosen. *A Fire in Her Bones: Mary Lyon*

Russell. *Frederick Douglass: Abolitionist Editor*

Ryan. *Louisa May Alcott: Her Girlhood Diary*

Sandak. *The Jacksons*

Sandak. *The Lincolns*

Sandburg. *Abe Lincoln Grows Up*

Schleichert. *The Life of Dorothea Dix*

Schleichert. *The Life of Elizabeth Blackwell*

Schomp. *Frederick Douglass*

Scott. *John Brown of Harper's Ferry*

Stefoff. *Abraham Lincoln: 16th President*

Stefoff. *Andrew Jackson: 7th President*

Stefoff. *William Henry Harrison: 9th President*

Stevens. *Chester Arthur: 21st President*

Swain. *The Road to Seneca Falls: Elizabeth Cady Stanton*

Trump. *Lincoln's Little Girl: A True Story*

Viola. *Andrew Jackson*

Weiner. *The Story of Frederick Douglass: Voice of Freedom*

Weisberg. *Susan B. Anthony*

Wilson. *The Ingenious Mr. Peale*

Collective Biography

Altman. *Extraordinary Black Americans*

Beard. *The Presidents in American History*

Blassingame. *The Look-It-Up Book of Presidents*

Clements. *The Picture History of Great Inventors*

Faber. *Great Lives: American Government*

Fleming. *Women of the Lights*

Hazell. *Heroines: Great Women Through the Ages*

Jacobs. *Great Lives: Human Rights*

Katz. *Proudly Red and Black: Stories of African and Native Americans*

King. *First Facts About American Heroes*

McKissack. *Rebels Against Slavery: American Slave Revolts*

Morin. *Women Who Reformed Politics*

Myers. *Now Is Your Time*

Pascoe. *First Facts About the Presidents*

Provensen. *The Buck Stops Here: The Presidents*

Provensen. *My Fellow Americans*

Rappaport. *Escape from Slavery: Five Journeys to Freedom*

Rennert. *Pioneers of Discovery*

Rubel. *The Scholastic Encyclopedia of the Presidents*

Presidents of a Young Republic

Sullivan. *Black Artists in Photography, 1840-1940*

History

Ash. *The Story of the Women's Movement*

Barboza. *Door of No Return: The Legend of Gorée Island*

Barrett. *Harpers Ferry: John Brown's Raid*

Bial. *The Underground Railroad*

Blue. *The White House Kids*

Bolick. *Mail Call!*

Bowler. *Trains*

Brill. *Let Women Vote!*

Burns. *Money*

Caulkins. *Pets of the Presidents*

Climo. *City! Washington, DC*

Colman. *Strike: The Bitter Struggle of American Workers*

Colman. *Toilets, Bathtubs, Sinks, and Sewers*

Connell. *Tales from the Underground Railroad*

Cosner. *The Underground Railroad*

Davies. *Transport: On Land, Road and Rail*

Emert. *Top Lawyers and Their Famous Cases*

English. *Transportation: Automobiles to Zeppelins*

Fisher. *Tracks Across America: The Story of the American Railroad, 1825-1900*

Frank. *The Birth of Black America: The Age of Discovery and the Slave Trade*

Giblin. *Be Seated: A Book About Chairs*

Goldish. *Our Supreme Court*

Gorrell. *North Star to Freedom: The Story of the Underground Railroad*

Guiberson. *Lighthouses: Watchers at Sea*

Guzzetti. *The White House*

Hakim. *Liberty for All?*

Hamilton. *Many Thousand Gone: African Americans*

Herda. *The Dred Scott Case*

Hirsch. *Taxation: Paying for Government*

Jones. *The President Has Been Shot*

Kalman. *Customs and Traditions*

Kalman. *Early Artisans*

Kalman. *Early Christmas*

Kalman. *Early Health and Medicine*

Kalman. *Early Schools*

Kalman. *Early Stores and Markets*

Kalman. *Early Travel*

Kalman. *Early Village Life*

Kalman. *19th Century Clothing*

Kalman. *Old-Time Toys*

Kalman. *A One-Room School*

Karl. *America Alive: A History*

Katz. *Breaking the Chains: African-American Slave Resistance*

Kurtz. *U.S. Army*

Lampton. *Epidemic*

Leiner. *First Children: Growing Up in the White House*

Lucas. *Civil Rights: The Long Struggle*

Markham. *Inventions That Changed Modern Life*

McKissack. *Christmas in the Big House, Christmas in the Quarters*

McNeese. *America's Early Canals*

McNeese. *America's First Railroads*

Medearis. *Come This Far to Freedom*

Meltzer. *The Black Americans*

Morley. *Clothes: For Work, Play and Display*

Patrick. *The Young Oxford Companion to the Supreme Court*

Paulson. *Days of Sorrow; Years of Glory*

Philip. *Singing America: Poems That Define a Nation*

Platt. *The Smithsonian Visual Timeline of Inventions*

Pleasant. *Kirsten's Cookbook*

Pollard. *The Nineteenth Century*

Reef. *The Supreme Court*

Rowland-Warne. *Costume*

Sandler. *Presidents*

St. George. *The White House: Cornerstone of a Nation*

Sherrow. *The Big Book of U.S. Presidents*

Stein. *The Story of the Powers of the Supreme Court*

Steins. *Our Elections*

Stepto. *Our Song, Our Toil: The Story of American Slavery as Told by Slaves*

Stern. *The Congress: America's Lawmakers*

Sullivan. *Children of Promise: African-American Literature and Art*

Taylor. *Black Abolitionists and Freedom Fighters*

Toynton. *Growing Up in America: 1830-1860*

Ventura. *Clothing*

Ventura. *Food: Its Evolution Through the Ages*
Weber. *Our Congress*
Wheeler. *Events That Changed American History*

White. *Let My People Go: African Americans 1804-1860*
Whitman. *Get Up and Go: American Road Travel*

Multimedia

CD-ROM

American History Explorer
Campaigns, Candidates and the Presidency
Eyewitness Encyclopedia of Science

Her Heritage: A Biographical Encyclopedia of American History
Portraits of American Presidents

SkyTrip America
Total History
The Way Things Work

Video

Abraham Lincoln
African American Life
African Americans
Black Is My Color: The African American Experience
Blind Tom
Causes of the Civil War
Democracy and Reform

Equal Rights for All
The Life and Times of Abraham Lincoln
Lincoln: A Photobiography
Old Sturbridge Village: Growing Up in New England
Presenting Mr. Frederick Douglass

Reading Terminal Market
The Sellin' of Jamie Thomas
Slavery and Freedom
The Steam Engine: G. Stephenson
Susan B. Anthony Story
Who Owns the Sun?

THE CIVIL WAR, 1861-1865

KINDERGARTEN THROUGH SECOND GRADE

Historical Fiction

Ackerman. *The Tin Heart*
Bunting. *The Blue and the Gray*
Gauch. *Thunder at Gettysburg*
Lyon. *Cecil's Story*
Monjo. *Gettysburg: Tad Lincoln's Story*
Monjo. *Me and Willie and Pa*
Monjo. *The Vicksburg Veteran*
Whittier. *Barbara Frietchie*
Winnick. *Mr. Lincoln's Whiskers*

Biography

Adler. *A Picture Book of Abraham Lincoln*
Adler. *A Picture Book of Frederick Douglass*
Adler. *A Picture Book of Harriet Tubman*
Adler. *A Picture Book of Sojourner Truth*
Benjamin. *Young Harriet Tubman*
Brenner. *Abe Lincoln's Hat*
Fritz. *Just a Few Words, Mr. Lincoln*
Greene. *Abraham Lincoln: President of a Divided Country*
Greene. *Robert E. Lee*
Gross. *True Stories About Abraham Lincoln*
Kunhardt. *Honest Abe*
Lawrence. *Harriet and the Promised Land*
Livingston. *Abraham Lincoln*
McKissack. *Frederick Douglass: Leader Against Slavery*
Rose. *Clara Barton: Soldier of Mercy*

Collective Biography

Marzollo. *My First Book of Biographies*

History

Medearis. *Our People*

Multimedia

Video

Equal Rights for All
President's Day

GRADE THREE

Historical Fiction

Ackerman. *The Tin Heart*
Bunting. *The Blue and the Gray*
Gauch. *Thunder at Gettysburg*
Lyon. *Cecil's Story*
Monjo. *Gettysburg: Tad Lincoln's Story*
Monjo. *Me and Willie and Pa*
Monjo. *The Vicksburg Veteran*
Porter. *Meet Addy: An American Girl*
Reeder. *Across the Lines*
Steele. *The Perilous Road*
Whittier. *Barbara Frietchie*
Winnick. *Mr. Lincoln's Whiskers*

66

Biography

Adler. *A Picture Book of Abraham Lincoln*

Adler. *A Picture Book of Frederick Douglass*

Adler. *A Picture Book of Harriet Tubman*

Anderson. *Mary Todd Lincoln: President's Wife*

Ash. *The Story of Harriet Beecher Stowe*

Banta. *Douglass: Voice of Liberty*

Benjamin. *Young Harriet Tubman*

Bennett. *Abraham Lincoln: Healing a Divided Nation*

Bennett. *Frederick Douglass and the War Against Slavery*

Bland. *Harriet Beecher Stowe: Antislavery Author*

Brenner. *Abe Lincoln's Hat*

Burns. *Harriet Tubman*

Colver. *Abraham Lincoln: For the People*

D'Aulaire. *Abraham Lincoln*

Ferris. *Go Free or Die*

Ferris. *Walking the Road to Freedom*

Fritz. *Just a Few Words, Mr. Lincoln*

Fritz. *You Want Women to Vote, Lizzie Stanton?*

Graves. *Robert E. Lee*

Greene. *Abraham Lincoln: President of a Divided Country*

Gross. *True Stories About Abraham Lincoln*

Jacobs. *Lincoln*

Jakoubek. *The Assassination of Abraham Lincoln*

Kent. *Jefferson Davis*

Kerby. *Samuel Morse*

Kunhardt. *Honest Abe*

Latham. *Samuel F. B. Morse*

Lawrence. *Harriet and the Promised Land*

Levin. *Susan B. Anthony*

Livingston. *Abraham Lincoln*

Lyons. *Deep Blues: Bill Traylor, Self-Taught Artist*

Malone. *Dorothea L. Dix*

McKissack. *Frederick Douglass: Leader Against Slavery*

McKissack. *Sojourner Truth: A Voice for Freedom*

Patterson. *Frederick Douglass: Freedom Fighter*

Peterson. *Henry Clay: Leader in Congress*

Rose. *Clara Barton: Soldier of Mercy*

Schomp. *Frederick Douglass*

Swain. *The Road to Seneca Falls: Elizabeth Cady Stanton*

Weiner. *The Story of Frederick Douglass: Voice of Freedom*

Collective Biography

King. *First Facts About American Heroes*

Marzollo. *My First Book of Biographies*

Provensen. *The Buck Stops Here: The Presidents*

History

Caulkins. *Pets of the Presidents*

English. *Transportation: Automobiles to Zeppelins*

Evert. *Addy's Cook Book*

Hopkins. *Hand in Hand: An American History Through Poetry*

Johnson. *The Battle of Gettysburg*

Kent. *The Battle of Chancellorsville*

Kent. *The Battle of Shiloh*

Kent. *The Story of the Battle of Bull Run*

Kent. *The Story of the Surrender at Yorktown*

Maestro. *The Story of Money*

Medearis. *Our People*

Paananen. *The Military: Defending the Nation*

Pleasant Company. *Addy's Cook Book 1864*

Read. *Sheridan's Ride*

Reef. *Gettysburg*

Reef. *The Lincoln Memorial*

Richards. *The Gettysburg Address*

Sherrow. *The Big Book of U.S. Presidents*

Stern. *The Congress: America's Lawmakers*

Multimedia

Video

Equal Rights for All

President's Day

The Rebel Slave

GRADE FOUR

Historical Fiction

Alphin. *The Ghost Cadet*

Blos. *A Gathering of Days: A New England Girl's Journal, 1830-32*

Donahue. *An Island Far from Home*

Gauch. *Thunder at Gettysburg*

Hansen. *Which Way Freedom?*

Holland. *The Promised Land*

Monjo. *Gettysburg: Tad Lincoln's Story*

Monjo. *Me and Willie and Pa*

Monjo. *The Vicksburg Veteran*

Nixon. *A Dangerous Promise*

Polacco. *Pink and Say*

Porter. *Meet Addy: An American Girl*

Reeder. *Across the Lines*
Shura. *Gentle Annie: The True Story of a Civil War Nurse*

Steele. *The Perilous Road*
Whittier. *Barbara Frietchie*

Wisler. *Mr. Lincoln's Drummer*

Biography

Adler. *A Picture Book of Frederick Douglass*
Adler. *A Picture Book of Harriet Tubman*
Anderson. *Mary Todd Lincoln: President's Wife*
Ash. *The Story of Harriet Beecher Stowe*
Banta. *Douglass: Voice of Liberty*
Bennett. *Abraham Lincoln: Healing a Divided Nation*
Bennett. *Frederick Douglass and the War Against Slavery*
Bentley. *Ulysses S. Grant*
Bland. *Harriet Beecher Stowe: Antislavery Author*
Burns. *Harriet Tubman*
Cannon. *Robert E. Lee*
Casey. *Millard Fillmore: Thirteenth President*
Clinton. *Benjamin Harrison: Twenty-Third President*
Colver. *Abraham Lincoln: For the People*
Connell. *They Shall Be Heard: Susan B. Anthony and Elizabeth Cady Stanton*

D'Aulaire. *Abraham Lincoln*
Ferris. *Go Free or Die*
Ferris. *Walking the Road to Freedom*
Fritz. *Harriet Beecher Stowe and the Beecher Preachers*
Fritz. *You Want Women to Vote, Lizzie Stanton?*
Graves. *Robert E. Lee*
Greene. *Louisa May Alcott: Author, Nurse, Suffragette*
Gross. *True Stories About Abraham Lincoln*
Hargrove. *Abraham Lincoln: Sixteenth President*
Jacobs. *Lincoln*
Jakoubek. *The Assassination of Abraham Lincoln*
Kent. *Andrew Johnson: Seventeenth President*
Kent. *Jefferson Davis*
Kerby. *Frederick Douglass*
Kerby. *Samuel Morse*
Latham. *Samuel F. B. Morse*
Levin. *Susan B. Anthony*
Lyons. *Deep Blues: Bill Traylor, Self-Taught Artist*
Macht. *Sojourner Truth: Crusader for Civil Rights*

Malone. *Dorothea L. Dix*
Marston. *Isaac Johnson: From Slave to Stonecutter*
McKissack. *Frederick Douglass: Leader Against Slavery*
McKissack. *Frederick Douglass: The Black Lion*
McKissack. *Sojourner Truth: A Voice for Freedom*
McPherson. *I Speak for the Women: A Story About Lucy Stone*
Patterson. *Frederick Douglass: Freedom Fighter*
Peterson. *Henry Clay: Leader in Congress*
Rose. *Clara Barton: Soldier of Mercy*
Schomp. *Frederick Douglass*
Stevens. *Frank Thompson: Her Civil War Story*
Swain. *The Road to Seneca Falls: Elizabeth Cady Stanton*
Weiner. *The Story of Frederick Douglass: Voice of Freedom*

Collective Biography

Altman. *Extraordinary Black Americans*
King. *First Facts About American Heroes*
Pascoe. *First Facts About the Presidents*

Provensen. *The Buck Stops Here: The Presidents*
Provensen. *My Fellow Americans*
Reef. *Black Fighting Men: A Proud History*

Rubel. *The Scholastic Encyclopedia of the Presidents*

History

Bolick. *Mail Call!*
Burns. *Money*
Carter. *The Battle of Gettysburg*
Caulkins. *Pets of the Presidents*
English. *Transportation: Automobiles to Zeppelins*
Evert. *Addy's Cook Book*
Hopkins. *Hand in Hand: An American History Through Poetry*
Johnson. *The Battle of Gettysburg*
Jones. *The President Has Been Shot*
Kent. *The Battle of Chancellorsville*

Kent. *The Battle of Shiloh*
Kent. *The Story of the Battle of Bull Run*
Kent. *The Story of the Surrender at Yorktown*
Kurtz. *U.S. Army*
Maestro. *The Story of Money*
Moss. *Forts and Castles*
Paananen. *The Military: Defending the Nation*
Pleasant Company. *Addy's Cook Book 1864*
Pollard. *The Nineteenth Century*
Read. *Sheridan's Ride*
Reef. *Gettysburg*

Reef. *The Lincoln Memorial*
Reef. *The Supreme Court*
Richards. *The Gettysburg Address*
Rowland-Warne. *Costume*
Sandler. *Presidents*
Sherrow. *The Big Book of U.S. Presidents*
Stern. *The Congress: America's Lawmakers*
Sullivan. *Children of Promise: African-American Literature and Art*
Weiner. *The Civil War*

Multimedia

CD-ROM

SkyTrip America   *Total History*

Video

Abraham Lincoln   *Elizabeth Cady Stanton and*   *President's Day*
African Americans   *Susan B. Anthony*   *The Rebel Slave*
Black Is My Color: The   *Equal Rights for All*
African American   *Presenting Mr. Frederick*
Experience   *Douglass*

GRADE FIVE

Historical Fiction

Alphin. *The Ghost Cadet*
Beatty. *Charley Skedaddle*
Beatty. *Eben Tyne,*
Powdermonkey
Beatty. *Turn Homeward,*
Hannalee
Beatty. *Wait for Me, Watch*
for Me, Eula Bee
Beatty. *Who Comes with*
Cannons?
Blos. *A Gathering of Days: A*
New England Girl's
Journal, 1830-32
Clapp. *The Tamarack Tree*
Climo. *A Month of Seven*
Days

Denenberg. *When Will This*
Cruel War Be Over?
Diary, 1864
Donahue. *An Island Far from*
Home
Duey. *Emma Eileen Grove:*
Mississippi
Fleischman. *Bull Run*
Gauch. *Thunder at Gettysburg*
Hansen. *Which Way*
Freedom?
Holland. *The Promised Land*
Houston. *Mountain Valor*
Monjo. *Gettysburg: Tad*
Lincoln's Story
Monjo. *Me and Willie and Pa*
Monjo. *The Vicksburg*
Veteran

Nixon. *A Dangerous Promise*
Nixon. *Keeping Secrets*
Polacco. *Pink and Say*
Porter. *Meet Addy: An*
American Girl
Reeder. *Across the Lines*
Reeder. *Shades of Gray*
Rinaldi. *The Last Silk Dress*
Shura. *Gentle Annie: The*
True Story of a Civil War
Nurse
Steele. *The Perilous Road*
Whittier. *Barbara Frietchie*
Wisler. *The Drummer of*
Vicksburg
Wisler. *Mr. Lincoln's*
Drummer
Wisler. *Red Cap*

Biography

Anderson. *Mary Todd*
Lincoln: President's Wife
Ash. *The Story of Harriet*
Beecher Stowe
Bennett. *Abraham Lincoln:*
Healing a Divided Nation
Bentley. *Ulysses S. Grant*
Bland. *Harriet Beecher*
Stowe: Antislavery Author
Brown. *Elizabeth Blackwell:*
Physician
Brown. *Robert E. Lee*
Bruns. *Abraham Lincoln*
Burchard. *Charlotte Forten:*
A Black Teacher in the
Civil War
Burke. *Louisa May Alcott*
Burns. *Harriet Tubman*
Cannon. *Robert E. Lee*
Carlson. *Harriet Tubman:*
Call to Freedom
Casey. *Millard Fillmore:*
Thirteenth President

Clinton. *Benjamin Harrison:*
Twenty-Third President
Colver. *Abraham Lincoln:*
For the People
Connell. *They Shall Be*
Heard: Susan B. Anthony
and Elizabeth Cady Stanton
Cooper. *From Slave to Civil*
War Hero: Robert Small
D'Aulaire. *Abraham Lincoln*
Dubowski. *Andrew Johnson:*
Rebuilding the Union
Ferris. *Go Free or Die*
Ferris. *Walking the Road to*
Freedom
Fritz. *Harriet Beecher Stowe*
and the Beecher Preachers
Fritz. *You Want Women to*
Vote, Lizzie Stanton?
Graves. *Robert E. Lee*
Greene. *Louisa May Alcott:*
Author, Nurse, Suffragette
Hamilton. *Clara Barton*

Hargrove. *Abraham Lincoln:*
Sixteenth President
Jacobs. *Lincoln*
Jakoubek. *Harriet Beecher*
Stowe
Jakoubek. *The Assassination*
of Abraham Lincoln
Kent. *Andrew Johnson:*
Seventeenth President
Kerby. *Frederick Douglass*
King. *Jefferson Davis*
Krass. *Sojourner Truth:*
Antislavery Activist
Latham. *Samuel F. B. Morse*
Lindop. *James K. Polk,*
Abraham Lincoln,
Theodore Roosevelt
Lyons. *Deep Blues: Bill*
Traylor, Self-Taught Artist
Macht. *Sojourner Truth:*
Crusader for Civil Rights
Malone. *Dorothea L. Dix*
Marston. *Isaac Johnson:*
From Slave to Stonecutter

McKissack. *Frederick Douglass: The Black Lion*

McKissack. *Sojourner Truth: Ain't I a Woman?*

McPherson. *I Speak for the Women: A Story About Lucy Stone*

Morris. *The Lincoln Way*

O'Brien. *Ulysses S. Grant*

O'Neal. *The Assassination of Abraham Lincoln*

Patterson. *Frederick Douglass: Freedom Fighter*

Peterson. *Henry Clay: Leader in Congress*

Rose. *Clara Barton: Soldier of Mercy*

Russell. *Frederick Douglass: Abolitionist Editor*

Rutberg. *Mary Lincoln's Dressmaker*

Ryan. *Louisa May Alcott: Her Girlhood Diary*

Sandak. *The Lincolns*

Schomp. *Frederick Douglass*

Stefoff. *Abraham Lincoln: 16th President of the United States*

Stevens. *Frank Thompson: Her Civil War Story*

Swain. *The Road to Seneca Falls: Elizabeth Cady Stanton*

Trump. *Lincoln's Little Girl: A True Story*

Weiner. *The Story of Frederick Douglass: Voice of Freedom*

Weisberg. *Susan B. Anthony*

Collective Biography

Aaseng. *You Are the General II: 1800-1899*

Altman. *Extraordinary Black Americans*

Beard. *The Presidents in American History*

Blassingame. *The Look-It-Up Book of Presidents*

Faber. *Great Lives: American Government*

King. *First Facts About American Heroes*

Myers. *Now Is Your Time*

Pascoe. *First Facts About the Presidents*

Provensen. *The Buck Stops Here: The Presidents*

Provensen. *My Fellow Americans*

Reef. *Black Fighting Men: A Proud History*

Rennert. *Pioneers of Discovery*

Rubel. *The Scholastic Encyclopedia of the Presidents*

Sheafer. *Women in America's Wars*

Wilkinson. *Generals Who Changed the World*

History

Ashabranner. *A Memorial for Mr. Lincoln*

Biel. *The Civil War*

Bolick. *Mail Call!*

Bolotin. *For Home and Country: A Civil War Scrapbook*

Burns. *Money*

Carter. *The Battle of Gettysburg*

Caulkins. *Pets of the Presidents*

Chang. *A Separate Battle: Women and the Civil War*

Cosner. *War Nurses*

Currie. *Music in the Civil War*

Czech. *Snapshot: America Discovers the Camera*

Damon. *When the Cruel War Is Over: The Civil War Home Front*

Davies. *Transport: On Land, Road and Rail*

English. *Transportation: Automobiles to Zeppelins*

Evert. *Addy's Cook Book*

Fisher. *Tracks Across America: The Story of the American Railroad, 1825-1900*

Hirsch. *Taxation: Paying for Government*

Hopkins. *Hand in Hand: An American History Through Poetry*

Johnson. *The Battle of Gettysburg*

Jones. *The President Has Been Shot*

Karl. *America Alive: A History*

Katz. *Breaking the Chains: African-American Slave Resistance*

Kent. *The Battle of Chancellorsville*

Kent. *The Battle of Shiloh*

Kent. *The Story of the Battle of Bull Run*

Kent. *The Story of the Surrender at Yorktown*

Kurtz. *U.S. Army*

Maestro. *The Story of Money*

Medearis. *Come This Far to Freedom*

Meltzer. *The Black Americans*

Mettger. *Till Victory Is Won: Black Soldiers in the Civil War*

Morley. *Clothes: For Work, Play and Display*

Moss. *Forts and Castles*

Paananen. *The Military: Defending the Nation*

Platt. *The Smithsonian Visual Timeline of Inventions*

Pleasant Company. *Addy's Cook Book 1864*

Pollard. *The Nineteenth Century*

Ray. *A Nation Torn: The Story of How the Civil War Began*

Read. *Sheridan's Ride*

Reef. *Gettysburg*

Reef. *The Lincoln Memorial*

Reef. *The Supreme Court*

Richards. *The Gettysburg Address*

Rowland-Warne. *Costume*

Sandler. *Presidents*

Sherrow. *The Big Book of U.S. Presidents*

Steins. *The Nation Divides: The Civil War, 1820-1880*

Stern. *The Congress: America's Lawmakers*

Sullivan. *Children of Promise: African-American Literature and Art*

Warner. *The U.S. Marine Corps*

Weiner. *The Civil War*

Multimedia

CD-ROM

American History Explorer

Portraits of American Presidents

SkyTrip America
Total History

Video

Abraham Lincoln
African Americans
Black Is My Color: The African American Experience
Causes of the Civil War

Elizabeth Cady Stanton and Susan B. Anthony
Equal Rights for All
The Life and Times of Abraham Lincoln
Lincoln: A Photobiography

Presenting Mr. Frederick Douglass
Susan B. Anthony Story

GRADE SIX

Historical Fiction

Alphin. *The Ghost Cadet*
Armstrong. *The Dreams of Mairhe Mehan: A Novel of the Civil War*
Beatty. *Charley Skedaddle*
Beatty. *Eben Tyne, Powdermonkey*
Beatty. *Turn Homeward, Hannalee*
Beatty. *Wait for Me, Watch for Me, Eula Bee*
Beatty. *Who Comes with Cannons?*
Blos. *A Gathering of Days: A New England Girl's Journal, 1830-32*
Clapp. *The Tamarack Tree*
Climo. *A Month of Seven Days*

Collier. *With Every Drop of Blood*
Denenberg. *When Will This Cruel War Be Over? Diary, 1864*
Donahue. *An Island Far from Home*
Duey. *Emma Eileen Grove: Mississippi*
Fleischman. *Bull Run*
Forrester. *Sound the Jubilee*
Hansen. *Out from This Place*
Hansen. *Which Way Freedom?*
Holland. *Behind the Lines*
Holland. *The Promised Land*
Houston. *Mountain Valor*
Hunt. *Across Five Aprils*
Kassem. *Listen for Rachel*
Lyon. *Here and Now*

Monjo. *Me and Willie and Pa*
Monjo. *The Vicksburg Veteran*
Nixon. *A Dangerous Promise*
Nixon. *Keeping Secrets*
Polacco. *Pink and Say*
Reeder. *Across the Lines*
Reeder. *Shades of Gray*
Rinaldi. *The Last Silk Dress*
Shura. *Gentle Annie: The True Story of a Civil War Nurse*
Steele. *The Perilous Road*
Whittier. *Barbara Frietchie*
Wisler. *The Drummer of Vicksburg*
Wisler. *Mr. Lincoln's Drummer*
Wisler. *Red Cap*

Biography

Adler. *A Picture Book of Frederick Douglass*
Anderson. *Mary Todd Lincoln: President's Wife*
Ash. *The Story of Harriet Beecher Stowe*
Banta. *Douglass: Voice of Liberty*
Bennett. *Abraham Lincoln: Healing a Divided Nation*
Bennett. *Frederick Douglass and the War Against Slavery*
Bentley. *Ulysses S. Grant*
Bland. *Harriet Beecher Stowe: Antislavery Author*
Brown. *Elizabeth Blackwell: Physician*
Brown. *Robert E. Lee*
Bruns. *Abraham Lincoln*

Burchard. *Charlotte Forten: A Black Teacher in the Civil War*
Burke. *Louisa May Alcott*
Burns. *Harriet Tubman*
Cannon. *Robert E. Lee*
Carlson. *Harriet Tubman: Call to Freedom*
Casey. *Millard Fillmore: Thirteenth President*
Claflin. *Sojourner Truth and the Struggle for Freedom*
Clinton. *Benjamin Harrison: Twenty-Third President*
Colver. *Abraham Lincoln: For the People*
Connell. *They Shall Be Heard: Susan B. Anthony and Elizabeth Cady Stanton*

Cooper. *From Slave to Civil War Hero: Robert Small*
Cullen-DuPont. *Elizabeth Cady Stanton and Women's Liberty*
D'Aulaire. *Abraham Lincoln*
Dubowski. *Andrew Johnson: Rebuilding the Union*
Dubowski. *Clara Barton: Healing The Wounds*
Dubowski. *Robert E. Lee*
Ferris. *Go Free or Die*
Ferris. *Walking the Road to Freedom*
Freedman. *Lincoln: A Photobiography*
Fritz. *Harriet Beecher Stowe and the Beecher Preachers*
Fritz. *You Want Women to Vote, Lizzie Stanton?*

Gehre. *Susan B. Anthony*

Graves. *Robert E. Lee*

Greene. *Louisa May Alcott: Author, Nurse, Suffragette*

Hamilton. *Clara Barton*

Hargrove. *Abraham Lincoln: Sixteenth President*

Jacobs. *Lincoln*

Jakoubek. *The Assassination of Abraham Lincoln*

Jakoubek. *Harriet Beecher Stowe*

Johnston. *Harriet: The Life and World of Harriet Beecher Stowe*

Kendall. *Susan B. Anthony*

Kent. *Andrew Johnson: Seventeenth President*

Kent. *Jefferson Davis*

Kerby. *Frederick Douglass*

Kerby. *Robert E. Lee*

Kerby. *Samuel Morse*

King. *Jefferson Davis*

Krass. *Sojourner Truth: Antislavery Activist*

Latham. *Samuel F. B. Morse*

Levin. *Susan B. Anthony*

Lindop. *James K. Polk, Abraham Lincoln, Theodore Roosevelt*

Lyons. *Deep Blues: Bill Traylor, Self-Taught Artist*

Macht. *Sojourner Truth: Crusader for Civil Rights*

Malone. *Dorothea L. Dix*

Marrin. *Virginia's General: Robert E. Lee*

Marston. *Isaac Johnson: From Slave to Stonecutter*

McClard. *Harriet Tubman: Slavery and the Underground Railroad*

McHale. *Dr. Samuel Mudd and the Lincoln Assassination*

McKissack. *Frederick Douglass: The Black Lion*

McKissack. *Sojourner Truth: Ain't I a Woman?*

McPherson. *I Speak for the Women: A Story About Lucy Stone*

Morris. *The Lincoln Way*

O'Brien. *Ulysses S. Grant*

O'Neal. *The Assassination of Abraham Lincoln*

Patterson. *Frederick Douglass: Freedom Fighter*

Peterson. *Henry Clay: Leader in Congress*

Pflueger. *Stonewall Jackson*

Potter. *Jefferson Davis: Confederate President*

Randolph. *Woodrow Wilson: President*

Rose. *Clara Barton: Soldier of Mercy*

Russell. *Frederick Douglass: Abolitionist Editor*

Ryan. *Louisa May Alcott: Her Girlhood Diary*

Sandak. *The Lincolns*

Schomp. *Frederick Douglass*

Stefoff. *Abraham Lincoln: 16th President*

Stevens. *Frank Thompson: Her Civil War Story*

Sullivan. *Matthew Brady: His Life and Photographs*

Swain. *The Road to Seneca Falls: Elizabeth Cady Stanton*

Trump. *Lincoln's Little Girl: A True Story*

Weiner. *The Story of Frederick Douglass: Voice of Freedom*

Weisberg. *Susan B. Anthony*

Zeinert. *Elizabeth Van Lew: Southern Belle, Union Spy*

Collective Biography

Sullivan. *Black Artists in Photography, 1840-1940*

History

Anderson. *Battles That Changed the Modern World*

Ashabranner. *A Memorial for Mr. Lincoln*

Biel. *The Civil War*

Bolick. *Mail Call!*

Bolotin. *For Home and Country: A Civil War Scrapbook*

Burns. *Money*

Carter. *The Battle of Gettysburg*

Caulkins. *Pets of the Presidents*

Chang. *A Separate Battle: Women and the Civil War*

Colman. *Spies! Women in the Civil War*

Corrick. *The Battle of Gettysburg*

Cosner. *War Nurses*

Currie. *Music in the Civil War*

Czech. *Snapshot: America Discovers the Camera*

Damon. *When the Cruel War Is Over: The Civil War Home Front*

Davies. *Transport: On Land, Road and Rail*

English. *Transportation: Automobiles to Zeppelins*

Evert. *Addy's Cook Book*

Fisher. *Tracks Across America: The Story of the American Railroad, 1825-1900*

Hakim. *War Terrible War*

Hirsch. *Taxation: Paying for Government*

Hopkins. *Hand in Hand: An American History Through Poetry*

Johnson. *The Battle of Gettysburg*

Jones. *The President Has Been Shot*

Karl. *America Alive: A History*

Katz. *Breaking the Chains: African-American Slave Resistance*

Kent. *The Battle of Chancellorsville*

Kent. *The Battle of Shiloh*

Kent. *The Story of the Battle of Bull Run*

Kent. *The Story of the Surrender at Yorktown*

Kurtz. *U.S. Army*

Leiner. *First Children: Growing Up in the White House*

Medearis. *Come This Far to Freedom*

Meltzer. *The Black Americans*

Mettger. *Till Victory Is Won: Black Soldiers in the Civil War*

Morley. *Clothes: For Work, Play and Display*

Moss. *Forts and Castles*

Murphy. *The Boys' War*

Murphy. *The Long Road to Gettysburg*

Paananen. *The Military: Defending the Nation*

Patrick. *The Young Oxford Companion to the Supreme Court*

Philip. *Singing America: Poems That Define a Nation*

Platt. *The Smithsonian Visual Timeline of Inventions*

Pleasant Company. *Addy's Cook Book 1864*

Pollard. *The Nineteenth Century*

Ray. *A Nation Torn: The Story of How the Civil War Began*

Read. *Sheridan's Ride*

Reef. *Gettysburg*

Reef. *The Lincoln Memorial*

Reef. *The Supreme Court*

Rowland-Warne. *Costume*

Sandler. *Presidents*

Sherrow. *The Big Book of U.S. Presidents*

St. George. *The White House: Cornerstone of a Nation*

Steins. *The Nation Divides: The Civil War, 1820-1880*

Stern. *The Congress: America's Lawmakers*

Sullivan. *Children of Promise: African-American Literature and Art*

Warner. *The U.S. Marine Corps*

Weiner. *The Civil War*

Wheeler. *Events That Changed American History*

Williams. *Forts and Castles*

Multimedia

CD-ROM

American History Explorer Campaigns, Candidates and the Presidency

Portraits of American Presidents

SkyTrip America

Total History

The Way Things Work

Video

Abraham Lincoln

African Americans

Black Is My Color: The African American Experience

Causes of the Civil War

Elizabeth Cady Stanton and Susan B. Anthony

Equal Rights for All

Gettysburg

The Life and Times of Abraham Lincoln

Lincoln: A Photobiography

Presenting Mr. Frederick Douglass

The Rebel Slave

Susan B. Anthony Story

RECONSTRUCTION, THE PROGRESSIVE ERA, AND THE EARLY TWENTIETH CENTURY, 1866-1916

KINDERGARTEN THROUGH SECOND GRADE

Historical Fiction

Bartone. *Peppe the Lamplighter*
Bedard. *Emily*
Bird. *The Blizzard of 1896*
Blake. *Spray*
Carrick. *Two Very Little Sisters*
Conrad. *Call Me Ahnighito*
Christiansen. *The Ice Horse*
Cooney. *Hattie and the Wild Waves*
Cooney. *Island Boy*
De Angeli. *The Lion in the Box*
Dionetti. *Coal Mine Peaches*
Goldin. *Fire!*
Griest. *Lost at the White House: A 1909 Easter Story*
Hall. *Lucy's Christmas*
Hall. *Lucy's Summer*
Hall. *Old Home Day*
Harvey. *Immigrant Girl: Becky of Eldridge Street*

Hendershot. *Up the Tracks to Grandma's*
Howard. *Chita's Christmas Tree*
Howard. *Papa Tells Chita a Story*
Johnston. *How Many Miles to Jacksonville?*
Levinson. *Clara and the Bookwagon*
Littlefield. *Fire at the Triangle Factory*
Martin. *Day of Darkness, Night of Light*
McCully. *The Ballot Box Battle*
McKenzie. *Stargone John*
McKissack. *Ma Dear's Aprons*
Medearis. *Treemonisha*
Monjo. *The One Bad Thing About Father*
Porte. *When Aunt Lucy Rode a Mule & Other Stories*

Precek. *Penny in the Road*
Rand. *The Cabin Key*
Ray. *Pianna*
Ray. *Shaker Boy*
San Souci. *Kate Shelley: Bound for Legend*
Sanders. *A Place Called Freedom*
Schotter. *Dreamland*
Schroeder. *Satchmo's Blues*
Selznick. *The Houdini Box*
Shea. *First Flight: The Story of Tom Tate and the Wright Brothers*
Spedden. *Polar the Titanic Bear*
Stevens. *Anna, Grandpa, and the Big Storm*
Welch. *Clouds of Terror*
Wetterer. *The Snow Walker*
Whiteley. *Only Opal: The Diary of a Young Girl*

Biography

Adler. *A Picture Book of Frederick Douglass*
Adler. *A Picture Book of Harriet Tubman*
Adler. *A Picture Book of Sojourner Truth*
Adler. *A Picture Book of Thomas Alva Edison*
Adler. *A Picture Book of Thurgood Marshall*
Adler. *Thomas Alva Edison: Great Inventor*
Behrens. *Juliette Low: Founder of the Girl Scouts of America*

Benjamin. *Young Harriet Tubman*
Benjamin. *Young Helen Keller*
Blos. *The Heroine of the Titanic: Molly Brown*
Blos. *Nellie Bly's Monkey*
Bradby. *More than Anything Else*
Brown. *Belva Lockwood Wins Her Case*
Brown. *Ruth Law Thrills a Nation*
Cooney. *Eleanor*
Giblin. *Edith Wilson*
Gleiter. *Booker T. Washington*

Greene. *Emily Dickinson: American Poet*
Greene. *John Philip Sousa: The March King*
Greene. *Mark Twain: Author of Tom Sawyer*
Greene. *Robert E. Lee*
Latham. *Elizabeth Blackwell: Pioneer Woman Doctor*
Lawrence. *Harriet and the Promised Land*
Lindbergh. *Nobody Owns the Sky: The Story of Brave Bessie Coleman*

McKissack. *Booker T. Washington*

McKissack. *Frederick Douglass: Leader Against Slavery*

McKissack. *Ida B. Wells-Barnett*

McKissack. *James Weldon Johnson: "Lift Every Voice and Sing"*

McKissack. *Mary Church Terrell: Leader for Equality*

McKissack. *Mary McLeod Bethune*

Rose. *Clara Barton: Soldier of Mercy*

Schott. *Will Rogers*

Schulz. *Will and Orv*

Towle. *The Real McCoy*

Venezia. *Mary Cassatt*

Wetterer. *Kate Shelley and the Midnight Express*

Collective Biography

Marzollo. *My First Book of Biographies*

History

Donnelly. *Titanic*

Goldish. *Our Supreme Court*

Maestro. *The Story of the Statue of Liberty*

Moser. *Fly!*

Swanson. *I Pledge Allegiance*

Multimedia

Video

African American Life

GRADE THREE

Historical Fiction

Bartone. *Peppe the Lamplighter*

Bedard. *Emily*

Bird. *The Blizzard of 1896*

Blake. *Spray*

Bland. *The Conspiracy of the Secret Nine*

Bylinsky. *Before the Wildflowers Bloom*

Carrick. *Two Very Little Sisters*

Christiansen. *The Ice Horse*

Cooney. *Hattie and the Wild Waves*

Cooney. *Island Boy*

De Angeli. *The Lion in the Box*

Goldin. *Fire!*

Griest. *Lost at the White House: A 1909 Easter Story*

Gross. *The Day It Rained Forever*

Hall. *Lucy's Summer*

Hall. *Old Home Day*

Harvey. *Immigrant Girl: Becky of Eldridge Street*

Hendershot. *Up the Tracks to Grandma's*

Howard. *Chita's Christmas Tree*

Hyatt. *Coast to Coast with Alice*

Johnston. *How Many Miles to Jacksonville?*

Krensky. *The Iron Dragon Never Sleeps*

Lawlor. *Come Away With Me*

Lawlor. *Take to the Sky*

Littlefield. *Fire at the Triangle Factory*

Martin. *Day of Darkness, Night of Light*

McCully. *The Ballot Box Battle*

McKenzie. *Stargone John*

Meacham. *Oyster Moon*

Medearis. *Treemonisha*

Monjo. *The One Bad Thing About Father*

Morpurgo. *The Wreck of the Zanzibar*

Naylor. *Maddie in the Middle*

Porte. *When Aunt Lucy Rode a Mule & Other Stories*

Porter. *Addy Saves the Day: A Summer Story, Book Five*

Porter. *Happy Birthday Addy!*

Precek. *Penny in the Road*

Rand. *The Cabin Key*

Rappaport. *Trouble at the Mines*

Ray. *Pianna*

Ray. *Shaker Boy*

Rose. *The Rose Horse*

San Souci. *Kate Shelley: Bound for Legend*

Sanders. *A Place Called Freedom*

Schotter. *Dreamland*

Schroeder. *Satchmo's Blues*

Selznick. *The Houdini Box*

Shea. *First Flight: The Story of Tom Tate and the Wright Brothers*

Spedden. *Polar the Titanic Bear*

Stevens. *Anna, Grandpa, and the Big Storm*

Stevens. *Lily and Miss Liberty*

Tripp. *Changes for Samantha*

Weber. *Forbidden Friendship*

Welch. *Clouds of Terror*

Wesley. *Freedom's Gifts*

West. *Fire in the Valley*

Wetterer. *The Snow Walker*

Whiteley. *Only Opal: The Diary of a Young Girl*

Wyman. *Red Sky at Morning*

Biography

Adler. *Our Golda: The Story of Golda Meir*

Adler. *A Picture Book of Frederick Douglass*

Adler. *A Picture Book of Harriet Tubman*

Adler. *A Picture Book of Sojourner Truth*

Adler. *A Picture Book of Thomas Alva Edison*

Adler. *A Picture Book of Thurgood Marshall*

Adler. *Thomas Alva Edison: Great Inventor*

Anderson. *Will Rogers: American Humorist*

Banta. *Douglass: Voice of Liberty*

Behrens. *Juliette Low: Founder of the Girl Scouts of America*

Benjamin. *Young Harriet Tubman*

Benjamin. *Young Helen Keller*

Bennett. *Frederick Douglass and the War Against Slavery*

Blos. *The Heroine of the Titanic: Molly Brown*

Blos. *Nellie Bly's Monkey*

Bradby. *More than Anything Else*

Brown. *Belva Lockwood Wins Her Case*

Brown. *Daisy and the Girl Scouts: Juliette Gordon Low*

Burford. *Chocolate by Hershey: Milton S. Hershey*

Burns. *Harriet Tubman*

Collins. *Mark T-W-A-I-N!: A Story About Samuel Clemens*

Colman. *Madam C. J. Walker*

Colman. *Mother Jones and the March of the Mill Children*

Cooney. *Eleanor*

Crofford. *Frontier Surgeons: A Story About the Mayo Brothers*

Dolan. *Matthew Henson: Arctic Explorer*

Ferris. *Go Free or Die*

Ferris. *Walking the Road to Freedom*

Fritz. *You Want Women to Vote, Lizzie Stanton?*

Giblin. *Edith Wilson*

Gleiter. *Booker T. Washington*

Graff. *Helen Keller: Toward the Light*

Graves. *Robert E. Lee*

Greene. *Emily Dickinson: American Poet*

Greene. *John Philip Sousa: The March King*

Greene. *Mark Twain: Author of Tom Sawyer*

Hunter. *Helen Keller*

Kelso. *Building a Dream: Mary Bethune's School*

Kent. *Jane Addams and Hull House*

Kent. *The Story of Admiral Peary at the North Pole*

Kerby. *Samuel Morse*

Kudlinski. *Helen Keller: A Light for the Blind*

Latham. *Elizabeth Blackwell: Pioneer Woman Doctor*

Latham. *George Goethals: Panama Canal Engineer*

Latham. *Samuel F. B. Morse*

Lawrence. *Harriet and the Promised Land*

Levin. *Susan B. Anthony*

Lindbergh. *Nobody Owns the Sky: The Story of Brave Bessie Coleman*

Lipsyte. *Jim Thorpe: Twentieth-Century Jock*

Lyons. *Deep Blues: Bill Traylor, Self-Taught Artist*

Lyons. *Stitching Stars: The Story Quilts of Harriet Powers*

Malone. *Dorothea L. Dix*

McKissack. *Booker T. Washington*

McKissack. *Frederick Douglass: Leader Against Slavery*

McKissack. *Ida B. Wells-Barnett*

McKissack. *James Weldon Johnson: "Lift Every Voice and Sing"*

McKissack. *Madam C. J. Walker*

McKissack. *Mary Church Terrell: Leader for Equality*

McKissack. *Mary McLeod Bethune*

McKissack. *Sojourner Truth: A Voice for Freedom*

McKissack. *The Story of Booker T. Washington*

McPherson. *The Workers' Detective: Dr. Alice Hamilton*

Mitchell. *We'll Race You, Henry*

Parker. *The Wright Brothers and Aviation*

Patterson. *Booker T. Washington*

Patterson. *Frederick Douglass: Freedom Fighter*

Quackenbush. *Mark Twain?*

Quackenbush. *Stop the Presses, Nellie's Got a Scoop!*

Rose. *Clara Barton: Soldier of Mercy*

Santella. *Jackie Robinson Breaks the Color Line*

Schomp. *Frederick Douglass*

Schott. *Will Rogers*

Schulz. *Will and Orv*

Swain. *The Road to Seneca Falls: Elizabeth Cady Stanton*

Taylor. *Madam C. Walker*

Towle. *The Real McCoy*

Turner. *Mary Cassatt*

Venezia. *Mary Cassatt*

Vernon. *Introducing Gershwin*

Weiner. *The Story of Frederick Douglass: Voice of Freedom*

Wetterer. *Kate Shelley and the Midnight Express*

Wolfe. *Mary McLeod Bethune*

Collective Biography

King. *First Facts About American Heroes*

Marzollo. *My First Book of Biographies*

Provensen. *The Buck Stops Here: The Presidents*

Rappaport. *Living Dangerously: American Women*

History

Ballard. *Exploring the Titanic*
Bowler. *Trains*
Burns. *Mail*
Caulkins. *Pets of the Presidents*
Donnelly. *Titanic*
English. *Transportation: Automobiles to Zeppelins*
Goldish. *Our Supreme Court*
Greene. *Our Century: 1900-1910*
Harvey. *Women's Voting Rights*
Johnson. *Our National Symbols*
Kalman. *A Child's Day*
Kalman. *Children's Clothing of the 1800s*
Kalman. *Early Artisans*
Kalman. *Early Christmas*
Kalman. *Early City Life*
Kalman. *Early Schools*
Kalman. *Early Stores and Markets*
Kalman. *Early Travel*
Kalman. *Early Village Life*
Kalman. *19th Century Clothing*
Kalman. *Old-Time Toys*
Kalman. *A One-Room School*
Kent. *The Lincoln Memorial*
Kent. *The Titanic*
Knight. *The Olympic Games*
Lawrence. *The Great Migration*
Libreatore. *Our Century: 1910-1920*
Maestro. *The Story of the Statue of Liberty*
Miller. *The Statue of Liberty*
Moser. *Fly!*
Parker. *Locks, Crocs, and Skeeters: The Story of the Panama Canal*
Pleasant. *Samantha's Cookbook*
Sherrow. *The Big Book of U.S. Presidents*
Stein. *The Story of the Powers of the Supreme Court*
Stern. *The Congress: America's Lawmakers*
Swanson. *I Pledge Allegiance*
Tanaka. *On Board the Titanic*
Weber. *Our Congress*
Wilson. *Visual Timeline of Transportation*

Multimedia

Video

African American Life

GRADE FOUR

Historical Fiction

Avi. *Emily Upham's Revenge*
Avi. *Punch with Judy*
Beatty. *Eight Mules from Monterey*
Bird. *The Blizzard of 1896*
Blake. *Spray*
Bland. *The Conspiracy of the Secret Nine*
Bylinsky. *Before the Wildflowers Bloom*
Carrick. *The Elephant in the Dark*
Carrick. *Two Very Little Sisters*
De Angeli. *The Lion in the Box*
Edwards. *Little John and Plutie*
Fleischman. *The Midnight Horse*
Goldin. *Fire!*
Gross. *The Day It Rained Forever*
Hall. *Old Home Day*
Hamilton. *The Bells of Christmas*
Harvey. *Immigrant Girl: Becky of Eldridge Street*
Hill. *The Banjo Player*
Holmes. *For Bread 1893*
Houston. *Littlejim*
Howard. *Her Own Song*
Hyatt. *Coast to Coast with Alice*
Irwin. *I Be Somebody*
Johnston. *How Many Miles to Jacksonville?*
Krensky. *The Iron Dragon Never Sleeps*
Lawlor. *Come Away With Me*
Lawlor. *Take to the Sky*
Leonard. *Finding Papa*
Martin. *Day of Darkness, Night of Light*
McCully. *The Ballot Box Battle*
McKenzie. *Stargone John*
Meacham. *Oyster Moon*
Medearis. *Treemonisha*
Morpurgo. *The Wreck of the Zanzibar*
Naylor. *Maddie in the Middle*
Nixon. *Circle of Love*
Partridge. *Clara and the Hoodoo Man*
Porter. *Addy Saves the Day: A Summer Story, Book Five*
Porter. *Happy Birthday Addy!*
Rappaport. *Trouble at the Mines*
Ray. *Shaker Boy*
Roberts. *Jo and the Bandit*
Robinet. *Children of the Fire*
Rodowsky. *Fitchett's Folly*
Rose. *The Rose Horse*
San Souci. *Kate Shelley: Bound for Legend*
Schotter. *Dreamland*
Schroeder. *Satchmo's Blues*
Sebestyen. *Words by Heart*
Selznick. *The Houdini Box*
Smucker. *Incredible Jumbo*
Snyder. *And Condors Danced*
Spedden. *Polar the Titanic Bear*
Stevens. *Anna, Grandpa, and the Big Storm*
Stevens. *Lily and Miss Liberty*
Tripp. *Changes for Samantha*
Weber. *Forbidden Friendship*
Welch. *Clouds of Terror*
Wesley. *Freedom's Gifts*
West. *Fire in the Valley*
Whiteley. *Only Opal: The Diary of a Young Girl*
Wyman. *Red Sky at Morning*

Biography

Adler. *Our Golda: The Story of Golda Meir*

Adler. *A Picture Book of Frederick Douglass*

Adler. *A Picture Book of Harriet Tubman*

Adler. *A Picture Book of Sojourner Truth*

Adler. *Thomas Alva Edison: Great Inventor*

Anderson. *Will Rogers: American Humorist*

Banta. *Douglass: Voice of Liberty*

Behrens. *Juliette Low: Founder of the Girl Scouts of America*

Benjamin. *Young Helen Keller*

Bennett. *Frederick Douglass and the War Against Slavery*

Bennett. *Will Rogers: Quotable Cowboy*

Bentley. *Ulysses S. Grant*

Blos. *The Heroine of the Titanic: Molly Brown*

Blos. *Nellie Bly's Monkey*

Brooks. *Mary Cassatt: An American in Paris*

Brown. *Belva Lockwood Wins Her Case*

Brown. *Chester Arthur: Twenty-First President*

Brown. *Daisy and the Girl Scouts: Juliette Gordon Low*

Burford. *Chocolate by Hershey: Milton S. Hershey*

Burns. *Harriet Tubman*

Cannon. *Robert E. Lee*

Casey. *Millard Fillmore: Thirteenth President*

Casey. *William H. Taft: Twenty-Seventh President*

Charleston. *Peary Reaches the North Pole*

Clinton. *Benjamin Harrison: Twenty-Third President*

Collins. *Mark T-W-A-I-N!: A Story About Samuel Clemens*

Colman. *Madam C. J. Walker*

Colman. *Mother Jones and the March of the Mill Children*

Connell. *They Shall Be Heard: Susan B. Anthony and Elizabeth Cady Stanton*

Crofford. *Frontier Surgeons: A Story About the Mayo Brothers*

Davidson. *Getting the Real Story: Nellie Bly and Ida B. Wells*

DeStefano. *Theodore Roosevelt: Conservation President*

Dolan. *Matthew Henson: Arctic Explorer*

Ferris. *Go Free or Die*

Ferris. *Walking the Road to Freedom*

Freedman. *Ida B. Wells and the Antilynching Crusade*

Freedman. *The Wright Brothers: How They Invented the Airplane*

Fritz. *Harriet Beecher Stowe and the Beecher Preachers*

Fritz. *You Want Women to Vote, Lizzie Stanton?*

Giblin. *Edith Wilson*

Gormley. *Maria Mitchell: The Soul of an Astronomer*

Graff. *Helen Keller: Toward the Light*

Graves. *Robert E. Lee*

Greene. *John Philip Sousa: The March King*

Greene. *Louisa May Alcott: Author, Nurse, Suffragette*

Greene. *Thomas Alva Edison: Bringer of Light*

Hunter. *Helen Keller*

Kelso. *Building a Dream: Mary Bethune's School*

Kent. *Andrew Johnson: Seventeenth President*

Kent. *Calvin Coolidge: Thirtieth President*

Kent. *Grover Cleveland: Twenty-Second and Twenty-Fourth President*

Kent. *Jane Addams and Hull House*

Kent. *The Story of Admiral Peary at the North Pole*

Kent. *Theodore Roosevelt: Twenty-Sixth President*

Kent. *Ulysses S. Grant: Eighteenth President*

Kerby. *Frederick Douglass*

Kerby. *Samuel Morse*

Kittredge. *Jane Addams*

Kudlinski. *Helen Keller: A Light for the Blind*

Latham. *Elizabeth Blackwell: Pioneer Woman Doctor*

Latham. *George Goethals: Panama Canal Engineer*

Latham. *Samuel F. B. Morse*

Levin. *Susan B. Anthony*

Lillegard. *James Garfield: Twentieth President*

Lindbergh. *Nobody Owns the Sky: The Story of Brave Bessie Coleman*

Lipsyte. *Jim Thorpe: Twentieth-Century Jock*

Lipsyte. *Joe Louis: A Champ for all America*

Lyons. *Deep Blues: Bill Traylor, Self-Taught Artist*

Lyons. *Stitching Stars: The Story Quilts of Harriet Powers*

Macht. *Sojourner Truth: Crusader for Civil Rights*

Malone. *Dorothea L. Dix*

Marston. *Isaac Johnson: From Slave to Stonecutter*

McKissack. *Frederick Douglass: Leader Against Slavery*

McKissack. *Frederick Douglass: The Black Lion*

McKissack. *Ida B. Wells-Barnett*

McKissack. *James Weldon Johnson: "Lift Every Voice and Sing"*

McKissack. *Madam C. J. Walker*

McKissack. *Mary Church Terrell: Leader for Equality*

McKissack. *Mary McLeod Bethune*

McKissack. *Sojourner Truth: A Voice for Freedom*

McKissack. *The Story of Booker T. Washington*

McPherson. *I Speak for the Women: Lucy Stone*

McPherson. *Peace and Bread: Jane Addams*

McPherson. *Rooftop Astronomer: Maria Mitchell*

McPherson. *The Workers' Detective: Dr. Alice Hamilton*

Meyer. *Mary Cassatt*

Mitchell. *The Wizard of Sound: Thomas Edison*

Mitchell. *We'll Race You, Henry*

O'Connor. *Barefoot Dancer: Isadora Duncan*

Parker. *The Wright Brothers and Aviation*

Parker. *Thomas Edison and Electricity*

Patterson. *Booker T. Washington*

Patterson. *Frederick Douglass: Freedom Fighter*

Pfeifer. *Henry O. Flipper*

Quackenbush. *Mark Twain?*

Quackenbush. *Stop the Presses, Nellie's Got a Scoop!*

Quiri. *Alexander Graham Bell*

Rose. *Clara Barton: Soldier of Mercy*

Santella. *Jackie Robinson Breaks the Color Line*

Schleichert. *The Life of Dorothea Dix*

Schleichert. *The Life of Elizabeth Blackwell*

Schomp. *Frederick Douglass*

Simon. *Franklin Pierce*

St. George. *Dear Dr. Bell. . . Your Friend, Helen Keller*

Swain. *The Road to Seneca Falls: Elizabeth Cady Stanton*

Taylor. *The First Flight: Wright Brothers*

Taylor. *The First Flight Across the United States: Calbraith Perry Rodgers*

Taylor. *Madam C. Walker*

Towle. *The Real McCoy*

Turner. *Mary Cassatt*

Vernon. *Introducing Gershwin*

Weiner. *The Story of Frederick Douglass: Voice of Freedom*

Wolfe. *Mary McLeod Bethune*

Collective Biography

Altman. *Extraordinary Black Americans*

Clements. *The Picture History of Great Inventors*

Fireside. *Is There a Woman in the House. . . or Senate?*

Jacobs. *Great Lives: Human Rights*

King. *First Facts About American Heroes*

Krull. *Lives of the Artists: Masterpieces, Messes*

Krull. *Lives of the Musicians: Good Times, Bad Times*

Krull. *Lives of the Writers: Comedies, Tragedies*

McKissack. *African-American Inventors*

Pascoe. *First Facts About the Presidents*

Provensen. *The Buck Stops Here: The Presidents*

Provensen. *My Fellow Americans*

Rappaport. *Living Dangerously: American Women*

Rubel. *The Scholastic Encyclopedia of the Presidents*

Vare. *Women Inventors and their Discoveries*

Wilkinson. *Scientists Who Changed the World*

History

Ballard. *Exploring the Titanic*

Berliner. *Before the Wright Brothers*

Blue. *The White House Kids*

Bolick. *Mail Call!*

Brill. *Let Women Vote!*

Burns. *Mail*

Burns. *Money*

Caulkins. *Pets of the Presidents*

Doherty. *The Statue of Liberty*

English. *Transportation: Automobiles to Zeppelins*

Ferrell. *The U.S. Air Force*

Fry. *The Orphan Train*

Giblin. *Be Seated: A Book About Chairs*

Goldish. *Our Supreme Court*

Greene. *Our Century: 1900-1910*

Harvey. *Women's Voting Rights*

The History of Moviemaking

Hoig. *It's the Fourth of July*

Johnson. *Our National Symbols*

Jones. *The President Has Been Shot*

Kalman. *A Child's Day*

Kalman. *Children's Clothing of the 1800s*

Kalman. *Early Artisans*

Kalman. *Early Christmas*

Kalman. *Early City Life*

Kalman. *Early Pleasures and Pastimes*

Kalman. *Early Schools*

Kalman. *Early Stores and Markets*

Kalman. *Early Travel*

Kalman. *Early Village Life*

Kalman. *19th Century Clothing*

Kalman. *Old-Time Toys*

Kalman. *A One-Room School*

Kent. *The Lincoln Memorial*

Kent. *The Titanic*

Knight. *The Olympic Games*

Kurtz. *U.S. Army*

Lawrence. *The Great Migration*

Libreatore. *Our Century: 1910-1920*

Miller. *The Statue of Liberty*

Moser. *Fly!*

Parker. *Locks, Crocs, and Skeeters: The Story of the Panama Canal*

Pleasant. *Samantha's Cookbook*

Pollard. *The Nineteenth Century*

Pollard. *The Red Cross and the Red Crescent*

Reef. *The Supreme Court*

Rowland-Warne. *Costume*

Sandler. *Presidents*

Scott. *Funny Papers: Behind the Scenes of the Comics*

Sherrow. *The Big Book of U.S. Presidents*

Stein. *The Story of the Powers of the Supreme Court*

Stern. *The Congress: America's Lawmakers*

The Story of Flight

Sullivan. *Children of Promise: African-American Literature and Art*

Swanson. *I Pledge Allegiance*

Tanaka. *On Board the Titanic*

Ventura. *Clothing*

Ventura. *Food: Its Evolution Through the Ages*

Ward. *Who Invented The Game?*

Weber. *Our Congress*

Wilson. *Visual Timeline of Transportation*

Multimedia

CD-ROM

Exploring the Titanic

Her Heritage: A Biographical Encyclopedia of American History

SkyTrip America
Total History

Video

African American Life
African Americans
Alexander Graham Bell
Black Is My Color: The African American Experience

Elizabeth Cady Stanton and Susan B. Anthony
Great Black Innovators
Helen Keller
Making It Happen: Masters of Invention

Presenting Mr. Frederick Douglass
Thomas Alva Edison

GRADE FIVE

Historical Fiction

Avi. *Emily Upham's Revenge*
Avi. *Punch with Judy*
Beatty. *Be Ever Hopeful, Hannalee*
Beatty. *Eight Mules from Monterey*
Bland. *The Conspiracy of the Secret Nine*
Bylinsky. *Before the Wildflowers Bloom*
Calvert. *Bigger*
Carrick. *The Elephant in the Dark*
Collier. *My Crooked Family*
Conrad. *My Daniel*
Cross. *The Great American Elephant Chase*
De Angeli. *The Lion in the Box*
DeFelice. *Lostman's River*
Dexter. *Mazemaker*
Edwards. *Little John and Plutie*
Emerson. *Julia's Mending*
Fleischman. *The Midnight Horse*
Griffin. *Switching Well*
Gross. *The Day It Rained Forever*
Hall. *Old Home Day*
Hamilton. *The Bells of Christmas*
Hill. *The Banjo Player*
Holmes. *For Bread 1893*
Houston. *Littlejim*
Howard. *Edith Herself*

Howard. *Her Own Song*
Hurmence. *Dixie in the Big Pasture*
Hyatt. *Coast to Coast with Alice*
Irwin. *I Be Somebody*
Karr. *It Ain't Always Easy*
Karr. *Gideon and the Mummy Professor*
Kirkpatrick. *Keeping the Good Light*
Krensky. *The Iron Dragon Never Sleeps*
Lawlor. *Come Away With Me*
Lawlor. *Take to the Sky*
Lenski. *Strawberry Girl*
Leonard. *Finding Papa*
Leonard. *Saving Damaris*
Lowell. *I Am Lavina Cumming*
McCall. *Better Than a Brother*
Meacham. *Oyster Moon*
Medearis. *Treemonisha*
Morpurgo. *The Wreck of the Zanzibar*
Naylor. *Maddie in the Middle*
Nelson. *Devil Storm*
Neufeld. *Gaps in Stone Walls*
Nixon. *Circle of Love*
Partridge. *Clara and the Hoodoo Man*
Paulsen. *The Winter Room*
Peck. *Voices After Midnight*
Pendergraft. *Hear the Wind Blow*

Pfeffer. *Justice for Emily*
Pfeffer. *Nobody's Daughter*
Phillips. *A Haunted Year*
Porter. *Addy Saves the Day: A Summer Story, Book Five*
Porter. *Happy Birthday Addy!*
Rappaport. *Trouble at the Mines*
Riskind. *Apple Is My Sign*
Roberts. *Jo and the Bandit*
Robinet. *Children of the Fire*
Robinet. *Mississippi Chariot*
Rodowsky. *Fitchett's Folly*
Rose. *The Rose Horse*
Ross. *The Bet's On, Lizzie Bingman!*
Rossiter. *Moxie*
San Souci. *Kate Shelley: Bound for Legend*
Sebestyen. *Words by Heart*
Smucker. *Incredible Jumbo*
Snyder. *And Condors Danced*
Spedden. *Polar the Titanic Bear*
Stevens. *Lily and Miss Liberty*
Stolz. *Cezanne Pinto: A Memoir*
Tripp. *Changes for Samantha*
Weber. *Forbidden Friendship*
Wesley. *Freedom's Gifts*
West. *Fire in the Valley*
Whiteley. *Only Opal: The Diary of a Young Girl*
Winter. *The Christmas Tree Ship*
Wisler. *Mustang Flats*
Wyman. *Red Sky at Morning*

Biography

Adler. *Our Golda: The Story of Golda Meir*
Adler. *A Picture Book of Frederick Douglass*

Archbold. *Deep-Sea Explorer: Robert Ballard*
Banta. *Douglass: Voice of Liberty*

Beneduce. *A Weekend with Winslow Homer*
Bennett. *Frederick Douglass and the War Against Slavery*

Bennett. *Will Rogers: Quotable Cowboy*

Bentley. *Ulysses S. Grant*

Bernotas. *Jim Thorpe: Sac and Fox Athlete*

Berry. *Emily Dickinson*

Blos. *The Heroine of the Titanic: Molly Brown*

Blos. *Nellie Bly's Monkey*

Brooks. *Mary Cassatt: An American in Paris*

Brown. *Belva Lockwood Wins Her Case*

Brown. *Chester Arthur: Twenty-First President*

Brown. *Daisy and the Girl Scouts: Juliette Gordon Low*

Brown. *Elizabeth Blackwell: Physician*

Brown. *James Garfield: 20th President of the United States*

Brown. *Robert E. Lee*

Bundles. *Madam C. J. Walker*

Buranelli. *Thomas Alva Edison*

Burchard. *Charlotte Forten: A Black Teacher in the Civil War*

Burford. *Chocolate by Hershey: Milton S. Hershey*

Burke. *Louisa May Alcott*

Burns. *Harriet Tubman*

Cain. *Mary Cassatt*

Canadeo. *Warren G. Harding*

Cannon. *Robert E. Lee*

Carlson. *Harriet Tubman: Call to Freedom*

Casey. *Millard Fillmore: Thirteenth President*

Casey. *William H. Taft: Twenty-Seventh President*

Charleston. *Peary Reaches the North Pole*

Clinton. *Benjamin Harrison: Twenty-Third President*

Collins. *Mark T-W-A-I-N!: A Story About Samuel Clemens*

Collins. *William McKinley: 25th President of the United States*

Colman. *Madam C. J. Walker*

Colman. *Mother Jones and the March of the Mill Children*

Connell. *They Shall Be Heard: Susan B. Anthony and Elizabeth Cady Stanton*

Cooper. *From Slave to Civil War Hero: Robert Small*

Crofford. *Frontier Surgeons: A Story About the Mayo Brothers*

Davidson. *Getting the Real Story: Nellie Bly and Ida B. Wells*

Davis. *Frank Lloyd Wright: Maverick Architect*

DeStefano. *Theodore Roosevelt: Conservation President*

Dolan. *Matthew Henson: Arctic Explorer*

Dominy. *Katherine Dunham: Dancer and Choreographer*

Driemen. *Clarence Darrow*

Dubowski. *Andrew Johnson: Rebuilding the Union*

Dwyer. *Robert Peary and the Quest for the North Pole*

Ehrlich. *Nelly Bly: Journalist*

Falkof. *William H. Taft*

Ferris. *Go Free or Die*

Ferris. *Walking the Road to Freedom*

Freedman. *Ida B. Wells and the Antilynching Crusade*

Freedman. *The Wright Brothers: How They Invented the Airplane*

Fritz. *Bully for You, Teddy Roosevelt*

Fritz. *Harriet Beecher Stowe and the Beecher Preachers*

Fritz. *You Want Women to Vote, Lizzie Stanton?*

Gentry. *Paul Laurence Dunbar: Poet*

Gilman. *Matthew Henson: Explorer*

Gormley. *Maria Mitchell: The Soul of an Astronomer*

Graff. *Helen Keller: Toward the Light*

Graves. *Robert E. Lee*

Greene. *Louisa May Alcott: Author, Nurse, Suffragette*

Greene. *Thomas Alva Edison: Bringer of Light*

Hamilton. *Clara Barton*

Hunter. *Helen Keller*

Jakoubek. *Harriet Beecher Stowe*

Kaye. *The Life of Daniel Hale Williams*

Kelso. *Building A Dream: Mary Bethune's School*

Kent. *Andrew Johnson: Seventeenth President*

Kent. *Calvin Coolidge: Thirtieth President*

Kent. *Dorothy Day: Friend to the Forgotten*

Kent. *Grover Cleveland: Twenty-Second and Twenty-Fourth President*

Kent. *Jane Addams and Hull House*

Kent. *Rutherford B. Hayes: Nineteenth President*

Kent. *The Story of Admiral Peary at the North Pole*

Kent. *Theodore Roosevelt: Twenty-Sixth President*

Kent. *Ulysses S. Grant: Eighteenth President*

Kent. *William McKinley: Twenty-Fifth President*

Kerby. *Frederick Douglass*

Kerby. *Samuel Morse*

Kittredge. *Jane Addams*

Klots. *Ida Wells-Barnett: Civil Rights Leader*

Kozodoy. *Isadora Duncan: Dancer*

Kraft. *Mother Jones: One Woman's Fight for Labor*

Krass. *Sojourner Truth: Antislavery Activist*

Kudlinski. *Helen Keller: A Light for the Blind*

Latham. *Elizabeth Blackwell: Pioneer Woman Doctor*

Latham. *George Goethals: Panama Canal Engineer*

Latham. *Samuel F. B. Morse*

Leavell. *Woodrow Wilson*

Lefer. *Emma Lazarus*

Levin. *Susan B. Anthony*

Levinson. *I Lift My Lamp: Emma Lazarus and the Statue of Liberty*

Lillegard. *James Garfield: Twentieth President*

Lindop. *James K. Polk, Abraham Lincoln, Theodore Roosevelt*

Lipsyte. *Jim Thorpe: Twentieth-Century Jock*

Lipsyte. *Joe Louis: A Champ for all America*

Lyons. *Deep Blues: Bill Traylor, Self-Taught Artist*

Lyons. *Stitching Stars: The Story Quilts of Harriet Powers*

Macht. *Sojourner Truth: Crusader for Civil Rights*

Malone. *Dorothea L. Dix*

Markham. *Helen Keller*

Markham. *Theodore Roosevelt*

Marston. *Isaac Johnson: From Slave to Stonecutter*

McKissack. *Frederick Douglass: The Black Lion*

McKissack. *James Weldon Johnson: "Lift Every Voice and Sing"*

McKissack. *Mary McLeod Bethune*

McKissack. *Sojourner Truth: Ain't I A Woman?*

McKissack. *The Story of Booker T. Washington*

McPherson. *I Speak for the Women: Lucy Stone*

McPherson. *Peace and Bread: Jane Addams*

McPherson. *Rooftop Astronomer: Maria Mitchell*

McPherson. *The Workers' Detective: Dr. Alice Hamilton*

Meyer. *Mary Cassatt*

Mintz. *Thomas Edison: Inventing the Future*

Mitchell. *The Wizard of Sound: Thomas Edison*

Mitchell. *We'll Race You, Henry*

Muhlberger. *What Makes a Cassatt a Cassatt?*

Nicholson. *Helen Keller: Humanitarian*

Norman. *Lewis Latimer: Scientist*

O'Brien. *Ulysses S. Grant*

O'Connor. *Barefoot Dancer: Isadora Duncan*

Olsen. *Emily Dickinson: Poet*

Parker. *Thomas Edison and Electricity*

Parker. *The Wright Brothers and Aviation*

Patterson. *Booker T. Washington*

Patterson. *Frederick Douglass: Freedom Fighter*

Pfeifer. *Henry O. Flipper*

Quackenbush. *Mark Twain?*

Quiri. *Alexander Graham Bell*

Rose. *Clara Barton: Soldier of Mercy*

Russell. *Frederick Douglass: Abolitionist Editor*

Ryan. *Louisa May Alcott: Her Girlhood Diary*

Sandak. *The Tafts*

Sandak. *The Theodore Roosevelts*

Sandak. *The Wilsons*

Santella. *Jackie Robinson Breaks the Color Line*

Schleichert. *The Life of Dorothea Dix*

Schleichert. *The Life of Elizabeth Blackwell*

Schomp. *Frederick Douglass*

Schroeder. *Booker T. Washington*

Schroeder. *Jack London*

Simon. *Franklin Pierce*

Sonneborn. *Will Rogers: Cherokee Entertainer*

St. George. *Dear Dr. Bell. . . Your Friend, Helen Keller*

Stefoff. *Theodore Roosevelt: 26th President*

Stevens. *Andrew Johnson: 17th President*

Stevens. *Benjamin Harrison: 23rd President*

Swain. *The Road to Seneca Falls: Elizabeth Cady Stanton*

Taylor. *The First Flight: Wright Brothers*

Taylor. *The First Flight Across the United States: Calbraith Perry Rodgers*

Taylor. *Madam C. Walker*

Towle. *The Real McCoy*

Turner. *Lewis Howard Latimer*

Turner. *Mary Cassatt*

Vernon. *Introducing Gershwin*

Weiner. *The Story of Frederick Douglass: Voice of Freedom*

Weisberg. *Susan B. Anthony*

Wolfe. *Mary McLeod Bethune*

Collective Biography

Aaseng. *Close Calls*

Aaseng. *From Rags to Riches*

Altman. *Extraordinary Black Americans*

Blue. *People of Peace*

Clements. *The Picture History of Great Inventors*

Faber. *Great Lives: American Government*

Fireside. *Is There a Woman in the House. . . or Senate?*

Glubok. *Great Lives: Painting*

Jacobs. *Great Lives: Human Rights*

Katz. *Proudly Red and Black: Stories of African and Native Americans*

King. *First Facts About American Heroes*

Krull. *Lives of the Artists: Masterpieces, Messes*

Krull. *Lives of the Musicians: Good Times, Bad Times*

Krull. *Lives of the Writers: Comedies, Tragedies*

Mayberry. *Business Leaders Who Built Financial Empires*

McKissack. *African-American Inventors*

Pascoe. *First Facts About the Presidents*

Provensen. *The Buck Stops Here: The Presidents*

Provensen. *My Fellow Americans*

Rappaport. *Living Dangerously: American Women*

Rubel. *The Scholastic Encyclopedia of the Presidents*

Schraff. *American Heroes of Exploration and Flight*

Schraff. *Women of Peace: Nobel Peace Prize Winners*

Sills. *Visions: Stories About Women Artists*

Vare. *Women Inventors and their Discoveries*

Veglahn. *Women Scientists*

Wilkinson. *Scientists Who Changed the World*

History

Altman. *The Pullman Strike of 1894*

Ballard. *Exploring the Titanic*

Bartoletti. *Growing Up in Coal Country*

Berliner. *Before the Wright Brothers*

Blue. *The White House Kids*

Bolick. *Mail Call!*

Branch. *The Water Brought Us: The Story of the Gullah-Speaking People*
Brill. *Let Women Vote!*
Brown. *The Struggle to Grow (1880-1913)*
Burns. *Mail*
Burns. *Money*
Caulkins. *Pets of the Presidents*
Colman. *Strike: The Bitter Struggle of American Workers*
Colman. *Toilets, Bathtubs, Sinks, and Sewers*
Cooper. *Bound for the Promised Land: The Great Black Migration*
Cosner. *War Nurses*
Czech. *Snapshot: America Discovers the Camera*
Dash. *We Shall Not Be Moved: The Women's Factory Strike of 1909*
Davies. *Transport: On Land, Road and Rail*
Doherty. *The Statue of Liberty*
Dolan. *Panama and the United States: Their Canal, Their Stormy Years*
Emert. *Top Lawyers and their Famous Cases*
English. *Transportation: Automobiles to Zeppelins*
Ferrell. *The U.S. Air Force*
Freedman. *Kids at Work: Lewis Hine Against Child Labor*
Fry. *The Orphan Train*
Giblin. *Be Seated: A Book About Chairs*
Goldish. *Our Supreme Court*
Greene. *Child Labor: Then and Now*
Greene. *Our Century: 1900-1910*
Harvey. *Women's Voting Rights*
Hirsch. *Taxation: Paying for Government*
The History of Moviemaking
Hoig. *It's the Fourth of July*

Johnson. *Our National Symbols*
Jones. *The President Has Been Shot*
Kalman. *A Child's Day*
Kalman. *Children's Clothing of the 1800s*
Kalman. *Early Artisans*
Kalman. *Early Christmas*
Kalman. *Early City Life*
Kalman. *Early Pleasures and Pastimes*
Kalman. *Early Schools*
Kalman. *Early Stores and Markets*
Kalman. *Early Travel*
Kalman. *Early Village Life*
Kalman. *19th Century Clothing*
Kalman. *Old-Time Toys*
Kalman. *A One-Room School*
Karl. *America Alive: A History*
Kent. *The Lincoln Memorial*
Kent. *The Titanic*
Knight. *The Olympic Games*
Kurtz. *U.S. Army*
Lawrence. *The Great Migration*
Leuzzi. *Urban Life*
Libreatore. *Our Century: 1910-1920*
Lucas. *Civil Rights: The Long Struggle*
Mason. *Peary and Amundsen: Race to the Poles*
Maurer. *Airborne: The Search for the Secret of Flight*
Medearis. *Come This Far to Freedom*
Meltzer. *The Black Americans*
Mettger. *Reconstruction: America After the Civil War*
Miller. *The Statue of Liberty*
Morley. *Clothes: For Work, Play and Display*
Moser. *Fly!*
Murphy. *Across America on an Emigrant Train*
Murphy. *The Great Fire*

Parker. *Locks, Crocs, and Skeeters: The Story of the Panama Canal*
Platt. *The Smithsonian Visual Timeline of Inventions*
Pleasant. *Samantha's Cookbook*
Pollard. *The Nineteenth Century*
Pollard. *The Red Cross and the Red Crescent*
Reef. *The Supreme Court*
Rowland-Warne. *Costume*
Sandler. *Presidents*
Scott. *Funny Papers: Behind the Scenes of the Comics*
Sherrow. *The Big Book of U.S. Presidents*
Sherrow. *The Triangle Factory Fire*
St. George. *Panama Canal: Gateway to the World*
Stacey. *The Titanic*
Stein. *The Story of the Powers of the Supreme Court*
Stern. *The Congress: America's Lawmakers*
The Story of Flight
Sullivan. *Children of Promise: African-American Literature and Art*
Tanaka. *On Board the Titanic*
Ventura. *Clothing*
Ventura. *Food: Its Evolution Through the Ages*
Warburton. *The Chicago Fire*
Ward. *Who Invented the Game?*
Warner. *The U.S. Marine Corps*
Weber. *Our Congress*
Whitman. *Get Up and Go: American Road Travel*
Whitman. *This Land Is Your Land*
Wilson. *Visual Timeline of Transportation*
Yepsen. *City Trains: America's Cities by Rail*

Multimedia

CD-ROM

Air and Space Smithsonian Dreams of Flight
American History Explorer
Exploring the Titanic

Eyewitness Encyclopedia of Science
Her Heritage: A Biographical Encyclopedia of American History

Portraits of American Presidents
SkyTrip America
Total History

Video

African American Life
African Americans
Alexander Graham Bell
American Consumerism
(1890-1930)
Black Is My Color: The
African American
Experience
Elizabeth Cady Stanton and
Susan B. Anthony

Great Black Innovators
Helen Keller
Industrialization and
Urbanization (1870-1910)
Making It Happen: Masters
of Invention
Mary McLeod Bethune
A Nation in Turmoil
Presenting Mr. Frederick
Douglass

Progressive Movement
Reconstruction and
Segregation (1870-1910)
Susan B. Anthony Story
Thomas Alva Edison
Tragedy to Triumph: An
Adventure with Helen
Keller
U.S. and the World
(1865-1917)

GRADE SIX

Historical Fiction

Alexander. *The Philadelphia
Adventure*
Avi. *Emily Upham's Revenge*
Avi. *Punch with Judy*
Beatty. *Be Ever Hopeful,
Hannalee*
Beatty. *Eight Mules from
Monterey*
Bethancourt. *The Tomorrow
Connection*
Calvert. *Bigger*
Carrick. *The Elephant in the
Dark*
Collier. *My Crooked Family*
Conrad. *My Daniel*
Cross. *The Great American
Elephant Chase*
DeFelice. *Lostman's River*
Dexter. *Mazemaker*
Edwards. *Little John and
Plutie*
Emerson. *Julia's Mending*
Fleischman. *The Midnight
Horse*
Griffin. *Switching Well*
Gross. *The Day It Rained
Forever*
Hall. *Old Home Day*
Hamilton. *The Bells of
Christmas*
Hill. *The Banjo Player*
Holmes. *For Bread 1893*

Houston. *Littlejim*
Howard. *Edith Herself*
Howard. *Her Own Song*
Hurmence. *Dixie in the Big
Pasture*
Hyatt. *Coast to Coast with
Alice*
Irwin. *I Be Somebody*
Karr. *It Ain't Always Easy*
Karr. *Gideon and the Mummy
Professor*
Kirkpatrick. *Keeping the
Good Light*
Krensky. *The Iron Dragon
Never Sleeps*
Lawlor. *Come Away With Me*
Lawlor. *Take to the Sky*
Lenski. *Strawberry Girl*
Leonard. *Finding Papa*
Leonard. *Saving Damaris*
Lowell. *I Am Lavina
Cumming*
McCall. *Better Than a Brother*
Meacham. *Oyster Moon*
Medearis. *Treemonisha*
Nelson. *Devil Storm*
Neufeld. *Gaps in Stone Walls*
Nixon. *Circle of Love*
Partridge. *Clara and the
Hoodoo Man*
Paulsen. *The Winter Room*
Peck. *Voices After Midnight*

Pendergraft. *Hear the Wind
Blow*
Pfeffer. *Justice for Emily*
Pfeffer. *Nobody's Daughter*
Phillips. *A Haunted Year*
Rappaport. *Trouble at the
Mines*
Riskind. *Apple Is My Sign*
Roberts. *Jo and the Bandit*
Robinet. *Children of the Fire*
Robinet. *Mississippi Chariot*
Rodowsky. *Fitchett's Folly*
Rose. *The Rose Horse*
Ross. *The Bet's On, Lizzie
Bingman!*
Rossiter. *Moxie*
Rostkowski. *After the
Dancing Days*
Sebestyen. *Words by Heart*
Smucker. *Incredible Jumbo*
Snyder. *And Condors Danced*
Spedden. *Polar the Titanic
Bear*
Stolz. *Cezanne Pinto: A
Memoir*
Townsend. *The Ghost Flyers*
Wesley. *Freedom's Gifts*
Winter. *The Christmas Tree
Ship*
Wisler. *Mustang Flats*
Wyman. *Red Sky at Morning*
Yarbro. *Floating Illusions*

Biography

Adler. *Our Golda: The Story
of Golda Meir*
Andronik. *Prince of
Humbugs: A Life of P. T.
Barnum*
Archbold. *Deep-Sea
Explorer: Robert Ballard*
Beneduce. *A Weekend with
Winslow Homer*

Bennett. *Will Rogers:
Quotable Cowboy*
Bentley. *Ulysses S. Grant*
Bernotas. *Jim Thorpe: Sac
and Fox Athlete*
Berry. *Emily Dickinson*
Brooks. *Mary Cassatt: An
American in Paris*

Brown. *Belva Lockwood Wins
Her Case*
Brown. *Chester Arthur:
Twenty-First President*
Brown. *Daisy and the Girl
Scouts: Juliette Gordon
Low*
Brown. *Elizabeth Blackwell:
Physician*

Brown. *James Garfield: 20th President*
Brown. *Robert E. Lee*
Bundles. *Madam C. J. Walker*
Buranelli. *Thomas Alva Edison*
Burchard. *Charlotte Forten: A Black Teacher in the Civil War*
Burford. *Chocolate by Hershey: Milton S. Hershey*
Burke. *Louisa May Alcott*
Burns. *Harriet Tubman*
Cain. *Mary Cassatt*
Canadeo. *Warren G. Harding*
Cannon. *Robert E. Lee*
Carlson. *Harriet Tubman: Call to Freedom*
Casey. *Millard Fillmore: Thirteenth President*
Casey. *William H. Taft: Twenty-Seventh President*
Charleston. *Peary Reaches the North Pole*
Claflin. *Sojourner Truth and the Struggle for Freedom*
Clinton. *Benjamin Harrison: Twenty-Third President*
Collins. *Mark T-W-A-I-N!: A Story About Samuel Clemens*
Collins. *William McKinley: 25th President*
Colman. *Mother Jones and the March of the Mill Children*
Connell. *They Shall Be Heard: Susan B. Anthony and Elizabeth Cady Stanton*
Cooper. *From Slave to Civil War Hero: Robert Small*
Cullen-DuPont. *Elizabeth Cady Stanton and Women's Liberty*
Davidson. *Getting the Real Story: Nellie Bly and Ida B. Wells*
Davis. *Frank Lloyd Wright: Maverick Architect*
DeStefano. *Theodore Roosevelt: Conservation President*
Dolan. *Matthew Henson: Arctic Explorer*
Dominy. *Katherine Dunham: Dancer and Choreographer*
Driemen. *Clarence Darrow*
Dubowski. *Andrew Johnson: Rebuilding the Union*
Dubowski. *Clara Barton: Healing the Wounds*

Dubowski. *Robert E. Lee*
Dwyer. *Robert Peary and the Quest for the North Pole*
Ehrlich. *Nelly Bly: Journalist*
Falkof. *William H. Taft*
Ferris. *Go Free or Die*
Ferris. *Walking the Road to Freedom*
Fleming. *P. T. Barnum*
Freedman. *Ida B. Wells and the Antilynching Crusade*
Freedman. *The Wright Brothers: How They Invented the Airplane*
Fritz. *Bully for You, Teddy Roosevelt*
Fritz. *Harriet Beecher Stowe and the Beecher Preachers*
Fritz. *You Want Women to Vote, Lizzie Stanton?*
Gehre. *Susan B. Anthony*
Gentry. *Paul Laurence Dunbar: Poet*
Gilman. *Matthew Henson: Explorer*
Gormley. *Maria Mitchell: The Soul of an Astronomer*
Graff. *Helen Keller: Toward the Light*
Graves. *Robert E. Lee*
Greene. *Louisa May Alcott: Author, Nurse, Suffragette*
Greene. *Thomas Alva Edison: Bringer of Light*
Hamilton. *Clara Barton*
Hawxhurst. *Mother Jones: Labor Crusader*
Haynes. *Ida B. Wells*
Horton. *Mother Jones*
Hunter. *Helen Keller*
Jakoubek. *Harriet Beecher Stowe*
Johnston. *Harriet: The Life and World of Harriet Beecher Stowe*
Kaye. *The Life of Daniel Hale Williams*
Kelso. *Building a Dream: Mary Bethune's School*
Kendall. *Susan B. Anthony*
Kent. *Andrew Johnson: Seventeenth President*
Kent. *Calvin Coolidge: Thirtieth President*
Kent. *Dorothy Day: Friend to the Forgotten*
Kent. *Grover Cleveland: Twenty-Second and Twenty-Fourth President*
Kent. *Rutherford B. Hayes: Nineteenth President*

Kent. *The Story of Admiral Peary at the North Pole*
Kent. *Theodore Roosevelt: Twenty-Sixth President*
Kent. *Ulysses S. Grant: Eighteenth President*
Kent. *William McKinley: Twenty-Fifth President*
Kerby. *Frederick Douglass*
Kerby. *Robert E. Lee*
Kittredge. *Jane Addams*
Klots. *Ida Wells-Barnett: Civil Rights Leader*
Kozodoy. *Isadora Duncan: Dancer*
Kraft. *Mother Jones: One Woman's Fight for Labor*
Krass. *Sojourner Truth: Antislavery Activist*
Kudlinski. *Helen Keller: A Light for the Blind*
Latham. *Elizabeth Blackwell: Pioneer Woman Doctor*
Latham. *George Goethals: Panama Canal Engineer*
Latham. *Samuel F. B. Morse*
Leavell. *Woodrow Wilson*
Lefer. *Emma Lazarus*
Levinson. *I Lift My Lamp: Emma Lazarus and the Statue of Liberty*
Lillegard. *James Garfield: Twentieth President*
Lindop. *James K. Polk, Abraham Lincoln, Theodore Roosevelt*
Lipsyte. *Jim Thorpe: Twentieth-Century Jock*
Lipsyte. *Joe Louis: A Champ for all America*
Lyons. *Deep Blues: Bill Traylor, Self-Taught Artist*
Lyons. *Stitching Stars: The Story Quilts of Harriet Powers*
Macht. *Sojourner Truth: Crusader for Civil Rights*
Malone. *Dorothea L. Dix*
Malone. *Will Rogers: Cowboy Philosopher*
Markham. *Helen Keller*
Markham. *Theodore Roosevelt*
Marrin. *Virginia's General: Robert E. Lee*
Marston. *Isaac Johnson: From Slave to Stonecutter*
McClard. *Harriet Tubman: Slavery and the Underground Railroad*
McKissack. *Frederick Douglass: The Black Lion*

McKissack. *Mary McLeod Bethune*

McKissack. *Sojourner Truth: Ain't I a Woman?*

McKissack. *The Story of Booker T. Washington*

McPherson. *I Speak for the Women: Lucy Stone*

McPherson. *Peace and Bread: Jane Addams*

McPherson. *Rooftop Astronomer: Maria Mitchell*

McPherson. *The Workers' Detective: Dr. Alice Hamilton*

Meyer. *Mary Cassatt*

Mintz. *Thomas Edison: Inventing the Future*

Mitchell. *We'll Race You, Henry*

Mitchell. *The Wizard of Sound: Thomas Edison*

Muhlberger. *What Makes a Cassatt a Cassatt?*

Nicholson. *Helen Keller: Humanitarian*

Norman. *Lewis Latimer: Scientist*

O'Brien. *Ulysses S. Grant*

O'Connor. *Barefoot Dancer: Isadora Duncan*

Olsen. *Emily Dickinson: Poet*

Parker. *Thomas Edison and Electricity*

Parker. *The Wright Brothers and Aviation*

Pasachoff. *Alexander Graham Bell*

Patterson. *Booker T. Washington*

Patterson. *Frederick Douglass: Freedom Fighter*

Pfeifer. *Henry O. Flipper*

Plain. *Mary Cassatt: An Artist's Life*

Quackenbush. *Mark Twain?*

Quiri. *Alexander Graham Bell*

Rose. *Clara Barton: Soldier of Mercy*

Russell. *Frederick Douglass: Abolitionist Editor*

Ryan. *Louisa May Alcott: Her Girlhood Diary*

Sandak. *The Tafts*

Sandak. *The Theodore Roosevelts*

Sandak. *The Wilsons*

Sandomir. *Isadora Duncan: Revolutionary Dancer*

Schleichert. *The Life of Dorothea Dix*

Schleichert. *The Life of Elizabeth Blackwell*

Schomp. *Frederick Douglass*

Schroeder. *Booker T. Washington*

Schroeder. *Jack London*

Simon. *Franklin Pierce*

Sonneborn. *Will Rogers: Cherokee Entertainer*

St. George. *Dear Dr. Bell. . . Your Friend, Helen Keller*

Stefoff. *Theodore Roosevelt: 26th President*

Stevens. *Andrew Johnson: 17th President*

Stevens. *Benjamin Harrison: 23rd President*

Swain. *The Road to Seneca Falls: Elizabeth Cady Stanton*

Taylor. *The First Flight: Wright Brothers*

Taylor. *The First Flight Across the United States: Calbraith Perry Rodgers*

Taylor. *Madam C. Walker*

Turner. *Lewis Howard Latimer*

Turner. *Mary Cassatt*

Vernon. *Introducing Gershwin*

Weiner. *The Story of Frederick Douglass: Voice of Freedom*

Weisberg. *Susan B. Anthony*

Whitelaw. *Theodore Roosevelt Takes Charge*

Woog. *Harry Houdini*

Collective Biography

Aaseng. *Close Calls*

Aaseng. *From Rags to Riches*

Altman. *Extraordinary Black Americans*

Beard. *The Presidents in American History*

Blassingame. *The Look-It-Up Book of Presidents*

Blue. *People of Peace*

Camp. *American Astronomers: Searchers and Wonderers*

Clements. *The Picture History of Great Inventors*

Cush. *Artists Who Created Great Works*

Cush. *Women Who Achieved Greatness*

Faber. *Great Lives: American Government*

Fireside. *Is There a Woman in the House. . . or Senate?*

Fradin. *We Have Conquered Pain: The Discovery of Anesthesia*

Glubok. *Great Lives: Painting*

Jacobs. *Great Lives: Human Rights*

Katz. *Proudly Red and Black: Stories of African and Native Americans*

King. *First Facts About American Heroes*

Krull. *Lives of the Artists: Masterpieces, Messes*

Krull. *Lives of the Musicians: Good Times, Bad Times*

Krull. *Lives of the Writers: Comedies, Tragedies*

Mayberry. *Business Leaders Who Built Financial Empires*

Mayo. *Smithsonian Book of the First Ladies*

McKissack. *African-American Inventors*

Morin. *Women Who Reformed Politics*

Myers. *Now Is Your Time*

Pascoe. *First Facts About the Presidents*

Plowden. *Famous Firsts of Black Women*

Provensen. *The Buck Stops Here: The Presidents*

Provensen. *My Fellow Americans*

Rappaport. *Living Dangerously: American Women*

Rennert. *Book of Firsts: Leaders of America*

Rennert. *Pioneers of Discovery*

Rubel. *The Scholastic Encyclopedia of the Presidents*

Schraff. *American Heroes of Exploration and Flight*

Schraff. *Women of Peace: Nobel Peace Prize Winners*

Sills. *Visions: Stories About Women Artists*

Smith. *Presidents of a Growing Country*
Smith. *Presidents of a World Power*

Sullivan. *Black Artists in Photography, 1840-1940*
Vahn. *Women Scientists*
Vare. *Women Inventors and Their Discoveries*

Whitelaw. *They Wrote Their Own Headlines*
Wilkinson. *Scientists Who Changed the World*
Yount. *Black Scientists*

History

Altman. *The Pullman Strike of 1894*
Anderson. *Battles That Changed the Modern World*
Ballard. *Exploring the Titanic*
Bartoletti. *Growing Up in Coal Country*
Basinger. *American Cinema*
Berliner. *Before the Wright Brothers*
Blue. *The White House Kids*
Bolick. *Mail Call!*
Branch. *The Water Brought Us: The Story of the Gullah-Speaking People*
Brashler. *The Story of the Negro League Baseball*
Brill. *Let Women Vote!*
Brown. *The Struggle to Grow (1880-1913)*
Burns. *Money*
Caulkins. *Pets of the Presidents*
Colman. *Strike: The Bitter Struggle of American Workers*
Colman. *Toilets, Bathtubs, Sinks, and Sewers*
Cooper. *Bound for the Promised Land: The Great Black Migration*
Cosner. *War Nurses*
Cush. *Disasters That Shook the World*
Czech. *Snapshot: America Discovers the Camera*
Dash. *We Shall Not Be Moved: The Women's Factory Strike of 1909*
Davies. *Transport: On Land, Road and Rail*
Doherty. *The Statue of Liberty*
Dolan. *Panama and the United States: Their Canal, Their Stormy Years*
Emert. *Top Lawyers and their Famous Cases*
English. *Transportation: Automobiles to Zeppelins*
Ferrell. *The U.S. Air Force*
Freedman. *Kids at Work: Lewis Hine Against Child Labor*
Fry. *The Orphan Train*

Garfunkel. *On Wings of Joy: The Story of Ballet*
Giblin. *Be Seated: A Book About Chairs*
Goldish. *Our Supreme Court*
Greene. *Child Labor: Then and Now*
Greene. *Our Century: 1900-1910*
Gutman. *World Series Classics*
Hakim. *An Age of Extremes*
Hakim. *Reconstruction and Reform*
Hirsch. *Taxation: Paying for Government*
The History of Moviemaking
Hoig. *It's the Fourth of July*
Jones. *The President Has Been Shot*
Kalman. *Early Artisans*
Kalman. *Early Christmas*
Kalman. *Early City Life*
Kalman. *Early Schools*
Kalman. *Early Stores and Markets*
Kalman. *Early Travel*
Kalman. *Early Village Life*
Kalman. *19th Century Clothing*
Kalman. *Old-Time Toys*
Kalman. *A One-Room School*
Karl. *America Alive: A History*
Kurtz. *U.S. Army*
Lawrence. *The Great Migration*
Leiner. *First Children: Growing Up in the White House*
Leuzzi. *Urban Life*
Libreatore. *Our Century: 1910-1920*
Lucas. *Civil Rights: The Long Struggle*
Markham. *Inventions That Changed Modern Life*
Mason. *Peary and Amundsen: Race to the Poles*
Maurer. *Airborne: The Search for the Secret of Flight*
Medearis. *Come This Far to Freedom*
Meltzer. *The Black Americans*

Mettger. *Reconstruction: America after the Civil War*
Mizell. *Think About Racism*
Monceaux. *Jazz: My Music, My People*
Morley. *Clothes: For Work, Play and Display*
Moser. *Fly!*
Murphy. *Across America on an Emigrant Train*
Murphy. *The Great Fire*
Patrick. *The Young Oxford Companion to the Supreme Court*
Philip. *Singing America: Poems That Define a Nation*
Platt. *The Smithsonian Visual Timeline of Inventions*
Pleasant. *Samantha's Cookbook*
Pollard. *The Nineteenth Century*
Pollard. *The Red Cross and the Red Crescent*
Rappaport. *The Lizzie Borden Trial*
Reef. *The Supreme Court*
Rowland-Warne. *Costume*
Sandler. *Presidents*
Scott. *Funny Papers: Behind the Scenes of the Comics*
Sherrow. *The Big Book of U.S. Presidents*
Sherrow. *The Triangle Factory Fire*
St. George. *Panama Canal: Gateway to the World*
St. George. *The White House: Cornerstone of a Nation*
Stacey. *The Titanic*
Stein. *The Story of the Powers of the Supreme Court*
Stern. *The Congress: America's Lawmakers*
The Story of Flight
Sullivan. *Children of Promise: African-American Literature and Art*
Tanaka. *On Board the Titanic*
Time-Life. *African Americans: Voices of Triumph: Leadership*

Ventura. *Clothing*
Ventura. *Food: Its Evolution Through the Ages*
Walker. *Hand, Heart, and Mind*
Warburton. *The Chicago Fire*

Ward. *Who Invented the Game?*
Warner. *The U.S. Marine Corps*
Weber. *Our Congress*
Wheeler. *Events That Changed American History*

Whitman. *Get Up and Go: American Road Travel*
Whitman. *This Land Is Your Land*
Yepsen. *City Trains: America's Cities by Rail*

Multimedia

CD-ROM

American History Explorer
Air and Space Smithsonian Dreams of Flight
Campaigns, Candidates and the Presidency
Daring to Fly!
Exploring the Titanic

Eyewitness Encyclopedia of Science
Her Heritage: A Biographical Encyclopedia of American History
History Through Art: 20th Century

Portraits of American Presidents
SkyTrip America
Time Almanac of the 20th Century
Total History
The Way Things Work

Video

African American Life
African Americans
Alexander Graham Bell
All Aboard for Philadelphia!
American Consumerism (1890-1930)
Black Is My Color: The African American Experience
Elizabeth Cady Stanton and Susan B. Anthony

The Era of Segregation: A Personal Perspective
Great Black Innovators
Helen Keller
Industrialization and Urbanization (1870-1910)
Making It Happen: Masters of Invention
Mary McLeod Bethune
A Nation in Turmoil
Presenting Mr. Frederick Douglass

Progressive Movement
Reading Terminal Market
Reconstruction and Segregation (1870-1910)
Susan B. Anthony Story
Thomas Alva Edison
Tragedy to Triumph: An Adventure with Helen Keller
U.S. and the World (1865-1917)

WORLD WAR I AND THE DEPRESSION, 1917-1941

KINDERGARTEN THROUGH SECOND GRADE

Historical Fiction

Antle. *Hard Times: A Story of the Great Depression*
Armstrong. *Patrick Doyle Is Full of Blarney*
Bodkin. *The Banshee Train*
Clifford. *The Remembering Box*
Friedrich. *Leah's Pony*
Hall. *The Farm Summer 1942*
Hesse. *Lester's Dog*
Houston. *My Great-Aunt Arizona*
Houston. *The Year of the Perfect Christmas Tree*

Ketteman. *The Year of No More Corn*
Kinsey-Warnock. *The Wild Horses of Sweetbriar*
Kroeger. *Paperboy*
Kudlinski. *Hero over Here*
Levinson. *DinnieAbbieSister-r-r!*
McDonald. *The Potato Man*
Oneal. *A Long Way to Go*
Rabin. *Casey over There*
Rael. *What Zeesie Saw on Delancey Street*
Ringgold. *Bonjour, Lonnie*

Ringgold. *Tar Beach*
Rylant. *When I Was Young in the Mountains*
Say. *Grandfather's Journey*
Stroud. *Down Home at Miss Dessa's*
Taylor. *The Friendship*
Taylor. *Song of the Trees*
Turner. *Dust for Dinner*
Wells. *Waiting for the Evening Star*
Yolen. *Letting Swift River Go*

Biography

Adler. *Jackie Robinson: He Was the First*
Adler. *A Picture Book of Eleanor Roosevelt*
Adler. *A Picture Book of Helen Keller*
Adler. *A Picture Book of Jackie Robinson*
Adler. *A Picture Book of Jesse Owens*
Adler. *A Picture Book of Thurgood Marshall*
Adler. *Thomas Alva Edison: Great Inventor*
Aliki. *A Weed Is a Flower: The Life of George Washington Carver*
Behrens. *Juliette Low: Founder of the Girl Scouts of America*
Benjamin. *Young Helen Keller*
Burleigh. *Flight: The Journey of Charles Lindbergh*
Cavan. *W. E. B. Du Bois*
Cooney. *Eleanor*

Cooper. *Coming Home: From the Life of Langston Hughes*
Cwiklik. *Philip Randolph*
Cwiklik. *Malcolm X*
Demarest. *Lindbergh*
Faber. *Eleanor Roosevelt: First Lady of the World*
Greene. *George Washington Carver: Scientist and Teacher*
Greene. *Jacques Cousteau: Man of the Oceans*
Greene. *Katherine Dunham: Black Dancer*
Greenfield. *Mary McLeod Bethune*
Lindbergh. *Nobody Owns the Sky: The Story of Brave Bessie Coleman*
Livingston. *Keep On Singing: A Ballad of Marian Anderson*
MacKinnon. *Silent Observer*
McKissack. *Carter G. Woodson*
McKissack. *George Washington Carver*

McKissack. *Ida B. Wells-Barnett*
McKissack. *James Weldon Johnson: "Lift Every Voice and Sing"*
McKissack. *Louis Armstrong: Jazz Musician*
McKissack. *Marian Anderson: A Great Singer*
McKissack. *Mary Church Terrell: Leader for Equality*
McKissack. *Mary McLeod Bethune*
McKissack. *Paul Robeson: A Voice to Remember*
McKissack. *Ralph J. Bunche*
Meltzer. *Dorothea Lange: Life Through the Camera*
O'Connor. *Jackie Robinson*
Venezia. *Edward Hopper*
Venezia. *George Gershwin*
Venezia. *Georgia O'Keeffe*
Venezia. *Jackson Pollock*
Wetterer. *Clyde Tombaugh and the Search for Planet X*

Collective Biography

Marzollo. *My First Book of Biographies*

History

Goldish. *Our Supreme Court*
Medearis. *Our People*
Moser. *Fly!*

Ritter. *Leagues Apart: The Men and Times of the Negro Baseball Leagues*

Steins. *Our Elections*

Multimedia

Video

African American Life

Let Me Tell You All About Trains

GRADE THREE

Historical Fiction

Antle. *Hard Times: A Story of the Great Depression*
Armstrong. *Patrick Doyle Is Full of Blarney*
Bodkin. *The Banshee Train*
Clifford. *The Man Who Sang in the Dark*
Clifford. *The Remembering Box*
Friedrich. *Leah's Pony*
Greene. *Dotty's Suitcase*
Hall. *The Farm Summer 1942*
Hall. *When Willard Met Babe Ruth*
Hesse. *Lester's Dog*
Houston. *My Great-Aunt Arizona*
Houston. *The Year of the Perfect Christmas Tree*

Ketteman. *The Year of No More Corn*
Kinsey-Warnock. *The Wild Horses of Sweetbriar*
Kroeger. *Paperboy*
Kudlinski. *Hero over Here*
Lehrman. *The Store That Mama Built*
Levinson. *DinnieAbbieSister-r-r!*
Mitchell. *Uncle Jed's Barbershop*
Oneal. *A Long Way to Go*
Patrick. *A Missing Portrait on Sugar Hill*
Rabin. *Casey over There*
Ransom. *Jimmy Crack Corn*
Rael. *What Zeesie Saw on Delancey Street*

Reeder. *Moonshiner's Son*
Ringgold. *Bonjour, Lonnie*
Ringgold. *Tar Beach*
Rylant. *When I Was Young in the Mountains*
Say. *Grandfather's Journey*
Stroud. *Down Home at Miss Dessa's*
Taylor. *Song of the Trees*
Taylor. *The Friendship*
Taylor. *Song of the Trees*
Turner. *Dust for Dinner*
Uchida. *A Jar of Dreams*
Weaver. *Child Star: When Talkies Came to Hollywood*
Wells. *Waiting for the Evening Star*
Yolen. *Letting Swift River Go*

Biography

Adler. *Jackie Robinson: He Was the First*
Adler. *Our Golda: The Story of Golda Meir*
Adler. *A Picture Book of Eleanor Roosevelt*
Adler. *A Picture Book of Helen Keller*
Adler. *A Picture Book of Jackie Robinson*
Adler. *A Picture Book of Jesse Owens*
Adler. *A Picture Book of Thurgood Marshall*
Adler. *Thomas Alva Edison: Great Inventor*
Aliki. *A Weed Is a Flower: The Life of George Washington Carver*

Behrens. *Juliette Low: Founder of the Girl Scouts of America*
Benjamin. *Young Helen Keller*
Berkow. *Hank Greenberg: Hall-of-Fame Slugger*
Brown. *Daisy and the Girl Scouts: Juliette Gordon Low*
Burford. *Chocolate by Hershey: Milton S. Hershey*
Burleigh. *Flight: The Journey of Charles Lindbergh*
Calvert. *Zora Neale Hurston: Storyteller of the South*
Cavan. *W. E. B. Du Bois*
Coil. *George Washington Carver*

Collins. *Charles Lindbergh: Hero Pilot*
Colman. *A Woman Unafraid: Frances Perkins*
Cooney. *Eleanor*
Cooper. *Coming Home: From the Life of Langston Hughes*
Crofford. *Frontier Surgeons: A Story About the Mayo Brothers*
Cwiklik. *Philip Randolph*
Cwiklik. *Malcolm X*
Davies. *Amelia Earhart Flies Around the World*
Demarest. *Lindbergh*
Dolan. *Matthew Henson: Arctic Explorer*
Dunlap. *Eye on the Wild: A Story About Ansel Adams*

Everett. *Li'l Sis and Uncle Willie: William Johnson*
Faber. *Eleanor Roosevelt: First Lady of the World*
Graff. *Helen Keller: Toward the Light*
Greene. *George Washington Carver: Scientist and Teacher*
Greene. *Jacques Cousteau: Man of the Oceans*
Greene. *Katherine Dunham: Black Dancer*
Greenfield. *Mary McLeod Bethune*
Heiligman. *Barbara McClintock: Alone in Her Field*
Hunter. *Helen Keller*
Jakoubek. *Walter White and the Power of Organized Protest*
Kelso. *Building a Dream: Mary Bethune's School*
Kerby. *Amelia Earhart: Courage in the Sky*
Kudlinski. *Helen Keller: A Light for the Blind*
Latham. *George Goethals: Panama Canal Engineer*
Lindbergh. *Nobody Owns the Sky: The Story of Brave Bessie Coleman*
Lipsyte. *Jim Thorpe: Twentieth-Century Jock*
Livingston. *Keep On Singing: A Ballad of Marian Anderson*

Lorbiecki. *Of Things Natural, Wild, and Free*
Macht. *Babe Ruth*
MacKinnon. *Silent Observer*
McKissack. *Carter G. Woodson*
McKissack. *George Washington Carver*
McKissack. *Ida B. Wells-Barnett*
McKissack. *James Weldon Johnson: "Lift Every Voice and Sing"*
McKissack. *Jesse Owens: Olympic Star*
McKissack. *Langston Hughes: Great American Poet*
McKissack. *Louis Armstrong: Jazz Musician*
McKissack. *Marian Anderson: A Great Singer*
McKissack. *Mary Church Terrell: Leader for Equality*
McKissack. *Mary McLeod Bethune*
McKissack. *Paul Robeson: A Voice to Remember*
McKissack. *Ralph J. Bunche*
McPherson. *The Workers' Detective: A Story About Dr. Alice Hamilton*
Medearis. *Little Louis and the Jazz Band*
Meltzer. *Dorothea Lange: Life Through the Camera*
Mitchell. *We'll Race You, Henry*
Nicholson. *George Washington Carver*
O'Connor. *Jackie Robinson*

Prentzas. *Thurgood Marshall: Champion of Justice*
Rambeck. *Lou Gehrig*
Reiser. *Jackie Robinson: Baseball Pioneer*
Rivinus. *Jim Thorpe*
Sanford. *Babe Ruth*
Sanford. *Jackie Robinson*
Sanford. *Jesse Owens*
Sanford. *Jim Thorpe*
Santella. *Jackie Robinson Breaks the Color Line*
Schmidt. *Robert Frost*
Shirley. *Malcolm X: Racial Spokesman*
Shorto. *Jackie Robinson*
Stine. *The Story of Malcolm X: Civil Rights Leader*
Streissguth. *Say It with Music: A Story About Irving Berlin*
Swanson. *I've Got an Idea! Frederick McKinley Jones*
Tames. *Amelia Earhart: 1897-1937*
Turner. *Georgia O'Keeffe*
Venezia. *Edward Hopper*
Venezia. *George Gershwin*
Venezia. *Georgia O'Keeffe*
Venezia. *Jackson Pollock*
Vernon. *Introducing Gershwin*
Weidt. *Stateswoman to the World: Eleanor Roosevelt*
Wetterer. *Clyde Tombaugh and the Search for Planet X*
Wolfe. *Mary McLeod Bethune*

Collective Biography

King. *First Facts About American Heroes*
Marzollo. *My First Book of Biographies*

Provensen. *The Buck Stops Here: The Presidents*

Rappaport. *Living Dangerously: American Women*

History

Ash. *The Story of the Women's Movement*
Bowler. *Trains*
Burns. *Mail*
Caulkins. *Pets of the Presidents*
English. *Transportation: Automobiles to Zeppelins*
Goldish. *Our Supreme Court*
Guzzetti. *The White House*
Harvey. *Women's Voting Rights*
Hill. *Our Century: 1920-1930*
Humble. *Ships*
Kent. *The Lincoln Memorial*

Knight. *The Olympic Games*
Lawrence. *The Great Migration*
Libreatore. *Our Century: 1910-1920*
Medearis. *Our People*
Moser. *Fly!*
Munro. *Aircraft*
Owen. *Our Century: 1930-1940*
Paananen. *The Military: Defending the Nation*
Ritter. *Leagues Apart: The Men and Times of the Negro Baseball Leagues*

Stein. *The Great Depression*
Stein. *The Hindenburg Disaster*
Stein. *The Story of the Powers of the Supreme Court*
Steins. *Our Elections*
Stern. *The Congress: America's Lawmakers*
Weber. *Our Congress*
Wilson. *Visual Timeline of Transportation*

Multimedia

Video

African American Life

Let Me Tell You All About Trains

GRADE FOUR

Historical Fiction

Ames. *Grandpa Jake and the Grand Christmas*

Antle. *Hard Times: A Story of the Great Depression*

Armstrong. *Patrick Doyle Is Full of Blarney*

Clifford. *The Man Who Sang in the Dark*

Clifford. *The Remembering Box*

Clifford. *Will Somebody Please Marry My Sister?*

Cochrane. *Purely Rosie Pearl*

Corcoran. *The Private War of Lillian Adams*

Friedrich. *Leah's Pony*

Greene. *Dotty's Suitcase*

Hall. *When Willard Met Babe Ruth*

Horvath. *The Happy Yellow Car*

Houston. *My Great-Aunt Arizona*

Kinsey-Warnock. *The Night the Bells Rang*

Kudlinski. *Hero over Here*

Lehrman. *The Store That Mama Built*

Levinson. *DinnieAbbieSister-r-r!*

McKenzie. *Under the Bridge*

Mitchell. *Uncle Jed's Barbershop*

Myers. *Spotting the Leopard*

Oneal. *A Long Way to Go*

Patrick. *A Missing Portrait on Sugar Hill*

Ransom. *Jimmy Crack Corn*

Reeder. *Grandpa's Mountain*

Reeder. *Moonshiner's Son*

Ringgold. *Bonjour, Lonnie*

Taylor. *The Friendship*

Taylor. *Mississippi Bridge*

Taylor. *Song of the Trees*

Taylor. *The Well: David's Story*

Uchida. *A Jar of Dreams*

Weaver. *Child Star: When Talkies Came to Hollywood*

Whelan. *That Wild Berries Should Grow*

Whitmore. *The Bread Winner*

Biography

Adler. *Jackie Robinson: He Was the First*

Adler. *Our Golda: The Story of Golda Meir*

Adler. *A Picture Book of Jesse Owens*

Adler. *Thomas Alva Edison: Great Inventor*

Anderson. *Gifford Pinchot: American Forester*

Behrens. *Juliette Low: Founder of the Girl Scouts of America*

Benjamin. *Young Helen Keller*

Bennett. *Will Rogers: Quotable Cowboy*

Berkow. *Hank Greenberg: Hall-of-Fame Slugger*

Brooks. *Georgia O'Keeffe: An Adventurous Spirit*

Brown. *Daisy and the Girl Scouts: Juliette Gordon Low*

Burford. *Chocolate by Hershey: Milton S. Hershey*

Burleigh. *Flight: The Journey of Charles Lindbergh*

Butts. *May Chinn: The Best Medicine*

Calvert. *Zora Neale Hurston: Storyteller of the South*

Casey. *William H. Taft: Twenty-Seventh President*

Cavan. *W. E. B. Du Bois*

Chadwick. *Amelia Earhart: Aviation Pioneer*

Chadwick. *Anne Morrow Lindbergh: Pilot and Poet*

Clinton. *Herbert Hoover: Thirty-First President*

Coil. *George Washington Carver*

Collins. *Charles Lindbergh: Hero Pilot*

Colman. *Fannie Lou Hamer and the Fight for the Vote*

Colman. *A Woman Unafraid: Frances Perkins*

Cooper. *Coming Home: From the Life of Langston Hughes*

Crofford. *Frontier Surgeons: A Story About the Mayo Brothers*

Cwiklik, Robert. *Philip Randolph*

Cwiklik, Robert. *Malcolm X*

Davidson. *Getting the Real Story: Nellie Bly and Ida B. Wells*

Davies. *Amelia Earhart Flies Around the World*

Dolan. *Matthew Henson: Arctic Explorer*

Duggleby. *Artist in Overalls: Grant Wood*

Dunlap. *Aldo Leopold: Living with the Land*

Dunlap. *Birds in the Bushes: Margaret Morse Nice*

Dunlap. *Eye on the Wild: A Story About Ansel Adams*

Everett. *Li'l Sis and Uncle Willie: William Johnson*

Faber. *Eleanor Roosevelt: First Lady of the World*

Ferris. *What I Had Was Singing: Marian Anderson*

Freedman. *Ida B. Wells and the Antilynching Crusade*

Graff. *Helen Keller: Toward the Light*

Greene. *Jacques Cousteau: Man of the Oceans*

Greene. *Thomas Alva Edison: Bringer of Light*

Greenfield. *Mary McLeod Bethune*

Hart. *Up in the Air: Bessie Coleman*

Heiligman. *Barbara McClintock: Alone in Her Field*

Hunter. *Helen Keller*

Jakoubek. *Walter White and the Power of Organized Protest*

Kaye. *The Life of Benjamin Spock*

Kaye. *The Life of Florence Sabin*

Kelso. *Building a Dream: Mary Bethune's School*

Kent. *Calvin Coolidge: Thirtieth President*

Kerby. *Amelia Earhart: Courage in the Sky*

Kittredge. *Jane Addams*

Kudlinski. *Helen Keller: A Light for the Blind*

Latham. *George Goethals: Panama Canal Engineer*

Lazo. *Eleanor Roosevelt*

Lindbergh. *Nobody Owns the Sky: The Story of Brave Bessie Coleman*

Lipsyte. *Jim Thorpe: Twentieth-Century Jock*

Lipsyte. *Joe Louis: A Champ for all America*

Livingston. *Keep On Singing: A Ballad of Marian Anderson*

Lorbiecki. *Of Things Natural, Wild, and Free*

Lyons. *Starting Home: Horace Pippin, Painter*

Macht. *Babe Ruth*

MacKinnon. *Silent Observer*

McKissack. *Carter G. Woodson*

McKissack. *George Washington Carver*

McKissack. *Ida B. Wells-Barnett*

McKissack. *James Weldon Johnson: "Lift Every Voice and Sing"*

McKissack. *Jesse Owens: Olympic Star*

McKissack. *Langston Hughes: Great American Poet*

McKissack. *Louis Armstrong: Jazz Musician*

McKissack. *Marian Anderson: A Great Singer*

McKissack. *Mary Church Terrell: Leader for Equality*

McKissack. *Mary McLeod Bethune*

McKissack. *Ralph J. Bunche*

McPherson. *Peace and Bread: Jane Addams*

McPherson. *TV's Forgotten Hero: Philo Farnsworth*

McPherson. *The Workers' Detective: A Story About Dr. Alice Hamilton*

Medearis. *Little Louis and the Jazz Band*

Meltzer. *Dorothea Lange: Life Through the Camera*

Mitchell. *The Wizard of Sound: Thomas Edison*

Mitchell. *We'll Race You, Henry*

Nicholson. *George Washington Carver*

O'Connor. *Barefoot Dancer: Isadora Duncan*

O'Connor. *Jackie Robinson*

O'Connor. *The Soldier's Voice: Ernie Pyle*

Parker. *Thomas Edison and Electricity*

Pfeifer. *Henry O. Flipper*

Porter. *Jump at de Sun: Zora Neale Hurston*

Prentzas. *Thurgood Marshall: Champion of Justice*

Ptacek. *Champion for Children's Health: Dr. S. Josephine Baker*

Rambeck. *Lou Gehrig*

Reiser. *Jackie Robinson: Baseball Pioneer*

Rennert. *Jesse Owens: Champion Athlete*

Rivinus. *Jim Thorpe*

Rogers. *George Washington Carver*

Sanford. *Babe Ruth*

Sanford. *Jackie Robinson*

Sanford. *Jesse Owens*

Sanford. *Jim Thorpe*

Santella. *Jackie Robinson Breaks the Color Line*

Schmidt. *Robert Frost*

Shirley. *Malcolm X: Racial Spokesman*

Shorto. *Jackie Robinson*

Stine. *The Story of Malcolm X, Civil Rights Leader*

Streissguth. *Rocket Man: Robert Goddard*

Streissguth. *Say It with Music: A Story About Irving Berlin*

Swanson. *I've Got an Idea! Frederick McKinley Jones*

Tames. *Amelia Earhart: 1897-1937*

Taylor. *The First Solo Flight Around the World: Wiley Post*

Turner. *Dorothea Lange*

Turner. *Georgia O'Keeffe*

Venezia. *George Gershwin*

Vernon. *Introducing Gershwin*

Wade. *Warren G. Harding: Twenty-Ninth President*

Weidt. *Stateswoman to the World: Eleanor Roosevelt*

Whitelaw. *Grace Hopper*

Wolfe. *Charles Richard Drew, M.D.*

Wolfe. *Mary McLeod Bethune*

Collective Biography

Altman. *Extraordinary Black Americans*

Clements. *The Picture History of Great Inventors*

Fireside. *Is There a Woman in the House. . . or Senate?*

Hart. *Flying Free: America's First Black Aviators*

Jacobs. *Great Lives: Human Rights*

Jacobs. *They Shaped the Game: Ty Cobb, Babe Ruth, and Jackie Robinson*

King. *First Facts About American Heroes*

Krull. *Lives of the Artists: Masterpieces, Messes*

Krull. *Lives of the Musicians: Good Times, Bad Times*

Krull. *Lives of the Writers: Comedies, Tragedies*

McKissack. *African-American Inventors*

Pascoe. *First Facts About the Presidents*

Pile. *Top Entrepreneurs and Their Businesses*
Provensen. *The Buck Stops Here: The Presidents*
Provensen. *My Fellow Americans*

Rappaport. *Living Dangerously: American Women*
Reef. *Black Fighting Men: A Proud History*

Rubel. *The Scholastic Encyclopedia of the Presidents*
Vare. *Women Inventors and Their Discoveries*
Wilkinson. *Scientists Who Changed the World*

History

Ash. *The Story of the Women's Movement*
Blue. *The White House Kids*
Bolick. *Mail Call!*
Bowler. *Trains*
Brill. *Let Women Vote!*
Burns. *Mail*
Burns. *Money*
Caulkins. *Pets of the Presidents*
English. *Transportation: Automobiles to Zeppelins*
Ferrell. *The U.S. Air Force*
Giblin. *Be Seated: A Book About Chairs*
Goldish. *Our Supreme Court*
Guzzetti. *The White House*
Harvey. *Women's Voting Rights*
Hill. *Our Century: 1920-1930*
The History of Moviemaking
Humble. *Ships*
Kent. *The Lincoln Memorial*
Knight. *The Olympic Games*
Kurtz. *U.S. Army*
Lampton. *Epidemic*

Lawrence. *The Great Migration*
Libreatore. *Our Century: 1910-1920*
McKissack. *Black Diamond*
Moser. *Fly!*
Munro. *Aircraft*
Norrell. *We Want Jobs!*
Owen. *Our Century: 1930-1940*
Paananen. *The Military: Defending the Nation*
Reef. *The Supreme Court*
Ritter. *Leagues Apart: The Men and Times of the Negro Baseball Leagues*
Rosen. *The First Transatlantic Flight*
Rowland-Warne. *Costume*
Sandler. *Presidents*
Scott. *Funny Papers: Behind the Scenes of the Comics*
Sloan. *Bismarck!*
Stein. *The Great Depression*
Stein. *The Hindenburg Disaster*

Stein. *The Story of the Powers of the Supreme Court*
Steins. *Our Elections*
Stern. *The Congress: America's Lawmakers*
The Story of Flight
Sullivan. *Children of Promise: African-American Literature and Art*
Tessendorf. *Wings Around the World: The American World Flight of 1924*
Ventura. *Clothing*
Ventura. *Food: Its Evolution Through the Ages*
Ward. *Shadow Ball: The Negro Leagues*
Ward. *Who Invented the Game?*
Warren. *Orphan Train Rider: One Boy's True Story*
Weber. *Our Congress*
Wilson. *Visual Timeline of Transportation*

Multimedia

CD-ROM

Her Heritage: A Biographical Encyclopedia of American History

SkyTrip America
Total History

Video

African American Life
African Americans
Amelia Earhart
Black Is My Color: The African American Experience
Frontier Buildings

Great Black Innovators
Helen Keller
In Search of the North Pole
Jackie Robinson
Let Me Tell You All About Trains

Making It Happen: Masters of Invention
Malcolm X
The Sky's the Limit
Thomas Alva Edison
Tsiolkovski: The Space Age

GRADE FIVE

Historical Fiction

Ames. *Grandpa Jake and the Grand Christmas*
Amoss. *The Mockingbird Song*

Antle. *Hard Times: A Story of the Great Depression*
Armstrong. *Sounder*
Avi. *Shadrach's Crossing*

Beatty. *Billy Bedamned, Long Gone By*
Clifford. *The Man Who Sang in the Dark*

Clifford. *The Remembering Box*

Clifford. *Will Somebody Please Marry My Sister?*

Cochrane. *Purely Rosie Pearl*

Corbin. *Me and the End of the World*

Corcoran. *The Private War of Lillian Adams*

Crofford. *A Place to Belong*

Cuneo. *Anne Is Elegant*

Ducey. *The Bittersweet Time*

Greene. *Dotty's Suitcase*

Hall. *When Willard Met Babe Ruth*

Horvath. *The Happy Yellow Car*

Karr. *The Cave*

Karr. *In the Kaiser's Clutch*

Kinsey-Warnock. *The Night the Bells Rang*

Koller. *Nothing to Fear*

Kudlinski. *Hero over Here*

Lehrman. *The Store That Mama Built*

Lyon. *Borrowed Children*

Mazer. *Cave Under the City*

McKenzie. *Under the Bridge*

Mills. *What About Annie?*

Mitchell. *Uncle Jed's Barbershop*

Myers. *Spotting the Leopard*

Olsen. *The View from the Pighouse Roof*

Oneal. *A Long Way to Go*

Patrick. *A Missing Portrait on Sugar Hill*

Pendergraft. *As Far as Mill Springs*

Ransom. *Jimmy Crack Corn*

Reeder. *Grandpa's Mountain*

Reeder. *Moonshiner's Son*

Ross. *Hillbilly Choir*

Skurzynski. *Good-bye, Billy Radish*

Snyder. *Cat Running*

Taylor. *The Friendship*

Taylor. *Mississippi Bridge*

Taylor. *Roll of Thunder, Hear My Cry*

Taylor. *Song of the Trees*

Taylor. *The Well: David's Story*

Thesman. *The Ornament Tree*

Uchida. *A Jar of Dreams*

Voight. *Tree by Leaf*

Weaver. *Child Star: When Talkies Came to Hollywood*

Whelan. *That Wild Berries Should Grow*

Whitmore. *The Bread Winner*

Biography

Adler. *Jackie Robinson: He Was the First*

Adler. *Our Golda: The Story of Golda Meir*

Anderson. *Gifford Pinchot: American Forester*

Bennett. *Will Rogers: Quotable Cowboy*

Berkow. *Hank Greenberg: Hall-of-Fame Slugger*

Bernotas. *Jim Thorpe: Sac and Fox Athlete*

Berry. *Georgia O'Keeffe: Painter*

Berry. *Langston Hughes*

Brooks. *Georgia O'Keeffe: An Adventurous Spirit*

Brown. *Daisy and the Girl Scouts: Juliette Gordon Low*

Buranelli. *Thomas Alva Edison*

Burford. *Chocolate by Hershey: Milton S. Hershey*

Burleigh. *Flight: The Journey of Charles Lindbergh*

Butts. *May Chinn: The Best Medicine*

Cain. *Louise Nevelson: Sculptor*

Calvert. *Zora Neale Hurston: Storyteller of the South*

Canadeo. *Warren G. Harding*

Casey. *William H. Taft: Twenty-Seventh President*

Castiglia. *Margaret Mead*

Chadwick. *Amelia Earhart: Aviation Pioneer*

Chadwick. *Anne Morrow Lindbergh: Pilot and Poet*

Clinton. *Herbert Hoover: Thirty-First President*

Coil. *George Washington Carver*

Collier. *Duke Ellington*

Collier. *Louis Armstrong: An American Success Story*

Collins. *Charles Lindbergh: Hero Pilot*

Collins. *Woodrow Wilson: 28th President*

Colman. *A Woman Unafraid: Frances Perkins*

Colman. *Fannie Lou Hamer and the Fight for the Vote*

Crofford. *Frontier Surgeons: A Story About the Mayo Brothers*

Cwiklik. *Malcolm X*

Daffron. *Margaret Bourke-White: Photographer*

Darby. *Douglas MacArthur*

Darby. *Dwight D. Eisenhower*

Davidson. *Getting the Real Story: Nellie Bly and Ida B. Wells*

Davies. *Amelia Earhart Flies Around the World*

Davies. *Malcolm X*

Davis. *Frank Lloyd Wright: Maverick Architect*

Devane. *Franklin Delano Roosevelt: President*

Dolan. *Matthew Henson: Arctic Explorer*

Dominy. *Katherine Dunham: Dancer and Choreographer*

Driemen. *Atomic Dawn: A Biography of Robert Oppenheimer*

Driemen. *Clarence Darrow*

Duggleby. *Artist in Overalls: Grant Wood*

Dunlap. *Aldo Leopold: Living with the Land*

Dunlap. *Birds in the Bushes: Margaret Morse Nice*

Dunlap. *Eye on the Wild: A Story About Ansel Adams*

Erlich. *Paul Robeson: Singer and Actor*

Everett. *Li'l Sis and Uncle Willie: William Johnson*

Faber. *Eleanor Roosevelt: First Lady of the World*

Falkof. *William H. Taft*

Farley. *Robert H. Goddard*

Ferris. *What I Had Was Singing: Marian Anderson*

Freedman. *Franklin Delano Roosevelt*

Freedman. *Ida B. Wells and the Antilynching Crusade*

Freedman. *Louis Brandeis*

Gentry. *Jesse Owens: Champion Athlete*

Gourse. *Dizzy Gillespie and the Birth of Bebop*

Graff. *Helen Keller: Toward the Light*

Gray. *George Washington Carver*

Greenblatt. *Franklin D. Roosevelt*

Greene. *Thomas Alva Edison: Bringer of Light*

Greenfield. *Mary McLeod Bethune*

Halasa. *Elijah Muhammad: Religious Leader*

Halasa. *Mary McLeod Bethune: Educator*

Hanley. *Philip Randolph*

Hart. *Up in the Air: Bessie Coleman*

Heiligman. *Barbara McClintock: Alone in Her Field*

Hunter. *Helen Keller*

Israel. *Franklin Delano Roosevelt*

Jakoubek. *Joe Louis: Heavyweight Champion*

Jakoubek. *Walter White and the Power of Organized Protest*

James. *Julia Morgan: Architect*

Kallen. *Thurgood Marshall: A Dream of Justice for All*

Kaye. *The Life of Alexander Fleming*

Kaye. *The Life of Benjamin Spock*

Kaye. *The Life of Daniel Hale Williams*

Kaye. *The Life of Florence Sabin*

Keller. *Margaret Bourke-White: A Photographer's Life*

Kelso. *Building a Dream: Mary Bethune's School*

Kent. *Calvin Coolidge: Thirtieth President*

Kerby. *Amelia Earhart: Courage in the Sky*

Kittredge. *Barbara McClintock*

Kittredge. *Helen Hayes: Actress*

Kittredge. *Jane Addams*

Kliment. *Billie Holiday: Singer*

Kliment. *Count Basie: Bandleader and Musician*

Kliment. *Ella Fitzgerald: Singer*

Klots. *Ida Wells-Barnett: Civil Rights Leader*

Kozodoy. *Isadora Duncan: Dancer*

Kronstadt. *Florence Sabin: Medical Researcher*

Kudlinski. *Helen Keller: A Light for the Blind*

La Farge. *Pearl Buck*

Larsen. *Amelia Earhart: Missing, Declared Dead*

Latham. *George Goethals: Panama Canal Engineer*

Lauber. *Lost Star: The Story of Amelia Earhart*

Lawler. *Marcus Garvey: Black Nationalist Leader*

Lazo. *Eleanor Roosevelt*

Leavell. *Woodrow Wilson*

Lindop. *Woodrow Wilson, Franklin D. Roosevelt, Harry S. Truman*

Lipsyte. *Jim Thorpe: Twentieth-Century Jock*

Lipsyte. *Joe Louis: A Champ for all America*

Lorbiecki. *Of Things Natural, Wild, and Free*

Lynn. *Babe Didrikson Zaharias*

Lyons. *Starting Home: Horace Pippin, Painter*

Macht. *Babe Ruth*

Mahone-Lonesome. *Charles R. Drew*

Markham. *Helen Keller*

McKissack. *James Weldon Johnson: "Lift Every Voice and Sing"*

McKissack. *Mary McLeod Bethune*

McPherson. *Peace and Bread: Jane Addams*

McPherson. *TV's Forgotten Hero: Philo Farnsworth*

McPherson. *The Workers' Detective: A Story About Dr. Alice Hamilton*

Meltzer. *Dorothea Lange: Life Through the Camera*

Mintz. *Thomas Edison: Inventing the Future*

Mitchell. *The Wizard of Sound: Thomas Edison*

Mitchell. *We'll Race You, Henry*

Morris. *The FDR Way*

Myers. *Malcolm X: By Any Means Necessary*

Nicholson. *Babe Ruth: Sultan of Swat*

Nicholson. *George Washington Carver*

Nicholson. *Helen Keller: Humanitarian*

O'Connor. *Barefoot Dancer: Isadora Duncan*

O'Connor. *The Soldier's Voice: Ernie Pyle*

Osofsky. *Free to Dream: Langston Hughes*

Palmer. *Lena Horne: Entertainer*

Parker. *Thomas Edison and Electricity*

Pfeifer. *Henry O. Flipper*

Polikoff. *Herbert C. Hoover*

Porter. *Jump at de Sun: Zora Neale Hurston*

Potter. *Buckminster Fuller*

Prentzas. *Thurgood Marshall: Champion of Justice*

Probosz. *Martha Graham*

Ptacek. *Champion for Children's Health: Dr. S. Josephine Baker*

Rambeck. *Lou Gehrig*

Randolph. *Amelia Earhart*

Reiser. *Jackie Robinson: Baseball Pioneer*

Rennert. *Jesse Owens: Champion Athlete*

Rivinus. *Jim Thorpe*

Rogers. *George Washington Carver*

Sandak. *The Franklin Roosevelts*

Sandak. *The Wilsons*

Sanford. *Babe Ruth*

Sanford. *Jackie Robinson*

Sanford. *Jesse Owens*

Sanford. *Jim Thorpe*

Santella. *Jackie Robinson Breaks the Color Line*

Schmidt. *Robert Frost*

Schroeder. *Josephine Baker*

Schuman. *Eleanor Roosevelt*

Scott. *Jackie Robinson*

Shirley. *Malcolm X: Racial Spokesman*

Shore. *Amelia Earhart: Aviator*

Sloate. *Amelia Earhart*

Shorto. *Jackie Robinson*

Sonneborn. *Will Rogers: Cherokee Entertainer*

St. George. *Dear Dr. Bell. . . Your Friend, Helen Keller*

Stafford. *W. E. B. Dubois: Scholar and Activist*

Stevens. *Calvin Coolidge: 30th President*

Stine. *The Story of Malcolm X, Civil Rights Leader*

Streissguth. *Rocket Man: Robert Goddard*

Streissguth. *Say It with Music: A Story About Irving Berlin*

Swanson. *I've Got an Idea! Frederick McKinley Jones*

Talmadge. *The Life of Charles Drew*

Tames. *Amelia Earhart: 1897-1937*

Tanenhaus. *Louis Armstrong: Musician*

Taylor. *The First Solo Flight Around the World: Wiley Post*

Tedards. *Marian Anderson: Singer*

Toor. *Eleanor Roosevelt*

Turner. *Dorothea Lange*

Turner. *Georgia O'Keeffe*

Vernon. *Introducing Gershwin*

Wade. *Warren G. Harding: Twenty-Ninth President*

Weidt. *Stateswoman to the World: Eleanor Roosevelt*

Weisbrot. *Father Divine: Religious Leader*

Whitelaw. *Grace Hopper*

Witcover. *Zora Neale Hurston*

Wolfe. *Charles Richard Drew, M.D.*

Wolfe. *Mary McLeod Bethune*

Ziesk. *Margaret Mead*

Collective Biography

Aaseng. *Close Calls: From the Brink of Ruin to Business Success*

Aaseng. *From Rags to Riches*

Aaseng. *True Champions*

Altman. *Extraordinary Black Americans*

Blue. *People of Peace*

Clements. *The Picture History of Great Inventors*

Faber. *Great Lives: American Government*

Fireside. *Is There a Woman in the House. . . or Senate?*

Glubok. *Great Lives: Painting*

Hart. *Flying Free: America's First Black Aviators*

Haskins. *Black Eagles: African Americans in Aviation*

Haskins. *The Harlem Renaissance*

Hazell. *Heroines: Great Women Through the Ages*

Jacobs. *Great Lives: Human Rights*

Jacobs. *They Shaped the Game: Ty Cobb, Babe Ruth, and Jackie Robinson*

Katz. *Proudly Red and Black: Stories of African and Native Americans*

King. *First Facts About American Heroes*

Krull. *Lives of the Artists: Masterpieces, Messes*

Krull. *Lives of the Musicians: Good Times, Bad Times*

Krull. *Lives of the Writers: Comedies, Tragedies*

Mayberry. *Business Leaders Who Built Financial Empires*

McKissack. *African-American Inventors*

Morin. *Women of the U.S. Congress*

Pascoe. *First Facts About the Presidents*

Pile. *Top Entrepreneurs and Their Businesses*

Provensen. *The Buck Stops Here: The Presidents*

Provensen. *My Fellow Americans*

Schraff. *American Heroes of Exploration and Flight*

Rappaport. *Living Dangerously: American Women*

Reef. *Black Fighting Men: A Proud History*

Rennert. *Jazz Stars*

Rubel. *The Scholastic Encyclopedia of the Presidents*

Vare. *Women Inventors and Their Discoveries*

Veglahn. *Women Scientists*

Weitzman. *Great Lives: Human Culture*

Wilkinson. *People Who Changed the World*

Wilkinson. *Scientists Who Changed the World*

History

Andryszewski. *The Dust Bowl*

Ash. *The Story of the Women's Movement*

Ashabranner. *A Memorial for Mr. Lincoln*

Blue. *The White House Kids*

Bolick. *Mail Call!*

Bowler. *Trains*

Brill. *Let Women Vote!*

Brown. *Conflict in Europe and the Great Depression (1914-1940)*

Burns. *Mail*

Burns. *Money*

Caulkins. *Pets of the Presidents*

Clare. *First World War*

Colman. *Strike: The Bitter Struggle of American Workers*

Colman. *Toilets, Bathtubs, Sinks, and Sewers*

Cooper. *Bound for the Promised Land: The Great Black Migration*

Cooper. *Playing America's Game: Negro League Baseball*

Cosner. *War Nurses*

Davies. *Transport: On Land, Road and Rail*

Emert. *Top Lawyers and their Famous Cases*

English. *Transportation: Automobiles to Zeppelins*

Farris. *The Dust Bowl*

Ferrell. *The U.S. Air Force*

Gardner. *The Forgotten Players: The Story of Black Baseball in America*

Giblin. *Be Seated: A Book About Chairs*

Goldish. *Our Supreme Court*

Granfield. *In Flanders Fields: The Story of the Poem by John McCrae*

Greene. *Child Labor: Then and Now*

Guzzetti. *The White House*

Harvey. *Women's Voting Rights*

Hill. *Our Century: 1920-1930*

Hintz. *Farewell, John Barleycorn: Prohibition in the United States*

Hirsch. *Taxation: Paying for Government*
The History of Moviemaking
Humble. *Ships*
Karl. *America Alive: A History*
Kent. *The Lincoln Memorial*
Knight. *The Olympic Games*
Kurtz. *U.S. Army*
Lampton. *Epidemic*
Lawrence. *The Great Migration*
Leuzzi. *Urban Life*
Levi. *Cowboys of the Sky*
Libreatore. *Our Century: 1910-1920*
McKissack. *Black Diamond*
Medearis. *Come This Far to Freedom*
Meltzer. *The Black Americans*
Migneco. *The Crash of 1929*
Morley. *Clothes: For Work, Play and Display*
Moser. *Fly!*
Munro. *Aircraft*
Naden. *The U.S. Coast Guard*
Norrell. *We Want Jobs!*

Owen. *Our Century: 1930-1940*
Paananen. *The Military: Defending the Nation*
Platt. *The Smithsonian Visual Timeline of Inventions*
Rappaport. *The Sacco-Vanzetti Trial*
Reef. *The Supreme Court*
Rosen. *The First Transatlantic Flight*
Rowland-Warne. *Costume*
Sandler. *Presidents*
Scott. *Funny Papers: Behind the Scenes of the Comics*
Sloan. *Bismarck!*
Stanley. *Big Annie of Calumet*
Stein. *The Great Depression*
Stein. *The Hindenburg Disaster*
Stein. *The Story of the Powers of the Supreme Court*
Steins. *Our Elections*
Stern. *The Congress: America's Lawmakers*
The Story of Flight
Sullivan. *Children of Promise:*

African-American Literature and Art
Tanaka. *The Disaster of the Hindenburg*
Tessendorf. *Wings Around the World: The American World Flight of 1924*
Ventura. *Clothing*
Ventura. *Food: Its Evolution Through the Ages*
Ward. *Shadow Ball: The Negro Leagues*
Ward. *Who Invented the Game?*
Warner. *The U.S. Marine Corps*
Warren. *Orphan Train Rider: One Boy's True Story*
Weber. *Our Congress*
Whitman. *Get Up and Go: American Road Travel*
Whitman. *This Land Is Your Land*
Whitman. *V Is for Victory*
Wilson. *Visual Timeline of Transportation*
Yepsen. *City Trains: America's Cities by Rail*

Multimedia

CD-ROM

Air and Space Smithsonian Dreams of Flight
Eyewitness Encyclopedia of Science

Her Heritage: A Biographical Encyclopedia of American History
Portraits of American Presidents

SkyTrip America
Total History
Voices of the 30s

Video

African American Life
African Americans
Amelia Earhart
American Consumerism (1890-1930)
Black Is My Color: The African American Experience
Elijah Muhammad
Frontier Buildings
George Washington Carver: A Man of Vision

Great Black Innovators
The Great Depression and the New Deal
Helen Keller
In Search of the North Pole
Jackie Robinson
Jesse Owens
Let Me Tell You All About Trains
Making It Happen: Masters of Invention
Malcolm X

Mary McLeod Bethune
Matthew Henson
The Sky's the Limit
Thomas Alva Edison
Tragedy to Triumph: An Adventure with Helen Keller
Tsiolkovski: The Space Age
World War I

GRADE SIX

Historical Fiction

Ames. *Grandpa Jake and the Grand Christmas*
Amoss. *The Mockingbird Song*

Antle. *Hard Times: A Story of the Great Depression*
Armstrong. *Sounder*
Armstrong. *Steal Away*
Avi. *Shadrach's Crossing*

Beatty. *Billy Bedamned, Long Gone By*
Clifford. *Will Somebody Please Marry My Sister?*
Cochrane. *Purely Rosie Pearl*

Collier. *The Jazz Kid*
Corbin. *Me and the End of the World*
Corcoran. *The Private War of Lillian Adams*
Crew. *Fire on the Wind*
Crofford. *A Place to Belong*
Cuneo. *Anne Is Elegant*
Ducey. *The Bittersweet Time*
Fowler. *The Last Innocent Summer*
Greene. *Dotty's Suitcase*
Hesse. *A Time of Angels*
Hooks. *Circle of Fire*
Horvath. *The Happy Yellow Car*
Karr. *The Cave*
Karr. *In the Kaiser's Clutch*
Kinsey-Warnock. *The Night the Bells Rang*
Koller. *Nothing to Fear*

Kudlinski. *Hero over Here*
Lehrman. *The Store That Mama Built*
Lyon. *Borrowed Children*
Mazer. *Cave Under the City*
McKenzie. *Under the Bridge*
Mills. *What About Annie?*
Mitchell. *Uncle Jed's Barbershop*
Myers. *Red-Dirt Jessie*
Myers. *Spotting the Leopard*
Olsen. *The View from the Pighouse Roof*
Oneal. *A Long Way to Go*
Pendergraft. *As Far as Mill Springs*
Reeder. *Moonshiner's Son*
Reeder. *Grandpa's Mountain*
Ross. *The Dancing Tree*
Ross. *Hillbilly Choir*

Skurzynski. *Good-bye, Billy Radish*
Snyder. *Cat Running*
Taylor. *The Friendship*
Taylor. *Mississippi Bridge*
Taylor. *Roll of Thunder, Hear My Cry*
Taylor. *The Well: David's Story*
Thesman. *The Ornament Tree*
Thesman. *Rachel Chance*
Uchida. *A Jar of Dreams*
Voight. *Tree by Leaf*
Weaver. *Child Star: When Talkies Came to Hollywood*
Whelan. *That Wild Berries Should Grow*
Whitmore. *The Bread Winner*
Whittaker. *Angels of the Swamp*
Yep. *The Star Fisher*

Biography

Adler. *Our Golda: The Story of Golda Meir*
Anderson. *Aldo Leopold: American Ecologist*
Anderson. *Thomas Edison*
Andryszewski. *The Amazing Life of Moe Berg*
Appel. *Joe Dimaggio*
Bennett. *Will Rogers: Quotable Cowboy*
Berkow. *Hank Greenberg: Hall-of-Fame Slugger*
Bernotas. *Jim Thorpe: Sac and Fox Athlete*
Berry. *Georgia O'Keeffe: Painter*
Berry. *Gordon Parks*
Berry. *Langston Hughes*
Brooks. *Georgia O'Keeffe: An Adventurous Spirit*
Brown. *Daisy and the Girl Scouts: Juliette Gordon Low*
Buranelli. *Thomas Alva Edison*
Burford. *Chocolate by Hershey: Milton S. Hershey*
Burleigh. *Flight: The Journey of Charles Lindbergh*
Butts. *May Chinn: The Best Medicine*
Cain. *Louise Nevelson: Sculptor*
Calvert. *Zora Neale Hurston: Storyteller of the South*
Canadeo. *Warren G. Harding*
Casey. *William H. Taft: Twenty-Seventh President*

Castiglia. *Margaret Mead*
Chadwick. *Amelia Earhart: Aviation Pioneer*
Chadwick. *Anne Morrow Lindbergh: Pilot and Poet*
Clinton. *Herbert Hoover: Thirty-First President*
Coil. *George Washington Carver*
Collier. *Duke Ellington*
Collier. *Louis Armstrong: An American Success Story*
Collins. *Charles Lindbergh: Hero Pilot*
Collins. *Woodrow Wilson: 28th President*
Colman. *Fannie Lou Hamer and the Fight for the Vote*
Colman. *A Woman Unafraid: Frances Perkins*
Daffron. *Margaret Bourke-White: Photographer*
Dallard. *Ella Baker: A Leader Behind the Scenes*
Darby. *Douglas MacArthur*
Darby. *Dwight D. Eisenhower*
Davidson. *Getting the Real Story: Nellie Bly and Ida B. Wells*
Davies. *Amelia Earhart Flies Around the World*
Davies. *Malcolm X*
Davis. *Frank Lloyd Wright: Maverick Architect*
Devane. *Franklin Delano Roosevelt: President*

Dolan. *Matthew Henson: Arctic Explorer*
Dominy. *Katherine Dunham: Dancer and Choreographer*
Driemen. *Atomic Dawn: A Biography of Robert Oppenheimer*
Driemen. *Clarence Darrow*
Duggleby. *Artist in Overalls: Grant Wood*
Dunlap. *Aldo Leopold: Living with the Land*
Dunlap. *Birds in the Bushes: Margaret Morse Nice*
Dunlap. *Eye on the Wild: A Story About Ansel Adams*
Erlich. *Paul Robeson: Singer and Actor*
Everett. *Li'l Sis and Uncle Willie: William Johnson*
Faber. *Eleanor Roosevelt: First Lady of the World*
Falkof. *William H. Taft*
Farley. *Robert H. Goddard*
Ferris. *What I Had Was Singing: Marian Anderson*
Frankl. *Charlie Parker: Musician*
Fraser. *Walter White: Civil Rights Leader*
Freedman. *Eleanor Roosevelt: A Life of Discovery*
Freedman. *Franklin Delano Roosevelt*
Freedman. *Ida B. Wells and the Antilynching Crusade*
Freedman. *Louis Brandeis*

Garfunkel. *Letter to the World: The Life and Dances of Martha Graham*

Gentry. *Jesse Owens: Champion Athlete*

Gourse. *Dizzy Gillespie and the Birth of Bebop*

Graff. *Helen Keller: Toward the Light*

Gray. *George Washington Carver*

Greenblatt. *Franklin D. Roosevelt*

Greene. *Thomas Alva Edison: Bringer of Light*

Halasa. *Elijah Muhammad: Religious Leader*

Halasa. *Mary McLeod Bethune: Educator*

Hanley. *Philip Randolph*

Hart. *Up in the Air: Bessie Coleman*

Haskins. *Thurgood Marshall: A Life for Justice*

Haynes. *Ida B. Wells*

Heiligman. *Barbara McClintock: Alone in Her Field*

Hunter. *Helen Keller*

Israel. *Franklin Delano Roosevelt*

Jakoubek. *Joe Louis: Heavyweight Champion*

Jakoubek. *Walter White and the Power of Organized Protest*

James. *Julia Morgan: Architect*

Kallen. *Thurgood Marshall: A Dream of Justice for All*

Kaye. *The Life of Alexander Fleming*

Kaye. *The Life of Benjamin Spock*

Kaye. *The Life of Daniel Hale Williams*

Kaye. *The Life of Florence Sabin*

Keller. *Margaret Bourke-White: A Photographer's Life*

Kelso. *Building a Dream: Mary Bethune's School*

Kent. *Calvin Coolidge: Thirtieth President*

Kerby. *Amelia Earhart: Courage in the Sky*

Kittredge. *Barbara McClintock*

Kittredge. *Helen Hayes: Actress*

Kittredge. *Jane Addams*

Kliment. *Billie Holiday: Singer*

Kliment. *Count Basie: Bandleader and Musician*

Kliment. *Ella Fitzgerald: Singer*

Klots. *Ida Wells-Barnett: Civil Rights Leader*

Kozodoy. *Isadora Duncan: Dancer*

Kronstadt. *Florence Sabin: Medical Researcher*

Kudlinski. *Helen Keller: A Light for the Blind*

La Farge. *Pearl Buck*

Larsen. *Amelia Earhart: Missing, Declared Dead*

Larsen. *Paul Robeson: Hero Before His Time*

Latham. *George Goethals: Panama Canal Engineer*

Lauber. *Lost Star: The Story of Amelia Earhart*

Lawler. *Marcus Garvey: Black Nationalist Leader*

Lazo. *Eleanor Roosevelt*

Leavell. *Woodrow Wilson*

Leder. *Amelia Earhart: Opposing Viewpoints*

Lindop. *Woodrow Wilson, Franklin D. Roosevelt, Harry S. Truman*

Lipsyte. *Jim Thorpe: Twentieth-Century Jock*

Lipsyte. *Joe Louis: A Champ for all America*

Lorbiecki. *Of Things Natural, Wild, and Free*

Lynn. *Babe Didrikson Zaharias*

Lyons. *Starting Home: Horace Pippin, Painter*

Macht. *Babe Ruth*

Macht. *Lou Gehrig*

Mahone-Lonesome. *Charles R. Drew*

Malone. *Will Rogers: Cowboy Philosopher*

Markham. *Helen Keller*

McKissack. *Mary McLeod Bethune*

McPherson. *Peace and Bread: Jane Addams*

McPherson. *TV's Forgotten Hero: Philo Farnsworth*

McPherson. *The Workers' Detective: A Story About Dr. Alice Hamilton*

Meltzer. *Dorothea Lange: Life Through the Camera*

Mintz. *Thomas Edison: Inventing the Future*

Mitchell. *We'll Race You, Henry*

Mitchell. *The Wizard of Sound: Thomas Edison*

Morris. *The FDR Way*

Myers. *Malcolm X: By Any Means Necessary*

Nicholson. *Babe Ruth: Sultan of Swat*

Nicholson. *George Washington Carver*

Nicholson. *Helen Keller: Humanitarian*

O'Connor. *Barefoot Dancer: Isadora Duncan*

O'Connor. *The Soldier's Voice: Ernie Pyle*

Osofsky. *Free to Dream: Langston Hughes*

Palmer. *Lena Horne: Entertainer*

Parker. *Thomas Edison and Electricity*

Pfeifer. *Henry O. Flipper*

Polikoff. *Herbert C. Hoover*

Porter. *Jump at de Sun: Zora Neale Hurston*

Potter. *Buckminster Fuller*

Pratt. *Martha Graham*

Prentzas. *Thurgood Marshall: Champion of Justice*

Probosz. *Martha Graham*

Ptacek. *Champion for Children's Health: Dr. S. Josephine Baker*

Randolph. *Amelia Earhart*

Randolph. *Charles Lindbergh*

Randolph. *Woodrow Wilson: President*

Rennert. *Jesse Owens: Champion Athlete*

Rivinus. *Jim Thorpe*

Rogers. *George Washington Carver*

Sandak. *The Franklin Roosevelts*

Sandak. *The Wilsons*

Sandomir. *Isadora Duncan: Revolutionary Dancer*

Schmidt. *Robert Frost*

Schroeder. *Josephine Baker*

Schuman. *Eleanor Roosevelt*

Scott. *Jackie Robinson*

Shirley. *Malcolm X: Racial Spokesman*

Shore. *Amelia Earhart: Aviator*

Sloate. *Amelia Earhart*

Sonneborn. *Will Rogers: Cherokee Entertainer*

St. George. *Dear Dr. Bell. . . Your Friend, Helen Keller*

Stafford. *W. E. B. Dubois: Scholar and Activist*

Stevens. *Calvin Coolidge: 30th President*

Stine. *The Story of Malcolm X, Civil Rights Leader*

Streissguth. *Rocket Man: Robert Goddard*

Streissguth. *Say It with Music: A Story About Irving Berlin*

Swanson. *I've Got an Idea! Frederick McKinley Jones*

Talmadge. *The Life of Charles Drew*

Tames. *Amelia Earhart: 1897-1937*

Tanenhaus. *Louis Armstrong: Musician*

Taylor. *The First Solo Flight Around the World: Wiley Post*

Tedards. *Marian Anderson: Singer*

Toor. *Eleanor Roosevelt*

Turner. *Dorothea Lange*

Turner. *Georgia O'Keeffe*

Vernon. *Introducing Gershwin*

Wade. *Warren G. Harding: Twenty-Ninth President*

Weisbrot. *Father Divine: Religious Leader*

Whitelaw. *Grace Hopper*

Whitelaw. *Mr. Civil Rights: The Story of Thurgood Marshall*

Witcover. *Zora Neale Hurston*

Wolfe. *Charles Richard Drew, M.D.*

Woog. *Louis Armstrong*

Yannuzzi. *Zora Neale Hurston: Southern Storyteller*

Ziesk. *Margaret Mead*

Collective Biography

Aaseng. *Close Calls: From the Brink of Ruin to Business Success*

Aaseng. *From Rags to Riches*

Aaseng. *True Champions*

Aaseng. *You Are the General*

Altman. *Extraordinary Black Americans*

Anderson. *Explorers Who Found New Worlds*

Beard. *The Presidents in American History*

Blassingame. *The Look-It-Up Book of Presidents*

Blue. *People of Peace*

Camp. *American Astronomers: Searchers and Wonderers*

Clements. *The Picture History of Great Inventors*

Cush. *Artists Who Created Great Works*

Cush. *Women Who Achieved Greatness*

Faber. *Great Lives: American Government*

Fireside. *Is There a Woman in the House. . . or Senate?*

Fradin. *We Have Conquered Pain: The Discovery of Anesthesia*

Glenn. *Discover America's Favorite Architects*

Glubok. *Great Lives: Painting*

Hart. *Flying Free: America's First Black Aviators*

Haskins. Black *Eagles: African Americans in Aviation*

Haskins. *The Harlem Renaissance*

Hazell. *Heroines: Great Women Through the Ages*

Jacobs. *Great Lives: Human Rights*

Jacobs. *They Shaped the Game: Ty Cobb, Babe Ruth, and Jackie Robinson*

Katz. *Proudly Red and Black: Stories of African and Native Americans*

King. *First Facts About American Heroes*

Krull. *Lives of the Artists: Masterpieces, Messes*

Krull. *Lives of the Musicians: Good Times, Bad Times*

Krull. *Lives of the Writers: Comedies, Tragedies*

Mayberry. *Business Leaders Who Built Financial Empires*

McKissack. *African-American Inventors*

Morin. *Women of the U.S. Congress*

Morin. *Women Who Reformed Politics*

Myers. *Now Is Your Time*

Pascoe. *First Facts About the Presidents*

Pile. *Top Entrepreneurs and Their Businesses*

Plowden. *Famous Firsts of Black Women*

Provensen. *The Buck Stops Here: The Presidents*

Provensen. *My Fellow Americans*

Schraff. *American Heroes of Exploration and Flight*

Rappaport. *Living Dangerously: American Women*

Reef. *Black Fighting Men: A Proud History*

Rennert. *Book of Firsts: Leaders of America*

Rennert. *Civil Rights Leaders*

Rennert. *Female Writers*

Rennert. *Jazz Stars*

Rennert. *Pioneers of Discovery*

Rubel. *The Scholastic Encyclopedia of the Presidents*

Sheafer. *Women in America's Wars*

Smith. *Presidents of a World Power*

Sullivan. *Black Artists in Photography, 1840-1940*

Vare. *Women Inventors and their Discoveries*

Veglahn. *Women Scientists*

Weitzman. *Great Lives: Human Culture*

Whitelaw. *They Wrote Their Own Headlines*

Wilkinson. *People Who Changed the World*

Wilkinson. *Scientists Who Changed the World*

Yount. *Black Scientists*

Yount. *Women Aviators*

History

Andryszewski. *The Dust Bowl*
Ash. *The Story of the Women's Movement*
Ashabranner. *A Memorial for Mr. Lincoln*
Basinger. *American Cinema*
Blue. *The White House Kids*
Bolick. *Mail Call!*
Bowler. *Trains*
Brashler. *The Story of the Negro League Baseball*
Brill. *Let Women Vote!*
Brown. *Conflict in Europe and the Great Depression (1914-1940)*
Burns. *Money*
Caulkins. *Pets of the Presidents*
Clare. *First World War*
Colman. *Strike: The Bitter Struggle of American Workers*
Colman. *Toilets, Bathtubs, Sinks, and Sewers*
Cooper. *Bound for the Promised Land: The Great Black Migration*
Cooper. *Playing America's Game: Negro League Baseball*
Cosner. *War Nurses*
Davies. *Transport: On Land, Road and Rail*
Dolan. *America in World War I*
Emert. *Top Lawyers and their Famous Cases*
English. *Transportation: Automobiles to Zeppelins*
Farris. *The Dust Bowl*
Ferrell. *The U.S. Air Force*
Gardner. *The Forgotten Players: The Story of Black Baseball in America*
Garfunkel. *On Wings of Joy: The Story of Ballet*
Giblin. *Be Seated: A Book About Chairs*
Goldish. *Our Supreme Court*
Granfield. *In Flanders Fields: The Story of the Poem by John McCrae*
Greene. *Child Labor: Then and Now*
Gutman. *World Series Classics*
Guzzetti. *The White House*

Hakim. *An Age of Extremes*
Hakim. *War, Peace, and All That Jazz*
Hill. *Our Century: 1920-1930*
Hintz. *Farewell, John Barleycorn: Prohibition in the United States*
Hirsch. *Taxation: Paying for Government*
The History of Moviemaking
Humble. *Ships*
Karl. *America Alive: A History*
Kent. *World War I*
Kurtz. *U.S. Army*
Lampton. *Epidemic*
Lawrence. *The Great Migration*
Leiner. *First Children: Growing Up in the White House*
Leuzzi. *Urban Life*
Levi. *Cowboys of the Sky*
Libreatore. *Our Century: 1910-1920*
Markham. *Inventions That Changed Modern Life*
McKissack. *Black Diamond*
Medearis. *Come This Far to Freedom*
Meltzer. *The Black Americans*
Migneco. *The Crash of 1929*
Mizell. *Think About Racism*
Monceaux. *Jazz: My Music, My People*
Morley. *Clothes: For Work, Play and Display*
Moser. *Fly!*
Munro. *Aircraft*
Naden. *The U.S. Coast Guard*
Norrell. *We Want Jobs!*
Owen. *Our Century: 1930-1940*
Paananen. *The Military: Defending the Nation*
Patrick. *The Young Oxford Companion to the Supreme Court*
Philip. *Singing America: Poems That Define A Nation*
Platt. *The Smithsonian Visual Timeline of Inventions*
Rappaport. *The Sacco-Vanzetti Trial*
Reef. *The Supreme Court*

Rosen. *The First Transatlantic Flight*
Rowland-Warne. *Costume*
Sandler. *Presidents*
Scott. *Funny Papers: Behind the Scenes of the Comics*
Sloan. *Bismarck!*
St. George. *The White House: Cornerstone of a Nation*
Stanley. *Big Annie of Calumet*
Stanley. *Children of the Dust Bowl*
Stein. *The Great Depression*
Stein. *The Story of the Powers of the Supreme Court*
Steins. *Our Elections*
Stern. *The Congress: America's Lawmakers*
The Story of Flight
Sullivan. *Children of Promise: African-American Literature and Art*
Tanaka. *The Disaster of the Hindenburg*
Tessendorf. *Wings Around the World: The American World Flight of 1924*
Time-Life. *African Americans: Voices of Triumph: Leadership*
Ventura. *Clothing*
Ventura. *Food: Its Evolution Through the Ages*
Walker. *Hand, Heart, and Mind*
Ward. *Shadow Ball: The Negro Leagues*
Ward. *Who Invented the Game?*
Warner. *The U.S. Marine Corps*
Warren. *Orphan Train Rider: One Boy's True Story*
Weber. *Our Congress*
Wheeler. *Events that Changed American History*
Whitman. *Get Up and Go: American Road Travel*
Whitman. *This Land Is Your Land*
Whitman. *V Is for Victory*
Yepsen. *City Trains: America's Cities by Rail*

Multimedia

CD-ROM

Air and Space Smithsonian Dreams of Flight

Campaigns, Candidates and the Presidency

Daring to Fly!

Eyewitness Encyclopedia of Science

Her Heritage: A Biographical Encyclopedia of American History

History Through Art: 20th Century

Portraits of American Presidents

SkyTrip America

Time Almanac of the 20th Century

Total History

Voices of the 30s

The Way Things Work

Video

African American Life

African Americans

Amelia Earhart

American Consumerism (1890-1930)

Black Is My Color: The African American Experience

Elijah Muhammad

The Era of Segregation: A Personal Perspective

Frontier Buildings

George Washington Carver: A Man of Vision

Great Black Innovators

The Great Depression and the New Deal

Helen Keller

In Search of the North Pole

Jackie Robinson

Jesse Owens

Let Me Tell You All About Trains

Making It Happen: Masters of Invention

Malcolm X

Mary McLeod Bethune

Matthew Henson

The Sky's the Limit

Thomas Alva Edison

Tragedy to Triumph: An Adventure with Helen Keller

Tsiolkovski: The Space Age

Women with Wings

World War I

WORLD WAR II, 1941-1945

KINDERGARTEN THROUGH SECOND GRADE

Historical Fiction

Adler. *The Number on My Grandfather's Arm*
Adler. *One Yellow Daffodil*
Hoobler. *Aloha Means Come Back: The Story of a World War II Girl*
Houston. *But No Candy*
Kinsey-Warnock. *The Summer of Stanley*
Ray. *My Daddy Was a Soldier: A World War II Story*
Ringgold. *Bonjour, Lonnie*
Say. *Grandfather's Journey*
Shaffer. *The Camel Express*
Uchida. *The Bracelet*
Yolen. *All Those Secrets of the World*

Biography

Adler. *Jackie Robinson: He Was the First*
Adler. *A Picture Book of Eleanor Roosevelt*
Adler. *A Picture Book of Helen Keller*
Adler. *A Picture Book of Jackie Robinson*
Adler. *A Picture Book of Jesse Owens*
Adler. *A Picture Book of Thurgood Marshall*
Cavan. *W. E. B. Du Bois*
Cooney. *Eleanor*
Cooper. *Coming Home: From the Life of Langston Hughes*
Cwiklik. *Malcolm X*
Cwiklik. *Philip Randolph*
Faber. *Eleanor Roosevelt: First Lady of the World*
Greene. *Jacques Cousteau: Man of the Oceans*
Greene. *Katherine Dunham: Black Dancer*
Greenfield. *Mary McLeod Bethune*
Livingston. *Keep on Singing: A Ballad of Marian Anderson*
MacKinnon. *Silent Observer*
McKissack. *Carter G. Woodson*
McKissack. *Louis Armstrong: Jazz Musician*
McKissack. *Marian Anderson: A Great Singer*
McKissack. *Paul Robeson: A Voice to Remember*
McKissack. *Ralph J. Bunche*
O'Connor. *Jackie Robinson*
Parks. *I Am Rosa Parks*
Venezia. *Edward Hopper*
Venezia. *Georgia O'Keeffe*
Venezia. *Jackson Pollock*

Collective Biography

Marzollo. *My First Book of Biographies*

History

Goldish. *Our Supreme Court*
Medearis. *Our People*
Ritter. *Leagues Apart: The Men and Times of the Negro Baseball Leagues*
Swanson. *I Pledge Allegiance*

Multimedia

Video

African American Life

GRADE THREE

Historical Fiction

Adler. *The Number on My Grandfather's Arm*
Adler. *One Yellow Daffodil*
Avi. *"Who Was That Masked Man, Anyway?"*
Banim. *American Dreams*
Chaikin. *Friends Forever*
Herman. *A Summer on Thirteenth Street*
Hest. *Love You, Soldier*

Hoobler. *Aloha Means Come Back: The Story of a World War II Girl*
Houston. *But No Candy*
Kinsey-Warnock. *The Summer of Stanley*
Mochizuki. *Baseball Saved Us*
Ray. *My Daddy Was a Soldier: A World War II Story*
Ringgold. *Bonjour, Lonnie*

Say. *Grandfather's Journey*
Shaffer. *The Camel Express*
Tripp. *Changes for Molly*
Uchida. *The Bracelet*
Yep. *Hiroshima*
Yolen. *All Those Secrets of the World*

Biography

Adler. *Jackie Robinson: He Was the First*
Adler. *A Picture Book of Eleanor Roosevelt*
Adler. *A Picture Book of Helen Keller*
Adler. *A Picture Book of Jackie Robinson*
Adler. *A Picture Book of Jesse Owens*
Adler. *A Picture Book of Thurgood Marshall*
Berkow. *Hank Greenberg: Hall-of-Fame Slugger*
Calvert. *Zora Neale Hurston: Storyteller of the South*
Cavan. *W. E. B. Du Bois*
Collins. *Harry S. Truman*
Colman. *A Woman Unafraid: The Achievements of Frances Perkins*
Cooney. *Eleanor*
Cooper. *Coming Home: From the Life of Langston Hughes*
Cwiklik. *Malcolm X*
Cwiklik. *Philip Randolph*
Dunlap. *Eye on the Wild: A Story About Ansel Adams*
Faber. *Eleanor Roosevelt: First Lady of the World*
Graff. *Helen Keller: Toward the Light*
Greene. *Jacques Cousteau: Man of the Oceans*

Greene. *Katherine Dunham: Black Dancer*
Greenfield. *Mary McLeod Bethune*
Heiligman. *Barbara McClintock: Alone in Her Field*
Hunter. *Helen Keller*
Jacobs. *Dwight David*
Jakoubek. *Walter White and the Power of Organized Protest*
Kudlinski. *Helen Keller: A Light for the Blind*
Livingston. *Keep On Singing: A Ballad of Marian Anderson*
Macht. *Babe Ruth*
MacKinnon. *Silent Observer*
McKissack. *Carter G. Woodson*
McKissack. *Jesse Owens: Olympic Star*
McKissack. *Langston Hughes: Great American Poet*
McKissack. *Louis Armstrong: Jazz Musician*
McKissack. *Marian Anderson: A Great Singer*
McKissack. *Paul Robeson: A Voice to Remember*
McKissack. *Ralph J. Bunche*

McPherson. *The Workers' Detective: A Story About Dr. Alice Hamilton*
Medearis. *Little Louis and the Jazz Band*
O'Connor. *Jackie Robinson*
Parks. *I Am Rosa Parks*
Prentzas. *Thurgood Marshall: Champion of Justice*
Reiser. *Jackie Robinson: Baseball Pioneer*
Sanford. *Jackie Robinson*
Sanford. *Jesse Owens*
Sanford. *Jim Thorpe*
Santella. *Jackie Robinson Breaks the Color Line*
Shirley. *Malcolm X: Racial Spokesman*
Shorto. *Jackie Robinson*
Stine. *The Story of Malcolm X: Civil Rights Leader*
Streissguth. *Say It with Music: A Story About Irving Berlin*
Swanson. *I've Got an Idea! Frederick McKinley Jones*
Turner. *Georgia O'Keeffe*
Venezia. *Edward Hopper*
Venezia. *Georgia O'Keeffe*
Venezia. *Jackson Pollock*
Weidt. *Stateswoman to the World: Eleanor Roosevelt*

Collective Biography

King. *First Facts About American Heroes*

Marzollo. *My First Book of Biographies*

Provensen. *The Buck Stops Here: The Presidents*

History

Blue. *U.S. Air Force*
Burns. *Mail*
Caulkins. *Pets of the Presidents*
English. *Transportation: Automobiles to Zeppelins*
Goldish. *Our Supreme Court*

Hill. *Our Century: 1940-1950*
Humble. *Ships*
Medearis. *Our People*
Munro. *Aircraft*
Paananen. *The Military: Defending the Nation*

Ritter. *Leagues Apart: The Men and Times of the Negro Baseball Leagues*
Stein. *The Manhattan Project*
Stein. *The USS Arizona*
Swanson. *I Pledge Allegiance*

Multimedia

Video

African American Life

GRADE FOUR

Historical Fiction

Adler. *The Number on My Grandfather's Arm*
Avi. *"Who Was That Masked Man, Anyway?"*
Banim. *American Dreams*
Banks. *Under the Shadow of Wings*
Bauer. *Rain of Fire*
Chaikin. *Friends Forever*
Cormier. *Other Bells for Us to Ring*
Glassman. *The Morning Glory War*
Hahn. *Stepping on the Cracks*
Herman. *A Summer on Thirteenth Street*

Hest. *Love You, Soldier*
Holmes. *Dear Dad*
Hoobler. *Aloha Means Come Back: The Story of a World War II Girl*
Hotze. *Summer Endings*
Kudlinski. *Pearl Harbor Is Burning!*
Manley. *She Flew No Flags*
Marko. *Hang Out the Flag*
Mochizuki. *Baseball Saved Us*
Ray. *My Daddy Was a Soldier: A World War II Story*
Rinaldi. *Keep Smiling Through*

Ringgold. *Bonjour, Lonnie*
Ross. *Harper & Moon*
Savin. *The Moon Bridge*
Shaffer. *The Camel Express*
Towne. *Dive Through the Wave*
Tripp. *Changes for Molly*
Uchida. *Journey to Topaz*
Willis. *A Place to Claim as Home*
Yep. *Hiroshima*

Biography

Adler. *Jackie Robinson: He Was the First*
Adler. *A Picture Book of Jesse Owens*
Berkow. *Hank Greenberg: Hall-of-Fame Slugger*
Brooks. *Georgia O'Keeffe: An Adventurous Spirit*
Butts. *May Chinn: The Best Medicine*
Calvert. *Zora Neale Hurston: Storyteller of the South*
Cavan. *W. E. B. Du Bois*
Chin. *When Justice Failed: The Fred Korematsu Story*
Collins. *Harry S. Truman*
Colman. *Fannie Lou Hamer and the Fight for the Vote*
Colman. *A Woman Unafraid: The Achievements of Frances Perkins*
Cooper. *Coming Home: From the Life of Langston Hughes*

Cross. *Roosevelt and the Americans at War*
Cwiklik. *Malcolm X*
Cwiklik. *Philip Randolph*
Dunlap. *Birds in the Bushes: Margaret Morse Nice*
Dunlap. *Eye on the Wild: A Story About Ansel Adams*
Faber. *Eleanor Roosevelt: First Lady of the World*
Ferris. *What I Had Was Singing: Marian Anderson*
Graff. *Helen Keller: Toward the Light*
Greene. *Jacques Cousteau: Man of the Oceans*
Greenfield. *Mary McLeod Bethune*
Hargrove. *Dwight D. Eisenhower*
Hargrove. *Harry S. Truman: Thirty-Third President*

Heiligman. *Barbara McClintock: Alone in Her Field*
Hunter. *Helen Keller*
Jacobs. *Dwight David Eisenhower*
Jakoubek. *Walter White and the Power of Organized Protest*
Kaye. *The Life of Benjamin Spock*
Kaye. *The Life of Florence Sabin*
Kudlinski. *Helen Keller: A Light for the Blind*
Lazo. *Eleanor Roosevelt*
Livingston. *Keep On Singing: A Ballad of Marian Anderson*
Macht. *Babe Ruth*
MacKinnon. *Silent Observer*
McKissack. *Carter G. Woodson*

McKissack. *Jesse Owens: Olympic Star*

McKissack. *Langston Hughes: Great American Poet*

McKissack. *Louis Armstrong: Jazz Musician*

McKissack. *Marian Anderson: A Great Singer*

McKissack. *Ralph J. Bunche*

McPherson. *TV's Forgotten Hero: Philo Farnsworth*

McPherson. *The Workers' Detective: A Story About Dr. Alice Hamilton*

Medearis. *Little Louis and the Jazz Band*

O'Connor. *Jackie Robinson*

O'Connor. *The Soldier's Voice: Ernie Pyle*

Porter. *Jump at de Sun: Zora Neale Hurston*

Prentzas. *Thurgood Marshall: Champion of Justice*

Reef. *Benjamin Davis, Jr.*

Reiser. *Jackie Robinson: Baseball Pioneer*

Rennert. *Jesse Owens: Champion Athlete*

Sanford. *Jackie Robinson*

Sanford. *Jesse Owens*

Sanford. *Jim Thorpe*

Santella. *Jackie Robinson Breaks the Color Line*

Shirley. *Malcolm X: Racial Spokesman*

Shorto. *Jackie Robinson*

Stine. *The Story of Malcolm X, Civil Rights Leader*

Streissguth. *Rocket Man: Robert Goddard*

Streissguth. *Say It with Music: A Story About Irving Berlin*

Swanson. *I've Got an Idea! Frederick McKinley Jones*

Turner. *Dorothea Lange*

Turner. *Georgia O'Keeffe*

Weidt. *Stateswoman to the World: Eleanor Roosevelt*

Whitelaw. *Grace Hopper*

Wolfe. *Charles Richard Drew, M.D.*

Collective Biography

Altman. *Extraordinary Black Americans*

Fireside. *Is There a Woman in the House. . . or Senate?*

Hart. *Flying Free: America's First Black Aviators*

Jacobs. *Great Lives: Human Rights*

Jacobs. *They Shaped the Game: Ty Cobb, Babe Ruth, and Jackie Robinson*

King. *First Facts About American Heroes*

Pascoe. *First Facts About the Presidents*

Provensen. *The Buck Stops Here: The Presidents*

Provenson. *My Fellow Americans*

Reef. *Black Fighting Men: A Proud History*

Rubel. *The Scholastic Encyclopedia of the Presidents*

Wilkinson. *Scientists Who Changed the World*

History

Black. *Battle of the Atlantic*

Black. *Battle of the Bulge*

Blue. *U.S. Air Force*

Bolick. *Mail Call!*

Bowler. *Trains*

Burns. *Mail*

Burns. *Money*

Caulkins. *Pets of the Presidents*

Dolan. *America in World War II: 1943*

Dolan. *America in World War II: 1945*

English. *Transportation: Automobiles to Zeppelins*

Ferrell. *The U.S. Air Force*

Goldish. *Our Supreme Court*

Hamanaka. *On the Wings of Peace*

Hill. *Our Century: 1940-1950*

Hopkinson. *Pearl Harbor*

Humble. *Ships*

Humble. *A World War Two Submarine*

Kurtz. *U.S. Army*

McKissack. *Black Diamond*

Munro. *Aircraft*

Nicholson. *Pearl Harbor Child*

Paananen. *The Military: Defending the Nation*

Pfeifer. *The 761st Tank Battalion*

Reef. *The Supreme Court*

Ritter. *Leagues Apart: The Men and Times of the Negro Baseball Leagues*

Rowland-Warne. *Costume*

Stein. *The Manhattan Project*

Stein. *The USS Arizona*

Swanson. *I Pledge Allegiance*

Tunnell. *The Children of Topaz*

Ward. *Shadow Ball: The Negro Leagues*

Ward. *25 Great Moments*

Ward. *Who Invented the Game?*

Zeinert. *Those Incredible Women of World War II*

Multimedia

CD-ROM

Her Heritage: A Biographical Encyclopedia of American History

SkyTrip America

Total History

Video

African American Life

African Americans

Helen Keller

Jackie Robinson

Malcolm X

GRADE FIVE

Historical Fiction

Avi. *"Who Was That Masked Man, Anyway?"*

Banim. *American Dreams*

Banks. *Under the Shadow of Wings*

Barrie. *Lone Star*

Bauer. *Rain of Fire*

Beatty. *Blue Stars Watching*

Branscum. *Old Blue Tilley*

Chaikin. *Friends Forever*

Cormier. *Other Bells for Us to Ring*

Cutler. *My Wartime Summers*

Ford. *The Most Wonderful Movie in the World*

Giff. *Lily's Crossing*

Glassman. *The Morning Glory War*

Hahn. *Following My Own Footsteps*

Hahn. *Stepping on the Cracks*

Herman. *A Summer on Thirteenth Street*

Hest. *Love You, Soldier*

Holmes. *Dear Dad*

Hoobler. *Aloha Means Come Back: The Story of a World War II Girl*

Hotze. *Summer Endings*

Kudlinski. *Pearl Harbor Is Burning!*

Manley. *She Flew No Flags*

Marko. *Hang Out the Flag*

Mochizuki. *Baseball Saved Us*

Oughton. *The War in Georgia*

Paterson. *Jacob Have I Loved*

Rinaldi. *Keep Smiling Through*

Ross. *Harper & Moon*

Salisbury. *Under the Blood-Red Sun*

Savin. *The Moon Bridge*

Taylor. *Timothy of the Cay*

Thesman. *Molly Donnelly*

Towne. *Dive Through the Wave*

Tripp. *Changes for Molly*

Uchida. *Journey to Topaz*

Willis. *Out of the Storm*

Willis. *A Place to Claim as Home*

Wunderli. *The Blue Between the Clouds*

Yep. *Hiroshima: A Novella*

Biography

Adler. *Jackie Robinson: He Was the First*

Berkow. *Hank Greenberg: Hall-of-Fame Slugger*

Berry. *Georgia O'Keeffe: Painter*

Berry. *Langston Hughes*

Brooks. *Georgia O'Keeffe: An Adventurous Spirit*

Butts. *May Chinn: The Best Medicine*

Cain. *Louise Nevelson: Sculptor*

Calvert. *Zora Neale Hurston: Storyteller of the South*

Castiglia. *Margaret Mead*

Chin. *When Justice Failed: The Fred Korematsu Story*

Collier. *Duke Ellington*

Collier. *Louis Armstrong: An American Success Story*

Collins. *Harry S. Truman*

Colman. *Fannie Lou Hamer and the Fight for the Vote*

Colman. *A Woman Unafraid: The Achievements of Frances Perkins*

Cross. *Roosevelt and the Americans at War*

Cwiklik. *Malcolm X*

Daffron. *Margaret Bourke-White: Photographer*

Darby. *Douglas MacArthur*

Darby. *Dwight D. Eisenhower*

Davies. *Malcolm X*

Davis. *Frank Lloyd Wright: Maverick Architect*

Deitch. *Dwight D. Eisenhower*

Devane. *Franklin Delano Roosevelt: President*

Dominy. *Katherine Dunham: Dancer and Choreographer*

Driemen. *Atomic Dawn: A Biography of Robert Oppenheimer*

Dunlap. *Birds in the Bushes: Margaret Morse Nice*

Dunlap. *Eye on the Wild: A Story About Ansel Adams*

Ellis. *Dwight D. Eisenhower*

Erlich. *Paul Robeson: Singer and Actor*

Faber. *Eleanor Roosevelt: First Lady of the World*

Farley. *Robert H. Goddard*

Ferris. *What I Had Was Singing: Marian Anderson*

Freedman. *Franklin Delano Roosevelt*

Gentry. *Jesse Owens: Champion Athlete*

Gourse. *Dizzy Gillespie and the Birth of Bebop*

Graff. *Helen Keller: Toward the Light*

Greenblatt. *Franklin D. Roosevelt*

Greenfield. *Mary McLeod Bethune*

Halasa. *Elijah Muhammad: Religious Leader*

Halasa. *Mary McLeod Bethune: Educator*

Hanley. *Philip Randolph*

Hargrove. *Dwight D. Eisenhower*

Hargrove. *Harry S. Truman: Thirty-Third President*

Heiligman. *Barbara McClintock: Alone in Her Field*

Hunter. *Helen Keller*

Israel. *Franklin Delano Roosevelt*

Jacobs. *Dwight David Eisenhower*

Jakoubek. *Adam Clayton Powell, Jr*

Jakoubek. *Joe Louis: Heavyweight Champion*

Jakoubek. *Walter White and the Power of Organized Protest*

James. *Julia Morgan: Architect*

Kallen. *Thurgood Marshall: A Dream of Justice for All*

Kaye. *The Life of Alexander Fleming*

Kaye. *The Life of Benjamin Spock*

Kaye. *The Life of Florence Sabin*

Keller. *Margaret Bourke-White: A Photographer's Life*

Kittredge. *Barbara McClintock*
Kittredge. *Helen Hayes: Actress*
Kliment. *Count Basie: Bandleader and Musician*
Kliment. *Ella Fitzgerald: Singer*
Kronstadt. *Florence Sabin: Medical Researcher*
Kudlinski. *Helen Keller: A Light for the Blind*
La Farge. *Pearl Buck*
Lazo. *Eleanor Roosevelt*
Leavell. *Harry S. Truman*
Lindop. *Dwight D. Eisenhower*
Lindop. *Woodrow Wilson, Franklin D. Roosevelt, Harry S. Truman*
Lubetkin. *George Marshall*
Lynn. *Babe Didrikson Zaharias*
Macht. *Babe Ruth*
Mahone-Lonesome. *Charles R. Drew*
Markham. *Helen Keller*
McPherson. *TV's Forgotten Hero: Philo Farnsworth*
McPherson. *The Workers' Detective: A Story About Dr. Alice Hamilton*
Morris. *The FDR Way*
Myers. *Malcolm X: By Any Means Necessary*
Nicholson. *Helen Keller: Humanitarian*

O'Connor. *The Soldier's Voice: Ernie Pyle*
Osofsky. *Free to Dream: Langston Hughes*
Palmer. *Lena Horne: Entertainer*
Peifer. *Soldier of Destiny: A Biography of George Patton*
Porter. *Jump at de Sun: Zora Neale Hurston*
Potter. *Buckminster Fuller*
Prentzas. *Thurgood Marshall: Champion of Justice*
Probosz. *Martha Graham*
Reef. *Benjamin Davis, Jr.*
Reiser. *Jackie Robinson: Baseball Pioneer*
Rennert. *Jesse Owens: Champion Athlete*
Sandak. *The Franklin Roosevelts*
Sandak. *The Trumans*
Sandberg. *Dwight D. Eisenhower*
Santella. *Jackie Robinson Breaks the Color Line*
Schuman. *Eleanor Roosevelt*
Schuman. *Elie Wiesel*
Schuman. *Martin Luther King, Jr.*
Shirley. *Malcolm X: Racial Spokesman*
Shorto. *Jackie Robinson*

St. George. *Dear Dr. Bell. . . Your Friend, Helen Keller*
Stafford. *W. E. B. Dubois: Scholar and Activist*
Stine. *The Story of Malcolm X, Civil Rights Leader*
Streissguth. *Rocket Man: Robert Goddard*
Streissguth. *Say It with Music: A Story About Irving Berlin*
Swanson. *I've Got an Idea! Frederick McKinley Jones*
Talmadge. *The Life of Charles Drew*
Tanenhaus. *Louis Armstrong: Musician*
Tedards. *Marian Anderson: Singer*
Toor. *Eleanor Roosevelt*
Turner. *Dorothea Lange*
Turner. *Georgia O'Keeffe*
Weidt. *Stateswoman to the World: Eleanor Roosevelt*
Weisbrot. *Father Divine: Religious Leader*
Whitelaw. *Grace Hopper*
Witcover. *Zora Neale Hurston*
Wolfe. *Charles Richard Drew, M.D.*
Ziesk. *Margaret Mead*

Collective Biography

Aaseng. *Navajo Code Talkers*
Aaseng. *You Are the General*
Altman. *Extraordinary Black Americans*
Beard. *The Presidents in American History*
Blassingame. *The Look-It-Up Book of Presidents*
Blue. *People of Peace*
Cohen. *Prophets of Doom*
Cush. *Artists Who Created Great Works*
Cush. *Women Who Achieved Greatness*
Faber. *Great Lives: American Government*
Fireside. *Is There a Woman in the House. . . or Senate?*
Hart. *Flying Free: America's First Black Aviators*
Haskins. *Black Eagles: African Americans in Aviation*
Italia. *Courageous Crimefighters*

Jacobs. *Great Lives: Human Rights*
Jacobs. *They Shaped the Game: Ty Cobb, Babe Ruth, and Jackie Robinson*
King. *First Facts About American Heroes*
Mayberry. *Business Leaders Who Built Financial Empires*
Morin. *Women Who Reformed Politics*
Myers. *Now Is Your Time*
Pascoe. *First Facts About the Presidents*
Plowden. *Famous Firsts of Black Women*
Provensen. *The Buck Stops Here: The Presidents*
Provenson. *My Fellow Americans*
Reef. *Black Fighting Men: A Proud History*
Rennert. *Book of Firsts: Leaders of America*

Rennert. *Civil Rights Leaders*
Rennert. *Female Writers*
Rennert. *Jazz Stars*
Rennert. *Pioneers of Discovery*
Rubel. *The Scholastic Encyclopedia of the Presidents*
Sheafer. *Women in America's Wars*
Tunnell. *The Children of Topaz*
Veglahn. *Women Scientists*
Weitzman. *Great Lives: Human Culture*
Whitelaw. *They Wrote Their Own Headlines*
Wilkinson. *Generals Who Changed the World*
Wilkinson. *Scientists Who Changed the World*
Yount. *Black Scientists*
Yount. *Women Aviators*

History

Black. *America Prepares for War*

Black. *Bataan and Corregidor*

Black. *Battle of the Atlantic*

Black. *Battle of the Bulge*

Black. *D-Day*

Black. *Desert Warfare*

Black. *Flattops at War*

Black. *Guadalcanal*

Black. *Hiroshima and the Atomic Bomb*

Black. *Invasion of Italy*

Black. *Island Hopping in the Pacific*

Black. *Iwo Jima and Okinawa*

Black. *Jungle Warfare*

Black. *Pearl Harbor!*

Black. *Victory in Europe*

Black. *War Behind the Lines*

Blue. *U.S. Air Force*

Bolick. *Mail Call!*

Bowler. *Trains*

Burns. *Mail*

Burns. *Money*

Caulkins. *Pets of the Presidents*

Colman. *Rosie the Riveter*

Cooper. *Playing America's Game: Negro League Baseball*

Cosner. *War Nurses*

Cross. *Children and War*

Cross. *Technology of War*

Davies. *Transport: On Land, Road and Rail*

Dolan. *America in World War II: 1941*

Dolan. *America in World War II: 1942*

Dolan. *America in World War II: 1943*

Dolan. *America in World War II: 1944*

Dolan. *America in World War II: 1945*

English. *Transportation: Automobiles to Zeppelins*

Ferrell. *The U.S. Air Force*

Gardner. *The Forgotten Players: The Story of Black Baseball in America*

Goldish. *Our Supreme Court*

Hamanaka. *On the Wings of Peace*

Helmer. *Belles of the Ballpark*

Hill. *Our Century: 1940-1950*

Hirsch. *Taxation: Paying for Government*

Hopkinson. *Pearl Harbor*

Humble. *A World War Two Submarine*

Humble. *Ships*

Karl. *America Alive: A History*

Krull. *V Is for Victory: America Remembers World War II*

Kurtz. *U.S. Army*

Levine. *A Fence Away from Freedom: Japanese Americans and World War II*

Macy. *A Whole New Ballgame: All-American Girls Professional Baseball League*

Marrin. *The Airman's War: World War II in the Sky*

Marrin. *The Secret Armies: Spies, Counterspies, and Saboteurs*

McKissack. *Black Diamond*

McKissack. *Red-Tail Angels: Tuskegee Airmen of World War II*

Medearis. *Come This Far to Freedom*

Meltzer. *The Black Americans*

Morley. *Clothes: For Work, Play and Display*

Munro. *Aircraft*

Naden. *The U.S. Coast Guard*

Nicholson. *Pearl Harbor Child*

Paananen. *The Military: Defending the Nation*

Pfeifer. *The 761st Tank Battalion*

Platt. *The Smithsonian Visual Timeline of Inventions*

Reef. *The Supreme Court*

Rowland-Warne. *Costume*

Stanley. *I Am an American: A True Story of Japanese Internment*

Stein. *The Manhattan Project*

Stein. *The USS Arizona*

Steins. *The Allies Against the Axis: World War II (1940-1950)*

Taylor. *Air Raid-Pearl Harbor: The Story of December 7, 1941*

Ward. *Shadow Ball: The Negro Leagues*

Ward. *25 Great Moments*

Ward. *Who Invented The Game?*

Warner. *The U.S. Marine Corps*

Whitman. *Uncle Sam Wants You!*

Zeinert. *Those Incredible Women of World War II*

Multimedia

CD-ROM

Air and Space Smithsonian Dreams of Flight

Eyewitness Encyclopedia of Science

Her Heritage: A Biographical Encyclopedia of American History

Portraits of American Presidents

SkyTrip America

Total History

Video

African American Life

African Americans

Elijah Muhammad

Helen Keller

Hiroshima Maiden

Jackie Robinson

Jesse Owens

Malcolm X

Prejudice: Monster Within

Tragedy to Triumph: An Adventure with Helen Keller

GRADE SIX

Historical Fiction

Avi. *"Who Was That Masked Man, Anyway?"*

Banks. *Under the Shadow of Wings*

Barrie. *Lone Star*

Bauer. *Rain of Fire*

Beatty. *Blue Stars Watching*

Bethancourt. *The Tommorow Connection*

Branscum. *Old Blue Tilley*

Cormier. *Other Bells for Us to Ring*

Cutler. *My Wartime Summers*

Ford. *The Most Wonderful Movie in the World*

Glassman. *The Morning Glory War*

Green. *The War at Home*

Hahn. *Following My Own Footsteps*

Hahn. *Stepping on the Cracks*

Harrah. *My Brother, My Enemy*

Herman. *A Summer on Thirteenth Street*

Hotze. *Summer Endings*

Kudlinski. *Pearl Harbor Is Burning!*

Manley. *She Flew No Flags*

Marko. *Hang Out the Flag*

Mochizuki. *Baseball Saved Us*

Murphy. *Gold Star Sister*

Oughton. *The War in Georgia*

Paterson. *Jacob Have I Loved*

Poynter. *A Time Too Swift*

Rinaldi. *Keep Smiling Through*

Ross. *Harper & Moon*

Salisbury. *Under the Blood-Red Sun*

Savin. *The Moon Bridge*

Taylor. *The Cay*

Taylor. *Timothy of the Cay*

Thesman. *Molly Donnelly*

Towne. *Dive Through the Wave*

Uchida. *Journey to Topaz*

Willis. *Out of the Storm*

Willis. *A Place to Claim as Home*

Wunderli. *The Blue Between the Clouds*

Yep. *Hiroshima: A Novella*

Biography

Andryszewski. *The Amazing Life of Moe Berg*

Berkow. *Hank Greenberg: Hall-of-Fame Slugger*

Berry. *Georgia O'Keeffe: Painter*

Berry. *Gordon Parks*

Berry. *Langston Hughes*

Brooks. *Georgia O'Keeffe: An Adventurous Spirit*

Butts. *May Chinn: The Best Medicine*

Cain. *Louise Nevelson: Sculptor*

Calvert. *Zora Neale Hurston: Storyteller of the South*

Castiglia. *Margaret Mead*

Chin. *When Justice Failed: The Fred Korematsu Story*

Collier. *Duke Ellington*

Collier. *Louis Armstrong: An American Success Story*

Collins. *Harry S. Truman*

Colman. *Fannie Lou Hamer and the Fight for the Vote*

Colman. *A Woman Unafraid: The Achievements of Frances Perkins*

Cross. *Roosevelt and the Americans at War*

Daffron. *Margaret Bourke-White: Photographer*

Dallard. *Ella Baker: A Leader Behind the Scenes*

Darby. *Douglas MacArthur*

Darby. *Dwight D. Eisenhower*

Davies. *Malcolm X*

Davis. *Frank Lloyd Wright: Maverick Architect*

Deitch. *Dwight D. Eisenhower*

Devane. *Franklin Delano Roosevelt: President*

Dominy. *Katherine Dunham: Dancer and Choreographer*

Driemen. *Atomic Dawn: A Biography of Robert Oppenheimer*

Dunlap. *Birds in the Bushes: Margaret Morse Nice*

Dunlap. *Eye on the Wild: A Story About Ansel Adams*

Ellis. *Dwight D. Eisenhower*

Erlich. *Paul Robeson: Singer and Actor*

Faber. *Eleanor Roosevelt: First Lady of the World*

Farley. *Robert H. Goddard*

Ferris. *What I Had Was Singing: Marian Anderson*

Frankl. *Charlie Parker: Musician*

Fraser. *Walter White: Civil Rights Leader*

Freedman. *Eleanor Roosevelt: A Life of Discovery*

Freedman. *Franklin Delano Roosevelt*

Garfunkel. *Letter to the World: The Life and Dances of Martha Graham*

Gentry. *Jesse Owens: Champion Athlete*

Gourse. *Dizzy Gillespie and the Birth of Bebop*

Graff. *Helen Keller: Toward the Light*

Greenblatt. *Franklin D. Roosevelt*

Halasa. *Elijah Muhammad: Religious Leader*

Halasa. *Mary McLeod Bethune: Educator*

Hanley. *Philip Randolph*

Hargrove. *Dwight D. Eisenhower*

Hargrove. *Harry S. Truman: Thirty-Third President*

Haskins. *Thurgood Marshall: A Life for Justice*

Heiligman. *Barbara McClintock: Alone in Her Field*

Hunter. *Helen Keller*

Israel. *Franklin Delano Roosevelt*

Jacobs. *Dwight David Eisenhower*

Jakoubek. *Adam Clayton Powell, Jr*

Jakoubek. *Joe Louis: Heavyweight Champion*

Jakoubek. *Walter White and the Power of Organized Protest*

James. *Julia Morgan: Architect*

Kallen. *Thurgood Marshall: A Dream of Justice for All*

Kaye. *The Life of Alexander Fleming*

Kaye. *The Life of Benjamin Spock*

Kaye. *The Life of Florence Sabin*

Keller. *Margaret Bourke-White: A Photographer's Life*

Kittredge. *Barbara McClintock*

Kittredge. *Helen Hayes: Actress*

Kliment. *Count Basie: Bandleader and Musician*

Kliment. *Ella Fitzgerald: Singer*

Kronstadt. *Florence Sabin: Medical Researcher*

Kudlinski. *Helen Keller: A Light for the Blind*

La Farge. *Pearl Buck*

Larsen. *Paul Robeson: Hero Before His Time*

Lazo. *Eleanor Roosevelt*

Leavell. *Harry S. Truman*

Lindop. *Dwight D. Eisenhower*

Lindop. *Woodrow Wilson, Franklin D. Roosevelt, Harry S. Truman*

Lubetkin. *George Marshall*

Lynn. *Babe Didrikson Zaharias*

Macht. *Babe Ruth*

Mahone-Lonesome. *Charles R. Drew*

Markham. *Helen Keller*

McPherson. *TV's Forgotten Hero: Philo Farnsworth*

McPherson. *The Workers' Detective: A Story About Dr. Alice Hamilton*

Morris. *The FDR Way*

Morris. *The Truman Way*

Myers. *Malcolm X: By Any Means Necessary*

Nicholson. *Helen Keller: Humanitarian*

O'Connor. *The Soldier's Voice: Ernie Pyle*

Osofsky. *Free to Dream: Langston Hughes*

Palmer. *Lena Horne: Entertainer*

Peifer. *Soldier of Destiny: A Biography of George Patton*

Porter. *Jump at de Sun: Zora Neale Hurston*

Potter. *Buckminster Fuller*

Pratt. *Martha Graham*

Prentzas. *Thurgood Marshall: Champion of Justice*

Probosz. *Martha Graham*

Reef. *Benjamin Davis, Jr.*

Rennert. *Jesse Owens: Champion Athlete*

Sandak. *The Franklin Roosevelts*

Sandak. *The Trumans*

Sandberg. *Dwight D. Eisenhower*

Schuman. *Eleanor Roosevelt*

Schuman. *Elie Wiesel*

Schuman. *Martin Luther King, Jr.*

Shirley. *Malcolm X: Racial Spokesman*

St. George. *Dear Dr. Bell. . . Your Friend, Helen Keller*

Stafford. *W. E. B. Dubois: Scholar and Activist*

Stine. *The Story of Malcolm X, Civil Rights Leader*

Streissguth. *Rocket Man: Robert Goddard*

Streissguth. *Say It with Music: A Story About Irving Berlin*

Swanson. *I've Got an Idea! Frederick McKinley Jones*

Talmadge. *The Life of Charles Drew*

Tanenhaus. *Louis Armstrong: Musician*

Tedards. *Marian Anderson: Singer*

Toor. *Eleanor Roosevelt*

Turner. *Dorothea Lange*

Turner. *Georgia O'Keeffe*

Weisbrot. *Father Divine: Religious Leader*

Whitelaw. *Grace Hopper*

Whitelaw. *Mr. Civil Rights: The Story of Thurgood Marshall*

Witcover. *Zora Neale Hurston*

Wolfe. *Charles Richard Drew, M.D.*

Woog. *Louis Armstrong*

Yannuzzi. *Zora Neale Hurston: Southern Storyteller*

Ziesk. *Margaret Mead*

History

Anderson. *Battles That Changed the Modern World*

Black. *America Prepares for War*

Black. *Bataan and Corregidor*

Black. *Battle of the Atlantic*

Black. *Battle of the Bulge*

Black. *D-Day*

Black. *Desert Warfare*

Black. *Flattops at War*

Black. *Guadalcanal*

Black. *Hiroshima and the Atomic Bomb*

Black. *Invasion of Italy*

Black. *Island Hopping in the Pacific*

Black. *Iwo Jima and Okinawa*

Black. *Jungle Warfare*

Black. *Pearl Harbor!*

Black. *Victory in Europe*

Black. *War Behind the Lines*

Blue. *U.S. Air Force*

Bolick. *Mail Call!*

Bowler. *Trains*

Brashler. *The Story of the Negro League Baseball*

Burns. *Money*

Caulkins. *Pets of the Presidents*

Colman. *Rosie the Riveter*

Cooper. *Playing America's Game: Negro League Baseball*

Cosner. *War Nurses*

Cross. *Children and War*

Cross. *Technology of War*

Davies. *Transport: On Land, Road and Rail*

Dolan. *America in World War II: 1941*

Dolan. *America in World War II: 1942*

Dolan. *America in World War II: 1943*

Dolan. *America in World War II: 1944*

Dolan. *America in World War II: 1945*

English. *Transportation: Automobiles to Zeppelins*

Ferrell. *The U.S. Air Force*

Gardner. *The Forgotten Players: The Story of Black Baseball in America*

Goldish. *Our Supreme Court*

Hakim. *War, Peace, and All That Jazz*

Hamanaka. *On the Wings of Peace*

Harris. *The Tuskegee Airmen: Black Heroes of World War II*

Helmer. *Belles of the Ballpark*

Hill. *Our Century: 1940-1950*

Hirsch. *Taxation: Paying for Government*

Hopkinson. *Pearl Harbor*

Humble. *Ships*

Humble. *A World War Two Submarine*

Karl. *America Alive: A History*

Krull. *V Is for Victory: America Remembers World War II*

Kurtz. *U.S. Army*

Levine. *A Fence Away from Freedom: Japanese Americans and World War II*

Macy. *A Whole New Ballgame: All-American Girls Professional Baseball League*

Marrin. *The Airman's War: World War II in the Sky*

Marrin. *The Secret Armies: Spies, Counterspies, and Saboteurs*

McKissack. *Black Diamond*

McKissack. *Red-Tail Angels: Tuskegee Airmen of World War II*

Medearis. *Come This Far to Freedom*

Meltzer. *The Black Americans*

Mizell. *Think About Racism*

Morley. *Clothes: For Work, Play and Display*

Munro. *Aircraft*

Naden. *The U.S. Coast Guard*

Nicholson. *Pearl Harbor Child*

O'Neal. *President Truman and the Atomic Bomb*

Paananen. *The Military: Defending the Nation*

Patrick. *The Young Oxford Companion to the Supreme Court*

Pfeifer. *The 761st Tank Battalion*

Philip. *Singing America: Poems That Define a Nation*

Platt. *The Smithsonian Visual Timeline of Inventions*

Reef. *The Supreme Court*

Rowland-Warne. *Costume*

Stanley. *I Am an American: A True Story of Japanese Internment*

Stein. *World War II in Europe: America Goes to War*

Steins. *The Allies Against the Axis: World War II (1940-1950)*

Taylor. *Air Raid-Pearl Harbor: The Story of December 7, 1941*

Time-Life. *African Americans: Voices of Triumph: Leadership*

Tunnell. *The Children of Topaz*

Ward. *Shadow Ball: The Negro Leagues*

Ward. *25 Great Moments*

Ward. *Who Invented the Game?*

Warner. *The U.S. Marine Corps*

Wheeler. *Events That Changed American History*

Whitman. *Uncle Sam Wants You!*

Zeinert. *Those Incredible Women of World War II*

Multimedia

CD-ROM

Air and Space Smithsonian Dreams of Flight
Daring to Fly!
Eyewitness Encyclopedia of Science

Her Heritage: A Biographical Encyclopedia of American History
Portraits of American Presidents

SkyTrip America
Time Almanac of the 20th Century
Total History
The Way Things Work

Video

African American Life
African Americans
Elijah Muhammad
The Era of Segregation: A Personal Perspective

Helen Keller
Hiroshima Maiden
Jackie Robinson
Jesse Owens
Malcolm X

Prejudice: Monster Within
Tragedy to Triumph: An Adventure with Helen Keller
Women with Wings

THE MID-TWENTIETH CENTURY, 1946-1975

KINDERGARTEN THROUGH SECOND GRADE

Historical Fiction

Crews. *Bigmama's*
Haddon. *The Sea of Tranquillity*
Joosse. *The Morning Chair*
Rosenblum. *Brooklyn Dodger Days*
Rosenblum. *The Old Synagogue*
Schwartz. *Annabelle Swift, Kindergartner*
Smalls-Hector. *Irene and the Big, Fine Nickel*
Smucker. *No Star Nights*
Taylor. *The Gold Cadillac*
Von Ahnen. *Charlie Young Bear*
Weaver. *Close to Home: A Story of the Polio Epidemic*
Woodtor. *Big Meeting*

Biography

Accorsi. *Rachel Carson*
Adler. *Jackie Robinson: He Was the First*
Adler. *A Picture Book of Eleanor Roosevelt*
Adler. *A Picture Book of Helen Keller*
Adler. *A Picture Book of Jackie Robinson*
Adler. *A Picture Book of Jesse Owens*
Adler. *A Picture Book of John F. Kennedy*
Adler. *A Picture Book of Martin Luther King, Jr.*
Adler. *A Picture Book of Thurgood Marshall*
Bray. *Martin Luther King*
Cavan. *W. E. B. Du Bois*
Coles. *The Story of Ruby Bridges*
Cooper. *Coming Home: From the Life of Langston Hughes*
Cwiklik. *Malcolm X*
Cwiklik. *Philip Randolph*
Faber. *Eleanor Roosevelt: First Lady of the World*
Golenbock. *Teammates*
Greene. *Jackie Robinson*
Greene. *Jacques Cousteau: Man of the Oceans*
Greene. *Katherine Dunham: Black Dancer*
Greene. *Rachel Carson: Friend of Nature*
Greenfield. *Mary McLeod Bethune*
Greenfield. *Rosa Parks*
Krull. *Wilma Unlimited*
Latham. *Rachel Carson: Who Loved the Sea*
Livingston. *Keep On Singing: A Ballad of Marian Anderson*
MacKinnon. *Silent Observer*
Marzollo. *Happy Birthday, Martin Luther King*
McKissack. *Carter G. Woodson*
McKissack. *Louis Armstrong: Jazz Musician*
McKissack. *Marian Anderson: A Great Singer*
McKissack. *Martin Luther King, Jr.: Man of Peace*
McKissack. *Paul Robeson: A Voice to Remember*
McKissack. *Ralph J. Bunche*
Myers. *Young Martin's Promise*
O'Connor. *Jackie Robinson*
Pinkney. *Alvin Ailey*
Sanford. *Jackie Robinson*
Sanford. *Jesse Owens*
Sanford. *Jim Thorpe*
Venezia. *Edward Hopper*
Venezia. *Georgia O'Keeffe*
Venezia. *Jackson Pollock*
Weidt. *Oh, the Places He Went: A Story About Dr. Seuss*

Collective Biography

Marzollo. *My First Book of Biographies*

History

Donnelly. *A Wall of Names: The Story of the Vietnam Memorial*

Goldish. *Our Supreme Court*
Medearis. *Our People*

Multimedia

Video

African American Life

Holiday Facts and Fun: Martin Luther King Day

A Picture Book of Martin Luther King, Jr.

> GRADE THREE

Historical Fiction

Acierno. *Children of Flight Pedro Pan*
Crews. *Bigmama's*
Haddon. *The Sea of Tranquillity*
Hamilton. *Drylongso*
Herman. *Millie Cooper, Take a Chance*
Herman. *Millie Cooper, 3B*

Marino. *Eighty-eight Steps to September*
Mochizuki. *Heroes*
Nelson. *Mayfield Crossing*
Rosenblum. *Brooklyn Dodger Days*
Smalls-Hector. *Irene and the Big, Fine Nickel*
Strauch. *Hey You, Sister Rose*

Taylor. *The Gold Cadillac*
Uchida. *The Best Bad Thing*
Uchida. *The Happiest Ending*
Von Ahnen. *Charlie Young Bear*
Weaver. *Close to Home: A Story of the Polio Epidemic*
Woodtor. *Big Meeting*

Biography

Adler. *Jackie Robinson: He Was the First*
Adler. *A Picture Book of Eleanor Roosevelt*
Adler. *A Picture Book of Helen Keller*
Adler. *A Picture Book of Jackie Robinson*
Adler. *A Picture Book of Jesse Owens*
Adler. *A Picture Book of John F. Kennedy*
Adler. *A Picture Book of Martin Luther King, Jr.*
Adler. *A Picture Book of Rosa Parks*
Adler. *A Picture Book of Thurgood Marshall*
Berkow. *Hank Greenberg: Hall-of-Fame Slugger*
Birch. *Martin Luther King, Jr.*
Bray. *Martin Luther King*
Calvert. *Zora Neale Hurston: Storyteller of the South*
Caras. *A World Full of Animals: The Roger Caras Story*
Cavan. *W. E. B. Du Bois*
Charleston. *Armstrong Lands on the Moon*
Coles. *The Story of Ruby Bridges*
Collins. *Harry S. Truman*

Collins. *To the Point: A Story About E. B. White*
Colman. *A Woman Unafraid: The Achievements of Frances Perkins*
Cooper. *Coming Home: From the Life of Langston Hughes*
Cwiklik. *Malcolm X*
Cwiklik. *Philip Randolph*
Dunlap. *Eye on the Wild: A Story About Ansel Adams*
Erdrich. *Maria Tallchief*
Faber. *Eleanor Roosevelt: First Lady of the World*
Goldberg. *Rachel Carson*
Golenbock. *Teammates*
Graff. *Helen Keller: Toward the Light*
Greene. *Jacques Cousteau: Man of the Oceans*
Greene. *Katherine Dunham: Black Dancer*
Greene. *Rachel Carson: Friend of Nature*
Greenfield. *Mary McLeod Bethune*
Greenfield. *Rosa Parks*
Hakim. *Martin Luther King, Jr.*
Hargrove. *The Story of Jonas Salk*

Heiligman. *Barbara McClintock: Alone in Her Field*
Hunter. *Helen Keller*
Jacobs. *Dwight David Eisenhower*
Jakoubek. *Walter White and the Power of Organized Protest*
Krull. *Wilma Unlimited*
Kudlinski. *Helen Keller: A Light for the Blind*
Latham. *Rachel Carson: Who Loved the Sea*
Livingston. *Keep On Singing: A Ballad of Marian Anderson*
MacKinnon. *Silent Observer*
McKissack. *Carter G. Woodson*
McKissack. *Jesse Owens: Olympic Star*
McKissack. *Langston Hughes: Great American Poet*
McKissack. *Louis Armstrong: Jazz Musician*
McKissack. *Marian Anderson: A Great Singer*
McKissack. *Martin Luther King, Jr.: Man of Peace*
McKissack. *Paul Robeson: A Voice to Remember*
McKissack. *Ralph J. Bunche*

McPherson. *The Workers' Detective: A Story About Dr. Alice Hamilton*

Medearis. *Dare to Dream: Coretta Scott King*

Medearis. *Little Louis and the Jazz Band*

Milton. *Marching to Freedom: Martin Luther King, Jr.*

Myers. *Young Martin's Promise*

O'Connor. *Jackie Robinson*

Patrick. *Martin Luther King, Jr.*

Pinkney. *Alvin Ailey*

Prentzas. *Thurgood Marshall: Champion of Justice*

Reiser. *Jackie Robinson: Baseball Pioneer*

Sanford. *Jackie Robinson*

Sanford. *Jesse Owens*

Sanford. *Jim Thorpe*

Shirley. *Malcolm X: Racial Spokesman*

Shirley. *Satchel Paige*

Shorto. *Jackie Robinson*

Stine. *The Story of Malcolm X: Civil Rights Leader*

Streissguth. *Say It with Music: A Story About Irving Berlin*

Swanson. *I've Got an Idea! Frederick McKinley Jones*

Swertka. *Rachel Carson*

Tolan. *Ralph Nader*

Turner. *Georgia O'Keeffe*

Venezia. *Edward Hopper*

Venezia. *Georgia O'Keeffe*

Venezia. *Jackson Pollock*

Walker. *Pride of Puerto Rico: The Life of Roberto Clemente*

Weidt. *Oh, the Places He Went: A Story About Dr. Seuss*

Weidt. *Stateswoman to the World: Eleanor Roosevelt*

Collective Biography

King. *First Facts About American Heroes*

Marzollo. *My First Book of Biographies*

Provensen. *The Buck Stops Here: The Presidents*

Rappaport. *Living Dangerously: American Women*

History

Alvarez. *The Official Baseball Hall of Fame Answer Book*

Ash. *The Story of the Women's Movement*

Blue. *U.S. Air Force*

Bowler. *Trains*

Burns. *Mail*

Caulkins. *Pets of the Presidents*

Donnelly. *A Wall of Names: The Story of the Vietnam Memorial*

English. *Transportation: Automobiles to Zeppelins*

Goldish. *Our Supreme Court*

Graham. *Spacecraft*

Guzzetti. *The White House*

Hill. *Our Century: 1940-1950*

Hill. *Our Century: 1970-1980*

Humble. *Ships*

Jones. *Our Century: 1950-1960*

Kelso. *Walking for Freedom: The Montgomery Bus Boycott*

Kent. *The Freedom Riders*

Knight. *The Olympic Games*

Lane. *Our Century: 1960-1970*

Medearis. *Our People*

Munro. *Aircraft*

Paananen. *The Military: Defending the Nation*

Stein. *The Assassination of John F. Kennedy*

Stein. *The Story of the Powers of the Supreme Court*

Stein. *The United Nations*

Stern. *The Congress: America's Lawmakers*

Weber. *Our Congress*

Wilson. *Visual Timeline of Transportation*

Wright. *The Story of the Vietnam Memorial*

Multimedia

Video

African American Life

Let Me Tell You All About Trains

GRADE FOUR

Historical Fiction

Acierno. *Children of Flight Pedro Pan*

Antle. *Tough Choices: A Story of the Vietnam War*

Barnes. *The Baby Grand, the Moon in July, & Me*

Bellairs. *The Drum, the Doll, and the Zombie*

Belton. *Ernestine and Amanda*

Bolden. *Just Family*

Cameron. *The Court of the Stone Children*

Hamilton. *Drylongso*

Harding. *The Leaving Summer*

Herman. *Millie Cooper, Take a Chance*

Herman. *Millie Cooper, 3B*

Kinsey-Warnock. *The Canada Geese Quilt*

Marino. *Eighty-eight Steps to September*

Mochizuki. *Heroes*

Nelson. *Mayfield Crossing*

Reese. *Katie Dee and Katie Haw*

Rorby. *Dolphin Sky*

Rosenblum. *Brooklyn Dodger Days*
Salisbury. *Blue Skin of the Sea*
Schotter. *Rhoda, Straight and True*
Smothers. *Moriah's Pond*
Strauch. *Hey You, Sister Rose*

Talbert. *The Purple Heart*
Taylor. *The Gold Cadillac*
Uchida. *The Best Bad Thing*
Uchida. *The Happiest Ending*
Von Ahnen. *Charlie Young Bear*

Von Ahnen. *Heart of Naosaqua*
Weaver. *Close to Home: A Story of the Polio Epidemic*
White. *Come Next Spring*

Biography

Adler. *Jackie Robinson: He Was the First*
Adler. *A Picture Book of Jesse Owens*
Adler. *A Picture Book of John F. Kennedy*
Adler. *A Picture Book of Martin Luther King, Jr.*
Adler. *A Picture Book of Rosa Parks*
Anderson. *Jackie Kennedy Onassis*
Anderson. *John F. Kennedy*
Ashabranner. *The Times of My Life: A Memoir*
Ayers. *Chuck Yeager: Fighter Pilot*
Berkow. *Hank Greenberg: Hall-of-Fame Slugger*
Birch. *Martin Luther King, Jr.*
Bray. *Martin Luther King*
Brooks. *Georgia O'Keeffe: An Adventurous Spirit*
Bryant. *Marjory Stoneman Douglas: Voice of the Everglades*
Butts. *May Chinn: The Best Medicine*
Calvert. *Zora Neale Hurston: Storyteller of the South*
Caras. *A World Full of Animals: The Roger Caras Story*
Cavan. *W. E. B. Du Bois*
Charleston. *Armstrong Lands on the Moon*
Chin. *When Justice Failed: The Fred Korematsu Story*
Collins. *Harry S. Truman*
Collins. *To the Point: A Story About E. B. White*
Colman. *A Woman Unafraid: The Achievements of Frances Perkins*
Colman. *Fannie Lou Hamer and the Fight for the Vote*
Cooper. *Coming Home: From the Life of Langston Hughes*
Cwiklik. *Malcolm X*
Cwiklik. *Philip Randolph*
Dunlap. *Birds in the Bushes: Margaret Morse Nice*

Dunlap. *Eye on the Wild: A Story About Ansel Adams*
Elish. *James Meredith and School Desegregation*
Erdrich. *Maria Tallchief*
Faber. *Eleanor Roosevelt: First Lady of the World*
Ferris. *What I Had Was Singing: Marian Anderson*
Goldberg. *Rachel Carson*
Golenbock. *Teammates*
Graff. *Helen Keller: Toward the Light*
Greene. *Jacques Cousteau: Man of the Oceans*
Greenfield. *Mary McLeod Bethune*
Greenfield. *Rosa Parks*
Hakim. *Martin Luther King, Jr.*
Hamilton. *The Assassination of a Candidate: Robert F. Kennedy*
Hamilton. *The Assassination of a Leader: Martin Luther King, Jr.*
Hargrove. *Dwight D. Eisenhower*
Hargrove. *Harry S. Truman: Thirty-Third President*
Hargrove. *Lyndon B. Johnson: Thirty-Sixth President*
Hargrove. *The Story of Jonas Salk*
Harlan. *Sounding the Alarm: A Biography of Rachel Carson*
Heiligman. *Barbara McClintock: Alone in Her Field*
Hunter. *Helen Keller*
Jacobs. *Dwight David Eisenhower*
Jakoubek. *Walter White and the Power of Organized Protest*
Kaye. *The Life of Benjamin Spock*
Kaye. *The Life of Florence Sabin*

Kehret. *Small Steps: The Year I Got Polio*
Kent. *John F. Kennedy: Thirty-Fifth President*
Krohn. *Elvis Presley: The King*
Krull. *Wilma Unlimited.*
Kudlinski. *Helen Keller: A Light for the Blind*
Latham. *Rachel Carson: Who Loved the Sea*
Lazo. *Eleanor Roosevelt*
Levinson. *Chuck Yeager: The Man Who Broke the Sound Barrier*
Lillegard. *Richard Nixon: Thirty-Seventh President*
Livingston. *Keep On Singing: A Ballad of Marian Anderson*
Lyons. *Painting Dreams: Minnie Evans*
MacKinnon. *Silent Observer*
McKissack. *Carter G. Woodson*
McKissack. *Jesse Owens: Olympic Star*
McKissack. *Langston Hughes: Great American Poet*
McKissack. *Louis Armstrong: Jazz Musician*
McKissack. *Marian Anderson: A Great Singer*
McKissack. *Martin Luther King, Jr.: Man of Peace*
McKissack. *Ralph J. Bunche*
McPherson. *TV's Forgotten Hero: Philo Farnsworth*
McPherson. *The Workers' Detective: A Story About Dr. Alice Hamilton*
Medearis. *Dare to Dream: Coretta Scott King*
Medearis. *Little Louis and the Jazz Band*
Milton. *Marching to Freedom: Martin Luther King, Jr.*
Myers. *Young Martin's Promise*
O'Connor. *Jackie Robinson*
Parks. *Rosa Parks: My Story*

Patrick. *Martin Luther King, Jr.*

Patrick-Wexler. *Barbara Jordan*

Porter. *Jump at de Sun: Zora Neale Hurston*

Prentzas. *Thurgood Marshall: Champion of Justice*

Reef. *Benjamin Davis, Jr.*

Reiser. *Jackie Robinson: Baseball Pioneer*

Rennert. *Jesse Owens: Champion Athlete*

Sanford. *Jackie Robinson*

Sanford. *Jesse Owens*

Sanford. *Jim Thorpe*

Shirley. *Malcolm X: Racial Spokesman*

Shirley. *Satchel Paige*

Shorto. *Jackie Robinson*

Simmons. *Ben Carson*

Stine. *The Story of Malcolm X, Civil Rights Leader*

Streissguth. *Say It with Music: A Story About Irving Berlin*

Swanson. *I've Got an Idea! Frederick McKinley Jones*

Swertka. *Rachel Carson*

Tolan. *Ralph Nader*

Turner. *Dorothea Lange*

Turner. *Georgia O'Keeffe*

Wade. *James Carter: Thirty-Ninth President*

Walker. *Pride of Puerto Rico: The Life of Roberto Clemente*

Weidt. *Oh, the Places He Went: A Story About Dr. Seuss*

Weidt. *Stateswoman to the World: Eleanor Roosevelt*

Whitelaw. *Grace Hopper*

Wolfe. *Charles Richard Drew, M.D.*

Wright. *Arthur Ashe: Breaking the Color Barrier in Tennis*

Collective Biography

Altman. *Extraordinary Black Americans*

Clements. *The Picture History of Great Inventors*

Fireside. *Is There a Woman in the House. . . or Senate?*

Hart. *Flying Free: America's First Black Aviators*

Jacobs. *Great Lives: Human Rights*

Jacobs. *Great Lives: World Religions*

Jacobs. *They Shaped the Game: Ty Cobb, Babe Ruth, and Jackie Robinson*

King. *First Facts About American Heroes*

Krull. *Lives of the Artists: Masterpieces, Messes*

Krull. *Lives of the Musicians: Good Times, Bad Times*

Krull. *Lives of the Writers: Comedies, Tragedies*

McKissack. *African-American Inventors*

Pascoe. *First Facts About the Presidents*

Pile. *Top Entrepreneurs and Their Businesses*

Provensen. *The Buck Stops Here: The Presidents*

Provensen. *My Fellow Americans*

Rappaport. *Living Dangerously: American Women*

Reef. *Black Fighting Men: A Proud History*

Rubel. *The Scholastic Encyclopedia of the Presidents*

Vare. *Women Inventors and their Discoveries*

Wilkinson. *Scientists Who Changed the World*

History

Alvarez. *The Official Baseball Hall of Fame Answer Book*

Ash. *The Story of the Women's Movement*

Ashabranner. *Always to Remember: Vietnam Veteran's Memorial*

Blue. *U.S. Air Force*

Blue. *The White House Kids*

Bolick. *Mail Call!*

Bowler. *Trains*

Burns. *Mail*

Burns. *Money*

Caulkins. *Pets of the Presidents*

Donnelly. *A Wall of Names: The Story of the Vietnam Memorial*

Duncan. *The Circus Comes Home*

English. *Transportation: Automobiles to Zeppelins*

Ferrell. *The U.S. Air Force*

Fichter. *The Space Shuttle*

Giblin. *Be Seated: A Book About Chairs*

Goldish. *Our Supreme Court*

Graham. *Spacecraft*

Guzzetti. *The White House*

Hill. *Our Century: 1940-1950*

Hill. *Our Century: 1970-1980*

The History of Moviemaking

Humble. *Ships*

Jones. *Our Century: 1950-1960*

Jones. *The President Has Been Shot*

Kelso. *Days of Courage: The Little Rock Story*

Kelso. *Walking for Freedom: The Montgomery Bus Boycott*

Kent. *The Freedom Riders*

Kerr. *Keeping Clean*

Knight. *The Olympic Games*

Kurtz. *U.S. Army*

Lane. *Our Century: 1960-1970*

McKissack. *Black Diamond*

Munro. *Aircraft*

O'Neill. *Little Rock: The Desegregation of Central High*

Paananen. *The Military: Defending the Nation*

Reef. *The Supreme Court*

Rosen. *The Conquest of Everest*

Rowland-Warne. *Costume*

Sandler. *Presidents*

Scott. *Funny Papers: Behind the Scenes of the Comics*

Siegel. *The Year They Walked: Rosa Parks and the Montgomery Bus Boycott*

Smith. *The Korean War*

Stein. *The Assassination of John F. Kennedy*

Stein. *The Story of the Powers of the Supreme Court*

Stein. *The United Nations*

Stern. *The Congress: America's Lawmakers*

Sullivan. *Children of
Promise:
African-American
Literature and Art*
Super. *Vietnam War Soldiers*

Ventura. *Clothing*
Ventura. *Food: Its Evolution
Through the Ages*
Ward. *25 Great Moments*
Ward. *Who Invented the Game?*

Weber. *Our Congress*
Wilson. *Visual Timeline of
Transportation*
Wright. *The Story of the
Vietnam Memorial*

Multimedia

CD-ROM

*Her Heritage: A Biographical
Encyclopedia of American
History*

*SkyTrip America
Total History*

Video

*African American Life
African Americans
Black Is My Color: The
African American
Experience
Great Black Innovators*

*Helen Keller
Holiday Facts and Fun:
Martin Luther King Day
Jackie Robinson
Making It Happen: Masters
of Invention*

*Malcolm X
Martin Luther King, Jr.
The Times and Dreams of
Martin Luther King, Jr.*

GRADE FIVE

Historical Fiction

Acierno. *Children of Flight
Pedro Pan*
Antle. *Tough Choices: A
Story of the Vietnam War*
Barnes. *The Baby Grand, the
Moon in July, & Me*
Barnes. *Promise Me the Moon*
Bellairs. *The Drum, the Doll,
and the Zombie*
Belton. *Ernestine and Amanda*
Bolden. *Just Family*
Cameron. *The Court of the
Stone Children*
Cole. *The Final Tide*
Cormier. *Tunes for Bears to
Dance To*
Curtis. *The Watsons Go to
Birmingham—1963*
Fromm. *Monkey Tag*
Hamilton. *Drylongso*
Harding. *The Leaving Summer*
Hausman. *Night Flight*
Herman. *Millie Cooper, Take
a Chance*

Herman. *Millie Cooper, 3B*
High. *The Summer of the
Great Divide*
Johnston. *Hero of Lesser
Causes*
Kinsey-Warnock. *The
Canada Geese Quilt*
Lelchuk. *On Home Ground*
Levin. *Fire in the Wind*
Levinson. *Your Friend,
Natalie Popper*
Marino. *The Day That Elvis
Came to Town*
Marino. *Eighty-eight Steps to
September*
Marino. *For the Love of Pete*
Martin. *Night Riding*
Mochizuki. *Heroes*
Myers. *Rosie's Tiger*
Nelson. *Mayfield Crossing*
Paulsen. *The Cookcamp*
Pendergraft. *Brushy Mountain*
Reese. *Katie Dee and Katie
Haw*

Rorby. *Dolphin Sky*
Salisbury. *Blue Skin of the Sea*
Schotter. *Rhoda, Straight and
True*
Smothers. *Down in the Piney
Woods*
Smothers. *Moriah's Pond*
Strauch. *Hey You, Sister Rose*
Strickland. *The Hand of the
Necromancer*
Talbert. *The Purple Heart*
Taylor. *The Gold Cadillac*
Uchida. *The Best Bad Thing*
Uchida. *The Happiest Ending*
Uchida. *Journey Home*
Von Ahnen. *Heart of
Naosaqua*
Weaver. *Close to Home: A
Story of the Polio Epidemic*
White. *Belle Prater's Boy*
White. *Come Next Spring*
Young. *Learning by Heart*

Biography

Adler. *Jackie Robinson: He
Was the First*
Anderson. *Jackie Kennedy
Onassis*
Anderson. *John F. Kennedy*
Ashabranner. *The Times of
My Life: A Memoir*
Ayers. *Chuck Yeager: Fighter
Pilot*

Barr. *Richard Nixon*
Berkow. *Hank Greenberg:
Hall-of-Fame Slugger*
Bernstein. *Judith Resnick:
Challenger Astronaut*
Berry. *Georgia O'Keeffe:
Painter*
Berry. *Langston Hughes*
Birch. *Martin Luther King, Jr.*

Bishop. *Ralph Ellison: Author*
Blau. *Betty Friedan: Feminist*
Blue. *Barbara Jordan:
Politician*
Bray. *Martin Luther King*
Bredeson. *Jonas Salk:
Discoverer of the Polio
Vaccine*

Brooks. *Georgia O'Keeffe: An Adventurous Spirit*

Brown. *Romare Bearden: Artist*

Bryant. *Marjory Stoneman Douglas: Voice of the Everglades*

Butts. *May Chinn: The Best Medicine*

Cain. *Louise Nevelson: Sculptor*

Calvert. *Zora Neale Hurston: Storyteller of the South*

Castiglia. *Margaret Mead*

Charleston. *Armstrong Lands on the Moon*

Chin. *When Justice Failed: The Fred Korematsu Story*

Cole. *John Glenn: Astronaut and Senator*

Collier. *Duke Ellington*

Collier. *Louis Armstrong: An American Success Story*

Collins. *Gerald R. Ford*

Collins. *Harry S. Truman*

Collins. *To the Point: A Story About E. B. White*

Colman. *Fannie Lou Hamer and the Fight for the Vote*

Colman. *A Woman Unafraid: The Achievements of Frances Perkins*

Conord. *John Lennon*

Curson. *Jonas Salk*

Cwiklik. *Malcolm X*

Daffron. *Margaret Bourke-White: Photographer*

Darby. *Douglas MacArthur*

Darby. *Dwight D. Eisenhower*

Darby. *Martin Luther King, Jr.*

Davies. *Malcolm X*

Davis. *Frank Lloyd Wright: Maverick Architect*

Deitch. *Dwight D. Eisenhower*

Denenberg. *John Fitzgerald Kennedy: America's 35th President*

Dunlap. *Birds in the Bushes: Margaret Morse Nice*

Dunlap. *Eye on the Wild: A Story About Ansel Adams*

Elish. *James Meredith and School Desegregation*

Ellis. *Dwight D. Eisenhower*

Erdrich. *Maria Tallchief*

Erlich. *Paul Robeson: Singer and Actor*

Faber. *Eleanor Roosevelt: First Lady of the World*

Falkof. *John F. Kennedy*

Falkof. *Lyndon B. Johnson*

Ferris. *What I Had Was Singing: Marian Anderson*

Gentry. *Dizzy Gillespie: Musician*

Gentry. *Jesse Owens: Champion Athlete*

Goldberg. *Rachel Carson*

Golenbock. *Teammates*

Gourse. *Dizzy Gillespie and the Birth of Bebop*

Graff. *Helen Keller: Toward the Light*

Greenfield. *Mary McLeod Bethune*

Greenfield. *Rosa Parks*

Hakim. *Martin Luther King, Jr.*

Halasa. *Elijah Muhammad: Religious Leader*

Halasa. *Mary McLeod Bethune: Educator*

Hanley. *Philip Randolph*

Hargrove. *Dwight D. Eisenhower*

Hargrove. *Harry S. Truman: Thirty-third President*

Hargrove. *Lyndon B. Johnson: Thirty-sixth President*

Hargrove. *The Story of Jonas Salk*

Harlan. *Sounding the Alarm: A Biography of Rachel Carson*

Harrison. *A Ripple of Hope: The Life of Robert F. Kennedy*

Heiligman. *Barbara McClintock: Alone in Her Field*

Henry. *Betty Friedan: Fighter for Women's Rights*

Hull. *Rosa Parks: Civil Rights Leader*

Hunter. *Helen Keller*

Jacobs. *Dwight David Eisenhower*

Jakoubek. *Adam Clayton Powell, Jr.*

Jakoubek. *Joe Louis: Heavyweight Champion*

Jakoubek. *Martin Luther King, Jr.*

Jakoubek. *Walter White and the Power of Organized Protest*

James. *Julia Morgan: Architect*

Jezer. *Rachel Carson: Biologist and Author*

Kallen. *Thurgood Marshall: A Dream of Justice for All*

Kaye. *Lyndon B. Johnson*

Kaye. *The Life of Alexander Fleming*

Kaye. *The Life of Benjamin Spock*

Kaye. *The Life of Florence Sabin*

Kehret. *Small Steps: The Year I Got Polio*

Keller. *Margaret Bourke-White: A Photographer's Life*

Kent. *John F. Kennedy: Thirty-Fifth President*

Kittredge. *Barbara McClintock*

Kittredge. *Helen Hayes: Actress*

Kliment. *Count Basie: Bandleader and Musician*

Kliment. *Ella Fitzgerald: Singer*

Krohn. *Elvis Presley: The King*

Kronstadt. *Florence Sabin: Medical Researcher*

Krull. *Wilma Unlimited.*

Kudlinski. *Helen Keller: A Light for the Blind*

La Farge. *Pearl Buck*

Latham. *Rachel Carson: Who Loved the Sea*

Lazo. *Eleanor Roosevelt*

Leavell. *Harry S. Truman*

Levinson. *Chuck Yeager: The Man Who Broke the Sound Barrier*

Lillegard. *Richard Nixon: Thirty-Seventh President*

Lindop. *Richard M. Nixon, Jimmy Carter, Ronald Reagan*

Lindop. *Woodrow Wilson, Franklin D. Roosevelt, Harry S. Truman*

Loewen. *Elvis*

Lubetkin. *George Marshall*

Lynn. *Babe Didrikson Zaharias*

Lyons. *Painting Dreams: Minnie Evans*

Markham. *Helen Keller*

McPherson. *TV's Forgotten Hero: Philo Farnsworth*

McPherson. *The Workers' Detective: A Story About Dr. Alice Hamilton*

Medearis. *Dare to Dream: Coretta Scott King*

Meltzer. *Betty Friedan: A Voice for Women's Rights*

Milton. *Marching to Freedom: Martin Luther King, Jr.*

Myers. *Malcolm X: By Any Means Necessary*

Myers. *A Place Called Heartbreak: A Story of Vietnam*

Myers. *Young Martin's Promise*

Nicholson. *Helen Keller: Humanitarian*

Oneal. *Grandma Moses: Painter of Rural America*

Osofsky. *Free to Dream: Langston Hughes*

Palmer. *Lena Horne: Entertainer*

Parks. *Rosa Parks: My Story*

Patrick. *Martin Luther King, Jr.*

Patrick-Wexler. *Barbara Jordan*

Porter. *Jump at de Sun: Zora Neale Hurston*

Potter. *Buckminster Fuller*

Prentzas. *Thurgood Marshall: Champion of Justice*

Probosz. *Martha Graham*

Randall. *John F. Kennedy*

Reef. *Benjamin Davis, Jr.*

Reiser. *Jackie Robinson: Baseball Pioneer*

Rennert. *Jesse Owens: Champion Athlete*

Richman. *James E. Carter*

St. George. *Dear Dr. Bell. . . Your Friend, Helen Keller*

Sandak. *The Eisenhowers*

Sandak. *The Lyndon Johnsons*

Sandak. *The Nixons*

Sandak. *The Trumans*

Sandberg. *Dwight D. Eisenhower*

Schroeder. *Josephine Baker*

Schuman. *Eleanor Roosevelt*

Schuman. *Elie Wiesel*

Scott. *Jackie Robinson*

Shirley. *Malcolm X: Racial Spokesman*

Shirley. *Satchel Paige*

Shorto. *Jackie Robinson*

Simmons. *Ben Carson*

Sklansky. *James Farmer*

Smith. *Coming out Right: Jacqueline Cochran*

Speaker-Yuan. *Agnes de Mille: Choreographer*

Stafford. *W. E. B. Dubois: Scholar and Activist*

Stefoff. *Richard M. Nixon*

Stine. *The Story of Malcolm X, Civil Rights Leader*

Streissguth. *Say It with Music: A Story About Irving Berlin*

Swanson. *I've Got an Idea! Frederick McKinley Jones*

Swertka. *Rachel Carson*

Talmadge. *The Life of Charles Drew*

Tanenhaus. *Louis Armstrong: Musician*

Tedards. *Marian Anderson: Singer*

Tingum. *E. B. White*

Tolan. *Ralph Nader*

Tomlinson. *Jonas Salk*

Toor. *Eleanor Roosevelt*

Turner. *Dorothea Lange*

Turner. *Georgia O'Keeffe*

Wade. *James Carter: Thirty-Ninth President*

Wadsworth. *Rachel Carson: Voice for the Earth*

Walker. *Pride of Puerto Rico: The Life of Roberto Clemente*

Weidt. *Oh, the Places He Went: A Story About Dr. Seuss*

Weidt. *Stateswoman to the World: Eleanor Roosevelt*

Weisbrot. *Father Divine: Religious Leader*

Whitelaw. *Grace Hopper*

Witcover. *Zora Neale Hurston*

Wolfe. *Charles Richard Drew, M.D.*

Wolfe. *Mahalia Jackson: Gospel Singer*

Wright. *Arthur Ashe: Breaking the Color Barrier in Tennis*

Ziesk. *Margaret Mead*

Collective Biography

Aaseng. *Close Calls: From the Brink of Ruin to Business Success*

Aaseng. *From Rags to Riches*

Aaseng. *True Champions: Great Athletes and Their off-the Field Heroics*

Altman. *Extraordinary Black Americans*

Blue. *People of Peace*

Clements. *The Picture History of Great Inventors*

Faber. *Great Lives: American Government*

Fireside. *Is There a Woman in the House. . . or Senate?*

Glubok. *Great Lives: Painting*

Hart. *Flying Free: America's First Black Aviators*

Haskins. *Black Eagles: African Americans in Aviation*

Jacobs. *Great Lives: Human Rights*

Jacobs. *Great Lives: World Religions*

Jacobs. *They Shaped the Game: Ty Cobb, Babe Ruth, and Jackie Robinson*

King. *First Facts About American Heroes*

Krull. *Lives of the Artists: Masterpieces, Messes*

Krull. *Lives of the Musicians: Good Times, Bad Times*

Krull. *Lives of the Writers: Comedies, Tragedies*

Mayberry. *Business Leaders Who Built Financial Empires*

McKissack. *African-American Inventors*

Morin. *Women of the U.S. Congress*

Pascoe. *First Facts About the Presidents*

Pile. *Top Entrepreneurs and Their Businesses*

Pile. *Women Business Leaders*

Provensen. *The Buck Stops Here: The Presidents*

Provensen. *My Fellow Americans*

Rappaport. *Living Dangerously: American Women*

Reef. *Black Fighting Men: A Proud History*

Rennert. *Jazz Stars*

Rochelle. *Witnesses to Freedom: Young People Who Fought for Civil Rights*

Rubel. *The Scholastic Encyclopedia of the Presidents*

Schraff. *American Heroes of Exploration and Flight*
Vare. *Women Inventors and their Discoveries*
Veglahn. *Women Scientists*

Weitzman. *Great Lives: Human Culture*
Wilkinson. *People Who Changed the World*
Wilkinson. *Scientists Who Changed the World*

Wilkinson. *Statesmen Who Changed the World*
Young. *Cy Young Award Winners*

History

Alvarez. *The Official Baseball Hall of Fame Answer Book*
Ash. *The Story of the Women's Movement*
Ashabranner. *Always to Remember: Vietnam Veteran's Memorial*
Blue. *The White House Kids*
Blue. *U.S. Air Force*
Bolick. *Mail Call!*
Bortz. *Catastrophe!: Great Engineering Failure—and Success*
Bowler. *Trains*
Brown. *The Nation in Turmoil: 1960-1973*
Burns. *Mail*
Burns. *Money*
Caulkins. *Pets of the Presidents*
Colman. *Strike: The Bitter Struggle of American Workers*
Colman. *Toilets, Bathtubs, Sinks, and Sewers*
Cosner. *War Nurses*
Cross. *Aftermath of War*
Davies. *Transport: On Land, Road and Rail*
Duncan. *The Circus Comes Home*
Emert. *Top Lawyers and their Famous Cases*
English. *Transportation: Automobiles to Zeppelins*
Ferrell. *The U.S. Air Force*
Fichter. *The Space Shuttle*
Gardner. *The Forgotten Players: The Story of Black Baseball in America*
Garrett. *The Seventies*
Giblin. *Be Seated: A Book About Chairs*
Gibson. *The War in Vietnam*
Goldish. *Our Supreme Court*
Graham. *Spacecraft*
Guzzetti. *The White House*
Helmer. *Belles of the Ballpark*
Hill. *Our Century: 1940-1950*

Hill. *Our Century: 1970-1980*
Hirsch. *Taxation: Paying for Government*
The History of Moviemaking
Humble. *Ships*
Jones. *Our Century: 1950-1960*
Jones. *The President Has Been Shot*
Karl. *America Alive: A History*
Kelso. *Days of Courage: The Little Rock Story*
Kelso. *Walking for Freedom: The Montgomery Bus Boycott*
Kent. *The Freedom Riders*
Kerr. *Keeping Clean*
Knight. *The Olympic Games*
Kurtz. *U.S. Army*
Lane. *Our Century: 1960-1970*
Levi. *Cowboys of the Sky*
Lucas. *Civil Rights: The Long Struggle*
Macy. *A Whole New Ballgame: All-American Girls Professional Baseball League*
McKissack. *Black Diamond*
Medearis. *Come This Far to Freedom*
Meltzer. *The Black Americans*
Morley. *Clothes: For Work, Play and Display*
Munro. *Aircraft*
Naden. *The U.S. Coast Guard*
O'Neill. *Little Rock: The Desegregation of Central High*
Paananen. *The Military: Defending the Nation*
Platt. *The Smithsonian Visual Timeline of Inventions*
Rappaport. *Tinker vs. Des Moines*
Reef. *The Supreme Court*
Rosen. *The Conquest of Everest*
Rowland-Warne. *Costume*

Sandler. *Presidents*
Scott. *Funny Papers: Behind the Scenes of the Comics*
Siegel. *The Year They Walked: Rosa Parks and the Montgomery Bus Boycott*
Smith. *The Korean War*
Stamper. *Save the Everglades*
Stein. *The Assassination of John F. Kennedy*
Stein. *The Story of the Powers of the Supreme Court*
Stein. *The United Nations*
Steins. *The Postwar Years: 1950-1959*
Stern. *The Congress: America's Lawmakers*
Sullivan. *Children of Promise: African-American Literature and Art*
Sullivan. *Slave Ship: The Story of the Henrietta Marie*
Super. *Vietnam War Soldiers*
Ventura. *Clothing*
Ventura. *Food: Its Evolution Through the Ages*
Ward. *25 Great Moments*
Ward. *Who Invented the Game?*
Warner. *The U.S. Marine Corps*
Weber. *Our Congress*
Westerfeld. *The Berlin Airlift*
Whitman. *Get Up and Go: American Road Travel*
Whitman. *This Land Is Your Land*
Wilson. *Visual Timeline of Transportation*
Wright. *The Story of the Vietnam Memorial*
Yepsen. *City Trains: America's Cities by Rail*

Multimedia

CD-ROM

Air and Space Smithsonian Dreams of Flight
Apollo Interactive: The Complete Insider's Guide

Eyewitness Encyclopedia of Science
Her Heritage: A Biographical Encyclopedia of American History

Portraits of American Presidents
SkyTrip America
Total History

Video

African American Life
African Americans
Black Is My Color: The African American Experience
Elijah Muhammad
Great Black Innovators

Helen Keller
Jackie Robinson
Jesse Owens
Making It Happen: Masters of Invention
Malcolm X
Martin Luther King, Jr.

Post War U.S.A.
The Times and Dreams of Martin Luther King, Jr.
Tragedy to Triumph: An Adventure with Helen Keller

GRADE SIX

Historical Fiction

Antle. *Tough Choices: A Story of the Vietnam War*
Barnes. *The Baby Grand, the Moon in July, & Me*
Barnes. *Promise Me the Moon*
Bellairs. *The Drum, the Doll, and the Zombie*
Belton. *Ernestine and Amanda*
Bolden. *Just Family*
Boutis. *Looking Out*
Cameron. *The Court of the Stone Children*
Cleaver. *Dust of the Earth*
Cole. *The Final Tide*
Cormier. *Tunes for Bears to Dance To*
Curtis. *The Watsons Go to Birmingham—1963*
Freeman. *The Cuckoo's Child*
Fromm. *Monkey Tag*
Hall. *Halsey's Pride*
Harding. *The Leaving Summer*
Hausman. *Night Flight*
Herman. *Millie Cooper, Take a Chance*
Herman. *Millie Cooper, 3B*

High. *The Summer of the Great Divide*
Hite. *It's Nothing to a Mountain*
Johnston. *Hero of Lesser Causes*
Kinsey-Warnock. *The Canada Geese Quilt*
Lelchuk. *On Home Ground*
Levin. *Fire in the Wind*
Levinson. *Your Friend, Natalie Popper*
Lyon. *Red Rover, Red Rover*
Marino. *The Day That Elvis Came to Town*
Marino. *Eighty-eight Steps to September*
Marino. *For the Love of Pete*
Martin. *Night Riding*
Mochizuki. *Heroes*
Myers. *Rosie's Tiger*
Nelson. *Mayfield Crossing*
Oughton. *Music from a Place Called Half Moon*
Paulsen. *The Cookcamp*
Paulsen. *Harris and Me: A Summer Remembered*

Pendergraft. *Brushy Mountain*
Reese. *Katie Dee and Katie Haw*
Rorby. *Dolphin Sky*
Salisbury. *Blue Skin of the Sea*
Schotter. *Rhoda, Straight and True*
Slepian. *Risk n' Roses*
Smothers. *Down in the Piney Woods*
Smothers. *Moriah's Pond*
Strauch. *Hey You, Sister Rose*
Strickland. *The Hand of the Necromancer*
Talbert. *The Purple Heart*
Taylor. *The Gold Cadillac*
Uchida. *The Best Bad Thing*
Uchida. *The Happiest Ending*
Uchida. *Journey Home*
Von Ahnen. *Heart of Naosaqua*
Weaver. *Close to Home: A Story of the Polio Epidemic*
White. *Belle Prater's Boy*
White. *Come Next Spring*
White. *Sweet Creek Holler*
Young. *Learning by Heart*

Biography

Anderson. *Jackie Kennedy Onassis*
Anderson. *John F. Kennedy*
Ashabranner. *The Times of My Life: A Memoir*
Ayers. *Chuck Yeager: Fighter Pilot*
Barr. *Richard Nixon*

Berkow. *Hank Greenberg: Hall-of-Fame Slugger*
Bernstein. *Judith Resnick: Challenger Astronaut*
Berry. *Georgia O'Keeffe: Painter*
Berry. *Gordon Parks*
Berry. *Langston Hughes*
Birch. *Martin Luther King, Jr.*

Bishop. *Ralph Ellison: Author*
Blau. *Betty Friedan: Feminist*
Blue. *Barbara Jordan: Politician*
Bredeson. *Jonas Salk: Discoverer of the Polio Vaccine*
Brooks. *Georgia O'Keeffe: An Adventurous Spirit*

Brown. *Romare Bearden: Artist*

Bryant. *Marjory Stoneman Douglas: Voice of the Everglades*

Butts. *May Chinn: The Best Medicine*

Cain. *Louise Nevelson: Sculptor*

Calvert. *Zora Neale Hurston: Storyteller of the South*

Castiglia. *Margaret Mead*

Charleston. *Armstrong Lands on the Moon*

Chin. *When Justice Failed: The Fred Korematsu Story*

Cole. *John Glenn: Astronaut and Senator*

Collier. *Duke Ellington*

Collier. *Louis Armstrong: An American Success Story*

Collins. *Gerald R. Ford*

Collins. *Harry S. Truman*

Collins. *To the Point: A Story About E. B. White*

Colman. *Fannie Lou Hamer and the Fight for the Vote*

Colman. *A Woman Unafraid: The Achievements of Frances Perkins*

Conord. *John Lennon*

Curson. *Jonas Salk*

Daffron. *Margaret Bourke-White: Photographer*

Dallard. *Ella Baker: A Leader Behind the Scenes*

Darby. *Douglas MacArthur*

Darby. *Dwight D. Eisenhower*

Darby. *Martin Luther King, Jr.*

Davies. *Malcolm X*

Davis. *Frank Lloyd Wright: Maverick Architect*

Deitch. *Dwight D. Eisenhower*

Denenberg. *John Fitzgerald Kennedy: America's 35th President*

Dunlap. *Birds in the Bushes: Margaret Morse Nice*

Dunlap. *Eye on the Wild: A Story About Ansel Adams*

Elish. *James Meredith and School Desegregation*

Ellis. *Dwight D. Eisenhower*

Erlich. *Paul Robeson: Singer and Actor*

Faber. *Eleanor Roosevelt: First Lady of the World*

Falkof. *John F. Kennedy*

Falkof. *Lyndon B. Johnson*

Ferris. *What I Had Was Singing: Marian Anderson*

Frankl. *Charlie Parker: Musician*

Fraser. *Walter White: Civil Rights Leader*

Freedman. *Eleanor Roosevelt: A Life of Discovery*

Friese. *Rosa Parks: The Movement Organizes*

Garfunkel. *Letter to the World: Martha Graham*

Gentry. *Dizzy Gillespie: Musician*

Gentry. *Jesse Owens: Champion Athlete*

Gherman. *E.B. White: Some Writer!*

Goldberg. *Rachel Carson*

Golenbock. *Teammates*

Gourse. *Dizzy Gillespie and the Birth of Bebop*

Graff. *Helen Keller: Toward the Light*

Halasa. *Elijah Muhammad: Religious Leader*

Halasa. *Mary McLeod Bethune: Educator*

Hanley. *Philip Randolph*

Hargrove. *Dwight D. Eisenhower*

Hargrove. *Harry S. Truman: Thirty-third President*

Hargrove. *Lyndon B. Johnson: Thirty-sixth President*

Hargrove. *The Story of Jonas Salk*

Harlan. *Sounding the Alarm: A Biography of Rachel Carson*

Harrison. *A Ripple of Hope: The Life of Robert F. Kennedy*

Haskins. *Thurgood Marshall: A Life for Justice*

Heiligman. *Barbara McClintock: Alone in Her Field*

Henry. *Betty Friedan: Fighter for Women's Rights*

Henry. *Coretta Scott King: Keeper of the Dream*

Hull. *Rosa Parks: Civil Rights Leader*

Hunter. *Helen Keller*

Jacobs. *Dwight David Eisenhower*

Jakoubek. *Adam Clayton Powell, Jr.*

Jakoubek. *Joe Louis: Heavyweight Champion*

Jakoubek. *Martin Luther King, Jr.*

Jakoubek. *Walter White and the Power of Organized Protest*

James. *Julia Morgan: Architect*

Jezer. *Rachel Carson: Biologist and Author*

Kallen. *Thurgood Marshall: A Dream of Justice for All*

Kaye. *The Life of Alexander Fleming*

Kaye. *The Life of Benjamin Spock*

Kaye. *The Life of Florence Sabin*

Kaye. *Lyndon B. Johnson*

Kehret. *Small Steps: The Year I Got Polio*

Keller. *Margaret Bourke-White: A Photographer's Life*

Kent. *John F. Kennedy: Thirty-Fifth President*

Kittredge. *Barbara McClintock*

Kittredge. *Helen Hayes: Actress*

Kliment. *Count Basie: Bandleader and Musician*

Kliment. *Ella Fitzgerald: Singer*

Krohn. *Elvis Presley: The King*

Kronstadt. *Florence Sabin: Medical Researcher*

Kudlinski. *Helen Keller: A Light for the Blind*

La Farge. *Pearl Buck*

Larsen. *Paul Robeson: Hero Before His Time*

Larsen. *Richard Nixon: Rise and Fall of a President*

Latham. *Rachel Carson: Who Loved the Sea*

Lazo. *Eleanor Roosevelt*

Leavell. *Harry S. Truman*

Levinson. *Chuck Yeager: The Man Who Broke the Sound Barrier*

Lillegard. *Richard Nixon: Thirty-Seventh President*

Lindop. *Richard M. Nixon, Jimmy Carter, Ronald Reagan*

Lindop. *Woodrow Wilson, Franklin D. Roosevelt, Harry S. Truman*

Loewen. *Elvis*

Lubetkin. *George Marshall*

Lynn. *Babe Didrikson Zaharias*

Lyons. *Painting Dreams: Minnie Evans*

Markham. *Helen Keller*

McPherson. *TV's Forgotten Hero: Philo Farnsworth*

McPherson. *The Workers' Detective: A Story About Dr. Alice Hamilton*

Meltzer. *Betty Friedan: A Voice for Women's Rights*

Meryman. *Andrew Wyeth*

Milton. *Marching to Freedom: Martin Luther King, Jr.*

Morris. *The Truman Way*

Myers. *Malcolm X: By Any Means Necessary*

Myers. *A Place Called Heartbreak: A Story of Vietnam*

Nicholson. *Helen Keller: Humanitarian*

Oneal. *Grandma Moses: Painter of Rural America*

Osofsky. *Free to Dream: Langston Hughes*

Palmer. *Lena Horne: Entertainer*

Parks. *Rosa Parks: My Story*

Patrick. *Coretta Scott King*

Patrick. *Martin Luther King, Jr.*

Patrick-Wexler. *Barbara Jordan*

Patterson. *Martin Luther King and the Montgomery Bus Boycott*

Pollack. *Shirley Chisholm*

Porter. *Jump at de Sun: Zora Neale Hurston*

Potter. *Buckminster Fuller*

Pratt. *Martha Graham*

Prentzas. *Thurgood Marshall: Champion of Justice*

Presnal. *Rachel Carson*

Probosz. *Martha Graham*

Randall. *John F. Kennedy*

Reef. *Benjamin Davis, Jr.*

Rennert. *Jesse Owens: Champion Athlete*

Richman. *James E. Carter*

Rowland. *Martin Luther King, Jr.*

Rubel. *Fannie Lou Hamer*

Sandak. *The Eisenhowers*

Sandak. *The Lyndon Johnsons*

Sandak. *The Nixons*

Sandak. *The Trumans*

Sandberg. *Dwight D. Eisenhower*

Sawyer. *Marjory Stoneman Douglas*

Scheader. *Shirley Chisholm*

Schroeder. *Josephine Baker*

Schuman. *Eleanor Roosevelt*

Schuman. *Elie Wiesel*

Scott. *Jackie Robinson*

Shirley. *Malcolm X: Racial Spokesman*

Shirley. *Satchel Paige*

Simmons. *Ben Carson*

Sklansky. *James Farmer*

Smith. *Coming out Right: Jacqueline Cochran*

Speaker-Yuan. *Agnes de Mille: Choreographer*

St. George. *Dear Dr. Bell. . . Your Friend, Helen Keller*

Stafford. *W. E. B. Dubois: Scholar and Activist*

Stefoff. *Richard M. Nixon*

Stine. *The Story of Malcolm X, Civil Rights Leader*

Streissguth. *Say It with Music: A Story About Irving Berlin*

Swanson. *I've Got an Idea! Frederick McKinley Jones*

Swertka. *Rachel Carson*

Talmadge. *The Life of Charles Drew*

Tanenhaus. *Louis Armstrong: Musician*

Tedards. *Marian Anderson: Singer*

Tingum. *E. B. White*

Tolan. *Ralph Nader*

Tomlinson. *Jonas Salk*

Toor. *Eleanor Roosevelt*

Turner. *Dorothea Lange*

Turner. *Georgia O'Keeffe*

Wade. *James Carter: Thirty-Ninth President*

Wadsworth. *Rachel Carson: Voice for the Earth*

Walker. *Pride of Puerto Rico: The Life of Roberto Clemente*

Weidt. *Oh, the Places He Went: A Story About Dr. Seuss*

Weisbrot. *Father Divine: Religious Leader*

Whitelaw. *Grace Hopper*

Whitelaw. *Mr. Civil Rights: The Story of Thurgood Marshall*

Williams. *Patrick Desjarlait*

Witcover. *Zora Neale Hurston*

Wolfe. *Charles Richard Drew, M.D.*

Wolfe. *Mahalia Jackson: Gospel Singer*

Woog. *Duke Ellington*

Woog. *Louis Armstrong*

Wright. *Arthur Ashe: Breaking the Color Barrier in Tennis*

Yannuzzi. *Zora Neale Hurston: Southern Storyteller*

Ziesk. *Margaret Mead*

Collective Biography

Aaseng. *Close Calls: From the Brink of Ruin to Business Success*

Aaseng. *From Rags to Riches*

Aaseng. *Genetics: Unlocking the Secrets of Life*

Aaseng. *True Champions: Great Athletes and Their off-the Field Heroics*

Allen. *Black Women Leaders of the Civil Rights Movement*

Altman. *Extraordinary Black Americans*

Beard. *The Presidents in American History*

Blassingame. *The Look-It-Up Book of Presidents*

Blue. *People of Peace*

Camp. *American Astronomers: Searchers and Wonderers*

Clements. *The Picture History of Great Inventors*

Cohen. *Prophets of Doom*

Cush. *Artists Who Created Great Works*

Cush. *Women Who Achieved Greatness*

Faber. *Great Lives: American Government*

Fireside. *Is There a Woman in the House. . . or Senate?*

Glenn. *Discover America's Favorite Architects*

Glubok. *Great Lives: Painting*

Hart. *Flying Free: America's First Black Aviators*

Haskins. *Black Eagles: African Americans in Aviation*

Italia. *Courageous Crimefighters*

Jacobs. *Great Lives: Human Rights*

Jacobs. *Great Lives: World Religions*

Jacobs. *They Shaped the Game: Ty Cobb, Babe Ruth, and Jackie Robinson*

King. *First Facts About American Heroes*

Krull. *Lives of the Artists: Masterpieces, Messes*

Krull. *Lives of the Musicians: Good Times, Bad Times*

Krull. *Lives of the Writers: Comedies, Tragedies*

Mayberry. *Business Leaders Who Built Financial Empires*

McKissack. *African-American Inventors*

Morin. *Women of the U.S. Congress*

Morin. *Women Who Reformed Politics*

Myers. *Now Is Your Time*

Pascoe. *First Facts About the Presidents*

Pile. *Top Entrepreneurs and Their Businesses*

Pile. *Women Business Leaders*

Plowden. *Famous Firsts of Black Women*

Provensen. *The Buck Stops Here: The Presidents*

Provensen. *My Fellow Americans*

Rappaport. *Living Dangerously: American Women*

Reef. *Black Fighting Men: A Proud History*

Rennert. *Book of Firsts: Leaders of America*

Rennert. *Civil Rights Leaders*

Rennert. *Female Writers*

Rennert. *Jazz Stars*

Rennert. *Pioneers of Discovery*

Rochelle. *Witnesses to Freedom: Young People Who Fought for Civil Rights*

Rubel. *The Scholastic Encyclopedia of the Presidents*

Schraff. *American Heroes of Exploration and Flight*

Smith. *Presidents in a Time of Change*

Vare. *Women Inventors and their Discoveries*

Veglahn. *Women Scientists*

Weitzman. *Great Lives: Human Culture*

Whitelaw. *They Wrote Their Own Headlines*

Wilkinson. *People Who Changed the World*

Wilkinson. *Scientists Who Changed the World*

Wilkinson. *Statesmen Who Changed the World*

Young. *Cy Young Award Winners*

Yount. *Black Scientists*

Yount. *Women Aviators*

History

Alvarez. *The Official Baseball Hall of Fame Answer Book*

Anderson. *Battles That Changed the Modern World*

Ash. *The Story of the Women's Movement*

Ashabranner. *Always to Remember: Vietnam Veteran's Memorial*

Basinger. *American Cinema*

Blue. *The White House Kids*

Blue. *U.S. Air Force*

Bolick. *Mail Call!*

Bortz. *Catastrophe!: Great Engineering Failure—and Success*

Bowler. *Trains*

Brown. *The Nation in Turmoil: 1960-1973*

Burns. *Money*

Caulkins. *Pets of the Presidents*

Clements. *An Illustrated History of the World*

Colman. *Strike: The Bitter Struggle of American Workers*

Colman. *Toilets, Bathtubs, Sinks, and Sewers*

Cosner. *War Nurses*

Cross. *Aftermath of War*

Davies. *Transport: On Land, Road and Rail*

Duncan. *The Circus Comes Home*

Emert. *Top Lawyers and their Famous Cases*

English. *Transportation: Automobiles to Zeppelins*

Ferrell. *The U.S. Air Force*

Fichter. *The Space Shuttle*

Fireside. *Brown V. Board of Education*

Gardner. *The Forgotten Players: The Story of Black Baseball in America*

Garfunkel. *On Wings of Joy: The Story of Ballet*

Garrett. *The Seventies*

Giblin. *Be Seated: A Book About Chairs*

Gibson. *The War in Vietnam*

Goldish. *Our Supreme Court*

Graham. *Spacecraft*

Gutman. *World Series Classics*

Guzzetti. *The White House*

Haas. *Engel V. Vitale*

Hakim. *All the People*

Haskins. *Freedom Rides*

Helmer. *Belles of the Ballpark*

Herda. *Furman V. Georgia*

Herda. *Roe V. Wade*

Herda. *United States V. Nixon*

Hill. *Our Century: 1940-1950*

Hill. *Our Century: 1970-1980*

Hirsch. *Taxation: Paying for Government*

The History of Moviemaking

Humble. *Ships*

Jones. *Our Century: 1950-1960*

Jones. *The President Has Been Shot*

Karl. *America Alive: A History*

Kelso. *Days of Courage: The Little Rock Story*

Kelso. *Walking for Freedom: The Montgomery Bus Boycott*

Kerr. *Keeping Clean*

Kurtz. *U.S. Army*

Lane. *Our Century: 1960-1970*

Leiner. *First Children: Growing Up in the White House*

Levi. *Cowboys of the Sky*

Lucas. *Civil Rights: The Long Struggle*

Macy. *A Whole New Ballgame: All-American Girls Professional Baseball League*

Markham. *Inventions That Changed Modern Life*

McKissack. *Black Diamond*

Medearis. *Come This Far to Freedom*

Meltzer. *The Black Americans*

Mizell. *Think About Racism*

Morley. *Clothes: For Work, Play and Display*

Munro. *Aircraft*

Naden. *The U.S. Coast Guard*

O'Neill. *Little Rock: The Desegregation of Central High*

Paananen. *The Military: Defending the Nation*

Patrick. *The Young Oxford Companion to the Supreme Court*

Philip. *Singing America: Poems That Define A Nation*

Platt. *The Smithsonian Visual Timeline of Inventions*

Rappaport. *The Alger Hiss Trial*

Rappaport. *Tinker vs. Des Moines*

Reef. *The Supreme Court*

Riley. *Miranda V. Arizona*

Rosen. *The Conquest of Everest*

Rowland-Warne. *Costume*

Sandler. *Presidents*

Scott. *Funny Papers: Behind the Scenes of the Comics*

Siegel. *The Year They Walked: Rosa Parks and the Montgomery Bus Boycott*

Smith. *The Korean War*

St. George. *The White House: Cornerstone of a Nation*

Stamper. *Save the Everglades*

Stein. *The Korean War*

Stein. *The Story of the Powers of the Supreme Court*

Steins. *The Postwar Years: 1950-1959*

Stern. *The Congress: America's Lawmakers*

Sullivan. *Children of Promise: African-American Literature and Art*

Sullivan. *Slave Ship: The Story of the Henrietta Marie*

Super. *Vietnam War Soldiers*

Time-Life. *African Americans: Voices of Triumph: Leadership*

Ventura. *Clothing*

Ventura. *Food: Its Evolution Through the Ages*

Walker. *Hand, Heart, and Mind*

Warburton. *Railroads: Bridging the Continents*

Ward. *25 Great Moments*

Ward. *Who Invented the Game?*

Warner. *The U.S. Marine Corps*

Weber. *Our Congress*

Weisbrot. *Marching Toward Freedom: 1957-1965*

Westerfeld. *The Berlin Airlift*

Wheeler. *Events That Changed American History*

Whitman. *Get Up and Go: American Road Travel*

Whitman. *This Land Is Your Land*

Yepsen. *City Trains: America's Cities by Rail*

Multimedia

CD-ROM

Air and Space Smithsonian Dreams of Flight

Apollo Interactive: The Complete Insider's Guide

Campaigns, Candidates and the Presidency

Daring to Fly!

Eyewitness Encyclopedia of Science

Her Heritage: A Biographical Encyclopedia of American History

History Through Art: 20th Century

Portraits of American Presidents

SkyTrip America

Time Almanac of the 20th Century

Total History

The Way Things Work

Video

African American Life

African Americans

Black Is My Color: The African American Experience

Elijah Muhammad

The Era of Segregation: A Personal Perspective

Great Black Innovators

Helen Keller

Jackie Robinson

Jesse Owens

Making It Happen: Masters of Invention

Malcolm X

Martin Luther King, Jr.

Post War U.S.A.

The Times and Dreams of Martin Luther King, Jr.

Tragedy to Triumph: An Adventure with Helen Keller

Women with Wings

SINCE 1975

KINDERGARTEN THROUGH SECOND GRADE

Biography

Coles. *The Story of Ruby Bridges*
Goble. *Hau Kola Hello Friend*
Krull. *Wilma Unlimited*
Liestman. *Columbus Day*

Livingston. *Keep On Singing: A Ballad of Marian Anderson*
Lowery. *Wilma Mankiller*
McKissack. *Marian Anderson: A Great Singer*
Pinkney. *Alvin Ailey*

Polacco. *Firetalking*
Ringgold. *Bonjour, Lonnie*
Simon. *Wilma P. Mankiller*
Weidt. *Oh, the Places He Went: A Story About Dr. Seuss*

Collective Biography

Marzollo. *My First Book of Biographies*

History

Adler. *A Picture Book of Jewish Holidays*
Cashman. *Jewish Days and Holidays*
Donnelly. *A Wall of Names: The Story of the Vietnam Memorial*

Fisher. *Stars and Stripes: Our National Flag*
Fradin. *The Flag of the United States*
Gibbons. *The Great St. Lawrence Seaway*
Krementz. *A Visit to Washington, DC*

Medearis. *Our People*
Spencer. *A Flag for Our Country*
Swanson. *I Pledge Allegiance*
Waters. *The Story of the White House*

Multimedia

Video

Adventures Behind the Scenes: At the Newspaper
African American Life
Christmas
Columbus Day

Independence Day
National Observances
Old Glory
Rosh Hashanah/Yom Kippur
U.S. Songs and Poems

United States Flag
Valentine's Day
Washington, D.C.

GRADE THREE

Biography

Anderson. *Maria Martinez: Pueblo Potter*
Applegate. *Benjamin O. Davis and Colin Powell*
Caras. *A World Full of Animals: The Roger Caras Story*

Carrigan. *Jimmy Carter: Beyond the Presidency*
Charleston. *Armstrong Lands on the Moon*
Coles. *The Story of Ruby Bridges*
Goble. *Hau Kola Hello Friend*

Hargrove. *The Story of Jonas Salk*
Krull. *Wilma Unlimited*
Liestman. *Columbus Day*
Livingston. *Keep On Singing: A Ballad of Marian Anderson*

Lowery. *Wilma Mankiller*
McKissack. *Marian Anderson: A Great Singer*
Medearis. *Dare to Dream: Coretta Scott King*
Milton. *The Story of Hillary Rodham Clinton*

Peet. *Bill Peet: An Autobiography*
Pinkney. *Alvin Ailey*
Polacco. *Firetalking*
Prentzas. *Thurgood Marshall: Champion of Justice*
Rand. *Wilma Mankiller*

Ringgold. *Bonjour, Lonnie*
Simon. *Wilma P. Mankiller*
Thomson. *Katie Henio: Navajo Sheepherder*
Tolan. *Ralph Nader*
Weidt. *Oh, the Places He Went: A Story About Dr. Seuss*

Collective Biography

Cohen. *The Ghost of Elvis*
King. *First Facts About American Heroes*

Marzollo. *My First Book of Biographies*
Provensen. *The Buck Stops Here: The Presidents*

Rappaport. *Living Dangerously: American Women*

History

Adler. *A Picture Book of Jewish Holidays*
Alvarez. *The Official Baseball Hall of Fame Answer Book*
Ballard. *Exploring the Titanic*
Blue. *U.S. Air Force*
Bowler. *Trains*
Braine. *Drumbeat. . . Heartbeat, the Powwow*
Burns. *Mail*
Cashman. *Jewish Days and Holidays*
Caulkins. *Pets of the Presidents*
Chrisp. *The Farmer Through History*
Chrisp. *The Soldier Through History*
Climo. *City! New York*
Climo. *City! San Francisco*
Climo. *City! Washington, DC*

Donnelly. *A Wall of Names: The Story of the Vietnam Memorial*
English. *Transportation: Automobiles to Zeppelins*
Fisher. *Stars and Stripes: Our National Flag*
Fradin. *The Flag of the United States*
Gibbons. *The Great St. Lawrence Seaway*
Graham. *Spacecraft*
Hicks. *The Big Book of America*
Hill. *Our Century: 1970-1980*
Hopkins. *Hand in Hand: An American History Through Poetry*
Knight. *The Olympic Games*
Krementz. *A Visit to Washington, DC*
Maestro. *The Story of Money*
Maestro. *The Voice of the People*

Medearis. *Our People*
Munro. *Aircraft*
Reef. *The Lincoln Memorial*
Shuker-Haines. *Rights and Responsibilities: Using Your Freedom*
Spencer. *A Flag for Our Country*
Stein. *The Story of the Powers of the Supreme Court*
Stein. *The United Nations*
Stern. *The Congress: America's Lawmakers*
Suter. *Our Century: 1980-1990*
Swanson. *I Pledge Allegiance*
Waters. *The Story of the White House*
Weber. *Our Congress*
Wilson. *Visual Timeline of Transportation*
Wright. *The Story of the Vietnam Memorial*

Multimedia

CD-ROM

Children's Atlas of the United States

Inside the White House

Video

Adventures Behind the Scenes: At the Newspaper
African American Life
Christmas
Columbus Day

Independence Day
National Observances
Old Glory
Rosh Hashanah/Yom Kippur
U.S. Songs and Poems

United States Flag
Valentine's Day
Washington, D.C.

GRADE FOUR

Biography

Anderson. *Jackie Kennedy Onassis*

Anderson. *Maria Martinez: Pueblo Potter*

Applegate. *Benjamin O. Davis and Colin Powell*

130 Since 1975

Ashabranner. *The Times of My Life: A Memoir*
Bryant. *Marjory Stoneman Douglas: Voice of the Everglades*
Butts. *May Chinn: The Best Medicine*
Caras. *A World Full of Animals: The Roger Caras Story*
Carrigan. *Jimmy Carter: Beyond the Presidency*
Charleston. *Armstrong Lands on the Moon*
Chin. *When Justice Failed: The Fred Korematsu Story*
Ferris. *What I Had Was Singing: Marian Anderson*
Glassman. *Wilma Mankiller: Chief of the Cherokee Nation*

Goble. *Hau Kola Hello Friend*
Hargrove. *The Story of Jonas Salk*
Kent. *George Bush: Forty-First President*
Kent. *Ronald Reagan: Fortieth President*
Krull. *Wilma Unlimited*
Lazo. *Wilma Mankiller*
Livingston. *Keep On Singing: A Ballad of Marian Anderson*
McKissack. *Marian Anderson: A Great Singer*
Medearis. *Dare to Dream: Coretta Scott King*
Milton. *The Story of Hillary Rodham Clinton*
Patrick-Wexler. *Barbara Jordan*

Peet. *Bill Peet: An Autobiography*
Pemberton. *George Bush*
Polacco. *Firetalking*
Prentzas. *Thurgood Marshall: Champion of Justice*
Rand. *Wilma Mankiller*
Simon. *Wilma P. Mankiller*
Sipiera. *Gerald Ford: Thirty-Eighth President*
Thomson. *Katie Henio: Navajo Sheepherder*
Tolan. *Ralph Nader*
Wade. *James Carter: Thirty-Ninth President*
Wadsworth. *Susan Butcher: Sled Dog Racer*
Weidt. *Oh, the Places He Went: A Story About Dr. Seuss*

Collective Biography

Altman. *Extraordinary Black Americans*
Fireside. *Is There a Woman in the House. . . or Senate?*
King. *First Facts About American Heroes*
Krull. *Lives of the Writers: Comedies, Tragedies*
McKissack. *African-American Inventors*

Pascoe. *First Facts About the Presidents*
Pile. *Top Entrepreneurs and Their Businesses*
Provensen. *The Buck Stops Here: The Presidents*
Provensen. *My Fellow Americans*

Rappaport. *Living Dangerously: American Women*
Rubel. *The Scholastic Encyclopedia of the Presidents*
Wilkinson. *Scientists Who Changed the World*

History

Almonte. *Get Inside Baseball*
Alvarez. *The Official Baseball Hall of Fame Answer Book*
Ashabranner. *Always to Remember: Vietnam Veteran's Memorial*
Avakian. *A Historical Album of Massachusetts*
Avakian. *A Historical Album of New York*
Ballard. *Exploring the Titanic*
Blue. *The White House Kids*
Blue. *U.S. Air Force*
Bowler. *Trains*
Braine. *Drumbeat. . . Heartbeat, the Powwow*
Burke. *Food and Fasting*
Burns. *Mail*
Burns. *Money*
Carlson. *A Historical Album of Minnesota*

Cashman. *Jewish Days and Holidays*
Caulkins. *Pets of the Presidents*
Chrisp. *The Farmer Through History*
Chrisp. *The Soldier Through History*
Climo. *City! New York*
Climo. *City! San Francisco*
Climo. *City! Washington, DC*
Cocke. *A Historical Album of Virginia*
Cocke. *A Historical Album of Washington*
Compton. *Marriage Customs*
Donnelly. *A Wall of Names: The Story of the Vietnam Memorial*
Doubleday. *Salt Lake City*
English. *Transportation: Automobiles to Zeppelins*
Fichter. *The Space Shuttle*

Fisher. *Stars and Stripes: Our National Flag*
Fradin. *The Flag of the United States*
Gibbons. *The Great St. Lawrence Seaway*
Giblin. *Chimney Sweeps: Yesterday and Today*
Graham. *Spacecraft*
Hicks. *The Big Book of America*
Hill. *Our Century: 1970-1980*
The History of Moviemaking
Hoig. *It's the Fourth of July*
Hopkins. *Hand in Hand: An American History Through Poetry*
Kerr. *Keeping Clean*
Knight. *The Olympic Games*
Kurtz. *U.S. Army*
Lampton. *Epidemic*
Lawlor. *Where Will This Shoe Take You?*

Maestro. *The Story of Money*
Maestro. *The Voice of the People*
Munro. *Aircraft*
Prior. *Initiation Customs*
Prior. *Pilgrimages and Journeys*
Reef. *The Lincoln Memorial*
Reef. *The Supreme Court*
Richardson. *Inside the Metropolitan Museum*
Rowland-Warne. *Costume*
Rushton. *Birth Customs*
Rushton. *Death Customs*
Scott. *Funny Papers: Behind the Scenes of the Comics*
Shuker-Haines. *Rights and Responsibilities: Using Your Freedom*
Sloan. *Bismarck!*
Spencer. *A Flag for Our Country*

Stein. *The Story of the Powers of the Supreme Court*
Stein. *The United Nations*
Stern. *The Congress: America's Lawmakers*
Stones and Bones: How Archaeologists Trace Human Origins
Sullivan. *Children of Promise: African-American Literature and Art*
Suter. *Our Century: 1980-1990*
Swanson. *I Pledge Allegiance*
Topper. *A Historical Album of New Jersey*
Ward. *25 Great Moments*
Ward. *Who Invented the Game?*
Weber. *Our Congress*

Wilkinson. *Building*
Wills. *A Historical Album of Alabama*
Wills. *A Historical Album of California*
Wills. *A Historical Album of Connecticut*
Wills. *A Historical Album of Florida*
Wills. *A Historical Album of Illinois*
Wills. *A Historical Album of Nebraska*
Wills. *A Historical Album of Oregon*
Wills. *A Historical Album of Texas*
Wilson. *Visual Timeline of Transportation*
Wright. *The Story of the Vietnam Memorial*

Multimedia

CD-ROM

Children's Atlas of the United States
Exploring the Titanic

Her Heritage: A Biographical Encyclopedia of American History

Inside the White House
SkyTrip America
Total History

Video

Adventures Behind the Scenes: At the Newspaper
African American Life
African Americans
Christmas
Columbus Day

Great Black Innovators
Independence Day
Making It Happen: Masters of Invention
National Observances
Old Glory

Rosh Hashanah/Yom Kippur
U.S. Songs and Poems
United States Flag
Valentine's Day
Washington, D.C.

GRADE FIVE

Biography

Anderson. *Jackie Kennedy Onassis*
Anderson. *Maria Martinez: Pueblo Potter*
Applegate. *Benjamin O. Davis and Colin Powell*
Archbold. *Deep-Sea Explorer: Robert Ballard*
Arginteanu. *The Movies of Alfred Hitchcock*
Ashabranner. *The Times of My Life: A Memoir*
Bishop. *Ralph Ellison: Author*
Blau. *Betty Friedan: Feminist*
Blue. *Barbara Jordan: Politician*

Bredeson. *Jonas Salk: Discoverer of the Polio Vaccine*
Brown. *Romare Bearden: Artist*
Bryant. *Marjory Stoneman Douglas: Voice of the Everglades*
Butts. *May Chinn: The Best Medicine*
Cain. *Louise Nevelson: Sculptor*
Carrigan. *Jimmy Carter: Beyond the Presidency*
Charleston. *Armstrong Lands on the Moon*
Chin. *When Justice Failed: The Fred Korematsu Story*

Cole. *John Glenn: Astronaut and Senator*
Collins. *Farmworker's Friend: Cesar Chavez*
Conord. *John Lennon*
Curson. *Jonas Salk*
Dolan. *Susan Butcher and the Iditarod Trail*
Ferris. *What I Had Was Singing: Marian Anderson*
Glassman. *Wilma Mankiller: Chief of the Cherokee Nation*
Goble. *Hau Kola Hello Friend*
Hargrove. *The Story of Jonas Salk*
Heiss. *Barbara Bush*

Henry. *Betty Friedan: Fighter for Women's Rights*
Johnson. *Stokely Carmichael: The Story of Black Power*
Kallen. *Thurgood Marshall: A Dream of Justice for All*
Kent. *George Bush: Forty-First President*
Kent. *Ronald Reagan: Fortieth President*
Kittredge. *Barbara McClintock*
Kittredge. *Helen Hayes: Actress*
Kliment. *Ella Fitzgerald: Singer*
Krull. *Wilma Unlimited*
Lazo. *Wilma Mankiller*
Lewis-Ferguson. *Alvin Ailey, Jr.: A Life in Dance*
Meltzer. *Betty Friedan: A Voice for Women's Rights*
Milton. *The Story of Hillary Rodham Clinton*

Palmer. *Lena Horne: Entertainer*
Patrick-Wexler. *Barbara Jordan*
Peet. *Bill Peet: An Autobiography*
Pemberton. *George Bush*
Polacco. *Firetalking*
Prentzas. *Thurgood Marshall: Champion of Justice*
Probosz. *Martha Graham*
Rand. *Wilma Mankiller*
Richman. *James E. Carter*
Robbins. *Ronald W. Reagan*
Sandak. *The Reagans*
Schuman. *Elie Wiesel*
Schwartzberg. *Ronald Reagan*
Schwarz. *Wilma Mankiller*
Selfridge. *John F. Kennedy: Courage in Crisis*
Simon. *Wilma P. Mankiller*
Sipiera. *Gerald Ford: Thirty-Eighth President*
Slavin. *Jimmy Carter*

Speaker-Yuan. *Agnes de Mille: Choreographer*
Stefoff. *George H. Bush*
Sullivan. *Ronald Reagan*
Super. *Daniel "Chappie" James*
Tedards. *Marian Anderson: Singer*
Thomson. *Katie Henio: Navajo Sheepherder*
Tolan. *Ralph Nader*
Tomlinson. *Jonas Salk*
Wade. *James Carter: Thirty-Ninth President*
Wadsworth. *Susan Butcher: Sled Dog Racer*
Weidt. *Oh, the Places He Went: A Story About Dr. Seuss*
Yannuzzi. *Wilma Mankiller: Leader of the Cherokee Nation*

Collective Biography

Aaseng. *Close Calls: From the Brink of Ruin to Business Success*
Aaseng. *From Rags to Riches*
Aaseng. *True Champions: Great Athletes and Their Off-the-Field Heroics*
Altman. *Extraordinary Black Americans*
Blue. *People of Peace*
Faber. *Great Lives: American Government*
Fireside. *Is There a Woman in the House. . . or Senate?*
Glubok. *Great Lives: Painting*
Haskins. *Black Eagles: African Americans in Aviation*
King. *First Facts About American Heroes*

Krull. *Lives of the Writers: Comedies, Tragedies*
Mayberry. *Business Leaders Who Built Financial Empires*
McKissack. *African-American Inventors*
Morin. *Women of the U.S. Congress*
Pascoe. *First Facts About the Presidents*
Pile. *Top Entrepreneurs and Their Businesses*
Pile. *Women Business Leaders*
Provensen. *The Buck Stops Here: The Presidents*
Provensen. *My Fellow Americans*

Rappaport. *Living Dangerously: American Women*
Rennert. *Jazz Stars*
Rubel. *The Scholastic Encyclopedia of the Presidents*
Schraff. *American Heroes of Exploration and Flight*
Sills. *Inspirations: Stories About Women Artists*
Sills. *Visions: Stories About Women Artists*
Veglahn. *Women Scientists*
Wilkinson. *Scientists Who Changed the World*
Young. *Cy Young Award Winners*

History

Almonte. *Get Inside Baseball*
Alvarez. *The Official Baseball Hall of Fame Answer Book*
Ashabranner. *Always to Remember: Vietnam Veteran's Memorial*
Avakian. *A Historical Album of Massachusetts*
Avakian. *A Historical Album of New York*
Ballard. *Exploring the Titanic*
Biel. *The Challenger*

Blue. *U.S. Air Force*
Blue. *The White House Kids*
Bortz. *Catastrophe!: Great Engineering Failure—and Success*
Bowler. *Trains*
Braine. *Drumbeat. . . Heartbeat, the Powwow*
Burke. *Food and Fasting*
Burns. *Mail*
Burns. *Money*

Capek. *Artistic Trickery: The Tradition of the Trompe L'oeil Art*
Capek. *Murals: Cave, Cathedral, to Street*
Carlson. *A Historical Album of Minnesota*
Caulkins. *Pets of the Presidents*
Chrisp. *The Farmer Through History*
Chrisp. *The Soldier Through History*
Climo. *City! New York*

Climo. *City! San Francisco*
Climo. *City! Washington, DC*
Cocke. *A Historical Album of Virginia*
Cocke. *A Historical Album of Washington*
Colman. *Toilets, Bathtubs, Sinks, and Sewers*
Compton. *Marriage Customs*
Davies. *Transport: On Land, Road and Rail*
Doubleday. *Salt Lake City*
Emert. *Top Lawyers and their Famous Cases*
English. *Transportation: Automobiles to Zeppelins*
Fichter. *The Space Shuttle*
Garrett. *The Seventies*
Gibbons. *The Great St. Lawrence Seaway*
Giblin. *Chimney Sweeps: Yesterday and Today*
Giblin. *When Plague Strikes*
Graham. *Spacecraft*
Green. *Women in American Indian Society*
Greene. *Child Labor: Then and Now*
Grey. *The Eighties*
Hicks. *The Big Book of America*
Hill. *Our Century: 1970-1980*
Hirsch. *Taxation: Paying for Government*
The History of Moviemaking
Hoig. *It's the Fourth of July*
Hopkins. *Hand in Hand: An American History Through Poetry*
Hull. *Breaking Free*
Karl. *America Alive: A History*
Kerr. *Keeping Clean*
King. *The Gulf War*
Knight. *The Olympic Games*

Kurtz. *U.S. Army*
Lampton. *Epidemic*
Lawlor. *Where Will This Shoe Take You?*
Levi. *Cowboys of the Sky*
Lucas. *Civil Rights: The Long Struggle*
Maestro. *The Story of Money*
Maestro. *The Voice of the People*
Medearis. *Come This Far to Freedom*
Meltzer. *The Black Americans*
Morley. *Clothes: For Work, Play and Display*
Munro. *Aircraft*
Nash. *The Baseball Hall of Shame*
Perl. *From Top Hats to Baseball Caps, from Bustles to Blue Jeans*
Platt. *The Smithsonian Visual Timeline of Inventions*
Prior. *Initiation Customs*
Prior. *Pilgrimages and Journeys*
Reef. *The Lincoln Memorial*
Reef. *The Supreme Court*
Richardson. *Inside the Metropolitan Museum*
Ride. *To Space and Back*
Rowland-Warne. *Costume*
Rushton. *Birth Customs*
Rushton. *Death Customs*
Scott. *Funny Papers: Behind the Scenes of the Comics*
Shuker-Haines. *Rights and Responsibilities: Using Your Freedom*
Sloan. *Bismarck!*
Spencer. *A Flag for Our Country*
Steele. *Censorship*
Steele. *Kidnapping*
Stein. *The Iran Hostage Crisis*

Stein. *The Story of the Powers of the Supreme Court*
Stein. *The United Nations*
Stern. *The Congress: America's Lawmakers*
Stones and Bones: How Archaeologists Trace Human Origins
Sullivan. *Children of Promise: African-American Literature and Art*
Suter. *Our Century: 1980-1990*
Topper. *A Historical Album of New Jersey*
Turvey. *Inventions: Inventors and Ingenious Ideas*
Ward. *25 Great Moments*
Ward. *Who Invented The Game?*
Weber. *Our Congress*
Whitman. *Get Up and Go: American Road Travel*
Wilkinson. *Building*
Wills. *A Historical Album of Alabama*
Wills. *A Historical Album of California*
Wills. *A Historical Album of Connecticut*
Wills. *A Historical Album of Florida*
Wills. *A Historical Album of Illinois*
Wills. *A Historical Album of Nebraska*
Wills. *A Historical Album of Oregon*
Wills. *A Historical Album of Texas*
Wilson. *Visual Timeline of Transportation*
Wright. *The Story of the Vietnam Memorial*
Yepsen. *City Trains: America's Cities by Rail*

Multimedia

CD-ROM

Air and Space Smithsonian Dreams of Flight
Children's Atlas of the United States
Exploring the Titanic

Eyewitness Encyclopedia of Science
Her Heritage: A Biographical Encyclopedia of American History

Inside the White House
Portraits of American Presidents
SkyTrip America
Total History

Video

Adventures Behind the Scenes: At the Newspaper
African American Life
African Americans
Great Black Innovators
Making It Happen: Masters of Invention

National Observances
Old Glory
Our Federal Government: The Legislative Branch
Our Federal Government: The Presidency

Our Federal Government: The Supreme Court
U.S. Songs and Poems
United States Flag
Washington, D.C.
Western Europe: Our Legacy

GRADE SIX

Biography

Anderson. *Jackie Kennedy Onassis*

Applegate. *Benjamin O. Davis and Colin Powell*

Archbold. *Deep-Sea Explorer: Robert Ballard*

Ashabranner. *The Times of My Life: A Memoir*

Bishop. *Ralph Ellison: Author*

Blau. *Betty Friedan: Feminist*

Blue. *Barbara Jordan: Politician*

Bredeson. *Jonas Salk: Discoverer of the Polio Vaccine*

Brown. *Romare Bearden: Artist*

Bryant. *Marjory Stoneman Douglas: Voice of the Everglades*

Butts. *May Chinn: The Best Medicine*

Cain. *Louise Nevelson: Sculptor*

Carrigan. *Jimmy Carter: Beyond the Presidency*

Charleston. *Armstrong Lands on the Moon*

Chin. *When Justice Failed: The Fred Korematsu Story*

Cole. *John Glenn: Astronaut and Senator*

Conord. *John Lennon*

Curson. *Jonas Salk*

Dolan. *Susan Butcher and the Iditarod Trail*

Ferris. *What I Had Was Singing: Marian Anderson*

Fleischman. *The Abracadabra Kid: A Writer's Life*

Glassman. *Wilma Mankiller: Chief of the Cherokee Nation*

Hargrove. *The Story of Jonas Salk*

Haskins. *Thurgood Marshall: A Life for Justice*

Heiss. *Barbara Bush*

Henry. *Betty Friedan: Fighter for Women's Rights*

Henry. *Coretta Scott King: Keeper of the Dream*

Johnson. *Stokely Carmichael: The Story of Black Power*

Kallen. *Thurgood Marshall: A Dream of Justice for All*

Kent. *George Bush: Forty-First President*

Kent. *Ronald Reagan: Fortieth President*

Kittredge. *Barbara McClintock*

Kittredge. *Helen Hayes: Actress*

Kliment. *Ella Fitzgerald: Singer*

Lazo. *Wilma Mankiller*

Lewis-Ferguson. *Alvin Ailey, Jr.: A Life in Dance*

Meltzer. *Betty Friedan: A Voice for Women's Rights*

Meryman. *Andrew Wyeth*

Milton. *The Story of Hillary Rodham Clinton*

Morris. *The Reagan Way*

Palmer. *Lena Horne: Entertainer*

Patrick. *Coretta Scott King*

Patrick-Wexler. *Barbara Jordan*

Paulsen. *Woodsong*

Peet. *Bill Peet: An Autobiography*

Pemberton. *George Bush*

Pollack. *Shirley Chisholm*

Prentzas. *Thurgood Marshall: Champion of Justice*

Probosz. *Martha Graham*

Richman. *James E. Carter*

Robbins. *Ronald W. Reagan*

Sandak. *The Reagans*

Sawyer. *Marjory Stoneman Douglas*

Schuman. *Elie Wiesel*

Schwartzberg. *Ronald Reagan*

Schwarz. *Wilma Mankiller*

Selfridge. *John F. Kennedy: Courage in Crisis*

Sipiera. *Gerald Ford: Thirty-Eighth President*

Slavin. *Jimmy Carter*

Speaker-Yuan. *Agnes de Mille: Choreographer*

Stefoff. *George H. Bush*

Sullivan. *George Bush*

Sullivan. *Ronald Reagan*

Super. *Daniel "Chappie" James*

Tedards. *Marian Anderson: Singer*

Thomson. *Katie Henio: Navajo Sheepherder*

Tolan. *Ralph Nader*

Tomlinson. *Jonas Salk*

Wade. *James Carter: Thirty-Ninth President*

Wadsworth. *Susan Butcher: Sled Dog Racer*

Weidt. *Oh, the Places He Went: A Story About Dr. Seuss*

Whitelaw. *Mr. Civil Rights: The Story of Thurgood Marshall*

Yannuzzi. *Wilma Mankiller: Leader of the Cherokee Nation*

Collective Biography

Aaseng. *Close Calls: From the Brink of Ruin to Business Success*

Aaseng. *From Rags to Riches*

Aaseng. *Genetics: Unlocking the Secrets of Life*

Aaseng. *True Champions: Great Athletes and Their Off-the-Field Heroics*

Altman. *Extraordinary Black Americans*

Beard. *The Presidents in American History*

Blassingame. *The Look-It-Up Book of Presidents*

Blue. *People of Peace*

Burns. *Black Stars in Orbit: NASA's African American Astronauts*

Camp. *American Astronomers: Searchers and Wonderers*

Cush. *Artists Who Created Great Works*

Cush. *Women Who Achieved Greatness*

Faber. *Great Lives: American Government*

Fireside. *Is There a Woman in the House. . . or Senate?*

Glenn. *Discover America's Favorite Architects*

Glubok. *Great Lives: Painting*

Haskins. *Black Eagles: African Americans in Aviation*

King. *First Facts About American Heroes*

Krull. *Lives of the Writers: Comedies, Tragedies*

Mayberry. *Business Leaders Who Built Financial Empires*

McKissack. *African-American Inventors*

Morin. *Women of the U.S. Congress*

Morin. *Women Who Reformed Politics*

Myers. *Now Is Your Time*

Pascoe. *First Facts About the Presidents*

Pile. *Top Entrepreneurs and Their Businesses*

Pile. *Women Business Leaders*

Plowden. *Famous Firsts of Black Women*

Provensen. *The Buck Stops Here: The Presidents*

Provensen. *My Fellow Americans*

Rappaport. *Living Dangerously: American Women*

Rennert. *Book of Firsts: Leaders of America*

Rennert. *Jazz Stars*

Rennert. *Pioneers of Discovery*

Rubel. *The Scholastic Encyclopedia of the Presidents*

Schraff. *American Heroes of Exploration and Flight*

Sills. *Inspirations: Stories About Women Artists*

Sills. *Visions: Stories About Women Artists*

Smith. *Presidents in a Time of Change*

Veglahn. *Women Scientists*

Whitelaw. *They Wrote Their Own Headlines*

Wilkinson. *Scientists Who Changed the World*

Young. *Cy Young Award Winners*

Yount. *Women Aviators*

History

Almonte. *Get Inside Baseball*

Alvarez. *The Official Baseball Hall of Fame Answer Book*

Anderson. *Battles That Changed the Modern World*

Ashabranner. *Always to Remember: Vietnam Veteran's Memorial*

Avakian. *A Historical Album of Massachusetts*

Avakian. *A Historical Album of New York*

Ballard. *Exploring the Titanic*

Basinger. *American Cinema*

Biel. *The Challenger*

Blue. *U.S. Air Force*

Blue. *The White House Kids*

Bortz. *Catastrophe!: Great Engineering Failure—and Success*

Bowler. *Trains*

Braine. *Drumbeat. . . Heartbeat, the Powwow*

Burke. *Food and Fasting*

Burns. *Money*

Capek. *Artistic Trickery: The Tradition of the Trompe L'oeil Art*

Capek. *Murals: Cave, Cathedral, to Street*

Carlson. *A Historical Album of Minnesota*

Caulkins. *Pets of the Presidents*

Clements. *An Illustrated History of the World*

Climo. *City! New York*

Climo. *City! San Francisco*

Climo. *City! Washington, DC*

Cocke. *A Historical Album of Virginia*

Cocke. *A Historical Album of Washington*

Colman. *Toilets, Bathtubs, Sinks, and Sewers*

Compton. *Marriage Customs*

Cush. *Disasters That Shook the World*

Davies. *Transport: On Land, Road and Rail*

Doubleday. *Salt Lake City*

Emert. *Top Lawyers and their Famous Cases*

English. *Transportation: Automobiles to Zeppelins*

Fichter. *The Space Shuttle*

Garfunkel. *On Wings of Joy: The Story of Ballet*

Garrett. *The Seventies*

Gibbons. *The Great St. Lawrence Seaway*

Giblin. *Chimney Sweeps: Yesterday and Today*

Giblin. *When Plague Strikes*

Graham. *Spacecraft*

Green. *Women in American Indian Society*

Greene. *Child Labor: Then and Now*

Grey. *The Eighties*

Hakim. *All the People*

Hill. *Our Century: 1970-1980*

Hirsch. *Taxation: Paying for Government*

The History of Moviemaking

Hoig. *It's the Fourth of July*

Hopkins. *Hand in Hand: An American History Through Poetry*

Hull. *Breaking Free*

Karl. *America Alive: A History*

Kerr. *Keeping Clean*

Kimmel. *Bar Mitzvah: A Jewish Boy's Coming of Age*

King. *The Gulf War*

Kurtz. *U.S. Army*

Lampton. *Epidemic*

Lang. *Extremist Groups in America*

Lawlor. *Where Will This Shoe Take You?*

Leiner. *First Children: Growing Up in the White House*

Levi. *Cowboys of the Sky*

Lucas. *Civil Rights: The Long Struggle*

Maestro. *The Voice of the People*

Markham. *Inventions That Changed Modern Life*

Medearis. *Come This Far to Freedom*

Meltzer. *The Black Americans*

Mizell. *Think About Racism*

Morley. *Clothes: For Work, Play and Display*

Munro. *Aircraft*

Nash. *The Baseball Hall of Shame*

Patrick. *The Young Oxford Companion to the Supreme Court*

Perl. *From Top Hats to Baseball Caps, from Bustles to Blue Jeans*

Philip. *Singing America: Poems That Define A Nation*

Platt. *The Smithsonian Visual Timeline of Inventions*

Prior. *Initiation Customs*

Prior. *Pilgrimages and Journeys*

Reef. *The Lincoln Memorial*

Reef. *The Supreme Court*

Richardson. *Inside the Metropolitan Museum*

Ride. *To Space and Back*

Rowland-Warne. *Costume*

Rushton. *Birth Customs*

Rushton. *Death Customs*

Scott. *Funny Papers: Behind the Scenes of the Comics*

Shuker-Haines. *Rights and Responsibilities: Using Your Freedom*

Sloan. *Bismarck!*

St. George. *The White House: Cornerstone of a Nation*

Steele. *Censorship*

Steele. *Kidnapping*

Stein. *The Iran Hostage Crisis*

Stein. *The Story of the Powers of the Supreme Court*

Stern. *The Congress: America's Lawmakers*

Stones and Bones: How Archaeologists Trace Human Origins

Sullivan. *Children of Promise: African-American Literature and Art*

Suter. *Our Century: 1980-1990*

Time-Life. *African Americans: Voices of Triumph: Leadership*

Topper. *A Historical Album of New Jersey*

Turvey. *Inventions: Inventors and Ingenious Ideas*

Walker. *Hand, Heart, and Mind*

Warburton. *Railroads: Bridging the Continents*

Ward. *25 Great Moments*

Ward. *Who Invented The Game?*

Weber. *Our Congress*

Wheeler. *Events That Changed American History*

Whitman. *Get Up and Go: American Road Travel*

Wilkinson. *Building*

Wills. *A Historical Album of Alabama*

Wills. *A Historical Album of California*

Wills. *A Historical Album of Connecticut*

Wills. *A Historical Album of Florida*

Wills. *A Historical Album of Illinois*

Wills. *A Historical Album of Nebraska*

Wills. *A Historical Album of Oregon*

Wills. *A Historical Album of Texas*

Yepsen. *City Trains: America's Cities by Rail*

Multimedia

CD-ROM

Air and Space Smithsonian Dreams of Flight

Campaigns, Candidates and the Presidency

Daring to Fly!

Exploring the Titanic

Eyewitness Encyclopedia of Science

Her Heritage: A Biographical Encyclopedia of American History

History Through Art: 20th Century

Inside the White House

Portraits of American Presidents

SkyTrip America

Time Almanac of the 20th Century

Total History

The Way Things Work

Video

Adventures Behind the Scenes: At the Newspaper

African American Life

African Americans

Choosing a President

Great Black Innovators

Making It Happen: Masters of Invention

National Observances

Our Federal Government: The Legislative Branch

Our Federal Government: The Presidency

Our Federal Government: The Supreme Court

U.S. Songs and Poems

United States Flag

Washington, D.C.

Western Europe: Our Legacy

Women with Wings

BOOKS: AN ANNOTATED BIBLIOGRAPHY

A

1. Aaseng, Nathan. **Close Calls: From the Brink of Ruin to Business Success**. Minneapolis, MN: Lerner, 1990. 80p. $18.95. ISBN 0-8225-0682-3. 5 up

Many people who start businesses go bankrupt before their ideas take hold. Among the people who were unsuccessful in business (some starting several times) discussed here are Du Pont and his gunpowder production in the mid-1800s; Folger and his coffee after the Civil War; in the late 1800s, Heinz and his "57 varieties," Woolworth and his five-and-dime chain stores, and Dow and his chemical company; and in the twentieth century, 3M, Etch-a-Sketch, Hallmark, and Chrysler. Aaseng defines terms such as *stock*, *debt*, and *controlling interest* in the margins. Further Reading and Index.

2. Aaseng, Nathan. **From Rags to Riches: People Who Started Businesses from Scratch**. Minneapolis, MN: Lerner, 1990. 80p. $18.95. ISBN 0-8225-0679-3. 5-7

Many big businesses in the United States began when people tried to overcome their poor circumstances. Both James Gamble and William Procter came to the United States in the mid-eighteenth century as immigrants with no money. They met in Cincinnati, pooled their resources in candles and soap, and eventually created Ivory, a very pure floating soap. Dow and Jones became partners while reporting mining stocks before creating the Dow-Jones. In 1863, Richard Sears started a business selling watches rejected by a jeweler. Milton Hershey, son of a man who could not support his family, established himself with caramel candy and then decided to risk all on chocolate; when he died, he left millions to an orphanage he had founded. J. C. Penney refused to sell merchandise he could not endorse, and his business flourished before the Depression; later, he lost 40 million dollars but began again and died in 1971 at 95 as chairman of many stores. John Willard Marriott, born in 1900 in Utah, first sold soda on Washington, D.C., streets before opening Hot Shoppes, serving food on airplanes, and investing in motels. Other stories include Packard of Hewlett-Packard and Sculley of Apple Computer. For Further Reading and Index.

3. Aaseng, Nathan. **Genetics: Unlocking the Secrets of Life**. Minneapolis, MN: Oliver Press, 1996. 144p. $14.95. ISBN 1-881508-27-7. 6 up

The study of genetics has been a science for only 100 years. Not until the work of Charles Darwin in the nineteenth century and his publication of *The Origin of Species* was an explanation for heredity given other than what Aristotle had posited during the fifth century BC. The text looks at the nineteenth- and twentieth-century figures who developed the theories behind this science. They include Gregor Mendel and the discovery of dominant and recessive traits, Thomas Hunt Morgan and the chromosome, Oswald Avery and the transforming principle, James Watson and Francis Crick with their work on the double helix of DNA, and Har Gobind Khorana and synthetic genes. Nobel Prize Winners, Glossary, Bibliography, and Index.

4. Aaseng, Nathan. **Navajo Code Talkers**. New York: Walker, 1992. 128p. $14.95. ISBN 0-8027-8182-9. 5-9

In World War II, Navajo Marines devised and used a code against the Japanese that they based on their native language. The text recounts their story and adds information on Indian culture, Indian lore, the reservations, and the treatment of Indians in the military. The text includes details about the code creation as well as how the messages were sent. Photographs, Bibliography, and Index.

5. Aaseng, Nathan. **True Champions: Great Athletes and Their Off-the-Field Heroics**. New York: Walker, 1993. 130p. $15.85. ISBN 0-8027-8246-9. 5 up

The newspaper sports pages tell of heroics on courts, tracks, and fields. However, knowing that great athletes have sacrificed for others by being brave, generous, or caring off the field may be more important. Aaseng has found inspiring stories about many athletes, including Babe Ruth, Jackie Robinson, Jesse Owens, and other contemporary sports figures that he has incorporated in this text. Sources and Further Reading and Index.

6. Aaseng, Nathan. **You Are the General**. Minneapolis, MN: Oliver Press, 1994. 160p. $14.95. ISBN 1-881508-11-0. (Great Decisions). 6 up

The text presents the decisions that several twentieth-century generals had to make in the middle of battle. Readers can decide what they would do in the same situation. What they decide will help them understand those who had to make real and life-threatening decisions in the past. Generals include those from the Kaiser's army in August 1914, the German Reich in the summer of 1940, the Imperial Japanese Navy in June 1942, the Allied Forces in June 1944, the United Nations Forces in July 1950, the Vietnamese Communist Forces in July 1967, and the Coalition Forces of Operation Desert Storm in February 1991. Source Notes, Bibliography, and Index.

7. Aaseng, Nathan. **You Are the General II: 1800-1899**. Minneapolis, MN: Oliver Press, 1995. 160p. $14.95. ISBN 1-881508-25-0. (Great Decisions). 6 up

Battles are carefully created patterns of military strategy to gain territory, erode an enemy army's morale, and win a broader war. The text presents eight battles and the generals who fought them. The battles are the British Army at New Orleans in 1815, the Prussian Army at Waterloo in 1815, the U.S. Army in Mexico in August of 1847, the Allied Army in Crimea in September 1854, the Army of Northern Virginia at Chancellorsville in May 1863, the U.S. Army at Little Bighorn in June 1876, and the Boer Army in Natal in December 1899. Source Notes, Bibliography, and Index.

8. Abbink, Emily. **Missions of the Monterey Bay Area: San Carlos Borromeo de Carmelo, San Juan Bautista, Santa Cruz**. Minneapolis, MN: Lerner, 1996. 80p. $17.21. ISBN 0-8225-1928-3. (California Missions). 4-6

In the 1700s, Spain sent Roman Catholic priests to establish missions and presidios (forts) along the coast of Baja California and other areas of New Spain (present-day Southwestern United States and Mexico). Spain wanted the Indians to accept the Spanish ways and become loyal subjects. The Ohlone who lived in Monterey Bay lived a stable life until the Spanish arrived. Mission San Carlos Borromeo de Carmelo was Father Serra's headquarters. Santa Cruz struggled from the beginning, but San Juan Bautista was among the most productive of the 21 missions. Glossary, Chronology, and Index.

9. Accorsi, William, author/illustrator. **My Name Is Pocahontas**. New York: Holiday House, 1992. Unpaged. $14.95. ISBN 0-8234-0932-5. K-2

This fictional biography in first person tells the story of Pocahontas (1595?-1617). She talks of her early years, her friendship with John Smith, and her voyage to England with her husband, John Rolfe. Folk art illustrations complement the text.

10. Accorsi, William, author/illustrator. **Rachel Carson**. New York: Holiday House, 1993. Unpaged. $15.95. ISBN 0-8234-0994-5. K-2

The text introduces Rachel Carson (1907-1964), the environmentalist trained as a biologist, who realized that the world needed to conserve its natural resources before they were destroyed. The book presents highlights of her childhood and career. A note tells that financial and health problems plagued her. Chronology.

11. Acierno, Maria Armengol. **Children of Flight Pedro Pan**. New York: Silver Moon Press, 1994. 80p. $12.95. ISBN 1-881889-52-1. (Stories of the States). 3-5

In 1961, Maria, 10, and her younger brother José escape Fidel Castro's Cuba on the Pedro Pan ("Peter Pan") flight to the United States. They have to leave their parents and live with their cousin in Miami. Maria tries to adjust to this new culture but is especially disheartened when she hears that her parents may never be able to join them. Endpaper Maps, Historical Postscript, and Recommended Reading.

12. Ackerman, Karen. **Araminta's Paint Box**. Betsy Lewin, illustrator. New York: Atheneum, 1990. 32p. $12.95. ISBN 0-689-31462-0. 2-4

In 1847, Araminta and her family travel from Boston to California on a covered wagon. She is distressed when she discovers that her paint box has fallen off the wagon. On a journey of its own, it eventually arrives in her father's San Francisco office with gold pieces inside as payment for a snake-bite treatment that her father had given.

13. Ackerman, Karen. **The Tin Heart**. Michael Hays, illustrator. New York: Atheneum, 1990. 32p. $13.95. ISBN 0-689-31461-2. K-3

Mahaley's father operates a ferry on the northern side of the Ohio River, and Flora's father has a store on the opposite side in Kentucky. The two girls play with each other when Mahaley's father's ferry docks in Kentucky. They both wear half of a tin heart on a necklace that Flora's father made that symbolizes their friendship. When the Civil War begins, the fathers support opposite sides, but the girls want to see each other. After Mahaley falls overboard one night while her father is rescuing escaped slaves, the situation shows the fathers that the girls understand friendship better than they do.

14.   Adler, David A. **Benjamin Franklin: Printer, Inventor, Statesman**. Lyle Miller, illustrator. New York: Holiday House, 1992. 48p. $15.95. ISBN 0-8234-0929-5. (First Biography). 2-4

By using Franklin's maxims written in *Poor Richard's Almanack*, Adler attempts to illustrate the various lessons that events probably taught the young boy. When Franklin became apprenticed to his brother, a printer, he read voraciously, including a book proclaiming the virtues of vegetarianism; he promptly stopped eating meat. His brother's circumstances led him to give Benjamin his freedom, and Ben left for Philadelphia. Adler recounts his successes (and failures), including Franklin's illegitimate son and Franklin's approval of George III in 1761 when he attended the king's coronation in London. In France, Franklin wore a fur cap down to his eyebrows to cover severe eczema on his scalp, and the French unknowingly copied it as fashion. Franklin was a fair man, against slavery and Native American stereotypes. Index.

15.   Adler, David A. **George Washington: Father of Our Country**. Jacqueline Garrick, illustrator. New York: Holiday House, 1988. 48p. $14.95. ISBN 0-8234-0717-9. (First Biography). 3-5

Chapters in the text on George Washington (1732-1799) show the various foci of the biography. They include young George, the surveyor, commander of Virginia's army, his marriage, his readiness to fight, the Revolution, and his time as President. Index.

16.   Adler, David A. **Jackie Robinson: He Was the First**. Robert Casilla, illustrator. New York: Holiday House, 1989. 48p. $15.95; $5.95pa. ISBN 0-8234-0734-9; 0-8234-0799-3pa. (First Biography). 2-5

Born in Georgia in 1919, the grandson of a slave and son of a sharecropper, Jackie Robinson became the first Black man to play modern-day major league baseball. The adversity of his childhood (his father disappeared when Jackie was around six months old, and he moved with his mother and siblings to California soon after) made him aware of the need for family harmony. He excelled in sports like his brother Mack, who won a silver medal behind Jesse Owens at the 1936 Berlin Olympics. At UCLA he lettered in baseball, track, basketball, and football—the first student to do so. After serving in World War II, he began to play professional baseball in the Negro Leagues. In 1946, the Brooklyn Dodgers decided to integrate, and his promise that he would ignore verbal taunts gave him the position as first Black man in the modern major leagues. Before his death in 1972 at 50, he had experienced much heartache but also the pleasure of induction into the Baseball Hall of Fame. Index.

17.   Adler, David A. **The Number on My Grandfather's Arm**. New York: UAHC Press, 1987. 28p. $9.95. ISBN 0-8074-0328-8. 2-4

A young girl asks her grandfather about the number tattooed across his forearm. He tells her his story of World War II, not in graphic detail, but so that she can understand that he had a terrible time and almost lost his life during his imprisonment in Auschwitz, a concentration camp.

18.   Adler, David A. **One Yellow Daffodil**. Lloyd Bloom, illustrator. San Diego, CA: Gulliver, Harcourt Brace, 1995. Unpaged. $16. ISBN 0-15-200537-4. K-3

When children come into Mr. Kaplan's shop to buy flowers for *Shabbat* and then for Hanukkah, they invite him to dinner on the first night of the celebration. He does not want to come, but he does, and he begins to remember his childhood in Poland when he lost almost everything during World War II. He remembers seeing a yellow daffodil outside the concentration camp and thinking that if the flower could live, so could he. What he did not lose was a box with his menorah in it, and he gives the menorah to the children. *Notable Children's Trade Books in the Field of Social Studies*.

19.   Adler, David A. **Our Golda: The Story of Golda Meir**. Donna Ruff, illustrator. New York: Viking, 1984. 52p. $4.99pa. ISBN 0-14-032104-7pa. 3-7

Golda Meir (1898-1978) lived in Kiev, Russia, outside the Pale of Settlement where only skilled Jews, like her carpenter father, were allowed. At five, Golda had to return to the Pale when her father left for America. In Pinsk, amid the Cossacks and pogroms, they heard talk of a Jewish homeland. Meir's family went to Milwaukee to join her father, and she left for Denver to live with her sister before she and her husband went to Palestine in the 1920s. Meir spoke to crowds about Jewish causes from the time she was 11, and during the rest of her life she led others in the fight for Israel. In 1956, she became the Foreign Minister, and then Prime Minister in 1969. Before her death in 1978, she met with Anwar Sadat in one of many attempts to find peace between the Arabs and the Jews.

20.   Adler, David A. **A Picture Book of Abraham Lincoln**. John and Alexandra Wallner, illustrators. New York: Holiday House, 1990. Unpaged. $15.95. ISBN 0-8234-0731-4. (Picture Book Biography). 1-3

The text presents major ideas about the life of Abraham Lincoln (1809-1865), showing a man who loved to read, called his stepmother his "angel mother," built a flatboat, was distressed at seeing a slave auction, and led the nation as President. Important Dates.

21. Adler, David A. **A Picture Book of Benjamin Franklin**. John and Alexandra Wallner, illustrators. New York: Holiday House, 1990. Unpaged. $15.95; $5.95pa. ISBN 0-8234-0792-6; 0-8234-0882-5pa. (Picture Book Biography). 2-4

In 1706, another of the Franklin's 17 children was born, Benjamin. An inventor when very young, he devised swimming paddles to fit over his hands and increase his speed. And he always enjoyed writing—an endeavor that led to his success as a printer and newspaper publisher. After retirement, he invented the Franklin stove, bifocals, and the lightning rod. Additionally, he served the American colonies in England for 10 years before the Revolution, and in 1776 went to France to plead support from Louis XVI. At 81 in 1787, Franklin was the Constitutional Convention's oldest delegate. Before his death in 1790, he recorded his dislike of slavery in his autobiography. Important Dates.

22. Adler, David A. **A Picture Book of Davy Crockett**. John and Alexandra Wallner, illustrators. New York: Holiday House, 1996. Unpaged. $15.95. ISBN 0-8234-1212-1. (Picture Book Biography). K-3

Davy Crockett (1786-1836) lived a life that became a legend. The text looks at the facts and fiction about a man who boasted but who was also forthright and honest. Important Dates.

23. Adler, David A. **A Picture Book of Eleanor Roosevelt**. Robert Casilla, illustrator. New York: Holiday House, 1991. Unpaged. $15.95; $5.95pa. ISBN 0-8234-0856-6; 0-8234-1157-5pa. (Picture Book Biography). K-2

Born to wealthy parents in 1884, Eleanor Roosevelt seemed destined to a life of happiness, but both her parents died before she was 10, and she had to live with her stern grandmother. As a young woman, she married a distant cousin, Franklin Delano Roosevelt. The most famous man in her family at that time was her uncle, President Theodore Roosevelt. When her husband became President during the Depression, she publicly spoke for women's rights and the rights of Indians, the homeless, young people, and minorities. She even severed her membership with the Daughters of the American Revolution when the group refused to let the African American singer Marian Anderson perform in Constitution Hall. Roosevelt arranged for Anderson to sing at the Lincoln Memorial instead. President Truman called her "First Lady of the World." Important Dates. *Notable Children's Trade Books in the Field of Social Studies.*

24. Adler, David A. **A Picture Book of Frederick Douglass**. Samuel Byrd, illustrator. New York: Holiday House, 1993. Unpaged. $15.95; $6.95pa. ISBN 0-8234-1002-1; 0-8234-1205-9pa. (Picture Book Biography). 2-5

Born around 1817, Frederick Bailey had a slave mother and an unidentified white father, but he was orphaned at seven. His new female owner, evidently unaware of the law against slaves learning to read, taught him. When he eventually escaped via the Underground Railroad to New Bedford, Massachusetts, he took the name Johnson and then Douglass. His reading of an antislavery newspaper led to a job and his writing an autobiography. But fear of capture as a runaway slave sent him to England. There, people bought his freedom, and when he returned to Massachusetts, he started his own antislavery newspaper, *The North Star.* He wrote two more books and married a white woman after the death of his first wife, "like my father," as he said. Important Dates.

25. Adler, David A. **A Picture Book of George Washington**. John and Alexandra Wallner, illustrators. New York: Holiday House, 1989. Unpaged. $15.95; $6.95pa. ISBN 0-8234-0732-2; 0-8234-0800-0pa. (Picture Book Biography). 2-4

This account of George Washington's life (1732-1799) lists its public highlights. Illustrations complement the text. Important Dates.

26. Adler, David A. **A Picture Book of Harriet Tubman**. Samuel Byrd, illustrator. New York: Holiday House, 1991. Unpaged. $15.95; $6.95pa. ISBN 0-8234-0926-0; 0-8234-1065-Xpa. (Picture Book Biography). 2-4

Born in either 1820 or 1821 in Maryland, Harriet Tubman heard about Nat Turner's Rebellion in 1831 and that he was hanged. She later married a free man but lived near her owner before she decided to follow the Underground Railroad to Pennsylvania. There she got jobs, but she returned to the South 19 times between 1850 and 1860 to lead more than 300 slaves to freedom. John Brown called her "General Tubman," and others called her "Moses." None of her "passengers" died on the way. She was more than 90 years old when she died in 1913. Important Dates.

27. Adler, David A. **A Picture Book of Helen Keller**. John and Alexandra Wallner, illustrators. New York: Holiday House, 1990. Unpaged. $15.95; $5.95pa. ISBN 0-8234-0818-3; 0-8234-0950-3pa. (Picture Book Biography). 1-3

Left blind and deaf from an illness when she was one-and-a-half years old, Helen Keller (1880-1968) was fortunate to have parents who could find a teacher for her. Anne Mansfield Sullivan dedicated her life to Keller and gave her words with which to communicate. Keller published several books and received the Presidential Medal of Freedom. Important Dates.

28.   Adler, David A. **A Picture Book of Jackie Robinson**. Robert Casilla, illustrator. New York: Holiday House, 1994. Unpaged. $15.95; $5.95pa. ISBN 0-8234-1122-2; 0-8234-0799-3pa. (Picture Book Biography). 1-3

Jack Roosevelt Robinson (1919-1972), youngest of five, was born in Georgia. His father left home for Florida when Jackie was six months old and never returned. The family had to leave their sharecropping home and moved to California. Jackie starred in sports throughout school and college, becoming the first four-letter winner at the University of California at Los Angeles. His army career ended after World War II because he was mistreated. He played baseball for a Negro League team, and soon the president of the Brooklyn Dodgers hired him to be the first Black player in modern major league baseball. In spite of fierce opposition from players and fans, Robinson became Rookie of the Year in 1947 and Most Valuable Player in 1949. He retired in 1956, and in 1962 was the first African American inducted into the Baseball Hall of Fame. Author's Note and Important Dates.

29.   Adler, David A. **A Picture Book of Jesse Owens**. Robert Casilla, illustrator. New York: Holiday House, 1992. Unpaged. 15.95; $5.95pa. ISBN 0-8234-0966-X; 0-8234-1066-8pa. (Picture Book Biography). 2-4

Born in Alabama as a grandson of slaves and a son of sharecroppers, Jesse (actually J. C.) Owens (1913-1980) achieved international recognition when he won four gold medals at the 1936 Berlin Olympics. He owed his success to his junior high track coach, who encouraged him to run not for the day but for "four years from Friday." Victories at Ohio State and three world records and a tie for a fourth in 1935 led to Berlin. At the games, Hitler refused to recognize the achievements of Black athletes. Owens bravely faced more prejudice before his death. Important Dates.

30.   Adler, David A. **A Picture Book of Jewish Holidays**. Linda Heller, illustrator. New York: Holiday House, 1981. 32p. $14.95; $5.95pa. ISBN 0-8234-0396-3; 0-8234-0756-Xpa. K-3

This book introduces terms and explanations for important holidays in the Jewish tradition for people of all religions. They include the Sabbath, Rosh Hashanah, Yom Kippur, Sukkot, Simhat Torah, Hanukkah, Tu bi-Shevat, Purim, Passover, Yom Ha-Azma'ut, Tishah Bov, and others. Glossary.

31.   Adler, David A. **A Picture Book of John F. Kennedy**. New York: Holiday House, 1991. Unpaged. $15.95; $5.95pa. ISBN 0-8234-0884-1; 0-8234-0976-7pa. (Picture Book Biography). 2-4

One of nine children from a wealthy Catholic family, John Kennedy (1917-1963) had various illnesses as a youngster but enjoyed athletics and disliked studying until his third year at Harvard. Before he became President of the United States, he wrote two books about the state of the world and his service in World War II. As President, he was concerned about civil rights, the arts, the space program, and establishing the Peace Corps. Important Dates.

32.   Adler, David A. **A Picture Book of Martin Luther King, Jr.** Robert Casilla, illustrator. New York: Holiday House, 1989. Unpaged. $15.95; $5.95pa. ISBN 0-8234-0770-5; 0-8234-0847-7pa. (Picture Book Biography). 2-4

In Atlanta, Georgia, on January 15, 1929, Martin Luther King, Jr. began his journey through a segregated world. His intelligence led him through Morehouse College and Boston University on his way to preach in Montgomery, Alabama, where Rosa Parks had been arrested for sitting in the whites-only section of a bus. King's peaceful marches for freedom there and in Atlanta culminated in 1963 with the March on Washington, where he gave his "I Have a Dream" speech. In 1964, he won the Nobel Peace Prize. James Earl Ray assassinated him in 1968. Important Dates. *Notable Children's Trade Books in the Field of Social Studies*.

33.   Adler, David A. **A Picture Book of Patrick Henry**. John C. Wallner, illustrator. New York: Holiday House, 1995. Unpaged. $15.95. ISBN 0-8234-1187-7. (Picture Book Biography). K-3

The text looks at the life of Patrick Henry (1736-1799), who gained the support of his Virginia colleagues and led them to form a militia to fight for the colonies by declaring "Give me liberty or give me death." He also served in the Continental Congress and as Virginia's governor. Important Dates.

34.   Adler, David A. **A Picture Book of Paul Revere**. New York: Holiday House, 1995. Unpaged. $15.95; $6.95pa. ISBN 0-8234-1144-3; 0-8234-129-4pa. (Picture Book Biography). 1-3

Paul Revere (1735-1818) left school at 13 to work for his silversmith father and was soon praised for the sound of bells he created. He added other trades such as cleaning and making teeth and goldsmithing to support his ever-growing family. His first wife died after giving birth to eight children; his second wife had eight more. Six of the children died young. Revere never reached Lexington (the "ride" for which he is famous), but he served in the army in Boston until 1781. Author's Note and Important Dates.

35.   Adler, David A. **A Picture Book of Robert E. Lee**. John and Alexandra Wallner, illustrators. New York: Holiday House, 1994. Unpaged. $15.95. ISBN 0-8234-1111-7. (Picture Book Biography). 3-4

Robert Edward Lee, son of "Light-Horse Harry" Lee and Ann Hill Carter Lee, was born in 1807, three years before his father lost all of the family's fortune. His father left when Lee was six and died while returning home. Robert Lee attended West Point, and soon after he began his military career, he showed his brilliance in the Mexican War. He hated war, however, because of its destruction of families. When the states disagreed over slavery, Lee sided with those who were against it, having freed all of his own slaves. But he was loyal to Virginia and did not want to fight against his family and friends, so he fought for the South in the Civil War. He preferred to attack rather than wait. At the end of the war, he realized that one more day would be too much of a sacrifice, so he surrendered. Always admired and dignified, he died in 1870 after serving as president of Washington College (now Washington and Lee) in Lexington, Virginia.

36.   Adler, David A. **A Picture Book of Rosa Parks**. Robert Casilla, illustrator. New York: Holiday House, 1993. Unpaged. $15.95; $5.95pa. ISBN 0-8234-1041-2; 0-8234-1177-Xpa. (Picture Book Biography). 2-4

In 1955, Rosa Parks (b. 1913) confronted a bus driver before she refused to move to the back of the bus. Twelve years before, she would not reenter a bus in the back after paying at the front door—and the bus driver was the same one both times. For many African Americans, her silent clash was the beginning of the Civil Rights movement because her action that day resulted in the year long Montgomery bus boycott (organized by Dr. Martin Luther King, Jr.). Parks is often called the "Mother of the Civil Rights Movement" because she continued to fight discrimination from Detroit until she was too old. Illustrations, including one of the Ku Klux Klan, enhance the text. Author's Notes.

37.   Adler, David A. **A Picture Book of Sitting Bull**. Samuel Byrd, illustrator. New York: Holiday House, 1993. 28p. $15.95. ISBN 0-8234-1044-7. (Picture Book Biography). K-3

Sitting Bull (1834?-1890) was the Sioux chief who worked to maintain the rights of Native Americans and who led the defeat of General Custer at the Little Bighorn in 1876. He was a Hunkpapa of the Dakota Sioux.

38.   Adler, David A. **A Picture Book of Sojourner Truth**. Gershom Griffith, illustrator. New York: Holiday House, 1994. Unpaged. $15.95; $6.95pa. ISBN 0-8234-1072-2; 0-8234-1262-9pa. (Picture Book Biography). 2-4

Sojourner Truth (1797-1883) was born a slave named Isabella, but she renamed herself after she became free. When accused of poisoning the leader of a religious community that she had joined, she decided to leave New York and "sojourn" or visit different places and preach against the evils of slavery, for the rights of women, and about her religious views. She raised money to feed African American soldiers during the Civil War and helped care for slaves who had escaped north to freedom. Important Dates. *Notable Children's Trade Books in the Field of Social Studies.*

39.   Adler, David A. **A Picture Book of Thomas Alva Edison**. John Wallner and Alexandra Wallner, illustrators. New York: Holiday House, 1996. Unpaged. $15.95. ISBN 0-8234-1246-6. (Picture Book Biography). 1-3

The text provides background on Thomas Alva Edison (1847-1931) and his dedication to his experiments and his inventions. Important Dates.

40.   Adler, David A. **A Picture Book of Thomas Jefferson**. John Wallner and Alexandra Wallner, illustrators. New York: Holiday House, 1990. Unpaged. $15.95; $6.95pa. ISBN 0-8234-0791-8; 0-8234-0881-7pa. (Picture Book Biography). 2-4

This overview of Thomas Jefferson's life (1743-1826) emphasizes his main achievements, including his education. He invented the swivel chair and the folding ladder, wrote the Declaration of Independence, and established the University of Virginia. Some call him the "Father of Our Democracy" because he believed people should govern themselves and be free.

41.   Adler, David A. **A Picture Book of Thurgood Marshall**. Robert Casilla, illustrator. New York: Holiday House, 1997. Unpaged. $6.95pa. ISBN 0-8234-1308-Xpa. (Picture Book Biography). 1-3

Thurgood Marshall (1908-1993) became a justice of the Supreme Court after helping to establish the Civil Rights movement. The text introduces his life and his accomplishments. Important Dates.

42.   Adler, David A. **Remember Betsy Floss: And Other Colonial Riddles**. John Wallner, illustrator. New York: Holiday House, 1987. 64p. $12.95. ISBN 0-8234-0664-4. 2-6

Although the text is a collection of riddles with illustrations of people who lived during colonial times, it gives solid history underneath the humor. It is an entertaining view of the times, and to understand the riddles, one must know something of the history itself. *International Reading Association Children's Choices.*

43. Adler, David A. **Thomas Alva Edison: Great Inventor**. Lyle Miller, illustrator. New York: Holiday House, 1990. 48p. $14.95. ISBN 0-8234-0820-5. (First Biography). 2-4

Thomas Alva Edison (1847-1931) worked as a telegraph operator before he became a full-time inventor. After he opened his laboratory in Menlo Park, New Jersey, he invented the phonograph and the electric light bulb as well as a thousand other items for which he received patents. Index.

44. Alexander, Lloyd. **The Philadelphia Adventure**. New York: Dutton, 1990. 150p. $12.95. ISBN 0-525-44564-1. 6-9

Before the 1876 Centennial Exposition in Philadelphia, the President calls Vesper Holly and asks her to help stop an expected kidnapping. Don Pedro, a Brazilian leader in town, has brought his children, and someone has threatened them. Vesper and her friends find the children and reach the convention hall just in time to defuse dynamite set to explode.

45. Aliki, author/illustrator. **The Many Lives of Benjamin Franklin**. New York: Simon & Schuster, 1988. 32p. $12.95; $5.95pa. ISBN 0-671-66119-1; 0-671-66491-3pa. K-3

Aliki illustrates her text with cartoons that embellish the events and inventions from Benjamin Franklin's life (1706-1790), including sayings from *Poor Richard's Almanack*. Through loaning books to his friends, Franklin started the first lending library. Aliki clarifies his interests, profession, family, and statesmanship.

46. Aliki, author/illustrator. **The Story of Johnny Appleseed**. New York: Aladdin, 1963. 32p. $5.95pa. ISBN 0-671-6746-7pa. K-3

John Chapman, born in Massachusetts in the 1700s, decided to walk west, planting apple trees. He believed in the friendliness of humans, and Indians confirmed his trust when they nursed him back to health after finding him ill. He continued to plant trees in his travels until his death.

47. Aliki, author/illustrator. **A Weed Is a Flower: The Life of George Washington Carver**. New York: Simon & Schuster, 1988. Unpaged. $14; $5.95pa. ISBN 0-671-66118-3; 0-671-66490-5pa. K-3

Born the son of slaves in 1860 and soon separated from his parents by death and deviousness, Carver asked questions about almost everything in the homes of those who raised him. Neighbors called him the "Plant Doctor" when he was very young and asked his advice because his own garden grew so beautifully. Although unable to save enough money for college until he was 30, he finally went, and decided not to be an artist but to be an agriculturist. He taught and researched at Tuskegee, finding more than 100 things that could be made from sweet potatoes and dispelling the idea that peanuts were only "monkey food." He worked until he died at 80.

48. Allen, John Logan. **Jedediah Smith and the Mountain Men of the American West**. New York: Chelsea House, 1991. 120p. $19.95. ISBN 0-7910-1301-4. (World Explorers). 5 up

Among the men who were called mountain men were John Colter, George Drouillard, Andrew Henry, Edward Rose, Wilson Price Hunt, Robert Stuart, Jim Bridger, Thomas "Peg Leg" Smith, "old" Hugh Glass, James Ohio Pattie, Kit Carson, and Joseph Walker. When Jedediah Smith went on an expedition to Santa Fe in 1831, a band of Comanche Indians killed him. Photographs and reproductions enhance the text. Chronology, Further Reading, and Index.

49. Allen, Paula Gunn, and Patricia Clark Smith. **As Long as the Rivers Flow: The Stories of Nine Native Americans**. New York: Scholastic, 1996. 328p. $15.95. ISBN 0-590-47869-9. 5-8

This collective biography covers nine Native Americans who lived from the seventeenth century to the present. From a variety of professions, they include Geronimo (1829-1909), Will Rogers (1879-1935), Maria Tallchief, Wilma Mankiller (b. 1945), Michael Naranjo, and Louise Erdich. Photographs, Bibliography, and Index.

50. Allen, Zita. **Black Women Leaders of the Civil Rights Movement**. New York: Franklin Watts, 1996. 128p. $22.70. ISBN 0-531-11271-3. (African-American Experience). 6 up

Included here are women whose efforts are often overlooked in texts devoted to the contributions of men in the Civil Rights movement. These women participated in the desegregation of schools, buses, lunch counters, and other facilities and represented sharecroppers, students, domestics, teachers, and college professors. Some of them are nationally known such as Charlayne Hunter Gault and Marian Wright Edelman. Photographs, Notes, and Index.

51. Almonte, Paul. **Get Inside Baseball**. Donna Salvini, illustrator. New York: Silver Moon Press, 1994. 74p. $13.95. ISBN 1-881889-55-6. (Get Inside). 4-6

Almonte suggests that baseball came from England and evolved from the game called "rounders," although Abner Doubleday is often credited with inventing it. A poem called "Base Ball," published in England in 1744, supports this idea. Alexander Cartwright invented modern baseball. The text discusses the various types of leagues, the seasons, memorabilia, and the World Series. An appendix lists baseball records. Glossary and Bibliography.

52. Alphin, Elaine Marie. **The Ghost Cadet**. New York: Henry Holt, 1991. 160p. $13.95. ISBN 0-8050-1614-7. 4-6

In this historical fantasy, Benjy, 12, and his sister Fran, 16, have to spend their spring vacation with their grandmother, whom they have not previously met. Benjy likes history so he goes to the nearby battlefield. There he finds a friend, Hugh, a Virginia military cadet. Benjy discovers that Hugh was killed in the 1864 Battle of New Market in the Civil War. Hugh looks for a gold watch he had hidden just before he died, and Benjy helps him find it.

53. Alter, Judith. **Eli Whitney**. New York: Franklin Watts, 1990. 64p. $18.43. ISBN 0-531-10875-9. (A First Book). 4-6

Although he is best known for his invention of the cotton gin in 1793, Eli Whitney (1765-1825) also invented and established the concept of standardized parts when he began to produce muskets for the military. Self-taught, he learned enough Latin and Greek to pass Yale's arduous entrance exams, and after graduation he planned to take a teaching job in South Carolina. He never reached that state because he found out about cotton in Georgia. Most of his life, he fought violations of his cotton gin patents but eventually gave up those pursuits to become the Father of the American system of interchangeable manufacturing. Not until late in life did he marry and have children. He died of poor health while his sons were still young. Further Reading, Glossary, and Index.

54. Alter, Judith. **Growing Up in the Old West**. New York: Franklin Watts, 1989. 64p. $18.43. ISBN 0-531-10746-9. (A First Book). 4-6

Beginning in the 1840s, families took wagon trains across the United States. They got up at 4 AM and traveled from 8 AM until evening. The main dangers were not Indians but accidental shootings and disease. Those settling in the North built log houses, and those on the prairie took an acre of sod to build a 16 x 20-foot home. Males worked outside, hauling water and fuel (either wood or cow "patties" and buffalo "chips"), and females spent much time cooking and sewing. Everyone worked to survive. They feared fire, locusts, Indians (until the 1880s), and outlaws. No one had time to be bored. Further Reading and Index.

55. Alter, Judith. **Women of the Old West**. New York: Franklin Watts, 1989. 64p. $18.43. ISBN 0-531-10756-6. (A First Book). 4-6

Not until the 1830s did the first white men go west, and by the 1840s women rode wagon trains going to California or Oregon. Among the women who went were homesteaders' wives, laundresses, officers' wives, teachers, physicians, lawyers, actresses, reformers, outlaws, and cowgirls. Each of the nine chapters introduces a group. Revealing a slightly different Old West are such women as Fanny Keely (captured by the Indians), Biddy Mason (a slave who became a wealthy woman), Libbie Custer (wife of General Custer), Georgia Arbuckle Fix (physician), Clara Shortridge Foltz (lawyer), Lola Montez (actress born in Ireland who commanded ticket prices of $65 during the 1850s in San Francisco), Esther Hobart McQuigg Morris (woman's suffragette), Carry Nation (alcohol reformation), Calamity Jane and Belle Starr (outlaws), and Molly Goodnight ("Mother of the Panhandle"). Further Reading and Index.

56. Altman, Linda. **The Pullman Strike of 1894: Turning Point for American Labor**. Brookfield, CT: Millbrook Press, 1994. 63p. $15.40. ISBN 1-56294-346-4. 5-8

In 1894, Pullman Palace Car announced pay cuts for everyone, but did not lower prices in the company store where employees shopped. The company continued to pay dividends to stockholders, and workers decided to strike because of the unfair practices. The strike began on May 11, 1894, and by the end of June it had become a historical event. In addition to discussing the strike and the major figures involved, Altman also examines the beginning of industrialization in the nation and the people who made the most money from it. Chronology, Further Reading, Sources, and Index.

57. Altman, Susan. **Extraordinary Black Americans: From Colonial to Contemporary Times**. Chicago: Childrens Press, 1989. 240p. $33.80; $15.95pa. ISBN 0-516-00581-2; 0-516-40851-0pa. 4 up

From the slave Estevanico, who helped guide the first expedition through the American Southwest on its way to the Seven Cities of Cibola, to Jesse Jackson and Toni Morrison, these vignettes pinpoint the contributions of 85 Black Americans. Short essays introduce the historical periods and topics—slave uprisings, Black Seminoles, the Underground Railroad, the Emancipation Proclamation, Black Civil War soldiers, Reconstruction, the Little Rock Nine, sit-ins, Freedom Riders, the 1963 march on Washington, the Black Power movement, and the "I Have a Dream" speech. Bibliography and Index.

58. Alvarez, Mark. **The Official Baseball Hall of Fame Answer Book**. New York: Simon & Schuster, 1989. 96p. $6.95pa. ISBN 0-671-67377-7pa. 3 up

In his answers to 76 questions on baseball, Alvarez tells anecdotes about each situation, sometimes dispelling myths, sometimes offering suggestions on how to shape the statistics. Questions on hitters, runners, types of pitches, the "Black Sox," ballparks, crowds, uniforms, plays, and other topics reveal baseball facts.

59. Ames, Mildred. **Grandpa Jake and the Grand Christmas**. New York: Scribner's, 1990. 96p. $12.95. ISBN 0-684-19241-1. 4-7

After her mother dies, Lizzie, 12, worries about her father finding work during the Depression, about the rising costs of her ballet lessons, and about she and her sister and father having to go to Aunt Mary Margaret's home for Christmas. Their aunt gives them hand-me-downs and thinks they should be grateful. Then Lizzie's Grandpa Jake, a man she has never known, arrives unexpectedly, saying they will have the best Christmas ever, with cookies and presents. Grandpa Jake does make cookies, but he leaves before Christmas without fulfilling all of his promises. His influence, however, encourages Lizzie to tell her father that she and her sister prefer a Christmas at home with only the three of them. *School Library Journal Best Book.*

60. Amoss, Berthe. **The Mockingbird Song**. New York: HarperCollins, 1988. 123p. $12.95. ISBN 0-06-020062-6. 5-7

Lindy, 11, mourns for her mother, who deserted her in the 1930s, and takes out her frustration on her step-mother Millie. When Millie becomes pregnant, Lindy goes to live with her neighbor, Miss Ellie, who is confined to a wheelchair. When the baby arrives prematurely, Millie stays weak, and Lindy goes to the house after school to help her. Miss Ellie reveals why she never married. She helps Lindy realize that her mother did not leave because of anything Lindy did, and Lindy begins to adjust to her new family.

61. Anderson, Catherine Corley. **Jackie Kennedy Onassis**. Minneapolis, MN: Lerner, 1995. 88p. $18.95; $6.95pa. ISBN 0-8225-2885-1; 0-8225-9714-4pa. 4-9

Jacqueline Kennedy Onassis (1929-1994) grew up in wealthy New England society, where she learned to be an excellent horsewoman. Then she attended Vassar and studied in France at the Sorbonne. She became fluent in French, Italian, and Spanish. She spent her senior year at George Washington University in Washington, D.C. After graduation, she became an Inquiring Reporter for the *Washington Times-Herald* (much to her mother's dismay). She met John Fitzgerald Kennedy, a congressman, and they married. She became the First Lady of the United States when he became president. His assassination in 1963 made her a widow with a son and daughter, John and Caroline. In 1968, she married Aristotle Onassis, a Greek shipping magnate. When he died in 1975, her inheritance guaranteed financial comfort. As an editor at Viking and Doubleday, she became close friends with Maurice Tempelsman. Always in the public eye but disliking scrutiny, she persevered. Perhaps she remembered her mother's warning to remount the horse as soon as she fell. Epilogue.

62. Anderson, Catherine Corley. **John F. Kennedy: Young People's President**. Minneapolis, MN: Lerner, 1991. 144p. $22.95. ISBN 0-8225-4904-2. 5-7

John Fitzgerald Kennedy (1917-1963) served as President of the United States from 1961 to 1963, when he was assassinated in Dallas. He was lively and witty, and the text shows these attributes. Bibliography and Index.

63. Anderson, Dale. **Battles That Changed the Modern World**. Austin, TX: Raintree/Steck-Vaughn, 1994. 48p. $15.96. ISBN 0-8114-4928-9. (20 Events Series). 6 up

Since the beginning of the nineteenth century, 20 battles have had a great impact on the world. In two-page spreads, Anderson presents the important aspects of these battles. They are Waterloo (1812), Antietam (1862), Gettysburg (1863), Sedan (1870), Little Bighorn (1875), Tsushima Strait (1905), the Marne (1914), Guernica (1937), Nanking (1937), Britain (1940), El Alamein (1942), Midway (1942), Stalingrad (1941-1943), Normandy (1944), the Chinese Civil War (1947-1949), Inchon (1950), Dien Bien Phu (1954), the Six-Day War (1967), the Tet Offensive (1968), and Desert Storm (1991). Glossary, Suggested Readings, and Index.

64. Anderson, Dale. **Explorers Who Found New Worlds**. Austin, TX: Raintree/Steck-Vaughn, 1994. 48p. $15.96. ISBN 0-8114-4931-9. (20 Events Series). 6 up

Anderson identifies 20 explorers who have found places that changed the lives of people throughout the world and presents profiles of them in two-page spreads. The explorers discussed here start with Marco Polo (Venice) in the thirteenth century. In the fifteenth century, Christopher Columbus (Portugal) and Vasco da Gama (Portugal) set forth. Their work continued in the sixteenth century with Vasco Nuñez de Balboa (Spain), Ferdinand Magellan (Portugal), Francisco Vasquez de Coronado (Spain), and Jacques Cartier (France). In the seventeenth century, Henry Hudson (England), Louis Jolliet and Jacques Marquette (France), and René-Robert Cavelier, Sieur de La Salle (France) explored North America. The eighteenth-century explorers were Vitus Bering (Denmark), James Cook (England), and Alexander Mackenzie (Scotland). The nineteenth century began with Americans Meriwether Lewis and William Clark, and continued with David Livingstone (Scotland), Richard Francis Burton and John Hanning Speke (England), John McDouall Stuart (Scotland and Australia), Sven Hedin (Sweden), and Robert Peary (America). The twentieth century boasts Roald Amundsen (Norway). Glossary, Suggested Readings, and Index.

65.   Anderson, Joan. **Christmas on the Prairie**. George Ancona, photographs. New York: Clarion, 1985. 48p. $14.95. ISBN 0-89919-307-2. 2-6

In 1836, the schoolmaster refuses to cancel school on Christmas Eve because he considers it a heathen celebration. But the Curtis children take cookies to the neighbors, and on Christmas morning they find presents in their stockings and in their father's wooden shoes.

66.   Anderson, Joan. **The First Thanksgiving Feast**. George Ancona, photographs. New York: Clarion, 1984. Unpaged. $15.95; $5.95pa. ISBN 0-89919-287-4; 0-395-51886-5pa. K-3

The text re-creates the first harvest festival that the pilgrims celebrated after arriving in Plymouth. The photographs accompanying the text feature the living history museum of Plimouth Plantation. Re-creations feature John Alden, Elizabeth Hopkins, Miles Standish, and Governor Bradford.

67.   Anderson, Joan. **Spanish Pioneers of the Southwest**. George Ancona, photographs. New York: Dutton, 1989. 48p. $14.95. ISBN 0-525-67264-8. 3-6

In this photo essay about the 1700s, a young boy near Santa Fe is asked to guard the pueblo. He sees someone in the distance and calls for the gates to be closed until the inhabitants find that the newcomer is a friend.

68.   Anderson, Joan. **A Williamsburg Household**. George Ancona, photographs. New York: Clarion, 1988. 48p. $15.95; $5.95pa. ISBN 0-89919-516-4; 0-395-54791-1pa. 3-7

In the Williamsburg of 1770, Rippon and his family are slaves in different families. Although they have difficult lives, they enjoy doing errands in town because they have a chance to see each other. Photographs from the Williamsburg living history museum complement the text.

69.   Anderson, Kelly. **Thomas Edison**. San Diego, CA: Lucent, 1994. 112p. $16.95. ISBN 1-56006-041-7. (The Importance Of). 6-9

Thomas Edison (1847-1931) is perhaps the most famous inventor who ever lived. He was not a scientist, which probably hindered him, but he was very logical in his approach to problems and willing to experiment endlessly. He also hired people who had the expertise he lacked. Newspapers early in his career referred to him as the "Wizard of Menlo Park" (the New Jersey town where he lived). The age of Edison covers the invention of the telegraph in the mid-1800s to the mid-1900s when he died. His phonograph and electric light are only two of his 1,093 patents. Notes, For Further Reading, Additional Works Consulted, and Index.

70.   Anderson, Kelly C. **Immigration**. San Diego, CA: Lucent, 1993. 112p. $16.95. ISBN 1-56006-140-5. (Overview). 4-8

The text discusses the difficulties for immigrants trying to adjust to life in America. Problems of illegal immigration, being refugees, and border disputes often complicate their lives as well. They also have to decide to accept either the "salad bowl" or the "melting pot" attitude toward assimilation into American culture.

71.   Anderson, LaVere. **Martha Washington: First Lady of the Land**. Cary, illustrator. New York: Chelsea Juniors, 1991. 80p. $14.95. ISBN 0-7910-1452-5. (Discovery). 3-7

After a childhood in Virginia, marriage, and the death of that husband, Martha Dandridge Custis (1731-1802) met George Washington and married him in 1759. Their marriage spanned the American Revolution and his presidency.

72.   Anderson, LaVere. **Mary Todd Lincoln: President's Wife**. Cary, illustrator. New York: Chelsea Juniors, 1991. 80p. $14.95. ISBN 0-7910-1415-0. (Discovery). 3-7

Mary Todd Lincoln (1818-1882) grew up in a Kentucky family that helped runaway slaves. After Lincoln started courting her and they married, he gave her a ring with "Love is Eternal" engraved on it; she wore it until she died. After she and Lincoln moved into the White House, she faced several family tragedies. One son died from pneumonia, her husband was assassinated, and another son died at 18 after she had left Washington. The text gives an overview of her life.

73.   Anderson, Peter. **Aldo Leopold: American Ecologist**. New York: Franklin Watts, 1995. 64p. $19.90; $5.95pa. ISBN 0-531-20203-8; 0-531-15759-8pa. (First Book). 3-6

In the beginning of the twentieth century, Aldo Leopold (1886-1948) worked out West after graduating from the Yale school of forestry. Aware of the beauty of the land, he devoted himself to helping conserve it. He published a survey of his work in 1931 that showed that the wildlife habitats such as woodlots and wetlands were disappearing. He moved to Wisconsin and wrote a book of essays called *A Sand County Almanac*. He was a naturalist, forester, wildlife manager, professor, and ecologist as well as a writer before he died. Photographs, For Further Reading, and Index.

74. Anderson, Peter. **Charles Eastman: Physician, Reformer, Native American Leader**. Chicago: Childrens Press, 1992. 111p. $19.30; $5.95pa. ISBN 0-516-03278-X; 0-516-43278-8pa. (People of Distinction). 4-6

As a child, Ohiyesa (1858-1939) thought his father had died in the Sioux Uprising of 1862, but his father had actually been sent to a federal prison for three years. When his father reappeared, he had found Christianity and taken the family name Eastman from Ohiyesa's mother, who had died in childbirth. Ohiyesa went with his father, who renamed him "Charles." In the world of the white man, Charles trained as a physician. But when he returned to the people in his native Sioux tribe, he tried to help them with their health while also lobbying for their rights. With the books that he wrote, he showed that a Native American could be intelligent and productive, contrary to what many whites believed. Timeline and Index.

75. Anderson, Peter. **Gifford Pinchot: American Forester.** New York: Franklin Watts, 1995. 64p. $19.90. ISBN 0-531-20205-4. 4-6.

In this wealthy family, Gifford Pinchot (1865-1946) had a chance to enjoy the lovely woods, and he did. His father suggested that he become a forester, and he attended Yale's school of forestry. He completed his education apprenticed to a Swiss forester in France. He knew that few Americans understood forestry and that he had much to learn. When he returned to America, he took a job looking after the Biltmore estate in North Carolina. He suggested selective logging, and after proving that it could be profitable, he set up his own business. He then headed the government's first Department of Forestry. With Theodore Roosevelt, he was able to conserve some of America's forests before he became governor of Pennsylvania. For Further Reading and Index.

76. Anderson, Peter. **John James Audubon: Wildlife Artist**. New York; Franklin Watts, 1995. 64p. $19.90; $5.95pa. ISBN 0-531-20202-X; 0-531-15762-8pa. (First Book). 3-6

John James Audubon (1785-1851) came to the United States from France. He loved the outdoors, and when he found so many exciting species of birds available, he began to paint them. His collection of accurate, beautiful bird illustrations was printed first in England. Further Reading and Index.

77. Anderson, Peter. **Maria Martinez: Pueblo Potter**. Chicago: Childrens Press, 1992. 31p. $16.70. ISBN 0-516-04184-3. 3-5

The story describes the life and accomplishments of the Pueblo Indian, Maria Martinez, who made pottery in the traditional way of her people and achieved renown as an artist.

78. Anderson, Peter. **Will Rogers: American Humorist**. Chicago: Childrens Press, 1992. 32p. $16.70; $3.95pa. ISBN 0-516-04183-5; 0-516-44183-3pa. (Picture-Story Biography). 3-4

Will Rogers (1879-1935) loved to rope things as a child, and his skill helped him get many jobs as he traveled around the world. In New York, he gained fame when he roped a steer that got loose in one of his company's performances. Soon he started adding humor to his act, and eventually he wrote a newspaper column. By the time he died in an airplane crash, he was a beloved performer and writer. Index.

79. Anderson, William. **Laura Ingalls Wilder: A Biography**. New York: HarperCollins, 1992. 240p. $16; $5.95pa. ISBN 0-06-020113-4; 0-06-446103-3pa. 4-7

Laura Ingalls Wilder (1867-1957) wrote books about her own life. In this biography, Anderson divides the chapter headings into the time periods that relate to her fiction. Wilder and her pioneer family lived in Indian territory, Plum Creek, Burr Oak, and Dakota Territory. She was a prairie girl who married and lived with her own family in Big Red Apple, on Rocky Ridge Farm, and in Gem City of the Ozarks. Her family encouraged her to write the stories that she told so vividly, and she won many awards for them. Index.

80. Andrews, Elaine. **Indians of the Plains**. New York: Facts on File, 1992. 96p. $21.95. ISBN 0-8160-2387-5. (First Americans). 6 up

The text presents the history of the Plains Indians, their way of life, their rituals, and the changes they have endured. The tribes known as the Plains Indians include the farmer-hunter tribes of the Arikara, Kansa, Mandan, Osage, Pawnee, and Wichita. The hunters are the Arapaho, Assiniboin, Blackfoot, Cheyenne, Comanche, Crow, Kiowa, and Sioux. Photographs enhance the text. Index.

81. Andronik, Catherine M. **Prince of Humbugs: A Life of P. T. Barnum**. New York: Atheneum, 1994. 136p. $15.95. ISBN 0-689-31796-4. 6-9

Phineas Taylor Barnum (1810-1891) had as many setbacks as he had successes, but he discovered that people would pay to see George Washington's nurse, who claimed to be 160 years old. He promoted Tom Thumb and Jenny Lind and showcased Jumbo the elephant. In later life, he met circus owner James A. Bailey, and with him brought to Americans "The Greatest Show on Earth." Notes, For More Information, and Index.

82. Andryszewski, Tricia. **The Amazing Life of Moe Berg: Catcher, Scholar, Spy**. Brookfield, CT: Millbrook Press, 1996. 127p. $16.40. ISBN 1-56294-610-2. 5-8

Moe Berg, an intellectual trained in linguistics at Princeton with a law degree from Columbia, played professional baseball for 20 years on a variety of teams. He was not a particularly effective batter or runner, but he was an excellent catcher. In World War II, he became a spy for the OSS. He traveled throughout Latin America and Europe making propaganda speeches in Japanese because he had gone to Japan before the war as a baseball player and knew the language. The text looks at the life of this unusual man. Photographs, Notes, and Index.

83. Andryszewski, Tricia. **The Dust Bowl: Disaster in the Plains**. Brookfield, CT: Millbrook Press, 1993. 64p. $15.90; $5.95pa. ISBN 1-56294-272-7; 1-56294-747-8pa. (Spotlight on American History). 5-7

The text presents the 1930s drought that turned the Great Plains into a "dust bowl." Both human and natural forces caused this disaster. The lack of rain coupled with the Great Depression led to enormous economic and emotional loss. Bibliography and Index.

84. Angell, Judie. **One-Way to Ansonia**. New York: Bradbury, 1985. 183p. $11.95. ISBN 0-02-705860-3. 5-8

After escaping from Russian pogroms, Rose, 11, and her siblings arrive at Ellis Island in 1893 to meet their father and his new wife. When Rose chooses to add the effort of night school to her long days of work, she surprises her family, but she realizes that she must work to escape the poverty of a New York tenement life.

85. Antle, Nancy. **Beautiful Land: A Story of the Oklahoma Land Rush**. John Gampert, illustrator. New York: Viking, 1994. 54p. $12.99. ISBN 0-670-85304-6. (Once Upon America). 3-6

On April 22, 1889, Annie Mae's family plans to begin a new life where they will have their own farm and not have to work for others. They participate in the race to claim land in the newly opened Oklahoma Territory. Although illegal squatters try to take their land first, they reach the land claim office and pay before anyone else does.

86. Antle, Nancy. **Hard Times: A Story of the Great Depression**. James Watling, illustrator. New York: Viking, 1993. 59p. $12.99. ISBN 0-670-84665-1. (Once Upon America). 2-6

During the Depression in 1933, Charlie's father loses his job, and the family can no longer afford the mortgage. After they move, Charlie's father is able to find a temporary job. They are all happy that they can stay together.

87. Antle, Nancy. **Sam's Wild West Show**. Simms Taback, illustrator. New York: Dial, 1995. 40p. $12.99. ISBN 0-8037-1532-3. 1-3

Sam brings his show to town with its cowgirls, cowboys, and horses. While he is there, the outlaws Flo and Bo come to town, and because the marshal and the mayor flee, Sam gets elected as marshal. He saves the town and flies away in his hot-air balloon.

88. Antle, Nancy. **Tough Choices: A Story of the Vietnam War**. Michele Laporte, illustrator. New York: Viking, 1993. 64p. $12.99. ISBN 0-670-84879-4. 4-6

After Mitch comes home from Vietnam in 1968, he has to face the young people who are protesting the war at the airport. At home, his brother Sam expresses his own hostile opinions. The war experience has changed Mitch, and Sam has to find out why he is different.

89. Appel, Marty. **Joe DiMaggio**. New York: Chelsea House, 1990. 64p. $14.95; $4.95pa. ISBN 0-7910-1183-6; 0-7910-1198-4pa. (Baseball Legends). 6-9

In addition to information about DiMaggio, son of an Italian immigrant, Appel presents a brief history of baseball on the West Coast. DiMaggio's fame began in 1933, when he had a 61-game hitting streak for his San Francisco team. In 1936, DiMaggio left for New York and the Yankees, the team of Babe Ruth and Lou Gehrig. His record there astounded baseball fans, and he played consistently until injuries sidelined him. Appel includes photographs of DiMaggio with his family and his ex-wife, Marilyn Monroe. Statistics, Chronology, Further Reading, and Index.

90. Appelbaum, Diana. **Giants in the Land**. Michael McCurdy, illustrator. Boston: Houghton Mifflin, 1993. Unpaged. $14.95. ISBN 0-395-64720-7. 1-6

Giant trees more than 250 feet tall once covered New England. These trees, branded the property of the king before the Revolutionary War, were good for Royal Navy ship masts. A few men using simple tools chopped down these trees and transported them across land. The text tells how they did it. *Bulletin Blue Ribbon Book.*

91. Applegate, Katherine. **Benjamin O. Davis, Jr., and Colin L. Powell: The Story of Two American Generals**. Minneapolis, MN: Gareth Stevens, 1995. 112p. $13.95. ISBN 0-8368-1380-4. (Famous Lives). 3 up

As the first Black cadet at the U.S. Military Academy at West Point, no one would speak to Benjamin O. Davis (b. 1912) for a while. But in 1941, he became the commander of the first all-Black Air Corps, and in 1967 he became the commander of the 13th Air Force. Following him is Colin L. Powell (b. 1937). Powell joined the ROTC at the City University of New York and from there went into service in Vietnam. His rise through the army ranks led him to become Chairman of the Joint Chiefs of Staff, America's highest military office. Photographs included. For Further Study and Index.

92. Archbold, Rick. **Deep-Sea Explorer: The Story of Robert Ballard, Discoverer of the Titanic**. New York: Scholastic, 1994. 144p. $13.95. ISBN 0-590-47232-1. 5-10

Growing up on the Pacific Coast in California gave Bob Ballard (b. 1942) a love for the sea. This influence, along with the fact that his sister was unable to talk (although she was otherwise normal), made Ballard realize that he must use his full faculties to improve the world. Intrigued with submarines through reading Jules Verne, he won an internship before his senior year in high school with the Scripps Institution of Oceanography. After setbacks, he attended graduate school and eventually had his first dive in a submersible in 1969 in Woods Hole, Massachusetts. Diving led to his 1986 discovery of the *Titanic*, wrecked in 1912. Since then he has run electronic educational programs to share with people his knowledge of what exists below sea level. Epilogue, Glossary, and Index.

93. Arginteanu, Judy. **The Movies of Alfred Hitchcock**. Minneapolis, MN: Lerner, 1994. 80p. $9.50. ISBN 0-8225-1642-X. 5-9

Alfred Hitchcock (1899-1980) made some of the scariest movies of the twentieth century. Knowing about the man and his movies gives insight into his decisions. He saw suspense as something that the audience must feel while the character seems to be unaware that anything might be wrong, and he used this situation in unexpected ways. The movies discussed here are *The 39 Steps*, *The Lady Vanishes*, *Shadow of a Doubt*, *Strangers on a Train*, *Vertigo*, *North by Northwest*, *Psycho*, and *The Birds*. For Further Reading and Index.

94. Armstrong, Jennifer. **Black-Eyed Susan**. Emily Martindale, illustrator. New York: Crown, 1995. 96p. $15. ISBN 0-517-70107-3. 3-5

Susie, 10, and her father try to entice her mother with a gift to make her like the vast prairie on which they live. But her mother stays inside the sod house, refusing to look at the land and coping with bugs that fall from the ceiling. Susie and her father opt to buy more land and commit the family to another five years. When an Icelandic family comes to the area, they help Susie's mother acclimate to her situation.

95. Armstrong, Jennifer. **The Dreams of Mairhe Mehan: A Novel of the Civil War**. New York: Knopf, 1996. 119p. $18. ISBN 0-679-88152-2. 6 up

Living in Washington, D.C., during the Civil War, Mairhe watches her brother Mike go off to fight and her Da lose his mind. She tries to make enough lace to buy Mike's place in the army. Mairhe meets Walt Whitman while he nurses the soldiers, and he encourages her. *Bulletin Blue Ribbon Book*.

96. Armstrong, Jennifer. **Patrick Doyle Is Full of Blarney**. Krista Brauckmann-Towns, illustrator. New York: Random House, 1996. 80p. $16. ISBN 0-679-87285-X. (Stepping Stone). 2-4

Patrick Doyle thinks that one way for his Hell's Kitchen gang to keep the baseball field behind the brewery away from the Copperheads is for Larry Doyle, a New York Giants player, to hit a home run over the fence. The Doyle who hits the homer happens to be Patrick, and his action saves the turf for his group.

97. Armstrong, Jennifer. **Steal Away**. New York: Orchard, 1992. 207p. $14.95. ISBN 0-531-05983-9. 6-9

Mary, 13, describes her 1896 trip from New York to Toronto with her grandmother. In Toronto, she meets Bethlehem Reid, Gran's friend since 1855, with whom Gran fled Virginia and her uncle's home as a young orphan. Beth had been given to Gran as her own slave, and although Beth would not normally trust a white person, she had gone with Gran because Gran said that she hated slavery. Beth, a retired teacher, tells Mary the story of their journey north.

98. Armstrong, William O. **Sounder**. New York: HarperCollins, 1969. 128p. $14.95; $2.25pa. ISBN 0-06-020143-6; 0-06-447153-5pa. 5 up

During the Depression, a Black boy's father steals a ham to feed his starving family. A white man accuses him, and he goes to jail. The boy has to work to support his family, but in his searches for his father, a man he meets teaches him to read. The dog Sounder is the only one in the story to have a name, and he waits faithfully for his master's return just as Argus, the dog of Odysseus, waited. When the father returns, Sounder dies peacefully. *Newbery Award, Lewis Carroll Shelf Award, American Library Association Notable Children's Books of 1940-1970, Horn Book Fanfare Honor List, School Library Journal "Best of the Best" Children's Books 1966-1978, New York Times Outstanding Children's Book, Publishers Weekly Select Children's Books*.

99.   Arnold, Caroline. **The Ancient Cliff Dwellers of Mesa Verde**. Richard Hewett, illustrator. New York: Clarion Books, 1992. 64p. $15.95. ISBN 0-395-56241-4. 4-6

The Native Americans known as the Anasazi migrated to southwestern Colorado in the first century AD. After constructing extensive dwellings in the walls of the steep canyon cliffs, they mysteriously disappeared around AD 1300. Their impressive dwellings still stand in Mesa Verde National Park, Colorado.

100.   Arnold, Caroline. **Stories in Stone: Rock Art Pictures by Early Americans**. Richard Hewett, illustrator. New York: Clarion Books, 1996. 48p. $15.95. ISBN 0-395-72092-3. 4-6

The text looks at the images inscribed on the canyon walls of the Coso Range in California's Mojave Desert, the largest display of rock art in the Western Hemisphere. It also discusses the methods that ancient peoples used to make the pictures and the ways that archaeologists have been able to date their origins.

101.   Ash, Maureen. **The Story of Harriet Beecher Stowe**. Chicago: Childrens Press, 1990. 32p. $17.30; $4.95pa. ISBN 0-516-04746-9; 0-516-44746-7pa. (Cornerstones of Freedom). 3-6

A powerful beginning using the second person "you" puts the reader on the slave auction block as a child of 11 soon to be separated from mother and younger brother. Such scenes viewed after she turned 21 and moved to Cincinnati influenced Harriet Beecher Stowe's great contribution to society, *Uncle Tom's Cabin*. Born in 1811 in Connecticut into a large family, she met Mr. Stowe in Cincinnati. Across the river in Kentucky, where slavery was legal, she saw slaves endure harsh and evil treatment. She and her husband moved to Maine, and her brother suggested that she use her writing talents to expose slavery. Because she had six children, including a baby, the book took a year to write. First published as a magazine serial, the book sold 5,000 copies in two days. It soon gave the Stowes much-needed money and international renown, but most important, it aided in the emancipation of slaves, although a terrible war had to come first. Index.

102.   Ash, Maureen. **The Story of the Women's Movement**. Chicago: Childrens Press, 1989. 32p. $16.40; $4.95pa. ISBN 0-516-04724-8; 0-516-44724-6pa. (Cornerstones of Freedom). 3-6

This excellent overview of the struggle of women to gain legal rights begins with a historical perspective. In England, around 1827, Caroline Norton fought the laws that allowed an abusive husband to leave her, take their sons, and legally get the money she had earned from her writing to support herself. In 1839, the Infants Custody Act passed, and in 1857 women deserted by their husbands gained the right to keep their earnings. Not until 1860 did the Married Woman's Property Act pass in New York. Emily Davis, Norton's contemporary, fought for equal education for women so that by 1921, women could enroll in all 12 British universities. Work in antislavery societies in the United States made women realize that they needed to vote, and Elizabeth Cady Stanton began her crusade, along with Lucretia Mott and Susan B. Anthony. Only after their deaths was the Nineteenth Amendment passed, giving women the right to vote in 1920. In 1963, Betty Friedan's *The Feminine Mystique* revealed that women were underused and mistreated in the workplace through lower salaries and lack of positions of authority. In Congress in 1964, Martha Griffiths of Michigan and Margaret Chase Smith of Maine refused to allow the word "sex" to be removed from Title VII, the equal employment bill, and it passed. Index.

103.   Ashabranner, Brent. **Always to Remember: The Story of the Vietnam Veteran's Memorial**. New York: Putnam, 1988. 40p. $14.95. ISBN 0-399-22031-3. New York: Scholastic, 1992. 40p. $2.95pa. ISBN 0-590-44590-1pa. 4-7

Although supposedly a tribute to the Vietnam Memorial in Washington, D.C., this book covers background about the war, including its inception and that it was the longest war in American history. Of the Americans who served—2.5 million men and 8,000 women—58,000 were killed and more than 300,000 wounded with 74,000 more having more than 50 percent disabilities. From the war's beginning in 1966 until its end in 1975, it cost 140 billion dollars. Some 7,500 people went to prison rather than serve, and more than 425,000 deserted. One man, Jan Scruggs, became obsessed with the creation of a memorial, and oversaw its construction, based on Maya Lin's design, by Veterans Day, 1982. Photographs of the memorial and the memorabilia left at the wall accent the power of this place for almost everyone who stands before it. Facts, Bibliography, and Index.

104.   Ashabranner, Brent. **An Ancient Heritage: The Arab-American Minority**. Paul S. Conklin, photographer. New York: HarperCollins, 1991. 148p. $14.89. ISBN 0-06-020049-9. 5 up

In the text, Ashabranner interviews many young people who were either born in the United States or immigrated because of troubles in their countries. Christians, Muslims, and Jews are represented. But regardless of their current status, they bring the traditions of their cultures into this country and have to balance the old with the new as they face the future. Bibliography and Index.

105.   Ashabranner, Brent. **Dark Harvest: Migrant Farmworkers in America**. Paul Conklin, illustrator. 1985. Hamden, CT: Linnet, Shoe String Press, 1993. 114p. $18.50. ISBN 0-208-02391-7. 5 up

Invisible workers, or migrants, drive around America following the crops, living inside shacks within huge farms where members of the surrounding communities rarely see them. Close to 1 million probably work the fields, but they remain uncounted and unrepresented by government officials. The large crops of California, Texas, and Florida seem to attract the largest number of migrants, whose median income for a family of six was $4,000 in 1982 while the average American family income was $22,000. Additionally, child labor laws do not apply to those who work with their families on these farms. The concern of teachers who periodically encounter these children helps the workers feel appreciated, but the teachers alone cannot change the system.

106.   Ashabranner, Brent. **A Memorial for Mr. Lincoln**. Jennifer Ashabranner, photographs. New York: Putnam, 1992. 113p. $15.95. ISBN 0-399-22273-1. 5 up

On Memorial Day, 1922, President Warren G. Harding dedicated the Lincoln Memorial. At the ceremony, gray-clad Confederate veterans sat with blue-clad Union veterans in the place of honor. Henry Bacon, an architect, spent much of his life trying to design the memorial, and Daniel Chester French, a sculptor with little formal training, created the extraordinary statue of Lincoln. The text looks at Lincoln's contribution to the union and the great care that the monument's creators took to make an appropriate memorial for this man. Bibliography and Index.

107.   Ashabranner, Brent K. **A Strange and Distant Shore: Indians of the Great Plains in Exile**. New York: Cobblehill, 1996. 54p. $16.99. ISBN 0-525-65201-9. 5-8

In 1875, the Red River War led to the imprisonment of 72 Indians of the Great Plains in St. Augustine, Florida, for three years. Their "jailer," Captain Richard Henry Pratt, realized that they deserved deference instead of disdain, and his attitude led to their freedom. However, he thought they should assimilate themselves rather than retain their culture. They refused. Bibliography and Index.

108.   Ashabranner, Brent. **The Times of My Life: A Memoir**. New York: Cobblehill, 1990. 114p. $14.95. ISBN 0-525-65047-4. 4-7

Some of the main issues of the twentieth century come to life in this autobiography. Ashabranner's Oklahoma boyhood during the Depression, his opportunities to write in college, his World War II Navy service, and his experiences in Africa and India as a Peace Corps official show his humanitarian interests. Ashabranner also discusses the roles of U.S. Presidents in aiding the development of less-fortunate countries. Bibliography and Index.

109.   Asimov, Isaac, and Elizabeth Kaplan. **Henry Hudson: Arctic Explorer and North American Adventurer**. Minneapolis, MN: Gareth Stevens, 1991. 48p. $14.95. ISBN 0-8368-0558-5. (Isaac Asimov's Pioneers of Exploration). 2-5

Henry Hudson (d. 1611) searched for a short route from Europe to the Orient, but he never found it. His sailors mutinied, and he disappeared. Hudson, an expert navigator, explored the Arctic regions north of Russia and the eastern coast of North America, and was the first European to enter the body of water now known as Hudson Bay. Chronology, Glossary, Things to Read, Places to Write, Other Activities, and Index.

110.   Auch, Mary Jane. **Journey to Nowhere**. New York: Henry Holt, 1997. 224p. $15.95. ISBN 0-8050-4922-3. 4-7

In 1815, Remembrance "Mem," 11, moves with her family from Hartford, Connecticut, to the wilderness of western New York State. On the journey, she becomes separated from her family members, and after finding them, almost loses them again. In addition to terrain, they must fight bears, wolves, and mountain lions before settling in the new community.

111.   Avakian, Monique. **A Historical Album of Massachusetts**. Brookfield, CT: Millbrook Press, 1994. 64p. $16.40; $6.95pa. ISBN 1-56294-481-9; 1-56294-762-1pa. (Historical Album). 4-8

The text presents the land of Massachusetts before it became a state, beginning with Native American civilizations and continuing through exploration and settlement. Early statehood developments and issues and the role of large cities in the state's livelihood lead to the present day. Prints, maps, and photographs illustrate the text. Gazetteer: Quick Facts, Key Events, Personalities, and Index.

112.   Avakian, Monique, and Carter Smith III. **A Historical Album of New York**. Brookfield, CT: Millbrook Press, 1994. 64p. $16.40; $6.95pa. ISBN 1-56294-005-8; 1-56294-758-3pa. (Historical Album). 4-8

The text presents the land of New York before it became a state, beginning with Native American civilizations and continuing through exploration and settlement. Early statehood developments and issues and the role of large cities in the state's livelihood lead to the present day. Prints, maps, and photographs illustrate the text. Gazetteer: Quick Facts, Key Events, Personalities, and Index.

113.   Avi. **The Barn**. New York: Orchard, 1994. 106p. $13.95. ISBN 0-531-06861-7. 3-6

When Ben is nine and away in school during 1855, his sister arrives unexpectedly. She takes him home, and he discovers that the illness his father has contracted has left him unable to speak or care for himself. Because their mother is dead, the three children nurse him and work the farm. Ben gets his father to respond by asking him to blink if he agrees with him or wants something. Ben thinks if the three children build the barn that his father wanted before his illness, his father will get well. The opposite occurs, and Ben must face questions about his own intentions. *ABC Children's Booksellers' Choices*, *American Library Association Notable Books for Children*, *Book Links*, *Booklist Editors' Choices*, and *IRA Teachers' Choices*.

114. Avi. **Beyond the Western Sea, Book Two: Lord Kirkle's Money**. New York: Jackson, Orchard, 1996. 380p. $18.95. ISBN 0-531-09520-7. 5-8

Patrick and his sister, Maura O'Connell, sail with their friends, Mr. Horatio Drabble and Laurence Kirkle, on the *Robert Peel* from England to Boston in 1851. They all go to Lowell, Massachusetts, where they discover that the O'Connell father has died. The characters must endure prejudice and hardship, but they eventually overcome the evil forces that would ruin their lives.

115. Avi. **Captain Grey**. 1977. New York: Beech Tree, Morrow, 1993. 160p. $15; $3.95pa. ISBN 0-688-12233-7; 0-688-12234-5pa. 5-9

When Kevin and Cathleen Cartwright meet Captain Grey during a journey from Philadelphia to New Jersey in 1783, Captain Grey and his men kill their father and convince Kevin that his sister is also dead. Captain Grey starves Kevin long enough so that the boy does as he wants, which includes helping his men kill a crew and sink a ship in the name of helping America defeat the British. With Grey's trust, Kevin begins to roam the island on which Grey is quartered and discovers his sister hiding in a cave. They plan an escape, aided by a schooner crew coming to get revenge on Grey for his evil deeds. Kevin understands but does not condone Grey, who has turned inhumane after the death of his wife and son.

116. Avi. **Emily Upham's Revenge**. 1978. New York: Beech Tree, Morrow, 1992. 192p. $15; $3.95pa. ISBN 0-688-11898-4; 0-688-11899-2pa. 4-6

In 1875, Emily Upham, only seven, journeys to Boston after her father disappears. She plans to stay with her uncle, but he ignores her. She and a young boy she meets decide to rob her uncle's bank for the money to pay her return to Boston. Another robber, however, beats them to the job. While Emily hides under the desk, Seth identifies the robber as Emily's father from a picture she showed him. They do get the money in an unusual way, return to Boston, and give it away to charities after Emily says she burned it.

117. Avi. **Encounter at Easton**. 1980. New York: Beech Tree, Morrow, 1994. 144p. $14; $4.95pa. ISBN 0-688-05295-9; 0-688-05296-7pa. 5 up

A sequel to *Night Journeys*, *Encounter at Easton* presents the story of Elizabeth Mawes and Robert Linnly through the first-person narratives of Robert and Nathaniel Hill, the man hired to find Elizabeth. Not until Mad Moll tries to save Elizabeth and Robert finds out that Hill has papers in his saddlebag to capture Elizabeth does Robert realize that he must fear Hill. The ensuing flight and discovery cause one death and one improvement of fortune even though both young people have done nothing for which they should suffer.

118. Avi. **The Fighting Ground**. Ellen Thompson, illustrator. New York: HarperCollins, 1984. 160p. $14.89; $4.50pa. ISBN 0-397-32074-4; 0-06-440185-5pa. 4 up

Jonathan, 11, spends a day fighting Hessians in 1778 near Trenton, New Jersey. After Hessians capture him, they shelter him in a deserted farmhouse where he sees a young boy hiding near his dead parents. Thinking the Hessians have killed the couple, Jonathan escapes to the group he had joined earlier in the day. He finds that they, not the Hessians, had killed the couple because they were Tories. When Jonathan leads the same group to the Hessians, they are pleased to kill them too. *American Library Association Notable Books for Children*, *American Library Association Recommended Books for Reluctant Young Adult Readers*, *Horn Book Fanfare Honor List*, *New York Public Library's Books for the Teen Age*, and *Lesbian and Gay Children's/YA Award*.

119. Avi. **Finding Providence: The Story of Roger Williams**. James Watling, illustrator. New York: HarperCollins, 1997. 48p. $14.95. ISBN 0-06-025179-4. (An I Can Read Chapter Book). 3-4

Mary tells the story of her father's trial in Massachusetts Bay Colony during 1635. After Roger Williams (1603?-1683) was condemned for his beliefs, he had to escape. Mary tells of his brave exit from home in the middle of the night, unafraid because he spoke the language of the Narragansett Indians. Indeed, they helped him and gave him land for his family and his followers, which he called Providence, his way of thanking God for saving him.

120. Avi. **The Man Who Was Poe**. New York: Orchard, 1989. 208p. $13.95. ISBN 0-531-08433-7. New York: Flare, 1991. 208p. $4.50pa. ISBN 0-380-71192-3pa. 4-8

In 1848, Edmund, 11, must find his sister, who disappears soon after his aunt. He must search Providence, Rhode Island, to find her. He meets a man who helps him look, but the man seems to think Edmund's difficulties are part of a story he is writing. When Edmund finds his mother, who has been gone for the past year, and his sister, who is sailing away in a boat, the man, Edgar Allan Poe, finally seems to understand that the situation is real.

121.   Avi. **Night Journeys**. 1979. New York: Beech Tree, Morrow, 1994. 160p. $14; $4.95pa. ISBN 0-688-05298-3; 0-688-13628-1pa. 5 up

In this novel, two bondservants escape from their master in 1767. When Peter York, an orphan of 12, discovers them, he has to decide whether to help them or to turn them in to the authorities and claim the reward money near Trenton, New Jersey. Because he had once been an avid searcher, his realization that he had befriended the bound girl while searching for her makes him wonder if a person has the right to sell another person. His Quaker guardian will not advise him, but because the guardian is also a justice of the peace, he cannot legally tell Peter to hide them. Peter's decision, however, pleases the Quaker. *Scott O'Dell Award for Historical Fiction*.

122.   Avi. **Punch with Judy**. New York: Bradbury, 1993. 167p. $14.95. ISBN 0-02-707755-1. New York: Avon, 1994. 167p. $3.99pa. ISBN 0-380-72253-4pa. 4-7

In 1870, when Punch is eight, the owner of a traveling medicine show sees him trying to earn bits of money by dancing for anyone who will watch. He lets Punch accompany the troop. They play to rural audiences, but soon they see that humor is the only thing that continues to entertain a hardworking but poor group of people. Punch has to accept the change in fortunes, but someone from the show helps him.

123.   Avi. **Shadrach's Crossing**. New York: Pantheon, 1983. 192p. $10.99. ISBN 0-394-95816-0. 5 up

Shadrach and his parents are bystanders cowed by bullies in a Prohibition smuggling operation on their island in 1932. The Depression forces many of the residents to help the smugglers because they need the money. When Shadrach begins talking to a man whom he hopes will reveal the operation to the government, he makes a risky decision.

124.   Avi. **Something's Upstairs: A Tale of Ghosts**. New York: Orchard, 1988. 120p. $14.95. ISBN 0-531-05782-8. New York: Flare, 1990. 120p. $4.50pa. ISBN 0-380-70853-1pa. 4-7

In this historical fantasy, Kenny's family moves to Providence, Rhode Island, and live in a house built in 1792. When Kenny sees a bloodstain on the floor of his bedroom closet, he is surprised to see a figure rising out of it. He helps the spirit of the dead slave, murdered in 1800, to uncover his killer. They must change memory before they can escape the past.

125.   Avi. **The True Confessions of Charlotte Doyle**. New York: Orchard, 1990. 215p. $15.95. ISBN 0-531-05893-X. New York: Avon, 1992. 215p. $4.50pa. ISBN 0-380-71475-2pa. 5-8

When Charlotte is 13 in 1832, she sails from England on the *Seahawk* to Rhode Island, where her family awaits her. As she is the only passenger on board, guilty crew members blame her for a murder she did not commit. She eventually realizes her plight and escapes it. But when she reaches her family, they cannot know what she has endured. They continue to treat her like a child and a female who must be confined to the home according to social norms—two conditions she can no longer accept. She runs away from them, back to sea. *Newbery Honor*, *Boston Globe-Horn Book Award*, *Golden Kite Award*, and *Judy Lopez Memorial Award*.

126.   Avi. **"Who Was That Masked Man, Anyway?"** New York: Orchard, 1992. 142p. $14.95. ISBN 0-531-08607-0. New York: Camelot, 1994. 142p. $3.99pa. ISBN 0-380-72113-9pa. 3-7

During World War II, Frankie, 11, prefers to pretend he is part of the radio programs to which he listens, such as *The Lone Ranger*, rather than do his homework. But when his brother returns home from war wounded, the war becomes more real to Frankie. Then his teacher's boyfriend is killed abroad. Drawing on his knowledge of plot from his favorite radio shows, Frankie creates a scheme through which his brother and teacher may meet. They do meet, but not as Frankie has imagined.

127.   Ayer, Eleanor H. **The Anasazi**. New York: Walker, 1993. 124p. $14.95. ISBN 0-8027-8184-5. 6-9

In covering the development of the Anasazi civilization, from the prehistoric Basket Makers approximately 14,000 years ago to the Pueblo peoples, Ayer describes archaeologists' finds in architecture and artifacts and what they reveal. Possible explanations of daily life also appear. Bibliography and Index.

128.   Ayers, Carter M. **Chuck Yeager: Fighter Pilot**. Minneapolis, MN: Lerner, 1988. 48p. $15.95. ISBN 0-8225-0483-9. (Achievers). 4-9

On October 14, 1947, when he was 24, Chuck Yeager (b. 1925) became the first person to fly faster than the speed of sound. He had already earned medals for bravery during World War II. Afterward, he spent a long career as a test pilot while the space program developed. He received both a Congressional Medal of Honor and the Presidential Medal of Freedom.

B

129. Bader, Bonnie. **East Side Story**. New York: Silver Moon Press, 1993. 80p. $12.95; $4.95pa. ISBN 1-881889-22-X; 1-881889-71-8pa. (Stories of the States). 3-5

At 10, Rachel Boganovich is a Russian immigrant in New York's Lower East Side. She befriends Antonio Russo, an Italian immigrant, in the early 1900s. Their sisters work together in the Triangle Shirtwaist Factory. Together they watch the battles for safety that their sisters and others undergo in an attempt to have union protection from the factory owners. Endpaper Maps, Historical Postscript, and Recommended Reading.

130. Bader, Bonnie. **Golden Quest**. New York: Silver Moon Press, 1993. 64p. $12.95; $4.95pa. ISBN 1-881889-30-0; 1-881889-74-2pa. (Stories of the States). 3-5

Some people want California to be a free state in 1850; others prefer it to be a slave state. David and Celia Taylor help their parents manage a dining hall for the prospectors looking for gold in the hills north of San Francisco. Everyone they know is intensely involved in the debate as to whether California should enter the Union as a free state. Endpaper Maps, Historical Postscript, and Recommended Reading.

131. Badt, Karin Luisa. **Charles Eastman: Sioux Physician and Author**. New York: Chelsea House, 1995. 112p. $18.95. ISBN 0-7910-2048-7. (North American Indians of Achievement). 5 up

In 1858, Hadakah was born and raised as a Santee Sioux who learned about white society in South Dakota's schools. After winning at lacrosse when a teenager, he earned his adult name, Ohiyesa, "The Winner." When he went to live with his father, he took yet a third name, Charles Eastman. He became a graduate of Dartmouth College and of medical school. He was on the scene at Wounded Knee when the U.S. Army attacked the Sioux, and he gave equal help to Native Americans and white soldiers. He then worked as an educator, fought against corruption in the government's Indian services, began the Young Men's Christian Association for Indian youths, started a summer camp for white children to learn about Indians, gave lectures to mixed audiences, and held government jobs to help relations. Thus, he was a civil rights activist and a believer in a multicultural approach to life. Photographs and reproductions enhance the text. Chronology, Further Reading, and Index.

132. Baker, Betty. **Walk the World's Rim**. New York: HarperCollins, 1965. 192p. $14.89. ISBN 0-06-020381-1. 5-9

Of 600 men who sailed from Cuba to Florida in 1527, only four survived. One, the black slave Esteban, encourages a young Indian, Chako, to go with him to Mexico. While their leaders petition for money to go to the seven cities of Cíbola, they wait separately in Tenochtitlán. Chako is disturbed that Esteban has not come to tell him what will happen. When Cortez tells Chako to feed his horse, he finds Esteban confined to the stables. Although taught not to respect slaves, Chako soon realizes that he respects Esteban's character despite his social class. When the Cíbolans murder Esteban, Chako dejectedly returns to his Florida home, having lost his friend.

133. Baldwin, Robert F. **New England Whaler**. Richard Erickson, illustrator. Minneapolis, MN: Lerner, 1996. 48p. $14.96. ISBN 0-8225-2978-5. (American Pastfinder). 3-6

New Englanders began to hunt whales so that they could have smokeless light from whale oil. Before electric and kerosene lamps, whale oil was the cleanest and brightest fuel for lamps. Because whale hunters could earn much money, they were willing to risk their lives at sea. In the 1840s, more than 700 sailing ships cruised the world to find whales and kill them with hand-thrown harpoons. The text looks at life on ship, the daily experience of the whale hunters during the hunt and cleaning of the whale, and other aspects of this time. Glossary and Index.

134. Ballard, Robert D. **Exploring the Titanic**. Ken Marschall, illustrator. New York: Madison, Scholastic, 1988. 96p. $14.95; $6.95pa. ISBN 0-590-41953-6; 0-590-41952-8pa. 4-7

Dr. Robert Ballard became fascinated with the story of the *Titanic*. When the tiny submarine *Alvin*'s tether was extended to 13,000 feet, Ballard realized that he could reach the wreck two and one-half miles under the sea. In July 1986, he saw the ship that had last been above the water on April 14, 1912. On that night, only 705 of the 1,500 people on board the magnificent ship reached the safety of a rescue vessel, the *Carpathia*, after an iceberg tore through the hull. Ballard returned to the Titanic eight times, going inside and reliving the scene based on what he had read or heard from survivors of that doomed voyage. Further Reading, Glossary, and *Titanic* Timeline. *American Library Association Best Books for Young Adults*, *School Library Journal Best Books of the Year*, and *Horn Book Fanfare*.

135. Bandon, Alexandra. **Asian Indian Americans**. New York: New Discovery, Silver Burdett, 1994. 112p. $14.95. ISBN 0-02-768144-0. (Footsteps to America). 5-8

Bandon examines the lives of Asian Indian Americans after they began to arrive in America around 1965. For them to leave their country was a major decision; therefore, Bandon tries to identify what in the history of the country would have precipitated such a move. Using personal narratives as a basis, she shows what the journey to America was like, what life in America has been like for those who came, the prejudice they faced, and the opportunities they found. For Further Reading and Index.

136. Bandon, Alexandra. **Chinese Americans**. New York: New Discovery, Silver Burdett, 1994. 112p. $14.95. ISBN 0-02-768149-1. (Footsteps to America). 5-8

Bandon examines the lives of Chinese Americans. For them to leave their country was a major decision; therefore, Bandon tries to identify what in the history of the country would have precipitated such a move. Using personal narratives as a basis, she shows what the journey to America was like, what life in America has been like for those who came, the prejudice they faced, and the opportunities they found. For Further Reading and Index.

137. Bandon, Alexandra. **Dominican Americans**. New York: New Discovery, Silver Burdett, 1994. 112p. $14.95. ISBN 0-02-768152-1. (Footsteps to America). 5-8

Bandon examines the lives of Dominican Americans after they began to arrive in America around 1965. For them to leave their country was a major decision, so Bandon tries to identify what in the history of their country would have precipitated such a move. Using personal narratives as a basis, she shows what the journey to America was like, what life in America has been like for those who came, the prejudice they faced, and the opportunities they found. For Further Reading and Index.

138. Bandon, Alexandra. **Filipino Americans**. New York: New Discovery, Macmillan, 1993. 112p. $14.95. ISBN 0-02-768143-2. (Footsteps to America). 5-8

Bandon examines the lives of Filipino Americans. For them to leave their country was a major decision; therefore, Bandon tries to identify what in the history of their country would have precipitated such a move. Using personal narratives as a basis, she shows what the journey to America was like, what life in America has been like for those who came, the prejudice they faced, and the opportunities they found. For Further Reading and Index.

139. Bandon, Alexandra. **Korean Americans**. New York: New Discovery, Silver Burdett, 1994. 111p. $14.95. ISBN 0-02-768147-5. (Footsteps to America). 5-8

Bandon examines the lives of Korean Americans. For them to leave their country was a major decision; therefore, Bandon tries to identify what in the history of their country would have precipitated such a move. Using personal narratives as a basis, she shows what the journey to America was like, what life in America has been like for those who came, the prejudice they faced, and the opportunities they found. For Further Reading and Index.

140. Bandon, Alexandra. **Mexican Americans**. New York: New Discovery, Macmillan, 1993. 110p. $14.95. ISBN 0-02-768412-4. (Footsteps to America). 5-8

Bandon examines the lives of Mexican Americans. For them to leave their country was a major decision; therefore, Bandon tries to identify what in the history of their country would have precipitated such a move. Using personal narratives as a basis, she shows what the journey to America was like, what life in America has been like for those who came, the prejudice they faced, and the opportunities they found. For Further Reading and Index.

141. Bandon, Alexandra. **Vietnamese Americans**. New York: New Discovery, Silver Burdett, 1994. 112p. $14.95. ISBN 0-02-768146-7. (Footsteps to America). 5-8

Bandon examines the lives of Vietnamese Americans. For them to leave their country was a major decision; therefore, Bandon tries to identify what in the history of their country would have precipitated such a move. Using personal narratives as a basis, she shows what the journey to America was like, what life in America has been like for those who came, the prejudice they faced, and the opportunities they found. For Further Reading and Index.

142. Bandon, Alexandra. **West Indian Americans**. New York: New Discovery, Silver Burdett, 1994. 112p. $14.95. ISBN 0-02-768148-3. (Footsteps to America). 5-8

In this text, Bandon examines the lives of West Indian Americans. For them to decide to leave their country was a major decision; therefore, Bandon tries to identify what in the history of their country would have precipitated such a move. Using personal narratives as a basis, she shows what the journey to America was like, what life in America has been like for those who have come, the prejudices they faced, and the opportunities they found. For Further Reading and Index.

143. Banim, Lisa. **American Dreams**. New York: Silver Moon Press, 1993. 80p. $12.95; $4.95pa. ISBN 1-881889-34-3; 1-881889-68-8pa. (Stories of the States). 3-5

Jeannie Bosold and Amy Mochida, a Japanese American, have gone to the movies and spent hours discussing their favorite movie stars. Then the government takes Amy and her family away from their home in southern California after the bombing of Pearl Harbor in 1941. Jeannie does not understand why children must suffer for adult problems. Endpaper Maps, Historical Postscript, and Recommended Reading.

144.   Banim, Lisa. **Drums at Saratoga**. New York: Silver Moon Press, 1993. 58p. $12.95; $4.95pa. ISBN 1-881889-20-3; 1-881889-70-Xpa. (Stories of the States). 3-5

Disgusted with the drudgery of a Canadian foundry apprenticeship, Nathaniel Phillips leaves it in 1777 to fight with the British general "Gentleman Johnny" Burgoyne. He follows him to the battle of Saratoga, where he has to endure the realities of colonial life. The experience matures him and gives him a different perspective about working in the foundry. Endpaper Maps, Historical Postscript, and Recommended Reading.

145.   Banim, Lisa. **A Spy in the King's Colony**. Tatyana Yuditskaya, illustrator. New York: Silver Moon Press, 1994. 76p. $12.95. ISBN 1-881889-54-8. (Mysteries in Time). 3-5

In 1776, Emily Parker, 11, finds herself followed by someone who may be a thief. Although she does not know the person's identity, she begins to suspect almost everyone of being a spy. She is especially concerned to know if her older sister's boyfriend is a loyalist or a patriot. What she discovers is a great relief.

146.   Banks, Sara Harrell. **Under the Shadow of Wings**. Chris Sheban, illustrator. New York: Simon & Schuster, Atheneum, 1997. 160p. $16. ISBN 0-689-81207-8. 4-8

Tattnall, 11, lives in the South near the end of World War II. She takes care of her cousin Obie, 16, who is developmentally disabled. She decides that she no longer wants this responsibility, but when Obie tragically dies, she has to cope with her feelings of relief and of intense grief at a major loss in her life.

147.   Banta, Melissa. **Frederick Douglass: Voice of Liberty**. New York: Chelsea Juniors, 1993. 78p. $14.95; $4.95pa. ISBN 0-7910-1765-6; 0-7910-1973-Xpa. (Junior World Biographies). 3-5

Although born a slave, Frederick Douglass (1817-1895) learned how to read and write while dreaming of becoming free. He escaped in 1838 and began to speak publicly against slavery. By 1845, he had written a book about his life as a slave, and in 1847 he began publishing *The North Star*, a newspaper. He approached President Lincoln about freeing the slaves and letting them join the Union armies in the Civil War. After the war, he worked for Black civil liberties. Photographs, Further Reading, Chronology, Glossary, and Index.

148.   Barboza, Steven. **Door of No Return: The Legend of Gorée Island**. New York: Cobblehill, Dutton, 1994. 42p. $14.99. ISBN 0-525-65188-8. 5 up

As early as 1433, Africans captured other Africans and sold them to Portuguese traders. They assembled the captured slaves on Gorée Island, two miles west of Dakar, Senegal. According to records in Lisbon, 3,589 slaves arrived there between 1486 and 1493. In 1619, a Dutch ship sailed into Jamestown, Virginia, with 20 slaves. Many Africans also owned slaves, and by the late 1800s slaves comprised two-thirds of many African societies. On Gorée, the wealthy kept slave houses. Anne Pepin, a *signare* who acted as the wife of the French governor of Senegal (although unmarried to him), had more than 35 slaves. The island today is a place of pilgrimage for Americans wanting to see where their ancestors started their long journey to servitude. Index.

149.   Barnes, Joyce Annette. **The Baby Grand, the Moon in July, and Me**. New York: Dial, 1994. 130p. $14.99. ISBN 0-8037-1586-2. 4-6

In July 1969, Annie Armstrong, 10, excitedly waits for Neil Armstrong (no relation) to walk on the Moon. At the same time, her brother Matty arranges for a baby grand piano to arrive at their house on credit so he can pursue his dream of becoming a jazz musician. The Armstrong father is upset, but Annie helps him see Matty's talent as she continues her own dream of being an astronaut.

150.   Barnes, Joyce Annette. **Promise Me the Moon**. New York: Dial, 1997. 176p. $14.99. ISBN 0-8037-1798-9. 5-8

Annie from *The Baby Grand, the Moon in July, and Me* is 13 in 1972 and having problems in eighth grade. She is losing her boyfriend and her best friend at the same time she is having trouble in her Enriched Science class. She wants to become an astronaut, and she thinks that attending one of Ohio's best high schools will help her. But she worries about being accepted and whether she really wants the added academic pressure.

151.   Barr, Roger. **The American Frontier**. San Diego, CA: Lucent, 1995. 111p. $16.95. ISBN 1-56006-282-7. (World History). 6-9

By focusing on concerns such as Manifest Destiny and the treatment of Native Americans, the text gives a view of westward expansion in the 1800s. Quotes from primary sources allow those on all sides of the debates to state their cases. The last chapter explains the significance of the time period to American history and development of the nation. Bibliography, Chronology, Further Reading, Notes, and Index.

152.   Barr, Roger. **Richard Nixon**. San Diego, CA: Lucent, 1992. 112p. $16.95. ISBN 1-56006-035-2. (The Importance Of). 5-8

Richard Milhaus Nixon (1913-1994) won his second term in the White House by a landslide. Two years later, he had to resign in ignominy because of his implication in the burglary of the Democratic National Party office at the Watergate Hotel. While in office, he improved relations with China and the Soviet Union. However, his less-favorable moments in office seem to be his legacy. Notes, For Further Reading, Works Consulted, and Index.

153.   Barrett, Katherine, and Richard Greene. **The Man Behind the Magic: The Story of Walt Disney**. New York: Viking, 1990. 208p. $18.99. ISBN 0-670-82259-0. 6 up

Walt Disney (1901-1966) grew up on a Missouri farm and built an animation empire through his vision and his willingness to try new ideas. He was determined to make the Disney studio work, and his brother Roy helped support his efforts. In the early years, artists left the studio, taking ideas with them. Making enough money to pay those who stayed was difficult, but Disney eventually built an empire that continues after his death. Index.

154.   Barrett, Tracy. **Harpers Ferry: The Story of John Brown's Raid**. Brookfield, CT: Millbrook Press, 1993. 64p. $15.90; $5.95pa. ISBN 1-56294-380-4; 1-56294-745-1pa. 5-8

John Brown led a raid on the U.S. arsenal at Harpers Ferry, West Virginia, in 1859. Although very religious, he believed that he had to use force, if necessary, to end slavery. His raid failed, and he was hung. Chronology, Further Reading, Bibliography, and Index.

155.   Barrett, Tracy. **Nat Turner and the Slave Revolt**. Brookfield, CT: Millbrook Press, 1993. 32p. $13.90. ISBN 1-56294-275-1. (Gateway Civil Rights). 2-4

At 21, Nat Turner (1800-1831) ran away from his Virginia owner, but returned later of his own free will. In 1828 and 1831, he reported visions from God, and they led him to begin a slave revolt on August 22, 1831. Two months later he was caught for the failed attempt and within two weeks, he was executed. Important Dates, Find Out More, and Index.

156.   Barrie, Barbara. **Lone Star**. New York: Delacorte, 1990. 182p. $13.95. ISBN 0-385-30156-1. 5-8

In 1944, 10-year-old Jane and her family move from Chicago to Corpus Christi, Texas, after her father is convicted of defrauding insurance customers. Lacking the support of her Jewish family and friends in Chicago, she decides that she would like a Christmas tree. Her grandfather discovers the tiny tree in her bedroom at the same time the family hears of the Nazi concentration camps. He is furious that she has not been true to her Jewish heritage. But she has to cope with her brother's threats to join the army, her parents' bickering, her grandfather's prejudices against Gentiles, and her teacher's prejudice against Yankees. And she wants her new friend's approval.

157.   Bartoletti, Susan C. **Growing Up in Coal Country**. Boston: Houghton Mifflin, 1996. 112p. $15.95. ISBN 0-395-77847-6. 5-8

Oral history, archival documents, and black-and-white photographs help to re-create life in a mining town in northeastern Pennsylvania at the beginning of the twentieth century. Among the hostile aspects were the difficult working conditions, the squalor, and the poverty that children had to endure in such situations. Not until unions and child labor laws did the families begin to escape their plights. Bibliography and Index.

158.   Bartone, Elisa. **American Too**. Ted Lewin, illustrator. New York: Lothrop, Lee & Shepard, 1996. Unpaged. $16. ISBN 0-688-13278-2. K-3

In New York City, after World War I, Rosina, an immigrant from Italy, is unhappy to be named queen of the San Gennaro feast. She wants to be an American, not an Italian. She solves her dilemma by coming to the feast dressed as Lady Liberty rather than in the white taffeta dress her mother made. She wants to feel comfortable in her American life, and she adapts her situation according to her needs.

159.   Bartone, Elisa. **Peppe the Lamplighter**. Ted Lewin, illustrator. New York: Lothrop, Lee & Shepard, 1993. 32p. $15. ISBN 0-688-10268-9. K-3

Peppe's mother is dead, and his father is sick. With eight sisters, he needs to make money to help support them. He gets a job as a lamplighter in New York's Little Italy, and his father belittles the job. Peppe refuses to light the lamps one night, and his father realizes how important Peppe's job is because the lit lamps help people reach home safely, including Peppe's little sister. *Caldecott Honor.*

160.   Basinger, Jeanine. **American Cinema: One Hundred Years of Filmmaking**. New York: Rizzoli, 1994. 300p. $50. ISBN 0-8478-1814-4. 6 up

This survey of the American cinema covers filmmaking from 1894, when Thomas Edison first photographed a man sneezing, to current-day full-length features. The text corresponds to the PBS series on American cinema. Among the varied topics included are technical tricks, the movie star, screwball comedy, *film noire*, and the rise and fall of the major studio system. Photographs, Bibliography, and Index.

161. Bauer, Marian. **Rain of Fire**. New York: Clarion, 1983. 160p. $10.95. ISBN 0-89919-190-8. 4-8
Steve, 12, does not understand why his brother has returned from World War II a different person, one who will not discuss his experiences. An older bully calls Steve's brother a "Jap lover." Steve starts lying, and when his brother finally intervenes in the fight that results, he tells Steve about the horror of Hiroshima and how he hates knowing that he killed people. *Jane Addams Book Award.*

162. Bealer, Alex W. **Only the Names Remain: The Cherokees and the Trail of Tears**. Kristina Rodanas, illustrator. Boston: Little, Brown, 1972, 1996. 96p. $15.95; $4.95pa. ISBN 0-316-08518-9; 0-316-08519-7pa. 6 up
On a forced march from Georgia to Oklahoma in 1837 and 1838, thousands of Cherokee Indians died. The text looks at the U.S. government's treatment of them as the troops took the Cherokees from their homes during mealtime and demanded that they leave their possessions, including land the Cherokees rightfully owned. Bibliography and Index.

163. Beard, Charles, and Detlev Vagts. **The Presidents in American History**. New York: Julian Messner, 1981. 240p. $14.98. ISBN 0-671-44026-8. 6-10
Brief vignettes on each President of the United States give insight on their backgrounds, achievements, and personalities. Three pages of text per man give a clear understanding of his integrity (or lack thereof) and the behaviors he exhibited in the highest office one can win in America. One wonders how some of the men ever got elected. Biographical Digest.

164. Beatty, Patricia. **Be Ever Hopeful, Hannalee**. New York, Morrow, 1988. 208p. $15. ISBN 0-688-07502-9. Mahwah, NJ: Troll, 1990. 208p. $3.95pa. ISBN 0-8176-2259-5pa. 5-9
After the Civil War ends in this sequel to *Turn Homeward, Hannalee*, Hannalee, now 13, and her mother and two brothers move to Atlanta. Because Hannah's brother has only one arm, he has difficulty finding work, and she is too young to work. In desperation, he almost becomes involved with criminals. People accuse him of misconduct, but he never does anything wrong. Their life finally becomes better after a difficult period.

165. Beatty, Patricia. **Behave Yourself, Bethany Brant**. New York: Morrow, 1986. 172p. $15. ISBN 0-688-05923-6. 5-9
In 1898, when she is 11, Bethany goes to live with relatives while her father becomes a circuit rider minister in Texas. Her mother died when she was born, and she worries about her father. Tempted to spend money on a fortune-teller, she does, but feels guilty. When someone gambles away her father's money to build a new church, she swallows her guilt and gambles again to win it back. Her seemingly righteous cousin understands her decision and supports it.

166. Beatty, Patricia. **Billy Bedamned, Long Gone By**. New York: Morrow, 1977. 223p. $9.95. ISBN 0-688-22101-7. 5-8
In 1929, Merle and her brother and grandmother travel from Pasadena to New Orleans with her mother driving. When they stop at the family home in MacRae, Texas, Merle is never sure which of the family stories her two great uncles tell are actually true.

167. Beatty, Patricia. **Blue Stars Watching**. New York: Morrow, 1969. 191p. $7.95. ISBN 0-688-21110-0. 5-9
When Will finds Rab, a hired hand, dead, his father tells him that Confederates have killed Rab because he has been running an Underground Railway station. In 1861, Will and his sister find safety with relatives in San Francisco. He gets a job at the newspaper so that he can find out about his father's Maryland Union army unit. What he hears from his former schoolteacher-turned-spy is that his relatives are supporting the Confederates from San Francisco by stuffing gold into dolls that are then transported via the Panama Canal to the Confederacy. Their detective work gives grounds for the government to stop the ship for piracy.

168. Beatty, Patricia. **Bonanza Girl**. 1968. New York: Beech Tree, Morrow, 1993. 224p. $4.95pa. ISBN 0-688-12280-9pa. 5 up
Ann, her widowed mother, and brother go to Idaho Territory in 1884. Although planning to open a school, her mother meets Helga Storkersen, who convinces her to open a tent restaurant for the miners in the town and a second one in the claim area of a silver mine. To get money to hire a preacher and open a church, the two collect money in the saloons.

169. Beatty, Patricia. **By Crumbs, It's Mine!** New York: Morrow, 1976. 254p. $7.25. ISBN 0-688-22062-2. 5-9
Damaris, an independent female of 13 in 1882, and her aunt take a traveling hotel, a cardboard building capable of being erected anywhere, and run it while her mother is ill and her father mines for gold. Among their customers are Chinese and Irish railroad workers. When Damaris realizes that her mother looks weaker every day, she persuades an Apache working at the hotel to accompany her on a five-day journey to retrieve her father.

170. Beatty, Patricia. **Charley Skedaddle**. New York: Morrow, 1987. 192p. $15. ISBN 0-688-06687-9. Mahwah, NJ: Troll, 1988. 192p. $4.95pa. ISBN 0-8167-1317-0pa. 5-9

When Charley's sister decides to marry an older man whom he dislikes, he stows away on a ship, leaving New York in 1864. He finds himself in the South with Union soldiers and becomes a drummer boy. So much death sickens him, especially because his brother was killed at Gettysburg. He runs away a second time into the mountains. There he meets a woman, once a member of the Underground Railway, and bravely helps her when she needs it. *Scott O'Dell Award.*

171. Beatty, Patricia. **The Coach That Never Came**. New York: Morrow, 1985. 164p. $11.95. ISBN 0-688-05477-3. 5-8

When Paul, 13, visits his grandmother in Colorado during the summer, his investigation of a gaudy belt buckle in the shape of a heart reveals information about his family. He discovers that an outlaw in the family ambushed a stagecoach in 1873, and after he killed the passengers, Ute Indians killed him for desecrating their sacred cave.

172. Beatty, Patricia. **Eight Mules from Monterey**. New York: Morrow, 1982. 224p. $15; $4.95pa. ISBN 0-688-01047-4; 0-688-12281-7pa. 4-7

When Fayette's widowed mother graduates from library school and begins a job taking books into the mountains of Monterey, California, Fayette and her brother go with her. They have a variety of experiences, but most important, they learn that they can survive together without a man's help. Her mother can safely reject the proposal of a man whom none of them like.

173. Beatty, Patricia. **Hail Columbia**. New York: Morrow, 1970. 251p. $12.88. ISBN 0-688-31371-X. 4-8

When Louisa's widowed Aunt Columbia comes from Philadelphia to Washington State in 1893, Louisa is delighted to find an aunt who graduated from Oberlin, uses her maiden name, and advertises her support of suffragettes Susan B. Anthony and Elizabeth Cady Stanton. Louisa's father refuses to speak with Columbia, but she befriends the town's Finnish immigrants, congratulating them on their contribution of poetic meter from the Finnish *Kalevala* to Longfellow's *Hiawatha*. She teaches English to the Chinese workers and cleans the bars of Swill Town as a temperance worker. Then she succeeds in having her brother nominated and elected mayor. He realizes her value and starts speaking to her when she announces plans to return to Philadelphia.

174. Beatty, Patricia. **How Many Miles to Sundown?** New York: Morrow, 1974. 222p. $6.95. ISBN 0-688-20102-4. 5-9

Beulah, 13, travels with two boys across New Mexico and Arizona in 1881, searching for the town of Sundown. They have a variety of adventures, and in them, Beulah tries to do the best thing for the group.

175. Beatty, Patricia. **Jayhawker**. New York: Morrow, 1991. 214p. $13.95. ISBN 0-688-09850-9. 5 up

When Lije is 12, his father goes with the abolitionist John Brown in 1858 on a raid from Kansas into Missouri against slave owners. The slave owners kill father, and in his stead, Lije becomes a Jayhawker spy, someone who tries to find other slave owners or "bushwackers" in Missouri after the Civil War begins. Lije has to fight and is wounded before he reunites with his mother and sweetheart in Kansas. *School Library Journal Best Book.*

176. Beatty, Patricia. **Jonathan Down Under**. New York: Morrow, 1982. 219p. $10.25. ISBN 0-688-01467-4. 5-9

Jonathan Cole's father, crazy for gold in 1851, goes to Australia after little success in California and takes Jonathan with him. After Jonathan recovers from "sandy blight," a disease during which he stayed inside for several months and had his eyes scraped daily to keep him from going blind, he hears that his father's partner has left with their gold. Then a mine cave-in kills his father. Jonathan begins working for an Irish woman who has come to Australia to escape the potato famine, but she soon dies. When he helps others find gold, they give him money to return home because he is interested in neither gold nor Australia.

177. Beatty, Patricia. **Just Some Weeds from the Wilderness**. New York: Morrow, 1978. 254p. $10.75. ISBN 0-688-22137-8. 4-8

In 1874, 13-year-old Lucinda helps her aunt make a tonic from plants so that she can sell it in Oregon. Her uncle disapproves, but her aunt's proceeds lead him to change his mind. She must tell him about the project because as a woman, she cannot enter a bank to deposit her money.

178. Beatty, Patricia. **Lacy Makes a Match**. New York: Morrow, 1979. 222p. $13. ISBN 0-688-22183-1. 4-8

Tired of keeping house for her brothers in 1893 after her mother's death, Lacy decides that she will find mates for them. She tries various tactics, including writing letters to women advertising in lovelorn columns, but eventually succeeds in an unexpected way. In one episode, she visits San Francisco, and the electric lights in the Palace Hotel's Palm Court, electric trolleys, telephone, dental laughing gas, and seven-story buildings amaze her.

179. Beatty, Patricia. **A Long Way to Whiskey Creek**. New York: Morrow, 1971. 224p. $7.75. ISBN 0-688-31427-9. 5-7

In 1879, Parker, an orphan, has to travel 400 miles to retrieve his brother's body. Another orphan, Nate, accompanies him on the journey. They argue about Confederates and Yankees, and Nate tries to teach Parker to read, but Parker does not think that a horse breaker needs to know. After several adventures, a former criminal helps them, encouraging Nate to teach them both to read.

180. Beatty, Patricia. **Melinda Takes a Hand**. New York: Morrow, 1983. 197p. $10.25. ISBN 0-688-02422-X. 5-9

When Sarah Jane and her fiancé Edgar have a misunderstanding in 1893, Sarah Jane's sister Melinda helps to reunite them. Sarah Jane misreads Edgar's letter to say "lonely," and she refuses to see him while the sisters stay in the Colorado town where she has gone to marry him. Among the people in town are Melinda's Jewish friend Esther, who wants to be a rabbi, and two remittance men paid to remain away from England; they are having the family castle shipped to them, piece by piece. When Melinda lets Edgar know about the "lonely," he rushes to explain that he had written "lovely."

181. Beatty, Patricia. **The Nickel-Plated Beauty**. 1964. New York: Beech Tree, Morrow, 1993. 272p. $4.95pa. ISBN 0-688-12279-5pa. 5 up

In Washington Territory during 1886, Hester decides that she and her siblings should work digging clams, picking berries, and gathering oysters so that they can buy their mother a stove. Hester also works at her aunt's hotel. Although they are poor, they learn that pooling their resources allows them to do much more than if they plan separately.

182. Beatty, Patricia. **O the Red Rose Tree**. 1972. New York: Beech Tree, Morrow, 1994. 222p. $4.95pa. ISBN 0-688-13627-3pa. 4-8

Lonely old Mrs. Hankinson wants pieces of red material to build a quilt that she has designed. Amanda and four other girls, with almost no money, manage to find the materials. The articles they commandeer are a chest protector, flotsam, a doll dress, a union suit, gift dress material, and a petticoat. These contribute to the seven roses in the pattern. The girls have to finish the quilt when Mrs. Hankinson becomes ill, and she notes that their ingenuity means more than the final effort.

183. Beatty, Patricia. **Red Rock over the River**. New York: Morrow, 1973. 253p. $7.50. ISBN 0-688-20065-6. 4-8

Dorcas befriends Hattie when she comes to Fort Yuma, Arizona, in 1881. They do "good works" by going to the local prison where they write letters for the tubercular prisoners. After Hattie loads one of the prisoners on a hot-air balloon owned by a traveling circus and rushes him away, Dorcas finds that he is Hattie's half-brother whom she is trying to keep from dying in prison. He dies from a lack of oxygen, they crash, and Hattie disappears in the desert while Dorcas returns to her boring home.

184. Beatty, Patricia. **Sarah and Me and the Lady from the Sea**. New York: Morrow, 1989. 182p. $11.95; $4.95pa. ISBN 0-688-08045-6; 0-688-13626-5pa. 5 up

When Marcella is 12, an 1894 flood destroys her father's dry goods store in Portland, Oregon. Her formerly wealthy family has to move to their summer beach home and learn everyday survival without servants to pamper them. At first they think themselves better than the peninsula residents, but they soon learn that they have no skills and must depend on the locals for advice. They learn to clean and cook and find that such simple knowledge gives them a feeling of independence and achievement that they did not have before.

185. Beatty, Patricia. **Something to Shout About**. New York: Morrow, 1976. 254p. $6.95. ISBN 0-688-22078-9. 4-8

In 1875, Hope Foster's family moves from Oregon to Idaho Territory to manage the Whole Shebang Store. When the new schoolteacher arrives, he is shocked to see that the school is a former chicken coop and that the mayor plans to build a town hall and a jail before improving the school. The teacher, however, is a woman masquerading as a man so she can have the job. She convinces the women in town to collect money in the saloons for a prefabricated school. Her persistence helps improve the situation for the women and children after several unexpected situations are resolved.

186. Beatty, Patricia. **That's One Ornery Orphan**. New York: Morrow, 1980. 222p. $11.75. ISBN 0-688-22227-7. 4-8

After her grandfather dies in 1889, Hallie has to go to an orphan asylum in Texas. She tries to adjust to three sets of foster parents but makes mistakes that cause each of them to take her back to the asylum. She finally goes to live with a family she has tried to avoid because they are farmers. What she finds is unexpected pleasure in their baby and their horses.

187. Beatty, Patricia. **Turn Homeward, Hannalee**. New York: Morrow, 1984. 208p. $15. ISBN 0-688-03871-9. Mahwah, NJ: Troll, 1991. 208p. $3.95pa. ISBN 0-8167-2260-9pa. 5-9

In 1864, the Yankees accuse Hannalee and her brother of treason and export them from Georgia to Indiana. They have to work, but Hannalee pretends to be male and escapes. She finds her brother and uses her mill wages to pay for train tickets to Nashville. On their long journey home, they go through a horrible battle, but a peddler helps them traverse the last segment. Their brother returns, unlike their father, but missing one arm. The family survives the war, but barely.

188. Beatty, Patricia. **Wait for Me, Watch for Me, Eula Bee**. 1978. New York: Beech Tree, Morrow, 1990. 221p. $3.95pa. ISBN 0-688-10077-5pa. 5-9

In 1861, Comanches kill the family of and capture three-year-old Eula Bee and her brother Lewtie. Lewtie's bravery earns him the privilege of herding horses, and with a horse, he escapes. He and a neighbor whose two children are missing go to search for them and Eula Bee. Yankee soldiers thwart their rescue by stampeding the Comanche-Kiowa camp just as they arrive. Lewtie eventually finds Eula Bee, but she shows no recognition, having adapted to her Indian mother. Months later, she calls him by name, having overcome her shock.

189. Beatty, Patricia. **Who Comes with Cannons?** New York: Morrow, 1992. 192p. $14. ISBN 0-688-11028-2. 5-9

Twelve-year-old Truth travels from Indiana in 1861 to stay with her North Carolina relatives. They, like her, are Quakers who hate slavery. Truth is surprised to discover that her uncle is hiding a runaway slave, but she is relieved to know that she can work for freedom in a peaceable way while the horrible war continues around them.

190. Beatty, Patricia, and Phillip Robbins. **Eben Tyne, Powdermonkey**. New York: Morrow, 1990. 227p. $12.95. ISBN 0-688-08884-8. 5-9

In 1862, during the Civil War, Eben obtains a job as a powdermonkey on a ship, the *Merrimack*, which sails from Norfolk, Virginia. Then Union forces capture it. He has to decide if he will join the Northern forces and try to stop Confederate pirates, or stay a prisoner for the duration of the war. He decides to help the North even though he has no way of knowing if he made the correct decision.

191. Beckman, Pat Ramsey. **From the Ashes**. Boulder, CO: Roberts Rinehart, 1996. 160p. $9.95pa. ISBN 1-57098-011-Xpa. 3-6

In Ohio during 1794, Shawnee Indians burn Davey's family's cabin, and he is unable to save his parents or stop the Shawnee from kidnapping his brother. While he searches for his brother, two Shawnee half-brothers kidnap him. Their tribe eventually adopts him, and he begins to feel Shawnee. When the Battle of Fallen Timbers begins between General Anthony Wayne and the federal troops and Chief Blue Jacket and the Shawnee, Davey tries to make peace. He sees his brother again and realizes that he could never have saved the family, and he might have to relinquish his brother to the life to which he has become accustomed.

192. Bedard, Michael. **Emily**. Barbara Cooney, illustrator. New York: Doubleday, 1992. 36p. $16. ISBN 0-385-30697-0. K-3

When a little girl moves to Amherst, Massachusetts, in the 1880s, she lives on the same street as an odd woman who does not have visitors and whom the neighbors call "The Myth." When the girl's mother goes to play the piano for the lady, the girl goes with her and sneaks upstairs, where she meets Emily Dickinson. They exchange unusual gifts.

193. Behrens, June. **Juliette Low: Founder of the Girl Scouts of America**. Chicago: Childrens Press, 1988. 32p. $16.70. ISBN 0-516-04171-1. (Picture-Story Biographies). 2-4

Juliette Gordon Low (1860-1927), called Daisy throughout her life, grew up in a wealthy Georgian family, married a man from England, and lived alternately in both countries. In England, she met Lord Baden-Powell, the man who had started the Boy Scouts. He told her about his Girl Guides, and she returned to Georgia to start a similar group so that girls could become socially involved with their communities. Her movement grew and became the Girl Scouts of America.

194. Behrens, June. **Missions of the Central Coast: Santa Bárbara, Santa Inés, La Purísima Concepción**. Minneapolis, MN: Lerner, 1996. 80p. $17.21. ISBN 0-8225-1930-5. (California Missions). 4-6

In the 1700s, Spain sent Roman Catholic priests to establish missions and presidios (forts) along the coast of Baja California and other areas of New Spain (present-day Southwestern United States and Mexico). Spain wanted the Indians to accept the Spanish ways and become loyal subjects. The Santa Barbara presidio protected the Santa Bárbara, La Purísíma, and Santa Inés missions, which the Spanish built among the Chumash villages. When drought caused famine, the Chumash families eventually moved into the missions and lost touch with some of their old customs. Glossary, Chronology, and Index.

195.   Bellairs, John. **The Drum, the Doll, and the Zombie**. New York: Dial, 1994. 123p. $14.99. ISBN 0-8037-1462-9. 4-7

During the mid-1950s, the folklore professor Dr. Coote goes to a party with 12-year-old Johnny Dixon, his friend Fergie, and Professor Childermass. Dr. Coote quiets the party when he tells what he learned on a recent visit to New Orleans. To accentuate his story, he beats on a drum as he tells about voodoo cults in Haiti and the Caribbean. The beats start a chain of events that releases a zombie. A woman and her grandson come to kill Dr. Coote and to make the others into zombies, but their little bit of knowledge helps them resist.

196.   Beller, Susan Provost. **Woman of Independence: The Life of Abigail Adams**. White Hall, VA: Shoe Tree Press, 1992. 128p. $5.95pa. ISBN 1-55870-237-7pa. 6-9

Abigail Adams (1735-1826) was a woman of strong will and character who played the roles of wife, mother, teacher, correspondent, and First Lady when her husband John Adams was elected President of the United States. She faced public dismay as well as approval for her willingness to say what she thought. Bibliography and Index.

197.   Belton, Sandra. **Ernestine and Amanda**. New York: Simon & Schuster, 1996. 160p. $16. ISBN 0-689-80848-8. 4-7

In the 1950s, Ernestine and Amanda, both 10, live in the same community. They become more and more irritated with each other as they meet at piano lessons, in church, at the Delta Sigma Theta Jabberwock, and at a party. When Ernestine steals Amanda's best friend, their tempers increase. Because they are so much alike, their hostility eventually turns into friendship.

198.   Benchley, Nathaniel. **Sam the Minuteman**. New York: HarperCollins, 1969. 64p. $14.89; $3.75pa. ISBN 0-06-020480-X; 0-06-444107-5pa. (I Can Read Books). 2-4

Sam's father decides that he may go with him to fight with the Minutemen if the British appear, as Paul Revere has rushed to tell them. After a friend is wounded, Sam goes to sleep that night worried about him, but he is ready to fight again.

199.   Beneduce, Ann Keay. **A Weekend with Winslow Homer**. New York: Rizzoli, 1993. 64p. $19.95; $9.95pa. ISBN 0-8478-1622-2; 0-8478-1919-1pa. (Weekend With). 5-8

With reproductions of his works, Winslow Homer (1836-1910) talks about his paintings and how the events in his life influenced the subjects he chose to paint.

200.   Benjamin, Anne. **Young Harriet Tubman: Freedom Fighter**. Ellen Beier, illustrator. Mahwah, NJ: Troll, 1992. 32p. $10.79; $2.95pa. ISBN 0-8167-2538-1; 0-8167-2539-Xpa. (First Start Biography). 1-3

This biography of Harriet Tubman (1820?-1913) tells how she helped more than 300 slaves escape through the Underground Railroad without being caught.

201.   Benjamin, Anne. **Young Helen Keller: Woman of Courage**. Julie Durrell, illustrator. Mahwah, NJ: Troll, 1992. 32p. $10.79; $2.95pa. ISBN 0-8167-2530-6; 0-8167-2531-4pa. (First Start Biography). 2-4

Helen Keller (1880-1968) was an extraordinary woman who overcame deafness and blindness with the help of a teacher, Annie Sullivan. She was able to attend college, become a speaker, and write books. This simple biography introduces her life.

202.   Benjamin, Anne. **Young Pocahontas: Indian Princess**. Christine Powers, illustrator. Mahwah, NJ: Troll, 1992. 32p. $10.79; $2.95pa. ISBN 0-8167-2534-9; 0-8167-2535-7pa. (First Start Biography). 1-3

Pocahontas (d. 1617), a Powhatan Indian, befriended Captain John Smith and the English settlers of Jamestown, Virginia, which helped them to survive. This biography tells her story.

203.   Bennett, Barbara J. **Stonewall Jackson: Lee's Greatest Lieutenant**. Englewood Cliffs, NJ: Silver Burdett, 1991. 135p. $12.95; $8.95pa. ISBN 0-382-09939-7; 0-382-24048-0pa. (The History of the Civil War). 5 up

Thomas Jackson (1824-1863) was always serious and shy. Students made fun of his stodginess when he was a teacher at the Virginia Military Institute. When the Civil War began, however, he had had experience in the Mexican War and knew that two important preparations for battle were scouting and flanking (not meet the enemy directly). He showed his brilliance in battle with daring maneuvers and his refusal to allow anyone to contradict him. General Barnard Bee gave him his nickname by saying "There is Jackson standing like a stone wall." He died at Chancellorsville. Epilogue, Time Table, Selected Sources, Suggested Reading, and Index.

204.   Bennett, Cathereen L. **Will Rogers: Quotable Cowboy**. Minneapolis, MN: Runestone Press, 1995. 96p. $18.95. ISBN 0-8225-3155-0. 4-6

In this biography, Bennett uses quotes to tell the life of Will Rogers (1879-1935). Among the things he said as an entertainer were, "I can't tell you where to write for I don't know where I will be"; "Personally, I have always felt that the best doctor in the world is the veterinarian. He can't ask his patients what is the matter—he's got to just know"; and before he died in a plane crash, "We are living in great times. A fellow can't afford to die now with all this excitement going on." Sources and Index.

205. Bennett, Evelyn. **Frederick Douglass and the War Against Slavery**. Brookfield, CT: Millbrook Press, 1993. 32p. $13.90; $4.95pa. ISBN 1-56294-341-3; 1-56294-790-7pa. (Gateway Civil Rights). 3-5

Frederick Douglass (1817?-1895) escaped from slavery and became an orator, writer, and leader in the abolitionist movement during the nineteenth century. This biography describes his role.

206. Bennett, Russell, and Anna Sproule. **Abraham Lincoln: Healing a Divided Nation**. Milwaukee, WI: Gareth Stevens, 1992. 68p. $16.95. ISBN 0-8368-0620-4. (People Who Made a Difference). 3-6

Abraham Lincoln's (1809-1865) stepmother encouraged his reading and writing, unlike his father, who had little use for learning. Perhaps the most important thing that Lincoln accomplished was signing the Emancipation Proclamation on January 1, 1963, which freed 4 million slaves. Lincoln faced happiness and heartbreak, including the death of a son while he lived in the White House. To Find Out More, List of New Words, Important Dates, and Index.

207. Bentley, Bill. **Ulysses S. Grant**. New York: Franklin Watts, 1993. 64p. $12.90. ISBN 0-531-20162-7. (First Book). 4-6

Ulysses S. Grant (1822-1885) left Ohio to attend West Point. After fighting in the Mexican War and failing at business, he reenlisted during the Civil War and served so well that Lincoln appointed him commander of the Union forces. During his second term in the presidency, he went on a world tour and enjoyed the acclaim given him and his wife. He needed money after his terms ended, so he began to write a book, *Personal Memoirs*, which he finished two days before his death from throat cancer. The book, published by his friend Mark Twain, financed the old age of his wife as he had hoped. For Further Reading and Index.

208. Bentley, Judith. **Brides, Midwives, and Widows**. New York: Twenty-First Century Books, 1995. 96p. $16.98. ISBN 0-8050-2994-X. (Settling the West). 5-8

The scarcity of women in the West during the nineteenth century gave them an exalted status in such places as San Francisco. The lively text, replete with photographs and drawings, looks at their roles through marriages of convenience, falling in love and marrying, as midwives for other women, as neighbors, and as women on their own. Source Notes, Further Reading, and Index.

209. Bentley, Judith. **"Dear Friend": Thomas Garrett and William Still, Collaborators on the Underground Railroad**. New York: Cobblehill, 1997. 128p. $15.99. ISBN 0-525-65156-X. 5-9

Two men who helped slaves escape on the Underground Railroad were a white Quaker, Thomas Garrett, from the slave state of Delaware, and a free Black, William Still, of Philadelphia. Garrett was the chief operator on the eastern line and led slaves across the dangerous Mason-Dixon line. William Still met his passengers and helped them to resettle in the North or continue their journeys to Canada. The basis of the text is their correspondence, which reveals their work and their friendship. Black-and-white photographs enhance the text. Notes and Index.

210. Bentley, Judith. **Explorers, Trappers, and Guides**. New York: Twenty-First Century Books, 1995. 96p. $16.98. ISBN 0-8050-2995-8. (Settling the West). 5-8

The importance of explorers, trappers, and guides for settling the West cannot be underestimated. The explorers found the places, the trappers used the natural resources to feed and cloth the settlers, and the guides helped the settlers find new land. The lively text with photographs and drawings looks at their roles. Source Notes, Further Reading, and Index.

211. Berkow, Ira. **Hank Greenberg: Hall-of-Fame Slugger**. Philadelphia: Jewish Publication Society, 1991. 108p. $12.95. ISBN 0-8276-0376-2. (JPS Young Biography). 3-7

Hank Greenberg (1911-1986) played baseball during the time the Nazis were killing Jews throughout Europe. He wanted to be the greatest Jewish baseball player, but the prejudice he experienced led him to establish a friendship with the first Black baseball player, Jackie Robinson. Greenberg hit the grand slam home run that won the pennant for the Tigers in 1945. In 1956, he became the first Jewish member of the Baseball Hall of Fame. The text looks at his life and his career in baseball.

212. Berleth, Richard. **Mary Patten's Voyage**. Ben Otero, illustrator. Niles, IL: Albert Whitman, 1994. 40p. $14.95. ISBN 0-8075-4987-8. 3-6

As the ship *Neptune's Car* rounds Cape Horn in 1856, Captain Joshua Patten falls unconscious from tuberculosis, the first mate is locked in his cabin, and the second mate can neither read nor plot a course. The captain's wife, Mary Patten, takes the responsibility for commanding the ship on its course to San Francisco. Although she shows great courage through the storms and as a leader, some of the crew rejects her guidance because she is female, and the first mate tries to mutiny. An epilogue comments that a similar episode occurred in real life, and that the captain died the next year, with his wife dying a few years later.

213. Berleth, Richard. **Samuel's Choice**. James Watling, illustrator. Niles, IL: Albert Whitman, 1990. 36p. $13.95. ISBN 0-8075-7218-7. 3-6

In a first-person narration, Samuel, 14 in 1775, tells of his decision as a Black slave to fight the British by sailing the Sons of Liberty across Gowanus Creek in the Battle of Long Island. Although owned by a man who opposes the patriots, Samuel makes a choice to support them, which helps the Sons of Liberty win the battle. He performs so well that the Maryland commander requests his services as an orderly. He gains his freedom.

214. Berliner, Don. **Before the Wright Brothers**. Minneapolis, MN: Lerner, 1990. 72p. $19.95. ISBN 0-8225-1588-1. 4-6

After discussing several theories about flying that have developed through the centuries, Berliner notes that the air screw principle, used by the Chinese in making toys as early as 400 BC, and propeller-driven windmills in the Middle Ages were what finally worked rather than the ornithopter (flapping wings) approach. Without the many inventors before them, the Wright brothers probably could not have piloted their plane in 1903. Men upon whom they relied included George Cayley, who in the late eighteenth and early nineteenth centuries originated the airplane. Others after him were William Henson, John Stringfellow, Felix du Temple, Alexander Mozhaiski, Hiram Maxim, Clement Ader, Otto Lilienthal, Octave Chanute, Augustus Herring, Gustave Whitehead, Karl Jatho, and Samuel Langley. For Further Reading and Index.

215. Bernotas, Bob. **Jim Thorpe: Sac and Fox Athlete**. New York: Chelsea House, 1992. 110p. $18.95. $7.95pa. ISBN 0-7910-1722-2; 0-7910-1695-1pa. (North American Indians of Achievement). 5 up

Jim Thorpe (1887-1953) was both an Olympic champion and an All-American football player. He attended the Carlisle Indian School in Carlisle, Pennsylvania, after leaving Oklahoma and the farm. He continued to work for Indian rights and remains the concept of a true champion, an Indian hero. Photographs complement the text. Chronology, Further Reading, and Index.

216. Bernotas, Bob. **Sitting Bull: Chief of the Sioux**. New York: Chelsea House, 1992. 111p. $18.95; $7.95pa. ISBN 0-7910-1703-6; 0-7910-1968-3pa. (North American Indians of Achievement). 5 up

As chief of the Sioux Indians, Sitting Bull (1834?-1890) led his warriors against Custer in the Battle of Little Bighorn. The author shows Sitting Bull as a military strategist and statesman. Black-and-white photographs supplement the text. Further Reading, Glossary, and Index.

217. Bernstein, Joanne, and Rose Blue with Alan Jay Gerber. **Judith Resnick: Challenger Astronaut**. New York: Lodestar, Dutton, 1990. 144p. $14.95. ISBN 0-525-67305-9. 5-7

In the first and last chapters, where the authors discuss the explosion of the *Challenger* space shuttle, they use present tense that intensifies the immediacy of the tragedy. The remainder of the book follows Resnick's life chronologically until January 28, 1986. Throughout her life, from her religious and academic education through her Ph.D. in engineering, her intelligence and perseverance show. Resnick was an especially private person; therefore, reasons for her divorce and her response to her parents' difficulties are unknown. Suggested Reading and Index.

218. Berrill, Margaret. **Mummies, Masks, & Mourners**. Chris Molan, illustrator. New York: Lodestar, Dutton, 1990. 48p. $14.95. ISBN 0-525-67282-6. (Time Detectives). 4-7

The "grave goods" that archaeologists find buried with the dead often reveal something about the culture and its burial customs. Berrill presents an unusual group of "finds." First are two Stone Age excavations: Çatal Hüyük in Turkey, found in 1958, and Haddenham, near Ely in England, the oldest wooden building ever discovered. From investigations of the pyramids in Egypt come mummies searching for the Field of Reeds. Recent excavations reveal Sumerians in 2500 BC. Other places excavated include the Siberian Altai horsemen from 400 BC; the Lindow Man, who died 2,000 years ago and was recently discovered in a peat bog; the Lady Dai from the Han Dynasty in China, buried 2,100 years previously; Roman memorials in Ephesus; Basket Makers in the American Southwest at Four Corners; Hopewell mounds in the Ohio/Tennessee area; Viking Ship burials; Qilakitsoq of the Inuits, buried in 1475 and found in Greenland; and the Kalabar Ijaw funeral screens from Africa. Fact boxes give additional information about each burial place and its culture. Drawings and photographs, one of a piece of 2,000-year-old preserved tattooed skin, augment the text. Glossary and Index.

219. Berry, Michael. **Georgia O'Keeffe: Painter**. New York: Chelsea House, 1988. 110p. $18.95; $7.95pa. ISBN 1-55546-673-7; 0-7910-0420-1pa. (American Women of Achievement). 5 up

As one of the first to express a woman's viewpoint in her painting, Georgia O'Keeffe (1887-1986) was a pioneer of modern art. She used beautiful flowers, scenes from the deserts, and cityscapes as her main subjects. Alfred Steiglitz "discovered" her, brought her to New York, and convinced her to marry him. Her independence continued, however, and after his death, she lived mainly in New Mexico, continuing to use the colors of the desert in her paintings. Photographs and reproductions enhance the text. Chronology, Further Reading, and Index.

220. Berry, S. L. **Emily Dickinson**. Stermer Dugald, illustrator. Mankato, MI: Creative Education, 1994. 45p. $17.95. ISBN 0-88682-609-8. (Voices in Poetry). 5 up

Emily Dickinson (1830-1886) lived in Amherst, Massachusetts, and rarely left her home. Her most innovative poetry about the world around her, written in the nineteenth century, rivals the best poetry composed before or since. Bibliography and Index.

221. Berry, S. L. **Langston Hughes**. Mankato, MN: Creative Education, 1994. 44p. $17.95. ISBN 0-88682-616-0. (Voices in Poetry). 5 up

This biography of Langston Hughes (1902-1967) shows a versatile poet who spent his career writing about the experiences of African Americans in their dialects. He went to Columbia, lived in Harlem, and flirted with socialism. Bibliography and Index.

222. Berry, Skip. **Gordon Parks**. New York: Chelsea House, 1990. 111p. $18.95. ISBN 1-55546-604-4. (Black Americans of Achievement). 6 up

As a poor young man in Kansas, Gordon Parks (b. 1912) worked as a pianist and a semipro basketball player. In 1937, he saw photographs of life in the Depression, and he knew that he could express his feelings about deprivation and racial discrimination with a camera. He won a fellowship to study and gained a position on the *Life* magazine staff in 1949. He wrote books, composed musical scores, directed films, and showed that one can overcome limited opportunities by using one's talents. Photographs enhance the text. Chronology, Further Reading, and Index.

223. Bethancourt, T. Ernesto. **The Tomorrow Connection**. New York: Holiday House, 1984. 134p. $10.95. ISBN 0-8234-0543-5. 6-9

When Richie and Mattie, both 18, travel through time to 1906, they stop in 1942 and 1912. In their attempts to find the gate that will take them back to the future, they meet Houdini. After they tell him about all of his tricks, even the ones not yet invented in 1906, he has them travel with him to San Francisco, where they finally find the key to return them to the future and their lives as the first Black President of the United States and an important historian.

224. Beyer, Don E. **The Totem Pole Indians of the Northwest**. New York: Franklin Watts, 1989. 64p. $19.90; $5.95pa. ISBN 0-531-10750-7; 0-531-15607-9pa. (A First Book). 4-7

Archaeological digs in the ruins of Ozette, a Makah village buried in a mudslide more than 500 years ago along the coast of Washington State, reveal some of the habits of the seven groups who have lived along the coasts of Canada and Alaska for the last 10,000 years. These groups include the Coast Salish, Nootka, Kwaki-utl, Bella Coola, Haida, Tsimshian, and Tlingit (easy pronunciation guides in the text). Totem poles, some more than 80 feet high, marked their existence. Photographs emphasize the importance of carvings not only for the totem but also for masks, spirit figures, canoes, body decorations, and homes (Big-Houses). The people also had slaves, either captured or purchased, and leaders held *potlatches* (celebrations for gift giving), some taking years to plan. White explorer Juan de Fuca arrived in 1592, and Captain James Cook came in 1777-1779 and wrote about the natives in his log. Other whites came later, bringing disease and change. Further Reading and Index.

225. Bial, Raymond, author/illustrator. **Amish Home**. Boston: Houghton Mifflin, 1993. 40p. $14.95. ISBN 0-395-59504-5. 4-6

The photographs of Amish homes today would be the same if taken when photography was in its infancy. The Germanic culture of the Amish people has stayed the same through the decades they have lived in the United States, mainly in Pennsylvania. Further Reading.

226. Bial, Raymond, author/illustrator. **Frontier Home**. Boston: Houghton Mifflin, 1993. 40p. $15.95. ISBN 0-395-64046-6. 4-6

Photographs help to illustrate the kinds of homes in which settlers who left the farms and towns of the East found themselves living in the West. Some were not much better than their Conestoga wagons until they had time to build permanent houses and to create furnishings to fill them. Further Reading.

227. Bial, Raymond. **Shaker Home**. Boston: Houghton Mifflin, 1994. 37p. $15.95. ISBN 0-395-64047-4. 3-8

Although 6,000 Shakers lived in the United States during the Civil War, none survive today. Seven Shakers, or Shaking Quakers, came with Mother Ann Lee to the American colonies and Watervliet, New York, in 1774 after they were persecuted in England. The text presents their history and beliefs with accompanying photographs. Further Reading.

228.   Bial, Raymond. **The Underground Railroad**. Boston: Houghton Mifflin, 1995. 48p. $14.95. ISBN 0-395-69937-1. 4-8

Before he tells the story of the Underground Railroad in the nineteenth century, Bial gives a chronology of the antislavery movement starting in 1775. Among the artifacts telling people where to find stations on the railroad were signal lamps in upper windows, false-bottomed wagons, and hand-dug tunnels lit with lanterns. Photographs of people and of memorabilia augment the verbal history of the abolitionists. Further Reading. *Notable Children's Trade Books in the Field of Social Studies.*

229.   Biel, Timothy L. **The Challenger**. San Diego, CA: Lucent, 1991. 64p. $12.95. ISBN 1-56006-013-1. (World Disasters). 5-8

On January 28, 1986, the *Challenger* space shuttle disintegrated almost immediately after it lifted off from the launch pad. Investigation showed that the O-ring seals were faulty. Among those who died was a schoolteacher who had won the right to be the first teacher in space, Christa McAuliffe. The text documents the tragedy, which was deeply shocking after the previous successes of the space program. Photographs enhance the text. Bibliography and Index.

230.   Biel, Timothy L. **The Civil War**. San Diego, CA: Lucent, 1991. 144p. $16.95. ISBN 1-56006-404-8. (America's Wars). 5-8

The text looks at the Civil War (1861-1865) in terms of its political, cultural, and military aspects and how it divided the Union. Bibliography and Index.

231.   Birch, Beverley, and Valerie Schloredt. **Martin Luther King, Jr.: Leader in the Struggle for Civil Rights**. Milwaukee, WI: Gareth Stevens, 1990. 68p. $16.95. ISBN 0-8368-0392-2. (People Who Made a Difference). 3-6

Starting with discussions on slavery, Jim Crow laws, and the Ku Klux Klan, the text leads to Martin Luther King, Jr.'s birth on January 15, 1929, in Atlanta, Georgia. King excelled in school, entered Morehead College at 15, and decided to be a minister, preaching his first sermon in his father's church when 17. In school, the philosophies of the American Henry David Thoreau and the Indian Mahatma Gandhi impressed him. In 1955, he finished his Ph.D. from Boston University while working full-time as a minister in Montgomery, Alabama. That same year, Rosa Parks refused to relinquish her bus seat, and King, Ralph Abernathy, and E. D. Nixon organized the Montgomery bus boycott. Although threatened, he persevered and gave his famous "I Have a Dream" speech on August 28, 1963. In 1964, he won the Nobel Peace Prize, only to be assassinated four years later. Organizations, Books, List of New Words, Important Dates, and Index.

232.   Bird, E. J., author/illustrator. **The Blizzard of 1896**. Minneapolis, MN: Carolrhoda, 1990. 72p. $9.95. ISBN 0-8761-4651-5. 2-4

Uncle Tim tells the incredible things that happened to people and animals during the blizzard of 1896 in the western part of the United States.

233.   Bird, E. J. **The Rainmakers**. Minneapolis, MN: Carolrhoda, 1993. 120p. $17.50. ISBN 0-87614-748-1. 4-6

Cricket, 11, finds an orphaned bear cub around AD 1250 in the Anasazi tribal area of Mesa Verde, Colorado. While the bear dances, Cricket plays his flute like the Anasazi god of mischief Kokopelli, and rains come. Their rain dances become famous in the area, and other groups seek their skills. At one place where Cricket and the bear dance, Cricket finds his sister whom the family had thought kidnapped by enemies.

234.   Bishop, Jack. **Ralph Ellison: Author**. New York: Chelsea House, 1988. 110p. $18.95. ISBN 1-55546-585-4. (Black Americans of Achievement). 5 up

Although he won a scholarship to study music at Tuskegee Institute, Ralph Ellison (1914-1994) became a writer instead. He wrote one book on which his literary merit stands, *Invisible Man*. Afterward, he wrote shorter pieces, but he was mainly a spokesman for the importance of individual excellence and Black culture. Photographs enhance the text. Chronology, Further Reading, and Index.

235.   Bisson, Terry. **Nat Turner: Slave Revolt Leader**. New York: Chelsea House, 1988. 112p. $18.95; $7.95pa. ISBN 1-55546-613-3; 0-7910-0214-4pa. (Black Americans of Achievement). 5 up

Nat Turner (1800-1831) was a fiery preacher and a militant leader whose slave uprising struck a blow against slavery 30 years before the Civil War began. He had mystical visions and began to preach in local churches when he was not in the fields. In 1831, he began his revolt, and the men who were with him left people dead in their wake as they fought against the slave system. They dispelled the myth that slaves were content with their lives. Photographs and engravings enhance the text. Chronology, Further Reading, and Index.

236.   Black, Shelia. **Sitting Bull and the Battle of the Little Bighorn**. Ed Lee, illustrator. Englewood Cliffs, NJ: Silver Burdett, 1989. 123p. $12.95. ISBN 0-382-09572-3. (Biography of American Indians). 5-8

Known for the Battle of Little Bighorn where he defeated Custer, Sitting Bull (1834?-1890) escaped to Canada but was offered amnesty when he returned in 1881 to live on a reservation. In 1890, friends tried to rescue him, and someone (supposedly shooting at someone else) killed him. The Sioux, instead of rising against the whites, embraced Ghost Dancing. Bibliography and Index.

237.   Black, Wallace B., and Jean F. Blashfield. **America Prepares for War**. New York: Crestwood House, 1991. 48p. $12.95. ISBN 0-89686-554-1. (World War II 50th Anniversary). 5-8

The text describes the military preparations that occurred before the United States actually entered World War II in 1941 and the other ways in which the country was already unofficially involved in the war. Black-and-white photographs supplement the text. Glossary and Index.

238.   Black, Wallace B., and Jean F. Blashfield. **Bataan and Corregidor**. New York: Crestwood House, 1991. 48p. $12.95. ISBN 0-89686-557-6. (World War II 50th Anniversary). 5 up

After the attack on Pearl Harbor, the Japanese went to the Philippines. Japanese air attacks led the United States to use Corregidor in Manila Bay as the command post while Bataan, part of the island of Luzon across from Manila, was the stronghold for troops to hold off the invading Japanese. The Battle of Bataan under General MacArthur failed, and on April 9, 1942, the Allies surrendered it to the Japanese. Then Corregidor was surrendered on May 6, 1942. Black-and-white photographs supplement the text. Glossary and Index.

239.   Black, Wallace B., and Jean F. Blashfield. **Battle of the Atlantic**. New York: Crestwood House, 1991. 48p. $12.95. ISBN 0-89686-558-4. (World War II 50th Anniversary). 4-9

This account of the Battle of the Atlantic tells of the struggle that the Allied forces had in trying to keep the North Atlantic free of German U-boats, or submarines, during World War II. On September 3, 1939, when the Germans torpedoed the *Athenia*, a British ocean liner with 1,300 passengers, they claimed that they thought it was an armed merchant ship. Photos and diagrams show the blitzkrieg at sea. U-boats and bombers, along with convoys to Russia, appeared before the U.S. Navy joined the battle, and the Allies fought back. Although U-boats were discovered off the coast of New York, antisubmarine warfare helped control them. Black-and-white photographs augment the text. Closer Look at German U-Boats and Allied Ships and Planes, Glossary, and Index.

240.   Black, Wallace B., and Jean F. Blashfield. **Battle of the Bulge**. New York: Crestwood House, 1992. 48p. $12.95. ISBN 0-89686-568-1. (World War II 50th Anniversary). 4-9

The road to Ardennes started in 1944. The Watch on the Rhine was Hitler's plan to divide the American and British attack before the Battle of the Bulge, December 16, 1944. He failed, but with Bastogne under siege, the German commander asked for an Allied surrender. The Allied commander, McAuliffe, replied, "Nuts!" On December 26, General Patton broke through the German lines and stopped the siege. Nordwind and Bodenplatte were two plans of the German offense that failed, and the Germans withdrew by January 22, 1945. The Bridge at Remagen was where the Allies crossed into German territory on March 7, 1945. Black-and-white photographs highlight the text. Glossary and Index.

241.   Black, Wallace B., and Jean F. Blashfield. **D-Day**. New York: Crestwood House, 1992. 48p. $12.95. ISBN 0-89686-566-6. (World War II 50th Anniversary). 5 up

In planning for D-Day, the Allies decided to invade the Normandy beaches to retake France. Operation Neptune called for naval operations to land on the Normandy beaches while protected from the air by the Allied forces. The Germans delayed in their pursuit, and the June 6, 1944, Allied invasion was successful. Black-and-white photographs supplement the text. Glossary and Index.

242.   Black, Wallace B., and Jean F. Blashfield. **Desert Warfare**. New York; Crestwood House, 1992. 48p. $12.95. ISBN 0-89686-561-4. (World War II 50th Anniversary). 5 up

Italy had a disaster in Africa when the British took control of East Africa in February 1941. The German army came to rescue Italians with General Rommel, the Desert Fox, in charge. The British retreated to El Alamein, 240 miles from Egypt, but General Montgomery took charge and defeated Rommel. The Allied Operation Torch invasion led to the race for Tunis. Next was the Battle of Kasserine Pass, which was won because the Germans could not agree on the best plan of attack. The resources of the Allies helped them win. Victory at Hill 609 prepared the way for the May 13, 1943, invasion of Italy. Black-and-white photographs supplement the text. Glossary and Index.

243. Black, Wallace B., and Jean F. Blashfield. **Flattops at War**. New York: Crestwood House, 1992. 48p. $12.95. ISBN 0-89686-559-2. (World War II 50th Anniversary). 5 up

After Pearl Harbor, the Battle of Coral Sea took place in February 1942. The Battle of Midway followed in June 1942. In these battles, the flattops (aircraft carriers) were most important. They continued to escort U-boats and participated in the Marianas "Turkey Shoot," June 19-21, 1944. Photographs of the war with flattops and planes of the U.S. Navy correlate with the text. Glossary and Index.

244. Black, Wallace B., and Jean F. Blashfield. **Guadalcanal**. New York: Crestwood House, 1992. 48p. $12.95. ISBN 0-89686-560-6. (World War II 50th Anniversary). 5 up

The Japanese attacked Midway Island on June 4, 1942. Following the attack, the Allies decided to invade Guadalcanal in August. Land battles ensued, as did sea battles, culminating with the Battle of the Solomon Islands on November 12, 1942. The Air Force helped, and the Japanese finally withdrew from Guadalcanal in February 1943. Black-and-white photographs augment the text. Index.

245. Black, Wallace B., and Jean F. Blashfield. **Hiroshima and the Atomic Bomb**. New York: Crestwood House, 1993. 48p. $12.95. ISBN 0-89686-571-1. (World War II 50th Anniversary). 5 up

In 1939, the Manhattan Project in Los Alamos and uranium manufacturing at Oak Ridge, Tennessee, simultaneously allowed the creation of the atomic bomb. After Iwo Jima and Okinawa, the Allies firebombed Tokyo in March 1945. Although the Japanese were starving, they kept fighting. The Enola Gay dropped "Little Boy," the first atomic bomb ordered by President Truman, on August 6, 1945, at 8:16 AM. After the second bomb ("Fat Man") on Nagasaki three days later, Japan surrendered. Black-and-white photographs supplement the text. Glossary and Index.

246. Black, Wallace B., and Jean F. Blashfield. **Invasion of Italy**. New York: Crestwood House, 1992. 48p. $12.95. ISBN 0-89686-565-7. (World War II 50th Anniversary). 5 up

In 1943, Operation Husky marked the invasion of Sicily to gain control of the Mediterranean Sea. The Allied forces landed there on July 10, 1943, under British Field Marshal Sir Harold Alexander, and Italy surrendered on September 1. Then the Allies invaded southern Italy. The Italian fleet surrendered, and the Germans retreated toward Rome. The Allies became temporarily trapped at Anzio because of misunderstandings and delays. The Battle for Monte Cassino occurred in late 1944, and Rome finally fell on June 4, 1944. The Germans made their new line 150 miles north of Rome before they surrendered Italy on April 29, 1945, after Mussolini's assassination. Black-and-white photographs augment the text. Glossary and Index.

247. Black, Wallace B., and Jean F. Blashfield. **Island Hopping in the Pacific**. New York: Crestwood House, 1992. 48p. $12.95. ISBN 0-89686-567-3. (World War II 50th Anniversary). 5 up

Japan threatened Australia in 1942, and the first encounter with naval forces occurred at the Battle of the Coral Sea. The strategy of island-hopping began from Guadalcanal and Papua, New Guinea. The Japanese had Rabaul, a fortress on the island of New Britain, that the Allies decided to capture after taking the Solomons and New Guinea. In 1944, the Allies' target date for retaking Philippines and Formosa (Taiwan) was February 1945, but they succeeded by June 1944. General MacArthur returned to the Philippines in October 1944 and plotted to take Iwo Jima. Black-and-white photographs augment the text. Glossary and Index.

248. Black, Wallace B., and Jean F. Blashfield. **Iwo Jima and Okinawa**. New York: Crestwood House, 1993. 48p. $12.95. ISBN 0-89686-569-X. (World War II 50th Anniversary). 5 up

The battles of Coral Sea and Midway occurred in 1945 before the Marines began landing on Iwo Jima beaches. They captured Mount Suribachi on February 23, 1945. Then they continued until victory on June 20 with Operation Iceberg. The Allied forces needed Okinawa for a base from which to launch other attacks on the Japanese. Black-and-white photographs highlight the text. Glossary and Index.

249. Black, Wallace B., and Jean F. Blashfield. **Jungle Warfare**. New York: Crestwood House, 1992. 48p. $12.95. ISBN 0-89686-563-0. (World War II 50th Anniversary). 5 up

In January 1942, Japan invaded Burma. The Allied commanders Vinegar Joe Stillwell, Chiang Kai-Shek, and Claire Chennault of the Flying Tigers in France disagreed about approaches to the difficult jungle terrain. Then Wingate's Chindit Raiders, British guerrilla forces, completed daring missions so that Wingate earned the label of "half genius and half mad." Merrill's Marauders were America's jungle fighters. Also in this area were the U.S. Air Force and the OSS, forerunner of the CIA. The last campaigns in the China-India-Burma area occurred in 1945. Black-and-white photographs supplement the text. Glossary and Index.

250. Black, Wallace B., and Jean F. Blashfield. **Pearl Harbor!** New York: Crestwood House, 1991. 48p. $12.95. ISBN 0-89686-555-X. (World War II 50th Anniversary). 5-8

In 1941, when the Japanese bombed the Pacific fleet at Pearl Harbor, America was ill-prepared for combat but still declared war on Japan. This account discusses the Japanese strategy and tactics and why the American forces were surprised by the attack. Black-and-white photographs complement the text. Glossary and Index.

251. Black, Wallace B., and Jean F. Blashfield. **Victory in Europe**. New York: Crestwood House, 1992. 48p. $12.95. ISBN 0-89686-570-3. (World War II 50th Anniversary). 5 up

The text gives an overview of World War II in Europe, the trek eastward from the Rhine, the Russian thousand-mile front, Germany surrounded, the Battle of Berlin in 1945, and the unconditional German surrender on May 7, 1945. The book also covers the Holocaust, starting with *Kristallnacht* (Crystal Night), as it looks at the cost of the war to all. Capsule biographies of Allied leaders end the information. Black-and-white photographs supplement the text. Glossary and Index.

252. Black, Wallace B., and Jean F. Blashfield. **War Behind the Lines**. New York: Crestwood House, 1992. 48p. $12.95. ISBN 0-89686-564-9. (World War II 50th Anniversary). 5 up

During World War II, battles behind the lines helped win the war. The text looks at the British Secret Services, the OSS of the Americans, the organization of the Resistance against the Nazis, the *Maquis* or Resistance heroes, women and the underground war, the Resistance in Norway, *Chetniks* (Yugoslavians) and Partisans (Communists against Hitler in other countries), and Russian Partisans. Heroes of the Resistance include Major General William Donovan, Marshal Tito, and General Charles de Gaulle. Glossary and Index.

253. Blair, Gwenda. **Laura Ingalls Wilder**. Thomas B Allen, illustrator. New York: Putnam, 1981. 64p. $9.99; $6.95pa. ISBN 0-399-61139-8; 0-399-20953-0pa. 1-4

For fans of Wilder, this book adds little information not available in the *Little House* books, but it rapidly covers the facts of Wilder's life (1867-1957), pointing out that she did not start to write her books until she was 63.

254. Blake, Arthur, and Pamela Dailey. **The Gold Rush of 1849: Staking a Claim in California**. Brookfield, CT: Millbrook Press, 1995. 64p. $15.90. ISBN 1-56294-483-5. (Spotlight on American History). 5-8

James Marshall, a carpenter, found gold in front of a sawmill belonging to John Sutter on January 24, 1848. His discovery led to the beginning of the gold rush as people scurried to the spot. They came by sea and by land from everywhere. The text looks at this migration and the camps set up to house the people, the ways they dug for the gold, the ways they spent their leisure time, and the results of their quests for wealth. Chronology, Further Reading, Bibliography, and Index.

255. Blake, Robert J. **Spray**. New York: Philomel, 1996. Unpaged. $15.95. ISBN 0-399-22770-9. 2-4

Justin, a newcomer in Martha's Vineyard, goes sailing and capsizes. Another Justin rescues him, and he happens to be Justin Slocum, the first man to sail around the world alone in 1898 on his sloop *Spray*. The Justins sail on *Spray* as the younger one learns to sail and encounters a pirate ship.

256. Blakely, Martha. **Native Americans and the U.S. Government**. New York: Chelsea House, 1995. 59p. $14.95. ISBN 0-7910-2475-X. (Junior Library of American Indians). 5-9

The U.S. government has made policies that have affected the lives of Native Americans throughout the history of the nation. The government took possession of Indian lands and placed the Indians on reservations. The General Allotment Act of 1887, the Dawes Act, divided the reservations into individual allotments of land assigned to families, which conflicted with tribal concepts of land ownership. The text looks at some of the questions that the government asked before it made decisions as well as at the Bureau of Indian Affairs, a government organization that has tried to change some of the past mistakes while simultaneously making new ones. Glossary, Chronology, and Index.

257. Bland, Celia. **The Conspiracy of the Secret Nine**. New York: Silver Moon Press, 1995 80p. $12.95. ISBN 1-881889-67-X. (Mysteries in Time). 3-5

In 1898, in Wilmington, North Carolina, two young boys see torches burning in a cemetery and menacing letters signed with "The Secret Nine." They try to find out who the group is and whether it is related to the cemetery phenomenon.

258. Bland, Celia. **Harriet Beecher Stowe: Antislavery Author**. New York: Chelsea House, 1993. 79p. $14.95; $4.95. ISBN 0-7910-1773-7; 0-7910-1968-3pa. (Junior World Biographies). 3-6

Harriet Beecher Stowe (1811-1896) expressed her convictions against slavery when such opinions were generally unacceptable and dangerous. This biography tells about Stowe's ideas and how they grew into the novel *Uncle Tom's Cabin*, a book denouncing slavery and intensifying the disagreement between the North and South. Bibliography and Index.

259. Bland, Celia. **Osceola: Seminole Rebel**. New York: Chelsea House, 1993. 110p. $18.95. ISBN 0-7910-1716-8. (North American Indians of Achievement). 5 up

Osceola's (1804-1838) resistance against the U.S. Army for seven years in Florida during the Second Seminole War showed his intelligence, his courage, and his strength of purpose. When he was 10, he fled to Florida from Alabama with his family because the government wanted the land. When the government declared that the Seminoles had to leave Florida, Osceola persuaded the Seminoles to resist, and they foiled the government. Engravings and reproductions enhance the text. Chronology, Further Reading, and Index.

260. Bland, Celia. **Pontiac: Ottawa Rebel**. New York: Chelsea House, 1994. 110p. $18.95; $7.95pa. ISBN 0-7910-1717-6; 0-7910-2043-6pa. (North American Indians of Achievement). 5 up

In 1763, Pontiac (1725-1769) led one of the smartest campaigns that a Native American had ever waged against the whites up to that time. His people and the French fur traders together had tried to defend their lands from the British. The British declared victory in 1760 but broke their treaty terms in 1762. Pontiac inspired nearly 18 tribes to fight against them, and for six months, the Indians and the French struggled against the British for the land between the Great Lakes and the Ohio Valley. Although the Indians lost, they showed their strength. Photographs and engravings enhance the text. Chronology, Further Reading, and Index.

261. Blassingame, Wyatt. **Jim Beckwourth: Black Trapper and Indian Chief**. Vestal Herman, illustrator. New York: Chelsea Juniors, 1991. 80p. $14.95. ISBN 0-7910-1404-5. (Discovery Biography). 2-6

Jim Beckwourth (1798-1866), born to a Black mother and a white father, became a great hunter and trapper. He was famous among mountaineers after he began his career at 14 by becoming a hunter for a group of soldiers. He trapped beaver in the Rocky Mountains, learned the ways of the Crow Indians, and earned the name Chief Medicine Calf for his leadership.

262. Blassingame, Wyatt. **The Look-It-Up Book of Presidents**. New York: Random House, 1990. 159p. $7.99pa. ISBN 0-679-80358-0pa. 6-9

Short biographies of two to four pages and portraits or photographs give insight into the characters of each man who led the United States, from George Washington through George Bush. Presidents at a Glance and Index.

263. Blau, Justine. **Betty Friedan: Feminist**. New York: Chelsea House, 1990. 102p. $18.95. ISBN 1-55546-653-2. (American Women of Achievement). 5 up

Elizabeth Naomi Goldstein (b. 1921) graduated near the top of her class in Smith College and won a prestigious research fellowship. Then she went to New York with her new husband to raise a family. The emptiness of being at home without intellectual stimulation led her to write *The Feminine Mystique* (1963), about men denying women the chance to perform meaningful work. Her book spurred the creation of the National Organization for Women (NOW), and she became its first president. As a senior citizen, she transferred her concerns to America's treatment of the aged. She talks about taboo subjects that force people to examine what they really think. Photographs enhance the text. Chronology, Further Reading, and Index.

264. Blos, Joan. **Brothers of the Heart: A Story of the Old Northwest, 1837-38**. New York: Scribner's, 1985. 176p. $14.95. ISBN 0-684-18452-4. 6 up

In a flashback while celebrating his 50th wedding anniversary, Shem remembers the one year that he lived away from Millfield, Michigan. His legs crippled, Shem needed to go to Detroit to find work. He kept accounts so well that his employer asked him to go on a fur expedition to keep records. When in trouble, the other men had to leave him in the woods, but they did not return as promised. An old woman, abandoned by her tribe to die, found him and taught him how to survive the Canadian winter. In turn, he befriended her and buried her when she died. His story, told by those who knew of her secrecy, made him a hero and a worthy mate for the woman he had always loved.

265. Blos, Joan. **A Gathering of Days: A New England Girl's Journal, 1830-32**. New York: Scribner's, 1979. 144p. $14. ISBN 0-684-16340-3. New York: Aladdin, 1990. 144p. $3.95pa. ISBN 0-689-71419-Xpa. 4-7

Catherine keeps a journal of her 14th year, 1830-1832, during which a friend dies; another departs for the Lowell, Massachusetts, factories; her father remarries; she gives one of her deceased mother's quilts to a runaway slave hiding in the woods; and she leaves home to tend someone else's child. She sends a letter and the journal to her great-granddaughter during her own 14th year in 1899. Her great granddaughter asks questions, and in a second letter, Catherine responds. The story reveals the time and life in New England. *Newbery Medal*.

266. Blos, Joan. **The Heroine of the Titanic: A Tale Both True and Otherwise of the Life of Molly Brown**. Tennessee Dixon, illustrator. New York: Morrow, 1991. Unpaged. $14.95. ISBN 0-688-07546-0. 2-4

Molly Brown left home at 19 in 1886 to search for gold in Leadville, Colorado. She met Jim Brown and told him that she wanted to have fun, do good, and have a lot of money. They married, became wealthy, and moved to Denver. After their children grew up, they separated, and Molly began traveling. She took the *Titanic* on its maiden voyage, and when it sank on April 14, 1912, she survived on one of the lifeboats and kept up the spirits of those who were with her. Before she died in New York, she sent presents to people in Leadville because they had lost their tourist and gold trade.

267. Blos, Joan W. **Brooklyn Doesn't Rhyme**. Paul Birling, illustrator. New York: Atheneum, 1994. 86p. $12.95. ISBN 0-684-19694-8. 4-6

Rosey Sachs has to write family stories for her sixth grade class in 1907. In her vignettes she reveals her Polish-Austrian-Jewish family and how they are learning to understand the American economy and culture as they help even newer immigrants adjust to Brooklyn. As Rosey's teacher suggested, Rosey learns about herself as she writes about her family.

268. Blos, Joan W. **Nellie Bly's Monkey: His Remarkable Story in His Own Words**. Catherine Stock, illustrator. New York: Morrow, 1996. 40p. $15. ISBN 0-688-12677-4. 2-5

McGinty, a monkey that Nelly Bly (1867-1922) purchased in Singapore, tells the story of the last leg of her 72-day trip around the world in 1889. He recalls their adventures and the various places they visited as well as the difficulties they encountered along the way. Bly herself wrote about the trip when she returned.

269. Blue, Rose, and Corinne Naden. **Barbara Jordan: Politician**. New York: Chelsea House, 1991. 110p. $18.85. ISBN 0-7910-1131-3. (Black Americans of Achievement). 5 up

Barbara Jordan (1936-1996), native of one of the poorest Black neighborhoods in Texas, became the South's first Black U.S. congresswoman. She went to school and established a law firm in Houston before she started campaigning for state office. In Congress, she helped investigate Watergate, and in 1976 she gave the keynote address at the Democratic National Convention. She retired to become a professor and to cope with a neurological disease that confined her to a wheelchair, but she always displayed intelligence and compassion toward her country. Photographs enhance the text. Chronology, Further Reading, and Index.

270. Blue, Rose, and Corrine Naden. **People of Peace**. Brookfield, CT, Millbrook Press, 1994. 80p. $18.90. ISBN 1-56294-409-6. 5-8

Because some people refused to compromise with the status quo and instead worked for peace, they made the world better than before. Some of these people won the Nobel Peace Prize for their efforts, but they have all saved lives. The people presented here are Andrew Carnegie (United States, 1835-1919), Jane Addams (United States, 1860-1935), Woodrow Wilson (United States, 1856-1924), Mohandas Gandhi (India, 1869-1948), Ralph Bunche (United States, 1904-1971), Dag Hammarskjöld (Sweden, 1905-1961), Jimmy Carter (United States, b. 1924), Desmond Tutu (South Africa, b. 1931), Oscar Arias Sanchez (Costa Rica, b. 1941), Betty Williams (Northern Ireland, b. 1943), and Mairead Corrigan Maguire (Northern Ireland, b. 1944). Conclusion, For Further Reading, and Index.

271. Blue, Rose, and Corinne J. Naden. **U.S. Air Force**. Brookfield, CT: Millbrook Press, 1993. 64p. $15.90; $5.95pa. ISBN 1-56294-217-4; 1-56294-754-0pa. (Defending Our Country). 3-6

Starting with a good historical background, the text discusses the role of the Air Force, its planes, its weapons, its command structure, and its work for the defense of the country. Bibliography and Index.

272. Blue, Rose, and Corinne J. Naden. **The White House Kids**. Brookfield, CT: Millbrook Press, 1995. 96p. $17.90. ISBN 1-56294-447-9. 4-6

Because the White House was not built when George Washington was president, he is one of the few presidents who had no children in it even though he did adopt children and have grandchildren. The text divides the commentary on children who were associated with the White House into six groups: the founding families through John Quincy Adams, the pre–Civil War families from Jackson to Buchanan, the Civil War and afterward from Lincoln to Arthur, the turn of the century from Cleveland to Taft, a growing America from Wilson to Johnson, and late-twentieth-century kids. Presidential Families, For Further Reading, and Index.

273. Blumberg, Rhoda. **Bloomers!** Mary Morgan, illustrator. New York: Bradbury, 1993. 32p. $14.95. ISBN 0-02-711684-0. New York: Aladdin, 1996. 32p. $5.95pa. ISBN 0-689-80455-5pa. K-5

When Libby Miller visits Seneca Falls, New York, in 1851, she wears blousy pants. A woman wrote about them in a magazine, and they got the name "bloomers." Elizabeth Cady Stanton wanted a pair, but men thought the clothes were indecent. The women who were campaigning to get the vote thought the pants were wonderful inventions that made climbing stairs easier. They decided to wear the pants even if men did not like them.

274. Blumberg, Rhoda. **The Incredible Journey of Lewis and Clark**. New York: Lothrop, Lee & Shepard, 1987. 144p. $18; $9.95pa. ISBN 0-688-06512-0; 0-688-14421-7pa. 4-10

Blumberg's scholarly and interesting background is complemented with photographs of documents and clear maps. Blumberg traces the Lewis and Clark expedition from its inception by Thomas Jefferson through its successful end. Jefferson, fearing that the British would settle the West and spurred on by Alex MacKenzie's reports of its wealth, requested that Congress fund a secret expedition. He asked for only a small amount of money so that Congress would agree, and selected his personal secretary, Lewis, 28, to head the group. Lewis chose a former military colleague, Clark, to join him as the map maker. They departed on August 31, 1803, from St. Louis, and returned on September 23, 1806. For the first time, those in the East became aware of the Yankton, Sioux, Teton Sioux, Arikara, Mandan, Crow, Hidatsa, Shoshoni, Nez Perce, Flathead, Blackfeet, Walla Walla, Wanapam, Clatsop, and Chinook Indian tribes plus 25 others. The expedition found 122 animals and 178 plants new to science. Aftermath, Notes, Bibliography, and Index.

275. Bodkin, Odds. **The Banshee Train**. Ted Rose, illustrator. New York: Clarion, 1995. Unpaged. $14.95. ISBN 0-395-69426-4. K-3

In 1929, spring storms and flooding make the railroad from Denver to Troublesome and Steamboat Springs dangerous, but Train Number 1 also has a mysterious train pursuing it to Gore Canyon, where a train and all its passengers were lost 20 years ago. The train escapes destruction at the last minute.

276. Bodow, Steven. **Sitting Bull: Sioux Leader**. Austin, TX: Raintree/Steck-Vaughn, 1994. 128p. $16.98. ISBN 0-8114-2328-X. (American Troublemakers). 6 up

Returns Again's son was born in 1831 into the Hunkpapa Sioux tribe but did not earn the name Sitting Bull until 1845. Throughout his life, he helped his people, eventually becoming their chief and medicine man. He worked to maintain the rights of Native Americans and encouraged the Sioux so that they defeated George Custer at the Battle of Little Bighorn in 1876. Although he took his people into Canada, lack of food forced them to return. The U.S. Army captured Sitting Bull and killed him in 1890. Maps, Photographs, Key Dates, Glossary, Places to Visit, Bibliography and Recommended Readings, and Index.

277. Bolden, Tonya. **Just Family**. New York: Cobblehill, 1996. 152p. $14.99. ISBN 0-525-65192-6. 4-7

Beryl, 10, and her older sister Randy are close friends as they grow up in the 1960s in a stable Harlem home with loving parents. Beryl discovers that Randy's father is different from hers and that Randy was born out of wedlock. That Randy knows this secret but never mentioned it before disturbs Beryl. Not until they attend a family reunion in South Carolina does Beryl begin to understand that family love and support are more important than people measuring up to others' criteria.

278. Bolick, Nancy O'Keefe. **Mail Call! The History of the U.S. Postal Service**. New York: Franklin Watts, 1995. 63p. $19.90. ISBN 0-531-20170-8. (First Books). 4-6

Although mail delivery of some kind has existed for many centuries throughout the world, mail delivery as it is currently known in the United States began in 1775, when the Second Continental Congress decided that the country should have a postmaster general. The first man appointed to the job was Benjamin Franklin, known as the father of the United States Postal Service. With complementary photographs, the text discusses ways the mail has been moved, such as by dog sled and the Pony Express; what happened during the Civil War; stamps and postmarks; and the contemporary postal service. For Further Reading and Index.

279. Bolick, Nancy O'Keefe, and Sallie G. Randolph. **Shaker Inventions**. Melissa Francisco, illustrator. New York: Walker, 1990. 96p. $12.95. ISBN 0-8027-6933-0. 4-6

Although all the Shakers are dead, the culture survives. The Shakers were a utopian society based on cleanliness, order, purity, good health, hard work, simplicity, and avoidance of waste. The text shows the ingenuity of their daily lives, including inventions such as a pill-making machine, window design, and chairs with tilting devices, as well as the motives behind their lifestyle. Index.

280. Bolick, Nancy O'Keefe, and Sally G. Randolph. **Shaker Villages**. Laura LoTurco, illustrator. New York: Walker, 1993. 79p. $13.85. ISBN 0-8027-8209-4. 4-8

After the Shakers came to America, they developed 19 communities. The sect was unusual because it kept the sexes separated and preached celibacy. While they thrived, the Shakers had their villages well organized. The text presents the architecture, industry, life, and worship of the Shakers. Time Line of Shaker History and Index.

281. Bolotin, Norman, and Angela Herb. **For Home and Country: A Civil War Scrapbook**. New York: Lodestar, Dutton, 1995. 98p. $16.99. ISBN 0-525-67495-0. (Young Readers History of the Civil War). 5 up

Sidebar text complements well-labeled photographs and reproductions showing aspects of the Civil War. Among the topics covered are outfitting the troops, the rigors of the war, food, coping, destruction of the armies as they marched, the sick and wounded, prisoners of war, news of the war, photographing the war, trying to escape boredom, and marching home at the end. Glossary and Bibliography.

282. Bolton, Jonathan, and Claire Wilson. **Joseph Brant: Mohawk Chief**. New York: Chelsea House, 1992. 112p. $18.95. ISBN 0-7910-1709-5. (North American Indians of Achievement). 5 up

As a member of two worlds, Joseph Brant (1743-1807) used his knowledge to help his country. He was a Thayendanega as a boy, reared as a Mohawk, and schooled by the British, where he gained praise for his mastery of English and understanding of European customs. He chose to be a missionary but had to abandon his plans when the American Revolution broke out. In 1775, he went on a diplomatic mission to England, and George III hosted a dinner in his honor. After England's defeat, Brant moved to Canada and tried to keep the whites from seizing Native American lands. His negotiations were so important that George Washington solicited his help. Photographs enhance the text. Chronology, Further Reading, and Index.

283.   Bonvillain, Nancy. **Black Hawk: Sac Rebel**. New York: Chelsea House, 1994. 110p. $18.95 ISBN 0-7910-1711-7. (North American Indians of Achievement). 5 up

Black Hawk (1767-1838) grew up in the Indian village of Saukenuk, now called Rock Island, Illinois. He learned to hunt, trade, and lead his people in battle so that he earned the rank of war chief. When the United States tried to get Sac and Fox Indians to give up their homelands, Black Hawk defied them by leading, at age 65, a protest of more than 2,000 people against the government order. Although the movement began in peace, the military drove them into retreat. They lost the Black Hawk war, but he offered a model of wisdom and idealism. Reproductions enhance the text. Chronology, Further Reading, and Index.

284.   Bonvillain, Nancy. **The Haidas: People of the Northwest Coast**. Brookfield, CT: Millbrook Press, 1994. 64p. $15.90. ISBN 1-56294-491-6. (Native Americans). 5-8

The Haida ancestors settled on the Queen Charlotte Islands in British Columbia, Canada, c. 1000. Many died in Alaska after 1750 from smallpox. Part of their culture was the celebration of potlatches and ceremonial dances that Canada outlawed in 1884. In the twentieth century, the Haidas joined with the Tlingits to file a land claim against the United States in Alaska, which they won. As they have become integrated into Alaskan and Canadian life, they have tried to preserve their identity through their traditions and artifacts. Important Dates, Glossary, Bibliography, and Index.

285.   Bonvillain, Nancy. **Hiawatha: Founder of the Iroquois Confederacy**. New York: Chelsea House, 1992. 120p. $18.95; $7.95. ISBN 0-7910-1707-9; 0-7910-1693-5pa. (North American Indians of Achievement). 5 up

In his attempt to create peace more than 500 years ago, Hiawatha was first thwarted by his enemy Thadodaho, an Onondaga chief. Probably Thadodaho killed Hiawatha's three daughters, but Hiawatha continued his pursuit of peace with the help of the Huron Indian, Deganawida. They convinced the Onondaga, Mohawk, Oneida, Cayuga, and Seneca nations to stop their conflicts and to create a common rule so that they would not destroy each other. Drawings and reproductions highlight the text. Chronology, Further Reading, and Index.

286.   Bortz, Fred. **Catastrophe!: Great Engineering Failure—and Success**. New York: W. H. Freeman, 1995. 80p. $19.95; $13.95pa. ISBN 0-7167-6538-1; 0-7167-6539-Xpa. (Scientific American's Mystery of Science). 5-9

Six engineering debacles have changed the lives of people who experienced them and lived as well as the families of those who died. The six discussed in the text are the collapse of the Kansas City Hyatt skywalk in 1980; the Tacoma Narrows Bridge in 1940; the crash of Eastern Airlines Flight 401 in Florida in 1972; the U.S. Space Shuttle *Challenger* disaster in 1986; nuclear power plant accidents (Three-Mile Island in 1979 and Chernobyl in 1986); and "The Great Northeast Blackout" of 1965. By explaining the science behind each disaster, the text shows how inadequate planning caused the problems and how engineers have corrected them. Photographs and Index.

287.   Borzendowski, Janice. **John Russwurm**. New York: Chelsea House, 1989. 110p. $18.95. ISBN 1-55545-610-9. (Black Americans of Achievement). 5 up

John Russwurm (1799-1851), son of a wealthy Jamaican landowner, came to America when he was 13. He attended private schools and was one of the first Black Americans to earn a college degree (Bowdoin College). He was a journalist and publisher who helped found *Freedom's Journal*, through which he attacked slavery and promoted Black pride. He also helped establish the Maryland Colony in Liberia, Africa, for former slaves to govern themselves. There he supervised the school system and started a newspaper before becoming the governor. Engravings and reproductions enhance the text. Chronology, Further Reading, and Index.

288.   Bosco, Peter I. **Roanoke: The Story of the Lost Colony**. Brookfield, CT: Millbrook Press, 1992. 72p. $13.90. ISBN 1-56294-111-9. (Spotlight on American History). 4-6

The people in the Roanoke colony, the first English settlement in the New World (established in 1585), disappeared 400 years ago. Where they went remains a mystery. Two colonists, scientist Thomas Hariot and Governor John White, wrote journals, and Bosco uses them to reveal what the group discovered about the Native Americans. Full-color maps and illustrations complement the text. Bibliography and Index. *Child Study Association Children's Books of the Year*.

289.   Boutis, Victoria. **Looking Out**. New York: Four Winds, 1988. 139p. $11.95. ISBN 0-02-711830-4. 6-9

In 1953, Ellen, 12, wants to be an ordinary girl like those in her class, but she hides a secret: Her parents are Communists. She fears that her parents will go to jail and be executed like the Rosenbergs for giving the Russians secrets about the atomic bomb. But she also resents her parents' attitude that Communism is more important to them than she is. She knows she can never be the average person she wants to be. *Jane Addams Book Award*.

290. Bowen, Andy Russell. **A World of Knowing: A Story About Thomas Hopkins Gallaudet**. Elaine Wadsworth, illustrator. Minneapolis, MN: Carolrhoda, 1995. 64p. $13.13; $5.95pa. ISBN 0-87614-871-2; 0-87614-954-9pa. (Creative Minds). 3-6

Thomas Gallaudet (1787-1851) suffered from poor health for most of his life, but he became the principal of the first school for the deaf and helped develop American Sign Language. When he was young, he met Alice Cogswell, a young deaf girl, with whom he began to work. Her father sent Gallaudet to Europe so that he could study deaf education. He returned and led a new school in Hartford, Connecticut. He fell in love with one of his students, who was 11 years younger than him, and married her in 1821. She feared that their children would be deaf, but none were. American Manual Alphabet, Bibliography, and Index.

291. Bowen, Gary, author/illustrator. **Stranded at Plimoth Plantation 1626**. New York: HarperCollins, 1994. 81p. $19.95. ISBN 0-06-022542-4. 2-6

In this journal kept by Christopher, a 13-year-old orphan waiting at Plimoth Plantation for passage to Jamestown, the reader finds a description of life in 1626-1627. Woodcuts illustrate Christopher's visits with Indians, the people planting and gathering food, their homes and businesses, and celebrations or losses. His experience enlightens readers about the New World.

292. Bowler, Mike. **Trains**. Steve Herridge, Paul Higgens, and Martin Woodward, illustrators. Austin, TX: Raintree/Steck-Vaughn, 1995. 32p. $13.98. ISBN 0-8114-6192-0. (Pointers). 3-7

The first locomotive ran along tracks in 1804. Two-page spreads of text and illustration present the history of trains. Topics and trains discussed are early railroads (c. 1825), the first inter-city railroad (1829), American locomotives (mid-nineteenth century), long-distance express trains (c. 1900), express steam trains, the largest steam engine, long-distance diesels, diesel-electric trains, high-speed diesels, subways, and the fastest trains currently in use. Glossary and Index.

293. Bradby, Marie. **More than Anything Else**. Chris K. Soentpiet, illustrator. New York: Jackson, Orchard, 1995. 32p. $14.95. ISBN 0-531-09464-2. K-3

When Booker T. Washington (1856-1915) hears a Black man read aloud, he has hope that he too can learn. His mother gets him an alphabet book, but he is unable to understand anything until the man he heard read shows him how. He spends time reading after working all day as he pursues his goal. *School Library Journal Starred Review*.

294. Brady, Philip. **Reluctant Hero: A Snowy Road to Salem in 1802**. New York: Walker, 1990. 159p. $16.95. ISBN 0-8027-6972-1. (Walker American History). 6-8

Cutting Favour, 13, has to travel from New Hampshire to Salem, Massachusetts, in snowy weather to sell furs and shingles so his family will have money for food. He has to defend a girl from a bully and then elude his new enemy, and he has to protect the money that he makes with his shrewd salesmanship and his ability to carve wood. By the time he returns home, he has been reluctantly successful in several ways.

295. Braine, Susan. **Drumbeat . . . Heartbeat: A Celebration of the Powwow**. Minneapolis, MN: Lerner, 1995. 48p. $19.95; $6.95pa. ISBN 0-8225-2656-5; 0-8225-9711-Xpa. (We Are Still Here: Native Americans Today). 3-6

At a powwow, the participants dance to celebrate, to share ancient cultures, to meet old and new friends, and to honor everyone, including the spirits of ancestors. The text, complemented with photographs, describes the powwow, the various dances, and the ceremonial rituals. Word List and For Further Reading.

296. Branch, Muriel Miller. **The Water Brought Us: The Story of the Gullah-Speaking People**. New York: Cobblehill, Dutton, 1995. 106p. $16.99. ISBN 0-525-65185-3. 5 up

Off the coast of South Carolina are 35 Sea Islands where the Gullah, descendants of slaves who stayed after the Emancipation, have become landowners, farmers, teachers, nurses, and other leaders in the community. The origin of their language traces to the castles and forts along the West African coast, where captured Africans awaited transport to the West Indies and America to be sold into slavery. The text presents their history through slavery, their religious traditions, and their language. Bibliography and Index.

297. Branscum, Robbie. **Old Blue Tilley**. New York: Macmillan, 1991. 96p. $11.95. ISBN 0-02-711931-9. 5-7

Hambone, a 14-year-old orphan, lives alone until he joins a circuit-riding preacher, Old Blue. He travels with Old Blue through the Ozarks as World War II begins in 1941. After a revival meeting, Old Blue's influence helps Hambone realize that he must assert himself by demanding his inheritance from his uncles and by returning to revive the family farm.

298. Brashler, William. **The Story of the Negro League Baseball**. New York: Ticknor & Fields, 1994. 166p. $15.95. ISBN 0-395-67169-8. 6 up

From 1890 to 1947, major league baseball was not an option for Black and Latino players. They formed their own leagues and teams such as the Black Yankees, the Homestead Grays, and the Kansas City Monarchs. Their wool uniforms and night lights were new, but they could not go into restaurants or hotels because of Jim Crow segregation laws. The text tells their stories. Box Score, Bibliography, and Index.

299. Bratman, Fred. **Becoming a Citizen: Adopting a New Home**. Austin, TX: Raintree/Steck-Vaughn, 1993. 48p. $15.49; $6.64. ISBN 0-8114-7354-6; 0-8114-5582-3pa. (Good Citizenship). 4-9

The text looks at the origins of citizenship as it discusses immigration, illegal aliens, and political asylum. Citizenship has been important throughout history. In America, citizenship began when immigrants arrived on the Mayflower in 1620. Four waves of immigrants have come to this country. The first wave occurred during the 1700s with many indentured servants. The second wave, mostly Germans and Irish, lasted from 1820 until 1870. In 1881, the third wave began and lasted for 40 years when 23 million arrived. The fourth wave began in 1965. Because of all these new people, learning the requirements for citizenship has been important. Photographs highlight the text. Further Reading, Glossary, and Index.

300. Bray, Rosemary. **Martin Luther King**. New York: Greenwillow, Morrow, 1995. 47p. $16. ISBN 0-688-13131-X. 2-5

Martin Luther King, Jr.'s father changed his name from Michael to Martin. Influences during King's youth appear along with his decision to attend college and graduate school, where he first heard about Gandhi and nonviolent resistance. When he went to Montgomery, Alabama, Rosa Parks sat in the front of the bus, and King wrote about the bus boycott that he helped organize in *Stride Toward Freedom*. He believed in civil disobedience—better to go to jail for breaking an unjust law than to submit to that law. On August 28, 1963, he led the march on Washington that attracted more than 250,000 people and gave his "I Have a Dream" speech. In 1964, at 35, he was awarded the Nobel Peace Prize, the youngest person ever to receive it. Before his assassination on April 4, 1968, he declared that the United States' involvement in Vietnam was immoral. Dates.

301. Bredeson, Carmen. **Jonas Salk: Discoverer of the Polio Vaccine**. Springfield, NJ: Enslow, 1993. 112p. $17.95. ISBN 0-89490-415-9. (People to Know). 5-9

Jonas Salk (b. 1914) found a vaccine to stop polio. At first people were leery of the serum, but desperate individuals were willing to try anything to avoid the horror of this disease, which damaged the cells of the brain and the spinal cord, leaving its sufferers paralyzed. Salk has also worked with other viruses such as HIV and influenza. His goal has always been the prevention of disease rather than fame. The text looks at his life and accomplishments. Chronology, Notes, Further Reading, and Index.

302. Brenner, Barbara, author/illustrator. **If You Were There in 1492**. New York: Bradbury, 1991. 112p. $13.95. ISBN 0-02-712321-9. 3-5

The text contains much information about the world during 1492, including statistics, descriptions of lifestyles, and expectations of the time. It also covers the world situation, including the expulsion of the Jews from Spain as Columbus sailed and background on the Arawak cultures that he enslaved and decimated. Notes, Bibliography, and Index.

303. Brenner, Barbara, author/illustrator. **If You Were There in 1776**. New York: Macmillan, 1994. 112p. $14.95. ISBN 0-02-712322-7. 3-6

During 1776 in the American colonies, the experiences people had influenced the concepts and principles incorporated into the Declaration of Independence. Brenner looks at the lives of families on a New England farm, a southern plantation, and the frontier to see what different people talked about, believed, ate, played, created, and felt about the Revolutionary War. Photographs complement the text. Notes, Sources, and Index.

304. Brenner, Barbara. **On the Frontier with Mr. Audubon**. New York: Coward, McCann, & Geoghegan, 1977. 96p. $6.95. ISBN 0-698-20385-2. 6-9

Joseph Mason travels down the Ohio and Mississippi Rivers and through the swamplands of Louisiana with John James Audubon (1785-1851) for 18 months. He sketches 50 of the 435 plates that Audubon later includes in his book but for which he does not give Mason credit. Mason is surprised and angered, but by the time the book is published, he has established himself as a portrait painter in Philadelphia and no longer needs Audubon's approval or acknowledgment.

305. Brenner, Barbara. **Wagon Wheels**. Don Bolognese, illustrator. New York: HarperCollins, 1978. 64p. $14.95; $3.75pa. ISBN 0-06-020668-3; 0-06-444052-4pa. (I Can Read Book). K-3

Ed Muldie takes his African American family west in 1878, but his wife dies on the journey, leaving him three boys. Johnny, 11, has to stay with the other two boys in Nicodemus, Kansas, while his father goes ahead to find better land. Osage Indians help the townspeople survive a famine; the boys have to help extinguish a prairie fire; and they have to protect themselves from a poisonous snake warming by their campfire before their father returns. *American Library Association Notable Books for Children* and *Notable Children's Trade Books in the Field of Social Studies.*

306. Brenner, Martha. **Abe Lincoln's Hat**. Donald Cook, illustrator. New York: Random House, 1994. 48p. $3.99pa. ISBN 0-679-84977-7pa. (Step into Reading). 1-3
     Abraham Lincoln (1809-1865) appears in this biography as a disorganized lawyer with common sense who succeeds because people like him. A court case where Lincoln had a colt turned loose to go to its mother showed who was the rightful owner of the horse. He also defended a slave who thought that he should be free in Illinois because it was a free state. Lincoln used his stovepipe hat not only to protect his head but also to protect important papers. Lincoln seems very human in this presentation.

307. Bresnick-Perry, Roslyn. **Leaving for America**. Mira Reisberg, illustrator. Chicago: Childrens Press, 1992. 28p. $13.95. ISBN 0-829239-105-7. 1-3
     The author left her home of Wysokie-Litewskie, Belarus, to come to America when she was very young because of Russian persecution of Jews. She recalls her days there before she and her mother had to leave relatives to join her father in the United States.

308. Brighton, Catherine, author/illustrator. **Dearest Grandmama**. New York: Doubleday, 1991. 28p. $13.95. ISBN 0-385-41843-4. 1-3
     In 1830, Maudie-Ann sails with her father, a naturalist, on the *Meralda*. She writes her grandmother about a boy who appears one night and who does not eat or sleep or have a shadow. She gives other strange details about the boy, but in a last letter to her grandmother, her father says that she has been sick.

309. Brill, Marlene Targ. **Allen Jay and the Underground Railroad**. Janice Lee Porter, illustrator. Minneapolis, MN: Carolrhoda, 1993. 47p. $15.95: $5.95pa. ISBN 0-87614-776-7; 0-87614-605-1pa. (On My Own). 2-4
     Allen Jay, 11, a young Quaker boy living in Randolph, Ohio, helps a slave flee his master on July 1, 1842. The experience helps him understand the dangers as well as the importance of his efforts.

310. Brill, Marlene Targ. **John Adams**. Chicago: Childrens Press, 1986. 100p. $17.27. ISBN 0-516-01384-X. (Encyclopedia of Presidents). 4-9
     John Adams (1735-1826) was the second president of the United States. He grew up in Braintree, Massachusetts, and trained to be a lawyer. After becoming involved in the rebellion against the English and taxation, he served abroad in Paris because he wanted to leave public life. Then he became the President because he was encouraged by his wife to do what needed to be done for the new country. Chronology and Index.

311. Brill, Marlene Targ. **Let Women Vote!** Brookfield, CT: Millbrook Press, 1996. 64p. $15.90. ISBN 1-56294-589-0. (Spotlight on American History). 4-6
     The text retells the struggle of women in their pursuit of the right to vote since before the Civil War. Even on the days before the final decision in 1920, women such as Carrie Chapman Catt had to continue their crusading. Other important advocates included Susan B. Anthony, Lucy Stone, Lucretia Mott, and Elizabeth Cady Stanton. Recollections of situations for which women had to fight also appear, such as the right to attend school. Chronology, Bibliography, Further Reading, and Index.

312. Brill, Marlene Targ. **The Trail of Tears: The Cherokee Journey from Home**. Brookfield, CT: Millbrook Press, 1995. 64p. $15.90. ISBN 1-56294-486-X. (Spotlight on American History). 6-9
     When the U.S. government removed Cherokees from their homes, people who once had plantations, animals, slaves, and gristmills were made to leave without taking anything with them. The Cherokees under John Ross were the last group forced to walk to Oklahoma from their lands in Georgia and North and South Carolina. Georgia passed the Indian Code in 1829 that abolished all Cherokee rights, and in 1830 Congress passed the Indian Removal Bill. In 1831, the government decided not to recognize the Cherokee as a separate nation. In 1838 and 1839, the Cherokee removal began, and the long road to Oklahoma became known as the Trail of Tears. Although the government promised to furnish supplies, the contractors delivered rancid meat and grain filled with weevils. Merchants charged inflated prices along the way, and farmers charged tolls for crossing their lands. Chronology, Further Reading, and Bibliography.

313. Brink, Carol Ryre. **Caddie Woodlawn**. Trina S. Hyman, illustrator. 1935. New York: Macmillan, 1974. 288p. $16. ISBN 0-02-713670-1. New York: Aladdin, 1990. 288p. $3.95pa. ISBN 0-689-71370-3pa. 4-6
     Unaffected by the American Civil War in 1864—her father in Wisconsin having paid someone to fight for him—Caddie enjoys playing with the boys. When 11, she realizes that her "prissy" female cousin may be reasonable. Having no alternatives, Caddie accepts the standards appropriate for females, and her family members show loyalty to their Indian friends and their patriotism toward America. *Newbery Medal.*

314. Brooks, Philip. **Georgia O'Keeffe: An Adventurous Spirit**. New York: Franklin Watts, 1995. 62p. $19.90. ISBN 0-531-20182-1. (First Book). 4-6

One of Georgia O'Keeffe's (1887-1986) most famous paintings, *Horse's Skull with White Rose*, first exhibited in 1931, shows her unique style. Her interest in shape and color come through in this work as well as in her paintings of flowers, deserts, and cities. The chapters highlight her life as she moved from Wisconsin to Georgia to New York and then to New Mexico, along with her family relationships and her marriage to Alfred Steiglitz. Color Reproductions, Further Reading, and Index.

315. Brooks, Philip. **Mary Cassatt: An American in Paris**. New York: Franklin Watts, 1995. 64p. $19.90. ISBN 0-531-20183-X. (First Book). 4-6

The text chapters divide the periods in painter Mary Cassatt's life (1844-1926). Their topics are "spirited child," Europe, the Salon, in Paris, in Italy, with the Independents, the Impressionists, refining her work, and returning to America. For Further Reading and Index. Reproductions.

316. Brower, Pauline. **Missions of the Inland Valleys: San Luis Obispo de Tolosa, San Miguel Arcángel, San Antonio de Padua, and Nuestra Señora de la Soledad**. Minneapolis, MN: Lerner, 1996. 80p. $17.21. ISBN 0-8225-1929-1. (California Missions). 4-6

In the 1700s, Spain sent Roman Catholic priests to establish missions and presidios (forts) along the coast of Baja California and other areas of New Spain (present-day Southwestern United States and Mexico). Spain wanted the Indians to accept the Spanish ways and become loyal subjects. In an attempt to reach Indians inland after settling the coast, Father Serra chose a site in the valley of the Coast Ranges for San Antonio de Padua, which at first faltered but then grew prosperous. Neophytes and Indians at San Luis Obispo de Tolosa, a second mission, developed durable clay tiles to replace tule reed as roofing materials. Other missions were Nuestra Señora de la Soledad, so isolated that it was called the "Forgotten Mission," and San Miguel Arcángel, which gained a reputation for its frescoes painted by talented neophytes. Glossary, Chronology, and Index.

317. Brown, Charnan. **Chester A. Arthur: Twenty-First President of the United States**. Chicago: Childrens Press, 1989. 110p. $19.80. ISBN 0-516-01369-6. (Encyclopedia of Presidents). 4-9

Chester A. Arthur (1829-1886) became president when James Garfield was assassinated. He had been appointed to the vice presidency in order to appease the New York City faction under Conkling and his Stalwart branch of the party. Additionally, Garfield's assassin stated that he was a Stalwart, and he wanted Arthur to be president. Garfield was neither the best nor the worst president in office. The text looks at this man and his life. Chronology of American History and Index.

318. Brown, Don, author/illustrator. **Ruth Law Thrills a Nation**. New York: Ticknor & Fields, 1993. Unpaged. $13.95. ISBN 0-395-66404-7. K-2

In 1916, Ruth Law attempted to fly from Chicago to New York in one day. She slept in a tent on the roof of a Chicago hotel so that she would be ready to go. The wind died late in the day while she was flying over New York State, and she had to land because her gas gave out. She did not reach New York until the following day, but she broke the record for a nonstop flight, 590 miles. The text includes details of her flight.

319. Brown, Drollene P. **Belva Lockwood Wins Her Case**. James Watling, illustrator. Morton Grove, IL: Albert Whitman, 1987. 64p. $11.95. ISBN 0-8075-0630-3. 3-7

Belva Lockwood (1830-1917) was a teacher, a suffragette, a lawyer, and a peace activist. She became the first woman to practice law before the Supreme Court. Additionally, she ran for President of the United States in 1884 and 1888. Afterword and Sources.

320. Brown, Drollene P. **Sybil Rides for Independence**. Niles, IL: Albert Whitman, 1985. 48p. $11.95. ISBN 0-8075-7684-0. 2-5

In 1777, when she was 16, Sybil Ludington (b. 1761) rode her horse on a stormy night to gather the minutemen after the British attack on Danbury, Connecticut. She rode more than 30 miles, but she accomplished her goal and lived to tell her grandchildren. More About Sybil Ludington.

321. Brown, Fern G. **Daisy and the Girl Scouts: The Story of Juliette Gordon Low**. Marie Dejohn, illustrator. Morton Grove, IL: Albert Whitman, 1996. 111p. $14.95. ISBN 0-8075-1440-3. 3-6

Juliette Gordon Low (1860-1927) founded the American Girl Scouts. Her wealthy Georgian background allowed her the luxury of travel, and she met Lord Baden Powell, founder of the Boy Scouts, in England. This encounter gave her the idea of establishing the Girl Scouts. The text looks at her life as well as the organization of the group. Chronology and Index.

322. Brown, Fern G. **Franklin Pierce: 14th President of the United States**. Ada, OK: Garrett Educational, 1989. 122p. $17.26. ISBN 0-944483-25-9. (Presidents of the United States). 5-9

As a trial lawyer from New Hampshire, Franklin Pierce (1804-1869) had great success. He was able to deliver his inauguration address from memory. He served in the presidency as the North and the South became increasingly bitter. During his administration, his minister to Mexico negotiated the Gadsden Purchase, buying the land now known as New Mexico and Arizona and completing the current map of the United States. Some of Pierce's secret plans to buy Cuba or take it by force made him undesirable, and he did not run for a second term. Bibliography and Index.

323. Brown, Fern G. **James A. Garfield: 20th President of the United States**. Ada, OK: Garrett Educational, 1990. 124p. $17.26. ISBN 0-944483-63-1. (Presidents of the United States). 5-9

His father dead when he was young, James A. Garfield (1831-1881) had to help his mother, and children taunted him for being poor and having no father. He left home to study but missed his mother. He returned, however, but soon left again to go to sea. Illness thwarted that career, and he spent his last two years of college at Williams, where his interest in the Republican Party began. He served in Congress and was elected President, but his presidency lasted only four months before Charles Julius Guiteau assassinated him. Bibliography and Index.

324. Brown, Gene. **Conflict in Europe and the Great Depression: World War I (1914-1940)**. New York: Twenty-First Century Books, 1994. 64p. $15.98. ISBN 0-8050-2585-5. (First Person America). 5-9

Brown posits that the period between World Wars I and II was when modern America was born. He discusses the rugged individualism that characterized many Americans at the time, but the government became a major force in everyday lives during and after the Great Depression of the 1930s. Most Americans were moving to cities, and mass media was growing in importance. From a nation of ballplayers and performers, Americans became watchers. Among people presented are John Reed, Gordon Parks, Al Capone, Marcus Garvey, and Lillian Gish. Photographs enhance the text. Timeline, For Further Reading, and Index.

325. Brown, Gene. **Discovery and Settlement: Europe Meets the "New World," 1490-1700**. New York: Twenty-First Century Books, 1993. 64p. $15.95. ISBN 0-8050-2574-X. (First Person America). 5-8

With primary source materials and illustrations, the text presents the discovery and settlement of America and daily life in the colonies, including the experiences of Native Americans, African Americans, and women. Bibliography and Index.

326. Brown, Gene. **The Nation in Turmoil: Civil Rights and the Vietnam War (1960-1973)**. New York: Twenty-First Century Books, 1994. 64p. $15.98. ISBN 0-8050-2588-X. (First Person American). 5-9

At the beginning of the 1960s, America had a new, young President, John F. Kennedy, who gave idealistic college students the Peace Corps. Integration began to be a reality. But the assassination of Kennedy in 1963 changed the mood of the country. The Cuban Missile Crisis, the Vietnam War, and the assassinations of Robert Kennedy and Martin Luther King, Jr. changed the nation again. Riots shook the cities. In the early 1970s, social changes for women and homosexuals gained momentum while the Arab nations imposed an oil embargo. Then Richard Nixon compromised the presidency and resigned in 1972. Photographs enhance the text. Timeline, For Further Reading, and Index.

327. Brown, Gene. **The Struggle to Grow: Expansionism and Industrialization (1880-1913)**. New York: Twenty-First Century Books, 1993. 64p. $15.95. ISBN 0-8050-2584-7. (First Person America). 5-8

The text uses letters, poems, broadsides, speeches, lyrics, and newspaper articles to present life on the western frontier as it began to urbanize and to absorb immigrants. It also faced social reformers who disapproved of western lifestyles, and contemporary technology that changed the modes of work. Bibliography and Index.

328. Brown, Jane Clark, author/illustrator. **George Washington's Ghost**. Boston: Houghton Mifflin, 1994. 86p. $13.95. ISBN 0-395-69452-3. 3-5

In the Noodle family, youngest child Celinda has to hold the horses while everyone else performs in their traveling marionette show during the late eighteenth century. When their General Washington puppet disappears, Celinda gets a chance to help recover the popular puppet by operating the most difficult puppet, the skeleton.

329. Brown, Jordan. **Elizabeth Blackwell: Physician**. New York: Chelsea House, 1989. 110p. $18.95. ISBN 1-55546-642-7. (American Women of Achievement). 5 up

Elizabeth Blackwell (1821-1910) decided to become a doctor after a brief stint as a teacher. Twenty-eight medical schools rejected her before New York State's Geneva College said "yes," and she began her practice in 1851. She lost an eye from disease, which prevented her from becoming a surgeon. Instead, she opened a clinic for poor women and children in 1857; established America's first visiting nurse service; managed the Union's Civil War nursing corps; and, in 1868, founded the Women's Medical College of the New York infirmary, the first medical school in the world for women. Photographs and reproductions enhance the text. Chronology, Further Reading, and Index.

330. Brown, Kevin. **Romare Bearden: Artist**. New York: Chelsea House, 1995. 112p. $18.95. ISBN 0-7910-1119-4. (Black Americans of Achievement). 5 up

Romare Bearden (1911-1987), a North Carolinian, wanted "to redefine the image of man" in terms of his experience as an African American. He knew Countee Cullen and Paul Robeson during the Harlem Renaissance and played semiprofessional baseball. He graduated from New York University in 1935 with a degree in mathematics, but he wanted to be an artist. He took a chance and became an art historian, teacher, author, curator, and gallery founder as well as a member by election of the National Institute of Arts and Letters. He also received the National Medal of Arts. Photographs and reproductions enhance the text. Chronology, Further Reading, and Index.

331. Brown, Marion Marsh. **Sacagawea: Indian Interpreter to Lewis and Clark**. Chicago: Childrens Press, 1988. 119p. $17.27. ISBN 0-516-03262-3. (People of Distinction). 4 up

After being captured by an enemy tribe, the Hidatsas, Sacagawea (1786?-1812) had to leave her peaceful Shoshone home. She married a French fur trader who went with Lewis and Clark on their famous journey to survey the Louisiana Purchase. Sacagawea and their child accompanied him. She acted as translator for the expedition, which was a basis for its success. Time Line and Index.

332. Brown, Marion Marsh. **Susette La Flesche: Advocate for Native American Rights**. Chicago: Childrens Press, 1992. 117p. $19.30; $5.95pa. ISBN 0-516-03277-1; 0-516-43277-Xpa. (People of Distinction). 4-6

Susette La Flesche (1854-1903), daughter of the Omaha Indian chief Iron Eyes, became an unwilling speaker about the plight of the Indians after her relatives, the Ponca Indians, had been taken from their homes on a forced march. Because she had been educated in the East, she spoke English very well. A Chicago reporter talked her into going on a speaking tour to tell her story to the whites. Even after many speeches, she never overcame the stage fright that accompanied her presentations about a subject so important to her, the rights of her people. The reporter also got her to write newspaper articles. The text looks at her life and her concerns for her people. Timeline and Index.

333. Brown, Warren. **Robert E. Lee**. New York: Chelsea House, 1992. 111p. $18.95; $7.95pa. ISBN 1-55546814-4; 0-7910-0698-0pa. (World Leaders Past and Present). 5 up

Robert E. Lee (1807-1870), long recognized as the most important Confederate general in the Civil War, not only commanded the discipline of his army but also gained its love and respect. Bibliography and Index.

334. Bruchac, Joseph. **A Boy Called Slow: The True Story of Sitting Bull**. Rocco Baviera, illustrator. New York: Philomel, 1995. 32p. $15.95. ISBN 0-399-22692-3. 1-5

A young Lakota boy called "slow" became the man who defeated the Crow and earned himself the name, which his father's vision had revealed, of Tatan'ka Iyota'ke or Sitting Bull (1834?-1890). The text looks at the battle actions that earned his name. *American Library Association Notable Books for Children*.

335. Bruchac, Joseph. **Children of the Longhouse**. New York: Dial, 1996. 150p. $14.99. ISBN 0-8037-1793-8. 5-8

When a small group of Mohawk adolescents decide to raid their peaceful neighbors, the Amen:taks, to gain glory as warriors, Ohkwa'ri, 11, tells the tribal council. Grabber, the leader of the group, wants revenge, and he plots when he can harm Ohkwa'ri. When the two boys find themselves on opposite sides during a game of Tekwaarathon (similar to lacrosse), Ohkwa'ri has to defend his life. Fortunately, family, including Ohkwa'ri's twin sister, Otsi:stia, and neighbors want to protect Ohkwa'ri, and they contrive ways to help him. The story includes information about Mohawk habits such as communal sleeping, name giving, government, family relationships, and the matrilineal hierarchy.

336. Bruns, Roger. **Abraham Lincoln**. New York: Chelsea House, 1986. 128p. $18.95; $7.95pa. ISBN 0-87754-597-9; 0-7910-0649-2pa. (World Leaders Past and Present). 5 up

Almost entirely self-educated, Abraham Lincoln (1809-1865) read for the law and became a lawyer in 1837. In 1856, he joined the Republican Party and ran for Congress against Stephen Douglas. Although he lost, he established himself as a campaigner of great integrity and intelligence. His skill as an orator and his humor got him the presidential nomination in 1860. He issued the Emancipation Proclamation in 1863, abolishing slavery and promising freedom to slaves in southern states. He confronted issues and tried to solve them. Photographs, engravings, and reproductions enhance the text. Chronology, Further Reading, and Index.

337. Bruns, Roger. **George Washington**. New York: Chelsea House, 1987. 116p. $18.95; $7.95pa. ISBN 0-87754-584-7; 0-7910-0668-9pa. (World Leaders Past and Present). 5 up

George Washington (1732-1799) valued his private life and tried to keep it that way. Trained as a surveyor, he became a military officer, a representative in Virginia's legislature, and a delegate to the nation's

First Continental Congress. People saw him as a leader, and he had to become one even though he did not want the glory. He had administrative skill and sometimes an explosive temper. Engravings enhance the text. Chronology, Further Reading, and Index.

338. Bruns, Roger. **John Wesley Powell: Explorer of the Grand Canyon**. New York: Enslow, 1997. 128p. $18.95. ISBN 0-89490-783-2. (Historical American Biographies). 6-9
John Wesley Powell (1834-1902) was the first explorer of the Grand Canyon. The biography looks at his impact on American history as it examines his life. Fact boxes and maps augment the text.

339. Bruns, Roger. **Thomas Jefferson**. New York: Chelsea House, 1986. 112p. $18.95; $7.95pa. ISBN 0-87754-583-9; 0-7910-0644-1pa. (World Leaders Past and Present). 5 up
Thomas Jefferson (1743-1826) wrote the Declaration of Independence for the colonies when he was only 33 years old, using language to make all men equal before the law. He then became, in succession, the minister to France, the Secretary of State, and the President. His ideas still inspire students of political science; his diplomacy is a guide to the modern statesperson; and his name is still linked to the concept of an ideal republic. Photographs and reproductions enhance the text. Chronology, Further Reading, and Index.

340. Bryant, Jennifer. **Marjory Stoneman Douglas: Voice of the Everglades**. Larry Raymond, illustrator. New York: Twenty-First Century Books, 1992. 72p. $14.98. ISBN 0-8050-2113-2. 4-6
Marjory Stoneman Douglas (b. 1890) refused to believe that the Everglades in Florida should be drained so that farms, homes, and roads could be built there. She saw the Everglades as part of a larger ecosystem in which wildlife, water, and weather worked together. She spent more than 60 years protecting this land and became known as "Grandmother of the Glades." Glossary and Index.

341. Bulla, Clyde Robert. **A Lion to Guard Us**. Michele Chessare, illustrator. New York: HarperCollins, 1981. 118p. $14.89. ISBN 0-690-04097-0. 2-5
In 1609, Amanda, Meg, and Jemmy sail from England to meet their father in Jamestown. Although their ship is wrecked in Bermuda, they survive. During their struggle, they keep a door knocker shaped like a lion from their old home, and it gives them hope that their father still protects them. They eventually reunite with him in Jamestown. *Notable Children's Trade Books in the Field of Social Studies.*

342. Bulla, Clyde Robert. **Pocahontas and the Strangers**. Peter Burchard, illustrator. 1971. New York: Scholastic, 1995. 180p. $3.99pa. ISBN 0-590-43481-0pa. 2-6
Pocahontas decides to claim Captain John Smith as her prisoner, an act that saves him as she becomes the liaison between the white settlers and her tribe in 1612. The settlers then take her as a hostage, and during the time she lives with them, she meets and marries John Rolfe. After she sails to England with him and their child, she dies. Her conciliatory efforts were a key to the settlers surviving in their Virginia homes.

343. Bulla, Clyde Robert. **Squanto, Friend of the Pilgrims**. Peter Burchard, illustrator. 1954. New York: Scholastic, 1990. 112p. $3.50. ISBN 0-590-44055-1. 3-6
Squanto goes to London in the early 1600s and learns about the white man's culture. He wants to return to his own people, and Captain John Smith takes him back to America in 1614. As soon as he arrives, another captain kidnaps him and takes him to Spain to sell into slavery. Because he speaks English, he gains his freedom, and in 1619 he again returns home. What he finds is a tribe killed by a disease that the white settlers brought to the New World.

344. Bundles, A'Lelia, and Perry Bundles. **Madam C. J. Walker: Entrepreneur**. New York: Chelsea House, 1989. 112p. $18.95; $7.95pa. ISBN 1-55546-615-X; 0-7910-0251-9pa. (Black Americans of Achievement). 5 up
As the daughter of former slaves, Madam C. J. Walker (1867-1919) became America's first Black female millionaire. She was widowed at 20 and worked as a laundress for 20 years afterward. In 1905, she invented a hair care product for Black women and began to sell it door-to-door. When it became successful, she started her own company. With her money, she made contributions to Black schools, orphanages, and civil rights organizations. She campaigned for the rights of Black war veterans and for federal antilynching legislation while insisting that Blacks had to defend themselves. Photographs enhance the text. Chronology, Further Reading, and Index.

345. Bunting, Eve. **The Blue and the Gray**. Ned Bittinger, illustrator. New York: Scholastic, 1996. Unpaged. $14.95. ISBN 0-590-60197-0. K-3
The narrator's family is building a new home near his best friend's house. His father tells him about the land on which he will live, once a battlefield for soldiers fighting the Civil War in 1862. His father explains how the battle raged and that men who died left their bones in the field. The narrator and his friend, one Black and the other white, are surprised that friends and families fought against each other, and they decide to memorialize the area in their minds.

346.   Bunting, Eve. **Dandelions**. Greg Shed, illustrator. San Diego, CA: Harcourt Brace, 1995. 48p. $15. ISBN 0-15-200050-X. K-5

In the spring, Zoe and her family come to Nebraska Territory from Illinois. Her mother is very lonely in the emptiness as her father tries to make a home for them. Neighbors only three hours away help, but building a new life cannot be easy. They plant two dandelions on the roof of the house, which mama thinks may also die of loneliness. *Notable Children's Trade Books in the Field of Social Studies*.

347.   Bunting, Eve. **Train to Somewhere**. Ronald Himler, illustrator. New York: Clarion, 1996. 32p. $14.95. ISBN 0-395-71325-0. 1-4

Marianne leaves on the Orphan Train from St. Christopher's Orphanage in 1877. Her mother had left her there saying that she would come get her after making a life out West. Marianne hopes that she will find her mother before someone adopts her. At the train's last stop, called Somewhere, her mother has not appeared, and a couple who had wanted a boy takes her because she is the only remaining child. The woman says later that sometimes people get better than what they thought they wanted.

348.   Buranelli, Vincent. **Thomas Alva Edison**. Englewood Cliffs, NJ: Silver Burdett, 1989. 133p. $13.98. ISBN 0-382-09522-7. (Pioneers in Change). 5-7

When asked when he planned to retire, Thomas Alva Edison (1847-1931) said "the day before the funeral." He did continue working, with more than 1,000 inventions to his credit, including the electric light, the phonograph, and the motion picture. The text looks at his life and work. Important Dates, Bibliography, and Index.

349.   Burby, Liza N. **The Pueblo Indians**. New York: Chelsea House, 1994. 79p. $14.95; $6.95pa. ISBN 0-7910-1669-2; 0-7910-2485-7pa. (Junior Library of American Indians). 3-7

The text presents the interaction of the Pueblo with Europeans as the Europeans came into the American Southwest. An essay on Pueblo architecture and photographs illustrate the text. Glossary and Index.

350.   Burchard, Peter. **Charlotte Forten: A Black Teacher in the Civil War**. New York: Crown, 1995. 106p. $16. ISBN 0-517-59242-8. 5-8

A child in a prominent Philadelphia family, Charlotte Forten (1837-1914) grew up as the United States was moving toward the Civil War. She saw the uproar surrounding the arrest of the fugitive slave Anthony Burns in Boston and the results of the war from South Carolina's Sea Islands, where she worked as a teacher and nurse. Her uncle's farm was a stop on the Underground Railroad; her grandfather had been a leading abolitionist; and her aunt had championed the rights of both women and Blacks. Charlotte was friendly with William Lloyd Garrison, John Greenleaf Whittier, and, later, Frederick Douglass when she moved to Washington, D.C. She also knew Harriet Tubman and Robert Gould Shaw, the commander of the first Black regiment. She showed that Black women could live full lives even in adversity. Bibliography and Index.

351.   Burford, Betty. **Chocolate by Hershey: A Story About Milton S. Hershey**. Loren Chantland, illustrator. Minneapolis, MN: Carolrhoda, 1994. 64p. $13.13; $5.95pa. ISBN 0-87614-830-5; 0-87614-641-8pa. (Creative Minds). 3-6

When Milton Hershey (1857-1945) was 13, he began to learn about candy making. As he kept trying to make his own candy, his businesses failed. Then he developed Crystal A Caramels, and his success began. When he experimented with chocolate, he created the town of Hershey in Pennsylvania and founded the Milton Hershey School for orphaned and disadvantaged young people. Bibliography.

352.   Burke, Deirdre. **Food and Fasting**. New York: Thomson Learning, 1993. 32p. $13.95. ISBN 1-56847-034-7. (Comparing Religions). 4-8

Six major religions—Buddhism, Christianity, Hinduism, Judaism, Islam, and Sikhism—have rules about what some foods mean and which foods they may eat. The text looks at what they eat, how they eat it, what and when they cannot eat, what foods appear at religious festivals, and what foods (e.g., bread and wine) appear in places of worship. Photographs enhance the information. Glossary, Books to Read, and Index.

353.   Burke, Kathleen. **Louisa May Alcott**. New York: Chelsea House, 1988. 109p. $18.95. ISBN 1-55546-637-0. (American Women of Achievement). 5 up

Louisa May Alcott (1832-1888) created a new genre of fiction when she authored *Little Women*. She began writing early to help support her family, and she continued throughout her life. She also developed a commitment to helping all needy people and volunteered as a nurse during the Civil War. In later life, she became active in the women's suffrage movement. Photographs and reproductions enhance the text. Chronology, Further Reading, and Index.

354. Burleigh, Robert. **Flight: The Journey of Charles Lindbergh**. Mike Wimmer, illustrator. New York: Philomel, 1991. Unpaged. $14.95. ISBN 0-399-22272-3. 1-6

In May 1927, Charles Lindbergh (1902-1974) attempted to fly solo nonstop from New York to Paris. He was the first person to achieve this remarkable feat. The story of his flight, from the first minute until the last, when he lands in Paris, is in this text.

355. Burleigh, Robert. **A Man Named Thoreau**. Lloyd Bloom, illustrator. New York: Atheneum, 1985. 48p. $15. ISBN 0-689-31122-2. 3 up

As Burleigh describes Henry Thoreau's (1817-1862) response to the world when he lived at Walden Pond for two years after graduating from Harvard, he uses Thoreau's own words from his book, *Walden Pond*, rather than creating unnecessary dialogue. The accompanying illustrations are almost surreal in their attempt to capture the concept of the "oneness" with nature that Thoreau sought and tried to practice. Thoreau's attempt to keep life simple runs counter to contemporary practices. Important Dates and Bibliography.

356. Burns, Bree. **Harriet Tubman**. New York: Chelsea House, 1992. 80p. $14.95; $4.95pa. ISBN 0-7910-1751-6; 0-7910-1995-0pa. (Junior World Biographies). 3-6

When she was only 15, Harriet Tubman (c. 1820-1913) refused to help an overseer recover a runaway slave; he hit her with a two-pound lead weight. She eventually escaped from slavery to the North, and began her work as a rescuer on the Underground Railroad before the Civil War. Photographs, paintings, and drawings complement the text. Bibliography, Glossary, and Index.

357. Burns, Khephra, and William Miles. **Black Stars in Orbit: NASA's African American Astronauts**. San Diego, CA: Gulliver, Harcourt Brace, 1995. 72p. $18.95; $8.95pa. ISBN 0-15-200432-7; 0-15-200276-6pa. 6 up

African Americans have been an important part of the Air Force since the inception of the Black Eagles, fighter pilots in World War II. Although others were accepted into the astronaut program, the first African American who ventured into space was Guion S. Bluford, Jr., in 1983. He was followed by others such as Ron McNair, Fred Gregory, and the first African American woman, Dr. Mae C. Jemison. These and others appear in the text with complementary photographs. Index. *Notable Children's Trade Books in the Field of Social Studies*.

358. Burns, Peggy. **The Mail**. New York: Thomson Learning, 1995. 32p. $13.95. ISBN 1-56847-249-8. (Stepping Through History). 3-5

In the past, people wrote letters on wax, clay, bronze tablets, or papyrus. Sometimes a messenger memorized the words and delivered them verbally. Around 500 BC, Cyrus created the longest postal route in ancient times so that he could send his decrees across the kingdom. Romans had postal routes, but they were discontinued after Rome fell. In the eleventh century, monasteries began messenger services. Other ancient cultures had their own systems. Topics include mailboxes, stamps, the Pony Express, international mail, and mail sorting. Time Line, Books to Read, Places to Visit, Further Information, Glossary, and Index.

359. Burns, Peggy. **Money**. New York: Thomson Learning, 1995. 32p. $13.95. ISBN 1-56847-248-X. (Stepping Through History). 4-6

The text looks at money by discussing barter and trade, the history of coins and paper money, banks and credit cards, and currency exchange between countries. Chronology, Glossary, Bibliography, and Index.

360. Butts, Ellen R., and Joyce R. Schwartz. **May Chinn: The Best Medicine**. Janet Hamlin, illustrator. New York: W. H. Freeman, 1995. 48p. $14.95; $4.95pa. ISBN 0-7167-6589-6; 0-7167-6590-Xpa. (Science Superstars). 4-8

May Chinn (1896-1980) was part African American, part Native American, and part Caucasian, although she called herself a "Negro." Even though her father believed she should marry, her mother wanted her to go to college and had secretly saved money from her jobs so that she could pay some of the tuition. Chinn loved music and played the piano beautifully, but she decided to change her major to science after successfully completing science courses. She played piano for Paul Robeson and was accepted into medical school based on an interview in which she talked about him with the interviewer. In 1926, she became the first African American woman to graduate from Bellevue Medical College. She developed a family clinic in Harlem and then began working at the Strang Clinics, trying to find out more about cancer. Index, Glossary, and Further Reading.

361. Byars, Betsy C. **The Golly Sisters Go West**. Sue Truesdell, illustrator. New York: HarperCollins, 1986. 58p. $15.89; $3.75pa. ISBN 0-06-020884-8; 0-06-444132-6pa. (An I Can Read Book). 1-3

May-May and Rose star in four stories while they make their way to the frontier of the West. They first have to figure out how to make their horse move. Then they give a road show but get lost afterwards. An argument precedes a nighttime scare. When they figure out how to get their horse in the act, their audiences enjoy their antics more.

362.   Byars, Betsy. **The Golly Sisters Ride Again**. Sue Truesdell, illustrator. New York: HarperCollins, 1994. 64p. $14; $3.75pa. ISBN 0-06-021563-1; 0-06-444207-1pa. (An I Can Read Book). 2-4

Although Rose and May-May have learned how to tell their horse to stop and go, they still have unexpected hitches with their traveling show. They argue over who should star in a drama with only one princess, and they worry that a goat in the audience will cause bad luck as they entertain on the western frontier.

363.   Byars, Betsy. **Hooray for the Golly Sisters**. Sue Truesdell, illustrator. New York: HarperCollins, 1990. 64p. $11.95; $3.75pa. ISBN 0-06-020898-8; 0-06-444256-3pa. (An I Can Read Book). 1-3

In the 1800s, Rose and May-May can drive their covered wagon with ease as they create new scenarios for their act. They try to use pigs instead of rabbits in a magic act and try to do high-wire walking on the ground. Even with their mistakes, they continue to improve their road show act.

364.   Bylinsky, Tatyana, author/illustrator. **Before the Wildflowers Bloom**. New York: Crown, 1989. 70p. $13.95. ISBN 0-517-57052-1. 3-5

Carmela, eight, lives in a coal mining community. In 1916, her father dies in a mine explosion, and her Italian family gathers for the funeral. Afterwards, her life changes even further when her grandfather says that he will take her mother and the five children to live on his ranch.

$$\boxed{C}$$

365. Cain, Michael. **Louise Nevelson: Sculptor**. New York: Chelsea House, 1989. 109p. $18.95. ISBN 155546-671-0. (American Women of Achievement). 5 up

Louise Berliawsky Nevelson (1899-1988) immigrated with her Russian family to the United States. She married a wealthy man as soon as she graduated from high school, moved to New York, had a child, and nine years later divorced her husband. The rest of her life she devoted to her sculpture. Her "environments" define her style: scrap lumber assembled and painted black or huge steel sculptures. She also produced paintings, lithographs, and works in ceramics, Plexiglas, and aluminum. She refused to be categorized, and lived and created in the way she preferred. Photographs of her work enhance the text. Chronology, Further Reading, and Index.

366. Cain, Michael. **Mary Cassatt**. New York: Chelsea House, 1989. 112p. $18.95. ISBN 1-55546-647-8. (American Women of Achievement). 5 up

Mary Cassatt (1844-1926), an Impressionist painter, was one of her era's finest artists. She went to Europe in 1866, where she developed her bold brushwork and bright palette. Japanese prints inspired her, and she liked to paint portraits of mothers and children. Photographs and reproductions enhance the text. Chronology, Further Reading, and Index.

367. Calvert, Patricia. **Bigger**. New York: Atheneum, 1994. 144p. $14.95. ISBN 0-684-19685-9. 5-8

Tyler, 12, hears that his father has gone to Mexico after the end of the Civil War instead of returning to his Missouri family. With the help of his Uncle Matt, Tyler goes to look for him, and on the way, makes friends with a mistreated dog that Tyler names Bigger. After he finds his father, he realizes that his father is not what he expected. Tyler returns and Bigger dies, but Tyler begins to understand things that lessen the pain a little.

368. Calvert, Roz. **Zora Neale Hurston: Storyteller of the South**. New York: Chelsea House, 1992. 80p. $14.95. ISBN 0-7910-1766-4. (Junior Black Americans of Achievement). 3-6

Born in Florida, Zora Neale Hurston (1891-1960) loved to read and listen to stories about the people in her area. She decided to write, started to support herself at age 14, and attended Howard University and Barnard College. She collected Black folklore and traveled in Jamaica, Honduras, and other Caribbean countries, as well as the American South, to find it. She published 10 books in her lifetime, but people condemned her for activities other than her work (many of their accusations were untrue), so she died in poverty. Further Reading, Chronology, Glossary, and Index.

369. Cameron, Eleanor. **The Court of the Stone Children**. 1973. Magnolia, MA: Peter Smith, 1983. 208p. $18.05. ISBN 0-8446-6757-9. New York: Puffin, 1992. $4.99pa. ISBN 0-14-034289-3pa. 4 up

Nina wants to become a museum curator because she finds solace in San Francisco's French Museum, a place where Chagall's painting *Time Is a River Without Banks* greets her. In this historical fantasy, Nina meets Dominique, a figure in an early-nineteenth-century painting. Dominique says that she dreamed about Nina as a girl and wants Nina to help her find out what happened to her father. Nina solves the puzzle by guessing about a painting and shows Dominique that her father was innocent of charges made against him by Napoleon's army. *American Book Award*.

370. Camp, Carole Ann. **American Astronomers: Searchers and Wonderers**. Springfield, NJ: Enslow, 1996. 104p. $17.95. ISBN 0-89490-631-3. (Collective Biographies). 6-9

The text profiles five men and five women who have contributed to the advancement of American astronomy. Included in the profiles are information about their lives, beginning with an exciting event and a brief overview of history to show why their particular contribution was important. Among those included are Maria Mitchell (1818-1889) and the late Carl Sagan. Notes and Index.

371. Canadeo, Anne. **Warren G. Harding: 29th President of the United States**. Ada, OK: Garrett Educational, 1990. 128p. $17.26. ISBN 0-944483-64-X. (Presidents of the United States). 5-8

Before he became president, Warren G. Harding (1865-1923) taught school, read law, worked in insurance and for a newspaper, and lost his first political race for county auditor. He won election to the Ohio state senate and then served as lieutenant governor of Ohio. After he became chairman of the Republican National Convention and a U.S. senator from Ohio, he won the nomination for the presidency after many ballots. In 1923, he died in office. After his death, scandals and convictions showed that some of his friends had been receiving bribes. Bibliography and Index.

372.   Cannon, Marian G. **Robert E. Lee**. New York: Franklin Watts, 1993. 64p. $12.90. ISBN 0-531-20120-1. (First Books). 4-6

In this presentation of Robert E. Lee (1807-1870), Cannon discusses his birth as a southerner, his happy marriage, his service during the Mexican War, his decision not to head the Union army when Lincoln asked him to, his life as a Confederate general, and his time after the War Between the States ended. Photographs, For Further Reading, and Index.

373.   Capek, Michael. **Artistic Trickery: The Tradition of the Trompe L'Oeil Art**. Minneapolis, MN: Lerner, 1995. Unpaged. $21.50. ISBN 0-8225-2064-8. (Art Beyond Borders). 5 up

An enjoyable type of art is *trompe l'oeil*, paintings that confuse the eye so that the viewer sees a scene that doesn't really exist. *Trompe l'oeil* is not realism because realism tries to represent objects truthfully; *trompe l'oeil* is a visual game. The text looks at several contemporary artists who make *trompe l'oeil* paintings and the subjects that have intrigued these artists through the years. These themes include damaged goods, money and stamps, food, people, animals and bugs, slates and letter racks, doors, landscapes, and murals. The earliest illustration comes from 1475, and other illustrations cover each century since. Glossary and Index. *IRA Children's Choices*.

374.   Capek, Michael. **Murals: Cave, Cathedral, to Street**. Minneapolis, MN: Lerner, 1996. 72p. $17.21. ISBN 0-8225-2065-6. (American Pastfinder). 5 up

The text looks at murals, huge drawings that decorate caves, walls, ceilings, and the sides of buildings. In an unusual order, the text looks at contemporary murals first and goes backward in history; the last chapter examines cave paintings. Among the topics are contemporary community murals, historical murals in the United States, Mexican murals, Italian Renaissance murals, early Christian murals, murals of ancient Rome and Egypt, and cave paintings. Glossary, For Further Reading, and Index.

375.   Caras, Roger. **A World Full of Animals: The Roger Caras Story**. San Francisco: Chronicle, 1994. 45p. $13.95. ISBN 0-8118-0682-0. (Great Naturalists). 3-4

Roger Caras (b. 1928) was the first television correspondent to devote his career to environmental issues. He has related stories from all over the world about animals and endangered species. Here he discusses snakes, penguins, Africa, and Sri Lanka. Photographs enhance the text. Afterword, Organizations, Glossary, and Index.

376.   Carlson, Jeffrey D. **A Historical Album of Minnesota**. Brookfield, CT: Millbrook Press, 1994. 64p. $16.40; $6.95pa. ISBN 1-56294-006-6; 1-56294-757-5pa. (Historical Album). 4-8

The text presents the land of Minnesota before it became a state, beginning with Native American civilizations and continuing through exploration and settlement. Early statehood developments and issues and the role of large cities in the state's livelihood lead to the present day. Prints, maps, and photographs illustrate the text. Gazetteer: Quick Facts, Key Events, Personalities, and Index.

377.   Carlson, Judy. **Harriet Tubman: Call to Freedom**. New York: Fawcett, 1989. 118p. $4.99pa. ISBN 0-449-90376-1pa. (Great Lives). 5-9

This fictional biography begins with Harriet running for freedom around the age of 20. Then it returns to the beginning of Harriet's life and recounts most of the known facts about her life, although no notes indicate sources. One point on which Carlson elaborates is that Tubman was lonely in Philadelphia, and when she found out about the Philadelphia Vigilance Committee, she was probably very happy to have support when she returned to the South to free other slaves, including all of her family except a sister and her two children. Carlson says that slavery began in the early 1500s on the East Coast, with 15 million to 100 million slaves being transported from Africa. Other Books to Read.

378.   Carlson, Laurie M. **Westward Ho!: An Activity Guide to the Wild West**. New York: Chicago Review, 1996. 149p. $12.95. ISBN 1-55652-271-1. 3-6

A variety of different activities such as crafts, songs, recipes, and games help young readers learn about the Old West in the nineteenth century. The stories and trivia will draw them into the time and teach them how to create a field book like Lewis and Clark's. Bibliography and Further Reading.

379.   Carrick, Carol. **The Elephant in the Dark**. Donald Carrick, illustrator. New York: Clarion, 1988. 135p. $13.95. ISBN 0-89919-757-4. 4-6

Will, 12, lives alone with his mother in Cadbury, Massachusetts, in the 1800s, and takes care of an elephant, Toong, that has come to town. Will's mother dies, and he develops an even stronger bond with Toong. After the new owner takes Toong away and rejects Will's request to join them, Will follows anyway. The owner accepts Will when he realizes that only the boy can soothe Toong when the elephant is distressed.

380. Carrick, Carol. **Stay Away from Simon!** Donald Carrick, illustrator. New York: Clarion, 1985. 64p. $13.95; $5.95pa. ISBN 0-89919-343-9; 0-89919-849-Xpa. 2-6

In the 1800s, Lucy, 11, is afraid of Simon, the boy who seems to be very slow. During a snowstorm, Lucy leaves school with her brother, only to become lost. Simon finds her and guides them home because he wants to share his new ability to count to 10.

381. Carrick, Carol. **Two Very Little Sisters**. Erika Weihs, illustrator. New York: Clarion, 1993. 64p. $14.95. ISBN 0-395-60927-5. K-4

Near the beginning of the twentieth century, P. T. Barnum finds two sisters in Martha's Vineyard who have not grown above the height of four feet. He asks Lucy and Sarah if they would like to travel with his circus. They decide that they would like to see the different places he visits, so they join. Soon they tire of the crowds who look at them, and they return to their home and start a tea shop.

382. Carrick, Carol. **Whaling Days**. David Frampton, illustrator. New York: Clarion, 1993. 40p. $15.95. ISBN 0-395-50948-3. 3-6

Although emphasizing the golden days of the whaling industry and the Yankee whalers, Carrick begins with the twelfth-century Basque whale hunters. She discusses harpooning, hard life on a whaling vessel, and the modern whaling methods that developed in the nineteenth century. Bibliography and Index. *Bulletin Blue Ribbon Book.*

383. Carrigan, Mellonee. **Jimmy Carter: Beyond the Presidency**. Chicago: Childrens Press, 1995. 32p. $16.70. ISBN 0-516-04193-2. 3-6

Since Jimmy Carter (b. 1924) was defeated for a second term as president of the United States in 1980, he has shown a regality that many did not spot while he was in office. He has volunteered much of his time to groups such as Habitats for Humanity and served as an elder statesman in various negotiations around the globe. Photographs, Timeline, and Index.

384. Carter, Alden R. **The Battle of Gettysburg**. New York: Franklin Watts, 1990. 64p. $10.40. ISBN 0-531-10852-X. (First Books). 4-6

With background on the key individuals in the Confederate army's northern campaign, the text presents the army's activities and its subsequent defeat at the Battle of Gettysburg. It also discusses the effect of this battle on the course of the Civil War. Historical photographs, paintings, and maps complement the text. Bibliography and Index.

385. Carter, Alden R. **The Colonial Wars: Clashes in the Wilderness**. New York: Franklin Watts, 1992. 63p. $12.40. ISBN 0-531-20079-5. (First Books). 4-8

With a general focus on the military and political strategies, the text gives the history of the Colonial Wars, also called the French and Indian Wars, which gave the British control of North America. These four wars were King William's War, 1689-1697; Queen Anne's War, 1702-1713; King George's War, 1744-1748; and the French and Indian War, 1755-1763. Bibliography and Index.

386. Carter, Alden R. **Last Stand at the Alamo**. New York: Franklin Watts, 1990. 64p. $19.90. ISBN 0-531-10888-0. (First Books). 4-6

Napoleon conquered Spain and its territories in 1800, then in 1803 sold the Louisiana Purchase to the United States for $15 million. Texas was still part of Mexico but attracted many people who had reasons for wanting to leave the country. Three of these, William Travis, Jim Bowie, and Davy Crockett, led the defense of the Alamo against Santa Anna on March 6, 1836, but they lost when no reinforcements arrived as they fought for Texas's freedom. By April 19, Sam Houston was ready to fight Santa Anna and his tired troops. In an 18-minute battle, Houston won freedom for Texas and became its president. Period paintings, maps, and flags of Texas complement the text. Suggested Reading and Index.

387. Carter, Alden R. **The Mexican War: Manifest Destiny**. New York: Franklin Watts, 1992. 63p. $12.40. ISBN 0-531-20081-7. (First Books). 4-8

With a general focus on military and political strategies, the text gives the history of the Mexican War, which lasted from 1846 to 1848. It discusses events, personalities, and the aftermath of the war as well. Reproductions enhance the text. Bibliography and Index.

388. Carter, Alden R. **The Spanish-American War: Imperial Ambitions**. New York: Franklin Watts, 1992. 64p. $12.40. ISBN 0-531-20078-7. (First Books). 4-8

The text tells of the 10-week war in 1898 between the United States and Spain over the liberation of Cuba. Theodore Roosevelt and his Rough Riders gained stature when the fight ended the Spanish colonial empire, and other countries recognized the United States as a world power. Bibliography and Index.

389. Casey, Jane Clark. **Millard Fillmore: Thirteenth President of the United States**. Chicago: Childrens Press, 1988. 100p. $19.80. ISBN 0-516-01353-X. (Encyclopedia of Presidents). 4-9

Most people have forgotten Millard Fillmore (1800-1874), a self-made man who tried to leave public office four different times. He was devoted to the Union and hated the Republican Party. He was opposed to slavery, but because the Fugitive Slave Act passed while he was in office, those who opposed slavery began to hate him. He always tried to support what he believed in, but he also had to negotiate to get the best result for the weak and unprotected. Chronology of American History and Index.

390. Casey, Jane Clark. **William H. Taft: Twenty-Seventh President of the United States**. Chicago: Childrens Press, 1989. 100p. $19.80. ISBN 0-516-01366-1. (Encyclopedia of Presidents). 4-9

As President, William Taft (1857-1930) was unlucky, but he followed his lonely stint in that office with teaching at Yale and a coveted position on the Supreme Court. His mother realized that he wanted to go on the Court rather than be President, but his wife and sons pushed him to the presidency. His last years were devoted to the Court. Chronology and Index.

391. Cashman, Greer, and Alona Frankel. **Jewish Days and Holidays**. New York: Modan-Adama, 1986. 64p. $12.95. ISBN 0-915361-58-2. K-4

With Jewish history integrated into the definitions, the authors present Rosh Hashanah, Yom Kippur, Sukkot, Simchat Torah, Chanukah, Purim, Pesach, Yom-Ha-Atzmaut, Shavuot, Tisha B'Av, and Shabbat. Sidebars contain simple illustrations and further clarifications.

392. Castiglia, Julie. **Margaret Mead**. Englewood Cliffs, NJ: Silver Burdett, 1989. 137p. $13.95. ISBN 0-382-09525-1. (Pioneers in Change). 5-9

Margaret Mead (1901-1978), innovator, ethnologist, wife, mother, and friend, balanced her career with the other aspects of her life. Her grandmother taught her about the value of the past. Because her father set up extensions of a university, her family moved often, and the artifacts that she had from her grandmother were the few permanent fixtures in her life. Her parents, both highly educated, allowed her to come and go from school as she pleased, thinking that school was not the most important activity for her. Later, in college, she studied psychology, but she met Ruth Benedict and Franz Boas, anthropologists, who influenced her selection of anthropology as a career. The text continues with the important contributions she made to the way people perceive themselves in their societies. Important Dates, Bibliography, and Index.

393. Catalano, Julie. **The Mexican Americans**. New York: Chelsea House, 1995. 102p. $19.95; $8.95pa. ISBN 0-7910-3359-7; 0-7910-3381-3pa. (The Immigrant Experience). 5 up

When Mexico ceded territory to the United States in 1848, nearly 75,000 Mexicans claimed citizenship. Immigrants have crossed the border since that time, taking jobs as farmhands, ranchers, railroaders, and miners. During the World Wars they moved north and to the Midwest where skilled jobs were available. Among the Mexicans best known for contributing to American life is Cesar Chavez, who gained rights for migrant workers. The text, with accompanying photographs, tells about their history and their contribution to American culture. Further Reading and Index.

394. Caudill, Rebecca. **Tree of Freedom**. Dorothy Bayley, illustrator. 1949. New York: Viking, 1988. 284p. $17.50; $5.99pa. ISBN 0-8446-6401-4; 0-14-032908-0pa. 5-9

To escape taxes in the North Carolina colony in 1780, Stephanie Venable's father takes his family to Kentucky. Because he allows the children to bring only one of their favorite items, Stephanie takes an apple seed from a tree her great-grandmother transported from France. She plants the seed and names the resulting seedling "Tree of Freedom." Others try to take their land, and Stephanie's brother decides to become a lawyer in order to protect people like his father, who cannot read and write. He and Stephanie leave for Williamsburg to further their education. *Newbery Honor* and *New York Herald Tribune Award*.

395. Caulkins, Janet. **Pets of the Presidents**. Brookfield, CT: Millbrook Press, 1992. 72p. $16.40. ISBN 1-56294-060-0. 3-6

Many presidents and their children have had pets in the White House. Caulkins gives information about the Presidents as well as insights about them and their pets. Thomas Jefferson had a bird and Lincoln a goat. Teddy Roosevelt had a lizard and a guinea pig, while Calvin Coolidge had a raccoon. Many others had dogs, including Warren Harding, Franklin Roosevelt, John Kennedy, Lyndon Johnson, and George Bush. Bibliography and Index.

396. Cavan, Seamus. **Daniel Boone and the Opening of the Ohio Country**. New York: Chelsea House, 1990. 111p. $19.95. ISBN 0-7910-1309-X. (World Explorers). 5 up

The story of Daniel Boone (1734-1820) is the story of the settlement along the western frontier of the American colonies and later the states. His family always moved, and he continued the tradition by going to Kentucky after he fought with the British in the losing battle at Monongahela. He married Rebecca in 1756 when both were young. She and 10 children (later seven after Indians killed three) endured his long absences from home while exploring, until her death at 73. Boone earned and lost money enough times so that he lived both an extravagant life and a frugal one as he moved westward to St. Louis and then further west. Not until his mid-eighties did he begin to lose strength, and he died at 86. Paintings, drawings, photographs, and maps clarify the history of the times. Further Reading, Chronology, and Index.

397. Cavan, Seamus. **The Irish-American Experience**. Brookfield, CT: Millbrook Press, 1993. 64p. $14.90. ISBN 1-56294-218-2. 5-7

The text presents the history of Ireland with an emphasis on the last two centuries, when the Irish suffered the potato famine, and many had to leave Ireland in order to survive. Among the topics included are the Irish at sea on the way to America, tenement life in America, and the way that men started to take leadership roles in politics. Photographs, Bibliography, Notes, and Index. *Child Study Association Children's Books of the Year.*

398. Cavan, Seamus. **W. E. B. Du Bois and Racial Relations**. Brookfield, CT: Millbrook Press, 32p. $13.90; $4.95pa. ISBN 1-56294-288-3; 1-56294-794-Xpa. (Gateway Civil Rights). 2-4

W. E. B. Du Bois faced prejudice for the first time as a high school student. He visited a new girl in town with his friends, and when they left their calling cards, only his was rejected. He then buried himself in the library, reading and preparing for his adult life, when he would speak loudly against racial inequality. Important Events, Find Out More, and Index.

399. Cedeno, Maria E. **Cesar Chavez: Labor Leader**. Brookfield, CT: Millbrook Press, 1993. 32p. $13.90; $4.95pa. ISBN 1-56294-280-8; 1-56294-808-3pa. (Hispanic Heritage). 3-5

Cesar Chavez (1927-1993) fought to improve the lives of Mexican American farmworkers in California because, as a farmworker himself, he understood their needs. By working to create the United Farm Workers, a trade union for migrants, he eventually got migrants a better life. Bibliography and Index. *Child Study Association Children's Books of the Year.*

400. Chadwick, Roxane. **Amelia Earhart: Aviation Pioneer**. Minneapolis, MN: Lerner, 1987. 56p. $15.95; $4.95pa. ISBN 0-8225-0484-7; 0-8225-9515-Xpa. (The Achievers). 4-9

Because Amelia Earhart (1897-1937) was the daughter of parents who allowed her to do things that girls normally did not do, she refused to be limited. Her childhood prepared her to become a female aviator capable of breaking records. For a woman, she flew the highest, the fastest, and the farthest. She crossed the Atlantic as the first female passenger and as the first woman solo pilot. She disappeared while she was trying to fly around the world at the equator. *Outstanding Science Trade Book.*

401. Chadwick, Roxane. **Anne Morrow Lindbergh: Pilot and Poet**. Minneapolis, MN: Lerner, 1987. 56p. $4.95pa. ISBN 0-8225-9516-8pa. 4-9

Anne Morrow Lindbergh (1906-) married Charles Lindbergh after he became the first pilot to fly nonstop across the Atlantic. A shy daughter of a wealthy family, she loved to write and excelled in English at Smith College. After she met Charles Lindbergh and flew for the first time, she read all that she could about aviation. They courted and even married in secret before the press began to follow them everywhere. She continued to write throughout their life together as she raised their family on two continents.

402. Chaikin, Miriam. **Friends Forever**. Richard Egielski, illustrator. New York: HarperCollins, 1988. 120p. $11.95. ISBN 0-06-021204-7. 3-6

Molly overhears rumblings in her Brooklyn neighborhood about problems with Jews in Europe, especially Poland, where her mother's family remains during World War II. She focuses her worries on getting into advanced math in the seventh grade and decides to help herself do well on tests by writing formulas on her palm. However, she feels guilty for cheating. After her subsequent graduation from sixth grade, she gets a boyfriend and prepares to enjoy the summer.

403. Chang, Ina. **A Separate Battle: Women and the Civil War**. New York: Lodestar, 1991. 103p. $15.95. ISBN 0-525-67365-2. (Young Readers' History of the Civil War). 5-8

Through primary source materials like letters and diaries, Chang shows the women who rolled bandages, nursed the injured, fought disguised as men, or tried to protect their homes. Some of the well-known figures she presents are Clara Barton, Harriet Tubman, and Belle Boyd. Maps, photographs, and reproductions complement the text. Bibliography and Index.

404. Charleston, Gordon. **Armstrong Lands on the Moon**. New York: Dillon Press, 1994. 32p. $13.95. ISBN 0-87518-530-4. (Great Twentieth Century Expeditions). 3-6

On July 20, 1969, Neil Armstrong (b. 1930) became the first human to walk on the face of the moon. The text describes in detail the preparation for the space flight to the moon, starting with the space race with the Soviet Union and *Sputnik*. It discusses the first astronauts, shows a map of the moon, and displays the photographs of the moon following this amazing feat. Further Reading, Glossary, and Index.

405. Charleston, Gordon. **Peary Reaches the North Pole**. New York: Dillon Press, Macmillan, 1993. 32p. $13.95. ISBN 0-87518-535-5. (Great Twentieth Century Expeditions). 4-7

In 13 two-page discussions, the text describes Admiral Peary's attempts to reach the North Pole in the early twentieth century. Because his claim of reaching it first in 1909 has been disputed, the text discusses this aspect of his exploration. Maps and photographs enhance the text. Further Reading, Glossary, and Index.

406. Childress, Diana. **Prehistoric People of North America**. New York: Chelsea House, 1996. 79p. $15.95; $7.95pa. ISBN 0-7910-2481-4; 0-7910-2482-2pa. (Junior Library of American Indians). 4-6

This overview of prehistoric Native Americans includes a discussion of archaeology and the techniques that archaeologists use to study artifacts. Childress traces the Paleo-Indians across the Bering Strait and records what the weapons and utensils discovered from the time period reveal about them. Photographs, Reproductions, Glossary, and Index.

407. Chin, Steven A. **When Justice Failed: The Fred Korematsu Story**. David Tamura, illustrator. Austin, TX: Raintree/Steck-Vaughn, 1993. 105p. $15.49; $5.95pa. ISBN 0-8114-7236-1; 0-8114-8076-3pa. (Stories of America—Personal Challenge). 5-9

In 1967, Karen Korematsu listened to her friend give a report on World War II about a man who had challenged the U.S. government's decision to intern Americans of Japanese descent. What she heard was the story of her father, Fred Korematsu, who had decided that the edict was unfair. The American Civil Liberties Union represented Korematsu and took his case to the Supreme Court, where it failed. In 1982, it was discovered that at least two studies of Japanese Americans before the war had concluded that they were not a threat to U.S. security. Because this information was not initially revealed to the courts, a new review reversed the earlier decision. Afterword and Notes.

408. Chrisman, Abbott. **David Farragut**. Francis Balistreri, illustrator. Austin, TX: Raintree/Steck-Vaughn, 1993. 32p. $13.98; $5.95pa. ISBN 0-8172-2904-3; 0-8114-6754-6pa. (Hispanic Stories). 4-7

Born in Tennessee in 1801 to a Spanish father and an American mother, David Farragut's father allowed him to be adopted after David's mother died. At 10, Farragut left to sail around Cape Horn, trying to capture British ships. At 12, he was made commander of one of the captured ships. He continued to sail, and in 1862 he took charge of a Union fleet in the Gulf of Mexico supposed to gain control of the Mississippi River. In his fight for Mobile (which he won), he yelled "Damn the torpedoes! Full speed ahead!" For his efforts, he became the first admiral in the U.S. Navy. He died in 1870. Glossary. English and Spanish text.

409. Chrisp, Peter. **The Farmer Through History**. Tony Smith, illustrator. New York: Thomson Learning, 1993. 48p. $15.95. ISBN 1-56847-011-8. (Journey Through History). 3-5

Photographs, reproductions, and drawings show farmers through history as the text covers the change in society from the hunter-gatherer to the farmer. The periods examined are a farmer in Jericho (8000-6000 BC), an Egyptian peasant farmer (3100-2150 BC), a Roman slave farmer (300 BC-AD 300), a Mayan maize farmer (300-900), a Chinese rice farmer (960-1279); an English serf (1100-1400), a yam farmer of Benin (1400-1700), an improving farmer of Britain (1730-1830), a Soviet collective farmer (1928-1990), and a modern Western farmer (1990-). Glossary, Further Reading, Timeline, and Index.

410. Chrisp, Peter. **The Soldier Through History**. Tony Smith, illustrator. New York: Thomson Learning, 1993. 48p. $15.95. ISBN 1-56847-010-X. (Journey Through History). 3-5

With emphasis on ground soldiers, military tactics, and weaponry, the text looks at Greek hoplites from 500-300 BC, Roman soldiers, knight crusaders, Mongol horsemen, Aztecs, Prussians, and tank fighters in the Gulf War. Maps, illustrations, and sidebars complement the text. Further Reading, Glossary, and Index.

411. Chrisp, Peter. **The Spanish Conquests in the New World**. New York: Thomson Learning, 1993. 48p. $14.95. ISBN 1-56847-123-8. (Exploration & Encounters). 4-6

The text, using original maps and firsthand accounts, presents a history of the Spanish exploration and conquests in America. It emphasizes Cortés and Pizarro, whose search for gold made them ruthless toward Montezuma and Atahuallpa. Chrisp explains Aztec religious practices without moralizing and goes beyond the better-known stories of the explorers. Glossary, Books to Read, and Index.

412. Chrisp, Peter. **Voyages to the New World**. New York: Thomson Learning, 1993. 48p. $14.95. ISBN 1-56847-123-8. (Exploration & Encounters). 4-6

In the general background about the explorers who found the New World and exploited it, Chrisp gives information about the fifteenth and sixteenth centuries in Europe, especially Portugal and Spain. With firsthand accounts and original maps, he tries to show how the New World appeared to the first Europeans who saw it five centuries ago. Glossary, Books to Read, and Index.

413. Chrisp, Peter. **The Whalers**. New York: Thomson Learning, 1995. 47p. $15.95. ISBN 1-56847-421-0. (Remarkable World). 4-6

The text traces the history of whaling, beginning with the Inuits and the Basques. It describes the ships, men, and equipment, including the harpoon cannon (invented in 1868), and the early attempts to curb whaling before its end in 1986. Photographs, drawings, and diagrams augment the text.

414. Christian, Mary Blount. **Who'd Believe John Colter?** Laszlo Kubinyi, illustrator. New York: Macmillan, 1993. 64p. $13.95. ISBN 0-02-718477-3. 2-6

In this fictional biography, John Colter (1775-1813) joined the Lewis and Clark expedition from St. Louis, Missouri, in 1803. His job was to hunt for food, but he also became a storyteller. After this expedition ended, he conflicted with the Blackfoot Indians, and they tried to kill him several times. He escaped them and eventually found water erupting from the ground, making him the discoverer of the geyser now named Old Faithful in Yellowstone National Park. Sources.

415. Christiansen, Candace. **The Ice Horse**. Thomas Locker, illustrator. New York: Dial, 1993. Unpaged. $15.99. ISBN 0-8037-1400-9. K-3

In the nineteenth century, Jack looks forward to the ice harvest when the Hudson River freezes and everyone sharpens their saws to carve the blocks of ice. When the horse Max falls through the ice, Jack is very frightened and pulls the rope tight as his uncle told him to do if Max ever fell. Jack is surprised when his action saves the horse.

416. Chu, Daniel, and Bill Shaw. **Going Home to Nicodemus: The Story of an African American Frontier Town and the Pioneers Who Settled It**. New York: Julian Messner, 1995. 96p. $14.95; $5.95pa. ISBN 0-671-88723-8; 0-671-88722-0pa. 5-9

In 1877, African American pioneers dug a community out of the Great Plains in Kansas called Nicodemus. But as the railroads bypassed it and the storms rushed through it, Nicodemus became less prosperous and lost population in the 1930s. Some people returned because they missed its charm, and the text gives the history of the settlers who lived there and those who left. Chronology, Bibliography, and Index. *Notable Children's Trade Books in the Field of Social Studies*.

417. Claflin, Edward Beecher. **Sojourner Truth and the Struggle for Freedom**. Jada Rowland, illustrator. Hauppauge, NY: Barron's, 1989. 153p. $15. ISBN 0-8120-3919-X. 6 up

After being freed from slavery in 1827, Sojourner Truth (1797-1883) worked to help others find a better life. In her later years, people lined up to hear her speak. She had earned respect because of her years of traveling alone preaching freedom and equality. Glossary, References, and Index.

418. Clapp, Patricia. **The Tamarack Tree: A Novel of the Siege of Vicksburg**. New York: Morrow, 1986. 224p. $15. ISBN 0-688-02852-7. New York: Viking, 1988. 256p. $3.99pa. ISBN 0-14-032406-2pa. 5-9

As a British girl living in Vicksburg, Mississippi, during the Civil War, Rosemary, 14, matures as the battles come closer and people starve during the siege of Vicksburg. That she likes people who own slaves when she hates the idea of owning another human surprises her, and that her brother is involved with the Underground Railroad relieves her. She helps during the difficult times but returns to England after the siege ends in 1863, where she waits for her Union soldier love while her brother attends medical school.

419. Clapp, Patricia. **Witches' Children**. 1982. Magnolia, MA: Peter Smith, 1992. $18.25. ISBN 0-8446-6572-X. New York: Penguin, 1987. $4.99pa. ISBN 0-14-032407-0pa. 5-9

In Salem, Massachusetts, during 1692, Mary Warren, a bound girl, visits friends freely and meets Tituba, slave to the Parris family, who reads Tarot cards and palms. Tituba refuses to tell Abigail, 11, what she sees in her future, because Abigail wants excitement of any kind. After several meetings of the 10 friends, they begin having visions and proclaiming that women in the town are trying to "possess" them like witches. Their accusations make them the center of attention, but they begin the destruction of lives perpetrated by trials in Salem and judgments of death on innocent people. As she reflects on the situation 15 years later, Mary regrets her role in this dastardly affair. *American Library Association Best Books for Young Adults* and *Jefferson Cup*.

420. Clare, John D. **First World War**. San Diego, CA: Gulliver, Harcourt Brace, 1995. 64p. $16.95. ISBN 0-15-200087-9. (Living History). 5-8

Both real and reenactment photographs augment the text, giving an overview of World War I from its beginning, when Archduke Ferdinand and his wife Sophie were murdered in Sarajevo on June 28, 1914, until its end, on November 11, 1918. The text establishes a sense of the war by discussing why men joined the armed forces, life in the trenches, the use of gas and tanks, the fight from the air and the sea, shortages that occurred, women in the war, and the Treaty of Versailles in 1919. A concluding essay explores the ways that people today benefit from knowing what happened during that time. Index. *Notable Children's Trade Books in the Field of Social Studies*.

421. Claro, Nicole. **The Apache Indians**. New York: Chelsea House, 1992. 71p. $14.95; $6.95pa. ISBN 0-7910-1656-0; 0-7910-1946-2pa. (Junior Library of American Indians). 3-7

The text examines the history, culture, and future prospects of the Apache Indians, with illustrations complementing the text. Glossary, Chronology, and Index.

422. Claro, Nicole. **The Cherokee Indians**. New York: Chelsea House, 1992. 79p. $14.95; $6.95pa. ISBN 0-7910-1652-8; 0-7910-2030-4pa. (Junior Library of American Indians). 3-7

After beginning with the Cherokee legend of creation, the text gives the history of the Cherokees. The chapters cover their way of life, their exile during the Trail of Tears in 1838 when they were marched from southern states to Oklahoma, their artistic work, their life in the West, and their current concerns. Photographs and reproductions enhance the text. Glossary, Chronology, and Index.

423. Cleaver, Vera, and Bill Cleaver. **Dust of the Earth**. New York: Lippincott, 1975. 160p. $13.95. ISBN 0-397-31650-X. 6-8

When Fern's mother inherits a house in South Dakota in the 1950s, the family moves there. Expecting much more than a house and a flock of sheep, they have to readjust their lives to their new environment. They learn that working as a group helps them become more productive than when they function as individuals.

424. Clements, Gillian, author/illustrator. **An Illustrated History of the World: How We Got to Where We Are**. New York: Farrar, Straus & Giroux, 1992. 62p. $16. ISBN 0-374-33258-4. 6-8

In cartoons, Clements presents single and double-spread segments that cover the events in a period of world history, beginning with theories about the origin of the universe. She continues into the 1970s and ends with a timeline noting different epochs of history. Chronology.

425. Clements, Gillian. **The Picture History of Great Inventors**. New York: Knopf, 1994. 77p. $13pa. ISBN 0-679-84787-1pa. 4-6

Pages cover 60 major inventors, from Archimedes (287-212 BC) through inventors in Alexandria during the first century AD, to the medieval period with Gutenberg and da Vinci, and into the twentieth century. Illustrations of each inventor's contributions enhance the text. Glossary and Index.

426. Clifford, Eth. **The Man Who Sang in the Dark**. Mary Beth Owen, illustrator. Boston: Houghton Mifflin, 1987. 112p. $12.95. ISBN 0-395-43664-8. 3-5

In 1929, Leah, 10, her younger brother, and her mother live in a tiny apartment. Leah's mother gives up her brother for adoption because she cannot make enough money sewing to support all of them. But after Leah asks a blind musician, the landlord's nephew, to help her find Daniel, the musician and her mother fall in love, and they all reunite as a family, with the landlord couple acting as surrogate grandparents.

427. Clifford, Eth. **The Remembering Box**. Donna Diamond, illustrator. Boston: Houghton Mifflin, 1985. 70p. $15.95. ISBN 0-395-38476-1. New York: Beech Tree, Morrow, 1992. 70p. $4.95pa. ISBN 0-688-11777-5pa. 2-5

Joshua goes to see his grandmother for the Sabbath meal each Friday, from 1938, when he is five, until 1942, when she dies. She tells him stories about her past as she shares items that she has kept in a box. Before she dies, she gives him a box like hers with some of her own items already inside.

428. Clifford, Eth. **Will Somebody Please Marry My Sister?** Ellen Eagle, illustrator. Boston: Houghton Mifflin, 1992. 122p. $13.95. ISBN 0-395-58037-4. 4-6

Abel, a 12-year-old orphan living with his sisters and grandmother, decides that he will have to marry off his sisters so that he can have his own room. Because in 1925 custom declares that the oldest girl must marry first, Able brings home eligible bachelors for his 26-year-old sister to meet. But she is a doctor without much interest in marriage, and the men are skeptical about marrying her. She solves Abel's problem when she decides to move to the hospital, and the middle sister decides to marry anyway.

429. Clifford, Mary. **When the Great Canoes Came**. Joyce Haynes, illustrator. Gretna, LA: Pelican, 1993. 144p. $12.95. ISBN 0-88289-926-0. 4-7

The old members of the Pamunkey tribe tell the young ones about the arrival of the English settlers in Jamestown, Virginia. The promise of trinkets and English clothes lure the young members of the tribe to Jamestown before the queen can even finish telling the story. Lost Owl is angry at their defection, and he must learn to cope with it. But the tribe no longer has peace after the death of Pocahontas in England, because her father no longer seems particularly interested in tribal affairs. Bibliography.

430. Climo, Shirley. **City! New York**. George Ancona, photographs. New York: Macmillan, 1990. 59p. $16.95. ISBN 0-02-719020-X. (City!) 3-6

Much of this book recounts the history of New York City, beginning in 1524 when the first European, Giovanni Verrazano, arrived. The final two chapters suggest places to visit in the various areas of the city and give encyclopedic information about New York State. Photographs of contemporary New York complement the text. Map and Index.

431. Climo Shirley. **City! San Francisco**. George Ancona, photographs. New York: Macmillan, 1990. 59p. $16.95. ISBN 0-02-719030-7. (City!). 3-6

Climo, with Ancona's photographs, traces the history of San Francisco, from the Costanoan Indians approximately 4,000 years ago, Cabrillo's later investigation of the area in 1542, and Father Junípero Serra's missions in the eighteenth century. Sir Francis Drake might have claimed it in the 1500s for Queen Elizabeth if the fog had not shrouded it. The Russians might have taken it for Catherine II in the 1700s if they had stayed long enough to settle it. Men searching for gold and silver, the Pony Express, and Chinese workers finally made San Francisco and its 43 hills sloping to the Pacific a permanent city. Men associated with its success and whose names mark sites in the city include John C. Frémont, who declared California a state and flew The Bear Republic flag for a few days; Kit Carson; Levi Strauss; Charles Crocker; Collis P. Huntington; Mark Hopkins; and Leland Stanford. Two final chapters, "Exploring San Francisco" and "A Pocketful of Facts," relate current information about San Francisco and California. Index.

432. Climo, Shirley. **City! Washington, DC**. George Ancona, photographs. New York: Macmillan, 1991. 59p. $16.95. ISBN 0-02-719036-6. (City!). 3-6

Although beautiful color photographs of Washington as it appears today highlight the text, the book tells the history of Washington from the time George Washington decided to have a capital. Included is information about the federal buildings and the monuments. Index.

433. Climo, Shirley. **A Month of Seven Days**. New York: HarperCollins, 1987. 152p. $13.89. ISBN 0-690-04656-1. 5-7

Zoe, 12, stays with her younger brother and pregnant mother while her father serves in the Confederate army in Georgia during 1864. A Yankee captain and his men take over the house and demand services, including cooking. Zoe puts up with what she must, but she devises schemes to frighten the superstitious captain. Although the soldiers leave within a week, she learns that not all Yankees are despicable.

434. Clinton, Susan. **Benjamin Harrison: Twenty-Third President of the United States**. Chicago: Childrens Press, 1989. 100p. $19.80. ISBN 0-516-01370-X. (Encyclopedia of Presidents). 4-9

Benjamin Harrison (1833-1901) fought in the Civil War against Confederates and Copperheads (Northern members of the American Democratic Party who opposed Abraham Lincoln and wanted to compromise with the South). When he became president, he helped change the Monroe Doctrine so that future territorial and trade expansion could occur. After he left the presidency, people still respected him, and he became a senior statesman. Photos, Reproductions, Chronology of American History, and Index.

435. Clinton, Susan. **Herbert Hoover: Thirty-First President of the United States**. Chicago: Childrens Press, 1988. 100p. $19.80. ISBN 0-516-41355-4. (Encyclopedia of Presidents). 4-9

Herbert Hoover (1874-1964), a mining engineer graduated from Stanford, had experience managing mining properties in Australia and China, and he became a millionaire by age 40. At the beginning of World War I in 1914, his responsibility was to organize and assist the return of thousands of Americans stranded in Europe. He became the president just before the Depression began, and his policies, although misrepresented, caused some people to vote for Franklin Roosevelt instead of him when he ran for a second term. Photographs, Chronology of American History, and Index.

436. Clinton, Susan. **James Madison: Fourth President of the United States**. Chicago: Childrens Press, 1986. 100p. $19.80. ISBN 0-516-01382-3. (Encyclopedia of Presidents). 4-9

As Father of the Constitution, James Madison (1751-1836) had a major influence on the structure of government in the new nation. Son of a Virginia planter, he was well educated and believed that people should have freedom of religion in a complete separation of church and state. He went to the Constitutional Convention, served as Secretary of State under Thomas Jefferson, and was President during the War of 1812. Chronology of American History and Index.

437. Cobb, Mary. **The Quilt-Block History of Pioneer Days: With Projects Kids Can Make**. Jan Davey Ellis, illustrator. Brookfield, CT: Millbrook Press, 1995. 64p. $7.95pa. ISBN 1-56294-485-1pa. 2-6

An album quilt was a very special quilt made for a family moving west in the pioneer days. Because many people would never see each other again, the designs and materials they used had much meaning. The text presents the habits of pioneer-day travels and quilt patterns that have been popular through the years. Outlines of the patterns allow copying the designs. For Further Reading and Index.

438. Cochrane, Patricia A. **Purely Rosie Pearl**. New York: Delacorte, 1996. 135p. $14.95. ISBN 0-385-32193-7. 4-7

Rosie, 12, and her family have steady jobs as migrant fruit pickers on the West Coast during 1936, while the rest of the country still fights the Depression. She looks forward to seeing old friends as the family makes the circuit, but she also meets a new girl whose well-educated family has had to join the migrant workers because no other jobs are available. A hiring boss makes advances toward Rosie, and her sister loses her first child when the hospital will not accept her without a cash payment. The strawberry farm owner admires Rosie's family's hard work, and he asks her father to replace the hiring boss. This change in fortunes makes the family's future look brighter.

439. Cocke, William. **A Historical Album of Virginia**. Brookfield, CT: Millbrook Press, 1994. 64p. $16.40; $6.95pa. ISBN 1-56294-596-3; 1-56294-856-3pa. (Historical Album). 4-8

The text presents the land of Virginia before it became a state, beginning with Native American civilizations and continuing through exploration and settlement. Early statehood developments and issues, and the role of large cities in the state's livelihood, lead to the present day. Prints, maps, and photographs illustrate the text. Gazetteer: Quick Facts, Key Events, Personalities, and Index.

440. Cocke, William. **A Historical Album of Washington**. Brookfield, CT: Millbrook Press, 1994. 64p. $16.40; $6.95pa. ISBN 1-56294-508-4; 1-56294-851-2pa. (Historical Album). 4-8

The text presents the land of Washington before it became a state, beginning with Native American civilizations and continuing through exploration and settlement. Early statehood developments and issues, and the role of large cities in the state's livelihood, lead to the present day. Prints, maps, and photographs illustrate the text. Gazetteer: Quick Facts, Key Events, Personalities, and Index.

441. Codye, Corinn. **Luis W. Alvarez**. Bob Masheris, illustrator. Austin, TX: Raintree/Steck-Vaughn, 1993. 32p. $13.98; $5.95pa. ISBN 0-8114-8467-X; 0-8114-6750-3pa. (Hispanic Stories). 4-7

Luis Alvarez (1911-1988) grew up in California, where he started his scientific career as a youngster by building a radio. He became especially interested in physics, and when the atom bomb fell on Hiroshima in 1945, he and a team of men flew around the area to measure its impact. Later, he and colleagues built a hydrogen bubble chamber in which they discovered many new atomic particles. His work won him the Nobel Prize in Physics in 1968. A new interest in his later life was geology. He and his son studied rocks and hypothesized that a meteor crashing into the Earth had destroyed the dinosaurs because they identified iridium that would not otherwise have been found in Earth's rocks. Glossary.

442. Codye, Corinn. **Vilma Martinez**. Susi Kilgore, illustrator. Austin, TX: Raintree/Steck-Vaughn, 1993. 32p. $13.98; $5.95pa. ISBN 0-8172-3382-2; 0-8114-6762-7pa. (Hispanic Stories). 4-7

Vilma Martinez (b. 1943) grew up speaking Spanish in her Texas home, and teachers always discouraged her from attending the best public high school and college. She disproved their theories by graduating from law school. During her career, she worked with the Mexican-American Legal Defense Fund (MALDEF) to gain voting rights for Mexican Americans and to demand that schools provide young students a bilingual education when they had only heard Spanish at home. Glossary.

443. Coelho, Tony. **John Quincy Adams**. New York: Chelsea House, 1990. 112p. $18.95. ISBN 1-55546-802-0. (World Leaders Past and Present). 5 up

John Quincy Adams (1767-1848), son of John and Abigail Adams, witnessed the American Revolution and his father's involvement in the creation of the nation. He went with his father to Europe, where he was educated, and began his political career in 1794, when George Washington appointed him ambassador to the Netherlands. He served in a number of roles until he defeated Andrew Jackson for President in 1824. After his term ended, he served in the House of Representatives and tried to get the right of petition and a restriction on slavery in the West during his tenure. He was independent and a defender of democratic ideals. Reproductions enhance the text. Further Reading, Chronology, and Index.

444. Coerr, Eleanor. **Buffalo Bill and the Pony Express**. Don Bolognese, illustrator. New York: HarperCollins, 1995. 64p. $14; $3.75pa. ISBN 0-06-023372-9; 0-06-444220-9pa. (An I Can Read Book). K-3

In 1860, the Pony Express started with riders brave enough to face many dangers while they carried the mail across the country. Buffalo Bill Cody was one of the riders who survived Indians and wolves during the 18 months of the Pony Express's existence, before trains started taking the mail.

444a. Coerr, Eleanor. **Chang's Paper Pony**. Deborah Kogan Ray, illustrator. New York: HarperCollins, 1988. 63p. $15.89; $3.75pa. ISBN 0-06-021329-9; 0-06-444163-6pa. (An I Can Read Book). K-3

Around 1850, Chang and his grandfather run a hotel for the gold miners near San Francisco, California. The miners are rude to Chang, but he continues to work and study so that he can have a better life away from the war in China. Chang finds gold in one of the miner's cabins, and the miner buys Chang a pony, the one thing Chang wants badly. *John and Patricia Beatty Award.*

445. Coerr, Eleanor. **The Josefina Story Quilt**. Bruce Degen, illustrator. New York: HarperCollins, 1986. 64p. $14.95; $3.75pa. ISBN 0-06-021348-5; 0-06-444129-6pa. (An I Can Read Book). K-3

While on the wagon journey to California in 1850, Josefina, Faith's pet hen, saves the family from robbers. Then Faith makes her a patch on the quilt that tells the story of their trip.

446. Cohen, Daniel. **The Alaska Purchase**. Brookfield, CT: Millbrook Press, 1996. 64p. $15.90. ISBN 1-56294-528-9. (Spotlight on American History). 4-8

In 1867, the United States bought from Russia the land that became the 49th state, Alaska. The text looks at the events from 1728 through 1864 that led to the completion of the purchase. Other topics cover the discovery of Alaska, the sea-otter trade, the land of Alaska under Russian rule, the American takeover of the land, and what happened to Alaska after its purchase. Primary sources help to tell Alaska's story along with photographs and reproductions. Chronology, Bibliography, Further Reading, and Index.

447. Cohen, Daniel. **The Ghost of Elvis: And Other Celebrity Spirits**. New York: Putnam, 1994. 100p. $14.95. ISBN 0-399-22611-7. 3-5

The text entertains with selections about the various speculations that exist concerning the ghosts of Elvis, Edgar Allan Poe, and other celebrities.

448. Cohen, Daniel. **The Ghosts of War**. New York: Putnam, 1990. 95p. $13.95. ISBN 0-399-22200-6. New York: Minstrel, 1993. 95p. $2.99pa. ISBN 0-671-74086-5pa. 5-8

Reports of ghosts near battlefields have occurred in all times. The text recounts samurai ghosts from 1180 to 1185, the angel of Mons in 1914, a Polish mercenary of the Revolutionary War, Steven Decatur's ghost after 1820 in Washington, D.C., and Lieutenant Muir in Canada in 1812. Other ghosts also appear in these 13 ghost tales, which Cohen says are "true" to the people who related them. Whether the stories can be verified is perhaps not as important as the concepts of realism and the history they impart.

449. Cohen, Daniel. **Prophets of Doom**. Brookfield, CT: Millbrook Press, 1992. 144p. $15.90. ISBN 1-56294-068-6. 6-9

Taking a skeptical view that anyone can accurately predict the future, the text covers the Millerites, Jehovah's Witnesses, the Greek oracles, the Cumaean Sybil, Mother Shipton, the Bible, Nostradamus, and Edgar Cayce. By noting various prophecies and their failures, Cohen supports his thesis. Bibliography and Index.

450. Coil, Suzanne M. **George Washington Carver**. New York: Franklin Watts, 1990. 64p. $19.90. ISBN 0-531-10864-3. (First Books). 3-6

People looking after George Washington Carver (1864?-1943) during his childhood taught him to read. Coil reveals Carver's curiosity and shows his movement from one school to another in his quest for learning. Although he was an artist and a musician, a dream of a knife stuck in a watermelon and the sight of the real thing the next day led him to think that God had a purpose for him in agriculture. In his adult role at Tuskegee Institute, he found uses for the peanut and the sweet potato that gained him international renown. But he refused extra money because he thought the greatest wealth was in helping people succeed. Activities and Experiments, For Further Reading, and Index.

451. Cole, Michael D. **John Glenn: Astronaut and Senator**. Springfield, NJ: Enslow, 1993. 104p. $17.95. ISBN 0-89490-413-2. (People to Know). 5-8

In February 1962, John Glenn (b. 1921) rocketed into space to become the first American to orbit the Earth in a space capsule. The text chronicles Glenn's family background, influences on his life, and his military career as a pilot and astronaut. He eventually became a U.S. senator from Ohio. Notes, Glossary, Further Reading, and Index.

452. Cole, Norma. **The Final Tide**. New York: Macmillan, 1990. 153p. $14.95. ISBN 0-689-50510-8. 5 up

Geneva, 14, has to make her grandmother leave her rural Kentucky home in 1948 when the government decides to build a lake where the house sits. Geneva figures out how to coerce her grandmother into moving into town rather than die in the old home as she has promised she will.

453. Coleman, Evelyn. **The Foot Warmer and the Crow**. Daniel Minter, illustrator. New York: Macmillan, 1994. 32p. $14.95. ISBN 0-02-722816-9. 3-6

When Hezekiah runs away, his master catches him and beats him. Because he has been the master's favorite slave, Hezekiah asks to become the master's "footwarmer," the slave who sleeps at the foot of the master's bed. A crow advises Hezekiah to learn as much about the master as he can and to use it against him. When Hezekiah hears his master talking about his fears in the middle of the night, Hezekiah confronts him with his new knowledge and runs away. The crow protects Hezekiah by reminding the master that he had killed the crow's mother and had come back to the nest each day to see the chicks die one by one.

454.   Coles, Robert. **The Story of Ruby Bridges**. New York: Scholastic, 1995. Unpaged. $13.95. ISBN 0-590-43967-7. 1-3

Ruby Bridges, born in 1953, was selected to be the first Black child in her elementary school in 1960. For almost a year she had to be protected from angry crowds of white people as she walked to school. One day her teacher, watching from the window, saw her stop and talk to the group. When she entered the empty classroom whose other students were kept home by their parents, she told her teacher that she did not speak to the people; she had stopped to pray, as she did every day. *Notable Children's Trade Books in the Field of Social Studies.*

455.   Collier, Christopher, and James Collier. **Jump Ship to Freedom**. New York: Delacorte, 1981. 192p. $14.95. ISBN 0-385-28484-5. New York: Yearling, 1996. 192p. $4.50pa. ISBN 0-440-44323-7pa. 4-6

In 1787, Captain Ivers accuses Daniel of stealing when Dan retrieves the money left to his mother that his dead father earned while serving as a soldier in Ivers's place. Ivers captures Dan and keeps him on his ship, but Dan jumps ship during a storm. When the damaged ship returns to shore, Dan gets the money off the ship and establishes that his father had received his freedom from Ivers. Mr. Fraunces helps Dan, and Dan travels to Philadelphia, where he meets Alexander Hamilton, a man whom he sees as most unpleasant. After the war, Dan plans to buy his and his mother's freedom.

456.   Collier, Christopher, and James Collier. **War Comes to Willy Freeman**. 1983. Magnolia, MA: Peter Smith, 1992. 192p. $17.25. ISBN 0-8446-6596-7. New York: Yearling, 1991. 192p. $3.99pa. ISBN 0-440-49504-0pa. 4-6

After going with her father to Fort Griswold, Connecticut, and having to stay there during a British advance, Willy, 13, watches a British soldier gore her father. When she returns home, the British have taken her mother. She dresses like a male and goes to find her. In New York City, she obtains work at Sam Fraunces's tavern and searches the canvas towns during her free time. She hears where her mother has gone, and she follows her although she knows that her aunt's master will probably say that Willy belongs to him. After her mother dies, Ivers does try to claim her, but Sam Fraunces and his friends help her discredit him in court.

457.   Collier, Christopher, and James Collier. **Who Is Carrie?** New York: Delacorte, 1984. 192p. $14.95. ISBN 0-385-29295-3. New York: Yearling, 1987. 192p. $3.99pa. ISBN 0-440-49536-9pa. 4-6

While Carrie watches President Washington arrive at New York City's waterfront, Captain Ivers tries to kidnap her, but Dan (cousin of Willy in *War Comes to Willy Freeman*) and Mr. Fraunces, owner of a tavern, save her. She goes with Mr. Fraunces, President Washington's new steward, to Washington's home, but decides to go to Philadelphia to be with Willy. Even though Ivers continues to pursue her, people help her escape until they are able to reconstruct her origin. They realize that she is Willy's sister and therefore free.

458.   Collier, James Lincoln. **Duke Ellington**. New York: Macmillan, 1991. 144p. $12.95. ISBN 0-02-722985-8. 5-9

Duke Ellington (1899-1974) often told his mother that he was going to be great. He did become one of the major figures in twentieth-century American music, with some people thinking that he was "America's most important composer." Ellington taught himself to play piano and compose music, ignoring many rules of composition to develop jazz. His self-respect and refusal to clown helped destroy the stereotypical image of the Black entertainer. The text presents his life and analyzes some of his major compositions. For Further Study and Index.

459.   Collier, James Lincoln. **The Jazz Kid**. New York: Henry Holt, 1994. 216p. $15.95. ISBN 0-8050-2821-8. 6-9

When Paulie Horvath is 12 in 1922, he hears two bands playing during a parade and decides he wants to play in one of them. His father is against music, wanting Paulie to follow him in the plumbing business. One day Paulie helps his father fix pipes in a jazz club, and when he hears a cornet solo, he knows that he must learn to play. He defies his parents to learn jazz and gets into trouble with organized crime, but his parents decide, in the end, to bargain with him. If he does well in school, they will support his decision to become a musician.

460.   Collier, James Lincoln. **Louis Armstrong: An American Success Story**. New York: Macmillan, 1985. 165p. $5.95pa. ISBN 0-02-042555-4pa. 5-9

Born in abject poverty in a New Orleans shack with no toilet or running water, Louis Armstrong (1900-1971) became one of the greatest jazz musicians who ever lived. As a youngster, he sang on street corners for pennies, and after reform school, he played cornet. By hanging around musicians when he was a teenager, he learned by watching, and they eventually asked him to join their jam sessions. From these experiences, his career blossomed until he became America's ambassador for peace. Index.

461. Collier, James Lincoln. **My Crooked Family**. New York: Simon & Schuster, 1991. 181p. $15. ISBN 0-671-74224-8. 5-9

Roger, 13, and his little sister almost starve while their parents drink in 1910. When a man offers Roger a job, he decides that he prefers buying food to stealing it. However, he soon becomes involved in a robbery and finds that his father has also been a thief. When the gang asks him to join, Roger's mother begs him not to do it, but he indicates that he might.

462. Collier, James Lincoln, and Christopher Collier. **The Clock**. Kelly Maddox, illustrator. New York: Delacorte, 1992. 162p. $15. ISBN 0-385-30037-9. 6-9

Annie, 15 in 1810, goes to work in a textile mill when her Connecticut family needs money. The overseer propositions her, and because she has heard that he is stealing from the mill owner, she rebuffs his advance and tells him that she will investigate him. The overseer in turn has her friend with a mangled foot climb on a frozen waterwheel to free it from the ice; he dies when it turns before he is prepared for movement. Annie's father sacrifices her desire to be a teacher for quick money.

463. Collier, James Lincoln, and Christopher Collier. **With Every Drop of Blood: A Novel of the Civil War**. New York: Delacorte, 1994. 233p. $15.95. ISBN 0-385-32028-0. 6-9

Johnny, 12, breaks his promise to his dying father by leaving his Virginia family to carry supplies to Rebel troops. An ex-slave, Cush, captures him. Johnny goes against his breeding and becomes friends with Cush, although Johnny takes advantage of the situation by teaching Cush to read incorrectly at first so that the Gettysburg address will reflect Confederate ideals. But when Rebels capture Cush, Johnny risks his life to find him. He rescues him just as Lee and Grant begin their talks at Appomattox.

464. Collins, David. **To the Point: A Story About E. B. White**. Amy Johnson, illustrator. Minneapolis, MN: Carolrhoda, 1989. 56p. $17.50; $5.95pa. ISBN 0-87614-345-1; 0-87614-508-Xpa. (Creative Minds). 3-6

As the youngest of several children, E. B. White (1899-1985) spent his teenage years alone, but when he was 12, *St. Nicholas* magazine published his first story. He filled many days with writing but never became serious about it or anything until, while attending Cornell, he began to feel guilty that he was too small to join the army and fight in World War I. He learned from his professor, William Strunk, Jr., to be precise and witty but also serious when necessary. He never forgot this advice during his work at the *New Yorker* and *Harper's* or while he wrote *Stuart Little*, *Charlotte's Web*, and *The Trumpet of the Swan*. In his later years, he edited Strunk's book *The Elements of Style*, and it became a publication by Strunk *and* White. *Booklist*.

465. Collins, David R. **Charles Lindbergh: Hero Pilot**. New York: Chelsea Juniors, 1991. 80p. $14.95. ISBN 0-7910-1417-7. (Discovery Biography). 3-7

Charles Lindbergh saw his first plane when he was eight years old. He decided then that he would fly. And he did. He became the first pilot to fly solo across the Atlantic Ocean between New York and Paris in 1927.

466. Collins, David R. **Farmworker's Friend: The Story of Cesar Chavez**. Minneapolis, MN: Carolrhoda, 1996. 80p. $14.96. ISBN 0-87614-982-4. (Trailblazers). 4-7

Cesar Chavez (1927-1993) was himself a migrant worker with other members of his family. When he saw the overwork and the underpay of migrant workers, he became an activist to make life better for the others. He helped to build a union for farmworkers and continued to fight for their rights throughout his life. Important Dates.

467. Collins, David R. **Gerald R. Ford: 38th President of the United States**. Ada, OK: Garrett Educational, 1990. 120p. $17.26. ISBN 0-944483-65-8. (Presidents of the United States). 5-9

Gerald Ford's (b. 1913) youth prepared him for some of the difficulties of being president of the United States after Richard Nixon resigned in 1974. Among the anecdotes included in the text is one about Ford's visit to North Carolina to see a football game at the invitation of a rear admiral. They flew into the airport, but the pilot discovered he was on the wrong runway, something he could not determine beforehand during a severe storm. He landed as quickly as possible and rushed everyone out of the plane. The plane exploded from the impact with the runway as soon as all had escaped. This event and Ford's experiences as a football player, a law student, and congressman shaped his approach to the presidency and his later life. Bibliography and Index.

468. Collins, David R. **Grover Cleveland: 22nd and 24th President of the United States**. Ada, OK: Garrett Educational, 1988. 119p. $17.26. ISBN 0-944483-01-1. (Presidents of the United States). 5-9

Grover Cleveland (1837-1908) served two separate and distinct terms as president. After his first term, Benjamin Harrison defeated him. Then he was reelected in the next election. During his presidency, he was honest to a fault but also stubborn. He believed that public office was a "public trust," and he spent his life trying to fulfill that belief. He fought battles over the tariff system and suggested that Americans were too protectionist. He also helped to establish the gold standard. Bibliography and Index.

469.   Collins, David R. **Harry S. Truman: People's President**. Paul Frame, illustrator. New York: Chelsea Juniors, 1991. 80p. $14.95. ISBN 0-7910-1421-5. (Discovery). 3-7

This biography of Harry S. Truman (1884-1972) begins with his childhood at eight, when his father crawled on the roof to get the children up to learn that Grover Cleveland, their candidate, had won the election. It continues with Truman's life and his rise to the presidency at the death of Franklin Delano Roosevelt.

470.   Collins, David R. **Mark T-W-A-I-N!: A Story About Samuel Clemens**. Vicky Carey, illustrator. Minneapolis, MN: Carolrhoda, 1994. 64p. $13.13. ISBN 0-87614-801-1. (Creative Minds). 3-6

Samuel Clemens (1835-1910) grew up in Hannibal, Mississippi, but he left and became a newspaperman and a writer after experimenting with being a steamboat pilot, a soldier, and a gold prospector. He took his pseudonym from his experience as a steamboat pilot. Some people consider *Tom Sawyer* and *Huckleberry Finn* to be books for children; others believe they are for adults. Mark Twain was born the year that Halley's comet swept into the sky, and it came back the year he died. Books and Bibliography.

471.   Collins, David R. **Pioneer Plowmaker: The Story of John Deere**. Steve Michaels, illustrator. Minneapolis, MN: Carolrhoda, 1990. 63p. $9.95. ISBN 0-87614-424-5. (Creative Minds). 4-8

Not only is this a biography of John Deere, but it is also a history of the events and influences of the early 1800s. John Deere worked hard and produced one of the first self-scouring plows. Later, he refused to put his name on an implement that was not worthy of it. Customers could always be confident that his products were of the highest quality. Bibliography.

472.   Collins, David R. **William McKinley: 25th President of the United States**. Ada, OK: Garrett Educational, 1990. 120p. $17.26. ISBN 0-944483-55-0. (Presidents of the United States). 5-9

William McKinley (1843-1901) served in the Union army during the Civil War before he attended law school. The text begins with his assassination in Buffalo at a World's Fair gathering that his assistants had discouraged him from attending. There, a young man in the reception line uncovered a gun and shot him. McKinley died not from the shot but from the gangrene that set in after the operation to remove the bullet. About him Grover Cleveland said, "All our people loved their dead President. His kindly nature and lovable traits of character, his amiable consideration for all about him will long live...." His assassin, Leon Czolgosz, was convicted in one day and was electrocuted one month later. McKinley's passion for others continued even as he lay dying, but he sometimes lacked strength of leadership during his presidency. Bibliography and Index.

473.   Collins, David R. **Woodrow Wilson: 28th President of the United States**. Ada, OK: Garrett Educational, 1989. 120p. $17.26. ISBN 0-9444483-18-6. (Presidents of the United States). 5-9

Woodrow Wilson (1856-1924) was president for eight years. After World War I, he introduced the Fourteen Points for World Peace and worked tirelessly to establish the League of Nations, but senators in Congress voted against it. In 1920, his efforts won him the Nobel Peace Prize. At the time, he had the highest educational degrees of any man to be President and worked with people to try to get his ideas passed. He was a trained lawyer, a professor, a history scholar, and an orator. Bibliography and Index.

474.   Collins, David R. **Zachary Taylor: 12th President of the United States**. Ada, OK: Garrett Educational, 1989. 121p. $17.26. ISBN 0-944483-27-8. (Presidents of the United States). 5-9

Zachary Taylor (1784-1850), nicknamed "Old Rough and Ready," never lost a battle. He became president because people hoped that a good general would still be as good a president as George Washington had been. Taylor, however, died after 16 months in office, so no one was ever sure. During his tenure, he could not offer a resolution of the slavery issue, but he owned slaves. The Galphin Claim scandal tainted his honor even though he had nothing to do with it. He did not choose subordinates well. Bibliography and Index.

475.   Collins, James L. **John Brown and the Fight Against Slavery**. Brookfield, CT: Millbrook Press, 1991. 32p. $11.50. ISBN 1-56294-043-0. (Gateway Civil Rights). 3-6

John Brown (1800-1859) was an abolitionist who struggled to free American slaves. He resorted to murder when he led a raid on Harpers Ferry, West Virginia, in 1859. He was tried and hung. Among those he knew were Harriet Tubman and Harriet Beecher Stowe. Bibliography and Index.

476.   Colman, Penny. **Fannie Lou Hamer and the Fight for the Vote**. Brookfield, CT: Millbrook Press, 1993. 32p. $13.90; $4.95pa. ISBN 1-56294-323-5; 1-56294-789-3pa. (Gateway Civil Rights). 2-4

Fannie Lou Hamer (1917-1977) supported the civil rights workers who came to her Mississippi town and registered to vote. Whites in Mississippi had fired or economically punished Blacks who tried to vote. Fannie Lou took the chance and began speaking for civil rights at such places as the Democratic National Convention, and she even ran for the Mississippi state senate, though she lost.

477. Colman, Penny. **Madam C. J. Walker: Building a Business Empire**. Brookfield, CT: Millbrook Press, 1994. 48p. $13.90. ISBN 1-56294-338-3. (Gateway Biography). 3-5

Madam C. J. Walker, born Sarah Breedlove on 1867 in a cotton plantation cabin, began a business and built a factory at a time when women, especially Black women, had few rights. She moved from St. Louis to Denver, where she began her business selling hair care products for Black women. Other moves took her to Indianapolis and New York City. Her products gave Black women a sense of their own beauty as well as jobs in her factory. She used much of her money to help Black artists and civil rights causes. Her enormous achievement should not be underestimated. She died in 1919. Important Dates, Further Information, and Index.

478. Colman, Penny. **Mother Jones and the March of the Mill Children**. Brookfield, CT: Millbrook Press, 1994. 48p. $15.90. ISBN 1-56294-402-9. 3-6

In 1903, Mother Jones (Mary Harris Jones, born in Ireland perhaps in 1830) led a 125-mile, 20-day protest march against child labor to see the President of the United States. News of the march appeared in the newspapers daily, and her attempt put the problem of child labor into American minds. She has been called an agitator, a fanatic, an angel, a champion, and a humanitarian. About herself, Mother Jones said, "I'm a hell-raiser." Tragedies in her own life led her to protest for others after she was 40. Photographs, Important Dates, Find Out More, and Index. *Notable Children's Trade Books in the Field of Social Studies.*

479. Colman, Penny. **Rosie the Riveter: Women Working on the Home Front in World War II**. New York: Crown, 1995. 120p. $16. ISBN 0-517-59790-X. 5-9

Colman introduces World War II with the story of a woman who had saved for many years for a trip to Europe. She went in 1939 but had difficulty getting home. Although the child (now an adult) who overheard the story did not quite understand, she gathered that the woman's delayed return related to someone named Hitler and a war. Because men had to leave to fight the war, the importance of women and their work during World War II led to the nickname "Rosie the Riveter." Chapters include getting ready for the war and the opportunities for women, the concern during the war that led women to try all kinds of jobs, the final years of the war, and the loss of these jobs to the men when they returned from the war. What women did not lose was the knowledge that they could do well in the workplace. Photographs, Chronology, Bibliography, and Index. *Bulletin Blue Ribbon Book, American Library Association Notable Books for Children*, and *American Library Association Best Books for Young Adults.*

480. Colman, Penny. **Spies! Women in the Civil War**. Cincinnati, OH: Betterway, 1992. 96p. $6.95pa. ISBN 1-55870-267-9pa. 6-8

Many women took part in the Civil War, some of them serving as spies for the North and South. They include Belle "The Siren of the Shenandoah" Boyd, Elizabeth "Crazy Bet" Van Lew, and Harriet Tubman. Chronology, Further Reading, and Index.

481. Colman, Penny. **Strike: The Bitter Struggle of American Workers from Colonial Times to the Present**. Brookfield, CT: Millbrook Press, 1995. 80p. $16.90. ISBN 1-56294-459-2. 5-8

Worker struggles in the United States began before the colonies became states. When the Industrial Revolution started, the nature of work changed, but laws did not control the workplace. Children began working in factories instead of farms, and immigrants joined them. With poor working conditions, strikes offered the only chance of improvement. The text includes the strikes in 1677 by the carters; in 1768 by the tailors; in 1834 and 1859 by female factory workers in Lowell, Massachusetts; in 1867 by the Chinese railroad workers; the Great Uprising of 1877; Haymarket in 1885 for an eight-hour day; the Homestead strike in 1892; and the Pullman strike the following year. In the 1900s, the New York factory workers went on strike in 1910; in 1936, there was a General Motors strike; the migrant workers in California struck during the 1960s; and in 1973, the Harlan, Kentucky, coal miners went on strike. Important Dates, Find Out More, and Index.

482. Colman, Penny. **Toilets, Bathtubs, Sinks, and Sewers: A History of the Bathroom**. New York: Atheneum, 1994. 70p. $14.95. ISBN 0-689-31894-4. 5-8

The text looks at various civilizations, from ancient Mesopotamia through the Middle Ages and the Renaissance to contemporary America, and how they have solved waste removal, sanitation, and water management. Such sources as archaeological finds and letters have given insight into the methods of handling these plumbing problems. Bibliography and Index.

483. Colman, Penny. **A Woman Unafraid: The Achievements of Frances Perkins**. New York: Atheneum, 1993. 128p. $14.95. ISBN 0-689-31853-7. 5-8

Frances Perkins (1880-1965) was the first woman in the United States cabinet and the creator of important reforms and social legislation. She became involved in social causes, and after moving to Philadelphia, she worked to keep young women from being exploited. When she witnessed the Triangle Shirtwaist Company fire in Greenwich Village, where 146 workers lost their lives, she wanted to improve conditions for all workers. Franklin Roosevelt appointed her Secretary of Labor during the Great Depression. She helped establish safer working conditions, fairer wages, reasonable working hours, unemployment insurance, and Social Security. Chronology, Notes, Bibliography, and Index.

484. Colver, Anne. **Abraham Lincoln: For the People**. New York: Chelsea Juniors, 1992. 80p. $14.95. ISBN 0-7910-01414-2. (Discovery Biography). 3-7

This biography of Abraham Lincoln (1809-1865) begins with the story of Lincoln as a boy falling off a log into a stream one Sunday and making his friend swear that he would not tell. Lincoln engineered falling off the log so that he could go swimming without breaking the Sabbath. His friend did not tell the story until after Lincoln's death. Lincoln's religious background and the things he read led him to become the President of the United States. The text ends with his funeral train going across the country back to Springfield. He was thoughtful and just.

485. Compton, Anita. **Marriage Customs**. New York: Thomson Learning, 1993. 32p. $13.95. ISBN 1-56847-033-9. (Comparing Religions). 4-8

Six major religions—Buddhism, Christianity, Hinduism, Judaism, Islam, and Sikhism—have specific ceremonies for marriage. Some have signed contracts and ways of affirming the promises connected to the marriage. In all, marriage has its basis in the family's life. Photographs enhance the information. Glossary, Books to Read, and Index.

486. Conley, Kevin. **Benjamin Banneker: Scientist and Mathematician**. New York: Chelsea House, 1989. 109p. $18.95. ISBN 1-55546-573-0. (Black Americans of Achievement). 5 up

Benjamin Banneker (1751-1806), a free Black man whose grandmother had been an indentured servant and his grandfather her slave, taught himself astronomy with the help of books and a telescope that George Ellicott, a Quaker, loaned to him. His talents in mathematics surfaced early. When he was 21, he decided to build a clock, although he had never seen one. His clock fascinated his Maryland community, and it kept correct time for his entire life. In 1792, he helped Ellicott survey the land on which the District of Columbia now stands, and he published his first almanac, with calculations from his study of the stars. His achievements earned him the title of America's first Black man of science. Chronology, Further Reading, and Index.

487. Conlon-McKenna, Marita. **Wildflower Girl**. New York: Holiday House, 1992. 173p. $14.95. ISBN 0-8234-0988-0. 5-7

In this sequel to *Under the Hawthorn Tree*, Peggy, the youngest in her family at 13, decides to leave Ireland and her siblings to go to America. After suffering through 40 days in steerage class on a ship crossing the Atlantic, she reaches Boston. She first works for an alcoholic who beats her. She finds another position with a wealthy family where the work is hard but fair. Her relationship with her fellow workers makes her feel as if she has some family around her again.

488. Connell, Kate. **Tales from the Underground Railroad**. Debbe Heller, illustrator. Austin, TX: Raintree/Steck-Vaughn, 1993. 68p. $14.95; $4.95pa. ISBN 0-8114-7223-X; 0-8114-8063-1pa. (Stories of America—Against All Odds). 4-7

The Underground Railroad was a major force in getting slaves away from cruel masters to freedom. It worked because many whites were willing to risk themselves for something they knew was right. They learned to be crafty and inventive with their methods of getting slaves or even free Blacks away from the unscrupulous slave owners. The stories of William Minnis, Harriet Eglin and Charlotte Giles, and William Still appear in this book. Epilogue.

489. Connell, Kate. **These Lands Are Ours: Tecumseh's Fight for the Old Northwest**. Jan Naimo Jones, illustrator. Austin, TX: Raintree/Steck-Vaughn, 1993. 96p. $15.49; $4.95pa. ISBN 0-8114-7227-2; 0-8114-8067-4pa. (Stories of America—Stand Up and Be Counted). 4-8

When white settlers and the U.S. government began to take Indian lands, one of the leaders who emerged to help his people was Tecumseh (1768-1813). He was a warrior and orator of the Shawnee tribe who united a confederacy of Indians to save the Indian lands. At the Battle of Tippecanoe in 1811, the Long Knives (government soldiers) under Governor William Henry Harrison defeated the Indians. Tecumseh was furious at the setback and blamed his brother for the defeat while he had been trying to talk to other tribes. With Tecumseh's death in 1813 while fighting for the British against Harrison, the Indians lost their organizer. Epilogue, Afterword, and Notes.

490. Connell, Kate. **They Shall Be Heard: Susan B. Anthony & Elizabeth Cady Stanton**. Barbara Kiwak, illustrator. Austin, TX: Raintree/Steck-Vaughn, 1993. 85p. $15.49; $4.95pa. ISBN 0-8114-7228-0; 0-8114-8068-2pa. (Stories of America—Stand Up and Be Counted). 4-8

Susan B. Anthony (1820-1906) and Elizabeth Cady Stanton (1815-1902) both worked ceaselessly for women's rights. These two women met in 1851 in Seneca Falls, New York, at an antislavery meeting; they were introduced by Amanda Bloomer. Because Stanton was older, Anthony always called her Mrs. Stanton, and Stanton called her Susan. Their dedication to equality for women laid the ground for the passage in 1920 of the constitutional amendment allowing women to vote. Unfortunately, neither woman lived to see the day, but without their work, it might not have existed. Epilogue, Afterword, and Notes.

491.   Conord, Bruce W. **Cesar Chavez: Union Leader**. New York: Chelsea House, 1992. 79p. $14.95. ISBN 0-7910-1739-7. (Junior World Biographies). 4-7

Cesar Chavez's life is tied to the history of the United Farm Workers, which he founded to help migrant workers gain rights in their jobs. Black-and-white photographs enhance the text. Further Reading, Glossary, and Index.

492.   Conord, Bruce W. **John Lennon**. New York: Chelsea House, 1994. 127p. $18.95; $7.95pa. ISBN 0-7910-1739-7; 0-7910-1740-0pa. (Pop Culture Legends). 5 up

One of the Beatles, rock music's most famous group, John Lennon (1940-1980) was murdered outside of his New York apartment building. In addition to information about his life, the text includes a discography. Bibliography and Index.

493.   Conrad, Pam. **Call Me Ahnighito**. Richard Egielski, illustrator. New York: Laura Geringer, HarperCollins, 1995. Unpaged. $14.95. ISBN 0-06-023322-2. 1-2

The meteorite Ahnighito talks of its experiences in Greenland. It is picked up and eventually moved by boat to Brooklyn Naval Yard in 1897. Seven years later, it is moved to the American Museum of Natural History in New York City, where everyone knows its name.

494.   Conrad, Pam. **My Daniel**. New York: HarperCollins, 1989. 137p. $13.95; $4.50pa. ISBN 0-06-021313-2; 0-06-440309-2pa. 5 up

Ellie's grandmother Julia tells her of being 12 around 1910 and finding dinosaur bones on their Nebraska farm with her brother Daniel. Their father had hoped for such luck because he needed the money that the bones would bring to save the farm. Ellie hears the story as they visit the Natural History Museum in New York, where the dinosaurs are on display. After Julia and Daniel made their find, lightning struck Daniel, and Julia's life changed. Looking at the bones in the museum momentarily brings him back to her. *Notable Children's Trade Books in the Field of Social Studies, American Library Association Best Books for Young Adults, Booklist Children's Editors Choices, IRA Teachers' Choices, Silver Spur Award for Best Juvenile Fiction, New York Public Library Children's Books*, and *New York Public Library's Books for the Teen Age*.

495.   Conrad, Pam. **Prairie Songs**. Darryl Zudeck, illustrator. New York: HarperCollins, 1985. 167p. $14.89; $4.50pa. ISBN 0-06-021337-X; 0-06-440206-1pa. 5 up

Louisa loves the books that the doctor and his wife bring with them to Nebraska, especially the one with Tennyson's poem, "The Eagle." The wife lets her enjoy the books, but after her newborn dies, the wife can no longer cope with the loneliness of the prairie. Louisa and her family continue to adjust while mourning the losses. *Boston Globe Award, Golden Kite Honor Book, Western Heritage Award, Best Books for Young Adults, Booklist Best of the 80s, Judy Lopez Children's Book Award, New York Public Library's Books for the Teen Age, Society of Midland Authors Award*, and *Golden Spur Award*.

496.   Conrad, Pam. **Prairie Visions: The Life and Times of Solomon Butcher**. Solomon Butcher, photographer. New York: HarperCollins, 1991. 85p. $17; $9.95pa. ISBN 0-06-021373-6; 0-06-446135-1pa. 4-8

Solomon Butcher (1856-1927) wanted to capture the lives of the pioneers in Custer County, Nebraska, by recording their tales in writing and by capturing their images in photographs. He shows winds, locusts, outlaws, children, grand pianos in sod houses, Black homesteaders, and the vast sky. Photographs and text reveal his life and the scenes around him. Bibliography. *Notable Children's Trade Books in the Field of Social Studies, Orbis Pictus Award Honor Book*, and *New York Public Library's Books for the Teen Age*.

497.   Conway, Celeste, author/illustrator. **Where Is Papa Now?** Honesdale, PA: Boyds Mills Press, 1994. Unpaged. $14.95. ISBN 1-56397-130-5. 1-3

When the narrator is five in the mid-nineteenth century, her father sails away in the spring on a trading journey. Each season she asks her mother where he is until he returns six seasons later. Her mother responds that he is in Java, China, and Bombay as she names exotic purchases that he makes and his activities in each place before he spends many months sailing home. Illustrations reveal the time frame.

498.   Cooney, Barbara, author/illustrator. **Eleanor**. New York: Viking, 1996. Unpaged. $15.99. ISBN 0-670-86159-6. 1-3

Cooney begins the story of Eleanor Roosevelt's life (1884-1962) by noting her mother's disapppointment with her. She gives an overview of her life in boarding school and her achievements. The emphasis concerns Roosevelt's ability to overcome the difficulties and problems of her childhood. *School Library Journal Best Book*.

499.   Cooney, Barbara, author/illustrator. **Hattie and the Wild Waves**. New York: Viking, 1990. 40p. $14.95. ISBN 0-670-83056-9. K-3

In the nineteenth century, Hattie walks on the beach at Far Rockaway near Brooklyn and wonders what the waves say to each other. She likes to paint them in the winter and in the summer as the years pass. Her sister marries, her brother becomes a businessman, and her mother wonders what will become of Hattie. Hattie expects the waves to tell her, and they tell her to draw. *Lupine Award.*

500.   Cooney, Barbara. **Island Boy**. New York: Viking, 1988. 32p. $15. ISBN 0-670-81749-X. K-3

As a small boy in the nineteenth century, Matthais goes with his family to live on Tibbetts Island, off the coast of New England. He becomes a ship's captain and travels all over the world, but he always returns to the island. He raises his family, and his own grandson Matthais lives with him when he is old. *School Library Journal Best Book.*

501.   Cooper, Floyd, author/illustrator. **Coming Home: From the Life of Langston Hughes**. New York: Philomel, 1994. Unpaged. $15.95. ISBN 0-399-22682-6. K-4

Cooper takes information about the childhood of Langston Hughes (1902-1967) and tells it as if it were fiction. He notes that Hughes lived with his grandparents and aunt and uncle rather than his parents because his father left for Mexico. Cooper also discusses Hughes's early interest in writing and some of the poems he wrote while in school. The last page is a short summary of Hughes's lifetime achievements to show that Hughes finally discovered that "home" was within himself. Bibliography.

502.   Cooper, Michael L. **Bound for the Promised Land: The Great Black Migration**. New York: Lodestar, 1995. 86p. $15.99. ISBN 0-525-674476-4. 5-9

In the early twentieth century, the lure of industrial jobs and the distaste for Jim Crow laws in the South led many Blacks to migrate to the North. The text looks at the discrimination they faced, the new politics and social class, the building of Black communities in Harlem, Black-owned businesses, and cultural achievements. Not all Blacks approved migration; Booker T. Washington discouraged it. W. E. B. Du Bois openly opposed Marcus Garvey. This movement in the United States occurred against a backdrop of World War I and the Depression as well as immigration from Haiti. Photographs, Bibliography, Reading List, and Index. *Notable Children's Trade Books in the Field of Social Studies.*

503.   Cooper, Michael L. **From Slave to Civil War Hero: The Life and Times of Robert Smalls**. New York: Lodestar, 1994. 73p. $13.99. ISBN 0-525-67489-6. 5-8

Robert Smalls (1839-1915) became the first slave to be a widely known hero during and after the Civil War. Smalls piloted the cotton steamer Planter past Confederate forts in Charleston harbor and joined the Union forces. After fighting for the Union, he became a spokesperson for the rights of the newly freed slaves. He served in the South Carolina legislature, and then he was elected to the U.S. Congress. His service was cut short when, after Reconstruction ended, others accused him of taking a bribe, and he was convicted. But no one is certain if he did or not. He still fought for the rights of those who had gained them with the Union victory. Glossary, Chronology, and Index.

504.   Cooper, Michael L. **Playing America's Game: The Story of Negro League Baseball**. New York: Lodestar, 1993. 96p. $15.99. ISBN 0-525-674071-1. 5 up

By World War II, Negro League baseball rivaled major league baseball in popularity and ability to attract fans. The East-West All-Star Classic game that began in 1933 in Chicago was always a sellout, with such stars as Andrew "Rube" Foster, John Henry Lloyd, and James "Cool Papa" Bell playing in it. The main teams of the Kansas City Monarchs and the American Giants thrived until the major leagues started hiring minority baseball players. Photographs complement the text. Further Reading, Glossary, and Index.

505.   Coote, Roger. **The Sailor Through History**. Tony Smith, illustrator. New York: Thomson Learning, 1993. 48 p. $16.95. ISBN 1-56847-012-6. (Journey Through History). 3-5

Four-page chapters present details about a Polynesian mariner, a Roman oarsman, a Viking raider, a sixteenth-century Portuguese explorer, the crew on the Armada, and the Mayflower voyage. Types of ships that the sailors worked on include sails, steamers, liners, U-boats, and supertankers. Drawings, photographs, and information boxes enliven the text. Bibliography and Index.

506.   Corbin, William. **Me and the End of the World**. New York: Simon & Schuster, 1991. 222p. $15. ISBN 0-671-74223-X. 5-9

When Tim, 13, hears that the end of the world will arrive on May 1, 1928, he wants to complete four things just in case the news is true. He wants to fight a bully, to kiss a girl, to make amends to a neighbor for not defending him against a racial slur, and to hitch sled rides on a dangerous new route. As he sets out to accomplish his goals, he realizes at the end of the year that he no longer needs to risk danger in childish ways.

507. Corbishley, Mike. **Secret Cities**. Roger Walker, illustrator. New York: Lodestar, 1989. 47p. $14.95. ISBN 0-525-67275-3. (Time Detectives). 4-7

Covering a span of 8,000 years, the text speculates about the lives in cities that have been excavated or restored. The cities covered (with approximate dates) are Skara Brae in Scotland (3000 BC), Biskupin in Poland (750 BC), Jorvik in England (AD 800), Çatal Hüyük in Turkey (6500 BC), the Pyramid of Khufu in Egypt (2700 BC), Knossos in Greece (1500 BC), Pompeii and Herculaneum in Italy (AD 100), Mohenjo-Daro in China (AD 1400), Great Zimbabwe in Zimbabwe (AD 1400), Ch'in Shi-huang-ti in China (200 BC), Mesa Verde in the United States (AD 1200), Machu Picchu in Peru (AD 1400), and Williamsburg in the United States (AD 1800). Glossary and Index.

508. Corcoran, Barbara. **The Private War of Lillian Adams**. New York: Atheneum, 1989. 166p. $13.95. ISBN 0-689-31443-4. 4-6

When Lil and her parents move to a small town during World War I, she has to adjust to her new classmates in the fifth grade. But she also has to adjust to the town, and she suspects several people of being spies, including the cobbler, a Jewish refugee from Russia who speaks another language. She plays a Halloween prank on him that leads a crowd of adults to threaten him. She and her new friends then pretend that peace has come as a way to atone for her behavior.

509. Corcoran, Barbara. **The Sky Is Falling**. New York: Atheneum, 1988. 185p. $13.95. ISBN 0-689-31388-8. 7-9

The family must go their separate ways in 1931 to cope with the effects of the Depression. Annah's father goes to Chicago to search for work after losing his job; her mother goes to Florida to live with her parents; and her brother has to drop out of college. Staying with her Aunt Edna in rural New Hampshire, Annah is an outsider who makes friends with another newcomer, Dodie. Annah discovers that Dodie's stepfather abuses her and that Dodie protects her blind brother from him and her alcoholic mother. Concerned for Dodie, Annah wants her to live with a former servant in Annah's house while Annah stays with her aunt, whom she has begun to understand much better.

510. Cordoba, Maria. **Pre-Columbian Peoples of North America**. Chicago: Childrens Press, 1994. 34p. $20. ISBN 0-516-08393-7. (The World Heritage). 4-7

Photographs clearly augment the text in this discussion of the people who lived in North America before Columbus arrived. The main sites presented in Canada are Bison Cliff, where bison jumped; Anthony Island, where the Haida Indians built totem poles; and L'Anse aux Meadows National Historic Park, which holds definitive proof that the Vikings settled in America before Columbus. Two sites in the United States are Mesa Verde National Park, home to the Anasazi nearly 700 years ago, and Cahokia Mounds Historic Site, where remains of mounds that denoted the Mississippian culture are found. Glossary and Index.

511. Cormier, Robert. **Other Bells for Us to Ring**. New York: Delacorte, 1990. 137p. $15. ISBN 0-385-30245-2. New York: Yearling, 1992. 137p. $3.99pa. ISBN 0-440-40717-6pa. 4-7

When Darcy is 11, she and her parents move to the Frenchtown section of Monument, Massachusetts. Her father enlists to fight in World War II, and he is reported missing. The Irish Catholic girl with whom Darcy has become friends introduces Darcy to a nun who helps Darcy understand her own fears and find her religious identity.

512. Cormier, Robert. **Tunes for Bears to Dance To**. New York: Delacorte, 1992. 101p. $15. ISBN 0-385-30818-3. New York: Laurel, 1994. 101p. $3.99pa. ISBN 0-440-21903-5pa. 5 up

Henry, 11, works for a grocer in the new place that he and his mother and father move to after World War II. His parents wanted to leave their old home so that they could forget the pain of his brother's accidental death the previous year. The grocer wants to damage a wood carving created by a Holocaust survivor, and Henry almost becomes an unwitting accomplice before he understands the grocer's motive for offering him a large reward if he will perform the deed.

513. Corrick, James A. **The Battle of Gettysburg**. San Diego, CA: Lucent, 1996. 111p. $26.59. ISBN 1-56006-451-X. (Battles of the Civil War). 6 up

The text looks at what both Confederates and the Union soldiers experienced in the summer of 1863 before the Battle of Gettysburg took place in July. It also explains why a battle in a small Pennsylvania town had such an influence on the war. A chronological day-by-day re-creation of the battle appears as well as sidebars with biographical profiles and practical information, such as a soldier's daily rations. Bibliography, Chronology, Further Reading, and Index.

514. Cory, Steven. **Pueblo Indian**. Richard Erickson, illustrator. Minneapolis, MN: Lerner, 1996. 48p. $14.96. ISBN 0-8225-2976-9. (American Pastfinder). 4-7

Not until 1888 did two cowboys rounding up cattle discover the stone houses and towers built along the side of a massive cliff in southwestern Colorado. They found skeletons, pots, an ax, and other things that people who were leaving in a hurry might have forgotten. They had discovered the cliff dwellings of the Anasazi in Mesa Verde that had not been inhabited for nearly 600 years. The text looks at the history of this culture, their world, how a pueblo would have been built, clothes, lifestyle, food, medicine, and other pieces of information that archaeologists have been able to fit together about the Anasazi. Index.

515. Cosner, Shaaron. **The Underground Railroad**. New York: Franklin Watts, 1991. 128p. $19.70. ISBN 0-531-12505-X. (Venture). 6 up

The text gives a thorough background on the workings of the Underground Railroad since its beginning, when Quakers in 1794 encouraged one of George Washington's slaves to escape. A discussion of the economic and social reasons for slavery's long history accompanies capsule biographies of various agents of the railroad, including John Fairfield, John Brown, Laura Haviland, William McKeever, Frederick Douglass, and Harriet Tubman. Reproductions highlight the text. Glossary, Further Reading, and Index.

516. Cosner, Shaaron. **War Nurses**. New York: Walker, 1988. 106p. $16.95. ISBN 0-8027-6826-1. 5-9

The text includes chapters on war nurses and their activities in the Civil War, the Crimean War, the Spanish-American War, World Wars I and II, the Korean War, and the Vietnam War. Letters and stories about the various personalities, among them Clara Barton and Florence Nightingale, show what the nurses had to face in their quest to help the wounded. Among the other topics included are a brief history of war weapons, the wounds from each, and the medical developments that evolved from these types of wounds. These nurses were clearly war veterans, a status for which nurses have had to petition. Index.

517. Cox, Clinton. **Mark Twain: America's Humorist, Dreamer, Prophet: A Biography**. New York: Scholastic, 1995. 236p. $14.95. ISBN 0-590-45642-3. 5-9

Mark Twain (1835-1910), son of a slave owner, wrote some of the most powerful antislavery literature of his day. He said he hated capitalism, but he married an heiress and longed to be rich. He believed that laughter was the only way to cope, but near the end of his life, after his family had died, he was extremely lonely. He died, as he had foretold, when Halley's comet came around as it did during the year of his birth. Bibliography and Index.

518. Crew, Linda. **Fire on the Wind**. New York: Delacorte, 1995. 198p. $14.95. ISBN 0-385-32185-6. 6-9

In August 1933, Storie, 13, worries about the smoke that she smells; she is also concerned for her father and the young logger Flynn, who have left the Blue Star logging camp to fight fires in other areas of Oregon. Storie gives a sense of the everyday lives of those who lived in the camp, especially the women who wait endlessly.

519. Crews, Donald, author/illustrator. **Bigmama's**. New York: Greenwillow, 1991. 32p. $13.95. ISBN 0-688-09950-5. K-3

The narrator enjoyed spending summers with his grandmother Bigmama. His family would take the train south and ride overnight to get there. He tells about the various facets of his summer vacation, including the stars at night, the outhouse, the kerosene lamps, and the well, which he contrasts to the city skyline of his adult life. *American Library Association Notable Books for Children.*

520. Crofford, Emily. **Frontier Surgeons: A Story About the Mayo Brothers**. Karen Ritz, illustrator. Minneapolis, MN: Carolrhoda, 1989. 64p. $17.50; $5.95pa. ISBN 0-87614-381-8; 0-87614-553-5pa. (Creative Minds). 3-5

Will and Charlie Mayo were children in 1872 when their physician father ordered a microscope from Germany, paying for it by mortgaging the house. His experiences and his sons' aid helped to create the largest private medical group practice in the world. Their goals always included learning how other physicians had solved problems, going to see those people, and returning to their own patients better informed. Their selflessness and tirelessness saved many before both died in 1939, but their legacy remains as recounted in this fictional biography. Sources.

521. Crofford, Emily. **A Place to Belong**. Minneapolis, MN: Carolrhoda, 1994. 152p. $14.95. ISBN 0-87614-808-9. 5-7

Talmadge, a seventh grader, has to move with his family from Tennessee to Mississippi and then to Arkansas in 1935, where his father hopes to find work during the Depression. With a club foot, Talmadge has always been an outsider, but he has reached a higher level of education than either of his parents. He plans to continue, but both his mother and brother think that he leaves the work to them, while his sisters and father support him. When the youngest child contracts polio, they are quarantined and later leave for Memphis and the hope of a better economic situation.

522. Cross, Gillian. **The Great American Elephant Chase**. New York: Holiday House, 1993. 193p. $14.95. ISBN 0-8234-1016-1. 5-8

Tad, an orphan of 15 in the nineteenth century, has his life change when he hides in a rail car cage, and the train leaves the station before he emerges. His companion in the car is an elephant. He travels with Khush and his mistress Cissie after the death of her father up the Mississippi, on the Ohio, and across the prairie. They are trying to escape people who claim to be Khush's new owners. When someone tries to steal the elephant, it will not leave Tad. They continue their travels west to Nebraska, where Cissie hopes to find sanctuary.

523. Cross, Robin. **Aftermath of War**. New York: Thomson Learning, 1994. 48p. $14.95. ISBN 1-56847-178-5. (World War II). 5-7

Many books cover World War II, but this book looks at what happened after the war's end. It reports on the Nuremberg trials held to convict Nazi war criminals, the division of Germany and the Berlin airlift, the contrast in power between the United States and Great Britain, the beginning of the Cold War, and the shift of Japanese factories from producing war goods to peacetime items. An interesting aspect of the year immediately after the war is that in 1946-1947, Great Britain had the coldest winter in 53 years, with snows melting to flood the island in the spring, and the following summer conversely producing a drought. Such foibles of nature following those of humans must have been especially frustrating. Glossary, Books to Read, Chronology, and Index.

524. Cross, Robin. **Children and War**. New York: Thomson Learning, 1994. 48p. $14.95. ISBN 1-56847-180-7. (World War II). 5-7

By using the experiences of young people during the war, Cross presents a view of World War II. His subjects include a Polish boy imprisoned by Soviet police, a French girl who fought the Resistance, a messenger boy in Britain during bombing attacks, a child from Hiroshima, and an American who had no direct contact except through newsreels. Further Reading, Glossary, and Index.

525. Cross, Robin. **Roosevelt and the Americans at War**. New York: Gloucester, Franklin Watts, 1990. 62p. $11.90. ISBN 0-531-17254-6. (World War II Biographies). 4-8

This text presents an overview of the life of Franklin Delano Roosevelt (1882-1945) and a closer look at his military leadership during World War II before his death. Colored maps of the campaigns and historical photographs complement the text. Bibliography, Chronology, Glossary, and Index.

526. Cross, Robin. **Technology of War**. New York: Thomson Learning, 1994. 48p. $14.95. ISBN 1-56847-177-7. (World War II). 5-7

Many weapons used in World War II had been introduced in World War I, with the submarine almost winning both wars for Germany. Between 1918 and 1939, radio communications improved, and the civil aviation industry expanded. Cathode ray tubes appeared, vital for radar screens, and research into the nature of the atom progressed. In 1936-1939, the Soviet Union, Germany, and Japan tested their new weapons, fighter planes, dive bombers, and tanks. The ultimate weapon became the atom bomb that the Americans developed. Glossary, Books to Read, Chronology, and Index.

527. Cross, Verda. **Great-Grandma Tells of Threshing Day**. Gail Owens, illustrator. Morton Grove, IL: Albert Whitman, 1992. 40p. $16.95. ISBN 0-8075-3042-5. 1-6

For a long time, Laura and her brother have been looking forward to the late June day in the early 1900s when the neighbors will come to help with threshing the winter wheat on their Missouri farm. The steam-driven thresher fascinates everyone, but all of the food and fun that everyone has together makes it one of the best days of the year. And afterwards, Laura has a newly filled tick mattress.

528. Cullen-DuPont, Kathryn. **Elizabeth Cady Stanton and Women's Liberty**. New York: Facts on File, 1992. 133p. $16.95. ISBN 0-8160-2413-8. (Makers of America). 6-12

The text uses excerpts from Elizabeth Cady Stanton's (1815-1902) writings and letters that reveal a woman who wanted equality for all. Further Reading and Index.

529. Cuneo, Mary Louise. **Anne Is Elegant**. New York: HarperCollins, 1993. 167p. $14.89. ISBN 0-06-022993-4. 5-8

Anna, 12, suffers during 1935 in Chicago over the death of her infant brother. Her father buries his grief in work, and her mother keeps reminding her of painful memories. Her Aunt Maria and her budding love for a boy at school help her to heal, but not until the death of a relative at Christmas does everyone understand what the others have been thinking.

530. Currie, Stephen. **Music in the Civil War**. Cincinnati, OH: Betterway, 1992. 111p. $8.95. ISBN 1-55870-263-6. 5 up

Music reflected the responses of all people to their political passions, whether from the North or South. This history presents the music used to rally the troops during the Civil War and to keep them fighting, and that sung at home. In addition to actual scores are biographies of some of the better-known composers of the time, such as Julia Ward Howe, who wrote "The Battle Hymn of the Republic," and Patrick Gilmore, composer of "When Johnny Comes Marching Home." Bibliography and Index.

531. Curry, Jane Louise. **Moon Window**. New York: Margaret K. McElderry, 1996. 192p. $16. ISBN 0-689-80945-X. 5-9

JoEllen Briggs goes to stay with an elderly cousin living in a small New Hampshire castle called Winterbloom while her mother enjoys her honeymoon with her new husband. JoEllen climbs through a round window in a turret on the top floor of the castle and finds herself in a different time. When she sees 1809, she forgets her irritation at her mother and begins to solve the mystery of Winterbloom.

532. Curry, Jane Louise. **What the Dickens!** New York: Margaret K. McElderry, 1991. 153p. $13.95. ISBN 0-689-50524-8. 4-6

In 1842, three of the Dobbs children, including Cherry, 11, sometimes work on their father's freight boat floating the central Pennsylvania Juniata Canal. Charles Dickens is on the canal, and Cherry hears a plan to steal his manuscript of American Notes. She and her siblings diligently pursue the two thieves and the nasty bookseller so that Dickens does not lose his work.

533. Curson, Marjorie N. **Jonas Salk**. Englewood Cliffs, NJ: Silver Burdett, 1990. 137p. $13.95. ISBN 0-382-09966-4. (Pioneers in Change). 5-9

In 1914, under Franklin D. Roosevelt, the March of Dimes drives began and netted money for medical research on polio and other viral diseases. For Jonas Salk, who once thought of becoming a lawyer, such money eventually came to his laboratories and supported his new research. Much of the book presents the process of vaccine development, from the discoveries of Semmelweis in Austria and Louis Pasteur in France during the mid-eighteenth century, through the testing and approval of the Salk vaccine, and then the Sabin vaccine, for polio. The balanced account enumerates the successes and failures in this long procedure. Important Dates, Bibliography, and Index.

534. Curtis, Christopher Paul. **The Watsons Go to Birmingham—1963**. New York: Delacorte, 1995. 210p. $14.95. ISBN 0-385-32175-9. 5-8

Kenny, 10, narrates the story of his family living in Flint, Michigan. When his older brother Byron needs more discipline, his parents take him to his grandmother's in Birmingham, Alabama. Their trip south gets them to Birmingham before a bomb explodes in the church. Kenny thinks his sister may be one of the four children killed. Although she is not, he experiences the fear that she might be a victim, so the Civil Rights movement affects him personally. *Bulletin Blue Ribbon Book, Bank Street College's Children's Book Award, Newbery Honor, Coretta Scott King Honor Book, American Library Association Notable Books for Children, American Library Association Best Book for Young Adults,* and *Horn Book Fanfare.*

535. Cush, Cathie. **Artists Who Created Great Works**. Austin, TX: Raintree/Steck-Vaughn, 1995. 48p. $15.96. ISBN 0-8114-4993-5. (20 Events Series). 6 up

In two-page spreads, Cush creates a minihistory of art by presenting profiles on 20 artists spanning from Leonardo Da Vinci (Italy, 1452-1519) to Salvadore Dali (Spain, 1904-1989). Photographs of famous paintings accompany the text. Other artists included are Albrecht Dürer (Germany, 1471-1528), Michelangelo Buonarroti (Italy, 1475-1564), Gian Lorenzo Bernini (Italy, 1598-1680), Rembrandt van Rijn (Netherlands, 1606-1669), Christopher Wren (England, 1632-1723), Francisco Goya (Spain, 1746-1828), Joseph M. W. Turner (England, 1775-1851), Eugène Delacroix (France, 1798-1863), Auguste Rodin (France, 1840-1917), Claude Monet (France, 1840-1926), Henri Matisse (France, 1869-1954), Pablo Picasso (Spain, 1881-1973), Diego Rivera (Mexico, 1886-1957), Ludwig Mies van der Rohe (Germany, 1886-1969), Georgia O'Keeffe (United States, 1887-1986), Alexander Calder (United States, 1898-1976), Henry Moore (England, 1898-1986), and Ansel Adams (United States, 1902-1984). Glossary, Suggested Readings, and Index.

536. Cush, Cathie. **Disasters That Shook the World**. Austin, TX: Raintree/Steck-Vaughn, 1994. 48p. $15.96. ISBN 0-8114-4929-7. (20 Events Series). 6 up

Some of the major changes in perception that have occurred in the world have come as a result of a disaster. In two-page spreads, Cush discusses 20 situations that were never expected to happen. They are the explosion of Vesuvius (AD 79 in Pompeii, Italy), the Black Death (fourteenth-century Europe), the destruction of the Native Americans (fifteenth through nineteenth centuries), the Great London Fire (1666), the Irish Potato Famine (1845-1849), the Great Chicago Fire (1871), Krakatoa's eruption (Indonesia, 1883), the San Francisco earthquake (1906), the Titanic sinking (1912), the world flu epidemic (1917-1919), the Bangladesh cyclone (1970), famine in Ethiopia and Somalia (1984-1985; 1992), the AIDS epidemic (1980s), the Bhopal chemical disaster (India, 1984), the Challenger explosion (United States, 1986), the Chernobyl nuclear meltdown (Russia, 1986), the Exxon Valdez oil spill (1989), the death of the Aral Sea (between Kazakhstan and Uzbekistan, 1960-1990), the Gulf War oil disaster (Kuwait, 1991), and hurricanes Andrew (Atlantic, 1992) and Iniki (Hawaii, 1992). Glossary, Suggested Readings, and Index.

537. Cush, Cathie. **Women Who Achieved Greatness**. Austin, TX: Raintree/Steck-Vaughn, 1995. 48p. $15.96. ISBN 0-8114-4938-6. (20 Events Series). 6 up

Women have achieved greatness in a variety of ways, and some, though not all, have received recognition for it. In two-page spreads, Cush profiles some of these women. The women included are Maria Montessori (Italy, 1870-1952), Helen Keller (1880-1968) and Annie Sullivan (d. 1936), Eleanor Roosevelt (1884-1962), Amelia Earhart (1899-1937), Golda Meir (Israel, 1898-1978), Margaret Mead (1901-1978), Barbara McClintock (1902-1992), Marian Anderson (1900-1993), Margaret Bourke-White (1906-1971), Rachel Carson (1907-1964), Mother Teresa (Albania and India, b. 1910), Indira Gandhi (India, 1917-1984), Katharine Meyer Graham (b. 1917), Maya Angelou (b. 1928), Violeta Chamorro (Nicaragua, b. 1929), Jane Goodall (England, b. 1934), Barbara Jordan (1936-1996), Aung San Suu Kyi (Burma, b. 1944), Wilma Mankiller (b. 1945), and Oprah Winfrey (b. 1954). Glossary, Suggested Readings, and Index.

538. Cushman, Karen. **The Ballad of Lucy Whipple**. New York: Clarion, 1996. 210p. $14.95. ISBN 0-395-72806-1. 5-7

In Lucky Diggins, California, Lucy (California Morning Whipple) and her mother run a boardinghouse in a huge tent. She wants to return home to New England where people are civilized, but she has to earn the money for the journey. She writes letters to her relatives describing the horrors of the place, but after three years, during which her brother dies and her mother remarries, she grows used to the people and decides that California is her real home. *School Library Journal Best Book*.

539. Cutler, Jane. **My Wartime Summers**. New York: Farrar, Straus & Giroux, 1994. 153p. $15. ISBN 0-374-35111-2. 5-8

While her Uncle Bob is away fighting in Europe during World War II, Ellen finishes the sixth, seventh, and eighth grades from 1942 to 1945. She thinks that she changes a lot, but she does not change as much as Uncle Bob. When he returns, her best friends' parents, who are Jewish, want to know if he saw anyone from the concentration camps. Someone else asks how he survived when so many did not. He seems to wonder the same thing and leaves with an army friend to tell another buddy's wife about his death. Ellen understands that all changes are not visible.

540. Cwiklik, Robert. A. **Philip Randolph and the Labor Movement**. Brookfield, CT: Millbrook Press, 1993. 32p. $13.90. ISBN 0-395-683696. (Gateway Civil Rights). 2-4

A. Philip Randolph (1889-1979) went to New York and began to publish a magazine called The Messenger, which exposed wrongs suffered by the poor and African Americans. He was arrested for telling people not to join the army in the magazine. The judge did not believe that he and his partner had written the intelligent articles; so the judge would not condemn them for something he did not believe they could do. Randolph threatened to organize various marches in Washington, and he did organize the march on Washington in 1963. In 1964, President Johnson gave him the Medal of Freedom. Important Events, Find Out More, and Index.

541. Cwiklik, Robert. **King Philip and the War with the Colonists**. Robert L. Smith, illustrator. Englewood Cliffs, NJ: Silver Burdett, 1989. 144p. $12.98. ISBN 0-382-09573-1. (Biography of the American Indians). 5-8

King Philip (Metacum) took the leadership of his tribe of Wampanoag Indians when his father Massasoit died. He tried to keep the treaties that his father had made with the English, but they continued to encroach on tribal lands. Finally, his people would not tolerate the situation, and King Philip had to fight. King Philip's war started in 1675, but he and many in his tribe lost their lives, and the colonists drove the remainder into northern New England. Suggested Reading.

542. Cwiklik, Robert. **Malcolm X and Black Pride**. Brookfield, CT: Millbrook Press, 1991. 28p. $13.90; $4.95pa. ISBN 1-56294-042-2; 1-87884-173-4pa. (Gateway Civil Rights). 2-5

Malcolm X (1925-1965) and his difficult childhood, stint in prison, and conversion to Islam appear in this biography. He was intelligent and articulate, and in his role as leader of the Nation of Islam had ideas opposed to those in the mainstream. He taught that Blacks should take pride in and respect themselves. *Child Study Association Children's Books of the Year*.

543.   Cwiklik, Robert. **Sequoyah and the Cherokee Alphabet**. T. Lewis, illustrator. Englewood Cliffs, NJ: Silver Burdett, 1989. 123p. $12.95; $7.95pa. ISBN 0-382-09570-7; 0-382-09759-9pa. (Biography of American Indians). 5-8

Sequoyah (1773?-1843) lived as a Cherokee concerned that his people would lose their culture and adapt all the ways of the white settlers. His father was white, possibly a wealthy man named Nathanial Gist who was George Washington's friend, or possibly a drunkard known as George Gist. Gist left Sequoyah's mother before Sequoyah was born. Sequoyah overcame a disability by developing his artistic talents and by creating a written language for the Cherokees based on syllables. The text looks at his life and his development of the language. Suggested Reading.

544.   Cwiklik, Robert. **Tecumseh: Shawnee Rebel**. New York: Chelsea House, 1993. 110p. $18.95. ISBN 0-7910-1721-4. (North American Indians of Achievement). 5 up

Tecumseh (1768-1813) declared that Indians owned their land and that no individual could legally sell or buy any of it. He campaigned for a national confederation, and his movement was beginning to work when the British declared war on the United States in 1812. He sided with the British, recruiting warriors from Old Northwest tribes, and won battles. But the British betrayed him, as the American whites had. He was a diplomat, fighter, revolutionary, military genius, and idealist. Engravings enhance the text. Chronology, Further Reading, and Index.

545.   Czech, Ken. **Snapshot: America Discovers the Camera**. Minneapolis, MN: Lerner, 1996. 88p. $18.95. ISBN 0-8225-1736-1. (People's History). 5 up

Photography, invented in France in 1839, has been a force in American society since its arrival in the country. Matthew Brady realized that pictures of the Civil War would make him money, and George Eastman began selling lightweight cameras in 1888 for amateurs. Other developments in photography have led to television, movies, and unusual art styles. Photographs complement the text. Bibliography and Index.

D

546. Daffron, Carolyn. **Margaret Bourke-White: Photographer**. New York: Chelsea House, 1988. 110p. $18.95; $7.95pa. ISBN 1-55546-644-3; 0-7910-0411-2pa. (American Women of Achievement). 5 up

Margaret Bourke-White (1904-1971) photographed architecture and showed the beauty in industry. Her later photojournalistic work showed the horrors of the Deep South, Nazi concentration camps, and South African apartheid. As she grew up, she saw her amateur photographer father take, develop, and enlarge prints, and she decided to become a professional photographer. After college, she joined *Fortune* magazine and went to the Soviet Union, where she became the first Westerner to photograph Soviet industry. In World War II, she joined *Life* magazine and became the first female war correspondent. She covered the arrival of American bombers in England, went on a mission, and photographed General Patton and his troops as they marched through Germany. Her independent lifestyle set her apart as well. Her photographs augment the text. Chronology, Further Reading, and Index.

547. Daley, William. **The Chinese Americans**. New York: Chelsea House, 1995. 93p. $19.95; $8.95pa. ISBN 0-710-3357-0; 0-7910-3379-1pa. (The Peoples of North America). 4-7

The immigration of Chinese into the United States began to rise when the first Opium War between China and England (1839-1842) gave Hong Kong to England in the Treaty of Nanking and opened four other Chinese ports. The corrupt Manchu (Ch'ing Dynasty) rulers imposed higher taxes, causing the people to revolt in 1850 under the leadership of Hung Hsiu-ch'uan, a convert to Christianity, in the Taiping "Great Peace" Rebellion. But the Taipings were defeated in 1864. A second Opium War fought at the same time, from 1856 to 1860, caused even more turmoil. By 1848, only seven Chinese were recorded as living in San Francisco, but by 1851 the gold rush had attracted 25,000. The Chinese immigrants were prevented from voting, holding public office, and practicing certain trades. For these reasons, they started laundries and worked to build the railroads across the United States. Immigration laws tightened in 1882, keeping out many women who had stayed behind to look after their husbands' parents. In the twentieth century, other problems in China caused emigration. Sun Yat-Sen ruled from 1866 to 1925, when the Japanese began to trouble the Chinese. In 1949, Mao Zedong declared victory over Chiang and established his brand of Communism. Chinese Americans developed the Bing cherry and were the first to hatch eggs with artificial heat. They have cultural depth through their religions—Confucianism, Taoism, and Buddhism—and their artists and inventors, such as Wang, Yo-Yo Ma, Maya Lin, Maxine Hong Kingston, Lawrence Yep, and David Hwang. Selected References and Index.

548. Dalgliesh, Alice. **Adam and the Golden Cock**. New York: Scribner's, 1959. 64p. $5.95. ISBN 0-684-12438-6. 3-5

In 1781, Adam's father tells him that he cannot talk to his friend Paul because Paul's father is a Tory. Adam disobeys when he asks Paul to look after the sheep Adam is watching so that he may get a closer look at the soldiers coming into Newtown, Connecticut. After Adam leaves, he realizes that he has disobeyed both his father and the sheepherder who has asked him not to leave the sheep until he returns. Adam runs back and sees that French soldiers serving under Rochambeau have camped near the sheep. He talks to Pierre, the only soldier who can speak English, and learns about some of a soldier's problems. The next year, Paul and Adam visit Pierre when he returns and try to continue their friendship.

549. Dalgliesh, Alice. **The Thanksgiving Story**. Helen Sewell, illustrator. 1954. New York: Atheneum, 1988. 32p. $15. ISBN 0-684-18999-2. New York: Aladdin, 1978. 32p. $4.95pa. ISBN 0-689-71053-4pa. K-3

The Hopkins children sail from Holland to England on the *Speedwell* and then from England to America on the *Mayflower*. During their first year in Massachusetts, they and the other Plymouth settlers meet Samoset and Squanto, English-speaking Native Americans who advise them about planting. They and Massasoit join the settlers to celebrate their first Thanksgiving feast.

550. Dallard, Shyrlee. **Ella Baker: A Leader Behind the Scenes**. Englewood Cliffs, NJ: Silver Burdett, 1990. 130p. $12.95; $7.95pa. ISBN 0-382-09931-1; 0-382-24066-9pa. (History of the Civil Rights Movement). 6-9

As a key person who helped to form the SNCC (Student Nonviolent Coordinating Committee), Ella Baker (1903-1986) always stayed out of the limelight. A film about her was titled *Fundi*, which is Swahili for someone who gives unselfishly to others; Baker did spend her life trying to help others. Dallard recounts the life of a sharecropper who graduated first in her class. She went to New York during the Harlem Renaissance and lived through the Depression, the WPA, and lynching. In New York, Baker began working for the NAACP (National Association for the Advancement of Colored People), and continued to do so after the Civil Rights Act passed in 1964 by supporting Nelson Mandela and his bid to stop apartheid in South Africa. Civil Rights Timeline, Suggested Reading, Sources, and Index.

551.   Damon, Duane. **When the Cruel War Is Over: The Civil War Home Front**. Minneapolis, MN: Lerner, 1996. 88p. $14.21. ISBN 0-8225-1731-0. (People's History). 5 up

A group of people who suffered as much in the Civil War as the soldiers were the civilians who waited at home, lonely and often overworked. The text looks at backyards as battlefields; factory workers; nurses; the professions of writer, photographer, sketch artist, and musician; women and children who managed farms; and the African Americans who waited to be free. Bibliography and Index.

552.   Darby, Jean. **Douglas MacArthur**. Minneapolis, MN: Lerner, 1989. 112p. $22.95. ISBN 0-8225-4901-8. 5 up

Douglas MacArthur (1880-1964) led a soldier's life, graduating from West Point and serving in major wars during the early twentieth century. When the Japanese defeated him in the Philippines in 1942, he said "I shall return." He did return in 1944 when he stopped their advances. He is best known for defeating the Japanese and then helping them establish a democracy. Appendix, Glossary, For Further Reading, and Index.

553.   Darby, Jean. **Dwight D. Eisenhower: A Man Called Ike**. Minneapolis, MN: Lerner, 1989. 112p. $21.50. ISBN 0-8225-4900-X. 5 up

Complemented with photographs, this text on the life of Dwight David Eisenhower (1890-1969) covers the main aspects of his youth in Abilene, Kansas, and his attendance at West Point. He excelled in his military career, rising to commander of the Allied forces in Europe. He came back to the United States after the war as a hero and was elected to the presidency. He endured heartaches but rose to his responsibilities. Appendix, Glossary, For Further Reading, and Index.

554.   Darby, Jean. **Martin Luther King, Jr.** Minneapolis, MN: Lerner, 1990. 144p. $14.95; $6.95pa. ISBN 0-382-09931-1; 0-382-24066-9pa. 5-9

This fictional biography is almost a history of the Civil Rights movement in its look at Martin Luther King, Jr.'s life, from his Atlanta birth in 1929 until his assassination in 1964. Using examples to emphasize the situation, Darby shows segregation in the South as opposed to the North, how Gandhi influenced King, Rosa Parks's confrontation in Montgomery, the bus boycott, Woolworth's lunch counter sit-in in 1960, James Meredith's enrollment in the University of Mississippi, and the "I Have a Dream" speech in the 1963 march on Washington. Darby also recounts the events in Memphis leading up to the moment when James Earl Ray allegedly shot King. Glossary, Further Reading, Index.

555.   Dash, Joan. **We Shall Not Be Moved: The Women's Factory Strike of 1909**. New York: Scholastic, 1996. 176p. $15.95. ISBN 0-590-48409-5. 5-9

In 1909, female teenager factory workers between the ages of 16 and 18, mostly unskilled, united with college girls and older women with extra money to strike against the bundle system manufacturing shirtwaists. The text posits that these alliances were what allowed even the limited success of this strike and looks at the process that led to 30,000 laborers jeopardizing their futures by refusing to accept the status quo. Photographs, Bibliography, and Index.

556.   D'Aulaire, Ingri, and Edgar Parin D'Aulaire, author/illustrators. **Abraham Lincoln**. 1939. New York: Yearling, 1993. 56p. $10.95pa. ISBN 0-440-40690-0pa. 3-6

This biographical fiction tells Lincoln's story from his birth in 1809 until his last days in the White House; it does not mention his death or the deaths of his children. It features his stepmother as a helper who allowed Lincoln to lie by the fire at night in order to have light and more time to read in Black Hawk, Illinois. Then the authors tell of Lincoln's business failures and his competition with Judge Douglass over Mary Todd (Lincoln won) and the Senate (Douglass won). *Caldecott Medal, 1939.*

557.   D'Aulaire, Ingri, and Edgar Parin D'Aulaire, author/illustrators. **Benjamin Franklin**. 1950. New York: Zephyr-BFYR, Doubleday, 1987. 48p. $12.95pa. ISBN 0-385-24103-8pa. 3-6

Illustrations and framed sayings from *Poor Richard's Almanack* decorate the somewhat slangy ("knee-high to a grasshopper") fictional biography discussing Franklin's life (1706-1790). The general facts include 17-year-old Franklin leaving his apprenticeship with brother James when no longer allowed to write as "Widow Dogood." He chose Philadelphia because, in 1723, it was larger than New York. Additionally, he began attending the University of Pennsylvania before he became the postmaster of Philadelphia. This text emphasizes Franklin's renown throughout the colonies and in France and England because of *Poor Richard* and his statesmanship.

558.   D'Aulaire, Ingri, and Edgar Parin D'Aulaire, author/illustrators. **George Washington**. 1936. New York: Doubleday, 1987. 64p. $11.95pa. ISBN 0-385-24107-0pa. 4-6

In this fictional biography, the reader finds that Washington (1732-1799) began to study surveying when he was 11, after his father's death. His interest in the frontier developed, and he was able to survive there. The governor of Virginia asked him to defend the frontier dwellers from Indian raids. He eventually married

Martha Custis, and they moved to Mount Vernon when Washington inherited it because of his beloved half-brother Lawrence's death. Washington received help from the French Lafayette and the German von Steuben as he fought to overcome Cornwallis. Trite and effusive language such as "gorgeous wedding" and "spick and span" date the text, but the facts chosen are interesting.

559. D'Aulaire, Ingri, and Edgar Parin D'Aulaire, author/illustrators. **Pocahontas**. 1946. New York: Doubleday, 1985. 45p. $13.95pa. ISBN 0-385-07454-9pa. 2-4

Because this version of Pocahontas's story is 50 years old, it may not be the best choice for young readers. In it, a stereotyped Powhatan contrasts with the sweetness of his daughter Pocahontas, and the authors do not give any sources to verify these personality traits. The book is more fiction than biography, although the few facts present seem to be accurate. Pocahontas has thoughts and feelings in this book that the authors could never document unless they had her diaries.

560. Davidson, Mary R. **Dolly Madison: Famous First Lady**. New York: Chelsea Juniors, 1992. 80p. $14.95. ISBN 0-7910-1446-0. (Discovery Biography). 3-7

Dolley Madison (1768-1849) and her family were Quakers, and her first marriage to John Todd in Philadelphia was a sedate Quaker wedding. After he died of yellow fever, James Madison began courting her, and she married him. When she became Mrs. James Madison, the wedding was a huge party instead of a quiet Quaker event. She became the nation's hostess for Thomas Jefferson and the First Lady who saved artifacts from the White House when the British burned Washington during the War of 1812. She and her husband spent their later years at Montpelier.

561. Davidson, Sue. **Getting the Real Story: Nellie Bly and Ida B. Wells**. Seattle, WA: Seal Press, 1992. 152p. $8.95pa. ISBN 1-878067-16-8pa. (Women Who Dared). 4-6

Nellie Bly (1867-1922) and Ida B. Wells (1862-1931) were women journalists in a time when women were not journalists. They both accomplished many things, with Wells having the additional stigma of being a Black woman. The fictional biography makes their stories more readable than authentic biography, but an Outline of Life Events for each subject aids in the interpretation.

562. Davies, Eryl. **Transport: On Land, Road and Rail**. New York: Franklin Watts, 1992. 47p. $7.95pa. ISBN 0-531-15741-5pa. (Timelines). 5-8

Illustrations interspersed with text show a history of transport. The text covers the first wheels, Roman roads, Ancient China, Vikings, Medieval Europe, animal power, coaches, steam pioneers, the railroad age, pedal power, the first motorcycles, automobiles, underground trains, streetcars, delivery modes, racing cars, and the future in transportation. Timeline, Glossary, and Index.

563. Davies, Kath. **Amelia Earhart Flies Around the World**. New York: Dillon Press, Silver Burdett, 1994. 32p. $14.95. ISBN 0-87518-531-2. (Great Twentieth Century Expeditions). 3-6

The text focuses on Amelia Earhart (1897-1937) and her achievements in aviation. Color photographs highlight the text and show her standing next to the various airplanes in which she flew. She became a heroine in America because she dared to fly when women were not supposed to do such things, but she showed that women could and should choose to become aviators. The mystery of Earhart's disappearance continues with several theories about her and navigator Fred Noonan's fate. Glossary, Further Reading, and Index.

564. Davies, Mark. **Malcolm X: Another Side of the Movement**. Glenn Wolff, illustrator. Englewood Cliffs, NJ: Silver Burdett, 1990. 130p. $12.95; $7.95pa. ISBN 0-382-09925-7; 0-382-09925-7pa. (History of the Civil Rights Movement). 5-12

Malcolm Little (1925-1965) took the name Malcolm X after he joined the Nation of Islam. It symbolized his real African name, which he would never know, rather than the white man's name of "Little." He went to prison for seven years after hustling and selling drugs in Boston and New York. In prison, he educated himself so that he was prepared to lead people in the fight against racial discrimination. He saw white people as the devil over which Black people had to gain power. Throughout his career, he spoke loudly about his beliefs. After he returned from a visit to Mecca, he was assassinated. Timetable, Suggested Reading, Sources, and Index.

565. Davis, Frances A. **Frank Lloyd Wright: Maverick Architect**. Minneapolis, MN: Lerner, 1996. 128p. $22.95. ISBN 0-8225-4953-0. 5 up

Frank Lloyd Wright (1867-1959) wanted to create a distinctly American architecture. He experimented with shapes and materials as he developed the Prairie style. Sometimes insufferable, but always dedicated, Wright's designs integrated all aspects of topography and structure. Because he was also interested in finding less-expensive ways to build innovative homes, he developed the "Usonian" partially prefabricated method. Photographs, Bibliography, and Index.

566.   De Angeli, Marguerite. **The Lion in the Box**. 1975. New York: Yearling, 1992. 80p. $3.50pa. ISBN 0-385-03317-6pa. 2-5

In 1901, seven-year-old Lili's mother cleans offices to support Lili and her three sisters and brother. Lili wants a doll for Christmas but knows that her mother cannot afford it. Instead, the family makes paper decorations for their tree. On Christmas Eve, a man delivers a mysterious box that he says has a lion inside. They open the box on Christmas Day and find gifts for everyone, sent by a woman their mother had met. Lili gets her doll.

567.   De Angeli, Marguerite. **Skippack School**. 1939. New York: Doubleday, 1961. 92p. $3.50. ISBN 0-385-07913-3. 4-6

In 1700, Eli comes to Pennsylvania with his parents from Germany where they have been persecuted for their Mennonite (Amish) religion. He is unwilling to study. The schoolmaster surprises him, however, by not caning him for mistakes and by showing interest in his ability to carve. After a trip with the schoolmaster, Eli shows his appreciation for the experience by carving and painting a book cover in which to place his written account of the trip. Eli's education is much broader than he could have imagined.

568.   De Angeli, Marguerite. **Thee, Hannah!** 1940. New York: Doubleday, 1989. 96p. $15.95. ISBN 0-385-07525-1. 2-5

Unhappy with the drab clothing she must wear as a Quaker in 1850 Philadelphia, Hannah secretly wears the brightly colored sash of her friend. When she dirties it, however, she has to buy her a new one with the few pennies of her allowance. A runaway slave tells Hannah that if Hannah had not been wearing her Quaker bonnet, the slave would not have known where to get help. Hannah realizes that her bonnet is a symbol for others and something that she should wear with pride.

569.   de Ruiz, Dana Catharine. **To Fly with the Swallows: A Story of Old California**. Debbe Heller, illustrator. Austin, TX: Raintree/Steck-Vaughn, 1993. 53p. $15.49; $5.95pa. ISBN 0-8114-7234-5; 0-8114-8074-7pa. (Stories of America—Personal Challenge). 5-9

In 1806, Concha, 15, lived with her family in San Francisco, where her father was commander of the presidio defending Spain's New World empire on the northern border of Alta California. Nikolai Petrovich Rezanov arrived from St. Petersburg requesting supplies for his ship. He stayed long enough for Concha and him to want to marry, but Rezanov was not Catholic. He left, as requested, to get the permission of the czar, the King of Spain, and the pope in Italy. Concha waited, but after five years she received word of his death. She never married but spent her life dedicated to Saint Francis and helping those who needed her in childbirth, sickness, and death. At 60, she became California's first nun in Santa Catalina. Epilogue, Afterword, and Notes.

570.   de Ruiz, Dana Catharine, and Richard Larios. **La Causa: The Migrant Farmworkers' Story**. Rudy Gutierrez, illustrator. Austin, TX: Raintree/Steck-Vaughn, 1993. 92p. $15.49; $5.95pa. ISBN 0-8114-7231-0; 0-8114-8071-2pa. (Stories of America—Stand Up and Be Counted). 4-7

When a young boy in 1940, Cesar Chavez watched his father, a worker who had left his home to find work, faithfully fulfill a contract as he had promised, but remain unpaid when the contractor disappeared. Dolores Huerta watched workers, desperate to help their families survive, try to pay their rent. The two met and began fighting the inequity between workers and owners in the fields of California. Their efforts, including a nonviolent strike, finally led to the formation of the United Farm Workers in 1966. However, that was only the beginning of their work to preserve dignity and hope in this quest. Epilogue, Afterword, and Notes.

571.   de Varona, Frank. **Bernardo de Gálvez**. Tom Redman, illustrator. Austin, TX: Raintree/Steck-Vaughn, 1993. 32p. $13.98; $5.95pa. ISBN 0-8172-3379-2; 0-8114-6756-2pa. (Hispanic Stories). 4-7

As a Spanish soldier, Bernardo de Gálvez (1746-1786) was assigned first to duty in Mexico, where he fought the Apaches, and then the Louisiana Territory, where he fought France. He ordered the British to leave the territory and gave Americans freedom to use it. His greatest victory was in Pensacola (now Florida) in 1781, when he defeated the British. Glossary. English and Spanish text.

572.   Deem, James M. **How to Make a Mummy Talk**. True Kelley, illustrator. Boston: Houghton Mifflin, 1995. 184p. $14.95. ISBN 0-395-62427-4. 4-8

Entertaining illustrations and boxed questions guide the reader through this text about mummies. With the premise that mummies "talk" through what archaeologists discover about them, Deem explores fact and myth about how mummies were and are made, what mummies "say," and where to find them. Some of the more famous mummies discussed are the 5,000-year-old Iceman of Europe; Elmer McCurdy, an Oklahoma outlaw; mummies from California; a Bigfoot mummy from Minnesota; and an Egyptian mummy. Bibliography and Index.

573. DeFelice, Cynthia. **The Apprenticeship of Lucas Whitaker**. New York: Farrar, Straus & Giroux, 1996. 160p. $15. ISBN 0-374-34669-0. 5 up

After Lucas Whitaker's mother dies in 1849, he hears that he could have saved her from her fatal tuberculosis by exhuming a deceased relative, removing the heart, and burning it so that his mother could have breathed the smoke. Distressed that he did not know in time, he goes to Southwick, Connecticut, and becomes an apprentice to the local physician who is also a dentist, apothecary, undertaker, and barber. When he looks through a microscope for the first time, he learns the difference between superstition and science, and that he cannot blame himself for his mother's death. *School Library Journal Best Book.*

574. DeFelice, Cynthia. **Lostman's River**. New York: Macmillan, 1994. 160p. $14.95. ISBN 0-02-726466-1. 5-8

In 1900, 13-year-old Tyler's father runs away from New York to the Florida Everglades when he thinks he will be charged with a murder he did not commit. In 1906, after "plumers" (men who illegally kill native birds for their feathers) kill a man who pretends that he collects for a museum, and Tyler is almost lost in the swamps, Tyler's father decides to stop fleeing from something that he did not do.

575. DeFelice, Cynthia. **Weasel**. New York: Macmillan, 1990. 119p. $15. ISBN 0-02-726457-2. New York: Camelot, 1991. 119p. $3.99pa. ISBN 0-380-71358-6pa. 5 up

When Ezra arrives at 11-year-old Nathan's cabin in 1839, he shows Nathan his dead mother's locket and then leads him to his father, almost dead from gangrene. Nathan and his sister hear their father's story about Weasel, the man who has wounded his father, killed his mother, and caused Ezra intense emotional pain. Nathan has to cope with his feelings of hatred after he has his own encounter with Weasel.

576. DeFord, Deborah H., and Harry S. Stout. **An Enemy Among Them**. Boston: Houghton Mifflin, 1987. 203p. $13.95. ISBN 0-395-44239-7. 6-9

Margaret's brother is wounded in 1776, and when she goes to the hospital to tend him, she also helps an enemy Hessian. Christian, the Hessian, begins working for Margaret's father on the family farm instead of going to prison, and as Margaret begins to fall in love with him, she finds out that he wounded her brother. Christian, however, becomes a believer in the Patriot cause, and Margaret's German-American family begins to accept him.

577. Deitch, Kenneth M., and JoAnne B. Weisman. **Dwight D. Eisenhower: Man of Many Hats**. Jay Connolly, illustrator. Lowell, MA: Discovery Enterprises, 1990. 48p. $17.95. ISBN 1-878668-02-1. (Picture-Book Biography). 5-12

Although the illustrations are interesting and representative of Dwight David Eisenhower's life (1890-1969), the text is more difficult than the pictures imply. Among the hats that Eisenhower wore throughout his life are high school sports enthusiast, West Point cadet, general in the army, recipient of honorary degrees, president, and golfer. No table of contents or index.

578. Demarest, Chris L., author/illustrator. **Lindbergh**. New York: Crown, 1993. Unpaged. $15. ISBN 0-517-58718-1. K-3

Charles Lindbergh (1902-1974) always loved speed. His father had a motorcar, and Lindbergh got a motorcycle before he began flying. Lindbergh first saw an airplane when he was eight, and when he saw one, he knew that he wanted to fly, and for the rest of his life, he did. He became the first person to fly over the Atlantic, landing in Paris on May 22, 1927, more than 33 hours after he had started in New York. Resource Guide.

579. Denenberg, Barry. **John Fitzgerald Kennedy: America's 35th President**. New York: Scholastic, 1988. 112p. $3.25pa. ISBN 0-590-41344-9pa. 5-9

John F. (Fitzgerald) Kennedy (1917-1963) was America's 35th president. The text follows him from his childhood until his assassination in Dallas, covering the memorable events of his presidency.

580. Denenberg, Barry. **The True Story of J. Edgar Hoover and the FBI**. New York: Scholastic, 1993. 202p. $13.95; $5.99pa. ISBN 0-590-43168-4; 0-590-44157-4pa. 7 up

J. Edgar Hoover (1895-1972) led the Federal Bureau of Investigation from 1924 until 1972. The text looks at his background and his commitment to hard work. At the same time, it examines his personal arrogance, snobbery, and desire for power. Some of the FBI's most famous cases show that Hoover liked to prosecute kidnappers, bank robbers, and murderers rather than members of organized crime or violators of civil rights. He saw himself above the law, a place that offered its own kind of corruption. Photographs, Bibliography, Timeline, and Index.

581.   Denenberg, Barry. **When Will This Cruel War Be Over? The Diary of Emma Simpson, Gordonsville, Virginia, 1864**. New York: Scholastic, 1996. 157p. $9.95. ISBN 0-590-22862-5. (Dear America, 1). 5-9

Emma begins her journal on December 23, 1863, and ends it on December 25, 1864. Her family fights for the Confederacy during the Civil War, and they all endure terrible hardships and several deaths from the battle and from illness. At the end of the year, she recounts her sadness and wonders if the waste could possibly be worth the pain of the war. An epilogue gives information about her later life.

582.   DeStefano, Susan. **Theodore Roosevelt: Conservation President**. Antonio Castro, illustrator. New York: Twenty-First Century Books, 1993. 80p. $14.98. ISBN 0-8050-2122-1. (Earth Keepers). 4-6

Theodore Roosevelt (1858-1919) was always fascinated with nature and collected such things as insects, seashells, and other specimens by the time he was nine. When he became president, few people were interested in conserving nature. However, with the influence of John Muir, he found ways to preserve resources in the environment. Among his accomplishments was the creation of five national parks. He believed that the country must last for the ages rather than for his generation alone. Glossary and Index.

583.   Devaney, John. **Franklin Delano Roosevelt: President**. New York: Walker, 1987. 188p. $12.95. ISBN 0-8027-6713-3. 5-9

Franklin D. Roosevelt (1882-1945) accompanied his father to see Grover Cleveland and heard his father refuse an ambassadorship. Cleveland supposedly said to the five-year-old Franklin, "I am making a strange wish for you. It is that you may never be president of the United States." Cleveland's wish did not come true, and for the leadership that Roosevelt gave during his four terms as president, America can only be grateful. Roosevelt was able to give the country hope during the Great Depression and World War II. Photographs and Index.

584.   Dewey, Jennifer Owings, author/illustrator. **Stories on Stone: Rock Art, Images from the Ancient Ones**. Boston: Little, Brown, 1996. 32p. $16.95. ISBN 0-316-18211-7. 2-4

Although little can be known about the artistic intent of the Anasazi, the text tries to interpret the drawings found in the Southwest. The Anasazi celebrated their lives by leaving impressions on the stone around them, either through petroglyphs or pictographs. Map. *Notable Children's Trade Books in the Field of Social Sciences.*

585.   Dexter, Catherine. **Mazemaker**. New York: Morrow, 1989. 202p. $11.95. ISBN 0-688-07383-2. 5-7

Winnie, 12, thinks she sees a cat fade into a maze in the schoolyard, and she tries to see if she can do the same. She succeeds and finds herself in 1889 instead of 1989. She wants to return, but while she tries to find someone to help her, she observes the era's people and their superstitions. She decides to follow the cat, and she returns to 1989 to search for William, the mazemaker who disappeared into the future while she was caught in the past. When she finds him, she tells him he is welcome at home.

586.   Di Certo, Joseph J. **The Pony Express: Hoofbeats in the Wilderness**. New York: Franklin Watts, 1989. 64p. $19.90. ISBN 0-531-10751-5. (A First Book). 4-6

Seven chapters describe the process of getting the Pony Express started, its heyday, and its passing. Three months after 190 relay and home stations along the 2,000-mile route were created, the first Pony Express rider left St. Joseph, Missouri, on April 3, 1860, and the mail arrived in San Francisco 10 days later. Riders had to overcome such hazards as the Sierra Nevadas and raiding Indians as they tried to make San Francisco feel closer to the East Coast. Mark Twain's *Roughing It* catches the excitement of those who saw the dedicated Pony Express riders, including such men as Pony Bob and the most famous of all, William F. Cody, Buffalo Bill. Because the transcontinental telegraph line was completed the next year, the Pony Express stopped on October 21, 1861. Photographs and illustrations of landmarks and maps noting all the stops on the Pony Express enhance the text. For Further Reading and Index.

587.   Di Franco, J. Philip. **The Italian Americans**. New York: Chelsea House, 1988. 94p. $18.95; $7.95pa. ISBN 0-87754-886-2; 0-7910-0268-3pa. (Peoples of North America). 5 up

Although this book professes to discuss only Italian Americans, it recounts a brief history of Italy through its revolutions and the Italian unification movement, *Risorgimento*, led by Guiseppe Mazzini, G. Garibaldi, and Camillo Benso di Cavour. In the nineteenth century, however, the greed of the wealthy led to a difficult life for many southern Italians. The northern Italians emigrated first, with the southern Italians following them. The peak immigration years were 1900 to 1914, when more than 2 million Italians arrived in the United States. Not all of them remained, but by 1980, 12 million Italians had settled in the United States. Among those who influenced American life was Filippo Mazzei, a physician philosopher whom Thomas Jefferson translated and whose words closely resembled the Bill of Rights. In 1832, Lorenzo de Ponte brought opera to America. Wine growers from Italy established the Swiss Colony winery, and fruit growers began the Del Monte company. Famous Italian Americans include Fiorello La Guardia, Geraldine Ferraro, Mario Cuomo, Mother Cabrini (America's first saint), Joe DiMaggio, Mario Lanza, Frank Sinatra, Marconi, Fermi, Toscanini, Anne Bancroft, and Lee Iacocca. Selected References and Index.

588. Diamond, Arthur. **Paul Cuffe: Merchant and Abolitionist**. New York: Chelsea House, 1989. 109p. $18.95. ISBN 1-55546-579-X. (Black Americans of Achievement). 5 up

When townspeople would not join him in supporting a school, Paul Cuffe, free Black in Westport, Massachusetts, built one on his own land with his own money so that his seven children could get an education without having to travel to a neighboring town. He accepted the children of the townspeople in the school. Cuffe was born in 1759 on an island off the coast of Massachusetts to a Native American mother and an Ashanti father captured by slave traders at 10. His father worked for and won his freedom. Paul Cuffe fell in love with the sea and shipping and, after working aboard several frigates, realized that the only way he could avoid sailing into ports where people abused slaves was to form his own business with his own ship. He and his brother began running the British blockade in 1779. Because he was not allowed to vote, Cuffe protested taxation, and by 1783 he was absolved of most tax, and Massachusetts was the first state to forbid slavery. Cuffe realized that one could fight and defeat unfair laws. With aid and blessings from fellow Quakers, Cuffe decided to investigate creating a colony in Africa for slaves where they could be educated. In Sierra Leone he met many obstacles and many people, including members of the Muslim Mandingo tribe who wanted to continue slave trading. Although unable to start colonization before his death in 1817, Cuffe tried to help other American Blacks eventually do so. Chronology, Further Reading, and Index.

589. Diamond, Arthur. **Prince Hall: Social Reformer**. New York: Chelsea House, 1991. 102p. $18.95. ISBN 1-55546-588-9. (Black Americans of Achievement). 5 up

Prince Hall (1735-1807) was the first organizer of Blacks in American history. He was shipped to Boston when 14 and witnessed the early stages of the American Revolution while he was a slave. He became free in 1770 but realized that a free Black had little more freedom than a slave. He became a member of the Order of the Free and Accepted Masons in 1775 and established his own branch for Blacks called the African Lodge. He united other Blacks, and they campaigned for the Continental army to accept slaves as soldiers. They worked to end the slave trade in Massachusetts, and they petitioned for Blacks to be educated, with Hall turning his home into the first school for Blacks in Boston. Reproductions enhance the text. Chronology, Further Reading, and Index.

590. Diamond, Arthur. **Smallpox and the American Indian**. San Diego, CA: Lucent, 1991. 64p. $16.95. ISBN 1-56006-018-2. (World Disasters). 5-8

Between 1836 and 1840, smallpox extinguished several Native American tribes. They possessed no natural immunity to the disease and distrusted the white man's medicine. It was one of the ways that the Native Americans began to disappear from the continent. The text looks at the situation and its effect. Glossary, Further Reading, and Index.

591. Dionetti, Michelle. **Coal Mine Peaches**. Anita Riggio, illustrator. New York: Orchard, 1991. 32p. $14.95. ISBN 0-531-05948-0. K-2

When the young female narrator's grandfather came from Italy in the early twentieth century, he helped build Brooklyn Bridge in New York City. He tells her about the coal mine where he had worked in Italy and the lumps of coal that grew into "peaches" during the hot summer. He also tells her about meeting her grandmother, marrying her, and having five children, one of whom is the girl's father.

592. Doherty, Craig A., and Katherine M. Doherty. **The Erie Canal**. Woodbridge, CT: Blackbirch Press, 1996. 48p. $15.95. ISBN 1-56711-112-2. (Building America). 3-5

The text looks at the reasons people decided to build the Erie Canal and how they did it. The task was not easy, and those who participated in the construction endured unpleasant living conditions. The photographs and illustrations provide a sense of the times. Chronology, Further Reading, Glossary, and Index.

593. Doherty, Craig A., and Katherine M. Doherty. **The Statue of Liberty**. New York: Blackbirch Press, 1996. 48p. $14.95. ISBN 1-56711-111-4. (Building America). 4-6

For the nineteenth century, the Statue of Liberty was a marvel. The text expands on the history of its design and construction. Archival photographs trace the progress of its construction, and contemporary full-color photographs show it as it has become. Further Reading, Glossary, Bibliography, and Index.

594. Dolan, Edward F. **America in World War I**. Brookfield, CT: Millbrook Press, 1996. 96p. $19.90. ISBN 1-56294-522-X. 6-9

The text introduces World War I and emphasizes the participation of the United States. Boxed essays include titles such as "American Women Go to War," "At War on the Home Front," "The War in the Air," and "Weapons of World War I." The book also presents brief biographical profiles of participants who later played important roles in World War II. Photographs, Maps, Bibliography, and Index.

595. Dolan. Edward F. **America in World War II: 1941**. Brookfield, CT: Millbrook Press, 1991. 72p. $16.40; $6.95pa. ISBN 1-878841-05-X; 1-87884-181-5pa. 4-8

America entered World War II on December 8, 1941, after Japanese planes bombed six U.S. military installations on the Hawaiian island of Oahu at Pearl Harbor. Other places bombed were the Philippine Island bases, Wake, Guam, and Midway. Then Japan's allies, Germany and Italy, declared war on the United States, and the country answered with a return declaration. Great Britain, already at war with Italy and Germany, declared war on Japan. In the closing weeks of 1941, Japanese troops captured the islands of Wake and Guam and invaded the Philippines. Photographs and maps expand the text. Bibliography and Index.

596. Dolan. Edward F. **America in World War II: 1942**. Brookfield, CT: Millbrook Press, 1991. 72p. $15.90. ISBN 1-56294-007-4. 5-8

In early 1942, Japan won control of the Philippine Islands. In June, however, the United States won a victory at the island of Midway, deep in the North Pacific. In the next months, two major campaigns began, one by the Army under General Douglas MacArthur, and the other under the Navy's Admiral Chester W. Nimitz. On the European front, America began to participate in the war in North Africa. A joint invasion of U.S. and British troops on the north coast of Africa began to drive the Germans out of Morocco, Algeria, and Tunisia. Photographs and maps expand the text. Bibliography and Index.

597. Dolan, Edward F. **America in World War II: 1943**. Brookfield, CT: Millbrook Press, 1992. 64p. $15.90; $6.95pa. ISBN 1-56294-113-5; 1-87884-162-9pa. 4-7

This volume begins with Operation Torch, which extended from Morocco to Algeria, and finally gave the Allies a victory in May 1943. A campaign in Sicily began in July (Operation Husky), with success achieved in August. In the Pacific, MacArthur controlled the battles of New Guinea and the Solomon Islands, which had continued since 1942. Nimitz fought at Makin and Tarawa. During the year, those remaining on the mainland wanted news of the battles while they rationed food and continued war production. Roosevelt and Churchill met several times to discuss strategy. Capsule highlights of the generals include Eisenhower, Rommel, Patton, Harold Alexander, Mussolini, Mark W. Clark, MacArthur, and Nimitz. Bibliography and Index.

598. Dolan. Edward F. **America in World War II: 1944**. Brookfield, CT: Millbrook Press, 1993. 72p. $16.40. ISBN 1-56294-221-2. 5-8

Admiral Nimitz spent the first nine months of 1944 capturing islands on his way to Japan. He sent his ships to support MacArthur's attempts on the Philippines. In October 1944, they stormed ashore on the island of Leyte, then in December on Mindoro. At the end of the year, the general was preparing to invade Luzon, home of the Philippines' capital city Manila. Nimitz continued toward Japan with his ships. In Europe, on June 6, more than 5,300 ships landed on the beaches at Normandy, France. General Eisenhower and the troops drove back the German defenders. In August, other Allied troops landed on the southern coast of France, and they spread east to the German border and north into Belgium, Luxembourg, and Holland. In December, in the snow, Hitler sent a massive force of German troops against U.S. forces stationed along the Belgium and Luxembourg borders. He wanted to separate the U.S. troops from the British forces in the Battle of the Bulge; he failed. Bibliography and Index.

599. Dolan, Edward F. **America in World War II: 1945**. Brookfield, CT: Millbrook Press, 1994. 72p. $16.40. ISBN 1-56294-320-0. 4-7

In early 1945, U.S. troops stopped the German attack on the borders of Luxembourg and Belgium. General Dwight Eisenhower returned to his plan to reach the Rhine River in Germany. In April, the Germans fought back, and the Allies suffered heavy casualties. The fighting ended with German defeat on May 5. But the real shock was the horror of finding the extermination camps. In January in the Pacific, General Douglas MacArthur landed on Luzon in the Philippines and began his attempt to recapture Manila. In July, the fighting there ended. Far to the north, Admiral Chester Nimitz had invaded Iwo Jima and Okinawa. By July 3, the U.S. had captured both places. On August 6, 1945, the *Enola Gay* dropped an atom bomb on Hiroshima, and on August 9, another dropped on Nagasaki. With those terrible explosions the war ended in the Pacific; the Japanese formally surrendered on September 2, 1945. Photographs and maps expand the text. Bibliography and Index.

600. Dolan, Edward F. **The American Revolution: How We Fought the War of Independence**. Brookfield, CT: Millbrook Press, 1995. 110p. $19.90. ISBN 1-56294-521-1. 6-9

The text looks at the American Revolution through battles in chronological order, beginning with Lexington and Concord. It covers all the places, people, and situations pertinent to the war, supplemented with maps and reproductions. Sidebars include information on figures such as Betsy Ross and Benedict Arnold. Bibliography and Index. *Notable Children's Trade Books in the Field of Social Studies.*

601. Dolan, Edward F. **Panama and the United States: Their Canal, Their Stormy Years**. New York: Franklin Watts 1990. 160p. $19.86. ISBN 0-531-110911-9. 5 up

When Columbus arrived in what is now Panama on his fourth voyage in 1503, probably 750,000 people, from the Cuna tribe and others, lived there. But Balboa arrived first, in 1501. Not until 1513 did Balboa cross Panama to see the great body of water on the other side, the Pacific. Balboa realized that a waterway would make the journey much easier; thus, the idea of a canal began very early in Panama's recorded history. From 1799 to 1804, Alexander von Humbolt surveyed the area and found nine reasonable routes to cut across land to the Pacific. Because of battles, treaties, and misfortune, the United States was not free to complete the canal until the beginning of the twentieth century. The man who made it most possible was William Crawford Gorgas; he discovered that mosquitoes caused malaria and yellow fever and saved the lives of many workers. On August 15, 1913, the canal opened. A further series of treaties and disagreements between Panama and the United States have peppered the canal's history. Finally, Torrijos made an agreement with President Carter to take possession of the canal on December 31, 1999. Panama's new ruler at Torrijos's death, Noreiga, did nothing to further good relationships. Photographs show the progress of the canal's construction. Source Notes, Bibliography, and Index.

602. Dolan, Ellen. **Susan Butcher and the Iditarod Trail**. New York: Walker, 1993. 103p. $15.85. ISBN 0-8027-8211-6. 5-8

Of all the sports events in the world, the Iditarod race in Alaska is considered the hardest. It officially began as a yearly event in 1973. It covers more than 1,000 miles in the snow with the racer using 7 to 20 mushers (dogs) to pull a sleigh along the trail. The value of racing mushers became clear in 1925 when the "black death" broke out in Nome, Alaska. Children infected with diphtheria needed medicine, but the closest medicine during the winter was 25 days away. By using teams of sled dogs and drivers, the medicine reached Nome in five days, seven and one-half hours. From this event, the idea of the race evolved until it became reality in 1973. Susan Butcher and her mushers have won the race at least three times. Appendices and Index.

603. Dolan, Sean. **James Beckwourth: Frontiersman**. New York: Chelsea House, 1992. 118p. $18.95. ISBN 0-7910-1120-8. (Black Americans of Achievement). 5 up

As the only son of a white plantation master and a slave, James Beckwourth (1798-1866) was legally a slave himself, but his father never treated him as one. He went with his father to Missouri in 1810 and went to school in St. Louis. After training to become a blacksmith, he decided to become a fur trapper and mountain man. His story includes his fighting the Seminoles in Florida, serving in the U.S. Army in Colorado, and becoming a Crow Indian war chief. He had many experiences with diverse people. Photographs and reproductions enhance the text. Chronology, Further Reading, and Index.

604. Dolan, Sean. **Junípero Serra**. New York: Chelsea House, 1991. 110p. $18.95; $7.95pa. ISBN 0-7910-1255-7; 0-7910-1282-4pa. (Hispanics of Achievement). 5 up

Miguel José Serra (1713-1784), born in Majorca, began his religious training at 15. He became a Franciscan and in 1748 left his home and family to become a missionary in the New World. He served the Spanish missions built by the conquerors trying to convert Indians to Catholicism by either persuasion or force. In 1769, he joined the expeditions exploring California and established the string of missions that still stand today from San Diego to San Francisco. In 1988, the church began the process of making him a saint, although Native Americans accuse him of trying to destroy their culture. Engravings and reproductions enhance the text. Chronology, Further Reading, and Index.

605. Dolan, Sean. **Matthew Henson: Arctic Explorer**. New York: Chelsea Juniors, 1992. 80p. $14.95. ISBN 0-7910-1766-4. (Junior Black Americans of Achievement). 3-6

As a Black American, Matthew Henson (1886-1955) had few opportunities as a young man until he met Robert Peary. He went with him to Greenland, and the Eskimos, unlike his countrymen, thought Henson a hero. He then became a member of Peary's first expedition to reach the North Pole in 1909. His skills and courage made the discovery possible, but he has received little credit because Peary organized the expedition. Chronology and Glossary.

606. Dominy, Jeannine. **Katherine Dunham: Dancer and Choreographer**. New York: Chelsea House, 1992. 111p. $18.95. ISBN 0-7910-1123-2. (Black Americans of Achievement). 5 up

As a teenager, Katherine Dunham (1909-) realized that she wanted to dance. She saw links between modern American dances and ancient tribal dances in Africa that won her an anthropology fellowship to the Caribbean to observe dance. Afterward, she formed a touring company to introduce dance to everyone. In 1945, she opened her own school in New York that trained Black performers. In 1962, she moved to East St. Louis, Illinois, and opened the Performance Arts Training Center to give opportunities to the city's youth. She has had a full life of giving to her community as a performer, choreographer, teacher, and scholar. Photographs and reproductions enhance the text. Chronology, Further Reading, and Index.

607.   Donahue, John. **An Island Far from Home**. Minneapolis, MN: Carolrhoda, 1995. 179p. $14.96. ISBN 0-87614-859-3. (Adventures in Time). 4-7

A button emblazoned with an "A" found in an attic begins the story. In Tilton, Massachusetts, in 1864, when Joshua Loring is 12, he hopes he might be able to join the army to fight against the enemy who killed his father. His Uncle Robert, a civilian lawyer and a wartime deputy commander of a fort called George's Island, tries to convince him that war is terrible. Uncle Robert gets Joshua to write to John, a young rebel soldier imprisoned on George's Island. Joshua quickly understands that John is very much like him, and when he suggests that his class write to this prisoner of war, he loses his friends. *Notable Children's Trade Books in the Field of Social Studies*, *IRA Children's Book Award*, and *Society of School Librarians Outstanding Book*.

608.   Donahue, Marilyn Cram. **The Valley in Between**. New York: Walker, 1987. 227p. $15.85. ISBN 0-8027-6745-1. 5 up

Emmie, 13 in 1857, likes to take off her shoes and get her feet muddy. People chastise her for this behavior, but other tensions in her California town divert attention from her. The Mormons must return to Utah, someone discovers gold, the Indians begin attacking, and notice that a Civil War may begin overshadows all. Emmie likes being part of the events, including having the handsome Tad appreciate her.

609.   Donnelly, Judy. **Titanic: Lost and Found**. Keith Kohler, illustrator. New York: Random House, 1987. 47p. $5.99; $2.95pa. ISBN 0-394-98669-5; 0-394-88669-0pa. 1-3

The *Titanic* sank in 1912. In 1987, an expedition led by Robert Ballard discovered its remains. The text tells of these two events.

610.   Donnelly, Judy. **A Wall of Names: The Story of the Vietnam Memorial**. New York: Random House, 1991. 48p. $11.99; $3.99pa. ISBN 0-679-90169-8; 0-679-80169-3pa. (Step into Reading). 2-4

In this story of the creation of the wall honoring those who fought and died in Vietnam, the author discusses attitudes toward the war and the determination that Jan Scruggs exhibited to get the wall designed and built. Photographs complement the text.

611.   Dorris, Michael. **Sees Behind Trees**. New York: Hyperion, 1996. 96p. $14.95. ISBN 0-7868-0224-3. 4-8

In pre-Colonial America, Walnut has myopia and knows that he can never see well enough to become the kind of hunter admired by his tribe. His mother suggests that he "look with his ears." Because of his ability to "see" what the others cannot, the tribe chooses him to accompany the village elder, Gray Fire, on a journey to find the land of water. He fulfills this role by passing his universal and age-old tests of manhood. *School Library Journal Best Book*.

612.   Doss, Michael P. **Plenty Coups**. Yoshi Miyake, illustrator. Austin, TX: Raintree/Steck-Vaughn, 1993. 32p. $13.98; $5.95pa. ISBN 0-8172-3409-8; 0-8114-4089-3pa. (Native American Stories). 3-5

When Chief Plenty Coups (1848-1932) died, the Crow Nation honored him by deciding that no other Crow would be a chief because the achievements of Plenty Coups could never be matched. Since then, all leaders have been called "chairman." He performed 80 feats of valor in combat during his youth, and he promoted education among his people, but he never warred against the United States. History.

613.   Doubleday, Veronica. **Salt Lake City**. New York: Dillon Press, Silver Burdett, 1994. 46p. $14.95. ISBN 0-87518-574-6. (Holy Cities). 4-6

Salt Lake City, Utah, is the spiritual center of the Mormon Church. The text focuses on the religion and its ceremonies and traditions. Other topics include different uses of important places of worship such as the Mormon temple, history, culture, festivals, and concern for ancestors. Photographs enhance the text. Further Reading and Index.

614.   Douglass, Frederick. **Escape from Slavery: The Boyhood of Frederick Douglass in His Own Words**. Michael McCurdy, ed. New York: Knopf, 1994. 63p. $15. ISBN 0-679-84652-2. 5-8

More than 150 years ago, Frederick Douglass (1817-1895) escaped from slavery. During his boyhood, he was separated from his family, he learned to read, and he endured harsh treatment from cruel masters. McCurdy has taken excerpts from Douglass's longer book to make his experiences accessible to younger readers. Bibliography.

615.   Driemen, J. E. **Atomic Dawn: A Biography of Robert Oppenheimer**. New York: Dillon Press, 1988. 160p. $13.95. ISBN 0-87518-397-2. (People in Focus). 5 up

As a physicist, Robert Oppenheimer (1904-1967) knew the danger associated with the announcement that the Germans had learned how to split uranium and could possibly create an atomic bomb. When the military approached him about the practicality of making a bomb in World War II, he knew the answers. The security check on his past revealed his flirtation with the Communist Party, so the government did not want him to head the Los Alamos, New Mexico, research laboratory, but he was the best person for the job. He succeeded in building the bombs that destroyed Hiroshima and Nagasaki in 1945. Afterward, anti-Communist sentiment in the United States, and the ability of the Soviet Union to create nuclear weapons so quickly after the first were detonated, led to an accusation that Oppenheimer had spied for the Soviet Union. He was cleared of the charges, however, and he advocated treaties against the bomb. Bibliography and Index.

616. Driemen, John E. **Clarence Darrow**. New York: Chelsea House, 1992. 112p. $18.95. ISBN 0-7910-1624-2. (Library of Biography). 5 up

As one of America's most famous lawyers, Clarence Darrow (1857-1938) represented the defense in the 1925 Scopes Monkey trial. He had a special sympathy for the oppressed because his own parents had been ostracized for their liberal ideals. He defended miners in Pennsylvania, workers whose lives were being ruined for profit, Blacks, pacifists, socialists, and any others whose personal freedom was threatened. He also became one of America's humanitarians. The text tells his story with complementary photographs. Further Reading, Chronology, and Index.

617. Dubowski, Cathy East. **Andrew Johnson: Rebuilding the Union**. Englewood Cliffs, NJ: Silver Burdett, 1991. 126p. $12.95. ISBN 0-382-09945-1. (History of the Civil War). 5 up

At the beginning of the Civil War, Andrew Johnson (1808-1875) declared that he was a "Union man." The Northerners were delighted, but his Tennessee neighbors thought him a traitor. Although born into poverty, he rose in politics because he believed in the working man. After becoming president at Lincoln's assassination, he became involved in postwar politics and had to endure an impeachment trial. He was acquitted, and then he was elected to the U.S. Senate. Timetable, Suggested Reading, Selected Sources, and Index.

618. Dubowski, Cathy East. **Clara Barton: Healing the Wounds**. Kimberly Bulcken Root, illustrator. Englewood Cliffs, NJ: Silver Burdett, 1991. 133p. $12.95. ISBN 0-382-09940-0. (History of the Civil War). 6-9

Although she began her teaching career in a one-room schoolhouse, Clara Barton (1821-1912) became the head of nursing operations during the Civil War. She convinced surgeons that they needed clean and orderly field hospitals. After the war, she went to Europe to see the emergency help available there, and later established the American Red Cross. She also led a fight for women's suffrage. Timetable, Suggested Reading, Selected Sources, and Index.

619. Dubowski, Cathy East. **Robert E. Lee and the Rise of the South**. Kimberly Bulcken Root, illustrator. Englewood Cliffs, NJ: Silver Burdett, 1991. 133p. $12.95. ISBN 0-382-09942-7. (History of the Civil War). 6-9

Lincoln offered Robert E. Lee (1807-1870) the command of the Union armies on the same day that Lee heard that Virginia had seceded from the Union. He decided to fight for his state, and he led the Army of Northern Virginia from one brilliant campaign to another against better-equipped enemies. He served with honor although what he saw made him sad. Timetable, Suggested Readings, Sources, and Index.

620. Ducey, Jean Sparks. **The Bittersweet Time**. Grand Rapids, MI: William B. Eerdman, 1995. 115p. $13; $6pa. ISBN 0-8028-5096-0; 0-8028-5113-4pa. 5-8

In October 1929, when she is 14, Jane Hartley's life changes. Her father loses his job, and she can no longer have an allowance. In this first-person novel in diary form, she discusses her love for writing and her chance to work for Mr. Walz in his new bookstore. He encourages her to read, and she discovers that she learns more by reading as many different books as possible than she learns in school. He offers her a full-time job, so she quits school to take it because her salary will keep her mother from having to go out of town to work, as her father has had to do. By March 1930, all have jobs in the area, but they must continue to pay their bills. Jane prepares to send more manuscripts to magazines.

621. Duey, Kathleen. **Anisett Lundberg: California, 1851**. New York: Aladdin, 1996. 144p. $3.99pa. ISBN 0-689-80386-9pa. (American Diaries, 3). 5-7

When Anisett finds a piece of gold where she and her mother serve gold diggers their food in California, she wonders whom she should tell. Her father is dead, and her mother, with no friends, only wants to return to the East. Anisett carelessly tells what she has found, and she jeopardizes her family's safety. In two days, the family identifies their friends, including a Chinese man; knows that they can start digging their own gold; and will have money to establish a place like their father wanted.

622. Duey, Kathleen. **Emma Eileen Grove: Mississippi, 1865**. New York: Aladdin, 1996. 144p. $3.99pa. ISBN 0-689-80385-0pa. (American Diaries, 2). 5-7

While Emma, her sister, and her brother travel from Mississippi to St. Louis, 10 days after Lincoln was shot in 1865, they are on a steamboat with horrible Yankees. Emma is concerned because she has not heard from her father. The boilers on the boat burst, and the boat catches fire near Memphis. A Yankee who helps Emma get to safety dies, and she begins to realize that even enemies can be kind. She and her brother decide to send the Yankee's family one of their last two pieces of gold.

623.	Duey, Kathleen. **Mary Alice Peale**. New York: Aladdin, 1996. 144p. $3.99pa. ISBN 0-689-80387-7pa. (American Diaries, 4). 3-7

Mary Alice Peale lives in Philadelphia during 1777. While her Loyalist father entertains British officers at a dance, her brother, a rebel soldier fighting for the Colonies' freedom, lies wounded outside in their garden shed. She must find a way to help her brother without letting her father know. She records the difficulties of the year in her diary and the outcome that she helps to instrument.

624.	Duey, Kathleen. **Sarah Anne Hartford: Massachusetts, 1651**. New York: Aladdin, 1996. 144p. $3.99pa. ISBN 0-689-80384-2pa. (American Diaries, 1). 5-7

Sarah, 15, knows that merriment on the Sabbath in Massachusetts in 1650 is a punishable offense. She and her friend Elizabeth play in the snow, but people think that she is Elizabeth's brother Roger because she is wearing his coat. When the town officials announce public punishment for the two, Elizabeth must decide if she will confess that they should punish her instead of Roger. One of Sarah's main concerns is the woman her father is planning to marry—a person who warns Sarah that Elizabeth is a bad influence. Fortunately, her father realizes his mistake.

625.	Duffy, James. **Radical Red**. New York: Scribner's, 1993. 152p. $13.95. ISBN 0-684-19533-X. 5-8

Connor, 12, hears Susan B. Anthony's pleas for women to have the right to vote. Connor starts wearing a ribbon called a "radical red" in 1849 during the suffragette appeal in Albany, New York, at the state's constitutional convention to adopt universal suffrage. Connor and her mother are swayed by Aunt Susan's idea, but Connor's father, a policeman, thinks suffragettes are troublemakers. The family argues, but Connor and her mother decide to continue their support of the cause.

626.	Duggleby, John. **Artist in Overalls: The Life of Grant Wood**. New York: Chronicle, 1996. 57p. $15.95. ISBN 0-8118-1242-1. 4-7

One of the best-known American paintings is Grant Wood's *American Gothic*. The text looks at Grant Wood's life (1892-1942). He grew up in Iowa as a shy but stubborn boy; was educated in Minneapolis, Chicago, and Paris; and returned to Iowa, where he taught high school to support himself. He saw irony in the discrepancy between the romantic ideals of and realistic situations in American life, and he translated these concepts into his paintings. Included are reproductions of his paintings.

627.	Duggleby, John. **Impossible Quests**. Allan Eitzen, illustrator. New York: Crestwood House, 1990. 48p. $10.95. ISBN 0-89686-509-6. (Incredible History). 4 up

Various quests have attempted to prove the existence of Bigfoot in the Pacific Northwest of the United States and Canada, the Loch Ness Monster in Scotland, Noah's Ark in Turkey, Atlantis in the Mediterranean, and the lost continent of gold in the South Pacific. The text discusses these quests and illustrates them with black-and-white drawings. Bibliography and Index.

628.	Duncan, Dayton. **People of the West**. Boston: Little, Brown, 1996. 144p. $19.95; $10.95pa. ISBN 0-316-19627-4; 0-316-19633-9pa. 3-7

The text introduces 15 ordinary people who faced extraordinary circumstances in the West. They include people who lived there before the settlers from Europe arrived, the first white woman to cross the Continental Divide, one of the Chinese men who helped to build the railroad, an inhabitant of a prairie sod house, a gold prospector, and a Native American who faced the difficulty of keeping tribal traditions while adopting the ways of the white man. They are Sweet Medicine, Cabeza de Vaca, Kit Carson, Narcissa, Walt Whitman, Mariano Guadalupe Vallejo, William Swain, "John Chinaman," Teddy Blue Abbott, Uriah and Mattie Oblinger, Chief Joseph, Emmeline Wells, Pap Singleton, Buffalo Bird Woman, and Wolf Chief. Black-and-White Photographs, Principal Sources, and Index. *Notable Children's Trade Books in the Field of Social Sciences*.

629.	Duncan, Dayton. **The West: An Illustrated History for Children**. Boston: Little, Brown, 1996. 144p. $19.95; $10.95pa. ISBN 0-316-19628-2; 0-316-19632-0pa. 3-7

The text looks at the West, a land that for thousands of generations belonged to the Native Americans. When explorers began arriving from other countries in the sixteenth century, they began to take over the lands. But the Americans from the eastern coast were the ones who incorporated the land into their nation. Personal stories from the people who took over the land give its history, mainly from the early nineteenth through the twentieth centuries. Black-and-White Photographs, Principal Sources, and Index. *Notable Children's Trade Books in the Field of Social Sciences* and *New York Public Library Books for the Teen Age*.

630.	Duncan, Lois. **The Circus Comes Home: When the Greatest Show on Earth Rode the Rails**. New York: Doubleday, 1993. 62p. $16.95. ISBN 0-385-30689-X. 4-6

Duncan's father traveled with the Ringling Brothers Circus during the 1940s, when the Flying Wallendas, the Doll family of midgets, the fat lady, and 1,600 troupers and menagerie animals from 28 countries took a train to performances. Photographs give a true sense of the circus life, and they relate to stories and intriguing facts that personalize everyone in the photographs. One interesting note is that the fat lady received 50 cents for every pound she weighed on payday; to lose weight was to lose money. Index.

631.   Dunlap, Julie. **Aldo Leopold: Living with the Land**. Antonio Castro, illustrator. New York: Twenty-First Century Books, 1993. 80p. $14.98. ISBN 0-8050-2501-4. (Earth Keepers). 4-7

As a young boy, Aldo Leopold (1886-1948) loved the land. When he went to prep school and had to give a speech, he said that people were using the forests too rapidly. He continued this concern as he attended and graduated from Yale's school of forestry. Not until he was older was he able to develop his own farmland in a way that would restore it. He saw when young that land was worth more than its ability to provide crops or lumber. He became concerned about soil conservation, ecology, and game management, and taught others what to do. Glossary and Index.

632.   Dunlap, Julie. **Birds in the Bushes: A Story About Margaret Morse Nice**. Ralph L. Ramstad, illustrator. Minneapolis, MN: Carolrhoda, 1996. 64p. $13.31. ISBN 0-87614-006-4. (Creative Minds). 4-6

Margaret Morse Nice (1883-1974) attended Mount Holyoke College and majored in languages. She returned to school for a master's degree in psychology. One day, on a walk with her daughters, she realized that she wanted to study nature and birds. She began to do research on birds and amassed data to arrive at conclusions about their habits, including finding the ways that males established territories by fighting with other males. Scientists at first saw her research as the work of a mere housewife, but its integrity propelled her into a position as one of the world's best ornithologists. Bibliography and Index.

633.   Dunlap, Julie. **Eye on the Wild: A Story About Ansel Adams**. Kerry Maguire, illustrator. Minneapolis, MN: Carolrhoda, 1995. 64p. $17.50; $5.95pa. ISBN 0-87614-944-1; 0-87614-966-2pa. (Creative Minds). 3-6

Ansel Adams (1902-1984) received his first camera at 14 while on a trip to Yellowstone National Park with his family. Even though he continued to take pictures and work in a developing lab, piano was more important to him. As a young man, he made his first serious money as an artist from his photographs. After he met Paul Strand, a member of Alfred Steiglitz's group, who admired his photographs, Adams changed his career. He became very active in the Sierra Club while trying to save the environment from federal government officials who wanted to sell it or tear it up. He fought for the environment and photographed nature throughout his life. Bibliography.

634.   Dunn, John. **The Relocation of the North American Indian**. San Diego, CA: Lucent, 1995. 128p. $16.95. ISBN 1-56006-240-1. (World History Series). 6-9

When Europeans arrived in the New World, more than 300 separate tribes speaking as many languages already thrived there—most in the Pacific coastal area, the Southwest, and east of the Mississippi. Some tribes were nomadic, some were sedentary farmers, but each tribe tended to live in a group with a tribal elder serving an advisory capacity. The disagreements that transpired between the whites and Native Americans began a dispossession that lasted 400 years and reduced the lands occupied by Native Americans to 2.3 percent of the continent. This disturbing history of the relationship between whites and the Native Americans uses works written during the periods related, the research of recognized scholars, and other relevant sources. An abbreviated litany of displacement begins when the Puritans overcame the Pequots in 1637, while the English fought and finally defeated the Powhatans in 1646. The Wampanoags lost in 1676. By 1794, Indians had ceded parts of Ohio and Indiana. In 1811, Tecumseh's confederacy was smashed, Jackson defeated the Creeks in 1814 and won Alabama, and the Seminoles had to cede most of west Florida in 1823. From 1835 to 1843, Osceola led a Seminole uprising. In 1838, the Cherokees were expelled from Georgia to walk the Trail of Tears. In 1859, gold seekers in California used guns to force the Osage tribe from its lands. From 1863 to 1868, the Navajos tried to protect themselves, but they lost, and the army marched them off their lands and onto reservations. Custer massacred the Cheyenne in 1868. In 1871, Congress ceased to recognize the tribes as individual nations. Then in 1876, Custer fought the Sioux at Little Bighorn and lost. But in 1890, the U.S. Army massacred the Sioux at Wounded Knee. Not until 1924 did Native Americans earn the right to vote in their own country. Notes, For Further Reading, Additional Works Consulted, and Index.

635.   Durrant, Lynda. **Echohawk**. New York: Clarion, 1996. 190p. $14.95. ISBN 0-395-74430-X. 6-8

Mohicans raid four-year-old Jonathan's home in 1738 and carry him off after killing his family. He becomes Echohawk, member of a Mohawk family. Other members of the tribe, however, do not accept him. He has little interest in pursuing his relatives, and after he vaguely remembers the circumstances about his parents, he decides to stay with his Mohawk father and help him protect their land.

636.   Durwood, Thomas A. **John C. Calhoun and the Roots of the Civil War**. Englewood Cliffs, NJ: Silver Burdett, 1991. 160p. $12.95. ISBN 0-382-09936-2. (History of the Civil War). 5 up

John C. Calhoun (1782-1850), a South Carolinian senator, argued for the South's interest in slavery and helped keep it intact while he served in the U.S. Congress. The text looks at his life and the effect of his determination to keep the institution of slavery. Suggested Reading, Selected Sources, and Index.

637. Duvall, Jill. **The Cayuga**. Chicago: Childrens Press, 1991. 48p. $5.50. ISBN 0-516-41123-3. (New True Books). 2-4

The text presents the history, changing fortunes, and way of life of a tribe that was one of the original five tribes of the Iroquois, first in west central New York on Lake Cayuga. Words You Should Know and Index.

638. Duvall, Jill. **The Chumash**. Chicago: Childrens Press, 1994. 48p. $5.50. ISBN 0-516-41052-0. (New True Books). 2-4

The text presents the history, changing fortunes, and way of life of a tribe that lived near Santa Barbara in southern California. Words You Should Know and Index.

639. Duvall, Jill. **The Mohawk**. Chicago: Childrens Press, 1991. 48p. $5.50. ISBN 0-516-41115-2. (New True Books). 2-4

The text presents the history, changing fortunes, and way of life of a tribe that was one of the original five tribes in the Iroquois confederacy. One of its famous members is Hiawatha. Words You Should Know and Index.

640. Duvall, Jill. **The Oneida**. Chicago: Childrens Press, 1991. 48p. $5.50. ISBN 0-516-41125-X. (New True Books). 2-4

The text presents the history, changing fortunes, and way of life of a tribe that was one of the five original members of the Iroquois confederation. Words You Should Know and Index.

641. Duvall, Jill. **The Onondaga**. Chicago: Childrens Press, 1991. 48p. $5.50. ISBN 0-516-41126-8. (New True Books). 2-4

The text presents the history, changing fortunes, and way of life of a tribe that inhabited the shores of the Finger Lakes in New York and was one of the original five members of the Iroquois confederation. Words You Should Know and Index.

642. Duvall, Jill. **The Penobscot**. Chicago: Childrens Press, 1993. 48p. $5.50. ISBN 0-516-41194-2. (New True Books). 2-4

The text presents the history, changing fortunes, and way of life of a tribe that joined the Abenaki confederation in the eighteenth century. An Algonquian-speaking tribe, it lived in Maine on Penobscot Bay and River. Words You Should Know and Index.

643. Duvall, Jill. **The Seneca**. Chicago: Childrens Press, 1991. 48p. $5.50. ISBN 0-516-41119-5. (New True Books). 2-4

The text presents the history, changing fortunes, and way of life of a tribe that was the westernmost member of the original Iroquois confederacy between Seneca Lake and Lake Erie in New York State. Words You Should Know and Index.

644. Duvall, Jill. **The Tuscarora**. Chicago: Childrens Press, 1991. 48p. $5.50. ISBN 0-516-41128-4. (New True Books). 2-4

The text presents the history, changing fortunes, and way of life of a tribe that migrated north from North Carolina into New York and joined the Iroquois confederation in 1722. Words You Should Know and Index.

645. Dwyer, Christopher. **Robert Peary and the Quest for the North Pole**. New York: Chelsea House, 1992. 110p. $19.95. ISBN 0-7910-1316-2. (World Explorers). 5 up

Many people competed with Robert Peary (1856-1920) to become the first to reach the North Pole. Those explorers included Frederick Albert Cook, Elisha Kent Kane, Charles Francis Hall, Edward Parry, Fridtjof Nansen, and Adolphus Greely. They risked starvation, frostbite, scurvy, and various other maladies to reach their goal, but Peary sacrificed 23 years, his health, his money, some of his toes, and probably his sanity before he claimed the North Pole as his discovery in 1909. Photographs and reproductions enhance the text. Chronology, Further Reading, and Index.

646. Dwyer, Frank. **John Adams**. New York: Chelsea House, 1989. 112p. $18.95; $7.95pa. ISBN 1-55546-801-2; 0-7910-0608-5pa. (World Leaders Past and Present). 5 up

Reproductions highlight the text that tells the story of John Adams, second president of the United States (1735-1826). The chapters note his childhood in Braintree, Massachusetts, and continue through his life. He became a major figure in the creation of the United States and an unlikely diplomat who feared for his life as he crossed the ocean to Paris. Further Reading, Chronology, and Index.

E

647.   Earle, Alice. **Home Life in Colonial Days**. 1898. New York: Corner House, 1991. 470p. $29.95. ISBN 0-87918-063-8. Stockbridge, MA: Berkshire House, 1993. 470p. $14.95pa. ISBN 0-936399-28-8pa. 5 up

A thorough and well-documented text reveals the daily life of the settlers from the time they arrived in the early 1600s, when some had to live in caves, until they had lovely gardens surrounding permanent homes. Chapter topics include kitchens and serving meals, foods, making clothes and their styles, occupations, travel, transportation, overnight accommodations at taverns, Sunday activities, and neighborliness. Index.

648.   Edmonds, Walter. **The Matchlock Gun**. Paul Lantz, illustrator. 1941. New York: Doubleday, 1989. 50p. $16.95. ISBN 0-399-21911-0. Mahwah, NJ: Troll, 1991. 50p. $5.95pa. ISBN 0-8167-2367-2pa. 3-6

Edward, 10, has to help his mother defend their home in 1757 while his father is away fighting the Indians. When his mother and the other children see smoke in the distance, they know that the Indians are coming. Edward's mother quickly teaches him how to fire the Spanish matchlock gun. Although the gun is twice as long as he is tall, Edward fires at the enemy and kills two men who have thrown tomahawks at his mother. The Indians burn the house, but his bravery saves their lives. *Newbery Medal*.

649.   Edwards, Lillie J. **Denmark Vesey: Slave Revolt Leader**. New York: Chelsea House, 1990. 108p. $18.95. ISBN 1-55546-614-1. (Black Americans of Achievement). 5 up

Denmark Vesey (1767-1822), sold into slavery at 14, served as captain on voyages across the Atlantic, during which he saw the horrors of the slave trade. He started living in Charleston, South Carolina, in 1783, with an owner who permitted him to hire himself out as a carpenter. In 1799, he won a huge amount of money in a lottery and was able to buy his freedom. Then he began to try to liberate others from slavery. He read about the slave revolt in St. Dominique in 1804 and started to organize a similar uprising. In 1822, the Charleston militia crushed the uprising just before it was to begin. Although he did not succeed, his attempt frightened slave owners. Photographs and engravings enhance the text. Chronology, Further Reading, and Index.

649a.   Edwards, Pamela Duncan. **Barefoot: Escape on the Underground Railroad**. New York: HarperCollins, 1997. Unpaged. $14.95. ISBN 0-06-027137-X. K-4

Barefoot fears what is both before and behind him as he finds himself farther away than he has ever been from the plantation. The frog croaks to show water, and a mouse leads to fruit. The heron waits to hear the heavy boots, and when they come, the mosquitoes swarm them away. The animals protect Barefoot and guide him to a safe house on the Underground Railroad.

650.   Edwards, Pat. **Little John and Plutie**. Boston: Houghton Mifflin, 1988. 172p. $13.95. ISBN 0-395-48223-2. 4-6

Little John's mother is furious about having to move to town with his Gran in 1897 after his father drinks away money with which he had planned to buy mules. However, Little John is pleased because he meets Plutie, his first friend. Although two years older and Black, Plutie and Little John have fun together. When Plutie gets into trouble and Little John's father helps him, Little John realizes that his father is more compassionate than he had thought.

651.   Egger-Bovet, Howard, and Marlene Smith-Baranzini. **Book of the American Revolution**. Bill Sanchez, illustrator. Boston: Little, Brown, 1994. 96p. $19.95; $11.95pa. ISBN 0-316-96922-2; 0-316-22204-6pa. (Brown Paper School USKids History). 4-6

Drawings augment the text describing the events leading to the Revolutionary War, the life in the colonies during the war, and important figures in the war. Some events and people are the Boston Tea Party, John Robinson, the Sons of Liberty, Boston, Lexington, Concord, Joseph Palmer, the Battle of Breed's Hill, Daniel Boone, Benjamin Franklin, Phillis Wheatley, Tom Paine, Joseph Plumb Martin, the first flags, women in battle, and victory at Yorktown. Games and activities are included and illustrated. If You Want to Know More and Index.

652.   Ehrlich, Elizabeth. **Nelly Bly: Journalist**. New York: Chelsea House, 1989. 111p. $18.95. ISBN 1-55546-643-5. (American Women of Achievement). 5 up

As the most celebrated reporter of her day, Nelly Bly (1885-1922), born Elizabeth Cochran, was prosperous. After being educated at home, she moved to Pittsburgh where she discovered that she, as a female, could not be a journalist. In 1885, however, she wrote a rebuttal to an editorial about women working and won a job. She visited prisons and slums and became a factory worker so that she could write her stories. In 1887, she moved to New York and revealed the horror of an insane asylum. She wrote about political corruption, the defenseless, and outdated traditions before she married and became a businesswoman. Later she returned to journalism. In 1890, she made a record-breaking trip around the globe. Photographs and reproductions enhance the text. Chronology, Further Reading, and Index.

653. Elish, Dan. **James Meredith and School Desegregation**. Brookfield, CT: Millbrook Press, 1994. 32p. $13.40; $4.95pa. ISBN 1-56294-379-0; 1-56294-861-Xpa. (Gateway Civil Rights). 4-6

James Meredith (b. 1933) tried to enroll in the all-white University of Mississippi in September 1962. Federal marshals had to be called to Oxford to keep the peace, and President John F. Kennedy announced via television that he was horrified at the actions of American citizens. Meredith finished college, went to Nigeria, and came back to America to be a stockbroker and to fight for civil rights. Important Events in the Life Of, Find Out More, and Index.

654. Elish, Dan. **The Transcontinental Railroad: Triumph of a Dream**. Brookfield, CT: Millbrook Press, 1994. 64p. $15.90; $5.95pa. ISBN 1-56294-746-X; 1-56294-337-5pa. (Spotlight on American History). 5-8

When the president and the vice president of the Central Pacific Railroad tried to drive in the last spike on the railroad to mark its official beginning in 1869, they both missed. They had to ask one of the Irish or Chinese workers to do the job for them. With this inability to drive one spike, they showed the value of the workers who had toiled unceasingly to finish the transcontinental railroad. The text, with photographs and prints, traces the progress of this major accomplishment from its groundbreaking in 1863 to its completion in 1869. Chronology, Further Reading, Bibliography, and Index.

655. Ellis, Rafaela. **Dwight D. Eisenhower: 34th President of the United States**. Ada, OK: Garrett Educational, 1989. 122p. $17.26. ISBN 0-944483-13-5. (Presidents of the United States). 5-9

The great-great-great-grandson of a German immigrant, Dwight David Eisenhower (1890-1969) rose from a life of poverty and love in dusty Abilene, Kansas, to go to West Point, achieve the highest military rank during World War II in Europe, and become President of the United States. The text relates information about his childhood and his career, including the Suez crisis, civil rights and Little Rock, the race in space, Khrushchev, and the U-2 affair. Photographs and reproductions enhance the text. Bibliography and Index.

656. Ellis, Rafaela. **Martin Van Buren: 8th President of the United States**. Ada, OK: Garrett Educational, 1989. 118p. $17.26. ISBN 0-944483-12-7. (Presidents of the United States). 5-9

Martin Van Buren (1782-1862) read law in New York State before becoming the attorney general of New York and then going to the Senate. He returned to New York as governor, and Andrew Jackson chose him to be Vice President. Van Buren became President after Jackson. During his time in office, the first major depression in the United States kept him from being reelected. Called the "Fox of Kinderhook" and "Little Magician," he knew how to manipulate events behind closed doors, but he could not end the economic problems. Bibliography and Index.

657. Emerson, Kathy Lynn. **Julia's Mending**. New York: Orchard, Franklin Watts, 1987. 136p. $11.95. ISBN 0-531-08319-5. 5-7

Julia, 12, does not want to stay with her country relatives in 1887 while her parents are missionaries in China. Her condescending attitude alienates her cousins, and when Julia breaks her leg, she cannot leave. While she is less mobile, she has to start talking to the family. When she realizes that the baby took the journal in which she had written nasty comments about everyone, she begins to adjust and make friends. Afterward, they work together to rescue a classmate.

658. Emert, Phyllis Raybin. **Top Lawyers and Their Famous Cases**. Minneapolis, MN: Oliver Press, 1996. 160p. $14.95. ISBN 1-881508-31-5. (Profiles). 5 up

Lawyers have always used the law and courts to make social, political, and economic change in the United States. The text presents some of these lawyers and their famous cases. They include Andrew Hamilton (1676?-1741) and the freedom to write the truth, John Adams (1735-1826) and the importance of justice, Abraham Lincoln (1809-1865) and the chance of equality for all, Belva Lockwood (1830-1917) and rights for Cherokees, Clarence Darrow (1857-1938) and support of society's outcasts, Robert H. Jackson (1892-1954) and his term as an international prosecutor of World War II Nazi criminals, Joseph Welch (1890-1960) as a legal folk hero during the McCarthy era, and Morris Dees (b. 1936) fighting against prejudice and hatred. Bibliography and Index.

659. English, June. **Transportation: Automobiles to Zeppelins**. New York: Scholastic, 1995. 154p. $16.95. ISBN 0-590-27550-X. 3-6

The text covers each topic in a double-page spread with a picture, diagram, general information, notes on historic interest, and photographs. Among the items are balloons, bridges, engines, tunnels, submersibles, bicycles, snowmobiles, and zeppelins. Glossary and Index.

660. Erdrich, Heidi Ellen. **Maria Tallchief**. Rick Whipple, illustrator. Austin, TX: Raintree/Steck-Vaughn, 1993. 32p. $13.98; $5.95pa. ISBN 0-8114-6577-2; 0-8114-4099-0pa. (Native American Stories). 3-5

Maria Tallchief (b. 1925) was the daughter of a white mother and a full-blooded Osage Indian. As an adult ballet dancer, she became a member of the Ballet Russe de Monte Carlo, where she met George Balanchine and married him. She then became the lead dancer for the New York City Ballet. After other endeavors, she and her sister established the Chicago City Ballet in 1980. History.

661. Erlich, Scott. **Paul Robeson: Singer and Actor**. New York: Chelsea House, 1988. 110p. $18.95; $7.95pa. ISBN 1-55546-608-7; 0-7910-0206-3pa. (Black Americans of Achievement). 5 up

As an athlete and scholar, Paul Robeson (1890-1976) graduated first in his college class before becoming a lawyer. His fame rested, however, in his acting and singing abilities. Noted for his dignified portrayals of Black characters, including Othello, he had a beautiful voice with which he popularized "Ol' Man River." He spoke for the poor and the oppressed and condemned racial injustice. The government punished him for sympathizing with Communist ideals and blacklisted him during the Red Scare of the 1950s. He spent much of his later life in the Soviet Union. Photographs enhance the text. Chronology, Further Reading, and Index.

662. Everett, Gwen. **John Brown: One Man Against Slavery**. New York: Rizzoli, 1993. 32p. $15.95. ISBN 0-8478-1702-4. 4-6

Expressionist illustrations created in 1941 help focus on the life of John Brown (1800-1859), who so badly wanted to end slavery. His daughter Anne, in a first-person narrative, tells of her feelings about his desires that led him to attack the government arsenal in Harpers Ferry, West Virginia, on October 16, 1859. Some historians believe that his action was one of the most important events leading to the Civil War.

663. Everett, Gwen. **Li'l Sis and Uncle Willie: A Story Based on the Life and Paintings of William Johnson**. William H. Johnson, illustrator. New York: Rizzoli, 1992. Unpaged. $14.95. ISBN 0-8478-1462-9. New York: Hyperion, 1994. Unpaged. $4.95pa. ISBN 1-56282-593-3pa. 3-6

Reproductions of Johnson's work accompany this fictionalized biography of his life. A little girl remembers her uncle coming to visit the family in Florence, South Carolina, before World War II. He told them about his years in Europe studying art, and when he returned to Europe he asked them to come visit him. The war intervened, and the uncle returned to New York. Li'l Sis realized that his letters had stopped coming. Her mother told her that her uncle's wife had died, and that he had gone to a hospital to live because his mind was not as good as it had been.

664. Evert, Jodi, ed. **Addy's Cook Book: A Peek at Dining in the Past with Meals You Can Cook Today**. Middleton, WI: Pleasant, 1994. 44p. $7.95pa. ISBN 1-56247-123-6pa. (American Girls Pastimes). 4-8

Illustrations and text cover cooking in the Civil War and kitchens in the 1860s after Addy and her family escaped from slavery in the South. Menus and recipes for breakfast, dinner, and favorite foods appear.

665. Evitts, William J. **Early Immigration in the United States**. New York: Franklin Watts, 1989. 63p. $18.34. ISBN 0-531-10744-2. (First Books). 4-6

Between 1820 and 1930, 37 million immigrants came to the United States. They either could no longer stay where they lived or the promise of America attracted them. In a brief history of the New World, the text discusses immigrants, including slaves and peasant classes, and how the Immigrant Aid Society tried to help as many people integrate as it could. Many immigrants, however, could only find the most menial jobs in sweatshops, as miners, and in farming. Photographs highlight the text. Further Reading and Index.

F

666. Faber, Doris. **Calamity Jane: Her Life and Her Legend**. Boston: Houghton Mifflin, 1992. 62p. $14.95. ISBN 0-395-56396-8. 5-9

Martha Jane Cannary (1852-1903), later known as Calamity Jane, became so large a legend that no one is sure what she did. She was a heroine of the Old West, a sharpshooter, a scout for General Custer, and the bride of Wild Bill Hickok. Or perhaps she was not. Faber tries to decide who she was from the most reliable sources available. Photographs, Sources, and Index.

667. Faber, Doris. **Eleanor Roosevelt: First Lady of the World**. Donna Ruff, illustrator. New York: Viking, 1985. 58p. $10.95; $4.99pa. ISBN 0-670-80551-3; 0-14-032103-9pa. (Women of Our Time). 2-6

Although loved by her alcoholic father and held at a distance by her reserved mother, "Nell" (1884-1962) grew up in the home of her stern grandmother after her parents' early deaths. She then attended a superb boarding school in England where she learned a lot. When she came back, she married her cousin Franklin and bore five children. After Franklin became Assistant Secretary of War, Eleanor discovered love letters in his luggage from her own secretary. Rather than mope, she decided to become useful. FDR contracted polio in 1921 when 39, and she helped his campaigning by speaking at Democratic meetings and staying involved. FDR got elected governor of New York and then President of the United States in 1932. Through FDR's three terms and the beginning of a fourth, Eleanor served the people. Truman asked her to represent the United States at the United Nations after FDR's death, and she did. About This Book.

668. Faber, Doris, and Harold Faber. **Great Lives: American Government**. New York: Scribner's, 1988. 278p. $22.95. ISBN 0-684-18521-0. 5-9

Short biographical profiles of 36 individuals who made important contributions to public office and contributed to the development of the United States throughout its history appear here. Included are Presidents, judges, and leaders in Congress: John Adams (1735-1826), Benjamin Franklin (1706-1790), Albert Gallatin (1761-1849), Alexander Hamilton (1755-1804), Thomas Jefferson (1743-1826), James Madison (1751-1836), John Marshall (1755-1835), James Monroe (1758-1831), George Washington (1732-1799), John Quincy Adams (1767-1848), John Calhoun (1782-1850), Samuel Houston (1792-1863), Henry Clay (1777-1852), Andrew Jackson (1767-1845), James Polk (1795-1845), Daniel Webster (1782-1852), William Jennings Bryan (1860-1925), Jefferson Davis (1808-1889), Robert La Follette (1855-1925), Abraham Lincoln (1809-1865), Justin Morrill (1810-1898), Jeannette Rankin (1880-1973), Theodore Roosevelt (1858-1919), Woodrow Wilson (1856-1924), Dwight David Eisenhower (1890-1969), Oliver Wendell Holmes (1841-1935), George Marshall (1880-1959), Eleanor Roosevelt (1884-1962), Franklin Delano Roosevelt (1882-1945), Margaret Chase Smith (1897-1994), Robert Taft (1889-1953), Harry Truman (1884-1972), Thurgood Marshall (1908-1993), Richard Nixon (1913-1994), and George Norris (1861-1944). Bibliography, Chronology, and Index.

669. Falkof, Lucille. **John F. Kennedy: 35th President of the United States**. Ada, OK: Garrett Educational, 1988. 120p. $17.26. ISBN 0-944483-03-8. (Presidents of the United States). 5-9

The text begins with John F. Kennedy's experience on PT 109 in the Solomon Islands during World War II; he saved a man after the Japanese sank his ship. It continues with his education at Harvard (a family tradition) and his winning the Pulitzer Prize for his book *Profiles in Courage* in 1957. After he became the youngest President, he faced the Cuban Missile Crisis in 1962 and delivered a memorable speech in Berlin in June 1963 where he said, "Ich bin ein Berliner." In July 1963, the nuclear test ban treaty was concluded. Kennedy (b. 1917) was assassinated on November 22 of the same year. Bibliography and Index.

670. Falkof, Lucille. **John Tyler: 10th President of the United States**. Ada, OK: Garrett Educational, 1990. 122p. $17.26. ISBN 0-9444483-60-7. (Presidents of the United States). 5-9

After running with William Henry Harrison on the "Tippecanoe and Tyler, Too" campaign slogan, John Tyler (1790-1862) became Vice President. What he did not expect was that Harrison would die in office. Tyler became a reluctant President, but he did his job honestly, an unhappy proposition for many in Congress. He did not receive credit for saving the annexation of Texas to the Union; instead he was criticized. After he left office, he was only summoned once to Washington for advice. He wanted to return to public office but was never asked. He died before the Union divided because of the Civil War. Bibliography and Index.

671. Falkof, Lucille. **Lyndon B. Johnson: 36th President of the United States**. Ada, OK: Garrett Educational, 1989. 120p. $17.26. ISBN 0-944483-20-8. (Presidents of the United States). 5-9

Lyndon B. Johnson (1908-1973) grew up in Texas and was elected to the House of Representatives from that state in 1937. He then went to the Senate and served as both minority and majority leader. He became the Vice President and then the President when John F. Kennedy was assassinated in 1963. He won his own election in 1964. He served in Washington during World War II and the Korean War, and was President during the Vietnam War. The text looks closely at his life and his family. Bibliography and Index.

672. Falkof, Lucille. **William H. Taft: 27th President of the United States**. Ada, OK: Garrett Educational, 1990. 124p. $17.26. ISBN 0-944483-56-9. (Presidents of the United States). 5-9

William Taft (1857-1930) gained experience as a young lawyer trying to clean up immoral law practices. Juries thwarted him, but he gained respect from those who realized the type of work that he completed. He served in Benjamin Harrison's and Theodore Roosevelt's administrations before becoming President. As President, he was unable to get a federal budget established and was not reelected, but he did make good appointments to the Supreme Court. After his presidency, he became a professor at Yale, and then he became the Chief Justice of the United States Supreme Court. Bibliography and Index.

673. Farley, Karin Clafford. **Robert H. Goddard**. Englewood Cliffs, NJ: Silver Burdett, 1991. 138p. $13.95; $6.95pa. ISBN 0-382-24171-1; 0-382-24177-0pa. (Pioneers in Change). 5-9

One day when a teenager, Robert Goddard (1882-1945) climbed into a tree and started looking at the sky. Influenced by the H. G. Wells story *The War of the Worlds*, he thought about traveling to places such as Mars, and his life changed. His scientific experiments began to focus on a way for that travel to occur. He studied electricity and physics in school and began to experiment with rockets in 1914, when he obtained two patents on his work. Later he began to develop weapons for the U.S. Army. He designed the forerunner of the jet engine for airplanes and began the development of jet-assisted takeoff engines for the U.S. Navy before his death. He and his heirs (on his behalf) filed 214 patents. Bibliography and Index.

674. Farley, Karin Clafford. **Samuel Adams: Grandfather of His Country**. Austin, TX: Raintree/Steck-Vaughn, 1994. 128p. $16.98. ISBN 0-8114-2379-4. (American Troublemakers). 6 up

Samuel Adams (1722-1803) believed, as John Locke espoused, that everyone is entitled to the natural rights of life, liberty, and property. Although he failed in several careers, he found his life's mission in politics and trying to free the colonies from unfair British rule. He led the Boston Tea Party, became a member of the Continental Congress, and signed the Declaration of Independence. Maps, Photographs, Key Dates, Glossary, Places to Visit, Bibliography and Recommended Readings, and Index.

675. Farley, Karin Clafford. **Thomas Paine: Revolutionary Author**. Austin, TX: Raintree/Steck-Vaughn, 1994. 128p. $16.98. ISBN 0-8114-2329-8. (American Troublemakers). 6 up

Thomas Paine (1737-1809) led a motley career. Born in England, he came to America where he published *Common Sense* and other works. He tried to get money from the French for the Continental army, but both England and France accused him of various crimes, and he was imprisoned briefly for wanting to save the life of Louis XVI. His writing and political philosophy, which showed his ideas of liberty and equality, helped to foment both the American and French Revolutions. Photographs, Key Dates, Glossary, Places to Visit, Bibliography and Recommended Readings, and Index.

676. Farris, John. **The Dust Bowl**. Maurie Manning, illustrator. New York: Lucent, 1990. 64p. $19.93. ISBN 1-56006-005-0. (World Disasters). 5-7

The text re-creates life on the southern Great Plains during the early 1900s, when farmers and sharecroppers tried to live off the land. The drought of the 1930s and the devastating dust storms that ensued ruined homes and farms. Drawings augment the discussion of why the Dust Bowl happened, how people survived it, and its effects. Glossary, Further Reading, and Index.

677. Feldman, Eve B. **Benjamin Franklin: Scientist and Inventor**. New York: Franklin Watts, 1990. 64p. $19.90. ISBN 0-531-10867-8. (First Books). 5-8

The text about Benjamin Franklin (1706-1790) emphasizes his ideas and inventions before and after he discovered electricity with his kite experiment. They include the lightning rod, the Franklin stove, the harmonica, bifocals, writing tables, and public libraries. Experiments You Can Do with Electricity, Glossary, For Further Reading, and Index.

678. Ferrell, Nancy Warren. **The Battle of the Little Bighorn in American History**. Springfield, NJ: Enslow, 1996. 128p. $18.95. ISBN 0-89490-768-9. 5-9

After relating background information about events and people prior to the Battle of Little Bighorn in June 1876, Ferrell then recounts the combat and its aftermath through the massacre at Wounded Knee in 1890. Her balanced reporting presents several sides of the conflict and introduces figures such as Red Cloud, Sitting Bull, and Crazy Horse. Index.

679. Ferrell, Nancy Warren. **The U.S. Air Force**. Minneapolis, MN: Lerner, 1990. 72p. $22.95. ISBN 0-8225-1433-8. 4-8

Air Force history begins in 1910, when Benjamin Foulois and Henry "Hap" Arnold became interested in flying after the Wright brothers achieved their successes. In 1915, Fokker designed a timing device to keep bullets from hitting airplane propellers as they were shot through them, and the airplane became an important part of

World War I. In the United States, Eddie Rickenbacker gained fame for his "aces." In 1935, the first B-17, or "Flying Fortress," was tested, and by mid-1941 aviation production in the United States was the world's largest industry. Because of the importance of the airplane, the Air Force gained equal status with the Army and the Navy in 1947. Its first major effort was the Berlin Airlift in 1948, followed by Korea and Vietnam. Concluding sections discuss how to join the Air Force, information about the Air Force Academy, and the major commands of the Air Force. Appendix and Index.

680.   Ferris, Jeri. **Go Free or Die**. Karen Ritz, illustrator. Minneapolis, MN: Carolrhoda, 1988. 63p. $17.50; $5.95pa. ISBN 0-87614-317-6; 0-87614-504-7pa. (Creative Minds). 3-6

Harriet Tubman (1820?-1913) had her own cruel experiences as a slave that led her to seek her freedom by fleeing north. She then returned to guide other slaves through the Underground Railroad and help them gain freedom.

681.   Ferris, Jeri. **Native American Doctor: The Story of Susan La Flesche Picotte**. Minneapolis, MN: Carolrhoda, 1991. 88p. $19.95; $6.95pa. ISBN 0-87614-443-1; 0-87614-548-9pa. 5-8

Susan La Flesche (1865-1915) of the Omaha tribe went East for her education, and after high school, received a scholarship to Hampton Institute in Virginia. There she met a woman doctor, and she decided that she wanted to be a doctor herself. After medical school, she returned to help her people, although she had a recurring illness that began when she took long train rides between her home and Pennsylvania. She found that she had many roles in her relationship with her people; she was doctor, teacher, nurse, financial and legal advisor, translator, and fighter against alcohol. Before she died, she helped raise money so that the Omaha people could have their own hospital. Notes, Bibliography, and Index.

682.   Ferris, Jeri. **Walking the Road to Freedom**. Peter E. Hanson, illustrator. Minneapolis, MN: Carolrhoda, 1988. 64p. $17.50; $5.95pa. ISBN 0-87614-318-4; 0-87614-505-5pa. (Creative Minds). 3-6

Sojourner Truth, born into slavery, was freed in 1827. She then became an abolitionist, speaking for slaves and for the rights of women throughout New England and the Midwest. She died in 1883.

683.   Ferris, Jeri. **What I Had Was Singing: The Story of Marian Anderson**. Minneapolis, MN: Carolrhoda, 1994. 96p. $19.95; $6.95pa. ISBN 0-87614-818-6; 0-87614-634-5pa. (Trailblazers). 4-7

Marian Anderson (1897-1993) was one of the twentieth century's greatest singers. She had to overcome prejudice against her race to show that she was one of the best. Ironically, Europeans accepted her long before her own country did; in 1955, she finally became the first African American to sing at the Metropolitan Opera House. The text looks at her life and what she achieved. Legacy, Bibliography, and Index. *Notable Children's Trade Books in the Field of Social Studies* and *Carter G. Woodson Award*.

684.   Fichter, George S. **The Space Shuttle**. New York: Franklin Watts, 1990. 64p. $17.71. ISBN 0-531-10815-5. (First Books). 4-6

This straightforward history of flight and space gives names and dates augmented by photographs. Index.

685.   Field, Rachel. **Calico Bush**. Allen Lewis, illustrator. 1931. New York: Macmillan, 1987. 224p. $16. ISBN 0-02-734610-2. New York: Yearling, 1990. 224p. $4.50pa. ISBN 0-440-40368-5pa. 4-8

In 1740, Marguerite and her grandmother arrive in the American colonies from France. Her grandmother dies soon after, and she becomes bound to a family leaving Massachusetts to go to a northern seacoast town. When they arrive, they discover that Indians think the land on which they will live is sacred, and they have burned down the house. Marguerite misses the celebration of Christmas and has to use her ingenuity to solve various problems. With the help of an old Scottish woman who knows about herbs, she copes with her changed situation. *Newbery Honor*.

686.   Fireside, Bryna J. **Is There a Woman in the House . . . or Senate?** Morton Grove, IL: Albert Whitman, 1994. 144p. $14.95. ISBN 0-8075-3662-8. 4-8

After looking at how Congress works, Fireside highlights some of the women who have served Congress in the Senate and in the House of Representatives. The women are Jeannette Rankin, first woman in Congress (1880-1973); Margaret Chase Smith, congresswoman and senator from Maine (1897-1994); Shirley Chisholm, African American representative (b. 1924); Bella Abzug, congresswoman (b. 1920); Barbara Jordan, congresswoman (1936-1995); Patricia Schroeder, Colorado congresswoman (b. 1940); Millicent Fenwick, congresswoman (b. 1910); Barbara Mikulski, congresswoman and senator (b. 1936); Nancy Kassebaum, senator (b. 1932); and Geraldine Ferraro, congresswoman (b. 1935). Selected Bibliography and Index.

687.   Fireside, Harvey, and Sarah Betsy Fuller. **Brown v. Board of Education: Equal Schooling for All**. Springfield, NJ: Enslow, 1994. 128p. $17.95. ISBN 0-89490-469-8. (Landmark Supreme Court Cases). 6-9

This Supreme Court case occurred in 1954 because Oliver Brown's eight-year-old daughter could not go to a school reserved for white children. He sued, saying that the schools for white and Black were unequal. The text looks at the ideas and arguments behind this case as well as the people who brought it to court. Notes, Glossary, Further Reading, and Index.

688. Fisher, Leonard Everett. **Ellis Island: Gateway to the New World**. New York: Holiday House, 1986. 64p. $15.95. ISBN 0-8234-0612-1. 3-7

Between 1892 and 1954, 15 million immigrants were processed at Ellis Island. After World War I, immigrants had to read and write in one language before they would be admitted. But fewer than 300,000 were denied admittance during the entire life of Ellis Island. Before 1892, individual states had admitted immigrants, but so many people began to come to the United States that the immigration process had to be turned over to the federal government. After World War II, Ellis Island was no longer needed, but it was restored during the late 1980s as a historical landmark. Photographs of immigrants underscore the importance of this place to those who were seeking safety. Index.

689. Fisher, Leonard Everett. **The Oregon Trail**. New York: Holiday House, 1990. 64p. $14.95. ISBN 0-8234-0833-7. 5-9

Stunning photographs of the trail, along with maps and paintings by Albert Bierstadt and A. J. Miller, highlight the story of 300,000 people who braved terrible conditions to reach the Willamette Valley of Oregon, mainly during the 1840s and 1850s. These people wanted to find jobs; claim "free" land; gain wealth in timber, fur, fish, and ore; have an adventure; convert the heathens; escape the claustrophobia of the East; or improve their health. They called the worst conditions "seeing the elephant," and some, who did not want to go north to Wyoming where a flat "bridge" over the Rocky Mountains had been located, went south and suffered, like the Donners in 1846. They also fought Native Americans, who were furious at the pioneers for killing the buffalo. Fewer people took the journey after the Civil War began. Index.

690. Fisher, Leonard Everett, author/illustrator. **Stars and Stripes: Our National Flag**. New York: Holiday House, 1993. Unpaged. $15.95. ISBN 0-8234-1053-6. 1-4

Fisher illustrates the words to the Pledge of Allegiance, with pictures of different flags that have flown as the symbol of the United States. He tells the date on which the flag replaced a previous flag and gives brief information about the enactment of the new flag.

691. Fisher, Leonard Everett. **Tracks Across America: The Story of the American Railroad, 1825-1900**. New York: Holiday House, 1992. 192p. $17.95. ISBN 0-8234-0945-7. 5 up

The text discusses the first railroads, the railroads going west, their effect during the Civil War, the first transcontinental railroad and Native American resistance, the robbers versus the owners, those who worked on the railroad, the disasters, and the progress in building different types of cars. Photographs supplement the text. Bibliography and Index.

692. Fitz-Gerald, Christine A. **Meriwether Lewis and William Clark**. Chicago: Childrens Press, 1991. 128p. $28.20. ISBN 0-516-03061-2. (World's Great Explorers). 5-8

The text begins with Lewis and Clark in the Pacific Northwest in 1805, where they have been wet for two weeks but are soon rewarded with their first view of the Pacific Ocean. The topics covered are the reasons for the journey, the plans and preparations, the Mississippi River, Fort Mandan, the High Plains, across the Rockies and beyond, their homeward journey, and the paths they took when they returned. Photographs, Timeline, Glossary, Bibliography, and Index.

693. Fitz-Gerald, Christine Maloney. **James Monroe: Fifth President of the United States**. Chicago: Childrens Press, 1987. 100p. $19.80. ISBN 0-516-01383-1. (Encyclopedia of Presidents). 4-9

James Monroe (1758-1831) was a careful and honest president, but he was not brilliant. He seemed old-fashioned in 1823 while his new country was changing. The tin can had been introduced, the Erie Canal would soon open, horse racing was common, and football had arrived on American campuses. Because he was concerned that foreign countries would invade South America, he proposed to Congress that the United States must go to war with any foreign country that came to North or South America; that no foreign nation could claim any more land in the Western Hemisphere; and that the United States, in turn, would stay out of European wars. Although Congress did not see the value of this plan, European countries were annoyed that the small United States was telling them what to do. Not for 100 years, until World War I, did the United States fight abroad. Chronology of American History and Index.

694. Fitz-Gerald, Christine Maloney. **William Henry Harrison: Ninth President of the United States**. Chicago: Childrens Press, 1987. 100p. $19.80. ISBN 0-516-01392-0. (Encyclopedia of Presidents). 4-9

In 1836, the Whig Party misrepresented their candidate William Henry Harrison (1773-1841), claiming that he was born in a log cabin. He was actually a member of a wealthy Virginia family. They told him to be quiet, and he added to his reputation, gained during his military career (his subordinates had called him "General Mum"), for saying little. In 1840, the party ran him for President with a southern Democrat, John Tyler, and used the slogan "Tippecanoe and Tyler, Too" to signify Harrison's defeat of the Shawnee in 1811. He served in Congress from Ohio before he became president, but after one month in office, he died of pneumonia. His most important decision was the appointment of Daniel Webster as Secretary of State. Photographs, Chronology of American History, and Index.

695. Fleischman, Paul. **The Borning Room**. New York: HarperCollins, 1991. 112p. $13.95. ISBN 0-06-023762-7. 6 up

The room in the house set aside for having babies and for laying out the dead is the one that Georgina enters and exits from the time she is born in 1851 until she dies. As her death approaches, she remembers the times in the room when she was nine and when she had her first child at 19. Each story she remembers tells something more about her Ohio family of abolitionists who worry about runaway slaves, the siege of Vicksburg, chloroform, and electricity. *Bulletin Blue Ribbon Book, American Library Association Notable Books for Children, American Library Association Best Books for Young Adults, Horn Book Fanfare Honor List, School Library Journal Best Book, Booklist Books for Youth Editors' Choices, IRA Teachers' Choices, Notable Children's Trade Books in the Field of Social Studies, NCTE Notable Trade Books in the Language Arts, Golden Kite Award Honor, Publishers Weekly Year's Best Books*, and *New York Public Library's Books for the Teen Age.*

696. Fleischman, Paul. **Bull Run**. New York: HarperCollins, 1993. 104p. $14.95; $4.95pa. ISBN 0-06-021446-5; 0-06-440588-5pa. 5 up

At the beginning of the Civil War, 10 people on each side begin their participation. They all meet at the First Battle of Bull Run in 1861. Their views of the war as they start and finish the battle are very different. A photographer tells of capturing the expressions of men not expecting to be alive the next evening; another character thinks of a depressed woman who has considered suicide. Other characters are slaves, soldiers, and citizens from North and South who seem to be mere observers until the battle begins. *Scott O'Dell Award, American Library Association Notable Books for Children, American Library Association Best Books for Young Adults, Horn Book Fanfare Book, School Library Journal Best Books, Notable Children's Trade Books in the Field of Social Studies, Booklist Books for Youth Editors' Choices, IRA Teachers' Choices, Publishers Weekly Year's Best Books*, and *New York Public Library's Books for the Teen Age.*

697. Fleischman, Paul. **Coming-and-Going Men**. Randy Gaul, illustrator. New York: HarperCollins, 1985. 147p. $12.95. ISBN 0-06-021883-5. 6 up

In 1800, four traveling men pass through New Canaan, Vermont: Mr. Cyrus Snype, silhouette cutter; Mr. Hamby, ballad and broadside seller; Simeon Fyfe and his son, who hate heroes but exhibit a panorama of the life of Washington; and Jonathan Wardell, a peddler with dyes and a book. Each man either finds himself transformed or changes someone in the town during that unusual year.

698. Fleischman, Paul. **Graven Images**. Andrew Glass, illustrator. New York: Harper, 1982. 85p. $14.89. ISBN 0-06-021907-6. 6 up

Graven images influence three people in the eighteenth century: a binnacle boy, an apprentice, and a sculptor. In one story, a poisoner who killed an entire ship's crew lives with his secret. In a second, an apprentice finally attracts the girl whom he has admired from afar. In the third, a sculptor attempts to carve a ghost's image on a marble statue. *Newbery Honor, American Library Association Notable Books for Children*, and *School Library Journal Best Books.*

699. Fleischman, Paul. **Path of the Pale Horse**. New York: HarperCollins, 1983. 160p. $13.89. ISBN 0-06-021905-X. 6 up

After Lep Nye's sister goes to live in Philadelphia during 1793 with an old family friend and does not contact the family, Lep goes to search for her. People throughout the city are dying from yellow fever, and Lep worries about her health as he discovers several frauds that the family friend has made. He finds not only her but himself as he pledges to dedicate his life to medicine in hope of saving people from disease.

700. Fleischman, Paul. **Townsend's Warbler**. New York: HarperCollins, 1992. 52p. $12.89. ISBN 0-06-021875-4. 3-7

In 1834, John Townsend (1809-1851) began a journey across the United States. He faced starvation, sandstorms, and Indian war parties, but he also found a bird that no scientist had ever seen. This black-and-yellow-striped warbler became Townsend's warbler. The text tells of his experience with complementary pictures from the times.

701. Fleischman, Sid. **The Abracadabra Kid: A Writer's Life**. New York: Greenwillow, 1996. 198p. $16. ISBN 0-688-14859-X. 6-10

Trained as a magician as well as a writer, Fleischman tells the story of his life in the style of his fiction, with anecdotes and action. He learned to write after his World War II service, when he worked on scripts for John Wayne movies, and he gives tips for writing well. He also reveals his sense of humor with self-deprecating commentary appropriate for the content.

702. Fleischman, Sid. **The Ghost in the Noonday Sun**. Peter Sis, illustrator. 1965. New York: Greenwillow, 1989. 144p. $16. ISBN 0-688-08410-9. New York: Scholastic, 1995. 144p. $3.50pa. ISBN 0-590-43662-7pa. 4-7

On Oliver Finch's 12th birthday, he awaits his father's arrival from a three-year whaling voyage. Instead, another captain kidnaps Oliver, takes him on a voyage, and tells him to find the ghost hoarding the gold. He and a sailor eventually foil the captain by hitting him on the head, making him think he is dead and that they are ghosts he sees. They escape the ship with food instead of booty, and another ship rescues them.

703. Fleischman, Sid. **Humbug Mountain**. 1978. Eric Von Schmidt, illustrator. Boston: Little, Brown, 1988. 149p. $4.95pa. ISBN 0-316-28613-3pa. 3-7

At 13, Willy goes with his family to find Sunrise, the town on the Missouri River started by his grandfather. They find it, but the river has receded, and boats can no longer stop there. To get people to visit, Willy and his father publish a newspaper containing enticing stories about the area. The family works together on unusual schemes to rejuvenate the town. *Boston Globe—Horn Book Award.*

704. Fleischman, Sid. **Jim Ugly**. Marcia Sewall, illustrator. New York: Greenwillow, 1992. 130p. $15. ISBN 0-688-10886-5. New York: Yearling, 1994. 130p. $3.99pa. ISBN 0-440-40803-2pa. 4-7

Jake, 12, begins his story at his father's 1894 burial in the Old West when he tries to get his father's dog, Jim Ugly, to follow him. The uninterested dog leads Jake instead. He shows Jake that his father is still alive but hiding from someone who wants to kill him for diamonds that Jake's father does not have. Jim helps Jake and his father escape the villains and encourages a romance between Jake's father and a lovely actress.

705. Fleischman, Sid. **The Midnight Horse**. Peter Sis, illustrator. New York: Greenwillow, 1990. 84p. $12.95. ISBN 0-688-09441-4. 4-6

Touch, an orphan, goes to live with his great-uncle in New Hampshire during the 1870s. He sees a thief and saves his inheritance as well as Miss Sally's. With magic tricks and other events, he and the village unseat the unsavory Judge Wigglesworth, which helps him avoid the orphanage. *Edgar Allen Poe Award* and *School Library Journal Best Book.*

706. Fleischman, Sid. **Mr. Mysterious & Co**. Eric Von Schmidt, illustrator. Boston: Little, Brown, 1962. 152p. $14.95; $4.95pa. ISBN 0-316-28578-1; 0-316-28614-1pa. 4-7

In 1884, Paul and Jane accompany their father, Mr. Mysterious, as he travels across the West in a wagon performing a magic show. They have various encounters and problems, but they have fun. When they decide to stake a homestead, a man comes to tell Mr. Mysterious that he is building a local theater.

707. Fleischman, Sid. **The 13th Floor: A Ghost Story**. Peter Sis, illustrator. New York: Greenwillow, 1995. 144p. $14. ISBN 0-688-14216-8. 3-6

In this historical fantasy, a distress message on the answering machine calls Buddy and his sister Liz, a lawyer, to a building that has no 13th floor. Then Buddy finds himself aboard the *Laughing Mermaid,* boat of an ancestor who was a privateer, and Liz ends up in Boston during 1692, where she must save another ancestor from a witch hunter, allowing the family line to continue. Buddy recounts the adventures that include such episodes as Spanish class notes, a dead pirate, a talking fish, orphans, and mistaken identity.

708. Fleischner, Jennifer. **The Apaches: People of the Southwest**. Brookfield, CT: Millbrook Press, 1994. 64p. $15.90. ISBN 1-56294-464-9. (Native Americans). 5-8

On September 4, 1886, the final surrender of the Apaches occurred when Geronimo agreed to the terms of U.S. General Miles. The Apaches migrated from Canada to the southwestern United States in the thirteenth and fourteenth centuries. They raided Spanish and Mexican settlements and fought the Mexicans in the Mexican War. Since then, the Apaches had to fight the U.S. government as they attempted to keep their traditions alive. Glossary, Bibliography, and Index.

709. Fleming, Alice. **P. T. Barnum: The World's Greatest Showman**. New York: Walker, 1993. 160p. $14.95. ISBN 0-8027-8234-5. 6-9

P. T. Barnum (1810-1891) may be linked to the circus, but his life shows that he was actually a promoter. He promoted oddities, exhibits (some of them scams), and himself. He introduced America to Jumbo the elephant, the soprano Jenny Lind, and General Tom Thumb. But most important, he entertained the public, which is what it wanted. For Further Reading and Index.

710. Fleming, Candace. **Women of the Lights**. James Watling, illustrator. Niles, IL: Albert Whitman, 1996. 79p. $13.95. ISBN 0-8075-9165-3. 4-6

Five American female lighthouse keepers are the focus of this collective biography, which describes their rescues and lifestyles in the lighthouses. To live in such solitary circumstances, they needed a special type of personality. The women include Hannah Thomas, who protected the Massachusetts coast in 1768; Ida Lewis; Kate Walker; Harriet Colfax; and Emily Fish. Bibliography and Index.

711. Forbes, Esther. **Johnny Tremain**. Lynd Ward, illustrator. 1943. Magnolia, MA: Peter Smith, 1992. 272p. $19.75. ISBN 0-8446-6600-9. New York: Dell, 1995. $4.99pa. ISBN 0-440-44250-8pa. 5 up

Johnny is very proud of the beautiful silver designs he created during his apprenticeship and brags about his talents to the other apprentices. When he decides to work on Sunday to complete an order for John Hancock, he breaks the law. He suffers for this decision by burning his hand so severely that he can no longer work in silver. As the American Revolution begins, a friend interests him in the Whig causes, and he starts to help the movement toward independence in any way that he can. *Newbery Medal*.

712. Force, Eden. **John Muir**. Englewood Cliffs, NJ: Silver Burdett, 1990. 144p. $13.95. ISBN 0-382-09965-6. (Pioneers in Change). 5-9

As a boy, John Muir (1838-1914) lived in Scotland before his father decided to immigrate to America. In America, he rose at 1 AM every morning to work on his inventions because his father said he could spend time in the morning before chores on the farm doing what he wanted. He invented a sawmill, a waterwheel, locks for the doors, a thermometer, a barometer, and many clocks, including an "early rising" machine. As he began to see the beauty of the world, his focus changed to understanding the relationship of humans to nature. His experiences led him to write Theodore Roosevelt, pleading for him to save the land while he could. Roosevelt met him in Yosemite and realized that John Muir knew the value of conservation. Important Dates, Bibliography, and Index.

713. Ford, Barbara. **Howard Carter: Searching for King Tut**. Janet Hamlin, illustrator. New York: Freeman, 1995. 63p. $14.95. ISBN 0-7167-6587-X. (Science Superstars). 4-8

Howard Carter (1873-1939) assisted others at the excavation at Tell el-Amarna in Egypt in the 1890s. In 1922, in the Valley of the Tombs of the Kings in Luxor, Egypt, he and George Herbert discovered the tomb of Tutankhamen, a pharaoh who reigned in the fourteenth century BC. Because it was untouched by grave robbers or other archaeologists, it held numerous treasures that Carter cataloged for 10 years. He also discovered the tombs of the pharaoh Thutmose IV and Queen Hatshepsut. Afterword, Index, Glossary, and Further Reading.

714. Ford, Barbara. **The Most Wonderful Movie in the World**. New York: Dutton, 1996. 160p. $14.99. ISBN 0-525-45455-1. 5-7

In 1941, Moira, 11, wants to see *Gone with the Wind*, the film of her favorite book. The Catholic Legion of Decency says that Catholics are not to see it, so she cannot go to the movie without going against her religion—and her parents. When she mentions it to a young priest, he suggests that she consult her conscience. She has to decide what to do about both her conscience and going to the movie.

715. Ford, Barbara. **Paul Revere: Rider for the Revolution**. New York: Enslow, 1997. 128p. $18.95. ISBN 0-89490-779-4. (Historical American Biographies). 6-9

Paul Revere (1735-1818) had a reputation as the one who made a midnight ride, but he had a wider involvement with the seeds of the American Revolution than most histories discuss. This biography looks at his impact on American history as it examines his life. Fact boxes and maps augment the text. Notes, Glossary, Further Reading, and Index.

716. Forrester, Sandra. **Sound the Jubilee**. New York: Lodestar, 1995. 184p. $15.99. ISBN 0-525-67486-1. 6-9

In 1861, Maddie, 11, accompanies her mistress, who broke the law by teaching her to read, to the Outer Banks of North Carolina to escape the war. Thinking that she has lost her chance to escape, Maddie is surprised when Union soldiers turn Roanoke Island into a place for runaway slaves. Her family escapes, but they face more hardships. Maddie helps teach the children but is delighted when the Yankees send a real teacher to the island. She is even more pleased when the teacher asks her to help with the younger children. The family strives for a better life, eventually leaving the island when they hear rumors of former owners returning to claim their land. *Notable Children's Trade Books in the Field of Social Studies*.

717. Foster, Leila Merrell. **David Glasgow Farragut: Courageous Navy Commander**. Chicago: Childrens Press, 1991. 107p. $19.30. ISBN 0-516-03273-9. (People of Distinction). 4 up

Born in Tennessee in 1801, David Farragut moved to New Orleans, where he went to live with a commander after his mother died. He became a midshipman on the *Essex* at the age of 9 or 10 and never left the U.S. Navy. He helped during the War of 1812 and made his major contributions during the Civil War, when he won two sea battles against the Confederacy, including the capture of Mobile, Alabama. His famous response "Damn the torpedoes! Full speed ahead" still resounds in Navy lore. For his efforts, he was awarded the rank of admiral, the first in the history of the U.S. Navy. Glossary and Index.

718.   Fowler, Zinita. **The Last Innocent Summer**. Forth Worth, TX: Texas Christian University, 1990. 145p. $11.95pa. ISBN 0-87565-045-7pa. 6-9

When Skeeter is 10 in the summer of 1931, she learns that not everything is within the control of her family when two young girls in Harris, Texas, are murdered. The following scandal and trial surprise her, but understanding the motivations of self-centered, uncaring people is more difficult to accept.

719.   Fox, Mary Virginia. **Chief Joseph of the Nez Perce Indians: Champion of Liberty**. Chicago: Childrens Press, 1992. 111p. $19.30. ISBN 0-516-03275-5. (People of Distinction). 5-9

Chief Joseph (1840-1904) tried to keep peace among the different bands of his tribe, the Nimipu, or Nez Perce, but he was unable to stop one man from killing white settlers as retribution for another white man's murder of his father. This act started the serious war between the tribe and the American army in 1877. Chief Joseph could not save all of his people, and they were relocated in Oklahoma. He tried throughout his life to regain the land in Oregon where they had lived for centuries, but he could not. Time Line and Index.

720.   Fox, Paula. **The Slave Dancer**. Eros Keith, illustrator. New York: Simon & Schuster, 1973. 192p. $16. ISBN 0-02-735560-8. New York: Dell, 1996. 192p. $4.50pa. ISBN 0-440-96132-7pa. 5-8

In 1840, Jessie, 14, serves unwillingly on a ship for four months as a fife player after slavers capture him in New Orleans. He sees Black African *cabocieros* sell their own people to the slavers, and he has to play while the slaves dance to exercise as the ship returns home. When the ship wrecks, he and one of the slaves survive. They wash ashore, and a Black man guides them north. As an adult, Jessie cannot listen to music because of the horror of his experience. *Newbery Medal.*

721.   Fradin, Dennis. **The Flag of the United States**. Chicago: Childrens Press, 1988. 45p. $18; $5.50pa. ISBN 0-516-01158-8; 0-516-41158-6pa. 2-4

The text traces the history of the American flag after talking about flags in other countries throughout history. Stories about the American flag include Betsy Ross's input and the composition of "The Star-Spangled Banner." Photographs highlight the text. Words You Should Know and Index.

722.   Fradin, Dennis B. **The Connecticut Colony**. Chicago: Childrens Press, 1990. 159p. $24.70. ISBN 0-516-00393-3. 5-9

The Connecticut colony grew from 1638 to 1675. It faced and thwarted problems from 1675 to 1689. Following this were the colonial wars from 1689 to 1750. Capsule biographies of John Winthrop, Jr., Israel Putnam, Nathan Hale, Jonathan Trumbull and his family, Benedict Arnold, Joseph Plumb Martin, and Roger Sherman appear in the text. Prints and photographs supplement the text. Time Line and Index.

723.   Fradin, Dennis B. **The Delaware Colony**. Chicago: Childrens Press, 1992. 159p. $24.70. ISBN 0-516-00398-4. 5-9

Delaware was under Swedish rule from 1638 to 1655, Dutch rule from 1655 to 1664, and English rule from 1664 to 1704. From 1705 to 1760, it grew until the Revolutionary War period. People with capsule biographies in the text are Henry Hudson, Peter Minuit, Johan Printz, William Penn, Caesar Rodney, Thomas McKean, and John Dickinson. Prints and photographs highlight the information. Time Line and Index.

724.   Fradin, Dennis B. **The Georgia Colony**. Chicago: Childrens Press, 1990. 159p. $24.70. ISBN 0-516-00392-5. 5-9

The text covers the founding of the Georgia colony and its life through the early 1760s. With prints and photographs as illustration, the information also includes brief biographies of Tomochichi, James Oglethorpe, Mary Musgrove, George Whitefield, Henry Ellis, and Button Gwinnett. Time Line and Index.

725.   Fradin, Dennis B. **The Maryland Colony**. Chicago: Childrens Press, 1990. 159p. $24.70. ISBN 0-516-00394-1. 5-9

From 1634 to 1689, Maryland was an area growing in population. It was a royal colony from 1689 to 1715 and a proprietary colony during 1715-1760. Prints and photographs complement the history. The capsule biographies include George Calvert, Cecil Calvert, Margaret Brent, Thomas Cresap, Charles Carroll, Benjamin Banneker, Charles Willson Peale, and James McHenry. Time Line and Index.

726.   Fradin, Dennis B. **The Massachusetts Colony**. Chicago: Childrens Press, 1986. 159p. $24.70. ISBN 0-516-00386-0. 5-9

From the time of the first settlements, life in the Massachusetts colony was important for the birth of the United States. There are capsule biographies of Squanto, Massasoit, William Bradford, Anne Bradstreet, Cotton Mather, Phillis Wheatley, Samuel Adams, Paul Revere, John Hancock, and John Adams. Prints and photographs complement the text. Time Line and Index.

727.   Fradin, Dennis B. **The New Hampshire Colony**. Chicago: Childrens Press, 1988. 159p. $24.70. ISBN 0-516-00388-7. 5-9

In telling of the early life in New Hampshire through colonial times, the text gives background history and brief biographies of Passaconaway, Eleazar Wheelock, Robert Rogers, the Johnson family of Charlestown, Benning Wentworth, John Wentworth, John Stark, and John Sullivan. Prints and photographs reveal the era. Time Line and Index.

728.   Fradin, Dennis B. **The New Jersey Colony**. Chicago: Childrens Press, 1991. 159p. $24.70. ISBN 0-516-00395-X. 5-9

The English took over the colony of New Jersey between 1664 and 1702. For the years before the Revolutionary War began, 1702-1760, it stayed a royal colony. The work has capsule biographies of Lewis Morris, Patience Lovell Wright, William Franklin, Reverend John Witherspoon, Francis Hopkinson, Molly Pitcher, and William Livingston. Prints, photographs, and text. Time Line and Index.

729.   Fradin, Dennis B. **The New York Colony**. Chicago: Childrens Press, 1988. 159p. $24.70. ISBN 0-516-00389-5. 5-9

Early New York colony was colonized by the Dutch until the English took over. Brief biographies of Hiawatha, Henry Hudson, Peter Minuit, Peter Stuyvesant, Captain William Kidd, Joseph Brant, Margaret Corbin, John Jay, and Alexander Hamilton show New York before the Revolutionary War. Prints and photographs highlight the text, which covers the history of the times. Time Line and Index.

730.   Fradin, Dennis B. **The North Carolina Colony**. Chicago: Childrens Press, 1991. 159p. $24.70. ISBN 0-516-00396-8. 5-9

Prints, photographs, and text introduce the history of the North Carolina colony. Topics include the Native Americans who lived there when the Roanoke colony was established in 1585 (and later disappeared); the westward expansion from 1705 to 1760; the revolutionary aspects of 1764-1783; and the Declaration of Independence. Capsule biographies include Sir Walter Raleigh, Sir John White, John Lawson, Blackbeard, Daniel Boone, Cornelius Harnett, James Iredell, and Richard Dobbs Spaight. Time Line and Index.

731.   Fradin, Dennis B. **The Pennsylvania Colony**. Chicago: Childrens Press, 1988. 159p. $24.70. ISBN 0-516-00390-9. 5-9

From the first colonists, the Pennsylvania area began to grow from 1684 to 1750. Also included is the life in Pennsylvania from 1750 to 1754. Capsule biographies and accompanying prints and photographs give a sense of William Penn, Benjamin Franklin, John Dickinson, Robert Morriss, Haym Salomon, Betsy Ross, James Wilson, and *Gouverneur* Morris. Time Line and Index.

732.   Fradin, Dennis B. **The Rhode Island Colony**. Chicago: Childrens Press, 1989. 159p. $24.70. ISBN 0-516-00391-7. 5-9

The early years of the Rhode Island colony lasted from 1636 to 1660. During 1700-1756, important events involved planters, pirates, slaves, and ships. Afterward came the Revolutionary War. Brief biographies of Roger Williams, Anne Marbury Hutchinson, King Philip Metacomet, Stephen Hopkins, Esek Hopkins, Abraham Whipple, and Nathanael Greene reveal their contributions to the state. Prints and photographs highlight various aspects. Time Line and Index.

733.   Fradin, Dennis B. **The South Carolina Colony**. Chicago: Childrens Press, 1992. 159p. $24.70. ISBN 0-516-00397-6. 5-9

The early period in South Carolina lasted from 1680 to 1729, the golden age from 1730 to the 1760s, and the revolutionary period after that. Biographical capsules of Dr. Henry Woodward, Blackbeard, Eliza Lucas Pinckney, Dr. Alexander Garden, Henry Laurens, John Laurens, Christopher Gadsden, and Francis Marion have accompanying prints and photographs. Time Line and Index.

734.   Fradin, Dennis B. **The Virginia Colony**. Chicago: Childrens Press, 1986. 159p. $24.70. ISBN 0-516-00387-9. 5-9

Jamestown, Virginia's first settlement, had its years of turmoil and growth from 1609 to the mid-1700s, prior to the revolutionary period. Accented with prints and photographs are the history and brief biographies of Powhatan, John Smith, Pocahontas, John Rolfe, George Washington, Patrick Henry, Thomas Jefferson, and Henry "Light-Horse Harry" Lee. Time Line and Index.

735. Fradin, Dennis Brindell. **Hiawatha: Messenger of Peace**. New York: Margaret K. McElderry, 1992. 40p. $16. ISBN 0-689-50519-1. 2-4

Longfellow's Hiawatha is not the real man. The real one lived 500 years ago and was an Iroquois Indian. He overcame personal tragedy when his daughters were murdered by an enemy tribe, and he united with a Huron Indian, Degandawida, to create the Iroquois Federation, a league of five previously warring tribes—the Oneida, the Onondaga, the Mohawk, the Cayuga, and the Seneca. This union lasted for 300 years. Photographs, maps, and reproductions enhance the text. Bibliography and Index.

736. Fradin, Dennis Brindell. **Washington's Birthday**. Springfield, NJ: Enslow, 1990. 48p. $15.95. ISBN 0-89490-235-0. (Best Holiday Books). 2-4

Photographs and drawings complement the text, which tells about George Washington's (1732-1799) achievements and proves why he, as the first President of the United States, deserves a holiday in his honor. Glossary and Index.

737. Fradin, Dennis Brindell. **We Have Conquered Pain: The Discovery of Anesthesia**. New York: Margaret K. McElderry, 1996. 148p. $16. ISBN 0-689-50587-6. 6-9

The text looks at the four nineteenth-century men who claimed to popularize nitrous oxide and ether as ways of curbing pain through anesthetics. It shows the rivalries and the human greed and jealousy that have continually marred medical advances as it examines the claims of these men: Crawford Long, Horace Wells, William Morton, and Charles Jackson. Photographs, Bibliography, and Index.

738. Frank, Andrew. **The Birth of Black America: The Age of Discovery and the Slave Trade**. New York: Chelsea House, 1996. 111p. $19.95; $8.95pa. ISBN 0-7910-2257-9; 0-7910-2683-3pa. (Milestones in Black American History). 6-8

The text covers the history of slavery in the United States. It relates the beginning of slave usage in North America, the slave trade across the Atlantic, the middle passage, and what happened when the slaves arrived. Primary source accounts from people who endured the horror make this a powerful resource. Chronology, Further Reading, and Index.

739. Frankl, Ron. **Charlie Parker: Musician**. New York: Chelsea House, 1993. 127p. $18.95. ISBN 0-7910-1134-8. (Black Americans of Achievement). 6 up

Charlie Parker (1920-1955) perfected the musical style known as bebop. He grew up in Kansas City, learning to play the saxophone and joining a band when only 14. He then went to New York in 1942 and began to work out bebop's complex approach to harmony and rhythm. He found that its freedom allowed him to stress improvisation rather than melody. He was able to invent new variations of songs each time he played. He had begun shooting heroin at 17, and his dependency on drugs and alcohol marred his later life. Photographs enhance the text. Further Reading, Glossary, and Index.

740. Fraser, Jane. **Walter White: Civil Rights Leader**. New York: Chelsea House, 1991. 111p. $18.95. ISBN 1-55546-617-6. (Black Americans of Achievement). 6-9

Walter White (1893-1955) served as the director of the National Association for the Advancement of Colored People (NAACP) from 1931 to 1955. He risked his life to personally investigate 41 lynchings and eight race riots. The organization, under his leadership, began to overcome segregated housing, education, employment, military service, and public facilities. White also wrote several books. Photographs enhance the text. Chronology, Further Reading, and Index.

741. Fraser, Mary Ann, author/illustrator. **In Search of the Grand Canyon: Down the Colorado with John Wesley Powell**. New York: Redfeather, Holt, 1995. 70p. $14.95. ISBN 0-8050-3495-1. 3-6

Until May 24, 1869, when Major John Wesley Powell and nine men set out to explore the Colorado River, the area was a blank space on existing maps. The Anasazi people had once lived there, but trappers and guides had only passed by it. Powell thought it would be important as the nation grew. The text looks at each day of the exploration and tells of the rapids, whirlpools, and canyons that Powell found along the river. Photographs and drawings augment the text. Bibliography and Index.

742. Fraser, Mary Ann, author/illustrator. **Sanctuary: The Story of Three Arch Rocks**. New York: Henry Holt, 1994. Unpaged. $15.95. ISBN 0-8050-2920-6. 3-5

In 1903, William Finley and Herman Bohlman went to Three Arch Rocks to set up camp. They were trying to find ways to save the sea lions and nesting colonies that lived on the island from gunmen who were disturbing them. For two weeks they climbed the rocks and took photographs of the seabirds and mammals. When they showed their photographs to lawmakers, Theodore Roosevelt listened, and in 1907 he made Three Arch Rocks the West Coast's first wildlife sanctuary.

743. Fraser, Mary Ann, author/illustrator. **Ten Mile Day: And the Building of the Transcontinental Railroad**. New York: Henry Holt, 1993. Unpaged. $15.95; $6.95pa. ISBN 0-8050-1902-2; 0-8050-4703-4pa. 4-6

Theodore Judah had a dream of a transcontinental railway. The building began in 1863, but in 1868, after the Union Pacific team had built seven miles in one day, the leader of the Central Team said that it could build 10 miles in one day. Judah wagered $10,000 that they could not. On April 28, 1869, the men of the Central Team worked in various segments to lay as much track as they could, and they successfully completed more than 10 miles. Judah lost the bet, but on May 10, 1869, the transcontinental railroad of his dream was completed. Suggested Reading and Index.

744. Freedman, Russell. **Buffalo Hunt**. New York: Holiday House, 1988. 52p. $16.95. ISBN 0-8234-0702-0. 5-8

Freedman's introduction presents Native American lore about the buffalo and the importance of this animal to the Indians. Information covers the preparation for a hunt, techniques for approaching the herd, the attack, and the stripping of the dead buffalo. He concludes by noting that repeating rifles, railroad sports, and bounty hunters depleted the herds and, along with them, the food, clothing, and livelihoods that the buffalo provided for many Native Americans. Photographs and reproductions embellish the text. Bibliography and Index. *Booklist Starred Review, Bulletin Blue Ribbon Book, Horn Book Fanfare Honor List, Kirkus Pointer Review, Publishers' Weekly Starred Review*, and *School Library Journal Best Book*.

745. Freedman, Russell. **Cowboys of the Wild West**. New York: Clarion, 1985. 103p. $15.95; $7.95pa. ISBN 0-89919-301-3; 0-395-54800-4pa. 6-8

The cowboy trade began in Mexico during the sixteenth century, when the Spanish brought the first domesticated horses and cattle to North America. *Vaqueros*, barefoot Indian cow herders, were the first to work with these animals, and to keep them together, they used *la riata*, or the lariat. After the Civil War, men went to Texas, where the animals roamed free, and began rounding them up. The meat-packing industry in Chicago needed meat, and the men wanted the money, so they rode the herds to Kansas railroad towns for shipment to Chicago and Kansas City. The typical cowboy was rarely older than 30 because the long days and hard work tired even the strongest. Their clothes had to survive all weather conditions and protect them from thorns. Hats and bandannas were useful in a variety of ways, including as tourniquets for snakebite. Movie and television stereotypes ignore the difficulty of the job and the fact that most cowboys were either Black or Mexican. Bibliography.

746. Freedman, Russell. **Eleanor Roosevelt: A Life of Discovery**. New York: Clarion, 1993. 198p. $17.95. ISBN 0-89919-862-7. 6-12

"If anyone were to ask me what I want out of life I would say—the opportunity to do something useful, for in no other way, I am convinced, can true happiness be attained." Eleanor Roosevelt (1884-1962), who considered herself an "ugly duckling," showed her values with that statement. As a young girl, she was very serious and reserved. She had to change when she began to travel extensively and to go where her wheelchair-bound husband could not. After his death, she was an American delegate to the United Nations, and Harry Truman called her the "First Lady of the World." Photographs, Books About and by Eleanor Roosevelt, and Index. *Newbery Honor* and *Bulletin Blue Ribbon Book*.

747. Freedman, Russell. **Franklin Delano Roosevelt**. New York: Clarion, 1990. 200p. $16.95; $7.95pa. ISBN 0-89919-379-X; 0-395-62978-0pa. 5-8

Born in 1882 to a wealthy family, Franklin Delano Roosevelt (1882-1945) became a philatelist, naturalist, and photographer before he entered Harvard. His father's death while he was a freshman freed his mother to come to Boston and live near him. At Harvard, Roosevelt was happiest working on the *Crimson*. After graduation, he married Eleanor Roosevelt. He became the Secretary of the Navy during World War I, and his idea to mine the North Sea to stop German U-boats proved successful. Verdun and the 500,000 who died there horrified him, and he wanted to join the army, but the war ended too soon. Eleanor found out by 1920 that he had been unfaithful, and they began an emotional estrangement that probably lasted throughout their marriage. But in 1921, when polio struck Franklin, their lives changed. Eleanor encouraged and supported his continued public life, although his mother did not. His illness helped him understand the difficulties of people who found themselves in situations through no fault of their own. Roosevelt became President in 1932, during the height of the Depression, and his New Deal program, including the Works Progress Administration, helped save the country. The first part of his term is known as the "Hundred Days." During his fourth term, and near the end of World War II, his strength waned, and he died in 1945 at Warm Springs, Georgia. Places to Visit, FDR Photo Album, Books About FDR, and Index. *Bulletin Blue Ribbon Book*.

748. Freedman, Russell. **An Indian Winter**. Karl Bodmer, illustrator. New York: Holiday House, 1992. 88p. $21.95. ISBN 0-8234-0930-9. 4-6

In 1833, Prince Alexander Philip Maximillian, a German prince, and Karl Bodmer, a Swiss painter, went into the heart of Indian country up the Missouri River. They spent the winter with the People of the First Man, the Mandan Indians, in contemporary North Dakota. The prince kept a detailed journal, while the artist painted pictures of everyday scenes. The text tells their story and that of the Indians who fed and housed them. In 1837, smallpox almost eradicated the Mandans and the Hidatsas, and when the settlers began slaughtering buffalo in the 1860s and 1870s, the tribes vanished completely. Bibliography and Index.

749.   Freedman, Russell. **Kids at Work: Lewis Hine and the Crusade Against Child Labor**. Lewis Hine, photographs. New York: Clarion, 1994. 104p. $16.95. ISBN 0-395-58703-4. 5 up

Lewis Wickes Hine (1874-1940) photographed thousands of working children before World War I. In 1911, more than 2 million American children under 16 were a regular part of the workforce, many working 12 or more hours a day, six days a week, in hazardous conditions for pitiful wages. Hine risked his life to get his photos because no employer wanted pictures of their underage workers. Hine had learned photography to offer his students an after-school activity, but when he spent time at Ellis Island photographing immigrants, giving them the grace and dignity they deserved, he became a master photographer. His photos led the National Child Labor Committee to fight for and gain stronger laws against child labor. Hine, however, died in poverty, unable to get funding for his projects and finally having to sell all that he owned. But his pictures are part of America's memory. Declaration of Dependence, Child Labor Then and Now, Bibliography, and Index. *Orbis Pictus Honor Book* and *Jane Addams Children's Book Award*.

750.   Freedman, Russell. **Lincoln: A Photobiography**. New York: Clarion, 1987. 150p. $16.95; $7.95pa. ISBN 0-89919-380-3; 0-395-51848-2pa. 6 up

Abraham Lincoln (1809-1865) had wit and good humor that attracted crowds as much as his height did. He began his career as a country lawyer, courted and married Mary Todd, and had a difficult presidency in the White House trying to oversee the Civil War. Freedman uses photographs and prints to illustrate his text about Lincoln's life. *Newbery Medal*.

751.   Freedman, Russell. **The Wright Brothers: How They Invented the Airplane**. New York: Holiday House, 1990. 129p. $18.95. ISBN 0-8234-0875-2. 4-8

The two Wright brothers, Wilbur (1867) and Orville (1871), were extraordinarily close until Wilbur died of typhoid in 1912. Their first flight in 1904 for one minute and 36 seconds caused Amos Root to say, ". . . like [Columbus] . . . these two brothers have probably not even a faint glimpse of what their discovery is going to bring to the children of men." Their repeatedly longer flights attracted attention from other experimenters like the German Lilienthal, Langley, and Chanute. By 1905, they could stay in the air more than 30 minutes. In 1908, although the French were suspicious of their plane and considered themselves the aviation leaders, Wilbur went to France to help. He awed them with his plane's grace and reported to Orville that Blériot was ecstatic. Blériot flew across the English Channel in 1909. Orville began to make demonstration flights at Fort Meyer, Virginia. After their achievements, they received a hero's welcome when they returned home to Dayton, Ohio. At Wilbur's death, Orville seemed to lose interest in the air. Now wealthy, he spent his time tinkering with all types of mechanical things, including the toys of his nieces and nephews, until his own death in 1948. When *Apollo II* landed on the moon, Neil Armstrong carried a piece of the cotton wing from the 1903 flight that started it all. Places to Visit, For Further Reading, and Index. *Booklist Starred Review*, *Bulletin Blue Ribbon Book*, *Horn Book Fanfare Honor List*, *Kircus Pointer Review*, *Notable Children's Trade Books in the Field of Social Studies*, and *School Library Journal Best Book*.

752.   Freedman, Suzanne. **Ida B. Wells-Barnett and the Antilynching Crusade**. Brookfield, CT: Millbrook Press, 1994. 32p. $13.40; $4.95pa. ISBN 1-56294-377-4; 1-56294-859-8pa. (Gateway Civil Rights). 4-6

Ida Wells-Barnett (1862-1931) wrote about three murders in Memphis, Tennessee, in the Black newspaper for which she was editor and then left on a business trip. She heard that if she returned, she, too, would be murdered, so she decided to stay in New York and write against lynchings for a national newspaper. Her inflamed article concerned three Black men who had shot at white intruders in their store and been arrested. In the middle of the night, a group of white men took them from the jail to an area outside the city limits. They had arranged for a train whistle to blow as they shot the men so that others would not know what they had done. This act and many similar ones were what Wells-Barnett fought during her career as a journalist and a civil rights leader. Important Dates, Find Out More, and Index.

753.   Freedman, Suzanne. **Louis Brandeis: The People's Justice**. Springfield, NJ: Enslow, 1996. 104p. $18.95. ISBN 0-89490-678-X. (Justices of the Supreme Court). 5-8

Louis Brandeis (1856-1941) was the first Jew to serve on the Supreme Court. Woodrow Wilson nominated him in 1916. Brandeis was also the first progressive Justice, a social reformer. The text looks at his life and his contributions to the court. Bibliography, Glossary, Notes, and Index.

754. Freeman, Suzanne T. **The Cuckoo's Child**. New York: Greenwillow, 1996. 256p. $15. ISBN 0-688-14290-7. 6-9

In 1962, Mia wants to leave Beirut, and after her parents disappear on a sailing trip, she goes to stay with her mother's sister in Ionia, Tennessee. She finds that the town has little tolerance for outsiders, and although she tries to adjust, she has difficulty fitting into their mold. She misses her parents, who have not been found; dislikes her aunt's married boyfriend; and hates attending the summer Bible school. She had dreamed of living in America while still in Beirut, but she realizes that what she really wants is a home where she feels comfortable.

755. Friedrich, Elizabeth. **Leah's Pony**. Michael Garland, illustrator. Honesdale, PA: Boyds Mills Press, 1996. 32p. $14.95. ISBN 1-56397-189-5. 1-4

During the Great Depression of the 1930s, Leah and her family live in the Dust Bowl of the Midwest, where drought and grasshoppers keep all crops from growing. When her family's farm is to be sold at auction, she decides to sell her beloved pony in hope of getting enough money to buy her father's tractor for him. Her bid of one dollar stands at the auction, and other people begin bidding ridiculously low prices for items and then returning them to the family. The next day, Leah finds her pony in the barn where its buyer has placed it for her.

756. Friese, Kai Jabir. **Rosa Parks: The Movement Organizes**. Eric Velasquez, illustrator. Englewood Cliffs, NJ: Silver Burdett, 1990. 130p. $12.95. ISBN 0-382-09927-3. (History of the Civil Rights Movement). 6-9

Rosa Parks (b. 1913) is the woman who refused to move to the back of the Montgomery, Alabama, bus. This refusal started the bus boycott in 1956, which lasted more than a year. She paid for her decision by being arrested, but her sacrifice allowed others to sit as she did without anyone forcing them to move. Timetable, Suggested Reading, Sources, and Index.

757. Fritz, Jean. **And Then What Happened, Paul Revere?** Margot Tomes, illustrator. New York: Coward, 1973. 48p. $14.95; $5.95pa. ISBN 0-698-20274-0; 0-698-20541-3pa. 2-6

Paul Revere (1735-1818) seems scatterbrained, but Fritz shows that he actually was interested in many different things as he tried to support his large family. A silversmith by trade, he also rang the town's bells when anything occurred. On his ride, he advised John Hancock and Samuel Adams to leave Lexington, and the British actually caught Revere before becoming distracted by others arriving. Some of Revere's church bells still ring in New England steeples. Notes from the Author.

758. Fritz, Jean. **Around the World in a Hundred Years: From Henry the Navigator to Magellan**. Anthony Bacon Venti, illustrator. New York: Putnam, 1994. 128p. $17.95. ISBN 0-399-22527-7. 4-7

In 1400, map makers named the space around the edge of the areas they had drawn as the Unknown. Later that century, explorers ventured into the Unknown searching for routes to the gold of China. The text discusses explorations, beginning with Prince Henry the Navigator (1394-1460) and ending with Magellan (1480?-1521), whose ship (after he had died in the Philippines) continued around the world. The explorers include Bartholomew Diaz exploring from 1487 to 1500, Christopher Columbus (1492-1504), Vasco da Gama (1497-1502), Pedro Álvares Cabral (1500-1501), John Cabot (1497-1498), Amerigo Vespucci (1499-1501), Juan Ponce de León (1513), and Vasco Núñez de Balboa (1513). Notes, Bibliography, and Index.

759. Fritz, Jean. **Brady**. Lynd Ward, illustrator. 1960. New York: Penguin, 1987. 223p. $13.95. ISBN 0-14-032258-2. 4-7

Brady accidentally finds an Underground Railway site in 1836 and runs home to tell his parents. They tell him he is wrong and should not make such foolish claims. When his father is injured in a fire, Brady takes slaves to another station along the Railway without telling his father. When his father becomes aware of Brady's deed, he acknowledges his approval by writing in the family Bible that Brady has done a man's job.

760. Fritz, Jean. **Bully for You, Teddy Roosevelt**. Mike Wimmer, illustrator. New York: Putnam, 1990. 127p. $20.95. ISBN 0-399-21769-X. 5-9

Theodore Roosevelt (1858-1919) described things that he especially liked as "Bully!" Among the activities he pursued were studying birds, shooting lions, roping steers, writing books, exploring South American rivers, and battling in Cuba. He fought corruption and worked for peace, winning the Nobel Peace Prize. He met with John Muir, saw the beauty of America, and used his presidential power to preserve it. Notes, Bibliography, and Index.

761. Fritz, Jean. **The Cabin Faced West**. Feodor Rojankovsky, illustrator. New York: Coward-McCann, 1958. 124p. $14.95. ISBN 0-698-20016-0. New York: Puffin, Penguin, 1987. 124p. $4.99pa. ISBN 0-14-032256-6pa. 4-7

Ann and her family move from Gettysburg in 1784 to the wilderness frontier of Pennsylvania. She misses her friends, so her mother tells her that they will take time off from all their work when an occasion for a party arises. One evening a stranger comes to visit, and they have a wonderful party. When the guest leaves, she is happy that she lives on Hamilton Hill. Their guest was George Washington.

762. Fritz, Jean. **The Double Life of Pocahontas**. Ed Young, illustrator. New York: Putnam, 1983. 96p. $14.95. ISBN 0-399-21016-4. New York: Viking, 1987. 96p. $3.99pa. ISBN 0-14-032257-4pa. 6-9

In this story of Pocahontas (d. 1617), Fritz shows that all was not happy in the colony where Pocahontas met the English settlers. When she sponsored John Smith, she was probably taking a traditional role in the tribe to support someone who wanted to be accepted in the group. She was later probably kidnapped and had to stay with the English. Then she married John Rolfe and went with him to England. In England, she saw John Smith after a year because he neglected to see her sooner even though she had saved his life. Notes, Bibliography, and Index.

763. Fritz, Jean. **Early Thunder**. Lynd Ward, illustrator. 1967. New York: Penguin, 1987. 256p. $4.99pa. ISBN 0-14-032259-0pa. 5-9

When he is 14 in 1775 and living in the American colonies, Daniel West supports the British king. But when fellow Tories throw stones into a judge's window while the man lies dying of smallpox, he becomes infuriated. He begins to change his allegiance when he sees people he respects support the Rebel cause.

764. Fritz, Jean. **George Washington's Mother**. DyAnne DiSalvo-Ryan, illustrator. New York: Grosset, 1992. 48p. $7.99. ISBN 0-448-40385-4. 2-4

Fritz tells the story of George Washington's mother, Mary (1708-1789), and her relationship to her children, including her son George. The interesting approach gives a view of George Washington from a mother who is concerned about him, like any mother would be for her child.

765. Fritz, Jean. **The Great Little Madison**. New York: Putnam, 1989. 159p. $15.95. ISBN 0-399-21768-1. 5-8

James Madison (1751-1836) was always committed to the unity of the United States, but his weak voice and small stature kept him from speaking effectively. He clashed with Patrick Henry, had a romance with and married the young widow Dolley Payne Todd, and was friends with Thomas Jefferson. He made important intellectual contributions to the beginning of the nation. Notes, Bibliography, and Index.

766. Fritz, Jean. **Harriet Beecher Stowe and the Beecher Preachers**. New York: Putnam, 1994. 144p. $15.95. ISBN 0-399-22666-4. 4-8

Harriet Beecher Stowe (1811-1896) strongly opposed slavery but did not know what to do to get rid of it. Her sister-in-law encouraged her to do what she did best—write. In 1852, *Uncle Tom's Cabin* was published, and Stowe became an instant celebrity. Her father was the most renowned preacher in America, and because he wanted more preachers in the family, he had seven children. He expected little from his girls, but Harriet was probably the most successful of his children because she became known in Europe as well as the United States. People in England crowded the streets to see her. She was a nineteenth-century wife, mother, and daughter who said that "writing is my element." Photographs, Bibliography, and Index.

767. Fritz, Jean. **Just a Few Words, Mr. Lincoln: The Story of the Gettysburg Address**. Charles Robinson, illustrator. New York: Grosset, 1993. 48p. $7.99; $3.95pa. ISBN 0-448-40171-1; 0-448-40170-3pa. (All Aboard Reading). 2-3

Fritz explains that Abraham Lincoln (1809-1865) had much to do to run the country, but he decided to take the time to say a few words at the opening of the cemetery in Gettysburg after the big battle there in 1863. He never expected anyone to remember his 271 words. Also included is the text of the speech.

768. Fritz, Jean. **Make Way for Sam Houston**. Elise Primavera, illustrator. New York: Putnam, 1986. 109p. $14.95. ISBN 0-399-21303-1. 4-6

Sam Houston (1793-1863) was one of the founding fathers of Texas. He loved the limelight and dressed for every occasion as if he were playing a role on the stage. Before he got to Texas, he had been wounded in battle, elected as governor of Tennessee and to the U.S. Congress, and had left civilization to live with the Cherokees twice. He adopted an Indian name and wore a queue when he lived among the Cherokees. He had a number of nicknames such as the "Big Drunk," the "Old Dragon," the "Great Designer," and the "Hero of San Jacinto." After he went to Texas, he continued to serve his country in leadership roles. Notes, Bibliography, and Index.

769. Fritz, Jean. **Shh! We're Writing the Constitution**. Tomie dePaola, illustrator. New York: Putnam, 1987. 58p. $12.95; $5.95pa. ISBN 0-399-21403-8; 0-399-21404-6pa. K-2

Fritz describes the writing of the Constitution and the conflicts among the delegates in Philadelphia. To get the document finished, people had to decide the issues, compromise on various aspects, and worry about resolution and ratification. Notes.

770. Fritz, Jean. **Stonewall**. Stephen Gammell, illustrator. New York: Putnam, 1979. 160p. $15.95. ISBN 0-399-20698-1. New York: Viking, 1989. 160p. $4.99pa. ISBN 0-14-032937-4pa. 3-9

Tom Jackson (1824-1863) saw his mother work in menial jobs because his father had frittered away the family money and died. After her death, when Tom was seven, he determined that he would make something of his life. His rules for life were to tell the truth, not to break promises, and to do what he planned. After living with an uncle, Tom's break came when he had a chance to go to West Point even though he was not well educated. He graduated, became a hero in the Mexican war, taught at Virginia Military Institute, and fought for the South in the Civil War, where he earned the name "Stonewall." Strong religious convictions and strict rules governed his life until he died of pneumonia after one of his soldiers accidentally shot him in the arm. Bibliography.

771. Fritz, Jean. **Traitor: The Case of Benedict Arnold**. New York: Putnam, 1981. 192p. $16.95. ISBN 0-399-20834-8. New York: Viking, 1989. 192p. $4.99pa. ISBN 0-14-032940-4pa. 5-9

Using the metaphor of wheels that turn without going anywhere, Fritz recounts the life of Benedict Arnold (1741-1801), a boy whose alcoholic father led him to think that if one could display wealth, then one would be happy and respected by others. Every aspect of Arnold's life seemed based on this premise. His final compromise with truth was to "sell" the new United States to the British by surrendering West Point, which he commanded by the grace of his friend, George Washington. This act of treason, discovered before it was concluded, only brought him exile to England and unhappiness. His name is not even carved on his tombstone. Bibliography and Index.

772. Fritz, Jean. **What's the Big Idea, Ben Franklin?** Margot Tomes, illustrator. New York: Coward, 1982. 48p. $13.95; $5.95pa. ISBN 0-698-20365-8; 0-698-11372-1pa. 2-6

Benjamin Franklin's father decided that Ben (1706-1790) would not be a Leather Apron man (following a trade) and sent him to school. When school proved to be a big expense that might lead to a poor job, his father reversed himself. Ben had other ideas, and even while he suffered under his brother as an apprentice, he saved money and bought books that taught him how to do things. He applied his idea about electricity, discovered it, and invented the lightning rod. As Philadelphia's Postmaster General, he reduced the time for a letter to reach Boston from six weeks to six days. In his later life, he lived in London for 18 years (he returned to America for 2 years) and in Paris from age 70 to 79. Additionally, he helped create the new government of the United States. Although not all of his ideas worked, enough did so that he made major contributions to American life.

773. Fritz, Jean. **Why Don't You Get a Horse, Sam Adams?** Trina Schart Hyman, illustrator. New York: Coward, 1982. 48p. $13.95; $7.95pa. ISBN 0-698-20292-9; 0-698-20545-6pa. 2-6

Samuel Adams (1722-1803) spent most of his time walking and talking with people in Boston, trying to get them to consider claiming independence from England. John Adams finally got Sam Adams to learn to ride a horse in 1775, when he convinced Sam that riding would help the country. Because Sam Adams was so vocal about his concerns against England, he is sometimes called "The Father of Independence."

774. Fritz, Jean. **Will You Sign Here, John Hancock?** Trina Schart Hyman, illustrator. New York: Coward, 1982. 48p. $13.95; $7.95pa. ISBN 0-698-20308-9; 0-698-20539-1pa. 2-6

Although orphaned at a very young age, John Hancock (1737-1793) lived with a wealthy aunt and uncle and increased his wealth as an adult. His love of clothes and attention made him seem ostentatious. People in Boston such as Sam Adams (Patriot Party) realized that supporting John Hancock for political office would entice him to share some of his money with their cause. Hancock himself was very unhappy with the British after the Stamp Act in 1765. He owned 20 ships and saw no reason to pay the British taxes on the cargo unloaded from them, especially when the lemons were spoiled or the wine poorly corked. Thus, Hancock became part of the attempt to form a new government and served as president of the Second Continental Congress, where he was able to emblazon his name on the Declaration of Independence. Notes from the Author.

775. Fritz, Jean. **You Want Women to Vote, Lizzie Stanton?** DyAnne DiSalvo-Ryan, illustrator. New York: Putnam, 1995. 88p. $15.95. ISBN 0-399-22786-5. 3-6

Elizabeth Cady's (1815-1902) father wanted her to be a boy, but she realized that woman should have the same rights as men even after she married Henry Stanton and had seven children. She wore bloomers, spoke out about the right to vote at the Seneca Falls Convention in 1848, and traveled around the country expressing her opinions on equality for all, male and female, Black and white. Notes, Bibliography, and Index. *American Library Association Notable Books for Children.*

776. Fromm, Peter. **Monkey Tag**. New York: Scholastic, 1994. 336p. $14.95. ISBN 0-590-46525-2. 5-7

While Eli and Thad, both 12 in 1970, play monkey tag on the bleachers, Thad falls and hurts himself enough to have to go through rehabilitation. As twins, he and Eli are close, and not even their parents' protective attitude toward Thad can keep them apart. Eli helps Thad until he begins to walk again, but Eli can only question his Catholic faith through this trauma. Eli finds no answers to his questions, and he has not yet made his decision about the church when the novel ends.

777.   Fry, Annette R. **The Orphan Train**. New York: New Discovery, 1994. 96p. $14.95. ISBN 0-02-735721-X. (American Event). 4-8

Unwanted children have always been a concern of society. In the nineteenth century the Children's Aid Society placed orphaned, poor, and abandoned children from New York and Boston in western homes after taking them across the country on a train. Photographs enhance the text about these children, who traveled away from what they knew to unknown homes and futures. Further Reading and Index.

G

778. Gaeddert, Louann. **Breaking Free**. New York: Atheneum, 1994. 144p. $14.95. ISBN 0-689-31883-9. 5-8

Richard's uncle has no use for either school or music, Richard's two loves. His uncle also owns slaves. Richard walks 10 miles a day to school. He teaches a slave girl to read, which allows her and her father to escape, and soon Richard makes a contact that leads to his own departure.

779. Gaines, Anne. **John Wesley Powell and the Great Surveys of the American West**. New York: Chelsea House, 1992. 136p. $19.95. ISBN 0-7910-1318-9. (World Explorers). 5 up

In 1865, after the Civil War, the Homestead Act and the transcontinental railroad made settlement of the West a priority for many even though much of the land was only superficially mapped. People wanted to know if oil, gold, silver, copper, or iron was under the ground. Between 1867 and 1879, four men led surveys of the West. They were Clarence King, George Wheeler, Ferdinand Hayden, and John Wesley Powell (1834-1902), the one-armed explorer of the Grand Canyon. These surveys mapped and photographed the West from the Sierra Nevadas to the Missouri River and from Yellowstone to the Mexican border. Photographs enhance the text. Chronology, Further Reading, and Index.

780. Gardner, Robert, and Dennis Shortelle. **The Forgotten Players: The Story of Black Baseball in America**. New York: Walker, 1993. 120p. $13.85. ISBN 0-8027-8248-5. 5 up

Noting how America shortchanged its Black baseball players in the late nineteenth and early twentieth centuries, the text gives a history of this maltreatment. Among the Negro League teams were the Detroit Stars, the Indianapolis ABCs, the Kansas City Monarchs, and the Chicago American Giants; they played thousands of ballgames for sellout crowds. The topics include an overview of early baseball, Rube Foster and the Negro National League, Gus Greenlee and a new Negro League, life in the leagues, barnstorming with them, and the integration of baseball with Jackie Robinson. Notes, Bibliography, and Index.

781. Garfunkel, Trudy. **Letter to the World: The Life and Dances of Martha Graham**. Boston: Little, Brown, 1995. 92p. $16.95. ISBN 0-316-30413-1. 6 up

Growing up in Pennsylvania and California, Martha Graham (1894-1991) did not know that she wanted to ·dance until she was 16. The text gives information about the various influences on her life, including Ruth St. Denis, Erick Hawkins, Paul Taylor, and Merce Cunningham. Among the 200 dances she choreographed and performed with her unique principles of movement are "Letter to the World," "Frontier," and "Appalachian Spring." Photographs, Bibliography, and Index.

782. Garfunkel, Trudy. **On Wings of Joy: The Story of Ballet from the 16th Century to Today**. Boston: Little, Brown, 1994. 194p. $18.95. ISBN 0-316-30412-3. 6 up

Ballet began more than 400 years ago in the courts of Europe. In the seventeenth century, the English masque and the five positions of classical ballet were established. Although some changes occurred in the eighteenth century, Jean-Georges Noverre (1727-1810), the father of modern ballet, was the theorist of the times. Dancers received training commensurate with their body types. In the nineteenth century, Romanticism and Romantic ballet began. Famous dancers included Marie Taglioni, Jules Perrot, Carlotta Grisi, and Carlotta Brianza. During the twentieth century, modern dance arrived. Still, famous dancers preferred classical ballet. Names that dominate this century are Pavlova and Balanchine. Coda, Glossary, Bibliography, and Index.

783. Garland, Sherry. **Cabin 102**. San Diego, CA: Harcourt Brace, 1995. 243p. $11; $5pa. ISBN 0-15-238631-9; 0-15-200662-1pa. 5-9

Although set in the present, this historical fantasy couples the contemporary Dusty, 12, with Tahni, an Arawak Indian girl who is in the cabin next door to Dusty's on a cruise ship. Through a series of inquiries and situations where people think he is crazy, Dusty finds out that Tahni drowned when the Spanish galleon *Estrella Vespertina* capsized in 1511. Now she is trying to return to her island of Bogati. With her story comes historical background on the Spanish conquest in the Caribbean and the end of the Arawak Indians.

784. Garland, Sherry. **Indio**. San Diego, CA: Harcourt Brace, 1995. 291p. $11; $5pa. ISBN 0-15-38631-9; 0-15-200021-6pa. 6-10

When Ipa-tah-chi is 10 in the early sixteenth century, Apache raiders take her brother prisoner and kill her grandmother. When she is older and getting married, Spanish soldiers arrive in her Jumano pueblo near the Rio Grande and capture her and her cousin and take them to work in the Mexican silver mines. Her cousin is raped, and when the man who raped her is murdered, the man's brother blames Ipa because she is an *indio*. A kind Spanish soldier with whom she has fallen in love helps her escape. She returns to her village, waits for the soldier to summon her to Mexico City, and looks after her dead cousin's baby. *American Library Association Best Books for Young Adults* and *American Bookseller Pick of the Lists*.

785. Garrett, Michael. **The Seventies**. Austin, TX: Raintree/Steck-Vaughn, 1990. 48p. $22.80. ISBN 0-8114-4214-4. (Decades). 5-7

One of the most significant events during the 1970s was the world oil crisis in 1973. It led to the collapse of many businesses and much unemployment. Many young people expressed their disillusionment through music and fashions of the punk rock movement. At the same time, the Vietnam War ended, the women's movement gained support, and preserving the environment became a priority. The text looks at the music, clothes, media, leisure, youth culture, and styles of the time against the backdrop of the major historical, political, and technological events. Glossary, Further Reading, and Index.

786. Gates, Viola R. **Journey to Center Place**. Boulder, CO: Roberts Rinehart, 1996. 144p. $10.95pa. ISBN 1-57098-061-6pa. 3-7

Neekah, 12, must leave her home in Salapa, Colorado, after months without rain, so the family can find water in their world of AD 1250. They go to Center Place, the Anasazi center of the universe, in Chaco Canyon, New Mexico. The family follows the Anasazi road system that leads to Center Place and joins others who have faced the same dangers and hardships.

786a. Gauch, Patricia L. **This Time, Tempe Wick?** Margot Tomes. illustrator. 1974. New York: Putnam, 1992. 48p. $13.95. ISBN 0-399-21880-7. 1-4

Tempe Wick knows that she must keep General Washington's soldiers from taking her horse in 1781. She hides the horse inside her house in Pennsylvania while keeping the men away for over three days. Her wits save both her house and her horse from harm.

786b. Gauch, Patricia L. **Thunder at Gettysburg**. Stephen Gammell, illustrator. 1975. New York: Putnam, 1990. 46p. $14.95. ISBN 0-399-22201-4. New York: Bantam, 1991. 46p. $4.50pa. ISBN 0-440-71075-4pa. 2-5

On July 1, 1863, Tillie takes a chair to her attic window so she can watch the battle on Seminary Ridge in Gettysburg. By late afternoon, she finds herself in the middle of the fighting as she tries to escape. She stops to carry pails of water to wounded soldiers. After the battle ends, she is relieved to know that the Union has won and that her family is safe.

787. Gehret, Jeanne. **Susan B. Anthony: And Justice for All**. Fairport, NY: Verbal Images, 1994. 120p. $14.95; $6.95pa. ISBN 0-9625136-9-5; 09625136-8-7pa. 6-9

Susan B. Anthony (1820-1906) spent her adult life working for human rights. Among the things she did was "kidnap" an abused woman from her husband, talk to angry mobs, break laws she considered unfair, and gather 400,000 signatures on a petition asking Congress to outlaw slavery. Although she worked 50 years for women's suffrage, it did not happen until 14 years after she died. But without her work, it might have been longer. Glossary, Important Events, Selections for Young Readers, Further Reading, and Index.

788. Geis, Jacqueline, author/illustrator. **The First Ride: Blazing the Trail for the Pony Express**. Nashville, TN: Ideals, 1994. Unpaged. $13.95. ISBN 1-57102-004-7. 2-4

When an advertisement appeared in papers wanting expert riders who were skinny for $25 a week, it attracted many men. Billy Hamilton was one of those hired, and he started riding the Pony Express in 1860. Like the other riders, he promised to get the mail across the United States in 10 days. The arrival of the telegraph 18 months after the Pony Express started rendered the company bankrupt, and the rides stopped.

789. Genet, Donna. **Father Junípero Serra: Founder of California Missions**. Springfield, NJ: Enslow, 1996. 128p. $18.95. ISBN 0-89490-762-X. 4-6

Father Junípero Serra (1713-1784) was a dedicated missonary who founded the missions in California. Although the text does not present the furor surrounding his sainthood in 1988, it does show him as a man who was a peaceful advocate for humans during the time of the Spanish conquests. Photographs, Further Reading, Chronology, and Index.

790. Gentry, Tony. **Dizzy Gillespie: Musician**. New York: Chelsea House, 1991. 112p. $18.95; $7.95pa. ISBN 0-7910-1127-5; 0-7910-1152-6pa. (Black Americans of Achievement). 5 up

John Birks Gillespie (b. 1917) began playing the trumpet when he was 12. In South Carolina, people began asking him to join them on stage, and he became a swing band member soon after, where he earned the name "Dizzy" for his energy. He developed his own approach to harmony and rhythm and, along with several other musicians, created bebop. In 1945, he began his own band, and two years later, he introduced Afro-Cuban rhythms. Photographs and reproductions enhance the text. Chronology, Further Reading, and Index.

791. Gentry, Tony. **Jesse Owens: Champion Athlete**. New York: Chelsea House, 1990. 111p. $18.95; $7.95pa. ISBN 1-55546-603-6; 0-7910-0247-0pa. (Black Americans of Achievement). 5 up

Gentry first recounts Owens's experience at the 1936 Olympics in Berlin, when Hitler spurned him as non-Aryan while the crowds loved his fluid running style. Then Gentry turns to Owens's childhood in the South and in Cleveland, where he met his future wife and the Irish coach who encouraged him. After breaking track records, Owens (1913-1980) met Olympic gold medal winner Charlie Paddock and decided that he wanted to become an Olympian himself. In Berlin, Owens became good friends with his chief competitor in the long jump, Luz Long. The two seemed to bring out the best in each other as they exchanged jump after jump before Owens finally won the gold and Long the silver. Photographs, Chronology, Further Reading, and Index.

792. Gentry, Tony. **Paul Laurence Dunbar: Poet**. New York: Chelsea House, 1989. 112p. $18.95; $7.95pa. ISBN 1-55546-583-8; 0-7910-0223-3pa. (Black Americans of Achievement). 5 up

Paul Laurence Dunbar (1872-1906) was the first Black American to gain international recognition as a poet. As the only Black to graduate from his Dayton, Ohio, high school, he could not get a job because of his color, though he'd been a top student, and he had no money for college. He worked as an elevator operator and wrote poetry on the side. He was able to publish two collections, and his third collection, published when he was 24, established his reputation. In his work, which also includes essays and novels, he suggested that humor can exist in all lives, even the most difficult. Photographs and reproductions enhance the text. Chronology, Further Reading, and Index.

793. George, Jean Craighead. **The First Thanksgiving**. Thomas Locker, illustrator. New York: Philomel, 1993. Unpaged. $15.95. ISBN 0-399-21991-9. New York: Paper Star, 1996. Unpaged. $5.95pa. ISBN 0-698-11392-6pa. 2-5

After the Pilgrims arrived and spent a long winter with the help of Squanto and others during 1619 and 1620, they celebrated with the first Thanksgiving. The text is complemented by vibrant illustrations.

794. Gerrard, Roy. **Rosie and the Rustlers**. New York: Farrar, Straus & Giroux, 1989. Unpaged. $15. ISBN 0-575-04382-2. K-3

Rosie Jones and her cowhands work very hard on her ranch. When Greasy Ben comes to steal her cattle, her hands and the Cherokee are able to stop him and his greedy outlaw buddies.

795. Gerrard, Roy, author/illustrator. **Wagons West!** New York: Farrar, Straus & Giroux, 1996. 32p. $15. ISBN 0-374-38249-2. K-3

The guide Buckskin Dan convinces a group of eastern farmers that they should leave their barren ground and go to Oregon where the soil is fertile. He takes them across the country where they experience the usual frustrations and difficulties of crossing prairies and rivers. They stop in Fort Laramie for supplies. Then they return a lost Arapaho child to his family, and the tribe later saves them from a cattle rustler. The text, in rhyme, complements illustrations that reveal the historical aspects of the trail. *School Library Journal Best Book.*

796. Gherman, Beverly. **E. B. White: Some Writer!** New York: Atheneum, 1992. 136p. $13.95. ISBN 0-689-31672-0. 6 up

E. B. White (1899-1985), author of *Charlotte's Web*, *Stuart Little*, and *The Trumpet of the Swan*, said that Stuart came to him in a dream, but that Charlotte did not. White had lived in Maine for five years on a farm with a barn, and he knew the behavior of spiders, geese, rats, and pigs. With this experience, he created the realities of life within his fantasy world. He also wrote for adults by editing William Strunk's older work to create the definitive style manual for writers. White was shy and hated to speak in public as a young man, but he was also someone who enjoyed adventure, his wife, and his family. Photographs, Notes, Bibliography, and Index.

797. Gibbons, Gail, author/illustrator. **Beacons of Light: Lighthouses**. New York: Morrow, 1990. Unpaged. $16. ISBN 0-688-07379-4. 2-4

Using watercolors of various lighthouses, Gibbons gives a history of them since the Pharos at Alexandria, Egypt. She shows the first American lighthouse, erected in 1716 in Boston; the evolution of lights up to the Fresnel (invented in 1822); and the various sounds to warn ships of danger in the fog.

798. Gibbons, Gail, author/illustrator. **The Great St. Lawrence Seaway**. New York: Morrow, 1992. 40p. $15. ISBN 0-688-06984-3. 2-6

Among the explorers who wanted to find a waterway across the continent were Jacques Cartier, who turned back in 1535, and Samuel de Champlain in 1603, who had his boats ported over Niagara Falls. In 1666, Robert Cavelier de La Salle also failed, but he realized that the area would be good for trapping and colonization. The text continues with the history of the seaway and the various improvements that allow ships to sail along it from the Atlantic through canals to the Great Lakes.

799. Giblin, James. **Be Seated: A Book About Chairs**. New York: HarperCollins, 1993. 136p. $15. ISBN 0-06-021537-2. 4-8

The text gives a history of chairs beginning with the three-legged stools and chairs of the Egyptians, which were mortise- and tenon-joined. It includes the thrones of kings such as Solomon and the *klismos* of the Greeks with their curved lines. Giblin also discusses the Sheridan chair and the Shaker rocker. The chair becomes a part of social custom, art, and politics in the society that uses it. Bibliography, Notes, and Index.

800. Giblin, James. **When Plague Strikes: The Black Death, Smallpox, AIDS**. New York: HarperCollins, 1995. 212p. $14.95. ISBN 0-06-025854-3. 5-9

Three major plagues have hit the known world in the past 1,000 years: the Black Death, smallpox, and AIDS. They have killed millions of people and have left social, economic, and political havoc. Although each plague has helped to increase knowledge about the human body, each new one must be researched and tested for a cure. The text first recounts the Plague of Athens that struck in the summer of 430 BC. Those who lived had terrible scars or lost their eyesight or their memory. Today no one is sure what the disease might have been, although typhus, smallpox, and the bubonic plague are candidates. The sure thing is that doctors did not know how to treat it. Giblin continues with information about the three plagues that have ravaged the world since. Source Notes, Bibliography, and Index. *American Library Association Best Books for Young Adults*, *Notable Children's Trade Books in the Field of Social Studies*, and *American Library Association Notable Books for Children*.

801. Giblin, James Cross. **Chimney Sweeps: Yesterday and Today**. New York: Trophy, 1987. 64p. $6.95pa. ISBN 0-06-446061-4pa. 4-6

The text looks at the history and folklore surrounding the profession of chimney sweep in Europe and America from the fifteenth century to the present. *American Book Award Winner*, *American Library Association Notable Books for Children*, *Horn Book Fanfare Honor List*, *Booklist Children's Editors Choices*, and *Golden Kite Award*.

802. Giblin, James Cross. **Edith Wilson: The Woman Who Ran the United States**. Michele Laporte, illustrator. New York: Viking, 1992. 64p. $11; $3.99pa. ISBN 0-670-83005-4; 0-14-034249-4pa. (Women of Our Time). 2-4

Edith Wilson (1872-1961), the wife of Woodrow Wilson, helped him run the United States after he had a stroke in 1920-1921. In fact, many think she was completely in charge. Others, however, think she was merely an advisor. She supported Wilson's policies and traveled with him as he worked to get League of Nations support in the United States.

803. Giblin, James Cross. **George Washington: A Picture Book Biography**. Michael Dooling, illustrator. New York: Scholastic, 1992. 48p. $14.95. ISBN 0-590-42550-1. 3-5

George Washington was actually born on February 11, 1732, but 20 years later, 11 days were added to the calendar, and his birthday changed to February 22. Seven years before he married the widowed Martha Custis, he inherited Mount Vernon, the place where they lived with the children from her first marriage. When the American Revolutionary War began, Washington was elected general of the Continental army. He served his country in various capacities until he retired in 1797. At his death in 1799, his slaves were freed according to the directions in his will. Index.

804. Giblin, James Cross. **Thomas Jefferson: A Picture Book Biography**. Michael Dooling, illustrator. New York: Scholastic, 1994. 48p. $16.95. ISBN 0-590-44838-2. 3-5

Thomas Jefferson's father promised his dying friend William Randolph that he would move to his home to look after his motherless children. Then, when Thomas was 14, his father died. Thomas enjoyed the books willed to him so much that at 17, he decided to go to college at William and Mary in Virginia. Two years in college and years afterward studying law led him into a practice and then to the position of writer and revisionist of the Declaration of Independence in 1776. Before that, however, he built a home called Monticello, and he married Martha Skelton in 1772. She died after 10 years during the birth of their sixth child (only three lived), and Jefferson's grieving led him to agree to go to Paris as a diplomat, taking his oldest daughter. In Paris, he may have met someone he loved, but he had promised his wife on her deathbed not to remarry. In his later years, he became president and then established the University of Virginia. Important Dates in Thomas Jefferson's Life, The Words of Thomas Jefferson, A Visit to Monticello, and Index. *American Library Association Booklist Editors' Choices*.

805. Gibson, Michael. **The War in Vietnam**. New York: Bookwright Press, Franklin Watts, 1992. 63p. $19.14. ISBN 0-531-18408-0. (Witness History). 5-8

The text traces the history of Vietnam from 1887 until the French left in 1954. It discusses the United States's entry into the conflict after it began in 1961 and the country's exit before the fighting ended in 1975, as well as the current situation within the country. Black-and-white and a few color photographs highlight the text. Chronology, Glossary, and Index.

806. Giff, Patricia R. **Lily's Crossing**. New York: Delacorte, 1997. 176p. $14.95. ISBN 0-385-32142-2. 5-7

Lily looks forward to the summer at the family home in Far Rockaway, but after she arrives, she finds that her best friend in the summer is moving away. The only playmate around is Albert, a Hungarian boy who left Europe to escape World War II. When Lily hears that her father is going to Europe as an engineer to help clean up, she is fearful that he will not return. Lily dislikes Albert at first, but she soon realizes that he has his own fears, and the two become friends.

807. Gilman, Michael. **Matthew Henson: Explorer**. New York: Chelsea House, 1988. 112p. $18.95; $7.95pa. ISBN 1-55546-590-0; 0-7910-1158-5pa. (Black Americans of Achievement). 5 up

Matthew Henson (1886-1955) gained a chance to explore when Robert Peary walked into the hat shop where he was working and told his boss that he wanted someone to go with him to Nicaragua while he searched for a place to build a passage between the Atlantic and Pacific Oceans. The shop owner suggested his employee. Henson had traveled to major ports in his life, but as a Black in America, he had had no opportunity to continue his sailing career. Henson went with Peary to Nicaragua and then to the area of the North Pole several times before he became one of the first men to reach the Pole itself in 1909. Photographs enhance the text. Chronology, Further Reading, and Index.

808. Gintzler, A. S. **Cowboys**. Santa Fe, NM: John Muir, 1994. 46p. $12.95. ISBN 1-56261-152-6. (Rough and Ready). 5-9

Most cowboys lived during the nineteenth century. In two-page spreads complemented with photographs, maps, and prints, Gintzler discusses topics that reveal a cowboy's life. They include the plains, roundups, cattle drives, skills, gear, horses, Texas longhorns, cow towns, the workday, law and order, Indians, famous cowboys, working cowgirls, Black cowboys, the *vaquero*, the rodeo trail, cowboy songs and poetry, range wars, and the cowboy of today. Index.

809. Gintzler, A. S. **Homesteaders**. Santa Fe, NM: John Muir, 1994. 46p. $12.95. ISBN 1-56261-154-2. (Rough and Ready). 5-9

Homesteaders made their homes in the Great Plains, a grassland in the middle of the United States once called the "Great American Desert." They moved to this area during the nineteenth century and changed the face of the land. In two-page spreads complemented with photographs, maps, and prints, Gintzler discusses the topics that describe the homesteader's life. They include the trails they took, waterways, who they were, houses, farming, hardships, native peoples they met, range wars, law and disorder, frontier towns, African American homesteaders, women on the plains, day-to-day living, homestead diaries and letters, songs of the sodbusters, games and celebrations, traveling salesmen and entertainers, commerce, and plains ecology. Index.

810. Gintzler, A. S. **Prospectors**. Santa Fe, NM: John Muir, 1994. 46p. $12.95. ISBN 1-56261-153-4. (Rough and Ready). 5-9

The United States won California from Mexico in a war that lasted from 1846 to 1848. In 1848, John Marshall found gold on the American River in northern California on John Sutter's land. Although they agreed to keep the information a secret, someone heard, and the gold rush started. In two-page spreads complemented with photographs, maps, and prints, Gintzler describes the prospector's life. She looks at gold fever, routes to the gold, gold seekers, life in the diggings, the geology of gold, tools, hard-rock mining, dangers, mining towns, law and disorder, Indians, mule trains and muleteers, songs of the Forty-Niners, the miners' own words, tall tales, bonanza kings and paupers, ghost towns, mining and the environment, and prospecting today. Index.

811. Gipson, Fred. **Old Yeller**. 1956. Cutchogue, NY: Buccaneer, 1995. 184p. $15.95. ISBN 0-8996-6906-9. New York: HarperCollins, 1990. 184p. $4.50pa. ISBN 0-06-440382-3pa. 4-7

When Travis is 14 during the 1860s, his father departs for Florida and leaves him in charge of the Texas family homestead. When an old dog arrives, his brother and mother want to keep it, calling it "Old Yeller." Although Travis does not want the dog, Old Yeller saves him from wild hogs. However, a wild wolf bites Old Yeller, and Travis must kill him because he develops hydrophobia (rabies) after the bite. *Newbery Honor* and *American Library Association Notable Children's Books of 1940-1970*.

812. Girard, Linda Walvoord. **Young Frederick Douglass: The Slave Who Learned to Read**. Colin Bootman, illustrator. Morton Grove, IL: Albert Whitman, 1994. 40p. $14.95. ISBN 0-8075-9463-6. 3-5

Before she knew teaching slaves was illegal, the woman to whom Frederick Douglass (1817?-1895) was loaned taught him to read. After her husband's reprimand, she tried to keep Douglass from books, but he had already realized the power of reading and writing. He searched for ways to learn more, and he succeeded. His knowledge helped him, after several setbacks, to escape to freedom. About Frederick Douglass.

813. Glassman, Bruce. **Wilma Mankiller: Chief of the Cherokee Nation**. New York: Blackbirch Press, Rosen, 1992. 64p. $14.95. ISBN 0-8239-1208-6. (Library of Famous Women). 4-8

The text begins with the point that Hollywood's idea of Indians is unrelated to reality. Wilma Mankiller (b. 1945) neither rides a horse to work nor wears stripes on her face. She is intensely interested in her people and furthering the education of all children, not just Native Americans. The text looks at her life and the events that led her to become the head of her tribe. Glossary, For Further Reading, and Index.

814. Glassman, Judy. **The Morning Glory War**. New York: Dutton, 1990. 119p. $13.95. ISBN 0-525-44637-0. 4-6

Jeannie is in the fifth grade in Brooklyn during World War II. She begins corresponding with a soldier who thinks that she is older, cute, and probably a cheerleader. She likes these ideas, but the girl who seems to know and have everything finds the letter and gives it to the teacher. Then the same girl destroys Jeannie's morning glories. As a way to get even, Jeannie decides that she will collect more newspapers for their War Effort school campaign than the girl does. That, plus her working in a Victory Garden and making friends with an Italian boy, improves her year.

815. Gleiter, Jan, and Kathleen Thompson. **Annie Oakley**. Yoshi Miyake, illustrator. Austin, TX: Raintree/Steck-Vaughn, 1995. 32p. $19.97. ISBN 0-8114-8451-3. (First Biographies). K-3

Anne Mozee (1860-1926) worked while still a child to help her abandoned mother. When she discovered she could shoot with a gun, she killed quail for her family's food and sold the extras. She met her husband, Frank Butler, when she beat him in a shooting contest. They changed her stage name to "Annie Oakley," and in 1885 she joined Buffalo Bill's Wild West Show. Fans called her "The Little Girl of the Western Plains," and the Butlers traveled across the United States and Europe with the show. Key Dates.

816. Gleiter, Jan, and Kathleen Thompson. **Booker T. Washington**. Rick Whipple, illustrator. Austin, TX: Raintree/Steck-Vaughn, 1995. 32p. $19.97; $4.95pa. ISBN 0-8114-8454-8; 0-8114-9353-9pa. (First Biographies). K-3

After Booker T. Washington (1856-1915) moved to West Virginia with his family, he saw some people reading a newspaper and realized the importance of reading. He worked in the coal mines, but in 1871 he met the mine owner's wife, and she hired him to work in her home. Her desire for perfection helped him get a job at Hampton Institute, when the woman who interviewed him made him clean a room before she decided he could go there. He went to Tuskegee Institute in 1881 and was its president when he died. Key Dates.

817. Gleiter, Jan, and Kathleen Thompson. **Christopher Columbus**. Rick Whipple, illustrator. Austin, TX: Raintree/Steck-Vaughn, 1995. 32p. $19.97; $4.95pa. ISBN 0-8114-8456-4; 0-8114-9351-2pa. (First Biographies). K-3

In this fictional biography, 13-year-old Ferdinand tells about his father, Christopher Columbus, on his fourth voyage to the New World. As he recounts the other voyages, the son tries to protect his father from the men who want to go ashore against his father's orders. Key Dates.

818. Gleiter, Jan, and Kathleen Thompson. **Junípero Serra**. Charles Shaw, illustrator. Austin, TX: Raintree/Steck-Vaughn, 1993. 32p. $13.98; $5.95pa. ISBN 0-8172-2909-4; 0-8114-6765-1pa. (Hispanic Stories). 4-7

As a Franciscan teacher and scholar in Spain, Junípero Serra (1713-1784) decided to go to the New World and help the natives. He and a friend went to California and began to build missions—San Diego, San Francisco, San Antonio, and San Luis Obispo. He wanted to make Spanish settlement in the area easier. He convinced the viceroy that soldiers protecting the missions needed to have their families join them, which created the towns surrounding the missions. Glossary.

819. Gleiter, Jan, and Kathleen Thompson. **Kit Carson**. Rick Whipple, illustrator. Austin, TX: Raintree/Steck-Vaughn, 1995. 32p. $19.97; $4.95pa. ISBN 0-8114-8455-6; 0-8114-9352-0pa. (First Biographies). K-3

Kit Carson (1809-1868) and his family moved to various places with Daniel Boone's family, and Boone taught him hunting and respect for Native American ways. Carson eventually settled in Taos, New Mexico. He met and married an Arapaho woman who bore him a daughter before she died. He left his daughter in the care of others and became a guide for John Carlos Frémont's exploration between Missouri and the Rocky Mountains. Afterward, he lived with the Utes and believed that the federal government had betrayed the Indian tribes. Key Dates.

820. Gleiter, Jan, and Kathleen Thompson. **Paul Revere**. Francis Balistreri, illustrator. Austin, TX: Raintree/Steck-Vaughn, 1995. 32p. $19.97. ISBN 0-8114-8452-1. (First Biographies). K-3

Rather than a biography of Paul Revere (1735-1818), this story describes the beginning of the Revolutionary War and Paul Revere's attempt to warn people of the British arrival. The ride is a minor part of the text, with more emphasis placed on the circumstances surrounding the decision behind the "shot heard round the world" in 1775. Key Dates.

821. Gleiter, Jan, and Kathleen Thompson. **Pocahontas**. Deborah L. Chabrian, illustrator. Austin, TX: Raintree/Steck-Vaughn, 1995. 32p. $19.97; $4.95pa. ISBN 0-8114-8450-5; 0-8114-9350-4pa. (First Biographies). K-3

Pocahontas (1595?-1617), in this fictional biography, makes friends with the white men and John Smith and helps them during the "starving time." Completing the text are her marriage to John Rolfe, the birth of her son, and her voyage to England, where people called her Lady Rebecca Rolfe before she died of smallpox. Key Dates.

822. Gleiter, Jan, and Kathleen Thompson. **Sacagawea**. Yoshi Miyake, illustrator. Austin, TX: Raintree/Steck-Vaughn, 1995. 32p. $19.97. ISBN 0-8114-8453-X. (First Biographies). K-3

After being kidnapped from her tribe, Sacagawea (1786?-1812) became Lewis and Clark's translator to the Shoshones. The text notes that Lewis and Clark did not like her husband but included him in the expedition because they needed her help. The text also suggests that the expedition would not have been successful without Sacagawea's Shoshone connections, especially her brother as chief of the tribe. Key Dates.

823. Glenn, Patricia Brown. **Discover America's Favorite Architects**. Joe Stites, illustrator. New York: Preservation, 1996. 118p. $19.95pa. ISBN 0-471-14354-5pa. 6-9

The text presents short biographies of 10 architects, arranged in chronological order according to their birth. They are Thomas Jefferson (1743-1826), Frederick Law Olmsted (1822-1903), Henry Hobson Richardson (1838-1886), Louis Henri Sullivan (1856-1924), Frank Lloyd Wright (1867-1959), Julia Morgan (1872-1957), Ludwig Mies van der Rohe (1886-1969), Paul R. Williams (1894-1980), Philip Johnson (b. 1906), and I. M. Pei (b. 1917). Although some of these architects are not American by birth, their designs grace American cities. Each segment presents the architect's background, training, and major accomplishments. Photographs, Bibliography, Glossary, and Index.

824. Glubok, Shirley. **Great Lives: Painting**. New York: Scribner's, 1994. 238p. $24.95. ISBN 0-684-19052-4. (Great Lives). 5-9

Places where they live and experiences they have influence the subjects that artists choose to paint. Biographical profiles of 23 major painters appear in the text: Mary Cassatt, American (1844-1926); Marc Chagall, Russian (1887-1985); Frederick E. Church, American (1826-1900); Jacques-Louis David, French (1748-1825); Edgar Degas, French (1834-1917); Albrecht Dürer, German (1471-1528); Thomas Gainsborough, English (1727-1788); Paul Gaugin, French (1848-1903); El Greco, Greek (1541-1614); Winslow Homer, American (1836-1910); Leonardo da Vinci, Italian (1452-1519); Michelangelo, Italian (1475-1564); Claude Monet, French (1840-1926); Georgia O'Keeffe, American (1889-1986); Pablo Picasso, Spanish (1881-1973); Rembrandt van Rijn, Dutch (1606-1669); Diego Rivera, Mexican (1886-1957); Peter Paul Rubens, Flemish (1577-1640); Titian, Venetian (?-1576); Vincent van Gogh, Dutch (1853-1890); Diego de Veláquez, Spanish (1599-1660); Johannes Vermeer, Dutch (1632-1675); and James McNeill Whistler, American (1834-1903). Further Reading and Index.

825. Goble, Paul. **Hau Kola Hello Friend**. Gerry Perrin, photographs. Katonah, NY: Richard C. Owen, 1994. 32p. $13.95. ISBN 1-878450-44-1. (Meet the Author). 2-5

When a child in England, Goble liked the outdoors. During World War II, he collected bullet shells and pieces of German bombs that fell too close to his house. Because he always loved anything about Indians, he moved to the United States and has been painting about Indian legends and history throughout his adult life.

826. Goldberg, Jake. **Rachel Carson**. New York: Chelsea House, 1991. 79p. $14.95. ISBN 0-7910-1566-1. (Junior World Biography). 3-6

Rachel Carson (1907-1964) made valuable contributions to society as a biologist and environmentalist who warned that humans had to change their treatment of the environment if they wanted to save it. She also began a major dispute over the use of pesticides, about which she proved to be correct. Chronology, Glossary, and Index.

827. Goldin, Barbara Diamond. **Fire! The Beginnings of the Labor Movement**. James Watling, illustrator. New York: Viking, 1992. 54p. $12. ISBN 0-670-84475-6. (Once Upon America). 2-4

Rosie, 11, wants to work with her sister Freyda in the garment factory rather than attend school in 1911. In a tragic accident resulting from unsafe conditions, the Triangle Shirtwaist factory burns, and 146 people die, many of them Jewish immigrants like Rosie's cousin, who perishes. Instead of going to work, Rosie decides to stay in school and campaign for the International Ladies' Garment Workers' Union.

828. Goldin, Barbara Diamond. **Red Means Good Fortune: A Story of San Francisco's Chinatown**. Wenhai Ma, illustrator. New York: Viking, 1994. 54p. $12.99. ISBN 0-670-85352-6. (Once Upon America). 3-6

Jim Mun comes to America to be with his brothers and father as they try to earn money to help the rest of the family in China during the 1850s. He hopes to have a different future than is possible for him in China. Then he meets Wai Hing, a poor slave girl who can never leave the house where she works. He tries to help her, and when he finds her cousin, he tries to purchase her freedom.

829.   Goldish, Meish. **Immigration: How Should It Be Controlled?** New York: Twenty-First Century Books, 1994. 64p. $15.98. ISBN 0-8050-3182-0. (Issues of Our Time). 5-8

Immigration problems began as early as 1620, when the colonists wondered who should be allowed to come to the new land. These concerns continue as people grapple with the needs of foreigners who want better lives for themselves and their children and think they can have them in the United States. Citizens wonder if their taxes should pay for health care and education for people who cannot support themselves. Laws have changed through the years, but still people enter the country illegally, willing to gamble for a chance to come to America. The text discusses these problems and posits possible solutions. Glossary, For Further Reading, Source Notes, and Index.

830.   Goldish, Meish. **Our Supreme Court**. Brookfield, CT: Millbrook Press, 1994. 48p. $14.40. ISBN 1-56294-445-2. (I Know America). 2-6

The text discusses the purpose and powers of the Supreme Court, its history, how it works, some of the famous justices, and a few of the most influential rulings, including school integration (*Brown v. Board of Education of Topeka*), school prayer (*Engel v. Vitale*), suspect's rights (*Miranda v. Arizona*), book banning (*Board of Education v. Pico*), and flag burning (*Texas v. Johnson*). Chronology, For Further Reading, and Index.

831.   Goldman, Martin S. **Crazy Horse: War Chief of the Oglala Sioux**. New York: Franklin Watts, 1996. 208p. $22. ISBN 0-531-11258-6. (American Indian Experience). 6 up

Goldman posits that the image of Crazy Horse divides into two, the one that Native Americans have of him and the one that whites have. He tries to recreate both of these men through careful documentation. He also discusses the decline of the Sioux through this loner thought to be very strange, a good friend, a brave warrior, or a cruel conqueror. Goldman includes cultural information and biographical sketches of people who knew Crazy Horse, the man who became war chief of the Ogalas at 23 and whom the Shirt Wearers, or ruling council, cast out in the end. Bibliography and Index.

832.   Golenbock, Peter. **Teammates**. Paul Bacon, illustrator. San Diego, CA: Gulliver, Harcourt Brace, 1990. Unpaged. $15.95; $6pa. ISBN 0-15-200603-6; 0-15-284286-1pa. K-6

Branch Rickey of the Brooklyn Dodgers decided to hire the best player for his team, regardless of color, at a time when baseball teams were segregated. He chose Jackie Robinson after Robinson promised to try not to fight back when taunted by racist fans. One person who stood by Robinson was his teammate Pee Wee Reese.

833.   Gonzales, Doreen. **Cesar Chavez: Leader for Migrant Farm Workers**. Springfield, NJ: Enslow, 1996. 128p. $17.95. ISBN 0-89490-760-3. (Hispanic Biographies). 5-9

Cesar Chavez (1927-1993) helped establish the United Farm Workers Union so that migrant workers would have better working conditions and more rights. As the union became established and the workers more satisfied, the union began to lose members because Chavez hesitated to delegate responsibility to other people. Chronology, Further Reading, Notes, and Index.

834.   Goor, Ron, and Nancy Goor. **Williamsburg: Cradle of the Revolution**. New York: Atheneum, 1994. 90p. $15.95. ISBN 0-689-31795-6. 4-8

Williamsburg was an important part of the nation's life during the years preceding the American Revolution; Virginia's leaders gathered there. The text uses photographs of modern-day Williamsburg and its living history museum to show what life during that time was like for the people who lived and worked there, including the slaves. Bibliography and Index.

835.   Gormley, Beatrice. **Maria Mitchell: The Soul of an Astronomer**. Grand Rapids, MI: William B. Eerdman, 1995. 123p. $15; $8pa. ISBN 0-8028-5116-9; 0-8028-5099-5pa. (Women of Spirit). 4-8

Maria Mitchell (1818-1889) grew up in a Nantucket, Massachusetts, Quaker community that did not allow women to study mathematics. However, Mitchell's father, an amateur astronomer, decided to teach her both mathematics and what he knew about astronomy. Mitchell believed that women should refuse to follow authority if they did not agree with it. Only then would they be able to accomplish the things they were capable of. Mitchell was the first female professional astronomer in the United States and the first woman elected to the American Academy of Arts and Sciences; she also became Vassar's professor of astronomy. Additionally, she discovered Comet Mitchell and won a gold medal for it. Sources, Further Reading, and Index.

836.   Gorrell, Gena K. **North Star to Freedom: The Story of the Underground Railroad**. New York: Delacorte, 1997. 168p. $17.95. ISBN 0-385-32319-0. 6-8

The focus of this book, unlike other texts on the Underground Railroad, is Canada. Many of the slaves who took the railroad ended their journey in Canada with the help of abolitionists and Quakers along the way. Individual accounts from slaves who settled in Canada add new insights about this ordeal of American history. Reproductions, Bibliography, Further Reading, Notes, and Index.

837.   Gourley, Catherine. **Hunting Neptune's Giants: True Stories of American Whaling**. Brookfield, CT: Millbrook Press, 1995. 94p. $19.90. ISBN 1-56294-534-3. 4-7

Writings from whalers and some of their wives give an idea of life and work aboard an American whaling ship in the nineteenth century. Details of the hunting, harpooning, and processing help one understand the value of whales in their lives. Who went whaling and why gives additional insight into these people. The text relates the story of George H. Newton's 1880 traveling whale show, when citizens could smell the show coming in the spring and did not need newspaper advertisements. Photographs, prints, and paintings highlight the text. Bibliography, Further Reading, and Index.

838.   Gourse, Leslie. **Dizzy Gillespie and the Birth of Bebop**. New York: Atheneum, 1994. 150p. $14.95. ISBN 0-689-31869-3. 5-9

When he was 10, Dizzy Gillespie (b. 1917) was the last child to arrive in the instrument room when he first joined the school band. The only instrument left was the slide trombone. He was delighted with it, and his career began. As an adult, he contributed greatly to jazz music with new rhythms, harmonic color, and a style called bebop. Suggested Listening, Bibliography, and Index.

839.   Gourse, Leslie. **Pocahontas: Young Peacemaker**. Meryl Henderson, illustrator. New York: Aladdin, 1996. 192p. $4.99pa. ISBN 0-689-80808-9pa. (Childhood of Famous Americans Series). 3-6

Pocahontas (d. 1617) grew up in the area now called Virginia, near Jamestown. There she lived in peace with her tribe until settlers from England arrived. She then became a liaison between the settlers and her father, the chief of her tribe. This fictional biography looks at her childhood with an ending chapter that discusses her marriage to John Rolfe, the changing of her name to Rebecca, and her trip to England, where she died.

840.   Graff, Stewart, and Polly Anne Graff. **Helen Keller: Toward the Light**. Paul Frame, illustrator. New York: Chelsea Juniors, 1992. 80p. $14.95. ISBN 0-7910-1412-6. (Discovery Biography). 3-6

Helen Keller (1880-1968), blind and deaf, had become unruly and unmanageable by seven years of age. Then her father found her a teacher through Alexander Graham Bell. Anne Sullivan taught Helen a special sign language that allowed her to learn to read and write and ultimately to graduate from Radcliffe College. Then she began lecturing and working to establish special schools for the blind and deaf. She showed that people with disabilities can contribute to the betterment of all lives.

841.   Graham, Ian. **Spacecraft**. Roger Stewart, illustrator. Austin, TX: Raintree/Steck-Vaughn, 1995. 32p. $13.98. ISBN 0-8114-6193-9. (Pointers). 3-6

Two-page discussions on each type of spacecraft place it within its twentieth-century historical context. The first spacecraft, launched by the Russians, were *Sputnik I* and *II* in 1957. The United States followed in 1958 with *Explorer V*. After these were the space capsules, *Gemini, Apollo, Soyuz,* the space shuttle, modern satellites, deep space probes, the *Viking* lander, *Salyut,* Skylab, and *Mir.* Illustrations enhance the information. Glossary and Index.

842.   Graham, Lorenz. **John Brown: A Cry for Freedom**. New York: Crowell, HarperCollins, 1980. 180p. $12.89. ISBN 0-690-04024-5. 6 up

In 1859, John Brown (1800-1859) and his friends took direct action to end slavery, which some think was the real beginning of the Civil War. Regardless, he was hanged for his actions. As the son of strongly religious parents who believed that humans should never be attached to things, Brown became a fighter against slavery and injustice. He was a friend of Frederick Douglass and Harriet Tubman and a supporter of the Jayhawkers, people who fought against Kansas becoming a slave state. Books for Further Reading and Index.

843.   Granfield, Linda. **Cowboy: An Album**. New York: Ticknor & Fields, 1994. 96p. $18.95. ISBN 0-395-68430-7. 5-10

Photographs, engravings, and drawings illustrate this five-part look at cowboys. The parts are the historical cowboy, the roundup, the closing of the West, the building of the cowboy myth, and cowboys today. More specific topics discussed include the cowboy's uniform, the long drive, the end of the cattle boom, cowboys and their circuses, and the new generation of cowboys. Other Books and Index.

844.   Granfield, Linda. **In Flanders Fields: The Story of the Poem by John McCrae**. Janet Wilson, illustrator. New York: Doubleday, 1996. Unpaged. $15.95. ISBN 0-385-32228-3. 5 up

Using the poem "In Flanders Fields" as a base, the text discusses the poem, gives an overview of World War I, and briefly capsulizes the life of the Canadian poet, John McCrae. Sketches, photographs, and memorabilia add to the illustrations.

845. Graves, Charles P. **Annie Oakley: The Shooting Star**. New York: Chelsea Juniors, 1991. 80p. $14.95. ISBN 0-7910-1448-7. (Discovery Biography). 3-6

When Annie Oakley (1860-1926) was only seven, growing up in Ohio, she shot game in the woods. At 14, she helped support her family by hunting quail and selling her catch. At 15, she beat a trick shooter, and he married her. After Buffalo Bill Cody added her to his traveling Wild West Show, she became an international star. Sitting Bull, the Sioux chief, named her "Little Sureshot." She was probably the most famous trick shooter who ever lived.

846. Graves, Charles P. **John Smith**. Al Fiorentino, illustrator. New York: Chelsea Juniors, 1991. 80p. $14.95. (Discovery Biography). 2-6

John Smith (1579?-1631) came to Jamestown in 1607 and helped establish it as the first permanent English settlement in America. He worked with the Indians and explored the area surrounding Jamestown. After the Indian chief Powhatan captured him, the chief's daughter Pocahontas saved him from death. He eventually returned to England.

847. Graves, Charles P. **Robert E. Lee: Hero of the South**. Nathan Goldstein, illustrator. New York: Chelsea Juniors, 1991. 80p. $14.95. ISBN 0-7910-1462-2. (Discovery Biography). 3-6

Robert E. Lee (1807-1870) admired his father, "Light-Horse Harry," a general in the American Revolution, and his father's friend, George Washington. They exemplified his ideals of duty, courage, and honesty. He lived his life that way, and after fighting against friends in the Civil War, he wanted the two sides in the conflict to have peaceful relations again. He was brilliant and courageous.

848. Gray, James. **George Washington Carver**. Englewood Cliffs, NJ: Silver Burdett, 1991. 138p. $13.98. ISBN 0-382-09964-8. (Pioneers in Change). 5-9

Son of slaves, George Washington Carver (c. 1864-1943) earned educational degrees from Iowa State. While teaching at Tuskegee Institute after graduating, his research showed the value of crop rotation and the benefits of peanuts and soybeans as soil-enriching. The text presents his life. Photographs, Important Dates, Bibliography, and Index.

849. Green, Carl, and William Sanford. **Billy the Kid**. Springfield, NJ: Enslow, 1992. 48p. $14.95. ISBN 0-89490-364-0. (Outlaws and Lawmen of the Wild West). 5-6

Billy the Kid supposedly killed 21 men, one for each year of his life, but he probably killed nine. He was part of a gang known for stealing cattle and horses and having gunfights. He always managed to escape the law, but other aspects of his life are covered in the text with accompanying photographs. Glossary, More Good Reading, and Index.

850. Green, Carl, and William Sanford. **Wild Bill Hickock**. Springfield, NJ: Enslow, 1992. 48p. $14.95. ISBN 0-89490-366-7. (Outlaws and Lawmen of the Wild West). 5-6

Wild Bill Hickok (1837-1876) fought bandits, Indians, and disruptive cowboys as a lawman. He had such skill with a gun that people called him the "Prince of Pistoleers." His fame has spread since the 1860s through stories of saloon gunfights, scouting missions, and narrow escapes, but he made the West safe for new settlers. Glossary, More Good Reading, and Index.

851. Green, Carl R., and William R. Sanford. **Allan Pinkerton**. Springfield, NJ: Enslow, 1995. 48p. $14.95. ISBN 0-89490-592-9. (Outlaws and Lawmen of the Wild West). 4-6

As America's first detective (although born in Scotland), Allan Pinkerton (1819-1884) had spies, criminals, and terrorists all fearing him. He used the motto "We Never Sleep," and his National Detective Agency was the model for the Federal Bureau of Investigation when it was formed in 1918. He never closed a case until the suspect was apprehended or had died. Pinkerton actually saved Abraham Lincoln from an earlier assassination attempt. Notes, Glossary, More Good Reading, and Index.

852. Green, Carl R., and William R. Sanford. **Bat Masterson**. Springfield, NJ: Enslow, 1992. 48p. $14.95. ISBN 0-89490-362-4. (Outlaws and Lawmen of the Wild West). 4-6

As one of the tough lawmen of Dodge City, Kansas, Bat Masterson saw gunfights, murders, and robberies; Boot Hill cemetery was one of the most famous spots in town. He was, however, well known at gambling tables. In Tombstone, Arizona, he was both a deputy and a card dealer for Wyatt Earp. Among his professions were buffalo hunter, Indian fighter, lawman, gambler, saloonkeeper, boxing promoter, and sportswriter. Glossary, More Good Reading, and Index.

853. Green, Carl R., and William R. Sanford. **Belle Starr**. Springfield, NJ: Enslow, 1992. 48p. $14.95. ISBN 0-89490-363-2. (Outlaws and Lawmen of the Wild West). 4-6

Belle Starr was the "Bandit Queen." She hid outlaws at her ranch in Indian Territory (now Oklahoma) and married several gunmen, all notorious. She also rode through Dallas, Texas, shooting her guns in the air. She was the most feared woman in the West, although some of the stories that circulated about her are untrue. Glossary, More Good Reading, and Index.

854.   Green, Carl R., and William R. Sanford. **Butch Cassidy**. Springfield, NJ: Enslow, 1995. 48p. $14.95. ISBN 0-89490-587-2. (Outlaws and Lawmen of the Wild West). 5-8

Butch Cassidy (b. 1866) was an outlaw who had a gang, the Wild Bunch. Newspapers, magazines, and dime novels reported their exploits. The text presents him, his group, and what they did. Glossary, More Good Reading, and Index.

855.   Green, Carl R., and William R. Sanford. **The Dalton Gang**. Springfield, NJ: Enslow, 1995. 48p. $14.95. ISBN 0-89490-588-0. (Outlaws and Lawmen of the Wild West). 4-6

Grat, Bill, Bob, and Emmett Dalton were four outlaw brothers. They followed the model of their cousins, the Younger brothers, and robbed trains and banks during the 1890s. Their exploits, featured in newspapers, magazines, and dime novels, gave them fame. Most of them were gunned down in the Coffeyville, Kansas, raid of 1892, when they tried to rob two banks at once. Notes, Glossary, Bibliography, and Index.

856.   Green, Carl R., and William R. Sanford. **Doc Holliday**. Springfield, NJ: Enslow, 1995. 48p. $14.95. ISBN 0-89490-589-9. (Outlaws and Lawmen of the Wild West). 4-6

John Henry "Doc" Holliday (1851-1887), a gambler and gunslinger, always seemed to be interested in a gunfight. He and Wyatt Earp participated in the most famous gunfight of the 1800s, the Shootout at O.K. Corral. Holliday was a young dentist who traveled west because he wanted adventure. He abandoned his dental practice, however, so he could spend more time gambling. He found cheaters, but he may also have worked as a con man or a stagecoach robber himself. Notes, Glossary, More Good Reading, and Index.

857.   Green, Carl R., and William R. Sanford. **Jesse James**. Springfield, NJ: Enslow, 1992. 48p. $14.95. ISBN 0-89490-365-9. (Outlaws and Lawmen of the Wild West). 4-6

Jesse James (1847-1882) and his gang held up banks, robbed trains and stagecoaches, got caught, and made escapes from the law that became famous. Some have said that James robbed from the rich to give to the poor, but others say that he was a deliberate murderer who did whatever he wanted and kept the money for himself. The text tries to tell the facts. Glossary, More Good Reading, and Index.

858.   Green, Carl R., and William R. Sanford. **Judge Roy Bean**. Springfield, NJ: Enslow, 1995. 48p. $14.95. ISBN 0-89490-591-0. (Outlaws and Lawmen of the Wild West). 4-6

As a colorful figure in the Wild West, the "law west of Pecos," Roy Bean was a judge as well as a saloonkeeper known to shortchange customers and pocket court fines. He never hanged a man and kept the peace. He eventually settled in Langtry, Texas, where he gained fame for his exploits. Photographs highlight the text. Glossary, More Good Reading, and Index.

859.   Green, Carl R., and William R. Sanford. **Wyatt Earp**. Springfield, NJ: Enslow, 1992. 48p. $14.95. ISBN 0-89490-367-5. (Outlaws and Lawmen of the Wild West). 4-6

Wyatt Earp (1848-1929) fought in the Shootout at O.K. Corral against the Clanton gang. Earp and his brothers were trying to clean Tombstone, Arizona, of thieves. Earp first became a lawman in Dodge City, Kansas, where he kept the peace. He was known for hitting people with his gun rather than shooting them. He had friends such as Bat Masterson and Doc Holliday. When he died, he owned mines and oil fields. Photographs, Glossary, More Good Reading, and Index.

860.   Green, Connie Jordan. **The War at Home**. New York: Macmillan, 1989. 137p. $12.95. ISBN 0-689-50470-5. 6-8

In 1945, Mattie, 13, and her family move to Oak Ridge, Tennessee, where her father has a job working on a secret project for the government. Then her cousin Virgil, 12, comes to stay with them. At first, she resents his presence because he announces that boys are much better than girls at a lot of different things. He leaves, but when she learns that his father has abused him by making him work in adult jobs after his mother died, she is glad he returns. After the atom bomb drops in World War II, people in Oak Ridge find out that they had been making parts of the bomb.

861.   Green, Rayna. **Women in American Indian Society**. New York: Chelsea House, 1992. 111p. $19.95; $8.95pa. ISBN 1-55546-734-2; 0-7910-0401-5pa. (Indians of North America). 5 up

Women have long had a role of leadership in the Native American community. This text, a social history, looks at the Native American female after the arrival of the Europeans, on the reservation, and in contemporary society. It focuses on the average woman and her contributions to her people. Photographs and drawings enhance the text. Further Reading, Glossary, and Index.

862. Greenberg, Judith E. **Newcomers to America: Stories of Today's Young Immigrants (in Their Own Words)**. New York: Franklin Watts, 1996. 128p. $22. ISBN 0-531-11256-X. 6-10

The text looks at 14 immigrants who came to the United States as young people from various parts of the world. Among them are an Irish girl who came in the 1950s, a girl from Poland early in the twentieth century, a boy from Iran in the 1980s, and a girl from Liberia in the 1980s. Their stories illustrate a particular aspect of an immigrant's experience, such as changing countries while a teenager or trying to retain cultural identity in a foreign place. Photographs, Further Reading, and Index.

863. Greenblatt, Miriam. **Franklin D. Roosevelt: 32nd President of the United States**. Ada, OK: Garrett Educational, 1988. 120p. $17.26. ISBN 0-9444483-06-2. (Presidents of the United States). 5-9

Franklin D. Roosevelt (1882-1945) attended Harvard and Columbia Law School before marrying his cousin Eleanor. He served in New York State government, as the Assistant Secretary of the Navy, and as President of the United States for four terms. He established the New Deal to overcome the Great Depression and declared war on Japan in 1941. Bibliography and Index.

864. Greenblatt, Miriam. **James K. Polk: 11th President of the United States**. Ada, OK: Garrett Educational, 1988. 120p. $17.26. ISBN 0-944483-04-6. (Presidents of the United States). 5-9

James K. Polk (1795-1849) graduated from the University of North Carolina and became a lawyer in Tennessee. He served in the House of Representatives and became the Speaker. He was also governor of Tennessee. The text begins with the operation he had at 17 for gallstones before anesthetics or antiseptics were discovered; luckily, he survived. He continued to show through his life that he could achieve things even though odds were against him, including being elected President. He died of poor health within months after leaving the White House. Bibliography and Index.

865. Greene, Carol. **Abraham Lincoln: President of a Divided Country**. Chicago: Childrens Press, 1989. 45p. $15.90; $4.95pa. ISBN 0-516-04206-8; 0-516-44206-9pa. (Rookie Biography). K-3

This simple biography of Abraham Lincoln (1809-1865) tells about his childhood and his experiences before becoming the Civil War President. Index.

866. Greene, Carol. **Benjamin Franklin: A Man with Many Jobs**. Steve Dobson, illustrator. Chicago: Childrens Press, 1988. 48p. $17.70; $4.95pa. ISBN 0-516-04202-5; 0-516-44202-3pa. (Rookie Biography). K-3

Benjamin Franklin (1706-1790) had many jobs during his long life after he left school at the age of 10. He made soap and candles for his father and was a printing apprentice for his brother before he ran away. He started his own printing business in Philadelphia, a library, and a fire department, and he wrote *Poor Richard's Almanack* for 25 years. He also became a diplomat, representing the American colonies and then the United States while he continued to invent things. Time Line and Index.

867. Greene, Carol. **Black Elk: A Man with a Vision**. Chicago: Childrens Press, 1990. 48p. $17.70. ISBN 0-516-04213-0. (Rookie Biography). 2-4

Although Black Elk (1863-1950), an Oglala medicine man, had a vision of universal peace, he saw his tribe decimated during his lifetime. When his people were attacked at Wounded Knee in 1890, he saw how much they lost. He tells the story of his tribe in 1931. Index.

868. Greene, Carol. **Daniel Boone: Man of the Forests**. Steven Dobson, illustrator. Chicago: Childrens Press, 1990. 47p. $17.70; $4.95pa. ISBN 0-516-04210-6; 0-516-04210-4pa. (Rookie Biography). 2-4

Daniel Boone (1734-1820) explored the frontier of Kentucky. The biography tells of his life and his family in five short chapters. An illustration of Indians capturing Boone's daughter and two other girls raises further interest. Also appearing are pictures of colonial crafts and skills, including candle making and weaving. Index.

869. Greene, Carol. **Emily Dickinson: American Poet**. Chicago: Childrens Press, 1994. 47p. $17.70; $4.95pa. ISBN 0-516-04263-7; 0-516-44263-5pa. (Rookie Biography). 2-3

Emily Dickinson (1830-1886) lived a conventional life with an unconventional mind. Greene has captured her complexity within the simple text. She mentions that Dickinson was in love with Charles Wadsworth, who already had a wife, but that she loved him is not specifically documented. Photographs, drawings, and poems complement the text. Important Dates and Index.

870. Greene, Carol. **George Washington Carver: Scientist and Teacher**. Chicago: Childrens Press, 1991. 42p. $17.70; $4.95pa. ISBN 0-516-04250-5; 0-516-44250-3pa. (Rookie Biography). 2-3

George Washington Carver (1864-1943) was a scientist who experimented with sweet potatoes and peanuts, finding valuable ways to use these foods. He tried to help the people he knew and was an important force in the development of the Tuskegee Institute in Tuskegee, Alabama. Important Dates and Index.

871.   Greene, Carol. **George Washington, First President of the United States**. Chicago: Childrens Press, 1991. 42p. $17.70; $4.95pa. ISBN 0-516-04218-1; 0-516-44218-Xpa. (Rookie Biography). 2-3

George Washington (1732-1799) was a surveyor and a soldier before becoming President. The text looks at his life, his family, and his accomplishments. Important Dates and Index.

872.   Greene, Carol. **Jackie Robinson: Baseball's First Black Major-Leaguer**. Chicago: Childrens Press, 1990. 47p. $17.70; $4.95pa. ISBN 0-516-04211-4; 0-516-44211-2pa. (Rookie Biography). K-2

Jackie Robinson (1919-1972) was the first Black man to play baseball on a modern major league team. The text gives facts about his life as an athlete and discusses his civil rights activities. Chronology and Index.

873.   Greene, Carol. **Jacques Cousteau: Man of the Oceans**. Chicago: Childrens Press, 1990. 48p. $17.70. ISBN 0-516-04215-7. (Rookie Biography). 2-4

In five chapters, the text tells the story of Jacques Yves Cousteau (1910-1997), who had an early interest in the sea, in films, and in machinery. These avocations led to his life's work of revealing the oceans to people. Color and black-and-white illustrations enhance the text. Index.

874.   Greene, Carol. **John Chapman: The Man Who Was Johnny Appleseed**. Chicago: Childrens Press, 1991. 48p. $17.70; $4.95pa. ISBN 0-516-04223-8; 0-516-44223-6pa. (Rookie Biography). 1-3

John Chapman (1774-1845) was named Johnny Appleseed because he planted apple trees along the Pennsylvania frontier and sold them to the settlers. Then he went into Ohio and did the same. He went as far as Indiana planting his seed. He disliked killing any living thing and once apologized to a rattlesnake he killed after it bit him. He supposedly doused a fire because it was killing mosquitoes. He lived his life for the good of others. Important Dates and Index.

875.   Greene, Carol. **John Muir: Man of the Wild Places**. Chicago: Childrens Press, 1991. 42p. $17.70; $4.95pa. ISBN 0-516-04220-3; 0-516-44220-1pa. (Rookie Biography). 2-3

Before he came to the United States when he was 11, John Muir (1838-1914) lived in Scotland. After he had to help his family with the farm for several years, he decided to walk toward South America. After taking a boat to Cuba, he got sick and had to return home. Then he decided to go to California. He loved Yosemite and realized that the beautiful land had to be preserved from those who would develop and destroy it. He started the Sierra Club, and President Theodore Roosevelt helped pass laws that would preserve the country. Important Dates.

876.   Greene, Carol. **John Philip Sousa: The March King**. Chicago: Childrens Press, 1992. 48p. $4.95pa. ISBN 0-516-04226-0pa. (Rookie Biography). 2-4

John Philip Sousa (1854-1932) learned to play many musical instruments during his life. When he was 11, he started his own dance band. At 13, he enlisted in the United States Marine Band. Among his march compositions are "Semper Fidelis" and "Washington Post." They helped him earn the title of "March King." Important Dates and Index.

877.   Greene, Carol. **Katherine Dunham: Black Dancer**. Chicago: Childrens Press, 1992. 44p. $17.70; $4.95pa. ISBN 0-516-04252-1; 0-516-44252-Xpa. (Rookie Biography). 1-3

Katherine Dunham (b. 1910) wanted to dance as a young girl, but her father wanted her to work and attend school. She began to study African countries and places that had African American dances. When she went to Haiti, she realized she wanted to perform these dances. She and her husband started a troupe and traveled around the world. After arthritis kept her off the stage, she became a choreographer. In 1967, she began the Performing Arts School in St. Louis for children in the ghetto. Important Dates and Index.

878.   Greene, Carol. **Laura Ingalls Wilder: Author of the Little House Books**. Steven Dobson, illustrator. Chicago: Childrens Press, 1990. 46p. $17.70; $4.95pa. ISBN 0-516-04212-2; 0-516-44212-0pa. (Rookie Biography). 1-3

This biography introduces readers to Laura Ingalls Wilder (1867-1957) and the little houses in which she lived as her family moved along the frontier. Photographs and drawings of these dwellings may entice readers to seek her novels. Chronology, Further Reading, and Index.

879.   Greene, Carol. **Louisa May Alcott: Author, Nurse, Suffragette**. Chicago: Childrens Press, 1984. 126p. $19.30. ISBN 0-516-03208-9. (People of Distinction). 4-6

Louisa May Alcott (1832-1888) served in a number of roles. She penned the novel *Little Women*, worked as a nurse during the Civil War, and supported the right of women to vote during the later years of her life. She also helped support her family with her writing. Time Line and Index.

880. Greene, Carol. **Mark Twain: Author of Tom Sawyer**. Chicago: Childrens Press, 1992. 48p. $17.70. ISBN 0-516-04228-9. (Rookie Biography). 2-3

Samuel Langhorne Clemens (1835-1910) took the name Mark Twain when he became a professional writer. The text looks at the main events in his life, with photographs to illustrate. Important Dates and Index.

881. Greene, Carol. **Phillis Wheatley: First African American Poet**. Chicago: Childrens Press, 1995. 47p. $17.70; $4.95pa. ISBN 0-5160-4269-6; 0-516-44269-4pa. (Rookie Biography). 1-3

Phillis Wheatley (1753-1784) died when she was only 31 years old, but her poetry was recognized as some of the best in the colonies. As a slave who could read and write, she used her literary talents throughout the Revolution. Index.

882. Greene, Carol. **Rachel Carson: Friend of Nature**. Chicago: Childrens Press, 1992. 48p. $17.70. ISBN 0-516-04229-7. (Rookie Biography). K-3

Rachel Carson (1907-1965) sold her first story to *St. Nicholas* magazine when she was only 10 years old. She and her family thought she would be an English teacher, but a college professor interested her in biology. The meshing of writing with biology led to such books as *The Sea Around Us* and *Silent Spring*. Her realization that humans were destroying their planet is one of the major reasons that ecology has become such an important part of contemporary life. Important Dates and Index.

883. Greene, Carol. **Robert E. Lee: Leader in War and Peace**. Chicago: Childrens Press, 1989. 45p. $17.70. ISBN 0-516-04209-2. (Rookie Biography). 1-2

People who knew Robert E. Lee (1807-1870) considered him to be a great general and a good man. Educated at West Point, he fought in the Mexican War. Lincoln asked him to lead the Union army in the Civil War. Instead, Lee decided to fight for his home state, Virginia, and the South. Photographs show him in various places before he surrendered to Grant in 1865. Important Dates and Index.

884. Greene, Carol. **Thomas Alva Edison: Bringer of Light**. Chicago: Childrens Press, 1985. 128p. $19.30. ISBN 0-516-03213-5. (People of Distinction). 4-6

Thomas Alva Edison (1847-1931) was so inquisitive as a boy that he sat on a nest of eggs to see if he could get them to hatch. Although he had eggs all over his pants, he learned that humans cannot hatch eggs. He burned down the family's barn when he lit a fire inside. Among the inventions that resulted from his inquisitiveness were the stock printer, the quadruplex telegraph, the phonograph, the incandescent electric lamp, the first hydroelectric plant, and the kinetoscope, a motion picture camera. Photographs, Time Line, and Index.

885. Greene, Constance C. **Dotty's Suitcase**. 1980. New York: Puffin, 1991. 147p. $3.95pa. ISBN 0-14-034882-4pa. 3-7

In 1934, during the Depression, Dotty, 12, wants a suitcase because she thinks it will make her feel like she is going somewhere. She finds one on the side of the road that, unknown to her, bank robbers threw out of their car while running from a heist. She and Jud, eight, with whom she is walking, get a ride to a town where her best friend has moved. Although Dotty has felt sorry for herself because she must stay at home alone while her older sisters work, she realizes that she has a good life. She gives the money in the suitcase to her best friend, who lost everything when her father died.

886. Greene, Janice. **Our Century: 1900-1910**. Milwaukee, WI: Gareth Stevens, 1993. 64p. $23.93. ISBN 0-8368-1032-5. 3-10

The book is written as if it were a newspaper; short articles give an overview of the decade. Included are statistics, daily life in America, the Boxer Rebellion in China, Boers and British fighting in South Africa, Russia and Japan at war, Russia's workers and peasants revolting, McKinley assassinated, San Francisco's earthquake and fire, Admiral Peary at the North Pole, Henry Ford, Marie Curie, Ivan Pavlov, Albert Einstein, Sigmund Freud, the first World Series, Christy Mathewson, Ty Cobb, Jack Johnson, Jack London, Upton Sinclair, Rudyard Kipling, Isadora Duncan, Pablo Picasso, the Wright brothers, Helen Keller, J. P. Morgan, and Typhoid Mary. Glossary, Books for Further Reading, Places to Write or Visit, and Index.

887. Greene, Laura Offenhartz. **Child Labor: Then and Now**. New York: Franklin Watts, 1992. 144p. $20.60. ISBN 0-531-13008-8. (Impact). 5-10

Ever since the British, with their chimney sweeps in the 1700s, and the Industrial Revolution, with children working in factories, child labor has been a serious problem. In the early twentieth century, Lewis Hine photographed children, especially immigrants, working in the terrible conditions of mines, mills, factories, sweatshops, and farms. A change in the laws has helped the United States, but child labor still exists in countries from which America gets many goods. Engravings enhance the text. Selected Bibliography and Index.

888. Greenfield, Eloise. **Mary McLeod Bethune**. Jerry Pinkney, illustrator. 1977. New York: Trophy, 1994. 34p. $5.95pa. ISBN 0-06-446168-8pa. 1-5

Because she wanted to learn to read so badly, Mary McLeod (1875-1955) walked five miles to and from school as a young girl. Her siblings stayed on the farm working, and she taught them what she learned when she returned home. She continued her schooling with scholarships, but when denied the chance to serve as a missionary to Africa, she eventually started her own school in Florida. When she saw a need, she also started a hospital for Blacks. Her work led Franklin D. Roosevelt to ask her to head the National Youth Administration during the Depression to help young Blacks get jobs. Her work and care helped many throughout her life.

889. Greenfield, Eloise. **Rosa Parks**. Eric Marlow, illustrator. New York: HarperCollins, 1973. 34p. $14.89; $3.95pa. ISBN 0-690-71211-1; 0-06-442025-6pa. 1-5

Aware of injustice almost since her birth in 1913, but never actively planning to counter it, Rosa Parks, tired after a long day's work bending over a sewing machine, refused to move from her seat in the Black section of a Montgomery, Alabama, bus for a white man. She had paid the same fare as he. Her action got her arrested and fired from her job, but it began the bus boycott, led by Dr. Martin Luther King, that lasted long enough for the Supreme Court to rule that the bus company was unconstitutional in its actions. She has been called "Mother of the Civil Rights Movement." *Notable Children's Trade Books in the Field of Social Studies* and *Carter G. Woodson Award*.

890. Greenwood, Barbara. **A Pioneer Sampler: The Daily Life of a Pioneer Family in 1840**. Heather Collins, illustrator. New York: Ticknor & Fields, 1995. 240p. $18.95. ISBN 0-395-71540-7. 5-8

The text introduces the Robertsons, a pioneer family on a backwoods farm in 1840. Among the chores they must complete during the year are making maple syrup, planting crops, and shearing sheep. They attend a backwoods school, visit a country store, build a house, and go to a barn dance. They have to cook their food, churn their butter, slaughter hogs, and operate a grist mill. They also have to tell time by looking at the sun, and they have no one to tell them the next day's weather. Glossary and Index. *Notable Children's Trade Books in the Field of Social Studies*.

891. Greeson, Janet. **An American Army of Two**. Patricia Rose Mulvihill, illustrator. Minneapolis, MN: Carolrhoda, 1992. 48p. $15.95; $5.95pa. ISBN 0-87614-664-7; 0-87614-547-0pa. K-4

When Rebecca and Abigail see British ships in the harbor near their coastal home in Massachusetts, they hide behind a tree with their fife and drum to play "Yankee Doodle." The music tricks the British into thinking that American troops await nearby, and they leave.

892. Gregory, Kristiana. **Earthquake at Dawn**. San Diego, CA: Harcourt Brace, 1992. 192p. $15.95; $3.95pa. ISBN 0-15-200446-7; 0-15-200099-2pa. (Great Episodes). 3-7

In 1906, Daisy, 15, and Edith Irvine, a photographer, plan a journey around the world. On the day of their departure, a devastating earthquake shakes San Francisco, the city where they plan to disembark. Instead of traveling, they help others construct tents and rescue people during the aftershocks. When they return to Edith's home, they have both real and mental photographs of the severe damage suffered throughout the city. *American Library Association Best Books for Young Adults, Notable Children's Trade Books in the Field of Social Studies*, and *New York Public Library's Books for the Teen Age*.

893. Gregory, Kristiana. **Jenny of the Tetons**. San Diego, CA: Harcourt Brace, 1989. 120p. $13.95. ISBN 0-15-200480-7. 5-7

Carrie, 15 in 1875, refuses to have any dealings with Indians because they killed her family in a raid. "Beaver Dick," a trapper, befriends her, but his wife is a Shoshone. Jenny and her children remain friendly toward Carrie until she adjusts to the idea that not all Indians can be equated with the ones who destroyed her family. *Golden Kite Award*.

894. Gregory, Kristiana. **Jimmy Spoon and the Pony Express**. New York: Scholastic, 1994. 117p. $13.95. ISBN 0-590-46577-5. 5-7

Based on the true exploits of Elijah Nicholas Wilson is this story of Jimmy Spoon, a 17-year-old bored with working in his father's store after living with the Shoshoni (*The Legend of Jimmy Spoon*). In 1860, he sees an advertisement for an expert rider not more than 18 who is willing to risk death daily. The lure of adventure attracts him; he applies and is hired immediately for the Pony Express. However, he still remembers a beautiful Shoshoni girl, Nahanee, and after a year passes he goes to find her and his Shoshoni family. Glossary and Bibliography.

895. Gregory, Kristiana. **The Legend of Jimmy Spoon**. San Diego, CA: Harcourt Brace, 1990. 164p. $15.95; $6pa. ISBN 0-15-200506-4; 0-15-243812-2pa. (Great Episodes). 3-7

Bored with working in his father's store in the Mormon stronghold of Utah in 1854, Jimmy, 12, agrees to go with two Shoshoni boys to their home when they promise to give him a horse. He does not realize that they expect him to live with the tribe until he proves his manhood and earns the horse. He stays, and he eventually earns enough respect so that whether he leaves or stays becomes his own decision.

896. Gregory, Kristiana. **The Stowaway: A Tale of California Pirates**. New York: Scholastic, 1995. 144p. $14.95. ISBN 0-590-48822-8. 4-6

Carlito, 11, decides that he will burn the ship of Hippolyte de Bouchard, a privateer who killed his father. He does not succeed, but after adventures with the pirate, he returns safely home to his mother and his horse.

897. Gregory, Kristiana. **The Winter of Red Snow: The Diary of Abigail Jane Stewart, Valley Forge, Pennsylvania, 1777-1778**. New York: Scholastic, 1996. 170p. $9.95. ISBN 0-590-22653-3. (Dear America 2). 5-9

As Abigail looks out her window on December 19, 1777, she sees soldiers and runs outside with her family to cheer. The soldiers are "quiet and thin," and she sees that their bare feet leave footprints in the snow. Her journal covers the days from December 1, 1777, until July 4, 1778, when everyone is sure that the newly trained soldiers under George Washington will be able to defeat the British in the American Revolution. An epilogue gives information about Abby after her journal ends.

898. Grey, Edward. **The Eighties**. Austin, TX: Raintree/Steck-Vaughn, 1990. 48p. $22.80. ISBN 0-8114-4215-2. (Decades). 5-7

Among the disasters of this decade of the 1980s were famine, war, a space tragedy, a nuclear accident, and the AIDS virus. But the world also became safer as superpowers came closer together in their philosophical outlook. It marked the beginning of global communication when in 1985, more than 1.5 billion people in 160 countries watched the Live Aid charity concert. The text looks at the music, clothes, media, leisure, youth culture, and styles of the time against a backdrop of major historical, political, and technological events. Glossary, Further Reading, and Index.

899. Griest, Lisa. **Lost at the White House: A 1909 Easter Story**. Andrea Shine, illustrator. Minneapolis, MN: Carolrhoda, 1994. 48p. $15.95; $5.95pa. ISBN 0-87614-726-0; 0-87614-632-9pa. (On My Own). 1-3

In 1909, Rena goes with her sister to the Easter Egg Roll at the White House in Washington, D.C. With so many people wandering around the huge lawn, she loses her sister. A guard finds her and takes her inside, where she gets to meet the president, Theodore Roosevelt.

900. Griffin, Peni. **Switching Well**. New York: Margaret K. McElderry, 1993. 218p. $15.95. ISBN 0-689-50581-7. 5-8

Each girl, Ada and Amber, wishes that she lived in another time. Both shift their 12-year-old selves to another century. Ada moves from 1891 to 1991, and Amber goes from 1991 to 1891. Their change comes inside a well. The busy life of San Antonio shocks Ada, where she is almost accosted by a child molester, and the prejudice and lack of opportunity of 100 years earlier distresses Amber. She is disturbed that the deaf are considered no different than the retarded and that Christians have more rights than Jews. An African American girl helps them return to their times after an unexpected inheritance.

901. Gross, Ruth Belov. **True Stories About Abraham Lincoln**. Jill Kastner, illustrator. New York; Lothrop, Lee & Shepard, 1990. 46p. $12.95. ISBN 0-688-08797-3. 2-4

This view of Abraham Lincoln (1809-1865) comes from one-page chapters that describe events in his life, including the legendary footprints on the ceiling. More complex personality traits and relationships are omitted, but Lincoln the man is accessible.

902. Gross, Virginia T. **The Day It Rained Forever**. Ronald Himler, illustrator. New York: Viking, 1991. 52p. $11.95. ISBN 0-670-83552-8. (Once Upon America). 3-6

Tina's mother saves herself and a newborn baby, but Tina's uncle and his fiancé drown in the Johnstown, Pennsylvania, flood of 1887. Tina's brother is very bitter toward the greedy men who neglected a weak dam to make their local sports club more valuable. When the flood ends, somewhere between 2,000 and 7,000 people are dead, and no one claims the baby. Because Tina's mother had lost a baby only two months before, they decide to raise the child.

903. Guccione, Leslie Davis. **Come Morning**. Minneapolis, MN: Carolrhoda, 1995. 120p. $14.96. ISBN 0-87614-892-5. (Adventures in Time). 4-7

Freedom Newcastle, 12 in the 1850s, cuts willows on his free Black father's farm for the Delaware Du-Pont company to buy and make into charcoal. What he really wants is to help his father at night because he knows his father and the Quaker neighbors work for the Underground Railroad. He gets his chance sooner than expected when slavers from the South capture his father, thinking that he has helped other slaves. His father proves his free status, but their home is burned. Freedom, however, delivers the "cargo" to Moses (Harriet Tubman) before the slavers find them. *Society of School Librarians International Outstanding Book.*

904. Guiberson, Brenda Z., author/illustrator. **Lighthouses: Watchers at Sea**. New York: Henry Holt, Redfeather, 1995. 70p. $15.95. ISBN 0-8050-3170-7. 3-6

In 280 BC, the Egyptian lighthouse known as the Pharos helped guard the Mediterranean. Since then, lighthouses have sometimes been the only beacon to guide ships lost at sea. Lighthouse keepers have risked their lives to keep lights burning before electricity was discovered, and even afterward, when high winds have destroyed lines. The text relates tales of shipwrecks and near-shipwrecks stopped by the lighthouse signal as well as the lonely life of the lighthouse keeper. It includes technical information such as the design of the lighthouses, the lenses, and the modern methods that replace lighthouses. Other elements give a sense of the role that lighthouses have played in history.

905. Gutman, Dan. **World Series Classics**. New York: Viking, 1994. 240p. $14.99. ISBN 0-670-85286-4. 6-8

Five World Series competitions have been considered the best in history. Gutman discusses each one in detail, with summaries, baseball trivia, and box scores for each. The series examined are that of 1912, when the New York Giants played the Boston Red Sox; 1924, when the Washington Senators played the New York Giants; 1947, when the New York Yankees played the Brooklyn Dodgers; 1975, when the Boston Red Sox played the Cincinnati Reds; and 1991, when the Atlanta Braves played the Minnesota Twins. Index.

906. Guttmacher, Peter. **Crazy Horse: Sioux War Chief**. New York: Chelsea House, 1994. 120p. $18.85. ISBN 0-7910-1712-5. (North American Indians of Achievement). 5 up

Crazy Horse (1841-1877), born in Bear Butte, South Dakota, went through the rites of passage of his people and had a powerful vision that led him to try to save them many times. After his renowned victory over Custer, he tried to preserve their freedom, but was unsuccessful in the end. Photographs and reproductions enhance the text. Chronology, Further Reading, and Index.

907. Guzzetti, Paula. **The White House**. New York: Dillon Press, 1996. 72p. $15.95; $7.95pa. ISBN 0-87518-650-5; 0-382-39175-6pa. (Places in American History). 3-6

The White House has its own history in addition to the history of those who have lived in it. The text looks at the plans for its creation, the building and the rooms inside it, and the families who have lived there since it was completed. The White House: A Historical Timeline, Visitor Information, and Index.

H

908. Haas, Carol. **Engel v. Vitale: Separation of Church and State**. Springfield, NJ: Enslow, 1994. 128p. $17.95. ISBN 0-89490-461-2. (Landmark Supreme Court Cases). 6-9

This Supreme Court case occurred in 1962, when Stephen Engel and other parents complained that prayer in public school violated the constitutional rights of nonbelievers. William Vitale believed that prayer was an important aspect of moral and spiritual training in schools. On June 25, 1962, the Supreme Court declared that prayer in school was unconstitutional. The separation of church and state continues to be challenged. The text looks at the ideas and arguments behind this case as well as the people who brought it to court. Notes, Glossary, Further Reading, and Index.

909. Haddon, Mark. **The Sea of Tranquillity**. Christian Birmingham, illustrator. San Diego, CA: Harcourt Brace, 1996. Unpaged. $16. ISBN 0-15-201285-0. 1-3

A man remembers his childhood when he looked through binoculars at the moon, wondering if anyone would ever go there. Then he recalls the excitement of watching Armstrong and Aldrin walking on the Sea of Tranquility in 1969. He cements the idea of the walk by noting that the footprints of the astronauts will always stay on the moon, undisturbed by natural forces and other beings.

910. Hahn, Elizabeth. **The Blackfoot**. Katherine Ace, illustrator. Vero Beach, FL: Rourke, 1992. 31p. $11.95. ISBN 0-86625-395-5. (Native American People). 4-6

This brief text tells the story of the Blackfoot tribe and its origins, history, lifestyle, and daily rituals. Like other Native American tribes, it suffered when the whites overran the land, decimated the buffalo, and spread smallpox. Index.

911. Hahn, Mary Downing. **Following My Own Footsteps**. New York: Clarion, 1996. 190p. $13.95. ISBN 0-395-76477-7. 5-8

Gordy (from *Stepping on the Cracks*) goes with his mother to his grandmother's when they finally leave his abusive father during World War II. He becomes friends with the boy next door, William, whose polio has changed his life. When Gordy's brother returns from the front, he dispels Gordy's romantic ideas of war and intimates that their brother Stuart, who deserted and went to the mental ward of a veteran's hospital, might have been the only sane person around. Gordy has to digest this information, deal with his father's behavior, and decide his own values as he passes through puberty.

912. Hahn, Mary Downing. **The Gentleman Outlaw and Me—Eli: A Story of the Old West**. New York: Clarion, 1996. 212p. $14.95. ISBN 0-395-73083-X. 4-7

Eliza, 12 in 1887, runs away from cruel relatives to Tinville, Colorado, where she looks for her missing father. After a tramp approaches her, she disguises herself as a boy. She meets Calvin, 18, who calls himself the "Gentleman Outlaw." He also goes to Tinville in search of the sheriff who shot his father in the back. Calvin, however, has no idea how to do things, and Eliza has to take charge of their adventures.

913. Hahn, Mary Downing. **Stepping on the Cracks**. New York: Clarion, 1991. 216p. $13.95. ISBN 0-395-58507-4. 4-7

Elizabeth and her friend Margaret spend time riding bicycles and trying to avoid Gordy, a bully who annoys them in College Hill, Maryland, during 1944. When they follow him through the woods, they find that he is protecting a brother who has run away from the army because his abusive father will beat him if he returns home. They hear the brother coughing and decide that they must help. When Margaret's family receives word of the death of her brother, who had been fighting abroad, they have to cope with the ethical problems of helping a deserter. *Bulletin Blue Ribbon Book, Scott O'Dell Award, Joan G. Sugarman Children's Book Award, American Library Association Notable Books for Children*, and *School Library Journal Best Book*.

914. Hakim, Joy. **An Age of Extremes**. New York: Oxford University Press, 1993. 160p. $14.95; $9.95pa. ISBN 0-19-509513-8; 0-19-507760-1pa. (A History of US, Book 8). 6 up

Filled with photographs, prints, sidebars, boxed text, and running commentary, this story of the United States at the beginning of the twentieth century up to 1917 and World War I is lively, entertaining, and informative. Hakim covers all aspects of society and all cultures in her text. Chronology of Events, More Books to Read, and Index.

915.   Hakim, Joy. **All the People**. New York: Oxford University Press, 1994. 160p. $14.95; $9.95pa. ISBN 0-19-509515-4; 0-19-507762-8pa. (A History of US, Book 10). 6 up

Filled with photographs, prints, sidebars, boxed text, and running commentary, this story of the United States after World War II ended in 1945 is lively, entertaining, and informative. Hakim covers all aspects of society and all cultures in her text. Chronology of Events, More Books to Read, and Index.

916.   Hakim, Joy. **The First Americans**. New York: Oxford University Press, 1993. 160p. $14.95; $9.95pa. ISBN 0-19-509506-5; 0-19-507746-6pa. (A History of US, Book 1). 6 up

This story of the Americas and their inhabitants from the earliest times until the arrival of the first Europeans is lively and entertaining as well as informative. The book is filled with photographs, prints, sidebars, boxed text, and running commentary. Hakim covers all aspects of society and all cultures in her text. Chronology of Events, More Books to Read, and Index.

917.   Hakim, Joy. **From Colonies to Country**. New York: Oxford University Press, 1993. 192p. $14.95; $9.95pa. ISBN 0-19-509508-1; 0-19-507750-4pa. (A History of US, Book 3). 6 up

Filled with photographs, prints, sidebars, boxed text, and running commentary, this is the story of the colonies, beginning with the French and Indian War around 1755 and proceeding through the Constitutional Convention in 1787. The book is lively and entertaining as well as informative. Hakim covers all aspects of society and all cultures in her text. Chronology of Events, More Books to Read, and Index.

918.   Hakim, Joy. **Liberty for All?** New York: Oxford University Press, 1993. 160p. $14.95; $9.95pa. ISBN 0-19-509510-3; 0-19-507754-7pa. (A History of US, Book 5). 6 up

This lively, informative book covers the United States during the period of growth from 1848 until it began to disintegrate at the beginning of the Civil War in 1861. It is filled with photographs, prints, sidebars, boxed text, and running commentary. Hakim covers all aspects of society and all cultures in her text, as well as such figures as Jedediah Smith, Emily Dickinson, John James Audubon, and Sojourner Truth. Chronology of Events, More Books to Read, and Index.

919.   Hakim, Joy. **Making Thirteen Colonies**. New York: Oxford University Press, 1993. 160p. $14.95; $9.95pa. ISBN 0-19-509507-3; 0-19-507748-2pa. (A History of US, Book 2). 6 up

Filled with photographs, prints, sidebars, boxed text, and running commentary, this entertaining, informative story covers the colonization of the New World through the mid-eighteenth century until the French and Indian War around 1755. Hakim covers all aspects of society and all cultures in her text. Chronology of Events, More Books to Read, and Index.

920.   Hakim, Joy. **The New Nation**. New York: Oxford University Press, 1994. 176p. $14.95; $9.95pa. ISBN 0-19-509509-X; 0-19-507752-0pa. (A History of US, Book 4). 6 up

Filled with photographs, prints, sidebars, boxed text, and running commentary, this lively story of the newly formed United States from 1787 to 1848 is both entertaining and informative. Hakim covers all aspects of society and all cultures in her text. Chronology of Events, More Books to Read, and Index.

921.   Hakim, Joy. **Reconstruction and Reform**. New York: Oxford University Press, 1994. 192p; $14.95. 160p. $9.95pa. ISBN 0-19-509512-X; 0-19-507758-Xpa. (A History of US, Book 7). 6 up

Filled with photographs, prints, sidebars, boxed text, and running commentary, this story of Reconstruction after the Civil War and ensuing reform from 1865 to 1898 is lively and entertaining as well as informative. Hakim covers all aspects of society and all cultures in her text. Chronology of Events, More Books to Read, and Index.

922.   Hakim, Joy. **War, Peace, and All That Jazz**. New York: Oxford University Press, 1994. 192p. $14.95; $9.95pa. ISBN 0-19-509514-6; 0-19-507762-8pa. (A History of US, Book 9). 6 up

Filled with photographs, prints, sidebars, boxed text, and running commentary, this story of the United States from 1918 through World War II is lively and entertaining as well as informative. Hakim covers all aspects of society and all cultures in her text. Chronology of Events, More Books to Read, and Index.

923.   Hakim, Joy. **War Terrible War**. New York: Oxford University Press, 1994. 192p. $14.95; $9.95pa. ISBN 0-19-507755-5; 0-19-507756-3pa. (A History of US, Book 6). 6 up

Filled with photographs, prints, sidebars, boxed text, and running commentary, this story of the Civil War years shows the war's horror but is lively and entertaining as well. Hakim covers all aspects of society and all cultures in her text. Chronology of Events, More Books to Read, and Index.

924.   Hakim, Rita. **Martin Luther King, Jr. and the March Toward Freedom**. Brookfield, CT: Millbrook Press, 1991. 32p. $13.90; $4.95pa. ISBN 1-878841-13-0; 1-878841-33-5pa. (Gateway to Civil Rights). 3-5

This brief biography of Martin Luther King, Jr. (1929-1968) traces his involvement in the Civil Rights movement from his early years until his assassination. Photographs enhance the text. Chronology and Index.

925.   Halasa, Malu. **Elijah Muhammad: Religious Leader**. New York: Chelsea House, 1990. 110p. $18.95; $7.95pa. ISBN 1-55546-602-8; 0-7910-0246-2pa. (Black Americans of Achievement). 5 up

When a young boy, Elijah Poole (1897-1975) was forbidden to go into the woods on the way home from school. One day he did. He saw a man from his church lynched by a group of white men, and he never forgot the horror. He moved to the North, where he had to go on relief during the Depression before he could find a job to support his family. He was interested in Marcus Garvey's Black Nationalism and Ali's Moorish Temple of America. But when he heard Fard talk about his Nation of Islam, Elijah in turn eloquently proclaimed the values of Islam to the Black community. He became Elijah Muhammad, the father of the Black Muslims. Chronology, Further Reading, and Index.

926.   Halasa, Malu. **Mary McLeod Bethune: Educator**. New York: Chelsea House, 1989. 112p. $18.95; $7.95pa. ISBN 1-55546-574-9; 0-7910-0225-Xpa. (Black Americans of Achievement). 5 up

Awarded scholarships to schools in North Carolina and Chicago, Mary McLeod Bethune (1875-1955) returned to the South to become a teacher. She settled in Daytona Beach, Florida, and established a school for Black girls. She campaigned constantly to raise funds and saw the school merger with Cookman Institute, over which she presided for 40 years. She also fought for equal education for Blacks by leading the National Association of Colored Women and the National Council of Negro Women. Photographs and reproductions enhance the text. Chronology, Further Reading, and Index.

927.   Hall, Donald. **The Farm Summer 1942**. Barry Moser, illustrator. New York: Dial, 1994. Unpaged. $15.99. ISBN 0-8037-1501-3. K-3

In 1942, nine-year-old Peter travels from San Francisco to stay with his father's parents while his mother works on a secret war project in New York and his father fights in the South Pacific. He misses his parents but experiences many things that his father used to do—feeding the horse, raking hay, eating gingersnaps, riding in the horse-drawn buggy, watching the trains pass, and salting the sheep. When he has to leave, all his cousins come to tell him "goodbye," and he regrets leaving. But he looks forward to seeing his father.

928.   Hall, Donald. **Lucy's Christmas**. Michael McCurdy, illustrator. San Diego, CA: Browndeer, Harcourt Brace, 1994. 40p. $14.95. ISBN 0-15-276870-X. K-2

At the turn of the century, Lucy makes Christmas presents of a clothespin doll and a pen-wiper for her friends and family during the autumn in her New England town. She tells about the summer wagon with wheels and the winter one, a sleigh. When a new stove arrives, she is very interested because it is a major event in the family. *American Bookseller Pick of the Lists* and *Parents' Choice Awards*.

929.   Hall, Donald. **Lucy's Summer**. Michael McCurdy, illustrator. San Diego, CA: Browndeer, Harcourt Brace, 1995. 40p. $15. ISBN 0-15-276873-4. K-3

In 1910, when Lucy is seven, her mother opens a millinery shop in the front parlor of their New Hampshire home. She sells hats that she designed and takes old hats for remodeling. When her hat trade is slack in the summer, Lucy, her mother, and sister prepare food for canning so they will be ready for winter. While they work, a photographer comes; they celebrate July 4th; an organ grinder and his monkey visit; gypsies barter picture frames for hat decorations; and Lucy goes with her mother to Boston to buy new materials for winter hats. *American Bookseller Pick of the Lists* and *Parents' Choice Awards*.

930.   Hall, Donald. **Old Home Day**. Emily Arnold McCully, illustrator. San Diego, CA: Browndeer, Harcourt Brace, 1996. Unpaged. $16. ISBN 0-15-276896-3. 2 up

When people in the nineteenth century came to an area where Ice Age water had melted and formed ponds, they called the area Blackwater Pond. A village began, and then the railroad came, and finally a general store. The people began to prosper, but many moved away. In 1899, the governor of New Hampshire decided that people could celebrate "Old Home Day" on the last weekend in August, 100 years after Enoch Boswell had built the first cabin. Each year families come back to the town to see each other, and now the town has revitalized as a place where people have built homes that they visit in the summer.

931.   Hall, Donald. **When Willard Met Babe Ruth**. Barry Moser, illustrator. San Diego, CA: Browndeer, Harcourt Brace, 1996. 42p. $16. ISBN 0-15-200273-1. 3-5

When he is 12 in 1917, Willard and his father help Babe Ruth get his car out of a New Hampshire ditch. Ruth gives Willard his glove. When Willard becomes a father himself, he names his daughter Ruth. Willard meets Babe Ruth twice more before the ballplayer retires. The family members each take their turn at keeping the love of baseball in the family, including Willard's daughter Ruth.

932. Hall, Lynn. **Halsey's Pride**. New York: Scribner's, 1990. 119p. $12.95. ISBN 0-684-19155-5. 6-9

March Halsey remembers when she was 13 and living with her father in Illinois during 1955. Her father spends all his money on a dog kennel, hoping that his prize collie Pride will earn enough money as a stud to support the kennel. March spends her days hiding her epilepsy from her classmates and helping her father. But she also has to keep the kennel running after Pride's offspring die of torsion (being twisted), and Pride cannot support the investment. As she grows older, she begins breeding her own dogs.

933. Halliburton, Warren. **The West Indian-American Experience**. Brookfield, CT: Millbrook Press, 1994. 64p. $16.40. ISBN 1-56294-340-5. (Coming to America). 4-8

European settlers eradicated the Arawaks, original inhabitants of the Caribbean, but traces of the culture remain. In the centuries after Columbus, many of the inhabitants died from diseases or became slaves to their conquerors. Between 1640 and 1713 more than seven slave revolts occurred in the British islands. In 1760, Tacky's Rebellion broke out in Jamaica, and in 1831 another revolt led to the abolishment of slavers in 1833. More recent inhabitants of the islands have immigrated to the United States, looking for economic opportunities. They found them, along with racial discrimination, unlike any they had experienced in the West Indies. Between 1952 and the 1960s, few islanders were admitted to the country, but after that the laws changed. More About West Indian Americans and Index.

934. Hamanaka, Shelia, author/illustrator. **The Journey: Japanese Americans, Racism, and Renewal**. New York: Orchard, Franklin Watts, 1990. 39p. $19.99; $8.95pa. ISBN 0-531-08449-3; 0-531-07060-3pa. 4 up

Hamanaka painted a five-panel mural, 8x25-feet, in which she depicted Japanese American history. Lured to America by its wealth, the first Japanese immigrants (Issei) worked as "stoop laborers," picking vegetables, and fishing. They and the second generation (Nisei) faced intense prejudice, and during World War II, after the Japanese bombed Pearl Harbor, many lost everything when the U.S. government interred them in 10 camps. After the war, they eventually won reparations of $20,000 each, but many had already died, some by fighting for America against the Germans and the Japanese in the war. The author's family endured this indignity.

935. Hamanaka, Shelia. **On the Wings of Peace: Writers and Illustrators Speak Out for Peace, in Memory of Hiroshima and Nagasaki**. New York: Clarion, 1995. 144p. $21.95. ISBN 0-395-72619-0. 4 up

In commemoration of the bombing of Hiroshima and Nagasaki in 1945, 60 writers and illustrators agreed to have portions of old or new work published in a book. The diverse entries and pictures provide insight into how this event affected people from different parts of the world and in Japan. Bibliography. *Notable Children's Trade Books in the Field of Social Studies.*

936. Hamilton, Leni. **Clara Barton**. New York: Chelsea House, 1988. 112p. $18.95. ISBN 1-55546-641-9. (American Women of Achievement). 5 up

Clara Barton (1821-1912) founded the American Red Cross, an organization that helped victims during both wartime and peacetime. She was initially a teacher who helped set up New Jersey's first public school. Then she moved to Washington, D.C., and became the only female employee of the federal government. During the Civil War, she organized the distribution of supplies for solders and traveled to the battlefields to make sure that soldiers received nursing care. In 1869, after the war, she went to Europe, where she received the Cross of Imperial Russia and the Iron Cross of Germany for her work. Photographs and reproductions enhance the text. Chronology, Further Reading, and Index.

937. Hamilton, Sue L. **The Assassination of a Candidate: Robert F. Kennedy**. Bloomington, MN: Abdo, 1989. 32p. $10.95. ISBN 0-939179-57-1. (Days of Tragedy). 4

In 1968, Robert Kennedy (b. 1925) was assassinated after being nominated presidential candidate by the Democratic Party. The text looks at his life and his close relationship with his brother, John F. Kennedy, as well as at the life of Sirhan Sirhan, the man who killed him. Photographs and Sources.

938. Hamilton, Sue L. **The Assassination of a Leader: Martin Luther King, Jr.** Bloomington, MN: Abdo, 1989. 32p. $10.95. ISBN 0-939179-56-3. (Days of Tragedy). 4

The text presents a brief biography of Martin Luther King, Jr. (1929-1968) but focuses on the day that James Earl Ray assassinated him. It tells of King's activities that day and gives background on Ray. Sources.

939. Hamilton, Virginia. **Anthony Burns: The Defeat and Triumph of a Fugitive Slave**. New York: Knopf, 1988. 195p. $12.99; $3.99pa. ISBN 0-394-98185-5; 0-679-83997-6pa. 5 up

When he escaped to Boston in 1854, Anthony Burns was 20. But his former owner located him and held him under the Fugitive Slave Act. Burns, however, had many abolitionist friends, and Richard Dana, a superb lawyer, decided to defend him without charge. This case incited Boston, and many rioted, but Burns gained freedom. His health, however, had declined, and he died at age 28. Fugitive Slave Act, Bibliography, and Index.

940. Hamilton, Virginia. **The Bells of Christmas**. Lambert Davis, illustrator. San Diego, CA: Harcourt Brace, 1989. 64p. $16.95. ISBN 0-15-206450-8. 4-6

In 1890, Jason, 12, and his family, the Bells, look forward to celebrating Christmas at their Ohio home near the National Road. The whole family anticipates Christmas, when the relatives visit and they go to church together. Jason is especially happy this year because of the mechanical wooden leg that his uncle designed and made for his father. *Coretta Scott King Honor Book* and *American Library Association Notable Books for Children*.

941. Hamilton, Virginia. **Drylongso**. Jerry Pinkney, illustrator. San Diego, CA: Harcourt Brace, 1992. 56p. $18.95. ISBN 0-15-224241-4. 3-5

In 1975, west of the Mississippi, Lindy's family tries to cope with a dust storm when Drylongso arrives. Only a boy, Drylongso helps the family find water with his dowsing rod and has seed for them to plant near the spring. After the garden begins growing, Drylongso leaves Lindy's family and goes to find his own garden while they prepare for the next drought season expected in 20 years during the 1990s.

942. Hamilton, Virginia. **The House of Dies Drear**. Eros Keith, illustrator. New York: Macmillan, 1968. 247p. $17; $3.95pa. ISBN 0-02-742500-2; 0-02-043520-7pa. 5-7

Thomas and his family move into a house once owned by the wealthy abolitionist Dies Drear when his father takes a job teaching at an Ohio college. Drear had helped more than 40,000 slaves pass through the Underground Railway before he and two slaves were murdered. Strange things happen around the house. Thomas and his father investigate the tunnels and secret entrances even though the hostile caretaker Pluto tries to thwart their efforts. *Edgar Allen Poe Award*.

943. Hamilton, Virginia. **Many Thousand Gone: African Americans from Slavery to Freedom**. Leo and Diane Dillon, illustrators. New York: Knopf, 1993. 151p. $16. ISBN 0-394-82873-9. 4-9

Divided into three main parts, the text covers slavery in America, the runaways of the nineteenth century, and the exodus to freedom. Among the topics and people are the Quaker protests, Jenny Slew, Elizabeth Freeman, the Gabriel Prosser uprising, Josiah Henson, Nat Turner, Underground Railroad, Anthony Burns, Alexander Ross, Henry Box Brown (who mailed himself to liberty), Jackson (who came north dressed as his wife's maid), Eliza (who inspired *Uncle Tom's Cabin* as she crossed the frozen Ohio), and the tide of freedom. Bibliography and Index.

944. Hancock, Sibyl. **Old Blue**. Erick Ingraham, illustrator. New York: Putnam, 1980. 48p. $6.99. ISBN 0-399-61141-X. K-3

In 1878, on his first cattle drive with his father, a trail boss, Davy gets to ride in front of the cattle on the leading steer, Old Blue. When a bad snowstorm causes Old Blue to be invisible to the rest of the group, Davy suggests that Old Blue wear a bell around his neck, and Old Blue walks into Kansas City ringing his bell. *American Library Association Notable Books for Children*.

945. Hanley, Sally. **A. Philip Randolph**. New York: Chelsea House, 1989. 110p. $18.95; $7.95pa. ISBN 1-55546-607-9; 0-7910-0222-5pa. (Black Americans of Achievement). 5 up

A. (Asa) Philip Randolph (1889-1979) organized the Brotherhood of Sleeping Car Porters in 1925, which acted as the labor union for Pullman car porters. He was also a member of the Fair Employment Practices Committee in World War II. As a leading opponent of segregation in the armed forces and of racial discrimination in organized labor, he was appointed in 1955 as a vice president of the American Federation of Labor and Congress of Industrial Organizations. He also directed the March on Washington for Jobs and Freedom in 1963, at which Martin Luther King delivered his "I Have a Dream" speech. Bibliography and Index.

946. Hansen, Joyce. **The Captive**. New York: Scholastic, 1994. 195p. $13.95; $3.50pa. ISBN 0-590-41625-1; 0-590-41624-3pa. 5-8

Slavers capture Kofi, 12, when a family servant betrays him, and take him from his African home to America in 1788. There he works for a New England family of somber Puritans. Then he meets Paul Cuffe, an African American shipbuilder who wants to take Africans back to their homeland. He becomes a first mate on Cuffe's ship, which gives him a chance to go home. *Coretta Scott King Honor* and *Notable Children's Trade Books in the Field of Social Studies*.

947. Hansen, Joyce. **Out from This Place**. New York: Walker, 1988. 135p. $13.95. ISBN 0-8027-6817-2. 6-9

This sequel to *Which Way Freedom?* shows Easter at 14, the girl that Obi left behind, as she tries to escape from a Charleston, South Carolina, plantation and to remain free. She joins people recently emancipated from Sea Island, fighting for the land that the government refuses to grant although it had been promised to them. Easter continues her search for Obi and decides that she will go north to begin training as a teacher, after encouragement from another teacher who has watched her work with children. Easter hopes to find Obi there.

948.   Hansen, Joyce. **Which Way Freedom?** New York: Walker, 1986. 120p. $13.95. ISBN 0-8027-6623-4. New York: Camelot, 1992. $3.99pa. ISBN 0-380-71408-6pa. 4-7

After hearing that they will be sold, Obi and Easter escape from the plantation where they are slaves in 1861. Confederate soldiers stop them, but Obi escapes to the South Carolina coastal islands. There he joins Union troops and meets a "colored Yankee" who begins teaching him to read. At the end of the war, Obi is wounded but alive, and he starts searching for Easter and the little boy Easter stayed on the plantation to save.

949.   Harding, Donal. **The Leaving Summer**. New York: Morrow, 1996. 177p. $15. ISBN 0-688-13893-4. 4-6

When Austin is 11 in 1958, the housekeeper, Miss Dixie, and Miss Ada, his educated aunt, become his mentors. A convict escapes while working in Austin's father's North Carolina tomato field and is injured. Austin and Miss Ada hide the man in her basement and nurse him back to health. Although the convict is only guilty of fist fighting with the sheriff's son, his punishment is harsh. As Austin watches the growing attachment between the two, he also has to cope with his parents' separation from each other and detachment from him. Jeering neighbors suspect that they are hiding the man, and when they try to stop his escape, they wound Austin's mother. Austin learns much during this unusual summer.

950.   Hargrove, Jim. **Abraham Lincoln: Sixteenth President of the United States**. Chicago: Childrens Press, 1988. 100p. $19.80. ISBN 0-516-01359-9. (Encyclopedia of Presidents). 4-9

As a young man, Abraham Lincoln (1809-1865) prepared himself to face his role as the sixteenth president. The text begins with Lincoln reading a humorous Artemis Ward story to his cabinet before he told the members about the Emancipation Proclamation. When they did not laugh, he admonished them for not realizing the importance of a balanced approach to life. Everything could not be serious, or they would not survive. After reviewing Lincoln's youth and young adulthood, the text ends with his assassination on Good Friday. Chronology of American History and Index.

951.   Hargrove, Jim. **Dwight D. Eisenhower: Thirty-Fourth President of the United States**. Chicago: Childrens Press, 1987. 100p. $19.80. ISBN 0-516-01389-0. (Encyclopedia of Presidents). 4-9

Starting with Dwight David Eisenhower's (1890-1969) achievement on D-Day as the Supreme Commander of Allied Forces in Europe, the text recounts his life as a young boy in Abilene, Kansas, his career at West Point, and his role as the 34th President of the United States. Chronology of American History and Index.

952.   Hargrove, Jim. **Harry S. Truman: Thirty-Third President of the United States**. Chicago: Childrens Press, 1987. 100p. $19.80. ISBN 0-516-01388-2. (Encyclopedia of Presidents). 4-9

Harry S. Truman (1884-1972) became President in 1945 when Franklin Roosevelt died. Within five months, he had to decide if the country should use the atomic bomb on Japan. As soon as the war ended, he had to make decisions about the best way to thwart the Soviet Union and to simultaneously help the weakened Western European countries. The text looks at his life and the decisions he made in the Senate and as President. Chronology of American History and Index.

953.   Hargrove, Jim. **Lyndon B. Johnson: Thirty-Sixth President of the United States**. Chicago: Childrens Press, 1987. 100p. $19.80. ISBN 0-516-01396-3. (Encyclopedia of Presidents). 4-9

Beginning with Lyndon B. Johnson's (1908-1973) transfer to the presidency at the death of John F. Kennedy in 1963, the text then gives an overview of his life, from serving Texas to leading the United States during his days in Washington. Chronology of American History and Index.

954.   Hargrove, Jim. **Martin Van Buren: Eighth President of the United States**. Chicago: Childrens Press, 1987. 100p. $19.80. ISBN 0-516-01391-2. (Encyclopedia of Presidents). 4-9

Martin Van Buren (1782-1862) became president a few months after Andrew Jackson declared that all land in the West had to be purchased with gold or silver rather than paper money. Banks would no longer make easy loans, and times became hard. A few months after Van Buren took office, America entered its first great depression, called the Panic of 1837. It lasted for five years, throughout his administration. Although lacking in education, Van Buren was a skilled political organizer and earned the names "Red Fox" and "Little Magician." However, the depression was a problem he could not solve. Chronology of American History and Index.

955.   Hargrove, Jim. **The Story of Jonas Salk and the Discovery of the Polio Vaccine**. Chicago: Childrens Press, 1990. 32p. $9.45. ISBN 0-5160-4747-7. (Cornerstones of Freedom). 3-6

Jonas Salk (1914-1995) found the vaccine that conquered polio. This brief account of his life shows what led to this discovery and its importance for humans. Index.

956.   Hargrove, Jim. **Thomas Jefferson: Third President of the United States**. Chicago: Childrens Press, 1986. 100p. $19.80. ISBN 0-516-01385-8. (Encyclopedia of Presidents). 4-9

These six chapters about Thomas Jefferson (1743-1826) cover his childhood in colonial Virginia, his participation in the change of American government from colony to country, the difficulty of forming a democracy, his role as the third president, and his return to Monticello. Chronology of American History and Index.

957. Harlan, Judith. **Sounding the Alarm: A Biography of Rachel Carson**. New York: Dillon Press, 1989. 128p. $13.95. ISBN 0-87518-407-3. 4-6

Called America's first ecologist, Rachel Carson (1907-1964) became a science writer after serving the government. She published *The Silent Spring* in 1962, and wrote three books about the sea and the value of its life to humans. Instead of marrying, she supported various members of her family. Bibliography and Index.

958. Harness, Cheryl, author/illustrator. **The Amazing Impossible Erie Canal**. New York: Macmillan, 1995. Unpaged. $16. ISBN 0-02-742641-6. 2-6

The text, in two-page spreads, presents the history of the Erie Canal since its completion in 1825, when people lined the canal towpath to watch the boats float through. It discusses why the canal was built, who constructed it, the politics behind its creation, and how the locks work as well as the reasons that people stopped using it. Bibliography.

959. Harness, Cheryl. **They're Off: The Story of the Pony Express**. New York: Simon & Schuster, 1996. 32p. $16. ISBN 0-689-80523-3. 2-5

Stagecoaches took three weeks before 1860 to deliver mail from Missouri to California. On April 3, 1860, the Pony Express began and showed that a relay of 80 men and 500 horses could take the mail from east to west in 10 days. The text looks at this historical group of men and the dangers they faced. Bibliography.

960. Harness, Cheryl. **Young Abe Lincoln: The Frontier Days, 1809-1837**. Washington, DC: National Geographic, 1996. Unpaged. $15.95. ISBN 0-7922-2713-1. 3-6

The text looks at the life of Abraham Lincoln (1809-1865) while he remained on the frontier of Illinois. Maps.

961. Harness, Cheryl. **Young John Quincy**. New York: Bradbury Press, 1994. Unpaged. $15.95. ISBN 0-02-742644-0. 2-4

As a boy, young John Quincy Adams (1767-1848) is eager for news because his father is in Philadelphia as part of the Continental Congress, and soldiers are traveling on the road near the family farm. He wants to know if the Congress will decide to fight or not. His mother writes to his father, and one day in 1776 his mother receives a letter with the words of the Declaration of Independence. The family then knows that war will begin. John Quincy went to Europe with his father, and he later became the sixth President of the United States. Bibliography.

962. Harrah, Madge. **My Brother, My Enemy**. Sheldon Greenberg, illustrator. New York: Simon & Schuster, 1997. 144p. $16. ISBN 0-689-80968-9. 5-9

After Robert Bradford finds his home burning and his family massacred by the Susquehannocks around 1675, he sees an arrow that tells him his blood brother Naokan is involved in the destruction. When Nathaniel Bacon, a plantation owner, organizes a band to protect their land, Robert volunteers, vowing to avenge his family's deaths. When he finds, however, that Bacon also wants to sever ties with the English, his affiliation becomes more complicated.

963. Harris, Edward D. **John Charles Frémont and the Great Western Reconnaissance**. New York: Chelsea House, 1990. 112p. $18.95. ISBN 0-7910-1312-X. (World Explorers). 5 up

As a self-educated man, son of a mother not married to his father, John Charles Frémont (1813-1890) investigated whatever interested him. He led five exploratory surveys of the American West to find out about the area's suitability for settlement. He was a presidential candidate, scientist, explorer, governor, land baron, railroad magnate, Indian fighter, senator, and author. From the regions he explored came 13 states. Photographs and drawings enhance the text. Further Reading, Glossary, and Index.

964. Harris, Jacqueline L. **The Tuskegee Airmen: Black Heroes of World War II**. Englewood Cliffs, NJ: Silver Burdett, 1996. 144p. $13.95; $7.95pa. ISBN 0-382-39215-9; 0-382-39217-5pa. 6 up

In addition to telling about the Tuskegee Airmen, Harris tells about race relations in the mid-twentieth century of the United States. Testimonies from individuals and journal entries form a background to the training of this all-Black squadron and its leader, Benjamin O. Davis, as they prepared for fighting in World War II. Their courage and success contradicts the military's unjustified prior treatment of them.

965. Harrison, Barbara, and Daniel Terris. **A Ripple of Hope: The Life of Robert F. Kennedy**. New York: Lodestar, 1997. 144p. $16.99. ISBN 0-525-67506-X. 5-9

The authors researched a documentary for Home Box Office cable television and used recorded interviews, photographs, newspaper clippings, and films as a basis for this story of a man who worked to help his country. Robert F. Kennedy (1925-1968) served his brother John F. Kennedy as Attorney General, and after JFK's assassination, decided to run for president himself. The book looks at the life of this man, arrogant to some but committed to those less fortunate.

966. Hart, Philip S. **Flying Free: America's First Black Aviators**. Minneapolis, MN: Lerner, 1992. 64p. $19.95. ISBN 0-87614-1598-9. 4-6

Photographs and drawings help tell the story of the first African American aviators from the 1920s onward. People covered are Bessie Coleman, William J. Powell, James Herman Banning, Hubert Fauntleroy Julian, the Chicago Flyers, Tuskegee Airmen of World War II, and modern aviators. Further Reading and Index.

967. Hart, Philip S. **Up in the Air: The Story of Bessie Coleman**. Minneapolis, MN: Carolrhoda, 1996. 80p. $14.96. ISBN 0-87614-949-2. (Trailblazers). 4-7

Bessie Coleman (1896-1926), a Black woman growing up in the South in the early 1900s, had to stay at home to watch her sister while her mother worked, but she planned to make something of her life. In 1920, she became the first African American woman to fly an airplane, and built a career as a barnstorming pilot in the 1920s. She did not live long enough to open a school for Black aviators, but she became an inspiration to many who followed her into new and risky occupations. Notes, Bibliography, and Index.

968. Harvey, Brett. **Cassie's Journey: Going West in the 1860s**. Deborah Kogan Ray, illustrator. New York: Holiday House, 1988. 40p. $14.95; $5.95pa. ISBN 0-8234-0684-9; 0-8234-1172-9pa. 1-4

In the 1860s, Cassie's family leaves the harsh climate of Illinois for California's cheap land and easier farming. She describes their journey, including crossing the rising Platte River as it approaches flood stage and escaping a stampeding buffalo herd. On the rough crossing of the Sierra Nevadas, she gets to carve her initials on Independence Rock. Although the family suffered, they continued their journey and passed the "elephant."

969. Harvey, Brett. **Farmers and Ranchers**. New York: Twenty-First Century Books, 1995. 96p. $16.98. ISBN 0-8050-2999-0. (Settling the West). 5-8

Farmers and ranchers took advantage of the wide expanses of land in the West and went there to settle. The text, enhanced with photographs and drawings, looks at their roles. Source Notes, Further Reading, and Index.

970. Harvey, Brett. **Immigrant Girl: Becky of Eldridge Street**. Deborah Kogan Ray, illustrator. New York: Holiday House, 1987. 40p. $11.95. ISBN 0-8234-0638-5. 2-4

Becky, 10, and nine members of her family live over her parents' grocery store in Brooklyn during 1910 after escaping Grodno, Russia, and the Jewish pogroms. She does not want to be labeled "Greenie," so she studies hard, while her grandmother refuses to speak any language other than Yiddish. She wants the family to remember its heritage even though it has moved to Hester Street.

971. Harvey, Brett. **My Prairie Christmas**. Deborah Kogan Ray, illustrator. New York: Holiday House, 1990. 32p. $15.95; $5.95pa. ISBN 0-8234-0827-2; 0-8234-1064-1pa. K-3

Elenore is 10 in 1889 when she celebrates her first Christmas in Dakota Territory. All of the decorations remain in Maine, and they have no whole wheat flour for baking. Two days before Christmas, her dad leaves to cut down a tree, but a blizzard starts before he returns. Her best Christmas present ever is the return of her father on Christmas Day.

972. Harvey, Brett. **My Prairie Year**. Deborah Kogan Ray, illustrator. New York: Holiday House, 1986. 40p. $14.95; $5.95pa. ISBN 0-8234-0604-0; 0-8234-1028-5pa. K-3

When Elenore is nine in early 1889, her family moves from Maine to "homestead" in the Dakotas. They have specific things to accomplish each day of the week, but sometimes nature interrupts their schedules with tornadoes, fires, or blizzards. Their normal weeks include a trip to town to visit with their friends. The best times of the year tend to be the threshing events where everyone works together. *American Library Association Notable Books for Children*.

973. Harvey, Miles. **Women's Voting Rights**. Chicago: Children's Press, 1996. 32p. $18. ISBN 0-516-20003-8. (Cornerstones of Freedom). 3-5

The text looks at the long struggle of women to gain the right to vote before the Nineteenth Amendment was ratified in 1920. Chronology, Glossary, and Index.

974. Haskins, James. **Freedom Rides: Journey for Justice**. New York: Hyperion, 1995. 99p. $14.95. ISBN 0-7868-0048-8. 6-9

When the Supreme Court declared in 1960 that segregation of waiting rooms and rest rooms in bus and train stations was unconstitutional, people in parts of the South continued to ignore the law. In 1961, a group of Blacks and whites decided to take a bus ride through the South to test *Boynton v. Virginia*. They survived 700 miles through Virginia, but as they entered Alabama, they faced burning and beating. Haskins gives background history, starting with the 1947 Journey of Reconciliation, the *Brown v. Board of Education* decision, and the Montgomery Bus Boycott of 1955. Bibliography and Index.

975. Haskins, James. **The Harlem Renaissance**. Brookfield, CT: Millbrook Press, 1996. 192p. $21.90. ISBN 1-56294-565-3. 5-8

After background on the Harlem Renaissance, Haskins discusses the various groups of people who contributed to it in separate chapters. Among them are performing artists, writers, and fine artists. Individuals include Langston Hughes, Jean Toomer, Jessie Fauset, Countee Cullen, Aaron Douglas, Palmer Hayden, Augusta Savage, Josephine Baker, Duke Ellington, and Bill Robinson. Endnotes, Bibliography, and Index.

976. Haskins, James. **Thurgood Marshall: A Life for Justice**. New York: Henry Holt, 1992. 163p. $14.95; $7.95pa. ISBN 0-8050-2095-0; 0-8050-4256-3pa. 6 up

Among the activities in which Thurgood Marshall (1908-1993) participated in order to promote racial equality were quietly desegregating a movie theater, challenging the laws that Blacks were "separate but equal," and arguing for the rights of all. This biography looks at his background and his career. Bibliography and Index.

977. Haskins, Jim. **Black Eagles: African Americans in Aviation**. New York: Scholastic, 1995. 196p. $14.95. ISBN 0-590-45912-0. 5-8

Eugene Bullard, an African American, went to France in World War I and received highest honors flying for the French. Bessie Coleman, an African American woman, received her pilot's license in France. By 1921, Hubert Fauntleroy Julian had arrived in New York City and become known as the Black Eagle. Many others gained fame for their achievements as Black flyers through the twentieth century and into the Space Age. Dr. Mae C. Jemison was the first African American woman in space. Bibliography, Chronology, and Index. *Notable Children's Trade Books in the Field of Social Studies.*

978. Hausman, Gerald. **Night Flight**. New York: Philomel, 1996. 133p. $15.95. ISBN 0-399-22758-X. 5-8

Jeff Hausman and Max Maeder, both 12 in rural New Jersey during 1957, expect to have fun with their dogs during the summer. On their first camp-out, their dogs are fatally poisoned along with several other neighborhood dogs. Max insists that immigrant Jews have killed them, and Jeff does not want to admit that he is half Jewish. He knows that he must confront Max, a decision made more difficult because Max's father, a German immigrant, admires Hitler and keeps his photograph on his desk. As they investigate the mysterious poisonings further, their leads point to Max's father.

979. Hawxhurst, Joan C. **Mother Jones: Labor Crusader**. Austin, TX: Raintree/Steck-Vaughn, 1994. 128p. $16.98. ISBN 0-8114-2327-1. (American Troublemakers). 6 up

Mother Jones, born Mary Harris (1843?-1930), was once called "the most dangerous woman in America." She lost her husband and her four children to a yellow fever epidemic in 1867, and the Chicago Fire of 1871 destroyed her home and her business. She spent the rest of her life organizing coal miners, Mexican revolutionaries, brewery workers, and textile mill laborers. She helped improve their lives by getting them to demand their rights from callous employers. Maps, Photographs, Key Dates, Glossary, Places to Visit, Bibliography and Recommended Readings, and Index.

980. Haynes, Richard M. **Ida B. Wells: Antilynching Crusader**. Austin, TX: Raintree/Steck-Vaughn, 1994. 128p. $16.98. ISBN 0-8114-2326-3. (American Troublemakers). 6 up

Among the labels for Ida B. Wells (1862-1931) are journalist, educator, suffragist, and militant civil rights leader. Her voice was loudest to expose lynching so that its horror became known throughout the world. At 16, she became a teacher to support her family. When she verbally denounced the inferior education available to Black children, she was fired. In 1910, she helped found the NAACP. Maps, Photographs, Key Dates, Glossary, Places to Visit, Bibliography and Recommended Readings, and Index.

981. Hayward, Linda. **The First Thanksgiving**. James Watling, illustrator. New York: Random House, 1990. 48p. $6.99; $2.95pa. ISBN 0-679-90218-X; 0-679-80218-5pa. (Step into Reading). 1-3

The text includes a summary of the events that led to the first Thanksgiving celebration when Samoset and Squanto joined the Pilgrims. The Pilgrims know the Native Americans are around them although they never know exactly where they are. Samoset and Squanto speak English and help the Pilgrims survive in the New World.

982. Hazell, Rebecca, author/illustrator. **Heroines: Great Women Through the Ages**. New York: Abbeville, 1996. 79p. $19.95. ISBN 0-7892-0289-1. 5-8

The text covers 12 women from ancient Greece to contemporary times. In addition to the information about each woman is background on the culture and the history of the times in which she lived. Among those included are Lady Murasaki Shikibu (973?-1025?), Sacagawea (1786?-1812), Agnodice (c. 300 BC) of ancient Greece, Anna Akhmatova (1888-1966), Madame Sun Yat-Sen (1893-1931), Frida Kahlo (1907-1954), Eleanor of Aquitaine (1122-1202), Joan of Arc (1412?-1431), Queen Elizabeth I (1533-1603), Harriet Tubman (1820?-1913), Marie Curie (1867-1934), and Amelia Earhart (1897-1937). Further Reading.

983. Heiligman, Deborah. **Barbara McClintock: Alone in Her Field**. Janet Hamlin, illustrator. New York: W. H. Freeman, 1994. 64p. $14.95; $4.95pa. ISBN 0-7167-6536-5; 0-7167-6548-9pa. (Science Superstars). 3-7

Barbara McClintock (1902-1992) enrolled in Cornell University and loved her studies. She discovered genetics, but she could only enter the graduate school in botany because she was a woman. She researched cytogenetics, the study of cells in maize plants. She discovered that genes "jumped," but her colleagues throughout the world ignored her discovery for 30 years. When they replicated her experiments, they saw she was right. In 1983, she won the Nobel Prize for her work. Index/Glossary.

984. Heiss, Arleen McGrath. **Barbara Bush**. New York: Chelsea House, 1991. 128p. $18.95. ISBN 0-7910-1627-7. (Library of Biography). 5 up

Barbara Bush (b. 1925), as wife of the 41st President of the United States, accompanied her husband George on all of his missions for the United States, and fulfilled her role of mother of six as well. She campaigned for her husband and served as hostess in the White House. She also has volunteered for many important organizations, especially those concerned with illiteracy. Photographs, Further Reading, Chronology, and Index.

985. Helmer, Diana Star. **Belles of the Ballpark**. Brookfield, CT: Millbrook Press, 1993. 96p. $14.90. ISBN 1-56294-230-1. 5-9

During World War II, when Wrigley had the idea to form female teams, the All-American Girls Professional Baseball League came into existence. The text describes their recruitment, their training in baseball and etiquette, and the chaperoning necessary to take females on the road. The games continued for five years. Bibliography, Chronology, and Index. *New York Public Library's Books for the Teen Age*.

986. Hendershot, Judith. **Up the Tracks to Grandma's**. Thomas B. Allen, illustrator. New York: Knopf, 1993. Unpaged. $15. ISBN 0-679-81964-9. K-3

A young girl in the early part of the twentieth century looks after her grandmother's chores while her grandmother has to be in town helping Aunt Katy. The narrator goes up the tracks to her grandmother's to feed the chickens, construct daisy wreaths, and make chicken soup. Back at home, her grandmother wears her deceased husband's boots, mining helmet, and overalls to work in the garden.

987. Henry, Joanne L. **A Clearing in the Forest**. Charles Robinson, illustrator. New York: Four Winds, 1992. 64p. $14.95. ISBN 0-02-743671-3. 3-6

Although Elijah's older brother thinks that Indianapolis is no more than a clearing in the forest, Elijah, nine in 1833, thinks it is a wonderful place where he can go to the fair, ride a stagecoach, and have fun with his five brothers and little sister. El dislikes the schoolteacher so much that his parents send him to boarding school in a nearby town, a gesture that he appreciates.

988. Henry, Joanne Landers. **Elizabeth Blackwell: Girl Doctor**. Robert Doremus, illustrator. New York: Aladdin, 1996. 192p. $4.99pa. ISBN 0-689-80627-2pa. (Childhood of Famous Americans). 3-6

The text looks at the childhood of Elizabeth Blackwell (1821-1910) as she grew up in England before she and her family came to the United States. It ends with a chapter about her acceptance into medical school after many failures and having to teach two years to earn the money to pay for it.

989. Henry, Sondra, and Emily Taitz. **Betty Friedan: Fighter for Women's Rights**. Springfield, NJ: Enslow, 1990. 128p. $17.95. ISBN 0-89490-292-X. (Contemporary Women). 5-7

Betty Friedan excelled at her schoolwork during the 1930s and 1940s but wanted to have a family. After her children went to school, she saw her own lack of fulfillment and wrote about it in *The Feminine Mystique*. When she found that many others agreed with her, she established the National Organization for Women (NOW) to fight for women's rights. Chronology and Index.

990. Henry, Sondra, and Emily Taitz. **Coretta Scott King: Keeper of the Dream**. Springfield, NJ: Enslow, 1992. 128p. $17.95. ISBN 0-89490-334-9. (Contemporary Women). 6 up

In this biography of Coretta Scott King (b. 1927), the authors introduce her with a series of quotes as the chapter titles. They are "As good as anyone else"; "Wherever Martin lives, I will live there too"; "Much bigger than Montgomery"; "Our faith has now been vindicated"; "Lord, I hope this isn't the way Martin has to go"; "Everything we can to help"; "Watch it, man, that's Mrs. King"; "I have to resist worry"; "You must be prepared to continue"; "I am acting in the name of Martin Luther King, Jr."; "The right time and the right thing to do"; and "I have done things . . . most women could never do." Chronology, Further Reading, Sources, and Index.

991.   Henry, Sondra, and Emily Taitz. **Everyone Wears His Name: A Biography of Levi Strauss**. New York: Dillon Press, 1990. 128p. $13.95. ISBN 0-87518-375-1. (People in Focus). 5-9

An immigrant from Germany who arrived via steerage class in the United States, Strauss became a peddler of merchandise like other merchants whose names are now well known—Gimbel, Altman, and Marshall Field. He moved east and supplied gold rush participants with durable canvas pants. Another man discovered that rivets added to Strauss's canvas helped the pants last longer. He and Strauss patented the idea, and jeans took their place in American culture. Strauss never married but always took an interest in his family and society. He was fair and ethical to his employees. Selected Bibliography and Index.

992.   Herda, D. J. **The Dred Scott Case: Slavery and Citizenship**. Springfield, NJ: Enslow, 1994. 104p. $17.95. ISBN 0-89490-460-4. (Landmark Supreme Court Cases). 6-9

With background on the life of Dred Scott and his family, the reader can understand some of the aspects of the Dred Scott case that began in 1840 in Missouri. After a series of appeals, the Supreme Court under Justice Taney finally ruled in 1857 that Dred Scott, a slave, was not a citizen of the United States, and therefore had no rights in deciding where he would live. The case was one more decision that led to the Civil War. Drawings enhance the text. Notes, Further Reading, and Index.

993.   Herda, D. J. **Furman v. Georgia: The Death Penalty Case**. Springfield, NJ: Enslow, 1994. 104p. $17.95. ISBN 0-89490-489-2. (Landmark Supreme Court Cases). 6-9

In 1972, the Supreme Court was asked to judge whether the death penalty could be considered cruel and unusual punishment. William Furman had been convicted of murder in Georgia and hoped to get out of that penalty. The Court did declare that it was unconstitutional and spared his life and those of others on "death row." The text looks at the ideas and arguments behind this case as well as the people who brought it to court. Notes, Glossary, Further Reading, and Index.

994.   Herda, D. J. **Outlaws of the American West**. Brookfield, CT: Millbrook Press, 1995. 64p. $17.40. ISBN 1-56294-449-5. 5-7

As the American West grew, people began to take the law into their own hands. Some broke the law, while others tried to apprehend those that did. The text recounts stories of Frank and Jesse James, Billy the Kid, and Butch Cassidy and the Wild Bunch. Photographs augment the text. Further Reading and Index.

995.   Herda, D. J. **Roe v. Wade: The Abortion Question**. Springfield, NJ: Enslow, 1994. 104p. $17.95. ISBN 0-89490-459-0. (Landmark Supreme Court Cases). 6-9

In 1969, a woman in Texas needed an abortion after being raped, and lawyers wanted her to sue the state. In 1970, Jane Roe did sue, and the case went to the Supreme Court. When it was settled in 1973, women gained the right to have abortions under certain circumstances. Since then, the issue has continued to be controversial. Further Reading and Index.

996.   Herda, D. J. **United States v. Nixon: Watergate and the President**. Springfield, NJ: Enslow, 1996. 112p. $17.95. ISBN 0-89490-753-0. (Landmark Supreme Court Cases). 6-9

President Richard Nixon resigned from office in August 1974 after admitting that he had knowledge of the Watergate break-in. The text looks at presidential power and executive privilege as it explains how the Supreme Court decided unanimously that Nixon had to relinquish tapes made in his White House office to the special prosecutor assigned to his case. The book discusses various groups involved and activities relating to the scandal as well as biographical information about Nixon. Photographs, Appendix, Chronology, Further Reading, Glossary, Notes, and Index.

997.   Herman, Charlotte. **The House on Walenska Street**. Susan Avishai, illustrator. New York: Dutton, 1990. 80p. $11.95. ISBN 0-525-44519-6. 3-5

Leah, eight, lives in Russia during 1913. After her father dies, she writes to her relatives in Minnesota. She tells them about the Cossacks ransacking their house and that they wanted to come to America. Leah also tells about more normal events such as going to the store and taking care of her sisters and her mother. *Carl Sandburg Literary Arts Award.*

998.   Herman, Charlotte. **Millie Cooper, Take a Chance**. Helen Cogancherry, illustrator. New York: Dutton, 1988. 101p. $5. ISBN 0-525-44442-4. 3-7

In this sequel to *Millie Cooper, 3B*, Millie, a third grader in 1947, worries that she will not get any valentines at school. To keep from being disappointed, she tells people not to give her any. When getting only one hurts her, she realizes that she has to take risks in order to have pleasures. She recites her favorite poem for class, and her parents reward her by giving her a bicycle like one she had tried to win.

999. Herman, Charlotte. **Millie Cooper, 3B**. Helen Cogancherry, illustrator. New York: Dutton, 1985. 74p. $5. ISBN 0-525-44157-3. 3-7

What Millie Cooper wants in 1946, at the beginning of third grade in Chicago, is a ball-point pen. She thinks it will help her make her spelling tests neater. She also wants to write an especially good composition on "Why I Am Special." Her father gives her a pen that does not work as she expects. But when her teacher compliments her as artistic and the first snow comes, she begins to feel special.

1000. Herman, Charlotte. **A Summer on Thirteenth Street**. New York: Dutton, 1991. 181p. $13.95. ISBN 0-525-44642-7. 3-7

Shirley Cohen, 11, plants her victory garden during the summer of 1944 and meets her friends on their Chicago street. When the local druggist's son enlists in the army, the war becomes real although the boy dies from a vaccination before leaving Chicago. Shirley suspects a man as a spy, but she finds out that he left Germany because his wife, killed in an accident, was Jewish. Shirley spends the summer learning that not everything turns out as expected.

1001. Hermes, Patricia. **On Winter's Wind**. Boston: Little, Brown, 1995. 163p. $14.95. ISBN 0-316-35978-5. 4-6

When Genevieve is 11 in the mid-1850s, she is desperate to help her mother, who now constantly looks out the window toward the harbor. Genevieve's father has been at sea for two years, and the family needs help. Genevieve gets a job, highly unusual for her time, at the general store, and hears that returned runaway slaves will bring more than $100 in bounty. She thinks about this incredible amount of money, especially when she finds that the store is an Underground Railway station. Her Quaker friend Sarah introduces her to one of the slaves, and she realizes that all people have needs, and that she could never sell another human.

1002. Hesse, Karen. **Lester's Dog**. Nancy Carpenter, illustrator. New York: Crown, 1993. Unpaged. $15. ISBN 0-517-58357-7. 1-3

In the 1930s, the narrator, six years old, fears Lester's dog more than anything. The dog runs after all of the old Chevys driving up and down the street. But Corey, an older boy, makes the narrator walk by the dog. Corey also makes him take home a kitten that they find down the street. When Lester's dog almost bites the narrator on the way back, he sees Mr. Frank, depressed since the death of his wife, and gives him the kitten. As the narrator leaves Mr. Frank talking to the kitten, he knows the kitten will "fix" Mr. Frank.

1003. Hesse, Karen. **A Time of Angels**. New York: Hyperion Press, 1995. 224p. $15.95. ISBN 0-7868-0087-9. 6-8

Hannah Gold lives with her two sisters, Tanta Rose, and the herbalist Vashti in Boston during the influenza epidemic of 1918. Her mother is in Russia, detained by the war in which her father fights. Hannah feels responsible for her sisters, but they get sick, and Tanta Rose dies. When Hannah becomes sick, Vashti sends her to relatives, but Hannah takes the wrong train and finds herself in Vermont. There, the Red Cross helps her, and an old German farmer, ostracized by the town for his heritage, nurses her to health. When she returns home, she discovers that her sisters have miraculously survived.

1004. Hest, Amy. **Love You, Soldier**. New York: Four Winds, 1991. 48p. $12.95. ISBN 0-02-743635-7. 3-5

Katie, seven, stays with her mother and her mother's friend Louise in New York City while her father and Louise's husband fight in World War II. During the next two years, Katie exchanges letters with her father and gets Louise to the hospital in the snow when she goes into labor while Katie's mother is away. After the war ends, Katie's father does not return, and Katie resents her mother's growing interest in Louise's brother Sam. An elderly neighbor advises her that love is risky but worth the effort, and Katie slowly adjusts to the idea of moving to Texas.

1005. Hevly, Nancy. **Preachers and Teachers**. New York: Twenty-First Century Books, 1995. 96p. $16.98. ISBN 0-8050-2996-6. (Settling the West). 5-8

After settlers went west, those who wanted them to be religious and educated followed. People needed someone to organize their religious activities and to teach their children things for which they might be unprepared. The text, with photographs and drawings, looks at the influence of teachers and preachers in the settlement of the West. Source Notes, Further Reading, and Index.

1006. Hicks, Peter. **The Sioux**. New York: Thompson Learning, 1994. 32p. $14.95. ISBN 1-56847-172-6. (Look into the Past). 4-6

Hicks tells the story of the Sioux from their origins until European settlers tried to destroy them. Their complex cultural beliefs are complemented with color illustrations. Glossary, Important Dates, Books to Read, and Index.

1007.   Hicks, Roger, Sallie Reason, and Helen Ward. **The Big Book of America**. Philadelphia, PA: Courage Books, Running Press, 1994. 56p. $10.98. ISBN 1-56138-390-2. (A Young Person's Guide to American History). 3-5

One page on each state in the United States gives information about the state, including nickname and state motto, flag, bird, tree, animal, and flower, or other distinguishing characteristic. Also included is a map with main geographic areas, industries, and crops (if any) noted, along with a brief history of the events and people for which the state is famous. Index.

1008.   High, Linda Oatman. **The Summer of the Great Divide**. New York: Holiday House, 1996. 177p. $15.95. ISBN 0-8234-1228-8. 5-7

When she is 12 in 1969, Wheezie's parents consider separating, and they send her to her uncle's farm. She hates it and her cousin Slow Roscoe with his greasy hair. Among the traumas of the summer are the arrival of her period, Roscoe's speech impediment, the slaughter of farm animals, and news that their uncle, missing in action in Vietnam, is dead. Wheezie decides to run away to her parents so that she can get them back together. But she reconciles to her situation when she realizes that the "divide" will continue.

1009.   Highwater, Jamake. **Eyes of Darkness**. New York: Lothrop, Lee & Shepard, 1985. 189p. $13. ISBN 0-688-41993-3. 6 up

In 1890, Alexander East surveys the hundreds of dead Sioux Indians massacred at Wounded Knee, and he recalls his own life as a young Native American. He had gone to live with whites at his father's request and lost touch with his identity. He remembers hearing his name Yesa, or "Winner," when he was eight after leading his lacrosse team to victory. He also recalls dancing the Bear Dance for his dying friend. When he left the reservation, he attended white men's schools and became a physician. After Wounded Knee, he returned to the home of his youth.

1010.   Hildick, E. W. **Hester Bidgood: Investigatrix of Evill Deedes**. New York: Macmillan, 1994. 141p. $14.95. ISBN 0-02-743966-6. 4-7

In 1692, people in Willow Bend, Massachusetts, discuss the witch hunt in Salem. When someone finds an unconscious cat, they think the devil has come to their town. Hester, 13, and her friend Rob, who has lived with the Indians, begin their investigation. What they find shows that the cat's owner Mistress Willson has nothing to do with the cat's problems.

1011.   Hill, Elizabeth Starr. **The Banjo Player**. New York: Viking, 1993. 197p. $14.99. ISBN 0-670-84967-7. 4-8

Jonathan, 12, takes the Orphan Train to New Orleans in 1888 after he almost dies in New York City's Great Blizzard. A family adopts him, and he enjoys playing the banjo that a hired man on the farm gives him. When he meets another orphan who works in a restaurant, they decide to trade places. Soon Jonathan becomes a banjo player on a riverboat, where he meets another orphan whom he had known in New York.

1012.   Hill, Prescott. **Our Century: 1920-1930**. Milwaukee, WI: Gareth Stevens, 1993. 64p. $23.93. ISBN 0-8368-1034-1. 3 up

Written as if a newspaper, this book's short articles give an overview of the decade. Included are statistics, daily life in America, immigration quotas, the end of the Russian Civil War, Lenin's death, Fascists and *Il Duce* in Italy, Hitler gaining power, the refusal of the United States to join the League of Nations, Sacco and Vanzetti, Calvin Coolidge, the Scopes "Monkey Trial," the court martial of Billy Mitchell, Herbert Hoover, the stock market crash, the Egyptian treasures discovery, Charles Lindbergh, John McGraw, Babe Ruth, Red Grange, the Demsey-Tunney rematch, Charles Lindbergh, Lady Astor, Mohandas Gandhi, and Leon Trotsky. Glossary, Books for Further Reading, Places to Write or Visit, and Index.

1013.   Hill, Prescott. **Our Century: 1940-1950**. Milwaukee, WI: Gareth Stevens, 1993. 64p. $23.93. ISBN 0-8368-1036-8. 3 up

Written as if a newspaper, this book's short articles give an overview of the decade. Included are statistics, daily life in America, Germany sweeping Europe and the Soviet Union, the Japanese bombing of Pearl Harbor, America in World War II, Edward R. Murrow, Ernie Pyle, the Warsaw ghetto, the siege of Leningrad, the atomic bomb, the Nuremberg trials, the United Nations, Israel, India and independence, Gandhi assassinated, the Communist victory in the Chinese war, the Berlin airlift, Roosevelt's death, Admiral Byrd in Antarctica, Ted Williams, Joe DiMaggio, William Faulkner, Tennessee Williams, Arthur Miller, Dwight Eisenhower, Eleanor Roosevelt, and Jackie Robinson. Glossary, Books for Further Reading, Places to Write or Visit, and Index.

1014. Hill, Prescott. **Our Century: 1970-1980**. Milwaukee, WI: Gareth Stevens, 1993. 64p. $23.93. ISBN 0-8368-1039-2. 3 up

Written as if a newspaper, this book's short articles give an overview of the decade. Included are statistics, daily life in America, Vietnam, Arabs and Israelis at war, Chile's Allende overthrow, bombs in Beirut, the Guyana mass suicide, the Sandinistas taking control, the Islamic overthrow of the Shah of Iran, the Attica prison revolt, Jimmy Carter, the first test-tube baby, Arab terrorists, Hank Aaron, O. J. Simpson, Billie Jean King, Muhammad Ali, Golda Meir, George Wallace, and Barbara Jordan. Glossary, Books for Further Reading, Places to Write or Visit, and Index.

1015. Hilton, Suzanne. **Miners, Merchants, and Maids**. New York: Twenty-First Century Books, 1995. 96p. $16.98. ISBN 0-8050-2998-2. (Settling the West). 5-8

Miners went west when they heard about gold, and merchants went to sell the items that people could not make for themselves. Maids came for a variety of reasons, including the desire for adventure. The text looks at their roles with photographs and drawings. Source Notes, Further Reading, and Index.

1016. Hilton, Suzanne. **The World of Young Andrew Jackson**. Patricia Lynn, illustrator. New York: Walker, 1988. 118p. $13.85. ISBN 0-8927-6814-8. 5-8

In this biography, Hilton looks at the youth of Andrew Jackson (1767-1845) and tries to recreate it. She uses diaries and news reports from the times and from places where Jackson would have been during his youth. Jackson's father died two weeks before he was born, and his Irish mother's superstitions kept her from revealing his chosen name before he was baptized. He disliked school, preferring to fight during the Revolutionary War. He wore a saber scar from those battles all his life, but he was shrewd and courageous. As a young man, he won an inheritance that he spent frivolously. Then he decided to "read law," the beginning of his adult achievements. Andrew Jackson: The Man, Bibliography, and Index.

1017. Hilton, Suzanne. **The World of Young George Washington**. William Sauts Bock, illustrator. New York: Walker, 1987. 112p. $12.95. ISBN 0-8027-6657-9. 5-9

The text looks at the boyhood of George Washington (1732-1799) and places his life in the context of the times in which he lived. It gives a different insight on the very private George Washington who loved the outdoors, rather than the legends that have grown up about his childhood. George Washington: The Man and Index.

1018. Hilton, Suzanne. **The World of Young Tom Jefferson**. William Sauts Bock, illustrator. New York: Walker, 1986. 92p. $12.95. ISBN 0-8027-6621-8. 5-9

As a youngster, Tom Jefferson (1743-1826) lived in Virginia, where his father mastered woodlore and his mother learned herbal cures from their Indian friends. He hated school but loved the violin. He watched after younger siblings and decided early to study law. People he knew traded tobacco instead of money; the parson was the schoolmaster; and few could afford a carriage. Other facts reveal Jefferson's boyhood. Thomas Jefferson: The Man and Index.

1019. Hilts, Len. **Quanah Parker: Warrior for Freedom, Ambassador for Peace**. San Diego, CA: Harcourt Brace, 1987. 148p. $12.95; $4.95pa. ISBN 0-15-200565-X; 0-15-264447-4pa. (Great Episodes). 3-7

Quanah Parker (1854-1911) was a Comanche leader who fought white intruders to protect the buffalo hunting grounds on the Plains. He especially angered General Sherman when he attacked Adobe Walls and the army. Eventually the army found Parker and his band, and they had to go to a reservation. Parker went peacefully, but he refused to give up all of the Comanche traditions. Historical Note, Glossary, and Index.

1020. Hilts, Len. **Timmy O'Dowd and the Big Ditch: A Story of the Glory Days on the Old Erie Canal**. San Diego, CA: Gulliver, Harcourt Brace, 1988. 91p. $13.95. ISBN 0-15-200606-0. 3-5

When Dennis O'Dowd comes to stay with his cousins, his city ways annoy Timmy. But Timmy must explain everything about the new Erie Canal so that his cousin will understand this technological wonder of 1845. Timmy wants to become the captain of a passenger packet. As Timmy describes the canal, a storm causes serious problems, and Dennis's attitude helps them become friends. Glossary and Bibliography.

1021. Hintz, Martin. **Farewell, John Barleycorn: Prohibition in the United States**. Minneapolis, MN: Lerner, 1996. 88p. $14.21. ISBN 0-8225-1743-5. (People's History). 5 up

Before Prohibition began on January 17, 1920, people called liquor "John Barleycorn." Those who wanted a ban on alcohol hoped that Prohibition would improve society. Instead, people made their liquor in basements or in the woods, and gangsters bought and sold liquor, while speakeasies filled. The text looks at the various aspects of a period that lasted until its repeal by the Volstead Act on April 7, 1933. Bibliography and Index.

1022. Hirsch, Charles. **Taxation: Paying for Government**. Austin, TX: Blackbirch/Steck-Vaughn, 1993. 48p. $15.49. ISBN 0-8114-7356-2. (Good Citizenship). 5-9

After defining what taxes are, the text tells what the government uses taxes for and the kinds of taxes. A history shows that taxes were first mentioned in 3500 BC in Sumer (currently Iraq). Egyptians, Greeks, and Romans all paid taxes. Spanish taxes financed Columbus's trip to the New World. However, many have complained about unfair taxes, one of the major reasons that the American Revolution began. A final presentation on the Internal Revenue Service completes the information. Photographs and drawings supplement the text. Further Reading, Glossary, and Index.

1023. **The History of Moviemaking**. New York: Scholastic, 1995. 47p. $19.95. ISBN 0-590-47645-9. (Voyages of Discovery). 4-6

The text covers the development of motion pictures. Topics cover the making of movies from still pictures, the invention of the talkies, the incorporation of Technicolor, Hollywood, competition from television, the evolution of special effects, and animation. Capsule biographies introduce those figures who have been most important to the history of this genre. Pages are diverse, with a foldout showing a Hollywood backlot, a transparency that shows the construction of sets for *A Trip to the Moon*, and die-cut pages to reveal the differences in movies filmed in 35 mm, 70 mm, and Cinemascope. Chronology and Index.

1024. Hite, Sid. **It's Nothing to a Mountain**. New York: Henry Holt, 1994. 214p. $15.95. ISBN 0-8050-2769-6. 6-9

In 1969, Lisette, 14, and Riley, 12, live with their grandparents in the Virginia mountains after their parents die in a car accident. Lisette wears her mother's gold locket and sees it as good luck and symbolic of a guardian angel looking after her. Riley meets a boy who lives in the woods trying to survive after his mother went to prison. Riley tries to help him but has difficulty deciding what to do. Lisette searches for her guardian angel with the aid of an elderly neighbor, and Riley's friend becomes interested in Lisette from afar.

1025. Hoig, Stan A. **Capital for the Nation**. New York: Cobblehill, Dutton, 1990. 132p. $15.95. ISBN 0-525-6503-4. 3-6

The capital of the United States was carved out of Georgetown, Maryland, and a piece of Virginia. Pierre L'Enfant volunteered to design a plan, and when L'Enfant became annoyed by people complaining about his plan, he left with it. Benjamin Banneker, who had surveyed the land, had memorized the plan so he was able to reproduce it. In 1800, 3,000 people, including 623 slaves, lived in Washington. Hoig talks about them and creates an interesting story about the site location; the buildings including the Capitol, the White House, the Washington Monument, and Mount Vernon; and the national buildings, parks, statuary, and memorials. He also discusses the inaugural ceremony. Selected Bibliography and Index.

1026. Hoig, Stan. **It's the Fourth of July**. New York: Cobblehill, Dutton, 1995. 81p. $15.99. ISBN 0-525-65175-6. 4-8

Using old prints and photographs to complement the text, Hoig shows how people have celebrated and commemorated the Fourth of July since its first anniversary in 1777. He includes a chapter on the Centennial celebration in 1876 and another about the arrival of the Statue of Liberty. Bibliography and Index.

1027. Holland, Isabelle. **Behind the Lines**. New York: Scholastic, 1994. 194p. $13.95. ISBN 0-590-45113-8. 6-10

While the United States is torn apart in 1863, Katie O'Farrell, 14, must help keep her motherless Irish immigrant family together by working as a maid on New York City's Washington Square for the Lacey family. What disturbs her is that the wealthy can pay someone $300 to go to war for them. The rich buy the Irish, who do not see this war as theirs but need the money. The Irish, however, are fearful that the free Blacks will take their jobs while they are gone. What erupts are the New York Draft Riots of 1863, which last for four days. Katie helps one of the Blacks escape from certain hanging, and her kindness helps her gain something she has always wanted.

1028. Holland, Isabelle. **The Journey Home**. New York: Scholastic, 1990. 212p. $13.95. ISBN 0-590-43110-2. 4-6

Maggie, 12, and Annie, seven, are Irish Catholic orphans who travel on the orphan train of the Children's Aid Society of New York to Kansas in the late 1800s. They have to adjust to the parents who adopt them, to the strange customs, and to a new religion.

1029. Holland, Isabelle. **The Promised Land**. New York: Scholastic, 1996. 176p. $15.95. ISBN 0-590-47176-7. 4-6

Maggie and Annie Lavin, both on the orphan train in *The Journey Home*, have lived with Uncle James and Aunt Priscilla Russel for three years and see a baby boy born in their home. They also observe the neighbors on the prairie who have different views toward the Civil War, biases toward various ethnicities, and prejudices against people with different religions. Maggie and Annie's uncle arrives from Ireland, planning to take them and raise them as Catholics. When he sees their situation, he realizes that although their benefactors are not Catholics, they have better lives than he can offer.

1030.   Holler, Anne. **Pocahontas: Powhatan Peacemaker**. New York: Chelsea House, 1993. 103p. $18.95; $7.95pa. ISBN 0-7910-1705-2; 0-7910-1952-7pa. (North American Indians of Achievement). 5-8

As the favorite child of Powhatan, Pocahontas had all that she wanted when she was growing up. When she was 12 in 1607, however, the colonists arrived and changed her life. She began to visit them and developed close ties while learning the language and the customs. She took food to them, and Captain John Smith said that her kindness was the "instrument [saving] the colony from death, famine and utter confusion." She had to choose either her family or her friends, and she ended up marrying the colonist John Rolfe and going to London with him, where she died. Engravings and drawings enhance the text. Chronology, Further Reading, and Index.

1031.   Holmes, Burnham. **Cesar Chavez: Farm Worker Activist**. Austin, TX: Raintree/Steck-Vaughn, 1994. 128p. $16.98. ISBN 0-8114-2326-3. (American Troublemakers). 6 up

Although Cesar Chavez (1927-1993) only had an eighth grade education, he rose to defend the injustices imposed on migrant farmworkers. His own family lost its farm in 1937, and he had to work as a field hand doing backbreaking work for minimum compensation. He established the United Farm Workers in 1962 and organized the California grape pickers' strike. He won increases in pay and better working conditions for migrant workers. Maps, Photographs, Key Dates, Glossary, Places to Visit, Bibliography and Recommended Readings, and Index.

1032.   Holmes, Burnham. **Paul Robeson: A Voice of Struggle**. Austin, TX: Raintree/Steck-Vaughn, 1994. 128p. $16.98. ISBN 0-8114-2381-6. (American Troublemakers). 6 up

Paul Robeson (1898-1976) was multitalented. He excelled in athletics, went to law school, and became an internationally acclaimed singer and actor. When he increased his political involvement, his stage career declined. His association with Communists in the 1950s caused the United States to revoke his passport, but when he regained it, he went to England to pursue his career. After he returned and retired, he wrote a book called *Here I Stand*. Maps, Key Dates, Glossary, Places to Visit, Bibliography and Recommended Readings, and Index.

1033.   Holmes, Mary Z. **Cross of Gold**. Geri Strigenz, illustrator. Austin, TX: Raintree/Steck-Vaughn, 1992. 48p. $20.70. ISBN 0-8114-3507-5. (History's Children). 4-8

In 1615, Felipe, 14, lies ill in Santa Fe. He promises God that he will give him his newfound gold if he gets well. A friar sent by the Viceroy of Spain helps Felipe recover, and Felipe gives him the gold to make a cross for the town's church.

1034.   Holmes, Mary Z. **Dear Dad**. Geri Strigenz, illustrator. Austin TX: Raintree/Steck-Vaughn, 1992. 48p. $9.98. ISBN 0-8114-3503-2; 0-8114-6428-8pa. (History's Children). 4-5

In 1942, young Max and his family want to help the war effort after his father and admired older cousin enlist. Max and his uncle use their boat to help patrol the shoreline. They bump into a German submarine periscope and use their wits to escape. Max learns that war has less to do with uniforms and medals than with danger and death.

1035.   Holmes, Mary Z. **For Bread—1893**. Geri Strigenz, illustrator. Austin, TX: Raintree/Steck-Vaughn, 1992. 48p. $20.70. ISBN 0-8114-3501-6. (History's Children). 4-8

Stefan, 13, lives with his family in Buffalo, New York, during 1893. His Polish father loses his job, but rather than work as his father wants him to do, Stefan uses his artistic talent to make and sell drawings so that the family can survive the hard times. He draws pictures of business buildings and sells them to the owners.

1036.   Holmes, Mary Z. **See You in Heaven**. Rick Whipple, illustrator. Austin, TX: Raintree/Steck-Vaughn, 1992. 48p. $9.98. ISBN 0-8114-3502-4; 0-8114-6427-Xpa. (History's Children). 4-5

In 1836, Elsy, 12, begins her "adult" work in the Alabama cotton fields as her master prepares to sell Elsy's sister to a Texan. Her family endures the hard plantation life as best it can by telling stories so that each one can remember the others regardless of what happens to them.

1037.   Holmes, Mary Z. **Thunder Foot—1730**. Geri Strigenz, illustrator. Austin, TX: Raintree/Steck-Vaughn, 1992. 48p. $20.70. ISBN 0-8114-3500-8. (History's Children). 4-8

In 1730, Running Dog, 14, finds a horse, an animal his Cheyenne Indian tribe has never seen. He brings it back, and it guides him on his vision quest. When he learns how to ride the horse, he earns the name Wind Chaser.

1038.   Holmes, Mary Z. **Two Chimneys**. Rick Whipple, illustrator. Austin TX: Raintree/Steck-Vaughn, 1992. 48p. $9.98. ISBN 0-8114-3506-7; 0-8114-6431-8pa. (History's Children). 4-5

Katherine Eastwood loves her new home in Jamestown, Virginia. She and her family of five have 12 indentured servants in 1628. What she does not like is the idea of returning to England to marry the man with whom her parents have arranged a marriage. Her brother Robert becomes ill, and she nurses him back to health so that he can return to England as he desires. Her father realizes that she would be happier in Jamestown living at "Two Chimneys," married to her brother Robert's friend instead.

1039.   Holmes, Mary Z. **Year of the Sevens—1777**. Geri Strigenz, illustrator. Austin, TX: Raintree/Steck-Vaughn, 1992. 48p. $20.70. ISBN 0-8114-3505-9. (History's Children). 4-8

In 1777, Polly and her family move to the Kentucky frontier. The country is fighting the Revolutionary War on the East Coast, and the Indians are at war near Polly's home. They raid and burn the house and kill her mother. She has to adjust to her father's remarriage and the new wife, who has lost a husband and a daughter.

1040.   Hoobler, Dorothy, and Thomas Hoobler. **Aloha Means Come Back: The Story of a World War II Girl**. Cathie Bleck, illustrator. Englewood Cliffs, NJ: Silver Burdett, 1991. 55p. $12.95. ISBN 0-382-24156-8. (Her Story). 2-5

In 1941, Laura and her mother go to Hawaii to be with Laura's Navy father. Laura and an islander, Michiko, become friends, and Michiko teaches Laura how to surf and Hawaiian customs. As tensions rise between the Japanese and the Americans, Laura's parents encourage her to end the friendship even though Michiko was born in Hawaii. After the Japanese bomb Pearl Harbor and Laura thinks her mother is hurt, Michiko's family helps her contact her father.

1041.   Hoobler, Dorothy, and Thomas Hoobler. **The Chinese American Family Album**. New York: Oxford University Press, 1994. 128p. $22.95. ISBN 0-19-509123-X. (American Family Albums). 5 up

In the 1830s, Chinese sugarcane workers arrived in Hawaii, and Chinese sailors entered New York City's harbor. From then to the present, the Chinese culture has enriched the experiences of all Americans. Chinese Americans have endured serious prejudice, including a law in 1924 that prohibited Chinese American citizens from bringing their wives and children into the country. The act was not repealed until 1943, after the United States and China became allies during World War II. The text, complemented by photographs, traces the history of Chinese immigrants, indicating that most have continued to live in groups or Chinatowns as they worked in laundries, restaurants, and sweatshops. Without the Chinese workers in the nineteenth century, the transcontinental railroad might not have been completed so rapidly. The diary entries of immigrants, tracing families as they live, work, and rest in America, enliven the text. Chinese American Timeline, Further Reading, and Index.

1042.   Hoobler, Dorothy, and Thomas Hoobler. **The Irish American Family Album**. New York: Oxford University Press, 1995. 128p. $19.95. ISBN 0-19-509461-1. (American Family Albums). 5 up

Using diary entries, letters, clippings, and interviews, the authors present the story of Irish Americans. More than 39 million Americans claim their ancestry to be Irish. Between 1841 and 1850, more than 800,000 Irish arrived, and another 900,000 followed in the next decade. During that 20-year period, one in five Irish natives left for the United States. First employed as laborers, miners, and servants, the Irish soon formed political organizations that became major forces throughout the country. The Irish count among their numbers the Kennedy family, John Wayne, Georgia O'Keeffe, F. Scott Fitzgerald, and Sandra Day O'Connor. Irish American Timeline, Further Reading, and Index.

1043.   Hoobler, Dorothy, and Thomas Hoobler. **The Italian American Family Album**. New York: Oxford University Press, 1994. 127p. $22.95. ISBN 0-19-509124-8. (American Family Albums). 5 up

Italian influences in all areas of society have helped create America since Cristofor Colombo arrived in 1492. The text traces the lives of individuals through their diaries and photographs of those who immigrated to America, especially during the nineteenth and early twentieth centuries: their work, living environment, religious activities, and burden of prejudice. Italian American Timeline, Further Reading, and Index.

1044.   Hoobler, Dorothy, and Thomas Hoobler. **The Japanese American Family Album**. New York: Oxford University Press, 1996. 127p. $22.95. ISBN 0-19-508131-5. (American Family Albums). 4-10

Through their own words and scrapbook pictures, Japanese American immigrants tell their stories. The first wave of Japanese immigration occurred in the nineteenth century, with another in the twentieth century. The text looks at treatment of Japanese Americans, including the deplorable chapter of internment during World War II. Japanese American Timeline, Further Reading, and Index.

1045. Hoobler, Dorothy, and Thomas Hoobler. **The Jewish American Family Album**. New York: Oxford University Press, 1995. 128p. $22.95. ISBN 0-19-508135-8. (American Family Albums). 6-9

Through their own words and scrapbook pictures, Jewish immigrants tell their stories. A brief history of Jewish life through the centuries precedes chapters that describe special taxes, the limit on Jewish marriages, and occupational restrictions that caused many Ashkenazi Jews to flee central Europe from 1840 to 1860. Other waves followed in the early twentieth century. Chapters include the earliest arrivals in the sixteenth century, new life in New York in the garment trade, going west, the neighborhoods and Yiddish theater, Jewish religious rituals, and becoming part of America. Jewish American Timeline, Further Reading, and Index.

1046. Hoobler, Dorothy, and Thomas Hoobler. **Next Stop, Freedom: The Story of a Slave Girl**. Cheryl Hanna, illustrator. Englewood Cliffs, NJ: Silver Burdett, 1991. 55p. $12.95. ISBN 0-382-24152-5. (Her Story). 2-5

When Emily is 10 during the 1850s, she works as a house slave while her brother works in the field. Her aunt tells them about Moses, a guide who helps people get their freedom. One night Moses (Harriet Tubman) arrives, sets a fire in the barn to distract the master, and leads Emily and others along the Underground Railroad. When they arrive at one of the stops, a Quaker shows Emily her letters and starts teaching her to read.

1047. Hoobler, Dorothy, and Thomas Hoobler. **The Sign Painter's Secret: The Story of a Revolutionary Girl**. Donna Ayers, illustrator. Englewood Cliffs NJ: Silver Burdett, 1991. 55p. $12.95. ISBN 0-382-24150-9. (Her Story). 2-5

In 1777, British soldiers come into Annie's home and use it as their Philadelphia headquarters. Her mother encourages her to get messages to George Washington at Valley Forge because no one else can go without being suspected. Her efforts help force the British out of Philadelphia.

1048. Hoobler, Dorothy, and Thomas Hoobler. **Treasure in the Stream: The Story of a Gold Rush Girl**. Nancy Carpenter, illustrator. Englewood Cliffs, NJ: Silver Burdett, 1991. 55p. $12.95. ISBN 0-382-24151-7. (Her Story). 2-5

Amy records the gold fever that hit California from 1848 to 1850 in her diary. She helps her family by finding gold, and the family decides to use the gold they find for something more concrete than speculation. They move from John Sutter's property to their own store selling Levi Strauss jeans in San Francisco.

1049. Hooks, William H. **The Ballad of Belle Dorcas**. Brian Pinkney, illustrator. New York: Knopf, 1990. 40p. $13.95. ISBN 0-394-84645-1. 2-5

Belle Dorcas, free-issue daughter of a slave mother and her white master, falls in love with another slave whom the new master prepares to sell after her father dies. Belle Dorcas gets a potion from a conjure woman that turns her new husband into a tree during the day and back to a man at night. When Belle Dorcas dies, they grow side by side as cedar trees. Although this is a historical fantasy, the plight of slaves who are born free because of their father but have few choices because of their color becomes clear in this story.

1050. Hooks, William H. **Circle of Fire**. New York: Atheneum, 1982. 147p. $15. ISBN 0-689-50241-9. 5-9

Harrison, 11 in 1936, sees two disparate happenings at Christmas in North Carolina. He watches the gypsies' lovely candlelight mummer's play as well as the Ku Klux Klan burn one of their crosses on the way to punish a man married to a South Carolina woman. Because his two best friends are Black, he cannot understand the Klan's hatred toward Blacks, Catholics, and Jews.

1051. Hooks, William H. **Freedom's Fruit**. James Ransome, illustrator. New York: Knopf, 1996. Unpaged. $16. ISBN 0-679-82438-3. 2-5

The master of a pre–Civil War plantation asks the slave Mama Marina, a conjure woman, to keep the slaves from stealing his grapes. She realizes that she might be able to earn freedom for her daughter and her daughter's boyfriend if she works the situation correctly.

1052. Hooks, William H. **The Legend of the White Doe**. Dennis Nolan, illustrator. New York: Macmillan, 1988. 48p. $13.95. ISBN 0-02-744350-7. 5-7

The first English child born in the colonies was Virginia Dare in North Carolina during 1587. This historical fantasy suggests that she escaped the hostile Indians who raided the settlement, and the Croatan Indians raised her after her mother walked into the sea. She refused to marry the medicine man who claimed her in favor of a brave whom she loved. She ran away with him, was killed, and supposedly roams through the Great Dismal Swamp as a white deer.

1053. Hopkins, Lee Bennett, comp. **Hand in Hand: An American History Through Poetry**. Peter Fiore, illustrator. New York: Simon & Schuster, 1994. 194p. $19.95. ISBN 0-671-73315-X. 3-6

The sections into which poems divide chronologically follow the history of America. Segments include the Pilgrims, the Revolution, and individual events and people such as "Paul Revere's Ride" and "Barbara Frietchie." The poems are more notable for their subject matter than for their quality, but they give insight into the historical topics they cover.

1054. Hopkinson, Deborah. **Pearl Harbor**. New York: Macmillan, 1991. 72p. $13.95. ISBN 0-87518-475-8. (Places in American History). 4-6

While noting the importance of Pearl Harbor, the text emphasizes the monument of the USS *Arizona* honoring those who died there at the beginning of U.S. involvement in World War II on December 7, 1941. Chronology and Index.

1055. Hopkinson, Deborah. **Sweet Clara and the Freedom Quilt**. James Ransome, illustrator. New York: Knopf, 1993. 32p. $15. ISBN 0-679-82311-5. K-3

Clara, 11, sews a pattern in a quilt that is actually a map to help her escape via the Underground Railway. She has worked her way into the Big House out of the fields because she can sew. She uses her talent to her advantage as she waits to find each piece of material that will illustrate the instructions that she hears from returned runaways or slaves who have traveled. When she has the pieces together and knows the direction, she leaves.

1056. Hopkinson, Deborah, and Kimberly Bulcken Root. **Birdie's Lighthouse**. New York: Simon & Schuster, Atheneum, 1997. 32p. $16. ISBN 0-679-86998-0. K-3

In the early 1800s, Birdie watches her father tend the lighthouse on their tiny and desolate island home. When he becomes sick, she is able to keep the lights burning. Her bravery keeps lost ships from wrecking.

1057. Horton, Madelyn. **Mother Jones**. San Diego, CA: Lucent, 1996. 95p. $16.95. ISBN 1-56006-057-3. (The Importance Of). 6-9

In addition to telling about the life of Mary Harris or "Mother" Jones (1830-1930), the text also gives an overview of the labor movement in the United States, in which Mother Jones played a prominent role. She was imprisoned for activities on behalf of West Virginia and Colorado coal miners, and she exposed some of the abuses in child labor. Among them were that children who had been wounded, such as losing a limb in the mines, were the only ones who went to school. Primary source documents give an immediacy to the information. Bibliography, Chronology, Further Reading, Notes, and Index.

1058. Horvath, Polly. **The Happy Yellow Car**. New York: Farrar, Straus & Giroux, 1994. 150p. $15. ISBN 0-374-32845-5. 4-7

Living in Missouri during the 1930s Depression with her family, Betty Grunt cannot get the dollar she needs for flowers so she can be crowned Pork-Fry Queen of her sixth grade class. A story of family money hidden in the area leads Betty and her brothers on a big search. When her father comes home with a yellow car, everyone wonders where he will find money to pay for the gas. Then her sister Gretel says that she is going to marry Clarence but has told him her family is in Italy and cannot come to the wedding. They do not find the family money, but the family's positive attitudes contrast to most stories set in the Depression.

1059. Hotze, Sollace. **A Circle Unbroken**. New York: Clarion, 1988. 224p. $13.95. ISBN 0-89919-733-7. 6 up

When she is 17, Rachel's father steals her back from the Dakota Sioux tribe that had taken her when she was 10. He wants to hear nothing about her life as Kata Wi and refuses to acknowledge that her kidnapping ever occurred. She enjoys her siblings and her stepmother but remembers the kindness and love of her other family. She becomes ill and fears that she will die like her Aunt Sarah, who died after she returned from being captured for the same seven years. Rachel realizes that she must go back to her Indian family in order to save her life. *Carl Sandburg Literary Arts Award*.

1060. Hotze, Sollace. **Summer Endings**. New York: Clarion, 1991. 176p. $13.95. ISBN 0-395-56197-3. 4-7

Christine Kosinski, 12, has a mixed summer in 1945. World War II ends, and her sister gets married. Christine enjoys watching the Chicago Cubs play baseball from her apartment window that overlooks the field, and she gets her first job working in the drugstore. She and her sister worry about their father, who has been a political prisoner in Poland during the war, but as the summer ends, they hear that he has survived Dachau. Finally, Christine gets her first kiss at Rosie's wedding.

1060a. Houston, Gloria. **But No Candy**. Lloyd Bloom, illustrator. New York: Putnam, 1992. 32p. $14.95. ISBN 0-399-22142-5. K-3

Lee enjoys sitting in her hiding place eating one square of her Hershey bar at a time. But when her Uncle Ted leaves to fight in a place called Europe, and the family talks about Axis and Allies all the time, things change. Her uncle returns four years later, and he brings her a candy bar. But she has discovered that the pleasure of eating the candy is nothing compared to having him safely back home.

1061. Houston, Gloria. **Littlejim**. New York: Philomel, 1990. 172p. $14.95. ISBN 0-399-22220-0. 4-6

Littlejim, 12, wants to read and write, but his father, Bigjim, thinks that boys in the early days of the twentieth century should work on the farm. Littlejim's teacher thinks he has talent, and Littlejim wants to win the newspaper essay contest so his father will change his mind about Littlejim's ideas for becoming a man.

1062. Houston, Gloria. **Mountain Valor**. Thomas B. Allen, illustrator. New York: Philomel, 1994. 227p. $14.95. ISBN 0-399-22519-6. New York: Paper Star, 1996. 227p. $5.95pa. ISBN 0-698-11383-7pa. 5-8

While Valor's father fights with a North Carolina regiment and her uncle with a Tennessee cavalry, Valor has to stay home with her mother and her cousin Jed. Jed is one year younger but recognized as the master of the house because he is a boy. When a soldier threatens her family's safety, Valor decides to pretend she is a Southern boy and join the army. She brings home the family's stolen livestock but catches pneumonia. Everyone hears of her exploits and knows that she is properly named.

1063. Houston, Gloria. **My Great-Aunt Arizona**. Susan Condie Lamb, illustrator. New York: HarperCollins, 1992. Unpaged. $14.89. ISBN 0-06-022607-2. 1-4

Great-Aunt Arizona, named for the state because her brother said it was so beautiful, wanted to travel from her home in the Blue Ridge Mountains, but she never did. She stayed, married, and taught all of the children who grew up there. She always encouraged those who could to go out and see the world.

1063a. Houston, Gloria. **The Year of the Perfect Christmas Tree**. Barbara Cooney, illustrator. New York: Dial, 1988. 32p. $15.99. ISBN 0-8037-0299-X. New York: Puffin, 1996. 32p. $4.99pa. ISBN 0-14-055877-2pa. K-3

Ruthie's father leaves Appalachia for World War I in the spring of 1918, but before he goes, he and Ruthie pick out a Christmas tree. When he has not returned by Christmas Eve, Ruthie and her mother cut down the tree and take it to the church for the pageant. Ruthie has a part as an angel, but the best aspect of the evening is that her father arrives just before the celebration begins.

1064. Howard, Elizabeth Fitzgerald. **Chita's Christmas Tree**. Floyd Cooper, illustrator. New York: Bradbury, 1989. 32p. $13.95. ISBN 0-02-744621-2. K-3

On Saturday before Christmas in Baltimore at the turn of the twentieth century, Chita and her father go to the nearby woods to look for a tree that they want Santa to bring on Christmas. Chita's father carves her name on the tree, but Chita worries that Santa will not find it. She is relieved on Christmas to see that Santa brought the right tree. *American Library Association Notable Books for Children.*

1065. Howard, Elizabeth Fitzgerald. **Papa Tells Chita a Story**. Floyd Cooper, illustrator. New York: Simon & Schuster, 1995. Unpaged. $15. ISBN 0-02-744623-9. K-2

After dinner one night, Chita's father tells her about his army days in the Spanish-American War, when he delivered a secret message to troops on the other side of Cuba. He had to worry about snakes, alligators, predatory birds, thorns, and brambles, but he successfully arrived and earned a medal for his bravery.

1066. Howard, Ellen. **The Cellar**. Patricia Rose Mulvihill, illustrator. New York: Atheneum, 1992. 52p. $12.95. ISBN 0-689-31724-7. 2-4

Faith has many difficulties for a little girl in 1900. The hen pecks her, she falls into the cellar, she gets burrs in her feet, and she makes uneven sampler stitches. Her family asks her to go into the scary cellar for apples, and when she returns with the fruit, her success pleases her, and she forgets her other problems.

1067. Howard, Ellen. **The Chickenhouse House**. New York: Atheneum, 1991. 52p. $11.95. ISBN 0-689-31695-X. 2-4

At the beginning of the twentieth century, Alena, around six, moves with her family an hour away from her grandfather's big house. At first, Alena has a hard time adjusting to living in the chicken house while her father builds a large farmhouse. Then, when the house is ready, she regrets having to leave the cozy chicken house.

1068. Howard, Ellen. **Edith Herself**. Ronald Himler, illustrator. New York: Atheneum, 1987. 132p. $12.95. ISBN 0-689-31314-4. 5-7

Edith's mother dies around 1890, and Edith has to move in with her sister and her strict Christian husband John as well as his sour-smelling mother. Edith has blackouts, later diagnosed as epilepsy, and her sister wants her to stay home from school in case she has a seizure in front of the other children. But Edith wants to go to school, and, ironically, John supports her desire. *School Library Journal Best Book.*

1069. Howard, Ellen. **Her Own Song**. New York: Atheneum, 1988. 160p. $12.95. ISBN 0-689-31444-2. 4-6

Mellie, 11, wants the acceptance of other girls, so she joins them in abusing the local Chinese laundry man, Geem-Wah. She lives with her adoptive father and his sister, and after the sister goes on a vacation, her father injures himself and has to stay in the hospital. Mellie comes to know Geem-Wah's family when he helps her during her difficult times. She finds out that her first adoptive parents were Chinese but that authorities took her away and gave her to white parents in 1908 because the government forbade interracial adoptions. She has mistreated people who once loved and cared for her as Mei-Le.

1070. Howard, Ellen. **The Log Cabin Quilt**. Ronald Himler, illustrator. New York: Holiday House, 1996. 32p. $15.95. ISBN 0-8234-1247-4. K-2

Although Elvirey's father does not want to bring anything on their journey to Michigan from Carolina that will remind him of his deceased wife, her grandmother decides to bring her bag of scraps for quilting. After their arrival and construction of a cabin, Elvirey's father goes to hunt. During his absence, the mud freezes and falls out of the chinks in the wall. Elvirey uses the scraps to fill the holes, and when her father returns and sees her ingenuity, he declares that her mother would be proud of her.

1071. Howard, Ellen. **Sister**. New York: Atheneum, 1990. 148p. $12.95. ISBN 0-689-31653-4. 5-7

In 1886 in the Midwest, Alena wants to stay in school, but the birth and death of her sister depresses her mother so much that Alena has to stay home to help her. Because Alena delivered the baby, she also grieves over the child's death. Her teacher knows her desires and helps her find a way to get a diploma and to help her mother. *American Library Association Notable Books for Children.*

1072. Howarth, Sarah. **Colonial People**. Brookfield, CT: Millbrook Press, 1994. 47p. $15.40. ISBN 1-56294-512-2. (People and Places). 4-8

Quotations and case studies provide insight into the everyday lives of 13 people typical of those who settled in North America. Each chapter shows how this person would have fit (or not) into society. The people are governor, newcomer, Puritan, planter, servant, goodwife, Native American, apprentice, slave, fur trader, constable, smuggler, and patriot. Glossary, Further Reading, and Index.

1073. Howarth, Sarah. **Colonial Places**. Brookfield, CT: Millbrook Press, 1994. 47p. $15.40. ISBN 1-56294-513-0. (People and Places). 4-8

Each chapter shows a typical place in the early days of European settlement in North America and how it fit into the life of the community. Places covered are the colony, cornfield, meetinghouse, church, tobacco field, hunting ground, street post office, harbor, governor's house, college, and the Old World (because many people spoke of it as "home"). Glossary, Further Reading, and Index.

1074. Hoyt-Goldsmith, Diane. **Day of the Dead: A Mexican-American Celebration**. New York: Holiday House, 1994. 30p. $15.95; $6.95pa. ISBN 0-8234-0194-3; 0-8234-1200-8pa. 3-6

For the Aztecs, the way a person died indicated the type of afterlife he or she would have. When the Spanish came to the Mexican peninsula, they brought All Saints' Day, which was then combined with the Aztec acknowledgment of the dead. The text gives the history of and details on the preparation for the modern celebration each November 1 and 2. The author notes that Frida Kahlo, the Mexican artist, collected *Día de Muertos* objects that keep Aztecs beliefs as part of the present as well as the past. Glossary and Index.

1075. Hull, Mary. **Rosa Parks: Civil Rights Leader**. New York: Chelsea House, 1994. 110p. $18.95; $7.95pa. ISBN 0-7910-1881-4; 0-7910-1910-1pa. (Black Americans of Achievement). 5 up

This biography of Rosa Parks (b. 1913) traces her life from the eventful day in 1955, when she refused to move from her seat on the bus because she "had had enough," through her life afterward. It is also a story of the Civil Rights movement from her perspective. Photographs and reproductions enhance the text. Chronology, Further Reading, and Index.

1076. Hull, Robert, sell. **Breaking Free: An Anthology of Human Rights Poetry**. New York: Thomson Learning, 1994. 64p. $17.95. ISBN 1-56847-196-3. All ages

This anthology of international poems written over several centuries presents such themes as imprisonment, liberation, slavery, hunger, education, and family and human relations. Photographs and drawings illustrate the text. Poet Biographies, Glossary, Bibliography, and Index.

1077. Humble, Richard. **Ships**. Peter Cornwall, illustrator. Austin, TX: Raintree/Steck-Vaughn, 1994. 32p. $21.40. ISBN 0-8114-6158-0. (Pointers). 3-7

Two-page spreads on each type of ship tell its structure and give historical information and an illustration. The types of ships presented are Egyptian warships, Greek triremes, Viking long ships, man-of-war ships, ships of the Line, early steamships, clipper ships, ironclads, turret rams, submarines, aircraft carriers, and ocean liners. Glossary and Index.

1078.   Humble, Richard. **A World War Two Submarine**. Mark Bergin, illustrator. New York: Peter Bedrick, 1991. 48p. $18.95. ISBN 0-87226-351-7. (Inside Story). 4-7

The very first submarine used in the United States was in 1776, when the *Turtle* was put to service to explode British ammunition. It failed, but it caused engineers to began searching for a submarine that would work. The text looks at submarine warfare during the World Wars and how they were designed and built. Diagrams and drawings show the midships, bow tubes, sleeping and eating arrangements, sonar, torpedoes and guns, and uniforms worn by the crew. A brief discussion of the Battle of the Atlantic from 1940 to 1943 describes subs in action. Chronology, Glossary, and Index.

1079.   Hunt, Irene. **Across Five Aprils**. 1965. Parsippany, NJ: Silver Burdett, 1994. 190p. $12.95. ISBN 0-382-24358-7. New York: Berkley, 1990. 190p. $3.99pa. ISBN 0-425-10241-6pa. 6 up

Jethro turns nine in 1861, and his life changes. The story traces the activities of his Illinois family during the four years of the Civil War, where brothers fight on opposite sides of the conflict. Jethro assumes the male responsibilities of the household when his father has a heart attack, and he learns about Abraham Lincoln and Robert E. Lee, both greatly respected by some and greatly reviled by others. When one of his brothers deserts, Jethro writes to Lincoln requesting amnesty. At Lincoln's death, the family mourns along with the nation. *Newbery Honor* and *Society of Midland Authors Book Award*.

1080.   Hunter, Nigel. **Helen Keller**. Richard Hook, illustrator. New York: Bookwright Press, Franklin Watts, 1986. 32p. $11.90. ISBN 0-531-18031-X. 3-6

In two-page chapters, Hunter presents some of the main events in Helen Keller's life (1880-1968). He discusses the main points that Keller herself presented in her autobiography about her illness when she was 19 months old, causing her to become blind and deaf.

1081.   Hurmence, Belinda. **Dixie in the Big Pasture**. New York: Clarion, 1994. 169p. $13.95. ISBN 0-395-52002-9. 5-7

In 1907, Dixie, 12, and her family move to Oklahoma with its wide plains. After her dog disappears, her father buys her a horse from a Kiowa Indian, but the Indian's son believes the horse still belongs to him. After this experience, plus a prairie fire, Dixie is unconvinced that the move from Tennessee was the right thing to do. But her family gains respect for being good neighbors and for her mother's medicinal knowledge.

1082.   Hurmence, Belinda. **A Girl Called Boy**. 1982. New York: Clarion, 1990. 180p. $5.95pa. ISBN 0-395-55698-8pa. 3-6

Boy, 11, is a Black girl who shifts in time from a picnic with her family in the late twentieth century to 1853. In 1853, slaves thinks she is a runaway, but they take her with them because she can read, an illegal activity. After several escapes, she reaches the stream that she crossed into 1853, but the slaves with her will not cross. When she returns to her family, she has only been gone 10 minutes, but her attitude toward her slave heritage has changed forever. *Parents' Choice Award*.

1083.   Hyatt, Patricia Rusch. **Coast to Coast with Alice**. Minneapolis, MN: Carolrhoda, 1995. 72p. $13.13. ISBN 0-87614-789-9. 3-6

In 1909, Hermine (Minna) Jahns, 16, rides with her friend Alice Ramsey from New York City to San Francisco, California. Ramsey is trying to become the first woman to cross the country in a motorcar. Using first-person diary form, Minna tells the story of the journey that takes 59 days, one day shorter than the first two attempts made by men. They ride in a Maxwell for 3,800 miles with 11 tire changes and three axle replacements. Afterword, A Few Car Questions, and Bibliography.

I

1084. IlgenFritz, Elizabeth. **Anne Hutchinson**. New York: Chelsea House, 1990. 111p. $18.95. ISBN 1-55546-660-5. (American Women of Achievement). 5 up

Born in Alford, England, in 1591 during the reign of Queen Elizabeth I, Anne Marbury was the daughter of a dissident clergyman. He gave her an excellent education, and after her marriage to William Hutchinson, she spent 20 years as his wife and a village folk medicine expert. During the reign of James I, religious turmoil changed their lives, and they joined the earliest settlers in the Massachusetts Bay Colony. There, Anne criticized the ministers and spoke about religion in her home. Although some people supported her ideas, the issues she raised divided the settlement. Because women had no power, the governor in Boston, John Winthrop, called her to trial and condemned her. At her trial, she spoke with intelligence and integrity, never shrinking from her beliefs. She was one of the first settlers to request religious tolerance in this new land, and she and her followers moved to Rhode Island where Roger Williams had earlier been banished. She went to New York after her husband died. She and five of her children, caught in a Native American and Dutch war, were killed in 1643. Photographs and reproductions enhance the text. Chronology, Further Reading, and Index.

1085. Irwin, Haley. **I Be Somebody**. New York: Macmillan, 1984. 170p. $13.95. ISBN 0-689-50308-3. Bergenfield, NJ: New American Library, 1988. 170p. $2.50pa. ISBN 0-4511-5303-0pa. 4-8

Rap, 10, lives with his Aunt Spicy in Oklahoma. In 1910, she decides that the two will move with others from their town to Athabasca, Canada. On the train north, she dies, but before she dies, she tells Rap his father's identity. With that information, he can be "somebody" who has both a past and a future.

1086. Irwin, Hadley. **Jim-Dandy**. New York: Margaret K. McElderry, 1994. 144p. $14.95. ISBN 0-689-50594-9. 5-8

In the late 1860s, Caleb, 12, hates life with his stepfather on the empty Kansas plains after his mother dies. A foal, Dandy, is born and gives Caleb a new interest. His stepfather has to sell Dandy to Custer's Seventh Cavalry at nearby Fort Hays, and Caleb follows. He sees their campaign against the Cheyenne when they massacre Black Kettle at Washita and realizes the horrible results of the Indian Wars.

1087. Israel, Fred L. **Franklin Delano Roosevelt**. New York: Chelsea House, 1985. 112p. $18.95. ISBN 0-87754-573-1. (World Leaders Past and Present). 5 up

Elected in 1932 to the presidency, Franklin D. Roosevelt (1882-1945) ignored those who disagreed with his New Deal programs to stop the economic devastation throughout the country. Not everything worked, but the United States entered World War II, and then true recovery could begin. Roosevelt was a great leader in both war and peace. Photographs enhance the text. Chronology, Further Reading, and Index.

1088. Italia, Robert. **Courageous Crimefighters**. Minneapolis, MN: Oliver Press, 1995. 160p. $14.95. ISBN 1-881508-21-8. (Profiles). 6-9

People who lived the adventures that make mystery and detective books so appealing risk their lives to catch criminals. The text looks at eight of these people: Sir Robert Peel (1788-1850) of Scotland Yard in England; Allan Pinkerton (1819-1884), the original private eye in America; Samuel Steele (1851-1919), a Canadian mountie; Leander H. McNelly (1844-1877), captain of the Texas Rangers; Melvin Purvis (1903-1960) and Eliot Ness (1902-1957), top agents in the Federal Bureau of Investigation; Estes Kefauver (1903-1963), a crusader in Congress; and Simon Wiesenthal (b. 1908), hunter of Nazis. Bibliography and Index.

J

1089. Jackson, Ellen. **The Winter Solstice**. Jan Davey Ellis, illustrator. Brookfield, CT: Millbrook Press, 1994. Unpaged. $15.40. ISBN 1-56294-400-2. 3-4

The winter solstice was a time of ritual and tradition for the Celts, the Romans, and the Native Americans. Its magic has had an influence throughout history and is reflected in the present with the celebration of Halloween and All Souls' Day. A Cherokee legend ends the presentation.

1090. Jacobs, Francine. **The Tainos: The People Who Welcomed Columbus**. Patrick Collins, illustrator. New York: Putnam, 1992. 103p. $15.95. ISBN 0-399-22116-6. 5-9

The Indians who met Christopher Columbus and his crews in 1492 were called Tainos. They had no written language, so all that survives about them are the writings made during the time of Columbus and pictographs discovered in caves on the islands. They were peaceful farming people whose ancestors had come from South America hundreds of years before. Although the Tainos welcomed Columbus and his men, the visitors called them Indians because they thought they were in India. Then they destroyed the Taino culture in their greed for gold. In 50 years, the Tainos became extinct. Notes, Museums, Bibliography, and Index.

1091. Jacobs, William. **War with Mexico**. Brookfield, CT: Millbrook Press, 1994. 64p. $15.90; $5.95pa. ISBN 1-56294-366-9; 1-56294-776-1pa. (Spotlight on American History). 5-8

War between Mexico and the United States started in 1846 over territories that both claimed. Battles occurred at Monterey and Buena Vista as the United States drove toward Mexico City. When the United States won the war, many thought the boundaries of the country would extend with the Treaty of Guadalupe Hidalgo. What ensued after 1848 was anything but peaceful because of the bills in Congress to keep slavery from being legal in the new territories. The text discusses these various aspects of this war. Chronology, Further Reading, Bibliography, and Index.

1092. Jacobs, William Jay. **Dwight David Eisenhower: Soldier and Statesman**. New York: Franklin Watts, 1995. 64p. $19.90. ISBN 0-531-20191-0. (First Book). 3-6

Dwight David Eisenhower (1890-1969) grew up in a large, poor Kansas family. He almost had his leg amputated after a football accident, but he recovered then and continued to recover from various adversities throughout his life. His son died, and he was one of the first to see the Holocaust victims at the end of World War II in Germany. He became the commander of Allied forces in Europe during the war, which propelled him into the public eye. His accomplishments after he became 34th President of the United States included ending the Korean War, sending economic aid to the Middle East, and strengthening the North American Treaty Organization (NATO). He retired to Gettysburg, Pennsylvania. His dream was "the promise of American Life." Photographs, Important Dates, For Further Reading, and Index.

1093. Jacobs, William Jay. **Ellis Island: New Hope in a New Land**. New York: Scribner's, 1990. 34p. $16. ISBN 0-684-19171-7. 2-5

Photography of people and buildings complement the present tense text, which gives the sense of what arriving at Ellis Island was like for many immigrants who landed there after passing the Statue of Liberty in New York Harbor. Index.

1094. Jacobs, William Jay. **Great Lives: Human Rights**. New York: Scribner's, 1990. 278p. $22.95. ISBN 0-684-19036-2. 4-7

People concerned with the rights of all humans have been expressing their beliefs throughout history. The text chronologically organizes profiles of some of these people. In the early New World, human rights advocates included Anne Hutchinson and Roger Williams. In the nineteenth century, such people as Dorothea Dix and Frederick Douglass professed their beliefs. In the Industrial Age, Susan B. Anthony and Andrew Carnegie are examples. The twentieth century contained such figures as Emma Goldman, Jacob Riis, Cesar Chavez, and Martin Luther King, Jr. For Further Reading and Index.

1095. Jacobs, William Jay. **Great Lives**: World Religions. New York: Atheneum, 1996. 280p. $23. ISBN 0-689-80486-5. 4-7

The text covers religions and religious leaders throughout world history. Beginning with the religions of ancient Egypt and Persia, it continues with Asian religions, Judaism, Christianity, and Islam. Among the figures presented are Amenhotep IV, Zarathustra, Confucius, Buddha, Muhammad, Mahavira, Gandhi, Jesus, Khomeini, Moses, Jeremiah, Meir, Erasmus, Thomas Aquinas, John Calvin, John Wesley, George Fox, Roger Williams, Anne Hutchinson, Martin Luther King, Jr., Mother Teresa, and Joseph Smith. If appropriate, a brief interpretation of a person's theology also appears. Further Reading and Index.

1096.   Jacobs, William Jay. **Lincoln**. New York: Scribner's, 1991. 42p. $12.95. ISBN 0-684-19274-8. 3-6

Raised on the words of the Bible, Abraham Lincoln (1809-1865) believed that life should be lived according to God's will and that people had to face losses and successes. He did both, as Jacobs records in this biography, using quotes from primary sources. For Further Reading and Index.

1097.   Jacobs, William Jay. **They Shaped the Game: Ty Cobb, Babe Ruth, and Jackie Robinson**. New York: Scribner's, 1995. 85p. $15.95. ISBN 0-684-19734-0. 4-6

Three great players shaped the game of baseball, all for different reasons. Ty Cobb (1886-1961) played aggressively and fiercely; his lifetime batting average of .367 may never be equaled. Babe Ruth (1895-1948) was an outstanding home run hitter and also an important major league pitcher. Jackie Robinson (1919-1972) had such natural talent that he was the first Black athlete in the modern major leagues. For Further Reading and Index.

1098.   Jaffe, Steven. **Who Were the Founding Fathers?: Two Hundred Years of Reinventing American History**. New York: Henry Holt, 1996. 227p. $16.95. ISBN 0-8050-3102-2. 6 up

The text looks at the way generations have reinterpreted history based on their own needs and politics. It examines the decisions of the founders such as Jefferson and Adams and uses cartoons and reproductions to enhance the idea that values taken for granted may not be as old or as entrenched as one supposes. Bibliography, Notes, and Index.

1099.   Jakes, John. **Susanna of the Alamo**. San Diego, CA: Gulliver, Harcourt Brace, 1986. Unpaged. $13.95. ISBN 0-15-200592-0. 2-4

Susanna Dickinson survived the massacre at the Alamo in 1836, unlike Davy Crockett, Jim Bowie, and William Barrett Travis. Mexico's General Santa Anna spared her so that she could see his might over Sam Houston's rebel Texas army. She refused to become his emissary, and her report that he had burned instead of buried the fallen men inspired the Texans enough to defeat Santa Anna at San Jacinto.

1100.   Jakoubek, Robert. **Adam Clayton Powell, Jr.** New York: Chelsea House, 1988. 112p. $18.95; $7.95pa. ISBN 1-55546-606-0; 0-7910-0213-6pa. (Black Americans of Achievement). 5 up

Adam Clayton Powell, Jr. (1908-1972) was a minister of the Abyssinian Baptist Church in Harlem. He gave impassioned sermons and organized protests against racial discrimination in business practices. He won election to the New York City Council in 1941 and to the U.S. House of Representatives in 1944. He wanted civil rights legislation and social welfare programs. When he became chair of the House Education and Labor Committee in the 1960s, he was in a position to guide civil rights bills through Congress. He remained committed to racial equality even while being maligned by others in the latter part of his career. Photographs enhance the text. Chronology, Further Reading, and Index.

1101.   Jakoubek, Robert. **Joe Louis: Heavyweight Champion**. New York: Chelsea House, 1990. 128p. $18.95. ISBN 0-7910-0244-6. (Black Americans of Achievement). 5 up

Joe Louis Barrow (1914-1981) grew up in Alabama and a Detroit ghetto, where he began boxing. He was soundly defeated in his first two bouts and spent the next six months shoving truck bodies onto a conveyor belt. Then he returned to the ring, winning 50 of his next 53 fights. He became the leading contender for the heavyweight title in 1935, but in 1936 his loss to Hitler's favorite, Max Schmeling, cost him approval. In 1937, however, he won the championship, and a year later fought Schmeling again, knocking him out in the first round. His victory was a blow to the myth of racial inferiority. Photographs enhance the text. Chronology, Further Reading, and Index.

1102.   Jakoubek, Robert. **Martin Luther King, Jr.** New York: Chelsea House, 1989. 143p. $18.95; $7.95pa. ISBN 1-55546-597-8; 0-7910-0243-8pa. (Black Americans of Achievement). 5 up

Martin Luther King, Jr. (1929-1968) grew up in the South, where he attended Atlanta's Morehead College and then went to Crozer Seminary and Boston University for advanced theological degrees. He returned to the South in 1954 to begin his pastorate in Montgomery, Alabama, and his fight for civil rights. The text tells of his important affiliations and his philosophy of nonviolence. Photographs enhance the text. Chronology, Further Reading, and Index.

1103.   Jakoubek, Robert E. **The Assassination of Abraham Lincoln**. Brookfield, CT: Millbrook Press, 1993. 64p. $14.40. ISBN 1-56294-239-5. (Spotlight on American History). 3-5

The text uses "standard accounts" of the day Lincoln was shot, April 14, 1865, to recount what Lincoln did throughout the day before he attended Ford's Theater in the evening. The event included the weeks afterward when the manhunt for John Wilkes Booth occurred and the conviction of the co-conspirators. Many details make this work memorable. Bibliography and Index. *Child Study Association Children's Books of the Year.*

1104. Jakoubek, Robert E. **Harriet Beecher Stowe**. New York: Chelsea House, 1989. 110p. $18.95. ISBN 1-55546-683-4. (American Women of Achievement). 5 up

Harriet Beecher Stowe (1811-1896) grew under the guidance of a stern religious father. She moved with her family to Cincinnati, Ohio, where she met the theologian Calvin Stowe and married him. She began publishing articles after talking to both abolitionists and fugitive slaves who lived across the Ohio River in the slave state of Kentucky. When she, her husband, and five children left for Maine, she was convinced that slavery had to be abolished. Abraham Lincoln commented that her book, *Uncle Tom's Cabin*, was one of the factors leading to the Civil War. After the war, she spoke on various topics, including feminism. Photographs, engravings, and reproductions enhance the text. Chronology, Further Reading, and Index.

1105. Jakoubek, Robert E. **Walter White and the Power of Organized Protest**. Brookfield, CT: Millbrook Press, 1994. 32p. $13.90; $4.95pa. ISBN 1-56294-378-2; 1-56294-697-8pa. (Gateway Civil Rights). 3-6

In 1906, when Walter White (1893-1955) was 13 in his hometown of Atlanta, Georgia, a race riot ensued when the white candidates for governor said that they planned to abolish many of the rights that Blacks had gained. Although Walter and his family looked white, they lived in Atlanta's Black section. When the rioters came searching for his father, someone else stopped them with a gunshot. Afterward, White knew he would try to improve conditions for his people. Important Dates, Find Out More, and Index.

1106. James, Betsy. **The Mud Family**. Paul Morin, illustrator. New York: Putnam, 1994. Unpaged. $15.95. ISBN 0-399-22549-8. K-3

The young Anasazi girl Sosi makes a family out of mud and plays with it while her real family prepares to move during a drought. The eleventh-century girl dances with her mud family, the winds blow, and the rains come. Her real family celebrates her for the success of her dance in bringing the rain when they originally would not let her participate.

1107. James, Cary. **Julia Morgan: Architect**. New York: Chelsea House, 1988. 110p. $18.95. ISBN 1-55546-669-9. (American Women of Achievement). 5 up

Julia Morgan (1872-1957) was the first well-known female architect. She received many commissions for women's organizations and private homes as she developed her style. In 1919, she started building William Randolph Hearst's private estate, San Simeon, and worked on it for 20 years. By the end of her career, she had designed more than 700 buildings. Photographs enhance the text. Chronology, Further Reading, and Index.

1108. Jeffery, David. **Geronimo**. Tom Redman, illustrator. Austin, TX: Raintree/Steck-Vaughn, 1990. 32p. $4.95pa. ISBN 0-8172-3404-7pa. (Native American Stories). 3-5

An Apache child, Goyahkla (1829-1909) enjoyed life in his tribe. After his marriage, Mexicans murdered his wife and children. He fought them and any others who tried to take away his heritage. His name changed to "Geronimo" because of his fierceness in battle, but in 1886 he surrendered to General Nelson Miles in order to save the remaining Apaches. History of Geronimo.

1109. Jeffredo-Warden, Louise V. **Ishi**. Kim Fujiwara, illustrator. Austin, TX: Raintree/Steck-Vaughn, 1993. 32p. $19.97; $4.95pa. ISBN 0-8114-6578-0; 0-8114-4096-6pa. (Native American Stories). 3-5

Ishi, the last of the Yahi Indian tribe, lived from the early 1860s until 1916. No one knows his real name because he never told; he was called Ishi because Ishi means "man" in Yahi. From 1911, when he met white people, until his death, he helped people in a California museum learn how to chip out an arrowhead and shape a bow and to understand his tribe's values. History.

1110. Jensen, Dorothea. **The Riddle of Penncroft Farm**. San Diego, CA: Harcourt, 1989. 180p. $14.95. ISBN 0-15-200574-9. 4-6

Lars and his parents move to Philadelphia from Minnesota to be with Lars's 90-year-old aunt. When she dies, a man claims her property, but her will cannot be located. Even though Lars had not wanted to come, he has an unsettling experience when a family ghost from the Revolutionary War era visits and tells him family history and the roles of his ancestors in the first civil war, the American Revolution. With the ghost's information, Lars finds the will and becomes the family heir.

1111. Jezer, Marty. **Rachel Carson: Biologist and Author**. New York: Chelsea House, 1988. 112p. $18.95. ISBN 1-55546-646-X. (American Women of Achievement). 5 up

An environmentalist who realized that people were destroying the Earth, Rachel Carson (1907-1964) wrote a book, *The Silent Spring*, in 1962. Its publication caused an uproar by companies who tried to convince the public that pesticides were not as dangerous as she claimed. However, the public believed her, and the ecology movement gained much momentum from her words. She died of cancer. Photographs enhance the text. Chronology, Further Reading, and Index.

1112. Johnson, Dolores, author/illustrator. **Now Let Me Fly: The Story of a Slave Family**. New York: Macmillan, 1993. Unpaged. $14.95; $5.99pa. ISBN 0-02-747699-5; 0-689-80966-2pa. 1-4

Minna hears drums on the African savanna and thinks there will be dancing and stories. Instead, a member of her own tribe kidnaps her and marches her toward slavery. She travels for three months on a ship to a place called America, where she is sold at auction to a plantation owner. She and Amadi, the boy she meets on the ship, eventually marry and have children, but they have no chance of freedom.

1113. Johnson, Dolores, author/illustrator. **Seminole Diary: Remembrances of a Slave**. New York: Macmillan, 1994. Unpaged. $14.95. ISBN 0-02-747848-3. 3-5

Gina's mother and Gina find and read Libbie's diary, and together they discover a family member who escaped slavery with her father and sister in 1834 to join the Seminoles in Florida. Libbie's father decides they will join the resettlement by going to Oklahoma, but Libbie's sister escapes with one of the Seminole families into the Everglades instead. The diary ends as Libbie and her father begin their long march, and Libbie laments the loss of her sister.

1114. Johnson, Jacqueline. **Stokely Carmichael: The Story of Black Power**. Eric Velasquez, illustrator. Englewood Cliffs, NJ: Silver Burdett, 1990. 130p. $12.95. ISBN 0-382-09920-6. (History of the Civil Rights Movement). 5-12

Stokely Carmichael (b. 1941) raised his fist when he was 20 years old and said the words "Black power." He grew up in Trinidad in a well-off family and felt sympathy for those who did not have what he had. When he was 12, the family came to the United States and Harlem, a different world where his color mattered more than anything. The text continues with Carmichael's life as the originator of the Black Panthers and as a leader in the Civil Rights movement. Timetable, Suggested Reading, Sources, and Index.

1115. Johnson, James E. **The Irish in America**. Minneapolis, MN: Lerner, 1981. 80p. $17.50; $5.95pa. ISBN 0-8225-1954-2; 0-8225-3475-4pa. 5-8

More people of Irish descent live in the United States than in Ireland. The potato blight, which began in 1845 and lasted for five years, was a turning point in the history of the country. People either had to stay and starve or leave their homes for another country. Many men who came fought in the Civil War, mainly for the North, in the Irish Brigade. After the war, some men working in the coalfields of Pennsylvania formed the Molly Maguires, a secret organization that terrorized cruel bosses who exploited them. Other difficulties the Irish faced stemmed from their Catholicism. Notable Americans of Irish descent are Eugene O'Neill, F. Scott Fitzgerald, John O'Hara, Mary McCarthy, John McCormack, the Barrymore family, Helen Hayes, John Wayne, Louis Henry Sullivan, John F. Kennedy, and Ronald Reagan. Index.

1116. Johnson, Janice. **Rosamund**. Deborah Haeffele, illustrator. New York: Simon & Schuster, 1994. Unpaged. $15. ISBN 0-671-79329-2. 1-3

When a young woman hears about the tradition of the rose in her family, she decides to name her unborn daughter Rosamund. What she discovers is that during the twelfth century in England, the rose bloomed in one of her ancestor's gardens. Cuttings survived during the Crusades, the Wars of the Roses, the migration to the New World, and the trek across America to Oregon.

1117. Johnson, Linda Carlson. **Our National Symbols**. Brookfield, CT: Millbrook Press, 1992. 48p. $12.90. ISBN 1-56294-108-9. (I Know America). 3-5

After the country was established in 1776, symbols evolved that have national significance. Among those are the Liberty Bell, bald eagle, Uncle Sam, and the Statue of Liberty. The text discusses the importance of each of these. Chronology and Index.

1118. Johnson, Neil. **The Battle of Gettysburg**. New York: Four Winds, 1989. 56p. $16. ISBN 0-02-747831-9. 3-6

Photographs in this text were taken at the reenactment of the Battle of Gettysburg on its 125th anniversary in 1988. Lee led the Army of Northern Virginia on a crusade toward Gettysburg in hopes of winning the war at the end of June 1863. A brief overview of the war until 1863 indicates that the cavalier attitudes of the armies changed in 1861 after the bloody First Battle of Manassas (Bull Run). But after three days against the Union soldiers at Gettysburg, the Confederates were defeated—22,000 men lost through death, serious wounds, or capture. The Gettysburg Address Delivered on November 19, 1863, and Bibliography.

1119. Johnson, Neil. **The Battle of Lexington and Concord**. New York: Four Winds, 1992. 40p. $15.95. ISBN 0-02-747841-6. 3-6

Using photographs of a reenactment of the battle, Johnson explains that the situation on April 18, 1775, was more an accident than a planned combat. He traces the warning rides of Revere, Dawes, and Prescott, and describes the fighting at Lexington, Concord, and on the road to Boston. To balance the story, he relates that the British bayoneted minutemen, but a minuteman hacked a British soldier with an ax.

1120. Johnston, Julie. **Hero of Lesser Causes**. Boston: Joy Street, 1993. 192p. $14.95. ISBN 0-316-46988-2. 5-8

Keely Connor, 12, loves to imagine that she is a knight riding a steed instead of a breadwagon horse. When her brother becomes paralyzed from polio in 1946, she spends the next year trying to interest him in living. He nearly dies before he realizes the value of his life.

1121. Johnston, Norma. **Harriet: The Life and World of Harriet Beecher Stowe**. New York: Four Winds, 1994. 239p. $16.95. ISBN 0-02-747714-2. 6 up

In 1852, after the passage of the Fugitive Slave Law and in the years preceding the Civil War, Harriet Beecher Stowe (1811-1896) and her book *Uncle Tom's Cabin* were important lights in the culture. As a middle-class white Calvinist, Stowe believed that everyone had equal rights under God. She faced the knowledge that her parents had wanted a boy, the loss of her mother and her sons, depression and physical illnesses, a husband who loved and respected her but could never quite support their family, and the misuse of her book when people retold it in a pejorative manner. Books for Further Reading and Index.

1122. Johnston, Tony. **How Many Miles to Jacksonville?** Bart Forbes, illustrator. New York: Putnam, 1996. Unpaged. $15.95. ISBN 0-399-22615-X. 1-4

During the 1920s, the narrator's family enjoys the wealthy visitors who arrive on the new train passing through their town and stop to eat at their restaurant. The story reveals the connections and the fantasy that the train bought to the children and the adults in east Texas.

1123. Jones, Rebecca C. **The President Has Been Shot: True Stories of the Attacks on Ten U.S. Presidents**. New York: Dutton, 1996. 134p. $14.99. ISBN 0-525-45333-4. 4-6

The text looks at four assassinations and another seven attacks that were unsuccessful. It presents a chronology of these attacks and the resulting changes in security for the presidents. It also notes that when doctors could not find the bullet in President McKinley, they did not think to use the latest medical advance, the x-ray machine. Further Reading and Index.

1124. Jones, S. D. **Our Century: 1950-1960**. Milwaukee, WI: Gareth Stevens, 1993. 64p. $23.93. ISBN 0-8368-1037-6. 3 up

Written as if a newspaper, the book's short articles give an overview of the decade. Included are statistics, daily life in America, Red China entering the Korean conflict, the Hungarian revolt, Fidel Castro in Cuba, Joseph McCarthy, civil rights, Edmund Hillary, Albert Schweitzer, Sputnik, Jonas Salk, Evita Peron, and Marilyn Monroe. Glossary, Books for Further Reading, Places to Write or Visit, and Index.

1125. Joosse, Barbara M. **The Morning Chair**. Marcia Sewall, illustrator. New York: Clarion, 1995. 32p. $14.95. ISBN 0-395-62337-5. K-2

In 1950, Bram and his family leave Holland for America, where his father hopes to get a job. When he was in Holland, he sat in his mother's lap in the morning chair to have tea. Not until the furniture arrives in their New York apartment and the morning chair reappears does Bram feel comfortable.

1126. Jumper, Moses, and Ben Sonder. **Osceola: Patriot and Warrior**. Patrick Soper, illustrator. Austin, TX: Raintree/Steck-Vaughn, 1993. 76p. $22.83; $4.95pa. ISBN 0-8114-7222-1; 0-8114-8062-3pa. (Stories of America—Against All Odds). 4-6

Osceola (1804-1838) fought to keep his people on their land in Florida. The United States, however, wanted the Seminoles off the land so it could be opened for white settlement. The United States also wanted to find the runaway slaves who had found refuge with Seminoles and return them to their owners. In the Second Seminole War, Osceola helped some of the Seminoles flee into the Everglades, but other leaders betrayed him. Epilogue, Afterword, and Notes.

K

1127. Kallen, Stuart A. **Thurgood Marshall: A Dream of Justice for All**. Minneapolis, MN: Abdo, 1993. 40p. $14.96. ISBN 1-56239-258-1. (I Have a Dream). 5-9

This biography of Thurgood Marshall (1908-1993) begins with his boss ordering him to go to the White House to see Lyndon Johnson in 1967. He did, and when he arrived, Johnson told him, "I'm going to put you on the Supreme Court." Marshall's response was "Oh, yippee, what did you say?" The rest of the text presents Marshall's life as a civil rights lawyer who helped diminish racial injustice. Glossary and Index.

1128. Kalman, Bobbie. **Children's Clothing of the 1800s**. Antoinette "Cookie" DeBiasi, illustrator. New York: Crabtree, 1992. 32p. $17.95; $7.95pa. ISBN 0-86505-480-0; 0-86505-519-Xpa. (Historic Communities). 3-6

Most settler children had two outfits, and when they wore one outfit for a week, they washed it only once. Girls wore petticoats and crinolines. Males wore skeleton suits and knickers. Photographs from living museums and drawings augment the text.

1129. Kalman, Bobbie. **Colonial Crafts**. New York: Crabtree, 1992. 32p. $17.95; $7.95pa. ISBN 0-6505-490-8; 0-86505-510-6pa. (Historic Communities). 3-6

Photographs from living museums illustrate the various craftspeople and their trades as they were practiced in the eighteenth century. They include leather workers, cabinetmakers, coopers, wheelwrights, gunsmiths, blacksmiths, founders, silversmiths, papermakers, printers, bookbinders, milliners, wig makers, building trades, home industries, and crafts in the classroom. Glossary and Index.

1130. Kalman, Bobbie. **Colonial Life**. New York: Crabtree, 1992. 32p. $17.95; $7.95pa. ISBN 0-86505-491-6; 0-86505-511-4pa. (Historic Communities). 3-5

Using photographs from a living museum, the text tells of settlements, homes, newcomers, the family, school, play, men's clothing and women's fashions, travel, taverns, work and fun, and prejudice in the lives of colonial people during the eighteenth century. Glossary and Index.

1131. Kalman, Bobbie. **A Colonial Town: Williamsburg**. Antoinette "Cookie" DeBiasi, illustrator. New York: Crabtree, 1992. 32p. $17.95; $7.95pa. ISBN 0-86505-489-4; 0-86505-509-2pa. 3-6

Using photographs of the historic community of Williamsburg, the text looks at the beginning of the settlement and its development, the Governor's Palace, public buildings, Bruton Parish Church, the College of William and Mary, the apothecary, the windmill, the shops and their signs, and the people. Williamsburg was a thriving town, and the text shows the various levels of society, what they wore, where they worked, and how they entertained themselves. Map, Glossary, and Index.

1132. Kalman, Bobbie. **Early Artisans**. New York: Crabtree, 1994. 32p. $17.95; $7.95pa. ISBN 0-86505-023-6; 0-86505-022-8pa. (Early Settler Life). 3-6

Although people had to build or make everything that they used as pioneers in the eighteenth and nineteenth centuries, many still wanted beautiful things. People made silver and gold jewelry and flatware. They painted pictures and designed and wove beautiful fabric. They created artifacts for the home and decorated the exteriors as well as the interiors of buildings and homes. The amount of decoration that a person had signified his or her economic class. Living photographs and drawings illustrate the text. Glossary and Index.

1133. Kalman, Bobbie. **Early Christmas**. Antoinette "Cookie" DeBiasi, illustrator. New York: Crabtree, 1994. 32p. $17.95; $7.95pa. ISBN 0-86505-001-5; 0-86505-003-1pa. (Early Settler Life). 3-6

As a celebration, Christmas has had a history based on where those settlers who celebrated it had lived before. From these various traditions, the American celebration of Christmas evolved. The text talks about the history of Christmas in the eighteenth and nineteenth centuries, and it covers almost all topics, from food to church celebrations, in the customs of the French, Germans, Mennonites, Scots, Dutch, Swedes, and Ukrainians. Photographs and reproductions highlight the text. Glossary and Index.

1134. Kalman, Bobbie. **Early City Life**. Antoinette "Cookie" DeBiasi, illustrator. New York: Crabtree, 1994. 32p. $17.95; $7.95pa. ISBN 0-86505-029-5; 0 -86505-028-7pa. (Early Settler Life). 3-6

Cities and towns grew in the nineteenth century, especially in the latter half. The type of life one found in these areas appears in the text, including buildings, schools, homes, stores, and other aspects of city life. Glossary and Index.

1135. Kalman, Bobbie. **The Early Family Home**. New York: Crabtree, 1994. 32p. $17.95; $7.95pa. ISBN 0-86505-017-1; 0-86505-016-3pa. (Early Settler Life). 3-6

Living history photographs and drawings tell about the frontier life of families. The text includes information about their dwellings: the rooms in them, their size, how they were furnished, and the materials available for home construction. Glossary and Index.

1136. Kalman, Bobbie. **Early Farm Life**. New York: Crabtree, 1994. 32p. $17.95; $7.95pa. ISBN 0-86505-027-9; 0-86505-026-0pa. (Early Settler Life). 3-6

Living history photographs and drawings tell about the frontier life of families on farms. The text includes information about the various aspects of farming, from planting to harvesting, as well as the difficulties of this life. Glossary and Index.

1137. Kalman, Bobbie. **Early Health and Medicine**. New York: Crabtree, 1994. 32p. $17.95; $7.95pa. ISBN 0-86505-031-7; 0-86505-030-9pa. (Early Settler Life). 3-6

Medicine for the early settlers lacked scientific basis, and people had to survive as best they could. Herbs and other medicines helped some ailments. The text looks at the habits and practices of this early time. Photographs and drawings enhance the text. Glossary and Index.

1138. Kalman, Bobbie. **Early Loggers and the Sawmill**. New York: Crabtree, 1994. 32p. $17.95; $7.95pa. ISBN 0-86505-005-8; 0-86505-006-6pa. (Early Settler Life). 3-6

Living history photographs and drawings tell about the frontier life of loggers as they worked in the forests and took their logs to the sawmill for shaping. The text includes information about their lives and work. Additionally, it discusses what the millers and the loggers did with the wood. Glossary and Index.

1139. Kalman, Bobbie. **Early Pleasures and Pastimes**. Antoinette DeBiasi, illustrator. New York: Crabtree, 1992. 95p. $15.95; $7.95pa. ISBN 0-86505-025-2; 0-86505-024-4pa. (Early Settler Life). 4-5

The text presents the recreation and amusements of families on the American and Canadian frontiers during the nineteenth century. Living photographs and drawings illustrate the text. Glossary and Index.

1140. Kalman, Bobbie. **Early Schools**. Antoinette "Cookie" DeBiasi, illustrator. New York: Crabtree, 1994. 32p. $17.95; $7.95pa. ISBN 0-86505-015-5; 0-86505-014-7pa. (Early Settler Life). 3-6

For the settlers, schools were usually one room, and children had to travel far to get to them. The text describes the schools, the subjects taught, and their roles in the lives of settler children. Photographs and drawings enhance the text. Glossary and Index.

1141. Kalman, Bobbie, comp. **Early Settler Storybook**. New York: Crabtree, 1992. 64p. $17.95; $7.95pa. ISBN 0-86505-021-X; 0-86505-020-1pa. (Early Settler Life). 3-6

Before families had electricity, when they lived on the frontier as pioneers, reading was a significant form of entertainment. The text includes various stories and poems that nineteenth-century families read together. Drawings highlight the text. Glossary and Index.

1142. Kalman, Bobbie. **Early Stores and Markets**. Antoinette "Cookie" DeBiasi, illustrator. New York: Crabtree, 1994. 32p. $17.95; $7.95pa. ISBN 0-86505-002-3; 0-86505-004-Xpa. (Early Settler Life). 3-6

During the eighteenth and nineteenth centuries peddlers sold people merchandise as they traveled house-to-house, but stores and markets also sold goods in towns, cities, and villages. The text tells about the different kinds of stores and markets and the products that they sold. Photographs and drawings highlight the text. Glossary and Index.

1143. Kalman, Bobbie. **Early Travel**. New York: Crabtree, 1994. 32p. $17.95; $7.95pa. ISBN 0-86505-007-4; 0-86505-008-2pa. (Early Settler Life). 3-6

To get from one place to another, settlers and pioneers had to walk, ride horseback, take a coach of some kind, or board a boat. The text describes travel, where one rested along the road, and the routes available for the traveler. Drawings enhance the story. Glossary and Index.

1144. Kalman, Bobbie. **Early Village Life**. New York: Crabtree, 1994. 32p. $17.95; $7.95pa. ISBN 0-86505-009-0; 0-86505-010-4pa. (Early Settler Life). 3-6

In the nineteenth century, villages allowed people to live more closely together than did farms around the countryside. The text discusses the types of stores in the villages, who lived there, what they did for work and entertainment, and other aspects. Living history photographs and drawings augment the text. Glossary and Index.

1145. Kalman, Bobbie. **18th Century Clothing**. Antoinette "Cookie" DeBiasi, et al., illustrators. New York: Crabtree, 1993. 32p. $17.95; $7.95pa. ISBN 0-86505-492-4; 0-86505-512-2pa. (Historic Communities). 3-6

Photographs of the living museum in Williamsburg, Virginia, illustrate the types of clothing worn during the eighteenth century. The items include making clothes from sheep's wool, carding flax for linen, and tanning leather; shoes and boots; various fashions for men and women as well as accessories like muffs and wigs; hair and hats; underclothes; unhealthy habits for teeth and skin; children's clothing; and different social classes made obvious by clothes worn. Glossary and Index.

1146. Kalman, Bobbie. **Food for the Settler**. New York: Crabtree, 1994. 32p. $17.95; $7.95pa. ISBN 0-86505-013-9; 0-86505-012-0pa. (Early Settler Life). 3-6

Early setters and pioneers had to grow and prepare their own food. If they drank milk, they had to milk cows. If they ate meat, they had to kill the cows. The text presents the various types of food that people liked and what they prepared for special occasions. Glossary and Index.

1147. Kalman, Bobbie. **Games from Long Ago**. Antoinette "Cookie" DeBiasi, illustrator. New York: Crabtree, 1995. 32p. $17.95; $7.95pa. ISBN 0-86505-482-7; 0-86505-521-1pa. (Historic Communities). 3-6

The text looks at the board games, parlor games, and other games of the 1800s. Children still play some of them today, such as duck duck goose, charades, and baseball. But few people remember some of the others, such as shinny and jackstraws. Photographs from living museums and drawings augment the text.

1148. Kalman, Bobbie. **The Grist Mill**. Antoinette "Cookie" DeBiasi, illustrator. New York: Crabtree, 1994. 32p. $17.95; $7.95pa. ISBN 0-86505-486-X; 0-86505-506-8pa. (Historic Communities). 3-6

When pioneers and those on the frontier wanted bread, they had to first grow the wheat. Then they had to grind the wheat into flour. The text discusses the gristmills and water mills where settlers took their wheat. Photographs and drawings highlight the text. Glossary and Index.

1149. Kalman, Bobbie. **Home Crafts**. Antoinette "Cookie" DeBiasi, illustrator. New York: Crabtree, 1994. 32p. $17.95; $7.95pa. ISBN 0-86505-485-1; 0-86505-505-Xpa. (Historic Communities). 3-6

When people wanted various items as pioneers, they had to make them. Some of the crafts they produced were candles, baskets, cloth, quilts, and samplers. These crafts sometimes became the center of social events, such as quilting bees. Photographs and drawings augment the text. Glossary and Index.

1150. Kalman, Bobbie. **The Kitchen**. Antoinette "Cookie" DeBiasi, illustrator. New York: Crabtree, 1993. 32p. $17.95; $7.95. ISBN 0-86505-484-3; 0-86505-504-1pa. (Historic Communities). 3-6

Photographs and drawings show the various aspects of a pioneer kitchen where people cooked food over an open fire. The types of food, wood and iron utensils, methods of preserving foods, and facts about the kitchen fill the text. Glossary and Index.

1151. Kalman, Bobbie. **19th Century Clothing**. Antoinette "Cookie" DeBiasi, illustrator. New York: Crabtree, 1993. 32p. $17.95; $7.95pa. ISBN 0-86505-493-2; 0-86505-513-0pa. (Historic Communities). 3-6

Drawings and engravings illustrate the clothing styles worn in the nineteenth century. Among the items considered are pioneer clothing, working clothes, women's fashions, men's fashions, underwear, footwear, hats and hairstyles, bathing, sportswear, children's clothes, and mass-produced clothing toward the end of the century. Glossary and Index.

1152. Kalman, Bobbie. **Old-Time Toys**. Antoinette "Cookie" DeBiasi, illustrator. New York: Crabtree, 1992. 32p. $17.95; $7.95pa. ISBN 0-86505-481-9; 0-86505-520-3pa. (Historic Communities). 3-6

Until the mid-1800s, adults made most children's toys in their homes. People often whittled them from wood while they sat in front of the fire in the winter. In the nineteenth century, toy makers chose porcelain for dolls, created rocking horses, and devised such toys as automated coin banks and magic lanterns. Photographs from toy museums and drawings augment the text.

1153. Kalman, Bobbie. **A One-Room School**. Antoinette "Cookie" DeBiasi, illustrator. New York: Crabtree, 1994. 32p. $17.95; $7.95pa. ISBN 0-86505-497-5; 0-86505-517-3pa. (Historic Communities). 3-6

With photographs of people acting as frontier students in the nineteenth century, the text shows what school was like. Teachers were never left-handed, and the school had one room. Other items are the subjects studied, supplies, transportation to school (walking or horseback), daily routine, lunch, recess, pranks, punishment, special events like spelling bees and pageants, and games. Glossary and Index.

1154.   Kalman, Bobbie. **Settler Sayings**. Antoinette "Cookie" DeBiasi, illustrator. New York: Crabtree, 1992. 32p. $17.95; $7.95pa. ISBN 0-86505-498-3; 0-86505-518-1pa. (Historic Communities). 3-6

Many sayings still uttered today were part of the vernacular of the early settlers. They told people to "show your mettle" and believed that someone was "the apple of one's eye." They also commented about a "flash in the pan." The text looks at these and other phrases that began in the mill, in the kitchen, on the farm, in battle, and in the workshops. Photographs from living museums and drawings augment the text.

1155.   Kalman, Bobbie. **Tools and Gadgets**. Antoinette "Cookie" DeBiasi, illustrator. New York: Crabtree, 1992. 32p. $17.95; $7.95pa. ISBN 0-86505-488-6; 0-86505-508-4pa. (Historic Communities). 3-6

Tools assist a person in getting work done, and a gadget is a clever device that helps with a small job. In the pioneer days, both were extremely important. Those covered in the text are home and food gadgets, mills, metalworking tools, woodworking tools, printing shop items, medical gadgets, children's toys and gadgets, cards, hackles, wheels, and shuttles. Photographs from living museums and drawings augment the text. Glossary and Index.

1156.   Kalman, Bobbie, and David Schimpky. **Fort Life**. New York: Crabtree, 1994. 32p. $17.95; $7.95pa. ISBN 0-86505-496-7; 0-86505-516-5pa. (Historic Communities). 3-5

Photographs from living museums help re-create life on a fort during the early years of the colonies. The text looks at the fort garrison, life in the barracks, the officers' quarters, drilling and music, guarding the fort, food, the infirmary, and other buildings. The text takes a close look at Fort Niagara and Fort George during the War of 1812. Glossary and Index.

1157.   Kalman, Bobbie, and Tammy Everts. **A Child's Day**. Antoinette DeBiasi, illustrator. New York : Crabtree, 1994. 32p. $17.95; $7.95pa. ISBN 0-86505-494-0; 0-86505-514-9pa. (Historic Communities). 3-5

Using living history photographs, the text tells about a child's day in nineteenth-century America. Included are recipes, daily chores and rituals, schools, books read, games (e.g., hoop with stick), parties (e.g., blindman's buff), Sunday and church in good clothes, visitors, a country fair, and town merchants and their goods. Glossary and Index.

1158.   Kalman, Bobbie, and Tammy Everts. **Customs and Traditions**. New York: Crabtree, 1994. 32p. $17.95; $7.95pa. ISBN 0-86505-495-9; 0-86505-515-7pa. (Historic Communities). 3-6

After an overview of customs and traditions, including a picture of a Chinese man eating with chopsticks, the chapters cover nineteenth-century social life and customs. Included are community customs, Sundays for the settlers, telling and remembering stories, predicting the weather, kitchen customs, health and cleanliness, holidays, courtship and marriage, a new baby, and various other habits. Photographs and reproductions highlight the text. Glossary, Further Reading, and Index.

1159.   Karl, Jean. **America Alive: A History**. Ian Schoenherr, illustrator. New York: Philomel, 1994. 120p. $22.95. ISBN 0-399-22013-5. 5-8

This history of the United States, tagged as a personal history, touches on almost every subject, from the crossing of the Bering Strait to the election of Bill Clinton as President. Karl sees history as a continuum and writes about it as if it occurs sequentially. She tries to give an overall view, such as telling what the Blacks and Indians were doing while the whites fought in battles. Illustrations, including pictures of appropriate individuals, appear in the borders of the pages. Bibliography and Index.

1160.   Karr, Kathleen. **The Cave**. New York: Farrar, Straus & Giroux, 1994. 165p. $16. ISBN 0-374-31230-3. 5-7

Christine, 12, and her family cope with dust during the Depression in the Black Hills of South Dakota. She finds a cave with white fish swimming in a stream inside. She reluctantly tells her brother, and the two visit the cave repeatedly without telling their parents. When her father decides that they will have to leave if it does not rain, she tries to show him the cave, but a tornado has destroyed it. However, she and her brother saved the perfectly formed geodes that they found on prior visits to the cave and can sell them for the family's survival.

1161.   Karr, Kathleen. **Gideon and the Mummy Professor**. New York: Atheneum, 1993. 137p. $16. ISBN 0-374-32563-4. 5-8

In the mid-nineteenth century, Gideon, 12, and his father travel through the South in Mississippi with a mummy that intermittently sheds jewels from its wrappings. Gideon grew up in Egypt while his father was in diplomatic service, and when George, the mummy, and his father are at odds, Gideon joins George. George saves them by producing a scarab. They are pursued by jewel thieves and a criminal from New Orleans, but a voodoo queen rescues them during their adventures.

1162. Karr, Kathleen. **Go West, Young Women!** New York: HarperCollins, 1996. 160p. $14.95; $4.50pa. ISBN 0-06-027151-5; 0-06-440495-1pa. (The Petticoat Party, Book 1). 4-7

Because falling buffalo have killed the ineffectual men in the wagon party going to Oregon, their women have to finish the journey without them. Phoebe, 12, tells about their humorous escapades and the romance that begins between two teenage girls and two Pawnee braves that they meet on the trail. The group finally arrives in Fort Laramie, but the journey is not complete.

1163. Karr, Kathleen. **In the Kaiser's Clutch**. New York: Farrar, Straus & Giroux, 1995. 144p. $15. ISBN 0-374-33638-5. 5-8

The twins Fritz and Nelly, 15 in 1918, star in their mother's silent-movie serial, *In the Kaiser's Clutch*, after the mysterious death of their father in a munitions store explosion. Their real lives mirror their movie lives when they discover that someone is pursuing them and trying to keep them from finding out about their father's death. The story reveals the problems of making films on low budgets and the need to make money to pursue one's art.

1164. Karr, Kathleen. **It Ain't Always Easy**. New York: Farrar, Straus & Giroux, 1990. 229p. $14.95. ISBN 0-374-33645-8. 5-8

Jack, 11, tells the story of how the New York Children's Aid Society planned to take him and Mandy, eight, on the orphan train west in 1882. They miss the train and live in a coal bin. They then have problems in Pennsylvania that cause Jack to return to New York for help from Miss Blackman of the Children's Aid Society. Mandy goes west, and a farmer mistreats her, but Miss Blackman and her suitor rescue her. The four then go to Nebraska to become a family.

1165. Karr, Kathleen. **Phoebe's Folly**. New York: HarperCollins, 1996. 199p. $14.95; $4.50pa. ISBN 0-06-027153-1; 0-06-440496-Xpa. (The Petticoat Party, Book 2). 5 up

While in Fort Laramie, the women of the Petticoat Party arm themselves with rifles and show their ability to use them on the next leg of their Oregon Trail journey. Phoebe, 12, makes a comment that prompts the Snake Indians to challenge them to a shooting contest. They survive the challenge and eventually have the thrill of seeing Mount Hood rise in the distance.

1166. Kassem, Lou. **Listen for Rachel**. New York: Margaret K. McElderry, Macmillan, 1986. 176p. $11.95. ISBN 0-689-50396-2. 6-9

At 14, Rachel has to leave Nashville to live with her grandparents in Appalachia after her parents die in a fire. She adjusts to the new home because she loves to ride her grandfather's horses and thinks that the mountains are beautiful. But discord arrives when the Civil War looms; her cousins and her fiancé go to fight, and the "poor white trash" threaten to rape her. An old woman, however, encourages her ability to heal with herbs, and this reassurance comforts her.

1167. Katz, William Loren. **Black Women of the Old West**. New York: Atheneum, 1995. 84p. $18. ISBN 0-689-31944-4. 5-8

The text looks at African American women who helped settle the West since colonial times. Because finding documentation on their achievements is difficult, Katz presents vignettes of them. Among those discussed are Sarah Lester, expelled from a San Francisco school for being too bright by her white neighbors; Mary Pleasant, both a civil rights activist and a bordello owner; Harriet Scott, wife of Dred; and Lucy Parsons, wife of Alfred. Photographs, Bibliography, and Index. *Notable Children's Trade Books in the Field of Social Studies*.

1168. Katz, William Loren. **Breaking the Chains: African-American Slave Resistance**. New York: Atheneum, 1990. 194p. $16. ISBN 0-689-31493. 5 up

Katz posits that slavery in the New World began the day that Christopher Columbus arrived. Columbus bought with him the knowledge that other slave owners, including African slave holders, had: Slaves had to be removed from their homes because their kinsmen would fight to regain their freedom. For this reason (among others), Africans were shipped to America. The chapters cover the difficulties and deprivations slaves endured, those who attempted to escape, the abolitionists who tried to help, and the freedom that the Civil War brought. Bibliography and Index.

1169. Katz, William Loren, and Paula A. Franklin. **Proudly Red and Black: Stories of African and Native Americans**. New York: Atheneum, 1993. 88p. $13.95. ISBN 0-689-31801-4. 5-8

Because official birth and death records were not kept for people of color for many years, the ancestry of African and Native Americans is cloudy. The text looks at Black Indians who made contributions to society even though they faced many barriers. Those profiled include Paul Cuffe (1759-1817), a New England trader; Edward Rose (1780?-1830?), a frontiersman; John Horse (1812-1882), a Black Seminole leader; Edmonia Lewis (1845-1911?), sculptor; George Henry White (1852-1918), militant Congressman; and Bill Pickett (1870-1932), rodeo star. Bibliography and Index.

1170. Kaye, Judith. **The Life of Alexander Fleming**. New York: Twenty-First Century Books, 1993. 80p. $13.95. ISBN 0-8050-2300-3. (Pioneers in Health and Medicine). 5-7

Alexander Fleming (1881-1955) told people that he "played with microbes" for a living. He discovered penicillin, the first antibiotic, which increased lifespan by an average of 30 years for humans. Although he said that its discovery was a matter of chance and fortune, he was curious, creative, and dedicated to fighting infection and disease. For his work, he won the Nobel Prize. For Further Reading and Index.

1171. Kaye, Judith. **The Life of Benjamin Spock**. New York: Twenty-First Century Books, 1993. 80p. $13.95. ISBN 0-8050-2301-1. (Pioneers in Health and Medicine). 4-7

Benjamin Spock (b. 1903) told parents to trust themselves as they tried to raise their children. He first published his book, *Baby and Child Care*, in 1946, and it changed the way parents raised American children, for good or for bad. In his later life, he involved himself in larger issues, such as nuclear disarmament and world peace. He even went to jail for his beliefs. For Further Reading and Index.

1172. Kaye, Judith. **The Life of Daniel Hale Williams**. New York: Twenty-First Century Books, 1993. 80p. $13.95. ISBN 0-8050-2302-X. (Pioneers in Health and Medicine). 5 up

Daniel Hale Williams (1856-1931) was an African American doctor who performed the first surgery on the human heart in the nineteenth century and founded the first interracial hospital in the United States. Black-and-white photographs illustrate the text. For Further Reading and Index.

1173. Kaye, Judith. **The Life of Florence Sabin**. New York: Twenty-First Century Books, 1993. 80p. $13.95. ISBN 0-8050-2299-6. (Pioneers in Health and Medicine). 4-7

Florence Sabin (1871-1953) spent the first part of her life as a medical researcher and helped discover a cure for tuberculosis. Then she went back to her home state of Colorado, discovered the miserable state of public health, and began working to change the laws and the poor sanitary conditions. One of her last activities was to offer free x-rays on Denver streets so that doctors could identify tuberculosis early for easier treatment. For Further Reading and Index.

1174. Kaye, Tony. **Lyndon B. Johnson**. New York: Chelsea House, 1988. 112p. $18.95. ISBN 0-87754-536-7. (World Leaders Past and Present). 5 up

Lyndon B. Johnson (1908-1973) had a grand vision of the American society. He had seen the depressed farmers in Texas in his youth, and he wanted to help them by changing things in Washington. When he became an elected President (after finishing the term of John F. Kennedy), he started his "Great Society" program and brought reform to Medicare, civil rights, pollution laws, and federal aid for the poor. By 1966, the Vietnam War occupied him. He said that the United States was not at war while simultaneously ordering bombing raids and deploying ground troops. Although he achieved much on the national level, the Vietnam War scarred his legacy. Photographs enhance the text. Chronology, Further Reading, and Index.

1175. Keehn, Sally. **I Am Regina**. New York: Philomel, 1991. 240p. $14.95. ISBN 0-399-21797-5. 4-8

In 1755, Regina is 11. Allegheny Indians kidnap her and her sister after killing her father and brother. She spends eight years with them, forgets German, and speaks the Allegheny language. Within the tribe, she has both a helpful friend and a spiteful enemy. When they die of smallpox, she knows them well enough to grieve, but she and her sister still miss their mother, who sang a song they cannot forget.

1176. Keehn, Sally M. **Moon of Two Dark Horses**. New York: Putnam, 1995. 218p. $16.95. ISBN 0-399-22783-0. 4-8

The ghost of Coshmoo, a young Indian boy killed in the Revolutionary War, relates how he and his friend, son of a white settler, tried to end the hostilities between their people. When the Delaware need money to survive, the differences surge, and fighting begins that eventually kills Coshmoo.

1177. Kehret, Peg. **Small Steps: The Year I Got Polio**. Niles, IL: Albert Whitman, 1996. 179p. $14.95. ISBN 0-8075-7457-0. 4-6

In 1949, Kehret was one of the 42,000 polio cases nationwide, and the only person who got polio in her small town. She tells about the diagnosis and treatment, but more importantly, the frustration and the pain. What will surprise most is the totally unexpected arrival of the disease and the immediate paralysis accompanying it. Kehret tells what it was like to give up the dreams of youth to live in an artificial environment.

1178. Keller, Emily. **Margaret Bourke-White: A Photographer's Life**. Minneapolis, MN: Lerner, 1996. 128p. $17.21. ISBN 0-8225-4916-6. (Lerner Biographies). 5 up

The person who helped to develop the photo-essay style of *Life* magazine's news reporting was Margaret Bourke-White (1904-1971). Her photographs of industrial scenes and machinery, people coping during the Depression, World War II battlefields, and a variety of other subjects helped people see these things in a different way. Her work retains its timeless quality. Photographs, Sources, Bibliography, and Index.

1179. Kellogg, Steven, author/illustrator. **Johnny Appleseed**. New York: Morrow, 1988. 48p. $16; $4.95pa. ISBN 0-688-06417-5; 0-688-14025-4pa. 2-4

His mother dead within two years of his birth in Massachusetts in 1774 and his father away at war, John Chapman decided that when he was old enough to leave, he would. He took apple seeds and planted them from the Allegheny Mountains into Ohio and Indiana for the rest of his life, never settling in one place as far as anyone knew. His kindness before his death in 1845 prompted those who knew him to embellish their tales about him.

1180. Kelso, Richard. **Building a Dream: Mary Bethune's School**. Debbe Heller, illustrator. Austin, TX: Raintree/Steck-Vaughn, 1993. 46p. $22.83; $4.95pa. ISBN 0-8114-7217-5; 0-8114-8057-7pa. (Stories of America—Working Together). 3-6

In 1904, Mrs. Mary McLeod Bethune (1875-1955) arrived in Daytona Beach, Florida, with the dream to build a school for girls. She only had $1.50 and was Black, but she persevered. In 1907, she opened Faith Hall with money donated by a man who believed in her. Epilogue, Afterword, and Notes.

1181. Kelso, Richard. **Days of Courage: The Little Rock Story**. Mel Williges, illustrator. Austin, TX: Raintree/Steck-Vaughn, 1993. 88p. $24.96; $5.95pa. ISBN 0-8114-7230-2; 0-8114-8070-4pa. (Stories of America—Stand Up and Be Counted). 4-7

When Elizabeth Eckford was 15 in 1957, she was one of nine Black students chosen to integrate Little Rock High School in Alabama. She and the other eight faced danger from hostile white adults determined that their children would not attend school with Blacks. Governor Faubus of Alabama was no help because he supported the white parents, defying a Supreme Court order for immediate integration. Finally, President Eisenhower had to intervene so that these young people could go to school. Epilogue, Afterword, and Notes.

1182. Kelso, Richard. **Walking for Freedom: The Montgomery Bus Boycott**. Michael Newton, illustrator. Austin, TX: Raintree/Steck-Vaughn, 1993. 52p. $22.83; $4.95pa. ISBN 0-8114-7218-3; 0-8114-8058-5pa. (Stories of America—Working Together). 3-7

In 1949, Mrs. Robinson, who usually drove her car, rode a Montgomery, Alabama, bus instead and inadvertently sat in the whites-only section. The driver's hostile and rude treatment toward her led her to suggest a bus boycott to the Woman's Political Council. They waited six years until the time was right to put the plan into effect. When Rosa Parks refused to rise from her seat in the Black section of the bus for a white man in 1955, the boycott began. It lasted until November 1956, when Montgomery officials changed their laws. Epilogue, Afterword, and Notes.

1183. Kendall, Martha E. **Susan B. Anthony: Voice for Women's Voting Rights**. Springfield, NJ: Enslow, 1997. 128p. $18.95. ISBN 0-89490-780-8. (Historical American Biographies). 6-9

Susan B. Anthony (1820-1906) was an intelligent and educated woman who refused to accept a double standard for women, and she fought for women's rights. The biography looks at her impact on American history as it examines her life. Fact boxes and maps augment the text. Notes, Glossary, Further Reading, and Index.

1184. Kent, Deborah. **African-Americans in the Thirteen Colonies**. Chicago: Childrens Press, 1996. 30p. $18; $4.95pa. ISBN 0-516-06631-5; 0-516-20065-8pa. (Cornerstones of Freedom). 3-5

By looking at the slave trade and the economic situation behind it, Kent tells about Blacks in colonial times. She also discusses the ways that Native Americans and indentured servants were able to escape their bonds. Glossary and Index.

1185. Kent, Deborah. **The American Revolution: "Give Me Liberty, or Give Me Death!"** Springfield, NJ: Enslow, 1994. 128p. $17.95. ISBN 0-89490-521-X. (American War). 4-6

In addition to text, paintings and maps help tell the story of the American Revolution. Because colonists defied taxation without representation, they staged the Boston Tea Party. The British instigated the Boston Massacre, where Crispus Attucks was one of the first to die for independence. Then someone fired the "shot heard round the world" that began the war against Britain. Among the battles was that of Breed's Hill. People were concerned about who was loyalist and who was a patriot. George Washington led the fighting until General Cornwallis surrendered to him on October 19, 1781. Chronology, Notes, Further Reading, and Index.

1186. Kent, Deborah. **Dorothy Day: Friend to the Forgotten**. Grand Rapids, MI: William B. Eerdman, 1996. 137p. $15; $8pa. ISBN 0-8028-5117-7; 0-8028-5100-2pa. 5-9

Dorothy Day (1897-1980) became known throughout the world as the leader of the Catholic Worker movement. She was a journalist who thought that community service and social justice defined what it means to be human. In her work, she helped publish a newspaper, reached out to all in need, gave solace to the indigent, and guided those who wanted to pursue their inner life of contemplation. She went to jail many times in the 1950s for protesting against nuclear weapons. Photographs and Index.

1187.   Kent, Deborah. **The Freedom Riders**. Chicago: Childrens Press, 1993. 32p. $17.30; $4.95pa. ISBN 0-516-4662-5; 0-516-46662-3pa. (Cornerstones of Freedom). 3-5

The freedom riders, an interracial group, rode buses through the South in the early 1960s in an attempt to integrate the area. The text looks at this group, the Montgomery bus boycott of 1956, and the 1965 Voting Rights Act. Black-and-white photographs complement the text. Index.

1188.   Kent, Deborah. **Jane Addams and Hull House**. Chicago: Childrens Press, 1992. 32p. $17.30. ISBN 0-516-04852-X. (Cornerstones of Freedom). 3-5

Jane Addams (1860-1935) welcomed all to Hull House, the home she founded to help the sick, the poor, the oppressed, and the defenseless. She said in her autobiography that she decided to help those less fortunate when she was seven and found out that others had no one to help them or to educate them. For her work, she received a Nobel Prize. Her work to keep peace after World War I weakened her. When situations did not end as she expected, she revised her perceptions, and in some cases, changed rules that did not work. Index.

1189.   Kent, Deborah. **The Lincoln Memorial**. Chicago: Childrens Press, 1996. 32p. $18. ISBN 0-516-20006-2. (Cornerstones of Freedom). 3-5

The Lincoln Memorial was finished in 1922 after a long controversy about where to locate the memorial and what it should look like. The text examines this process from its inception until its dedication. Chronology, Glossary, and Index.

1190.   Kent, Deborah. **Salem, Massachusetts**. Englewood Cliffs, NJ: Dillon Press, 1996. 64p. $15.95. $7.95pa. ISBN 0-87518-648-3; 0-382-39174-8pa. (Places in American History). 3-6

One of the most surprising episodes in American history involved the tales that several young girls told about people in their town around 1692-1693. They led to accusations that these people were witches. Kent gives background about this situation and discusses other historical aspects of the town of Salem. A Salem Time Line, Visitor Information, and Index.

1191.   Kent, Deborah. **The Titanic**. Chicago: Childrens Press, 1993. 31p. $17.30; $4.95pa. ISBN 0-516-06672-2; 0-516-06672-2pa. (Cornerstones of Freedom). 3-5

The "nonsinkable" ocean liner *Titanic* sank after sailing in the Atlantic for four days because on April 14, 1912, she collided with an iceberg. The text recounts this situation and tells about some of those involved. Photographs and reproductions appear throughout the text. Index.

1192.   Kent, Zachary. **Andrew Johnson: Seventeenth President of the United States**. Chicago: Childrens Press, 1989. 100p. $19.80. ISBN 0-516-01363-7. (Encyclopedia of Presidents). 4-9

Andrew Johnson (1808-1875) lived a life filled with contradictions. He was born into extreme poverty, but apprenticed himself to a tailor and learned a trade to propel him into another life. He struggled to learn to read; he taught himself to give speeches; and he became President of the United States. People admired him for pardoning Confederates, but at the same time, they perceived him as a failure for being unable to engineer a speedy, peaceful reconstruction of the South. He was accused of misdeeds and suffered an impeachment trial, but emerged without guilt. Chronology of American History and Index.

1193.   Kent, Zachary. **The Battle of Chancellorsville**. Chicago: Childrens Press, 1994. 31p. $17.30; $4.95pa. ISBN 0-516-06679-X; 0-516-46679-8pa. (Cornerstones of Freedom). 3-7

The Battle of Chancellorsville, Virginia, May 2-4, 1863, was Robert E. Lee's last major victory in the Civil War. He fought Joseph Hooker's Union army with the help of Stonewall Jackson, but Jackson's own troops mortally wounded Jackson in the fray. Black-and-white photographs and engravings enhance the text. Index.

1194.   Kent, Zachary. **The Battle of Shiloh**. Chicago: Childrens Press, 1991. 32p. $4.95pa. ISBN 0-516-44754-8pa. (Cornerstones of Freedom). 3-7

The second great battle of the Civil War was the Battle of Shiloh fought in Tennessee on April 6-7, 1862. At the time, it was the bloodiest battle fought on American soil, with 10,000 men losing their lives before the Confederates retreated. Index.

1195.   Kent, Zachary. **Calvin Coolidge**. Chicago: Childrens Press, 1988. 100p. $19.80. ISBN 0-516-01362-9. (Encyclopedia of Presidents). 4-9

Calvin Coolidge (1872-1933), a shy man from Vermont, moved to Massachusetts, where he held state offices, including governor. When refusing reelection for president, he said "I do not choose to run." Photographs, Chronology of American History, and Index.

1196.   Kent, Zachary. **George Bush: Forty-First President of the United States**. Chicago: Childrens Press, 1993. 100p. $19.80. ISBN 0-516-01374-2. (Encyclopedia of Presidents). 4-9

Kent uses many of George Bush's direct quotes to give insight into his life. Bush (b. 1924) discusses his reactions to being shot down in World War II, his life as a father and as a Texas oilman, his service in the United States and China, his role as vice president when he was a "heartbeat" away from the presidency, and his life as president. Photographs, Chronology of American History, and Index.

1197.   Kent, Zachary. **Geronimo**. Chicago: Childrens Press, 1989. 31p. $4.95pa. ISBN 0-516-44743-2. (Cornerstones of Freedom). 3-7

In the 1870s and 1880s, Geronimo (1829-1909), the Apache chief, led attacks on settlers and soldiers in Mexico and the southwestern United States. He tried to protect his tribe, but he eventually had to surrender in 1886. The government took the Apaches as prisoners of war to Florida, but Geronimo returned to Fort Sill, Oklahoma, where he became a farmer and marched in Theodore Roosevelt's inaugural parade. Index.

1198.   Kent, Zachary. **Grover Cleveland: Twenty-Second and Twenty-Fourth President of the United States**. Chicago: Childrens Press, 1988. 100p. $19.80. ISBN 0-516-01360-2. (Encyclopedia of Presidents). 4-9

Grover Cleveland (1837-1908) served as president during a depression that gripped the nation during 1893. He urged that the Sherman Act, which allowed gold to be drained from the national treasury, be repealed. At the same time, a cancerous growth discovered in his mouth had to be removed. He demanded secrecy, and the operation took place on a yacht near his Buzzards Bay, Massachusetts, home. Part of his jaw was removed, and during public appearances he wore a rubber jaw. Not until nine years after he died did the public find out about his ordeal. This was one case in which Cleveland did not tell the truth, but he did not otherwise lie. He believed that one must always be truthful, and he never changed. Chronology of American History and Index.

1199.   Kent, Zachary. **Jefferson Davis**. Chicago: Childrens Press, 1993. 31p. $4.95pa. ISBN 0-516-46664-Xpa. (Cornerstones of Freedom). 3-5

Interesting quotes from people who lived during the Civil War and Jefferson Davis's tenure as president of the Confederacy help the reader to sense the tension during that time. Davis (1808-1889) was both a soldier and a statesman who tried to lead the Confederates as best he could. Photographs enhance the text. Index.

1200.   Kent, Zachary. **John F. Kennedy: Thirty-Fifth President of the United States**. Chicago: Childrens Press, 1987. 100p. $19.80. ISBN 0-516-01390-4. (Encyclopedia of Presidents). 4-9

John Fitzgerald Kennedy (1917-1963) was in a boat sunk by the Japanese in World War II, and the chapter covering this event in his life is "They sank my boat." The text looks at his youth, his experience in the war that made him a hero, his political races, his book *Profiles of Courage*, the call for "Let's Back Jack!" as the president, his time in the White House, space as the new frontier, and the eternal flame still burning on his grave. Photographs, Chronology of American History, and Index.

1201.   Kent, Zachary. **Ronald Reagan: Fortieth President of the United States**. Chicago: Childrens Press, 1989. 100p. $19.80. ISBN 0-516-01373-4. (Encyclopedia of Presidents). 4-9

Ronald Reagan (b. 1911) was shot as he left a Washington, D.C., hotel in 1981, and this biography begins with that story. It returns to his childhood and his life, from actor to politician in California to president of the United States. Chronology of American History and Index.

1202.   Kent, Zachary. **Rutherford B. Hayes: Nineteenth President of the United States**. Chicago: Childrens Press, 1989. 100p. $19.80. ISBN 0-516-01365-3. (Encyclopedia of Presidents). 5-8

Born prematurely in Ohio, Rutherford Hayes (1822-1893) had his uncle persuade his overprotective mother to let him have more freedom, and he left home for boarding school and college. Encouraged to do the best that he could, he attended Harvard Law School. When he returned to Ohio, he gave legal advice to those working for the Underground Railway. He fought in the Civil War for the Union and was much loved and respected by the soldiers in the 23rd Regiment. He became the nineteenth president in 1876 (winning by one electoral vote), a job in which he served as conscientiously as possible but hated so much that he never considered running for a second term. At his death he was looking forward to joining his beloved wife. Chronology of American History and Index.

1203.   Kent, Zachary. **The Story of Admiral Peary at the North Pole**. Chicago: Childrens Press, 1988. 30p. $4.95pa. ISBN 0-516-44738-6pa. (Cornerstones of Freedom). 3-6

Robert E. (Edwin) Peary (1856-1920) endured a grueling expedition across the Arctic to become the first person to reach the North Pole in 1909. Although Frederick Cook disputed his claim, the United States recognized Peary for his achievement in 1911. The text traces his life, with illustrations complementing the text. Index.

1204.   Kent, Zachary. **The Story of John Brown's Raid on Harpers Ferry**. Chicago: Childrens Press, 1988. 30p. $4.95pa. ISBN 0-516-44734-3pa. (Cornerstones of Freedom). 3-6

In 1859, John Brown (1800-1859) led a raid on the U.S. arsenal at Harpers Ferry. During the raid, his group killed some people. As an abolitionist, John Brown felt that he had to stop slavery in any way that he could. He suffered the consequences of his decision. Index.

1205.   Kent, Zachary. **The Story of the Battle of Bull Run**. Chicago: Childrens Press, 1986. 30p. $4.95pa. ISBN 0-516-44703-3pa. (Cornerstones of Freedom). 3-7

The first Battle of Bull Run occurred on July 21, 1861, near Manassas, Virginia. It was also the first battle of the Civil War, a war not expected to last very long. Because people only expected a minor skirmish at Bull Run, sightseers went there with picnic baskets. The text presents the events that led to that battle and its aftermath. Index.

1206.   Kent, Zachary. **The Story of the Surrender at Yorktown**. Chicago: Childrens Press, 1989. 32p. $14.60. ISBN 0-516-04723-X. (Cornerstones of Freedom). 3-7

On October 25, 1781, the announcement of Cornwallis's surrender on October 19 at Yorktown reached Philadelphia. With a brief overview of the American Revolution and its most significant dates, Kent leads to Washington's unification with the French soldiers as he neared the British stronghold at Yorktown. The text, with accompanying illustrations, gives a good summary of the situation before the surrender.

1207.   Kent, Zachary. **Tecumseh**. Chicago: Childrens Press, 1992. 31p. $11.45. ISBN 0-516-06660-9. (Cornerstones of Freedom). 3-5

Tecumseh (1768-1813), a Shawnee chief, tried to establish a confederacy that would unify Native Americans against the white settlers. In 1812, he sided with the British and died in the Battle of the Thames. The text looks at his life and his concerns. Reproductions and Index.

1208.   Kent, Zachary. **Theodore Roosevelt: Twenty-Sixth President of the United States**. Chicago: Childrens Press, 1988. 100p. $19.80. ISBN 0-516-01354-8. (Encyclopedia of Presidents). 4-9

Theodore Roosevelt (1858-1919) led a volunteer regiment of western cowboys and Indians along with Ivy League college graduates up San Juan Hill during the Cuban war of independence from Spain. He helped Cuba win. With his relentless charging ahead, he became America's new folk hero. Roosevelt said to America, "Get action, do things; be sane; don't fritter away your time; create, act, take a place wherever you are, and be somebody!" He took his own advice while serving in various roles, including President. Chronology of American History and Index.

1209.   Kent, Zachary. **Ulysses S. Grant: Eighteenth President of the United States**. Chicago: Childrens Press, 1989. 100p. $19.80. ISBN 0-516-01364-5. (Encyclopedia of Presidents). 4-9

Ulysses S. Grant (1822-1885) experienced years of glory followed by years of failure and repeated the cycle. He graduated from West Point and served ably in the Mexican War, but he left the army at a low point in his life. He returned and became a Civil War hero, which led to his election as President of the United States. Chronology of American History and Index.

1210.   Kent, Zachary. **William McKinley: Twenty-Fifth President of the United States**. Chicago: Childrens Press, 1988. 100p. $19.80. ISBN 0-516-01361-0. (Encyclopedia of Presidents). 3 up

William McKinley (1843-1901) served Ohio as a representative in Congress and as its governor before he became President of the United States. During his second term, an assassin's bullet killed him, and Theodore Roosevelt took his place. He had a reputation as a kind man, concerned about everyone. Chronology of American History and Index.

1211.   Kent, Zachary. **Williamsburg**. Chicago: Childrens Press, 1992. 32p. $17.30; $4.95pa. ISBN 0-516-04854-6; 0-516-44854-4pa. (Cornerstones of Freedom). 3-5

In 1699, when fire destroyed Jamestown, the capital of Virginia shifted to Middle Plantation, where the College of William and Mary had been established six years previously. The town's name was changed to honor King William III of England. The text looks at the creation of Williamsburg, from its first buildings to its renovation in the early twentieth century. Index.

1212.   Kent, Zachary. **World War I: "The War to End Wars."** Springfield, NJ: Enslow, 1994. 128p. $17.95. ISBN 0-89490-523-6. (American War). 6 up

Starting with the sinking of the *Lusitania* in 1915, the text relates the progress of World War, I from its beginning in Sarajevo in August 1914 until its end in November 1918. It presents the major battles starting with the Hindenburg Line marked by the Germans, Belleau Wood, the Marne, Saint-Mihiel, and the Meuse-Argonne offensive. Among the leaders on both sides were Captain Baron Manfred von Richthofen,

"The Red Baron"; Sergeant York; General Douglas MacArthur; and General John J. (Black Jack) Pershing. During the war, more than 116,000 American soldiers died, and 4 million more from other nations. Afterward, President Woodrow Wilson tried to start the League of Nations, but American isolationism defeated his plan. Photographs complement the text. Chronology, Notes, Further Reading, and Index.

1213.   Kent, Zachary. **Zachary Taylor: Twelfth President of the United States**. Chicago: Childrens Press, 1988. 100p. $19.80. ISBN 0-516-01352-1. (Encyclopedia of Presidents). 4-9

Zachary Taylor (1784-1850) attacked Buena Vista in the Mexican War, and against great odds, he won. His many years of experience and his fearless leadership earned him the name "Old Rough and Ready." His popularity spread, and his fame swept him into the White House in 1849. As president, he tried to help domestic policy, but he had no solution to the problem of slavery. Chronology of American History and Index.

1214.   Kerby, Mona. **Amelia Earhart: Courage in the Sky**. Eileen McKeating, illustrator. New York: Viking, 1990. 57p. $10.95; $3.99pa. ISBN 0-670-83024-0; 0-14-034263-Xpa. (Women of Our Time). 3-6

Amelia Earhart (1897-1937) was the first woman to cross the Atlantic by herself in a plane. The text presents her life and how she became interested in flight. While flying over the Pacific, she disappeared; no one knows what became of her and her plane. Bibliography and Index.

1215.   Kerby, Mona. **Frederick Douglass**. New York: Franklin Watts, 1995. 63p. $19.90. ISBN 0-531-20173-2. (First Books). 4-6

Frederick Douglass (1817-1895) was an abolitionist. The text looks at his escape from slavery after he secretly learned to read and the importance of literacy to his success as a free man. He was able to help many others who were incapable of helping themselves while still enslaved. Photographs, Reproductions, Bibliography, and Index.

1216.   Kerby, Mona. **Robert E. Lee: Southern Hero of the Civil War**. Springfield, NJ: Enslow, 1997. 128p. $18.95. ISBN 0-89490-782-4. (Historical American Biographies). 6-9

Robert E. Lee (1807-1870) had a reputation as a gentleman general, and he fought only for the South because he lived in Virginia. He owned no slaves. This biography looks at his impact on American history as it examines his life. Fact boxes and maps augment the text. Notes, Glossary, Further Reading, and Index.

1217.   Kerby, Mona. **Samuel Morse**. New York: Franklin Watts, 1991. 60p. $19.90. ISBN 0-531-20023-X. (First Book). 3-5

Samuel Morse (1791-1872) kept a journal throughout his life and wrote many letters. This recording of his thoughts gave a good view of his attitudes while he worked to invent the telegraph. As he returned home from a European trip on a ship, he realized, listening to passengers talk about electricity, that an electromagnet producing an electric current could transmit messages. He began working on an electric telegraph system and made the first telegraph soon after. He continued painting to support himself, but not for 12 years could he get enough money to demonstrate the value of his invention. Index.

1218.   Kerr, Daisy. **Keeping Clean**. New York: Franklin Watts, 1995. 48p. $14.42. ISBN 0-531-15353-8. 4-7

This text relates a history of bathing, plumbing, and waste removal. Each two-page spread deals with a different time or region as they cover such topics as the ancient world, the Middle Ages, Roman baths, spaceship hygiene, and lavatories on board ships. Illustrations augment the text. Glossary and Index.

1219.   Ketchum, Liza. **The Gold Rush**. Boston: Little, Brown, 1996. 144p. $19.95; $10.95pa. ISBN 0-316-59133-5; 0-316-49047-4-0pa. 3-7

On January 24, 1848, someone discovered a tiny nugget of gold about the size of a dime. Thousands of people all over the world heard about this event and rushed to California hoping to find gold for themselves. Many lost money or even their lives, but others found adventure and new hope for the future. The text tells the story of some of the people whose lives changed, and what they did for themselves and others after the height of the gold rush ended. Black-and-White Photographs, Bibliography, and Index. *Notable Children's Trade Books in the Field of Social Studies* and *New York Public Library's Books for the Teen Age*.

1220.   Ketteman, Helen. **The Year of No More Corn**. Robert Andrew Parker, illustrator. New York: Jackson/Orchard, 1993. 32p. $14.99. ISBN 0-531-08550-3. K-3

Young Beanie complains to his grandfather that he cannot help with the corn planting. Grampa laughs that Beanie is too young, while he is too old to help. Then he tells Beanie about 1928 when he planted corn four times. Each time something destroyed it—rain, wind, heat, and crows. But he kept planting corn, so he knows Beanie will have plenty of chances.

1221. Kherdian, David. **Bridger: The Story of a Mountain Man**. New York: Greenwillow, 1987. 147p. $11.75. ISBN 0-688-06510-4. 5-8

After fulfilling his duty as a bound-out servant, Jim Bridger journeys up the Missouri River when he is 18 and begins his life as a trapper. He becomes friends with the Crow Indians and "discovers" the Great Salt Lake (long known to the Indians). He delights in his experiences of freedom.

1222. Kimmel, Eric. **Bar Mitzvah: A Jewish Boy's Coming of Age**. Erika Weihs, illustrator. New York: Viking, 1995. 143p. $15. ISBN 0-670-85540-5. 6-8

The text presents the importance of the bar mitzvah in the life of a 13-year-old Jewish boy by comparing it to rituals in other cultures and describing it in detail. Kimmel includes the origins and teachings of Judaism, the place of the synagogue in worship, the structure of the prayer service, the Torah ritual, the bar mitzvah ceremony, and the importance of ritual objects. Glossary and Index.

1223. King, David C. **First Facts About American Heroes**. Woodbridge, CT: Blackbirch Press, 1996. 112p. $22.95. ISBN 1-56711-165-3. 3-6

The text looks at people who made major accomplishments in seven periods of American history. These periods are colonial America (John Smith, Squanto, Anne Hutchinson, William Penn, and Daniel Boone), the American Revolution (Paul Revere, Patrick Henry, Molly Pitcher, Francis Marion, and John Paul Jones), the early United States (Tecumseh, Stephen Decatur, Oliver Hazard Perry, Dolley Madison, and Andrew Jackson), the Civil War era (Harriet Tubman, Frederick Douglass, Robert E. Lee, Ulysses S. Grant, and Clara Barton), heroes of the West (Jim Beckwourth, Kit Carson, Wild Bill Hickok, Chief Joseph, and Annie Oakley), the early twentieth century (John J. Pershing, Jane Addams, Robert Peary, Mother Jones, Jim Thorpe, Charles A. Lindbergh, Douglas MacArthur, Audie Murphy, and Jackie Robinson), and America since 1950 (Jonas Salk, Rosa Parks, Martin Luther King, Jr., Cesar Chavez, Jacqueline Kennedy Onassis, Neil Armstrong, Rachel Carson, and H. Norman Schwarzkopf). Further Reading, Places to Visit, and Index.

1224. King, John. **The Gulf War**. New York: Dillon Press, Macmillan, 1991. 48p. $13.95. ISBN 0-87518-514-2. 5-10

Questions arise as to why the United States fought the Gulf War in 1991. The text looks at geography in the area, history, the role of oil, and Saddam Hussein's Iraq as it asks why Hussein initially invaded Kuwait. The crisis began in August 1990 and escalated to the attack in January 1991. Glossary, Key Events, Further Reading, and Index.

1225. King, Perry Scott. **Jefferson Davis**. New York: Chelsea House, 1990. 112p. $18.95 ISBN 1-55546-806-3. (World Leaders Past and Present). 5 up

In 1861, Jefferson Davis (1808-1889) left the U.S. Senate to join the revolt of the southern states. His West Point education prepared him to fight in the Mexican War, serve as Secretary of War for Franklin Pierce, and become the South's president while it fought the Civil War. He was the opposite of Lincoln as he tried to preserve the rights of slave owners in the South. The text, augmented by photographs and reproductions, looks at his life and influences. Chronology, Further Reading, and Index.

1226. Kinsey-Warnock, Natalie. **The Canada Geese Quilt**. Leslie W. Bowman, illustrator. New York: Dutton, 1989. 64p. $12.95. ISBN 0-525-65004-0. 4 up

When Ariel is 10 in 1946, she and her grandmother work on a quilt for the new baby. Her grandmother has a stroke and begins to act in ways that Ariel cannot understand, and Ariel refuses to talk to her for a while. Ariel does overcome her feelings and helps finish the Canada geese quilt before the baby arrives. But what makes her happiest is the quilt that her grandmother gives her that she secretly made. *American Library Association Notable Books for Children*.

1227. Kinsey-Warnock, Natalie. **The Night the Bells Rang**. Leslie W. Bowman, illustrator. New York: Cobblehill, 1991. 76p. $12.95. ISBN 0-525-65074-1. 4 up

In Vermont during 1918, Mason tries to avoid Aden, the big boy who knocks him down and fills his hat with snow. But Aden also helped Mason retrieve a drawing created for his father that flew out of his hand. Thus, Mason has mixed feelings when Aden enlists. His feelings change to sadness when he hears that Aden has died. As the bells ring to signal the end of the war, Mason knows that he has changed in his attitude toward Aden as well as others who have bothered him, including his younger brother.

1228. Kinsey-Warnock, Natalie. **The Summer of Stanley**. Donald Gates, illustrator. New York: Cobblehill, 1997. 32p. $14.99. ISBN 0-525-65177-2. K-3

Although Molly gets a goat named Stanley for her ninth birthday, what she really wants is a bicycle. Molly's father is at war in 1945, and Stanley causes a variety of problems for the family, including climbing on the car and eating her mother's victory garden and the neighbor's dress. Molly's brother Tyler likes Stanley until he takes the goat fishing.

1229. Kinsey-Warnock, Natalie. **The Wild Horses of Sweetbriar**. Ted Rand, illustrator. New York: Cobble-hill, Dutton, 1990. 32p. $14.99. ISBN 0-525-65015-6. K-3

The eight-year-old narrator lives on an island off Nantucket in 1903, where her father runs the lighthouse. She loves the area, but she worries about the 10 wild horses who need food in the winter.

1230. Kinsey-Warnock, Natalie. **Wilderness Cat**. Mark Graham, illustrator. New York: Dutton, 1992. 32p. $14. ISBN 0-525-65068-7. K-3

When Serena's father tells her that Moses, the cat, cannot move with the family from Vermont to Canada in the late 1700s, she is disappointed. In the Canadian wilderness, they have a hard life trying to find food, but the Indians sometimes supply them. Finally, Serena's father and brother have to go to town to get work so they will have money to survive. Serena and her mother hear a cry at the door while they are gone, and Moses awaits them, hauling a rabbit in his mouth.

1231. Kirby, Philippa. **Glorious Days, Dreadful Days: The Battle of Bunker Hill**. John Edens, illustrator. Austin, TX: Raintree/Steck-Vaughn, 1993. 88p. $24.26; $4.95pa. ISBN 0-8114-7226-4; 0-8114-8066-6pa. (Stories of America—Stand Up and Be Counted). 4-8

The Battle of Bunker Hill (actually Breed's Hill), which occurred in 1775, began the Revolutionary War. In that war, a group of ordinary citizens overcame the most powerful army in the world. The text presents the causes of the battle, its story, and its results. Epilogue, Afterword, and Notes.

1232. Kirkpatrick, Katherine. **Keeping the Good Light**. New York: Delacorte, 1995. 220p. $14.95. ISBN 0-385-32161-9. 5-9

Eliza Brown, 16 in 1903, thinks that her chores are endless at the Stepping Stones Lighthouse. She is isolated on the island with her quiet brother Sam, her father, and a mother who always criticizes her. She is happiest when she goes by rowboat to school on another island. After she goes out unchaperoned with a boyfriend at night and because she thinks independently—two unacceptable attributes in her closed society—she is expelled from school. As she tries to decide if she will accept a marriage without love, a job offer lets her escape the island's rigid expectations.

1233. Kirkpatrick, Patricia. **Plowie: A Story from the Prairie**. Joey Kirkpatrick, illustrator. San Diego, CA: Harcourt Brace, 1994. 32p. $14.95. ISBN 0-15-262802-9. K-3

When a little girl lives with her family on the Iowa prairie at the turn of the century, her father plows up a doll, and the little girl names it "Plowie." She keeps the doll and tells its story to her children and grandchildren until it becomes the last existing piece of the farm.

1234. Kitano, Harry. **The Japanese Americans**. New York: Chelsea House, 1988. 92p. $19.95; $8.95pa. ISBN 0-7910-3766-5; 0-7910-3380-5pa. (The Immigrant Experience). 5 up

The Japanese began to arrive in America in the late nineteenth century, and since their arrival, they have faced hostility. The text, with photographs, looks at their religion and politics, the situation in the West, their wartime evacuation in World War II, their traditions and the difficult transition from them, their contributions to the country, and their lives. Selected References and Index.

1235. Kittleman, Laurence R. **Canyons Beyond the Sky**. New York: Atheneum, 1985. 212p. $13.95. ISBN 0-689-31138-9. 4-6

Evan, 12, spends the summer with his father's archaeological dig in the Southwest. An experience takes him back 5,000 years, but he thinks he has been dreaming. When he is able to locate the exact place, and his father sees the ruins of a complete village that no one has ever discovered, he has to wonder about the origin of his dream.

1236. Kittredge, Mary. **Barbara McClintock**. New York: Chelsea House, 1990. 103p. $18.95. ISBN 1-55546-666-4. (American Women of Achievement). 5 up

As a young woman working for a male scientist studying genes in maize (corn), Barbara McClintock (1902-1992) realized that he was looking in the wrong places for the differences among the 10 genes. She looked in the right place, made him furious, and lost her job. But she began to establish her name in the study of cytogenetics. She worked mainly at the labs of Carnegie Institution in Cold Spring Harbor, New York, researching maize. She cross-pollinated various kinds of corn to see what happened to the offspring. Her major discovery that genetic material moved from place to place on chromosomes occurred 30 years before scientists realized that she was right. They refused to acknowledge her research at a time when they were more interested in the discovery of DNA. She won the Nobel Prize in 1983 for her work, and other awards and prizes followed. But none of them changed her methods or her appreciation of life. She said that her work had given her much pleasure through the years. Photographs enhance the text. Chronology, Further Reading, and Index.

1237.   Kittredge, Mary. **Helen Hayes: Actress**. New York: Chelsea House, 1988. 112p. $18.95. ISBN 1-55546-656-7. (American Women of Achievement). 5 up

Helen Hayes (1900-1993) began her theatrical career at the age of five and made a Broadway debut at nine, achieving major stardom before she was 20. She won two Oscars for her movie work and much acclaim for her stage work. Her daughter died at 19 from polio, and Hayes constantly publicized the new polio vaccine and encouraged parents to inoculate their children. When she retired at 85, she started a campaign to aid the elderly. Photographs and reproductions enhance the text. Chronology, Further Reading, and Index.

1238.   Kittredge, Mary. **Jane Addams**. New York: Chelsea House, 1990. 111p. $18.95. ISBN 1-55546-636-2. (American Women of Achievement). 4-7

As a pioneering social worker, Jane Addams (1860-1935) revolutionized America's attitude toward the poor. She was born into a prosperous family and went to college, graduating in 1881. When she could not find other avenues to help people, she moved into the Chicago slums and opened Hull House. She always defended poor and unpopular minorities, and in 1920 she was called "the most dangerous woman in America." Black-and-white photographs supplement the text. Bibliography and Index.

1239.   Klausmeier, Robert. **Cowboy**. Richard Erickson, illustrator. Minneapolis, MN: Lerner, 1996. 48p. $14.96. ISBN 0-8225-2975-0. (American Pastfinder). 4-7

The cowboy has domesticated cattle and horses, built empires, and helped open the West to settlement. The text looks at the daily routine of a cowboy, his uniform, the roundup, branding, trail drives, chuckwagon stops, winter on a ranch, and living in a bunkhouse. It shows that a cowboy's real life rarely resembles the romantic image created in movies and books. Glossary and Index.

1240.   Klausner, Janet. **Sequoyah's Gift: A Portrait of the Cherokee Leader**. New York: HarperCollins, 1993. 111p. $14.89. ISBN 0-06-021235-7. 4-8

When Sequoyah (1773?-1843) saw that Cherokees were losing land to white settlers, he noted that the whites communicated through symbols as well as through speech. He did not want the Cherokees to lose their culture by succumbing to all of the white customs. He then began working on a system of written Cherokee and eventually accomplished his goal. The text looks at his life as a man who overcame the physical disability of one leg shorter than the other, his achievements, and the times. The information about him comes from people who knew or met him. Photographs, Bibliography, and Index. *Notable Children's Trade Books in the Field of Social Studies*.

1241.   Kliment, Bud. **Billie Holiday: Singer**. New York: Chelsea House, 1990. 112p. $18.95; $7.95pa. ISBN 1-55546-592-7; 0-7910-0241-1pa. (Black Americans of Achievement). 5 up

Born Eleanor Fagan in 1915, Billie Holiday moved to New York City with her mother in 1927; she made her professional debut at age 15 in a Harlem nightclub. She toured with big bands such as Count Basie and Artie Shaw during the 1930s, and in the early 1940s she was a star attraction. In 1941, however, she became addicted to heroin, and by 1947 she was imprisoned for possession of narcotics. Regardless of her meteoric rise and fall, she was extremely talented. Photographs enhance the text. Chronology, Further Reading, and Index.

1242.   Kliment, Bud. **Count Basie: Bandleader and Musician**. New York: Chelsea House, 1992. 128p. $18.95. ISBN 0-7910-1118-6. (Black Americans of Achievement). 5 up

Count Basie (1904-1984) was a drummer who switched to playing the piano. He toured in vaudeville acts to sharpen his timing and to learn a variety of styles. In 1935, he formed his own group, backing such vocalists as Billie Holiday. Photographs and reproductions enhance the text. Chronology, Further Reading, and Index.

1243.   Kliment, Bud. **Ella Fitzgerald: Singer**. New York: Chelsea House, 1988. 112p. $18.95; $7.95pa. ISBN 1-55546-586-2; 0-7910-0220-9pa. (Black Americans of Achievement). 5 up

For more than 50 years, Ella Fitzgerald (1918-1996) entertained the world with her unique jazz vocal stylings. She grew up in Yonkers, in New York City, where she started her career at 14 by winning a contest. She became the featured singer in the Chick Webb orchestra, one of the country's best-known swing bands. Her recordings made her famous across the nation by the time she was 20. Eventually she toured with her own band while promoting racial equality around the world. Photographs and reproductions enhance the text. Chronology, Further Reading, and Index.

1244.   Klots, Steve. **Ida Wells-Barnett: Civil Rights Leader**. New York: Chelsea House, 1994. 128p. $18.95. ISBN 0-7910-1885-7. (Black Americans of Achievement). 5 up

Ida Wells-Barnett (1862-1931), born in Mississippi, decided when she was very young that she would help her people. She became a teacher and the editor of a Black newspaper in Tennessee. Her editorials upset the white population so much that they exiled her from the South. She continued to write in the *New York Age*, one of the country's leading Black newspapers. She wanted to expose the gruesome practice of lynching, and she continually attacked racial injustice. Neither women nor African Americans were expected to speak out about problems during Wells-Barnett's lifetime. She refused to stay quiet and became a fearless leader for civil rights. Photographs enhance the text. Chronology, Further Reading, and Index.

1245. Klots, Steve. **Richard Allen: Religious Leader and Social Activist**. New York: Chelsea House, 1990. 111p. $18.95. ISBN 1-55546-570-6. (Black Americans of Achievement). 5 up

When Methodist circuit rider preachers convinced Richard Allen's master that owning slaves was sinful, the master allowed his slaves to buy their freedom. Allen (1760-1831) went to Philadelphia and tried to use his strong Methodist beliefs to serve the Black community. The church grew until whites who still supported slavery infiltrated it, and the Black members suffered. Allen, after many years and many setbacks, established the American Methodist Episcopal Church with the first Black congregation of Bethel Church in Philadelphia. He was also the first Black ordained to the deaconate of the church and allowed to serve the sacraments. Those supporting him in his endeavors, especially after his service to the city during the yellow fever epidemic in 1793, included the vocal abolitionist William Lloyd Garrison. Chronology, Further Reading, and Index.

1246. Knight, Amelia Stewart, and Lillian Schlissel. **The Way West: Journal of a Pioneer Woman**. Michael McCurdy, illustrator. New York: Simon & Schuster, 1993. Unpaged. $15. ISBN 0-671-72375-8. 3-5

In diary form with entries for days during 1853, the text tells Amelia Stewart Knight's thoughts while she, her husband, and seven children journeyed from Iowa to the Oregon Territory. The entries heighten the suspense of the courageous journey.

1247. Knight, Theodore. **The Olympic Games**. San Diego, CA: Lucent, 1991. 112p. $12.95. ISBN 1-56006-119-7. (Overview). 3-5

The text gives a history of the Olympic Games, from the first games in Greece through the games in 1988. It highlights some of the records achieved as well as humorous and tragic moments. Because the games have sometimes been a place for political statements, the text also discusses boycotts and terrorism. Bibliography, Glossary, and Index.

1248. Koller, Jackie French. **Nothing to Fear**. San Diego, CA: Harcourt Brace, 1991. 279p. $14.95. ISBN 0-15-200544-7. 5-7

Danny worries about his pregnant mother and his father, who has left home in Manhattan to seek work during the Depression in 1932. When his mother goes to the hospital in a coma, Danny finds a letter saying that his father had died on the rails four months earlier. Another victim of the Depression from Oklahoma, whom they have nursed back to health, helps them in turn, and Danny's mother decides she will marry him. *IRA Young Adults' Choices*.

1249. Koller, Jackie French. **The Primrose Way**. San Diego, CA: Gulliver, Harcourt Brace, 1995. 352p. $15.95; $5pa. ISBN 0-15-256745-3; 0-15-200372-Xpa. 6 up

After Rebekah meets the Pawtucket people in 1633, she begins to make friends with them. Knowing that the colonists consider the Pawtuckets savages, Rebekah expects them to be very different. She sees that they have their own valid beliefs, especially when she falls in love with the Pawtucket medicine man, a defiant individualist. *American Library Association Best Books for Young Adults* and *New York Public Library's Books for the Teen Age*.

1250. Koral, April. **An Album of War Refugees**. New York: Franklin Watts, 1989. 96p. $13.90. ISBN 0-531-10765-5. (Picture Album). 6-9

The text presents refugees from different countries who have come to the United States since the Armenians arrived in 1915. The latest refugees have come from Central America. Personal stories bring immediacy to situations in which people have had to leave their homes, usually having lost all material items, in order to save their lives. In their land of exile, they have faced new political, social, and economic problems. Bibliography and Index.

1251. Koslow, Philip. **The Seminole Indians**. New York: Chelsea House, 1994. 79p. $14.95; $6.95pa. ISBN 0-7910-1672-2; 0-7910-2486-5pa. (The Junior Library of American Indians). 3-7

People trying to escape subjugation eventually banded together and ended up in the Florida Everglades. They called themselves "Seminoles," and they are the one Native American tribe that the U.S. government never defeated. Two bloody wars, the Seminole wars, showed that the government could not fight in the swamps of Florida. Other aspects of history appear as well. Photographs and engravings enhance the text. Glossary, Chronology, and Index.

1252.   Kozodoy, Ruth. **Isadora Duncan: Dancer**. New York: Chelsea House, 1988. 112p. $18.95. ISBN 1-55546-650-8. (American Women of Achievement). 5 up

Isadora Duncan (1878-1927) was a self-described "revolutionist" with an unconventional lifestyle. After dancing barefoot to classical music and rejecting orthodox ballet techniques throughout Europe and Russia, she created a new form of dance that evolved into modern expressive dance. Photographs enhance the text. Chronology, Further Reading, and Index.

1253.   Kraft, Betsy Harvey. **Mother Jones: One Woman's Fight for Labor**. New York: Clarion, 1995. 116p. $16.95. ISBN 0-395-67163-9. 5-9

Although Mary Harris Jones, known as Mother Jones (1843?-1930), looked like a grandmother wearing a modest black dress and glasses, she was one of America's most effective union organizers. An Irish immigrant, she used her oratorical gifts to help abused workers. She wanted children out of the coal mines, and while she bullied the officials, she lived with the coal miner families. Titles of the chapters give insight into her thoughts and those of her enemies: "I have been in jail more than once," "My people were poor," "I sat alone through nights of grief," "A quick brain and an even quicker tongue," "Just an old woman," "Good fight against wrong," and "I didn't come out on a stretcher." Additional topics include the miners' angel, coal wars in West Virginia, a march for the children, and the woman with an excess of courage. Photographs, Engravings, Notes, More About Mother Jones, and Index.

1254.   Krass, Peter. **Sojourner Truth: Antislavery Activist**. New York: Chelsea House, 1988. 110p. $18.95; $7.95pa. ISBN 1-55546-611-7; 0-7910-0215-2pa. (Black Americans of Achievement). 5 up

As a child, Isabella (1797-1883) was sold to another slave owner and separated from her family. She won her freedom in 1827 and became a traveling preacher who took the name Sojourner Truth. Eventually renowned throughout the East Coast for her beliefs, she published the story of her life as a slave in 1850. Afterward, she began lecture tours to advocate the end of slavery and the beginning of women's rights. She worked as a counselor to former slaves and started campaigns to help Blacks obtain federal grants for farmland. Photographs and engravings highlight the text. Chronology, Further Reading, and Index.

1255.   Krementz, Jill, author/illustrator. **A Visit to Washington, DC**. New York: Scholastic, 1987. 48p. $13.95. ISBN 0-590-40582-9. 1-3

Matt Wilson, six, a native of Washington, D.C., introduces the sights of his beautiful city. Those he chooses to discuss are of interest to someone his age, like the Discovery Room in the Smithsonian. Maps on endpapers indicate the location of the places he mentions, and photographs reveal what they look like.

1256.   Krensky, Stephen. **The Iron Dragon Never Sleeps**. John Fuleveiler, illustrator. New York: Delacorte, 1994. 85p. $13.95. ISBN 0-385-31171-0. 3-6

Winnie Tucker, 10, and her mother come to Cisco, California, in the summer of 1867, where Winnie's father works on the transcontinental railroad. She becomes friends with Lee Cheng, a young Chinese tea carrier, who tells her stories about the work—unlike those her father reports. She discovers that the Chinese workers are maltreated and that racial discrimination permeates the area. Afterword.

1257.   Krensky, Stephen. **The Printer's Apprentice**. Madeline Sorel, illustrator. New York: Delacorte, 1995. 103p. $13.95. ISBN 0-385-32095-7. 5-7

Gus Croft tells the story of the 1734 arrest and trial of New York printer Peter Zenger, indicted for slandering the colonial governor. Gus wonders why Zenger's words, which are true, should not be printed, and why his boss, a rival printer, does not report on the trial. Gus helps Zenger retain a lawyer from Philadelphia who thinks that slander will become the concern that leads to a discussion on the freedom of the press. Through Zenger's ordeal, the reader begins to understand the importance of free speech.

1258.   Krensky, Stephen. **Striking It Rich: The Story of the California Gold Rush**. Anna Divito, illustrator. New York: Simon & Schuster, 1996. 64p. $14; $3.99pa. ISBN 0-689-80804-6; 0-689-80803-8pa. (Ready-to-Read). 1-4

The text looks at the rush to California after 1849, when news traveled around the world that James Marshall had discovered gold at Sutter's Mill. It talks about the living conditions the prospectors found, the profiteers who sold supplies at inflated prices, and lawlessness in California until people decided to organize the new settlers. Cartoon illustrations enliven the text.

1259.   Krensky, Stephen. **Witch Hunt: It Happened in Salem Village**. James Watling, illustrator. New York: Random House, 1989. 48p. $6.99; $2.95pa. ISBN 0-394-91923-8; 0-394-81923-3pa. 3-5

The text begins with Betty Parris and her "fits" and describes the behavior of the other girls in her group who visited Tituba in Salem Village during the 1690s. It continues with the accusations, the trials, and the convictions. Some of the people seemed to be hired to testify against the witches, and they successfully achieved what they set out to do. Index.

1260. Kroeger, Mary Kay, and Louise Borden. **Paperboy**. Ted Lewin, illustrator. New York: Clarion, 1996. 34p. $16.95. ISBN 0-395-64482-8. K-3

Willie Brinkman likes delivering the Cincinnati, Ohio, *Times-Star* newspaper in 1927 and is pleased to bring home his pay for his family. He wants to be the first to shout that Jack Dempsey has beat Gene Tunney in the upcoming fight, but when Dempsey loses, Willie must adjust. He does learn other values through the defeat because Dempsey is the workingman's hero.

1261. Krohn, Katherine E. **Elvis Presley: The King**. Minneapolis, MN: Lerner, 1994. 64p. $15.95. ISBN 0-8225-2877-0. 4-8

In January 1956, Elvis Presley (1935-1977) recorded his first hit single, "Heartbreak Hotel." The next January, Ed Sullivan wanted to improve the ratings on his television show so he paid Elvis the huge sum of $50,000 to appear. Sullivan's assessment of the man was that he was polite and pleasant. Presley entered the army, but as soon as he exited, his career resumed. This poor boy became a millionaire and the focus of people all over the world. His fans created a shrine to his memory at Graceland, his home in Memphis, Tennessee.

1262. Kroll, Steven. **By the Dawn's Early Light: The Story of the Star-Spangled Banner**. New York: Scholastic, 1994. 40p. $15.95. ISBN 0-590-45054-9. 4-7

Francis Scott Key wrote a poem to verbalize his feeling of relief when he looked across the water at Fort McHenry in Baltimore, Maryland, at dawn in September 1814 and saw the Stars and Stripes still flying after a British attack. The text tells the story of Key's days after the British burned Washington. He was trying to save Dr. Beanes, a friend, from British injustice and found himself at Fort McHenry during the battle. Author's Note, Manuscript, Music, Maps, Bibliography, and Index. *Notable Children's Trade Books in the Field of Social Studies.*

1263. Kroll, Steven. **Ellis Island: Doorway to Freedom**. New York: Holiday House, 1995. 32p. $15.95. ISBN 0-8234-1192-3. 4-7

Until 1954, Ellis Island was a symbol of both hope and fear for immigrants arriving in New York Harbor. The text tells the island's history from its beginning in colonial times until it became an immigrant station for the federal government. More than 16 million foreigners began their quest for American citizenship at its gates. Now a national monument, the buildings house an immigration museum. Glossary and Index.

1264. Kroll, Steven. **Lewis and Clark: Explorers of the American West**. Richard Williams, illustrator. New York: Holiday House, 1994. 32p. $16.95. ISBN 0-8234-1034-X. 2-5

The Louisiana Purchase led to Thomas Jefferson asking Meriwether Lewis to lead an expedition to the West Coast. Jefferson want to find a water route to make trade and travel easier and also to learn about the Indians living there. The journey began on May 14, 1804, with the help of William Clark and others, and before it ended on September 23, 1806, it revealed much about the new country. Afterword, Important Dates, and Index.

1265. Kroll, Steven. **Mary McLean and the St. Patrick's Day Parade**. Michael Dooling, illustrator. New York: Scholastic, 1991. 32p. $13.95. ISBN 0-590-43701-1. K-3

In the fall of 1849, Mary and her family arrive in America from Ireland. She likes the stories that people tell in her New York neighborhood, especially the one about the St. Patrick's Day parade. She wants to ride on Mr. Finnegan's horse-drawn cart, but he will let her only if she can find a perfect shamrock. She finds a leprechaun, but she forgets that if she takes her eye off it, it will disappear.

1266. Kroll, Steven. **Pony Express!** Dan Andreasen, illustrator. New York: Scholastic, 1996. 40p. $16.95. ISBN 0-590-20239-1. 3-5

A background on the beginning of the Pony Express in 1860 leads to the first 10 days that it was in operation, when riders took the mail from Sacramento, California, to St. Joseph, Missouri. Among the hazards of those days were weather, difficult terrain, and mistakes made at connecting points. The end of the text focuses on the factors that stopped the Pony Express, the main ones being the development of the telegraph and the completion of the transcontinental railroad. Bibliography and Index.

1267. Kronstadt, Janet. **Florence Sabin: Medical Researcher**. New York: Chelsea House, 1990. 110p. $18.95. ISBN 1-55546-676-1. (American Women of Achievement). 5 up

Florence Sabin (1871-1953) was the first woman to be elected to the National Academy of Sciences and was recognized as the most eminent of living women scientists in the early twentieth century. After graduating from Smith College and going to Johns Hopkins, she began studying the lymphatic system. Her work allowed her to join a team of scientists that found how to control tuberculosis, the chief cause of death in the United States at the time. She spent her later years trying to improve public health in Colorado. Photographs enhance the text. Chronology, Further Reading, and Index.

1268. Krull, Kathleen. **Lives of the Artists: Masterpieces, Messes (and What the Neighbors Thought)**. Kathryn Hewitt, illustrator. San Diego, CA: Harcourt Brace, 1995. 96p. $19. ISBN 0-15-200103-4. 4-8

Vignettes on artists, arranged chronologically, give interesting insights into their lives and sometimes their relationships to each other. The artists are Leonardo da Vinci (Italy, 1452-1519), Michelangelo Buonarroti (Italy, 1475-1564), Peter Bruegel (Netherlands, 1525-1569), Sofonisba Anguissola who served King Philip II of Spain although Italian (1532-1625), Rembrandt van Rijn (Holland, 1606-1669), Katsushika Hokusai (Japan, 1760-1849), Mary Cassatt (American relocated in France, 1845-1926), Vincent van Gogh (Holland, 1853-1890), Käthe Kollwitz (Germany, 1867-1945), Henri Matisse (France, 1869-1954), Pablo Picasso (Spain 1881-1973), Marc Chagall (Russia, 1887-1985), Marcel Duchamp (France, 1887-1968), Georgia O'Keeffe (United States, 1887-1986), William H. Johnson (United States, 1901-1970), Salvador Dali (Spain, 1904-1989), Isamu Noguchi (United States, 1904-1988), Diego Rivera (Mexico, 1886-1957), Frida Kahlo (Mexico, 1907-1954), and Andy Warhol (United States, 1928-1987). Artistic Terms, Index of Artists, and For Further Reading and Looking. *IRA Teachers' Choices*, *American Bookseller Pick of the Lists*, and *New York Public Library's Books for the Teen Age*.

1269. Krull, Kathleen. **Lives of the Musicians: Good Times, Bad Times (and What the Neighbors Thought)**. Kathryn Hewitt, illustrator. San Diego, CA: Harcourt Brace, 1993. 96p. $18.95. ISBN 0-15-248010-2. 4-8

Vignettes on musicians, arranged chronologically, give interesting insights into their lives and sometimes their relationships to each other. The musicians included are Antonio Vivaldi (Italy, 1876-1741), Johann Sebastian Bach (Germany, 1685-1750), Wolfgang Amadeus Mozart (Austria, 1756-1791), Ludwig van Beethoven (Germany, 1770-1827), Frédéric Chopin (Poland, 1810-1849), Giuseppe Verdi (Italy, 1813-1901), Clara Schumann (Germany, 1819-1896), Stephen Foster (America, 1826-1864), Johannes Brahms (Germany, 1833-1897), Peter Ilich Tchaikovsky (Russia, 1840-1893), William Gilbert (England, 1836-1911) and Arthur Sullivan (England, 1842-1900), Erik Satie (France, 1866-1925), Scott Joplin (America, 1868-1917), Charles Ives (1874-1954), Igor Stravinsky (Russia, 1882-1971), Nadia Boulanger (France, 1887-1979), Sergei Prokofiev (Ukraine, 1891-1953), George Gershwin (America, 1898-1937), and Woody Guthrie (America, 1912-1967). Musical Terms, Index of Composers, and For Further Reading . . . and Listening. *Boston Globe-Horn Book Honor*, *American Library Association Notable Books for Children*, *Notable Children's Trade Books in the Field of Social Studies*, *PEN Center USA West Literary Award*, *IRA Teachers' Choices*, *New York Public Library's Books for the Teen Age*, and *Golden Kite Honor*.

1270. Krull, Kathleen. **Lives of the Writers: Comedies, Tragedies (and What the Neighbors Thought)**. Kathryn Hewitt, illustrator. San Diego, CA: Harcourt Brace, 1994. 96p. $19. ISBN 0-15-248009-9. 4 up

Vignettes on writers, arranged chronologically, give interesting insights into their lives and sometimes their relationships to each other. Writers covered are Murasaki Shikibu (Japan, 973?-1025?), Miguel de Cervantes (Spain, 1547-1616), William Shakespeare (England, 1564-1616), Jane Austen (England, 1775-1817), Hans Christian Anderson (Denmark, 1805-1875), Edgar Allan Poe (America, 1809-1849), Charles Dickens (England, 1812-1870), Charlotte Brontë (England, 1816-1855) and Emily Brontë (England, 1818-1848), Emily Dickinson (America, 1830-1886), Louisa May Alcott (America, 1832-1888), Mark Twain (America, 1835-1910), Frances Hodgson Burnett (England, 1849-1924), Robert Louis Stevenson (Scotland, 1850-1894), Jack London (America, 1876-1916), Carl Sandburg (America, 1878-1967), E. B. White (America, 1899-1985), Zora Neale Hurston (America, 1901?-1960), Langston Hughes (1902-1967), and Isaac Bashevis Singer (Poland and America, 1904-1991). Literary Terms, Index of Writers, and For Further Reading and Writing. *American Bookseller Pick of the Lists*, *NCTE Notable Children's Trade Books in the Language Arts*, and *IRA Teachers' Choices*.

1271. Krull, Kathleen. **V Is for Victory: America Remembers World War II**. New York: Apple Soup, Knopf, 1995. 116p. $24. ISBN 0-679-86198-X. 5-8

In this text, photographs of memorabilia such as postcards, posters, ration books, and newspapers give a view of life during World War II. The book covers many aspects of the war, including Pearl Harbor, weapons, soldiers, civilian life, Japanese American internment camps, and the Holocaust. It presents people from both the Axis and Allied sides. Chronology, Bibliography, Map, and Index.

1272. Krull, Kathleen. **Wilma Unlimited: How Wilma Rudolph Became the World's Fastest Woman**. David Diaz, illustrator. San Diego, CA: Harcourt Brace, 1996. 42p. $16. ISBN 0-15-201267-2. K-5

Wilma Rudolph (b. 1940) came into the world at a disadvantage by weighing only four pounds at birth, by being Black in the South, and by being poor. She added a point to this list when polio crippled her. But with her strong mother, 21 sisters and brothers, deep faith, and an inner strength to succeed, she recovered. After an athletic coach recognized her ability on the basketball court, she trained as a sprinter and won three Olympic gold medals. *American Bookseller Pick of the Lists, Bulletin Blue Ribbon Book*.

1273. Krupinski, Loretta, author/illustrator. **Bluewater Journal: The Voyage of the Sea Tiger**. New York: HarperCollins, 1995. Unpaged. $15. ISBN 0-06-023437-7. K-3

With his captain father, Benjamin Slocum and the rest of his family traveled around the world on the clipper ship, *Sea Tiger*, beginning in 1860. His grandfather gave him a journal in which he recorded his experiences and surroundings: the family's plants and animals on board and the race with another ship to reach Hawaii. Among the landmarks he recorded were Brazil, Cape Horn, Sandwich Islands, Honolulu, and Hong Kong. Afterword and Glossary.

1274. Kudlinski, Kathleen. **Earthquake! A Story of Old San Francisco**. Ronald Himler, illustrator. New York: Viking, 1993. 64p. $12.99. ISBN 0-670-84874-3. (Once Upon America). 2-6

When terrified dogs and horses awaken him on April 18, 1906, Phillip tries to calm them. Almost immediately, however, an earthquake topples him, and aftershocks follow. Soon exploding gas lines start fires, and the wind blows the fires over the city. Phillip and the animals escape, but others have to be helped during the destruction of San Francisco.

1275. Kudlinski, Kathleen. **Pearl Harbor Is Burning!: A Story of World War II**. Ronald Himler, illustrator. New York: Viking, 1991. 54p. $11.95. ISBN 0-670-83475-0. (Once Upon America). 4-7

Lonely and isolated from his friends while he lives in Hawaii during 1941, Frank, 10, meets Kenji, a Japanese American boy. As they play in Frank's tree house one morning, they see planes bomb the harbor below, and Kenji realizes that they are Japanese. During this time, the families have to learn how to deal with their conflicting emotions of loyalty to friends versus patriotism.

1276. Kudlinski, Kathleen V. **Facing West: A Story of the Oregon Trail**. James Watling, illustrator. New York: Viking, 1994. 58p. $12.99. ISBN 0-670-85451-4. (Once Upon America). 3-6

In 1845, Ben and his family begin their journey from Missouri to Oregon, a 2,000-mile trek via covered wagon. They have the same hazards as the other pioneer families before them, such as snakes, illness, bears, rolling off cliffs, or washing down rivers, and Ben has the added problem of being asthmatic. He worries about being able to cope.

1277. Kudlinski, Kathleen V. **Helen Keller: A Light for the Blind**. Donna Diamond, illustrator. New York: Viking, 1989. 56p. $10.95; $4.50pa. ISBN 0-670-82460-7; 0-14-032902-1pa. (Women of Our Time). 3-6

This fictional biography begins when Helen Keller (1880-1968) does not respond to her parents as they call her name and shine lights in her eyes. At the age of 19 months, an illness caused her to become deaf and blind. Frustration causes her to behave unpleasantly, but Annie Sullivan arrives and teaches her to understand words and love. Annie Sullivan dedicated her life to Helen, and at her death, Helen and a companion, Polly, go to Scotland to recover. Keller's accomplishments and failures are objectively presented.

1278. Kudlinski, Kathleen V. **Hero over Here**. Bert Dodson, illustrator. New York: Viking, 1990. 56p. $13. ISBN 0-670-83050-X. (Once Upon America). 2-6

In 1918, Theodore, 10, is alone with his sister and mother because his father and brother are in Europe fighting World War I. To his surprise, his mother and sister become sick during an influenza epidemic, and he has to care for them. He helps them and saves a man whom he must drag to the hospital for care. He does not think he has done much, but he is a hero in his hometown. This epidemic took 22 million lives, more than World War I killed.

1279. Kudlinski, Kathleen V. **Lone Star: A Story of the Texas Rangers**. Ronald Himler, illustrator. New York: Viking, 1994. 54p. $12.99. ISBN 0-670-85179-5. (Once Upon America). 3-6

After Comanche Indians attack his family, Clay wants to become a Texas Ranger so that he can take revenge. But when he sees two rangers unnecessarily kill a young girl and an old Comanche, he realizes that learning how to heal people is better than trying to seek revenge.

1280. Kudlinski, Kathleen V. **Shannon: A Chinatown Adventure, San Francisco, 1880**. Bill Farnsworth, illustrator. New York: Simon & Schuster, 1996. 72p. $13; $5.99pa. ISBN 0-689-81138-1; 0-689-80984-0pa. (Girlhood Journeys). 2-6

Shannon O'Brien and her family come to San Francisco from Ireland in 1880. When she goes on an errand, Shannon meets Mi Ling, a Chinese girl whom someone has frightened. When Shannon finds out about Mi Ling's situation, she rushes through San Francisco trying to help her.

1281. Kunhardt, Edith. **Honest Abe**. Malcah Zeldis, illustrator. New York: Greenwillow, 1993. Unpaged. $16. ISBN 0-688-11189-0. K-3

This simple biography, with illustrations in a primitive style, gives the highlights of Abraham Lincoln's life. The Life of Abraham Lincoln.

1282. Kunstler, James Howard. **Davy Crockett: The Legendary Frontiersman**. Steve Brodner, illustrator. New York: Simon & Schuster, 1995. Unpaged. $19.95. ISBN 0-689-80189-0. 2-5

Beginning with Davy Crockett's 1786 birth in Tennessee and ending with the battle of the Alamo in 1836, where he died, the text presents some of Crockett's exploits, such as luring a bear, running for Congress, and fighting a keelboatman.

1283. Kuropas, Myron B. **Ukrainians in America**. 1972. Minneapolis, MN: Lerner, 1996. 80p. $13.13. ISBN 0-8225-1043-X. (In America). 6 up

This revised edition includes the history of the Ukraine up through the country's recent independence in 1991. It discusses the periods under foreign rule of the Poles, Lithuanians, Austro-Hungarians, Hungarians, and Russians. As Ukrainians have come to the United States, they have found ways to organize themselves into communities. The text covers the concern over preservation of identity in the Ukrainian population. Photographs, Glossary, and Notes.

1284. Kurtz, Henry I. **U.S. Army**. Brookfield, CT: Millbrook Press, 1993. 64p. $15.90; $5.95pa. ISBN 1-56294-242-5; 1-56294-752-4pa. (Defending Our Country). 4-6

The text presents the history of the army in the United States. Featured is information on the various combat units and on the weapons used to protect the country. Bibliography and Index.

1285. Kvasnicka, Robert M. **Hole-in-the-Day**. Rick Whipple, illustrator. Austin, TX: Raintree/Steck-Vaughn, 1993. 32p. $19.97. ISBN 0-8172-3405-5. (Native American Stories). 3-5

Hole-in-the-Day (1828-1868) was chief of the Mississippi bands of the Chippewa in Minnesota. He became a leader at 19, and because he decided to follow the white man's way, the Chippewa still live on their lands. He was intelligent and brave, but because he did not fight against the U.S. government, he did not gain the fame of other Indian chiefs. History.

L

1286. La Farge, Ann. **Pearl Buck**. New York: Chelsea House, 1988. 111p. $18.95. ISBN 1-55546-645-1. (American Women of Achievement). 5 up

The first American woman to win the Nobel Prize for Literature, Pearl Buck (1892-1972) did more than write vivid stories about China (her best-known book is *The Good Earth*), where she grew up as the daughter of missionaries. When she returned to the United States, she opened a home for children of mixed American and Asian descent who were orphaned or abandoned, trying to help them have better lives. Photographs and reproductions enhance the text. Chronology, Further Reading, and Index.

1287. La Pierre, Yvette. **Native American Rock Art: Messages from the Past**. Lois Sloan, illustrator. Charlottesville, VA: Thomasson-Grant, 1994. 48p. $16.95. ISBN 1-56566-063-3. 3-7

The English settlers in the Massachusetts colony were the first to note prehistoric rock drawings in North America and wonder what they meant, but the first scientific study of rock art was not made until the late 1880s. Now archaeologists study the two types of rock art: *petroglyphs*, or images pecked or carved on stone surfaces, and *pictographs*, paintings on rocks. The first Americans who came across the Bering Sea land bridge may have left rock art that still exists. Scientists study where the art can be found, the pictures it presents, the culture of the Native Americans who created it, and what age it might be. Photographs of rock art in North America enhance the text. Rock Art Sites to Visit and Glossary.

1288. LaFarelle, Lorenzo G. **Bernardo de Gálvez: Hero of the American Revolution**. Austin, TX: Eakin Press, 1992. 76p. $14.95. ISBN 0-89015-849-5. 5-8

The family of Bernardo de Gálvez (1746-1786) lived in Spain during the time of Queen Isabel and Columbus's journey to the New World. Bernardo de Gálvez attended a military academy in Avila, Spain, before coming to New Spain with his father. Later, he became the commander of Spanish forces that supported the American Revolution. He directed the offense against the British in Louisiana, Alabama, and Florida. He first served in northern Mexico and the Spanish territory before he fought the British. Then he became the Viceroy of New Spain before he died in Mexico City. Galveston, Texas, is named for him. Glossary and Bibliography.

1289. Lampton, Christopher. **Epidemic**. Brookfield, CT: Millbrook Press, 1992. 64p. $13.40. ISBN 1-56294-126-7. (Disaster Book). 4-6

In a discussion about the start of epidemics and how they spread, the text recounts some of the most serious epidemics, with emphasis on the bubonic plague of the mid-fourteenth century. Although the text mentions AIDS, it does not dwell on it as a modern-day plague. Bibliography and Index.

1290. Landau, Elaine. **The Abenaki**. New York: Franklin Watts, 1996. 63p. $20.95; $5.95pa. ISBN 0-531-20227-5; 0-531-15782-2pa. (First Books). 3-6

The text gives a clear overview of tribal life, religion, government, food, clothing, and housing of the Abenaki, speakers of Algonquian who lived in the areas that are now Maine and Vermont. Some of the changes for the Abenaki such as migration to Quebec after the arrival of the French and the English also appear. Further Reading, Glossary, and Index.

1291. Landau, Elaine. **Cowboys**. New York: Franklin Watts, 1990. 64p. $19.90. ISBN 0-531-10866-X. (First Books). 5-8

Photographs and illustrations tell the story of the cowboys of the American West during the nineteenth century. Topics cover the range, the roundup, the trail drive, and cowboy social life until the end of the era. Glossary, Further Reading, and Index.

1292. Landau, Elaine. **The Hopi**. New York: Franklin Watts, 1994. 63p. $19.90; $5.95pa. ISBN 0-531-20098-1; 0-531-15684-2pa. (First Books). 3-6

The Hopi, still in northeast Arizona, resisted European influence more than the other Pueblo tribes and revolted against the Spanish in 1680. The Navajos began to encroach on their land by the 1820s, but the Hopis, farmers and sheepherders, retain their clan structure and ritual, including the Kachina ceremony and the snake dance. The text discusses these and other customs. Further Reading and Index.

1293. Landau, Elaine. **The Ottawa**. New York: Franklin Watts, 1996. 63p. $20.95; $5.95pa. ISBN 0-531-20226-7; 0-531-15783-0pa. (First Books). 3-6

The text gives a clear overview of tribal life, religion, government, food, clothing, and housing of the Ottawa speakers of the Ojibwa language who lived in the area of Lake Huron in Ontario, Canada. Some of the changes for the Ottawa including a migration south toward the area now known as Michigan after the arrival of the French and the English also appear. Further Reading, Glossary, and Index.

1294. Landau, Elaine. **Robert Fulton**. New York: Franklin Watts, 1991. 62p. $12.90. ISBN 0-531-20016-7. (First Books). 3-5

During his youth, Robert Fulton's family endured several setbacks, but he always wanted to be an artist. Fulton (1765-1815) continued drawing as he worked to help support the family and then went to England, where he found that little work for a young artist existed. He continued his inventions because the Industrial Revolution was at its height, and received acclaim for a machine to speedily spin flax into linen and a machine that sawed marble into smaller pieces. Earlier, he had created a mechanical paddle for a rowboat; thus, his design for a submarine, completed in 1797, was a natural progression of his interests. Then he met Robert Livingston, who wanted him to design a steamboat for use on New York's waterways. After several failures, Fulton succeeded. Although not the first to create a steamboat, he is often credited with their increased use in the early nineteenth century. Glossary, Further Reading, and Index.

1295. Lane, Joyce. **Our Century: 1960-1970**. Milwaukee, WI: Gareth Stevens, 1993. 64p. $23.93. ISBN 0-8368-1038-4. 3 up

Written as if a newspaper, the book's short articles give an overview of the decade. Included are statistics, daily life in America, Vietnam on television, Soviets and the U-2 spy plane, the Berlin Wall, Israel, the Czechoslovakian revolt, the Kennedy years, the riots of 1968, the first man on the moon, Roger Maris, Sandy Koufax, Robert Frost, Martin Luther King, Jr., and Malcolm X. Glossary, Books for Further Reading, Places to Write or Visit, and Index.

1296. Lang, Susan. **Extremist Groups in America**. New York: Franklin Watts, 1990. 174p. $12.90. ISBN 0-531-10901-1. 6 up

Extremist groups in the United States include religious, paramilitary, and racist factions. Among them are the White Aryan Resistance, Chicago Area Skinheads (CASH), Christian Patriots Defense League (CPDL), David Duke, Lyndon LaRouche, Louis Farrakhan, and others. The text looks at the history of these groups, how they recruit, and what effects they have on society as a whole. Bibliography and Index.

1297. Langley, Myrtle. **Religion**. New York: Knopf, 1996. 59p. $19. ISBN 0-679-88123-9. (Eyewitness Books). 4-7

The text looks at different religions or facets of religions and relates them in double-page spreads illustrated with photographs, drawings, and reproductions. Among the religions and beliefs introduced in this overview are the Egyptian, Greek, Primitive, Hindu, Buddhist, Confucian, Taoist, Jainist, Sikh, Zoroastrian, Judaic, Christian, and Islamic faiths. Index.

1298. Larsen, Anita. **Amelia Earhart: Missing, Declared Dead**. Marcy Ramsey, illustrator. New York: Crestwood House, 1992. 48p. $11.95. ISBN 0-89686-613-0. (History's Mysteries). 5 up

When Amelia Earhart and Fred Noonan disappeared in 1937 on their trip around the world at the equator, various theories arose as to what had happened to them. Some thought they were spying on the Japanese; others thought they might be lost at sea. The mystery continues because no one has found any remains of either the aviators or the plane. Chronology, Resources, and Index.

1299. Larsen, Rebecca. **Paul Robeson: Hero Before His Time**. New York: Franklin Watts, 1989. 158p. $13.95. ISBN 0-531-10779-5. 6-9

Paul Robeson (1890-1976) was an all-American football player, a Phi Beta Kappa member, a debater, and the class valedictorian at Rutgers University. He then graduated from Columbia University Law School. But he became famous as an actor and singer when he played in *Show Boat, Othello*, and *The Emperor Jones*. He was always outraged at the way Blacks were treated, and he was an early activist in many of the civil rights and labor movement struggles. He thought the Soviet Union must be better after he saw how poorly the United States treated Blacks. In the 1950s, during the Joseph McCarthy era, his pro-Soviet sentiments became targeted, and his career was ruined. He spent much of his later life in the Soviet Union. Notes, Bibliography, and Index.

1300. Larsen, Rebecca. **Richard Nixon: Rise and Fall of a President**. New York: Franklin Watts, 1991. 208p. $23.40. ISBN 0-531-10997-6. 6-9

Richard Milhous Nixon (1913-1994) was elected to the presidency in 1968 and reelected in 1972 only to resign in ignominy when found to have known about people breaking into the Democratic Committee's headquarters at the Watergate. The text looks at Nixon's life and the variety of influences that may have affected his choices during his political career. Notes, Sources, and Index.

1301. Lasky, Kathryn. **Beyond the Burning Time**. New York: Blue Sky, Scholastic, 1994. 272p. $13.95. ISBN 0-590-47331-X. 5-9

In 1691, Mary Chase, 12, works hard with her mother on their Salem farm while her brother Caleb serves his shipbuilding apprenticeship. At the same time, the strange actions of the girls who have been visiting Tituba, Reverend Parris's slave, begin to frighten the town. Then a boy who works for the family accuses Mary's mother Virginia of being a witch. Mary and Caleb threaten Mary Warren, and she tells them where their mother is hidden after she is taken from prison to be hanged. They save her and escape. The ending reveals that the story, in omniscient point of view, is a flashback. *American Library Association Best Books for Young Adults.*

1302. Lasky, Kathryn. **A Journey to the New World: The Diary of Remember Patience Whipple: Mayflower/Plimoth Colony, 1620**. New York: Scholastic, 1996. 173p. $9.95. ISBN 0-590-50214-X. (Dear America 3). 5-9

When Mem is 12, she and her family sail on the *Mayflower* to the New World. She writes in her journal beginning on October 1, 1620, and ends it on November 10, 1621, as she watches another ship come into the harbor and hopes that a girl her age will be arriving soon. She talks of the difficult times in the year as well as the Thanksgiving celebration, and dares to dream that someday their settlement will have a bakery. An epilogue gives further information about her after her diary ends.

1303. Lasky, Kathryn. **The Night Journey**. Trina. S. Hynam, illustrator. New York: Viking, 1986. 152p. $12.95. ISBN 0-670-80935-7. New York: Penguin, 1986. 152p. $4.99pa. ISBN 0-14-032048-2pa. 5-9

Not until she is 13 does Rache hear the story of Jewish pogroms and her grandmother's escape from Russia with her family in 1900. Her grandmother hid under chicken crates, paraded as a Purim player, and crossed the border with her cookies. The cookies held the family's gold. *National Jewish Awards, American Library Association Notable Books for Children, Association of Jewish Libraries Award*, and *Sydney Taylor Book Award.*

1304. Lasky, Kathryn, and Meribah Knight. **Searching for Laura Ingalls: A Reader's Journey**. Christopher G. Knight, illustrator. New York: Macmillan, 1993. Unpaged. $15.95. ISBN 0-02-751666-0. 3-6

When Lasky and Knight's daughter expresses interest in Laura Ingalls (1867-1957) and her "Little House" books, the family visits the sites where the Ingalls family pioneered. They find that Silver Lake no longer exists but that DeSmet, South Dakota, does. They swim in Plum Creek and see other sites in Wisconsin, Minnesota, and South Dakota. The photographs enhance the text.

1305. Latham, Jean Lee. **Carry On, Mr. Bowditch**. John O'Hara Cosgrave II, illustrator. Boston: Houghton Mifflin, 1955. 256p. $14.95; $6.95pa. ISBN 0-395-06881-9; 0-395-13713-6pa. 6 up

Several years after Nathaniel Bowditch was born in 1773, his sailing captain father ran aground and lost his ship. This reversed the family's fortunes, as recounted in this fictional biography, and when 12, Nat was indentured for nine years. He had desperately wanted to go to Harvard, but instead, he read widely and taught himself languages (including Latin word-by-word so that he could read Newton) with the help of mentors who were impressed with his enormous intelligence. His abilities helped him navigate by using the moon's position. He found mistakes in charts used by sailors and dedicated himself to checking every one of the entries and correcting the wrong ones that were published in *The New American Practical Navigator* (1802). He taught others how to navigate before his death in 1838. *Newbery Medal.*

1306. Latham, Jean Lee. **David Glasgow Farragut: Our First Admiral**. Paul Frame, illustrator. New York: Chelsea Juniors, 1991. 80p. $14.95. ISBN 0-7910-1428-X. (Discovery Biographies). 3-6

At 10, Farragut (1801-1870) was assigned to his adopted father's ship in the U.S. Navy. At 12, he was appointed prizemaster of a ship captured from the British. He worked to take forts for the Union during the Civil War and won the Battle of Mobile Bay. He is famous for saying, "Damn the torpedoes! Go ahead! Full speed." For his work, he became the first admiral in the U.S. Navy.

1307. Latham, Jean Lee. **Eli Whitney**. Cary, illustrator. New York: Chelsea Juniors, 1991. 80p. $14.95. ISBN 0-7910-1453-3. (Discovery Biographies). 3-6

Eli Whitney (1765-1825) loved tools and making things. He had a nail business until supplies started coming from England again after the American Revolution ended. Then he invented the cotton gin, a machine that helped the South. Later he made interchangeable parts for muskets, which led to mass production.

1308. Latham, Jean Lee. **Elizabeth Blackwell: Pioneer Woman Doctor**. New York: Chelsea Juniors 1991. 80p. $14.95. ISBN 0-7910-1406-1. (Discovery Biographies). 2-6

When her father lost his business in England, Elizabeth Blackwell (1821-1910) and her family moved to America. When her father died, she had to help make ends meet, and a visit to her mother's friend who was dying gave her a goal. At 24, she decided to become a doctor. After three years, she was finally admitted to the Geneva Medical College in western New York State when the student body voted that a woman could enter. She trained, succeeded, and graduated in 1849, becoming the first woman doctor in the United States. Her achievement opened the way for other women.

1309.　Latham, Jean Lee. **George Goethals: Panama Canal Engineer**. New York: Chelsea Juniors, 1991. 80p. $14.95. ISBN 0-7910-1440-1. (Discovery Biographies). 3-6

After attending West Point, George Goethals (1858-1928) went to Washington State to learn how to build bridges. Then the army transferred him to Panama to work on digging the Panama Canal. That process took many years, but he stayed with the job until it was completed during World War I. He wanted to fight in World War I, but his superiors wanted him to manage the distribution of supplies for the forces instead. He was always disappointed that he never got to fight in a war, but his contribution to the canal was a major victory for the United States.

1310.　Latham, Jean Lee. **Rachel Carson: Who Loved the Sea**. Victor Mays, illustrator. 1973. New York: Chelsea Juniors, 1991. 80p. $14.95. ISBN 0-7910-1408-8. (Discovery Biographies). 2-6

The first woman scientist employed by the United States Bureau of fisheries, Rachel Carson (1907-1964) eventually was able to stop working for the government and write full-time about the natural world that she loved. Her book, *The Silent Spring*, published in 1962, warned the public about pesticides. Other books followed.

1311.　Latham, Jean Lee. **Sam Houston: Hero of Texas**. 1965. New York: Chelsea Juniors, 1991. 80p. $14.95. ISBN 0-7910-1441-X. (Discovery Biographies). 2-6

Sam Houston (1793-1863) ran away from home when he was only 14 to join a tribe of Cherokee Indians. Later, his patriotism for his country compelled him to leave the wilderness and fight for it. He joined the army and General Andrew Jackson in the War of 1812. Then he became a politician in Tennessee, serving as governor, before he became President Jackson's advisor. He rejoined his Cherokee tribe when Jackson requested that Houston lead the new Texan army to fight for independence from Mexico. He led the victory at the Battle of San Jacinto. Then he became the President of the Republic of Texas and later a senator from and governor of the new state.

1312.　Latham, Jean Lee. **Samuel F. B. Morse: Artist-Inventor**. New York: Chelsea House, 1991. 80p. $14.95. ISBN 0-7910-1447-9. (Discovery Biographies). 3-6

Samuel Morse (1791-1872) painted most of his life. He liked drawing better than studying, and at the Royal Academy of Art in London, he won a gold medal for one of his works. When he returned to the United States, he struggled for a long while until he gained fame for his dramatic portraits. At 41, he thought of the telegraph, and worked on it for 12 more years before he successfully introduced it.

1313.　Lattimore, Deborah Nourse. **Frida María: A Story of the Old Southwest**. San Diego, CA: Browndeer, Harcourt Brace, 1994. Unpaged. $14.95. ISBN 0-15-276636-7. 2-4

In the author's note, the reader finds that Frida María lived during the nineteenth century near one of Padre Junípero Serra's missions. She loves to ride horses and do things unbecoming of a young lady, but when the fiesta finally arrives, her ability to ride horses saves her father from losing a large bet. A double-page illustration of the outside of the mission opens to reveal a quadruple-page spread of the inside with people doing different things. Glossary.

1314.　Lauber, Patricia. **Lost Star: The Story of Amelia Earhart**. New York: Scholastic, 1988. 106p. $3.50. ISBN 0-590-41615-4. 5-8

In 1937, Amelia Earhart (1897-1937) attempted to fly around the world at the equator. Her plane was lost, and no one has ever found a trace of it. Earhart's mother was the first woman to reach Pikes Peak and made bloomers for Amelia and her sister like those introduced by Amelia Jenks Bloomer. While alcoholism was destroying her father, Amelia became interested in airplanes and eventually flying. She married a publicist, George Putnam, who supported her interests. She was the first woman to cross the Atlantic and the first person to cross the Pacific. People speculate that Earhart might have crashed in the Pacific islands controlled by the Japanese, where no one was allowed to search. For Further Reading and Index.

1315.　Lavender, David. **Snowbound: The Tragic Story of the Donner Party**. New York: Holiday House, 1996. 87p. $16.95. ISBN 0-8234-1231-8. 4-8

In 1846, the Donner party became stranded in a blizzard in the Sierra Nevada Mountains as they tried to negotiate the Overland Trail. Lavender looks at their journey by focusing mainly on the group that stayed near the lake during the winter and tries to assess what caused the tragedy. He says that part of the blame belongs to the guidebook author Lanford Hastings, who misled the group. The other part belongs within the party because supplies were not equally distributed. Lavender downplays the accusations against those who survived for engaging in cannibalism by noting that it was the one means to keep themselves alive. Maps, Photographs, Bibliography, and Index.

1316.   Lavender, David Sievert. **The Santa Fe Trail**. New York: Holiday House, 1995. 64p. $15.95. ISBN 0-8234-1153-2. 4-6

The 775-mile-long wagon road between the frontier of Missouri and Santa Fe was risky to travel, but many made the trip, which took more than two months, between 1822 and 1879. On the way, traders carried cloth, cutlery, hardware, firearms, and more. On the way back, they had money and fur. Indians, the Mexican War, and the Civil War caused them problems. The trail traffic ended when the railroad was built. Reproductions and maps highlight the text. Index.

1317.   Law, Kevin J. **Milliard Fillmore: 13th President of the United States**. Ada, OK: Garrett Educational, 1990. 122p. $19.80. ISBN 0-944483-61-5. (Presidents of the United States). 5-9

Millard Fillmore (1800-1874) lived in poverty as a young boy. His father apprenticed him to a mill owner, a job that he hated. While there, he realized that he needed more education and began studying. His father secured another position for him to read law in the summer, and the kindness of the judge who saw his potential changed the course of his life. He went to Washington as a congressman and became Zachary Taylor's Vice President. When Taylor died in 1849, Fillmore rose to the presidency. He served in office during a difficult time and did not want to run again. His party members begged him, but because of various strategies by his enemies, he lost the nomination, and the Whigs lost the election to Franklin Pierce. Fillmore was not displeased with the results because he was able to leave a job he never really wanted. Bibliography and Index.

1318.   Lawler, Mary. **Marcus Garvey: Black Nationalist Leader**. New York: Chelsea House, 1988. 112p. $18.95; $7.95pa. ISBN 1-55546-587-0; 0-7910-0203-9pa. (Black Americans of Achievement). 5 up

Marcus Garvey (1887-1940) believed in the Back to Africa movement for Blacks to return to Africa and establish a central homeland. He began his fight for Black rights in 1914 as he tried to heighten racial pride and improve economics and education. People called him "Black Moses" for his efforts, but a failed business venture led to his loss of power. Photographs enhance the text. Chronology, Further Reading, and Index.

1319.   Lawlor, Laurie. **Addie Across the Prairie**. Gail Owens, illustrator. Niles, IL: Albert Whitman, 1986. 128p. $12.95. ISBN 0-8075-0165-4. New York: Minstrel, 1991. 128p. $3.99pa. ISBN 0-671-70147-9pa. 3-6

Addie does not want to travel across the prairie with her family, though her father decides to go to Dakota after the Civil War. On the long journey, she saves herself and her brother from a rapidly spreading fire, and she acts graciously to unwelcome Indians. She shows her bravery even in situations where she does not want to be.

1320.   Lawlor, Laurie. **Addie's Dakota Winter**. Toby Gowing, illustrator. Niles, IL: Albert Whitman, 1989. 160p. $12.95. ISBN 0-8075-0171-9. New York: Minstrel, 1992. 160p. $3.50pa. ISBN 0-671-70148-7pa. 3-6

In 1884, Addie goes to school in Dakota. She has a dream of what her best friend will be like, and Tilla, the Norwegian girl who enters class late, does not fulfill her expectations. As the year progresses and problems occur, Addie realizes that Tilla is the best friend she could have, and that Tilla has the right to be herself, not what Addie wants her to be.

1321.   Lawlor, Laurie. **Addie's Long Summer**. Toby Gowing, illustrator. Niles, IL: Whitman, 1992. 173p. $12.95. ISBN 0-8075-0167-0. New York: Minstrel, 1995. 173p. $3.50pa. ISBN 0-671-52607-3pa. 3-6

Addie, 12 in 1886, has to play hostess to her two cousins, 15 and 17, when they come to visit the sod house farm. Elizabeth's affectations impress her until she almost loses her best friend Tilla because of them. Addie has additional concerns: They have not had rain for weeks, and she fears that the family will lose the farm. When she hears that her cousins have their own problems, she realizes that looking sophisticated does not solve one's problems.

1322.   Lawlor, Laurie. **Come Away with Me**. New York: Pocket, Minstrel, 1996. 184p. $3.99pa. ISBN 0-671-53716-4pa. (Heartland, No. 1). 3-6

Moe, 12, lives in Luck, Wisconsin, around 1910. Her older sister is overbearing, and her younger ones want to go everywhere with her. When two older sophisticated cousins come to visit, Moe tries to save the family horse from replacement by an automobile.

1323.   Lawlor, Laurie. **Daniel Boone**. Bert Dodson, illustrator. Niles, IL: Albert Whitman, 1989. 160p. $13.95. ISBN 0-8075-1462-4. 4-8

Daniel Boone (1734-1820) would not want to be remembered as a man who fought the Native Americans. As a Quaker, he did not hold grudges, and he was not particularly tall or imposing. Shawnee Chief Blackfish adopted him as his son. What motivated Boone was a love of the wilderness and a desire to explore. He was a leader who moved beyond the Appalachian Mountains to open the area for others. Chronology, Bibliography, and Index.

1324. Lawlor, Laurie. **George on His Own**. Morton Grove, IL: Albert Whitman, 1993. 191p. $12.95. ISBN 0-8075-2823-4. New York: Minstrel, 1996. 191p. $3.50pa. ISBN 0-671-52608-1pa. 3-6

In 1887, George, 12, dreams of becoming a famous trombone player, but his father thinks that playing the trombone is a waste of time. His father wants him to be a farmer, but George hates farming. When his little sister dies and his family begins mourning and ignoring him, George buys a trombone with money saved from selling gopher tails and leaves home. His loneliness leads him back, and the family members must learn to adjust to their changed situation.

1325. Lawlor, Laurie. **Gold in the Hills**. New York: Walker, 1995. 146p. $15.95. ISBN 0-8027-8371-6. 4-7

Hattie, 10, and her brother Pheme, 12, go to live with a cousin after their mother dies, while their father goes to mine gold in the mountains around 1880. After a mine owner tries to get their cousin to commit them to slave labor, the two make friends with a neighbor, an old woodsman who teaches them the secrets of the Colorado forest. After Hattie nearly drowns and Pheme meets a nine-foot grizzly bear, they feel more comfortable with their changed life.

1326. Lawlor, Laurie. **The Real Johnny Appleseed**. Mary Thompson, illustrator. Niles, IL: Albert Whitman, 1995. 64p. $13.95. ISBN 0-8075-6909-7. 3-6

John Chapman (1775-1845), known as "Johnny Appleseed," was an eccentric but astute man who espoused the ideas of Emmanuel Swedenborg while buying and keeping much land. Lawlor says that he never wore a tin-pot hat nor had the name "Johnny," as the legend around him has asserted. The text also contains information about colonial times and the change to a nation. Bibliography, Further Reading, and Index.

1327. Lawlor, Laurie. **Take to the Sky**. New York: Pocket, Minstrel, 1996. 162p. $3.99pa. ISBN 0-671-53717-2pa. (Heartland, No. 2). 3-6

Moe and her best friend Otto Price build and fly an airplane, an adventure that becomes a disaster. The attempts and results relay an underlying humor in their situation.

1328. Lawlor, Laurie. **Where Will This Shoe Take You?: A Walk Through the History of Footwear**. New York: Walker, 1996. 132p. $17.95. ISBN 0-8027-8434-8. 4-8

Among a number of facts, Lawlor shows that footwear reflects economic class, social status, authority level, and sometimes political beliefs of the wearer. She presents the invention and development of shoes in seven categories: sandals, boots, oxfords, pumps, clogs, mules, and moccasins as well as shoe-related customs. Photographs, Bibliography, and Index.

1329. Lawlor, Veronica, selector/illustrator. **I Was Dreaming to Come to America: Memories from the Ellis Island Oral History Project**. New York: Viking, 1995. 40p. $14.99. ISBN 0-670-86164-2. 5 up

This collection of images and memories from children and adults who passed through Ellis Island from 1900 to 1925 gives a vibrant view of the immigrant experience. *Notable Children's Trade Books in the Field of Social Studies*.

1330. Lawrence, Jacob, author/illustrator. **The Great Migration**. New York: HarperCollins, 1993. Unpaged. $23.89; $6.95pa. ISBN 0-06-023038-X; 0-06-443428-1pa. 3-7

Around the time of World War I, African Americans began leaving their homes in the rural South and moving to the North. This sequence of paintings shows this Great Migration. The accompanying text tells about the movement of a people who wanted to improve their lives with better opportunities. *Notable Children's Trade Books in the Field of Social Studies, American Library Association Notable Books for Children, Booklist Books for Youth Editors' Choices, IRA Teachers' Choices, Carter G. Woodson Outstanding Merit Book*, and *New York Public Library's Books for the Teen Age*.

1331. Lawrence, Jacob, author/illustrator. **Harriet and the Promised Land**. New York: Simon & Schuster, 1993. Unpaged. $16; $5.99pa. ISBN 0-671-86673-7; 0-689-80965-4pa. K-3

This poem about the life of Harriet Tubman (1820-1913) presents her courageous desire to help others be free.

1332. Lawson, John. **If Pigs Could Fly**. Boston: Houghton Mifflin, 1989. 136p. $13.95. ISBN 0-395-50928-9. 6-9

During the War of 1812, innocent and naive Morgan James becomes involved with some interesting characters. Perhaps a Scottish regiment was defeated when bees flew under their kilts, but documentation may not be available. Morgan is moral and true and loves with great idealism in this entertaining rendition of the war.

1333. Lawson, Robert, author/illustrator. **Ben and Me**. Boston: Little, Brown, 1939. 114p. $15.95 ISBN 0-316-51732-1. 3-6

Amos, a mouse, describes himself as Dr. Benjamin Franklin's closest friend and advisor and the one responsible for the inventions and discoveries of Franklin, especially of his successes at the French court. In this biographical fiction, the mouse reveals Franklin's achievements.

1334.   Lawson, Robert. **Mr. Revere and I**. Boston: Little, Brown, 1953. 152p. $16.95. ISBN 0-316-51739-9. 3-6
Paul Revere's horse Scheherazade tells about the life of Paul Revere from her vantage point of the shed stall where she can look into the kitchen. She learns about the family, the silversmith trade, and the Sons of Liberty, and tells about them in this biographical fiction.

1335.   Lazar, Jerry. **Red Cloud: Sioux War Chief**. New York: Chelsea House, 1995. 111p. $18.95; $7.95pa. ISBN 0-7910-1718-4; 0-7910-2044-4pa. (North American Indians of Achievement). 6-9
Red Cloud (1822-1909) was an able warrior by the time the first settlers arrived in Sioux territory, where he lived as a Teton Sioux. To keep the lands, he united more than 2,000 Sioux, Cheyenne, and Arapaho to drive the U.S. Army from the Black Hills of South Dakota. He won, stopped fighting, and moved to the Sioux reservation. He spent the last 40 years of his life trying to keep the government from taking the remainder of his people's homeland and culture. Photographs enhance the text. Chronology, Further Reading, and Index.

1336.   Lazo, Caroline. **Eleanor Roosevelt**. New York: Dillon Press, 1993. 64p. $13.95. ISBN 0-87518-594-0. (Peacemakers). 4-8
Eleanor Roosevelt (1884-1962) had a sad childhood after her parents died, living with a strict grandmother. She went to study in England, however, and one of her teachers saw her potential and encouraged her. She became reacquainted with and married Franklin Roosevelt, her distant cousin, when she returned to the United States. Among the early disappointments of the marriage was finding love letters from another woman in his luggage and his bout with polio, which left him in a wheelchair. She spoke for issues in which she believed. Photographs, For Further Reading, and Index.

1337.   Lazo, Caroline. **Wilma Mankiller**. New York: Dillon Press, 1995. 64p. $13.95; $7.95pa. ISBN 0-87518-635-1; 0-382-24716-7pa. (Peacemakers). 4-8
Wilma Mankiller (b. 1945) became the leader of the Cherokee Nation when the chief for whom she worked resigned in 1985. Two years later, she was elected in her own right. The name "Mankiller" in the eighteenth century referred to a top military rank of the Cherokee's warring ancestors. Because of the pride associated with the name, Wilma Mankiller continued to use it after she was married. But contrary to what the name implies, she has been working for peace with her nation of 130,000 members. The text looks at her life. For Further Reading and Index.

1338.   Leathers, Noel L. **The Japanese in America**. Minneapolis, MN: Lerner, 1991. 64p. $17.50; $5.95pa. ISBN 0-8225-0241-0; 0-8225-1044-8pa. (In America). 5 up
Photographs, maps, and text tell about the Japanese immigration to America, their way of life, the prejudice they faced during World War II, and their contributions to American life. Index.

1339.   Leavell, J. Perry, Jr. **Harry S. Truman**. New York: Chelsea House, 1988. 112p. $18.95. ISBN 0-87754-558-8. (World Leaders Past and Present). 5 up
Harry S. Truman (1884-1972) became president when Franklin Roosevelt died in office. He first worked in the Senate for Missouri, where he earned a reputation for honesty and efficiency. He began the atomic age when he authorized the bombing of Hiroshima. After the war, he committed the United States to a program of economic aid for war-torn countries, even the enemies. Blacks and labor helped him win a second term, but Congress defeated most of his proposals. His last years in office saw the Korean War and Senator Joseph McCarthy's crusade against Communism. Photographs enhance the text. Chronology, Further Reading, and Index.

1340.   Leavell, J. Perry, Jr. **James Madison**. New York: Chelsea House, 1988. 112p. $18.95. ISBN 55546-815-2. (World Leaders Past and Present). 5 up
James Madison (1751-1836) is the father of the Constitution. He and Thomas Jefferson outlined the ideas of freedom and democracy that appear in that document. During his presidency, he established the second national bank, and the "era of good feeling," a time of economic growth, ensued. He was intelligent, philosophical, and democratic. Engravings and reproductions enhance the text. Chronology, Further Reading, and Index.

1341.   Leavell, J. Perry, Jr. **Woodrow Wilson**. New York: Chelsea House, 1987. 116p. $18.95. ISBN 0-87754-557-X. (World Leaders Past and Present). 5 up
Woodrow Wilson (1856-1924) was a college professor and university president before he became New Jersey's governor. Later, as President of the United States, he started "trust-busting." He helped create the federal reserve system and the graduated income tax. He was reelected in 1916 for keeping America out of the Great War, but he had to declare war on Germany in 1917. After the war, he could not get support at home for the League of Nations, but the United States became a military power during his terms of office. Wilson was alternately pragmatic, idealistic, pacifistic, and militaristic, but he was always dedicated to world peace. Photographs enhance the text. Further Reading, Glossary, and Index.

1342.   Ledbetter, Cynthia, and Richard C. Jones. **John Muir**. Vero Beach, FL: Rourke, 1993. 112p. $19.93. ISBN 0-86625-494-3. (Pioneers). 5-9

John Muir (1838-1914) was one of the first to speak out for the protection of the country's natural areas. He was an expert in botany and geology, largely self-taught. He observed nature closely and saw that glaciers had formed Yosemite's landscape. He saw that nature and humans were interconnected, and he wrote articles to ensure that humans would know their responsibilities to nature and to keep it healthy. As perhaps the first ecologist, he was able to influence Theodore Roosevelt to save as much land as he could. Time Line, Glossary, Bibliography, Media Resources, and Index.

1343.   Leder, Jane. **Amelia Earhart: Opposing Viewpoints**. San Diego, CA: Greenhaven, 1990. 111p. $19.95. ISBN 0-89908-070-7. (Great Mysteries—Opposing Viewpoints). 6-9

The text explores the mystery of the disappearance of Amelia Earhart, the first woman to cross the Atlantic, in 1937 when she was flying over the Pacific. Because no one knows what happened to her, the speculation continues as to whether she was lost at sea or survived and was unable to communicate her whereabouts. Quotes, black-and-white illustrations, and maps complement the text. Bibliography and Index.

1344.   Leder, Jane Mersky. **A Russian Jewish Family**. Alan Leder, photographs. Minneapolis, MN: Lerner, 1996. 64p. $21.50; $8.95pa. ISBN 0-8225-3401-0; 0-8225-9744-6pa. (Journey Between Two Worlds). 3-6

Although not a history book, the text includes the history of the Jewish people in Russia as a background for understanding the reasons that Jewish families have chosen to immigrate. Photographs and personal experiences explain Jewish social and religious traditions and how Jews have had to adapt to a new culture in order to survive as immigrants in a new world. Further Reading.

1345.   Lee, Kathleen. **Tracing Our Italian Roots**. Santa Fe, NM: John Muir, 1993. 46p. $12.95. ISBN 1-56261-148-8. 1-5

The text looks at the reasons people left Italy in the early part of the twentieth century to come to the United States. The book's two parts, the Old World and the New World, give an overview with two-page looks at topics such as crossing the Atlantic, Ellis Island, family life, prejudices faced, achievements in America, and famous people of Italian descent who have contributed to American culture. Archival photographs highlight the text. Index.

1346.   Lee, Sally. **San Antonio**. New York: Dillon Press, Macmillan, 1992. 63p. $12.95. ISBN 0-89686-510-X. (Downtown America). 4-6

The history of San Antonio includes the fight at the Alamo in 1836. The city also has festivals indigenous to the area and identifiable neighborhoods. Index.

1347.   Leeuwen, Jean Van. **A Fourth of July on the Plains**. Henri Sorensen, illustrator. New York: Dial, 1997. 32p. $14.99. ISBN 0-8037-1771-7. K-3

Jesse enjoys fording rivers, sleeping outside in a hailstorm, chasing buffalo, and seeing Indians on the Oregon Trail. As the members of the wagon train prepare for July 4, he has the idea that he and his friends will make a parade by marching to their own version of "Yankee Doodle Dandy."

1348.   Lefer, Diane. **Emma Lazarus**. New York: Chelsea House, 1988. 110p. $18.95. ISBN 1-55546-664-8. (American Women of Achievement). 5 up

The poet who made the Statue of Liberty a symbol of hope, Emma Lazarus (1849-1887) grew up in a wealthy New York Jewish family. She published her first poems at 18. Her strong beliefs surfaced 14 years later when she heard of the anti-Semitic violence abroad and realized that it was a part of her own heritage. She became a spokeswoman for Jewish unity, religious tolerance, and an "open-door" immigration policy in the United States. Not until 10 years after she died were her verses inscribed on the base of the Statue of Liberty: "Give me your tired, your poor, your huddled masses yearning to breathe free." Photographs and engravings enhance the text. Chronology, Further Reading, and Index.

1349.   Lehrer, Brian. **The Korean Americans**. New York: Chelsea House, 1988. 108p. $19.95. ISBN 0-87754-888-9. (The Immigrant Experience). 5 up

Although Koreans had migrated to Hawaii during the twentieth century, they did not began settling around New York and Los Angeles until 1965, when the anti-Asian quota system was abolished. At that time, many educated Koreans arrived. Recorded Korean history begins in the first century AD with the words of a Chinese scholar, Ki-tze. At the end of the Sino-Japanese war in 1895, troops of Japanese soldiers controlled Korean civilians until 1945. After World War II, Korea was split with the Communists in the north above the 38th parallel. Further Reading and Index.

1350. Lehrman, Robert. **The Store That Mama Built**. New York: Macmillan, 1992. 126p. $13.95. ISBN 0-02-754632-2. 3-7

Almost ready to open his grocery store in Harrisburg, Pennsylvania, in 1917, Birdie's father, a Russian Jewish immigrant, dies of influenza. Birdie's mother decides that she will open the store as planned, and the entire family helps. His mother decides that she will offer credit to Black families, and the store begins to make money even though the family closes it on Friday nights and Saturdays so that they can keep their Sabbath.

1351. Leighton, Maxinne Rhea. **An Ellis Island Christmas**. Dennis Nolan, illustrator. New York: Viking, 1992. 32p. $15. ISBN 0-670-83182-4. New York: Puffin, 1994. $4.99pa. ISBN 0-14-055344-4pa. 1-4

When she is six in the early twentieth century, Krysia, her mother, and her brother sail from Poland to Ellis Island to meet her father, already in New York. When they arrive and go into New York City, they all enjoy the beautiful Christmas tree, with the children relieved that Saint *Mikolaj* (Saint Nicholas) can also be found in America.

1352. Leiner, Katherine. **First Children: Growing Up in the White House**. Katie Keller, illustrator. New York: Tambourine, 1996. 224p. $20. ISBN 0-688-13341-X. 6-9

Leiner limits the text to information about 17 first families as she presents Presidents' children and grandchildren as well as the offspring of staff and visitors who stay in the White House for a long time. She also shows an angle such as Luci Johnson's wedding, Quentin Roosevelt and his gang, Letitia Tyler's response to her father's new wife being the same age as she, Caroline Kennedy's White House school, or Andrew Johnson's son Frank waiting to hear if his father has been impeached. Appendix and Bibliography.

1353. Leland, Dorothy Kupcha. **Sallie Fox: The Story of a Pioneer Girl**. Davis, CA: Tomato, 1995. 115p. $8.95. ISBN 0-9617357-6-7. 4-6

Sallie Fox, 12, goes with her family from Iowa to California in the mid-1800s. She expects an exciting trip, but it becomes an ordeal when she has to spend many days without water. Many in the group die of thirst. They also have to cope with illness and avoid Indian attacks as well as each other when they disagree.

1354. Lelchuk, Alan. **On Home Ground**. Merle Nacht, illustrator. San Diego, CA: Harcourt Brace, 1987. 72p. $9.95. ISBN 0-15-200560-9. 5-7

When Aaron is almost 10 in 1947, three males are important in his life. One, a veteran suffering from war wounds, takes him to baseball games. The second, Jackie Robinson, plays in those games. The third, his father, feels uncomfortable with his new life in the United States after leaving Russia. When Aaron sees his father in the country, galloping on a large horse, he understands that his father has a side to his personality that he had never seen.

1355. Lemieux, Margo. **Full Worm Moon**. Robert Andrew Parker, illustrator. New York: Tambourine, Morrow, 1994. Unpaged. $15. ISBN 0-688-12105-5. 1-3

From the author's note, the reader finds that the story is based on the knowledge that sometime in the New England March, the earth begins to thaw for spring planting. The Native Americans living there, probably until the late nineteenth century, knew the ground was ready because the full moon seemed to bring out the worms so that squiggly mounds of dirt appeared.

1356. Lemke, Nancy. **Missions of the Southern Coast: San Diego de Alcalà, San Luis Rey de Francia, San Juan Capistrano**. Minneapolis, MN: Lerner, 1996. 80p. $14.96. ISBN 0-8225-1925-9. (California Missions). 4-6

In the 1700s, Spain sent Roman Catholic priests to establish missions and presidios (forts) along the coast of Baja California and other areas of New Spain (present-day Southwestern United States and Mexico). Spain wanted the Indians to accept the Spanish ways and become loyal subjects. San Diego de Alcalà, the first mission, was established in 1769. Father Serra named it for Saint Didacus, a fifteenth-century monk who came to Spain's island colonies. The area's poor soil and raids from nearby Indians delayed the mission's start. San Juan Capistrano prospered from its location and especially beautiful architecture while Mission San Luis Rey de Francia flourished under its leader, Father Antonio Peyri. Glossary, Chronolgy, and Index.

1357. Lenski, Lois. **Indian Captive: The Story of Mary Jemison**. 1941. New York: Trophy, 1995. 304p. $16; $4.95pa. ISBN 0-397-30072-7; 0-06-446162-9pa. 5 up

This book is based on a true story. Seneca Indians captured Mary Jemison, 12, in 1758, and massacred her family in retaliation for white settlers killing their own people. After two years, she felt like she belonged to this group, which was mostly kind and courageous, and refused to go with the English conquerors of Quebec. Although the book was first published in 1941, Lenski presents a balanced view of Native American and white settlers—none of them all bad or all good. The blond Mary, first known as "Corn Tassel," earned her name "Little-Woman-of-Great-Courage" by realizing that being with people who loved her was more important than being with people of the same race who only saw her as a pawn in a distant war. *Newbery Honor.*

1358.   Lenski, Lois. **Strawberry Girl**. 1945. New York: HarperTrophy, 1995. 194p. $4.50pa. ISBN 0-06-440585-0pa. 5 up

Two families in Florida during the early 1900s, the Slaters and the Boyers, have to adjust to each other's ways. The Boyers strive to succeed through work and education, but the Slater family's father seems to thrive on destroying their efforts. When the Slater mother and children become ill while the father is away, Mrs. Boyer comes to nurse them back to health. Her kindness and the influence of an itinerant preacher help Mr. Slater realize the value of being a good neighbor and an honest employee. *American Library Association Notable Books for Children* and *Newbery Medal*.

1359.   Leonard, Laura. **Finding Papa**. New York: Atheneum, 1991. 185p. $14.95. ISBN 0-689-31526-0. 4-6

In 1905, this sequel to *Saving Damaris* features Abigail, 13, as the narrator. She, Damaris, and her brother take a train to San Francisco to join Papa, who is planning to marry. When they arrive, he has gone prospecting, so they get jobs. When he returns, he does marry, but he marries someone the children met on the train rather than the woman he had intended to marry before they arrived. The children continue to have their own adventures.

1360.   Leonard, Laura. **Saving Damaris**. New York: Jean Karl, Atheneum, 1989. 192p. $14.95. ISBN 0-689-31553-8. 5-7

Abby is 12 on July 4, 1904. That day she begins a diary in which she tells of her father leaving home, her sewing, and her sister Damaris, 16, taking a job in Mr. Buttenbacher's emporium. After their mother dies, Mr. Buttenbacher wants Damaris to marry him. Although Damaris does not love him, she knows she must accept the offer. Before Abby can figure out how to stop the engagement, Mr. Buttenbacher realizes he will have to care for the other two children as well as Damaris. He changes his mind.

1361.   Lepthien, Emilie U. **The Mandans**. Chicago: Childrens Press, 1989. 48p. $18; $5.50pa. ISBN 0-516-01180-4; 0-516-41180-2pa. (A New True Book). 2-4

Peaceful farmers who called themselves Mandans, or "Those Who Dwell by the River," believed that Lone Man saved them from a great flood. With no written history, the Mandans were thought to have settled first in South Dakota between AD 1000 and AD 1400 along the Missouri River. They eventually helped Lewis and Clark with their expedition. Several artists, including George Caitin in the early nineteenth century, painted the tribe. Today they have almost all disappeared, having become integrated into other Siouan tribes like the Hidatsa and the Arikara. Words You Should Know and Index.

1362.   Leuzzi, Linda. **Urban Life**. New York: Chelsea House, 1995. 104p. $18.95. ISBN 0-7910-2841-0. (Life in America One Hundred Years Ago). 5-9

Cities in the United States began to flourish only a century ago. In the second half of the nineteenth century, construction of huge buildings, electric lights, elevators, parks, suspension bridges, and mansions furthered their growth. At the same time, however, they became places of dingy tenements for poorly paid immigrants who worked long hours. Social workers and muckrakers had to expose their existence and the political system that allowed it. The text looks at all of these complexities underlying the growth of cities. Photographs, Further Reading, and Index.

1363.   Levi, Steven C. **Cowboys of the Sky: The Story of Alaska's Bush Pilots**. New York: Walker, 1996. 114p. $17.95. ISBN 0-8027-8331-7. 5-9

The size of the state of Alaska and the portions isolated by ice and snow in the winter have made the role of bush pilots important. The text looks at the history of pilots since the 1920s who have brought mail, supplies, and contact to citizens in the outer areas. Anecdotes about the adventures of men with such nicknames as "the craziest pilot in the world" or "Thrill 'Em, Chill 'Em, Spill 'Em, But No Kill 'Em" include encounters with weather, animals such as polar bears, planes barely holding together, and dangerous landing places. The people who fly these planes have their own unusual histories. Photographs, Bibliography, Glossary, and Index.

1364.   Levin, Betty. **Fire in the Wind**. New York: Greenwillow, 1995. 176p. $15. ISBN 0-688-14299-0. 5-7

Meg and her brother wait for the fire ravaging through the Maine woods to reach their two-room schoolhouse in 1947. Her slightly retarded cousin Orin knows the way to the school so well that he is able to beat the fire and rescue the two by thrusting them into a culvert. His quick response leads his parents to recognize his worth and stop revering their other son, a dead hero of World War II.

1365.   Levin, Pamela. **Susan B. Anthony: Fighter for Women's Rights**. New York: Chelsea House, 1993. 79p. $14.95. ISBN 0-7910-1762-1. (Junior World Biographies). 3-5

Susan B. (Susan Brownell) Anthony (1820-1906) became a crusader for a variety of causes in the nineteenth century. She led conventions to get women the right to vote and to get women rights that belonged to their husbands and fathers. She and Elizabeth Cady Stanton helped get women's rights over their children in New York. Without her tireless efforts, much of the gains that women claim today would not have happened. Bibliography and Index.

1366. Levine, Ellen. **A Fence Away from Freedom: Japanese Americans and World War II**. New York: Putnam, 1995. 288p. $17.95. ISBN 0-399-22638-9. 5 up

Using the memories of 35 people who lived in several different camps during the World War II internment of Japanese Americans, Levine tells a story about the people and the camps. The government even brought some Japanese from Peru and placed them in the camps, probably as a bait for exchange of prisoners of war. The text is arranged both chronologically and topically, with the stories of the 35 people appearing as parts in more than one chapter. Appendix and Index. *Notable Children's Trade Books in the Field of Social Studies.*

1367. Levine, Ellen. **If Your Name Was Changed at Ellis Island**. Wayne Parmenter, illustrator. New York: Scholastic, 1993. 80p. $15.95. ISBN 0-590-46134-6. 3-6

Ellis Island became a center for immigrants in 1892. During the 30 years after that, more than 12 million people entered the United States from its doors. When people arrived, they had to answer a series of questions before they could be allowed to settle in the country. The text answers 36 questions about such topics as why immigrants left their homes, what they had to do at Ellis Island to pass inspection, where they planned to work, and if they ever returned to their homes.

1368. Levinson, Nancy Smiler. **Chuck Yeager: The Man Who Broke the Sound Barrier**. New York: Walker, 1988. 132p. $13.95. ISBN 0-8027-6781-8. 4-6

In October 1947, Chuck Yeager (b. 1923) broke the sound barrier in a Bell X-1 rocket by flying faster than 761 miles per hour at sea level. The text begins with a detailed account of this experience and then discusses Yeager's life. Glossary, Bibliography, and Index.

1369. Levinson, Nancy Smiler. **Clara and the Bookwagon**. Carolyn Croll, illustrator. New York: HarperCollins, 1988. 64p. $9.95. ISBN 0-06-023838-0. (An I Can Read Book). 1-3

In 1905, Clara works with her family on the farm and wants a book. When they pass the general store's "book station," her father tells her that their family cannot afford to buy a book. When the first traveling bookwagon comes to the farm, the librarian persuades her father to let her borrow a book and begin learning to read. He agrees because the books are free.

1370. Levinson, Nancy Smiler. **I Lift My Lamp: Emma Lazarus and the Statue of Liberty**. New York: Lodestar, Dutton, 1992. 102p. $13.95. ISBN 0-525-67180-3. (Jewish Biography). 5-9

Emma Lazarus (1849-1887) grew up in a privileged family, but seeing Jewish refugees fleeing from persecution affected her so much that she began to write about their problems. She wrote her now-famous poem about the Statue of Liberty before the statue was unveiled. She had composed it as part of a portfolio of works created to entice people to contribute to a fund to pay for the statue's base. Not until 1903, when a woman discovered the portfolio in a book store, did the poem become famous. "The New Colossus," with its words, "Give me your tired, your poor," became symbolic of what the United States could offer to its immigrants. The text looks at Emma's life and the background of the statue's sculptor, Fréréric Auguste Bartholdi. Books for Further Reading and Index.

1371. Levinson, Nancy Smiler. **Snowshoe Thompson**. Joan Sandin, illustrator. New York: HarperCollins, 1992. 64p. $12.89; $3.75pa. ISBN 0-06-023802-X; 0-06-444206-3pa. (An I Can Read Book). K-3

Snowshoe Thompson (1827-1876) decides to make a pair of skis so that he can deliver Danny's letter to his father, who is 90 miles away, across the Sierra Nevadas. Thompson makes the trip and returns with a letter to Danny saying that his father will be home for Christmas. *Notable Children's Trade Books in the Field of Social Studies.*

1372. Levinson, Nancy Smiler. **Your Friend, Natalie Popper**. New York: Lodestar, 1991. 113p. $13.95. ISBN 0-525-67307-5. 5-7

After Natalie, 12, and her friend Corinne finish sixth grade, they go to camp. At first, Natalie clings to Corrine, who had attended camp the previous summer. But living in a different cabin, Natalie meets a variety of people, including a motherless girl, a girl who stutters, and a girl who makes anti-Semitic remarks. The latter girl contracts polio at camp, and the camp closes. What happened was very different from what Natalie had anticipated.

1373. Levinson, Rikki. **DinnieAbbieSister-r-r!** Helen Cogancherry, illustrator. New York: Bradbury, 1987. 90p. $11.95. ISBN 0-02-757380-X. 2-4

Along with her two brothers, Jennie, five, enjoys romping in the rain with her mother in the 1930s. Even though her brother gets a crippling disease in his leg that requires therapy treatment, the family does things together. One of her happiest times is going to yeshiva to see her brothers. She wants to attend the school too, but her mother tells her that girls are not allowed.

1374. Levinson, Rikki. **Soon, Annala**. Julie Downing, illustrator. New York: Orchard, 1993. Unpaged. $15.95. ISBN 0-531-05494-2. 1-3

Annala, her sister, and her parents come to live in New York. Annala goes to school and begins to learn English. She wants her brothers to join them. Finally, the family receives a letter saying that they will be arriving on a ship in September 1911. When they come from Ellis Island by ferry, the family is together again.

1375. Levinson, Rikki. **Watch the Stars Come Out**. Diane Goode, illustrator. New York: Dutton, 1985. Unpaged. $15. ISBN 0-525-44205-7. New York: Puffin, 1995. Unpaged. $4.99pa. ISBN 0-14-055506-4pa. K-3

A little girl and her brother cross the ocean to America to join their parents and sister. She becomes distressed when she cannot see the stars out at night over the ship and when her parents are not at Ellis Island waiting for them. She also does not know why the people wearing white jackets look at her body so carefully. But when she sees her parents at the ferry docks and looks out the window in their top floor apartment and sees the stars, she feels much better.

1376. Levitin, Sonia. **Annie's Promise**. New York: Atheneum, 1993. 192p. $14.95; $3.99pa. ISBN 0-689-31752-2; 0-689-80440-7pa. 5 up

In this sequel to *Journey to America* and *Silver Days*, Annie, 12 in 1945, wants to become independent from her parents and follow her older sisters. Still suffering from migraine headaches of the year before, she thinks that her parents are overly protective. In the summer, she has the opportunity to go to a Quaker camp in the mountains. Although not the expected solace, the camp offers her a chance to meet others and to personally combat the anti-Semitic sentiment lingering from World War II. *Publishers Weekly Starred Review*.

1377. Levitin, Sonia. **Nine for California**. Cat Bowman Smith, illustrator. New York: Kroupa, Orchard, 1996. Unpaged. $15.95. ISBN 0-531-09527-4. K-3

Amanda's father writes his family from the California gold mines to say that he is lonely. Her mother takes her five children west from Missouri to join him. Whenever Amanda becomes bored on the journey, something exciting happens such as the arrival of hungry Indians, a heavy rainfall, or a buffalo stampede. Levitin uses journals and letters as her sources.

1378. Levitin, Sonia. **A Piece of Home**. Juan Wijngaard, illustrator. New York: Dial, 1996. Unpaged. $14.99. ISBN 0-8037-1625-7. K-3

When Gregor's family leaves Russia, each person chooses one thing to take. His mother chooses the samovar and his father the small accordion called a *garmoshka*. Gregor wants the blanket that his great-grandmother made for him. On the journey, he realizes that his American cousin might laugh at him for such a silly item, but when he arrives, the blanket unites the two.

1379. Levitin, Sonia. **Silver Days**. New York: Atheneum, 1989. 186p. $13.95. ISBN 0-689-31563-5. 6-8

Lisa, 13, tells of her family's move from New York to California, where her father thinks that he can make money. They have had to leave all of their assets in Nazi Germany and are still concerned about Lisa's grandmother, whom they hear has had to go to Auschwitz. In this sequel to *Journey to America*, Lisa's father reenters the garment-making business, and she succeeds when she returns to her dancing.

1380. Lewis-Ferguson, Julinda. **Alvin Ailey, Jr.: A Life in Dance**. New York: Walker, 1994. 96p. $12.95. ISBN 0-8027-8239-6. 5-7

The text looks at Alvin Ailey's professional career in detail, from work with Lester Horton to the formation of his own ballet company. Quotes from Ailey and people with whom he was associated help reveal his personality and talent. Also included are interpretations of the dances that he choreographed. Bibliography and Reviews.

1381. Libreatore, Karen. **Our Century: 1910-1920**. Milwaukee, WI: Gareth Stevens, 1993. 64p. $23.93. ISBN 0-8368-1033-3. 3 up

Written as if a newspaper, this book's short articles give an overview of the decade. Included are statistics, daily life in America, the *Titanic* sinking, Archduke Ferdinand's murder, World War I, Nicholas I of Russia's overthrow, Bolsheviks, the flu epidemic, suffragettes, Prohibition, Pancho Villa's border town raids, the first assembly line, Panama Canal progress, the Black Sox baseball scandal, Woodrow Wilson, Vladimir Lenin, Louis B. Brandeis, Eugene Debs, Margaret Sanger, D. W. Griffith, Mary Pickford, and Charlie Chaplin. Glossary, Books for Further Reading, Places to Write or Visit, and Index.

1382. Liestman, Vicki. **Columbus Day**. Rick Hanson, illustrator. Minneapolis, MN: Carolrhoda, 1991. 52p. $9.95. ISBN 0-87614-444-X. 1-3

The simple text relates a general story of Christopher Columbus and the holiday celebrated in his name. Additional information includes reasons why the Europeans wanted to find new sea routes and that Columbus and his crew saw the natives as potential slaves. Although Columbus lost favor with his crew, his perseverance allowed him to find the New World.

1383. Lillegard, Dee. **James A. Garfield: Twentieth President of the United States**. Chicago: Childrens Press, 1987. 100p. $19.80. ISBN 0-516-01394-7. (Encyclopedia of Presidents). 4-9

Although James Garfield (1831-1881) liked Abraham Lincoln personally, he opposed some of his decisions. And when Lincoln died, Garfield mourned. Garfield attended Williams College before serving Ohio in the U.S. Senate. Then he went to the House of Representatives from which he was elected President of the United States in 1880. A disappointed office seeker, however, kept him from serving long because he assassinated him. Chronology of American History and Index.

1384. Lillegard, Dee. **James K. Polk: Eleventh President of the United States**. Chicago: Childrens Press, 1988. 100p. $19.80. ISBN 0-516-01351-3. (Encyclopedia of Presidents). 4-9

James K. Polk (1795-1849) of Tennessee wanted to be the vice president for Martin Van Buren, but he had been defeated for governor and various other positions. Andrew Jackson decided to support him, so Polk persuaded Democrats to write letters saying that if Henry Clay were elected, he would give the federal government too much control over the states. Instead of the nomination for vice president, Polk actually won the nomination for president because he favored immediate annexation of Texas even though it was a slave state. Jackson decided not to support Van Buren because he would not annex Texas. Polk was nominated on the ninth ballot as the first "dark horse" president. Although his accomplishment was not recognized for years, he was one of the great presidents. Chronology of American History and Index.

1385. Lillegard, Dee. **John Tyler: Tenth President of the United States**. Chicago: Childrens Press, 1987. 100p. $19.80. ISBN 0-516-01393-9. (Encyclopedia of Presidents). 4-9

John Tyler (1790-1862) became President after being a senator from Virginia and William Henry Harrison's vice presidential running mate. He did not plan to be President, but when he took office, he began to battle with the Whigs in Congress who expected him to pass their laws. But his friends had already nicknamed him "Honest John." After he left office, he did not leave politics. Seeing the Union moving toward civil war distressed him; he was trying to save the Union at his death. Chronology of American History and Index.

1386. Lillegard, Dee. **Richard Nixon: Thirty-Seventh President of the United States**. Chicago: Childrens Press, 1988. 100p. $19.80. ISBN 0-516-01356-4. (Encyclopedia of Presidents). 4-9

This biography of Richard Milhaus Nixon (1913-1994) presents Nixon's famous "Checkers" speech with his dog, his background, his marriage and family, and his service for California and as vice president. It also comments on his victories and defeats before he had to resign during the Watergate controversy. Chronology of American History and Index.

1387. Lincoln, Abraham. **The Gettysburg Address**. Michael McCurdy, illustrator. Boston: Houghton Mifflin, 1995. Unpaged. $14.95. ISBN 0-395-69824-3. K up

McCurdy has carefully illustrated the words of the Gettysburg Address so that they are accessible to all readers. By having only a few words per page, he shows the shortness of the speech as well as its power. *Notable Children's Trade Books in the Field of Social Studies.*

1388. Lincoln, Margarette. **The Pirate's Handbook: How to Become a Rogue of the High Seas**. New York: Cobblehill, 1995. 29p. $12.99. ISBN 0-525-65209-4. 3-6

Interspersed with ways to make costumes and food related to pirates, the text includes photographs and drawings along with specific information about different kinds of pirates. Among those included are the Muslim corsairs of the sixteenth century, the buccaneers of the seventeenth century, the pirates in East and West Africa of the early eighteenth century, and pirates from the Philippines in the nineteenth century. Additional topics are clothing, provisions, codes of conduct, charts and maps, types of ships such as the schooner and galley, flags, attacks, treasure, punishment, and language. Rogue's Gallery.

1389. Lindbergh, Reeve. **Nobody Owns the Sky: The Story of Brave Bessie Coleman**. Pamela Paparone, illustrator. New York: Candlewick, 1996. Unpaged. $15.99. ISBN 1-56402-533-0. 1-4

Highlighted with folk art illustrations, this narrative poem tells the life of Bessie Coleman (1896-1926) from her childhood in Texas through her days in Chicago during World War I and her life in Paris during the 1920s when she was flying airplanes.

1390. Lindop, Edmund. **Dwight D. Eisenhower, John F. Kennedy, Lyndon B. Johnson**. New York: Twenty-First Century Books, 1996. 64p. $15.98. ISBN 0-8050-3404-8. (Presidents Who Dared). 5-8

The text covers the childhood, educations, and prepresidential careers of Dwight Eisenhower, John Kennedy, and Lyndon Johnson. It then describes their administrations by noting their goals and their achievements in office. The inclusion of each man's strengths and weaknesses lends objectivity to the presentation. Bibliography, Further Reading, Notes, and Index.

1391. Lindop, Edmund. **George Washington, Thomas Jefferson, Andrew Jackson**. New York: Twenty-First Century Books, 1996. 64p. $15.98. ISBN 0-8050-3401-3. (Presidents Who Dared). 5-8

The text covers the childhood, educations, and prepresidential careers of George Washington, Thomas Jefferson, and Andrew Jackson. It then describes their administrations by noting their goals and their achievements in office. The inclusion of each man's strengths and weaknesses lends objectivity to the presentation. Washington set the major precedents for the government, while Jefferson established the Democratic-Republican Party and abolished slave trade. Jackson decided that the South had no right to nullify federal laws. Bibliography, Further Reading, Notes, and Index.

1392. Lindop, Edmund. **James K. Polk, Abraham Lincoln, Theodore Roosevelt**. New York: Twenty-First Century Books, 1996. 64p. $15.98. ISBN 0-8050-3402-1. (Presidents Who Dared). 5-8

The text covers the childhood, educations, and prepresidential careers of James Polk, Abraham Lincoln, and Theodore Roosevelt. It then describes their administrations by noting their goals and their achievements in office. The inclusion of each man's strengths and weaknesses lends an objectivity to the presentation. Polk pushed the idea of Manifest Destiny while Lincoln tried to guide the country through the Civil War. Roosevelt realized the importance of conservation and broke the trusts and monopolies of large businesses. Bibliography, Further Reading, Notes, and Index.

1393. Lindop, Edmund. **Richard M. Nixon, Jimmy Carter, Ronald Reagan**. New York: Twenty-First Century Books, 1996. 64p. $15.98. ISBN 0-8050-3405-6. (Presidents Who Dared). 5-8

The text covers the childhood, educations, and prepresidential careers of Richard Nixon, Jimmy Carter, and Ronald Reagan. It then describes their administrations by noting their goals and their achievements in office. Nixon had to resign or be impeached while Carter had to face the Iranian hostage crisis. Reagan kept office for eight years but left a huge budget deficit after his term ended. The inclusion of each man's strengths and weaknesses lends objectivity to the presentation. Bibliography, Further Reading, Notes, and Index.

1394. Lindop, Edmund. **Woodrow Wilson, Franklin D. Roosevelt, Harry S. Truman**. New York: Twenty-First Century Books, 1996. 64p. $15.98. ISBN 0-8050-3403-X. (Presidents Who Dared). 5-8

The text covers the childhood, educations, and prepresidential careers of Woodrow Wilson, Franklin D. Roosevelt, and Harry Truman. It then describes their administrations by noting their goals and their achievements in office. The inclusion of each man's strengths and weaknesses lends objectivity to the presentation. Wilson helped create the Federal Trade Commission and the Federal Reserve System. Roosevelt used the powers of the government to help lessen the horror of the Depression. Truman used the first atomic weapon while also supporting the Marshall Plan and the United States' involvement in Korea under the aegis of the United Nations. Bibliography, Further Reading, Notes, and Index.

1395. Lipsyte, Robert. **Jim Thorpe: Twentieth-Century Jock**. New York: HarperCollins, 1993. 103p. $13.89. ISBN 0-06-022988-8. 3-7

An American Indian, Jim Thorpe (1887-1953) surprised everyone with his athletic ability. He won two gold medals at the 1912 Olympics, but the next year someone reported that he had played professional baseball during the previous summer, so the medals were stripped from him. He won fairly, and many think that he was made a scapegoat for something that others also did. The National Football League Most Valuable Player award bears his name. Further Reading and Index.

1396. Lipsyte, Robert. **Joe Louis: A Champ for All America**. New York: HarperCollins, 1994. 64p. $13.89. ISBN 0-06-023410-5. (Superstar Lineup). 4-9

In this fictional biography, when Joe Louis (1914-1981) beat the German Max Schmeling on the eve of World War II after losing to him in 1936, he became a symbol of American power, although whites continued to discriminate against him in his home country. Louis's own hero was Jack Johnson, a Black boxer who won the heavyweight championship in 1908. When Louis served in the Armed Forces, he met and helped Jackie Robinson. In his own life, his mother, stepfather, and boxing trainer served as strong reminders that he must do the best that he could in order to represent his race well. For Further Reading and Index.

1397. Litowinsky, Olga. **The High Voyage: The Final Crossing of Christopher Columbus**. New York: Delacorte, 1991. 147p. $14.95. ISBN 0-385-30304-1. 5-8

In 1502, Fernando, 13, joins his father on another voyage trying to find India. They reach Jamaica instead. Several crew members mutiny against Columbus, but the others defeat them. Columbus eventually gets a ship to sail back to Spain. Fernando decides that he wants to stay in Spain rather than explore the world.

1398. Littlefield, Holly. **Fire at the Triangle Factory**. Mary O'Keefe Young, illustrator. Minneapolis, MN: Carolrhoda, 1996. 48p. $11.96. ISBN 0-87614-868-2. (On My Own History). K-3

On March 25, 1911, while Minnie and Tessa, 14, work in the Triangle Shirtwaist factory in New York City, the building catches fire. Minnie helps Tessa get out of the room, and Tessa finds water to pour on Minnie's dress when flames shoot out of the hemline. With all other exits blocked, they climb on the roof, and someone on the next building gets a ladder for them to crawl across and escape the quickly burning building. After the fire, when Minnie's Jewish father realizes that Tessa, an Italian Catholic, is a real friend, he helps her home because she has a sprained ankle. Afterword.

1399. Littlesugar, Amy. **The Spinner's Daughter**. Robert M. Quackenbush, illustrator. New York: Pippin, 1994. 30p. $14.95. ISBN 0-945912-22-6. K-3

Elspeth Allen, a Puritan living in the American colonies during the seventeenth century, wants to play ball with an Indian nearby, but her widowed mother tells her that she cannot take time to indulge herself. When the Indian boy makes Elspeth a cornhusk doll, she shows it to the village children, and they want one. She makes dolls for them, and the elders in the town decide that she must wear a sign to show her disobedience. A judge coming through town declares that her sign should read "Child."

1400. Livingston, Myra Cohn. **Abraham Lincoln: A Man for All the People: A Ballad**. Samuel Byrd, illustrator. New York: Holiday House, 1993. 32p. $15.95. ISBN 0-8234-1049-8. K-3

A ballad about Lincoln's life (1809-1865) gives some of the details and some of the famous lines with which people identify him. The beginning and ending quatrains are the same, "A man for all the people/A man who stood up tall/Abe Lincoln spoke of justice/And liberty for all." Two-page spreads have each of 18 stanzas with paintings balancing the text.

1401. Livingston, Myra Cohn. **Keep On Singing: A Ballad of Marian Anderson**. Samuel Byrd, illustrator. New York: Holiday House, 1994. Unpaged. $15.95. ISBN 0-8234-1098-6. 1-4

Marian Anderson's voice, the kind heard only once every 100 years according to one critic, was inside a Black skin; therefore, America denied her the respect and admiration she deserved until Eleanor Roosevelt declared that she would sing at the Lincoln Memorial. This story, in ballad form, recounts some of the situations Anderson (1897-1993) had to overcome before singing to the American public when Europe regaled her openly. She loved spirituals because they showed "simplicity and faith, humility and hope." She became the first Black woman to sing at the Metropolitan Opera house in 1955. Author's Notes.

1402. Lizon, Karen Helene. **Colonial Holidays and Entertainment**. New York: Franklin Watts, 1993. 111p. $19.60. ISBN 0-531-12546-7. (Colonial America). 4-6

The text looks at different holidays in America before 1775. It focuses on sports and recreation, games and toys, social amusements, entertainment and pastimes, and early American observances such as funerals, weddings, "raising days," and working bees. Illustrations and reproductions highlight the text. Appendix, Glossary, Bibliography, For Further Reading, and Index.

1403. Lobel, Arnold, author/illustrator. **On the Day Peter Stuyvesant Sailed into Town**. New York: HarperCollins, 1987. 48p. $4.95pa. ISBN 0-06-443144-4pa. K-3

In 1647, when Peter Stuyvesant arrives in New Amsterdam, he finds mud and garbage. The houses need repair, and animals roam free. As governor, he is furious, and he finally yells that the town must be cleaned immediately. The city slowly improves, but the inhabitants have no idea that the place will one day be New York City. *Christopher Award*.

1404. Lodge, Sally. **The Cheyenne**. Katherine Ace, illustrator. Vero Beach, FL: Rourke, 1992. 31p. $11.95. ISBN 0-86625-387-4. (Native American People). 4-6

In the nineteenth century, westward expansion by white pioneers decimated the lands of the Cheyenne and destroyed the buffalo, their main source of sustenance, housing, and clothing. Smallpox was a major factor in the tribe's destruction as well. The text presents the history, customs, and present-day status of this tribe. Chronology and Index.

1405. Lodge, Sally. **The Comanche**. Katherine Ace, illustrator. Vero Beach, FL: Rourke, 1992. 31p. $11.95. ISBN 0-86625-390-4. (Native American People). 4-6

The text recounts the origins and daily activities of the Comanche, who lived on the Plains and ranged across the Southwest during the eighteenth century. They were excellent horsemen and warriors who kept their territory unsafe for white settlers for as long as they could. They probably introduced peyote to the Plains tribes in their rituals. Photographs and maps highlight the text. Chronology and Index.

1406. Loewen, Nancy. **Elvis**. Vero Beach, FL: Rourke, 1989. 111p. $18.60. ISBN 0-86592-606-9. 5 up

One of the best-known entertainers in the twentieth century was Elvis Presley (1935-1977). The text looks at his life and career from his early years in Mississippi to his unexpected death. Index.

1407. Looby, Chris. **Benjamin Franklin**. New York: Chelsea House, 1990. 112p. $18.95. ISBN 1-55546-808-X. (World Leaders Past and Present). 5 up

Benjamin Franklin (1706-1790) is reported to have said to the signers of the Declaration of Independence in July 1776 that "Gentlemen, we must now all hang together, or we shall most assuredly hang separately." His wit and wisdom as a self-made man permeated all aspects of his life as statesman, revolutionary, publisher, philanthropist, and inventor. His many professions prepared him to represent the new government abroad. Photographs and reproductions enhance the text. Chronology, Further Reading, and Index.

1408. Lorbiecki, Marybeth. **Of Things Natural, Wild, and Free**. Kerry Maguire, illustrator. Minneapolis, MN: Carolrhoda, 1993. 64p. $17.50. ISBN 0-87614-797-X. (Creative Minds). 3-6

Aldo Leopold (1886-1948) always looked for adventure as a child living on the banks of the Mississippi River. He went to the Northeast to study at Lawrenceville Prep School and Yale before becoming a forester, a conservation pioneer, and a wildlife scientist. He convinced people that they had to protect the patches of wilderness for the future. Bibliography.

1409. Lord, Athena. **The Luck of Z.A.P. and Zoe**. Jean Jenkins, illustrator. New York: Macmillan, 1987. 154p. $13.95. ISBN 0-02-759560-9. 4-7

In 1940, Zach, 12, and his family move to Albany, New York, where many Greek Americans live. He has adventures with his little sister Zoe and becomes friends with a Jewish boy who lived in Austria and Cuba before coming to America. When his mother hears that Axis forces have bombed her Greek hometown, she worries about the people she knows. But the family has Greek friends who support them.

1410. Lord, Athena. **Today's Special: Z.A.P. and Zoe**. Jean Jenkins, illustrator. New York: Macmillan, 1984. 150p. $13.95. ISBN 0-02-761440-9. 4-7

Zach, 11, has to babysit for his sister in 1939 while his parents work in their Greek family restaurant. Because he teaches Zoe her letters and numbers, she is prepared to enter kindergarten at an earlier age. She also learns to take more responsibility for herself.

1411. Lord, Athena. **Z.A.P., Zoe, & the Musketeers**. New York: Macmillan, 1992. 157p. $13.95. ISBN 0-02-759561-7. 4-7

In 1941, Zach, 13, and his sister Zoe, Greek Americans, enjoy their friends in Albany, New York. But as Zach's body begins to change, he begins to worry about himself. He realizes that the changes have nothing to do with his tonsillectomy.

1412. Lord, Bette Bao. **In the Year of the Boar and Jackie Robinson**. New York: Trophy, 1986. 176p. $4.50pa. ISBN 0-06-440175-8pa. 3-7

In 1947, Bandit Wong immigrates to America from China. She tries to assimilate into the idea of the Chinese American Shirley Temple Wong but faces hostility from her classmates. When she makes friends with the toughest girl in class, she begins playing in stickball games and becomes a loyal fan of the Brooklyn Dodgers. *American Library Association Notable Books for Children*, *School Library Journal Best Book*, *Notable Children's Trade Books in the Field of Social Studies*, *New York Public Library's Children's Books*, and *Jefferson Cup Award*.

1413. Love, D. Anne. **Bess's Log Cabin Quilt**. Ronald Himler, illustrator. New York: Holiday House, 1995. 123p. $14.95. ISBN 0-8234-1178-8. 3-5

Bess, 10, decides to enter her log cabin quilt in the local fair's competition for a huge $25 entry fee in hopes that she can eventually win hundreds to help pay the family's bills. Her father is missing on the Oregon Trail, her mother has swamp fever, and the moneylender has threatened to evict them. Mama agrees to let her enter, and with the help of a neighbor she gets second prize. All resolves positively even though Indians threaten them at one point.

1414. Lowe, Felix C. **John Ross**. Patrick Soper, illustrator. Austin, TX: Raintree/Steck-Vaughn, 1993. 32p. $19.97; $4.99pa. ISBN 0-8172-3407-1; 0-8114-4093-1pa. (Native American Stories). 3-5

John Ross (1790-1866) was a Cherokee chief. He was the leader of his people who unsuccessfully tried to keep them in Georgia when the government forced them to march along the Trail of Tears to Oklahoma in 1838-1839. The government had found gold in Georgia in 1829 and determined that the Cherokee could not have it by enacting the Indian Removal Act. History.

1415. Lowell, Susan. **I Am Lavinia Cumming**. Paul Mirocha, illustrator. Minneapolis, MN: Milkweed Press, 1993. 198p. $14.95. ISBN 0-915943-39-5. 5-7

Lavinia, 10, loves the Bosque Ranch in Arizona Territory where she lives with her parents, five brothers, and pony. Her mother dies, and she has to go to California in 1905 to live with her aunt. Her aunt has a telephone and oak floors and an annoying eight-year-old child, Aggie. Lavinia has to deal with a new school, homesickness, Aggie, and the earthquake that nearly demolishes the city. But her aunt helps her see that life outside the ranch also has its value, and Lavinia decides to pursue her schooling.

1416. Lowery, Linda. **Wilma Mankiller**. Janice Lee Porter, illustrator. Minneapolis, MN: Carolrhoda, 1996. 56p. $11.96. ISBN 0-87614-880-1. (On My Own Biography). K-3

When Wilma Mankiller's family moved from Oklahoma to San Francisco when she was 11, she knew that she would return, but she needed the strength of her Cherokee heritage to help her succeed during the intervening years. She became the chief of the Cherokee in 1985, but she decided to relinquish her job in 1995. Important Dates.

1417. Lubetkin, Wendy. **George Marshall**. New York: Chelsea House, 1989. 112p. $18.95. ISBN 1-55546-843-8. (World Leaders Past and Present). 5 up

General George C. Marshall (1880-1959) distinguished himself under General Pershing in Europe during World War I. On the day that Nazi Germany invaded Poland, he became the U.S. Army chief of staff. After the Allies won, he became the Secretary of State. He introduced a plan for the reconstruction of Europe after the war that offered relief to the war-torn nations. For the Marshall Plan he received the Nobel Peace Prize in 1953, the first military man to do so. Photographs enhance the text. Chronology, Further Reading, and Index.

1418. Lucas, Eileen. **The Cherokees: People of the Southeast**. Brookfield, CT: Millbrook Press, 1993. 64p. $15.90. ISBN 1-56294-312-X. (Native Americans). 5-8

Four chapters of the text cover the origins of the Cherokee, their culture, their interaction with white settlers, and the current status of the Cherokee Nation. Photographs and maps enhance the text. Bibliography, Chronology, Glossary, and Index.

1419. Lucas, Eileen. **Civil Rights: The Long Struggle**. Springfield, NJ: Enslow, 1996. 112p. $18.95. ISBN 0-89490-729-8. 5-8

The text covers the long history of civil rights beginning with the first 10 amendments to the Constitution, the abolition of slavery, the desegregation of the South, and the most recent developments such as the Million Man March. It also looks at the activities of militias through this time. Photographs, Further Reading, Glossary, and Index.

1420. Luce, Willard, and Celia. **Jim Bridger: Man of the Mountains**. New York: Chelsea House, 1991. 80p. $14.95. ISBN 0-7910-1454-1. (Discovery Biography). 3-6

Jim Bridger (1804-1881) lived a life as a trapper after growing up in Virginia. He discovered the Great Salt Lake in Utah, thinking at first that it was the Pacific Ocean. He knew Indians well and sensed which men to trust and which ones would betray him. He finally married the daughter of a chief but, after her death, moved his family back to civilization. But he missed the mountains and returned after his children were grown to live there the remainder of his life.

1421. Lunn, Janet. **One Hundred Shining Candles**. Lindsay Grater, illustrator. New York: Scribner's, 1991. 32p. $12.95. ISBN 0-684-19280-2. 2-4

Lucy, 10, wants to make her family's 1800 Christmas memorable even though they have no money for presents. Her schoolmaster in Upper Canada tells about homes lit with many candles to brighten the season. Lucy and her young brother make five candles. Her parents are as pleased with her gift as she had hoped they would be.

1422. Lydon, Kerry Raines. **A Birthday for Blue**. Michael Hays, illustrator. Niles, IL: Albert Whitman, 1989. 32p. $14.95. ISBN 0-8075-0774-1. K-3

Blue and his family are traveling on the Cumberland Road toward Illinois on his seventh birthday. Because the family has no gift for him, his father plants trees in his honor. They carve Blue's name and his age in a big tree before they leave.

1423. Lynn, Elizabeth A. **Babe Didrikson Zaharias**. New York: Chelsea House, 1988. 108p. $18.95. ISBN 1-55546-684-2. (American Women of Achievement). 5 up

Babe Didrikson Zaharias (1911-1956) had an amazing athletic career, starring in basketball, baseball, swimming, tennis, and volleyball in high school. At the 1932 Olympics, she won three track and field medals. Then she added boxing, football, and hockey to her games as a professional before becoming a professional golfer. Dissatisfied with treatment given to women golfers, she helped establish the Ladies Professional Golf Association before succumbing to cancer. Some of her records remain unequaled. Photographs enhance the text. Chronology, Further Reading, and Index.

1424. Lyon, George Ella. **Borrowed Children**. New York: Orchard, 1988. 154p. $12.95. ISBN 0-532-08351-9. 5-7

Amanda, 12, the oldest in a Kentucky family suffering during the Depression, quits school to help her mother recover from a difficult childbirth. For all her work, she gets a vacation with her grandparents in Memphis. Although the Memphis family members have few worries, Mandy observes the unhappy marriage of her alcoholic aunt and appreciates her own home, sparse as it is, much more. *Golden Kite Award* and *School Library Journal Best Book*.

1425. Lyon, George Ella. **Cecil's Story**. Peter Catalanotto, illustrator. New York: Orchard, 1991. 32p. $14.95. ISBN 0-531-05912-X. K-3

Cecil's father goes to fight in the Civil War, and Cecil becomes concerned about his mother leaving to get his father if he becomes wounded. When his father returns home missing an arm, Cecil still knows that he is his dad.

1426. Lyon, George Ella. **Here and Then**. New York: Orchard, 1994. 114p. $14.95. ISBN 0-531-06866-8. 5-7

After Abby, 12, returns from a Civil War reenactment with her parents, she finds that in the journal in which she writes about her character Eliza, she "becomes" Eliza. Abby searches for supplies to help the wounded that Eliza Hoskins, 40, needed as the "Angel of Camp Robinson." In an interesting twist, Abby, with the help of her practical friend Harper, delivers them to 1861.

1427. Lyon, George Ella. **Red Rover, Red Rover**. New York: Jackson, Franklin Watts, 1989. 131p. $12.95. ISBN 0-531-05832-8. 6-9

In the early 1960s, Sumi, 12, reviews the year past when she has had to cope with two losses—the death of her grandfather and the departure of her favorite older brother for music school. She also starts her menstrual period; enjoys the music of Peter, Paul, and Mary; and gets a crush on her teacher. She admits that she has a hard time getting used to new things.

1428. Lyons, Mary E. **Deep Blues: Bill Traylor, Self-Taught Artist**. New York: Scribner's, 1994. 42p. $15.95. ISBN 0-684-19458-9. (African-American Artists and Artisans). 3-6

Born into slavery in 1856, Bill Traylor became a self-taught artist in the Alabama Black Belt. By the time he died c. 1948, he had created more than 1,200 pieces of art. In them were complexities that seemed beyond a man who did not learn how to write his name until late in his life. When Charles Shannon saw Traylor's drawings, he wanted to exhibit him, and he did in 1940. World War II curtailed the chance for more than one other exhibition while Traylor still lived. After his death, Shannon began cataloging the work, and today Traylor has become recognized as a major African American artist. Selected Sources and Index.

1429. Lyons, Mary E. **Master of Mahogany: Tom Day, Free Black Cabinetmaker**. New York: Scribner's, 1994. 42p. $15.95. ISBN 0-684-19675-1. (African-American Artists and Artisans). 3-5

Tom Day, born in Halifax County, Virginia, in 1801, was a free Black because his mother was a Native American, not a slave. Educated and apprenticed, he opened his own furniture store in Milton, North Carolina. He became wealthy, with white apprentices, and as a free Black, he owned two slaves of his own. Because the law for free Blacks changed during the 1830s, Day had to send his children to Massachusetts for schooling, and he had problems with his business. He probably died in 1860 or 1861, but no record exists because the Civil War occupied most newspapers. His place of business from 1848 to 1858, Yellow Tavern, has become a historic landmark. Afterword, Glossary, and Selected Sources.

1430. Lyons, Mary E. **Painting Dreams: Minnie Evans, Visionary Artist**. Boston: Houghton Mifflin, 1996. 47p. $14.95. ISBN 0-395-72032-X. 4-8

Minnie Evans (b. 1892) had tormenting visions. In her middle age, she began to paint with scrap materials using her imagination as a subject source for her pictures. Her family thought she was mentally unstable, and although the individual members accepted her need to paint, no one thought much of the results. In the 1960s, a photographer saw her work and helped her exhibit it. Interviews with people who knew the artist and reproductions of her work highlight the text. Index.

1431. Lyons, Mary E. **Starting Home: The Story of Horace Pippin, Painter**. New York: Scribner's, 1993. 42p. $14.95. ISBN 0-684-19534-8. (African-American Artists and Artisans). 4-7

Horace Pippin (1885-1946) once penciled pictures on a piece of cloth that he sold to a woman. She returned to tell him that they disappeared when she washed it. He had other memories of trying to work because each piece of art revealed a piece of his life. A disabling wound in World War I did not keep him from painting, especially the horrors he saw on the battlefield, and he continued to paint those memories as well as others. Index.

1432.   Lyons, Mary E. **Stitching Stars: The Story Quilts of Harriet Powers**. New York: Scribner's, 1993. 42p. $15.95. ISBN 0-684-19576-3. (African-American Artists and Artisans). 3-6

In 1886, Harriet Powers (d. 1911) was 49, living in Athens, Georgia. Mother of 11 children, she began a quilt that was to be a diary of her spiritual life. She used 299 pieces of appliquéd cloth, with each panel a scene from the Bible. The quilt is now on display in the Smithsonian. Twelve years later, she finished a second story-quilt that showed biblical incidents and local folktales. No one is certain where she learned to make the figures she used on the quilts, but the tradition has been traced back to Africa, where men made funeral quilts for many years. Selected Sources and Index.

M

1433.   MacBride, Roger Lea. **In the Land of the Big Red Apple**. David Gilleece, illustrator. New York: HarperCollins, 1995. 338p. $14.89. $4.50pa. ISBN 0-06-024964-1; 0-06-440574-5pa. (Little House: The Rocky Ridge Years). 3-6

The third in the series. Rose, eight, adjusts to life in the Ozarks in 1895 with her parents, Almanzo and Laura Ingalls Wilder. Rose battles an ice storm, helps with the construction of the family's new farmhouse, returns to school, and celebrates their first Christmas in their new home. But she also finds that others do not have as much as she has, and she has to decide if she wants to share.

1434.   MacBride, Roger Lea. **Little Farm in the Ozarks**. David Gilleece, illustrator. New York: HarperCollins, 1994. 286p. $15.95; $4.05pa. ISBN 0-06-024245-0; 0-06-440510-9pa. (Little House: The Rocky Ridge Years). 3-6

In 1894, Rose's family moves from the drought of DeSmet, South Dakota, to Mansfield, Missouri. They cross the Missouri River in a dust storm, adopt a dog found on the trail, and locate a missing $100 bill in time to purchase their house. This is the second in the series about Rose and her parents, Almanzo and Laura Ingalls Wilder.

1435.   MacBride, Roger Lea. **Little House on Rocky Ridge**. David Gilleece, illustrator. New York: HarperCollins, 1993. 353p. $15.95; $3.95pa. (Rocky Ridge Years). ISBN 0-06-020842-2; 0-06-440478-1pa. 3-7

Rose, Laura Ingalls Wilder's daughter, begins her story in 1894, when she is seven. She and her parents take their possessions on a covered wagon to southern Missouri. The farm needs a barn, and when the neighbors gather from around the area to raise the barn, the family begins to feel like a part of the community.

1436.   MacBride, Roger Lea. **Little Town in the Ozarks**. David Gilleece, illustrator. New York: HarperCollins, 1996. 338p. $14.89. $4.50pa. ISBN 0-06-024977-3; 0-06-440580-Xpa. (Little House: The Rocky Ridge Years). 3-6

The fourth in the series. Rose, 10, and her family have to move to Mansfield in 1897 because they cannot keep their farm functioning during the economic slump. The noisy trains and the streets crowded with people baffle her. She has to adjust to this new experience, but she makes friends at school who show her how to enjoy life in town.

1437.   Macht, Norman L. **Babe Ruth**. New York: Chelsea House, 1991. 64p. $14.95. ISBN 0-7910-1189-5. (Baseball Legends). 3-6

George Herman "Babe" Ruth (1895-1948) was perhaps the most talented and popular player in baseball history. He hit 714 home runs in his career, mainly playing for the New York Yankees. Bibliography and Index.

1438.   Macht, Norman L. **Lou Gehrig**. New York: Chelsea House, 1993. 64p. $14.95; $7.95pa. ISBN 0-7910-1176-3; 0-7910-1210-7pa. (Baseball Legends). 6-9

Lou Gehrig (1903-1941) played in 2,140 consecutive games, which earned him the nickname of "The Iron Man." He also hit 493 home runs. Black-and-white photographs complement the text. Chronology, Further Reading, and Index.

1439.   Macht, Norman L. **Sojourner Truth: Crusader for Civil Rights**. New York: Chelsea House, 1992. 79p. $14.95; $4.95pa. ISBN 0-7910-1754-0; 0-7910-1998-5pa. (Junior Black Americans of Achievement). 4-6

Sojourner Truth (d. 1883) was first promised freedom and then denied it, but she found out how to gain what was rightfully hers. She became an outspoken antislavery and women's rights activist in the United States. Her abolitionist voice helped slaves gain freedom.

1440.   MacKinnon, Christy, author/illustrator. **Silent Observer**. Washington, DC: Kendall Green, Gallaudet, 1993. 42p. $15.95. ISBN 1-56368-022-X. 2-4

Christy MacKinnon (1889-1981) became deaf when she was two years old as a result of whooping cough. She went to a special school in Halifax, Nova Scotia, and then received a scholarship to study at the Boston Museum of Fine Arts. She continued drawing and painting throughout her life, working both as a teacher and as a commercial artist. The text and complementary illustrations tell about her childhood of horse-drawn sleighs over frozen lakes, farming life, the one-room school, and her family.

1441. MacLachlan, Patricia. **Sarah, Plain and Tall**. New York: HarperCollins, 1985. 64p. ˝13.95. ISBN 0-06-024102-0. New York: Dell, 1986. $1.50pa. ISBN 0-440-84000-7pa. 3-6

Caleb and his sister Anna welcome Sarah, the woman who comes from Maine to meet their father and stay for a month to see if she likes the family. Because their own mother died at Caleb's birth, they have wanted a mother, and they are afraid that Sarah will not like them. Sarah loves the seacoast of Maine, but she tells them at the end of her visit that she will miss them more if she leaves. *Newbery Medal, Scott O'Dell Award, Golden Kite Award, Christopher Medal, Jefferson Cup Award, International Board of Books for Young People, American Library Association Notable Books for Children, Booklist Children's Editors' Choices, IRA Children's Choices, New York Times Outstanding Children's Books, NCTE Notable Trade Book in the Language Arts, Horn Book Fanfare Honor List*, and *School Library Journal Best Book*.

1442. MacLachlan, Patricia. **Skylark**. New York: HarperCollins, 1994. 80p. $12. ISBN 0-06-023328-1. 3-5

After a drought comes to the area where Anna and Caleb live with their father and Sarah, Sarah takes the children to her home in Maine in this sequel to *Sarah, Plain and Tall*. They fear that she will stay, but when their father comes to get them after rain finally dampens the prairie, she says she will make her home with them by writing her name in the dirt, a skylark that has "come to earth."

1443. MacLachlan, Patricia. **Three Names**. Alexander Pertzoff, illustrator. New York: HarperCollins, 1991. 32p. $14.95. ISBN 0-06-024035-0. K-4

A little boy at the end of the eighteenth century goes to school via prairie roads in a horse-drawn wagon, and his dog, Three Names, always goes with him. The boy plays games like fox-and-geese, hide-and-seek, and marbles. Although he enjoys the summer, he looks forward to school because he can see his friends. *School Library Journal Best Book*.

1444. MacMillan, Dianne. **Missions of the Los Angeles Area: San Gabriel Arcángel, San Fernando Rey de España, San Buenaventura**. Minneapolis, MN: Lerner, 1996. 80p. $14.96. ISBN 0-8225-1927-5. (California Missions). 4-6

In the 1700s, Spain sent Roman Catholic priests to establish missions and presidios (forts) along the coast of Baja California and other areas of New Spain (present-day Southwestern United States and Mexico). Spain wanted the Indians to accept the Spanish ways and become loyal subjects. San Gabriel Arcángel was the earliest mission in the Los Angeles area and suffered from poor crops and Indian rebellions, but became known as the Pride of Missions. San Bonaventure, called the Mission by the Sea, flourished while San Fernando Rey de España was one of the later settlements and eventually one of the largest in Alta California. Glossary, Chronology, and Index.

1445. MacMillan, Dianne M. **Chinese New Year**. Springfield, NJ: Enslow, 1994. 48p. $15.95. ISBN 0-89490-500-7. (Best Holiday Books). 2-5

Although Chinese people live all over the world, they observe their New Year as they have for thousands of years. The text presents the history of the holiday as well as the way it is currently celebrated. Glossary and Index.

1446. MacMillan, Dianne M. **Jewish Holidays in the Spring**. Springfield, NJ: Enslow, 1994. 48p. $15.95. ISBN 0-89490-503-1. (Best Holiday Books). 2-5

After a brief introduction to the Jewish religion, the text presents the history and current rituals of five Jewish holidays celebrated in the spring: Purim, Passover, Yom Ha-Azma'ut, Lag B'Omer, and Shavuot. Glossary and Index.

1447. MacMillan, Dianne M. **Ramadan and Id Al-Fitr**. Springfield, NJ: Enslow, 1994. 48p. $15.95. ISBN 0-89490-502-3. (Best Holiday Books). 2-5

A brief look at Muhammad's life, the pillars of Islam, and the role of the mosque in the life of Muslims precedes the discussion of Ramadan, the holiday during the ninth month of the Islamic lunar calendar. Ramadan ends on the first day of the tenth month with Id Al-Fitr, a celebration that lasts for a day. Glossary and Index.

1448. MacMillan, Dianne M. **Tet: Vietnamese New Year**. Springfield, NJ: Enslow, 1994. 48p. $15.95. ISBN 0-89490-501-5. (Best Holiday Books). 2-5

For the Vietnamese, Tet is like a birthday, Thanksgiving, Christmas, and New Year's all in one holiday that lasts for three days. It begins on the first day of the new lunar year, as it has for centuries. The text traces its history and the way it is currently celebrated. Glossary and Index.

1449. Macy, Sue. **A Whole New Ballgame: The Story of the All-American Girls Professional Baseball League**. New York: Henry Holt, 1993. 140p. $14.95. ISBN 0-8050-1942-1. 5-9

The All-American Girls Professional Baseball League played during World War II, but interest declined when the men and normality returned in the early 1950s. The text looks at some tense games and reconstructs them play-by-play while showing statistics for the best players. It notes that women players faced both encouragement and prejudice in their roles and tells what they did after the league play ended. Photographs, Notes, Further Reading, and Index.

1450. Maestro, Betsy. **Coming to America: The Story of Immigration**. Susannah Ryan, illustrator New York: Scholastic, 1996. Unpaged. $15.95. ISBN 0-590-44151-5. K-4

This history of immigration begins with the coming of Native Americans thousands of years ago across the Bering Strait land bridge. In more recent times, Annie Moore of Ireland, 15, was the first person to arrive at Ellis Island in New York. The United States has since adopted laws to control immigration either through Ellis Island or other venues. Additional inclusions in the text are commentary about the harsh treatment of Indians and the forced immigration of Africans. Chronology.

1451. Maestro, Betsy. **The Discovery of the Americas**. Giulio Maestro, illustrator. New York: Lothrop, Lee & Shepard, 1991. 48p. $16. ISBN 0-688-06837-5. 2-5

Beginning with the migration of peoples into North and South America more than 20,000 years ago, the text presents theories and facts about the settlements discovered on the two continents. Cultures and explorers before Columbus include the Mayans, possibly Saint Brendan from Ireland in the sixth century, the Vikings Bjarni Herjolfsson in the tenth century and Leif Ericsson in the eleventh, possibly Prince Madoc of Wales in the twelfth, and the Hopewell mound builders. Those explorers after Columbus mentioned in the text are Italians John Cabot in 1497 and Amerigo Vespucci in 1499, Vasco Nuñez de Balboa from Spain in 1513, and Ferdinand Magellan from Portugal in 1519. Additional Information, Some People of the Ancient and Early Americas, The Age of Discovery, How the Americas Got Their Name, and Other Interesting Voyages.

1452. Maestro, Betsy. **Exploration and Conquest: The Americas After Columbus: 1500-1620**. Giulio Maestro, illustrator. New York: Lothrop, Lee & Shepard, 1994. 48p. $16. ISBN 0-688-09267-5. 4-6

Noting that Spanish discovery of the New World ignored or exploited the people who had lived there for years, the authors describe the feats and effects of explorers after Columbus. Balboa (1513) saw the Pacific. Ponce de León (1513) found Florida. Magellan began his voyage around the world in 1519, while Cortés overpowered the Aztecs. Pizarro and deSoto (1532) conquered the Incas in Peru when Cabez de Vaca was in Texas. DeSoto went to Florida in 1539, and Coronado left Mexico in search of the Seven Cities of Gold in 1540. After Spain lost interest in America, European explorers arrived. John Cabot, Giovanni da Verrazano, Jacques Cartier, and John Hawkins (who began the slave trade) came. Britain's Francis Drake, Martin Frobisher, Humphrey Gilbert, John Davis, Walter Raleigh (at Roanoke), John White, and Virginia Dare added their names to history. After 1600, famous arrivals were John Smith, John Rolfe, Champlain, and Henry Hudson. Where these people arrived on shore, the indigenous cultures disappeared. Additional Information, Table of Dates, Some Other Explorers, North America—1500-1620, Contacts Between Native Americans and European Explorers, Impact of the European Arrival in the Americas, Native American Contributions to the World, and European Colonies and Settlements in the New World.

1453. Maestro, Betsy. **The Story of Money**. Giulio Maestro, illustrator. New York: Clarion, 1993. 48p. $15.95. ISBN 0-395-56242-2. 3-5

Among the objects used for money throughout history are tea leaves, shells, feathers, animal teeth, tobacco, blankets, barley, salt, feathers, and metal balls. When the Sumerians used metal bars of the same weight and stamped the amount on the bar, they invented the first known metal money. The text has other interesting information about money through the centuries and short chapters on American money, unusual money, and currencies of other countries. Illustrations complement the text.

1454. Maestro, Betsy. **The Story of the Statue of Liberty**. Giulio Maestro, illustrator. New York: Lothrop, Lee & Shepard, 1986. 40p. $16.93; $5.95pa. ISBN 0-688-05774-8; 0-688-08746-9pa. K-3

The building of the Statue of Liberty began in 1871 after Frédérick Auguste Bartholdi visited New York and saw Bedloe's Island in New York Harbor. He saw this place as the perfect setting for a statue that he would create for the French government to present as a gift to the United States on the occasion of its birthday. He completed it in 1884, and money raised by a New York newspaper funded the completion of the base so that it could be mounted when it arrived from France in 1885. Information About the Statue of Liberty.

1455. Maestro, Betsy. **The Voice of the People: American Democracy in Action**. Giulio Maestro, illustrator. New York: Lothrup, Lee & Shepard, 1996. 48p. $16. ISBN 0-688-10678-1. 3-6

The text looks at the election process and how Americans elect their Presidents. An appendix summarizes the Constitution and the amendments and contains a list of the Presidents.

1456. Magocsi, Paul R. **The Russian Americans**. New York: Chelsea House, 1995. 110p. $19.95 ISBN 0-7910-3367-8. (The Immigrant Experience). 6-9

Russians came to North America before the fur trade drew them to Alaska in the 1740s. In the early twentieth century, before World War I, more than 2 million Russians settled along the East Coast. After the Russian Revolution in 1917, a large wave of Russians came, and after World War II, another group arrived. Since the 1970s, a third group has come to America to escape the harsh life in the Soviet Union. Photographs and text tell their history and their contributions to American life. Further Reading and Index.

1457. Mahone-Lonesome, Robyn. **Charles R. Drew**. New York: Chelsea House, 1990. 109p. $18.95. ISBN 1-55546-581-1. (Black Americans of Achievement). 5 up

Charles Drew (1904-1950) became a surgeon and researcher. He helped establish blood banks and found out how to preserve blood plasma after studying its properties. Bibliography and Index.

1458. Malone, Mary. **Dorothea L. Dix: Hospital Founder**. New York: Chelsea Juniors, 1991. 80p. $14.95. ISBN 0-7910-1436-3. (Discovery Biography). 3-6

Always helping others, Dorothea Dix (1802-1887) opened a school when she was barely 14. When she began teaching a Sunday school class at a woman's prison, she saw the terrible treatment of the mentally ill. She then devoted herself to the improvement and enlargement of mental hospitals. She worked with people in almost every state and visited many hospitals. Her efforts helped the mentally ill gain better treatment.

1459. Malone, Mary. **Will Rogers: Cowboy Philosopher**. Springfield, NJ: Enslow, 1996. 128p. $17.95. ISBN 0-89490-695-X. (People to Know). 6-10

Will Rogers (1875-1935), part Cherokee, wanted to be a cowboy, but he became a performer in vaudeville, in Ziegfeld's Follies, and on his own. He twirled a lariat as he told jokes. He also traveled widely and wrote a newspaper column. When he died in an airplane crash, the nation mourned. Chronology, Further Reading, Notes, and Index.

1460. Manley, Joan B. **She Flew No Flags**. Boston: Houghton Mifflin, 1995. 269p. $15.95. ISBN 0-395-71130-4. 4-8

In 1944, Janet, 10, returns to the United States with her family after living in India for seven years. The ship travels through enemy waters with no lights or radio contact, zigzagging to avoid torpedoes. It has no name and flies no flag so that the enemy will not attack it. She and her brothers explore the ship, and she wonders about other people aboard. When she arrives in America, it is not what she expects, and she has to adjust not only to wartime but also to her new country.

1461. Manson, Ainslie. **A Dog Came, Too**. Anne Blades, illustrator. New York: Macmillan, 1993. 32p. $13.95. ISBN 0-689-50567-1. 1-5

In 1793, Alexander Mackensie travels across Canada to the Pacific Ocean, the first European to cross North America. Traveling with him is a dog that the group calls "Our Dog." Our Dog warns them of various dangers while walking alongside canoes with no room for him. After the group loses the dog near the Pacific Ocean, it finds him waiting, half-starved, when they return on the trip across the country. Mackensie writes about Our Dog in his journal.

1462. Marino, Jan. **The Day That Elvis Came to Town**. Boston: Little, Brown, 1991. 204p. $15.95. ISBN 0-316-54618-6. 5 up

In 1964, a new boarder, Mercedes Washington, moves into Wanda's family's boardinghouse. A jazz singer, Mercedes knows everyone, and Wanda, 13, is delighted that she even knows her hero, Elvis Presley. When Wanda hears that Elvis is coming to nearby Savannah, Georgia, for a concert, she expects Mercedes to take her backstage. Instead, Wanda finds out that Mercedes is not what she pretends to be. Most shocking of all, she is part Black, something that Wanda has difficulty accepting in her Southern home. *Bulletin Blue Ribbon Book* and *School Library Journal Best Book*.

1463. Marino, Jan. **Eighty-Eight Steps to September**. Boston: Little, Brown, 1989. 162p. $14.95. ISBN 0-316-54620-8. 3-6

In 1948, Amy, 11, enjoys racing her brother up the 88 steps on the way home from school. Robbie starts complaining about feeling tired, and Amy's parents take him to the hospital for various tests. Amy wants everyone to be home again so that they can have their summer cookouts. But Robbie goes into the hospital instead, and Amy waits for him to come home. Robbie has leukemia, and Amy refuses to believe that he will not come home to see the new puppy. When he dies, she responds honestly.

1464. Marino, Jan. **For the Love of Pete**. Boston: Little, Brown, 1993. 197p. $14.95. ISBN 0-316-54627-5. 5 up

Phoebe, nine in 1977, lives with her grandmother in Lubelle, Georgia, until the grandmother begins to grow senile and must go to a nursing home. Bertie, the cook; her brother Billy; and Bishopp, the English butler, take Phoebe north to meet her father whom she has never known except for the letter that she found in the attic. What she discovers is that her grandmother had never told him about her because her grandmother, once a famous opera singer, was afraid she would lose her granddaughter. The four have encounters on the journey including a racial incident and a restaurant owner's kindness.

1465. Markham, Lois. **Helen Keller**. New York: Franklin Watts, 1993. 64p. $12.90. ISBN 0-531-20101-X. (First Books). 5-8

Helen Keller (1880-1968) lived a remarkable life after Annie Sullivan taught her to talk, read, and write. Blind and deaf from disease at 18 months, the struggle Keller and her family endured was difficult. Sullivan helped her, and after Keller attended Radcliffe College, she continued to amaze people with what she was able to achieve. For Further Reading and Index.

1466. Markham, Lois. **Inventions That Changed Modern Life**. Austin, TX: Raintree/Steck-Vaughn, 1994. 48p. $15.96. ISBN 0-8114-4930-0. (20 Events Series). 6 up

In the late eighteenth century, James Watt's steam engine was produced for sale, Nicolas Appert began working with food preservation, and Eli Whitney designed interchangeable parts for guns. In the nineteenth century, Richard Trevithick and George Stephenson worked with locomotives. Photography began with experiments in France and England by Josiah Wedgwood, Joseph-Nicéphore Niepce, Louis Daguerre, and W. H. Fox Talbot. Cyrus McCormick began work on the combine harvester, and Isaac Singer patented the sewing machine begun by Elias Howe. Work on refrigeration, plastics, the telephone, electric light, and the automobile ended the century. In 1901, Marconi's radio worked. Also in the twentieth century, the airplane, assembly line, rocket, nuclear fission, television, computers, and lasers have changed the way people live. Each topic covers two pages. Glossary, Suggested Readings, and Index.

1467. Markham, Lois. **Theodore Roosevelt**. New York: Chelsea House, 1984. 112p. $18.95. ISBN 0-87754-553-7. (World Leaders Past and Present). 5 up

Theodore Roosevelt (1858-1919) was a sickly child, but he decided when he was 12 that he would become strong and active. He became a cowboy, a war hero, a cavalry officer, an author, a husband, a father, an explorer, a conservationist, a police commissioner, a governor, and a President. In all of his professions, he wanted Americans to have a "square deal." Photographs enhance the text. Chronology, Further Reading, and Index.

1468. Marko, Katherine. **Hang Out the Flag**. New York: Macmillan, 1992. 160p. $13.95. ISBN 0-02-762320-3. 4-6

In 1943, Leslie, 11, wants a welcome home present for her father, who has been training with the Seabees before he will go away to fight in the war. She settles on a huge flag painted on the town's water tower, and townspeople help create it. Discussions include rationing, victory gardens, and scrap drives. Leslie discovers that a local German man is a spy trying to sabotage the steel mill where Leslie's mother works.

1469. Marrin, Albert. **The Airman's War: World War II in the Sky**. New York: Atheneum, 1982. 213p. $11.95. ISBN 0-689-30907-4. 5 up

In 1939, German Reichsmarshal Hermann Goering boasted that no one would ever bomb Germany. He thought that Germany controlled the skies. He was wrong. The text looks at the importance of air power in World War II after many leaders of the American armed services had ignored the value of an air force in the early 1930s. Three men, "Hap" Arnold, "Tooey" Spaatz, and Ira Eaker, fulfilled "Billy" Mitchell's goal for a strong air fleet. The text tells their stories; the stories of pilots in the war flying bombers and fighter planes; the stories of the planes they flew, such as the B-17s, the Liberators, the Spitfires, and the Messerschmitts; and the battles they fought, some of them bombing raids that lasted around the clock. Photographs, Maps, Some More Books, and Index.

1470. Marrin, Albert. **Cowboys, Indians and Gunfighters: The Story of the Cattle Kingdom**. New York: Atheneum, 1993. 196p. $22.95. ISBN 0-689-31774-3. 6 up

The cattle industry began when horses arrived from Spain. Men used them to drive longhorn cattle across the plains where cowboys, Indians, and gunfighters merged in their dealings. The text looks at the drives; the different areas of the country; leisure time in town; and other facts about these people, who thrived through the reign of the cattle barons in the late nineteenth century. Photographs and reproductions enhance the text. Further Reading, Some More Books, and Index. *Bulletin Blue Ribbon Book.*

1471. Marrin, Albert. **1812: The War Nobody Won**. New York: Atheneum, 1985. 176p. $12.95. ISBN 0-689-31075-7. 5 up

While Dolley Madison was waiting for her husband to return from inspecting the U.S. troops defending Washington, she got word that the British were advancing. She had to flee the White House. She took George Washington's portrait and an original copy of the Declaration of Independence, but not her husband's bags. The British arrived and destroyed most of the buildings. The text looks at the events that led up to the "Second War of Independence" and the results. Neither country gained territory, but the United States proved to the British that it could retain what it had won in the Revolution. Some More Books and Index.

1472. Marrin, Albert. **Empires Lost and Won: The Spanish Heritage in the Southwest**. New York: Simon & Schuster, Atheneum, 1997. 224p. $19. ISBN 0-689-80414-8. 5 up

In 1540, Francisco Vásquez de Coronado left Mexico City to go north and claim the wealth of the fabled cities. Although only Pueblo villages awaited him, Santa Fe became their capital and the capital of New Mexico by 1610. The Texans voted for independence from Mexico in the nineteenth century, and the ensuing battle caused Mexico to lose all of its northern conquests. The text looks at the history of this process with accompanying photographs. Index.

1473. Marrin, Albert. **Plains Warrior: Chief Quanah Parker and the Comanches**. New York: Atheneum, 1996. 208p. $18. ISBN 0-689-80081-9. 6-9

Beginning with the Comanche kidnapping of Cynthia Ann Parker, Quanah Parker's mother, when she was nine, Marrin tells the story of the Comanches and their fight to preserve their land on the Great Plains during the nineteenth century. Without making the government all bad or the Comanches all good, Marrin uses eyewitness sources that describe many of the events during this time. Photographs, Notes, Further Reading, and Index.

1474. Marrin, Albert. **The Sea Rovers: Pirates, Privateers, and Buccaneers**. New York: Atheneum, 1984. 173p. $15.95. ISBN 0-689-31029-3. 5 up

In the early history of Europeans coming to American shores, pirates rode the seas in search of other peoples' wealth. English sea dogs such as Jack Hawkins and Francis Drake helped Queen Elizabeth declare war on Spain. Henry Morgan, Blackbeard, and Captain Kidd looked for booty on all the ships sailing the Atlantic. On the Mediterranean, the Barbary pirates patrolled the northern coast of Africa, but the U.S. Navy proved itself by thwarting their progress. The text looks at these pirates as well as women who also sailed under the pirate flag, the Jolly Roger. Some More Books and Index.

1475. Marrin, Albert. **The Secret Armies: Spies, Counterspies, and Saboteurs in World War II**. New York: Atheneum, 1985. 239p. $13.95. ISBN 0-689-31165-6. 5 up

Spies and counterspies worked in Europe during World War II under code names, such as Hedgehog, Zigzag, and Tricycle, to gather information behind German lines and pass misinformation to Nazi intelligence. People participated in the Resistance movement, in the Maquis in France, in the Netherlands, and in other conquered countries where people risked their lives. These undercover agents cracked the German secret code with the Enigma machine and helped ensure an Allied victory. The text looks at all aspects of these important participants in the war. Photographs, More Books, and Index.

1476. Marrin, Albert. **Struggle for a Continent: The French and Indian Wars: 1690-1760**. New York: Atheneum, 1987. 218p. $15.95. ISBN 0-689-31313-6. 5 up

On February 8, 1690, raiders entered the settlement of Schenectady on the Mohawk River in New York and murdered almost all of the members of 50 families. The Indians took the rest as prisoners. This massacre began the series of wars called King William's War, Queen Anne's War, King George's War, and the French and Indian War. However, they were all part of the same war, and Marrin presents them as he narrates this episode in American history. Some More Books and Index.

1477. Marrin, Albert. **Virginia's General: Robert E. Lee and the Civil War**. New York: Atheneum, 1994. 218p. $19.95. ISBN 0-689-31838-3. 6 up

Robert E. Lee (1807-1870) attended West Point because it was free. His father, "Light-Horse Harry," Revolutionary War hero, had abandoned the family and left them with no money. Robert E. Lee, admired for his kindness, generosity, and courtesy, was also loyal to his family and to his own state of Virginia, even though he disliked slavery and opposed secession. His victory at Chancellorsville still intrigues military strategists with its masterful planning. Even as the loser at the end of the Civil War, however, he kept his dignity. Notes, Some More Books, and Index. *American Library Association Best Books for Young Adults*.

1478. Marsh, Joan. **Martha Washington**. New York: Franklin Watts, 1993. 64p. $19.90. ISBN 0-531-20145-7. (First Books). 4-6

Martha Washington (1731-1802) grew up in a time when women were not expected or encouraged to go to school. Her job was to become a good wife and mother. Eight years after she married, she had two children and lost a husband. She inherited a lot of money, and at 26 was an attractive widow. She soon met George Washington, who had money of his own, and the two married. She moved from her home, the White House, to Washington's Mount Vernon. She supported him in his career as general in the American Revolution and then as President. For Further Reading and Index.

1479. Marston, Hope Irvin. **Isaac Johnson: From Slave to Stonecutter**. Maria Magdalena Brown, illustrator. New York: Cobblehill, Dutton, 1995. 80p. $14.99. ISBN 0-525-65165-9. 4-7

When Isaac Johnson was seven, a sheriff came to the family farm while his father was away and took him, his mother, and brothers away and sold them into slavery. After the Civil War began, Johnson joined the Union army, and when the war ended, he went to Canada. There he became an accomplished stonecutter, with churches, bridges, and other structures to his credit. He wrote the story of his slave days, *Slavery Days in Old Kentucky*, to earn money for his children to attend college. The text, based on this book, also includes conversations with his descendants. Important Dates, For Further Reading, and Index.

1480. Martin, C. L. G. **Day of Darkness, Night of Light**. Victoria M. Williams, illustrator. Minneapolis, MN: Gemstone, 1989. 46p. $10.95. ISBN 0-87518-357-3. (It Really Happened!). 2-4

In 1871, Daniel, 13, helps the people in Menominee, Michigan, save the town from fires that sweep through the Great Lakes. When the women take refuge on a rescue ship, Daniel watches the boy who bullied him for his cowardice caught for being dressed as a woman and trying to get on the ship.

1481. Martin, Jacqueline Briggs. **Grandmother Bryant's Pocket**. Petra Mathers, illustrator. Boston: Houghton Mifflin, 1996. 48p. $14.95. ISBN 0-395-68984-8. K-4

Sarah, eight in 1787, enjoys playing on her family's Maine farm with her dog, but Patches dies in a fire that also burns down the barn. Sarah becomes distraught, and her parents send her to stay with her grandmother. She likes her grandmother's pocket, the bag that she wears on her belt where she keeps her herbs. After Sarah's grandmother gives her the pocket and a cat, Sarah is calmed by the smell of the rosemary and the cat's purrs. *School Library Journal Best Book*.

1482. Martin, Katherine. **Night Riding**. New York: Knopf, 1989. 197p. $12.95. ISBN 0-679-90064-0. 5-8

Prin's father has to go to the hospital for tuberculosis treatment in 1958 when she is 11. At the same time, new neighbors move in next door to their Tennessee home. Prin does not understand why her mother will not let her visit the neighbors, and her sister tells her that the girl is pregnant without being married. The girl's father makes overtures to Prin one night when she is out riding her horse, and she realizes that the father has abused his own daughter and would do the same to her.

1483. Martinello, Marian L., and Samuel P. Nesmith. **With Domingo Leal in San Antonio 1734**. San Antonio, TX: University of Texas Institute of Texas Culture, 1980. 78p. $6.95. ISBN 0-933164-40-8pa. 5-8

When he becomes bored with watching the cattle in 1734, Domingo, 10, happily takes an adze to the mission for repair. He loiters at the blacksmiths and finally rides his horse toward home in the company of a soldier. On the way, he sees enemy Indians stopping by the river for their horses to drink. He realizes that everyone must do boring chores in order to look after themselves and their animals.

1484. Marvin, Isabel R. **A Bride for Anna's Papa**. Minneapolis, MN: Milkweed Press, 1994. 136p. $6.95pa. ISBN 0-915943-93-Xpa. 5-7

At 13 in 1907, Anna Kallio has to manage the house and look after her nine-year-old brother and her father, who works in the dangerous Minnesota iron mines. Now that her mother is dead, she realizes that her father is very lonely, so she and her brother try to arrange a marriage for him, even with a mail-order bride from Finland. Although she wants her father to be happy, she still has to deal with her feelings about having someone else, someone unexpected, running the household.

1485. Marzollo, Jean. **Happy Birthday, Martin Luther King**. J. Brian Pinkney, illustrator. New York: Scholastic, 1993. Unpaged. $14.95. ISBN 0-590-44065-9. K-2

The national holiday on January 15 celebrates the birthday of Martin Luther King, Jr. (1929-1968), the man who advocated a peaceful solution to civil rights problems. The text looks at his life and comments that at his death, his body was put on a farm cart and pulled slowly through Atlanta by two mules because he had done so much to help the poor.

1486.   Marzollo, Jean. **My First Book of Biographies: Great Men and Women Every Child Should Know**. Irene Trivas, illustrator. New York: Cartwheel, Scholastic, 1994. 80p. $14.95. ISBN 0-590-45014-X. 2-3

The text highlights the reasons for fame in the lives of the 45 people presented. The capsule biographies cover two columns of one page opposite a portrait of the person. Included here are Neil Armstrong and Edwin Aldrin, Jr. (both 1930-), Rachel Carson (1907-1964), George Washington Carver (1864-1943), Cesar Chavez (1927-1993), Winston Churchill (1874-1965), Cleopatra (69-30 BC), Christopher Columbus (1451-1506), Marie Curie (1867-1934), Pierre Curie (1859-1906), Walt Disney (1901-1966), Amelia Earhart (1897-1937), Thomas Alva Edison (1847-1931), Albert Einstein (1879-1955), Elizabeth I (1533-1603), Duke Ellington (1899-1974), Benjamin Franklin (1706-1790), Mohandas Gandhi (1869-1948), Katsushika Hokusai (1760-1849), Thomas Jefferson (1743-1826), Helen Keller (1880-1968), Anne Sullivan (1866-1936), Martin Luther King, Jr. (1929-1968), Rosa Parks (1913-), Leonardo da Vinci (1452-1519), Abraham Lincoln (1809-1865), Yo-Yo Ma (1955-), Gabriela Mistral (1889-1957), Wolfgang Amadeus Mozart (1756-1791), Jesse Owens (1913-1980), Peter the Great (1672-1725), Beatrix Potter (1866-1943), Eleanor Roosevelt (1884-1962), Franklin Roosevelt (1882-1945), Sequoyah (c. 1760-1843), William Shakespeare (1564-1616), Elizabeth Cady Stanton (1815-1902), Lucretia Mott (1793-1880), Susan B. Anthony (1820-1906), Maria Tallchief (1925-); George Balanchine (1904-1983), Harriet Tubman (1820-1913), Frederick Douglass (1818-1895), George Washington (1732-1799), and Babe Didrikson Zaharias (1914-1956).

1487.   Mason, Antony. **Peary and Amundsen: Race to the Poles**. Austin, TX: Raintree/Steck-Vaughn. 1995. 46p. $15.96. ISBN 0-8114-3977-1. (Beyond the Horizons). 5-8

Robert Peary (1856-1920) tried to reach the North Pole first, and Roald Amundsen (1872-1928) raced for the South Pole. Peary tried for the North Pole in 1898 and 1899, when he lost several toes. He made further expeditions in 1902 and 1906 before reaching it in 1909. Another American, however, claimed to have gotten to it in 1908, having taken a year to return by dogsled. Amundsen reached the South Pole two weeks before Robert Scott, who arrived crestfallen to find that someone had already been there. He nor his companions survived, only his diary and photographs. The text also includes historical background, information about the people who live in the Arctic region, and what happened as a result of these expeditions. Photographs, paintings, drawings, and maps augment the text. Glossary, Further Reading, and Index.

1488.   Maurer, Richard. **Airborne: The Search for the Secret of Flight**. New York: Aladdin, 1990. 48p. $5.95pa. ISBN 0-671-69423-5pa. (NOVA). 5-8

A history of flight, the text begins with experiments and designs for various types of aircraft, gliders, and hot-air balloons from the 1600s. It continues through the history of experimentation until the Wright brothers flew their heavier-than-air craft in 1903. Drawings, photographs, and diagrams illustrate the principles of flight that had to be understood before flying became possible. When such terms as *aileron, elevator, rudder,* and *throttle* became attached to the principles, human flight began. Index.

1489.   Mayberry, Jodine. **Business Leaders Who Built Financial Empires**. Austin, TX: Raintree/Steck-Vaughn, 1995. 48p. $24.26. ISBN 0-8114-4934-3. (20 Events Series). 5-8

Two-page spreads with accompanying photographs and drawings give capsule biographies of Levi Strauss (1829?-1902), Andrew Carnegie (1835-1919), John D. Rockefeller (1839-1937), W. K. Kellogg (1860-1951), Richard Sears (1863-1914), William Randolph Hearst (1863-1951), Madame C. J. Walker (1867-1919), A. P. Giannini (1870-1949), Alfred Fuller (1885-1973), David Sarnoff (1891-1971), Roy Herbert Thomson (1894-1976), Walt Disney (1901-1966), Ray Kroc (1902-1984), Walter Annenberg (b. 1908), Sam Walton (1918-1992), Phil Knight (b. 1938), Ted Turner (b. 1938), Anita Roddick (b. 1942), Ben Cohen (b. 1951), Jerry Greenfield (b. 1951), and Steven Jobs (b. 1955). Glossary, Suggested Readings, and Index.

1490.   Mayberry, Jodine. **Eastern Europe**. New York: Franklin Watts, 1991. 64p. $20.30. ISBN 0-531-11109-1. (Recent American Immigrants). 4-6

The text details the history of the areas from which the Eastern Europeans emigrated to the United States. Many of them Jews, they came after World War II to begin new lives. The text spends less time on their assimilation into the new culture. Photographs and maps supplement the text. Bibliography and Index.

1491.   Mayo, Edith, ed. **Smithsonian Book of the First Ladies**. New York: Henry Holt, 1996. 302p. $24.95. ISBN 0-8050-1751-8. 6 up

The text gives a brief account of women who have married Presidents, from Martha Washington to Hillary Rodham Clinton, as well as those who have served as hostesses in the White House for unmarried Presidents. Also included is how the role has changed, the question of suffrage, temperance, and other historical movements that have affected these women. Bibliography, Further Reading, and Index.

1492.   Mazer, Harry. **Cave Under the City**. New York: Crowell, 1986. 152p. $13.89. ISBN 0-690-04559-X. New York: HarperCollins, 1986. 152p. $3.95pa. ISBN 0-06-440303-3pa. 5-8

During the early years of the Depression, Tolley, 12, and his younger brother decide to stay in the streets rather than go to the children's shelter when their father leaves New York to look for work and their mother is hospitalized for tuberculosis. They survive day by day doing little jobs, begging, and stealing until Tolley himself becomes sick. When they return home, they find their father waiting for them.

1493.   Mazzio, Joann. **Leaving Eldorado**. Boston: Houghton Mifflin, 1993. 170p. $13.95. ISBN 0-395-64381-3. 5-9

In 1896, Maude, 14, decides that she will stay in Eldorado, New Mexico, after her father goes to search for gold in the Yukon. She begins work at the boardinghouse, where she meets an unusual group of people, including a woman who calls herself Venus Adonna and a schoolteacher. In diary entries addressed to her deceased mother, she tells about her experiences. Maude is surprised that she likes a "fallen" woman and that she would rather take art lessons than marry. After she receives unexpected money for saving someone from a fire, she decides that she does not have to marry someone she does not love.

1494.   McCall, Edith. **Better than a Brother**. Minneapolis, MN: Walker, 1988. 133p. $13.95. ISBN 0-8027-6783-4. 5-7

Hughie, 13 and the oldest of six children in 1900, lives with her family in their house free because they board a team of ice cutters. Hughie loses a gold locket given her by her grandmother in the snow. When an ice cutter tells her he has found it, he says that he will give it to her for sexual favors. Hughie's friend, a boy whom she likes, hears about the proposition and finally gets her to tell her father.

1495.   McCall, Edith S. **Message from the Mountains**. New York: Walker, 1985. 122p. $11.95. ISBN 0-8027-6582-3. 6-9

In 1826, Jim, 15, tries to get information about his father when a caravan returns to Franklin, Missouri, from Santa Fe. Concerned, he decides to join Kit Carson on his caravan leaving soon, but Jim's boss breaks his leg before he can leave. Jim then finds a note from his father telling him to wait for his return. He does.

1496.   McClard, Megan. **Harriet Tubman: Slavery and the Underground Railroad**. Den Schofield, illustrator. Englewood Cliffs, NJ: Silver Burdett, 1991. 133p. $12.95; $7.95pa. ISBN 0-382-09938-9; 0-382-224047-2pa. (History of the Civil War). 6-9

As an illiterate slave, Harriet Tubman (1820-1913) fought one of the great battles against the power structure by conducting on the Underground Railroad and freeing more than 300 slaves. She also served as a nurse and scout in the South during the Civil War and later started speaking out for women's rights. John Brown, the abolitionist, called her "General Tubman," and her people called her "Moses." Time Table, Selected Sources, Suggested Reading, and Index.

1497.   McClard, Megan, and George Ypsilantis. **Hiawatha and the Iroquois League**. Frank Riccio, illustrator. Englewood Cliffs, NJ: Silver Burdett, 1989. 123p. $12.95; $7.95pa. ISBN 0-382-09568-5; 0-382-09757-2pa. (Biography of American Indians). 5-8

Hiawatha grew up as an Iroquois in the area of the current New York State during the fifteenth century. His concern over the blood feuds of tribes and the determination to avenge the death of anyone in the tribe led him to want peace. At great personal sacrifice, he eventually led, with the Huron Degandawida, the formation of the Iroquois League, consisting of five tribes, which became the example for the U.S. government. Suggested Reading.

1498.   McClung, Robert. **Hugh Glass, Mountain Man**. New York: Morrow, 1990. 142p. $12.95. ISBN 0-688-08092-8. 6 up

Hugh Glass has an amazing history of capture and escape from pirates and from death at the hands of Indians before he joins the Rocky Mountain Fur Company. In August 1823, on a hunting expedition for his new employer, a grizzly bear attacks him. Two trappers, Jim Bridger and John Fitzgerald, fearful of Indian attack, leave him for dead, without supplies, food, or weapons. He survives and begins to crawl toward the area of present-day South Dakota, 200 miles away, to the nearest settlement. He determines to reunite with the two who left him and get his retribution. He succeeds.

1499.   McClung, Robert M. **America's First Elephant**. Marilyn Janovitz, illustrator. New York: Morrow, 1991. Unpaged. $14.88. ISBN 0-688-08359-5. K-2

In 1796, according to a New York newspaper, the ship *America* transported an elephant from Bengal. A circus owner showed the elephant in New York, and after walking her to Philadelphia by night, exhibited her there. She was a huge success. On July 4, George Washington had a chance to see her.

1500. McClung, Robert M. **The True Adventures of Grizzly Adams**. New York: Morrow, 1985. 208p. $11.95. ISBN 0-688-05794-2. 5 up

Grizzly Adams (1812-1860) was one of the best-known frontiersmen in the Old West. He went to the gold-fields in California where the greed of the miners disillusioned him. He disappeared into the western wilderness of the Sierra Nevadas, where he confronted jaguars and bears. He captured the largest grizzly of his day, a 1,200-pound animal he named Samson. When his menagerie starred as one of P. T. Barnum's leading attractions, he became a legend. Bibliography and Index.

1501. McCully, Emily Arnold, author/illustrator. **The Ballot Box Battle**. New York: Knopf, 1996. Unpaged. $17. ISBN 0-679-87938-2. 2-4

In the summer of 1880 in Tenafly, New Jersey, Cordelia enjoys riding Mrs. Stanton's horse and listening to stories about her childhood when her family's main concern was not that Elizabeth Cady could speak Greek but that she was not a boy. When Cordelia goes with Mrs. Stanton to the ballot box where she attempts to vote, she sees Mrs. Stanton's courage in facing the taunts of the men, and Cordelia becomes brave herself.

1502. McCully, Emily Arnold, author/illustrator. **The Bobbin Girl**. New York: Dial, 1996. 34p. $14.99. ISBN 0-8037-1827-6. 3-5

The life of Harriet Hanson Robinson is the basis for this story. For 15 minutes each hour between 5:30 AM and 7:00 PM, Rebecca, 10, removes filled bobbins from spinning frames in the Lowell, Massachusetts, textile mills and replaces them with empty ones. She is happy to earn money to supplement the rent from girls who board at her mother's and work in the factories in 1836. She enjoys the friendship and conversations of the older girls when, in the evenings, they return to her house and discuss their problems. When injury to one of the girls leads the others to plan a walk-out, Rebecca's mother lets her decide if she will join the protest and lose her job or stay inside and save it.

1503. McDaniel, Melissa. **The Powhatan Indians**. New York: Chelsea House, 1995. 80p. $14.95; $6.95pa. ISBN 0-7910-2494-6; 0-7910-2495-4pa. (Junior Library of American Indians). 3-6

The best-known member of the Powhatan tribe is probably Pocahontas. This tribe consisted of 30 separate groups ruled by her father. Chiefs called *werowances* and priests who survived the *Huskenaw* initiation ruled their villages. When the British built Jamestown in their territory, they supplied the earliest colonists with food, but as the colony expanded, fighting between the two groups began. Through the years, the Powhatans have tried to keep their identity, and they have official recognition in Virginia today. The text, with reproductions, photographs, and maps, tells their history. Glossary, Chronology, and Index.

1504. McDonald, Megan. **The Potato Man**. Ted Lewin, illustrator. New York: Orchard, 1991. 32p. $14.95. ISBN 0-531-05914-6. K-2

When Grandpa was young, children would steal from the potato man who had lost one eye in the Great War of 1918. Over time, the man caught the boy taking potatoes that had fallen from the wagon, squeezing orange juice on his sister's hair, and breaking a window. But when Grandpa tried to return an apple that had fallen off the cart, the potato man gave it to him. *School Library Journal Best Book.*

1505. McGovern, Ann. **The Secret Soldier: The Story of Deborah Sampson**. Ann Grifalconi, illustrator. New York: Four Winds, 1987. 64p. $15. ISBN 0-02-765780-9. 1-5

As Robert Shurtliff, Deborah Sampson enlisted in the Continental army to fight against the British, who killed her fiancé during the American Revolution. She was a bound servant to his family and not allowed to attend school or learn a trade. The text tells of her attempts to keep her identity secret while she makes long tiring marches to fight the Tories.

1506. McGrath, Patrick. **The Lewis and Clark Expedition**. Englewood Cliffs, NJ: Silver Burdett, 1985. 64p. $14.95. ISBN 0-382-06828-9. 4-9

In 1803, Thomas Jefferson commissioned the expedition that sent Meriwether Lewis and William Clark to explore the Louisiana Purchase territory. During this journey across land, they and members of the group cataloged plant and animal life and established relations with Indian inhabitants while collecting information about their cultures. The leaders of the expedition were two Virginians who shared a similar military background but who had dissimilar personalities and temperaments. The text looks at them and their achievements. Index and Suggested Reading.

1507. McGraw, Eloise Jarvis. **Moccasin Trail**. 1952. New York: Penguin, 1986. 256p. $4.99pa. ISBN 0-14-032170-5pa. 6-10

A bear mauls Jim when he is 12, and the Crow tribe adopts him. He spends six years living with them and counting coup (the number of whites scalped), wearing his eagle feathers as a young brave. When he meets his younger siblings in a nearby settlement, they tell him that they need his signature as the oldest son. They need it to get the land that their father had identified in Willamette Valley, Oregon, before dying on the trail with their mother. Jim agrees, and he goes with them although they distrust each other. They eventually learn that each has talents that will help them all be successful. *Newbery Honor, Junior Literary Guild Selection,* and *Lewis Carroll Shelf Award.*

1508. McGugan, Jim. **Josepha: A Prairie Boy's Story**. Murray Kimber, illustrator. San Francisco: Chronicle, 1994. Unpaged. $11.95. ISBN 0-8118-0802-5. 2-5

In 1900, a younger boy admiringly tells of Josepha, a kind teenager who must stay with the elementary children during school because he cannot speak English very well. Although impoverished, he carves beautiful things and protects the children. His family is inexperienced at prairie farming and unable to produce. He stops school to work, but before he leaves, he gives the narrator his cherished possession, and the narrator responds by giving Josepha his own most treasured item.

1509. McHale, John E., Jr. **Dr. Samuel A. Mudd and the Lincoln Assassination**. New York: Dillon Press, Silver Burdett, 1995. 144p. $7.95. ISBN 0-87518-629-7. (People in Focus). 6-9

On April 15, 1865, two men, one with a broken leg, rode to the southern Maryland farmhouse of Dr. Samuel A. Mudd. As a doctor obligated to heal the sick, Dr. Mudd set the man's leg and gave the two a place to sleep for the night. Because the injured man was John Wilkes Booth, the man who had just assassinated Abraham Lincoln, Dr. Mudd was convicted and sent to prison for helping the criminals. The text looks at his story and asks questions such as whether he knew who the patient was, if he waited to tell authorities about the strangers, if he showed the men through the Zekiah Swamp as an escape route, if he hid the assassin's boots from War Department detectives, and if he lied when he said he did not recognize a picture of Booth after the incident. Bibliography and Index.

1510. McKenzie, Ellen Kindt. **Stargone John**. William Low, illustrator. New York: Henry Holt, Redfeather, 1990. 67p. $13.95. ISBN 0-8050-1451-9. 2-4

Liza, nine, has a younger brother John who will not talk to anyone but Lisa. In first grade, he refuses to learn how to read and write because he thinks that the new teacher is hostile toward him. Not until the former teacher, who is blind, reveals his intelligence does Lisa stop suffering for her brother's "stargone" ways. *Bulletin Blue Ribbon Book*.

1511. McKenzie, Ellen Kindt. **Under the Bridge**. New York: Henry Holt, 1994. 140p. $14.95. ISBN 0-8050-3398-X. 4-7

Ritchie, 10, and his little sister Rosie in Illinois during 1939 try to cope while their mother is away. She disappears one day, but their father does not tell them where she is. Someone finally says that she has had a nervous breakdown. Rosie gets sick, and she starts getting letters from a troll that she thinks might be living under a nearby bridge after hearing "Billy Goats Gruff." The letters help her get better, and they eventually stop when their mother returns and a musician who lives next to the bridge goes to fight in World War II. Although they never know who sent the letters, Ritchie realizes after the war in 1945, when they receive a letter from England saying "we won" and signed by the troll, that the musician is safe.

1512. McKissack, Pat. **Ma Dear's Aprons**. Floyd Cooper, illustrator. New York: Simon & Schuster, Atheneum, 1997. 32p. $16. ISBN 0-679-85099-6. K-2

In the early twentieth century, Ma Dear and David clean clothes for white folks using their rub board before they own washing machines. Among the other jobs that they work to earn money are making and selling pies from their fruit trees and running errands on a horse and buggy. Although their days are hard, their love makes life easier.

1513. McKissack, Patricia, and Frederick McKissack. **African-American Inventors**. Brookfield, CT: Millbrook Press, 1994. 96p. $18.40. ISBN 1-56294-468-1. (A Proud Heritage). 4-6

The short biographical profiles show the talent, creativeness, and resolve that African American inventors have used beginning with an introduction on patent law. The text covers free African American inventors, slave inventions, Norbert Rillieux's sugar refining (1806-1894), Jan Matzeliger's shoe-lasting machine (1852-1889), the railroad inventions of electricity pioneer Lewis Latimer (1848-1928), electric railways and Granville T. Woods (1856-1910), automotive inventions, and contemporary inventors. Bibliography and Index.

1514. McKissack, Patricia, and Frederick McKissack. **Booker T. Washington: Leader and Educator**. Michael Bryant, illustrator. Springfield, NJ: Enslow, 1992. 32p. $12.95. ISBN 0-89490-314-4. (Great African Americans). K-3

Booker T. Washington (1856-1915) was born a slave, but after he gained his freedom, he was determined to get an education. He walked many miles to college in Hampton, Virginia, and worked to stay there both physically and academically. The text looks at his childhood, his education, and his career at Tuskegee Institute, where he became the principal. He was determined to achieve, and he tried to help other African Americans make choices that would benefit their own lives. Photographs, Glossary, and Index.

1515. McKissack, Patricia, and Frederick McKissack. **Carter G. Woodson: The Father of Black History**. Ned O, illustrator. Springfield, NJ: Enslow, 1991. 32p. $12.95. ISBN 0-89490-309-8. (Great African Americans). 2-4

Carter G. Woodson (1875-1950) had a father who believed that it was never too late to do something. Woodson listened, and when he could not go to high school before he was 18, he went and graduated in 18 months. He went on to college and eventually received a Ph.D. from Harvard. He taught in Washington, D.C., and began to collect works written by African Americans because none of the history books included them. He began to celebrate contributions by African Americans one week of the year, the beginning of today's expanded Black History month. Words to Know and Index.

1516. McKissack, Patricia, and Frederick McKissack. **Frederick Douglass: Leader Against Slavery**. Ned O, illustrator. Springfield, NJ: Enslow, 1991. 32p. $12.95. ISBN 0-89490-306-3. (Great African Americans). 2-4

Frederick Douglass (1817-1895) showed his determination by escaping from slavery, traveling north, creating a newspaper, and doing many things to help African Americans. He also helped with the Underground Railroad and counted Harriet Tubman and Abraham Lincoln as his friends. Glossary and Index.

1517. McKissack, Patricia, and Frederick McKissack. **Frederick Douglass: The Black Lion**. Chicago: Childrens Press, 1987. 136p. $18.60; $5.95pa. ISBN 0-516-03221-6; 0-516-43221-4pa. (People of Distinction). 4 up

Frederick Douglass (1817-1895) had many important relationships in his life, including his family, when he was a young slave living with his grandparents. Among those who helped him to escape and joined in his fight against slavery are individuals who are the topics of the book's chapters. They include Lucretia and Sophia Auld, Thomas Auld and Edward Covey, William Freeland, Master Hugh, John Brown, and Abraham Lincoln. Photographs, Time Line, and Index.

1518. McKissack, Patricia, and Frederick McKissack. **George Washington Carver: The Peanut Scientist**. Edward Ostendorf, illustrator. Springfield, NJ: Enslow, 1991. 32p. $12.95. ISBN 0-89490-308-X. (Great African Americans). 2-4

George Washington Carver (1864?-1943) became a scientist who promoted the idea of crop rotation and found many uses for peanuts. Many initially thought his ideas were foolish. Black-and-white photographs and drawings enhance the text. Glossary and Index.

1519. McKissack, Patricia, and Frederick McKissack. **Ida B. Wells-Barnett: A Voice Against Violence**. Edward Ostendorf, illustrator. Springfield, NJ: Enslow, 1991. 32p. $12.95. ISBN 0-89490-301-2. (Great African Americans). 2-4

Ida B. Wells-Barnett (1862-1931), a Black woman journalist, campaigned for the civil rights of women and other minorities. She was also a founder of the National Association for the Advancement of Colored People in 1909. Black-and-white photographs and drawings enhance the text. Glossary and Index.

1520. McKissack, Patricia, and Frederick McKissack. **James Weldon Johnson: "Lift Every Voice and Sing"**. Chicago: Childrens Press, 1990. 31p. $15.80. ISBN 0-516-04174-6. 2-5

When James Weldon Johnson (1871-1938), a Black school principal, was asked to speak at a celebration for Abraham Lincoln's birthday, he wanted to do more than just speak. He talked to his brother, and his brother wrote music while Johnson wrote the words to "Lift Every Voice and Sing." Five hundred schoolchildren sang the song for the first time in 1900, and 20 years later, the National Association for the Advancement of Colored People (NAACP) chose it for their theme song. Johnson was an educator, a lawyer, a diplomat, and a civil rights leader. Index.

1521. McKissack, Patricia, and Frederick McKissack. **Jesse Owens: Olympic Star**. Springfield, NJ: Enslow, 1992. 32p. $12.95. ISBN 0-89490-312-8. (Great African Americans). 3-4

Jesse Owens (1913-1981) broke several world records when he ran for Ohio State University. When he ran in the 1936 Olympics held in Berlin during Hitler's regime, he won four gold medals and became an Olympic legend. Index.

1522. McKissack, Patricia, and Frederick McKissack. **Langston Hughes: Great American Poet**. Michael David Biegel, illustrator. Springfield, NJ: Enslow, 1992. 32p. $12.95. ISBN 0-89490-315-2. (Great African Americans). 3-4

Langston Hughes (1902-1967) lived with his father only briefly because his father moved to Mexico where he could practice law. When Hughes and his mother went to join him, an earthquake frightened his mother back to Kansas. Hughes lived mainly with his grandmother before he attended college in New York. He decided, against his father's will, to become a writer. He wrote drama, poetry, essays, and newspaper articles during his career, and he had the opportunity to travel to such places as Russia and Africa. Some have called him "Harlem's Poet" because he wrote so well about his own people. Words to Know and Index.

1523. McKissack, Patricia, and Frederick McKissack. **Louis Armstrong: Jazz Musician**. Edward Ostendorf, illustrator. Springfield, NJ: Enslow, 1991. 32p. $12.95. ISBN 0-89490-307-1. (Great African Americans). 2-4

Louis Armstrong (1900-1971) became a jazz trumpeter known as "Satchmo." Starting in New Orleans, Louisiana, his ability to play the trumpet increased interest in the instrument for solo performance. Black-and-white photographs and drawings enhance the text. Glossary and Index.

1524. McKissack, Patricia, and Frederick McKissack. **Madam C. J. Walker: Self-Made Millionaire**. Michael Bryant, illustrator. Springfield, NJ: Enslow, 1992. 32p. $12.95. ISBN 0-89490-311-X. (Great African Americans). 3-4

As the daughter of slaves, Sarah Breedlove (1867-1919) proved that she was free. She did something that no other American woman had done: start a business and become a millionaire. She created hair products to improve her own hair, and when they worked, she sold them to others who liked them. When she built a factory in Indiana, she hired people who could help her run her business properly. After one year, she had 950 salespeople. She continued to work and to support other Blacks by encouraging them to start their own businesses. Words to Know and Index.

1525. McKissack, Patricia, and Frederick McKissack. **Marian Anderson: A Great Singer**. Edward Ostendorf, illustrator. Hillside, NJ: Enslow, 1991. 32p. $12.95. ISBN 0-89490-303-9. (Great African Americans). 2-4

Marian Anderson (1897-1993), an African American singer, struggled against prejudice to become one of the great opera performers of the century. Black-and-white photographs and drawings enhance the text. Glossary and Index.

1526. McKissack, Patricia, and Frederick McKissack. **Martin Luther King, Jr.: Man of Peace**. Springfield, NJ: Enslow, 1991. 32p. $12.95. ISBN 0-89490-302-2. (Great African Americans). 2-4

Martin Luther King, Jr. (1929-1968) wanted to help his people have a better life. The text uses photographs and illustrations to augment the information about his determination. The racism he faced appears in the setting but is not the center of his story. Glossary and Index.

1527. McKissack, Patricia, and Frederick McKissack. **Mary Church Terrell: Leader for Equality**. Edward Ostendorf, illustrator. Springfield, NJ: Enslow, 1991. 32p. $12.95. ISBN 0-89490-305-5. (Great African Americans). 2-4

Mary Church Terrell (1863-1954) was a civil rights activist who helped her people see that they needed to gain their rights. She was also a suffragist and educator. Photographs and drawings enhance the text. Glossary and Index.

1528. McKissack, Patricia and Fredrick McKissack. **Mary McLeod Bethune**. Chicago: Childrens Press, 1991. 32p. $17.30; $4.95pa. ISBN 0-516-06658-7; 0-516-46658-5pa. (Cornerstones of Freedom). 3-6

Mary McLeod Bethune (1875-1955) wanted to start a school for young Black girls in Florida in 1904. With hard work raising money, this daughter of former slaves succeeded. After Franklin Roosevelt became President, he asked her to serve as the director of the Office of Minority Affairs, and she became the first Black woman to serve as a presidential advisor. Index.

1529. McKissack, Patricia, and Frederick McKissack. **Mary McLeod Bethune: A Great Teacher**. Ned O, illustrator. Springfield, NJ: Enslow, 1991. 32p. $12.95. ISBN 0-89490-304-7. (Great African Americans). K-2

The text introduces Mary McLeod Bethune (1875-1955) by focusing on her childhood, her education, and her leadership role in the U.S. government. With only $1.50, she opened a school for Black girls in Florida in 1904. Her determination led to the expansion of her school into an accredited four-year college. Photographs highlight the text. Glossary and Index.

1530. McKissack, Patricia, and Frederick McKissack. **Paul Robeson: A Voice to Remember**. Michael David Biegel, illustrator. Springfield, NJ: Enslow, 1992. 32p. $12.95. ISBN 0-89490-310-1. (Great African Americans). K-3

Paul Robeson (1898-1976), a baritone, became an actor. He performed in Eugene O'Neill's plays and *Show Boat*. His dismay at the treatment of African Americans caused him to support leftist ideals, and he suffered for his beliefs. The text looks at his childhood, his education, and his career as actor and singer. Photographs, Glossary, and Index.

1531. McKissack, Patricia, and Frederick McKissack. **Ralph J. Bunche: Peacemaker**. Springfield, NJ: Enslow, 1991. 32p. $12.95. ISBN 0-89490-300-4. (Great African Americans). 2-4

Ralph Bunche (1904-1971) worked to help his fellow African Americans have a better life. But he was also interested in the lives of other races. In 1950, he received the Nobel Prize for his work on the United Nations Palestine Commission. Photographs and illustrations augment the text. Glossary and Index.

1532. McKissack, Patricia, and Frederick McKissack. **Red-Tail Angels: The Story of the Tuskegee Airmen of World War II**. New York: Walker, 1995. 136p. $19.95. ISBN 0-8027-8292-2. 5-9

Because of prejudice, the United States denied African Americans the right to make contributions to various war efforts or shunned them when they returned home from fighting. The text looks at the history of African American participation in the U.S. military, including decisions, assignments, and experiences of those involved. For World War II, the text gives a chronological account of African American participation. The flying squadron of the Tuskegee Airmen showed that prior decisions to exclude African Americans were a mistake, and they helped others have a better chance for promotion in the military. Photographs, Bibliography, and Index. *American Library Association Best Books for Young Adults*, *IRA Teachers' Choices*, *Carter G. Woodson Book Award*, and *Notable Children's Trade Books in the Field of Social Studies*.

1533. McKissack, Patricia, and Frederick McKissack. **Sojourner Truth: A Voice for Freedom**. Springfield, NJ: Enslow, 1992. 32p. $12.95. ISBN 0-89490-313-6. (Great African Americans). 3-4

Sojourner Truth (1797?-1883) was an American abolitionist and feminist who preached against slavery and for women's rights after she obtained her freedom from slavery in 1827. The text looks at her early childhood, her struggles, and her extraordinary achievements. Reproductions, Glossary, and Index.

1534. McKissack, Patricia, and Frederick McKissack. **Sojourner Truth: Ain't I a Woman?** New York: Scholastic, 1992. 186p. $13.95; $3.50pa. ISBN 0-590-44690-8; 0-590-44691-6pa. 5-8

Isabella (1797-1883) was born a slave in New York and freed in 1827. Mother of five children, she sued because her son had been illegally sold to someone in the South and became one of the first Black women to win a lawsuit against a white. Not until later in her life did she choose the name Sojourner Truth. She wandered from place to place speaking against slavery to anyone who would listen. Six feet tall with a resonant voice, she was a visible and vocal fighter against injustice. Although she could not read, she was a preacher who could quote the Bible word-for-word, an abolitionist, and an activist for the rights of women. Bibliography and Index. *Coretta Scott King Honor Book*, *American Library Association Best Books for Young Adults*, *American Library Association Notable Books for Children*, and *Boston Globe/Horn Book Award*.

1535. McKissack, Patricia, and Frederick McKissack. **The Story of Booker T. Washington**. Chicago: Childrens Press, 1991. 31p. $17.30. ISBN 0-5160-4758-2. (Cornerstones of Freedom). 3-6

This brief biography of Booker T. Washington (1856-1915) discusses his life as an African American educator and leader associated with Tuskegee Institute. It also presents the view that he wanted to appease whites in order to gain rights while other African American leaders wanted to assert themselves. Photographs and drawings enhance the text. Index.

1536. McKissack, Patricia C., and Frederick L. McKissack. **Christmas in the Big House, Christmas in the Quarters**. John Thompson, illustrator. New York: Scholastic, 1994. 80p. $15.95. ISBN 0-590-43027-0. 4-6

Using 1859, two years before the Civil War, as their setting, the authors present a Christmas as it might have been celebrated on a Virginia plantation near the James River. They juxtapose the two societal segments, master and slave, by showing how each probably celebrated the season. The preparation for Christmas, food served and eaten; the giving of gifts both simple and elaborate; the anticipation of visiting other family members on different plantations for the slaves and the arrival of guests for masters; and the enjoyment of New Year's Eve contrasted with the slaves' disappointment that everything will again focus on work. Balancing the abandonment to the pleasure of the season on both sides are the undertones of slave conversations about who might have escaped, with slaves who could read reporting from Frederick Douglass's *North Star*, and a grandfather master grumbling that Virginia will secede. Looking Back, Notes, and Bibliography. *Coretta Scott King Award*, *Notable Children's Trade Books in the Field of Social Studies*, and *Orbis Pictus Honor Book*.

1537. McKissack, Patricia C., and Frederick L. McKissack. **Rebels Against Slavery: American Slave Revolts**. New York: Scholastic, 1996. 176p. $14.95. ISBN 0-590-45735-7. 5-8

The text looks at several slave revolts and posits that each one was more intense than the previous one with all leading to the organized attempts that eventually overcame slavery. Toussaint L'Ouverture, Cato, Denmark Vesey, Gabriel Prosser, Harriet Tubman, and John Brown led the way, with others operating on the fringes. Tubman was willing to shoot any runaway who could not complete the journey to freedom. But the McKissacks think that even the nonviolent resistance had its place because it helped the final goal. Photographs, Chronology, and Index.

1538. McKissack, Patricia C., and Fredrick McKissack, Jr. **Black Diamond: The Story of the Negro Baseball Leagues**. New York: Scholastic, 1994. 184p. $14.95; $3.99pa. ISBN 0-590-45809-4; 0-590-45810-8pa. 4-9

Because African Americans were not allowed to play in white baseball leagues for nearly a century, they formed leagues of their own. Many participants were superb players like Cool Papa Bell, Josh Gibson, and Satchel Paige. The text covers their history from the beginning of baseball through some of the first African Americans to play in the major leagues: Jackie Robinson, Willie Mays, and Hank Aaron. Player Profiles, Hall of Fame, Time Line, Bibliography, and Index. *Coretta Scott King Honor* and *Notable Children's Trade Books in the Field of Social Studies*.

1539.   McLerran, Alice. **The Year of the Ranch**. Kimberly Bulcken Root, illustrator. New York: Viking, 1996. 32p. $14.99. ISBN 0-670-85131-0. 1-4

In 1919, Emily's family moves into the desert because her father dreams of farming land near Yuma, Arizona, while keeping a day job in an office. She and her three sisters try to overcome the sandstorms, the scorpions, and the outhouse, but they eventually have to return to town. Her father decides he will try to build a college instead. After the father dies, the girls see the development in the desert and realize that their father's first dream has been realized by others.

1540.   McNeese, Tim. **America's Early Canals**. New York: Crestwood House, 1993. 48p. $11.95. ISBN 0-89686-730-7. (Americans on the Move). 4-8

By the 1790s, 30 canal companies were working on canals. One such place was Middlesex in Massachusetts, which connected the Merrimack River to Boston Harbor. The companies built hundreds of canals before the Civil War including the Potomac Canal, to connect the Potomac with the Ohio, and the Erie Canal, to connect the Hudson River with Lake Erie at Buffalo. After the war, canal travel began to decline. Drawings augment the text. Further Reading, Glossary, and Index.

1541.   McNeese, Tim. **America's First Railroads**. Chris Duke, illustrator. New York: Crestwood House, 1993. 48p. $11.95. ISBN 0-89686-729-3. (Americans on the Move). 4-8

In 1828, work began on the Baltimore and Ohio Railroad, and its first miles were completed in 1830. It stretched to Cumberland, Maryland, by 1842. During that time and after, locomotives changed. Matthias Baldwin designed and made a full-size locomotive nicknamed "Old Ironsides" in the 1830s. Then railroads began to stretch to the West after the transcontinental line was finished. Drawings highlight the text. Further Reading, Glossary, and Index.

1542.   McNeese, Tim. **Clippers and Whaling Ships**. Chris Duke, illustrator . New York: Crestwood House, 1993. 48p. $11.95. ISBN 0-89686-735-8. (Americans on the Move). 4-8

In the mid-1840s and for 30 years, privateers changed to clipper ships. Some of those built were the *Ann McKim*, *Rainbow*, and *Sea Witch*. American whalers traveled the world. The text covers life on ship, killing and carving the whales, and the sources for oil. Drawings and diagrams highlight the text. Further Reading, Glossary, and Index.

1543.   McNeese, Tim. **Conestogas and Stagecoaches**. Chris Duke, illustrator. New York: Crestwood House, 1993. 48p. $11.95. ISBN 0-89686-732-3. (Americans on the Move). 4-8

Among those vehicles carrying passengers and mail during the eighteenth and nineteenth centuries were Conestoga wagons and stagecoaches. The text discusses the differing functions of wagons and stagecoaches along with the facilities for passengers along the travel routes, like sleeping and eating at taverns. Among the trails were the National Road from Cumberland, Maryland, to Wheeling, Virginia (West Virginia today). Some of the companies were the Butterfield Overland mail, which traveled 2,000 miles across Texas, New Mexico, and Arizona; the Western Stage Trail; and the Colorado stages. By 1920, mass-produced vehicles took over the roads. Drawings enhance the text. Further Reading, Glossary, and Index.

1544.   McNeese, Tim. **Early River Travel**. New York: Crestwood House, 1993. 48p. $11.95. ISBN 0-89686-733-1. (Americans on the Move). 4-8

The earliest ships were canoes, but when Americans moved west, people needed new crafts. Flatboats and keelboats floated the Mississippi, and steamboats became the mode of travel for passengers. Men who helped develop the steamboat were John Fitch in 1790 and Robert Fulton, who, after an initial failure, built the Clermont in New York in 1807. Helping Fulton was Robert Livingston. Drawings enhance the text. Further Reading, Glossary, and Index.

1545.   McNeese, Tim. **From Trails to Turnpikes**. New York: Crestwood House, 1993. 48p. $11.95. ISBN 0-89686-731-5. (Americans on the Move). 4-8

Buffalo and the Native Americans created paths that became colonial roads. In 1775, Daniel Boone built the Wilderness Road into Kentucky. Other turnpikes were Lancaster Pike, first opened in Philadelphia in 1797. The National Road from Maryland to Ohio was built between 1827 and 1850 with Conestogas, pack trains, and stagecoaches taking advantage of its convenience. In the early 1800s, western trails included the Santa Fe, the Oregon, and the California. Drawings enhance the text. Further Reading, Glossary, and Index.

1546.   McNeese, Tim. **West by Steamboat**. Chris Duke, illustrator. New York: Crestwood House, 1993. 48p. $11.95. ISBN 0-89686-728-5. (Americans on the Move). 4-8

Once the first steamboat became a vessel, rivers became two-way streets because boats could travel against the current. Nicholas J. Roosevelt constructed the first western steamer and launched it in 1811. Others followed, and the text chronicles the golden age of the steamboat, which took passengers on the Mississippi. With the advent of the locomotive, the boats lost their attraction. Illustrations enhance the text. Glossary, Further Reading, and Index.

1547. McPhail, David, author/illustrator. **Farm Boy's Year**. New York: Atheneum, 1992. 32p. $13.95. ISBN 0-689-31679-8. K-3

In a series of entries, one for each month of a year, a 12-year-old boy in Maine during the 1800s recreates the seasons and rituals of the year. The ice blocks from the pond, cut in winter to sell in summer; the maple syrup; the scythe forging; the swimming pond; the Fourth of July parade; apple picking; and the Thanksgiving goose all make up the year.

1548. McPherson, Stephanie Sammartino. **I Speak for the Women: A Story About Lucy Stone**. Brian Liedahl, illustrator. Minneapolis, MN: Carolrhoda, 1990. 64p. $17.50. ISBN 0-87614-740-6. (Creative Minds). 4-6

Lucy Stone (1818-1893), the eighth child in her family, always asked questions about the work that her mother had to do as a woman, with no rights for herself. When Lucy was 12, she tried to help her mother as much as possible without sacrificing her schoolwork, but it exhausted her to try to accomplish both. She realized for the first time what not being counted was like when a vote was called in her church, and although she was a member, she was not a man or "voting member." She worked to change that for the rest of her life. When she married, her husband supported her decision to drop his name from hers, although others were shocked.

1549. McPherson, Stephanie Sammartino. **Peace and Bread: The Story of Jane Addams**. Minneapolis, MN: Carolrhoda, 1993. 96p. $19.95. ISBN 0-87614-792-9. (Trailblazers). 4-7

As a child, Jane Addams (1860-1935) helped her neighbors. As an adult, she saw a problem and tried to solve it. She rented a house in one of the poorest areas of Chicago, on Halsted Street, and in it she created the first settlement house for the poor. She spent more than 40 years at Hull House, and her years with the Women's International League for Peace and Freedom led her to become one of the leading figures battling for the less fortunate. Photographs, Bibliography, and Index.

1550. McPherson, Stephanie Sammartino. **Rooftop Astronomer: A Story About Maria Mitchell**. Hetty Mitchell, illustrator. Minneapolis, MN: Carolrhoda, 1990. 64p. $17.50. ISBN 0-8761-4410-5. (Creative Minds). 4-6

Maria Mitchell (1818-1889) became a professor at Vassar in astronomy, the subject she loved, and was the first woman elected to the American Academy of Arts and Sciences. She also fought for women's rights and served as president of the Women's Congress. Her family encouraged her to think for herself, and her decisions show that she honored their support. Bibliography and Index.

1551. McPherson, Stephanie Sammartino. **TV's Forgotten Hero: The Story of Philo Farnsworth**. Minneapolis, MN: Carolrhoda, 1996. 96p. $19.95. ISBN 1-57505-017-X. 4-7

In the 1920s, Philo Farnsworth (1906-1971) developed the basic components for electronic television. When he was 12, he saw electric lines for the first time, and he began experimenting. What he created changed the twentieth century. He needed to control electrons so that they would change speed or direction, change light into electricity, and change electricity into pictures. After much effort, he succeeded. In honor of his achievement, children from Utah voted to have him be the subject of the second statue from their state to be displayed in the capitol building. Notes, Bibliography, and Index.

1552. McPherson, Stephanie Sammartino. **The Workers' Detective: A Story About Dr. Alice Hamilton**. Janet Schulz, illustrator. Minneapolis, MN: Carolrhoda, 1992. 64p. $17.50. ISBN 0-87614-699-X. (Creative Minds). 3-6

Alice Hamilton (1869-1970) followed her mother's advice to be the one who tries to change things rather than to say that someone else ought to be responsible. She decided to be a doctor, and after her studying, she went to live at Jane Addams's Hull House in Chicago. Of Hull House residents who had worked in factories, Hamilton saw the kinds of injuries and illnesses that could come from an industrialized society. She fought to change laws so that workers would be protected, and she succeeded in that as well as in helping orphans who had no one to support them. She stated her opinions throughout her life, and at 94 she picketed against the war in Vietnam. Bibliography.

1553. Meacham, Margaret. **Oyster Moon**. Marcy Dunn Ramsey, illustrator. New York: Cornell Maritime, 1996. 112p. $9.95pa. ISBN 0-87033-459-Xpa. 3-6

Anna and Toby, 14-year-old twins, live in Maryland during the late nineteenth century. Toby leaves home to work on an oyster dredge, and Anna begins finding little notes that she has written while sleeping. She thinks that Toby has dictated them to her. When she receives a letter in his handwriting but in a foreign language, she is certain that he is in danger. She goes to save him and finds abused immigrants and a murder on board the dredge.

1554. Medearis, Angela Shelf. **Come This Far to Freedom: A History of African Americans**. New York: Atheneum, 1993. 148p. $14.95. ISBN 0-689-31522-8. 5 up

Medearis divides the history of African Americans into five parts: coming from Africa to the hardships of slavery, the fight for freedom, the fresh start during Reconstruction after the Civil War, the movement for equality, and the people who have continued to break down the barriers in politics, the military, the sciences, and other fields. Important Dates, Bibliography, and Index.

1555. Medearis, Angela Shelf. **Dare to Dream: Coretta Scott King and the Civil Rights Movement**. Anna Rich, illustrator. New York: Lodestar, 1994. 42p. $13.99. ISBN 0-525-67426-8. (Rainbow Biography). 3-4

Coretta Scott King (b. 1927) wanted to be an opera singer. She worked hard enough to earn a scholarship to the Boston Conservatory of Music, but before she finished, she met Martin Luther King, Jr. He wanted a wife who would help him in his ministry, and after falling in love with him, she agreed to put aside her career. She continued to support his ideas for equal rights after his assassination. The text looks at her childhood and her life after marriage. Selected Bibliography, Further Reading, and Index.

1556. Medearis, Angela Shelf. **Little Louis and the Jazz Band: The Story of Louis "Satchmo" Armstrong**. Anna Rich, illustrator. New York: Lodestar, 1994. 42p. $13.99. ISBN 0-525-67424-1. (Rainbow Biography). 3-4

Louis Armstrong (1900-1971) grew up in New Orleans. He lived with his mother and sister until he shot blanks from a pistol one New Year's Eve. Then the police placed him in the Colored Waifs' Home for Boys. There he joined a brass band and soon became the leader. When he left at 13, he planned to be the best coronet player of all time. Eventually, he drove a coal cart during the day while playing jazz around town at night, where he got the name "Satchmo" for his large, toothy smile. He started traveling and then formed his own band. With his talent, he became the first African American to have his own radio show, and he appeared in more than 28 movies. Chronology, End Notes, Further Reading for Children, Bibliography, and Index.

1557. Medearis, Angela Shelf. **Our People**. Michael Bryant, illustrator. New York: Atheneum, 1994. 32p. $14.95. ISBN 0-689-31826-X. K-3

This brief overview lists some of the many accomplishments of African Americans throughout history, from the construction of the pyramids in Egypt to contemporary scientists. Among the professions included are royalty, mathematicians, artists, explorers, Underground Railroad conductors, cowboys, businesspeople, doctors, farmers, politicians, and inventors. The narrator has her father's assurance that she can do anything she wants.

1558. Medearis, Angela Shelf, and Scott Joplin. **Treemonisha**. Michael Bryant, illustrator. New York: Henry Holt, 1995. 37p. $15.95. ISBN 0-8050-1748-8. 2-6

With former slaves as parents, Treemonisha is well educated. In 1884, after she returns from college to her Arkansas home, she disagrees with a conjure man who has been misleading the townspeople for his own profit. He kidnaps her and threatens to throw her into a wasps' nest. The story is adapted from Scott Joplin's opera.

1559. Meltzer, Milton. **Betty Friedan: A Voice for Women's Rights**. Stephen Maarchesi, illustrator. New York: Viking, 1985. 58p. $9.95. ISBN 0-670-80786-9. (Women of Our Lifetime). 5 up

Betty Friedan (b. 1921) grew up in Peoria, Illinois, and left her unhappy family to attend Smith College. After college, she began graduate school at Berkeley, and then went to New York to work as a writer. She met a man whom she married. After she gave up her work to raise his children in the suburbs, she felt she had given up her self. As she became more and more unhappy and talked to others like her, she found out that many women wanted to work. She wrote a book called *The Feminine Mystique* in 1963, which furthered the feminist movement. She saw that women had more to offer than roles as housecleaners and babysitters, and this book led them to recognize and use their abilities.

1560. Meltzer, Milton. **The Black Americans: A History in Their Own Words**. 1964. New York: Trophy, 1987. 306p. $9.95pa. ISBN 0-06-446055-Xpa. 5 up

Meltzer has collected documents showing 350 years of Black life in America. His subjects range from the sharecropper's struggle to the scholar Maya Angelou. Using the words of those who endured, he relates a history that stretches from 1619 to 1983. Sources and Index. *American Library Association Notable Books for Children* and *Notable Children's Trade Books in the Field of Social Studies*.

1561. Meltzer, Milton. **Dorothea Lange: Life Through the Camera**. Donna Diamond, illustrator. New York: Puffin, Penguin, 1986. 64p. $3.95pa. ISBN 0-14-032105-5pa. 2-6

Dorothea Lange (1895-1965) suffered polio as a child, which made her limp for the rest of her life. She disliked school and stayed away as much as possible while a teenager. She lived with her grandparents after her parents divorced. When she was 17, she knew she wanted to be a photographer, although she had never taken a picture. She had seen poor people in the street, and she wanted to record their lives. While working, she traveled across the country and took photographs of the hungry and homeless during the Great Depression. Those photographs today give insight into a difficult time in history. *Booklist Editor's Choice*.

1562. Meltzer, Milton. **Gold: The True Story of Why People Search for It, Mine It, Trade It, Steal It, Mint It, Hoard It**. New York: HarperCollins, 1993. 167p. $15. ISBN 0-06-022983-7. 4-8

Photographs complement the text, which tells of humankind's 5,000-year quest for gold. Included are such topics as shekels, bezants, florins, ducats, and guineas. Other chapters look at where to get gold in the mines and the slaves who mined it, African empires built on gold, the gold rush in California, the search from Australia to South Africa, and what people endured when others came to their lands looking for gold. Bibliography and Index.

1563. Mendez, Adriana. **Cubans in America**. Minneapolis, MN: Lerner, 1994. 80p. $17.50; $5.95pa. ISBN 0-8225-1953-4; 0-8225-1039-1pa. (In America). 5-9

Cuba's position at 90 miles from Florida puts it at a location strategic to the United States. When Columbus arrived, he wrote about its beauty, and other explorers landed there. Cuba's history has been one of people who have had to survive. The Taino Indians, natives when Columbus came, were conquered and became slaves to the Spanish. In the nineteenth century, José Martí finally helped free the country from Spain. In 1959, Batista lost Cuba to Fidel Castro. Castro set up a socialist government from which people now want to escape. The text compares the different Cubas that have existed on this beautiful island. Glossary, Selected Bibliography, and Index.

1564. Meryman, Richard. **Andrew Wyeth**. New York: Harry N. Abrams, 1991. 92p. $19.95. ISBN 0-8109-3956-8. (First Impressions). 6-9

Andrew Wyeth (b. 1917) was born into a family of artists. Not until his father died was he able to develop his own painting and become an artist in his own right, with pictures such as *Christina's World*. Reproductions and Index.

1565. Mettger, Zak. **Reconstruction: America After the Civil War**. New York: Lodestar, 1994. 122p. $16.99. ISBN 0-525-67490-X. (Young Readers' History of the Civil War). 5-9

After the Civil War, not only were cities and farms ruined but also the South's entire way of life. The years 1865-1877 are known as Reconstruction. Northern politicians discussed whether to punish Southern traitors before allowing them to rejoin the United States. Freed slaves had to fight for their rights in the South to vote, own land, and earn wages. Mettger discusses these problems and how the people confronted them as they tried to rebuild their lives. Glossary, Further Reading, and Index.

1566. Mettger, Zak. **Till Victory Is Won: Black Soldiers in the Civil War**. New York: Lodestar, 1994. 118p. $16.99. ISBN 0-525-67412-8. (Young Readers' History of the Civil War). 5-9

Photographs, prints, and reproductions of newspaper notices complement the text, which presents the attempts of Black men to fight in the Civil War. At first their services were refused in the "white man's war," but they finally gained the right to fight. Their enormous contribution helped the Union win. In addition, they fought for equal pay and equal rights. Mettger discusses their recruitment, their battles behind the lines, the treatment of women and children, and how Black occupation forces helped to both liberate and protect the slaves in the South. Glossary, Selected Bibliography, and Index.

1567. Meyer, Carolyn. **Where the Broken Heart Still Beats: The Story of Cynthia Ann Parker**. San Diego: Gulliver, Harcourt Brace, 1992. 196p. $16.95; $7pa. ISBN 0-15-200639-7; 0-15-295602-6pa. 6-9

When Cynthia Parker was nine in 1836, a raiding band of Comanche warriors kidnapped her. Lucy tells the story of her aunt after Texas rangers recapture her and her daughter in 1861. Called Naduah, she has no desire to live with whites because she is happily married with two other children. She almost escapes twice, and she lives with the hope that her son Quanah will find her and return her to the people she loves and understands. After fever kills her daughter, she also dies. *American Library Association Best Books for Young Adults*, *Notable Children's Trade Books in the Field of Social Studies*, *IRA Teachers' Choices*, and *New York Public Library's Books for the Teen Age*.

1568. Meyer, Susan E. **Mary Cassatt**. New York: Harry N. Abrams, 1990. 92p. $19.95. ISBN 0-8109-3154-0. (First Impressions). 4-8

Born into a wealthy family during the Victorian age, Mary Cassatt (1844-1926) became a painter when "nice girls didn't do that sort of thing." She went to Paris to work and study, met the Impressionists, and began to work in a similar style. Photographs and reproductions enhance the text. Index.

1569. Migneco, Ronald, and Timothy Levi Biel. **The Crash of 1929**. Maurie Manning, et al., illustrators. San Diego, CA: Lucent, 1990. 64p. $12.95. ISBN 1-56006-003-4. (World Disasters). 5-7

After the "Roaring Twenties," with stocks on Wall Street rising in a bull market, the market crashed on October 29, 1929. With its fall began the Depression, which finally ended after Franklin Delano Roosevelt instituted the New Deal and America entered World War II. The text discusses aspects of the stock market and why it fell so radically. Additionally, it considers the market today and whether it could do the same thing. Photographs augment the text. Further Reading, Glossary, Other Works Consulted, and Index.

1570. Miller, Brandon Marie. **Buffalo Gals: Women of the Old West**. Minneapolis, MN: Lerner, 1995. 88p. $18.95. ISBN 0-8225-1730-2. 4-8

Reproductions and text give a good view of women who went west during the nineteenth century. Topics covered include why they left home, the homes they tried to create, their use of leisure time, their hopes for the future, falling in love, and the clash between Native American and white women. Bibliography and Index. *Notable Children's Trade Books in the Field of Social Studies*, *IRA Teachers' Choices*, *Scientific American Young Readers Book Award*, and *Society of School Librarians Outstanding Book*.

1571. Miller, Natalie. **The Statue of Liberty**. Rev. ed. Chicago: Childrens Press, 1992. 31p. $11.45. ISBN 0-516-06655-2. (Cornerstones of Freedom). 3-5

The text tells the story of the Statue of Liberty from its creation in France, the plan to get money for its pedestal, and the restoration necessary for its centennial. Photographs complement the story. Index.

1572. Miller, Robert. **Buffalo Soldiers: The Story of Emanuel Stance**. Michael Bryant, illustrator. Englewood Cliffs, NJ: Silver Press, 1995. Unpaged. $12.95; $4.95pa. ISBN 0-382-24400-1; 0-382-24395-1pa. 1-4

After the Civil War ended, Congress voted to add four all-Black infantry units to the army. They went out West to protect white settlers from Indian raids, and their effectiveness earned the respect of the Indians they defeated. Named buffalo soldiers because their hair resembled buffalo's hair, they earned several Medals of Honor, with the first going to Emanuel Stance at the age of 19. The text tells his story.

1573. Miller, Robert. **The Story of Nat Love**. Michael Bryant, illustrator. Englewood Cliffs, NJ: Silver Press, 1994. Unpaged. $12.95. ISBN 0-382-24398-6. 1-3

Nat Love (1854-1921) learned how to herd, rope, and brand cows and horses as a slave in Tennessee. After the Civil War, he went west and became one of the most famous of the 8,000 African Americans who drove cattle on the Chisholm Trail. After he won a riding, roping, and shooting contest in Deadwood, South Dakota, he was given the nickname "Deadwood Dick."

1574. Miller, William. **Frederick Douglass: The Last Day of Slavery**. Cedric Lucas, illustrator. New York: Lee & Low, 1995. 32p. $14.95. ISBN 1-880000-17-2. 1-4

Frederick Douglass faced a slave breaker when he was 17. The man supposedly struck Douglass with a whip while the other slaves watched in disbelief. In his autobiography, however, Douglass says that he struck the first blow and other slaves joined him in the resistance. Regardless, the story of Douglass before he escaped slavery is a dramatic moment in history.

1575. Mills, Claudia. **What About Annie?** New York: Walker, 1985. 68p. $9.95. ISBN 0-8027-6573-4. 5 up

When Annie is 13 in 1931, her father loses his job, and her family has to find support during the Depression. Her friends and their families have similar problems during this difficult period. As she passes through her teenage years toward 18, she becomes intrigued with flying. The Lindbergh baby's kidnapping and murder sadden her, but Amelia Earhart's achievements in the air are delightful. Becoming interested in this whole new aspect of life helps her cope with daily difficulties.

1576. Milton, Joyce. **Marching to Freedom: The Story of Martin Luther King, Jr.** 1987. Minneapolis, MN: Gareth Stevens, 1995. 112p. $13.95. ISBN 0-8368-1382-0. (Famous Lives). 3-6

In 1943, "M. L." faced Jim Crow laws when he was riding on a bus. Martin Luther King, Jr. (1929-1968) became a major voice in the Civil Rights movement by advocating nonviolence rather than force as African Americans tried to overturn Jim Crow laws. His courage has been a guide to many after him. Photographs, Highlights in the Life, For Further Study, and Index.

1577. Milton, Joyce. **The Story of Hillary Rodham Clinton: First Lady of the United States**. Minneapolis, MN: Gareth Stevens, 1995. 112p. $13.95. ISBN 0-8368-1381-2. (Famous Lives). 3-6

Hillary Rodham Clinton (b. 1947) cannot be considered merely the president's wife. She is also a woman with her own mind. She graduated from Wellesley, went to Yale Law School, and worked in a firm before her husband was elected President in 1992. She is also a mother who takes time to be with her daughter. Balancing public and private life while keeping a strong character take much effort. Photographs, Highlights in the Life, For Further Study, and Index.

1578. Minahan, John A. **Abigail's Drum**. Robert Quackenbush, illustrator. New York: Pippin, 1995. 64p. $14.95. ISBN 0-945912-25-0. 2-5

Rebecca Bates, 11, and her sister Abigail are bored at the Scituate, Massachusetts, lighthouse that their father tends. As entertainment, they try to sound like the Home Guard corps when they play their fife and drum. In 1812, the British stage a supply raid and take their father captive. Rebecca and Abigail start playing their music in the lighthouse, and the echoes make them sound like a much larger group. Because the British think that many soldiers are coming, they retreat.

1579. Mintz, Penny. **Thomas Edison: Inventing the Future**. New York: Fawcett, 1990. 118p. $3.95pa. ISBN 0-449-90378-8pa. (Great Lives). 5-8

Although this look at Thomas Edison (1847-1931) covers his entire life, it emphasizes the years during which he was trying to develop the incandescent light bulb. He was a man focused on his work to such an extent that he could be unpleasant in his relationships with others. Bibliography.

1580. Mitchell, Barbara. **We'll Race You, Henry**. Kathy Haubrich, illustrator. Minneapolis, MN: Carolrhoda, 1986. 56p. $17.50. ISBN 0-87614-291-9. (Creative Minds). 3-6

People twice wanted to put money on Henry Ford's cars, but Ford (1863-1947) refused to start production until he thought the car was ready. Not until he had built racing prototypes, one that lasted through a hard race, did he think that cars with his name should be sold. Another man offered to put money into the business, and on June 13, 1903, Ford Motor Company started and is still functioning today. The text looks at the influences that caused Ford to want to develop horseless carriages, including his early interest in mechanical things like springs and gears and cogs. *Outstanding Science Trade Books for Children.*

1581. Mitchell, Barbara. **The Wizard of Sound: A Story About Thomas Edison**. Hetty Mitchell, illustrator. Minneapolis, MN: Carolrhoda, 1991. 64p. $17.50. ISBN 0-87614-445-8. (Creative Minds). 4-6

Thomas A. (Alva) Edison (1847-1931) was a sickly child who became a shy and inept student. Most of the text discusses Edison's favorite invention, the phonograph. Other inventions are listed in the back of the book. Bibliography.

1582. Mitchell, Margaree King. **Uncle Jed's Barbershop**. James Ransome, illustrator. New York: Simon & Schuster, 1993. 34p. $15. ISBN 0-671-67969-3. 3-6

As the only Black barber in his county of the segregated South during the 1920s, five-year-old Sarah Jean's Uncle Jed has to travel around to cut people's hair. He wants to open his own barbershop and is saving money for it. When Sarah Jean needs an emergency operation, he gives his money to the doctor. When the Depression comes, he loses his money in a bank failure. Finally he opens his shop when he is 79; the adult Sarah Jean gets to twirl around in his new barber's chair. *Coretta Scott King Honor.*

1583. Mizell, Linda. **Think About Racism**. New York: Walker, 1992. 230p. $15.85. ISBN 0-8027-8113-6. (Think). 6-10

Mizell's theory is that the history of racism in the United States is actually the history of people of color. Among the topics she presents are an assessment of Christopher Columbus, an overview of the slave trade and slavery laws, the Jim Crow laws, lynching, white supremacist groups, and relationships with Mexican and Japanese Americans, including the Japanese internment during World War II. She focuses on African Americans, Native Americans, Latinos, and Asian Americans through the Civil Rights movements of the 1960s. Glossary, Bibliography, and Index.

1584. Mochizuki, Ken. **Baseball Saved Us**. Dom Lee, illustrator. New York: Lee & Low, 1993. Unpaged. $14.95. ISBN 1-880000-01-6. 3-6

Shorty goes with his family to the internment camp during World War II because he is Japanese. When the young people start acting insolent to the adults, his father realizes that they need baseball. The adults create a field, and soon people of all ages are playing. Shorty gets better at his game, and when he leaves the camp and people call him "Jap," he gets angry and proves he can play baseball as well as anyone. *Parents' Choice Award.*

1585. Mochizuki, Ken. **Heroes**. Dom Lee, illustrator. New York: Lee & Low, 1995. Unpaged. $14.95. ISBN 1-880000-16-4. 3-6

Donnie hates to play war in the 1960s because his friends want him to be the enemy because he looks like "them." When he tells his friends that his father and uncle both served in the army, his friends refuse to believe it. Donnie continues to suffer until his father and uncle realize they must help him. Then he becomes the leader rather than the quarry.

1586. Moeri, Louise. **Save Queen of Sheba**. 1981. New York: Puffin, 1994. 116p. $3.99pa. ISBN 0-14-037148-6pa. 5-8

After a Sioux raid on their portion of the wagon train, King David, 12, and Queen of Sheba, six, cannot find their father or his wagon. Although almost scalped himself, King David looks after Queen of Sheba as they walk along the trail. He eventually recovers and becomes reunited with his father.

1587. Mohr, Nicholasa. **All for the Better: A Story of El Barrio**. Rudy Gutierrez, illustrator. Austin, TX: Raintree/Steck-Vaughn, 1993. 56p. $22.83; $4.95pa. ISBN 0-81147-220-5; 0-81147-060-7pa. (Stories of America). 2-5

Evalina Lopez Antonetty came alone from Puerto Rico to New York and the Bronx during the Depression. She adjusted to English and to a new school and then convinced her proud neighbors to accept food stamps from the federal government so they could survive. She eventually formed the United Bronx Parents group to help the Hispanic community.

1588. Monceaux, Morgan. **Jazz: My Music, My People**. New York: Knopf, 1994. 64p. $18. ISBN 0-679-85618-8. 6 up

The text looks at the history of jazz through profiles of its greatest performers. The first segment covers the early years when jazz was taking shape under such talents as W. C. Handy, Leadbelly, Jelly Roll Morton, Ma Rainey, and Louis Armstrong. The second part continues with the swing years and dance music from Duke Ellington, Billie Holiday, Ella Fitzgerald, and Dorothy Dandridge. The third section on bebop and modern jazz poses questions about what will come next in the jazz world. Some of the performers mentioned here are Charlie Parker, Nat King Cole, Sarah Vaughan, and Pearl Bailey. Glossary and Index.

1589. Monjo, F. N. **The Drinking Gourd**. Fred Brenner, illustrator. 1970. New York: HarperCollins, 1993. 64p. $14.95; $3.75pa. ISBN 0-06-024329-5; 0-06-444042-7pa. K-3

Tommy misbehaves in church, and his father sends him home alone. In the barn, he finds four escaped slaves who tell him that they are following the "drinking gourd," or the North Star, to Canada. When Tommy's father hides them in the hay wagon and takes them to the river, Tommy realizes that his father is breaking the law. He also knows that the reward money for reporting on escaped slaves is very high. He has to adjust to the idea that some laws and some rewards are damaging rather than helpful. *American Library Association Notable Books for Children*.

1590. Monjo, F. N. **Gettysburg: Tad Lincoln's Story**. Douglas Gorsline, illustrator. New York: Simon & Schuster, 1976. 45p. ISBN 0-671-96143-8. 2-5

In first-person point of view, Tad Lincoln tells the story of Gettysburg as his father told it to him after returning from his speech in 1863. Tad had to wait to hear it because his father got smallpox as soon as he returned to the White House. But when his father tells Tad about the battle, he shows him maps with red pins stuck in spots representing the Rebels and blue pins for the Union soldiers. Bibliography.

1591. Monjo, F. N. **Grand Papa and Ellen Aroon**. Richard Cuffari, illustrator. New York: Henry Holt, 1974. 58p. $5.50. ISBN 0-03-012091-8. 2-5

Ellen Aroon (Ellen Wayles Randolph), Thomas Jefferson's nine-year-old granddaughter, tells about visiting her grandfather at Monticello, his home, or in Washington, where he works at the White House. She tells about his accomplishments as statesman, astronomer, inventor, architect, writer, and gardener. About This Story and Bibliography.

1592. Monjo, F. N. **The House on Stink Alley: A Story About the Pilgrims in Holland**. Robert Quackenbush, illustrator. New York: Henry Holt, 1978. 64p. ISBN 0-03-016651-9. 2-5

Love-of-God Brewster, or Love, eight, tells about his life in Leyden, Holland, before coming on the *Mayflower* in 1620. His family and their friends worshipped as Saints of the Holy Disciples. Their people had had to leave England because James I would not let them choose the pastor of their congregation. Love's father adopted an orphan, William Bradford, who later became the governor of Plymouth Colony after those who escaped persecution were able to go to the American colonies.

1593. Monjo, F. N. **King George's Head Was Made of Lead**. Margot Tomes, illustrator. New York: Coward, McCann & Geoghegan, 1974. 48p. $5.95. ISBN 0-698-20298-8. 2-5

The statue of King George III on New York City's Bowling Green tells the story of the 13 colonies who will not listen to him and do as he has requested. He establishes the Stamp Tax and then the Tea Tax, but they refuse to pay. Because the statue's head is made of lead, he does not listen to those who advise him otherwise, and the colonists revolt against him.

1594. Monjo, F. N. **Me and Willie and Pa: The Story of Abraham Lincoln and His Son Tad**. New York: Simon & Schuster, 1973. 94p. $8.95. ISBN 0-671-65211-7. 2-6

Tad, Abraham Lincoln's son, tells what he observed about his father. This unusual point of view gives an innocence to situations loaded with various kinds of emotionally charged information. The usual facts about Abraham Lincoln (1809-1865) appear, but Tad remembers Washington as being a sad place because his brother and father both died there. Bibliography.

1595. Monjo, F. N. **A Namesake for Nathan**. Eros Keith, illustrator. New York: Coward, McCann & Geoghegan, 1977. 48p. $6.95. ISBN 0-698-20411-5. 4-7

Joanna Hale, 12, and her family prepare for her brother Nathan's leave from the army during 1776. The women support the six family men serving in the Continental army by spinning, weaving, and knitting. As the story progresses, Joanna and her family learn that the British have executed Nathan, 21, for spying.

1596. Monjo, F. N. **The One Bad Thing About Father**. 1970. Rocco Negri, illustrator. New York: Trophy-Harper, 1987. 64p. $3.50pa. ISBN 0-06-444110-5pa. (I Can Read Book). K-3

The text, a fictional account of Theodore Roosevelt (1858-1919) as related by his children, gives an insight into the character of the 26th President of the United States.

1597. Monjo, F. N. **Poor Richard in France**. Brinton Turkle, illustrator. New York: Henry Holt, 1973. 58p. $4.95. ISBN 0-03-088598-1. 2-6

Benny Bache, Benjamin Franklin's grandson, goes with him to France in 1769 and 1770. Benny observes his grandfather's behavior in Paris and sees that it is different from home. Everyone already knows his grandfather, and his grandfather's picture adorns many items. Franklin wears plain clothes and a fur cap like Daniel Boone because the French want to think he has lived close to the frontier. Like a good diplomat, Franklin fulfills the expectations of those from whom he would like help. About This Story.

1598. Monjo, F. N. **The Vicksburg Veteran**. Douglas Gorsline, illustrator. New York: Simon & Schuster, 1971. 62p. $5.95. ISBN 0-671-65156-0. 2-6

Fred Grant, 12, accompanies his father, General Ulysses S. Grant, to Vicksburg, Mississippi, in 1863. Fred tells the story of the siege there that lasted from April to July and the importance of this victory, which cut the Confederacy into two parts and gave the North full control over the Mississippi River. He also tells how good a general his father is.

1599. Monroe, Jean Guard, and Ray A. Williamson. **First Houses: Native American Homes and Sacred Structures**. Susan Johnston Carlson, illustrator. Boston: Houghton Mifflin, 1993. 160p. $14.95. ISBN 0-395-51081-3. 5-9

The text, with pen-and-ink drawings, presents the homes of various Native American tribes while noting that their different creation myths served as patterns for how the homes and ritual structures would be built. The dwellings also relate closely to the climate and the local building materials. Buildings discussed include the Iroquois longhouse, the Pueblo kiva, the Navajo hogan, Mohave houses, Pawnee earth lodges, the Plains tipi, Northwest Coast dwellings, and the sweatlodge, an important structure in many tribes. Bibliography and Index.

1600. Mooney, Martin J. **The Comanche Indians**. New York: Chelsea House, 1993. 71p. $14.95; $6.95pa. ISBN 0-7910-1653-6; 0-7910-1957-8pa. (Junior Library of American Indians). 3-6

The Comanches settled in Texas, New Mexico, Oklahoma, Colorado, and Kansas in the early 1700s, and the area became known as the *Comanchería*. Many of them were killed in the battle at Adobe Walls, which was their last great effort in 1874 to get rid of Americans in their homeland. Much of their land became the state of Oklahoma in 1907. Photographs and drawings enhance the text. Glossary, Chronology, and Index.

1601. Moore, Ruth Nulton. **Distant Thunder**. Allan Eitzen, illustrator. Scottdale, PA: Herald, 1991. 160p. $5.95pa. ISBN 0-8361-3557-1pa. 4-8

When the War of Independence begins, prisoners of war come to Bethlehem, Pennsylvania, in 1777, where Kate, 15, lives with her aunt's family while her parents serve in the mission field. The Moravians do not believe in war, but they know they must help with peaceful ways. They welcome wounded soldiers to their buildings and try to feed as many as possible. Kate, her cousin, and their Indian friend help a Hessian drummer boy escape capture by the American guards and meet the young Marquis de Lafayette, a French nobleman come to help the fight. It is a difficult year, but Kate's mother reunites with her brother, adopted years before by the Seneca Indians.

1602. Morin, Isobel V. **Women of the U.S. Congress**. Minneapolis, MN: Oliver Press, 1994. 160p. $14.95. ISBN 1-881508-12-9. (Profiles). 5-7

This book looks at 11 of the women voted into Congress during the twentieth century: Jeannette Rankin (1880-1973); Margaret Chase Smith (1897-1994); Helen Gahagan Douglas (1900-1980); Shirley Chisholm (b. 1924); Barbara Jordan (1936-1996); Nancy Landon Kassebaum (b. 1932); Barbara Mikulski (b. 1936); and the women elected in 1992, who were Dianne Feinstein, Barbara Boxer, Patty Murray, and Carol Moseley Braun. Women Who Served in the U.S. Congress, Bibliography, and Index.

1603. Morin, Isobel V. **Women Who Reformed Politics**. Minneapolis, MN: Oliver Press, 1994. 160p. $14.95. ISBN 1-881508-16-1. (Profiles). 6 up

Women who saw connections between social problems, the second-class status of women, and racial justice worked for reforms in politics. The women included in this text are Abby Kelley Foster, crusader against slavery (1811-1887); Frances Willard, temperance fighter (1839-1898); Ida Wells-Barnett, intolerant of mob violence (1862-1931); Carrie Chapman Catt, right to vote (1859-1947); Molly Dewson, political boss (1874-1962); Pauli Murray, for integration (1910-1985); Fannie Lou Hamer, civil rights (1917-1977); and Gloria Steinem, women's rights (b. 1934). Major Reforms in U.S. History, Bibliography, and Index.

1604.   Morley, Jacqueline. **Clothes: For Work, Play and Display**. Vanda Baginskia, Mark Bergin, John James, Carolyn Scrace, and Gerald Wood, illustrators. New York: Franklin Watts, 1992. 48p. $7.95pa. ISBN 0-531-15740-7pa. (Timelines). 5-8

Two-page spreads divide the text into minichapters with many illustrations to show clothes throughout history. The time periods covered are the first clothes people wore; classical clothes of the Minoans, Greeks, and Romans; the Dark Ages; armor and tournament gear; medieval and Renaissance Italy; farthingales with Spanish influence in the sixteenth century; seventeenth-century Cavaliers and Puritans in England; court clothes and politics of France; crinoline petticoats introduced in 1857; folk costumes; dress reforms like bloomers; sportswear; between the World Wars; work clothes; clothes today; and clothes of the future. Timeline, Glossary, and Index.

1605.   Morley, Jacqueline. **Exploring North America**. David Antram, illustrator. New York: Peter Bedrick, 1996. 48p. $18.95. ISBN 0-87226-488-2. (Voyages of Discovery). 3-6

The text covers the four centuries of exploration beginning with Columbus, Cabot, and the Conquistadores and continues through Cartier, Champlain, Lewis and Clark, Mackenzie, and Fremont. The entries that give an overview of the topic cover double-page spreads and contain illustrations. Maps, Glossary, and Index.

1606.   Morpurgo, Michael. **Twist of Gold**. New York: Viking, 1993. 246p. $14.99. ISBN 0-670-84851-4. 5-9

When Sean O'Brien's mother is too sick from hunger to travel during the 1850s, he and his sister leave Ireland to join their father in America. They carry with them the symbol of their clan: the golden torc (necklace) of their ancestors. Thieves who know of their possession try to steal it, and twice they lose it. But twice they find it again as they travel from Boston to California to meet their father, and surprisingly, their mother, who has been able to make a quicker, safer journey.

1607.   Morpurgo, Michael. **The Wreck of the Zanzibar**. François Place, illustrator. New York: Viking, 1995. 64p. $14.99. ISBN 0-670-86360-2. 3-5

Laura Perryman's great-nephew inherits her diary at her death, and he finds that she had an amazing story. When she had been a young girl, she had wanted to help her father salvage ships wrecked at sea. One day in 1907, she had her chance, and the *Zanzibar* rescue changed the town for a long time. The story includes characterizations of family members and their needs as well as her own.

1608.   Morris, Gilbert. **The Dangerous Voyage**. Minneapolis, MN: Bethany House, 1995. 104p. $5.99pa. ISBN 1-55661-395-4pa. (Time Navigators, 1). 4-6

Time travelers Danny and Dixie Fortune find themselves in seventeenth-century London boarding the *Mayflower*. Because one of their shipmates steals the Recall Unit that will return them home, they must stay on the ship for its entire journey to the colonies. They meet figures known through history, such as John Alden, as well as those who seek freedom to worship, known as the "saints," and those who want a better life, the "strangers." The Fortunes' Christian values become clear during the plot development.

1609.   Morris, Jeffrey. **The FDR Way**. Minneapolis, MN: Lerner, 1996. 128p. $22.95. ISBN 0-8225-2929-7. (Great Presidential Decisions). 5 up

Franklin Delano Roosevelt was elected President for four terms. During those years, he had to make many decisions, beginning with what to do about the Depression, which had destroyed many lives before he took office in 1933. The text looks at his style, the first 100 days of his presidency, his fight for social security, his choices for the Supreme Court, how he traded destroyers to Great Britain in World War II for 99-year leases in the Western Hemisphere, his decision to seek a third term, his creation of the United Nations, and his death. Index.

1610.   Morris, Jeffrey. **The Jefferson Way**. Minneapolis, MN: Lerner, 1994. 128p. $23.95. ISBN 0-8225-2926-2. (Great Presidential Decisions). 6-9

The text presents some of the major decisions, good and bad, that Thomas Jefferson (1743-1826) made as President. These decisions and their effects on the country's life are part of the examination of his presidency. Photographs and reproductions enhance the text. Glossary, Further Reading, and Index.

1611.   Morris, Jeffrey. **The Lincoln Way**. Minneapolis, MN: Lerner, 1996. 136p. $22.95. ISBN 0-8225-2930-0. (Great Presidential Decisions). 5 up

The text looks at Lincoln while he was President and the decisions that he had to make. The chapter topics include the election of 1860, Lincoln's qualifications for the presidency, how Lincoln made decisions, what kind of man he was, the decision he made to preserve the Union and to back down in the *Trent* affair, the decision not to change the cabinet but to free the slaves, his attempt to find a general, his final days, and his questions about how to reconstruct the South. Index.

1612. Morris, Jeffrey. **The Truman Way**. Minneapolis, MN: Lerner, 1995. 128p. $22.95. ISBN 0-8225-2927-0. (Great Presidential Decisions). 7-9

The first decision that Harry Truman made as President when Franklin Delano Roosevelt died on April 12, 1945, was that the conference for creating the United Nations would proceed as planned. Morris looks at other decisions that Truman had to make while President such as dropping the atomic bomb on Japan, aiding Europe after the end of World War II, and standing against Communist aggression with the Truman Doctrine. Morris asks what led to the decisions, what other options the President might have had, and what the long-term effects have been. Photographs complement the text. Index. *Society of School Librarians International Outstanding Book.*

1613. Morris, Jeffrey. **The Washington Way**. Minneapolis, MN: Lerner, 1994. 128p. $22.95. ISBN 0-8225-2928-9. 6-9

As the first President, George Washington set many precedents. He established traditions that have influenced the role of the Presidents throughout the years. Most of his decisions worked well, and the text looks at his time in office and examines the situations and the solutions that he offered. Photographs and reproductions enhance the text. Glossary, Further Reading, and Index.

1614. Morris, Jeffrey Brandon. **The Reagan Way**. Minneapolis, MN: Lerner, 1995. 124p. $22.95. ISBN 0-8225-2931-9. (Great Presidential Decisions). 6-9

Beginning with a biographical overview of Ronald Reagan's life, the text looks at the major decisions that he made during his presidency from 1980 to 1988. He cut taxes and increased defense spending, sent American troops to Lebanon, supported tax reform, traded arms for hostages in the Iran-Contra situation, and talked to the Soviets about arms reduction. In his attempt to be fair, Morris decides not to assess Reagan's decisions because time has not yet proven them either good or bad. Index.

1615. Morris, Juddi. **The Harvey Girls: The Women Who Civilized the West**. New York: Walker, 1994. 101p. $15.95. ISBN 0-8027-8302-3. 6-9

Fred Harvey started railroad restaurants and hotels in the American West at such places as Dodge City, Topeka, Santa Fe, and Albuquerque. To staff these establishments, he imported young, single white women who had character references as spotless as their uniforms. The text discusses what being a "Harvey girl" meant and why the women went west initially. Economic circumstances were usually the prime reason that the women took jobs with Harvey. After World War II, the chain began to decline, and Morris discusses reasons why this might have happened. Photographs, Notes, Bibliography, and Index.

1616. Morrison, Dorothy Nafus. **Chief Sarah: Sarah Winnemucca's Fight for Indian Rights**. New York: Atheneum, 1980. 170p. $9.95. ISBN 0-689-30752-7. 6-8

An Indian woman with only three weeks of formal education, Sarah Winnemucca (1844-1891) became a successful lecturer, wrote the first book published in English by any Native American, and started the first school taught and administered by Indians. Her people, the Paiutes, suffered when miners and settlers moved into Nevada, taking their land and resources. Sarah often argued with the corrupt Bureau of Indian Affairs about the rights of Indians. The text relies on her autobiography, newspaper accounts, and her letters. She is sometimes called the Indian Joan of Arc because of her willingness to support the cause of her people. Photographs and prints enhance the text. Bibliography and Index.

1617. Morrow, Barbara, author/illustrator. **Edward's Portrait**. New York: Macmillan, 1991. 32p. $13.95. ISBN 0-02-767591-2. K-3

Having a daguerreotype made requires that Edward stay still for a minute in the mid-1800s. He dreads the ordeal, but the photographer tells stories about Indians in the West, which focuses his attention on something else.

1618. Morrow, Barbara, author/illustrator. **Help for Mr. Peale**. New York: Macmillan, 1990. 32p. $14.95. ISBN 0-02-767590-4. 2-3

In 1794, Rubens, 10, one of Charles Willson Peale's children, helps his father move their taxidermy collection from one home to another in Philadelphia. Rubens decides that the move will be a parade, with each of his friends carrying an animal to the new house, also to be a museum. He and his brothers Rembrandt, Titian, and Raphaelle ready the items for removal.

1619. Morrow, Honoré. **On to Oregon!** 1927. New York: Beech Tree, Morrow, 1991. 239p. $4.95pa. ISBN 0-688-10494-0pa. 5-9

John, 13, leaves Missouri with his family in 1844 for a journey to Oregon. Both of his parents die on the way, and he takes the other six children the remaining 1,000 miles through snow and mountains.

1620.   Morrow, Mary Frances. **Sarah Winnemucca**. Ken Bronikowski, illustrator. Austin, TX: Raintree/Steck-Vaughn, 1992. 32p. $19.97. ISBN 0-8172-3402-0. (Native American Stories). 3-5

Sarah Winnemucca (1844-1891), a full-blooded Paiute Indian, became a spokesperson for Indian rights at a time when few women or Indians became leaders. White people called her "Princess Sarah," a name she liked because it drew attention to her causes. She met with President Rutherford B. Hayes about her people, and in 1881 she opened a school for Indian children. History.

1621.   Moscinski, Sharon. **Tracing Our Irish Roots**. Santa Fe, NM: John Muir, 1993. 46p. $12.95. ISBN 1-56261-148-8. 3-6

The text looks at life in Ireland for people who decided to emigrate to the United States. Many had to leave after the potato famine because they had no way to support themselves, but they have contributed much to American culture. The two parts of the text, the Old World and the New World, give an overview, with two-page spreads on such topics as crossing the Atlantic, Ellis Island, family life, prejudices faced, achievements in America, and famous people of Irish descent. Archival photographs highlight the text. Index.

1622.   Moseley, Elizabeth R. **Davy Crockett: Hero of the Wild Frontier**. New York: Chelsea Juniors, 1991. 80p. $14.95. ISBN 0-7910-1409-6. (Discovery Biography). 3-6

As a boy, Davy Crockett (1786-1836) became a skillful hunter, a hard worker, and a good storyteller. He went to Congress, where he fought for the rights of the Indian and for property rights of homesteaders. He believed that one should be sure of being correct and then going ahead. He kept moving west and ended up in Texas, where he died fighting for the dream of an independent Texas.

1623.   Moser, Barry. **Fly! A Brief History of Flight Illustrated**. New York: Willa Perlman, HarperCollins, 1993. Unpaged. $16. ISBN 0-06-022893-8. 2-6

This brief history of flight has illustrations of airplanes and their famous pilots who have contributed to the history of flight in the nineteenth and twentieth centuries. Bibliography.

1624.   Moss, Miriam. **Forts and Castles**. Chris Forsey, illustrator. Austin, TX: Raintree/Steck-Vaughn, 1994. 32p. $21.40. ISBN 0-8114-6157-2. (Pointers). 3-3

The brief text and labeled illustrations on two-page spreads discuss the history and architecture of several forts and castles, focusing on their ability to protect themselves in times of siege. The various types are a Bronze Age citadel, an Iron Age hill fort, Herod's fort, a Norman keep, a Crusader castle, a medieval castle, a fourteenth-century castle, a French château, a Japanese castle, an Indian fortress, a Civil War fort, and a romantic castle, Neuschwanstein. Glossary and Index.

1625.   Muggamin, Howard. **The Jewish Americans**. New York: Chelsea House, 1995. 128p. $19.95; $8.95pa. ISBN 0-7910-3365-1; 0-7910-3387-2pa. (The Immigrant Experience). 6-9

The first Jewish immigrants to settle in America came in 1654 because they wanted to worship in their own congregations. In the eighteenth century, more than 150,000 Jews arrived from Germany. In the decades following, more than 4 million came, fleeing the anti-Semitism of their homelands. The text, with accompanying photographs, tells of their history and their contribution to American culture. Further Reading and Index.

1626.   Muhlberger, Richard. **What Makes a Cassatt a Cassatt?** New York: Viking, 1994. 48p. $11.99. ISBN 0-670-85742-4. 5-9

Although born an American, Mary Cassatt (1844-1926) lived most of her life in Paris, painting in the style of the French Impressionists. She traveled to Spain, and her study of the work of Velásquez and Goya led her to focus on people and eliminate almost all background detail. Japanese work inspired her to use contrasting colors and tilted perspective. She used solid lines and clear colors to present relationships between people. Included are reproductions and discussions of *Offering the Panale to the Bullfighter*, *Little Girl in a Blue Armchair*, *At the Opéra*, *Lydia Crocheting in the Garden at Marly*, *Five O'Clock Tea*, *Reading Le Figaro*, *Children Playing on the Beach*, *The Letter*, *Baby Reaching for an Apple*, *The Boating Party*, *Breakfast in Bed*, and *Mother and Child*.

1627.   Munro, Bob. **Aircraft**. Ian Moores, illustrator. Austin, TX: Raintree/Steck-Vaughn, 1994. 32p. $21.40. ISBN 0-8114-6161-0. (Pointers). 3-6

The two-page spreads of brief text and labeled illustrations describe different types of aircraft. They include a long-range airliner, commuter airline, medium-range airline, supersonic airliner, helicopter, tilt-rotor aircraft, jump jet, supersonic fighter, swing-wing interceptor, stealth fighter, aerobatic airplane, and glider. Glossary and Index.

1628.   Murdoch, David. **North American Indian**. New York: Dorling Kindersley, 1995. 62p. $19. ISBN 0-679-096169-0. 4 up

In conjunction with the artifacts of the American Museum of Natural History, the text gives an overview of the North American Indian. Two-page spreads cover such topics as the peopling of the Americas, medicine and the spirit world, the League of the Iroquois, the Mid-Atlantic Seaboard, the Ohio River Valley, the western Great Lakes, the Southeast, the Great Plains, the Dakota Sioux, Mandan and Hidatsa, war and peace, the Sun Dance, the Plateau, the Great Basin, California, the Southwest, the Pueblo peoples, Apache and Navajo, Papago and Pima, totem pole land, art, the potlatch, northern hunters, the Arctic, and modern times. Index.

1629.   Murdoch, David H. **Cowboy**. New York: Dorling Kindersley, 1993. 64p. $19. ISBN 0-679-84014-1. (Eyewitness). 3 up

This overview of cowboys includes brief topics on dress such as hats, boots, chaps, and spurs. It also looks at the *charros* and *vaqueros*, the best horses, saddles, life on the ranch, cattle and branding, ranges, trail drives, law and order, guns and gunslingers, the South American gaucho, Camargue *Gardians* of France, cowgirls, cowboys in Australia, the rodeo, and the culture of the cowboy. Index.

1630.   Murphy, Claire Rudolf. **Gold Star Sister**. New York: Lodestar, 1994. 166p. $14.99. ISBN 0-525-67492-6. 6-9

In a first-person narrative, Carrie, 13, describes her pleasure at her Gram coming to live with the family and her consternation at Gram's rapid surrender to the cancer invading her body. She and Gram spend time looking at Gram's memorabilia. She discovers letters from Billy Sweeney, a brother killed by friendly fire in a World War II Aleutian Islands battle. She also finds a letter that Billy was supposed to give to a dying soldier's baby son, but his own death prevented the delivery. Carrie determines that she must find the son and give him the letter before Gram dies.

1631.   Murphy, Jim. **Across America on an Emigrant Train**. New York: Clarion, 1993. 150p. $16.95. ISBN 0-395-63390-7. 5-8

The text looks at a journey that the young writer Robert Louis Stevenson made in 1879 when he traveled from Scotland to see the woman he loved in California. He took the cheapest transportation and wrote about it. Murphy uses Stevenson's words to tell about the construction of the transcontinental railroad and steam travel. Photographs, Drawings, Bibliography, and Index. *Orbis Pictus Award.*

1632.   Murphy, Jim. **The Boys' War: Confederate and Union Soldiers Talk About the Civil War**. New York: Clarion, 1990. 110p. $15.95. ISBN 0-89919-893-7. 6 up

Using quotes from boys who actually fought in the Civil War, Murphy shows that they left home at 16 or even younger for what they thought would be an exciting adventure. What they found was different, a savage slaughter of humans and animals from which many, if they survived, never psychologically recovered. The text looks at the thrill of enlistment, the rigors of camp life, and the terror of the battlefield. Bibliography and Index.

1633.   Murphy, Jim. **The Great Fire**. New York: Scholastic, 1995. 144p. $16.95. ISBN 0-590-47267-4. 5 up

One of the major disasters in American history was the Great Fire of 1871, when Chicago became a wasteland. The damage was so widespread that few believed the city could ever recover. It began when a small fire broke out in O'Leary's barn on a Sunday evening. The fire department could not locate the fire, and no one was particularly concerned. But the city's wooden sidewalks and roads burned when a steady wind fueled the flames. The text includes personal accounts of survivors and facts about this devastation as the people began to rebuild the city. Bibliography and Sources and Index. *Bulletin Blue Ribbon Book, American Library Association Notable Books for Children, American Library Association Best Books for Young Adults, Newbery Honor Book, Orbis Pictus Award, American Library Association Booklist Editors' Choices, Horn Book Fanfare Books, American Library Association Quick Picks for Reluctant Young Adult Readers, Notable Children's Trade Books in the Field of Social Studies, School Library Journal Best Book,* and *Boston Globe-Horn Book Honor.*

1634.   Murphy, Jim. **Into the Deep Forest with Henry David Thoreau**. Kate Kiesler, illustrator. New York: Clarion, 1995. 39p. $14.95. ISBN 0-395-60522-9. 3-6

Henry David Thoreau (1817-1862) went other places besides Walden Pond. The text looks at his life and works, with an emphasis on his three trips to Mount Katadn (now Katahdin) in Maine with two other travelers. Thoreau's journal gives the basis of the descriptions. Index.

1635.   Murphy, Jim. **The Long Road to Gettysburg**. New York: Clarion, 1992. 116p. $15.95. ISBN 0-395-55965-0. 6 up

This story of the Battle of Gettysburg, fought in 1863, includes firsthand accounts by young soldiers and others. It reveals the hardships, the anxieties accompanying the preparation and wait for the battle, the long days of the actual battle, and the anguish of treating the wounded and burying the dead. The address that President Lincoln delivered helped the families of the dead to think of their losses as being a sacrifice for liberty and equality. Photographs, Bibliography, and Index.

1636. Murphy, Jim. **Young Patriot: The American Revolution as Experienced by One Boy**. New York: Clarion, 1996. 101p. $15.95. ISBN 0-395-60523-7. 6 up

Joseph Plumb Martin, a 15-year-old from Connecticut, enlisted in the Continental army in 1776. Murphy uses Martin's self-published memoir to tell about his fears, boredom, and hardships in winter camp as well as other aspects of the American Revolution. Figures known to history, including Burgoyne, Cornwallis, and Washington, become indivduals in this intriguing view of the Revolution. Bibliography, Chronology, and Index. *School Library Journal Best Book.*

1637. Murphy, Virginia Reed. **Across the Plains in the Donner Party**. Karen Zeinert, ed. New York: Linnet, 1996. 112p. $19.50. ISBN 0-208-02404-2. 5-10

Virginia Reed, 12, went with her stepfather and her family to California with the Donners in 1846. Zeinert uses Reed's account of the ordeal published in a magazine after her marriage, along with information from Patrick Breen and notes from Virginia's stepfather James. The memoirs show that people in the group enjoyed their hunting parties, each other's company, and the scenery until they decided to take the Hastings Cutoff, advertised by Lanford Hastings as the quickest way through the Sierra Nevadas. As she keeps record of the increasing snow, Virginia Reed promises God that she will become a Catholic if she survives. Index.

1638. Myers, Anna. **Red-Dirt Jessie**. New York: Walker, 1992. 107p. $13.95. ISBN 0-8027-8172-1. 6-9

After Jessie's baby sister dies in 1930, Jessie's father stops talking. Her aunt and uncle leave for California, and when Jessie tries to get their dog to come home with her, the dog will not move. Only when the dog becomes wounded and cannot walk can she get it away from its house. But when the dog arrives and becomes part of the family, it saves Jessie from a wild dog and helps her father escape from his depression. *Oklahoma Book Award, Parents' Choice Award, Sequoyah Children's Book Award Masterlist, Volunteer State Book Ward Masterlist*, and *Land of Enchantment Book Award Masterlist.*

1639. Myers, Anna. **Rosie's Tiger**. New York: Walker, 1994. 121p. $14.95. ISBN 0-8027-8305-8. 5-7

Rosie adores her brother Ronny, especially after her mother dies, and she misses him while he is fighting in Korea during the 1950s. When she and her father hear that he is coming home, not alone but with a Korean wife who has a child, Rosie is distressed. Her new friend Cassandra tells her that she makes magic, and Rosie depends on Cassandra to help her get rid of the two extra people after they arrive. Rosie's wish almost comes true when the child Yong So falls into a cemetery cistern. But Rosie is surprised at what she learns about herself and her friend during the rescue and its aftermath.

1640. Myers, Anna. **Spotting the Leopard**. New York: Walker, 1996. 176p. $15.95. ISBN 0-8027-8459-3. 4-8

Jessie, from *Red-Dirt Jessie*, wants to go to college, but her father cannot afford to send her even though he has recovered from his Depression losses. Her brother H. J. knows that Jessie feels caged and wants to be free, just like the leopard named Lucky he has seen in the Oklahoma City zoo. When Lucky escapes, zoo officials search for him in fields near H. J. and Jessie's home. H. J. wants to find Lucky before the hunters kill him. He seems to think that saving Lucky will somehow help him save Jessie.

1641. Myers, Walter Dean. **Malcolm X: By Any Means Necessary**. New York: Scholastic, 1993. 210p. $13.95. ISBN 0-590-46484-1. 5 up

Malcolm Little's father died during the Depression, and his mother slowly went insane trying to feed her children and keep shelter over their heads. After she was committed to an asylum, he resented having to live in a foster home. He left for Boston and New York, where he was eventually arrested for theft and imprisoned for 10 years. After he was released, he began working with the Nation of Islam and Elijah Muhammad. Malcolm (1925-1965) took the last name "X" and spoke out against racial discrimination. When the two men split because Malcolm refused to curb his comments, Malcolm went on a *hajj* to Mecca. When he returned, he established his own group, but he was soon assassinated as he prepared to give a public speech. Chronology, Bibliography, and Index. *Coretta Scott King Honor Book, American Library Association Best Books for Young Adults, American Library Association Notable Books for Children*, and *Horn Book Fanfare Books.*

1642. Myers, Walter Dean. **Now Is Your Time: The African-American Struggle for Freedom**. New York: HarperCollins, 1991. 292p. $17.95; $10.95pa. ISBN 0-06-024370-8; 0-06-446120-3pa. 6 up

The text looks at three centuries of African American life with many individual stories. It includes anecdotes about Ibrahima, an educated Islamic scholar and Fula prince who was abducted into slavery; Meta Vaux Warrick, an artist; Dolly Dennis, Myers's great-grandmother; and many others. Myers shows how a group of people has been kept from its rightful heritage for several centuries. Photographs, Bibliography, and Index. *Coretta Scott King Author Award, American Library Association Notable Books for Children, American Library Association Best Books for Young Adults, Horn Book Fanfare Honor List, Orbis Pictus Honor Book, Golden Kite Honor Book for Nonfiction, Carter G. Woodson Book Award Outstanding Merit Book, Jane Addams Children' Honor Book Award*, and *New York Public Library's Books for the Teen Age.*

1643.   Myers, Walter Dean. **A Place Called Heartbreak: A Story of Vietnam**. Frederick Porter, illustrator. Austin TX: Raintree/Steck-Vaughn, 1993. 71p. $24.26; $6.64pa. ISBN 0-8114-7237-X; 0-8114-8077-1pa. (Stories of America—Personal Challenge). 5-9

In 1965, Major Fred Cherry was shot down on a routine mission near Hanoi in North Vietnam. He was the 43rd American and the first Black American to be captured. The Viet Cong beat him for 92 days straight even though his arm and ankle were broken. They finally hospitalized him, and afterward, he lived in solitary for almost a year before being imprisoned with other Americans. To communicate, the prisoners used a code of tapping on the walls that the guards could not hear. After being a prisoner for seven-and-a-half years, the war ended, and Fred Cherry became free. Epilogue, Afterword, and Notes.

1644.   Myers, Walter Dean. **The Righteous Revenge of Artemis Bonner**. New York: HarperCollins, 1992. 140p. $14. ISBN 0-06-020846-5. 5-9

At 15 in 1880, Artemis leaves New York City to avenge the murder of his uncle, Ugly Ned Bonner, and find a gold mine. He has a map his uncle made on his deathbed. Artemis travels from Mexico to the Alaskan Territory tracking Catfish Grimes and his female companion, Lucy Featherdip. In New Mexico he meets half-Cherokee Frolic, 12, who aids him in his search. *American Library Association Best Books for Young Adults* and *New York Public Library's Books for the Teen Age*.

1645.   Myers, Walter Dean. **Young Martin's Promise**. Barbara Higgins Bond, illustrator. Austin, TX: Raintree/Steck-Vaughn, 1993. 32p. $21.40; $6.64pa. ISBN 0-8114-7210-8; 0-8114-8050-Xpa. (Stories of America—Holidays). 2-5

When Martin Luther King, Jr. (1929-1968) was a young boy, he did not understand why he could no longer play with his white friends after they started elementary school. Other situations kept his parents from doing certain things. This background led to his strong support of civil rights as an adult and shows why the nation now celebrates a holiday in his honor.

N

1646. Naden, Corinne J., and Rose Blue. **John Muir: Saving the Wilderness**. Brookfield, CT: Millbrook Press, 1992. 48p. $11.90; $5.95pa. ISBN 1-56294-110-0; 1-56294-797-4pa. (Gateway Biography). 4-6

John Muir (1838-1914), a young immigrant from Scotland, loved to explore nature. As an adult, he realized the wilderness would disappear if someone did not save it from greedy developers who would destroy it. He began the Sierra Club and wrote about his explorations and the danger of losing the wilderness. Theodore Roosevelt went to visit him in Yosemite, California, and decided to establish national parks afterward. Photographs and Index.

1647. Naden, Corinne J., and Rose Blue. **The U.S. Coast Guard**. Brookfield, CT: Millbrook Press, 1993. 64p. $14.90. ISBN 1-56294-321-9. (Defending Our Country). 5-8

The text gives the origins of the U.S. Coast Guard and traces its combat history in America's wars. Chapters on weapons, equipment, personnel, organization, and work give an overview of this branch of the U.S. military. Photographs and drawings enhance the text. Further Reading, Glossary, and Index.

1648. Nardo, Don. **Jim Thorpe**. San Diego, CA: Lucent, 1994. 95p. $16.95. ISBN 1-56006-045-X. (The Importance Of). 7 up

During the first half of the twentieth century, Jim Thorpe (1887-1953) was perhaps the world's greatest athlete. He could kick a field goal from the 50-yard line and high jump more than six feet. At the 1912 Olympic Games in Sweden, he competed in both the decathlon and pentathlon, 15 grueling events, and won both. Because he had played semiprofessional baseball in the summer, his medals were taken from him, but they were posthumously restored in 1983. A Sac and Fox Indian, he and others on his Native American football team at the Indian School in Carlisle, Pennsylvania, showed their abilities only 14 years after the massacre at Wounded Knee. Whites had difficulty accepting the notion of an American Indian hero. Photographs, Notes, For Further Reading, Works Consulted, and Index.

1649. Nardo, Don. **Thomas Jefferson**. San Diego, CA: Lucent, 1993. 112p. $16.95. ISBN 1-56006-037-9. (The Importance Of). 5-8

Chapter headings in this biography of Thomas Jefferson (1743-1826) include topics that show his thirst for knowledge, his role in the colonies' rebellion, his writing of the Constitution, his reluctance to become a diplomat, his realization that he had to serve as President, his return to Monticello, and his legacy. Notes, For Further Reading, Works Consulted, and Index.

1650. Nash, Bruce, and Allan Zullo. **The Baseball Hall of Shame: Young Fans Edition**. New York: Archway, Pocket, 1990. 133p. $2.99pa. ISBN 0-671-69354-9pa. 5-8

The authors think that one of the reasons baseball is such an interesting sport is "the losers, the flakes, the buffoons, the boneheads, and the outrageous." Twenty-three chapters include topics such as coaching mistakes, misplayed games, and inept fielding. The text also recalls other entertaining mistakes, mainly in the twentieth century, that have made baseball fun to watch.

1651. Naylor, Phyllis Reynolds, and Lura Shield Reynold. **Maddie in the Middle**. Judith Gwyn Brown, illustrator. New York: Atheneum, 1988. 161p. $13.95. ISBN 0-689-31395-0. 3-5

Maddie, eight, feels she is either too old or too young to do anything with the other six children in her family because she is in the middle. In 1908, her parents have to leave for five weeks to help her father's sister. While they are gone, Maddie has to comfort the baby in the family when it gets a fever. She is very happy that someone needs her.

1652. Nelson, Sharlene, and Ted Nelson. **Bull Whackers to Whistle Punks: Logging in the Old West**. New York: Franklin Watts, 1996. 63p. $20.95. ISBN 0-531-20228-3. (First Books—Western U.S. History). 4-6

In examining the early days of logging, the text looks at the tools used, the animals needed for hauling the equipment, and the loggers' language. These men spent many dangerous moments before steam locomotives or trucking became available for transporting the logs. Also included is an account of their daily lives. Further Reading, Glossary, and Index.

1653. Nelson, Theresa. **Devil Storm**. New York: Orchard, 1987. 214p. $12.95. ISBN 0-531-08311-X. 5-8

Walter, 13, and his sister befriend old Tom in 1900, even though their father has told them not to talk to the man, who says he is the son of pirate Jean LaFitte. They like his stories, and in return they give him food. When a hurricane begins blowing through their Texas town, old Tom rushes to help the family escape while Walter's father is away on business.

1654.   Nelson, Vaunda M. **Mayfield Crossing**. Leonard Jenkins, illustrator. New York: Putnam, 1993. 96p. $14.95. ISBN 0-399-22331-2. 3-7

In 1960, Meg looks forward to going to a new school that has a larger baseball field. When she and her friends arrive, they find that they are outsiders, and no one wants them at the school because they are Black. When Meg and her friends challenge the others to a baseball game, one of the Parkview students refuses to continue the hostility and joins their team so they will have enough players.

1655.   Neufeld, John. **Gaps in Stone Walls**. New York: Atheneum, 1996. 192p. $16. ISBN 0-689-80102-5. 5-8

In this nineteenth-century story Merry Skiffe, 12, finds herself a suspect for the murder of Ned Nickerson, the most despised man in her town. She cannot verify where she was when he died, and her deafness makes it difficult to communicate with the investigator. Her town of Chilmark on Martha's Vineyard has an unusually high population of deaf people. She has to devise a way to prove her innocence.

1656.   Nichols, Joan Kane. **A Matter of Conscience: The Trial of Anne Hutchinson**. Dan Krovatin, illustrator. Austin, TX: Raintree/Steck-Vaughn, 1993. 101p. $24.26; $6.64pa. ISBN 0-8114-7233-7; 0-8114-8073-9pa. (Stories of America—Personal Challenge). 5-9

Because she wanted to follow John Cotton and his teachings, Anne Hutchinson (1591-1643) left England in 1634 for the New World. On board ship, she disagreed with the preaching of Reverend Symmes. He refused to think that anyone not a minister, much less a woman, could know what God wanted. After they landed, he accused her of being a witch. Eventually even John Cotton turned against her, and in 1838 she and her husband moved outside the colony to Rhode Island because the Boston Puritan community would not tolerate different beliefs. Epilogue, Afterword, and Notes.

1657.   Nicholson, Dorinda Makanaonalani Stagner. **Pearl Harbor Child: A Child's View of Pearl Harbor—From Attack to Peace**. Honolulu, HI: Woodson House, Arizona Memorial Museum Association, 1993. 64p. $9pa. ISBN 0-9631388-6-3pa. 4-8

In 1941, Nicholson was in first grade in Pearl Harbor when the Japanese bombs fell. She remembers that the noise of the planes kept her from hearing the incendiary bullets, but they found their targets because her family's kitchen and parts of the roof burned. She tells of the evacuation afterward, the increase in military personnel, blackouts, and rationing. Her mother would rub pieces of newspaper together so they would soften enough to become effective toilet paper. Photographs.

1658.   Nicholson, Lois. **Babe Ruth: Sultan of Swat**. Woodbury, CT: Goodwood, 1995. 119p. $17.95. ISBN 0-9625427-1-7. 5-9

George Herman Ruth (1895-1948) was one of the greatest ballplayers who ever lived. He said of his childhood that he was a bum, and he continued to resist authority throughout his adulthood, an attitude that cost him the chance to manage the Yankees after he retired from playing. But he loved children, and his honest appreciation of them showed in his personality. The text looks at this man and what he accomplished. Chronology, Statistical Record, Further Readings, and Index.

1659.   Nicholson, Lois. **George Washington Carver**. New York: Chelsea Juniors, 1994. 80p. $14.95; $4.95pa. ISBN 0-7910-1763-X; 0-7910-2114-9pa. (Junior Black Americans of Achievement). 3-6

As a young man, George Washington Carver (c. 1864-1943) worked for his education. As an adult working at Tuskegee Institute, he developed more than 300 products from peanuts and 118 from sweet potatoes. His concerns for his community led people to revere him as a folk hero. Photographs enhance the text. Chronology, Further Reading, and Index.

1660.   Nicholson, Lois. **Helen Keller: Humanitarian**. New York: Chelsea House, 1996. 111p. $18.95. ISBN 1-55546-662-1. (American Women of Achievement). 5 up

Helen Keller (1880-1968) said that "Life is either a daring adventure or nothing." She was blind and deaf from a childhood illness at 18 months, but her teacher Anne Sullivan gave her the world by teaching her to read and write. She became one of the best-educated and most influential women in the world. She graduated from Radcliffe College in 1904 and became an author, lecturer, and political activist. Mark Twain said that the two most interesting people in the nineteenth century were Napoleon and Helen Keller. Photographs enhance the text. Chronology, Further Reading, and Index.

1661.   Nirgiotis, Nicholas. **Erie Canal: Gateway to the West**. New York: Franklin Watts, 1993. 64p. $19.90. ISBN 0-531-20146-5. (First Books). 4-7

The text describes the construction of the Erie Canal, begun in 1817, to connect the Hudson River in Albany to Lake Erie in Buffalo. This transportation route had political, historical, economic, and sociological impact on the area and on the country. Photographs, maps, and drawings enhance the text. Further Reading, Glossary, and Index.

1662.   Nixon, Joan L. **A Family Apart**. New York: Bantam, 1987. 163p. $13.95. ISBN 0-553-05432-5. 5-7

When Frances is 13 in 1860, her mother relinquishes her and her five siblings to the Children's Aid Society so they can be adopted by people in the West who have enough money to care for them. Frances cuts her hair and pretends to be a boy so she can be placed with her little brother. The family with whom they live soon discovers that she is not "Frankie," but they are pleased. She works hard and courageously when she helps her new family transport slaves along the Underground Railway. *Western Writers of America Spur Award.*

1663.   Nixon, Joan Lowery. **Caught in the Act: The Orphan Quartet Two**. New York: Bantam, 1988. 151p. $13.95. ISBN 0-553-05443-0. 5-7

When Mike, 11, leaves his brothers and sisters after they take the orphan train to the West, he goes to live with the Friedrichs in Missouri. The father is harsh and hostile, always willing to believe his natural son Gunter instead of Mike, whom he knows once stole money in New York. When Gunter makes problems on the farm, he blames Mike, but Mike has a chance to prove he is innocent before he goes to live with another family.

1664.   Nixon, Joan Lowery. **Circle of Love**. New York: Bantam, 1997. 160p. $15.95. ISBN 0-385-32280-1. (Orphan Train Adventures). 4-8

After the Civil War, Frances Mary Kelly's love returns home. He, however, is reluctant to marry her, and to escape from her distress, she decides to go to New York City to accompany a group of orphans out west. During the journey, she has to cope with her memories and with the threats of a stranger.

1665.   Nixon, Joan Lowery. **A Dangerous Promise**. New York: Delacorte, 1994. 148p. $15.95; $3.99pa. ISBN 0-385-32073-6; 0-440-21965-5pa. (Orphan Train Adventures). 4-8

In 1861, Mike Kelly and his friend Todd practice to become army drummers. They run away to join the Kansas Infantry and fight for the Union. In a Missouri battle, Mike is left for dead and Todd is killed. After Mike watches a thief steal Todd's watch, someone he met on the orphan train to the Midwest from New York finds and rescues him. Because Mike had promised to return Todd's watch to his sister, he spends much time behind Confederate lines looking for the thief. He eventually locates the watch, and after being accused of stealing, returns it and fulfills a second promise as well.

1666.   Nixon, Joan Lowery. **Keeping Secrets**. New York: Delacorte, 1995. 163p. $15.95; $3.99pa. ISBN 0-385-32139-2; 0-440-21992-2pa. (Orphan Train Adventures). 5-8

When she is 11 in 1863, Peg Kelly thinks her mother should treat her like the young woman she almost is. Peg meets and helps a woman escaping from the Confederates, Violet Hennessey. Violet needs Peg to pretend to be her daughter so she can safely deliver secrets to the Union army. Peg agrees, and their efforts help the army win, but not quickly enough to save Peg's brother from the Confederates.

1667.   Nordstrom, Judy. **Concord and Lexington**. New York: Dillon Press, 1993. 72p. $14.95. ISBN 0-875-18567-3. (Places in American History). 4-6

The first battles of the Revolutionary War were the battles of Concord and Lexington in 1775. The text describes these battles and the events leading up to them. It also details the monuments and commemorations that currently exist at these Massachusetts sites. Photographs and drawings enhance the text. Chronology and Index.

1668.   Norman, Winifred Latimer, and Lily Patterson. **Lewis Latimer: Scientist**. New York: Chelsea House, 1993. 100p. $18.95. ISBN 0-7910-1977-2. (Black Americans of Achievement). 5 up

Lewis Latimer (1848-1928), the son of fugitive slaves living in Boston, worked closely with Alexander Graham Bell and Thomas Edison. He became a master draftsman, engineer, and inventor. Because Blacks went unrecognized, his name was not associated with his achievements, which included the creation and design of electric street lighting. Photographs and reproductions enhance the text. Chronology, Further Reading, and Index.

1669.   Norrell, Robert J. **We Want Jobs! A Story of the Great Depression**. Jan Naimo Jones, illustrator. Austin, TX: Raintree/Steck-Vaughn, 1993. 40p. $24.26; $5.95pa. ISBN 0-8114-7229-9; 0-8114-8069-0pa. (Stories of America—Stand Up and Be Counted). 4-8

In 1929, John Waskowitz, a Pennsylvania steelworker, loses his job like millions of others during the Great Depression. His family and the others suffer while everyone looks for nonexistent jobs. Some despair, but all call for government intervention. Not until 1933 does work start to become more available. Epilogue, Afterword, and Notes.

O

1670. Oberman, Sheldon. **The Always Prayer Shawl**. Ted Lewin, illustrator. Honesdale, PA: Caroline House, Boyds Mills Press, 1994. Unpaged. $14.95. ISBN 1-878093-22-3. K-3

In Russia during the late nineteenth century, Adam gets his eggs from chickens and his heat from wood, and he travels on a horse. But when the czar's soldiers start destroying towns nearby, Adam and his family leave Russia and Adam's grandfather, who had been his tutor. The grandfather gives Adam his own prayer shawl, which had belonged to his grandfather Adam. Although everything is different in his new home across the ocean, Adam has two things the same: his name and his prayer shawl. Throughout his life he keeps them, and when an old man, he promises to give his grandson Adam the prayer shawl. *National Jewish Book Award, Notable Children's Trade Books in the Field of Social Studies, Children's Bookseller's Choice, IRA Teachers' Choice, American Booksellers' Pick of the List, Reading Rainbow Review Book*, and *Sydney Taylor Award*.

1671. O'Brien, Steven. **Alexander Hamilton**. New York: Chelsea House, 1988. 112p. $18.95. ISBN 1-55546-810-1. (World Leaders Past and Present). 5 up

Alexander Hamilton (1757-1804), a political thinker, essayist, and statesman, devoted his life to building the nation. But his volatile personality led him to bitter feuds with Thomas Jefferson and John Adams. He arrived in New York at 17 to study at Columbia after an impoverished life as an illegitimate child on the island of St. Croix. He later joined the Continental army and became Washington's trusted personal aide. He favored a strong national government and, as a lawyer able to articulate many of the Constitution's central principles, led the fight with John Madison to ratify the Constitution. He was the first secretary of the Treasury, but his policies advocating expansion of the nation's economy drew opposition. He died in a duel with Aaron Burr, the Vice President. Reproductions enhance the text. Chronology, Further Reading, and Index.

1672. O'Brien, Steven. **Ulysses S. Grant**. New York: Chelsea House, 1991. 112p. $18.95. ISBN 1-55546-809-8. (World Leaders Past and Present). 5 up

Ulysses S. Grant (1822-1885), a graduate of West Point, fought in the Mexican War, but he was discharged from the army in 1854 suffering from alcoholism and depression. He reenlisted during the Civil War, and he rose to become the Union's boldest commander, taking charge of the Union forces in 1864. He refused to accept any type of surrender in the Civil War except an unconditional one. That decree led to a longer war, but he received the surrender in 1865. From 1869 to 1877, he served as President of the United States, but he remains best known as the man who defeated Robert E. Lee. Photographs and reproductions enhance the text. Chronology, Further Reading, and Index.

1673. O'Connor, Barbara. **Barefoot Dancer: The Story of Isadora Duncan**. Minneapolis, MN: Carolrhoda, 1994. 96p. $13.13. ISBN 0-87614-807-0. 4-6

Isadora Duncan (1877-1927) said that she began dancing in her mother's womb. By the time she was 12, she was a student, a teacher, and a performer. She eventually began her ascent in the Budapest dance world where the Hungarians loved her creativity. She refused to marry because she did not want to give up her dancing, but by different fathers, she had two children who tragically drowned. Most of her adult life she lived abroad. Bibliography and Index.

1674. O'Connor, Barbara. **The Soldier's Voice: The Story of Ernie Pyle**. Minneapolis, MN: Carolrhoda, 1996. 80p. $14.96. ISBN 0-87614-942-5. (Trailblazers). 4-7

Ernie Pyle (1900-1945) grew up on a farm in Indiana, but he wanted to travel. When he discovered his talent for newspaper writing, he was able to see the world. He wrote the first daily aviation column and then used his words to take people across America to visit a variety of places. In World War II, he began to speak for the soldiers by sharing their thoughts and experiences with the people who waited for them at home. President Truman complemented him for being the voice of "American fighting [men] as [they] wanted [their story] told." The text looks at Pyle's life and accomplishments. Notes, Bibliography, and Index.

1675. O'Connor, Jim. **Jackie Robinson and the Story of All-Black Baseball**. New York: Random House, 1989. 48p. $7.99; $3.50pa. ISBN 0-394-92456-8; 0-394-82456-3pa. (Step into Reading). 2-4

Jackie Robinson (1919-1972), the first Black baseball player in the modern major leagues, joined the Brooklyn Dodgers in 1947. His abilities showed the strength of the all-Black baseball teams that existed before the major leagues integrated.

1676.   O'Dell, Scott. **Island of the Blue Dolphins**. Ted Lewin, illustrator. 1960. Boston: Houghton Mifflin, 1990. 192p. $18.95. ISBN 0-395-53680-4. New York: Scholastic, 1994. 192p. $3.95pa. ISBN 0-590-22165-5pa. 5 up

Karana is the only remaining human on her island after Aleuts kill most of the men and the others sail to the mainland. Her brother survives for a while, but a wild dog kills him. Karana learns how to live by overcoming tribal taboos such as women not making weapons. Her experiences as she lives each day show that people can adapt to and work with nature. *Newbery Medal, Southern California Council on Literature for Children and Young People Awards, International Board of Books for Young People, Friends of Children and Literature Award, American Library Association Notable Books for Children,* and *School Library Journal Best Book.*

1677.   O'Dell, Scott. **The Serpent Never Sleeps: A Novel of Jamestown and Pocahontas**. Ted Lewin, illustrator. Boston: Houghton Mifflin, 1987. 240p. $15.95. ISBN 0-395-4424-7. 6-9

Serena Lynn, supposed to come to the court of King James in London, decides instead to join the company sailing from Plymouth to Jamestown in 1609. The king has given her a ring engraved with a serpent that supposedly will protect her. As she follows the man she loves, she can only hope that the ring will perform if necessary. Serena arrives in Jamestown, gets to know Pocahontas, and experiences the tragedy of the colony.

1678.   O'Dell, Scott. **Sing Down the Moon**. Boston: Houghton Mifflin, 1970. 137p. $14.95. ISBN 0-395-10919-1. New York: Dell, 1992. 137p. $3.99pa. ISBN 0-400-40673-0pa. 5 up

Spanish slavers enter the Canyon de Chelly in 1864 and take the Navajo girl Bright Morning and her friend south with them to sell. Soon after, the white soldiers burn the crops and force the remaining Navajos to march toward Fort Sumner. The boy she intends to marry, Tall Boy, helps her escape from the slavers, but the soldiers retake them all. Bright Morning and Tall Boy have to endure the ignominy of the camp before they escape and return to live in the crevices of their canyon with their son. *Newbery Honor.*

1679.   O'Dell, Scott. **Zia**. Ted Lewin, illustrator. Boston: Houghton Mifflin, 1976. 224p. $14.95. ISBN 0-395-24393-9. New York: Laurel, 1996. 144p. $4.50pa. ISBN 0-440-21956-6pa. 4-8

Karana's niece Zia tries to rescue her in this sequel to *Island of the Blue Dolphins*. Zia and her brother get a boat to sail to the island, but a ship sees and captures them, and the captain enslaves them on board. They steal another boat and return to the Santa Barbara mission. When Zia tells her story to another captain, he promises to bring Karana back to the mainland on his next trip. He does as he promised, but Karana cannot adjust to mission life and its rules after living alone for so many years and learning to survive without anyone else around.

1680.   O'Dell, Scott, and Elizabeth Hall. **Thunder Rolling in the Mountains**. Boston: Houghton Mifflin, 1992. 128p. $14.95. ISBN 0-395-59966-0. 6-9

Sound of Running Feet, daughter of Chief Joseph of the Nez Perce Indians, tells about the Blue Coats (American soldiers) pursuing her people in 1877. The army forces them to leave their Oregon valley and then attacks them so that they have to fight. She walks toward Canada with her intended husband, but another tribe, the Assiniboin, betray them. She escapes again and goes to join Sitting Bull. *Notable Children's Trade Books in the Field of Social Studies.*

1681.   Oleksy, Walter. **The Boston Tea Party**. New York: Franklin Watts, 1993. 64p. $19.90. ISBN 0-531-20147-3. 4-6

As a response to increased taxes, men in Boston destroyed tea in 1773 instead of buying it. The text, enhanced with reproductions, looks at "taxation without representation," the Boston Massacre, the Boston Tea Party, and freedom. For Further Reading and Index.

1682.   Olsen, Victoria. **Emily Dickinson: Poet**. New York: Chelsea House, 1990. 110p. $18.95. ISBN 1-55546-649-4. (American Women of Achievement). 5 up

Emily Dickinson (1830-1886) lived her entire life in Amherst, Massachusetts. She left only to visit Washington, D.C., and Boston. She had strong convictions about Christianity and nature that seemed contrary to many who knew her. After she was 30 years old, she avoided society, choosing to stay inside her home. Because only seven of her poems were published during her lifetime, she gained most of her fame in the twentieth century, when the originality and thoughtfulness of her poems were better understood. Photographs and reproductions enhance the text. Chronology, Further Reading, and Index.

1683.   Olsen, Violet. **The View from the Pighouse Roof**. New York: Atheneum, 1987. 176p. $13.95. ISBN 0-689-31324-1. 5-7

Marie, 12, misses her older sister Rosie, who has left the home of her Danish-American farm family with her husband and child to go around the country looking for a job during the Great Depression. But Rosie dies in a motorcycle accident. Marie plans not to attend high school so she can look after Rosie's two-year-old child, but Marie's mother says that she must. Marie realizes that her view of life has changed and equates it with looking from the pighouse roof. *Society of Midland Authors' Award.*

1684. Olson, Arielle. **The Lighthouse Keeper's Daughter**. Elaine Wentworth, illustrator. Boston: Little, Brown, 1987. 32p. $16.95. ISBN 0-316-65053-6. K-3

On a rocky island off the coast of Maine in the 1850s, Miranda has to keep the 14 lamps of the lighthouse lit while her father is stranded ashore during a blizzard. Because they have just moved to the island, Miranda already has had difficulty adjusting to the harsh life. But the fishermen whom she helped with her efforts reward her with gifts of dirt in which she can plant summer flowers among the rocks. *Friends of American Writers Juvenile Book Merit Award.*

1685. O'Neal, Michael. **The Assassination of Abraham Lincoln**. San Diego, CA: Greenhaven, 1991. 96p. $13.95. ISBN 0-89908-092-8. (Great Mysteries). 5-9

A prologue gives the facts behind the assassination of Abraham Lincoln on April 14, 1865. In two-page spreads, the text presents the theories behind the murder at Ford's Theater in Washington. Captions and quotes from sources, as well as black-and-white photographs and drawings, enhance the text. Bibliography and Index.

1686. O'Neal, Michael. **President Truman and the Atomic Bomb: Opposing Viewpoints**. San Diego, CA: Greenhaven, 1990. 112p. $13.95. ISBN 0-89908-079-0. (Great Mysteries—Opposing Viewpoints). 6-9

When President Truman gave the command to drop the atomic bomb on Hiroshima in 1945, he relied on information from various sources to assist him in reaching the decision. The text examines the events and the facts that Truman might have used as his basis for initiating this situation. Bibliography and Index.

1687. Oneal, Zibby. **Grandma Moses: Painter of Rural America**. Donna Ruff, illustrator. New York: Puffin, 1986. 58p. $4.99pa. ISBN 0-14-032220-5pa. (Women of Our Time). 5 up

Called a primitive painter because she never had formal lessons, Anna Mary Moses (1860-1961) began painting after she was 70 years old. She gave her landscapes away as gifts, and her first "show" was in the local drugstore window. A man saw her paintings in the drugstore, bought them, and eventually got them displayed in the Museum of Modern Art in New York City. The year she was 80, she had a real gallery show.

1688. Oneal, Zibby. **A Long Way to Go**. Michael Dooling, illustrator. New York: Viking, 1990. 64p. $11.95. ISBN 0-670-82532-8. 2-6

In 1917, Lila, 10, does not understand why her brother but not she is allowed to vote, because she is smarter than him. She sees her grandmother go to jail after picketing for women's suffrage in Washington, and Lila begins to notice how laws prohibit women from doing many things. She disagrees with the laws and tells her father that he should not oppose letting women vote.

1689. O'Neill, Laurie. **Little Rock: The Desegregation of Central High**. Brookfield, CT: Millbrook Press, 1994. 64p. $15.40. ISBN 1-56294-354-5. (Spotlight on American History). 4-8

On September 25, 1957, nine Black teenagers entered high school in Little Rock, Arkansas. Little Rock's white citizens refused to accept that Blacks and whites were equal, and a mob shouted for them to go home and leave the white school alone. In fact, they closed the high school during 1958-1959 to avoid integration. The text tells about these nine students and what they had to endure as they tried to take their rightful places in the classroom. Photographs illustrate the text. Chronology, Sources, Further Reading, and Index.

1690. O'Neill, Laurie. **Wounded Knee: The Death of a Dream**. Brookfield, CT: Millbrook Press, 1993. 64p. $14.40. ISBN 1-56294-253-0. (Spotlight on American History). 3-7

In 1890, U.S. Cavalry troops massacred men, women, and children at Wounded Knee, South Dakota. The text places the incident in a historical context by looking at the relationships between whites and the Lakota Sioux, the early Sioux Plains settlements in the 1700s and their interaction with nature, the reservation plan, the ghost dance ceremony, and other topics. Archival photographs and drawings enhance the text. Further Reading, Glossary, and Index. *Child Study Association Children's Books of the Year.*

1691. O'Rear, Sybil J. **Charles Goodnight: Pioneer Cowman**. New York: Eakin, 1990. 69p. $10.95. ISBN 0-89015-741-3. 5-8

Charles Goodnight (1836-1929) lived in the Texas panhandle all his life and served his state by remaining there to fight during the Civil War. He developed the idea of the chuckwagon, and he improved the sidesaddle for women. He experimented with plants and fought against cattle diseases, trying to have laws passed protecting cattle. He loved children, and he helped the people of his state in any way he could. Glossary and Bibliography.

1692. Osborne, Angela. **Abigail Adams: Women's Rights Advocate**. New York: Chelsea House, 1989. 112p. $18.95; $7.95pa. ISBN 1-55546-635-4; 0-7910-0405-8pa. (American Women of Achievement). 5 up

As America's First Lady from 1796 to 1800, Abigail Adams (1744-1818) was a political advisor, dedicated wife and mother, and defender of women. She insisted that women deserved the same rights as men, and in many letters she makes these assertions. She lived in five world capitals, raised four children, and enjoyed more than 50 years of marriage. Photographs and reproductions enhance the text. Further Reading, Chronology, and Index.

1693.   Osborne, Mary Pope. **George Washington: Leader of a New Nation**. New York: Dial, 1991. 117p. $14. ISBN 0-8037-0947-1. 4-7

Osborne believes that the greatness of George Washington (1732-1799) lay in his courage and humility. When offered the chance to be the leader of a new country, he refused to become either a dictator or a king. He did not capitalize on his popularity to become an absolute ruler. When he was elected president, he felt that he had to serve even though he preferred life on his Virginia farm. He gained power by giving it up and, in turn, laid the foundation for America to become a free and self-governing nation. The text looks at his life and his choices. Timeline, Bibliography, and Index.

1694.   Osborne, Mary Pope. **The Many Lives of Benjamin Franklin**. New York: Dial, 1990. 129p. $13.95. ISBN 0-8037-0679-0. 4-7

When Benjamin Franklin was a small boy, his family gave him some money. He spent it on a whistle that he bought from another boy. His family laughed and said that he had spent too much. He never forgot the lesson because he was frugal for the rest of his life. He was an apprentice, a journeyman, and a printer; a scientist and inventor; an agent to England; the oldest revolutionary; and one of the founding fathers of the nation. The text looks at his contributions, including his tenure as the president of the first abolitionist society. Timeline, Bibliography, and Index.

1695.   Osinski, Alice. **Andrew Jackson: Seventh President of the United States**. Chicago: Childrens Press, 1987. 100p. $19.80. ISBN 0-516-01387-4. (Encyclopedia of Presidents). 4-9

The 6′1″ Andrew Jackson (1767-1845) became president of the United States in 1829. Face scarred by smallpox and battle wounds, he told his audience, "I will not fail you." People were invited to the White House for a reception, but they destroyed the furniture. Others said that Jackson was beginning "the reign of King Mob." He was the first president since George Washington not to have a college education, and he was determined to govern for all people. Chronology of American History and Index.

1696.   Osofsky, Audrey. **Free to Dream: The Making of a Poet, Langston Hughes**. New York: Lothrop, Lee & Shepard, 1996. 112p. $16. ISBN 0-688-10605-6. 5-9

This biography of Langston Hughes (1902-1967) concentrates on the childhood influences that shaped his life when he was interested in writing, and his absent father who was against his choice. He accomplished extraordinary things as a Black author who wrote in a variety of genres while establishing the unique language of the African American. Bibliography, Notes, and Index.

1697.   Oughton, Jerrie. **Music from a Place Called Half Moon**. Boston: Houghton Mifflin, 1995. 160p. $13.95. ISBN 0-395-70737-4. 6-9

Edie Jo, 13, realizes that the prejudice between the Indians and the whites in Half Moon, North Carolina, during 1956 affects all of them when her father suggests that the church allow Indians to attend. She becomes even more involved when she falls in love with Cherokee Fish, a local Indian boy. That year, however, a fire in the town causes enormous hostility. Cherokee dies when his brother, who started the fire but wants Cherokee to protect him, hits him in a fight. After a few months, Edie Jo's family seems to forget the incident, but she retains her changed attitude. *Bank Street College's Children's Book Award*.

1698.   Oughton, Jerrie. **The War in Georgia**. Boston: Houghton Mifflin, 1997. 192p. $14.95. ISBN 0-395-81568-1. 5-8

Shanta, 13, lives with her grandmother and her bedridden uncle during World War II. They have difficult times during the summer of 1945, and she learns about helping others during a time of local war in Georgia that creeps through her town.

1699.   Owen, Marna. **Our Century: 1930-1940**. Milwaukee, WI: Gareth Stevens, 1993. 64p. $23.93. ISBN 0-8368-1035-X. 3-10

Written as if a newspaper, the book's short articles give an overview of the decade. Included are statistics, daily life in America, the Spanish king's abdication and civil war in Spain, General Franco, Edward of England abdicating, the Nazis' rise, Stalin and Hitler, Hoover, Roosevelt, the end of Prohibition, the Scottsboro case, the rise of the Empire State Building, Boulder Dam, New York's World Fair, Babe Didrikson, Lou Gehrig, Joe Louis, Eugene O'Neill, Jane Addams, Huey Long, and Amelia Earhart. Glossary, Books for Further Reading, Places to Write or Visit, and Index.

P

1700.   Paananen, Eloise. **The Military: Defending the Nation**. Austin, TX: Raintree/Steck-Vaughn, 1993. 48p. $15.49. ISBN 0-8114-7353-8. (Good Citizenship). 3-6

The text examines the history of the military, from the colonial militia through the various wars. It also considers what the military does in both peace and war, its chain of command, and its process for preparing for a war. Photographs augment the text. Bibliography, Glossary, and Index.

1701.   Palmer, Leslie. **Lena Horne: Entertainer**. New York: Chelsea House, 1989. 127p. $18.95. ISBN 1-55546-594-3. (Black Americans of Achievement). 5 up

Lena Horne, born into a privileged family in 1917, grew up in Brooklyn and several towns in the racially segregated South. She made her professional debut as a singer at 16 at the Cotton Club in Harlem, a place that featured Black performers. Her career as a solo nightclub performer began in 1941, and she became the first Black singer to be promoted by the movie industry. She has crossed color barriers while pushing civil rights issues. Photographs, Chronology, Further Reading, and Index.

1702.   Parker, Nancy Winslow, author/illustrator. **Locks, Crocs, and Skeeters: The Story of the Panama Canal**. New York: Greenwillow, 1996. 32p. $16. ISBN 0-688-12241-8. 3-5

After acknowledging the large number of West Indian, Chinese, and Jamaican workers who made the Panama Canal possible, Parker focuses on the well-known people who supported, designed, and engineered the canal. She also includes the history of the area since the Spaniards arrived 400 years earlier. William Gorgas suppressed the yellow fever that was killing the workers. George Goethals had the engineering knowledge and managerial skills to complete the canal. Charts and Index.

1703.   Parker, Steve. **Benjamin Franklin and Electricity**. New York: Chelsea House, 1995. 32p. $14.95. ISBN 0-7910-3006-7. (Science Discoveries). 3 up

The text gives a brief overview of Benjamin Franklin's life (1706-1790) while emphasizing the contributions he made to science through inventions that have influenced contemporary life. He was the first person to use the terms "positive" and "negative" when referring to electricity. In addition to inventing bifocals, the Franklin stove, and a musical instrument, he also studied oceans and their water currents. His most famous experiments occurred in the field of static electricity. The World in Franklin's Time, Glossary, and Index.

1704.   Parker, Steve. **Thomas Edison and Electricity**. New York: Chelsea House, 1995. 32p. $14.95. ISBN 0-7910-3012-1. (Science Discoveries). 4-8

Through his understanding of science, Thomas A. (Alva) Edison (1847-1931) made major contributions to humanity. Some see him as the greatest inventor in history because of electricity. The text examines his wizardry and perseverance. Glossary, Timeline, and Index.

1705.   Parker, Steve. **The Wright Brothers and Aviation**. Tony Smith, illustrator. New York: Chelsea House, 1995. 32p. $14.95. ISBN 0-7910-3013-X. (Science Discoveries). 3-7

The text presents the early years of the Wright brothers, Wilbur and Orville, and their gliding skills learned from their early experiments with bicycles. They taught themselves much about machines and mechanics and even made a small combustion engine. Although they were not the first to attempt powered flight, they were the first to be successful when they overcame the three basic problems in flying: designing wings that would lift the craft, figuring out how to control it in the air, and building a power plant that would propel it. The final chapter looks at aviation after the Wrights made their flight on December 17, 1903. The World in the Wrights' Time, Glossary, and Index.

1706.   Parks, Rosa, and James Haskins. **I Am Rosa Parks**. Wil Clay, illustrator. New York: Dial, 1997. 48p. $12.99. ISBN 0-8037-1206-5. (Easy to Read). K-3

Rosa Parks, the woman who refused to give up her seat on an Alabama bus one day in 1955, tells her story, covering her childhood up to the present. Her decision led to the Montgomery bus boycott and led to the Supreme Court ruling that Montgomery buses could not segregate passengers.

1707.   Parks, Rosa, with Jim Haskins. **Rosa Parks: My Story**. New York: Dial, 1992. 192p. $17. ISBN 0-8037-0673-1. 4-6

Rosa Parks (b. 1913) said about her decision not to give up her bus seat, "The only tired I was, was tired of giving in." Her action started the Montgomery bus boycott in 1955, which lasted more than a year and led to a federal injunction against segregation on buses. She was always proud of her heritage and her family and believed that all races were equal. She was an activist before sitting on the bus, and afterward she became a speaker for civil rights. Her husband encouraged her to complete her education and register to vote. She has earned the title "Mother to a Movement." Chronology and Index.

1708. Parlin, John. **Andrew Jackson: Pioneer and President**. New York: Chelsea Juniors, 1991. 80p. $14.95. ISBN 0-7910-1442-8. (Discovery Biography). 3-6

Andrew Jackson (1767-1845) believed in fighting for what he thought was right. Although born into a very poor family, he used his fighting abilities in the American Revolution and later in the War of 1812. He also used his brains to become a lawyer. He was tough and often refused to change his mind, so he earned the name "Old Hickory." He was also very hot tempered, sometimes frightening his friends. He was the first President to come from the frontier, and he tried to make government work for all Americans, not just the rich.

1709. Partridge, Elizabeth. **Clara and the Hoodoo Man**. New York: Dutton, 1996. 168p. $14.99. ISBN 0-525-45403-9. 4-6

In the beginning of the century in Tennessee, when Clara breaks her mother's bowl, she has to earn money to pay for it. Her main occupation becomes gathering ginseng in the hills. While working, Clara and her younger sister Bessie encounter the local hoodoo man, whom their mother dislikes. Her mother thinks that Bessie's subsequent illness is the result of their meeting, but Clara realizes that the man may have a medicine to help Bessie, and she goes to ask. He helps, and all is well.

1710. Pasachoff, Naomi. **Alexander Graham Bell: Making Connections**. New York: Oxford University Press, 1996. 140p. ISBN 0-19-509908-7. 6-9

The text looks at Alexander Graham Bell (1847-1922) and his contributions as an educator and inventor more than at his personal life. Clear explanations of his experiments and the scientific principles behind them enliven the text and clarify his work, especially as a teacher of the deaf. Photographs and reproductions highlight the text. Further Reading and Index.

1711. Pascoe, Elaine. **First Facts About the Presidents**. New York: Blackbirch, 1996. 112p. $22.95. ISBN 1-56711-167-X. (First Facts). 4-8

Four main sections in the text introduce the first presidents, the presidents as America grew, the Civil War and after, and the twentieth century. Within each area, full-page portraits of each President appear with personal statistics and paragraphs about the term of office. Also included are sidebars listing contemporary events and information about family and cabinet members. Chronology, Further Reading, and Index.

1712. Patent, Dorothy Hinshaw. **West by Covered Wagon: Retracing the Pioneer Trails**. William Muñoz, photographer. New York: Walker, 1995. 32p. $15.95. ISBN 0-8027-8377-5. 3-5

Contemporary Montana Wagoneers recreate the experiences along the Oregon Trail on the weekends. Patent explains the difference between actual life on the trail and the easy life of the re-creators, who know they will return to civilization when they finish their trip. She discusses the differences in gear that each group packs, today's horses versus the mules and oxen of the original trail riders, and the value of plastic liners for contemporary rain barrels as opposed to the leaky contraptions of the nineteenth century. The text gives an introduction to life on the trail through this recreation with accompanying photographs of the Wagoneers. *School Library Journal Starred Review*.

1713. Paterson, Katherine. **Jacob Have I Loved**. New York: HarperCollins, 1980. 256p. $14.95; $4.50pa. ISBN 0-690-04078-4; 0-06-447059-8pa. 5 up

Louise (Wheeze) grows up in the early 1940s on her Chesapeake Bay island thinking that everyone loves her younger twin Caroline more than they do her. Wheeze learns about crabbing and being a waterman from her father, while Caroline sings and wins money to go to school on the mainland. Not until Wheeze leaves the island herself does she understand that everyone has always thought she was strong but that Caroline needed help. *Newbery Medal, American Book Award for Children's Literature Nominee, American Library Association Notable Children's Books of 1976-1980, American Library Association Best Books for Young Adults, Horn Book Fanfare Honor List, School Library Journal Best Book, Booklist Children's Editors' Choices, New York Times Outstanding Books of 1980*, and *New York Public Library's Children's Books*.

1714. Paterson, Katherine. **Jip: His Story**. New York: Lodestar, 1996. 181p. $15.99. ISBN 0-525-67543-4. 5-9

Jip works for lazy Vermont farm owners in the late 1850s. They told him that he fell out of a wagon near the house when a toddler, and they have supported him since. A stranger arrives and tells Jip that his father might be looking for him, and Jip wants to leave the farm. The stranger turns out to be a slave catcher, and to give the story an acceptable ending, Lyddie, from Paterson's book of the same title, now Jip's teacher, and her Quaker sweetheart Luke help Jip escape to Canada. The complex story presents the dark times before the Civil War. *School Library Journal Best Book*.

1715. Paterson, Katherine. **Lyddie**. New York: Lodestar, 1991. 192p. $15. ISBN 0-525-67338-5. New York: Puffin, 1994. 192p. $3.99pa. ISBN 0-14-037389-6pa. 6-9

Lyddie, 13, has to take charge of the family after her father dies because her mother seems to have lost her mind. Without economic support, the family must separate, and Lyddie goes to the mills in Lowell, Massachusetts, to work in 1843. There she has to overcome the Quaker prejudice instilled by her mother and begin to assert her rights as a worker and a woman. Because she refuses to comply with the overseer's advances, she loses her job, but by that time she has enough money to save the farm. She also knows that the Quaker in love with her will wait until she finishes college for them to marry. *Bulletin Blue Ribbon Book.*

1716. Patrick, Diane. **Coretta Scott King**. New York: Franklin Watts, 1991. 128p. $22.10. ISBN 0-531-13005-3. (Impact Biographies). 6-9

As the wife of Martin Luther King, Jr., Coretta Scott King (b. 1927) has spent her life supporting a man who was always at the forefront of controversy. When she met King, she was studying in New England to be a concert singer. She works today for civil rights and for world peace. The text examines her early life, her education, her courtship and marriage, her early years of marriage, her work for civil rights with her husband, and her continued endeavors. Notes, Bibliography, and Index.

1717. Patrick, Diane. **Martin Luther King, Jr.** New York: Franklin Watts, 1990. 64p. $10.90. ISBN 0-531-10892-9. (First Books). 3-6

Martin Luther King, Jr. (1929-1968) was a major leader in the Civil Rights movement. The text traces his life, from his education and his decision to become a Baptist minister to his activities as an important figure who called for the nonviolent achievement of rights. Photographs supplement the text. Index.

1718. Patrick, Diane. **A Missing Portrait on Sugar Hill**. New York: Silver Moon Press, 1995. 80p. $12.95. ISBN 1-881889-66-1. (Mysteries in Time). 3-5

In the late 1920s, Charles Broomfield's paintings are finally selling in Harlem. But his paintings are also disappearing. Harriet, Broomfield's young friend, tries to figure out what is happening to the paintings, which she thinks are stolen.

1719. Patrick, John J. **The Young Oxford Companion to the Supreme Court of the United States**. New York: Oxford University Press, 1994. 368p. $40. ISBN 0-19-507877-2. 6 up

Alphabetically arranged articles include biographies of all chief justices and associate justices of the Supreme Court, from John Jay in 1789 through Ruth Ginsberg. There are discussions of 100 of the most historically significant cases and decisions with their official citations. Other essays present the core concepts of constitutionalism, ideas and issues, and the procedures and practices of the Court. Each article has cross-references and a recommendation for further reading. Photographs and drawings complement the text. The appendices list the justices in chronological order since the beginning of the Court, with their terms, and information about visiting the Supreme Court. Further Reading and Index.

1720. Patrick-Wexler, Diane. **Barbara Jordan**. Austin, TX: Raintree/Steck-Vaughn, 1996. 48p. $16.98. ISBN 0-8172-3976-6. (Contemporary African Americans). 4-6

Barbara Jordan (1936-1996) became a U.S. congresswoman from Texas who worked to help the poor and minorities. She overcame all kinds of adversity to become successful in her field. The texts look at her life. Bibliography, Chronology, Glossary, and Index.

1721. Patterson, Charles. **Thomas Jefferson**. New York: Franklin Watts, 1987. 95p. $10.40. ISBN 0-531-10306-4. (First Book). 5-9

Before becoming the third President of the United States, Thomas Jefferson (1743-1826) had participated fully in the life of the new government. The text includes a discussion of his beliefs and their influence on the Declaration of Independence. Index.

1722. Patterson, Lillie. **Booker T. Washington: Leader of His People**. New York: Chelsea Juniors, 1991. 80p. $14.95. ISBN 0-7910-1427-4. (Discovery Biography). 3-6

Booker T. Washington (1856-1915) was born into slavery and became free at the end of the Civil War. He worked to go to school and later became the head of Tuskegee Institute. He thought that the best way for African Americans to gain rights was to work hard and get an education.

1723. Patterson, Lillie. **Francis Scott Key: Poet and Patriot**. New York: Chelsea Juniors, 1991. 80p. $14.95. ISBN 0-7910-1461-4. (Discovery Biography). 3-6

Francis Scott Key (1799-1843) grew up in Washington, D.C., where he became a lawyer who tried to help slaves and the poor. He was a good father, and when he had time, he wrote poetry. Key wanted to help his country, however, as his father had done during the American Revolution. He had the chance in 1812, when the ship on which he was held in Chesapeake Bay outside Baltimore gave him a view of the battle at Fort McHenry. When he saw the American flag still flying over the fort at dawn, he wrote the words to the poem now known as "The Star-Spangled Banner."

1724. Patterson, Lillie. **Martin Luther King and the Montgomery Bus Boycott**. New York: Facts on File, 1989. 178p. $17.95; $8.95pa. ISBN 0-8160-1605-4; 0-8160-2997-0pa. (Makers of America). 6-9

Martin Luther King, Jr. (1929-1968) reflected the times in which he lived. Primary sources such as his letters, speeches, documents, and diaries help to define him in this text. He believed that America's moral progress was much behind its scientific progress because Americans so often failed to see others as human beings. He led the Civil Rights movement, but from that came other movements—for women, for peace, and for the survival of the planet. Chapters cover the Montgomery bus boycott, King's childhood, his trip to India, the sit-ins, the Freedom Ride, Albany and Birmingham, Washington, the Selma Protest, and his Nobel Peace Prize. Significant Events, For Further Reading, and Index.

1725. Paulsen. Gary. **Call Me Francis Tucket**. New York: Delacorte, 1995. 97p. $14.95. ISBN 0-385-32116-3. 4-8

While Francis Tucket, 14, is taking a wagon train from Missouri to Oregon in 1848, Pawnee Indians kidnap him. A mountain man helps him escape and teaches him to survive. When he is on his own, he thinks he can handle anything. But he has not considered the difficulties of caring for two abandoned children, Lottie and Billy. When he tries to leave them, he realizes he has made a mistake and returns to find that their benefactor beat them for not working hard enough.

1726. Paulsen, Gary. **The Cookcamp**. New York: Orchard, 1991. 116p. $13.95. ISBN 0-531-05927-8. 5-8

In this 1944 story, when the five-year-old unnamed protagonist's mother comes home with a man whom she identifies as his uncle and makes sounds with the man on the couch that bother him, his mother sends him to stay with his grandmother in Minnesota, who cooks for a group of men building a road into Canada. The huge men frighten the boy at first, but then they invite him to sit in their trucks and tractors with them, and he begins to feel comfortable in their company. He regrets having to leave. *School Library Journal Best Book*.

1727. Paulsen, Gary. **Harris and Me: A Summer Remembered**. San Diego, CA: Harcourt Brace, 1993. 157p. $13.95. ISBN 0-15-292877-4. 6-8

The nameless protagonist, victim of alcoholic parents who have abused him, travels in a 1949 pickup to live on his uncle's farm. The dirty farm disgusts him, but he meets Harris, a boy who leads him into surprising adventures. They pretend to be Tarzan in the hayloft, GI Joes in the pigpen with its mire, and Gene Autry riding his horse. The protagonist learns that a real farm and those associated with it can give him a sense of belonging.

1728. Paulsen, Gary. **Mr. Tucket**. New York: Delacorte, 1994. 176p. $14.95. ISBN 0-385-31169-9. 6-9

Jason Grimes, a mountain man, finds and frees Francis Alphonse Tucket, 14, after Pawnee Indians kidnap him. Grimes calls Francis "Mr. Tucket" and teaches him how to survive on the frontier. Francis meets Jim Bridger and fights the Pawnee while serving his apprenticeship in which he learns to shoot, ride, trap, and trade with the Indians.

1729. Paulsen, Gary. **Tucket's Ride**. New York: Bantam, 1997. 112p. $15.95. ISBN 0-385-32199-6. 5-8

Francis Tucket and his adopted family of Lottie and Billy head west to look for Francis's parents on the Oregon Trail. When they turn south to avoid the early winter, they enter enemy territory during the war between the United States and Mexico. Outlaws capture them, and their loyalty to each other, ability to endure, and intelligence give them hope of escape.

1730. Paulsen, Gary. **The Winter Room**. New York: Orchard, Franklin Watts, 1989. 103p. $11.95. ISBN 0-531-08439-6. 5-8

Eldon, 11, discusses the various events of the seasons on the family's Minnesota farm at the turn of the twentieth century. Although Eldon enjoys his uncle's stories in winter the best, his brother Wayne challenges them. He does not believe that anyone can cut wood the way that his uncle describes. However, from a hiding place, they watch Uncle David prove that he can still perform as he said he could. *Newbery Honor, American Library Association Notable Books for Children*, and *Judy Lopez Memorial Award*.

1731. Paulsen, Gary, with Ruth Wright Paulsen. **Woodsong**. New York: Bradbury, 1990. 132p. $15. ISBN 0-02-770221-9. New York: Puffin, 1991. 132p. $4.99pa. ISBN 0-14-034905-7pa. 6 up

Gary Paulsen tells his story of participating in the Iditarod Race for 1,180 miles through Alaska. He describes the physical endurance needed to complete the race across ice and snow and the importance of the sled dogs as a team and individually.

1732. Paulson, Timothy J. **Days of Sorrow; Years of Glory: 1831-1850: From the Nat Turner Revolt to the Fugitive Slave Law**. New York: Chelsea House, 1994. 111p. $18.95; $7.95pa. ISBN 0-7910-2263-3; 0-7910-2552-7pa. (Milestones in Black American History). 6-9

In 1831, Nat Turner led a slave revolt in Virginia. In 1850, the Fugitive Slave Law passed, allowing masters to hunt for fugitive slaves in other states. Among the topics presented about the years in between are the Underground Railway, the abolitionist movement, and the Seminoles in Florida, who harbored escaped slaves in the Everglades. The text shows the desperate desire of people wanting to be free at any cost. Black-and-white reproductions enhance the text. Further Reading and Index.

1733. Peck, Richard. **Voices after Midnight**. New York: Delacorte, 1989. 182p. $14.95. ISBN 0-385-29779-3. New York: Yearling, Dell, 1990. 182p. $3.99pa. ISBN 0-440-40378-2pa. 5-8

Three contemporary children, Chad, Luke, and Heidi, spend two weeks in New York City at a house built in 1888. The three children find themselves in 1888 with the people who lived in the house then. Luke, eight, is fascinated, and his intense love of history shows through the experience. He understands how the people felt then, and he wants to know more about them.

1734. Peet, Bill. **Bill Peet: An Autobiography**. Boston: Houghton Mifflin, 1989. 190p. $17.95; $10.95pa. ISBN 0-395-50932-7; 0-395-68982-1pa. 3-6

In his autobiography, Bill Peet describes life in twentieth-century America, including the Depression, when he tried to get work using his artistic ability. He had enormous success by working for Disney Studios and helping create the animation for *Dumbo*, *Fantasia*, *Cinderella*, *Song of the South*, *Peter Pan*, *Alice in Wonderland*, *The Sword in the Stone*, and *101 Dalmatians*. His humorous illustrations interact with the text. *Caldecott Honor Book*.

1735. Peifer, Charles, Jr. **Soldier of Destiny: A Biography of George Patton**. New York: Dillon Press, 1989. 126p. $13.95. ISBN 0-87518-395-6. (People in Focus). 5 up

George Patton (1885-1945) knew he wanted to be a soldier very early in life because he loved the stories his father read to him about military men in history and literature. Although he had a reading disability, he was able to go to West Point, where his athleticism propelled him into the 1912 Olympics and a fifth-place finish in the pentathlon. His 3rd Army in World War II became an important key to winning the war, spurred onward by his inspiring (and scatological) speeches earning him the nickname "Old Blood and Guts." The text looks at his life and his burial in Luxembourg as he requested. Appendix, Major Events, Bibliography, and Index.

1736. Pellowski, Anne. **First Farm in the Valley: Anna's Story**. Wendy Watson, illustrator. New York: Philomel, 1982. 192p. $9.95. ISBN 0-399-20887-9. 4-7

In 1876, Anna and her family live on their Wisconsin farm. She is happy to have a friend of her age who is also Polish. She helps her mother do chores and enjoys the Fourth of July fireworks, but does not understand what the adults mean when they talk about a Polish government ruled by people who speak German. She wonders how the Kaiser and Bismarck can have more power than kings and queens, but she knows that the reason influences why some of the Polish immigrants have come to Wisconsin.

1737. Pelta, Kathy. **Discovering Christopher Columbus: How History Is Invented**. Minneapolis, MN: Lerner, 1991. 112p. $19.95. ISBN 0-8225-4899-2. 6-9

The text looks at the life of Christopher Columbus and his voyages beginning in 1492 and ending in 1506. Additional chapters examine the historical response to his discovery in the subsequent centuries. An ending chapter titled "You, the Historian" shows how information can be disseminated, even when it is wrong, because historians copy what another historian has written without trying to get the information from as original a source as possible. Sometimes even primary sources are unreliable. Pelta comments about a letter from Columbus that washed ashore in a barrel. It would have been interesting, except that it was written in modern English, a language that was not even spoken during Columbus's lifetime. Sources and Information. *Notable Children's Trade Books in the Field of Social Studies* and *American Library Association Notable Books for Children*.

1738. Pemberton, William E. **George Bush**. Vero Beach, FL: Rourke, 1993. 112p. $22.60. ISBN 0-86625-478-1. 4 up

The text starts with the 1990s crisis that led to the Persian Gulf War and returns to George Bush's childhood, when he was a child of privilege in New England born in 1924. It looks at his achievements in business and public service before he became vice president and then president. Photographs, Time Line, Glossary, Bibliography, Media Resources, and Index.

1739.   Pendergraft, Patricia. **As Far as Mill Springs**. New York: Philomel, 1991. 153p. $15.95. ISBN 0-399-22102-6. 5 up

After living most of his life in foster homes and enduring much abuse, Robert hears adults talking through a closed door in 1932. They say that his biological mother lives in a nearby town. He and one of the girls from the home leave for the town by riding in boxcars with hobos. They become separated but find each other on Christmas, the day after Robert turns 13. Robert does not find his mother, but he finds an old woman who needs him as much as he needs her.

1740.   Pendergraft, Patricia. **Brushy Mountain**. New York: Philomel, 1989. 207p. $14.95. ISBN 0-399-21610-3. 5-7

Arney, 13, lives with his mother and sister in a tiny mountain town after his father died in World War II. He hates one of the town's old men and wants to kill him, but instead, he ends up saving him three times: from drowning, from a fire, and from an explosion. He also helps his sister deliver Old Man Hooker's twin grandsons, one of them dead. The mother names the remaining one Arney.

1741.   Pendergraft, Patricia. **Hear the Wind Blow**. New York: Philomel, 1988. 208p. $14.95. ISBN 0-399-21528-X. New York: Point, Scholastic, 1989. 208p. $2.75pa. ISBN 0-590-42273-1pa. 5 up

Isadora, 12, attends school in a small town near the beginning of the twentieth century. Various things happen in the town, and people talk about the male schoolteacher, who marries a woman already pregnant, and Isadora's best friend, who dies when her parents choose herbal over medicinal treatment. One of the good things that happens is that Isadora gets her wish, which is to take dancing lessons.

1742.   Perl, Lila. **From Top Hats to Baseball Caps, from Bustles to Blue Jeans: Why We Dress the Way We Do**. New York: Clarion, 1990. 118p. $14.95. ISBN 0-899-19872-4. 5-9

Perl thinks that through the years in Western Europe and the United States such things as social class, women's liberation, war, and technology have influenced styles of clothing. She includes chapters on pants, skirts, shoes, and hats. The text is complemented with photographs and drawings. Bibliography and Index.

1743.   Petersen, David. **Ishi: The Last of His People**. Chicago: Childrens Press, 1991. 30p. $9.95. ISBN 0-516-04179-7. (Picture-Story Biography). 2-5

By 1911, Ishi was the only survivor of his Native American tribe, the Yahi. The other four individuals who had survived persecution by white Americans had died. When Ishi was found, dogs surrounded him at a slaughterhouse in Oroville, California. Eventually he was brought to the Museum of Anthropology at the University of California to live. Chronology and Index.

1744.   Petersen, David. **Meriwether Lewis and William Clark: Soldiers, Explorers, and Partners in History**. Chicago: Childrens Press, 1988. 152p. $19.30. ISBN 0-516-03264-X. 6 up

Meriwether Lewis (1774-1809) and William Clark (1770-1838) explored Thomas Jefferson's new addition to the United States, the Louisiana Purchase. They traveled from St. Louis to the mouth of the Columbia River in the Pacific Northwest. This biography of their lives emphasizes the value of the many scientific contributions of their expedition. Timeline and Index.

1745.   Peterson, Helen Stone. **Abigail Adams: "Dear Partner"**. Betty Frasier, illustrator. New York: Chelsea Juniors, 1991. 80p. $14.95. ISBN 0-7910-1402-9. (Discovery Biography). 2-6

Abigail Adams (1744-1818) and her family survived an earthquake in Massachusetts when she was a young girl. She grew up to be a president's wife and a president's mother. The accessible text presents aspects of her life that show she was a good mother and wife and that she also believed in the rights of women and anyone else who needed help.

1746.   Peterson, Helen Stone. **Henry Clay: Leader in Congress**. New York: Chelsea Juniors, 1991. 80p. $14.95. ISBN 0-7910-1457-6. (Discovery Biography). 3-7

After growing up on a farm in Virginia and moving to Kentucky, Henry Clay became a lawyer whose intelligence allowed him to speak with authority. He became the youngest senator in Congress, Speaker of the House, and Secretary of State. He tried to save the country from civil war by proposing compromise plans but was unsuccessful.

1747.   Pfeffer, Susan B. **Justice for Emily**. New York: Delacorte, 1997. 160p. $14.95. ISBN 0-385-32259-3. 5-7

In the sequel to *Nobody's Daughter*, Emily has to face a town that dislikes her because she has told the truth about the death of a child in the orphan home where she once stayed. Her best friend is also an outcast because her father is a mill labor organizer and her mother a suffragette in this early-twentieth-century New England town. The school board has to decide whether it will expel Emily for misdeeds that she did not commit.

1748. Pfeffer, Susan Beth. **Nobody's Daughter**. New York: Delacorte, 1995. 154p. $14.95. ISBN 0-385-32106-6. 4-7

Emily, 11, has to go to the Austen Home for Orphaned Girls when her great-aunt Mabel dies. She expects to join her sister, adopted at birth, but the sister's family refuses her. After enduring the taunts of the town's wealthy young girls, having her braids cut, knowing how one of the orphans died, and not being able to play her beloved piano, she finds a home with the librarian, who has one of the new automobiles, and the librarian's mother in the early twentieth century.

1749. Pfeifer, Kathryn. **The 761st Tank Battalion**. New York: Twenty-First Century Books, 1994. 80p. $14.98. ISBN 0-8050-3057-3. (African-American Soldiers). 4-6

The 761st Tank Battalion went to Europe during World War II and began serving in October 1944. It was the first African American armored unit to be committed to combat in the war. When the average life of a separate tank battalion on the front lines was approximately 10 to 12 days, the 761st stayed in combat for 183 and 83 consecutive days. As members continued to serve under General George Patton, they exhibited courage as they faced some of Germany's elite troops. When they returned to their homes, they faced racism and segregation until 33 years later, when the surviving members received the Presidential Unit Citation from the Carter administration. Chronology of African Americans in the U.S. Armed Forces, Index, and Bibliography.

1750. Pfeifer, Kathryn Browne. **Henry O. Flipper**. New York: Twenty-First Century Books, 1993. 80p. $14.95. ISBN 0-8050-2351-8. (African-American Soldiers). 4-7

Henry Ossian Flipper (1856-1940) was the first African American graduate of West Point, but he was dishonorably discharged from the army in 1881. Nearly 100 years later, attempts were made to have this decision reversed. Photographs supplement the text. Bibliography, Chronology, and Index.

1751. Pflueger, Lynda. **Stonewall Jackson: Confederate General**. New York: Enslow, 1997. 128p. $18.95. ISBN 0-89490-783-2. (Historical American Biographies). 6-9

Stonewall Jackson (1824-1863) led Confederate troops who followed him faithfully because he planned carefully and was fearless in battle. This biography looks at his impact on American history as it examines his life. Fact boxes and maps augment the text. Notes, Glossary, Further Reading, and Index.

1752. Phelan, Mary Kay. **The Story of the Boston Massacre**. Allan Eitzen, illustrator. New York: Crowell/HarperCollins, 1990. 160p. $13.89. ISBN 0-690-04883-1. 4-7

On the evening of March 5, 1770, angry Boston citizens stormed the Custom House. Soldiers began to fire on the crowd, and five men are killed, along with six others wounded. People, however, think the men must have a fair trial, and John Adams decides to defend them. The text looks at the actions prior to the killings and the trial and verdict after. Bibliography and Index.

1753. Philip, Neil, ed. **Singing America: Poems That Define a Nation**. Michael McCurdy, illustrator. New York: Viking, 1995. 160p. $19.99. ISBN 0-670-86150-2. 6 up

This collection of American poems that give different views of the country begins with Walt Whitman's "I Hear America Singing" and ends with Woody Guthrie's "This Land Is Your Land." In between are poems about cities, tribes, animals, people, and places. The overview of American life collected in such a way is varied and interesting. Index of Poets, Index of First Lines and Titles, Subject Index, and Further Reading.

1754. Phillips, Ann. **A Haunted Year**. Teresa Flavin, illustrator. New York: Macmillan, 1994. 175p. $14.95. ISBN 0-02-774605-4. 5-8

Florence, bored with Sunday life in 1910, finds 12-year-old George's photograph in a family album. Her aunts do not want to talk about him. With the photograph and a magic-circle ritual, she calls up the ghost of George, and he becomes her playmate. But George soon realizes that he can come to her whenever he wants, and he takes control of the situation by coming at night and keeping her up. With the help of cousins who become friends, she finally rids herself of the unexpected burden.

1755. Pile, Robert B. **Top Entrepreneurs and Their Businesses**. Minneapolis, MN: Oliver Press, 1993. 159p. $14.95. ISBN 1-881508-04-8. 4-7

In this collective biography are several profiles of twentieth-century Americans who have created their own businesses. They are Lewis Brittin, a Connecticut Colonel, and his flying; L. L. Bean, who hated wet feet; Walt Disney and his animation; Bruce Barton, an advertising wizard; Nathan Cummings and his Sara Lee brand; Bud Hillerich, who made baseball bats; Sam Walton and Walmart Drugs; Rose Totino and her pizza; and John Johnson, an African American who founded a publishing company and who said "don't get mad, get smart."

1756.   Pile, Robert B. **Women Business Leaders**. Minneapolis, MN: Oliver Press, 1995. 160p. $14.95. ISBN 1-881508-24-2. (Profiles). 5 up

The women included here actively pursued their goals to create businesses of significance in the economy. Some of them had to overcome physical impairments as well as gender bias. They are Mary Kay Ash (cosmetics), Helen Boehm (porcelain figures), Leeann Chin (Chinese food products), Ellen Terry (real estate), Ella Musolina-Alber (sports and entertainment promoter), Louise Woerner (health care), Masako Boissonnault (commercial design), and Marilyn Hamilton (wheelchair design). More Notable Twentieth-Century Businesswomen, Bibliography, and Index.

1757.   Pinchot, Jane. **The Mexicans in America**. Minneapolis, MN: Lerner, 1989. 94p. $17.50; $5.95pa. ISBN 0-8225-0222-4; 0-8225-1016-2pa. (In America). 5 up

This brief history of the Mexicans in the United States tells about their life in the American Southwest before statehood, the United States's acquisition of their land, and their individual contributions to American life. Index.

1758.   Pinkney, Andrea Davis. **Alvin Ailey**. Brian Pinkney, illustrator. New York: Hyperion Press, 1993. Unpaged. $13.95; $4.95pa. ISBN 1-56282-414-7; 0-7868-1077-7pa. K-3

After Alvin Ailey and his mother moved to San Francisco, Ailey saw Katherine Dunham's dance troupe from outside the stage door. He knew then that he wanted to dance. After many lessons, he and his friends danced *Blues Suite* on March 30, 1958, in New York. The reviews hailed this introduction, and the theater asked the group to return. From that time, his troupe has been a major presenter of African American dances and dancers.

1759.   Pinkney, Andrea Davis. **Bill Pickett: Rodeo-Ridin' Cowboy**. Brian Pinkney, illustrator. San Diego, CA: Gulliver, Harcourt Brace, 1996. Unpaged. $16. ISBN 0-15-200100-X. K-3

Bill Pickett (c. 1860-1932) lived with his family in Texas after they became free during the Civil War. He wanted to be a cowboy, and when he saw a dog tame a bull by biting its lower lip, he thought he could do the same thing. He did, and his reputation for "bulldogging" grew. As he developed his riding abilities and his lariat skills, he became famous. Soon he became the star of the 101 Ranch Wild West Show and traveled to Europe and South America as its best performer while his family waited for him at the 101 Ranch. More about Black Cowboys and For Further Reading.

1760.   Pinkney, Andrea Davis. **Dear Benjamin Banneker**. J. Brian Pinkney, illustrator. San Diego, CA: Gulliver, Harcourt Brace, 1994. Unpaged. $14.95. ISBN 0-15-200417-3. 1-5

A self-taught mathematician and astronomer, free Black Benjamin Banneker (1731-1806) was also one of the first to speak loudly for civil rights in a 1791 letter to the Secretary of State, Thomas Jefferson. Banneker's grandmother had taught him to read and write, and he studied and experimented while developing his skills as a builder and farmer. His highest goal was to calculate and publish an almanac that would be different from others. It was finally published in 1792. In it he included the cycles of the full moons and new moons, sunrise and sunset, Chesapeake Bay tide tables, and news about festivals and horse habits. He published new almanacs every year through 1797. His skill led George Washington to hire him as a surveyor for the nation's new capital in Washington, D.C. *Notable Children's Trade Books in the Field of Social Studies* and *American Bookseller Pick of the Lists*.

1761.   Plain, Nancy. **George Catlin: The Man Who Painted Indians**. Miami, FL: Benchmark, 1997. 48p. $14.95. ISBN 0-7614-0486-4. 3-6

George Catlin (1796-1872) loved the American wilderness and the natives who lived in it enough that he quit his law career and became a painter. Although undocumented, the text presents a view of Catlin and his art so that his contribution to preserving images of the people is clear. Further Reading, Glossary, and Index.

1762.   Plain, Nancy. **Mary Cassatt: An Artist's Life**. New York: Dillon Press, 1994. 168p. $13.95; $7.95pa. ISBN 0-87518-597-5; 0-382-24720-5pa. (People in Focus). 6 up

Mary Cassatt (1844-1926) knew by the time she was 16 that she wanted to become a professional artist. She was willing to take what she viewed as the narrow and hard path to achieve her goal. In Paris, she initially found a stuffy, aristocratic view of painting. In rebellion, she joined Degas and other Impressionists in creating a different style of painting. Photographs and reproductions of her work highlight the text. Bibliography and Index.

1763.   Platt, Richard. **Pirate**. Tina Chambers, illustrator. New York: Knopf, 1995. 64p. $19. ISBN 0-679-87255-8. (Eyewitness). 5-8

Photographs of artifacts and drawings complement the text, presented in two-page spreads that cover different topics. They include the pirates of ancient Greece and Rome, the raiders of the north, the Barbary Coast in the eleventh century, the corsairs of Malta during the sixteenth and seventeenth centuries, and the privateers, buccaneers, and pirates of the Caribbean. Other topics are women pirates like Mary Read, the Jolly Roger flag, pirate life, pirates in the Indian Ocean, American privateers, the French corsairs, and pirates of the China Sea. Index.

1764. Platt, Richard. **The Smithsonian Visual Timeline of Inventions**. New York: Dorling Kindersley, 1994. 64p. $16.95. ISBN 1-56458-675-8. 5-9

Each segment contains an overview of the period followed by a timeline presenting inventions helpful to counting and communication, daily life and health, agriculture and industry, and travel and conquest. A brief list of world events correlates to the inventions. For example, the closed-eye needle appeared in 1450. Time segments are 600,000 BC (Fire, etc.) to AD 1299 for the first inventions; 1300-1779 for inventions motivated by printing and the spread of ideas; 1780-1869 and the rise of steam power and the Industrial Revolution; 1870-1939 and the use of electric power in the modern world; and 1940-2000, when transistors and information seem most important. Index of Inventions and Index of Inventors.

1765. Pleasant Company. **Addy's Cook Book 1864**. Middleton, WI: Pleasant, 1994. 44p. $5.95pa. ISBN 1-56247-123-6pa. (American Girls Pastimes). 3-7

Addie cooks the foods available during the Civil War using recipes and cooking utensils then in use. The recipes for breakfast and dinner are updated for contemporary kitchens and include such foods as pork sausage and gravy, sweet potato pone, and hoppin' John (a mixture of black-eyed peas, bacon, and other ingredients).

1766. Pleasant Company. **Kirsten's Cookbook**. Middleton, WI: Pleasant, 1994. 44p. $5.95pa. ISBN 1-56247-111-2pa. (American Girls Pastimes). 3-7

In 1854, Kirsten lives in a one-room log cabin on the Minnesota frontier. Her family came from Sweden and joined other immigrants who had come to the new land. Their recipes and menus reflect their Swedish heritage. After the breakfast and dinner recipes, the favorite foods presented are potato soup, Swedish meatballs, fresh applesauce, Swedish pancakes, St. Lucia buns, and *pepparkakor* cookies.

1767. Pleasant Company. **Samantha's Cookbook**. Middleton, WI: Pleasant, 1994. 44p. $5.95pa. ISBN 1-56247-114-7pa. (American Girls Pastimes). 3-7

In 1904, when Samantha, an orphan, lives with her grandmother, she follows strict rules of etiquette in setting the table and serving the food. Menus and recipes for breakfast, dinner, and tea show that the favorite foods are apple brown betty, jelly biscuits, cream cheese and walnut sandwiches, chicken salad sandwiches, gingerbread, and lemon ice.

1768. Plowden, Martha Ward. **Famous Firsts of Black Women**. Ronald Jones, illustrator. Gretna, LA: Pelican, 1993. 155p. $15.95. ISBN 0-88289-973-2. 6-9

The text focuses on notable African American women who have helped shape American life, including contributors in the fields of politics, sports, and the arts. The women selected are Marian Anderson (1902-1993), Mary McLeod Bethune (1875-1955), Gwendolyn Brooks (b. 1917), Diahann Carroll (b. 1935), Shirley Chisholm (b. 1924), Althea Gibson (b. 1927), Patricia Roberts Harris (1924-1985), Barbara Jordan (1936-1996), Elizabeth Duncan Koontz (b. 1919), Edmonia Lewis (1845-1890), Hattie McDaniel (1898-1952), Constance Baker Motley (b. 1920), Rosa Parks (b. 1913), Leontyne Price (b. 1927), Wilma Rudolph (b. 1940), Sojourner Truth (1797?-1883), Harriet Tubman (1820-1913), Maggie Lena Walker (1867-1934), Ida B. Wells-Barnett (?-1931), and Phillis Wheatley (1753-1784). Illustrations complement the text. Further Reading.

1769. Polacco, Patricia. **Firetalking**. Lawrence Migdale, photographer. Katonah, NY: Richard C. Owen, 1994. 32p. $13.95. ISBN 1-878450-55-7. (Meet the Author). 2-5

A look at the influences on Patricia Polacco's life gives insight as to how she chooses her stories and why she incorporates certain figures in her drawings. The title comes from her Ukrainian grandmother's name for telling stories by the fire that were always true but may not have happened. As a child, Polacco and her brother lived with their Irish father in the summer, while the rest of the year they lived with their mother. Polacco married an Italian Jewish immigrant from Poland. The accessible text and photographs introduce Polacco's family and friends as well as her environs.

1770. Polacco, Patricia, author/illustrator. **Pink and Say**. New York: Philomel, 1994. Unpaged. $15.95. ISBN 0-399-22671-0. 4 up

Pinkus (Pink) Aylee saves Sheldon (Say), 15, after he has been shot in the leg for deserting his unit of the Union army during the Civil War. Pink takes him home to his mother, a slave still living on the plantation after everyone else has left. While they are healing, marauders come and murder Pink's mother, the woman who has made Say feel like he belonged to her. The two boys, almost immediately captured, end up at Andersonville, where Say survives; Pink is most likely hung hours after they arrive. *Jefferson Cup Award*.

1771. Polikoff, Barbara G. **Herbert C. Hoover: 31st President of the United States**. Ada, OK: Garrett Educational, 1990. 120p. $17.26. ISBN 0-944483-58-5. (Presidents of the United States). 5-9

Herbert C. Hoover (1874-1964) attended Stanford University and became a mining engineer. He served presidents Wilson, Harding, and Coolidge before being elected to the presidency himself. As the Depression developed, people accused Hoover of refusing to pay hungry veterans and then routing them with army troops. What Hoover did not know was that MacArthur, charged with looking after the veterans, was disobeying Hoover's directions and choosing to act as he wanted. Hoover, in turn, dismayed by the harsh charges, accused many rebellious veterans of being Communists. These and other problems led to Roosevelt defeating him in his bid for a second term. Bibliography and Index.

1772. Polikoff, Barbara G. **James Madison: 4th President of the United States**. Ada, OK: Garrett Publications, 1989. 118p. $17.26. ISBN 0-944483-22-4. (Presidents of the United States). 5-9

James Madison (1751-1836), born in Virginia, attended Princeton University (then the College of New Jersey), and returned home to serve on the Virginia Council of State under Governors Thomas Jefferson and Patrick Henry. He was a delegate to the Second Continental Congress, where he advocated separation of church and state and a strong central government. He wrote the *Federalist* essays, married Dolley Payne Todd, and served as President for two terms. Bibliography and Index.

1773. Pollack, Jill S. **Shirley Chisholm**. New York: Franklin Watts, 1994. 64p. $19.90. ISBN 0-531-20168-6. (First Book). 6 up

In her grandparents' Barbados home, Shirley St. Hill (Chisholm) learned to read by age four. She stayed with them until 1934, when she went to be with her parents in Brooklyn during the Depression. There, she heard her father discussing politics with friends, and became interested in it herself. Although she became a teacher after college, she still loved politics. Soon she ran for office and went to the state capital of New York as an assemblywoman. She followed this job by becoming a representative to Congress. She retired in 1982, and in 1985 became the first president of the national Political Congress of Black Women.

1774. Pollard, Michael. **The Nineteenth Century**. New York: Facts on File, 1993. 78p. $17.95. ISBN 0-8160-2791-9. (Illustrated History of the World). 4-7.

In the nineteenth century, towns and the cities showed changes from the old way of life. The British went into India and Americans went West in attempts to build empires. The slave trade led to the Civil War in the United States. Other changes affected Europe, Africa, Australia, and New Zealand as steamships reshaped travel, the oil age began, and the communication revolution started. Illustrations highlight the text. Glossary, Further Reading, and Index.

1775. Pollard, Michael. **The Red Cross and the Red Crescent**. New York: New Discovery, 1994. 64p. $7.95. ISBN 0-02-774720-4. (Organizations That Help the World). 4-8

The Red Cross and the Red Crescent are two organizations created in the nineteenth century to help soldiers on the battlefield receive help more quickly. Neutral emergency units became available that could offer medical aid without threatening the enemy. In Europe, Jean-Herni Dunant watched the Battle of Solferino in 1859. In 1862, he wrote a book about it in which he suggested ways to alleviate some of the deaths. At the same time, Clara Barton in America had become interested in helping prisoners and the wounded. In 1863, an international conference to launch the Red Cross movement opened in Geneva with representatives from 16 countries. On August 22, 1964, the first Geneva Convention had signatures from 12 countries. During the Franco-Prussian war of 1870-1871, the Red Cross helped trace and report on prisoners of war, and Clara Barton provided relief on the battlefields. In 1873, Barton returned to the United States to begin setting up the Red Cross in America. Various other treaties and disagreements continued to refine the process. Since then, the Red Cross (Red Crescent in Islamic countries) has been a major relief organization. Glossary, Important Dates, How You Can Help, and Index.

1776. Porte, Barbara Ann. **When Aunt Lucy Rode a Mule & Other Stories**. Maxie Chambliss, illustrator. New York: Orchard, 1994. Unpaged. $15.95. ISBN 0-531-06816-1. 1-3

When Stella and Zelda visit their Aunt Lucy, they ask her to tell them a story. She says she does not know any stories and then proceeds to talk nonstop about her and the girls' grandmother's childhood adventures. They are amazed at the entertainment.

1777. Porter, A. P. **Jump at de Sun: The Story of Zora Neale Hurston**. Minneapolis, MN: Carolrhoda, 1992. 95p. $19.95; $6.95pa. ISBN 0-87614-667-1; 0-87614-546-2pa. (Trailblazers). 4-6

As a young girl in Eatonville, Florida, Zora Neale Hurston (1891-1960) used to hear her mother say "Jump at de Sun," but her mother died when Hurston was 13. Hurston had to work to pay for school. She went to Howard University and then Barnard to study anthropology. She wanted to write and collect African American folklore. Her 10 books urged people to be African American and stop trying to be something they were not, which was white. Her work won acclaim during her lifetime, but she died penniless because she refused to compromise. Notes, Bibliography, and Index.

1778.   Porter, Connie. **Addy Saves the Day: A Summer Story, Book Five**. Bradford Brown, illustrator. Middleton, WI: Pleasant, 1994. 60p. $12.95; $5.95pa. ISBN 1-56247-084-1; 1-56247-083-3pa. 3-5

In Philadelphia, after the Civil War ends in 1865, people are trying to reunite with their families. Addy works at the church fair beside her conceited friend Harriet to raise money for those hurt by the war. Something happens that makes them forget their arguing, and Addy has to find the money raised at the fair when it is stolen. A Peek into the Past.

1779.   Porter, Connie. **Happy Birthday Addy! A Springtime Story, Book Four**. Bradford Brown, illustrator. Middleton, WI: Pleasant, 1994. 60p. $12.95; $5.95pa. ISBN 1-56247-082-5; 1-56247-081-7pa. (American Girls Collection). 3-5

In Philadelphia during the spring, Addy and her family move to a boardinghouse where she meets a friend, M'dear. Because Addy, like many others who grew up in slavery, does not know her birthday, her friend suggests that she claim one day as her own. A Peek into the Past.

1780.   Porter, Connie. **Meet Addy: An American Girl**. Melodye Rosales, illustrator. Madison, WI: Pleasant, 1993. 69p. $12.95; $5.95pa. ISBN 1-56247-076-0; 1-56247-075-2pa. 3-5

In the summer of 1864, Addy's parents decide to escape from the plantation where they are slaves. Before they can leave, the master sells some of the family. Addy, disguised as a boy, makes her way to Philadelphia. On one part of the journey, she almost enters a camp of Confederate soldiers. She arrives safely, and after the war, the family reunites in the city.

1781.   Potter, Robert R. **Benjamin Franklin**. Englewood Cliffs, NJ: Silver Burdett, 1991. 138p. $10.95; $6.95pa. ISBN 0-382-24173-8; 0-382-24178-9pa. (Pioneers in Change). 5-9

This text on Benjamin Franklin (1706-1790) starts with his firsts: flying the kite to test electricity; suggesting that the union begin with the 13 original colonies; and inventing the lightning rod, bifocal glasses, and the Franklin stove. He also wrote documents for publication and for the public good in the Declaration of Independence and the Constitution. As a youth, he and his family faced one of the main enemies of the time: disease, and the losses there helped prepare him for his future disappointments. His humor and intelligence as a self-made man propelled him into a prominent role during the creation of the new country. Engravings, Important Dates, Bibliography, and Index.

1782.   Potter, Robert R. **Buckminster Fuller**. Englewood Cliffs, NJ: Silver Burdett, 1990. 152p. $13.98. ISBN 0-382-09967-2. (Pioneers in Change). 5-9

Buckminster Fuller (1895-1983) attributed his interest in shapes to the poor eyesight he had as a child, when he saw everything in large squares, triangles, or circles. He was, therefore, always interested in "the big picture." Among his accomplishments were 25 inventions, one of them the famous geodesic dome; 52 trips around the world; 17 books; 47 honorary degrees; and many other things. He was a scientist, an inventor, an architect, a mathematician, a historian, a philosopher, an economist, and a prophet. The text looks at this many-faceted man and his interests. Bibliography and Index.

1783.   Potter, Robert R. **Jefferson Davis: Confederate President**. Austin, TX: Raintree/Steck-Vaughn, 1994. 128p. $16.98. ISBN 0-8114-2330-1. (American Troublemakers). 6 up

Jefferson Davis (1808-1889) was born eight months before and only 100 miles from Abraham Lincoln. He went to West Point but resigned to become a plantation owner where he became thoroughly committed to the aristocratic Southern way of life and the value of states' rights. He was selected to be president of the Confederacy after the South seceded from the Union, was imprisoned without trial after the South's defeat, and refused to swear allegiance to the United States. Maps, Photographs, Key Dates, Glossary, Places to Visit, Bibliography and Recommended Readings, and Index.

1784.   Potter, Robert R. **John Brown: Militant Abolitionist**. Austin, TX: Raintree/Steck-Vaughn, 1994. 128p. $16.98. ISBN 0-8114-2378-6. (American Troublemakers). 6 up

As a member of a religious family, John Brown (1800-1859) first became a minister. When that line of work failed him, he ran a tannery. In 1836 at an Ohio church meeting, he vowed to dedicate his life to end slavery in America, a practice he had always abhorred. In 1855, he went to Kansas Territory to help antislavery forces, and the next year led a massacre in a proslavery settlement. In 1859, he led the Harper's Ferry raid and was tried for treason, convicted, and hanged. Maps, Photographs, Key Dates, Glossary, Places to Visit, Bibliography and Recommended Readings, and Index.

1785. Poynter, Margaret. **A Time Too Swift**. New York: Atheneum, 1990. $12.95. 216p. ISBN 0-689-31146-X. 6-9

In 1941, Marjorie, 15, undergoes several experiences. She meets a boy whom she likes, but he has to go to Pearl Harbor after the bombing. Her brother enlists in the Marines, and her friend's father is killed. She has Japanese-American friends who have to go to an internment camp, and she has to listen to her father's prejudiced remarks. Eventually the strands resolve as her brother returns injured but alive, and Marjorie falls in love with her brother's best friend, who is not physically fit to fight in the war.

1786. Pratt, Paula. **Martha Graham**. San Diego, CA: Lucent, 1995. 112p. $16.95. ISBN 1-56006-056-5. (Importance Of). 6 up

Martha Graham (1894-1991), a pioneer in dance and choreography, exposed the hard work of the dancer to the audience rather than hiding it, as in traditional ballet, and became the creator of modern dance. Most of her major work was begun in the 1930s and 1940s. Modern dancers work into the ground rather than leap into the air. To her, every dancer was trying to show the trials of the human spirit and the triumphs over those trials. She showed courage by being different, and today her methods are taught worldwide. Notes, For Further Reading, Additional Works Consulted, and Index.

1787. Precek, Katharine Wilson. **Penny in the Road**. Patricia Cullen-Clark, illustrator. New York: Macmillan, 1989. 32p. $14.95. ISBN 0-02-774970-3. K-3

As a boy in 1913, a grandfather remembers finding a penny on the way to school dated 1793. He thinks about the person who had the penny and what kind of life that the person had enjoyed more than a century before.

1788. Prentzas, G. S. **Thurgood Marshall: Champion of Justice**. New York: Chelsea Juniors, 1994. 80p. $14.95; $4.95pa. ISBN 0-7910-1769-9; 0-7910-1969-1pa. (Junior Black Americans of Achievement). 3-6

In 1954, Thurgood Marshall (1908-1993) argued before the U.S. Supreme Court that all children should receive the same education. The Court agreed, and *Brown v. Board of Education of Topeka* was a victory for Brown. The text begins with the story of this case and continues with other information about Marshall's life. He was a lawyer, a civil rights leader, a judge, and the first African American on the Supreme Court. Further Reading, Chronology, Glossary, and Index.

1789. Presnall, Judith Janda. **Rachel Carson**. San Diego, CA: Lucent, 1995. 96p. $16.95. ISBN 1-56006-052-2. (Importance Of). 6 up

Although a biologist by training, Rachel Carson (1907-1964) loved writing; her first published story appearing in *St. Nicholas* magazine when she was only 12. Her talent led to *The Sea Around Us* (1951), a bestseller that introduced readers to the life under the ocean surface. Her intense concern with the proliferation of pesticides between 1947 and 1960, when the number of them increased fivefold, led her to write *Silent Spring* (1962). The public had been unaware of the dangers of chemicals being sprayed almost everywhere and on almost everything. Her book caused a furor in the chemical industry, but it led to the passage of more than 40 bills controlling the use of chemicals in daily life. She is the founder of today's ecology movement. Notes, For Further Reading, Additional Works Consulted, and Index.

1790. Press, Skip. **Mark Twain**. San Diego, CA: Lucent, 1994. 112p. $16.95. ISBN 1-56006-043-3. (Importance Of). 6-9

Born in 1835 when Halley's comet blazed through the sky, Mark Twain (Samuel Langhorne Clemens) was arguably the most recognized man in America by the time of his death, when Halley's comet reappeared in 1910. His bushy white hair and mustache, white suits, and cigar on the lecture circuit had made him famous. His friends included Nikola Tesla (discoverer of alternating current), Andrew Carnegie, and Thomas Edison. Twain's life, filled with writing and traveling, had moments of intense happiness and intense sadness. He seemed to recover from the bad and regain his composure, but his writing became more cynical in his later years. Still, he is the dean of American letters because he wrote the first truly American novel, *Huckleberry Finn*. Notes, For Further Reading, Additional Works Consulted, and Index.

1791. Prior, Katherine. **Initiation Customs**. New York: Thomson Learning, 1993. 32p. $13.95. ISBN 1-56847-035-5. (Comparing Religions). 4-8

Six major religions—Buddhism, Christianity, Hinduism, Judaism, Islam, and Sikhism—have specific ideas about the introduction to adulthood. The text examines the age for initiation ceremonies, how much study and preparation each requires, the special clothing worn, and the symbols that represent the religion. Topics such as baptism and confirmation for Christians, bar mitzvah for Jews, *uanayana* for Hindus, *anint* for Sikhs, and *pravrajya* for Buddhists show these rituals.

1792.   Prior, Katherine. **Pilgrimages and Journeys**. New York: Thomson Learning, 1993. 32p. $13.95. ISBN 1-56847-032-0. (Comparing Religions). 4-8

Six major religions—Buddhism, Christianity, Hinduism, Judaism, Islam, and Sikhism—have used pilgrimages and journeys as part of their faith. The text looks at why people go on pilgrimages, where they go, how they behave and dress, and what journeys they took in the past. Photographs of holy sites such as Jerusalem augment the text. Glossary, Books to Read, and Index.

1793.   Probosz, Kathilyn Solomon. **Martha Graham**. Englewood Cliffs, NJ: Dillon Press, 1995. 184p. $13.95. ISBN 0-87518-568-1. 5 up

As a child, Martha Graham (1894-1991) preferred to jump rope in a tree rather than on the ground. At 16, she saw Ruth St. Denis perform and knew that she wanted to dance. People thought she was too old to begin lessons, but she proved them wrong as she became accomplished. She revolutionized the dance world by choreographing nearly 200 dances and creating a dance company. Although her beliefs cost her personal relationships, she thought that a person should listen to their inner voice in deciding what to do with life. Chapter Notes, For Further Reading, and Index.

1794.   Provensen, Alice, author/illustrator. **The Buck Stops Here: The Presidents of the United States**. New York: HarperCollins, 1990. Unpaged. $18. ISBN 0-06-024786-X. 3-6

The text is a poem about the first 41 presidents of the United States. The pictures include anecdotes about the presidents' lives and about things happening in the country during their terms that give an entertaining view of history. Notes About the Presidents and Selected Bibliography.

1795.   Provensen, Alice, author/illustrator. **My Fellow Americans**. San Diego, CA: Browndeer, Harcourt Brace, 1995. 64p. $19.95. ISBN 0-15-276642-1. 4 up

Provensen says that her fellow Americans are the people who have created the country. To have names or portraits included in the book, however, they must be deceased, because "today's heroes may become tomorrow's fools." Some of the categories of people are Pilgrims, Quakers, ministers, equal rights fighters, warriors, patriots, industrialists, writers, expatriates, architects, superstars, composers, groundbreakers, scoundrels, and visionaries. Obligations and Reflections and Selected Bibliography. *Notable Children's Trade Books in the Field of Social Studies* and *American Bookseller Pick of the Lists*.

1796.   Pryor, Bonnie. **The Dream Jar**. Mark Graham, illustrator. New York: Morrow, 1996. Unpaged. $15. ISBN 0-688-13061-5. K-3

Valentina and her family immigrate from Russia at the beginning of the twentieth century. Papa has to lay bricks instead of peel vegetables, which tires him too much. Mama and Aunt Katherine sew piecework, and Michael drops out of school to earn money. Their earnings go into a dream jar, but Valentina worries because she cannot contribute any money. She works hard in school, however, and she soon teaches the family and neighbors how to speak and write English.

1797.   Ptacek, Greg. **Champion for Children's Health: A Story About Dr. S. Josephine Baker**. Lydia M. Anderson, illustrator. Minneapolis, MN: Carolrhoda, 1994. 64p. $13.13. ISBN 0-87614-806-2. (Creative Minds). 4-6

Distressed by the deaths of her brother and father in 1890, S. Josephine Baker (1873-1945) announced that she wanted to become a doctor. She became the first woman to hold a doctor's degree in public health, the first woman to hold an executive position in the U.S. government, and the first woman to be a professional representative in the League of Nations. She was also one of the first to state that preventive medicine for children was important. She fought for women's rights and helped win the right to vote. Bibliography.

Q

1798. Quackenbush, Robert, author/illustrator. **Benjamin Franklin and His Friends**. New York: Pippin Press, 1991. 36p. $14.95. ISBN 0-945912-14-5. 2-4

With quotes on each page from *Poor Richard's Almanack*, the text gives information about Benjamin Franklin (1706-1790), the man who was always a good friend. That he was a philosopher, an inventor, a printer, a scientist, a reformer, and a writer become clear in the text and accompanying illustrations.

1799. Quackenbush, Robert, author/illustrator. **James Madison and Dolley Madison and Their Times**. New York: Pippin, 1992. 36p. $14.95. ISBN 0-945912-18-8. 2-5

James and Dolley Madison were already in Washington when he was elected the fourth President of the United States in 1809. Dolley Madison loved to entertain and was hostess for Thomas Jefferson while he was President. The text looks at their contributions to the history of the new nation.

1800. Quackenbush, Robert. **Mark Twain? What Kind of a Name Is That?** New York: Prentice Hall, 1984. 36p. $13. ISBN 0-13-55570-00-X. 3-6

Samuel Langhorne Clemens (1835-1910) pursued a variety of careers such as typesetter, riverboat pilot, gold miner, and frontier reporter before he settled into writing full time. He became a performer who delighted his audiences. The text looks at his life, some of it not as humorous as his work because he suffered a variety of setbacks. He died as he had been born, in a year that Halley's comet returned.

1801. Quackenbush, Robert, author/illustrator. **Pass the Quill, I'll Write a Draft: A Story of Thomas Jefferson**. New York: Pippin, 1989. 36p. $12.95. ISBN 0-945912-07-2. 2-4

This biography features information about Thomas Jefferson rather than a chronological guide to his life. The cartoon illustrations add to the information about his life and accomplishments, from his birth in 1743 until his retirement to Monticello, his Virginia home. Jefferson died in 1826.

1802. Quackenbush, Robert, author/illustrator. **Stop the Presses, Nellie's Got a Scoop! A Story of Nellie Bly**. New York: Simon & Schuster, 1992. 36p. $13. ISBN 0-671-76090-4. 3-4

Elizabeth Cochrane (1864-1922) became famous as Nelly Bly, the first crusading woman reporter. She got her first job because she wrote a letter to a newspaper, furious with the comments it made about women who wanted to work. She needed a job, and the editor asked through the paper for the "Poor Lonely Orphan Girl" to reveal herself. She did, and he hired her. Because she wrote such strong opinions, her editor suggested that she use a pen name so her family would escape harm from people angry with what she said. With her undercover work as an investigative reporter, she exposed injustices that led to important reforms.

1803. Quiri, Patricia Ryon. **Alexander Graham Bell**. New York: Franklin Watts, 1991. 62p. $11.90. ISBN 0-531-20022-1. (First Books). 4-6

Alexander Graham Bell (1847-1922) invented the telephone and developed instruments to help the hearing-impaired. His own mother was deaf, a situation that influenced his interests. Photographs and drawings enhance the text. Bibliography and Index.

1804. Quiri, Patricia Ryon. **Dolley Madison**. New York: Franklin Watts, 1993. 64p. $12.90. ISBN 0-531-20097-3. (First Books). 4-6

Dolley Payne (1768-1849) moved from North Carolina to Philadelphia with her Quaker family and was relieved that the Quakers there were a little less strict in their practices. She married John Todd, and they lived together happily until he died in the yellow fever epidemic that hit Philadelphia in 1793. Aaron Burr eventually introduced her to James Madison, 17 years older than her. She decided to marry him when he asked, and he adopted her son. While Madison served as Secretary of State, Dolley became Thomas Jefferson's official hostess, a role that she carried into her husband's term as President. At her request, Madison sent Francis Scott Key to rescue Dr. Beane aboard a British ship; Key wrote "The Star Spangled Banner" when he saw the flag flying over Fort McHenry early the next morning. Dolley also organized the first White House Easter Egg Roll. After Madison left the presidency, they had financial problems because of entertainment expenses and the irresponsibility of her son. For Further Reading and Index.

R

1805. Rabin, Staton. **Casey over There**. Greg Shed, illustrator. San Diego, CA: Harcourt Brace, 1994. Unpaged. $14.95. ISBN 0-15-253186-6. 1-3

Aubrey, seven, writes his brother Casey, who is fighting the Great War in France during 1917. While Aubrey waits for a response, he visits New York's Coney Island and plays kick the can in the street. Discouraged, he eventually writes Uncle Sam to ask where Casey is. Uncle Sam, alias President Woodrow Wilson, replies. A Note from the Author. *Marion Vannett Ridgway Award* and *Notable Children's Trade Books in the Field of Social Studies*.

1806. Rael, Elsa Okon. **What Zeesie Saw on Delancey Street**. Marjorie Priceman, illustrator. New York: Simon & Schuster, 1996. 40p. $16. ISBN 0-689-80549-7. K-3

Zeesie gets to attend her first package party in the 1930s where people gather to dance, sing, and eat while raising funds for other members of their New York City Jewish community. She hears about the "money" room where adults leave or take money according to their needs. Although she has been told not to go into the room, she looks inside and sees a transaction that causes her to contribute her most precious item, her birthday dollar. *Bulletin Blue Ribbon Book*.

1807. Rambeck, Richard. **Lou Gehrig**. Chicago: Child's World, 1994. 31p. $21.36. ISBN 1-56766-073-8. 3-5

Lou Gehrig (1903-1941) played for the Yankees in the 1930s. People called him the "Iron Horse" because he played regardless of injuries, relying instead on his strong build. He also won the triple crown of baseball: highest batting average, most home runs, and most RBIs in 1934. By 1939, he began to lose his reflexes, and he was diagnosed with the muscle disease that killed him and was later named after him.

1808. Rand, Gloria. **The Cabin Key**. Ted Rand, illustrator. San Diego, CA: Harcourt Brace, 1994. Unpaged. $14.95. ISBN 0-15-213884-6. 1-3

Although not officially historical fiction, this story tells of a little girl's experience at the cabin that her family has owned for decades. When the family comes to the cabin, it cooks on the open fire, uses the toilet outside, sees by the light of kerosene lamps, and carries water to drink from the nearby stream. Some items in the cabin date from pioneer days. The reader gets a sense of the past from the inhabitants of the cabin.

1809. Rand, Jacki Thompson. **Wilma Mankiller**. Wayne Anthony Still, illustrator. Austin, TX: Raintree/Steck-Vaughn, 1993. 32p. $19.97; $4.95pa. ISBN 0-8114-6576-4; 0-8114-4097-4pa. (Native American Stories). 3-5

Wilma Mankiller (b. 1945) was the first woman to be elected Principal Chief of the Oklahoma Cherokees. After getting a college education and becoming active in Indian Rights groups, she returned to Oklahoma from California where she had grown up and assisted the Bell, Oklahoma, community in its quest for water pipes. In 1985, she became the head of the Cherokee Nation. History.

1810. Randall, Marta. **John F. Kennedy**. New York: Chelsea House, 1988. 112p. $18.95; $7.95pa. ISBN 0-87754-586-3; 0-7910-0580-1pa. (World Leaders Past and Present). 5 up

John F. Kennedy (1917-1963) was full of determination and competitiveness. As President, he created the Peace Corps and the Alliance for Progress, revamped the space program, and instituted welfare reforms. His first foreign policy foray, the invasion at the Bay of Pigs in 1961, was a disaster. Photographs enhance the text. Chronology, Further Reading, and Index.

1811. Randolph, Blythe. **Amelia Earhart**. New York: Franklin Watts, 1987. 121p. $11.90. ISBN 0-531-10331-5. (Impact). 5-8

Amelia Earhart refused to accept traditional feminine roles in order to pursue her interest in flying. When she married George Putnam, he promoted her relentlessly. The text looks at her life and the records that she broke before she attempted to fly around the world. She disappeared in the Pacific. Bibliography and Index.

1812. Randolph, Blythe. **Charles Lindbergh**. New York: Franklin Watts, 1990. 160p. $11.90. ISBN 0-531-10918-6. 6-12

Charles Lindbergh (1902-1974) gained fame when he became the first person to fly across the Atlantic Ocean. Five years later, he and his wife suffered the kidnapping and death of their firstborn son. With emotions from the highest jubilation to the lowest despair, his demeanor became well known to the American public. When he went to Germany in 1936 and professed admiration for Hitler and his country, many accused him of being a traitor. The text looks at the controversies in Lindbergh's life. Bibliography and Index.

1813.   Randolph, Sallie G. **Woodrow Wilson: President**. New York: Walker, 1992. 124p. $15.85. ISBN 0-8027-8143-8. 6-9

Woodrow Wilson (1856-1924) made massive labor reforms, overhauled the banking system, and solved problems in international trade and tariffs while facing the threat of world war. He changed from an allegiance to his privileged social class to a fighter for the common people, a decision that shocked his political associates. Although a dreamer and an idealist, he declared war on Germany when he had to save Great Britain. He worked for a lasting peace and was disappointed when the United States would not ratify the League of Nations charter. Index.

1814.   Ransom, Candice F. **Jimmy Crack Corn**. Shelly O. Hass, illustrator. Minneapolis, MN: Carolrhoda, 1994. 72p. $14.21. ISBN 0-87614-786-4. 3-5

In 1932, Jimmy, nine, goes with his father from their Virginia farm into Washington, D.C., to join other veterans of World War I trying to get the bonus money they had been promised after World War I. Although this march is unsuccessful, Jimmy, who likes to sing, befriends Mr. Morris, who has a harmonica, and learns that sometimes friendship is more important than being right.

1815.   Raphael, Elaine, and Don Bolognese. **Daniel Boone: Frontier Hero**. New York: Cartwheel, Scholastic, 1996. Unpaged. $14.95. ISBN 0-590-47900-8. (Drawing America). 3-5

This brief biography of Daniel Boone (1734-1820) shows how much people liked and trusted him as well as his love of nature. It also discusses his daughter and her kidnapping by Indians. Directions for drawing Boone, his daughter, a Conestoga wagon, and a log cabin add a different approach to the frontier background presented here.

1816.   Raphael, Elaine, and Don Bolognese. **Sacajawea: The Journey West**. New York: Cartwheel, Scholastic, 1994. Unpaged. $12.95. ISBN 0-590-47898-2. (Drawing America). 1-3

This fictional biography recounts Sacajawea's life with her Shoshoni family before Minnetaree raiders captured her at 10. They sold Sacajawea (1790-1812) to the French-Canadian fur trader Toussaint Charbonneau, and she became his wife at 13. In 1804, Lewis and Clark found her and took her, her husband, and her child on their expedition across the western half of the United States so she could translate between them and the Shoshoni Indians. Following the text are segmented drawings so readers can easily learn to sketch Sacajawea, a trader, a horse, and other elements of the story.

1817.   Rappaport, Doreen. **The Alger Hiss Trial**. New York: HarperCollins, 1993. 184p. $14.89. ISBN 0-06-025120-4. (Be the Judge/Be the Jury). 6 up

In 1948, Whittaker Chambers, a former Communist, accused Alger Hiss of giving him secret documents. In 1949, a second trial began after the first jury could not reach a verdict. In 1950, Alger Hiss was declared guilty, and he had to go to prison. However, he never stopped trying to clear his name. The text looks at all the facts available from the trial and asks the reader to make a decision before reading the verdict. Photographs and drawings enhance the text. Bibliography and Stenographer's Notes.

1818.   Rappaport, Doreen. **The Boston Coffee Party**. Emily A. McCully, illustrator. New York: HarperCollins, 1988. 64p. $14.89; $3.50pa. ISBN 0-06-024825-4; 0-06-444141-5pa. (An I Can Read Book). K-3

Sarah and her sister want sugar in 1775, but the only merchant who has it in stock overcharges for it. The same man hides coffee, waiting for the prices to go up before he sells it. A group of women decide to show the merchant that he cannot succeed with such a plan. They meet and take it from him.

1819.   Rappaport, Doreen. **Escape from Slavery: Five Journeys to Freedom**. Charles Lilly, illustrator. New York: HarperCollins, 1991. 117p. $13.95. ISBN 0-06-021631-X. 4-6

The text tells five stories of slaves who escaped their bondage. They were Eliza, who tried to cross a melting river of ice to save her two-year-old daughter; Selena and Cornelia Jackson, who deceived their master with a plan for a free Black settlement in Cabin Creek, Indiana; Henry Brown, who shipped himself out of slavery in a box; Jane Johnson, who faced her master in a Philadelphia courtroom; and Ellen and William Craft, who dressed as an invalid white master and slave as they traveled to the North by steamship, train, and coach. Bibliography.

1820.   Rappaport, Doreen. **The Flight of the Red Bird**. New York: Dial, 1997. 208p. $15.99. ISBN 0-8037-1438-6. 5 up

Gertrude Bonnin was a writer, lecturer, and activist known as Zitkala-Sa, one of the most important Native American reformers of the early twentieth century. After authorities took her from her South Dakota home, she went to a Quaker school in Indiana where she was forced to abandon her Yankton Sioux language and other aspects of her heritage. She spent her adulthood trying to inform white audiences of her distressful childhood and to encourage them to better the lives of Native Americans in ways not previously practiced. Photographs and Index.

1821.   Rappaport, Doreen. **Living Dangerously: American Women Who Risked Their Lives for Adventure**. New York: HarperCollins, 1991. 117p. $13.95. ISBN 0-06-025108-5. 3-6

In the twentieth century, women have defied expectations and become adventurers. Annie Edson Taylor became the first person to go over Niagara Falls in a barrel when she was 63 in 1901. Annie Smith Peck made her sixth attempt to conquer Huascarán, the highest peak in Peru, in 1908. Delia Akeley lived with the pygmies of Central Africa in 1925 and went on a dangerous elephant hunt. Bessie Coleman, the world's first Black pilot, performed stunts in the 1920s. Eugenie Clark dove underwater to bring back prehistoric skeletons in 1959; and in 1990, Thecla Mitchell, a triple amputee, participated in the New York City Marathon. The text looks at these women and their accomplishments. Appendix: Women Adventurers, Bibliography, and Index.

1822.   Rappaport, Doreen. **The Lizzie Borden Trial**. New York: HarperCollins, 1992. 175p. $15. ISBN 0-06-025114-X. (Be the Judge/Be the Jury). 6 up

Eight days after Andrew and Abby Borden were bludgeoned to death with an ax, Lizzie Borden (1860-1927) was accused of the murder. Because she was wealthy and a regular church attendee, the jury acquitted her. Although she was declared not guilty, the town thought that she was, and she was ostracized. The text looks at all the facts available from the trial and asks the reader to make a decision before reading the verdict. Photographs and drawings enhance the text. Bibliography and Stenographer's Notes.

1823.   Rappaport, Doreen. **The Sacco-Vanzetti Trial**. John Palencar, illustrator. New York: HarperCollins, 1992. 175p. $15. ISBN 0-06-0251116-6. (Be the Judge/Be the Jury). 5 up

When a paymaster and a guard were shot and killed on April 15, 1920, the two men accused of the crime were Italian immigrants Sacco and Vanzetti. Most likely, the trial that convicted them of the murders was not fair because of their background. They were electrocuted on August 22, 1927, after appeals failed. The text looks at all the facts available from the trial and asks the reader to make a decision before reading the verdict. Photographs and drawings enhance the text. Bibliography and Stenographer's Notes.

1824.   Rappaport, Doreen. **Tinker vs. Des Moines: Student Rights on Trial**. New York: HarperCollins, 1993. 153p. $15. ISBN 0-06-025118-2. (Be the Judge/Be the Jury). 5 up

In 1965, John Frederick Tinker and two other students protested the Vietnam War by wearing black armbands in memory of those who had died. They were expelled from school. Appeals to this decision reached the Supreme Court, which decided in favor of the students in 1969 because they were exercising their freedom of speech according to the First Amendment. The text looks at all the facts available from the trial and asks the reader to make a decision before reading the verdict. Photographs and drawings enhance the text. Bibliography and Law Clerk's Notes.

1825.   Rappaport, Doreen. **Trouble at the Mines**. Joan Sandin, illustrator. New York: HarperCollins, 1987. 96p. $14.89. ISBN 0-690-04446-1. 3-7

When they get neither improvement in working conditions nor pay raises in the Arnot, Pennsylvania, mines by 1898, Mother Jones comes to the area and helps the miners strike. The wives and daughters keep the men from succumbing to the mine owners' demands and stand by their needs. They also have to keep them from hurting their friends who choose to support the mine owners.

1826.   Rawls, Jim. **Dame Shirley and the Gold Rush**. John Holder, illustrator. Austin, TX: Raintree/Steck-Vaughn, 1993. 55p. $22.83; $6.64pa. ISBN 0-8114-7222-1; 0-8114-8062-3pa. (Stories of America—Against All Odds). 3-7

Louise Amelia Knapp Smith Clappe (1819-1906) called herself Dame Shirley when she wrote letters in which she described the truth about the California Gold Rush of the early 1850s. Rumors said gold was everywhere for anyone who wanted it, but that was not the reality. Epilogue, Afterword, and Notes.

1827.   Rawls, Jim. **Never Turn Back: Father Serra's Mission**. George Guzzi, illustrator. Austin, TX: Raintree/Steck-Vaughn, 1993. 54p. $22.83; $6.64pa. ISBN 0-8114-7221-3; 0-8114-8061-5pa. (Stories of America—Against All Odds). 5-9

In 1749, Father Serra and a friend left Spain to become missionaries to New Spain. They established a mission in San Xavier, Baja California. But in April 1769, Father Serra left there to help the Tipais Indians in Alta California. He established San Diego de Alacalá, where he lived until his death five years later. Epilogue, Afterword, and Notes.

1828.   Ray, Deborah Kogan, author/illustrator. **My Daddy Was a Soldier: A World War II Story**. New York: Holiday House, 1990. 40p. $12.95. ISBN 0-8234-0795-0. 2-4

Jeanne, eight, has to say good-bye to her father in 1943 when he goes to the Pacific theater in World War II. Her mother works as a welder, and the two of them have to deal with food shortages and lack of necessities. After two years, they are fortunate to reunite.

1829.   Ray, Delia. **A Nation Torn: The Story of How the Civil War Began**. New York: Lodestar, 1990. 102p. $15.95. ISBN 0-525-67308-3. 5-8

In the mid-1800s, the North and South were very different. They had contrasting economies and differing ideas about slavery. The text looks at the various events that led to the beginning of the war over slavery on April 12, 1861, when the rebels attacked Union troops at Fort Sumter, South Carolina. It also presents influential figures of the time, such as Henry Clay, Harriet Tubman, and John Brown. Photographs, letters, diaries, and eyewitness accounts help tell this story. Glossary, Bibliography, and Index.

1830.   Ray, Mary Lyn. **Pianna**. Bobbie Henba, illustrator. San Diego, CA: Harcourt Brace, 1994. Unpaged. $14.95. ISBN 0-15-261357-9. K-3

An unidentified narrator tells the story of Anna, who lives in the same house her father built 80 years before. When she was a young girl, after the turn of the century, she had both an organ and a piano in her house. Because she loved to play, her father sent her to Boston to take lessons each week. She played for everyone, and they called her "Pianna" until she fell in love at 17 and married. She played on Sundays at churches and one other night a week, but most of the time she played for herself.

1831.   Ray, Mary Lyn. **Shaker Boy**. Jeanette Winter, illustrator. San Diego, CA: Browndeer, Harcourt Brace, 1994. Unpaged. $15.95. ISBN 0-15-276921-8. 1-4

After the Civil War, when Caleb is six, his mother, a widow, goes to work in the Lowell factories and places him in a Shaker colony. He learns the ways of the Shakers, which include work and singing. He makes brooms, fills buckets at sugaring time, and studies. When he is 19, he gains responsibility for the apple orchard, which he continues to keep until he is an old man. Author's Note About Shakers. *Notable Children's Trade Books in the Field of Social Studies*.

1832.   Read, Thomas Buchanan. **Sheridan's Ride**. Nancy Winslow Parker, illustrator. New York: Greenwillow, 1993. 31p. $14. ISBN 0-688-10873-3. 3-6

On the morning of October 19, 1864, Major General Philip H. Sheridan, commander of the Union Army of the Shenandoah, was preparing to destroy the Confederates' food supply. But General Early of the Confederate Army of the Valley was planning a surprise attack at Cedar Creek, Virginia. When Sheridan heard artillery fire at eight in the morning, he started riding south toward his men and stopped them from retreating. He rallied his troops and formed a battle line to attack the Confederate army. At four o'clock that afternoon, they drove the Confederates off the field. Many were killed and wounded, but the Confederate army left the Shenandoah Valley for the rest of the war. This poem commemorates that feat. Military and Historical Notes.

1833.   Reeder, Carolyn. **Across the Lines**. Robin Moore, illustrator. New York: Simon & Schuster, Atheneum, 1997. 224p. $16. ISBN 0-689-81133-0. 3-7

Edward, 12, is surprised when his young slave, Simon, runs away at the Union army's arrival. Edward's family flees to Petersburg, and the constant shell bombardment frays Edward's nerves. Simon finds that being free and serving in the army can also be lonely. The two points of view in the novel give differing perspectives on the same conflict.

1834.   Reeder, Carolyn. **Grandpa's Mountain**. New York: Macmillan, 1991. 171p. $13.95. ISBN 0-02-775811-7. 4-6

Carrie, 11, has always enjoyed her summers with her grandparents in Virginia's Shenandoah Mountains. But this summer during the Depression is different because the government is trying to take Grandpa's land for a national park. He fights to save it and is disappointed that so many of the neighbors gladly take the money rather than keep their land. When he fails, Carrie realizes that he has done the best he can.

1835.   Reeder, Carolyn. **Moonshiner's Son**. New York: Macmillan, 1993. 208p. $14.95. ISBN 0-02-775805-2. 3-7

Because Tom, 12, only wants to please his father, he tries to make whiskey as best as he can even though it is illegal during Prohibition in 1919. A new preacher arrives and speaks against the liquor, and police arrest Tom's father. Tom observes wife beating and fighting, both caused by drunkenness. He slowly realizes that his wood carvings, which he can sell to the townsfolk, will fulfill his creative urges. His father, remorseful at having beaten his son, stops running the still.

1836.   Reeder, Carolyn. **Shades of Gray**. New York: Macmillan, 1989. 152p. $12.95. ISBN 0-02-775810-9. New York: Camelot, 1992. 152p. $3.99pa. ISBN 0-380-71232-6pa. 5-7

During the Civil War, Jed's sisters die of typhoid, Yankees kill his father and brother, and his mother dies of grief. At 12, he must go to his mother's sister's home. There he has to adjust to the rural life of Virginia and to an uncle who refuses to fight for the South or the North. Jed has to overcome his own prejudices and ignore the neighbors' jeers as he begins to understand the strength that his uncle shows in standing firm to his own convictions. *Scott O'Dell Award, Child Study Children's Book Award, Jefferson Cup Award*, and *American Library Association Notable Books for Children*.

1837.   Reef, Catherine. **Benjamin Davis, Jr.** New York: Twenty-First Century Books, 1992. 80p. $14.95. ISBN 0-8050-2137-X. (African-American Soldiers). 4-6

Benjamin Davis, Jr., graduated from West Point with a strong record, but he was refused the right to be a pilot because no Black flying units existed. He overcame this difficulty by commanding the Tuskegee Airmen, the first Black flying unit, in 1941. He served a distinguished career in the military while forwarding the cause of his race. Photographs, Chronology, Index, and Bibliography.

1838.   Reef, Catherine. **Black Fighting Men: A Proud History**. New York: Twenty-First Century Books, 1994. 80p. $14.98. ISBN 0-8050-3106-5. (African-American Soldiers). 4-6

Men who have fought for the United States have been from all races. Reef looks at African Americans who have distinguished themselves in wars through the centuries. These men are Crispus Attucks (Revolutionary War); Jordan B. Noble (War of 1812); Robert Smalls and William Carney (Civil War); Augustus Wally (Indian Wars and Spanish-American War); Henry Johnson and Freddie Stowers (World War I); Benjamin Davis, Sr., Dorie Miller, and Ruben Rivers (World War II); William Thompson (Korean War); Lawrence Joel and Fred V. Cherry (Vietnam War); and Lonnie Davis (Persian Gulf War). Chronology, Index, and Bibliography.

1839.   Reef, Catherine. **Ellis Island**. New York: Dillon Press, 1991. 72p. $13.95. ISBN 0-87518-473-1. (Places in American History). 4-6

The text looks at the background and historical significance of Ellis Island, the place from which immigrants either looked forward to a new life in America or faced rejection and return to their homelands because of disease. Photographs and illustrations augment the text. Chronology and Index.

1840.   Reef, Catherine. **Gettysburg**. New York: Dillon Press, 1992. 72p. $13.95. ISBN 0-87518-503-7. (Places in American History). 3-6

In July 1863, the Civil War battle at Gettysburg was a major loss for the South, but it was also a loss for the Union because of the number of men who died. The text describes the battle, the results of the battle, and the military park that currently commemorates this event. Photographs and drawings enhance the text. Chronology and Index.

1841.   Reef, Catherine. **Henry David Thoreau: A Neighbor to Nature**. Larry Raymond, illustrator. New York: Twenty-First Century Books, 1992. 72p. $14.98. ISBN 0-941477-39-8. (Earth Keepers). 4-8

Henry David Thoreau (1817-1862) believed that many answers to life could be found by observing nature. His most famous account of nature appears in *Walden Pond*, a book he wrote about his two-year stay on its shores. Glossary and Index.

1842.   Reef, Catherine. **The Lincoln Memorial**. New York: Dillon Press, 1994. 72p. $14.95. ISBN 0-87518-624-6. (Places in American History). 3-6

An aerial view of the Lincoln Memorial shows the people who gathered there in 1963 at the March for Freedom where Martin Luther King, Jr., gave his "I Have a Dream" speech. The choice to give the speech in front of the memorial to the man who made the dream possible, was fitting. The text looks at the reasons for building a monument honoring Lincoln, its design, and some of the events that have occurred there. The Lincoln Memorial: A Historical Timeline, Visitor Information, and Index.

1843.   Reef, Catherine. **Mount Vernon**. New York: Dillon Press, 1992. 72p. $13.95. ISBN 0-87518-474-X. (Places in American History). 3-6

George Washington (1732-1799), the first President of the United States, lived at Mount Vernon, overlooking the Potomac River in Virginia. The text looks at the historical background of this lovely home and its current position as a historic site. Photographs and drawings enhance the text. Chronology and Index.

1844.   Reef, Catherine. **The Supreme Court**. New York: Dillon Press, 1991. 72p. $14.95. ISBN 0-87518-626-2. (Places in American History). 4-6

The Supreme Court first met on February 1, 1790, in New York City. By 1801, the Court was meeting in Washington, D.C., and John Marshall was the chief justice. Under him, the Court decided *Marbury v. Madison*, which established the Supreme Court as the nation's authority on constitutional matters. The text covers the general history of the Supreme Court and some of the important cases up to the present. Supreme Court Justices and Index.

1845.   Reese, Joe. **Katie Dee and Katie Haw: Letters from a Texas Farm Girl**. Melissa James, illustrator. Lubbock, TX: Cotten, 1995. 178p. $8.95. ISBN 0-925854-13-1. 4-6

In 1967, Katie Hawkins, 10 and in fifth grade, moves to her mother's childhood sheep farm in Texas after her father dies. She writes letters to her friend Katie Dee back in Vermont. Each of the letters tells about an event in Katie's life, from possums loose in the house to her success at baseball to her fears of going to her first dance. Fortunately, she and her mother are close, so she has someone nearby to comfort her during this difficult year.

1846. Reiser, Howard. **Jackie Robinson: Baseball Pioneer**. New York: Franklin Watts, 1992. 64p. $12.90. ISBN 0-531-20095-7. (First Book). 3-5

Jackie Robinson (1919-1972) left the South for California with his mother, attended UCLA, played in the Negro Leagues, and became the first Black to play in the modern major leagues. The author spent time with Jackie Robinson in his office after the end of his baseball career, and Robinson gave him advice about playing with a team. Robinson's advice was his philosophy for living his life. Glossary, For Further Reading, and Index.

1847. Reit, Seymour. **Guns for General Washington: A Story of the American Revolution**. San Diego, CA: Harcourt Brace, 1990. 144p. $15.95. ISBN 0-15-200466-1. 4-6

In the winter of 1775, men transferred large arms from Fort Ticonderoga to Massachusetts. Colonel Henry Knox planned the transfer over the rough ground, and his organization gave Boston guns to free themselves from the British in the spring of 1776. The story of those who participated is re-created in this historical fiction.

1848. Rennert, Richard, ed. **Book of Firsts: Leaders of America**. New York: Chelsea House, 1994. 63p. $14.95; $5.95pa. ISBN 0-7910-2065-7; 0-7910-2066-5pa. (Profiles of Great Black Americans). 6-9

This collection of succinct biographies gives an overview of African American leaders. Those profiled are Blanche K. Bruce (1841-1898), Ralph Bunche (1904-1971), Shirley Chisholm (b. 1924), Benjamin O. Davis (1877-1970), William H. Hastie (1904-1976), Thurgood Marshall (1908-1993), Colin Powell (b. 1937), and L. Douglas Wilder (b. 1931). Black-and-white illustrations highlight the text. Bibliography and Index.

1849. Rennert, Richard, ed. **Civil Rights Leaders**. New York: Chelsea House, 1993. 63p. $14.95; $5.95pa. ISBN 0-7910-2051-7; 0-7910-2052-5pa. (Profiles of Great Black Americans). 6-9

This collection of biographical profiles gives an overview of African Americans who led the Civil Rights movement. Those presented are James Weldon Johnson (1871-1938), Martin Luther King, Jr. (1929-1968), Thurgood Marshall (1908-1993), Malcolm X (1925-1965), Adam Clayton Powell, Jr. (1908-1972), Asa Philip Randolph (1889-1979), Walter White (1893-1955), and Jesse Jackson (b. 1941). Black-and-white illustrations highlight the text. Bibliography and Index.

1850. Rennert, Richard, ed. **Female Writers**. New York: Chelsea House, 1994. 63p. $14.95; $5.95pa. ISBN 0-7910-2063-0; 0-7910-2064-9pa. (Profiles of Great Black Americans). 6-9

This collection of biographical profiles gives an overview of African American female writers. Those included are Maya Angelou (b. 1928), Gwendolyn Brooks (b. 1917), Nikki Giovanni (b. 1943), Lorraine Hansberry (1930-1965), Zora Neale Hurston (1901?-1960), Toni Morrison (b. 1931), Alice Walker (b. 1944), and Phillis Wheatley (1753?-1784). Black-and-white illustrations highlight the text. Bibliography and Index.

1851. Rennert, Richard, ed. **Jazz Stars**. New York: Chelsea House, 1993. 63p. $14.95; $5.95pa. ISBN 0-7910-2059-2; 0-7910-2060-6pa. (Profiles of Great Black Americans). 5-8

The text looks at people who starred in the jazz music world of the twentieth century. Given are an account of each performer's life, his or her early interest in music, and career development. The book includes capsule biographies of Louis Armstrong (1900-1971), Count Basie (1904-1984), John Coltrane (1926-1967), Duke Ellington (1899-1974), Ella Fitzgerald (1918-1996), Dizzy Gillespie (1917-1993), Billie Holiday (1915-1959), and Charlie Parker (1920-1955). Bibliography and Index.

1852. Rennert, Richard, ed. **Pioneers of Discovery**. New York: Chelsea House, 1994. 63p. $14.95; $5.95pa. ISBN 0-7910-2067-3; 0-7910-2068-1pa. (Profiles of Great Black Americans). 6-9

This collection of biographies gives an overview of African American scientists. Those profiled are Benjamin Banneker (1731-1806), George Washington Carver (1864?-1943), James Beckwourth (1798-1867?), Guion Bluford (b. 1942), Charles Drew (1904-1950), Matthew Henson (1866-1955), Ernest Everett Just (1883-1941), and Lewis Latimer (1848-1928). Black-and-white illustrations highlight the text. Bibliography and Index.

1853. Rennert, Rick. **Jesse Owens: Champion Athlete**. New York: Chelsea House, 1991. 79p. $14.95; $4.95pa. ISBN 0-7910-1570-X; 0-7910-1955-1pa. (Junior Black Americans of Achievement). 4-6

As the 10th child in an Alabama home, Jesse Owens (1913-1980) realized when he was very young that the only place for real victory was from within himself. Pop Riley became his mentor and encouraged him to join the track team in school. Owens became the nation's top high school sprinter and broke five world records at one college track meet. Then he won four gold medals at the 1936 Olympic Games in Berlin, a feat that contradicted Hitler's proclamation that all races other than Aryan were inferior. Owens believed that people who worked could succeed. Further Reading, Chronology, Glossary, and Index.

1854. Richards, Kenneth. **The Gettysburg Address**. Chicago: Childrens Press, 1992. 31p. $17.30; $4.95pa. ISBN 0-516-06654-4; 0-516-46654-2pa. (Cornerstones of Freedom). 3-5

The text tells of the battle at Gettysburg, Pennsylvania, between the Confederate and Union armies during the Civil War, July 3-5, 1863. In the autumn after this battle, where the North lost 23,000 men and the South lost 28,000, Abraham Lincoln took the train to Gettysburg to deliver a speech at a cemetery dedication. Although very short in comparison to the other speech made that day, the address remains a strong statement for the importance of supporting one's beliefs in freedom. Index.

1855. Richards, Norman. **Monticello**. Rev. ed. Chicago: Childrens Press, 1995. 30p. $17.30; $4.95pa. ISBN 0-516-06695-1; 0-516-46695-Xpa. (Cornerstones of Freedom). 2-5

Thomas Jefferson (1743-1826) was 14 when he inherited the little mountain that he called Monticello. Around 10 years later, he began building his 35-room home, expecting to take many years to complete his own plans for it. The text looks at unusual additions he made that were unusual for the time, including revolving doors, a weathervane, a clock for the hall with one face outside, a folding ladder to wind the clock, dumbwaiters, and other pieces of furniture. He eventually finished the house but continued architectural design by working on the central buildings for the nearby University of Virginia in Charlottesville.

1856. Richardson, Joy. **Inside the Metropolitan Museum**. New York: Metropolitan Museum of Art, Harry N. Abrams, 1993. 72p. $12.95pa. ISBN 0-8109-2561-3pa. 4-8

Photographs and reproductions show what one might see on a visit to the Metropolitan Museum in New York. An aerial photograph locates the museum's position in New York City. Inside the book, one may look behind the scenes and then visit some of the exhibits, including Egyptian art, Ancient Near Eastern art, Asian art, Islamic art, Greek and Roman art, medieval art, arms and armor, European sculpture and decorative arts, arts of Africa, Oceania, and the Americas, musical instruments, American art, European paintings, costumes, and twentieth-century art. Quiz.

1857. Richman, Daniel A. **James E. Carter: 39th President of the United States**. Ada, OK: Garrett Educational, 1989. 122p. $17.26. ISBN 0-944483-24-0. (Presidents of the United States). 5-9

As a farm boy from Georgia, Jimmy Carter (b. 1924) grew up to become state senator, governor, and President of the United States. The text tells his story and gives information about his family. Bibliography and Index.

1858. Richmond, Merle. **Phillis Wheatley**. New York: Chelsea House, 1987. 111p. $18.95; $7.95pa. ISBN 1-55546-683-4; 0-7910-0218-7pa. (American Women of Achievement). 5 up

Before Phillis Wheatley (1753-1784) became America's first Black poet, slavers captured her when she was seven and brought her from Africa. The prosperous Wheatley family in Boston bought her in 1761 and taught her Latin and English. The neighbors knew her talents when she was a teenager, and she recited poems for the elite even though she could not sit at their tables. After the American Revolution, people seemed no longer interested in poetry, and she had to struggle to be recognized. She died penniless at 31, but today people realize that she was an important colonial poet. Engravings enhance the text. Chronology, Further Reading, and Index.

1859. Richter, Conrad. **The Light in the Forest**. 1953. Cutchogue, NY: Buccaneer, 1996. 180p. $21.95. ISBN 1-568-49064-X. New York: Juniper, Fawcett, 1995. 180p. $4.50pa. ISBN 0-449-70437-8pa. 5 up

True Son, 15 in 1765, has lived with the Cuyloga (Delaware Indians) for 11 years and thinks of himself as a Cuyloga. When the whites demand that the Cuyloga release the white captives living with them, True Son has to leave. He cannot adjust to the whites, whom he has learned to hate, including his biological parents.

1860. Ride, Sally. **To Space and Back**. New York: Lothrop, Lee & Shepard, 1986. 96p. $19. ISBN 0-688-06159-1. 5-9

The text and photographs help describe what it is like to be an astronaut on the space shuttle through Sally Ride's experiences. Glossary.

1861. Riley, Gail Blasser. **Miranda v. Arizona: Rights of the Accused**. Springfield, NJ: Enslow, 1994. 128p. $17.95. ISBN 0-89490-504-X. (Landmark Supreme Court Cases). 6 up

Ernesto Miranda was arrested and questioned about a rape and kidnapping. He was charged without being advised that he had the right to an attorney. The case came before the Supreme Court in 1966, and on June 13 of that year, the court said that police must tell all people being questioned that they have a right to remain silent. The text looks at the background of this case and what brought it to the Supreme Court. Notes, Further Reading, Glossary, and Index.

1862.   Rinaldi, Ann. **Keep Smiling Through**. San Diego, CA: Harcourt Brace, 1996. 208p. $11; $5pa. ISBN 0-15-200768-7; 0-15-201072-6pa. 4-7

Kay, a fifth grader in 1943, thinks that World War II gives her penurious father another reason not to spend money, and because her stepmother uses any excuse, the rationing does not cause her much stress. Her problems come from the death of her stepmother's baby and deciding who is on what side during the war. A German neighbor is kind and helpful, while her own grandfather's comments let her know that he sympathizes with the Germans. Ann has to learn that nationality does not automatically reveal one's political or moral direction and that she is not guilty for the baby's death.

1863.   Rinaldi, Ann. **The Last Silk Dress**. New York: Holiday House, 1988. 350p. $15.95. ISBN 0-8234-0690-3. New York: Bantam, 1996. 350p. $4.99pa. ISBN 0-553-28315-4pa. 5 up

At 14, Susan wants to do something meaningful in support of the Confederacy during the Civil War. Her mother, however, worries that Susan's older brother's scandalous reputation will hurt Susan, so she makes her stay home. When the Yankees approach Richmond, Susan and her friend convince their mothers to let them collect silk dresses to make a balloon that will help spy on the Yankees. In the meantime, Susan has met her brother, banished from the house, and he has told her family secrets. When she almost faces treason for her actions and falls in love with a Yankee, she knows she must hurt someone she loves.

1864.   Ringgold, Faith, author/illustrator. **Bonjour, Lonnie**. New York: Hyperion. Unpaged. $15.95. ISBN 0-7868-0076-3. 2-4

In this fantasy that reveals a historical past, Lonnie, a red-haired and green-eyed orphan, is in Paris where he follows a "Love Bird," which leads him to people who tell him his family's history. He discovers an African American grandfather in Paris since the 1920s, a French grandmother, a father killed in World War II, and a Jewish mother who died in the Holocaust. He wants to stay, but his family convinces him that he would be happier back in the United States with his adoptive family.

1865.   Ringgold, Faith, author/illustrator. **Tar Beach**. New York: Crown, 1991. 32p. $14.95. ISBN 0-517-58030-6. K-3

Cassie, eight, dreams of flying above the George Washington Bridge in New York City in 1939. When she flies, Cassie realizes that she can go anywhere or have anything she wants. In her fantasy flights over Brooklyn and Tar Beach, she also imagines that she is helping others. *Caldecott Honor; California Children's Book, Video, and Software Award; Coretta Scott King Award; New York Times Best Illustrated Book of the Year; Parents' Choice Award; American Library Association Notable Books for Children;* and *School Library Journal Best Book*.

1866.   Riskind, Mary. **Apple Is My Sign**. Boston: Houghton Mifflin, 1981. 146p. $14.95; $4.95pa. ISBN 0-395-30852-6; 0-395-65747-4pa. 5-9

Harry, 10, bravely travels to Philadelphia in 1899 by train to enter the school for the deaf. Worried about being accepted, he soon finds a place for himself when he begins to play football and make clever drawings for the people around him. He thrives in an environment that accepts him as he is, and he carries his newly found confidence home with him. *American Library Association Notable Children's Book*.

1867.   Ritchie, David. **Frontier Life**. New York: Chelsea House, 1996. 104p. $18.95. ISBN 0-7910-2842-9. (Life in America 100 Years Ago). 5-7

The frontier more than 100 years ago was not the romantic wild place that people imagine. To live there and survive, one had to be a farmer or rancher, a gunslinger or a lawman. These people and the army waged a war against Native Americans, taking their lands. Then they fought the railroad monopolies to lower the rates for freight. The Industrial Revolution at the end of the nineteenth century led to new factories and businesses. The shift to more people in industry than agriculture changed the frontier. Photographs and drawings enhance the text. Further Reading and Index.

1868.   Ritter, Lawrence S. **Leagues Apart: The Men and Times of the Negro Baseball Leagues**. Richard Merkin, illustrator. New York: Morrow, 1995. Unpaged. $15. ISBN 0-688-13316-9. 2-4

The text gives the history of the Negro Leagues until 1947, how it differed from the major leagues, and the contributions of various players to the sport. It focuses on 21 men who played for the Negro Leagues, including Oscar Charleston, known as the Ty Cobb of the Negro Leagues; Smokey Joe Williams; Cool Papa Bell; and Jackie Robinson. Pastel illustrations complement the brief profiles. *Notable Children's Trade Books in the Field of Social Studies*.

1869. Rivinus, Edward F. **Jim Thorpe**. Bob Masheris, illustrator. Austin, TX: Raintree/Steck-Vaughn, 1992. 32p. $19.97. ISBN 0-8172-3403-9. (Native American Stories). 3-5

Jim Thorpe (1887-1953) earned a reputation as a great all-around athlete. In 1950, the Associated Press named him the best athlete of the past 50 years. He was a mixed blood Sac and Fox Indian from Oklahoma. He won two Olympic gold medals in 1912, which were taken away because he had played semipro baseball. In 1920, he was elected president of the American Professional Football League. In 1982, the International Olympic Committee posthumously restored his gold medals and records.

1870. Roach, Marilynne K. **In the Days of the Salem Witchcraft Trials**. Boston: Houghton Mifflin, 1996. 92p. $14.95. ISBN 0-395-69704-2. 4-6

With beginning chapters covering the law, punishment, and system of beliefs in Puritan New England around 1692, Roach then looks at the people who were convicted of witchcraft. In her account, she shows that the culture was more diversified than is usually recognized by discussing such things as the land, government, making a living, farming, and leisure-time activities. She thinks that the witchcraft "panic" came from personal fears that grew in a variety of ways until they permeated the entire society. Maps, Bibliography, and Index.

1871. Robbins, Neal E. **Ronald W. Reagan: 40th President of the United States**. Ada, OK: Garrett Educational, 1990. 124p. $17.26. ISBN 0-944483-66-6. (Presidents of the United States). 5-9

Ronald Reagan (b. 1911) grew up in Illinois before he began to work in radio and the movies in Hollywood. He married Nancy Davis, became the governor of California, and then the President of the United States. His ability to communicate with people helped his negotiations with Gorbachev in Moscow. Bibliography and Index.

1872. Roberts, Wills Davis. **Jo and the Bandit**. New York: Atheneum, 1992. 185p. $15. ISBN 0-689-31745-X. 4-7

While Jo and her brother are taking the stagecoach to Texas in the late 1860s, a gang robs it. She remembers details about the men because she is an artist who looks at things very carefully. Her drawings cover the wanted posters, and her ideas for capturing the men succeed. Her intelligence impresses her uncle, a judge, as he realizes she has unusual talents.

1873. Robinet, Harriette Gillem. **Children of the Fire**. New York: Atheneum, 1991. 144p. $12.95. ISBN 0-689-31655-0. 4-6

Hallelujah, an 11-year-old orphan of a slave who escaped on the Underground Railway, lives with a Chicago couple who promise her that she can go watch the next fire. This fire is the worst and earns the name of the Chicago Fire of 1871. She helps save people, including a wealthy white girl lost from her home. While helping others, they begin a friendship. *Friends of American Writers Juvenile Book Merit Award* and *Notable Children's Trade Books in the Field of Social Studies*.

1874. Robinet, Harriette Gillem. **Mississippi Chariot**. New York: Jean Karl, Atheneum, 1994. 116p. $14.95. ISBN 0-689-31960-6. 5-7

Shortning Bread Jackson's father, innocent of the crime for which he was convicted, serves on a Mississippi chain gang in 1936. Shortning, 12, wants to help his family, but first he saves Hawk Baker, a white boy, from drowning. Then he starts a rumor that he hopes will save his father. He and Hawk become friends, and Hawk's father saves Shortning's father when he tells how officials have hidden the truth. *New York Public Library's Books for the Teen Age* and *Notable Children's Trade Books in the Field of Social Studies*.

1875. Robinet, Harriette Gillem. **Washington City Is Burning**. New York: Atheneum, 1996. 160p. $16. ISBN 0-689-80773-2. 4-6

Virginia lives in the White House as a slave whose master is President Madison. She has good food and nice clothes, but she is concerned about the welfare of other slaves who have nothing. She becomes part of a conspiracy to help those slaves reach freedom, and as a child, she helps hundreds of slaves escape when the British soldiers set fire to the White House during the War of 1812. Instead of leaving with them, she decides to stay in the White House where she can continue her work for the freedom of others.

1876. Rochelle, Belinda. **Witnesses to Freedom: Young People Who Fought for Civil Rights**. New York: Lodestar, Dutton, 1993. 97p. $15.99. ISBN 0-525-67377-6. 5-8

Adults are not the only people who have fought for civil rights. The text tells the stories of several children who defied Jim Crow laws in the 1950s and 1960s. Claudette Colvin, 15, refused to give her bus seat to a white passenger. Elizabeth Eckford faced a crowd spitting on her and calling her names as she tried to enter Little Rock High School in Arkansas. Sheyann Webb, nine, marched in Selma, Alabama, to protest racism. Others profiled are Barbara Johns, Spottswood Thomas Bolling, Jr., Rosa Parks, Harvey Gantt, Dianne Nash, and Raymond Greene. Sources, Further Reading for Children, and Index.

1877.   Rockwood, Joyce. **Groundhog's Horse**. Victor Kalin, illustrator. New York: Henry Holt, 1978. 115p. $12.95. ISBN 0-8050-1173-0. 4-7

In 1750, Groundhog goes to rescue his horse Midnight from the Creeks who stole it. His brother and their friends had refused to help him because they did not think the horse was worth the effort. But in addition to his horse, Groundhog is able to rescue a Cherokee boy, Duck, kidnapped two years before. He gets lost on his return, but Midnight brings him and Duck safely home.

1878.   Rodowsky, Colby F. **Fitchett's Folly**. New York: Farrar, Straus & Giroux, 1987. 165p. $15. ISBN 0-374-32342-9. 4 up

When Sarey's father drowns around 1890 off the eastern coast of the United States, he is trying to save a child from a shipwreck in which all others died. Sarey resents the girl, Faith, even though the girl has lost both parents, and dislikes her staying in the house with Sarey's family. Faith runs away, and Sarey realizes that in their grief, they both need each other.

1879.   Rodriguez, Consuelo. **Cesar Chavez**. New York: Chelsea House, 1991. 112p. $18.95. ISBN 0-7910-1232-8. (Hispanics of Achievement). 5 up

Cesar Chavez (1927-1993) helped win a contract for migrant farmworkers and thereby upheld some of the dignity of Mexican Americans. After the Depression, he and his own family had become migrant workers, so he knew their plight. He became a community organizer, and in 1965 the United Farm Workers, the union he began, went on strike against the grape growers. He organized a national boycott of grapes rather than resort to violence and fasted for 25 days. In 1970, the grape growers relented. Photographs enhance the text. Chronology, Further Reading, and Index.

1880.   Roessel, Monty. **Songs from the Loom: A Navajo Girl Learns to Weave**. Minneapolis, MN: Lerner, 1995. 48p. $19.95; $6.95pa. ISBN 0-8225-2657-3; 0-8225-9712-8pa. (We Are Still Here: Native Americans Today). 3-6

Using the stories behind the designs in rugs that the Navajos weave, the author tells a story of the tribe and its background as well as how it weaves its rugs today. Photographs complement the text. Word List and For Further Reading. *Society of School Librarians International Outstanding Book.*

1881.   Rogers, Teresa. **George Washington Carver: Nature's Trailblazer**. Antonio Castro, illustrator. New York: Twenty-First Century Books, 1992. 72p. $14.98. ISBN 0-8050-2115-9. (Earth Keepers). 4-7

George Washington Carver (c. 1864-1943), an American botanist, was the son of slave parents. He worked to gain an education. Among other achievements, he learned the value of crop diversification, which he promoted to Southern farmers. He also taught at Tuskegee Institute for many years. Glossary and Index.

1882.   Roman, Joseph. **King Philip: Wampanoag Rebel**. New York: Chelsea House, 1991. 110p. $18.95. ISBN 0-7910-1704-4. (North American Indians of Achievement). 5 up

As the son of Massasoit, the leader of the Wampanoag Indians, Metacom became the chief when his father died. The English had named him "Philip," and when he took leadership of the tribe, they called him "king." He tried to relieve the growing tension between his tribe and the English, but to do so, he had to give away acres of land. In 1675, he tried to stop the continued encroachment, and King Philip's War began. He asked for help from other tribes, but they could not defeat the English. The colonists killed many people, including Philip, and the balance of power shifted to the colonists. Photographs and reproductions enhance the text. Chronology, Further Reading, and Index.

1883.   Roop, Peter. **The Buffalo Jump**. Bill Farnsworth, illustrator. Flagstaff, AZ: Northland, 1996. 32p. $14.95. ISBN 0-87358-616-6. 1-4

Little Blaze, a Blackfoot, wants to lead the buffalo jump, but tribal leaders ask his older brother Curly Bear instead. When his brother trips after luring the herd of buffalo, Little Blaze rescues him so that the buffalo will not stampede him as they fall over the cliff.

1884.   Roop, Peter, and Connie Roop, eds. **Capturing Nature: The Writings and Art of John James Audubon**. Rick Farley, illustrator. New York: Walker, 1993. 39p. $16.95. ISBN 0-8027-8204-3. 4-8

Beautiful illustrations of birds accompany the story of John James Audubon (1785-1851) through his journal. He traveled around America painting birds, but he had to go to England to be published.

1885.   Roop, Peter, and Connie Roop. **Keep the Lights Burning, Abbie**. Peter E. Hanson, illustrator. Minneapolis, MN: Carolrhoda, 1985. 40p. $15.95; $5.95pa. ISBN 0-87614-275-7; 0-87614-454-7pa. 1-4

In 1856, Abbie Burgess has to keep the island lighthouse lights burning while her father is caught on the mainland in a storm that lasts four weeks. During this endless time, she has to clean the lamps and trim the wicks while she and her sisters look after their sick mother. She does not know if her father will return, but she realizes that he or someone else might wreck if the lights are not steady.

1886. Roop, Peter, and Connie Roop. **Off the Map: The Journals of Lewis and Clark**. New York: Walker, 1993. 40p. $15.85. ISBN 0-8027-8207-8. 3-6

Lewis and Clark kept journals on their journey across the Louisiana Purchase without a map from May 13, 1804, to March 23, 1806. The text looks at some of the entries and the information they relate about this trip. In February 1806, Clark completed a map of the country from Missouri to the Pacific. The expedition then turned around for the long trek home. Epilogue.

1887. Roop, Peter, and Connie Roop. **Pilgrim Voices: Our First Year in the New World**. Shelley Prichett, illustrator. New York: Walker, 1995. 48p. $16.95. ISBN 0-8027-8314-7. 3-6

The pilgrims tell about their first year in the colonies through their journals and diaries. Hearing what they say makes the experience much more understandable. Bibliography, Glossary, Further Reading, and Index. *Notable Children's Trade Books in the Field of Social Studies.*

1888. Rorby, Ginny. **Dolphin Sky**. New York: Putnam, 1996. 246p. $16.95. ISBN 0-399-22905-1. 4-6

That Buddy's father thinks she is stupid disturbs her, but she appreciates her grandfather's support in her world of 1968. A biologist befriends her and recognizes her learning disability. After tests show that she has dyslexia, she develops a relationship with the mistreated dolphins at Stephens Everglade Eden. Through the biologist, she becomes aware of animal rights.

1889. Rose, Deborah Lee. **The Rose Horse**. Greg Shed, illustrator. San Diego, CA: Harcourt Brace, 1995. 60p. $16. ISBN 0-15-200068-2. 3-6

In 1909, Lily's baby sister is born prematurely, and her mother goes with the baby to Dr. Martin Couney's incubator clinic on Coney Island in New York. Lily and her father follow, and her father begins helping in the carousel shop where her uncle carves beautiful animals for carousels. She meets Mae and enjoys her new friend while keeping an *omer* calendar where she counts the seven weeks from the holiday of *Pesach* (when the Jews escaped from Egypt) to *Shevuos* (when God gave them the Torah). When the baby comes home, Lily expects to return to their home, but she finds that the family will stay. To help her adjust to the new plans, her father gives her a tiny replica of the beautiful rose horse that she watched her uncle carve in his shop and that was sent to a carousel in California. Glossary (Yiddish Words).

1890. Rose, Mary Catherine. **Clara Barton: Soldier of Mercy**. E. Harper Johnson, illustrator. New York: Chelsea Juniors, 1991. 80p. $14.95. ISBN 0-7910-1403-7. (Discovery Biography). 2-6

In this fictional biography, Clara Barton (1821-1912) appears as a shy girl growing up on a New England farm and learning things about animals that would help her for the rest of her life. She rode horses bareback, cooked, sewed, and nursed her brother after a difficult accident. She became the most famous nurse in the Civil War, cooked for the soldiers, and rode horseback to escape from the enemy. She was a major force in the establishment of the American Red Cross.

1891. Rosen, Dorothy Schack. **A Fire in Her Bones: The Story of Mary Lyon**. Minneapolis, MN: Carolrhoda, 1995. 88p. $19.95. ISBN 0-87614-840-2. 4-8

When Mary Lyon (1797-1849) had to give up schooling to work on the family farm, she found ways to save money so that she could return to school, an unusual desire for a female in her time. She wanted to make going to school easier for other females than it had been for her, and she wanted to start a school for young women. This desire was like "a fire, shut up in my bones." In 1837, she opened Mount Holyoke Female Seminary in South Hadley, Massachusetts. One of the students at this very demanding school was Emily Dickinson. Bibliography and Index. *Notable Children's Trade Books in the Field of Social Studies.*

1892. Rosen, Michael J. **A School for Pompey Walker**. Aminah Brenda Lynn Robinson, illustrator. San Diego, CA: Harcourt Brace, 1995. 48p. $16. ISBN 0-15-200114-X. 3-7

When Pompey Bibb is barely a teen in the 1840s, a white man, Jeremiah Walker, buys him and sets him free. But Black men could still be caught and accused of running away even if they were free. Jeremiah and Pompey decide that Jeremiah will sell him and help him escape enough times so that Pompey can earn the money to build a school for Black children in Ohio. He tells his story at the dedication of the school and explains that he changed his last name to "Walker" because Jeremiah Walker, although dead more than 30 years, was his best friend. *American Library Association Notable Books for Children.*

1893. Rosen, Mike. **The Conquest of Everest**. New York: Bookwright Press, Franklin Watts, 1990. 32p. $12.90. ISBN 0-531-18319-X. (Great Journeys). 4-6

Each two-page chapter highlights a topic, with four chapters devoted to Hillary and Tenzing's successful climb to the top of Mount Everest in 1953. Other topics include the difficulties and personal stories of others who tried to reach the top of the mountain straddling China and Nepal. Photographs and drawings enhance the text. Bibliography, Glossary, and Index.

1894. Rosen, Mike. **The First Transatlantic Flight**. Richard Scollins, illustrator. New York: Bookwright Press, Franklin Watts, 1989. 32p. $17. ISBN 0-53118303-3. (Great Journeys). 4-6

John Alcock (1892-1919) and Arthur Whitten Brown (1886-1948) made the first flight over the Atlantic from Canada to Great Britain. Charles Lindbergh (1902-1974) made the first solo flight from New York to Paris in 1927. These two achievements changed the concept of travel around the globe. Photographs highlight the text. Bibliography, Glossary, and Index.

1895. Rosenblum, Richard, author/illustrator. **Brooklyn Dodger Days**. New York: Atheneum, 1991. 32p. $12.95. ISBN 0-689-31512-0. 2-4

Five Brooklyn boys attend the Dodgers-Giants game at Ebbets Field in 1946. Only one of the boys, Buddy, is a Giants' fan, and he catches the Dodger home run ball. When the Dodgers win, Buddy says that he would prefer to have his team win than to catch a home run ball.

1896. Rosenblum, Richard, author/illustrator. **The Old Synagogue**. Philadelphia, PA: Jewish Publication Society, 1989. Unpaged. $12.95. ISBN 0-8276-0322-3. K-2

Jews who had immigrated to a New York neighborhood worked hard to build a synagogue where they could worship. Years after they created the building, they began to move away, and the synagogue became a factory. Then Jews began returning to the neighborhood. When they needed a place to worship, they discovered the old factory, and they began saving money to buy it. They succeeded and again had a place to worship in their own neighborhood. *New York Times Notable Children's Book*.

1897. Rosenburg, John M. **William Parker: Rebel Without Rights**. Brookfield, CT: Millbrook Press, 1996. 141p. $15.90. ISBN 1-56294-139-9. 4-8

On September 11, 1851, Maryland slave owner Edward Gorsuch tried to reclaim his human property of former slaves. William Parker and the others fought back, and Gorsuch died. Parker escaped to Canada via the Underground Railroad, but several of the men were arrested and tried for treason against the Fugitive Slave Act. The response to this act depended upon which side the person supported.

1898. Ross, Ramon Royal. **The Dancing Tree**. New York: Atheneum, 1995. 59p. $14. ISBN 0-689-80072-X. 6-9

In 1934, Zeenie senses that her mother will leave, which she does when Zeenie is 12, after World War II starts. Although Zeenie does not tell her grandmother about the departure, her grandmother seems to know. She tells Zeenie of a day when she had been near Zeenie's age. She danced with the gypsies who once camped by a tree in the backyard and felt a love that she had not experienced since she was five before her mother died. Zeenie realizes that she will survive the desertion.

1899. Ross, Ramon Royal. **Harper & Moon**. New York: Atheneum, 1993. 181p. $14.95. ISBN 0-689-31803-0. 4 up

Harper, 12, has enjoyed his friends Moon, 17, and Olinger, an old storekeeper who lived alone up in the Blue Mountains of Washington. But during World War II, Moon enlists in the army, and that winter Olinger dies. Moon, whose parents abused him, cannot speak clearly, but he is very artistic. After he returns from the war, a hero and wounded, Moon tells Harper that Olinger lived alone in remorse over the young boy he killed during World War I and the medal he did not want.

1900. Ross, Rhea Beth. **The Bet's On, Lizzie Bingman!** Boston: Houghton Mifflin, 1988. 186p. $13.95; $4.95pa. ISBN 0-395-44472-1; 0-395-64375-9pa. 5-9

Elizabeth, 14, makes a bet with her brother in 1914 that she will remain self-sufficient for the entire summer. If she does, he will have to change his speech for a statewide oratory contest so that it promotes women's rights rather than denies them. Among the things that happen to her is that she witnesses a murder and has to testify in court, but she wins the bet. He changes the speech.

1901. Ross, Rhea Beth. **Hillbilly Choir**. Boston: Houghton Mifflin, 1991. 166p. $13.95. ISBN 0-395-53356-2. 5-7

Laurie, 15, returns to rural Arkansas in 1932 when her mother decides to relinquish her hope for an acting career in New York City. Laurie starts her career as a hillbilly musician, which helps her adjust to the different way of life. Various characters respond to her choices and admire her progress in her singing.

1902. Ross, Stewart. **Bandits & Outlaws**. Brookfield, CT: Copper Beach, Millbrook Press, 1995. 48p. $15.90; $5.95pa. ISBN 1-56294-649-8; 1-56294-189-5pa. (Fact or Fiction). 4-6

The text includes historical facts about 20 individuals or groups who have been considered bandits and outlaws. Among them are Spartacus, Ali Baba, Robin Hood, Rob Roy, Jesse James, Zapata, and Bonnie Parker. It describes the acts these people committed and the unpleasant ways that many of them died. Chronology and Index.

1903.   Ross, Stewart. **Witches**. Brookfield, CT: Copper Beach, 1996. 48p. $16.90; $6.95pa. ISBN 0-7613-0452-5; 0-7613-0467-3pa. (Fact or Fiction). 4-6

The text looks at witches in a variety of ways, including double-page spreads on topics such as "Ministers of Magic" and "Popes and Pagans." It includes information about people accused of being witches, such as Joan of Arc. Diverse illustrations highlight the text. Chronology and Index.

1904.   Rossiter, Phyllis. **Moxie**. New York: Four Winds, 1990. 192p. $14.95. ISBN 0-02-777831-2. 5 up

Drew, 13, raises sheep in the Kansas dust bowl area during 1934. But the lack of rain to grow crops causes his family to have almost no money, and they worry about paying for their land. By using his mule Moxie, Drew helps save the family farm.

1905.   Rostkowski, Margaret. **After the Dancing Days**. New York: HarperCollins, 1986. 217p. $14.89; $4.50pa. ISBN 0-06-025078-X; 0-06-440248-7pa. 6-9

Annie, 13, is delighted that her physician father is returning from World War I after her favorite uncle has been killed. She is surprised when he announces that he is going to work with returning wounded veterans in a nearby hospital. Annie's mother, a concert pianist, wants Annie to have nothing to do with the hospital, but Annie visits anyway and meets Andrew, a young man who lost part of his face when gassed without wearing his mask. She helps him regain confidence and finally her mother's acceptance. *American Library Association Notable Books for Children, American Library Association Best Books for Young Adults, USA Through Children's Books, Booklist Children's Editors' Choices, IRA Children's Book Award, IRA Young Adult Choices, Notable Children's Trade Books in the Field of Social Studies, NCTE Teachers' Choices, Golden Kite Award for Fiction, Judy Lopez Memorial Certificate of Merit*, and *Jefferson Cup Award Winner*.

1906.   Rounds, Glen. **Sod Houses on the Great Plains**. New York: Holiday House, 1995. Unpaged. $15.95. ISBN 0-8234-1162-1. K-3

The Great Plains settlers found no trees suitable for building houses. When their tents were insecure, they discovered that prairie sod was tough enough to be chopped into blocks and stacked to build houses. Animals and rain could penetrate the roofs of ridge poles covered with grass and dirt. Others built houses into the sides of hills, but they always feared that animals would fall through the roof. Most "soddies" lasted four to five years, with plants and grass often growing out of the sides and roof.

1907.   Rowland, Della. **Martin Luther King, Jr.: The Dream of Peaceful Revolution**. Englewood Cliffs, NJ: Silver Burdett, 1990. 138p. $12.95. ISBN 0-382-09924-9. (History of the Civil Rights Movement). 6-9

Martin Luther King, Jr. (1929-1968), along with others, helped shape the Civil Rights movement with some of the highlights being his "I Have a Dream" speech at the Lincoln Memorial in 1963, the beginning of the Poor People's Campaign in 1967, and his "I've Been to the Mountaintop" speech in 1968. Photographs, Timetable, Suggested Reading, Sources, and Index.

1908.   Rowland, Della. **The Story of Sacajawea: Guide to Lewis and Clark**. Richard Leonard, illustrator. 1989. Minneapolis, MN: Gareth Stevens, 1995. 112p. $13.95. ISBN 0-8368-1385-5. (Famous Lives). 3-6

When Sacajawea (1788-1812) was 12, Minnetarees captured her from her Shoshoni Indian tribe and sold her to a French fur trader. Because she could translate for Lewis and Clark, she and her husband accompanied them on their journey to survey the current United States when she was only 16. Highlights in the Life, For Further Study, and Index.

1909.   Rowland-Warne, L. **Costume**. New York: Knopf, 1992. 64p. $19. ISBN 0-679-81680-1. 4-6

The topics here cover all aspects of clothes from shoes to hats. The illustrations and photographs give a good sense of dress in the eighteenth through twentieth centuries, although references to prehistory, Roman times, and the Viking era are included. Index.

1910.   Rubel, David. **America's War of Independence: A Concise Illustrated History of the American Revolution**. New York: Silver Moon Press, 1993. 48p. $6.95pa. ISBN 1-881889-39-4pa. 3-6

In this illustrated text, Rubel presents the major battles, their strategies, and the people who fought them in clear detail. The paintings, photographs, and maps offer further clarification. Endpaper Maps.

1911.   Rubel, David. **Fannie Lou Hamer: From Sharecropping to Politics**. Englewood Cliffs, NJ: Silver Burdett, 1990. 130p. $12.95. ISBN 0-8335-9870-8. (History of the Civil Rights Movement). 6-9

When Civil Rights workers came to her Mississippi town in 1962, Fannie Lou Hamer (1917-1977) was 45. She knew that any African American who registered to vote would suffer consequences, but she was one of the first to volunteer and spent the last 15 years of her life as a civil rights activist. She said "I'm sick and tired of being sick and tired!" She testified before the Democratic National Convention in 1968 and founded Freedom Farm Cooperative in 1969. She then ran unsuccessfully for the Mississippi state senate. Suggested Reading, Sources, and Index.

1912. Rubel, David. **The Scholastic Encyclopedia of the Presidents and their Times**. New York: Scholastic, 1994. 224p. $16.95. ISBN 0-590-49366-3. 4 up

Each page of the text corresponds to one year, beginning with 1789 and ending in 1994. In the first year of a President's term appears a list of statistics about him, including his nickname. Campaign information corresponds to the year in which the campaign occurred. Information on important events and people appears in boxed text during the appropriate year. At the end of the text, a chart gives results of every presidential election. Index.

1913. Ruby, Lois. **Steal Away Home**. New York: Simon & Schuster, 1994. 192p. $15.95. ISBN 0-02-777883-5. 5-8

Dana, 12, in contemporary Kansas, reluctantly strips away wallpaper, and she finds a secret room with a skeleton and a black book inside. As she studies the black book, she pieces together the mystery of the skeleton and the life inside the house before the Civil War. The Quaker inhabitants protected a young Underground Railroad conductor who died in the house while guards were outside searching for runaway slaves.

1914. Rushton, Lucy. **Birth Customs**. New York: Thomson Learning, 1993. 32p. $13.95; $5.95pa. ISBN 1-56847-034-7; 1-56847-502-0pa. (Comparing Religions). 4-8

Six major religions—Buddhism, Christianity, Hinduism, Judaism, Islam, and Sikhism—have customs surrounding the birth of a child. The text looks at the choosing of a name, the prayers said over the child, the ceremonies, and gifts to the child and family. Photographs enhance the information. Glossary, Books to Read, and Index.

1915. Rushton, Lucy. **Death Customs**. New York: Thomson Learning, 1993. 32p. $13.95; $5.95pa. ISBN 1-56847-031-2; 1-56847-503-9pa. (Comparing Religions). 4-8

Six major religions—Buddhism, Christianity, Hinduism, Judaism, Islam, and Sikhism—have specific rituals for approaching death. The text looks at the practices, the attitudes toward death, mourning customs, and ways to remember the dead. Glossary, Books to Read, and Index.

1916. Russell, Marion, and Ginger Wadsworth. **Along the Santa Fe Trail: Marion Russell's Own Story**. James Watling, illustrator. Morton Grove, IL: Albert Whitman, 1993. Unpaged. $16.95. ISBN 0-8075-0295-2. 2-3

In 1852, seven-year-old Marion Sloan (1845-1936) kept a diary while traveling with her mother and older brother in a wagon train along the Santa Fe Trail. The story of her journey, with its hardships and the things she noticed, such as spiders, rainbows, and campfires, appears here. She also describes the abode walls of Santa Fe strung with red peppers.

1917. Russell, Sharman. **Frederick Douglass: Abolitionist Editor**. New York: Chelsea House, 1988. 110p. $18.95; $7.95pa. ISBN 1-55546-580-3; 1-7910-0204-7pa. (Black Americans of Achievement). 5 up

Frederick Douglass (1817?-1895) escaped slavery and became an orator, writer, and leader in the antislavery movement during the early nineteenth century. His newspaper, *The North Star*, helped others learn what was happening in the abolitionist movement. Black-and-white illustrations enhance the text. Bibliography, Chronology, and Index.

1918. Rutberg, Becky. **Mary Lincoln's Dressmaker**. New York: Walker, 1994. 176p. $15.95. ISBN 0-8027-8224-5. 5 up

Elizabeth Keckley (c. 1818-1907) was a servant in the Lincoln White House, and she kept a diary. But she was much more than a servant; she was also Mary Lincoln's confidante. The text uses information from her writing and facts about the times to recreate a story of Mary Lincoln, Abraham Lincoln's wife. It also reveals the life of a slave before and after freedom and the perils of a Black businesswoman. Bibliography, Further Reading, and Index. *Notable Children's Trade Books in the Field of Social Studies*.

1919. Ryan, Cary, ed. **Louisa May Alcott: Her Girlhood Diary**. Mark Graham, illustrator. Mahwah, NJ: Troll, BridgeWater, 1993. 42p. $14.95; $4.95pa. ISBN 0-8167-3139-X; 0-8167-3140-3pa. 5 up

Through her diaries, Louisa May Alcott (1832-1888) reveals the influences of her father, her mother, and her sisters in her life. She confides about her moods as a young girl and shows her feelings of doubt as she grew up.

1920. Ryan, Peter. **Explorers and Mapmakers**. Chris Molan, illustrator. New York: Lodestar, 1990. 48p. $14.95. ISBN 0-525-67285-0. (Time Detective). 4-6

Before a place can be mapped, someone needs to explore it to find where it is and what is in it. The text looks at a variety of explorers, including Ptolemy (d. 283 BC), Christopher Columbus (1451-1506), Marco Polo (1254-1324), Francisco de Orellana (c. 1490-1546, discoverer of the Amazon), Cheng Ho (c. 1371-c. 1433, saw the east coast of Africa 70 years before Vasco da Gama arrived), and Meriwether Lewis (1774-1809) and William Clark (c. 1771-c. 1833), as well as the maps their travels helped them create.

1921. Rylant, Cynthia. **When I Was Young in the Mountains**. Diane Goode, illustrator. New York: Dutton, 1982. 32p. $14.99; $4.99pa. ISBN 0-525-42525-X; 0-525-44198-0pa. K-3

The narrator recalls the times in the mountains during the mid-twentieth century when grandfather came home covered with coal dust from the mines, as well as the rituals of school and church. A photograph of four children with a long, dead black snake draped around their necks also brings many memories. Although they have no modern conveniences, their lives are full and happy. *American Library Association Notable Books for Children.*

S

1922. Sabin, Francene. **Young Abigail Adams**. Yoshi Miyake, illustrator. New York: Troll, 1992. 48p. $10.79; $2.95pa. ISBN 0-8167-2503-9; 0-8167-2504-7pa. (Easy Biography). 2-5

The text looks at Abigail Adams (1744-1818), wife to John Adams and mother of John Quincy Adams, both presidents of the United States. It examines her life as a youth and the influences that prevailed during her adulthood, about which she wrote in her letters to her husband when the colonies were fighting the American Revolution almost on her doorstep.

1923. Salisbury, Graham. **Blue Skin of the Sea**. New York: Delacorte, 1992. 215p. $15.95. ISBN 0-385-30596-6. New York: Laurel, 1994. 215p. $3.99pa. ISBN 0-440-21905-1pa. 4-7

In 1953, Sonny at six fears the sea, and he lives in Hawaii. He does not know why he hates it until after his father disappears in his sampan. Then Sonny remembers falling into the water at the age of one. A yachter finds his father and brings him home. Sonny realizes that he must get to know his father, although they are very different, and learn something about his mother, who died when Sonny was only a few months old.

1924. Salisbury, Graham. **Under the Blood-Red Sun**. New York: Delacorte, 1994. 246p. $15.95. ISBN 0-385-32099-X. 5-8

When Tomi Nakaji is in eighth grade in Hawaii, the Japanese bomb Pearl Harbor. As the son and grandson of Japanese immigrant workers who have been proud of their heritage but who are interred as a result of the bombing, Tomi becomes an enemy himself. He, his sister, and mother live through the trauma of the times with the help of others who know that they are not guilty for decisions made by others who happen to be of the same heritage. *Scott O'Dell Award.*

1925. San Souci, Robert. **N. C. Wyeth's Pilgrims**. San Francisco, CA: Chronicle, 1991. Unpaged. $13.95. ISBN 0-87701-806-5. 3 up

The text uses the beautiful illustrations by N. C. Wyeth (1882-1945), completed in the 1940s, of the Pilgrims coming to America. The pictures are a way of retelling the story of their arrival at New Plymouth, Massachusetts, in 1620. The facts are less important than the pictures in this text.

1926. San Souci, Robert D. **Kate Shelley: Bound for Legend**. Max Ginsburg, illustrator. New York: Dial, 1995. Unpaged. $14.99. ISBN 0-8037-1289-8. 2-5

Kate Shelley (1866-1912) risked her life when she was 15 to warn an oncoming train that another train had wrecked before it and blocked the track. A terrible storm caused the first wreck, and Kate, afraid of trestles, had to climb across in the storm to tell the stationmaster to stop the midnight express. She arrived in time and then took the men in the station back to the wreck so that they could help the wounded. Her exploit cost her three months of bed rest from sickness and exhaustion, but it also won her admiration for years to come. *Notable Children's Trade Books in the Field of Social Studies.*

1927. Sandak, Cass R. **The Eisenhowers**. New York: Crestwood House, 1993. 48p. $12.95. ISBN 0-89686-653-X. (First Families). 5 up

The text examines the life of the World War II general Dwight D. Eisenhower (1890-1969), who became the 34th President of the United States. It describes his relationship with his wife, Mamie. Illustrations highlight the text. Bibliography and Index.

1928. Sandak, Cass R. **The Franklin Roosevelts**. New York: Crestwood House, 1992. 48p. $12.95. ISBN 0-89686-639-4. (First Families). 5 up

Franklin Delano Roosevelt (1882-1945) became the 32nd President of the United States during the Depression. He and his wife Eleanor (1884-1962) had an unusual partnership during his unprecedented four terms in the White House. Illustrations highlight the text. Bibliography and Index.

1929. Sandak, Cass R. **The Jacksons**. New York: Crestwood House, 1992. 48p. $12.95. ISBN 0-89686-636-X. (First Families). 5 up

Andrew Jackson (1767-1845), the 7th President of the United States from 1829 until 1837, was married to Rachel Jackson (1767-1828), who died as he took office. The text emphasizes his years in office. Illustrations highlight the text. Bibliography and Index.

1930. Sandak, Cass R. **The Jeffersons**. New York: Crestwood House, 1992. 48p. $12.95. ISBN 0-89686-637-8. (First Families). 5 up

Thomas Jefferson (1743-1826) was the 3rd President of the United States. Jefferson was a widower when he reached office. The text gives an overview of the private and political situations in which he was involved, including the Louisiana Purchase. Illustrations highlight the text. Bibliography and Index.

1931. Sandak, Cass R. **The John Adamses**. New York: Crestwood House, 1992. 48p. $12.95. ISBN 0-89686-640-8. (First Families). 5 up

John Adams (1735-1826), the second American president, and Abigail Adams (1744-1818) were happily married for many years. Their letters revealed much about their relationship. The text also discusses other periods of Adams's life. Illustrations highlight the text. Bibliography and Index.

1932. Sandak, Cass R. **The Lincolns**. New York: Crestwood House, 1992. 48p. $12.95. ISBN 0-89686-641-6. (First Families). 5 up.

Abraham Lincoln (1809-1865) had a stormy marriage to Mary Todd Lincoln (1818-1882), but reports indicate that Lincoln was devoted to his family. The text examines his family life and political career. Illustrations highlight the text. Bibliography and Index.

1933. Sandak, Cass R. **The Lyndon Johnsons**. New York: Crestwood House, 1993. 48p. $12.95. ISBN 0-89686-644-0. (First Families). 5 up

Lyndon Baines Johnson (1908-1973) was the 36th President of the United States, taking his post after John Kennedy was assassinated in 1963. He, his wife, and his two daughters lived in the White House. Although Johnson had a long career in Congress, the text discusses his family's life in the White House. Bibliography and Index.

1934. Sandak, Cass R. **The Madisons**. New York: Crestwood House, 1992. 48p. $12.95. ISBN 0-89686-642-4. (First Families). 5 up

James Madison (1751-1836), known as the "Father of the Constitution," was the 4th President of the United States. Dolley Madison (1768-1849), his wife, was beloved by those who knew her and served as the hostess for Thomas Jefferson when he occupied the White House. The text emphasizes the White House years of the Madison family. Illustrations highlight the text. Bibliography and Index.

1935. Sandak, Cass R. **The Nixons**. New York: Crestwood House, 1992. 48p. $12.95. ISBN 0-89686-638-6. (First Families). 5 up

Richard Nixon (1913-1994) became the 37th President of the United States. When he was in the White House, his wife Pat was with him, and he had a close relationship with his two daughters. The text emphasizes their time in the White House until Nixon resigned from his office in 1974. Illustrations highlight the text. Bibliography and Index.

1936. Sandak, Cass R. **The Reagans**. New York: Crestwood House, 1993. 48p. $12.95. ISBN 0-89686-646-7. (First Families). 5 up

Ronald Reagan (b. 1911) was President from 1982 until 1990. He and his wife, Nancy Davis Reagan, lived in the White House while his older children were elsewhere. The text discusses his life and his relationship with his wife. Illustrations highlight the text. Bibliography and Index.

1937. Sandak, Cass R. **The Tafts**. New York: Crestwood House, 1993. 48p. $12.95. ISBN 0-89686-647-5. (First Families). 5 up

William Howard Taft (1857-1930) occupied the White House as the 27th President from 1909 to 1913. He was the only president to also serve as Supreme Court justice. The text discusses his life, especially his time in the White House, and his relationship with his wife Nellie Herron Taft (1861-1943).

1938. Sandak, Cass R. **The Theodore Roosevelts**. New York: Crestwood House, 1991. 48p. $12.95. ISBN 0-89686-634-3. (First Families). 5 up

Theodore Roosevelt (1858-1919) became President of the United States in 1901 when William McKinley was assassinated. He initiated lawsuits against big companies in order to "trust bust." He met John Muir and created important conservation legislation. He wanted to help people who had little power, and this commitment reelected him in 1904. He also mediated the end of the Russo-Japanese War, and for these efforts, he won the Nobel Peace Prize. While he was working internationally, he also had a family with him, and the text presents these important people in his life. Illustrations highlight the text. Bibliography and Index.

1939. Sandak, Cass R. **The Trumans**. New York: Crestwood House, 1992. 48p. $12.95. ISBN 0-89686-643-2. (First Families). 5 up

The text focuses on Harry Truman (1884-1972), his wife, and his daughter Margaret as well as his years in the presidency, from 1945 to 1952 after the beginning of the Cold War. Illustrations highlight the text. Bibliography and Index.

1940. Sandak, Cass R. **The Washingtons**. New York: Crestwood House, 1991. 48p. $12.95. ISBN 0-89686-635-1. (First Families). 5 up

George Washington (1732-1799), the first president of the United States, inherited Mount Vernon in Virginia when his half-brother died. He married Martha Custis, and they lived on the estate. The text emphasizes Washington's years as president and his relationship with his family. Illustrations enhance the text. Bibliography and Index.

1941. Sandak, Cass R. **The Wilsons**. New York: Crestwood House, 1993. 48p. $12.95. ISBN 0-89686-651-3. (First Families). 5 up

Woodrow Wilson (1856-1924) was the 28th president of the United States. The text describes his time in office as well as his relationship with his family. Illustrations highlight the text. Bibliography and Index.

1942. Sandberg, Peter Lars. **Dwight D. Eisenhower**. New York: Chelsea House, 1986. 116p. $18.95. ISBN 0-87754-521-9. (World Leaders Past and Present). 5 up

In 1911, Dwight David Eisenhower (1890-1969) entered West Point and began his illustrious career in the military. Franklin D. Roosevelt appointed him to lead the Allied Forces in Europe, where he controlled the Normandy landing on June 6, 1944, known as D-Day. He was elected to the U.S. presidency in 1952 and reelected in 1956, but while becoming a shrewd Cold War negotiator, he did little to curb the anti-Communist hysteria throughout the country. Photographs highlight the text. Chronology, Further Reading, and Index.

1943. Sandburg, Carl. **Abe Lincoln Grows Up**. James Daugherty, illustrator. 1928. San Diego, CA: Harcourt Brace, 1985. 222p. ISBN 0-15-201037-8. 4-8

The first 27 chapters of Carl Sandburg's biography of Abraham Lincoln (1809-1865) concern his years of maturity. As a boy, Lincoln walked four miles to school, did chores on the family farm, helped his father cut down trees, and shot wild turkeys. At 17, he split rails and became a champion "rassler" as well as an expert at skinning animals and curing hides. He saw a slave auction in New Orleans, and at 19 he set off to make his fortune. Throughout all, he always read as much as he could.

1944. Sanders, Scott R. **Aurora Means Dawn**. Jill Kastner, illustrator. New York: Bradbury, 1989. 32p. $15. ISBN 0-02-778270-0. 1-5

In 1800, a family with seven children travels from Connecticut to Aurora, Ohio, to find cheaper land. When a terrible storm blocks their way, people from the next two towns gather to free their wagon from fallen trees. Although they travel alone, they realize that they need others for success.

1945. Sanders, Scott R. **A Place Called Freedom**. Thomas B. Allen, illustrator. New York: Simon & Schuster, Atheneum, 1997. 32p. $16. ISBN 0-689-80470-9. K-3

James Starman and his slave family get their freedom, and they travel north to Indiana and begin a new life. His father keeps returning to Tennessee and bringing relatives back with him so that soon they have a community of family members. They decide to call their new home "Freedom."

1946. Sanders, Scott Russell. **Here Comes the Mystery Man**. Helen Cogancherry, illustrator. New York: Bradbury, 1993. Unpaged. $15.95. ISBN 0-02-778145-3. 2-4

In the Midwest in the early eighteenth century, the news travels ahead of the peddler that he will be arriving. Everyone looks forward to his visits because he brings all kinds of wonderful things from faraway places and tells exciting stories.

1947. Sandin, Joan, author/illustrator. **The Long Way to a New Land**. New York: HarperCollins, 1981. 64p. $14.89; $3.75pa. ISBN 0-06-025194-8; 0-06-444100-8pa. (An I Can Read Book). K-3

Carl Erik's family leaves Sweden in 1868 during a famine to come to America. They sail to America via England and find that Carl Erik's father has a job for the winter. *American Library Association Notable Books for Children, Booklist Children's Editor's Choices, Notable Children's Trade Books in the Field of Social Studies*, and *American Library Association USA Children's Books of International Interest*.

1948. Sandin, Joan, author/illustrator. **The Long Way Westward**. New York: HarperCollins, 1989. 64p. $15.89; $3.50pa. ISBN 0-06-025207-3; 0-06-444198-9pa. (An I Can Read Book). K-3

In the sequel to *The Long Way to a New Land*, also in 1868, Carl Erik and his family arrive in New York and take the train to Anoka, Minnesota. The train moves so slowly that the children sometimes run along next to it. They meet all kinds of people as they journey to their new home from Sweden. *American Library Association Notable Books for Children, USA Through Children's Books*, and *New York Public Library's Children's Books*.

1949. Sandler, Martin. **Immigrants**. New York: HarperCollins, 1995. 92p. $19.95. ISBN 0-06-024507-7. (Library of Congress Books). 4-8

Using photographs and paintings from the Library of Congress collection, Sandler tells a story of America's immigrants since the late 1800s as they entered Ellis Island, settled in New York and other cities, and worked hard. Some became pioneers and went west. Immigration continues, but immigrants go to a variety of places throughout the country. The Library of Congress and Index. *Notable Children's Trade Books in the Field of Social Studies*.

1950. Sandler, Martin. **Presidents**. New York: HarperCollins, 1995. 94p. $19.95. ISBN 0-06-024534-3. (Library of Congress Books). 4-8

In a text complemented by photographs and paintings available in the Library of Congress collection, the reader meets many of the presidents and their wives and children, sees them relaxing, and hears about their pets. The Library of Congress and Index.

1951. Sandomir, Larry. **Isadora Duncan: Revolutionary Dancer**. Austin, TX: Raintree/Steck-Vaughn, 1994. 128p. $16.98. ISBN 0-8114-2380-8. (American Troublemakers). 6 up

Isadora Duncan (1877-1927) grew up in a fatherless household, and to earn money, she and her sister taught children to dance. She revolutionized the art of ballet by moving away from the rigidity of the classical to find other forms of expressing the music. She loved Greek art and unsullied nature, but her choice of immodest costumes to represent these ideas upset her audiences. Thus, her innovation in dance and in her private life caused both acclaim and criticism. Maps, Photographs, Key Dates, Glossary, Places to Visit, Bibliography and Recommended Readings, and Index.

1952. Sandoz, Mari. **The Horsecatcher**. 1957. Lincoln, NE: University of Nebraska Press, 1986. 192p. $7.95pa. ISBN 0-8032-4166-6pa. 6 up

Young Elk's Cheyenne tribe expects him to be a warrior in the 1830s, but he prefers to catch and tame mustangs. The idea of killing makes him ill. As he proves his ability to find horses, he captures the Ghost Horse, a beautiful white horse that he wants more than anything. But he sees Kiowa warriors on the way to invade his village, so he must free the horses he has caught, including the white one, to rush home and warn his people. The Kiowa tell that he had caught and freed the Ghost Horse, and his village gives him his new name, "Horsecatcher."

1953. Sanford, William R. **Chief Joseph: Nez Percé Warrior**. Springfield, NJ: Enslow, 1994. 48p. $14.95. ISBN 0-89490-509-0. (Native American Leaders of the Wild West). 5-7

A Nez Percé warrior was urged by his friends to take retribution because a white man killed his father. He killed four whites who had harmed the Indians but were not the ones responsible for his father's death, and triggered government retaliation. Although this warrior was not a member of Chief Joseph's band, Chief Joseph (1840-1904) knew that the army would not care who had killed the whites because soldiers would kill any group of Indians that they saw. He was right. He led his people during this warring period, the Nez Percé-American War, all the while trying to get peace. He led his tribe toward safety in Canada but was detained 30 miles from the border. He spent the rest of his life in Washington State working to get his people back to their Oregon land, but whites who had settled on it would not leave. Glossary, More Good Reading, and Index.

1954. Sanford, William R. **Crazy Horse: Sioux Warrior**. Springfield, NJ: Enslow, 1994. 48p. $14.95. ISBN 0-89490-511-2. (Native American Leaders of the Wild West). 5-7

As one of the greatest chiefs of the Oglala Sioux, Crazy Horse (1842-1877) led his warriors against the U.S. Army and won many battles. His famous victory at the Battle of the Little Bighorn caused the defeat of the 7th Cavalry and Lt. Colonel George A. Custer, but Sanford believes he should be remembered for his wise leadership of his people. He was eventually forced to surrender, and he died mysteriously in Fort Robinson, Nebraska. Photographs and reproductions highlight the text. Notes, More Good Reading, Glossary, and Index.

1955. Sanford, William R. **Geronimo: Apache Warrior**. Springfield, NJ: Enslow, 1994. 48p. $14.95. ISBN 0-89490-510-4. (Native American Leaders of the Wild West). 5-7

Geronimo (1829-1909) spent much of his life trying to avenge the deaths of his wife, mother, and children by Mexicans after they had promised peace in 1848. He became a leader of the Apaches as they fought against the U.S. Army in the later half of the nineteenth century and escaped from several reservations where the army had imprisoned him with other Apaches. Geronimo told his life story in 1906, and he lived in depression until his death in 1909. Glossary, More Good Reading About Geronimo, and Index.

1956. Sanford, William R. **Osceola: Seminole Warrior**. Springfield, NJ: Enslow, 1994. 48p. $14.95. ISBN 0-89490-535-X. (Native American Leaders of the Wild West). 4-10

Osceola (1804-1838), once known as Billy Powell, tried to keep the U.S. government from removing Seminoles from their land in Florida. He led the Second Seminole War, which began in 1835, but the white Jesup betrayed Osceola when he tried to negotiate. Glossary, Notes, More Good Reading, and Index.

1957. Sanford, William R. **Quanah Parker: Comanche Warrior**. Springfield, NJ: Enslow, 1994. 48p. $14.95. ISBN 0-89490-512-0. (Native American Leaders of the Wild West). 5-7

Quanah Parker (1854-1911) was the last great Comanche chief. He led his people in their resistance to resettlement in Texas when white ranchers wanted the land on which they lived. They survived the onslaught of the U.S. Army trying to take their lands, but the cavalry destroyed Parker's herd of more than 1,400 horses before he stopped the Comanche protest. After he took his people on a reservation, he taught them to acquiesce as necessary but to keep their traditional ways as well. Photographs, Notes, More Good Reading, Glossary, and Index.

1958. Sanford, William R. **Red Cloud: Sioux Warrior**. Springfield, NJ: Enslow, 1994. 48p. $14.95. ISBN 0-89490-513-9. (Native American Leaders of the Wild West). 5-7

Red Cloud (1822-1909) led the Oglala Sioux against the U.S. government in Bozeman, Montana, when they began to build forts for white settlers after gold was discovered around 1863. Red Cloud fought many battles, but the one remembered is the Fetterman Fight, which forced the United States to abandon its forts. Notes, Glossary, More Good Reading, and Index.

1959. Sanford, William R. **Sitting Bull: Sioux Warrior**. Springfield, NJ: Enslow, 1994. 48p. $14.95. ISBN 0-89490-514-7. (Native American Leaders of the Wild West). 4-10

Sitting Bull, the Hunkpapa Sioux chief (1834?-1890), led the Plains Sioux for many years and helped to defeat Custer at Little Bighorn. Before his death (while white soldiers were taking him away from his home), he toured with Buffalo Bill Cody. Glossary, Notes, More Good Reading, and Index.

1960. Sanford, William R., and Carl R. Green. **Babe Ruth**. New York: Crestwood House, 1992. 48p. $11.95. ISBN 0-89686-741-2. (Sports Immortals). 3-5

Babe Ruth (1895-1948), according to *Life* magazine in 1990, was one of two sports figures to be the century's most important Americans. He hit 714 home runs in his career, and people called him the "Sultan of Swat." The text continues with information about Ruth's life and career with trivia questions interspersed. Photographs, Glossary, More Good Reading, and Index.

1961. Sanford, William R., and Carl R. Green. **Bill Pickett: African-American Rodeo Star**. Springfield, NJ: Enslow, 1997. 48p. $14.95. ISBN 0-89490-676-3. (Legendary Heroes of the Wild West). 4-6

Bill Pickett (c. 1860-1932) was a rodeo star who invented bulldogging, a rodeo stunt that involved biting a bull on the lip. Because of his talent, he was the first African American cowboy to be inducted into the Rodeo Cowboy Hall of Fame. The text looks at both the facts and the legends that developed about this man. Glossary, Notes, More Good Reading, and Index.

1962. Sanford, William R., and Carl R. Green. **Brigham Young: Pioneer and Mormon Leader**. Springfield, NJ: Enslow, 1996. 48p. $14.95. ISBN 0-89490-672-0. (Legendary Heroes of the Wild West). 4-6

Brigham Young (1801-1877) directed the Mormon Church after Joseph Smith, its founder, was assassinated in 1884. He led Mormons from their settlement in Illinois, where they had conflicts with prior settlers, to Salt Lake City, Utah, where they were able to establish a permanent home for the Mormons in 1847. The text looks at both the facts and the legends that developed about this man. Glossary, Notes, More Good Reading, and Index.

1963. Sanford, William R., and Carl R. Green. **Buffalo Bill Cody: Showman of the Wild West**. Springfield, NJ: Enslow, 1996. 48p. $14.95. ISBN 0-89490-646-1. (Legendary Heroes of the Wild West). 4-6

Buffalo Bill Cody (1846-1917) was initially a scout on the American frontier. Later he established his Wild West Show, which toured the United States and Europe after 1883 with such stars as Sitting Bull and Annie Oakley. The text looks at both the facts and the legends that developed about this man. Glossary, Notes, More Good Reading, and Index.

1964. Sanford, William R., and Carl R. Green. **Calamity Jane: A Frontier Original**. Springfield, NJ: Enslow, 1996. 48p. $14.95. ISBN 0-89490-647-X. (Legendary Heroes of the Wild West). 4-6

Martha Jane Burk or Burke (1852?-1903), known as Calamity Jane, dressed like a man, could do difficult manual labor, could outshoot most men, and could ride better than them. The text looks at both the facts and the legends that developed about this woman. Glossary, Notes, More Good Reading, and Index.

1965. Sanford, William R., and Carl R. Green. **Daniel Boone: Wilderness Pioneer**. Springfield, NJ: Enslow, 1996. 48p. $14.95. ISBN 0-89490-674-7. (Legendary Heroes of the Wild West). 4-6

Daniel Boone (1734-1820) was an American frontiersman who was a central figure in the settlement of Kentucky. He also became a folk hero. The text looks at both the facts and the legends about this man. Glossary, Notes, More Good Reading, and Index.

1966. Sanford, William R., and Carl R. Green. **Davy Crockett: Defender of the Alamo**. Springfield, NJ: Enslow, 1996. 48p. $14.95. ISBN 0-89490-648-8. (Legendary Heroes of the Wild West). 4-6

David or Davy Crockett (1786-1836) was an American frontiersman who became a politician and the Tennessee representative to the U.S. Congress (1827-1831 and 1833-1835). He then joined the Texas revolutionaries fighting against Mexico and died at the siege of the Alamo. The text looks at both the facts and the legends that developed about this man. Glossary, Notes, More Good Reading, and Index.

1967. Sanford, William R., and Carl R. Green. **Jackie Robinson**. New York: Crestwood House, 1992. 48p. $11.95. ISBN 0-89686-743-9. (Sports Immortals). 3-5

Jackie Robinson (1919-1972) excelled at sports when he was growing up, and he began to play in the All-Negro baseball league. The Brooklyn Dodgers owner decided to offer him a position because he thought Robinson would be able to handle the intense prejudice that the first African American playing major league baseball would face. Robinson fulfilled this expectation and became an active voice for equal rights. Black-and-white photographs highlight the text. Bibliography and Index.

1968. Sanford, William R., and Carl R. Green. **Jesse Owens**. New York: Crestwood House, 1992. 48p. $11.95. ISBN 0-89686-742-0. (Sports Immortals). 3-5

Jesse Owens (1913-1981) was a noted African American track star whose record-breaking performances in college and four gold medals in the 1936 Berlin Olympics assured him a place in sports history. Black-and-white photographs highlight the text. Bibliography and Index.

1969. Sanford, William R., and Carl R. Green. **Jim Thorpe**. New York: Crestwood House, 1992. 48p. $11.95. ISBN 0-89686-740-4. (Sports Immortals). 3-5

Jim Thorpe (1887-1953), a Native American, proved himself to be one of the greatest all-around athletes in history. He won events in the pentathlon and decathlon in the 1912 Olympics and played both baseball and football. Black-and-white photographs highlight the text. Bibliography and Index.

1970. Sanford, William R., and Carl R. Green. **John C. Frémont: Soldier and Pathfinder**. Springfield, NJ: Enslow, 1996. 48p. $14.95. ISBN 0-89490-649-6. (Legendary Heroes of the Wild West). 4-6

John Charles Frémont (1813-1890) was an American explorer, soldier, and politician. He mapped much of the American West and Northwest before serving as a U.S. senator from California (1850 and 1851) and running for President in 1856. The text looks at both the facts and the legends that developed about this man. Glossary, Notes, More Good Reading, and Index.

1971. Sanford, William R., and Carl R. Green. **Kit Carson: Frontier Scout**. Springfield, NJ: Enslow, 1996. 48p. $14.95. ISBN 0-89490-650-X. (Legendary Heroes of the Wild West). 4-6

Kit Carson (1809-1868) was an American frontiersman who went from Kentucky to Taos, New Mexico, in 1825. He began working as a cook, guide, and hunter for exploring parties, including those of John C. Frémont. In 1853, he became an Indian agent, and then he served in the Civil War as a Union general. One of Carson's solutions for survival on the frontier was building a campfire and then sleeping two miles away from it. The text looks at both the facts and the legends that developed about this man. Glossary, Notes, More Good Reading, and Index.

1972. Sanford, William R., and Carl R. Green. **Richard King: Texas Cattle Rancher**. Springfield, NJ: Enslow, 1996. 48p. $14.95. ISBN 0-89490-673-9. (Legendary Heroes of the Wild West). 4-6

Richard King (1825-1885) was a steamboat captain who became a rancher in Texas. His 600,000-acre ranch was the largest in the United States. The text looks at both the facts and the legends that developed about this man. Glossary, Notes, More Good Reading, and Index.

1973. Sanford, William R., and Carl R. Green. **Sacagawea: Native American Hero**. Springfield, NJ: Enslow, 1997. 48p. $14.95. ISBN 0-89490-675-5. (Legendary Heroes of the Wild West). 4-6

Sacagawea (1786?-1812) was a Shoshone woman whom hostile Indians captured and sold to the Mandans. They traded her to Toussaint Charbonneau, the interpreter for the Lewis and Clark expedition. When the group reached the upper Missouri River region, she was in her home country and could translate and guide. The text looks at both the facts and the legends that developed about her. Glossary, Notes, More Good Reading, and Index.

1974. Sanford, William R., and Carl R. Green. **Sam Houston: Texas Hero**. Springfield, NJ: Enslow, 1996. 48p. $14.95. ISBN 0-89490-651-8. (Legendary Heroes of the Wild West). 4-6

Sam Houston (1793-1863) was an American general and politician who fought in the Texas battle for independence from Mexico. He became the president of the Texas Republic and served from 1836 to 1838 and from 1841 to 1844. After Texas became a state, he served as a U.S. senator from 1845 to 1859 and as governor of Texas from 1859 until 1861. The text looks at both the facts and the legends that developed about this man. Glossary, Notes, More Good Reading, and Index.

1975. Sanford, William R., and Carl R. Green. **Zebulon Pike: Explorer of the Southwest**. Springfield, NJ: Enslow, 1996. 48p. $14.95. ISBN 0-89490-671-2. (Legendary Heroes of the Wild West). 4-6

Zebulon Pike (1779-1813) was an American army officer and explorer who became famous for his expedition up the Arkansas River to the Rocky Mountains beginning in 1806. Pikes Peak was named for him. The text looks at both the facts and the legends that developed about this man. Glossary, Notes, More Good Reading, and Index.

1976. Santella, Andrew. **Jackie Robinson Breaks the Color Line**. Chicago: Childrens Press, 1996. 30p. $18; $4.95pa. ISBN 0-516-06637-4; 0-516-26031-6pa. (Cornerstones of Freedom). 3-5

Santella recalls the situation when Jackie Robinson (1919-1972) began to play Major League baseball for the Brooklyn Dodgers and what it meant at the time. Because of Robinson's strength of character, his behavior became an example to all. Glossary and Index.

1977. Sattler, Helen Roney. **The Earliest Americans**. Jean Day Zallinger, illustrator. New York: Clarion, 1993. 125p. $16.95. ISBN 0-395-54996-5. 5-9

The text looks at the earliest people known to have been on the American continent. Chapters include discussions of the Paleo-Indians in Beringia before they came across the Bering Strait, the Paleo-Indians in North America approximately 12,500-22,000 years ago, the big game hunters approximately 7,000-12,000 years ago, the beginnings of civilization from 2,000 to 8,000 years ago, and the rise of empires and nations from 500 to 2,000 years ago. Time Chart, Bibliography, and Index.

1978. Sattler, Helen Roney. **Hominids: A Look Back at Our Ancestors**. Christopher Santoro, illustrator. New York: Lothrop, Lee & Shepard, 1988. 125p. $15.95. ISBN 0-688-06061-7. 4-8

Drawings of early fossil remains decorate this story of our early ancestors: the Australopithecines, Genus Homo, Homo Habilis, Homo Erectus, Homo Sapiens Neanderthalensis, and modern humans (Homo Sapiens). Time Chart, Species Chart, Bibliography, and Index.

1979. Savage, Jeff. **Cowboys and Cow Towns of the Wild West**. Springfield, NJ: Enslow, 1995. 48p. $14.95. ISBN 0-89490-603-8. (Trailblazers of the Wild West). 4-7

The text looks at the personal experiences of the cowboys, ranchers, and businesspeople who started the cattle trails and the towns that sprang up to serve them. Among the trails that cowboys followed were the Goodnight-Loving Trail, the Western Trail, the Chisholm Trail, and the Shawnee Trail. A gunshot could start a stampede, and these men (and some women) had to be prepared for such situations. Among the topics discussed are dangers, equipment, cattle drives, the boredom between drives, and roundups. Notes, Glossary, Further Reading, and Index.

1980. Savage, Jeff. **Gold Miners of the Wild West**. Springfield, NJ: Enslow, 1995. 48p. $14.95. ISBN 0-89490-601-1. (Trailblazers of the Wild West). 4-7

The California gold rush period began in 1849 and ended with the Yukon gold rush in 1897. People from all over the world came to the western United States hoping to find money. The text tells of those who found hoards and those who found nothing, of claim-jumpers and of people who helped or hindered the miners. Notes, Glossary, Further Reading, and Index.

1981. Savage, Jeff. **Gunfighters of the Wild West**. Springfield, NJ: Enslow, 1995. 48p. $14.95. ISBN 0-89490-600-3. (Trailblazers of the Wild West). 4-7

In the second half of the nineteenth century, gunfighters were notorious in the Wild West. The text looks at some of these men, from the Shootout at O.K. Corral until their end. The topics include background on the gunfighters, the outlaws, the gangs, and the lawmen who eventually put them out of business. Notes, Glossary, Further Reading, and Index.

1982. Savage, Jeff. **Pioneering Women of the Wild**. Springfield, NJ: Enslow, 1995. 48p. $14.95. ISBN 0-89490-604-6. (Trailblazers of the Wild West). 4-7

Many women lived on the frontier in America. To survive, they had to exhibit great courage. They were teachers, homesteaders, ranchers, outlaws, miners, and reformers. They included such women as Sacajawea, Carrie Nation, Calamity Jane, Belle Starr, Carrie Chapman Catt, and Anna Howard Shaw. Notes, Glossary, Further Reading, and Index.

1983. Savage, Jeff. **Pony Express Riders of the Wild West**. Springfield, NJ: Enslow, 1995. 48p. $14.95. ISBN 0-89490-602-X. (Trailblazers of the Wild West). 4-7

On April 3, 1860, the Pony Express began carrying mail the 2,000 miles between St. Joseph, Missouri, and Sacramento, California. In only 18 months, the telegraph put it out of business, but during that time, men showed that they could ride fast enough to get the mail delivered within 10 days. The text looks at these riders, who dodged angry Native Americans and thieves. Notes, Glossary, Further Reading, and Index.

1984. Savage, Jeff. **Scouts of the Wild West**. Springfield, NJ: Enslow, 1995. 48p. $14.95. ISBN 0-89490-605-4. 4-7

Pioneers and settlers in the Wild West of the 1800s needed people to find out what was in the territory before they came. Scouts such as Kit Carson and Jim Bridger helped them find their way by leading trapping parties and mapping expeditions and guiding wagon trains. They also protected them from wild animals and bandits. Notes, Glossary, Further Reading, and Index.

1985. Savin, Marcia. **The Moon Bridge**. New York: Scholastic, 1992. 232p. $13.95. ISBN 0-590-45873-6. 4-7

The war does not affect Ruthie in 1942 until her best friend tells her not to make friends with the new girl in school, Mitzi Fujimoto. Because Ruthie dislikes being told what to do, she defies her friend and begins to talk with Mitzi. What she discovers is a "better" best friend until Mitzi and her family disappear, having been taken to the internment camps. While she is gone, Ruthie writes her about her life, but does not mail the letters. As the end of the war arrives, Mitzi writes and asks to meet Ruthie. When they meet, Mitzi tells her that she had stopped talking during the war. After her family convinced her that to hate would make her the same as those who had imprisoned her, she changed. However, she can never recover the years lost behind the chain fences.

1986. Sawyer, Kem Knapp. **Marjory Stoneman Douglas: Guardian of the Everglades**. Lowell, MA: Discovery, 1992. 72p. $14.95; $7.95pa. ISBN 1-878668-20-X; 1-878668-28-5pa. 6-8

Marjory Stoneman Douglas (b. 1890) was born into a privileged household in New England, and she attended Wellesley College. Among her jobs was working with the Red Cross. When she moved to Florida, she realized the Everglades were unique, and she has spent much of her life trying to protect the area from poachers and developers. The text looks at her life and the events that made her become the advocate of the Everglades. Index.

1987. Saxon-Ford, Stephanie. **The Czech Americans**. New York: Chelsea House, 1989. 110p. $14.95. ISBN 0-87754-870-6. (Peoples of North America). 5 up

In the 1880s and 1890s, nearly 100,000 Czechs came to America from central Europe and regions of Bohemia and Moravia. They were skilled, literate, and able to function in many areas of society. The text looks at their arrival, their history, what they did after they came, their religion and community, and their future. Photographs augment the text. Further Reading and Index.

1988. Say, Allen, author/illustrator. **El Chino**. Boston: Houghton Mifflin, 1990. 32p. $14.95. ISBN 0-395-52023-1. 2-5

Bill Wong, a Chinese American, became a famous bullfighter in Spain. Say tells his story using first person to give a sense of immediacy to Wong's experiences as he won over the Spanish crowd through his exploits with the bull. *Bulletin Blue Ribbon Book*.

1989. Say, Allen, author/illustrator **Grandfather's Journey**. Boston: Houghton Mifflin, 1993. 32p. $16.95. ISBN 0-395-57035-2. K-3

The narrator's grandfather left Japan as a young man to see America in the early twentieth century. He travels around the country wearing Western clothes. After he returns to Japan, he marries. Then he brings his bride to San Francisco and raises his daughter. They go to Japan to live, with the grandfather planning to return for a visit. But World War II destroys his plans as well as his home and his city. The narrator carries on his grandfather's dream by living in America and raising his own daughter there. *Bulletin Blue Ribbon Book* and *Caldecott Medal*.

1990. Scarf, Maggi. **Meet Benjamin Franklin**. 1968. New York: Random House, 1989. 64p. $3.99pa. ISBN 0-394-81961-6pa. (Step Up Book). 2-4

Before the Colonies began to fight against the British, Benjamin Franklin (1706-1790) made two trips to England to discuss the matter of taxes. He thought at first that the people of his colony, the Penns, should pay their taxes, but he eventually realized that life would not improve as long as the colonies remained under British rule. This service to his country is only one of the many contributions that Franklin made during his long life. The text gives an overview of his years as inventor and representative of the country.

1991. Scheader, Catherine. **Shirley Chisholm: Teacher and Congresswoman**. Springfield, NJ: Enslow, 1990. 138p. $17.95. ISBN 0-89490-285-7. (Contemporary Women). 6 up

Shirley Chisholm (b. 1924) was the first Black woman elected to Congress and the first to make a serious bid for the presidency when George McGovern won the nomination. She has always wanted to be known as a woman who fought for women and for Blacks. Chronology and Index.

1992. Schleichert, Elizabeth. **The Life of Dorothea Dix**. Antonio Castro, illustrator. New York: Twenty-First Century Books, 1992. 80p. $13.98. ISBN 0-941477-68-1. (Pioneers in Health and Medicine). 4-7

When Dorothea Dix (1802-1887) visited a prison in 1841, she found women in cells with no furniture, no heat, and no sanitary facilities. When she asked why they were there, the jailer told her that they were insane. For women who had no money and no one to care for them, they had no place to go but to the jails. Dix began to try to establish mental hospitals to look after those who could not help themselves. When the Civil War started, she came to Washington, where she was appointed the Superintendent of U.S. Army Nurses, the highest post in the nation held by a woman. After her death, the study of the mentally ill became a significant branch of medicine. For Further Reading and Index.

1993. Schleichert, Elizabeth. **The Life of Elizabeth Blackwell**. New York: Twenty-First Century Books, 1992. 80p. $14.95. ISBN 0-941477-66-5. (Pioneers in Health and Medicine). 4-7

Elizabeth Blackwell (1821-1910) became the first female physician in the United States in 1849 and opened the medical field to women. In 1857, she founded the Hospital for Women and Children in New York and announced her desire to have women medical students living there. For Further Reading and Index.

1994. Schlein, Miriam. **I Sailed with Columbus**. Tom Newsom, illustrator. New York: HarperCollins, 1991. 136p. $14.95. ISBN 0-06-022513-0. 3-7

Julio, 12, leaves the monastery in which he was raised and sails with Christopher Columbus (Cristóbal Colón) in 1492 on the *Santa Maria*. As the monks had requested, he keeps a diary in which he records events and facts about the voyage. He never loses faith in Columbus, but he looks forward to returning to Spain and becoming a farmer with money earned on the voyage.

1995. Schmidt, Gary D., ed. **Robert Frost**. Henri Sorensen, illustrator. New York: Sterling, 1994. 48p. $14.95. ISBN 0-8069-0633-2. (Poetry for Young People). 3 up

After an introductory biographical sketch of Robert Frost (1874-1963), the editor arranges some of Frost's more famous poems thematically according to summer, autumn, winter, and spring. Index.

1996. Schomp, Virginia. **Frederick Douglass: Voice of Freedom.** Miami, FL: Benchmark, 1997. 48p. $14.95. ISBN 0-7614-0488-0. 3-6

Contemporary paintings and illustrations augment this thorough view of Fredrick Douglass's life from his childhood through his adult life (1818-1895). It clarifies the horror of slavery and the contribution that Douglass made to helping slaves to freedom. Further Reading, Glossary, and Index.

1997. Schott, Jane A. **Will Rogers**. David Charles Brandon, illustrator. Minneapolis, MN: Carolrhoda, 1996. 48p. $11.96. ISBN 0-87614-983-2. (On My Own Biography). K-3

Will Rogers (1879-1935) wanted to make people laugh, and he achieved that with his rope tricks and his writing. As a boy, he had wanted to be a cowboy, but he found out that being a cowboy was hard work. He always enjoyed rope throwing, even as he stood on stage and told jokes. The text looks at his life and mentions his death in the afterword.

1998. Schotter, Roni. **Dreamland**. Kevin Hawkes, illustrator. New York: Orchard, 1996. Unpaged. $15.95. ISBN 0-531-09508-8. K-4

Theo idealizes his uncle, who is always trying to create something new in his tailor's shop. His uncle admires the drawings of "dream machines" that Theo creates in his free time. When the family starts a new life in California during the early 1900s, Theo creates an amusement park.

1999. Schotter, Roni. **Rhoda, Straight and True**. New York: Lothrop, Lee & Shepard, 1986. 184p. $10.25. ISBN 0-688-06157-5. 4-6

Rhoda and her friends, in sixth grade in Brooklyn during 1953, decide that Mr. and Mrs. Rose are spies. They also dislike the Mancy family because it contains 13 children. Rhoda, however, slowly learns that preconceived ideas may not be correct. She discovers that the Mancys are poor but kind and that the Roses are both actors.

2000. Schouweiler, Tom. **The Lost Colony of Roanoke: Opposing Viewpoints**. San Diego, CA: Greenhaven, 1991. 80p. $16.95. ISBN 0-89908-093-6. (Great Mysteries—Opposing Viewpoints). 5-9

The Colony of Roanoke on the coast of North Carolina disappeared without much of a trace between 1587 and 1590. The text tries to piece together the mystery by examining the colony's founding by Sir Walter Raleigh and what might have happened based on the members' relationships to each other and to the Native Americans who lived in the area. Reproductions highlight the information. For Further Exploration, Works Consulted, and Index.

2001. Schraff, Anne. **Women of Peace: Nobel Peace Prize Winners**. Springfield, NJ: Enslow, 1994. 112p. $17.95. ISBN 0-89490-493-0. (Collective Biographies). 5-9

The first Nobel Peace Prize was awarded in 1901, and since then, nine women have been named winners for their attempts to establish peace in the world. They are Baroness von Suttner (1905), Jane Addams (1931), Emily Green Balch (1946), Mairead Corrigan and Betty Williams (1976), Mother Teresa (1979), Alva Myrdal (1982), Daw Aung San Suu Kyi (1991), and Rigoberta Menchu (1992). Index.

2002. Schraff, Anne E. **American Heroes of Exploration and Flight**. Springfield, NJ: Enslow, 1996. 112p. $17.95. ISBN 0-89490-619-4. (Collective Biographies). 5-9

The text profiles 10 people who have contributed to exploration and flight in America. Included in the profiles are information about their lives, beginning with an exciting event and a brief overview of history to show why their particular contribution was important. Those profiled include Matthew Henson (1866-1955) and Robert Peary (1856-1920), who discovered the North Pole together; Amelia Earhart (1897-1937); Jacqueline Cochran (1910-1980); Sally Ride (b. 1951); and Christa McAuliffe (d. 1986). Notes and Index.

2003. Schroeder, Alan. **Booker T. Washington: Educator and Racial Spokesman**. New York: Chelsea House, 1992. 142p. $18.95; $7.95pa. ISBN 1-55546-616-8; 0-7910-0252-7pa. (Black Americans of Achievement). 5 up

Booker T. Washington (1856-1915) was born a slave on a Virginia farm and got his freedom when the Civil War ended. He then went to work in the salt furnaces and coal mines of West Virginia. At 16, he walked 200 miles to enroll at Virginia's Hampton Institute. He became a teacher, and in 1881 he went to Tuskegee, Alabama, where he founded a school that became one of the largest and best-endowed of the Black institutions. He worked for a better life for Blacks and wanted them to accept white society in their attempts to raise themselves economically. Photographs enhance the text. Chronology, Further Reading, and Index.

2004. Schroeder, Alan. **Jack London**. New York: Chelsea House, 1991. 127p. $18.95. ISBN 0-7910-1623-4. (Library of Biography). 5-8

Jack London (1876-1916) was one of the highest paid and most widely read American authors in the early twentieth century, with such novels as *Call of the Wild* and stories like "To Build a Fire." After growing up in the San Francisco area, he started working in a pickle cannery at 13. He became an oyster pirate two years later, then a sailor, next a hobo. By 21, he was a gold miner. When he returned from the Klondike gold rush in 1898, he had much material for future stories but no gold. He was known for many things, including being a socialist and a correspondent during the Russo-Japanese War. Photographs enhance the text. Chronology, Further Reading, and Index.

2005. Schroeder, Alan. **Josephine Baker**. New York: Chelsea House, 1991. 127p. $18.95. ISBN 0-7910-1116-X. (Black Americans of Achievement). 5 up

Josephine Baker (1906-1975) tried to escape her poverty in St. Louis, Missouri, by entertaining her friends and visiting the city's Black vaudeville houses. At 13, when she made her debut, she realized that she should make an ill-fitting costume be the focus of her act and thus began her comedy. In 1925, she sailed to France, and the French loved both her beauty and her dancing. During World War II, the French Resistance recruited her to be a secret agent. After the war, she turned her estate in southern France into a tourist resort. She was one of the first civil rights crusaders, and she adopted 12 children from different nations to show that people of different backgrounds could live in peace. Photographs complement the text. Chronology, Further Reading, and Index.

2006. Schroeder, Alan. **Minty: A Story of Young Harriet Tubman**. Jerry Pinkney, illustrator. New York: Dial, 1996. 40p. $16.99. ISBN 0-8037-1888-8. K-3

When Minty (Araminta) was too clumsy to work in the house, Mistress Brodas sent her to work in the fields. Even when the field hands warned her to avoid any confrontations, she freed muskrats from traps she had been ordered to empty. The overseer whipped her and threatened to sell her "downstream." Knowing that she would probably not change, her father taught her how to cope in the outdoors and how to navigate. These skills helped her survive when she attempted to escape and later became the Harriet Tubman who led the Underground Railroad.

2007. Schroeder, Alan. **Satchmo's Blues**. Floyd Cooper, Illustrator. New York: Doubleday, 1996. Unpaged. $15.95. ISBN 0-385-32046-9. 1-4

Louis Armstrong works in any job he can find to earn the five dollars to buy a cornet that he sees in a pawn shop window. In Armstrong's archival autobiography, he says that he bought the horn; he did not get one for free at the Colored Waif's Home for Boys in New Orleans. This fictional story traces Armstrong's quest to make music as a young boy.

2008. Schulz, Walter A. **Will and Orv**. Janet Schulz, illustrator. Minneapolis, MN: Carolrhoda, 1991. 46p. $15.95. ISBN 0-87614-669-8. (On My Own). 1-3

On December 17, 1903, Wilbur and Orville Wright flew an aircraft powered by a motor and changed the history of the world. The text presents this day from the point of view of "young Johnny Moore of Nag's Head [North Carolina]," one of the five people who witnessed the first flight.

2009. Schuman, Michael A. **Eleanor Roosevelt: First Lady and Humanitarian**. Springfield, NJ: Enslow, 1995. 128p. $17.95. ISBN 0-89490-547-3. (People to Know). 5-9

Among the titles used to describe Eleanor Roosevelt (1884-1962) are First Lady, journalist, activist, and delegate to the United Nations. Her concern for others showed in her attempts to help people of all races and economic levels although she had a wealthy and privileged background. She was an early advocate of women's rights, child labor laws, the eight-hour workday, and equality for African Americans. Chronology, Notes, and Index.

2010. Schuman, Michael A. **Elie Wiesel: Voice from the Holocaust**. Springfield, NJ: Enslow, 1994. 128p. $17.95. ISBN 0-89490-428-0. (People to Know). 5-8

In 1986, Elie Wiesel (b. 1928) won the Nobel Peace Prize. After growing up in Rumania, he almost died because he and his family were taken to Auschwitz, Poland, in 1944, to Hitler's death camp because they were Jewish. He was later transferred to Buchenwald, where he was rescued when the U.S. Army liberated the prisoners. The rest of his family died. He has written books and lectured on his experience while trying to get people to reject bigotry, hatred, and violence. Chronology, Further Reading, and Index.

2011. Schuman, Michael A. **Martin Luther King, Jr.: Leader for Civil Rights**. Springfield, NJ: Enslow, 1996. 128p. $18.95. ISBN 0-89490-687-9. 5-8

The text begins with Martin Luther King, Jr.'s (1929-1968) "I Have a Dream" speech delivered in 1963. It has enough detail and information about collections at museums and historical sites that the text is worthwhile. Other information is standard and available in other places.

2012. Schwartz, Amy, author/illustrator. **Annabelle Swift, Kindergartner**. New York: Orchard, Franklin Watts, 1988. $12.95. ISBN 0-531-05737. K-2

In 1950s California, Annabelle asks a lot of questions as Lucy, her sister, has told her to do. She only confuses her teacher. But delighted to be chosen milk monitor, she is especially happy when she counts the money properly. She and Lucy are loyal to each other, and Lucy gives her much advice.

2013. Schwartzberg, Renée. **Ronald Reagan**. New York: Chelsea House, 1991. 134p. $18.95. ISBN 1-55546-849-7. (World Leaders Past and Present). 5 up

Ronald Reagan (b. 1911) became President after many things had disturbed the United States during the 1970s. As an actor, he had learned to communicate with people, and he made them believe in his conservative vision for a better United States. When he ran for President, he had already demonstrated his abilities as the governor in California. Concerns about his presidency included the reduction in help for the poor and education and the increase in the military budget. He said he would not deal with terrorists, but his subordinates secretly sold arms to Iran and the Nicaraguan rebels. Photographs enhance the text. Chronology, Further Reading, and Index.

2014. Schwarz, Melissa. **Cochise, Apache Chief**. New York: Chelsea House, 1992. 119p. $18.95; $7.95pa. ISBN 0-7910-1706-0; 0-7910-1694-3pa. (North American Indians of Achievement). 5 up

Cochise (c. 1805-1874) was one of the greatest chiefs in Apache history. He earned respect from his people and fear from his enemies. He was an honest man whom soldiers called a liar when he denied their accusation that he had kidnapped a white boy. When the soldiers murdered his brother and two nephews, he vowed war and made revenge attacks against white settlers for a decade. During the Cochise wars, he became "public enemy number one" to Tucson officials. He continued attacking until 1872, when he concluded a peace treaty with the military. He became the only Apache ever to be granted a reservation for his people. Photographs and reproductions enhance the text. Chronology, Further Reading, and Index.

2015. Schwarz, Melissa. **Geronimo: Apache Warrior**. New York: Chelsea House, 1991. 128p. $18.95; $7.95pa. ISBN 0-7910-1701-X; 0-7910-1691-9pa. (North American Indians of Achievement). 5 up

The Apaches thought that Geronimo (1823-1909) was a war shaman with mystical power, but the Mexicans and Americans, his enemies, thought he was a fearless and terrifying warrior. He led killing raids against his foes, and during the raids, he lost many family members, including his wife, mother, and children. Four times the U.S. Army forced Geronimo to surrender, and three times he escaped. The fourth time, he was imprisoned and not allowed to return to his homeland. He was relocated to an Oklahoma reservation where he died. Photographs and reproductions enhance the text. Chronology, Further Reading, and Index.

2016. Schwarz, Melissa. **Wilma Mankiller: Principal Chief of the Cherokees**. New York: Chelsea House, 1994. 110p. $18.95. ISBN 0-7910-1715-X. (North American Indians of Achievement). 5 up

Wilma Mankiller (b. 1945) moved to San Francisco at 12 when a drought struck her family's Oklahoma region. In 1969, when Native Americans seized Alcatraz Island to protest U.S. government policy on Indians, Mankiller became a supporter. In 1976, she returned to Oklahoma and continued community development work. Then in 1985, she became the first woman to head the Cherokee Nation. She continues to encourage her people to work together. Photographs enhance the text. Chronology, Further Reading, and Index.

2017. Scordato, Ellen. **Sarah Winnemucca: Northern Paiute Writer and Diplomat**. New York: Chelsea House, 1992. 126p. $18.95; $7.95pa. ISBN 0-7910-1710-9; 0-7910-1696-Xpa. (North American Indians of Achievement). 5 up

Sarah Winnemucca (1844-1891), a Northern Paiute, grew up in what is now the state of Nevada, where she learned English. She became an ambassador between the tribal and the non-Indian world by arguing against the displacement of her people, the taking of their lands, and the theft of their property. She served as a guide during the Bannock War of 1878 and tried to get Indians and whites to live together peacefully. To tell their story, she wrote *Life Among the Paiutes*, published in 1883, as the first book about Indians by an Indian woman. She traveled across the country trying to raise money for education and was able to start one of the first Indian-run schools. Photographs and engravings enhance the text. Chronology, Further Reading, and Index.

2018. Scott, Elaine. **Funny Papers: Behind the Scenes of the Comics**. Margaret Miller, photographer. New York: Morrow, 1993. 90p. $15. ISBN 0-688-11575-6. 4-8

The first cartoon appeared in 1895 in a New York newspaper. Since that time, the comics have been newspaper features. The text looks at Hank Ketcham and *Dennis the Menace*, Charles Schulz and *Peanuts*, and Dean Young and *Blondie* to give insight about this aspect of our culture. Photographs supplement the text. Index.

2019. Scott, John Anthony, and Robert Alan Scott. **John Brown of Harper's Ferry**. New York: Facts on File, 1988. 184p. $16.95. ISBN 0-8160-1347-0. (Makers of America). 5 up

John Brown (1800-1859) is best known for his raid on the arms factories in Harpers Ferry, West Virginia, in 1859. He was trying to spark a slave rebellion, but it ended unsuccessfully when most of his men were killed, and he had to surrender to the federal troops. He and seven of his men who survived were hanged because of their insurrection. The text shows that Brown's love of humans and his belief that all people were equal propelled him toward violence when he saw no other way. Maps, Bibliography, and Index.

2020. Scott, Lynn H. **The Covered Wagon and Other Adventures**. Lincoln, NE: University of Nebraska Press, 1987. 134p. $15. ISBN 0-8032-4179-8. 4-7

Before 1910, Lynn Scott lived in the West when it was underdeveloped. He illustrated his stories about family experiences on their covered wagon in 1906, and other stories about encounters with Indians, sheepmen, and freighters; crises with rattlesnakes, black ants, and rock avalanches; and Rocky Mountain spotted fever. His story gives a view of life in western America at that time.

2021. Scott, Richard. **Jackie Robinson**. New York: Chelsea House, 1987. 110p. $18.95; $7.95pa. ISBN 1-55546-609-5; 0-7910-0200-4pa. (Black Americans of Achievement). 5 up

Jackie Robinson (1919-1972), former All-American football player and army officer, was playing for the Kansas City Monarchs when asked to join the Brooklyn Dodgers as the first African American baseball player in the modern major leagues. After he stopped playing, he became vice president of Chock Full O'Nuts and a spokesman for the NAACP. He wanted equal opportunity at work, condemned drug use, and urged people to return to family values. Photographs and reproductions enhance the text. Chronology, Further Reading, and Index.

2022. Scott, Robert A. **Chief Joseph and the Nez Percés**. New York: Facts on File, 1993. 134p. $17.95. ISBN 0-8160-2475-8. (Makers of America). 5 up

The American government attacked Chief Joseph's (1840-1904) Nez Percé tribe in June 1877, trying to kill the people before they could start another Sioux uprising as they marched from Oregon to a new home chosen by the government in Idaho. Women and children were slaughtered in their tipis, with soldiers saying later that they had to kill them because they were going to fight back. Chief Joseph tried to protect his people, but by October of that year, he knew they could not win. Even after this defeat, he continued to try to regain the ancestral home of his people, but he could not. A description of Chief Joseph at that time by a man who later regretted the horrible treatment of the Native Americans said that he was "a splendid looking man . . . fully six feet high . . . . His forehead is high, his eyes bright yet kind, his nose finely cut . . . ." Bibliography and Index.

2023. Sebestyen, Ouida. **Words by Heart**. Boston: Little, Brown, 1979. 144p. $15.95. ISBN 0-316-77931-8. New York: Bantam, 1991. 144p. $3.99pa. ISBN 0-553-27179-2pa. 4-8

Lena Sills, 12 in 1910, wins a spelling contest instead of a white boy and refuses the first prize of a bow tie. Someone upset that a Black family lives in the small town leaves a big butcher knife stabbed through bread on their table. Because Lena has only been concerned with making her father proud, she has been unaware of the prejudice surrounding her. A tragedy causes the white sharecropper family to understand that they must all work together to be successful. *International Children's Books Awards* and *American Book Award*.

2024. Selfridge, John W. **John F. Kennedy: Courage in Crisis**. New York: Fawcett Columbine, 1989. 120p. $3.95pa. ISBN 0-449-90399-0pa. 5-9

The text looks at the life of John Fitzgerald Kennedy (1917-1963), the youngest man to be elected president of the United States. Included are chapters on the Cuban crisis, what being a "Kennedy" meant, his heroic action in World War II, the beginning of his political career, his role as president and the "New Frontierism," his fight against the Cold War, his arguments for civil rights, and his death in Dallas. Glossary.

2025. Selznick, Brian, author/illustrator. **The Houdini Box**. New York: Knopf, 1991. 56p. $12.95. ISBN 0-679-81429-9. 2-4

The feats of Harry Houdini enthrall Victor, and he tries to recreate them in his home by locking himself in a trunk, holding his breath underwater, and trying to walk through walls. He happens to meet Houdini, and when Houdini invites Victor to his house, Victor expects to learn some of the magician's secrets.

2026. Sewall, Marcia, author/illustrator. **People of the Breaking Day**. New York: Atheneum, 1990. 48p. $14.95. ISBN 0-689-31407-8. 2-5

The Wampanoag tribe of Native Americans greeted the settlers at Plimoth Plantation in 1620. Their leader Massasoit helped the Pilgrims when they needed food during their first months on land. The text looks at the tribal structure and respect for the leader as well as the customs throughout the year within the tribe and the families. Glossary.

2027. Sewall, Marcia, author/illustrator. **The Pilgrims of Plimoth**. New York: Atheneum, 1996. 48p. $15.95. ISBN 0-689-31250-4. 2-5

In a first-person narrative, the text shows the language and thoughts of the people who came from England to build new homes in America in 1620. The men, women, and children speak about their experiences on the *Mayflower* and their daily lives in the new settlement. The accompanying illustrations enhance the text. Glossary. *Boston Globe-Horn Book Award, School Library Journal Best Book, Horn Book Fanfare Honor List, IRA Children's Choices*, and *Notable Children's Trade Books in the Field of Social Studies*.

2028. Sewall, Marcia, author/illustrator. **Thunder from the Clear Sky**. New York: Atheneum, 1995. 56p. $17. ISBN 0-689-31775-1. 3-5

The text looks at King Philip's War in 1675-1676 between the Wampanoags and the Pilgrims from each side's point of view by giving alternating responses to the intrigues and betrayals. When the Pilgrims killed three Native Americans, the Native Americans retaliated, and the war between the two groups began. The same situation with two peoples reacting so differently shows how people misunderstand each other. *Notable Children's Trade Books in the Field of Social Studies*.

2029. Seymour-Jones, Carole. **Refugees**. New York: New Discovery, 1992. 48p. $12.95. ISBN 0-02-735402-4. (Past and Present). 5-7

People have had to flee their homes because of war, poverty, starvation, or government persecution. Among the historical flights of people included in the text are the dispersions under Genghis Khan and the Mongols around 1214, the Trail of Tears in 1838 when the Cherokees had to leave their homes, the boat people fleeing to Thailand following the fall of Saigon in 1975, and the escape of the Israelites from Egypt around 1280 BC. The text looks at the way these people coped and how other societies have tried to help. Key Dates, Glossary, and Index.

2030. Shaffer, Ann. **The Camel Express**. Robin Cole, illustrator. Minneapolis, MN: Gemstone, 1989. 46p. $10.95. ISBN 0-87518-400-6. (It Really Happened!). 2-4

An old man takes his granddaughter with him on a camel when he has to quickly deliver a Pony Express bag in 1861. Three foes make the trip more dangerous than expected: wolves, Indians, and bandits.

2031. Shaw, Janet. **Changes for Kirsten**. Renée Graef and Keith Skeen, illustrators. Madison, WI: Pleasant, 1988. 65p. $12.95; $5.95pa. ISBN 0-937295-44-2; 0-937295-45-0pa. (American Girls Collection). 4-6

In 1854, Kirsten wants to go trapping with her brother and his friend in the Minnesota woods. Although they do not want a young girl with them, they let her go because she knows the animals' habits. After their house burns, she and her brother go to visit the best trapper in the area but find him dead. Because he has no family, they sell his furs and use the money to buy a new house.

2032. Shea, George. **First Flight: The Story of Tom Tate and the Wright Brothers**. Don Bolognese, illustrator. New York: HarperCollins, 1997. 46p. $14.95. ISBN 0-06-024503-4. (An I Can Read Chapter Book). 1-3

Tom Tate met Orville and Wilbur Wright in Kitty Hawk, North Carolina, in 1900 when he was 12. He saw them when they came each year, and they let him try to fly the glider once when not enough wind was blowing to support an adult. The dialogue recreates the excitement that flying engendered in Tom.

2033. Sheafer, Silvia Anne. **Women in America's Wars**. Springfield, NJ: Enslow, 1996. 112p. $17.95. ISBN 0-89490-553-8. (Collective Biographies). 6-9

The text profiles 10 women who have helped America during times of war. Included in the profiles are information about their lives, beginning with an exciting event and a brief overview of history to show why their contribution was important. They include Mary Hays, known as Molly Pitcher (1754-1832), and Pamela Davis Dorman, the first female U.S. chaplain to serve in the Marines. Notes and Index.

2034. Sherman, Eileen B. **Independence Avenue**. Philadelphia, PA: Jewish Publication Society, 1990. 145p. $13.95. ISBN 0-8276-0367-3. 5-8

In 1907, Elias, 14, arrives in Kansas City from Russia, alone and with no job. He talks his way into a job in a department store, hoping to become a tailor, his family's trade. He meets the boss's daughter, but her aunt sees him as an immigrant, beneath Rebecca's attentions. He must learn how to cope in this new environment. He does, but he first hears of his parents' deaths in a pogrom, and his six-year-old brother arrives to live with him.

2035. Sherrow, Victoria. **The Aztec Indians**. New York: Chelsea House, 1993. 79p. $14.95; $6.95pa. ISBN 0-7910-1658-7; 0-7910-1963-2pa. (Junior Library of American Indians). 3-6

The Aztec empire began in 1325 when the wandering Mexica Indians settled near present-day Mexico City. They grew in strength by establishing a trade network. Despite their wealth and daily rituals, the capital fell to the Spanish in 1521. Photographs and reproductions enhance the text. Glossary, Chronology, and Index.

2036. Sherrow, Victoria. **The Big Book of U.S. Presidents**. Philadelphia, PA: Courage, Running Press, 1994. 56p. $10.98. ISBN 1-56138-427-5. (A Young Person's Guide to American History). 3-5

In an introduction, Sherrow tells how presidents are elected. Then she covers information about each president on one page, including family matters and what he did of note while in office. Portraits of each president and his wife appear. The Presidents and Vice Presidents, Famous Quotes, Fun Facts, and Index.

2037. Sherrow, Victoria. **The Iroquois Indians**. New York: Chelsea House, 1992. 79p. $14.95; $7.95pa. ISBN 0-7910-1655-2; 0-7910-2027-4pa. (Junior Library of American Indians). 3-6

Around 1500, Hiawatha and the Peacemaker founded the Iroquois Confederacy. They drove others from their territory in the next century and became the most powerful Native Americans at the time. During the American Revolution, colonial forces destroyed many of their villages. The text examines their past in detail. Photographs and drawings enhance the text. Glossary, Chronology, and Index.

2038. Sherrow, Victoria. **The Nez Percés: People of the Far West**. Brookfield, CT: Millbrook Press, 1994. 64p. $15.90. ISBN 1-56294-315-4. (Native Americans). 4-6

The Nez Percés, an independent people, found horses in the 1700s and began to hunt buffalo on horseback. They were self-sufficient and intelligent, with public-speaking skills and peaceful ways. The text talks about their practice of a democratic style of government that honored both men and women in their communities. It also discusses traditional life in a village, the fighting with the U.S. government, and Chief Joseph's desire to one day return to his home. The work is augmented with photographs and illustrations. Important Dates, Glossary, Bibliography, and Index. *Science Books and Films Annual Best Children's Science Book List.*

2039. Sherrow, Victoria. **Phillis Wheatley: Poet**. New York: Chelsea Juniors, 1992. 80p. $14.95; $4.95pa. ISBN 0-7910-1753-2; 0-7910-2036-3pa. (Junior Black Americans of Achievement). 3-6

While working for the Wheatley family in Boston, Phillis Wheatley (1753-1784) learned Latin and English. The family liked her poetry enough to have a book of it published in London in 1773. Wheatley was only the second woman in America with a published book and the first Black. Afterward, the family freed her. She married but died alone and without money when she was only 31.

2040. Sherrow, Victoria. **The Triangle Factory Fire**. Brookfield, CT: Millbrook Press, 1995. 64p. $15.90. ISBN 1-56294-572-6. (Spotlight on American History). 5-8

The text begins with an account of the 1911 fire in the Triangle factory, which killed young female workers trapped inside by doors locked from the outside. It then gives the background to the calamity in a chronological order of events, including dismal working conditions and the beginnings of the labor movement. Bibliography, Chronology, Further Reading, and Index.

2041. Shirley, David. **Malcolm X: Racial Spokesman**. New York: Chelsea Juniors, 1994. 80p. $14.95; $4.95pa. ISBN 0-7910-2106-8; 0-7910-2112-2pa. (Junior Black Americans of Achievement). 3-6

After growing up in Lansing, Michigan, Malcolm Little (1925-1965) went first to Boston, where he became a street hustler, and then to New York. At 20, he went to prison. There he learned about the Nation of Islam, a Black religious group, from his brother. When he left prison, he became one of the Nation's ministers. The head of the group, Elijah Muhammad, saw him as second in command. In 1964, Malcolm (having taken the name Malcolm X) disagreed with Muhammad and traveled to Mecca, the Holy City of Islam. When he returned, he attempted to unite Blacks all over the world, but someone assassinated him on February 21, 1965. Further Reading, Glossary, Chronology, and Index.

2042. Shirley, David. **Satchel Paige**. New York: Chelsea House, 1993. 100p. $18.95; $7.95pa. ISBN 0-7910-1880-6; 0-7910-1983-7pa. (Black Americans of Achievement). 5 up

LeRoy "Satchel" Paige (1906-1982) was a great pitcher in the Negro Leagues. He got his nickname from carrying satchels at the local train station when he was seven. He learned to pitch while attending reform school and began playing baseball at 17. When he became the American League's first Black pitcher in 1948, he was also the oldest rookie ever. He had 2,000 lifetime victories before he quit playing in 1968. He was the first Negro League star to enter the Baseball Hall of Fame, and some consider him "the World's Greatest Pitcher." Photographs enhance the text. Chronology, Further Reading, and Index.

2043. Shore, Nancy. **Amelia Earhart: Aviator**. New York: Chelsea House, 1987. 110p. $18.95; $7.95pa. ISBN 1-55546-651-6; 0-7910-0415-5pa. (American Women of Achievement). 5 up

Amelia Earhart (1897-1937) received her pilot's license in 1922 and began to break many records as a female flyer. In 1932, she became the first woman to pilot a small plane across the Atlantic Ocean. In 1937, she planned to fly around the world at the equator. She left on June 1. On July 3, while she was flying over the Pacific, communication with her plane ceased. No trace of pilot or plane has been found. She believed in being an individualist throughout her life. Photographs, Chronology, Further Reading, and Index.

2044. Shorto, Russell. **David Farragut and the Great Naval Blockade**. Englewood Cliffs, NJ: Silver Burdett, 1991. 128p. $12.95. ISBN 0-382-09941-9. (History of the Civil War). 5 up

David Farragut (1801-1870) became a midshipman for the U.S. Navy at the age of nine, helping to capture pirates in the Caribbean and journeying around the world in the War of 1812. At the beginning of the Civil War, he rose to the rank of captain and led two of the major sea battles of the war, the Battle of New Orleans and the Battle of Mobile Bay. History remembers his response to the cry "Torpedoes ahead!" as "Damn the torpedoes! Full speed ahead!" His achievements earned him the rank as the first admiral in the U.S. Navy's history. Timetables, Suggested Reading, Selected Sources, and Index.

2045. Shorto, Russell. **Geronimo and the Struggle for Apache Freedom**. Englewood Cliffs, NJ: Silver Burdett, 1989. 131p. $12.95; $7.95pa. ISBN 0-382-09571-5; 0-382-09760-2pa. (Biography of the American Indians). 5-8

Named Goyathlay at his birth (1823-1909), he became Geronimo after he proved his manhood to his Apache tribe. Geronimo's life changed when he saw the bodies of his wife, mother, and children mutilated in the dirt where U.S. Army soldiers had left them. He began planning revenge with Cochise and others. He continued to fight for Apache freedom until the army finally captured and imprisoned him. They would not allow him to return to his homeland. Suggested Reading.

2046. Shorto, Russell. **Jackie Robinson and the Breaking of the Color Barrier**. Brookfield, CT: Millbrook Press, 1991. 32p. $10.90. ISBN 1-878841-15-7. (Gateway to Civil Rights). 3-5

As the first Black player in modern major league baseball, Jackie Robinson (1919-1972) had the responsibility to make his role a success. The text looks at Robinson's recruitment, Negro League baseball, the man who asked Robinson to play, and Robinson's contribution to civil rights. Photographs, Chronology, and Index.

2047. Shorto, Russell. **Tecumseh and the Dream of an American Indian Nation**. Tim Sisco, illustrator. Englewood Cliffs, NJ: Silver Burdett, 1989. 123p. $12.95; $7.95pa. ISBN 0-382-09569-3; 0-382-09758-0pa. (Biography of American Indians). 5-8

Tecumseh (1768-1813) was a bold and talented Shawnee warrior as well as a statesman and powerful speaker who cared about others. He wanted a united Indian nation in the present Midwest, and tried to use European ways to his advantage. If he had not been killed during the War of 1812, he might have been successful. Suggested Reading.

2048. Shub, Elizabeth. **Cutlass in the Snow**. Rachel Azoturia, illustrator. New York: Greenwillow, 1986. 48p. $13.93. ISBN 0-688-05928-7. 1-4

In 1797, Sam and his grandfather sail to Fire Island off Long Island, New York, to pick Christmas holly. The area has unusual land and tree formations, and rumors say that pirates have used it to hide their loot. When a snowstorm strands Sam and his grandfather on the island, they see unexplained lights in the night. The next day, they find a chest of gold coins.

2049. Shuker-Haines, Frances. **Rights and Responsibilities: Using Your Freedom**. Austin, TX: Raintree/Steck-Vaughn, 1993. 48p. $15.49. ISBN 0-8114-7355-4. (Good Citizenship). 3-6

This brief history of citizenship, including quotes from the Declaration of Independence and comments about people like John Brown, discusses the importance of being a citizen and an adult. With rights as a citizen come responsibilities to protect one's self and government. Photographs enhance the text. Further Reading, Glossary, and Index.

2050. Shumate, Jane. **Chief Gall: Sioux War Chief**. New York: Chelsea House, 1995. 118p. $18.95. ISBN 0-7910-1713-3. (North American Indians of Achievement). 5 up

Chief Gall (1840-1894), born in Dakota Territory, rose to a position of power in his tribe when U.S. officials began to pressure his people, the Hunkpapa Sioux, to let white settlers live on their lands. In 1863, he fought the U.S. Army. For the next 20 years, he continued to defend his home and culture until he had to surrender his weapons to the army during the winter of 1881. The army called him "the fighting cock of the Sioux." Photographs and reproductions enhance the text. Chronology, Further Reading, and Index.

2051. Shumate, Jane. **Sequoyah: Inventor of the Cherokee Alphabet**. New York: Chelsea House, 1994. 112p. $18.95. ISBN 0-7910-1720-6. (North American Indians of Achievement). 5 up

Sequoyah (1773?-1843) was an artist, an inventor, and a Cherokee patriot. He developed a system of writing for the Cherokee language based on syllables. He worked many years on his efforts, and eventually his people recognized his great contribution and gave him the respect he deserved. Engravings and reproductions enhance the text. Chronology, Further Reading, and Index.

2052. Shura, Mary Francis. **Gentle Annie: The True Story of a Civil War Nurse**. New York: Scholastic, 1991. 184p. $12.95; $3.50pa. ISBN 0-590-44367-4; 0-590-43500-0pa. 4-7

Annie, 16, enlists as one of 18 female volunteers from Michigan to defend the Union in the Civil War. She prepares to cook and sew but hopes to be a nurse. She is the only one who stays when the Army of the Potomac goes to battle. She becomes known for her letters and for her bravery as a nurse in almost every battle fought by this army.

2053. Shura, Mary Francis. **Kate's Book**. New York: Scholastic, 1989. 204p. $2.75pa. ISBN 0-590-42381-9pa. 3-7

When her family decides to move from Ohio to Oregon in 1843, Kate, 11, has to go although her older brother stays to study medicine. Not many of the women seemed to want to be on the trip, but they have to go with their husbands and fathers. On the long journey, Kate finds a friend, Tildy, who helps her endure the trials of the journey. Kate is lonely when Tildy and her family go in a different direction.

2054. Shura, Mary Francis. **Kate's House**. New York: Scholastic, 1990. 183p. $3.25pa. ISBN 0-590-42380-0pa. 4-7

In 1843, Kate's family arrives in Oregon. To escape the animals roaming in the night, they have to build a house as quickly as they can. They have other problems, such as Kate's friend's brother's disappearance and another dying after falling off a horse. When they find out that Kate's mother will have a baby, they start to see Oregon as a place for new life.

2055. Shuter, Jane, ed. **Charles Ball and American Slavery**. Austin, TX: Raintree/Steck-Vaughn, 1995. 48p. $15.96. ISBN 0-8114-8281-2. (History Eyewitness). 6 up

Slavery started in the Americas about 1502, when the Spanish used slaves instead of hired labor in the silver mines of Mexico and on the sugar plantations of the West Indies. While slavery declined in South America during the early seventeenth century, it began growing in North America. Charles Ball grew up in the 1790s, when most slaves lived in Maryland and Virginia, working on tobacco plantations. His owner sold him away from his family to a Georgia landowner. Ball escaped, walking back to Maryland, and reunited with his family. Eventually he was recaptured and returned to Georgia, only to escape again, going to Philadelphia via ship. Once there, he found that his family had been sold to someone in the South; he never saw any of them again. He narrated his story to an abolitionist, who published it, with its detailed description of plantation life, during the early nineteenth century. Glossary and Index.

2056. Shuter, Jane, ed. **Parkman and the Plains Indians**. Austin, TX: Raintree/Steck-Vaughn, 1995. 48p. $15.96. ISBN 0-8114-8280-4. (History Eyewitness). 5 up

Although Francis Parkman (1823-1893) went to Harvard and enjoyed chemistry and acting, he always seemed to have "Indians on the brain." In 1846, he set off on the Oregon Trail. This text is a description of the summer of 1847, when he stayed with a group of Sioux Indians. He relates many of the customs and beliefs of these Plains Indians, including their dependence on the buffalo. Although Parkman had a weakness of the nervous system and was in bed for months at a time, he kept working on his American history books throughout his life. Glossary and Index.

2057. Shuter, Jane, ed. **Sarah Royce and the American West**. Austin, TX: Raintree/Steck-Vaughn, 1996. 48p. $15.96. ISBN 0-8114-8286-3. (History Eyewitness). 5-8

In 1849, Sarah Royce traveled with her husband and daughter across the western territories. She described illnesses, high rivers, drought, and difficult mountain passes that others experienced as well as more personalized events such as a cattle stampede and an encounter with tarantulas. In California her family moved from camp to camp, living in a portable tent, as she had several more children. Photographs, Reproductions, Glossary, and Index.

2058. Siegel, Beatrice. **The Year They Walked: Rosa Parks and the Montgomery Bus Boycott**. New York: Four Winds, 1992. 103p. $13.95. ISBN 0-02-782631-7. 4-7

With photographs and maps to highlight the text, Siegel recounts the year 1956, during which the Blacks of Montgomery, Alabama, refused to ride the public buses in protest of their treatment on board. They won a public victory, but privately many of them suffered personal consequences that Siegel documents. Bibliography, Suggested Titles for Young Readers, and Index.

2059. Sills, Leslie. **Inspirations: Stories About Women Artists**. Ann Fay, illustrator. Morton Grove, IL: Albert Whitman, 1989. Unpaged. $16.95. ISBN 0-8075-4649-0. 5-8

Georgia O'Keeffe (1887-1986), Frida Kahlo (1907-1954), Alice Neel (1900-1984), and Faith Ringgold (b. 1930) have found different inspirations for their work. O'Keeffe loved nature and repeatedly painted the same subjects. Kahlo looked inward for her inspiration and painted what she thought about. Neel called herself a "collector of souls" and tried to capture the inner life of her subjects as well as the vulnerability of human nature. Ringgold tries to express the sense of community in Harlem, her relationships to other women, and life within her family.

2060. Sills, Leslie. **Visions: Stories About Women Artists**. Morton Grove, IL: Albert Whitman, 1993. 58p. $18.95. ISBN 0-8075-8491-6. 5-8

The text presents the works of and biographical information about Mary Cassatt, an American Impressionist living in Paris; Betye Saar, an African American assemblage artist; Leonora Carrington, a British surrealist painter; and Mary Frank, an American sculptor. Chapter Bibliographies.

2061. Silverman, Jerry. **Songs and Stories from the American Revolution**. Brookfield, CT: Millbrook Press, 1994. 71p. $18.90. ISBN 1-56294-429-0. 7 up

In the days of the American Revolution, balladeers sang songs and spread the music around the country. They sold broadsides with the printed words for the songs, and everyone sang those they liked best. Songs featured in the text, including the music and the stories behind them, are "The Drum," "The Wars of America," "The Sergeant," "Yankee Doodle," "Ballad of Bunker Hill," "The Riflemen of Bennington," "The Battle of Saratoga," "The Swamp Fox," "The Surrender of Cornwallis," and "In the Days of Seventy-Six." Further Reading and Index.

2062. Silverstein, Herma. **The Alamo**. New York: Dillon Press, 1992. 72p. $13.95. ISBN 0-87518-502-9. (Places in American History). 3-6

The Alamo in San Antonio, Texas, was the sight of the famous battle between the Texans and the Mexicans in 1836. The text talks about some of the people involved in the battle, such as Davey Crockett and Jim Bowie. Photographs and drawings enhance the text. Chronology and Index.

2063.   Simmons, Alex. **Ben Carson**. Austin, TX: Raintree/Steck-Vaughn, 1996. 48p. $22.83. ISBN 0-817239-75-8. (Contemporary African Americans). 4-6

Ben Carson overcame his poverty and overt racism to become a brain surgeon. He became the first to successfully separate Siamese twins joined at the head. The text looks at his life and his contributions to society. Bibliography, Chronology, Glossary, and Index.

2064.   Simon, Charnan. **Franklin Pierce**. Chicago: Childrens Press, 1988. 100p. $17.27. ISBN 0-516-01357-2. (Encyclopedia of Presidents). 4-9

As the 14th president, Franklin Pierce (1804-1869) wanted states to have more rights, with federal authority lessened. Stephen Douglas from Illinois put the idea into practice by negotiating with Kansas and Nebraska so that he could have the transcontinental railroad come through his state rather than through the South. Pierce served in the House and the Senate but loved the idea of going to war so much that he enlisted in 1846 to fight the Mexicans. He rose to the rank of general in little more than a year. On a personal level, Pierce's son died two months before Pierce took office, and the White House never had much happiness while he lived in it. Chronology of American History and Index.

2065.   Simon, Charnan. **Wilma P. Mankiller: Chief of the Cherokee**. Chicago: Childrens Press, 1991. 31p. $9.95. ISBN 0-516-04181-9. (Picture Story Biography). 2-5

Wilma Pearl Mankiller (b. 1945) became the first woman Principal Chief of the Cherokee Nation. She was an activist for Native American rights before her tribe honored her, like women in their past, with selection as its highest official. The text tells her story as a child in Oklahoma before she moved to San Francisco and as an adult preparing to lead. Photographs and drawings enhance the text. Index.

2066.   Sinnott, Susan. **Chinese Railroad Workers**. New York: Franklin Watts, 1995. 63p. $19.30. ISBN 0-531-20169-4. (First Books). 5-8

By the 1850s, people realized that finding a way to get from coast to coast other than wagon train, stagecoach, or the Isthmus of Panama was going to be important. They began planning and constructing a transcontinental railroad. Theodore Dehone Judah was the visionary who began it, but Californians who forced it through were Collis P. Huntington, Mark Hopkins, Leland Stanford, and Charles Crocker. Those who made it exist were Chinese workers who worked through some of the worst snow ever, 44 blizzards, in the Sierra Nevada winter of 1866-1867. The railroad was finished and dedicated in 1869, carrying 30,000 passengers that year. For Further Reading and Index.

2067.   Sinnott, Susan. **Extraordinary Asian Pacific Americans**. Chicago: Childrens Press, 1993. 270p. $33.80; $15.95pa. ISBN 0-516-03052-X; 0-516-43152-8pa. (Extraordinary People). 5 up

The text looks at topics and people of Asian Pacific descent who are now Americans. The 83 topics include people as well as groups of people. Brief biographies of individuals complement the lives of Gold Mountain travelers, Chinese benevolent associations, inmates in detention camps, and Korean-American grocery and convenience store businesspeople. Notes, Further Reading, and Index.

2068.   Sinnott, Susan. **Zebulon Pike**. Chicago: Childrens Press, 1990. 128p. $28.20. ISBN 0-516-03058-2. (World's Great Explorers). 5-8

Zebulon Pike (1779-1813) was an army officer who explored the upper Mississippi, the Great Plains, and the Colorado area before the War of 1812. Jefferson sent him to look for the source of the Arkansas River. When he saw Cheyenne Mountain in Colorado, he climbed it to see the beauty of the Grand Peak, which was too far to reach in the cold Rocky Mountain winter. Although he did not know, the larger peak would become known as Pikes Peak. He returned to the army and died at the Battle of York. Timeline, Glossary, Bibliography, and Index.

2069.   Sipiera, Paul P. **Gerald Ford: Thirty-Eighth President of the United States**. Chicago: Childrens Press, 1989. 100p. $19.80. ISBN 0-516-01371-8. (Encyclopedia of Presidents). 4-9

Gerald Ford (b. 1913) became President of the United States after Richard Nixon resigned on August 8, 1974, as a result of wrongdoing in the Watergate break-in before the 1972 election. Ford was not reelected to a second term. During his youth he was an Eagle Scout, a football player, and a member of the National Honor Society. He received a football scholarship to the University of Michigan, but instead of playing professional football, he decided to study law at Yale. In 1948, he was elected to Congress, and he served 25 years in that role before becoming Vice President and then President of the United States. Photographs, Chronology of American History, and Index.

2070.   Sita, Lisa. **The Rattle and the Drum: Native American Rituals and Celebrations**. Brookfield, CT: Millbrook Press, 1994. 71p. $18.40. ISBN 1-56294-420-7. 4-6

Although Native American ceremonies continue today, they are part of a tradition spanning many years. The timeless rituals and celebrations described are initiation ceremonies, such as the girls' puberty rite of the Apache and the Hamatsa Society of the Kwakiutl; Lakota sweat rituals and tobacco offerings; the Creek Green Corn dance; the Hopi Snake ceremony; Navajo chants; the Iroquois False Face Society; and powwows. Also included are descriptions of Native American crafts, games, and recipes. Glossary, For Further Reading, and Index.

2071.   Sklansky, Jeff. **James Farmer: Civil Rights Leader**. New York: Chelsea House, 1991. 112p. $18.95. ISBN 0-7910-1126-7. (Black Americans of Achievement). 5 up

James Farmer (1920-) was one of the most influential leaders in the fight against racial discrimination. He organized the first nonviolent protests after becoming a Methodist minister educated at Howard University in Washington, D.C. He formed the Congress of Racial Equality (CORE) in 1942 to end segregation in housing, restaurants, and other public facilities. He held boycotts, marches, sit-ins, jail-ins, Freedom Rides, and other demonstrations that filled the news. He has served the government and education since his departure from CORE in 1966. Photographs and reproductions enhance the text. Chronology, Further Reading, and Index.

2072.   Skurzynski, Gloria. **Good-Bye, Billy Radish**. New York: Bradbury, 1992. 137p. $15. ISBN 0-02-782921-9. New York: Aladdin, 1996. 137p. $3.99pa. ISBN 0-689-80443-1pa. 5 up

Although Billy Radish (Bazyli Radichevych) is two years older than Hank, they are best friends living in Canaan, Pennsylvania, where their fathers work in the steel mills. Because Billy is Ukrainian, the two share their cultures and a love of beauty. They go to Pittsburgh to see the Greek sculptures, and they share each others' triumphs, such as Hank's successful delivery of his sister-in-law's baby and Billy's naturalization as a U.S. citizen. What they do not expect is for Billy to get influenza in 1917 and die. *School Library Journal Best Book*, *New York Public Library's Books for the Teen Age*, and *Jefferson Cup Honor Book*.

2073.   Slavin, Ed. **Jimmy Carter**. New York: Chelsea House, 1989. 112p. $18.95. ISBN 1-55546-828-4. (World Leaders Past and Present). 5 up

Jimmy Carter (b. 1924), when president of the United States, allowed the exiled Shah of Iran into the United States for medical treatment, and Iranians took Americans as hostages. This crisis contributed to the problems that kept Carter from serving for more than one term. Before the presidency, Carter was a Georgia state senator and Georgia's governor. Some think he is an idealist who forgot the realities of the world while in office. Photographs and reproductions enhance the text. Chronology, Further Reading, and Index.

2074.   Slepian, Jan. **Risk n' Roses**. New York: Philomel, 1990. 175p. $14.95. ISBN 0-399-22219-7. 6 up

In 1948, 11-year-old Skip wants to be accepted into the family's new neighborhood. She meets Jean, who has a group of followers, and Jean accepts her into the group. Jean manipulates all of them until even Angela, Skip's retarded sister, does what she asks. Angela tells her a secret that hurts the kind man in the neighborhood who keeps searching for any family who might have survived the Nazi concentration camps in World War II. Skip must choose, and she realizes that Jean has misled them all. *Bulletin Blue Ribbon Book*.

2075.   Sloan, Frank. **Bismarck!** New York: Franklin Watts, 1991. 63p. $18.43. ISBN 0-531-20002-7. (First Books). 4-6

On June 8, 1989, the search for the *Bismarck* ended when the tiny submarine *Argo* found it under the Atlantic Ocean. The *Bismarck*, launched on February 14, 1939, was one of Hitler's U-boats pitted against the British. It was one-sixth of a mile long and suited for battle, weighing 7,000 tons more than the World War I peace treaty allowed. The text, with photographs and illustrations, talks about the building of the ship, the chase and battle with the *Hood*, and the sinking of the *Bismarck* in May 1941. Glossary, Finding Out More, and Index.

2076.   Sloate, Susan. **Amelia Earhart: Challenging the Skies**. New York: Fawcett, 1990. 118p. $3.95pa. ISBN 0-449-90396-6pa. (Great Lives). 5-8

Amelia Earhart (1897?-1937) disappeared during her attempt to fly around the world. Sloate considers the idea that the Japanese took her prisoner and that she might have lived a quiet life with another identity somewhere else. Although this idea is interesting, it is insupportable. The rest of the text sees Earhart as a woman exuding feminism and compassion while she broke records in a field considered to be reserved for men. Bibliography.

2077.   Smalls-Hector, Irene. **Irene and the Big, Fine Nickel**. Tyrone Geter, illustrator. Boston: Little, Brown, 1991. 32p. $14.95. ISBN 0-316-79871-1. K-3

Irene, seven, enjoys herself on a day in Harlem in 1957. She and her friends have a fight, climb rocks, and plant seeds for the future. Best of all, they find a nickel. They decide to purchase a raisin bun as a special treat.

2078.   Smalls-Hector, Irene. **Irene Jennie and the Christmas Masquerade**. Melodye Rosales, illustrator. Boston: Little, Brown, 1996. 32p. $15.95. ISBN 0-316-79878-9. K-3

In the slave quarters, Irene Jennie waits for the wild parade of the Knoners, known as the Johnkankus, that occurs on Christmas Day. The master, however, loans her father and mother to another plantation and almost spoils the day for her. But the excitement envelopes her and she has a special day with the music, dancing, and costumes. When her parents return early, she is especially pleased. *IRA Notable Books for a Global Society.*

2079.   Smith, Adam, and Katherine Snow Smith. **A Historical Album of Kentucky**. Brookfield, CT: Millbrook Press, 1994. 64p. $16.40; $6.95pa. ISBN 1-56294-507-6; 1-56294-850-4pa. (Historical Album). 4-8

The text presents the land of Kentucky before it became a state, beginning with Native American civilizations and continuing through exploration and settlement. Early statehood developments and issues, and the role of large cities in the state's livelihood, lead to the present day. Prints, maps, and photographs illustrate the text. Gazetteer: Quick Facts, Key Events, Personalities, and Index.

2080.   Smith, Carter, ed. **The Korean War**. Englewood Cliffs, NJ: Silver Burdett, 1990. 64p. $14.98; $7.95pa. ISBN 0-382-09953-2; 0-382-09949-4pa. (Turning Points in American History). 4-8

The text gives the background as to why the United States was involved in the Korean War and the surprise of the Chinese joining on the side of the North Koreans. It focuses on the battles and the strategy of the war, which lasted from 1950 to 1953. Photographs highlight the text. Bibliography and Index.

2081.   Smith, Carter, ed. **Presidents in a Time of Change: A Sourcebook on the U.S. Presidency**. Brookfield, CT: Millbrook Press, 1993. 96p. $18.90. ISBN 1-56294-362-6. (American Albums from the Collections of the Library of Congress). 6-9

Photographs and materials from the Library of Congress complement the text, which describes and illustrates the personal and political lives of the U.S. presidents from Harry Truman to Bill Clinton. Other presidents are Dwight Eisenhower, John F. Kennedy, Lyndon Johnson, Richard Nixon, Gerald Ford, Jimmy Carter, Ronald Reagan, and George Bush. Chronology, Notes, and Index.

2082.   Smith, Carter, ed. **Presidents of a Divided Nation: A Sourcebook on the U.S. Presidency**. Brookfield, CT: Millbrook Press, 1993. 96p. $18.90. ISBN 1-56294-360-X. (American Albums from the Collections of the Library of Congress). 6-9

Photographs and materials from the Library of Congress complement the text, which describes and illustrates the personal and political lives of the U.S. presidents during the time the nation was divided: Abraham Lincoln, Andrew Johnson, and Ulysses S. Grant. Chronology, Notes, and Index. *Notable Children's Trade Books in the Field of Social Studies.*

2083.   Smith, Carter, ed. **Presidents of a Growing Country: A Sourcebook on the U.S. Presidency**. Brookfield, CT: Millbrook Press, 1993. 96p. $18.90. ISBN 1-56294-358-8. (American Albums from the Collections of the Library of Congress). 6-9

Photographs and materials from the Library of Congress complement the text, which describes and illustrates the personal and political lives of the U.S. presidents from Rutherford Hayes to Grover Cleveland. Those in between were James Garfield and Chester Arthur. Chronology, Notes, and Index.

2084.   Smith, Carter, ed. **Presidents of a World Power: A Sourcebook on the U.S. Presidency**. Brookfield, CT: Millbrook Press, 1993. 96p. $18.90. ISBN 1-56294-361-8. (American Albums from the Collections of the Library of Congress). 6-9

Photographs and materials from the Library of Congress complement the text, which describes and illustrates the personal and political lives of the U.S. presidents from Theodore Roosevelt to Franklin Delano Roosevelt. Those in between were William Howard Taft, Woodrow Wilson, Warren Harding, Calvin Coolidge, and Herbert Hoover. Chronology, Notes, and Index.

2085.   Smith, Carter, ed. **Presidents of a Young Republic: A Sourcebook on the U.S. Presidency**. Brookfield, CT: Millbrook Press, 1993. 96p. $18.90. ISBN 1-56294-359-6. (American Albums from the Collections of the Library of Congress). 6-9

Photographs and materials from the Library of Congress complement the text, which describes and illustrates the personal and political lives of the U.S. presidents from John Quincy Adams to James Buchanan. Those in between were Andrew Jackson, Martin Van Buren, William Henry Harrison, John Tyler, James Polk, Zachary Taylor, Millard Fillmore, and Franklin Pierce. Chronology, Notes, and Index. *Notable Children's Trade Books in the Field of Social Studies.*

2086.   Smith, Elizabeth Simpson. **Coming Out Right: The Story of Jacqueline Cochran, the First Woman Aviator to Break the Sound Barrier**. New York: Walker, 1991. 114p. $14.95. ISBN 0-8027-6988-8. 5-8

Jacqueline Cochran (d. 1980) overcame a childhood of poverty in a foster home to become the first woman pilot to break the sound barrier after learning to pilot a plane in less than three weeks. At her death, she held more speed, altitude, and distance records than any pilot in history. In World War II, she headed WASP (the Women's Airforce Service Pilots), and she earned the Distinguished Service Medal and the Distinguished Flying Cross. In her later years, she owned a cosmetic company and was named American Business Woman of the Year. Appendices and Index.

2087.   Smith-Baranzini, Marlene, and Howard Egger-Bovet. **Book of the American Indians**. T. Taylor Bruce, illustrator. Boston: Little, Brown, 1994. 96p. $10.95pa. ISBN 0-316-22208-9pa. (Brown Paper School USKids History). 4-6

Before the arrival of the Europeans, North American Indian tribes had developed their beliefs. The text presents these beliefs by telling a myth indigenous to the tribe and describing ceremonies, games, and daily life that come from the myth and the tribe. Additional suggestions about items to make and how to make them enliven the text. General groups included are the people of the Northwest, the people of California, the people of the Southwest, the people of the Great Basin, the people of the Plains, the people of the Northeast, and the people of the Southeast. If You Want to Know More and Index.

2088.   Smith-Baranzini, Marlene, and Howard Egger-Bovet. **USKids History: Book of the New American Nation**. T. Taylor Bruce, illustrator. Covelo, CA: Yolla Bolly Press; Little, Brown, 1995. 94p. $21.95; $12.95pa. ISBN 0-316-96923-0; 0-316-2206-2pa. (Brown Paper School). 5-7

The text covers the beginning of the American nation. Among the topics are building a flatboat, playing a cabinet game, a dance, the first inauguration, America's "first granddaughter," Benjamin Banneker, the Louisiana Purchase, the burning of the Capitol, the Erie Canal, frontier towns, prairie schools, the cotton gin, mill girls, and Texas. If You Want to Know More and Index.

2089.   Smothers, Ethel Footman. **Down in the Piney Woods**. New York: Knopf, 1992. 151p. $14.99; $3.99pa. ISBN 0-679-90360-7; 0-679-84714-6pa. 5-9

Annie Rye, 10, loves her Georgia summers with her grandfather. In the 1950s, she is surprised by having to share her experiences of the rolling store and going possum hunting with half-sisters. She also has to adjust to a little white girl who visits and to finding rattlesnakes in the house that have to be smoked out.

2090.   Smothers, Ethel Footman. **Moriah's Pond**. New York: Knopf, 1995. 111p. $14. ISBN 0-679-84504-6. 4-6

In this sequel to *Down in the Piney Woods*, Annie, 10, in rural Georgia during the 1950s, sees her sister have to take the blame for something that a white girl does. Annie is angry, but her uncle helps her see that other attitudes are better. Annie's sisters disobey their great-grandmother Moriah and swim in a contaminated pond. When they confess, the doctor is able to treat their temporary blindness, but one has permanent scarring.

2091.   Smucker, Anna Egan. **No Star Nights**. Steve Johnson, illustrator. New York: Knopf, 1989. 48p. $12.95. ISBN 0-394-99925-8. K-2

When the narrator was a child living in the coal mine area of Pennsylvania, she remembers the red fires lighting the skies and the days while her father slept after working the night shift. She also loved going to baseball games with him in Pittsburgh. She remembers her school and her Catholic teachers with their habit collars still white in the smoky air, the holidays, and playing games with other children in the streets. *IRA Children's Book Award* and *American Library Association Notable Books for Children*.

2092.   Smucker, Barbara. **Incredible Jumbo**. New York: Viking, 1991. 177p. $12.95. ISBN 0-670-82970-6. 4-6

In 1865, Tod, 10, gets a job as assistant elephant keeper at the London Zoo. He becomes attached to Jumbo, but P. T. Barnum purchases Jumbo to take to America as a performer in his circus. Tod stows away so that he can follow Jumbo to the United States.

2093.   Smucker, Barbara. **Runaway to Freedom**. 1977. Magnolia, MA: Peter Smith, 1992. 154p. $17.55. ISBN 0-8446-6585-1. New York: Trophy, 1979. $4.50pa. ISBN 0-06-440106-5pa. 4-8

Julilly, 12, travels from Virginia to Mississippi after being sold and separated from her mother. The overseer on the journey whips the slaves without provocation. After they arrive at the new plantation, Julilly meets a white man who has come from Canada, and he leads her and three other slaves north to Canada. *IRA Children's Choices* and *Notable Children's Trade Books in the Field of Social Studies*.

2094.   Sneve, Virginia Driving Hawk. **The Cherokees**. Ronald Himler, illustrator. New York: Holiday House, 1996. 32p. $15.95. ISBN 0-8234-1214-8. (First Americans Book) 3-6

The Cherokees lived peacefully in the eastern states until President Andrew Jackson heard that their land might have gold on it. He decided that the Cherokees would walk to new land in Oklahoma. Famous leaders include John Ross, Sequoyah, Tsali, and Wilma Mankiller. The text recounts their creation myth and their history. Notes and Index.

2095.   Sneve, Virginia Driving Hawk. **The Cheyennes**. Ronald Himler, illustrator. New York: Holiday House, 1996. 32p. $15.95. ISBN 0-8234-1250-4. (First Americans Book). 1-4

In this text on the Cheyennes, Sneve covers cultural background and historical moments as she looks at the groups of men, women, and children in the tribe and the locations in which they lived. She includes the traits that make the Cheyenne unique from other tribes. Maps and Index.

2096.   Sneve, Virginia Driving Hawk. **The Hopis**. Ronald Himler, illustrator. New York: Holiday House, 1995. 32p. $15.95. ISBN 0-8234-1194-X. (First Americans Book). 3-6

Even though the U.S. government drove the Hopis to a reservation in 1882, the Hopis have kept their tribal traditions and beliefs. They have always believed that they must take care of the Earth and keep their ceremonies for all humans. They live on the First Mesa, Second Mesa, and Third Mesa in Arizona, and their arts and crafts appear worldwide. The text recounts their creation myth and their history. Index. *Notable Children's Trade Books in the Field of Social Studies*.

2097.   Sneve, Virginia Driving Hawk. **The Iroquois**. Ronald Himler, illustrator. New York: Holiday House, 1995. 32p. $15.95. ISBN 0-8234-1163-X. (First Americans Book). 3-6

The Iroquois, or *Haudenosaunee*, "those who build the longhouse," lived in New York State. Their Algonquian enemy may have given them the name of *Iroquois*, but the French adopted it in the 1600s. Between the 1400s and the 1600s, the five Iroquois tribes formed a league, or confederacy, which the Tuscarora later joined. They were warriors, hunters, craftsmen, and fishermen who played lacrosse. The women were the heads of the families and clans, with the heritage of the tribe traced through them. After the Revolutionary War, the government moved them further west and north. The text recounts their creation myth and their history. Index.

2098.   Sneve, Virginia Driving Hawk. **The Navajos**. Ronald Himler, illustrator. New York: Holiday House, 1993. 32p. $15.95. ISBN 0-8234-1039-0. (First Americans Book). 3-6

First the Utes and then the Pueblos affected the Navajo or *Dinhe* way of life. By the 1600s, the Spanish settlers took territory, and then the U.S. Army arrived in the nineteenth century. It walked the Navajos first to Fort Sumner, New Mexico, in 1863. In 1868, it permitted them to return to their former homeland, turned into a reservation, covering the corner where Utah, Arizona, and New Mexico meet. The text recounts their creation myth and their history. Index.

2099.   Sneve, Virginia Driving Hawk. **The Nez Percé**. Ronald Himler, illustrator. New York: Holiday House, 1993. 32p. $15.95. ISBN 0-8234-1090-0. (First Americans Book). 3-6

The Nez Percé, or "pierced nose," originally called themselves the "Chopunnish" or "Nimipu," the "real people." They lived in the mountains of western states with their villages spread over the area so that everyone would have plenty of animals to hunt and fish to catch. White settlers bringing diseases with them infected the Nez Percé with smallpox and measles, killing many. In 1877, the U.S. government forced them to Idaho, where most live today. The text recounts their creation myth and their history. Index.

2100.   Sneve, Virginia Driving Hawk. **The Seminoles**. Ronald Himler, illustrator. New York: Holiday House, 1994. 32p. $15.95. ISBN 0-8234-1112-5. (First Americans Book). 3-5

A group split from the Muskogee tribe in Georgia and Alabama in 1708, when the whites came, and went to Florida. The Seminoles, or "separatists," were Spanish citizens who owned their own slaves and offered protection to slaves running away from cruel Georgian masters. Because the Seminoles fought on the British side in the Revolutionary War, Andrew Jackson raided their villages during the War of 1812 and burned them. The First Seminole War lasted until 1819. The Second Seminole War occurred when the tribe refused to go to Oklahoma at the bidding of the 1828 Indian Removal Act. Two important leaders were Osceola and Coacoochee, and they led the Seminoles into the Everglades area. Bobek, or Billy Bowlegs, steered them through the Third Seminole War in 1855 against white settlers. Also incorporated are segments on daily life and ways of celebrating special occasions in the Seminole culture. Index.

2101. Sneve, Virginia Driving Hawk. **The Sioux**. Ronald Himler, illustrator. New York: Holiday House, 1993. 32p. $15.95. ISBN 0-8234-1017-X. (First Americans Book). 3-6

The text looks at the history, traditions, social structure, importance of the buffalo, and contemporary life in the Sioux tribe with its three divisions of the Dakota, the Lakota, and the Nakota. The Sioux used to live on the northern Great Plains and the western prairies, but in 1867 they agreed to a treaty that limited them to a reservation in North and South Dakota. When people discovered gold in the Black Hills, Sitting Bull, Red Cloud, and Crazy Horse resisted. In 1890, 200 Sioux died at Wounded Knee. Index.

2102. Snyder, Zilpha Keatley. **And Condors Danced**. New York: Delacorte, 1987. 216p. $14.95; $3.50pa. ISBN 0-385-29575-8; 0-440-40153-4pa. 4-7

Carly keeps a journal when she is 11 in California in 1907. In it she tells of the feud between her family and the wealthy Mr. Quigley. She worries about her invalid mother and the two people who look after her, her great-aunt Mehitabel and her servant Woo Ying. She also has to cope with a young Quigley who attends school with her. When her mother dies and she loses her favorite dog, her aunt and Woo Ying give her emotional support.

2103. Snyder, Zilpha Keatley. **Cat Running**. New York: Delacorte, 1994. 168p. $14.95. ISBN 0-385-31056-0. 5-8

Sixth-grader Cat, the fastest runner in her school, refuses to participate in the school's Play Day races during the Depression years because her father will not let her wear slacks like the other girls. She finds refuge in her secret spot by the river in California's Central Valley, where she hides her favorite things. When she goes there, she finds Sammy has invaded. Sammy, a young Okie girl with nothing of her own, has fallen in love with Cat's doll. Sammy's brother Zane wins a race in Cat's absence, and Cat struggles with disliking him and wanting to help Sammy. When Sammy catches pneumonia and nearly dies, Cat behaves honorably with Sammy's deprived family.

2104. Sonder, Ben. **The Tenement Writer: An Immigrant's Story**. Meryl Rossne, illustrator. Austin, TX: Raintree/Steck-Vaughn, 1993. 72p. $15.49. ISBN 0-8114-7235-3. (Stories of America—Personal Challenge). 5-9

Around 1890, Anzia Yezierska (1880?-1970) and her family arrived in New York from Poland to join her brother, renamed "Mayer." Taking the name Hattie Mayer, Anzia had to adjust to a new life in a tenement, safer than Poland but drearier. After she had worked for a long time and attended school, she began to write about the life of an immigrant who hated being poor. By the 1920s, she had become a well-known American immigrant writer. Epilogue, Afterword, and Notes.

2105. Sonneborn, Liz. **Will Rogers: Cherokee Entertainer**. New York: Chelsea House, 1993. 110p. $18.95; $7.95pa. ISBN 0-7910-1719-2; 0-7910-1988-8pa. (North American Indians of Achievement). 5 up

Will Rogers (1879-1935), born in Indian Territory (now the state of Oklahoma), was part Cherokee. He liked riding and roping as a youth and became a great lariat artist. He was also one of the most popular entertainers in the early twentieth century with his lariat and his humor. He said "I never met a man I didn't like." He lampooned the follies of the wealthy and powerful while showing concern for the rights of ordinary humans. Photographs enhance the text. Chronology, Further Reading, and Index.

2106. Sorensen, Henri, author/illustrator. **New Hope**. New York: Lothrop, Lee & Shepard, 1995. Unpaged. $15. ISBN 0-688-13925-6. 1-4

Jimmy's grandfather tells him the story of Lars Jensen, the Danish immigrant who founded his town of New Hope. When his axle broke, he and his family settled on the nearby riverbank. The next spring, he built a small ferry and transported settlers across the river. Then a blacksmith set up a forge. Others moved into the area, and Lars managed a general store that stocked goods that they all needed. Best of all, Lars is one of Jimmy's relatives. *Notable Children's Trade Books in the Field of Social Studies.*

2107. Speaker-Yuan, Margaret. **Agnes de Mille: Choreographer**. New York: Chelsea House, 1988. 112p. $18.95. ISBN 1-55546- 648-6. (American Women of Achievement). 5 up

Agnes de Mille (b. 1905) helped change American dance with her uniquely American dance patterns and rhythms. Her first success was *Rodeo*, presented in 1942. The next year, her choreography for *Oklahoma* delighted viewers. In the 1950s, she organized a dance troupe to introduce ballet to Americans around the country. She wanted to have a family and a career, and she did both. Photographs enhance the text. Chronology, Further Reading, and Index.

2108. Speare, Elizabeth George. **The Sign of the Beaver**. Boston: Houghton Mifflin, 1983. 144p. $14.95. ISBN 0-395-33890-5. New York: Bantam, 1995. 144p. $1.99pa. ISBN 0-440-21623-0pa. 4-7

Matt and his father go to Maine to build a new house in 1768. Matt's father has to leave him alone while he returns to Massachusetts for the rest of the family after the home is ready. Someone visits and steals Matt's gun, but his worst moment comes when bees sting him so badly that he loses consciousness. An Indian boy nearby hears him screaming and comes to nurse him back to health. Matt begins teaching the boy to read, and the boy teaches Matt how to trap, fish, and find trails. *Newbery Honor, Child Study Children's Book Committee and Bank Street College Award, Christopher Award, American Library Association Notable Books for Children, School Library Journal Best Book,* and *Scott O'Dell Award.*

2109. Speare, Elizabeth George. **The Witch of Blackbird Pond**. Boston: Houghton Mifflin, 1958. 256p. ISBN 0-395-07114-3. New York: Laurel, 1993. 256p. $4.99pa. ISBN 0-440-99577-9pa. 5 up

When Kit's grandfather dies in 1687, she has to leave Barbados and go to New England to live with her only relative, her deceased mother's sister. The bleak life with no entertainment or color depresses her, and she cannot adjust. A Quaker woman nearby, whom others in the community call a witch, helps her endure the agony. The people also decide that Kit is a witch when she tries to teach a child to read, and they try her in court. When the child reads for the court, the people can no longer condemn Kit. *Newbery Medal* and *International Board of Books for Young People*.

2110. Spedden, Daisy Corning Stone. **Polar the Titanic Bear**. Laurie McGaw, illustrator. Boston: Little, Brown, 1994. 64p. $16.95. ISBN 0-316-80625-0. 2 up

The story of Polar, a toy bear belonging to a little boy who survives the *Titanic* sinking in 1912, reveals the life of a wealthy family of the era that traveled to different homes and different parts of the world. Polar belongs to Douglas, six, and Douglas leaves Polar behind on the lifeboat when he is rescued. A sailor finds Polar and re-unites him with his master. Accompanying the text and illustrations are photographs of the family in places throughout the world, some of them including Polar, a Steiff toy.

2111. Spencer, Eve. **A Flag for Our Country**. Mike Eagle, illustrator. Austin, TX: Raintree/Steck-Vaughn, 1993. 32p. $13.98. ISBN 0-8114-7211-6. (Stories of America—Holidays). 2-5

In 1776, Betsy Ross continued to work in her shop making clothes in Philadelphia although her husband had recently died. According to a family story, George Washington saw her through the window and asked her to make a flag for the new country. He had a design, but she suggested the five-point stars placed in a circle. No proof exists that this actually happened, but none exists that it did not happen either. Flag Day.

2112. Spinka, Penina Keen. **White Hare's Horses**. New York: Atheneum, 1991. 154p. $12.95. ISBN 0-689-31654-2. 6-8

In 1522, the Aztecs threaten the calm of the Chumash village in the area now known as southern California. White Hare, 13, knows that the Aztecs are preparing for war and that they will offer human sacrifices. To stop their plan, White Hare frees their horses by imitating a frightened colt. Without horses, the Aztecs no longer have an advantage, and the Chumash drive them from the village.

2113. St. George, Judith. **Dear Dr. Bell . . . Your Friend, Helen Keller**. New York: Putnam, 1992. 95p. $15.95. ISBN 0-399-22337-1. 5-9

When Helen Keller (1880-1968) and her father met Alexander Graham Bell, the inventor of the telephone and a teacher of the deaf, her life changed. Bell recommended a teacher for her, Anne Sullivan, and Keller, after being deaf and blind from disease since she was 19 months old, learned to read and write because of her. Keller wrote one of her first letters to Bell, and they corresponded until he died. He advised her and encouraged her to speak about issues of importance to give a sense of accomplishment and bravery to others with disabilities. The text recounts their friendship. Photographs, Bibliography, and Index.

2114. St. George, Judith. **Mason and Dixon's Line of Fire**. New York: Putnam, 1991. 128p. $16.95. ISBN 0-399-22240-5. 4-8

Two English scientists came to America in 1763 to survey the line between Maryland and Pennsylvania. Trouble had already flared on that border before they arrived, and it continued after they left. Among those who fought along the line were William Penn, Lord Baltimore, George Washington, Chief Pontiac, Lafayette, Harriet Tubman, John Brown, Robert E. Lee, and Abraham Lincoln. Others included settlers, riverboat men, slaves, foot soldiers, and frontiersmen. The Line serves now as a landmark that signifies the growing pains of the nation with its bitter divisions. The text gives a history of the altercations along this boundary. Photographs, Bibliography, and Index.

2115. St. George, Judith. **Panama Canal: Gateway to the World**. New York: Putnam, 1989. 159p. $16.95. ISBN 0-399-21637-5. 5 up

The construction of the Panama Canal began in 1904. Unfortunately, it was not a simple cutting through of the isthmus from one side to the other. It took 10 years of transforming a swamp, a jungle, and mountain ranges to create the 50-mile-long waterway. It was the biggest human-made lake in the world and the longest earthen dam ever built. Part of the problem in the construction was the personalities of the men behind it, such as Teddy Roosevelt, William Howard Taft, William Gorgas, and three chief engineers—indecisive John Wallace, frontiers-man John Stevens, and professional George Goethals. The text, with photographs, tells the story of this difficult task. Bibliography and Index.

2116. St. George, Judith. **To See with the Heart: The Life of Sitting Bull**. New York: Putnam, 1990. 182p. $17.95. ISBN 0-399-22930-2. 5-9

Sitting Bull (1834?-1890), the leader of the Hunkpapa Sioux, tried to preserve his tribe's hunting grounds, but he was unsuccessful. His attempts to protect his people from the army representing the federal government led to a victory against Custer at the Little Bighorn as well as his own death under unexplained circumstances. The text looks at his life, the stresses among the tribal members, and the government's policies during his leadership.

2117. St. George, Judith. **The White House: Cornerstone of a Nation**. New York: Putnam, 1990. 160p. $15.95. ISBN 0-399-22186-7. 6 up

The text gives an anecdotal history of the White House, emphasizing times when history influenced the building. Statements from presidents, presidents' wives, servants, and architects tell about the construction, re-construction, and remodeling of the White House. Additional anecdotes include information about guests' re-quests and varied influences on the presidents who have resided there, such as the media or specific crises. Photographs, Bibliography, and Index.

2118. St. Pierre, Stephanie. **Our National Anthem**. Brookfield, CT: Millbrook Press, 1992. 48p. $12.90. ISBN 1-56294-106-2. (I Know America). 3-6

During the War of 1812, Francis Scott Key became stranded on a ship in Baltimore Harbor near the battle against the British. When he awoke the next morning and saw the American flag still flying, he wrote a poem. This poem became "The Star Spangled Banner," the national anthem. The text presents other information about the history and significance of this song and other patriotic songs. Photographs and drawings enhance the text. Glossary and Index.

2119. Stacey, Tom. **The Titanic**. Maurie Manning and Michael Spackman, illustrators. San Diego, CA: Lucent, 1990. 64p. $22.95. ISBN 1-56006-006-9. (World Disasters). 5-7

The *Titanic* was advertised as the ship that could not sink, but a few days into its maiden voyage, on April 14, 1914, icebergs sank it. The text recounts the story as it has been pieced together by rescue teams and survi-vors. In 1985, Robert Ballard and his submarine *Jason* discovered the wreckage of the *Titanic*, thereby allow-ing new information to become available. Diagrams and drawings augment the text. Further Reading, Glossary, Other Works, and Index.

2120. Stafford, Mark. **W. E. B. Du Bois: Scholar and Activist**. New York: Chelsea House, 1989. 127p. $18.95; $7.95pa. ISBN 1-55546-587-0; 0-7910-0238-1pa. (Black Americans of Achievement). 5 up

W. E. B. Du Bois (1868-1963) had degrees from Fisk and Harvard and studied at the University of Berlin in Germany. At 26, as a college professor, he began publishing a series of sociological studies on Black life. In *The Souls of Black Folk*, he attacked Booker T. Washington's position that Blacks should wait until their eco-nomic status rose before they began to seek equality. He cofounded the National Association for the Advance-ment of Colored People (NAACP). In 1961, he went to live in Africa because of his dissatisfaction with American society. Photographs enhance the text. Chronology, Further Reading, and Index.

2121. Stallones, Jared. **Zebulon Pike and the Explorers of the American Southwest**. New York: Chelsea House, 1991. $19.95. ISBN 0-7910-1317-0. (World Explorers). 5 up

Zebulon Pike (1779-1813) was sent to conduct a geographic survey of the Arkansas and Red Rivers. However, his boss, an army general and a double agent for Spain, may have directed his men into the Rocky Mountains during the winter so that he would not succeed. Pike's group finally reached the Rio Grande River, which Spain claimed, and Pike supposedly said, "What? Is this not the Red River?" Pike most likely conducted a secret surveillance of the Spanish, which may have been the real intent of his journey. Photographs and illus-trations enhance the text. Chronology, Further Reading, and Index.

2122. Stamper, Judith Bauer. **New Friends in a New Land: A Thanksgiving Story**. Chet Jezierski, illustrator. Austin, TX: Raintree/Steck-Vaughn, 1993. 32p. $13.98. ISBN 0-8114-7213-2. (Stories of America—Holidays). 2-5

In 1621, Damaris Hopkins and her family had sailed on the *Mayflower* to the colonies. Among the sur-prises she had were seeing three Indians try to establish friendships with the settlers at different times. She saw Samoset and Squanto, who spoke English, and Massasoit, who brought his tribespeople to celebrate the first Thanksgiving with Damaris and her neighbors.

2123. Stamper, Judith Bauer. **Save the Everglades**. Allen Davis, illustrator. Austin, TX: Raintree/Steck-Vaughn, 1993. 58p. $14.95. ISBN 0-8114-7219-1. (Stories of America—Working Together). 5-9

By 1969, the U.S. government had decided to build a huge jetport near Miami, Florida, which would de-stroy much of the wetlands of the Big Cypress Swamp near the Everglades. Joe Browder and Marjory Douglas fought together to keep the wetlands. Disagreement in Washington led President Nixon to send an emissary to the area. Julie Nixon realized that the loss of this area would be a loss for the nation and supported the Browder and Douglas dissent. Epilogue, Afterword, and Notes.

2124.   Standiford, Natalie. **The Bravest Dog Ever: The True Story of Balto**. Donald Cook, illustrator. New York: Random House, 1989. 47p. ISBN 0-394-99695-X; 0-394-89695-5pa. (Step into Reading). 1-3

In 1925, two children lay sick in Nome, Alaska. To bring serum to save their lives, a train rushed from Anchorage, Alaska, but a blizzard stopped it 700 miles away. Teams of sled dogs and their drivers decided to form a relay. Balto was the lead dog on the next to the last team. When his team got to the last stop, no one was there, and his team had to continue. They reached Nome in five-and-a-half days instead of the anticipated 15, after traveling for 20 hours nonstop. The team driver gave all the credit to Balto because he said he could not see in the blizzard, and only Balto could have gotten them back to Nome.

2125.   Stanley, Diane. **Saving Sweetness**. G. Brian Karas, illustrator. New York: Putnam, 1996. Unpaged. $15.95. ISBN 0-399-22645-1. K-3

Sweetness, the smallest orphan at Mrs. Sump's house, escapes, and the sheriff tries to save her from the horrors of the desert. However, when the sheriff is thirsty, Sweetness appears with water. When he is cold, she builds the fire and brings marshmallows. And when Coyote Pete tries to kill him, she holds a boulder over Coyote Pete's head. Sweetness refuses to return to the orphanage until the sheriff tells how he will save her "fer good." *School Library Journal Best Book*.

2126.   Stanley, Diane, author/illustrator. **The True Adventure of Daniel Hall**. New York: Dial Press, 1995. Unpaged. $15.95. ISBN 0-8037-1469-6. 3-6

Daniel Hall set sail in 1856 at the age of 14 on a whaling ship bound for the Arctic waters. He expected the bad weather, food, and difficulties of whale hunting, but not a moody captain who was also violent. Daniel stayed for two years and finally deserted the ship on the Siberian coast along with another boy named Elias. They had to survive hunger, bitter cold, and wild animals who saw them as food. When spring finally came, they went to the bay where they had come ashore, and a boat immediately responded to their calls. Daniel discovered that his father had sent a message to all whaling ships to look for the two boys on the coast. Daniel was gone for five years. When he returned, he was welcomed, while the captain who had abused him was brought to trial. *Notable Children's Trade Books in the Field of Social Studies*.

2127.   Stanley, Jerry. **Big Annie of Calumet: A True Story of the Industrial Revolution**. New York: Crown, 1996. 102p. $18. ISBN 0-517-70097-2. 5-8

In 1913, the copper miners working for Michigan's Calumet and Hecla Mining Company decided to strike for a shorter workday and safer working conditions. The woman who led their marches every morning for a year was a Croatian miner's wife, Annie Clemenc, who at 6'2" became a media attraction. She realized that families should help their husbands and fathers, and their participation might get the concessions that the strike wanted. The text looks at her contribution to the strike and presents the events that comprised the strike, including a stampede, probably started by company supporters, that caused the deaths of many children. Photographs and Index.

2128.   Stanley, Jerry. **Children of the Dust Bowl: The True Story of the School at Weedpatch Camp**. New York: Crown, 1992. 85p. $15. ISBN 0-517-57821-5. 6 up

Migrant workers who traveled from the Dust Bowl to California during the Depression were forced to live in federal labor camps. A school established in a camp helped the children. Photographs and maps augment the text, which talks about the situation in the camp. Index.

2129.   Stanley, Jerry. **I Am an American: A True Story of Japanese Internment**. New York: Crown, 1994. 102p. ISBN 0-517-59786-1. 5-10

When the Japanese bombed Pearl Harbor on December 7, 1941, the Japanese Americans who lived in the United States immediately attracted suspicion as possible Japanese spies. These Californians were taken from their homes and businesses and placed into internment camps where they lived through the war. The text looks at these 10 camps and what happened to the people who had neither home nor work after they were released. Photographs, Bibliographic Note, and Index.

2130.   Steedman, Scott. **A Frontier Fort on the Oregon Trail**. Mark Bergin, illustrator. New York: Peter Bedrick, 1993. 48p. $18.95; $9.95pa. ISBN 0-87226-371-1; 0-87226-264-2pa. 5 up

Settlers, prospectors, and soldiers met in the western frontier forts because they were places in which to fend off tribal attacks. The text, with many illustrations, looks at life in these forts. Two-page spreads present such topics as the first forts, the Oregon Trail, the site for a fort, building the fort, inside the fort, feeding the troops, a soldier's day, fur and gold traders, Plains Indians, trappers and traders, a pioneer cabin, a woman's day, the railway, Indian wars, and famous folk on the frontier. Glossary and Index.

2131. Steele, Philip. **Censorship**. New York: New Discovery, 1992. 48p. ISBN 0-02-735404-0. (Past and Present). 5-7

The text looks at the history of censorship, including the Chinese emperor who burned books in 213 BC, Roman censors, religion and the printing press, revolution, and private censorship. It examines the reasons stated for censorship and assesses freedom or control as a motive. Key Dates, Glossary, and Index.

2132. Steele, Philip. **Kidnapping**. New York: Discovery, Macmillan, 1992. 48p. ISBN 0-02-735403-2. (Past and Present). 5-7

The text looks at the history of kidnapping, including the hostages of Greeks and Romans, Joseph in the Bible, the Children's Crusade, and the ransoms for kings. It tries to account for the reasons behind kidnappings and abductions and ways to overcome or avoid them. Key Dates, Glossary, and Index.

2133. Steele, Philip. **Little Bighorn**. Richard Hook, illustrator. New York: New Discovery, 1992. 32p. ISBN 0-02-786885-0. (Great Battle and Sieges). 5 up

Plains wars in America began in 1854 and did not end until 1890. On June 25, 1876, Lieutenant Colonel George Armstrong Custer challenged the Cheyenne and Sioux Nations. Under Sitting Bull, they crushed him. The text covers events that led to the battle, including white settlers taking Native American lands. It looks at the weapons, the enemies, and the land on which the battle took place. It also tells about Ghost Dancers, who believed that their dances would cause warriors to rise from the dead, the Bluecoats (army) to disappear, and the buffalo to return. At Wounded Knee in 1890, they found that this was not true. Glossary, Further Reading, and Index.

2134. Steele, William O. **The Buffalo Knife**. Magnolia, MA: Peter Smith, 1992. 123p. $16.50. ISBN 0-8446-6505-3. San Diego, CA: Harcourt Brace, 1990. 123p. $3.95pa. ISBN 0-15-213212-0pa. 3-7

In 1782, nine-year-old Andy's uncle gives him a knife to mark the beginning of the family's flatboat journey down the Tennessee River. After whitewater rapids and Chickamauga Indian attacks, they reach the end of the journey. Andy cannot find the knife when they arrive. He feels bad for his carelessness, but his uncle arrives and tells him what happened to it.

2135. Steele, William O. **Flaming Arrows**. Paul Galdone, illustrator. 1958. Magnolia, MA: Peter Smith, 1992. 146p. $17. ISBN 0-8446-6506-1. San Diego, CA: Harcourt Brace, 1990. 146p. $3.95pa. ISBN 0-15-228427-3pa. 3-7

When the Chickamaugas raid Cumberland in 1784, Chad, 11, and other settlers go to the nearby fort for protection. People inside accuse one boy's father of betraying them to the Indians, but that boy risks his life for those inside the fort during the ensuing battle.

2136. Steele, William O. **The Lone Hunt**. Paul Galdone, illustrator. San Diego, CA: Harcourt Brace, 1957. 175p. ISBN 0-15-652983-1. $1.75pa. 3-7

In 1810, Yance, 11, finds buffalo tracks in the Cumberland Mountains. He knows that others will reach the buffalo before he has a chance, but he goes on the hunt anyway. He uses almost all his bullets before he sees a buffalo, and after he shoots it, a Cherokee helps him save his kill while he returns home for help.

2137. Steele, William O. **The Magic Amulet**. San Diego, CA: Harcourt Brace, 1976. 114p. $6.95. ISBN 0-15-250427-3. 3-7

In prehistoric times, Tragg's family abandons him because his wounded leg keeps him from walking fast enough while they are hunting mastodons and mammoths. As he watches an armadillo defend itself from a wolf, he realizes that he can defend himself as well. He joins another tribe, and they fully accept him when he leads them to food that he has previously found. They think Tragg's amulet has protected him.

2138. Steele, William O. **The Man with the Silver Eyes**. San Diego, CA: Harcourt Brace, 1976. 147p. $5.95. ISBN 0-15-251720-0. 4-7

Talatu, 11, hates to leave his home to go with the pale-eyed Quaker Shinn in 1780. Talatu thinks that the man must need him as a guide. When Cherokees capture Shinn, Talatu asks them, in Cherokee, to kill Shinn, but they respect Talatu's uncle and think that he must have a good reason for sending the two into enemy territory. During the winter with Shinn, Talatu gets smallpox, and Shinn saves him. Another man tries to kill the Quaker. As he dies, Shinn tells Talatu that he is his father. Talatu realizes that Shinn understood his request that the Cherokees kill him, and he begins to miss being with Shinn more than he could have imagined.

2139. Steele, William O. **The Perilous Road**. 1958. Magnolia, MA: Peter Smith, 1991. 156p. $16.50. ISBN 0-8446-6507-X. San Diego, CA: Harcourt Brace, 1990. 156p. $4.95pa. ISBN 0-15-260647-5pa. 3-7

The Union troops take all of Chris's family's food, which it has carefully stored in the winter during the Civil War. At 11, Chris decides that he will support the Rebels. But his brother joins the Union army in 1863 without telling Chris. Before Chris knows, he almost gets his brother killed by telling the Rebels that a federal wagon train has moved into the region. *Newbery Honor* and *Jane Addams Book Award*.

2140. Steele, William O. **Tomahawk Border**. Charles Beck, illustrator. San Diego, CA: Harcourt Brace, 1965. 120p. $3.95. ISBN 0-03-058050-1. 3-7

In 1716, Dalk tries to be a ranger on the Virginia border. He stops a Seneca Indian from crossing the border, and he takes an Indian captive to Williamsburg. What he and a friend discover is that one of the rangers is betraying the friendly Indians and causing much unnecessary conflict.

2141. Steele, William O. **Trail Through Danger**. Charles Beck, illustrator. San Diego, CA: Harcourt Brace, 1964. 186p. $4.95. ISBN 0-15-289661-9. 3-7

In 1775, Lafe Birdwell, 11, hires himself to Mr. Gibbs to hunt buffalo on the other side of the Carolina mountains. Of the men in the group, Lafe likes only Rice, and when he sees the other men trying to kill Rice, he becomes furious. The group collects many buffalo skins, but the Cherokees come and take everything because they have been hunting illegally on Cherokee lands. Rice advises Lafe to return to his father and forget that Lafe's father shamed Lafe by selling guns to the Shawnee.

2142. Steele, William O. **Wayah of the Real People**. Isa Barnett, illustrator. New York: Henry Holt, 1964. $3.95. ISBN 0-03-045220-1. 5-9

Wayah, 11, leaves his Cherokee home for Williamsburg to attend school in 1752. The customs and the buildings of the white people surprise him in many ways. He has never seen steps, and the bell frightens him. He thinks the piano has teeth. When he returns home, he has to use his knowledge and become a translator between the whites and the Cherokee in an attempt to keep peace.

2143. Steele, William O. **Wilderness Journey**. Paul Galdone, illustrator. San Diego, CA: Harcourt Brace, 1953. $6.75. ISBN 0-15-297318-4. 3-7

Flan's family leaves for Kentucky in 1782, but Flan, 10, remains behind to recover from an illness. After he recuperates, he goes with Chap to Kentucky, but without a gun to shoot, he feels useless. Chap teaches him how to shoot and how to survive when they escape from attacking Indians and save a trader. Flan also has to nurse Chap back to health after a fever, and they ride a raft on a swirling river. When he reaches his family, he has developed new confidence.

2144. Steele, William O. **Winter Danger**. Paul Galdone, illustrator. 1954. Magnolia, MA: Peter Smith, 1992. 131p. $16.50. ISBN 0-8446-6508-8. San Diego, CA: Harcourt Brace, 1990. 131p. $3.95pa. ISBN 0-685-51103-0pa. 3-7

After Caje's mother dies in the 1780s, his father takes him to his mother's sister's home for the winter. Caje, 11, worries about the family's meager food supply and decides to leave so he will not burden them further. He happens to see a bear hibernating, and he kills it and brings the carcass back to the house so they can have food for the rest of the winter.

2145. Steen, Sandra, and Susan Steen. **Colonial Williamsburg**. New York: Dillon Press, 1993. 71p. $14.95. ISBN 0-87518-546-0. (Places in American History). 3-6

Colonial Williamsburg has been preserved so that it gives tourists a view of history as a living museum. The text includes photographs of the people who work in Williamsburg so that the colonial times of the eighteenth century come alive. Index.

2146. Steen, Sandra, and Susan Steen. **Independence Hall**. New York: Dillon Press, 1994. 71p. $14.95. ISBN 0-87518-650-5. (Places in American History). 3-6

Independence Hall in Philadelphia became famous because the vote for independence from England took place inside its walls. The text looks at the building and the history that was made at it, the ensuing struggle for independence, and the Liberty Bell sitting outside. Independence Hall: A Historical Timeline, Visitor Information, and Index.

2147. Stefoff, Rebecca. **Abraham Lincoln: 16th President of the United States**. Ada, OK: Garrett Educational, 1989. 122p. $17.26. ISBN 0-944483-14-3. (Presidents of the United States). 5-9

This biography of Abraham Lincoln (1809-1865) begins with the Battle of Gettysburg, after which Lincoln made his memorable speech. The text then returns to his frontier boyhood, his becoming a self-made man, his introduction to politics, his career as a lawyer, and his love. He became Congressman Lincoln and then President Lincoln. During his presidency, he had to face the question of slavery, try to reunite a divided nation, and decide that the slaves should be emancipated. Bibliography and Index.

2148. Stefoff, Rebecca. **Andrew Jackson: 7th President of the United States**. Ada, OK: Garrett Educational, 1988. 119p. $17.26. ISBN 0-944483-08-9. (Presidents of the United States). 5-9

Andrew Jackson (1767-1845) served informally during the Revolutionary War before he became certified to practice law in North Carolina. He went to Tennessee and became both a congressman and a senator. He also became a judge. In 1812, he led a company from Tennessee in the war and defeated the British at New Orleans in 1815. Then he attacked the Seminoles in Florida. After losing his first presidential campaign to John Quincy Adams, he began serving as President in 1829. Bibliography and Index.

2149.   Stefoff, Rebecca. **Children of the Westward Trail**. Brookfield, CT: Millbrook Press, 1996. 96p. $16.90. ISBN 1-56294-582-3. 6-9

More than 500,000 people went west during the nineteenth century looking for gold, land, or adventure. The text focuses on one man: Martin Gay, a farmer from Springfield, Missouri, who took his family on a five-month journey to the Willamette Valley of Oregon. What they faced were problems experienced by all those who risked the trip. Bibliography and Index.

2150.   Stefoff, Rebecca. **George H. W. Bush: 41st President of the United States**. Ada, OK: Garrett Educational, 1992. 140p. $17.26. ISBN 1-56074-033-7. (Presidents of the United States). 5-9

The text examines George Bush's life (b. 1924) before he became the 41st President as well as after. Chapters cover his New England boyhood, his navy career, living in Texas, influence in the Republican Party, his service in China and as the Vice President, his campaign and election for president, his years in office, and his role in the Persian Gulf War. Bibliography and Index.

2151.   Stefoff, Rebecca. **James Monroe: 5th President of the United States**. Ada, OK: Garrett Educational, 1988. 120p. $17.26. ISBN 0-944483-11-9. (Presidents of the United States). 5-9

James Monroe (1758-1831) served General Washington in the American Revolution when his troops crossed the Delaware River. He also participated in the Battle of Trenton, when the Americans defeated the Hessians. He was wounded, and the farmer-doctor who gave the troops food soon after they crossed the river saved his life. Forty years after being wounded, he was elected President of the United States. Among his other achievements was buying the Louisiana Purchase for Thomas Jefferson and serving as a foreign ambassador. Bibliography and Index.

2152.   Stefoff, Rebecca. **John Adams: 2nd President of the United States**. Ada, OK: Garrett Educational, 1988. 118p. $17.26. ISBN 0-944483-10-0. (Presidents of the United States). 7 up

John Adams (1735-1826) had many roles as he grew up and served the nation. Two of these were husband to Abigail Adams and father to John Quincy Adams. The chapters identify him in the roles of Puritan, student, lawyer, patriot, ambassador, Vice President, President, and the "Old Man," the name he called himself. Bibliography and Index.

2153.   Stefoff, Rebecca. **Richard M. Nixon: 37th President of the United States**. Ada, OK: Garrett Educational, 1995. 129p. $17.26. ISBN 1-56074-063-9. (Presidents of the United States). 5-9

Richard Milhaus Nixon (1913-1994) served as President after being a congressman from California and Vice President of the United States. He had to resign from office or face impeachment for his implication in the Watergate burglary during the campaign for his second term in office. Bibliography and Index.

2154.   Stefoff, Rebecca. **Theodore Roosevelt: 26th President of the United States**. Ada, OK: Garrett Educational, 1988. 120p. $17.26. ISBN 0-944483-09-7. (Presidents of the United States). 5-9

Theodore Roosevelt (1858-1919) went to Harvard and served as New York legislative leader. After his wife died in 1884, he remarried and became the Assistant Secretary of the Navy in 1897-1898. He resigned to become a colonel in the Rough Riders, a volunteer cavalry in the Spanish-American War in Cuba, where he led the San Juan Hill battle. He returned, won the governorship of New York, and soon after, in 1900, became McKinley's Vice President. When President, he made the Panama Canal Treaty and started antitrust legislation. In his second term, he won the Nobel Peace Prize. In the last years of his life, he explored Brazil. Bibliography and Index.

2155.   Stefoff, Rebecca. **Thomas Jefferson: 3rd President of the United States**. Ada, OK: Garrett Educational, 1988. 122p. $17.26. ISBN 9-44483-07-0. (Presidents of the United States). 5-9

This text about Thomas Jefferson (1743-1826) includes chapters on the Declaration of Independence, the rebellion of the colonies, his role during the American Revolution, his accomplishments as a statesman at home and abroad, the politics in his party, his tendency to philosophize, and his late years at Monticello. Bibliography and Index.

2156.   Stefoff, Rebecca. **William Henry Harrison: 9th President of the United States**. Ada, OK: Garrett Educational, 1990. 120p. $17.26, ISBN 0-944483-54-2. (Presidents of the United States). 5-8

William Henry Harrison (1773-1841) fought in the Northwest Territory under General "Mad" Anthony Wayne before he became a delegate to the U.S. House of Representatives and defeated the Shawnee at the Battle of Tippecanoe in 1811. As a general in the War of 1812, he won a battle that secured American control of the western territory. He represented Ohio in the House from 1816 to 1829, lost his first bid for the presidency to Martin Van Buren, and beat Van Buren in 1840. One month after taking office in 1841, he died. Bibliography and Index.

2157.   Stefoff, Rebecca. **Women Pioneers**. New York: Facts on File, 1995. 126p. $17.95. ISBN 0-8160-3134-7. (American Profiles). 6 up

The text looks at several women who played important roles in the settling of the West during the nineteenth century. They include Rebecca Burlend, Clara Brown, Virginia Reed, Tabitha Brown, Polly Bemis, Elinore Pruitt Stewart, and Martha Gay Masterson. Rebecca Burlend was raised in England; Polly Bemis grew up in China; Clara Brown was a slave in Virginia. Chronology, Further Reading, and Index.

2158.   Stein, R. **The Great Depression**. 1985. Chicago: Childrens Press, 1993. 30p. $15.93. ISBN 0-516-06668-4. (Cornerstones of Freedom). 3-6

In a look at the time after the 1929 stock market crash, the text describes the Depression that followed and the attempts of Franklin Roosevelt to restore the economy with his New Deal programs. Photographs and drawings highlight the text. Index.

2159.   Stein, R. Conrad. **The Assassination of John F. Kennedy**. Chicago: Childrens Press, 1992. 31p. ISBN 0-516-06652-8. (Cornerstones of Freedom). 3-5

On November 22, 1963, Lee Harvey Oswald assassinated John F. Kennedy in Dallas, Texas. The deed shocked the entire world. The text starts by looking at the day Kennedy was shot, beginning with the comment that he made in the morning about being the man who accompanied the popular Mrs. Kennedy to Dallas. The text continues through his burial in Arlington Cemetery across the Memorial Bridge from Washington several days later. Photographs augment the information presented in the text. Index.

2160.   Stein, R. Conrad. **The Declaration of Independence**. Chicago: Childrens Press, 1995. 30p. $15.27. ISBN 0-516-06693-5. (Cornerstones of Freedom). 3-6

Facts about the writing and signing of the Declaration of Independence in July 1776, with photographs and reproductions, give a background for this important document. Included are sections on why troubles with England began, the voting by Congress, and a copy of the Declaration. Glossary and Index.

2161.   Stein, R. Conrad. **Ellis Island**. Chicago: Childrens Press, 1992. 32p. $18; $4.95pa. ISBN 0-516-06653-6. 0-516-46653-4pa. (Cornerstones of Freedom). 3-5

To many Europeans, Ellis Island was the "Isle of Tears." If immigrants did not pass the health tests, they had to return to their homes. They had all left their native countries, however, because they hoped for a better life in America. The text calls the country a "nation of immigrants" because immigrants include the Pilgrims and those who settled in Jamestown. A variety of laws have governed the acceptance of immigrants through the years, and the text also comments about them. Index.

2162.   Stein, R. Conrad. **The Hindenburg Disaster**. Chicago: Childrens Press, 1993. 30p. $15.27. ISBN 0-516-06663-3. (Cornerstones of Freedom). 3-5

With photographs and illustrations of aircraft before the passenger-dirigible flight of the Hindenburg, the text tells of the precautions made on this craft, designed mainly by Count Ferdinand von Zeppelin. It leads to the crash in New Jersey during 1937 and presents the text of the famous radio broadcast of the disaster. Photographs and drawings enhance the text. Index.

2163.   Stein, R. Conrad. **The Iran Hostage Crisis**. Chicago: Childrens Press, 1994. 32p. $15.27. ISBN 0-516-06681-1. (Cornerstones of Freedom). 5 up

On November 4, 1979, Iranian students seized 60 employees in the U.S. embassy in Tehran. They kept most of the hostages for 444 days in various places separated from each other. After Jimmy Carter lost the presidential election, Ronald Reagan took office on the same day the hostages were released, January 20, 1981. People displayed yellow ribbons everywhere so that others would not forget the hostages before the Iranians freed them. Index.

2164.   Stein, R. Conrad. **The Korean War: "The Forgotten War"**. Hillside, NJ: Enslow, 1994. 128p. ISBN 0-89490-526-0. (American War). 6-9

Although 54,000 Americans died in the Korean War, fought from 1950 to 1953, many Americans at home lost interest because they did not understand the threat of Communist control spreading when the North Koreans invaded South Korea. This war did not have the media coverage common today, and no major event such as Pearl Harbor caused it to start. The text, with photographs, looks at the war and its effects on those who fought and on their families. Chronology, Further Reading, and Index.

2165.   Stein, R. Conrad. **The Manhattan Project**. Chicago: Childrens Press, 1993. 30p. $15.27. ISBN 0-516-06670-6. (Cornerstones of Freedom). 3-5

The Manhattan Project was the program that resulted in the development of the atomic bomb during World War II. Its success led to the bombing of Hiroshima and Nagasaki in 1945. Photographs and drawings enhance the text. Index.

2166. Stein, R. Conrad. **The Story of the Powers of the Supreme Court**. Chicago: Childrens Press, 1995. 32p. $15.27. ISBN 0-516-06697-8. (Cornerstones of Freedom). 3-6

The text offers an overview of the history of the court, the important personalities who have served there, and some of the most important cases. Photographs and drawings enhance the text. Index.

2167. Stein, R. Conrad. **The United Nations**. Chicago: Childrens Press, 1994. 30p. $15.27. ISBN 0-516-06677-3; 0-516-46677-1pa. 3-5

Photographs of people from around the world highlight the text, which discusses the value of the United Nations in helping countries. It supported the United States during the Cuban Missile Crisis in 1962. Quotes help to personalize this mammoth organization. Index.

2168. Stein, R. Conrad. **The USS Arizona**. Chicago: Childrens Press, 1992. 32p. $18.00. ISBN 0-516-06656-0. (Cornerstones of Freedom). 3-5

Stein opens his book about the Japanese attack on Pearl Harbor, December 7, 1941, with comments from an 18-year-old sailor aboard the USS *Arizona* and with the information that Admiral Yamamoto, the planner of the Japanese bombing, was an excellent poker player who had once lived in Washington, D.C. He continues with the story of the bombing and the immediate aftermath for crew and families of the USS *Arizona*, sunk in Pearl Harbor that day. Photographs and Index.

2169. Stein, R. Conrad. **Valley Forge**. Chicago: Childrens Press, 1994. 28p. $16.40. ISBN 0-516-06683-8. (Cornerstones of Freedom). 3-8

After the British beat him at the Battle of Brandywine on September 11, 1777, George Washington and his soldiers retreated to Valley Forge, Pennsylvania. Soldiers who describe their loyalties and their frustration with struggling through the cold winter with few supplies give this account a personal touch. Black-and-white photographs and reproductions enhance the text. Index.

2170. Stein, R. Conrad. **World War II in Europe: "America Goes to War"**. Hillside, NJ: Enslow, 1994. 128p. $17.95. ISBN 0-89490-525-2. (American War). 6 up

Stein begins the text on World War II with the story of "Canned Goods." The Germans dressed convicts in Polish army uniforms, then killed them and announced that they were Polish invaders whom they had caught before they infiltrated Germany. Adolf Hitler used this farce to justify his invasion of Poland in 1939. Even though the German people were against war, Hitler declared it anyway. Many Germans were shocked that France and Great Britain supported Poland because they had refused to do anything when Hitler had previously broken the Treaty of Versailles. The other chapters follow the war across Europe. Chronology, Notes, Further Reading, and Index.

2171. Stein, Wendy. **Witches: Opposing Viewpoints**. San Diego, CA: Greenhaven, 1995. 112p. $19.95. ISBN 1-56510-240-1. (Great Mysteries—Opposing Viewpoints). 6-9

In an attempt to define "witch," the author asserts that witches either destroy or heal, depending upon intent. Some researchers trace the etymology of "witch" to *witan* (to know) in Old English, and others select *wiccian* (to cast a spell). The text presents a history of witches from the Western world, mentioning the Inquisition; a trial in Arras, France, from 1459 to 1460; witchcraft in England, especially Chelmsford in Essex; witch covens in sixteenth-century Scotland (1591); and the Salem witch hunt in the American colonies from 1620 to 1725. Some believe that misogyny (hatred of women) is a leading cause of witch hunts because more than 80 percent of the people persecuted as witches have been female. Contemporary witches worship a goddess that is said to have been worshipped more than 35,000 years ago. In history, the most overt worship of the goddess occured in Greece from approximately 1500 BC to 900 BC with Diana, Selene, and Hecate. But sources also indicate other pockets of goddess worship. For Further Exploration, Additional Works Consulted, and Index.

2172. Steins, Richard. **The Allies Against the Axis: World War II (1940-1950)**. New York: Twenty-First Century Books, 1994. 64p. $15.95. ISBN 0-8050-2586-3. (First Person America). 5-8

America entered World War II after the Japanese bombed Pearl Harbor in 1941, thus ending its isolationist policy. Steins looks at the war on both oceans and notes such situations as the challenges of army segregation, the fear and paranoia of the county according to a nisei (second-generation Japanese American), the women working in factories, soldiers returning to peacetime, and the descent of the Iron Curtain. Photographs enhance the text. Timeline, For Further Reading, and Index.

2173. Steins, Richard. **The Nation Divides: The Civil War, 1820-1880**. New York: Twenty-First Century Books, 1993. 64p. $15.95. ISBN 0-8050-2583-9. (First Person America). 5-8

The text uses letters, poems, broadsides, speeches, lyrics, and newspaper articles to present the different aspects of the Civil War, including the debate over slavery, the secession of the Confederate states, the war itself, and life for the slaves after emancipation. Bibliography and Index.

2174. Steins, Richard. **A Nation Is Born: Rebellion and Independence in America, 1700-1820**. New York: Twenty-First Century Books, 1993. 64p. $15.95. ISBN 0-8050-2582-0. (First Person America). 5-8

The text uses letters, poems, broadsides, speeches, lyrics, and newspaper articles to present the life of the settlers in the 13 colonies as they began to have problems with England and decided to fight for freedom. The pains of creating a new government of the United States are related. Bibliography and Index.

2175. Steins, Richard. **Our Elections**. Brookfield, CT: Millbrook Press, 1994. 48p. $14.40; $6.95pa. ISBN 1-56294-446-0; 0-7613-0092-9pa. (I Know America). 2-6

Steins thinks that four presidential elections shaped the history of the United States: the election of 1800, when Thomas Jefferson won; the election of 1860, when Abraham Lincoln won; the election of 1920, when women began to vote; and the election of 1932, when Franklin Delano Roosevelt became President during the Depression. Steins explains the democratic process, campaigns and elections, the two-party system, and how a President can be elected. Chronology, For Further Reading, and Index.

2176. Steins, Richard. **The Postwar Years: The Cold War and the Atomic Age (1950-1959)**. New York: Twenty-First Century Books, 1994. 64p. $15.95. ISBN 0-8050-2587-1. (First Person America). 5-8

During the 1950s, television took hold at the same time Joseph McCarthy was creating a climate of terror by blacklisting anyone who had ever made pro-Communist remarks. War had not ended because many were fighting in Korea. The country was "white" because ethnic groups were "invisible" until the Montgomery bus boycott in Alabama. People noted here include Lillian Hellman, the Rosenbergs, Elvis Presley, Dr. Spock, and Martin Luther King, Jr. Photographs enhance the text. Timeline, For Further Reading, and Index.

2177. Stepto, Michele, ed. **Our Song, Our Toil: The Story of American Slavery as Told by Slaves**. Brookfield, CT: Millbrook Press, 1985. 95p. $18.40. ISBN 1-56294-401-0. 5-9

Some masters taught their slaves how to read and write. Excerpts from autobiographies and other documents tell the story of slavery in this text. Chapters include "born a slave," enslaved families, work of slavery, resistance, literacy, escaping slavery, and freedom. Photographs and reproductions enhance the text. Sources, Further Reading, and Index. *Notable Children's Trade Books in the Field of Social Studies*.

2178. Stern, Gary M. **The Congress: America's Lawmakers**. Austin, TX: Raintree/Steck-Vaughn, 1993. 48p. $22.83; $6.64pa. ISBN 0-8114-7351-1; 0-8114-5579-3pa. (Good Citizenship). 3-6

Congress originated with British roots because its creators had that system in their backgrounds. The text gives the history of Congress; the requirements to become members of Congress; how Congress works with its committees, filibusters, and cloture rules; and some of its decisions. Among the most notable acts are the Missouri Compromise of 1820, the Civil Rights Bill of 1964, the Watergate hearings in 1973, the Bork hearings for the Supreme Court in 1987, and those for Clarence Thomas in 1991. Photographs and drawings highlight the text. Further Reading, Glossary, and Index.

2179. Stevens, Bernardine S. **Colonial American Craftspeople**. New York: Franklin Watts, 1993. 128p. $19.60. ISBN 0-531-12536-X. (Colonial America). 5 up

The text looks at the craftwork performed in the early years of the United States. Among the craftspeople highlighted are coopers, joiners, woodworkers, masons, sawyers, bricklayers, metalworkers, leather workers, papermakers, printers, and bookbinders. The sources of these crafts and the lives of those who practiced them give an insight into the daily life of the times. Reproductions and drawings enhance the text. Glossary, Further Reading, and Index.

2180. Stevens, Bryna. **Frank Thompson: Her Civil War Story**. New York: Macmillan, 1992. 144p. $13.95. ISBN 0-02-788185-7. 4-9

A Canadian-born woman, Emma Edmonds, 15, disguised herself as "Frank Thompson" to serve in the Union army during the Civil War. She was too short to be a foot soldier so she became a nurse, a mail carrier, and later a spy. She had to leave the army after becoming sick and injured because a hospital stay would have revealed her secret. She published an account of her life in 1865, entitled *Nurse and Spy*. Sources and Index.

2181. Stevens, Carla. **Anna, Grandpa, and the Big Storm**. Margot Tomes, illustrator. Boston: Houghton Mifflin, 1982. 60p. $13.95. ISBN 0-89919-066-9. New York: Penguin, 1989. 64p. $3.99pa. ISBN 0-14-031705-8pa. 1-4

When Anna is seven in 1888, she and her grandfather get caught on an elevated train in New York City during a blizzard. Her grandfather's kindness to everyone on the train helps them return safely to their homes.

2182.   Stevens, Carla. **Lily and Miss Liberty**. Deborah Kogan Ray, illustrator. New York: Scholastic, 1992. 80p. $12.95. ISBN 0-590-44919-2. 3-5

In New York in 1885, Lily, eight, waits for the statue soon to arrive on a French ship. The city wants to raise money for a pedestal. Because this statue will greet immigrants seeking freedom in the United States, Lily wants to help. She and her friend decide to make crowns, and they give the money they earn to the cause.

2183.   Stevens, Carla. **Trouble for Lucy**. Ronald Himler, illustrator. 1979. Boston: Houghton Mifflin, 1987. 80p. $5.95pa. ISBN 0-89919-523-7pa. 3-6

While the family travels to Oregon from Independence, Missouri, in 1843, Lucy's mother expects a baby any day. Her father worries and tells Lilly to keep her dog away from the oxen. When the dog disappears one day, she sneaks away from the wagon train to find him. She becomes lost, but someone locates her while her mother delivers a healthy baby girl.

2184.   Stevens, Rita. **Andrew Johnson: 17th President of the United States**. Ada, OK: Garrett Educational, 1989. 122p. $17.26. ISBN 0-944483-16-X. (Presidents of the United States). 5-9

On April 14, 1865, five days after Robert E. Lee had surrendered to Ulysses S. Grant at Appomattox, Virginia, John Wilkes Booth shot Abraham Lincoln. As the sitting Vice President, Johnson (1808-1875) was also a target of the conspiracy, but his would-be assassin was too drunk and too scared to carry out his assignment. Three hours after Lincoln died, Johnson became President. The text looks at the rest of his life, including charges of impeachment against him. Bibliography and Index.

2185.   Stevens, Rita. **Benjamin Harrison: 23rd President of the United States**. Ada, OK: Garrett Educational, 1989. 120p. $17.26. ISBN 0-944483-15-1. (Presidents of the United States). 5-8

The grandson of William Henry Harrison, Benjamin Harrison (1833-1901) was a member of the Ohio bar before he joined the Republican Party in 1856. During the Civil War, he served with the Indiana Infantry and reached the rank of brigadier general. At first a U.S. senator from Indiana, he was elected President in 1888. Because people disagreed with his policies, Grover Cleveland defeated him in 1892. Bibliography and Index.

2186.   Stevens, Rita. **Calvin Coolidge: 30th President of the United States**. Ada, OK: Garrett Educational, 1990. 124p. $17.26. ISBN 0-944483-57-7. (Presidents of the United States). 5-9

Calvin Coolidge (1872-1933) grew up in New England and served in the Massachusetts legislature and as the state's governor. He became Vice President under Warren G. Harding in 1921, and when Harding died in 1923, he became President. Many people blamed him for the Great Depression. Others thought that he was merely lazy. A mediocre President, he did not make any serious mistakes. War did not occur while he was in office, and business, science, and industry were free to grow. He was thrifty, honest, and moral. Bibliography and Index.

2187.   Stevens, Rita. **Chester A. Arthur: 21st President of the United States**. Ada, OK: Garrett Educational, 1989. 120p. $17.26. ISBN 0-944483-05-4. (Presidents of the United States). 5-9

At the death of James Garfield, Chester A. Arthur (1829-1886) became President. He had never been elected to an office, and no one knew what to expect, including himself. He chose good assistants and lived honorably while in office. He had never wanted to be President, but he did not succumb to any unsavory practices while serving his country. The text looks at his life and his presidency. Bibliography and Index.

2188.   Stevenson, Augusta. **Sitting Bull: Dakota Boy**. Robert Jenney, illustrator. New York: Aladdin, 1996. 192p. $4.99pa. ISBN 0-689-80628-0pa. (Childhood of Famous Americans). 4-7

While Sitting Bull (1834?-1890) was still called Jumping Badger as a boy of 10, boys pretending to be his friends started calling him "Slow" so that he would begin to think that he could not win races or games. His father talked with the tribe's witch, and she told Jumping Badger to start believing in himself. She gave him a tooth to wear as a lucky charm. He began winning, and people began asking him to tell them about their fates based on the tooth. By the time he was 12, he needed to earn his adult Sioux name. In a dream, he saw many buffalo sitting down as if they were wounded. His father gave him the name "Sitting Bull" because he expected him to become a great hunter. He did.

2189.   Stewart, Elizabeth J. **On the Long Trail Home**. New York: Clarion, 1994. $13.95. ISBN 0-395-68361-0. 4-6

Meli, nine, becomes separated from her Cherokee family in the 1830s when her family is forced out of their home in North Carolina and made to march to Oklahoma. She and her brother escape and find their father and younger brother. Their Cherokee customs stay intact, and other details of the times show the help that Quakers gave to those in need.

2190. Stewart, Gail. **Where Lies Butch Cassidy?** Yoshi Miyaki, illustrator. New York: Crestwood House, 1992. 48p. $11.95. ISBN 0-89686-618-1. (History's Mysteries). 5-8

Using pseudonyms such as Butch Cassidy, Billy Maxwell, and Jim Ryan, Robert Leroy Parker tried to spare his family shame while he continued his exploits. He robbed banks and trains but was only arrested once for cattle rustling, and he never killed anyone. Supposedly he and his partner, the Sundance Kid, died in Bolivia. Conflicting evidence arose during the 1930s, which indicated that he may have returned to the United States instead. The text examines what is known and what is guessed about Butch Cassidy. Chronology, For Further Reading, and Index.

2191. Stewart, Gail B. **Benjamin Franklin**. San Diego, CA: Lucent, 1992. 127p. $16.95. ISBN 1-560-06026-3. (The Importance Of). 6-9

Quotes from a variety of sources give insight into the importance of Benjamin Franklin (1706-1790) to American history and to intellectual advancement. As a scientist, statesman, printer, and leader, he was one of the fathers of the concept of American ingenuity. Photographs, reproductions, and drawings enhance the text. Further Reading and Index.

2192. Stewart, Gail B. **Cowboys in the Old West**. San Diego, CA: Lucent, 1995. 112p. $22.59. ISBN 1-56006-077-8. (The Way People Live). 6-8

The myth of the cowboy in American legend remains although the era of the cowboy only lasted from approximately 1865 until 1890. During that time, cowboys drove almost 8 million head of cattle north from Texas into Kansas and beyond. Their time ended with the increased use of trains across the country. Some of the details that Stewart presents are that cowboys were often Black and Mexican, but only white cowboys seemed to get raises and promotions. Their vocabulary included swearing and simple words, and they were likely to "shoot" at words they considered pretentious. Their guns made them all equal, and most cowboys had a sense of when to stay quiet. Their life on the trail was hard work, but they always tried to stay friendly with the cook, head of the chuckwagon (invented by Charles Goodnight). Notes, For Further Reading, Works Consulted, and Index.

2193. Stiles, T. L. **Jesse James**. New York: Chelsea House, 1993. 111p. $18.95; $7.95pa. ISBN 0-7910-1737-0; 0-7910-1738-9pa. (Library of Biography). 6-12

Jesse James (b. 1847) grew up in western Missouri, site of guerrilla fighting during the Civil War, where he fought for the Bushwhackers on the losing Confederate side. By 16, he was an experienced killer who was almost killed himself. He recovered and married the woman who nursed him, but he decided to get revenge by robbing banks and railroads. He and his brother Frank's band of robbers worked for more than 10 years, giving Missouri the name "the bandit state." A member of his gang, Bob Ford, finally killed him in 1882 to get the reward money. Photographs, Chronology, Further Reading, and Index.

2194. Stine, Megan. **The Story of Laura Ingalls Wilder, Pioneer Girl**. Marcy Dunn Ramsey, illustrator. New York: Dell, 1992. 101p. $3.25pa. ISBN 0-440-40578-5pa. 3-5

Laura Ingalls Wilder wrote her *Little House* books about her life, and this biography does not reveal much more except at the end, when it tells about her marriage to Almanzo Wilder. This book is a shorter version of her life than her own series.

2195. Stine, Megan. **The Story of Malcolm X: Civil Rights Leader**. Minneapolis, MN: Gareth Stevens, 1995. 112p. $13.95. ISBN 0-8368-1383-9. (Famous Lives). New York: Dell, 1994. 102p. $3.50pa. ISBN 0-440-40900-4pa. 4-7

The author notes that even in his autobiography, Malcolm X (1925-1965) wrote incorrect information, a situation that mirrors other different versions about him. Knowing what might be true is often difficult. His father might have been a criminal. His mother went insane when Malcolm was 13, and he went into a juvenile detention home. He committed crimes and went to prison, where he learned about the Nation of Islam and wrote to Elijah Muhammad, the leader. He began to read. In 1952, after being paroled, he met Elijah, and in a few months converted and changed his name to Malcolm X. He continued his work until he was assassinated in 1965. Photographs included. Highlights in the Life, For Further Study, and Index.

2196. Stolz, Mary. **Cezanne Pinto: A Memoir**. New York: Knopf, 1994. 252p. $15. ISBN 0-679-84917-3. 5-9

Cezanne Pinto, an old man around 90, recalls his life as a young man around 12, when he was a slave on a Virginia plantation. He escaped to the North in 1860. His mother had been sold before he left, and he went to search for her. He saw the beginnings of the Civil War, tended horses on a Canadian farm, and became a teenage cowboy who decided to move to Chicago when a longhorn steer looked him in the eye. He decides at his advanced age that he, like Zora Neale Hurston, does not mind being colored. *Jane Addams Honor Award*.

2197. Stone, Bruce. **Autumn of the Royal Tar**. New York: Laura Geringer, HarperCollins, 1995. 160p. $13.95. ISBN 0-06-021492-9. 5 up

In this first-person narrative, 12-year-old Nora tries to help the survivors of a ship, the *Royal Tar*, that sinks off the coast of her Maine home in 1835. Among them is a burned boy whose mother has died in the accident. Nora and Giles, a man working for her father, try to care for an elephant that survived, but it soon dies. Giles and the others mourn its death. More important, caring for the boy helps Nora empathize with the pain her mother has suffered since Nora's brother died three years before.

2198. **Stones and Bones: How Archaeologists Trace Human Origins**. Minneapolis, MN: Runestone Press, 1994. 64p. $11.95. ISBN 08225-3207-7. 4-9

Archaeology as a science is only a century old. During that time, scientists have learned a lot about prehistoric humans and ancient civilizations. The text explains the methodology of archaeology and gives theories that have sprung from this research. Glossary and Index.

2199. **The Story of Flight** New York: Scholastic, 1995. 45p. $19.95. ISBN 0-590-47643-2. (Voyages of Discovery). 4-6

The text discusses the dreams of flying that humans have had as it presents information on kites, gliders, balloons, and dirigibles. Discussions of modern flight include an introduction to the Wright brothers, the early flyers, flying aces, warplanes, and the functions of navigational systems. The text also contains a cross-section of an airship, a fold-out page showing the interior of the Wright brothers' workshop, and tracing-paper design sketches to place over the finished planes. Chronology and Index.

2200. Strauch, Eileen Walsh. **Hey You, Sister Rose**. New York: Tambourine, 1993. 159p. $13. ISBN 0-688-11829-1. 3-7

In Baltimore, Maryland, Arlene enters sixth grade in 1951 during the Korean War, fearful of her teacher, the terror Sister Rose. But as the year progresses, Arlene learns about herself and her talent that Sister Rose encourages: writing. Arlene realizes that people who demand hard work can also be some of the kindest.

2201. Streissguth, Tom. **Rocket Man: The Story of Robert Goddard**. Minneapolis, MN: Carolrhoda, 1995. 88p. $19.95. ISBN 0-87614-863-1. (Trailblazers). 4-7

One of the experiments that 16-year-old Robert Goddard (1882-1945) tried was to make diamonds. He did not succeed, but his interests led him to rockets and to becoming the man who thought about traveling in space and tried to find a way to do it. He always suffered from tuberculosis, but he did not let his health keep him from making major advancements in science while he worked as a professor. The text looks at his many achievements. Notes, Glossary, Bibliography, and Index.

2202. Streissguth, Tom. **Say It with Music: A Story About Irving Berlin**. Jennifer Hagerman, illustrator. Minneapolis, MN: Carolrhoda, 1994. 64p. $13.13. ISBN 0-87614-810-0. (Creative Minds). 3-6

Irving Berlin (1888-1989), born Israel Baline, came to the United States at the age of five with his family. He had to sell newspapers on the corner to help his family survive, and sometimes he would sing. People would give him extra money, and his singing led to an unexpected career, that of songwriter. He wrote "God Bless America" and "White Christmas" as well as many other songs during his long life. Afterword and Bibliography.

2203. Strickland, Brad. **The Hand of the Necromancer**. New York: Dial, 1996. 176p. $14.89. ISBN 0-8037-1830-6. 5-8

In the 1950s, John Dixon gets a job in the Gudge Museum with the help of his friend Professor Childermass and the professor's donation of artifacts created by the evil wizard Esdrias Blackleash during the Salem witch trials. Mattheus Mergal comes to town to steal the wooden hand from the collection, and with him come the supernatural beings that fill the rest of the story.

2204. Stroud, Bettye. **Down Home at Miss Dessa's**. Felicia Marshall, illustrator. New York: Lee & Low, 1996. Unpaged. $14.95. ISBN 1-880000-39-3. K-3

During the early twentieth century, two sisters help Miss Dessa when she falls and hurts her ankle. Miss Dessa has helped them, and they return the favor as they play together and read aloud to make her feel better.

2205. Sufrin, Mark. **George Catlin: Painter of the Indian West**. New York: Atheneum, 1991. 153p. $14.95. ISBN 0-689-31608-9. 5 up

To record the life of the Plains Indians through paintings became George Catlin's desire. During his life (1796-1872), he abandoned the study of law and started painting. Between 1831 and 1836, he traveled west by riverboat, canoe, and horseback. He saw and painted people in the Cheyenne, Sioux, Blackfeet, Crow, and Mandan tribes. He learned that these people were humans who had a variety of cultural backgrounds, and his work gave them an individuality that the public had never before seen. Bibliography and Index.

2206.   Sullivan, Charles, ed. **Children of Promise: African-American Literature and Art for Young People**. New York: Harry N. Abrams, 1991. 126p. $24.95. ISBN 0-8190-3170-2. 4 up

This book is a collection of poems, essays, speeches, and other writings by African Americans. Some of it is autobiographical, and some of it is fiction. All of it gives a picture of the lives of African Americans since Phillis Wheatley in the late eighteenth century. Photographs and drawings complement the text. Biographical Notes and Index.

2207.   Sullivan, George. **Black Artists in Photography, 1840-1940**. New York: Cobblehill, 1996. 104p. $16.99. ISBN 0-525-65208-6. 6-9

Among the Black photographers who have made successful professions are Jules Lion, Augustus Washington, James P. Ball, the Goodridge brothers, Cornelius M. Battey, and Addison Scurlock. Although not detailing the problems with photographic processing, the text gives interesting insights into the lives of these men along with high-quality representations of their work. Further Reading and Index.

2208.   Sullivan, George. **George Bush**. New York: Julian Messner, 1989. 170p. $12.98; $5.98pa. ISBN 0-671-64599-4; 0-671-67814-0pa. 6-10

George Bush (b. 1924) became the 41st president after serving as vice president under Ronald Reagan. Chapters look at his life in Texas, as a loyal member of the Republican Party, as a candidate, as vice president, and as president. Highlights of his public life include naval service, having the Japanese shoot down his plane in World War II, serving as a member of the House, becoming the U.S. ambassador to the United Nations, working as chief of the U.S. Liaison Office in the People's Republic of China in Beijing, and being the director of the Central Intelligence Agency. Photographs, Time Line, For Further Reading, and Index.

2209.   Sullivan, George. **Matthew Brady: His Life and Photographs**. New York: Cobblehill, Dutton, 1994. 136p. $15.99. ISBN 0-525-65186-1. 6-10

On Matthew Brady's tombstone are the words "Renowned Photographer of the Civil War." He realized early that photographs could give visual records of people and events, so he and his assistants photographed most of the people serving in public life during his times. In 1862, when he exhibited a show called "The Dead at Antietam," viewers were shocked at the reality of war. The text, with photographs, gives the life of Brady (c. 1823-1896), who left an important view of the nineteenth century in America. Sources and Index.

2210.   Sullivan, George. **Ronald Reagan**. New York: Julian Messner, 1991. 144p. $10.98. ISBN 0-671-74537-9. 5 up

Ronald Reagan (b. 1911) became the 40th president of the United States. The text covers his earlier years, life in Hollywood, the military, his family, his tenure as governor of California, the two terms as president, and his legacy. Important Dates, Further Reading, and Index.

2211.   Sullivan, George. **Slave Ship: The Story of the Henrietta Marie**. New York: Cobblehill, Dutton, 1994. 80p. $15.99. ISBN 0-525-65174-8. 5-8

In 1972, divers found the remains of a sunken ship in the Gulf of Mexico. One of the first items found was a pair of shackles, which indicated that the ship had been a slave ship. On the ship's bell was engraved the name *Henrietta Marie* and the date 1699. Records show that the ship had unloaded its human cargo in Jamaica and had sunk in a storm while returning to London. Background information about slavers and photographs of the items discovered in the ship give an insight into what the people on board might have endured. This ship is the only slaver to have been scientifically studied. Bibliography and Index.

2212.   Sullivan, Silky. **Grandpa Was a Cowboy**. Bert Dodson, illustrator. New York: Orchard, Jackson, 1996. Unpaged. $14.95. ISBN 0-531-09511-8. K-4

In the mid-1920s, Grandpa comes to visit his grandson and tells him about his life in the late 1800s, when he was a cowboy, a photographer, a farmer, and a father of 11 children. He also talks about his own parents: his father, who went to war, and his mother, who died soon after his birth. When the boy wants to return to the Ozarks with his Grandpa, he tells him that one of them is too young and the other too old for such an arrangement.

2213.   Super, Neil. **Daniel "Chappie" James**. New York: Twenty-First Century Books, 1992. 80p. $14.95. ISBN 0-8050-2138-8. (African-American Soldiers). 5-9

Last in a family of 17 children, Daniel James (b. 1920) grew up in Florida in a racially segregated society. His parents taught him to dream, and he turned his dreams into a reality by becoming a fighter pilot, a four-star general in the U.S. Air Force, and a commander of the nuclear air defenses. Chronology, Bibliography, and Index.

2214. Super, Neil. **Vietnam War Soldiers**. New York: Twenty-First Century Books, 1993. 80p. $14.95. ISBN 0-8050-2307-0. (African-American Soldiers). 4-7

In looking at the contribution of African Americans in the Vietnam War (1961-1975), the author sees that they served in all branches of the service. However, they were less likely to be promoted or awarded medals than their white counterparts. Additionally, they were more likely to receive disciplinary action. These conclusions give insight into the treatment of African Americans while they were serving their country. Photographs supplement the text. Bibliography, Chronology, and Index.

2215. Surat, Michele Maria. **Angel Child, Dragon Child**. Vo-Dinh Mai, illustrator. Austin, TX: Raintree/Steck-Vaughn, 1983. 32p. $19.97. ISBN 0-940742-12-8. New York: Scholastic, 1989. 32p. $3.95pa. ISBN 0-590-42271-5pa. 3-6

In the 1960s, Ut, seven, faces ridicule from the Americans when she wears her Vietnamese native dress to school. A boy at the school throws snowballs at her, so the principal isolates the two until they begin to understand each other. The school decides to raise money in an effort to help Ut's mother afford passage to America.

2216. Suter, Joanne. **Our Century: 1980-1990**. Milwaukee, WI: Gareth Stevens, 1993. 64p. $23.93. ISBN 0-8368-1040-6. 3-10

Written as if a newspaper, this book's short articles give an overview of the decade. Included are statistics, daily life in America, technology, American hostages in Iran, civil war in Lebanon, Contra forces in Nicaragua, assassins killing Indira Gandhi, the battle against apartheid, Philippine unrest, U.S. forces in Panama, Eastern Europe falling, AIDS, Ronald Reagan, John Lennon, the *Challenger* explosion, George Bush, Mount St. Helen's, Magic Johnson, Larry Bird, Steven Spielberg, George Lucas, Mikhail Gorbachev, Jesse Jackson, and Margaret Thatcher. Glossary, Books for Further Reading, Places to Write or Visit, and Index.

2217. Swain, Gwenyth. **The Road to Seneca Falls: A Story About Elizabeth Cady Stanton**. Mary O'Keefe Young, illustrator. Minneapolis, MN: Carolrhoda, 1996. 64p. $14.21; $5.95pa. ISBN 0-8225-947-6; 1-57505-025-0pa. 3-6

Elizabeth Cady Stanton (1815-1902) heard her father say many times that he wished she had been a boy. He was especially distressed after the death of her older brother. Elizabeth decided that she would try to be like a boy by working hard, and she studied Greek, Latin, and other rigorous subjects. She eventually started going to her father's law office. When Elizabeth heard a widow's distress over her son not letting her live in her own house, she discovered the discrimination against women in the laws. She devoted her life to changing those laws. After she met Lucretia Mott, she and her husband, Henry, became spokespersons for women and slaves. Bibliography and Index.

2218. Swanson, Diane. **Buffalo Sunrise: The Story of a North American Giant**. San Francisco, CA: Sierra Club, 1996. 58p. $16.95. ISBN 0-87156-861-6. 4-7

The text looks at the importance of bison in American history by discussing their role in the survival and culture of Native Americans and the way that European settlers indiscriminately destroyed them. Anecdotes set in boxes give a liveliness to the text, along with accompanying photographs and reproductions. Index.

2219. Swanson, Gloria M., and Margaret V. Ott. **I've Got an Idea! The Story of Frederick McKinley Jones**. Minneapolis, MN: Runestone Press, Lerner, 1994. 95p. $17.50; $7.95pa. ISBN 0-8225-3174-7; 0-8225-9662-8pa. 3-6

Son of an Irish American father and an African American mother, Frederick Jones (1893-1961) was always inquisitive. He never knew his mother, and he lived with his father, who worked on the railroads, until he was seven. Then his father left him at school and never returned. For the rest of his life, Jones had an obsessive desire to learn about machines. He taught himself about race cars, steam engines, radio transmitters, electronics, x-ray units, and air conditioners. He then invented such things as refrigerated trucks, boxcars, and transport containers. He had more than 60 patents at his death, and in 1991 he was posthumously awarded the National Medal of Technology. Notes, Bibliography, and Index.

2220. Swanson, June. **David Bushnell and His Turtle: The Story of America's First Submarine**. Mike Eagle, illustrator. New York: Atheneum, 1991. 40p. $13.95. ISBN 0-689-31628-3. 3-6

The first attempt to use a submarine occurred in the American Revolution. David Bushnell (1740-1824), a farmer who had attended Yale, developed a wooden craft that could go underwater and put a mine under a ship. Although the mine placed with the *Turtle* did not go off as it should have, Bushnell proved that it could be done. He also proved that gunpowder could explode in water, and he developed the first time bomb. Ships and boats today still use the screw propellers, ballast tanks, and conning tower that he developed. Bushnell disappeared into Georgia after his project failed, but he was the first. Bibliography.

2221.   Swanson, June. **I Pledge Allegiance**. Rick Hanson, illustrator. Minneapolis, MN: Carolrhoda, 1990. 39p. $9.95. ISBN 0-87614-393-1. 2-4

On the 400th birthday of Columbus's arrival in 1892, Francis Bellamy wrote the Pledge of Allegiance to the flag of the United States. In the twentieth century, various minor changes occurred before it received legal sanction in 1942. The text defines the words to the pledge and discusses the controversy that often surrounds it. One year after legalization, the Supreme Court ruled that no one could make other people say the pledge against their will.

2222.   Swertka, Eve. **Rachel Carson**. New York: Franklin Watts, 1991. 64p. $11.90. ISBN 0-531-20020-5. (First Book). 3-6

Rachel Carson (1907-1964) had to struggle for recognition in the scientific community because she was female, but she made an important contribution to the preservation of the Earth when she realized that pesticides were killing it. The text emphasizes her work and its importance to her, including the book that got her recognition not just from academics but from the entire world, *The Silent Spring*, published in 1962. For Further Reading, Glossary, and Index.

T

2223. Takaki, Ronald. **Democracy and Race: Asian Americans and World War II**. New York: Chelsea House, 1994. 126p. $18.95. ISBN 0-7910-2184-X. (Asian American Experience). 6 up

During World War II, the United States wanted other countries to think that it had no race problems, but for the Japanese community, the war intensified discrimination and resulted in loss of property and internment in concentration camps. However, young Japanese courageously fought on all fronts for the United States during the war. Chronology, Further Reading, and Index.

2224. Takaki, Ronald. **Ethnic Islands: The Emergence of Urban Chinese America**. New York: Chelsea House, 1994. 125p. $18.95. ISBN 0-7910-2180-7. (Asian American Experience). 6-10

When the Chinese first came to the United States in the second half of the nineteenth century, discrimination, language barriers, and their own needs kept them from mixing with the general population. They established Chinatowns, which were not exotic places, like white Americans thought, but often full of poverty, overcrowding, and the fear of whites. Takaki describes their development and how the people organized to protect themselves from prejudice and as a way to fight for their rightful places as American citizens.

2225. Takaki, Ronald. **From the Land of Morning Calm: The Koreans in America**. New York: Chelsea House, 1994. 125p. $18.95. ISBN 0-7910-2181-5. (Asian American Experience). 6-10

The Japanese began invading Korea in the 1890s. Through 1945, thousands had to leave the country they called "Land of the Morning Calm" to avoid political repression and poor economic conditions. They came first to Hawaii and then to the California coast. They formed Korean patriotic associations wherever they were, hoping someday to return home to an independent Korea. But as they raised their children, they began to think of themselves as Americans. In 1965, the Immigration Act allowed a second wave of Koreans to come. Photographs enhance the text. Chronology, Further Reading, and Index.

2226. Takaki, Ronald. **India in the West: South Asians in America**. New York: Chelsea House, 1994. 117p. $18.95. ISBN 0-7910-2186-6. (Asian American Experience). 5-10

In the early 1900s, Asian Indians came to Canada and the United States. Mainly Sikh men, they endured much prejudice. When the immigration laws became more liberal in 1965, more arrived. The text tells of the difficulties they encountered and how they have had to adjust their cultural expectations to their new country. Black-and-white photographs complement the text. Chronology, Further Reading, and Index. *New York Public Library's Best Books for the Teen Age.*

2227. Takaki, Ronald. **Issei and Nisei: The Settling of Japanese America**. New York: Chelsea House, 1994. 126p. $18.95. ISBN 0-7910-2179-3. (Asian American Experience). 6-10

The Issei are first-generation Japanese Americans, and the Nisei were their American-born children. In 1868, the Meiji Emperor of Japan returned to power and bankrupted thousands of farmers by imposing new taxes. To deal with the problem, the government encouraged emigration. From the 1880s to the 1920s, many Japanese immigrants came first to Hawaii and then to the mainland. They transformed California's marshes and deserts to orchards and gardens, but the discrimination they faced with laws made in 1913 kept them from buying their own farmland. In 1922, the Supreme Court said that they could not become naturalized citizens. In 1924, no new immigration from Asia was permitted. Photographs enhance the text. Chronology, Further Reading, and Index.

2228. Takaki, Ronald. **Journey to Gold Mountain: The Chinese in Nineteenth Century America**. New York: Chelsea House, 1994. 126p. $18.95. ISBN 0-7910-2177-7. (Asian American Experience). 5-10

When the Chinese came to America during the nineteenth century, they were searching for Gold Mountain, a way to gain success and money and return home to support their families. What they did was become the builders of the transcontinental railroad, farmers in California, or laundrymen. They also went to Mississippi and Massachusetts to work in the factories. They had to struggle against prejudice and for their few rights. They eventually settled, but Chinese men outnumbered women fourteen-to-one. Although the women had a variety of jobs, many were prostitutes in the early years while many of the men remained bachelors. Photographs supplement the text. Glossary, Further Reading, and Index.

2229. Takaki, Ronald. **Raising Cane: The World of Plantation Hawaii**. New York: Chelsea House, 1994. 125p. $18.95. ISBN 0-7910-2178-5. (Asian American Experience). 6-10

Many Asian immigrants coming to the United States stopped on the way in Hawaii, and many stayed. In the nineteenth century, sugarcane growers had a shortage of labor so they recruited Japanese, Chinese, Korean, and Filipino workers. The conditions were harsh with low wages, but workers from the different ethnic groups learned to work together. On Hawaii, unlike the United States, men could bring their spouses and children. These people helped to make Hawaii a multiracial society. Photographs enhance the text. Chronology, Further Reading, and Index.

2230. Takaki, Ronald. **Spacious Dreams: The First Wave of Asian Immigration**. New York: Chelsea House, 1994. 127p. $18.95. ISBN 0-7910-2176-9. (Asian American Experience). 5-10

In the early 1800s, the first Asian immigrants arrived in Hawaii and worked on the plantations. Others continued to the mainland United States, where they helped to build the transcontinental railroad. Asians from India arrived in the United States in the early twentieth century. Their difficulties as well as successes appear in the book. Photographs and reproductions enhance the text. Glossary, Further Reading, and Index.

2231. Takaki, Ronald. **Strangers at the Gates Again: Asian American Immigration after 1965**. New York: Chelsea House, 1995. 124p. $18.95. ISBN 0-7910-2190-4. (Asian American Experience). 6-10

In the United States, Asian citizens after World War II eventually won more rights through the Civil Rights movement. In 1965, Congress passed a new immigration act that permitted an increase in immigration from Asian countries. Many came from Japan, China, the Philippines, India, and Pakistan. After 1975, refugees came from Vietnam, Cambodia, and Laos. The old problems of racism, unequal employment, and cultural conflict continued, but America was more diverse and more democratic. Chronology, Further Reading, and Index.

2232. Talbert, Marc. **The Purple Heart**. New York: HarperCollins, 1992. 135p. $14. ISBN 0-06-020428-1. 4-8

Delighted that his father is returning early from Vietnam in 1967, Luke is surprised by his father's disinterest in everything around him. The Purple Heart his father won for being wounded fascinates Luke, and he thinks that in it lies the key to his father's attitude. Luke's father, however, dismisses the award as something one gets for being wounded—nothing special. Although his father needs much time to recover from the horrors of the war, he eventually learns to love his family again.

2233. Talmadge, Katherine. **The Life of Charles Drew**. Antonio Castro, illustrator. New York: Twenty-First Century Books, 1992. 84p. $13.98. ISBN 0-941477-65-7. (Pioneers in Health and Medicine). 5-8

Charles Drew (1904-1950), known as the "father of modern blood banking," was a surgeon and teacher who also fought for racial equality. He helped future generations of African Americans gain access to medical training. He devoted his life to helping others. For Further Reading and Index.

2234. Talmadge, Katherine S. **John Muir: At Home in the Wild**. Antonio Castro, illustrator. New York: Twenty-First Century Books, 1993. 80p. $14.98. ISBN 0-8050-2123-X. (Earth Keepers). 3-5

John Muir (1838-1914), born in Scotland, moved to the United States when he was around 12. He had already discovered the joy of nature, and he was happiest as an adult when he roamed in the Sierra Mountains or in Alaska with a few biscuits and a notebook. He became worried that the places he saw might be destroyed, so he began to write about their beauty. In 1892, he and others formed the Sierra Club, which was dedicated to protecting the wild from greedy development. Among the places named for him are the John Muir Trail in the Sierras and the Muir Glacier in Alaska. Glossary and Index.

2235. Tames, Richard. **Amelia Earhart: 1897-1937**. New York: Franklin Watts, 1989. 32p. $18.50. ISBN 0-531-10851-1. (Lifetimes). 3-6

Amelia Earhart (1897-1937) broke many flying records during her lifetime and was trying to break another when she disappeared over the Pacific. The text looks at her life and the influences that led her to the new profession of flying. Photographs of other flyers and those important in her life complement the text. Find Out More, Important Dates, Glossary, and Index.

2236. Tanaka, Shelley. **The Disaster of the Hindenburg: The Last Flight of the Greatest Airship Ever Built**. New York: Scholastic, 1993. 64p. $6.95pa. ISBN 0-590-45751-9pa. (Time Quest). 5 up

The Hindenburg was 804-feet long and the most fashionable and elite way to cross the Atlantic. The journey took only four-and-a-half days, half the time sailing on a ship. On May 3, 1937, it was in its second season when it burst into flames because it contained flammable hydrogen instead of nonflammable helium. Photographs and drawings of cross-sections show the inside and outside of the ship. Glossary, Chronology, and Further Reading.

2237. Tanaka, Shelley. **On Board the Titanic**. Ken Marshall, illustrator. New York: Hyperion, Madison Press, 1996. 48p. $16.95. ISBN 0-7868-0283-9. (I Was There). 3-6

Complementing the text are photographs and cross-sectional drawings of the *Titanic*, which sank in April 1912. The story recreates the surprise and shock of the passengers that the ship was actually sinking as well as the lack of preparation for such a situation. It discusses people who were on board, including those who heroically helped others.

2238. Tanenhaus, Sam. **Louis Armstrong: Musician**. New York: Chelsea House, 1989. 112p. $18.95; $7.95pa. ISBN 1-55546-571-4; 0-7910-0221-7pa. (Black Americans of Achievement). 5 up

Louis Armstrong (1900-1971) revolutionized jazz and helped establish it as one of the nation's most popular African American art forms. His father deserted the family, and his mother raised him until he was sent to reform school at 13. There he learned to play the coronet. He continued playing and perfecting his art as he watched others play in New Orleans' entertainment areas. He went to Chicago and then New York before he became America's official goodwill ambassador in 1960. Photographs complement the text. Chronology, Further Reading, and Index.

2239. Taylor, Kimberly Hayes. **Black Abolitionists and Freedom Fighters**. Minneapolis, MN: Oliver Press, 1996. 160p. $14.95. ISBN 1-881508-30-7. (Profiles). 5 up

The text looks at eight African American leaders of the abolitionist and freedom fighter movements in the United States. They are Richard Allen (1760-1831), Sojourner Truth (1797?-1883), Nat Turner (1800-1831), Henry Highland Garnet (1815-1882), Frederick Douglass (1818-1895), Harriet Ross Tubman (1820-1913), Booker T. Washington (1856-1915), and Mary Church Terrell (1863-1954). An additional chapter presents capsules of information on more leaders in this area. Bibliography and Index.

2240. Taylor, M. W. **Harriet Tubman: Antislavery Activist**. New York: Chelsea House, 1990. 110p. $18.95; $7.95pa. ISBN 1-55546-612-5; 0-7910-0249-pa. (Black Americans of Achievement). 5 up

Harriet Tubman (1820-1913) led more slaves to freedom than anyone else. She first tried to escape from slavery when she was seven, but was caught, beaten, and put in the fields to work. Twenty years later, she did reach the North, and she began her career on the Underground Railroad. She was able to guide more than 300 people, including her parents, to freedom. In the Civil War, she went to South Carolina as a nurse and led raids on Confederate positions. She continued to work after the war by helping people who needed homes. People call her "Moses." Photographs and engravings enhance the text. Chronology, Further Reading, and Index.

2241. Taylor, Marian W. **Chief Joseph: Nez Percé Leader**. New York: Chelsea House, 1993. 110p. $18.95. ISBN 0-7910-1708-7. (North American Indians of Achievement). 5 up

Chief Joseph (1840-1904) led the flight of the Nez Percé Indians from the government in 1877. His ancestors had lived in Oregon for centuries, but in 1874, the U.S. government decided that the tribe should move to Idaho. In 1877, he started leading his group of 800 toward resettlement, but an incident incited the army, and the U.S. cavalry pursued them, ambushing the group 42 miles from Canada. Joseph saved 418 of them. On October 5, 1877, he said "I will fight no more forever." He spent the next 27 years trying to get the Nez Percé back to their home, but he never succeeded. Photographs enhance the text. Chronology, Further Reading, and Index.

2242. Taylor, Marian W. **Madam C. J. Walker: Pioneer Businesswoman**. New York: Chelsea House, 1993. 80p. $14.95. ISBN 0-7910-2039-8. (Junior Black Americans of Achievement). 3-6

Madam C. J. Walker (1867-1919) had little money until she invented a hair care product for Black women in 1905. It was immediately successful, and she established a business with employees throughout the country. She became the first Black female millionaire. The text looks at her contributions, which also included speaking out for the rights of others and supporting causes with her money. Glossary, Chronology, Further Reading, and Index.

2243. Taylor, Mildred. **The Friendship**. Max Ginsburg, illustrator. New York: Dial, 1987. 56p. $13.95. ISBN 0-8037-0417-8. 2-6

In 1933, Aunt Callie sends Cassie, nine, and her brothers for medicine. The four children have to go to the Wallace store although their parents have warned them never to go there. The storekeeper has given an old Black man, Tom Bee, permission to call him by his first name because Old Tom saved his life twice. When Tom Bee calls him "John," the patrons tell him that Old Tom is being disrespectful. To make himself look important, John shoots Old Tom in the leg. The children witness this despicable act. *Boston Globe—Horn Book Award, Coretta Scott King Award,* and *American Library Association Notable Books for Children.*

2244. Taylor, Mildred. **The Gold Cadillac**. New York: Dial, 1987. 48p. $15.99. ISBN 0-8037-0342-2. 2-6

After 'lois's father buys a new 1950 gold Cadillac, he decides to take it from Toledo, Ohio, to Mississippi to visit the family. People warn 'lois's father that he should reconsider before appearing in the South in such a grand car, and police arrest him because they do not think that a Black person could own such a vehicle. 'lois and her family cannot stay in motels or eat in restaurants along the way, and for the first time she experiences the difficulties of being Black. Her father decides that the car is not worth the hassle. *Christopher Award.*

2245. Taylor, Mildred. **Mississippi Bridge**. New York: Dial, 1990. 64p. $15.99. ISBN 0-8037-0426-7. New York: Bantam, 1992. 64p. $3.50pa. ISBN 0-553-15992-5pa. 4-7

Jeremy Simms, 10, a white boy who wants to be friends with the Logan children of *Roll of Thunder, Hear My Cry* and *Let the Circle Be Unbroken,* watches a bus driver make Black people get off the bus in a heavy rainstorm for some late-arriving white passengers, even though the Black travelers urgently need to take the bus. What happens next shocks Jeremy: A bridge collapses under the bus, and people he knows on board drown. *Christopher Award.*

2246. Taylor, Mildred. **Roll of Thunder, Hear My Cry**. Jerry Pinkney, illustrator. New York: Dial, 1976. 210p. $15.99. ISBN 0-8037-7473-7. New York: Puffin, 1991. 210p. $4.99pa. ISBN 0-14-034893-Xpa. 5 up

In 1933, Cassie Logan, nine, lives in Mississippi with her family and goes to the school for Black children, which only has old books. A white boy, Jeremy, wants to play with the Logan children, but his family hates Blacks and degrades the Logans. Because the family owns land, Mr. Logan has to leave home during the Depression to find work in order to keep their land. Another Black boy tries to make friends with Jeremy's brothers, but they kill a man and blame him for the murder. The love that the family members have for each other and the loyalty they have for their community directs the choices they must make. *Newbery Medal* and *George C. Stone Center for Children's Books Recognition of Merit Award.*

2247. Taylor, Mildred. **Song of the Trees**. Jerry Pinkney, illustrator. New York: Dial, 1975. 56p. $15.99. ISBN 0-8037-5452-3. New York: Skylark, 1989. 56p. $3.50pa. ISBN 0-553-15132-0pa. 2-5

Cassie Logan, eight in 1932, loves to listen to the old pines and other trees outside her window talk to each other, even though her family says she is only hearing the wind. Her father has gone to Louisiana to work during the Depression so that he will have money to pay the mortgage on their land. While he is gone, Mr. Anderson comes and tries to cheat Cassie's grandmother out of their trees. Mr. Logan returns and threatens the man but cannot save the trees that Anderson has already cut.

2248. Taylor, Mildred D. **The Well: David's Story**. New York: Dial, 1995. 92p. $14.99. ISBN 0-8037-1803-9. 4-7

When the father of the Logan family (in *Roll of Thunder, Hear My Cry* and other books) was young, he and his brother Hammer had to cope with the Simms brothers, Charlie and Ed-Rose. As Black children in the early twentieth-century white world of Mississippi, their word was never as good as that of a white man, even if the white man was lying. The Logan well was the only one not to dry up during a long spell, and they allowed neighbors to use their water until the Simms boys poisoned it with parts of a coon, skunk, and possum. A half-wit sees them hunting and reports to people gathered at the well so that their mischief becomes clear. *American Library Association Notable Books for Children.*

2249. Taylor, Richard L. **The First Flight: The Story of the Wright Brothers**. New York: Franklin Watts, 1990. 64p. $19.90. ISBN 0-531-10891-0. 4-6

When the Wrights made their first flight in Kitty Hawk, North Carolina, on December 17, 1903, many had already made unsuccessful attempts to fly. The Wrights also had had their research difficulties, but they were able to solve them. The text looks at their research and some of the aeronautical puzzles they solved on their way to building and flying the "Wright Flyer." Facts, Figures, Important Dates, For Further Reading, and Index.

2250. Taylor, Richard L. **The First Flight Across the United States: The Story of Calbraith Perry Rodgers and His Airplane, the *Vin Fiz***. New York: Franklin Watts, 1993. 64p. $19.90. ISBN 0-531-20159-7. (First Book). 4-6

Calbraith Perry Rodgers (1879-1912) started from New York to cross the country in his airplane on September 17, 1911, and ended in Long Beach, California, on December 10, 1911. He had flown 4,231 miles in 82 hours and 40 minutes. His interest in airplanes began when he saw the Wright brothers' airplanes in Dayton, Ohio. He enrolled as a student with them, but in order to fly solo, he had to buy his own plane because the Wright brothers would not allow solo flights on their planes. He became the world's 49th pilot in 1911. Soon after, he died in a crash at Long Beach.

2251. Taylor, Richard L. **The First Solo Flight Around the World: The Story of Wiley Post and His Airplane, the *Winnie Mae***. New York: Franklin Watts, 1993. 64p. $19.90. ISBN 0-531-20160-0. (First Book). 4-6

When he was 15, Wiley Post (1898-1935) went to the Oklahoma State Fair, where he first saw a pilot perform with his airplane. Post decided to become a pilot, but he had to wait 13 years until World War I ended and he had enough money. He worked as an air-circus pilot and lost an eye on an oil rig. He used his insurance money from the accident to buy a plane and start a "barnstorming" business. He became licensed, began work as a pilot for oil drillers, and delivered their new plane from the Lockheed brothers. In the Depression, he went to work for Lockheed. In 1933, he became the first man to fly around the world twice, the first person to fly alone for 7 days, 18 hours, and 49-and-a-half minutes. Facts, Further Reading, and Index.

2252.   Taylor, Theodore. **Air Raid—Pearl Harbor: The Story of December 7, 1941**. Rev. ed. San Diego, CA: Odyssey, Harcourt Brace, 1991. 179p. $4.95pa. ISBN 0-15-201655-4pa. 5-8

This look at the Japanese raid on Pearl Harbor examines what was happening throughout the world at the time and the sequence of events that led to the bombing. Taylor lists key figures and discusses the situation. Bibliography.

2253.   Taylor, Theodore. **The Cay**. 1969. New York: Doubleday, 1989. 138p. $15.95. ISBN 0-385-07906-0. New York: Flare, 1995. 138p. $4.50pa. ISBN 0-380-01003-8pa. 6-9

In 1942, Phillip, 11, sails with his mother from Curaçao to Norfolk after German submarines begin torpedoing ships in the harbor. After Germans sink their ship, an old Black man, Timothy, saves Phillip and a cat. On the raft, Phillip finds that he is blind from a head injury sustained during the ship's explosion. On the island where they wash up, Timothy teaches Phillip how to be independent in spite of his disability so that Phillip can survive if Timothy dies. *Jane Addams Book Award.*

2254.   Taylor, Theodore. **Timothy of the Cay: A Prequel-Sequel**. San Diego, CA: Harcourt Brace, 1993. 160p. $13.95. ISBN 0-15-288358-4. New York: Camelot, 1995. 160p. $13.95pa. ISBN 0-380-72522-3pa. 5-8

A ship sees the smoke from Phillip's fire on the island where he stays after he was shipwrecked and blinded with Timothy in *The Cay* in 1942. He has survived because Timothy carefully taught him what he needed to know about the island before Timothy died. The ship rescues him, and Phillip, 12, tells what Timothy did. In alternate chapters, he tells Timothy's story, beginning in 1884 as a young cabin boy, and his own story as he hopes to regain his sight. After he is healed, his parents take him to the cay and Timothy's grave. *American Library Association Best Books for Young Adults, Notable Children's Trade Books in the Field of Social Studies,* and *New York Public Library's Books for the Teen Age.*

2255.   Taylor, Theodore. **Walking Up a Rainbow**. 1986. San Diego, CA: Harcourt Brace, 1994. 275p. ISBN 0-15-294512-1. New York: Flare, 1996. 275p. $4.50pa. ISBN 0-380-72592-4pa. 5 up

Susan's parents die in a buggy accident when she is 14 in 1852. To get the money to pay the debt her father left and keep the family home, she has to go across the United States, down through Panama, and back up to New Orleans and Iowa to achieve her goal. Along the way with her chaperone, she meets a variety of people.

2256.   Tedards, Anne. **Marian Anderson: Singer**. New York: Chelsea House, 1988. 111p. $18.95; $7.95pa. ISBN 1-55546-638-9; 0-7910-0216-0pa. (American Women of Achievement). 5 up

Marian Anderson (1897-1993) has been called the "voice of the American soul." Denied entrance to music school because she was African American, she began to perform for segregated audiences. By 1935, she was recognized as one of the century's greatest singers. When the Washington, D.C., Daughters of the American Revolution refused to let her sing in their hall, she sang for 75,000 Americans at the Lincoln Memorial, an event arranged by Eleanor Roosevelt. President Eisenhower appointed her to the U.S. Mission to the United Nations in 1958. Photographs, Further Reading, Chronology, and Index.

2257.   Tessendorf, K C. **Wings Around the World: The American World Flight of 1924**. New York: Atheneum, 1991. 104p. $14.95. ISBN 0-689-31550-3. 4-8

The first world flight occurred in 1924 from April 6 to September 28. The airmen of the U.S. Army's Air Service decided to be the first to accomplish this feat, but they had to have the support of other branches of the services to be successful. The flight began in Seattle, Washington, and continued over two oceans and three continents. They crossed 22 foreign nations with all types of climate. In every country, they had to accept invitations and attend celebrations. The text, with photographs, gives the details of the preparations and the execution of this journey. On Further Reading and Index.

2258.   Thaxter, Celia. **Celia's Island Journey**. Loretta Krupinski, illustrator and adapter. Boston: Little, Brown, 1992. Unpaged. $15.95. ISBN 0-316-83921-3. 1-4

In 1839, Celia Thaxter, a nineteenth-century writer and poet, lived on White Island where her father kept a lighthouse. Her journals written during that time create the story of a time of beauty, although the winters were long and tedious. Her love of nature and her family are clear in this presentation.

2259.   Thayer, Ernest Lawrence. **Casey at the Bat**. Gerald Fitzgerald, illustrator and adapter. New York: Atheneum, 1995. Unpaged. $15. ISBN 0-689-31945-2. K-3

In this narrative poem, the batter strikes out at an important point in the game. The illustrations complement the story by displaying the feelings the swaggering Casey had when he struck out.

2260.   Thesman, Jean. **Molly Donnelly**. Boston: Houghton Mifflin, 1993. 186p. $13.95. ISBN 0-395-64348-1. 5-9

Although her day in Seattle, Washington, begins normally, Molly Donnelly sees changes begin on December 7, 1941, after the Japanese bomb Pearl Harbor. That night, the blackouts begin. Her best friend Emily Tanaka and her family are taken away and placed in an internment camp. Her brother and father start to work longer shifts for Boeing Aircraft, and her mother begins working. During the war, two of her cousins die, she has her first date, and she becomes interested in a young soldier. What she realizes as she looks around is that getting a college education is the only way she can escape the limited choices for women.

2261.   Thesman, Jean. **The Ornament Tree**. Boston: Houghton Mifflin, 1996. 240p. $15.95. ISBN 0-395-74278-1. 5-8

Bonnie, 14, becomes an orphan and has to move to Seattle where her mother's relatives live. The women are well-educated liberals who distribute information on suffrage, birth control, and the horrors of child labor. They have no management skills, however, so they have to take in boarders to recover from World War I and survive the general strike of 1919. When Bonnie arrives, the Deveraux women have found out that they need kitchen skills, so she comes to their aid, and they, in turn, help her.

2262.   Thesman, Jean. **Rachel Chance**. Boston: Houghton Mifflin, 1990. 175p. $13.95. ISBN 0-395-50934-3. 6-9

In Seattle in the early 1940s, Rachel, 15, feels despair when someone kidnaps her four-year-old illegitimate brother Rider. Her grandfather, cousin, and widowed mother desperately search for him with the help of her grandfather's eccentric friend Druid Annie and a hired boy whom Rachel at first dislikes. Rachel suspects revivalists who have just left town. She finds them and Rider, as well as Rider's father, who did not know about his son.

2263.   Thomson, Peggy. **Katie Henio: Navajo Sheepherder**. New York: Cobblehill, 1995. 52p. $16.99. ISBN 0-525-65160-8. 3-6

Although Katie Henio is a modern Navajo who has been tending sheep in New Mexico throughout her long life, she represents the timeless occupations of her tribe. The text, with photographs, tells of her day tending sheep, cooking, or weaving. It also includes the customs of naming, umbilical cords, salt, coming-of-age, wedding pudding, wedding baskets, and plants for healing.

2264.   Time-Life. **African Americans: Voices of Triumph: Leadership**. Alexandria, VA: Time-Life, 1994. 256p. $18.95. ISBN 0-7835-2254-1. 6 up

The text and the accompanying photographs give a view of African leadership throughout history. Brief commentaries on the seventeenth-century Queen Nzingha and her contemporary Okomfo Anokye of the Ashanti nation, Makeda of Ethiopia (who may have been the Queen of Sheba), the Islamic Ahmed Baba in the sixteenth century, and Imhotep around 2600 BC introduce the heritage of African American leaders. Included are African American leaders in science and invention, business and industry, religion, education, and politics. Bibliography and Index.

2265.   Tingum, Janice. **E. B. White: The Elements of a Writer**. Minneapolis, MN: Lerner, 1995. 124p. $17.21. ISBN 0-8225-4922-0. 5 up

Elwyn Brooks White (1899-1985), known as Andy, loved to play with the animals in his farmyard when he was a boy. Their presence most likely led to the animals in *Charlotte's Web*, which he published in 1952. By the time he wrote the book, he had published in many other places but had worked continuously at the *New Yorker*, where he met his wife Katherine. As a writer, he also was concerned about style and vocabulary. Perhaps his most important other book is his revision of William Strunk's *The Elements of Style*. In it he continued the tradition of a love for good, correct writing. A private person, he was always devoted to his wife. Sources, Bibliography, and Index.

2266.   Toht, David W. **Sodbuster**. Richard Erickson, illustrator. Minneapolis, MN: Lerner, 1996. 48p. $14.96. ISBN 0-8225-2977-7. (American Pastfinder). 4-7

Between 1800 and 1850, many Americans went west because they wanted to own a farm of approximately 160 acres. With few tools and a team of oxen, they cleared land, raised barns, built fences, and started farms that began to thrive. Because breaking the prairie was the first job of these immigrants, they became known as "sodbusters." In two-page chapters the text looks at their efforts, their daily lives, home remedies, clothing, planting and harvesting, winter, going to market, celebrations, church, and school. Glossary and Index.

2267.   Tolan, Mary, and Kelli Peduzzi. **Ralph Nader: Crusader for Safe Consumer Products**. Milwaukee, WI: Gareth Stevens, 1991. 68p. $16.95. ISBN 0-8368-0455-4. (People Who Made a Difference). 3-6

Ralph Nader (b. 1934) studied cars and realized that General Motors' Corvair was dangerous to its drivers and passengers. Nader wrote a book about its problems, and sales fell. Nader won a court case when he found out that General Motors had hired people to spy on him, and he used the money to establish a firm to study consumer problems. He and his lawyers have revealed unfair business practices and shoddy products that have helped the average person make better choices. Organizations, Books, List of New Words, Important Dates, and Index.

2268. Tomlinson, Michael. **Jonas Salk**. Vero Beach, FL: Rourke, 1993. 112p. $19.93. ISBN 0-86625-495-1. (Pioneers). 5-9

Jonas Salk (b. 1914) was the first person to find a vaccine for the polio virus, but he refused to patent it. He was a great humanitarian who, throughout his research years, was always looking for a way to improve the human condition. The text looks at his life and work. Photographs, Time Line, Glossary, Bibliography, Media Resources, and Index.

2269. Toor, Rachel. **Eleanor Roosevelt**. New York: Chelsea House, 1989. 110p. $18.95. ISBN 1-55546-676-1. (American Women of Achievement). 5 up

Among the causes that Eleanor Roosevelt (1884-1962) espoused during her years in the public eye were feminism, labor reform, civil rights, and economic aid for the poor. After her husband died in 1945, she served two presidents as a delegate to the United Nations. Hers was a strong voice in the twentieth century. Photographs highlight the text. Chronology, Further Reading, and Index.

2270. Topper, Frank, and Charles A. Wills. **A Historical Album of New Jersey**. Brookfield, CT: Millbrook Press, 1994. 64p. $16.40; $6.95pa. ISBN 1-56294-505-X; 1-56294-849-0pa. (Historical Album). 4-8

The text presents the land of New Jersey before it became a state, beginning with Native American civilizations and continuing through exploration and settlement. Early statehood developments and issues, and the role of large cities in the state's livelihood, lead to the present day. Prints, maps, and photographs illustrate the text. Gazetteer: Quick Facts, Key Events, Personalities, and Index.

2271. Towle, Wendy. **The Real McCoy: The Life of an African-American Inventor**. Wil Clay, illustrator. New York: Scholastic, 1993. Unpaged. $14.95; $4.95pa. ISBN 0-590-43596-5; 0-590-48102-9pa. 2-5

After studying engineering in Scotland, the Canadian-born African American Elijah McCoy (1844-1929) patented more than 50 inventions. From his name came the expression "the real McCoy," because people knew that the automatic oil cup he invented for locomotives and heavy machinery was much better than the imitations.

2272. Towne, Mary. **Dive Through the Wave**. Mahwah, NJ: BridgeWater, 1994. 124p. $13.95. ISBN 0-8167-3478-X. 4-6

When she is 11 in 1943, Ruth feels inadequate. She worries about the killing in the war and the threat of polio. She meets a Jones Beach lifeguard on Long Island and finds that he has survived polio. His comments to her make life seem less traumatic, especially when he compares it to a wave through which one must dive to escape the sting of the spray.

2273. Townsend, Tom. **The Ghost Flyers**. Pat Finney, illustrator. Austin, TX: Eakin Press, 1993. 98p. $5.95pa. ISBN 0-89015-938-6pa. 6-8

Ghost flyers appeared in the night skies over the southwestern United States during 1896-1897. Harlin, 13, sees the ghost flyers while he shovels coal into the boiler of an engine.

2274. Toynton, Evelyn. **Growing Up in America**: **1830-1860**. Brookfield, CT: Millbrook Press, 1995. 96p. $16.90. ISBN 1-56294-453-3. 4-9

Toynton answers the question of what it was like to grow up in the years prior to the Civil War in the United States. Because children who lived in different parts of the country had different types of lives, she looks at children in New England, on the Plains, in the Sioux tribe, on the streets, and in bondage. Then she looks at the different activities they might have had at school, play, work, and reading. Further Reading, Bibliography, and Index. *Notable Children's Trade Books in the Field of Social Studies*.

2275. Trimble, Stephen. **The Village of Blue Stone**. Jennifer Owings, illustrator. New York: Macmillan, 1990. 58p. $15. ISBN 0-02-789501-7. 3-6

In December 1888, two cowboys discovered the Cliff Palace, a ruined village of the highly developed Anasazi civilization. The text recreates one year in the life of the Anasazi community and its Chaco culture around AD 1100 by beginning with the winter solstice and the predictions of the local astrologist. Arts and pottery, life, religion, and work are part of this year described by illustrations and text. Afterword, Author's Note, and Index.

2276. Tripp, Valerie. **Changes for Molly**. Nick Backes and Keith Skeen, illustrators. Middleton, WI: Pleasant, 1990. 67p. $12.95; $5.95pa. ISBN 0-937295-48-5; 0-937295-49-3pa. (American Girls). 3-5

In 1944, Molly, 10, wants to be Miss Victory for her dance recital. Concerns about her hair and other things do not overshadow her worry that her father will return safely from the war. On the day of the recital, Molly becomes ill. She stays at home, depressed, but her father appears unexpectedly, and the earlier problems of the day disappear.

2277. Tripp, Valerie. **Changes for Samantha**. Luann Roberts, illustrator. Middleton, WI: Pleasant, 1988. 72p. $12.95; $5.95pa. ISBN 0-937295-46-9; 0-937295-47-7pa. (American Girls). 3-5

In 1904, when Samantha goes to New York City to live with her aunt and uncle, she waits to hear from her friend Nellie, recently orphaned and planning to come to the city to live with her own uncle. She eventually finds Nellie abandoned in an orphanage. Samantha convinces Nellie to run away so that she will not have to go on the orphan train to the West. Samantha's aunt takes in Nellie and her sisters.

2278. Tripp, Valerie. **Meet Felicity: An American Girl**. Dan Andreasen, illustrator. Middleton, WI: Pleasant, 1991. 69p. $12.95; $5.95pa. ISBN 1-56247-003-5;1-56247-004-3pa. (American Girls). 3-5

In Williamsburg, Virginia, during 1774, Felicity, nine, rises early every morning to take care of a horse owned by an alcoholic owner who beats and starves it. He will not sell the horse to her father, so Felicity helps it escape by jumping it over the fence and deliberately falling off so that it can leave the area.

2279. Trump, Fred. **Lincoln's Little Girl: A True Story**. Kit Wray, illustrator. Honesdale, PA: Boyds Mills Press, 1994. 184p. $19.95. ISBN 1-56397-375-8. 5-8

When Grace Bedell (b. 1848 or 1849) was 11 in 1860, she wrote Abraham Lincoln a letter. She suggested that he grow whiskers because they would increase his chances of becoming president. Although details of Lincoln's life after this time are almost public record, only the letters that Bedell wrote document her husband's service in the Civil War and their life homesteading in Kansas, fighting grasshopper plagues, tornadoes, prairie fires, and other disasters.

2280. Tunbo, Frances G. **Stay Put, Robbie McAmis**. Charles Shaw, illustrator. Fort Worth, TX: Texas Christian University, 1988. 158p. $15.95. ISBN 0-87565-025-2. 4 up

In 1848, Robbie, 12, becomes separated from the rest of the wagons while crossing the Big Cypress River in East Texas. With him are an infant, three younger girls, a sickly boy of 10, and Grammie, a woman who seems to live in another world. He stays put, as his uncle told him to do, and the group begins surviving on the river's shore with their few provisions and the cow. Grammie regains her senses, and she and Robbie provide a loving environment for the children as they wait for a rescue. *Western Heritage Award.*

2281. Tunnell, Michael O., and George W. Chilcoat. **The Children of Topaz: The Story of a Japanese-American Internment Camp Based on a Classroom Diary**. New York: Holiday House, 1996. 74p. $16.95. ISBN 0-8234-1239-3. 4-7

A third grade teacher in the Topaz, Utah, internment camp recorded her students' responses to their situation in 1943. The authors use this diary as a basis for a discussion on the internment of Japanese Americans during World War II after the bombing of Pearl Harbor. They elaborate with information that clarifies the simple statements of the children. For Further Reading and Index.

2282. Turner, Ann. **Dakota Dugout**. New York: Macmillan, 1985. 32p. $15. ISBN 0-02-789700-1. New York: Aladdin, 1989. 32p. $3.95pa. ISBN 0-689-71296-0pa. K-3

A young girl thought her sod house in Dakota during the nineteenth century was very uncomfortable. But when the family has enough money to build a large house, she misses it. As a grandmother, she tells the story. *American Library Association Notable Books for Children.*

2283. Turner, Ann. **Dust for Dinner**. Robert Barrett, illustrator. New York: HarperCollins, 1995. 64p. $13.95; $3.75pa. ISBN 0-06-023377-X; 0-06-444225-Xpa. (An I Can Read Book). K-3

In the 1930s, Jake's family survives three years of dust and drought before his father decides that they will go to California. He finally gets a job as a watchman, and the family has a home again.

2284. Turner, Ann. **Grasshopper Summer**. New York: Macmillan, 1989. 166p. $12.95. ISBN 0-02-789511-4. 4-6

In 1874, Sam's younger brother Billy is the better student; he is also teaching an ex-slave to read, and both facts annoy Sam. Then Sam's father decides to leave Kentucky for the West, and the family journeys to Dakota Territory. They have to fight their way there, and after they arrive, they have to cope with a plague of grasshoppers that destroys their first efforts at pioneering.

2285. Turner, Ann. **Katie's Trunk**. Ronald Himler, illustrator. New York: Macmillan, 1992. 32p. $13.95. ISBN 0-02-789512-2. K-3

When someone yells "Tory!" at Katie's mother, and people dump tea into Boston Harbor, Katie knows something is wrong. Katie's father tells the family to hide in the woods if the rebels come, but when they do come, Katie gets mad and runs back into the house. She hides in her mother's wedding trunk, and her friend's father, a rebel, finds her. He tells the other men that no one is in the room, so she realizes that rebels are not all bad, even though they are her father's enemies.

2286. Turner, Ann. **Nettie's Trip South**. Ronald Himler, illustrator. New York: Macmillan, 1987. 32p. $14. ISBN 0-02-789240-9. New York: Aladdin, 1995. 32p. $4.95pa. ISBN 0-689-80117-3pa. 1-5

When Nettie is 10 in the 1850s, she goes south with her journalist brother. She writes her friend to tell her how disturbed she is by what she has seen. When she watches slaves sold at auction, she vomits because she realizes that if her skin were black, she would be treated in the same way. She also knows that she would have only one name and not be identified with her real family.

2287. Turner, Ann. **Sewing Quilts**. Thomas B. Allen, illustrator. New York: Macmillan, 1994. Unpaged. $14.95. ISBN 0-02-789285-9. K-3

The pastel drawings clarify the setting as the nineteenth century while the first-person text tells the story of a young girl who appreciates her mother's quilt because it makes her feel secure. Their new house, built after the last one burned, needs the quilt for its safety. The narrator creates her own quilt, a Bear Paw pattern, as a further protection, while her sister, born on July 4, sews a patriotic red, white, and blue quilt.

2288. Turner, Ann. **Shaker Hearts**. Wendell Minor, illustrator. New York: HarperCollins, 1997. Unpaged. $14.95. ISBN 0-06-025369-X. 3-7

Using Mother Ann Lee's phrase "hands to work; hearts to God," Turner creates a poetical look at the Shaker community, one of the most successful Utopian communities in America. The verses, which describe the daily activities, almost serve as short prayers with the illustrations revealing the life and the landscape of the Shaker people. An appendix discusses the contributions they made to society.

2289. Turner, Glennette Tilley. **Lewis Howard Latimer**. Englewood Cliffs, NJ: Silver Burdett, 1990. 128p. $13.95. ISBN 0-382-09524-3. (Pioneers in Change). 5-9

Lewis Latimer (1848-1928), born to parents in Boston who had escaped from slavery and were almost returned to the South after the Fugitive Slave Act, fought for the Union in the Civil War. He began his experimenting and received a patent for water closets on trains. Then he made drawings for Alexander Graham Bell's first telephone. When Thomas Edison made an incandescent light bulb, the filament lasted only 40 hours. Two years later, Latimer invented the improved long-burning carbon filament. Then he worked on the "Maxim lamp," which was installed in large cities in the northeastern states. He also wrote the first book on electrical lighting called *Incandescent Electric Lighting*. He continued his work and tried to help immigrants and others in New York during his later life. He is remembered as a draftsman, inventor, technical writer, poet, essayist, musician, linguist, artist, family man, veteran, citizen, and civil rights activist. Important Dates, Bibliography, and Index.

2290. Turner, Glennette Tilley. **Running for Our Lives**. Samuel Byrd, illustrator. New York: Holiday House, 1994. 198p. $15.95. ISBN 0-8234-1121-4. 4-8

In 1855, Luther and Carrie escape with their parents after their plantation owner leaves his Missouri home to fight abolitionists in Kansas. The family becomes separated by the Underground Railroad "conductor" when they are crossing the Mississippi, but they hope to reunite in Canada. Their difficult journey, with typical sibling arguments, leads them to an unknown aunt and, after four years, finally to their parents.

2291. Turner, Robyn Montana. **Dorothea Lange**. Boston: Little, Brown, 1994. 32p. $15.95. ISBN 0-316-85656-8. (Portraits of Women Artists for Children). 4-6

Dorothea Lange (1895-1965) grew up in New Jersey. After her father left her mother when Lange was in her early teens, they moved in with a grandmother who drank too much. Lange always tried to see the beauty in things, and when she saw photographs in a store window, she asked to work with the photographer even though she had never taken a picture. He gave her a camera, and she began. She and a friend went out west, and she stayed there. As she photographed, she wanted more than studio poses; she wanted to find the humanity in her subjects. Some of her best work was photographing people during the Great Depression of the 1930s. With the pictures, she showed the need for social change.

2292. Turner, Robyn Montana. **Georgia O'Keeffe**. Boston: Little, Brown, 1991. 32p. $16.95. ISBN 0-316-85649-5. (Portraits of Women Artists for Children). 3-6

Georgia O'Keeffe (1887-1986) grew up in Wisconsin thinking she would become an artist when women were rarely able to pursue their artistic talents. She used shape, color, and form to create the idea of her subject. Her images of giant flowers, cityscapes, and desert scenes show her perception of the world. Reproductions.

2293. Turner, Robyn Montana. **Mary Cassatt**. Boston: Little, Brown, 1992. 32p. $16.95. ISBN 0-316-85650-9. (Portrait of Women Artists for Children). 3-6

When Mary Cassatt began painting in the 1860s, few women had ever attempted to become artists. As a child, she had traveled in Europe with her family and visited important museums. These opportunities influenced her later life and her intense interest in recreating mothers and their children on her canvases.

2294. Turvey, Peter. **Inventions: Inventors and Ingenious Ideas**. New York: Franklin Watts, 1992. 48p. $13.95. ISBN 0-531-14308-2. (Timelines). 5-8

The text and illustrations combine to give the history of inventions, from the making of fire to the space stations of the future. Included are inventors and ingenious ideas during the classical period of the Greeks and Romans, the Middle Ages, the Renaissance, and the present. Chronology, Glossary, and Index.

2295. Twist, Clint. **Lewis and Clark: Exploring the Northwest**. Austin, TX: Raintree/Steck-Vaughn, 1994. 46p. $15.96. ISBN 0-8114-7255-8. (Beyond the Horizons). 5-8

Meriwether Lewis (1774-1809) and William Clark (1770-1838) led an expedition from 1804 to 1806 across the new land purchased by Thomas Jefferson. The text gives historical background, the preparation of the Corps of Discovery, the actual journey, the achievements of the expedition, information on Native North Americans, and what happened as a result of the expedition. Photographs, paintings, drawings, and maps augment the text. Glossary, Further Reading, and Index.

U

2296.   Uchida, Yoshiko. **The Best Bad Thing**. New York: Atheneum, 1983. 136p. $15; $4.95pa. ISBN 0-689-50290-7; 0-689-71745-8pa. 3-7

The second book of the trilogy beginning with *A Jar of Dreams* and ending with *The Happiest Ending* sees Rinko's mother wanting Rinko to work with Mrs. Hatta for the summer. Rinko thinks that Mrs. Hatta is slightly crazy, but when she calls Rinko outside to see the lovely spider webs floating in the air, Rinko begins to change her mind. An old man living nearby also helps the summer become the "best bad thing" when he gives Rinko a kite and calls it an extension of the sky. *American Library Association Notable Books for Children* and *School Library Journal Best Book.*

2297.   Uchida, Yoshiko. **The Bracelet**. Joanna Yardley, illustrator. New York: Philomel, 1993. 32p. $14.95. ISBN 0-399-22503-X. K-3

When Emi, seven, leaves her home in 1942 for the internment camp after the Japanese bomb Pearl Harbor, she takes a bracelet with a heart charm that her best friend Laurie gives her. When she arrives at the camp, she loses the bracelet. Her mother tells her that she can carry Laurie in her heart just as she does her father, whom the government has taken to be interred in a different place.

2298.   Uchida, Yoshiko. **The Happiest Ending**. New York: Macmillan, 1985. 120p. $15. ISBN 0-689-50326-1. 3-7

In the last book of the trilogy beginning with *A Jar of Dreams* and *The Best Bad Thing*, Rinko wants to be more American than Japanese, and she revolts against an arranged marriage between a young Japanese girl and an older man. When she sees the man's kindness and the appreciation that the girl has for this quality, she becomes more accepting of this traditional way to marry. *Bay Area Book Reviewers Association Award.*

2299.   Uchida, Yoshiko. **The Invisible Thread**. 1991. New York: Beechtree, 1992. 128p. $4.95pa. ISBN 0-688-13703-2pa. 5-8

Yoshiko Uchida (d. 1992) tells of her life growing up in America where her experiences included having to ask if someone cut "Japanese" hair and having another person complement her on her ability to speak English well while looking at her Japanese face. During World War II, when the Japanese bombed Pearl Harbor, she and her family were transported to Topaz, Utah, which she wrote about in *Journey to Topaz*. She eventually went to Smith College to graduate school and got a job teaching outside Philadelphia, where she could bring her parents from Topaz. Even with these indignities, Uchida managed to keep her integrity and her sense of humor as she created her award-winning books about the Japanese experience in America.

2300.   Uchida, Yoshiko. **A Jar of Dreams**. New York: Atheneum, 1981. 144p. $14; $3.95pa. ISBN 0-689-50210-9; 0-689-71672-9pa. 3-7

The first book in a trilogy with *The Best Bad Thing* and *The Happiest Ending* presents Rinko, 11, and her family with all their dreams for their future as Japanese Americans in 1935. When an aunt comes to visit, she influences each person to start working toward one of their goals. Rinko's mother opens a laundry, her father starts his garage, and her brother returns to college. *Commonwealth Club of California Book Award* and *Friends of Children and Literature Award (FOCAL).*

2301.   Uchida, Yoshiko. **Journey Home**. Charles Robinson, illustrator. New York: Macmillan, 1978. 144p. $15; $3.95pa. ISBN 0-689-50126-9; 0-689-71641-9pa. 5-9

In the sequel to *Journey to Topaz*, Yuki and her mother return from the internment camp to Berkeley, California, after World War II. They and the neighbors have to work together to restart their lives. They learn the meaning of forgiveness and acceptance when neighbors whose son was killed in Japan help them rebuild their firebombed store and invite them to celebrate Thanksgiving.

2302.   Uchida, Yoshiko. **Journey to Topaz**. Donald Carrick, illustrator. 1971. Berkeley, CA: Creative Arts Book, 1985. 160p. $8.95pa. ISBN 0-916870-85-5pa. 4 up

Yuki Sakane, 11, born in America as a Nisei and therefore a citizen, looks forward to Christmas in 1941, but the Japanese bomb Pearl Harbor. The FBI comes and takes her father away, and then they take her, her mother, and brother to Topaz, Utah, to an internment camp. She makes new friends but faces hardships such as dust storms and a tragedy that disturbs everyone. Eventually the family reunites in Topaz, but their lives have been altered permanently. *American Library Association Notable Books for Children.*

2303.   Uchida, Yoshiko. **Samurai of Gold Hill**. Ati Forberg, illustrator. 1972. Berkeley, CA: Creative Arts Books, 1985. 119p. $8.95pa. ISBN 0-916870-86- 3pa. 4 up

Although he wants to be a samurai, Koichi must leave Japan when he is 12 in 1869 to sail to the United States because his clan and the Shogun are defeated. In Gold Hill, his father and partners in the Wakamatsu colony try to start a tea and silk farm, but miners destroy their work. When Koichi sees a Maidu Indian celebrate a ritual, he realizes that it looks very much like a Japanese ritual. He knows that people are not as different as they might seem.

$$\boxed{V}$$

2304. Vail, John. **Thomas Paine**. New York: Chelsea House, 1990. 112p. $18.95. ISBN 1-55546-819-5. (World Leaders Past and Present). 5 up

Thomas Paine (1737-1809) grew up in an English Quaker family and did not come to America until he was almost 40. He worked as an editor in Pennsylvania and wrote numerous articles and political pamphlets arguing for independence from England. His writing inspired the colonists, and after the revolution, he helped found the new nation. In 1787, he went to France to help with that revolution. He rejected the idea of hereditary rule and became a proponent of popular rebellion. He was jailed for his views in France in 1793. Then he began to work on *The Age of Reason*, an attack on organized Christianity. He returned to America in 1802 at Thomas Jefferson's invitation, but he was out of favor because of his ideas. Photographs and engravings enhance the text. Chronology, Further Reading, and Index.

2305. Van Der Linde, Laurel. **Devil in Salem Village**. Brookfield, CT: Millbrook Press, 1992. 72p. $15.90. ISBN 1-56294-144-5. (Spotlight on America). 4-6

At her execution, Sarah Good said "God will give you blood to drink," and she was hanged as a witch on July 19, 1692. This time of witchcraft trials in the colonial period is hard to understand, but the trials occurred throughout 1692 in Salem. The text, with engravings and drawings highlighting, tells of those accused and how they were examined and convicted. Chronology, Further Reading, Bibliography, and Index.

2306. Van Der Linde, Laurel. **The Pony Express**. New York: New Discovery, 1993. 72p. $14.95. ISBN 0-02-759056-9. (Timestop). 6-9

The Pony Express began in 1860 and ran for only 18 months. During that time, it proved that mail could travel across the continent much faster than had been imagined. The text discusses the method of advertising for riders, the most famous riders (including Buffalo Bill Cody and Wild Bill Hickok), the Indian war in 1860, and other problems that riders had to overcome. Photographs and drawings enhance the text. Further Reading and Index.

2307. Van Leeuwen, Jean. **Across the Wide Dark Sea: The Mayflower Journey**. Thomas B. Allen, illustrator. New York: Dial, 1995. Unpaged. $15.99. ISBN 0-8037-1166-2. K-3

Love, a nine-year-old passenger on the *Mayflower*, tells of the journey and the first few months in the New World. He always fears the Indians and concentrates on what he observes, such as the crowding aboard ship and a ship's hand nearly drowning. He does not pay attention to the name of the settlement or other details that one usually expects in an account of Plymouth, but he does emphasize the things that would concern a boy of his age.

2308. Van Leeuwen, Jean. **Bound for Oregon**. James Watling, illustrator. New York: Dial, 1994. 167p. $14.89. ISBN 0-8037-1527-7. 4-6

When Mary Ellen Todd is around 13 in 1852, her father decides that the family will go west with a wagon train leaving Independence, Missouri. They leave with more than 100 other wagons, but when they arrive, only one other family remains. The river crossings, arguments, and disease either discourage or destroy the others. After they arrive, Mary Ellen writes to her grandmother, the woman who raised her for six years after her real mother died. As she recalls the hardship of the journey, she realizes that her grandmother will never be strong enough to endure the trip. That she will never see her grandmother again saddens her, but she begins to adjust to her stepmother and to their new life.

2309. Van Steenwyk, Elizabeth. **The California Gold Rush: West with the Forty-Niners**. New York: Franklin Watts, 1991. 63p. $19.90. ISBN 0-531-20032-9. (First Books). 5-7

The California Gold Rush around 1846-1850 was an important event in the nineteenth century. It changed more people's lives than any other episode except the Civil War. It opened new routes of transportation and changed the face of California and the West. These topics and the lives of the miners before, during, and after the event appear in the text, which is enhanced with photographs and reproductions. Glossary, Further Reading, and Index.

2310. Vare, Ethlie Ann, and Greg Ptacek. **Women Inventors and their Discoveries**. Minneapolis, MN: Oliver Press, 1993. 160p. $14.95. ISBN 1-88150-806-4. 4-7

The text presents 10 women throughout American history who invented things. One of them, Fannie Farmer, wrote a modern cookbook using standardized measurements rather than a "pinch of this" and a "handful of that." Other inventions include Liquid Paper correction fluid, cosmetics and hair products for Black women, fiber for bulletproof vests, an indigo plant capable of producing a superior dye, and the Barbie doll. The women are mostly unknown, but their creations have made a mark on American society. Photographs, Bibliography, and Index.

2311. Veglahn, Nancy. **Women Scientists**. New York: Facts on File, 1991. 134p. $17.95. ISBN 0-8160-2482-0. 5 up

Many women scientists have not been sufficiently recognized for their achievements. The text looks at 11 women who have made major contributions to their scientific fields. They are Alice Eastwood, botanist (1859-1953); Nettie Maria Stevens, cytologist (1861-1912); Annie Jump Cannon, astronomer (1863-1941); Alice Hamilton, industrial medicine physician (1869-1970); Edith Quimby, radiation physicist (1891-1982); Gerty Cori, biochemist (1896-1957); Margaret Mead, anthropologist (1901-1978); Barbara McClintock, geneticist (b. 1902); Rachel Carson, environmentalist (1907-1964); Rosalyn Yalow, physiologist (b. 1921); and Mildred Dresselhaus, physicist (b. 1930). Index.

2312. Venezia, Mike, author/illustrator. **Edward Hopper**. Chicago: Childrens Press, 1990. 32p. $5.95pa. ISBN 0-516-42277-4pa. (Getting to Know the World's Greatest Artists). K-3

Edward Hopper (1882-1967) was an American realist painter who painted scenes of cities in which the figures often represented the loneliness of society. Illustrations highlight the text.

2313. Venezia, Mike, author/illustrator. **George Gershwin**. Chicago: Childrens Press, 1994. 32p. $18.60. ISBN 0-516-04536-9. (Getting to Know the World's Greatest Composers). K-4

George Gershwin (1898-1937), born in New York City, was one of the first composers to mix popular music with symphonic music. As a young boy, after he became interested in music, he learned to play the piano. He got a job in Tin Pan Alley, playing songs for performers who might want them for their acts. Before radio, the only way someone could hear a song was if someone played it in person. When he played *Rhapsody in Blue* for the first time in 1924 on live radio, the public approved. He followed it with *An American in Paris* and *Porgy and Bess*, his favorite work.

2314. Venezia, Mike, author/illustrator. **Georgia O'Keeffe**. Chicago: Childrens Press, 1993. 32p. $5.95pa. ISBN 0-516-42297-9pa. (Getting to Know the World's Greatest Artists). K-3

Georgia O'Keeffe (1887-1986) is known for her paintings of flowers in the colors of Southwest American desert scenes, places that she loved. Illustrations augment the text.

2315. Venezia, Mike, author/illustrator. **Jackson Pollock**. Chicago: Childrens Press, 1994. 32p. $5.95pa. ISBN 0-516-42298-7pa. (Getting to Know the World's Greatest Artists). K-3

Jackson Pollock (1912-1956) was an American artist who splashed paint over his canvases to create non-representational scenes. One of his paintings, *Blue Poles*, sold to the Australian government for several million dollars. After that his paintings began to command high prices. Illustrations highlight the text.

2316. Venezia, Mike, author/illustrator. **Mary Cassatt**. Chicago: Childrens Press, 1993. 32p. $5.95pa. ISBN 0-516-42278-2pa. (Getting to Know the World's Greatest Artists). K-3

Mary Cassatt (1844-1926) was an American Impressionist painter who lived much of her life in France. She is especially known for the figures of mothers and children incorporated in her paintings. Illustrations supplement the text.

2317. Ventura, Piero, author/illustrator. **Clothing**. Boston: Houghton Mifflin, 1993. 64p. $16.95. ISBN 0-395-66791-7. 4-8

The text, with illustrations, gives a history of clothing. The periods and topics covered are prehistory, Egypt, the Ancient East, tanning leather, Crete, Greek styles, Rome, classical society, Byzantium, the barbarians, from sheep to cloth, pyramidal societies, late Middle Ages, thirteenth and fourteenth centuries, merchants and tailors in the 1400s, end of the Middle Ages, society in the 1500s, sixteenth century, the early 1600s, the style of the Sun King, the early 1700s and getting dressed in the noble ranks, the French revolution, the early 1800s, nineteenth-century society, a tailor's shop in the early 1900s, and the mid-twentieth century. Glossary.

2318. Ventura, Piero, author/illustrator. **Food: Its Evolution Through the Ages**. Boston: Houghton Mifflin, 1994. 64p. $16.95. ISBN 0-395-66790-9. 4-8

Illustrations and text tell the story of food through the centuries. Included are hunting with pits and snares, bows and arrows, and traps; fishing; gatherers; agriculture in ancient Egypt and Rome; making bread; grain transportation; beekeeping, spices, and cured meats; animals and vegetables in the New World; harvesters; steam engines; freezing; canning; cattle raising and breed selection; pasteurization and sterilization; diet; factory ships; and new foods and products. Glossary.

2319. Ventura, Piero, author/illustrator. **1492: The Year of the New World**. New York: Putnam, 1992. 96p. $19.95. ISBN 0-399-22332-0. 4 up

Illustrations and text present what was happening in the Old World during 1492 in Germany, Flanders, England, France, the Ottoman Empire, Genoa, Portugal, and Spain. It looks at Columbus's voyage and those people found in this world: the Tainos, Aztecs, Maya, and Inca. Other important voyages of discovery after 1492 were to the Orient. Some Important Dates in European History 1493-1558, Important Dates in Italian Renaissance Art, Native North and South Americans, Five Hundred Years Later, and Index.

2320. Vernon, Roland. **Introducing Gershwin**. Englewood Cliffs, NJ: Silver Burdett, 1996. 32p. $14.95; $7.95pa. ISBN 0-382-39161-6; 0-382-39160-8pa. 3-6

George Gershwin (1898-1937), son of an immigrant, changed ideas about music with his compositions. The double-page spreads of the text show various phases of his career with sidebars discussing the history of the times including Prohibition and the Great Depression. Photographs and reproductions highlight the text. Time Chart, Glossary, and Index.

2321. Viola, Herman J. **Andrew Jackson**. New York: Chelsea House, 1986. 112p. $18.95. ISBN 0-87754-587-1. (World Leaders Past and Present). 5 up

Andrew Jackson (1767-1845) was born poor and rose to become President of the country. His charismatic personality and popularity helped him preserve the Union against secession threats from South Carolina, curtail the power in the Bank of the United States, and encourage territorial expansion. Citizens mourned him at his death, but some of his decisions involving minorities, especially Native Americans, must be questioned. Reproductions enhance the text. Chronology, Further Reading, and Index.

2322. Viola, Herman J. **Osceola**. Yoshi Miyake, illustrator. Austin, TX: Raintree/Steck-Vaughn, 1993. 32p. $19.97; $4.95pa. ISBN 0-8114-6575-6; 0-8114-4098-2pa. (Native American Stories). 3-5

Osceola (1804-1838) had a rather unusual childhood: One of his grandfathers was white, and Osceola had a Christian name until his mother took him to Florida to join the Seminole Indian tribe, probably in 1814. He helped the Seminoles after the U.S. government put them on a reservation to keep order. But when the government tried to move the Seminoles out of Florida, Osceola decided to resist. He did until he was betrayed in 1837. History.

2323. Viola, Herman J. **Sitting Bull**. Charles Shaw, illustrator. Austin, TX: Raintree/Steck-Vaughn, 1992. 32p. $19.97. ISBN 0-8172-3401-2. (Native American Stories). 3-5

Sitting Bull (1831-1890) was a warrior, a statesman, a holy man, a showman, and a fighter. He fought as a young man to protect his family and his Sioux (Lakota) tribe from others. His greatest victory was the defeat of General Custer at the Battle of Little Bighorn on June 25, 1876. In later years, he was in Buffalo Bill's Wild West Show with Annie Oakley. Two weeks after he died, the U.S. cavalry killed most of the Sioux believers in the Ghost Dance religion, which wanted the Indians to return to their old ways. History.

2324. Vogt, Esther Loewen. **A Race for Land**. Scottdale, PA: Herald Press, 1992. 112p. $4.95pa. ISBN 0-8361-3575-Xpa. 4-7

Ben Martens, 12, and his family immigrate from Russia to Kansas in 1892. The next year they join the race for Cherokee land in Oklahoma Territory. Another man beats them to the claim that they especially wanted. But they find that other Mennonites live near their alternate claim, and a Cheyenne Indian helps Ben understand that God's love remains even when things seem hopeless.

2325. Voight, Cynthia. **Tree by Leaf**. New York: Atheneum, 1988. 192p. $13.95. ISBN 0-689-31403-5. 5-7

Clothilde, 12 in 1920, worries about her mother's difficulty with accepting responsibility; her older brother, who has run off to live with their paternal grandfather; and her father, when he returns from World War I and stays in the boathouse. Her father dreads the family's disgust when they see his disfigured face. Clothilde convinces him to come "home," and when he does, the family begins to look toward a more stable future.

2326. Von Ahnen, Katherine. **Charlie Young Bear**. Paulette Livers Lambert, illustrator. Boulder, CO: Roberts Rinehart, 1994. 42p. $4.95pa. ISBN 1-57098-001-2pa. (Council for Indian Education). 2-4

In 1955, the U.S. government finally pays the Mesquakie Indians for their land in Iowa. Charlie Young Bear wants a bicycle more than anything, but his family's share will go to his mother's new stove. He decides to appeal to the Great Spirit. When every child in the tribe gets a new red bicycle, Charlie goes to his private place to thank the Great Spirit for his own wonderful bicycle.

2327.   Von Ahnen, Katherine. **Heart of Naosaqua**. Paulette Livers Lambert, illustrator. Boulder, CO: Roberts Rinehart, 1996. 126p. $9.95pa. ISBN 1-57098-010-1pa. 4-8

Naosaqua, 12, lives with her grandmother in the Mesquakie village of Saukinek, on the Mississippi River in Missouri in 1823. When soldiers come one night and burn the village and the crops, the tribe must find a new place to live. They search and eventually settle on the Iowa River. Naosaqua vows to leave her true happiness in Saukinek and to one day return. She also worries about her father's absence, but when he returns, and Gray Beaver declares his love for her, she again has peace.

W

2328. Wade, Linda R. **James Carter: Thirty-Ninth President of the United States**. Chicago: Childrens Press, 1989. 110p. $17.26. ISBN 0-516-01372-6. (Encyclopedia of Presidents). 4-9

As the 39th president of the United States, James Carter (b. 1924) grew up in Plains, Georgia, and became the governor of Georgia. Carter served in the navy and was a businessman and civic leader before he became a politician and President. He served one term. Photographs, Chronology of American History, and Index.

2329. Wade, Linda R. **St. Augustine: America's Oldest City**. Vero Beach, FL: Rourke, 1991. 48p. $11.95. ISBN 0-86592-468-6. (Doors to America). 3-5

The nation's oldest city, St. Augustine, Florida, was established in 1565. It was the first permanent European settlement in America, with 600 colonists under the Spanish conquistador Pedro Menendez de Aviles. The text looks at its history from 1565 to the present. Photographs and Index.

2330. Wade, Linda R. **Warren G. Harding: Twenty-Ninth President of the United States**. Chicago: Childrens Press, 1989. 100p. $19.80. ISBN 0-516-01368-8. (Encyclopedia of Presidents). 4-9

Warren G. Harding (1865-1923) came to the presidency in 1921, after World War I. He wanted to return the country to "normalcy." He delegated power to his cabinet, among whom Herbert Hoover was Secretary of Commerce. Harding died in San Francisco while still serving as President. After his death, the revelations of corruption that occurred during his term tainted most of his successes. Photographs, Chronology of American History, and Index.

2331. Wade, Mary Dodson. **Benedict Arnold**. New York: Franklin Watts, 1994. 64p. $19.90. ISBN 0-531-20156-2. (First Book). 3-6

Benedict Arnold (1741-1801) served George Washington as one of his generals. Annoyed with Washington for not giving him the respect or command that he expected, Arnold decided to help the British instead. The text looks at Arnold's life as daredevil and career as merchant captain, colonial patriot, Continental army officer, and general, as well as his disaster in Philadelphia and his treason at West Point. Although George Washington called him "the bravest of the brave," Arnold's behavior afterward means that his name does not appear on his grave-stone on the grounds of West Point, nor on the monument at Saratoga dedicated to the general who won that battle. Photographs and reproductions enhance the text. Further Reading and Index.

2332. Wadsworth, Ginger. **John Muir: Wilderness Protector**. Minneapolis, MN: Lerner, 1992. 144p. $15.95. ISBN 0-8225-4912-3. 4-6

John Muir (1838-1914) came from Scotland to Wisconsin, and as an adult, lived in California. He was attuned to the potential destruction of the wilderness and influenced Theodore Roosevelt to start conservation of natural resources by instituting the national park system. He also helped found the Sierra Club. Photographs and drawings supplement the text. Bibliography and Index.

2333. Wadsworth, Ginger. **Rachel Carson: Voice for the Earth**. Minneapolis, MN: Lerner, 1992. 128p. $15.95. ISBN 0-8225-4907-7. 5-9

Portrayed as sensitive and passionate in this biography, Rachel Carson (1907-1964) grew up loving nature. She became a biologist whose literary success allowed her to leave her government job and devote her energy to research and see how humans were destroying the Earth. These findings propelled her to voice her concerns and become a leader of the environmental and conservation movement. Selections from her work pepper the text along with good black-and-white photographs. Bibliography and Index.

2334. Wadsworth, Ginger. **Susan Butcher: Sled Dog Racer**. Minneapolis, MN: Lerner, 1994. 63p. $15.95. ISBN 0-8225-2878-9. 4-9

Susan Butcher (b. 1954) won the Iditarod Race in Alaska four times. She and her training dogs, called "mushers," have completed the 1,049-mile trail by traveling 20 hours a day for more than 14 days straight. Her first win, in 1984, was an exciting moment in this grueling race. The texts tells about her life and the procedures for training dogs for such an ordeal. Statistics.

2335. Walker, Lou Ann. **Hand, Heart, and Mind: The Story of the Education of America's Deaf People**. New York: Dial, 1994. 144p. $14.99. ISBN 0-8037-1225-1. 6-9

The text focuses on the history of education for the deaf by looking at the "oralists" and the "manualists." The oralists, led by Alexander Graham Bell, believed that the deaf should communicate with lip-reading and speech. The manualists, under Edward Gallaudet, felt that signing was important because it allowed the deaf to speak in their own language. The attitude toward these two sides reveals a cultural history and a civil rights issue as well as information about the nuances in signing. Twentieth-Century Deaf People of Achievement, Bibliography, and Index.

2336.   Walker, Paul Robert. **Pride of Puerto Rico: The Life of Roberto Clemente**. San Diego, CA: Odyssey, Harcourt Brace, 1988. 157p. $4.95pa. ISBN 0-15-200562-5pa. 3-7

Roberto Clemente (1934-1972) was a right fielder for the Pittsburgh Pirates before he died in a plane crash while trying to help earthquake victims in Nicaragua. As a native of Puerto Rico, he made an enormous leap from the barrios of that area to the Baseball Hall of Fame soon after his untimely death. Bibliography and Roberto Clemente's Career Record.

2337.   Walker, Paul Robert. **Spiritual Leaders**. New York: Facts on File, 1994. 144p. $17.95. ISBN 0-8160-2875-3. (American Indian Lives). 5 up

Religion has always been at the center of Native American life. The people in this collective biography were at the core of their tribes in trying to provide spiritual advice. They are Passaconaway, Son of the Bear (early sixteenth century); Popé, prophet of the Pueblo Revolt (late seventeenth century); Neolin, the Delaware prophet (mid-eighteenth century); Handsome Lake, prophet of the Good Word (late eighteenth century); Tenskwatawa, the Shawnee prophet (1775-1836); Kenekuk, the Kickapoo prophet (c. 1790-1852); Smohalla, the Washani prophet (d. 1895); John Slocum, the Shaker prophet (c. 1840-c. 1897); Zotom, warrior, artist, and missionary (1853-1913); Wovoka, Ghost Dance prophet (c. 1856-1932); Black Elk, Lakota holy man (1863-1950); Mountain Wolf Woman, Winnebago visionary (1884-1960); and Ruby Modesto, desert Cahuilla medicine woman (1913-1980). Annotated Bibliography and Index.

2338.   Wallace, Bill. **Buffalo Gal**. New York: Holiday House, 1992. 185p. $15.95. ISBN 0-8234-0943-0. New York: Minstrel, 1993. 185p. $3.50pa. ISBN 0-671-79899-5pa. 5 up

In the summer of 1904, Amanda, nearly 16, looks forward to riding horseback with her boyfriend and to her coming-out party in San Francisco. Instead, her mother insists that she go with her to Texas to search for a herd of buffalo so she can help save them from extinction. Amanda hates the train journey but is more dismayed that the half-Comanche David Talltree will accompany them on their search. He goads her into a horseback race, and the two begin to respect each other as the summer continues. They fall in love, only to face separation while she returns home and he goes to Harvard Law School.

2339.   Wallner, Alexandra, author/illustrator. **Betsy Ross**. New York: Holiday House, 1994. 32p. $15.95. ISBN 0-8234-1071-4. 2-4

The text presents Betsy Ross (1752-1836) and her early life. She was first a Quaker, but left the faith during her three marriages and her business. She returned to her Quaker beliefs later in her life. Ross has kept a place in history because, as a seamstress, she supposedly made the first American flag in Philadelphia, her home. Additionally, the text gives information about life in colonial America.

2340.   Wallner, Alexandra, author/illustrator. **The First Air Voyage in the United States: The Story of Jean-Pierre Blanchard**. New York: Holiday House, 1996. 32p. $15.95. ISBN 0-8234-1224-5. K-3

After successfully flying a balloon in Germany and across the English Channel, Jean-Pierre Blanchard decided to come to America in 1793 and try to fly here. On January 9, 1793, he conducted several scientific experiments from his hot-air balloon and almost lost his dog overboard before landing in a field, where the farmer thought he was the devil. Among those who might have seen the lift off were Thomas Jefferson, John Adams, James Madison, and James Monroe.

2341.   Walter, Mildred Pitts. **Second Daughter: The Story of a Slave Girl**. New York: Scholastic 1996. 214p. $15.95. ISBN 0-590-48282-3. 6-9

Because her master's family likes her, Elizabeth Freeman, known as Mum Bet, hears the conversations that they have with their guests. She realizes that she can sue for cruel punishment in a court of law and possibly gain her freedom. Her sister Aissa (whom the family does not treat so favorably and who is fictional) tells the story of the court case in 1781. Her view of the American Revolution indicates that the men fight to preserve their property, including their slaves. To the astonishment of many, Mum Bet wins her case.

2342.   Wangerin, Walter, Jr. **The Crying for a Vision**. New York: Simon & Schuster, 1994. 278p. $16; $3.95pa. ISBN 0-671-79911-8; 0-689-80650-7pa. 6-10

As a little boy, Moves Walking or *Waskn Mani*, a Lakota Sioux in the nineteenth century, has to live with his grandmother, the wise woman of the tribe, because he has no parents. When Fire Thunder returns from gathering horses, he cuts off the child's ear, but no one understands why until Moves Walking finds out that Fire Thunder had loved Moves Walking's mother, who abandoned him. As the years progress, Moves Walking's life becomes more involved with Fire Thunder, a man who seems to have no mercy. Then Fire Thunder begins to prove himself when he admits that he has tried to stay near his mentally retarded sister so he could help her. However, after she is raped and dies in childbirth, he fails again. Moves Walking takes the place of his grandmother with his wisdom. *Publishers Weekly Starred Review* and *School Library Journal Starred Review*.

2343.   Warburton, Lois. **The Beginning of Writing**. San Diego, CA: Lucent, 1990. 128p. $16.95. ISBN 1-56006113-8. 6-10

Before people had writing, they had to communicate. The text looks at their attempts and how these cultures began to form alphabets in order to write. The text highlights the Egyptian, Mayan, Chinese, and American Indian societies. Photographs enhance the text. Bibliography, Glossary, and Index.

2344.   Warburton, Lois. **The Chicago Fire**. Maurie Manning, illustrator. San Diego, CA: Lucent, 1990. 64p. $12.95. ISBN 1-56006-002-6. (World Disasters). 5-7

The text places the Chicago Fire of 1871 into a historical and social setting. This huge fire destroyed about four square miles of central Chicago (nearly one-third of the total area). Some people thought the city had died, and they left. However, others quickly rebuilt it, and the city continued its rapid growth. Facts and anecdotes tell the story of this disaster. Bibliography, Chronology, and Index.

2345.   Warburton, Lois. **Railroads: Bridging the Continents**. San Diego, CA: Lucent, 1991. 96p. $16.95. ISBN 1-56006216-9. 6-9

In the text, period paintings, prints, and photographs from Library of Congress collections illustrate two-page spreads that present various topics. They include the major western trails, early railroads, and the inland and ocean waterways. The text examines the history, development, and technology of the steam engine and railroads; discusses the decline of rail transport in the United States; and describes the growth of railroads in Europe and Japan, focusing on their high-speed trains and magnetic levitation. Chronology and Index.

2346.   Ward, Geoffrey C., Ken Burns, and Jim O'Connor. **Shadow Ball: The History of the Negro Leagues**. New York: Knopf, 1994. 79p. $15. ISBN 0-679-86749-X. (Baseball, The American Epic). 4-6

Although Blacks played (briefly) on white baseball teams after the Civil War, the first Black professional team was the Cuban Giants, a group of waiters from the Argyle Hotel in Babylon, Long Island. Their story and that of the other teams appears in the text, complemented by photographs. The league ended soon after Jackie Robinson began playing in the major leagues. Index.

2347.   Ward, Geoffrey C., Ken Burns, and Paul Robert Walker. **Who Invented the Game?** New York: Knopf, 1994. 79p. $15. ISBN 0-679-96750-8. (Baseball, The American Epic). 4-6

Supposedly in 1839, a game of ball began in Cooperstown, New York. A player named Abner Doubleday created new rules and called it baseball—but that story is untrue, according to the text. Bats and balls were parts of games long before the Revolutionary War. Topics augmented with photographs include the Black Sox, Babe Ruth, the integration of baseball, the miracle of the Mets, free agents, and high salaries. Index.

2348.   Ward, Geoffrey C., Ken Burns, and Sydelle Kramer. **25 Great Moments in Baseball**. New York: Knopf, 1994. 79p. $15. ISBN 0-679-86751-1. (Baseball, The American Epic). 4-6

Photographs and text tell the story, which starts from the first baseball game on June 19, 1846, in New Jersey. Included are stars such as Fred Merkle in 1908, Bob Feller in 1938, Satchel Paige in 1942, Jackie Robinson in 1947, Don Larsen in 1956, Roberto Clemente in 1972, Carlton Fisk in 1975, and Joe Carter in 1993. Index.

2349.   Warner, J. F. **The U.S. Marine Corps**. Minneapolis, MN: Lerner, 1991. 88p. $22.95. ISBN 0-8225-1432-X. (Armed Services). 5-8

On November 10, 1775, the Marine Corps came into being. It fought its first battle on March 3, 1776, when Marines went ashore in the Bahamas and took the area from the British. In the twentieth century, large numbers of Marines fought in the wars. The text explains how to join the Marines and Marine life after boot camp. Photographs and drawings enhance the text. Index.

2350.   Warner, John F. **Colonial American Homelife**. New York: Franklin Watts, 1993. 127p. ISBN 0-531-12541-6. (Colonial America). 5 up

In looking at what the people in colonial America did every day, one sees their homes and furniture, their clothes and how they were made, their food, their schools and books, their games and leisure time, and how they got from one place to another. But some settlers did these things differently. The text looks at settlers from England, Sweden, Spain, and other countries as well as the Native Americans. Reproductions enhance the text. Glossary, Bibliography, and Index.

2351.   Warren, Andrea. **Orphan Train Rider: One Boy's True Story**. Boston: Houghton Mifflin, 1996. 80p. $15.95. ISBN 0-395-69822-7. 4-7

The text alternates chapters that contain information about orphan trains with the actual experience of Lee Nailling, who rode the train west in 1926. Along the way, he experienced several rejections before he eventually had a positive family placement. His emotional turmoil reflects that of the many children who took the orphan train to a new life, which for some did not fulfill their hopes. Bibliography and Index. *Boston-Globe Horn Book Award* and *School Library Journal Best Book*.

2352. Warren, Scott, author/photographer. **Cities in the Sand: The Ancient Civilizations of the Southwest**. San Francisco: Chronicle Books, 1992. 64p. $10.95. ISBN 0-8118-0021-1. 4-7

The text looks at the history of three Native American cultures: the Anasazi, the Hohokam, and the Mogollon. The first segment looks at the archaeological digs and the physical settings that have identified artifacts dating back 11,000 years. Photographs of the sites give a sense of the places where the people lived, and discussions of artifacts tell something about their lifestyles. Glossary and Index.

2353. Waters, Kate. **The Mayflower**. Russ Kendall, photographs. New York: Scholastic, 1996. 40p. $16.95. ISBN 0-590-67308-4. K-3

William Small takes his second voyage on the *Mayflower* as the master of the ship's apprentice. He learns all types of jobs to help sail the ship, and he meets one of the passengers, Ellen. The text looks at the journey through William's eyes. More About the *Mayflower* and Glossary.

2354. Waters, Kate. **The Mysterious Horseman: An Adventure in Prairietown, 1836**. Marjory Dressler, photographs. New York: Scholastic, 1994. 40p. $15.95. ISBN 0-590-45503-6. 2-4

While the boy Andrew McClure works at an inn in Prairie, Indiana, he hears a traveler talking about a headless rider following a schoolmaster. Not until his friend's father reads him Washington Irving's story "The Legend of Sleepy Hollow" does Andrew realize that traveler had been talking about that tale. Photographs taken at the Conner Prairie Living Museum show the various jobs at the inn during the nineteenth century. Glossary.

2355. Waters, Kate. **Samuel Eaton's Day: A Day in the Life of a Pilgrim Boy**. Russ Kendall, photographs. New York: Scholastic, 1993. 40p. $14.95. ISBN 0-590-46311-X. 1-6

On July 16, 1627, Samuel Eaton, seven, is delighted to be old enough to begin helping harvest the rye. He says that he came on the *Mayflower* and that his mother died during the voyage. Photographs of him at Plimoth Plantation show him getting dressed, fetching water, setting snares for game, and tying the stalks of rye. He discovers that binding rye is more difficult than it looks, and his skin blisters from the sun and his fingers blister from the rough stalks. He also itches. But when his father compliments his work, he is pleased. Glossary.

2356. Waters, Kate. **Sarah Morton's Day: A Day in the Life of a Pilgrim Girl**. Russ Kendall, photographs. New York: Scholastic, 1989. 32p. $12.95. ISBN 0-590-42634-6. K-4

In Plimoth Plantation during 1627, Sarah Morton's day begins at sunup when the cock crows. Sarah must build a fire, cook breakfast, feed the chickens, milk the goats, learn her letters, and memorize Scripture. Sometime she has time to play knickers (marbles) and talk to her friend. The photographs of the living history museum at Plymouth, Massachusetts, complement the text.

2357. Waters, Kate. **The Story of the White House**. New York: Scholastic, 1991. 40p. $12.95. ISBN 0-590-43335-0. K-3

The history of and trivia about the White House, an overview of its layout, the rooms, and some of the jobs available there are the focus of this simple book. Photographs and reproductions of old drawings augment the text. Bibliography and Index.

2358. Waters, Kate. **Tapenum's Day: A Wampanoag Indian Boy in Pilgrim Times**. Russ Kendall, photographs. New York: Scholastic, 1996. 40p. $16.95. ISBN 0-590-20237-5. 2-4

In 1627, while Samuel Eaton and Sarah Morton help the adults at the Pilgrims' stockade, Tapenum, a Wampanoag boy, learns from his elders nearby. His warrior counselors refuse to initiate him, and although he at first does not understand why, he soon finds out that he needs more skill, more strength, and more wisdom. Tapenum has little interest in the Pilgrims while he tries to fulfill the requirements to earn his position as a Wampanoag brave.

2359. Weaver, Lydia. **Child Star: When Talkies Came to Hollywood**. Michele Laporte, illustrator. New York: Viking, 1992. 52p. $12. ISBN 0-670-84039-4. (Once Upon America). 3-6

Trying to survive in Hollywood during the Depression becomes more and more difficult for Joey's mother when he is 10. Someone spots him as a new child star, and as Little Joey Norman, he makes money. When the talkies arrive, he adapts, but making movies has none of the glamour that people think it does, and he has to decide whether to continue.

2360. Weaver, Lydia. **Close to Home: A Story of the Polio Epidemic**. Aileen Arrington, illustrator. New York: Viking, 1993. 64p. $12.99. ISBN 0-670-84511-6. (Once Upon America). 2-6

Betsy, 10 in 1952, and her brother are inoculated against the fearful polio virus because her mother works in Dr. Jonas Salk's Pittsburgh laboratory. When one of her friends contracts the disease, Betsy has difficulty adjusting to the change in her. She eventually realizes that the change is only physical.

2361. Weber, Judith Eichler. **Forbidden Friendship**. New York: Silver Moon Press, 1993. 80p. $12.95. ISBN 1-881889-42-4. (Stories of the States). 3-5

Molly Bartlett, in North Adams, Massachusetts, finds herself in a strange predicament when she and Chen Li become friends during 1870. Her father owns a local shoe factory where the workers are striking. Chen's parents are some of the Chinese immigrants brought into town to break the strike. Molly has to learn about friendship as well as the realities of business and of other peoples' needs. Endpaper Maps and Historical Postscript.

2362. Weber, Michael. **Our Congress**. Brookfield, CT: Millbrook Press, 1994. 48p. $14.40; $6.95pa. ISBN 1-56294-443-6; 0-7613-0091-0pa. (I Know America). 3-6

Congress, one of the most powerful bodies in the United States, works by certain rules that have been in effect since its beginning. The text traces its history and explains the laws that govern it. Photographs of senators and congresspeople aid the understanding of these abstract concepts. Chronology, For Further Reading, and Index.

2363. Weidt, Maryann. **Mr. Blue Jeans: A Story About Levi Strauss**. Lydia M. Anderson, illustrator. Minneapolis, MN: Carolrhoda, 1990. 64p. $9.95. ISBN 0-87614-421-0. (Creative Minds Books). 4-6

Levi Strauss (1829-1902), a Jewish German businessman, moved from New York to San Francisco after the Gold Rush, where he made millions of dollars selling denim pants that would survive the stress of manual labor. Background about Strauss's life reveals him to have been a humane employer. Bibliography.

2364. Weidt, Maryann N. **Oh, the Places He Went: A Story About Dr. Seuss**. Kerry Maguire, illustrator. Minneapolis, MN: Carolrhoda, 1994. 64p. $13.13; $5.95pa. ISBN 0-87614-823-2; 0-87614-627-2pa. (Creative Minds Books). 2-6

Theodor Seuss Geisel (1904-1994) lived three blocks from the library and six blocks from the zoo as he was growing up in Springfield, Massachusetts. At first discouraged by his lack of success with his animal drawings, he wrote and illustrated 48 books during his life that sold more than 200 million copies. An award for aspiring illustrators has been established in his name and carries a large cash prize. Afterword and Bibliography.

2365. Weidt, Maryann N. **Stateswoman to the World: A Story About Eleanor Roosevelt**. Lydia Anderson, illustrator. Minneapolis, MN: Carolrhoda, 1991. 62p. $9.95. ISBN 0-87614-663-9. (Creative Minds Books). 3-5

Eleanor Roosevelt (1884-1962) had a lonely childhood, feeling out of favor until she went to England to boarding school. After her return, she married Franklin Delano Roosevelt. He became President, and she stood with him and supported many who were downtrodden, like women, African Americans, and the poor. After Franklin died, Eleanor became a delegate to the United Nations, a role that underscored her desire for peace. Photographs highlight the text. Bibliography.

2366. Weiner, Eric. **The Civil War**. New York: Smithmark, 1992. 64p. $9.95. ISBN 0-831-72312-2. (Facts America). 4-8

The text presents an overview of the Civil War, its causes, major events from 1861 to 1865, and the aftermath. Illustrations enhance the text. Further Reading, Glossary, and Index.

2367. Weiner, Eric. **The Story of Frederick Douglass: Voice of Freedom**. Steven Parton, illustrator. 1992. Milwaukee, WI : Gareth Stevens, 1996. 107p. $18.60. ISBN 0-8368-1464-9. (Famous Lives). 3-6

Frederick Douglass grew up in slavery but ran away to the North. Because he was literate, he edited a newspaper, the *North Star*. The text shows his life and his determination to be free and to contribute to society by helping his people become free. Pen-and-ink drawings highlight the text.

2368. Weisberg, Barbara. **Susan B. Anthony: Woman Suffragist**. New York: Chelsea House, 1988. 112p. $18.95; $7.95pa. ISBN 1-55546-639-7; 0-7910-0408-2pa. (American Women of Achievement). 5 up

Believing in the rights of all people, regardless of race or background, Susan B. Anthony (1820-1906) was one of the nineteenth century's greatest political crusaders. She grew up in a Quaker community and started her campaigns by condemning drunkenness and slavery. Over the next 50 years she fought for women's suffrage. Without her, the right of women to vote would most likely not have passed in 1920, 14 years after her death. Photographs and reproductions enhance the text. Glossary, Further Reading, and Index.

2369. Weisbrot, Robert. **Father Divine: Religious Leader**. New York: Chelsea House, 1992. 120p. $18.95. ISBN 0-7910-1122-4. (Black Americans of Achievement). 5 up

George Baker (1879-1965) moved from Maryland to Harlem around 1915, where he began calling himself Major J. Divine. He launched his Peace Mission movement in 1930 to provide Sunday food for the poor. In 1940, his group gathered 250,000 signatures on an antilynching bill. Then he supported Freedom Rides and other civil rights campaigns from his new headquarters in Philadelphia. His second wife, Mother Divine, took over his work at his death. Photographs and reproductions enhance the text. Chronology, Further Reading, and Index.

2370.   Weisbrot, Robert. **Marching Toward Freedom: 1957-1965**. New York: Chelsea House, 1994. 141p. $19.95; $7.95pa. ISBN 0-7910-2256-0; 0-7910-2682-5pa. (Milestones in Black American History). 6-9

The text relates the American Civil Rights movement with complementary photographs. The details reveal the various personalities involved in the struggle to change society. Glossary and Index.

2371.   Weitzman, David. **Great Lives: Human Culture**. New York: Scribner's, 1994. 294p. $22.95. ISBN 0-684-19438-4. (Great Lives). 5-9

Biographical profiles of 27 anthropologists and archaeologists describe their work and their motivations. They are Ruth Benedict (American, 1887-1948); Franz Boas (American, 1858-1942); James Henry Breasted (American, 1865-1935); Howard Carter (English, 1873-1939); Herbert, Fifth Earl of Carnarvon (English, 1866-1923); Jean-François Champollion (French, 1790-1832); Arthur Evans (English, 1851-1941); Alice Cunningham Fletcher (American, 1838-1923); Jane Goodall (English, b. 1934); Georg Fredrich Grotefend (German, 1775-1883); Zora Neale Hurston (American, 1891-1960); Alfred Kroeber (English, 1876-1960); Austen Henry Layard (French, 1817-1894); Louis S. B. Leakey (English, 1903-1972); Mary Nicol Leakey (English, b. 1913); Richard Leakey (Kenyan, b. 1944); Robert Harry Lowie (American, 1883-1957); Max Mallowan (English, 1904-1978); Margaret Mead (American, 1901-1978); Elsie Clews Parsons (American, 1875-1941); Hortense Powdermaker (American, 1900-1970); Mary Kawena Pukui (Hawaiian, 1895-1986); Heinrich Schliemann (German, 1822-1890); Michael Ventris (English, 1922-1956); Robert Eric Mortimer Wheeler (English, 1890-1976); Charles Leonard Woolley (English, 1880-1960); and Yigael Yadin (Israeli, 1917-1984). Further Reading and Index.

2372.   Weitzman, David. **The Mountain Man and the President**. Austin, TX: Raintree/Steck-Vaughn, 1993. 40p. $22.83; $4.95pa. ISBN 0-8114-7224-8; 0-8114-8064-Xpa. (Stories of America—Against All Odds). 4-6

John Muir (1838-1914) loved the California woods and mountains and wanted to save their beauty for everyone. After President Teddy Roosevelt (1858-1919) read Muir's articles, he arranged to walk with him in the Sierra Mountains in 1903. Because of what Muir showed him about the beauty of the land, Roosevelt, himself a naturalist trained at Harvard, created five new national parks and 16 national monuments. Afterword and Notes.

2373.   Weitzman, David, author/illustrator. **Thrashin' Time**: **Harvest Days in the Dakotas**. Boston: Godine, 1991. 80p. $24.95. ISBN 0-87923-910-7. 4-7

In 1912, Peter, 12, has his first encounter with a new steam engine thrasher. He and his father use the machine on their North Dakota farm and find that it finishes the job in much less time than their horses could do it.

2374.   Welch, Catherine A. **Clouds of Terror**. Laurie K. Johnson, illustrator. Minneapolis, MN: Carolrhoda, 1994. 48p. $15.95; $5.95pa. ISBN 0-87614-771-6; 0-87614-639-6. (On My Own). 2-4

Helga and Erik's family, immigrants from Sweden, face a plague of grasshoppers during the 1870s at their new Minnesota home. The grasshoppers eat everything, get into the water, and rest on top of the baby. Because no crops remain, their father has to go away to find work. The next year, the grasshoppers hatch from eggs left the previous summer, but they fly away. *Notable Children's Trade Books in the Field of Social Studies.*

2375.   Welch, Catherine A. **Danger at the Breaker**. Andrea Shine, illustrator. Minneapolis, MN: Carolrhoda, 1992. 48p. $15.95; $5.95pa. ISBN 0-87614-693-0; 0-87614-564-0pa. (On My Own History). K-3

Andrew is eight in the early 1800s when he has to stop school and start working in the breaker house of the Pennsylvania coal mines with his father. His family needs the money, but on the first day, an explosion occurs in the mine. Although his father is wounded, he survives.

2376.   Wells, Rosemary. **Waiting for the Evening Star**. Susan Jeffers, illustrator. New York: Dial Press, 1993. Unpaged. $15. ISBN 0-8037-1398-3. K-3

When Berty is 11 in 1917, his older brother Luke decides to join the military and go to France to fight in the war. Luke wants to travel after the war ends and see the world. Berty cannot understand why anyone would want to leave the Green Mountains of Vermont, an area that already has everything Berty could want. When Luke leaves on the train, Berty's grandmother suggests that Berty wait for the Evening Star so he can make his good luck wishes for Luke.

2377.   Wesley, Valerie Wilson. **Freedom's Gifts**. Sharon Wilson, illustrator. New York: Simon & Schuster, 1997. 32p. $16. ISBN 0-689-80269-2. 3-6

Juneteenth marks the day Texas slaves found out about their freedom, two years after the Emancipation Proclamation. The holiday is June's favorite, but she does not look forward to this celebration because her cousin Lillie is coming and may ruin the day because Lillie prefers July 4. But June's Aunt Marshall, who was June's age on June 19, 1865, the first Juneteenth, thinks that she can convince Lillie of the day's significance.

2378. West, Tracey. **Fire in the Valley**. New York: Silver Moon Press, 1993. 80p. $12.95; $4.95pa. ISBN 1-881889-32-7; 1-881889-73-4pa. (Stories of the States). 3-5

As an inhabitant of Owens Valley, California, in 1904, Sarah Jefferson shares her farming family's distress that a Los Angeles water company will divert water from their valley in central California into Los Angeles. The water loss causes problems for the valley, and Sarah writes a letter of protest to President Teddy Roosevelt. Additionally, Sarah helps her family when the barn catches fire. Endpaper Maps, Historical Postscript, and Recommended Reading.

2379. West, Tracey. **Mr. Peale's Bones**. New York: Silver Moon Press, 1994. 63p. $12.95; $4.95pa. ISBN 1-881889-50-5; 1-881889-75-0pa. (Stories of the States). 4-6

In 1801, Will Finch, 11, and his father have the opportunity to help the artist and scientist Charles Willson Peale excavate a mammoth in upstate New York. When he later hears that Peale has mounted his "Mammoth Exhibition" in Philadelphia, Will gains a new interest in science. Endpaper Maps, Historical Postscript, and Further Reading.

2380. West, Tracey. **Voyage of the Half Moon**. New York: Silver Moon Press, 1993. 64p. $12.95; $4.95pa. ISBN 1-881889-18-1; 1-881889-76-9pa. (Stories of the States). 3-5

In 1609, John Hudson accompanies explorer Henry Hudson, his father, on his first trip up a river in the New World. From the deck of the *Half Moon*, he sees the life of the river, including its animals and its plants. This eventful journey marks the discovery of the Hudson River for Europeans. Endpaper Maps, Historical Postscript, and Recommended Reading.

2381. Westerfeld, Scott. **The Berlin Airlift**. Englewood Cliffs, NJ: Silver Burdett, 1989. 64p. $16.98. ISBN 0-382-09833-1. (Turning Points). 5 up

Although the title indicates that the text covers the Berlin airlift in 1948 and 1949, it also discusses several other points important to the history of the time. It includes background on the Iron Curtain and on the Marshall Plan, with a biographical commentary on George Marshall, "Operation Vittles," and the rise of the Berlin Wall. Index and Suggested Reading.

2382. Wetterer, Margaret K. **Clyde Tombaugh and the Search for Planet X**. Laurie A. Caple, illustrator. Minneapolis, MN: Carolrhoda, 1996. 56p. $15.95; $5.95pa. ISBN 0-87614-893-3; 0-87614-969-7pa. (On My Own History). K-3

Clyde Tombaugh (b. 1906) was 12 when he first looked through a telescope. He became fascinated with what he saw and spent much time reading astronomy books and studying the stars. He did not have enough money to go to college, but after he made his own telescope, an astronomer at Lowell Observatory in Arizona hired him. In March 1930, on photographs taken with the Lowell telescope, he found a tiny dot of light that proved to be an unidentified planet body. His careful observation rewarded him with the discovery of Pluto, the ninth planet. Important Dates.

2383. Wetterer, Margaret K. **Kate Shelley and the Midnight Express**. Karen Ritz, illustrator. Minneapolis, MN: Carolrhoda, 1990. 48p. $15.95; $5.95pa. ISBN 0-87614-425-3; 0-87614-541-1pa. (On My Own History). K-3

When Kate Shelley is 15 in 1881, she notes a rickety wooden bridge that she is afraid to cross in the daytime. It has no hand railing, and some of the boards are loose. But a heavy storm destroys the bridge over Honey Creek, near her home. She rushes out and crosses the rickety bridge to get to the train station so that the midnight express train can be stopped before many lose their lives. Her railroad friends rewarded her bravery by letting her out in front of her house every time she rides the train.

2384. Wetterer, Margaret K., and Charles M. Wetterer. **The Snow Walker**. Mary O'Keefe Young, illustrator. Minneapolis, MN: Carolrhoda, 1996. 48p. $11.96. ISBN 0-87614-891-7. (On My Own History). K-3

Milton Daub, 12, awakens in 1888 to see snow everywhere around his home in the Bronx. He and his father make a pair of snowshoes from barrel hoops and old roller skates so that he can go out to buy milk for his family. Soon he buys supplies for everyone in the neighborhood, and they declare him a hero. *American Bookseller Pick of the List*.

2385. Wheeler, Jill, C. **Forest Diplomat: The Story of Hiawatha**. Bloomington, MN: Abdo, 1989. 32p. $17.08. ISBN 0-939179-71-7. 4

Around 1400, Hiawatha lived with his people, the Iroquois. As a boy, he watched while warring Mohawks retaliated against a young warrior in his tribe who had recently killed a Mohawk. Hiawatha could not understand why the bloodshed continued, and as a leader when older, he wanted peace. Some were against him, and one day when he left his village, enemies killed his wife and his "seven [sic] daughters." He joined with Degandawida, a Huron Indian, to unite the five tribes of the Iroquois: the Onondaga, the Mohawk, the Seneca, the Cayuga, and the Oneida. Their example influenced the designers of the American government, James Madison and Benjamin Franklin.

2386.   Wheeler, Jill. **Forest Warrior: The Story of Pontiac**. Bloomington, MN: Abdo, 1989. 32p. $17.08. ISBN 0-939179-69-5. 4

Because of friendships made throughout his life, Pontiac (1725-1769) was able to unite tribes to fight against the British when they reneged on terms of their agreement about the land between the Great Lakes and the Ohio Valley. Although Pontiac's forces faced defeat, they fought much longer than the British expected in 1763 and showed that the Native Americans were a force to be reckoned with.

2387.   Wheeler, Jill. **The Story of Sequoyah: The Lame One**. Bloomington, MN: Abdo, 1989. $17.08. ISBN 0-939179-70-9. (Famous Native American Leaders). 4

Sequoyah (1773?-1843), son of a Cherokee mother and a white father, was crippled as a child from a disease, but discovered in his teen years that he could draw and make things. He experimented and found that he especially liked to make silver items. While away fighting in the War of 1812, he had seen writing for the first time. He wanted to make writing leaves for his people, and after much thought, he realized that he could make symbols for sounds. When he began to work seriously, his wife disapproved, and he left home with his daughter. He discovered that he could make all the Cherokee sounds in 200 symbols, and later narrowed the number to 86. The first translation into Cherokee was the Gospel of John, and a full-blooded Cherokee minister translated the complete Bible a year later. Sequoyah began a newspaper in 1828, but whites destroyed it forcing the Cherokees out of their land on the Trail of Tears in 1829. He died on a journey to Mexico.

2388.   Wheeler, Leslie, and Judith Peacock. **Events That Changed American History**. Austin, TX: Raintree/Steck-Vaughn, 1994. 48p. $15.96. ISBN 0-8114-4927-0. (20 Events Series). 6 up

With two-page spreads, the authors have given an overview of American history showing the pivotal points of change that have occurred since the founding of the Plymouth colony in 1620. Other events included are the introduction of slavery in 1619 to Jamestown, Virginia; the Declaration of Independence in 1776; the ratification of the Constitution in 1787; the 1800 election of Thomas Jefferson over Alexander Hamilton; the Louisiana Purchase in 1803; the Seneca Falls Convention in 1848; secession in 1860; the Emancipation Proclamation of 1863; the transcontinental railroad completion in 1869; the Pullman strike of 1894; the Spanish-American War in 1898; the Treaty of Versailles ending World War I in 1919; the National Origins Act of 1924, closing America's open door to immigrants; the Great Depression of the 1930s; the Japanese attack on Pearl Harbor, December 7, 1941; the Montgomery bus boycott, 1955-1956; the Cuban Missile Crisis in 1962; the Vietnam war from 1965 to 1973; and the Reagan election in 1980. Glossary, Suggested Readings, and Index.

2389.   Whelan, Gloria. **Hannah**. Leslie Bowman, illustrator. New York: Knopf, 1991. 64p. $10.95. ISBN 0-679-91397-1. 3-5

In the fall of 1887, Hannah, nine, begins to attend school at the urging of her father and the new teacher, Miss Robbin, when the teacher comes to live with the family in Michigan. Hannah's mother opposes the idea because Hannah is blind. But Hannah learns to count with an acorn abacus, and other students help her win contest money so she can purchase a Braille writing machine.

2390.   Whelan, Gloria. **The Indian School**. Gabriela Dellosso, illustrator. New York: HarperCollins, 1996. 89p. $13.95. ISBN 0-06-027077-2. 3-6

In 1839, after the death of her parents, Lucy, 11, goes to live with her uncle and aunt at their Indian school in the Michigan woods. Her aunt shows no emotion and demands specific attitudes and work from her Indian pupils. When a small boy and his sister come to the school, the boy whom Aunt Emma calls Matthew rather than his Indian name wins Aunt Emma's affection. His sister Raven refuses to answer to the Christian name given her, but she stays so that she can watch over her brother. Raven teaches Lucy about nature as well. Lucy mourns her own loss, but she understands that the other children have had similar separations from their homes and parents.

2391.   Whelan, Gloria. **Next Spring an Oriole**. Pamela Johnson, illustrator. New York: Random House, 1987. 62p. $3.99pa. ISBN 0-394-89125-2pa. (Stepping Stone Book). 2-4

Libby, 10, journeys from Virginia to Michigan in 1837 with her parents. On the way, they have problems similar to those of people on other wagon trains. Her mother helps some Potawatomi Indians whom they meet by nursing the Indian children back to health after they get measles. Libby's father complains that whites treat the Indians unfairly. A member of the Indian family brings food to Libby's family during their first winter when they almost starve.

2392.   Whelan, Gloria. **Night of the Full Moon**. Leslie Bowman, illustrator. New York: Knopf, 1993. 64p. $15; $3.99pa. ISBN 0-679-94464-8; 0-679-87276-0pa. 3-5

In 1840, after the long winter in Michigan, Libby's friend Fawn, a Potawatomi *(Neshnabek)* Indian, visits with her. As the summer progresses, Fawn invites Libby and her family to her new brother's naming ceremony. The U.S. government's representatives warn Libby's father that Fawn's people will be moved from their land, and he tells them, but they do not go away. On the day of the naming ceremony, Libby's mother is having her own baby. Libby sneaks away without permission and goes to Fawn's home. The soldiers come the same day to move the people, and Libby has to go with them. Fawn's family escapes so they can return Libby to her home, and her father gives them land so that they can stay.

2393. Whelan, Gloria. **Once on This Island**. New York: HarperCollins, 1995. 186p. $14.95; $4.50pa. ISBN 0-06-026248-6; 0-06-440619-9pa. 4-8

Mary O'Shea, 12, and her brother and sister try to look after their Mackinac, Michigan, farm when their father has to join the army in its 1812 fight against the British. In her first-person narrative, she is surprised to see the British flag fly over the captured fort and even more surprised that the friendly Indians have banded together to support the British cause. When her father returns after three years, he is greatly relieved to find that his children have succeeded at keeping their land in order.

2394. Whelan, Gloria. **That Wild Berries Should Grow: The Diary of a Summer**. Grand Rapids, MI: William B. Eerdman, 1994. 122p. $13.99; $4.99pa. ISBN 0-8028-3754-9; 0-8028-5091-Xpa. 4-7

In 1933, the summer after Elsa, 12, gets sick, she leaves her Detroit home to stay with her grandparents at their "boring" Lake Huron summer home. With only the three of them on the land, she learns many things about the natural world around her, including how to eat tomatoes just picked from their vine. By the time her parents arrive to take her home, she knows she will return the next summer. *American Bookseller Pick of the Lists*.

2395. Whitcraft, Melissa. **Francis Scott Key**. New York: Franklin Watts, 1995. 63p. $19.90. ISBN 0-531-20163-5. (First Books). 3-6

Francis Scott Key (1779-1843) belonged to a wealthy colonial family. He graduated from St. John's College in Annapolis, Maryland, as valedictorian and became a lawyer. In this capacity, he was arguing for his clients when he had to go to Baltimore to try to get a family friend, Dr. Beane, released from a British warship during the War of 1812. A battle ensued, which Key watched from the distance. When he eventually saw the American flag flying over Fort McHenry, he recorded his happiness in a poem that became "The Star-Spangled Banner." Another concern was slavery, which he tried to solve through legal means, but failed. For Further Reading and Index.

2396. White, Alana. **Come Next Spring**. New York: Clarion, 1990. 170p. $13.95. ISBN 0-395-52593-4. 4-8

In 1949, Salina, 12, dislikes the new girl Scooter. Scooter thinks that a highway through the farmland is okay, but Salina does not like change. The taffy-pulls and church socials throughout Salina's year stay the same, but she has to adjust to the "Outlanders," and develops a new friend as she loses an old one.

2397. White, Deborah Gray. **Let My People Go: African Americans 1804-1860**. New York: Oxford University Press, 1996. 141p. $21. ISBN 0-19-508769-0. (Young Oxford History of African Americans, 4). 6 up

In looking at the years from 1804 to 1860, the text tells the story of the active roles of both slaves and free Blacks in trying to abolish slavery. Simultaneously, slave owners spent much time and money trying to retain the profitable system. The book reveals the harshness of the times and dispels any ideas that slaves wanted to remain in bondage. Chronology, Further Reading, and Index.

2398. White, Ruth. **Belle Prater's Boy**. New York: Farrar, Straus & Giroux, 1996. 208p. $16. ISBN 0-374-30668-0. 5-8

During the 1950s, Beauty (Gypsy Arbutus Leemaster) has lovely golden curls, while her cousin Woodrow is cross-eyed and ill-dressed. Otherwise, they have things in common, such as one missing parent and deep pain. When Woodrow's mother, Belle Prater, deserts him, and his alcoholic father cannot look after him, he comes to live with his grandparents next door to Gypsy in Coal Station, Virginia, on the best street in town. Meanwhile, Gypsy has to come to terms with the knowledge that her father committed suicide. But Woodrow and Gypsy enjoy each other's jokes and stories as they cope with situations neither one wants to admit. *Boston-Globe Horn Book Award, School Library Journal Best Book,* and *Newbery Honor*.

2399. White, Ruth. **Sweet Creek Holler**. New York: Farrar, Straus, & Giroux, 1988. 215p. $13.95. ISBN 0-374-37360-4. 6-8

In the Appalachian community of Sweet Creek Holler, Ginny and her mother try to survive after Ginny's father is murdered when she is six. The people in the community all have difficult problems, some that they cannot overcome. The local gossip slanders the family, and Ginny's mother takes her to Pennsylvania and a new life by the time Ginny is 12. *American Library Association Notable Books for Children*.

2400. White, Tekla. **Missions of the San Francisco Bay Area: Santa Clara de Asís, San José de Guadalupe, San Francisco de Asís, San Rafael Arcángel, San Francisco Solano**. Minneapolis, MN: Lerner, 1996. 80p. $14.96. ISBN 0-8225-1926-7. (California Missions). 4-6

In the 1700s, Spain sent Roman Catholic priests to establish missions and presidios (forts) along the coast of Baja California and other areas of New Spain (present-day Southwestern United States and Mexico). Spain wanted the Indians to accept the Spanish ways and become loyal subjects. San Francisco de Asís was the San Francisco Bay's first mission, and it had trouble keeping neophytes (recently baptized Indians). Santa Clara, however, was one of the most productive missions with the largest number of neophytes over a 25-year period. At Mission San José, the neophyte Estanislao led other Indians against mission soldiers. San Rafael Arcángel was originally a hospital, and San Francisco Solano was established after Spain no longer ruled Alta California. Glossary, Chronology, and Index.

2401. Whitelaw, Nancy. **Grace Hopper: Programming Pioneer**. Janet Hamlin, illustrator. New York: W. H. Freeman, 1996. 64p. $15.95; $5.95pa. ISBN 0-7167-6598-5; 0-7167-6599-3pa. (Science Superstars). 4-8

Grace Hopper served in the U.S. Navy, resigned, and returned to work on the first computer during World War II. She then rose to become an admiral. Her work on the ENIAC at Harvard helped to establish the computer. The text looks at her life and work. Further Reading, Glossary, and Index.

2402. Whitelaw, Nancy. **Mr. Civil Rights: The Story of Thurgood Marshall**. Greensboro, NC: Morgan Reynolds, 1995. 121p. $17.95. ISBN 1-883846-10-2. (Notable Americans). 6-9

Thurgood Marshall (1908-1993) devoted himself early in life to ending racial injustice. After he attended college and law school, he began working as an attorney for the NAACP. He helped to argue the case that led to the Supreme Court decision ending school segregation. He later served as the first African American on the Supreme Court. The text begins with an incident when a man accused Marshall, 14, of being a "nigga" who pushed a white woman. Marshall had not even seen the woman, and he beat up the man. His boss freed him on bail, telling him that he had done a good job trying to deliver hats in boxes over which he could not see. Timeline, Glossary, Notes, Bibliography, and Index.

2403. Whitelaw, Nancy. **Theodore Roosevelt Takes Charge**. Morton Grove, IL: Albert Whitman, 1992. 192p. $14.95. ISBN 0-8075-7849-5. 6-12

Theodore Roosevelt (1858-1919) wanted his daughters to be wise and his sons to fight on the side of righteousness. He said to his children, "Don't flinch, don't foul, hit the line hard." For his own exercise, he boxed with an army officer and led his children on "obstacle walks" where they had to walk exactly behind him, even if he traveled over a haystack. Roosevelt became President when William McKinley was assassinated. Among his achievements was the signing of the Panama Canal Treaty. The text looks at his life. Books by Theodore Roosevelt, Chronology, Bibliography, and Index.

2404. Whitelaw, Nancy. **They Wrote Their Own Headlines: American Women Journalists**. Greensboro, NC: Morgan Reynolds, 1994. 144p. $17.95. ISBN 1-883846-06-4. 6-10

American women journalists historically have had few chances to excel, but some of them have done so in the twentieth century, and the text talks about these women. They are Ida M. Tarbell (1857-1944), activist; Dorothy Thompson (1893-1961), foreign correspondent; Margaret Bourke-White (1905-1971), photojournalist; Alice Dunnigan (1906-1983), African American White House correspondent; Ann Landers (1918-), advice columnist; Marguerite Higgins (1920-1963), war correspondent; and Charlayne Hunter-Gault (1942-), African American TV journalist. Bibliography and Index.

2405. Whiteley, Opal. **Only Opal: The Diary of a Young Girl**. Jane Boulton, adapter. Barbara Cooney, illustrator. New York: Philomel, 1994. 32p. $14.95. ISBN 0-399-21990-0. 1-4

Opal, born in 1900, wrote in her diary when she was five and six after going to live with a new family after her parents died. She does many chores, including churning butter, sweeping floors, and bringing in the wood, but she still loves the Oregon countryside. She goes to school, likes animals, and enjoys naming things. The text ends when she leaves for a mill town.

2406. Whitman, Sylvia. **Get Up and Go: The History of American Road Travel**. Minneapolis, MN: Lerner, 1996. 88p. $18.95. ISBN 0-8225-1735-3. (People's History). 5-9

Americans have always traveled, and the text looks at their history from Native Americans to the present. It covers the development of superhighways from paths through the woods; the progression of vehicles from wagons to steam engines; and bicycles, cars, and trucks. Historic photographs highlight the text. Selected Bibliography and Index.

2407. Whitman, Sylvia. **This Land Is Your Land: The American Conservation Movement**. Minneapolis, MN: Lerner, 1994. 88p. $18.95. ISBN 0-8225-1729-9. (People's History). 5-9

In 1872, Yellowstone National Park was founded. After that, Theodore Roosevelt met John Muir, who influenced Roosevelt's policy toward the national natural resources. Among those mentioned in the text as having important roles in saving the environment and conserving land are Rachel Carson and the Sierra Club. Photographs augment the text. Bibliography and Index.

2408. Whitman, Sylvia. **Uncle Sam Wants You! Military Men and Women of World War II**. Minneapolis, MN: Lerner, 1993. 80p. $18.95. ISBN 0-8225-1728-0. (People's History). 5-9

Both men and women made major contributions during World War II. The text looks at their experiences in the draft, at boot camp, in stateside duty, and during combat in Europe and the Pacific. It describes battlefield conditions with eyewitness accounts and focuses on the role of African Americans and women during the war. Both groups had to cope with prejudice, while all participants dealt with homesickness and periods of fear. Photographs, Bibliography, and Index. *New York Public Library's Books for the Teen Age*.

2409. Whitman, Sylvia. **V Is for Victory: The American Homefront During World War I**. Minneapolis, MN: Lerner, 1992. 80p. $18.95. ISBN 0-8225-1727-2. (People's History). 5-9

Containing photographs of ordinary people on farms, in factories, in homes, and in the streets, the text shows what life was like during World War II in America. The chapter topics include the important roles of women (Rosie the Riveter) and Black workers, rationing and drives for scrap, separation and waiting for soldiers to return, growth in the defense industry, race riots, and optimism at the end of the war. Bibliography and Index. *Notable Children's Trade Books in the Field of Social Studies*.

2410. Whitmore, Arvella. **The Bread Winner**. Boston: Houghton Mifflin, 1990. 138p. $13.95. ISBN 0-395-53705-3. 4-6

Sarah, 12 in 1932, goes with her parents to live in town after they sell their farm. She looks forward to a different life, but her father cannot find a job. He even goes to California in search of work. Sarah decides to sell a few loaves of bread made with an award-winning family recipe as a way to help the family. People want more than a few loaves of her bread, and her business grows until the family decides to start a bakery in their small town.

2411. Whittaker, Dorothy. **Angels of the Swamp**. New York: Walker, 1991. 209p. $15.95. ISBN 0-8027-8129-2. 6-8

During the Depression in 1932, Taffy, 15; Jody, 12; and Jeff, 18, meet in a Florida swamp where Taffy and Jody have established a hideout on land that Jody's family owns. Both are orphans who are escaping from unpleasant situations. Jeff joins them because he has no money. As they establish bonds, they know that they will survive without Taffy having to go to a foster home or Jody back to his alcoholic uncle, because they can fish for a living.

2412. Whittier, John Greenleaf. **Barbara Frietchie**. Nancy Winslow Parker, illustrator. New York: Greenwillow, 1992. 32p. $14. ISBN 0-688-09829-0. 1-6

Accurate drawings illustrate the story of Barbara Frietchie, who on September 10, 1862, supposedly hung the flag of the United States from her Frederick, Maryland, home window. She embarrassed Stonewall Jackson, marching through town on his way to the Battle of Antietam at Sharpsburg, into leaving the flag alone rather than desecrating it.

2413. Wilder, Laura Ingalls. **By the Shores of Silver Lake**. Garth Williams, illustrator. 1939. New York: HarperCollins, 1953. 292p. 15.95; $4.50pa. ISBN 0-06-026416-0; 0-06-440005-0pa. 3-7

In Dakota Territory, Laura's pa works on the railroad until he finds a homestead and files a claim. They all spend the winter 60 miles from anyone. Laura, 13, and Mary get to ride on a train, but a payroll robbery attempt surprises them. In the spring of 1880, more homesteaders come and build a new town. *Newbery Medal* and *American Library Association Notable Children's Books of 1940-1954*.

2414. Wilder, Laura Ingalls. **Christmas in the Big Woods**. Renée Graef, illustrator. New York: HarperCollins, 1995. 40p. $12; $3.25pa. ISBN 0-06-024752-5; 0-694-00877-Xpa. K-1

Laura's family has Christmas with relatives, and Laura is especially happy with her new doll, which she names Charlotte. This text is adapted from *Little House in the Big Woods*.

2415. Wilder, Laura Ingalls. **Dance at Grandpa's**. Renée Graef, illustrator. New York: HarperCollins, 1994. 32p. $12; $3.25pa. ISBN 0-06-023878-X; 0-694-00885-0pa. K-1

The text for this adaptation comes from chapter 8 in Wilder's *Little House in the Big Woods*. Laura and her parents go to her grandparents for a big party. She enjoys the lovely dresses, the dancing, and the delicious food.

2416. Wilder, Laura Ingalls. **The Deer in the Woods**. Renée Graef, illustrator. New York: HarperCollins, 1995. 40p. $12; $3.25pa. ISBN 0-06-024881-5; 0-694-00879-6pa. K-1

Laura's father goes into the woods one night to shoot a deer so that the family can have meat. When he returns, he tells the girls that he saw three deer in the moonlight, but he could not make himself shoot the lovely animals. This text is adapted from *Little House in the Big Woods*.

2417. Wilder, Laura Ingalls. **Farmer Boy**. Garth Williams, illustrator. 1933. New York: HarperCollins, 1953. 372p. $15.95; $4.50pa. ISBN 0-06-026425-X; 0-06-440003-4pa. 3-7

While Laura grows up in the West around 1875, Almanzo Wilder lives on a big farm in New York State. Although he goes to school when he can, he has much work to do. His best times are when the cobbler or the tin peddler visit or during the annual county fair. Almanzo also has a colt that his father gives him to break in when he is only 10. *American Library Association Notable Children's Books of 1940-1954*.

2418. Wilder, Laura Ingalls. **The First Four Years**. Garth Williams, illustrator. New York: HarperCollins, 1971. 137p. $15.95; $4.50pa. ISBN 0-06-026426-8; 0-06-440031-Xpa. 3-7

Laura and Almanzo Wilder begin their married life living on a small prairie homestead. Each year, however, brings disasters. Storms destroy their crops, they have sickness, and a fire damages their property. Although they have unpaid debts and worries, their little daughter Rose brings them much happiness. *Notable Children's Trade Books in the Field of Social Studies*.

2419. Wilder, Laura Ingalls. **Going to Town**. Renée Graef, illustrator. New York: HarperCollins, 1994. 40p. $12; $3.50pa. ISBN 0-06-0230212-6; 0-06-443452-4pa. K-1

The text, adapted from *Little House in the Big Woods*, relates Laura's story of going to town for the first time, where all the buildings and the number of items from which her parents have to choose at the store amaze her. The family finishes the visit by eating their picnic lunch on the lakeshore.

2420. Wilder, Laura Ingalls. **Little House in the Big Woods**. Garth Williams, illustrator. 1932. New York: HarperCollins, 1953. 238p. $15.95; $4.50pa. ISBN 0-06-026430-6; 0-06-440001-8pa. 3-7

In 1872, Laura is five, and her family lives in the woods of Wisconsin. She loves the family togetherness of her father's stories and preparing meat, vegetables, and fruits for the long, snowy winter. But when spring comes, they enjoy the maple syrup rising from the trees and celebrate it with a dance. *American Library Association Notable Children's Books of 1940-1970, American Booksellers' Choices,* and *Lewis Carroll Shelf Award*.

2421. Wilder, Laura Ingalls. **Little House on the Prairie**. Garth Williams, illustrator. New York: Harper, 1953. 338p. $15.95; $4.50pa. ISBN 0-06-026445-4: 0-06-440002-6pa. 3-7

Laura, six, travels with her family to the Indian territory of Kansas on a covered wagon. They find a spot to build a log cabin, and the neighbors help them build it. The family has to plant their fields and plow them, hunt for their food, chop logs and find firewood, and gather grass to feed the cattle. A prairie fire burns too close, and they almost have an Indian uprising. Pa decides to leave when he hears that the U.S. government plans to move them. *American Library Association Notable Books for Children*.

2422. Wilder, Laura Ingalls. **Little Town on the Prairie**. Garth Williams, illustrator. New York: HarperCollins, 1953. 308p. $15.95; $4.50pa. ISBN 0-06-026450-0; 0-06-440007-7. 3-7

After the difficult winter in town, Laura enjoys the Fourth of July celebration and her first evening social. Life is good for the family because Laura wins a teaching certificate though she is only 15. She knows she can earn money to help send Mary to college in Iowa. And Almanzo Wilder asks to walk her home from church. *Newbery Honor* and *American Library Association Notable Children's Books of 1940-1954*.

2423. Wilder, Laura Ingalls. **The Long Winter**. Garth Williams, illustrator. 1940. New York: HarperCollins, 1953. 334p. $15.95; $4.50pa. ISBN 0-06-026460-8; 0-06-440006-9pa. 3-7

When the Indians warn that the winter of 1880-1881 will be difficult, Pa moves the family from the claim into town. Blizzards cut off all supplies to the outside world, and Mary and Laura are unable to go to school. When everyone needs food, Almanzo Wilder and another boy make a dangerous trip across the prairie for wheat. Not until May, when the train comes through, does the Ingalls family get their Christmas presents. *Newbery Honor* and *American Library Association Notable Children's Books of 1940-1954*.

2424. Wilder, Laura Ingalls. **On the Banks of Plum Creek**. Garth Williams, illustrator. 1937. New York: HarperCollins, 1953. 340p. $15.95; $4.50pa. ISBN 0-06-026471-3; 0-06-440004-2pa. 3-7

Laura, seven, and her family leave their Indian territory home and cross Kansas, Missouri, and Iowa, on their way to Minnesota, where they purchase land and move into a sod house beside Plum Creek. They eventually get a house with real windows, but grasshoppers destroy the wheat, and her father has to leave home to find work. *Newbery Honor* and *American Library Association Notable Children's Books of 1940-1954*.

2425.   Wilder, Laura Ingalls. **On the Way Home**. New York: HarperCollins, 1976. 101p. $1.95pa. ISBN 0-06-440080-8pa. 4-7

In 1894, Laura Ingalls Wilder traveled with her husband, Almanzo Wilder, and their daughter, Rose, seven, from their drought-stricken farm in South Dakota to the Ozarks. She describes the towns they passed, the rivers they crossed, and the people they met along the way. Not for 40 years would she begin to write the "Little House" books, which told about her own childhood. Her journal gives a clear glimpse of the prairie while many were having difficulty surviving.

2426.   Wilder, Laura Ingalls. **Summertime in the Big Woods**. Renée Graef, illustrator. New York: HarperCollins, 1996. 40p. $11.95. ISBN 0-06-025934-5. K-1

The text, adapted from *Little House in the Big Woods*, tells of Laura and Mary helping with chores on the farm and going to visit Mrs. Peterson who gives them each a cookie that they share with baby Carrie. In the summer, they also look forward to visitors who might come.

2427.   Wilder, Laura Ingalls. **These Happy Golden Years**. 1943. Garth Williams, illustrator. New York: HarperCollins, 1971. 289p. $15.95; $4.50pa. ISBN 0-06-026480-2; 0-06-440008-5pa. 5-9

At 15, Laura Ingalls goes to teach school 12 miles from home. The students are taller than her, and she has to board with an unpleasant family. She is unhappy, but she needs the money to help her blind sister Mary go to school. Almanzo Wilder arrives every Friday and takes her home and then returns her on Sunday night. After three years, she decides to marry him. *Newbery Honor* and *American Library Association Notable Children's Books of 1940-1970*.

2428.   Wilder, Laura Ingalls. **Winter Days in the Big Woods**. Renée Graef, illustrator. New York: HarperCollins, 1994. 32p. $12. ISBN 0-06-023022-3. K-1

The text for this adaptation comes from chapter 2 in Wilder's *Little House in the Big Woods*. Laura and her family have to entertain themselves during the cold winter after they have done their chores each day. Laura's father plays his fiddle, and they sing with him.

2429.   Wilkes, Maria D. **Little House in Brookfield**. New York: HarperCollins, 1996. 298p. $14.95; $4.50pa. ISBN 0-06-026459-4; 0-06-440610-5pa. 3-7

Caroline, five in 1845, lives in Brookfield, Wisconsin, with her mother, grandmother, and five brothers and sisters after her father was lost at sea. She helps her mother as much as she can, and they struggle through the winter. Then in the summer, the garden grows, and the family has enough food. Best of all, she goes to school and finds that she might be able to learn rapidly along with her first best friend. This story is the first about the mother of Laura Ingalls Wilder, who wrote the *Little House* books.

2430.   Wilkie, Katherine E. **Daniel Boone: Taming the Wilds**. New York: Chelsea Juniors, 1991. 72p. $14.95. ISBN 0-7910-1407-X. (Discovery Biographies). 2-6

Daniel Boone (1734-1820) moved with his Quaker family from the Pennsylvania area toward Kentucky, where he formed alliances with Native Americans and helped open the area in Kentucky to settlers.

2431.   Wilkinson, Philip. **Building**. Dave King and Geoff Dann, illustrators. New York: Knopf, 1995. 61p. $16.95. ISBN 0-679-97256-0. (Eyewitness). 4-12

Photographs and drawings give clear pictures of the various aspects of building. Topics covered in two-page spreads are structural engineering, house construction, and building materials. These include wood, earth, bricks, stone, timber frames, the roof, thatching, columns and arches, vaults, staircases, fireplaces and chimneys, doors and doorways, windows, stained glass, balconies, and building on unusual topography. Index.

2432.   Wilkinson, Philip, and Jacqueline Dineen. **People Who Changed the World**. Robert Ingpen, illustrator. New York: Chelsea House, 1994. 93p. $19.95. ISBN 0-7910-2764-3. (Turning Points in History). 5-10

Religious leaders, philosophers, and explorers have changed the world. Those presented in the text include Confucius (c. 551-479 BC), Gautama Buddha (c. 563-480 BC), Pericles (c. 495-429 BC), Jesus Christ (c. 6 BC-c. AD 30), Muhammad (c. AD 570-632), St. Benedict of Nursia (c. AD 480-550), Marco Polo (1215-1294), Lorenzo de Medici (1449-1492), Christopher Columbus (1451-1506), Martin Luther (1483-1546), Ferdinand Magellan (1480-1521), James Cook (1728-1779), Karl Marx (1818-1883), Henri Dunant (1828-1910), Sigmund Freud (1856-1939), Leopold II of Belgium (1835-1909) who colonized Africa, and Martin Luther King, Jr. (1929-1968). Events included are the Black Plague, the Irish Famine, and the Wall Street stock market crash. Further Reading and Index.

2433. Wilkinson, Philip, and Jacqueline Dineen. **Statesmen Who Changed the World**. Robert Ingpen, illustrator. New York: Chelsea House, 1994. 93p. $19.95. ISBN 0-7910-2762-7. (Turning Points in History). 5-10

Using the definition that a statesperson is someone who influences people around the world rather than only in their own country or neighborhood, the text looks at people who have had a vision of changes whether good or bad. Included are Asoka, the Buddhist emperor (270-232 BC); Shih Huang Ti, Emperor of China (259-210 BC); Julius Caesar, Consul of Rome (100-44 BC); Constantine of Byzantium (AD 285-337); King John and the Magna Carta (1167-1216); Isabella of Castille (1451-1504) and Ferdinand II of Aragon (1452-1516); Cortés and the Aztec Empire (1485-1547); Ivan IV of Russia (1530-1584); the Manchu Empire of China under Prince Dorgon (1612-1650); Prague's Frederick V (1596-1632); the fall of the Bastille in 1789 under Louis XVI (1754-1793) and Marie Antoinette of Austria (1755-1793); Simón Bolívar (1783-1830) in South America; Emperor Meiji (1852-1912) opening up Japan; Palmerston (1784-1865) and the opening of India; Bismarck (1815-1898) and German unity; Lenin (1870-1924) and the Russian Revolution; Gandhi (1869-1948) and Indian independence; Mao (1893-1976) and the Chinese Long March; Eleanor Roosevelt (1884-1962) and the United Nations; and Gorbachev (b. 1931) and the Berlin Wall. Further Reading and Index.

2434. Wilkinson, Philip and Michael Pollard. **Generals Who Changed the World**. Robert Ingpen, illustrator. New York: Chelsea House, 1994. 93p. $19.95. ISBN 0-7910-2761-9. (Turning Points in History). 5-10

Generals have changed the map of the Earth through the battles they have won or lost. The generals discussed in the text cover many centuries. They are Alexander of Macedonia (356-323 BC); the Vandals, Huns, and Visigoths under Alaric (c. AD 370-410); Viking raiders beginning in the eighth century; William I (c. 1027-1087) conquered England in 1066; Abu Bakr, leader of the Almoravids, who overcame Ghana in 1056; the first crusade in 1095 called by Urban II; Genghis Khan (c. 1162-1227) and the Mongols; Sultan Mehmet II (1432-1481) who overtook Byzantium; Babur (1483-1530), conqueror of India; the revolt of the Netherlands toward Spain under William the Silent (1533-1584); Drake and the defeat of the Spanish Armada in 1588 (1540-1596); John III Sobieski (1624-1696) saving Vienna from the Turks; James Wolfe (1727-1759) capturing Quebec; Washington (1732-1799) after Lexington; Napoleon (1769-1821) attacking Moscow; Robert E. Lee (1807-1870) and Sharpsburg; Paul Kruger's Boers (1825-1904) against Great Britain; the beginning of World War I under Kaiser Wilhelm II (1859-1941); Japan's bombing of Pearl Harbor with Hideki Tojo as prime minister (1884-1948); and Dwight Eisenhower (1890-1969) and D-Day. Further Reading and Index.

2435. Wilkinson, Philip, and Michael Pollard. **Scientists Who Changed the World**. Robert R. Ingpen, illustrator. New York: Chelsea House, 1994. 93p. $19.95. ISBN 0-7910-2763-5. (Turning Points in History). 4-6

People who have had an interest in why and how things happen have helped shape the world. Brief profiles of some of those scientists or groups appear in the text. They are Kaifung, Johannes Gutenburg (fifteenth century), Galileo Galilei (1564-1642), Isaac Newton (1642-1727), James Watt (1736-1819), Donkin and Hall (early nineteenth-century cannery), Louis Daguerre (1789-1851), Charles Darwin (1809-1882), Joseph Lister (1827-1912), Alexander Graham Bell (1847-1922), Marie Curie (1867-1934), the Wright brothers (early twentieth century), Henry Ford (1863-1947), Albert Einstein (1879-1955), John Logie Baird (1888-1946), Alan Turing (1912-1954), the Manhattan Project (early 1940s), Crick and Watson (twentieth century), Wilkins and Franklin (twentieth century), the launch of Sputnik I in 1957, and astronauts Aldrin, Armstrong, and Collins. Photographs enhance the text. Timeline and Index.

2436. Williams, Brian. **Forts and Castles**. New York: Viking, 1994. 48p. $15.99. ISBN 0-670-85898-6. (See Through History). 6-9

People began building forts and castles in prehistoric times when walled towns were important, and they continued through the Middle Ages. They helped kings control lands, protect their subjects, and impress their enemies. Armies tried to capture them and developed complex weapons to achieve their goals. See-through cutaways of a Mycenaean citadel in Greece, a besieged castle in the Middle Ages, the castle of a Japanese warlord, and a U.S. Army frontier fort highlight the text. Two-page topics cover information on Hattusas, Tiryns, the siege of Lachish, hill forts, the Great Wall of China, Roman forts, Masada, the Normans, Crusader castles, the Moors in Spain, the Renaissance, Japanese castles, Sacsayhuaman, Golconda, Vauban fortresses, cavalry fort, Fort Sumter, and the end of the age. Key Dates and Glossary and Index.

2437. Williams, Brian, and Brenda Williams. **The Age of Discovery: From the Renaissance to American Independence**. James Field, illustrator. New York: Peter Bedrick, 1994. 64p. $18.95. ISBN 0-87226-311-8. (Timelink). 5-8

The text presents history in 50-year segments and depicts discoveries from all cultures. Various aids such as comparative time charts, maps, charts, and graphs show the major historical events from 1491 to 1789 in the Americas, Asia, and Africa. Illustrations complement the text.

2438.   Williams, David. **Grandma Essie's Covered Wagon**. Wiktor Sadowski, illustrator. New York: Knopf, 1993. 41p. $16. ISBN 0-679-90253-8. K-3

When the narrator was a young girl, she and her family went by covered wagon from Missouri to Kansas. After her father's farm failed in the drought, the family went to Oklahoma where oil was booming. One of her siblings died, however, and the family, tired of all the hard work, returned to Kansas. The narrator describes their lives as they moved from place to place.

2439.   Williams, Neva. **Patrick Desjarlait: Conversations with a Native American Artist**. Minneapolis, MN: Runestone Press, 1994. 56p. $21.50. ISBN 0-8225-3151-8. 6 up

Patrick Desjarlait (1921-1972) created vivid watercolor paintings of Chippewa (Ojibway or Anishinabe) life in northwestern Minnesota to preserve the culture. As he tells his story, he gives excellent information about growing up with tribal rituals and celebrations. He also discusses his role in the relocation camps for the Japanese in World War II. Glossary and Pronunciation Guide.

2440.   Willis, Patricia. **Out of the Storm**. New York: Clarion, 1995. 188p. $14.95. ISBN 0-395-68708-X. 5-7.

Mandy's father does not return from World War II in 1945, and she, her mother, and brother have to move 40 miles away to live with an aunt where her mother can get a job to support them. Mandy, 12, hates the town but finds friends faster than she expected. When she saves sheep in a storm—more from guilt than from duty—she realizes that her father will not return and that staying in the town is okay.

2441.   Willis, Patricia. **A Place to Claim as Home**. New York: Clarion, 1991. 166p. $13.95. ISBN 0-395-55395-4. 4-7

Pretending to be 15 during World War II, Henry, 13, gets a job helping Sarah on her farm for the summer. As an orphan, he loves the farm and soon begins to like the quiet and preoccupied Sarah. As families hear either good or bad news from relatives fighting in the war, they try to harvest their crops with the few men available. Henry hopes that Sarah's home will soon become his as well. *Friends of American Writers Juvenile Book Merit Award.*

2442.   Wills, Charles. **The Battle of Little Bighorn**. Englewood Cliffs, NJ: Silver Burdett, 1990. 64p. $14.98; $7.95pa. ISBN 0-382-09952-4; 0-382-09948-6pa. (Turning Points in American History). 4-8

The text gives the background on the Battle of Little Bighorn and the shock when all of the U.S. soldiers were found dead on the ground. The relationship between whites and Native Americans becomes clear with additional information. Photographs highlight the text. Bibliography and Index.

2443.   Wills, Charles. **A Historical Album of Alabama**. Brookfield, CT: Millbrook Press, 1994. 64p. $16.40; $6.95pa. ISBN 1-56294-591-2; 1-56294-854-7pa. (Historical Album). 4-8

The text presents the land of Alabama before it became a state, beginning with Native American civilizations and continuing through exploration and settlement. Early statehood developments and issues, and the role of large cities in the state's livelihood, lead to the present. Prints, maps, and photographs illustrate the text. Gazetteer: Quick Facts, Key Events, Personalities, and Index.

2444.   Wills, Charles. **A Historical Album of California**. Brookfield, CT: Millbrook Press, 1994. 64p. $16.40; $6.95pa. ISBN 1-56294-479-7; 1-56294-759-1pa. (Historical Album). 4-8

Native Americans inhabited California for centuries before Columbus came to the New World in 1492. Disease, conflict, and loss of land when the settlers arrived destroyed life for these people. The Spanish came in the sixteenth century and settled in the eighteenth. In the early 1800s, Mexicans began to rule California. After the United States won the Mexican War, California became a territory in 1848, just as the gold rush started. Other information about California also appears in the text, which is complemented by photographs and reproductions. Gazetteer: Quick Facts, Key Events, Personalities, and Index.

2445.   Wills, Charles. **A Historical Album of Connecticut**. Brookfield, CT: Millbrook Press, 1994. 64p. $16.40; $6.95pa. ISBN 1-56294-506-8; 1-56294-848-2pa. (Historical Album). 4-8

The text presents the land of Connecticut before it became a state, beginning with Native American civilizations and continuing through exploration and settlement. Early statehood developments and issues, and the role of large cities in the state's livelihood, lead to the present day. Prints, maps, and photographs illustrate the text. Gazetteer: Quick Facts, Key Events, Personalities, and Index.

2446.   Wills, Charles. **A Historical Album of Florida**. Brookfield, CT: Millbrook Press, 1994. 64p. $16.40; $6.95pa. ISBN 1-56294-480-0; 1-56294-760-5pa. (Historical Album). 4-8

The text presents the land of Florida before it became a state, beginning with Native American civilizations and continuing through exploration and settlement. Early statehood developments, and issues and the role of large cities in the state's livelihood, lead to the present day. Prints, maps, and photographs illustrate the text. Gazetteer: Quick Facts, Key Events, Personalities, and Index.

2447. Wills, Charles. **A Historical Album of Illinois**. Brookfield, CT: Millbrook Press, 1994. 64p. $16.40; $6.95pa. ISBN 1-56294-482-7; 1-56294-761-3pa. (Historical Album). 4-8

The text presents the land of Illinois before it became a state, beginning with Native American civilizations and continuing through exploration and settlement. Early statehood developments and issues, and the role of large cities in the state's livelihood, lead to the present day. Prints, maps, and photographs illustrate the text. Gazetteer: Quick Facts, Key Events, Personalities, and Index.

2448. Wills, Charles. **A Historical Album of Nebraska**. Brookfield, CT: Millbrook Press, 1994. 64p. $16.40; $6.95pa. ISBN 1-56294-509-2; 1-56294-852-0pa. (Historical Album). 4-8

The text presents the land of Nebraska before it became a state, beginning with Native American civilizations and continuing through exploration and settlement. Early statehood developments and issues, and the role of large cities in the state's livelihood, lead to the present day. Prints, maps, and photographs illustrate the text. Gazetteer: Quick Facts, Key Events, Personalities, and Index.

2449. Wills, Charles. **A Historical Album of Oregon**. Brookfield, CT: Millbrook Press, 1994. 64p. $16.40; $6.95pa. ISBN 1-56294-594-7; 1-56294-855-5pa. (Historical Album). 4-8

The text presents the land of Oregon before it became a state, beginning with Native American civilizations and continuing through exploration and settlement. Early statehood developments and issues, and the role of large cities in the state's livelihood, lead to the present day. Prints, maps, and photographs illustrate the text. Gazetteer: Quick Facts, Key Events, Personalities, and Index.

2450. Wills, Charles. **A Historical Album of Texas**. Brookfield, CT: Millbrook Press, 1994. 64p. $16.40; $6.95pa. ISBN 1-56294-504-1; 1-56294-847-4pa. (Historical Album). 4-8

The text presents the land of Texas before it became a state, beginning with Native American civilizations and continuing through exploration and settlement. Early statehood developments and issues, and the role of large cities in the state's livelihood, lead to the present day. Prints, maps, and photographs illustrate the text. Gazetteer: Quick Facts, Key Events, Personalities, and Index.

2451. Wilson, Anthony. **Visual Timeline of Transportation**. New York: Dorling Kindersley, 1995. 48p. $16.95. ISBN 1-56458-880-7. 3-5

Brief essays introduce the four time periods identified as changes in modes of transportation. Following is a timeline divided into air and space, land, and water, with photographs of the different vehicles or animals that people used for travel. An additional category notes important milestones, such as the 1970 explosion of Apollo 13. The four segments are 10,000 BC to AD 1779, when humans could only go as fast as the fastest domesticated animal; 1780-1879, the age of steam; 1880-1959, the rise of powered flight and the automobile; and 1960 to 2000, the time of space travel. Future Trends and Index.

2452. Wilson, Claire. **Quanah Parker: Comanche Chief**. New York: Chelsea House, 1991. 112p. $18.95. ISBN 0-7910-1702-8. (North American Indians of Achievement). 5 up

Quanah Parker (1854-1911) was the son of a Comanche war leader and Cynthia Ann Parker, a captured white settler. Parker became a respected warrior who led a band of Quahadi fighters in battle against intruders on Comanche lands. In 1875, after years of eluding the army, they were forced to surrender, and Parker led his people onto the reservation. He cooperated with his former enemies and used them to best advantage so that he made much money dealing with Texas cattlemen. He decided that his people had to bend, but not break, if they were to survive. Photographs enhance the text. Chronology, Further Reading, and Index.

2453. Wilson, Janet. **The Ingenious Mr. Peale: Painter, Patriot and Man of Science**. New York: Atheneum, 1996. 128p. $16. ISBN 0-689-31884-7. 5-9

Charles Willson Peale (1741-1827) is best known for his paintings and his interest in natural history. He found the bones of a mammoth and displayed them in his Philadelphia museum. But he became an artist because he owed money, and he painted portraits of Franklin and Washington. His other interests included revolutionary politics, inventing, farming, and the idea of motion pictures, and he unwillingly served in the military. The text looks at this man and notes his dilettantish approach to life. Bibliography and Index. *School Library Journal Best Book.*

2454. Wilson, Kate. **Earthquake! San Francisco, 1906**. Richard Courtney, illustrator. Austin, TX: Raintree/Steck-Vaughn, 1993. 54p. $22.83; $4.95pa. ISBN 0-8114-7216-7; 0-8114-8056-9pa. (Stories of America—Working Together). 5-9

After an earthquake struck San Francisco, California, in 1906, fires began to destroy many buildings, but the quake had wrecked water pipes throughout the city, and firefighters were helpless. George Lowe reported for the *San Francisco Chronicle,* and Helen Dare (on vacation) reported for the *Los Angeles Examiner.* They realized that they must get the news to the outside world, so they took the ferry across the bay to Oakland from where they could send their stories. Others also rapidly began orderly actions to overcome the devastation. One of these was General Funston, a man who had mapped Death Valley. He organized a militia for rebuilding; others collected mail in all forms (such as writing on sleeve cuffs) and sent it to worried relatives. Epilogue, Afterword, and Notes.

2455.   Winnick, Karen, author/illustrator. **Mr. Lincoln's Whiskers**. Honesdale, PA: Boyds Mills Press, 1996. Unpaged. $15.95. ISBN 1-56397-485-1. K-3

When Grace's father brings her a picture of Abraham Lincoln (1809-1865), she thinks he looks thin. Although only 11, Grace decides to write him a letter. She sees a shadow across his face from the light outside, and she realizes he would look better with a beard. She tells him, and he answers her letter. When his train comes through Westfield, he thanks her for her advice, and she admires his new beard.

2456.   Winslow, Mimi. **Loggers and Railroad Workers**. New York: Twenty-First Century Books, 1995. 96p. $16.98. ISBN 0-8050-2997-4. (Settling the West). 5-8

Two groups helped make settling in the West possible. Loggers cut the trees, and railroad workers helped build the rails that transported both people and goods. The text presents first-person views from loggers, who worried about being 200 feet up in a tree and the tree not falling exactly right, and from railroad workers, who had other concerns. Notes, Further Reading, and Index.

2457.   Winter, Jeanette, author/illustrator. **The Christmas Tree Ship**. New York: Philomel, 1994. 32p. $14.95. ISBN 0-399-22693-1. 5-9

From 1887 until 1912, Captain Herman takes Christmas trees chopped in the Michigan woods on his schooner to the Clark Street Bridge in Chicago. In 1912, he encounters a fierce storm and sends a message in a bottle to his wife and daughters before he is lost at sea. The trees never arrive. The next year, after grieving for him, Captain Herman's wife and daughters know that they must take over the voyage so they can help the people waiting in Chicago have a happy Christmas season. *Bulletin Blue Ribbon Book*.

2458.   Winter, Jeanette, author/illustrator. **Cowboy Charlie: The Story of Charles M. Russell**. San Diego, CA: Harcourt Brace, 1995. 32p. $15. ISBN 0-15-200857-8. 2-4

As a young boy, Charles M. Russell (1864-1926) spent more time dreaming of the West than he did studying, so his parents let him go to Montana Territory with a family friend for the summer when he was 15. After two years, he got a job as a cowboy guarding horses during the night. During the day, he would sleep or draw everything that he saw. The West began to change, and Russell devoted the rest of his life to his paintings. The pictures include a triple-page spread showing a broad view of western scenery. *American Bookseller Pick of the Lists* and *Parents' Choice Awards*.

2459.   Winter, Jeanette, author/illustrator **Follow the Drinking Gourd**. New York: Knopf, 1988. 48p. $13.95. ISBN 0-394-99694-1. K-3

Peg Leg Joe, a white sailor, teaches the Drinking Gourd song to slaves so that they will know how to follow the Underground Railroad. In the text, a family follows his directions by escaping at night while looking at the stars leading them to the Ohio River. There an abolitionist waits to ferry them across to safe houses on their way to Canada.

2460.   Winter, Jeanette, author/illustrator **Klara's New World**. New York: Knopf, 1992. 41p. $15.99. ISBN 0-679-90626-6. 2-7

In 1852, Klara, eight, and her family have to leave Sweden during a famine. They go to America, where they hope to grow crops. They sail on an ocean, a river, and a lake as well as ride a train during the three months that they take to reach Minnesota.

2461.   Wisler, G. Clifton. **Caleb's Choice**. New York: Lodestar, 1996. 154p. $14.99. ISBN 0-525-67526-4. 4-6

Caleb, 13, goes to Houston, Texas, to live with his wealthy relatives. They quickly move him to his grandmother's Dallas boardinghouse. He finds out that Texas bounty hunters seek runaway slaves or take freemen without identification. After Caleb becomes friends with his grandmother's hired boy Micah, they unwittingly become involved in the Underground Railroad work of Caleb's family. Caleb has to go north after he decides that the family's association is morally proper and that he wants to participate.

2462.   Wisler, G. Clifton. **The Drummer of Vicksburg**. New York: Lodestar, 1997. 144p. $15.99. ISBN 0-525-67537-X. 5-8

The life of Orion Howe, a Medal of Honor–winning drummer boy in the Civil War, is the basis for this story about a brave 14-year-old. Howe risked his life by running through enemy fire to tell General Sherman that the regiment for which he played the drum needed ammunition.

2463.   Wisler, G. Clifton. **Jericho's Journey**. New York: Lodestar, 1993. 137p. $13.99; $3.99pa. ISBN 0-525-67428-4; 0-14-037065-Xpa. 4-8

Jericho, 11, wants to move to Texas because he has heard of Davy Crockett and Sam Houston as well as his Uncle Dan's tales after the battle of the Alamo. The reality of the journey to Texas does not include the ideal of his dreams, however, as the family, including his older brother, bossy sister, and two younger brothers, have encounters along the way. Wisler mentions in an afterword that some of the episodes come from entries in a frontier journal.

2464.   Wisler, G. Clifton. **Mr. Lincoln's Drummer**. New York: Lodestar, 1995. 131p. $14.99. ISBN 0-525-67463-2. 4-8

Willie Johnson, 10 when the Civil War starts in 1861, plays the drum for a captain in town trying to get recruits. He makes enough money to help his family, and when his father joins for the salary, Willie decides that he will go with the Vermont group as the drummer boy. He is transferred to be a nurse, and his bravery wins him the Congressional Medal of Honor in 1863. The real Willie Johnson was the seventh soldier to receive that honor.

2465.   Wisler, G. Clifton. **Mustang Flats**. New York: Lodestar, 1997. 144p. $14.99. ISBN 0-525-67544-2. 5-9

Alby Draper, 14, has to face a number of changes in his life when his father returns from the Civil War missing one leg. To lift the family from poverty, Alby and his father try to catch and tame wild mustangs and then sell them. During this process, they learn about each other, and Alby learns about himself.

2466.   Wisler, G. Clifton. **Piper's Ferry**. New York: Dutton, 1990. 131p. $14.95. ISBN 0-525-67303-2. 6-8

Tim, 14, goes to see relatives in Texas, and while he is there, he decides to join the fight for freedom from Mexico in 1836. Although he is with family, he is lonely, and he talks to the family's bound servant, who was once a slave. Tim realizes that regardless of his emotional situation, he has the choice to remain or leave a place, unlike those who belong to someone else.

2467.   Wisler, G. Clifton. **Red Cap**. New York: Dutton, 1991. 160p. $15. ISBN 0-525-67337-7. 5-9

Ransom J. Powell, 13 and four feet tall in 1862, runs away from his home in Frostburg, Maryland, to fight with the Union army in the Civil War. He becomes the drummer boy, but two years later, the Confederates capture him and take him to Camp Sumter, a prison in Andersonville, Georgia. He refuses to sign a parole that would release him from the stockade, and he again has the job of drummer boy, this time for the camp. This position and the kindness of a guard help him survive this terrible ordeal.

2468.   Wisler, G. Clifton. **This New Land**. New York: Walker, 1987. 125p. $13.95. ISBN 0-8027-6727-3. (American History for Young People). 5-7

Richard, 12, leaves the Netherlands with his family after escaping from England and James I's religious tyranny in 1620. They travel first on the *Speedwell* and then on the *Mayflower* as they journey to the new colony in America. Richard's mother dies on board the *Mayflower*, and Richard goes with Miles Standish to meet the Native Americans Samoset and Squanto. Richard describes the cold, the number of pilgrims who die, and the relief of the settlers to have food and to celebrate their first year in their new land.

2469.   Wisniewski, David, author/illustrator. **The Wave of the Sea-Wolf**. New York: Clarion, 1994. Unpaged. $16.95. ISBN 0-395-66478. 3-6

As a young girl, Kchokeen, a member of the Tlingit tribe on the coast of Alaska, goes looking for berries. Warned by her mother to stay away from the sea where she could be overcome by a huge wave that the tribe calls Gonakadet (Sea Wolf), she goes inland for her search. She falls into a huge tree, and a bear cub begins howling. She soon finds that the bear knows that Gonakadet is coming. The huge tree saves her, and after her father and brothers rescue her the following day, she becomes the tribe's warning for the arrival of Gonakadet by listening for the bear's howl. Traders come to the coast and demand more furs than the tribe can provide, so the men burn the longhouses. In this late-eighteenth-century story, the tribe rebuilds, but the traders continue to bother them. A canoe caught in a tree when Gonakadet kills the first traders helps Kchokeen keep hope that life will return to normal.

2470.   Witcover, Paul. **Zora Neale Hurston**. New York: Chelsea House, 1990. 119p. $18.95; $7.95pa. ISBN 0-7910-1129-1; 0-7910-1154-2pa. (Black Americans of Achievement). 5 up

Zora Neale Hurston (1891-1960) began to support herself at 14 and eventually attended Howard University. She dreamed of becoming a writer throughout her youth, and in 1925 she won a major literary contest. In the same year, she entered Barnard College to study anthropology with a specialty in African American folklore. In the 1930s, she became well known for *Jonah's Gourd Vine, Mules and Men,* and *Their Eyes Were Watching God.* She also wrote an autobiography, *Dust Tracks on a Road.* Among her friends were Langston Hughes and Countee Cullen. Untrue and unsavory accusations in the press destroyed her reputation, but her work has recently resurfaced to positive critiques. She was original, intelligent, independent, and hardworking. Photographs and reproductions enhance the text. Chronology, Further Reading, and Index.

2471.   Wolfe, Charles K. **Mahalia Jackson: Gospel Singer**. New York: Chelsea House, 1990. 103p. $18.95; $7.95pa. ISBN 1-55546-661-3; 0-7910-0440-6pa. (American Women of Achievement). 5 up

The drive of Mahalia Jackson (1912-1972) transformed gospel music by taking it from Black churches into the concert halls. She was orphaned at six but absorbed the music around her in New Orleans. At 15, her aunt sent her to Chicago to keep her away from the rowdy life. At 16, she started her career. She revolutionized gospel by adding blues inflections. Offstage, she had many friends in politics and knew Dr. Martin Luther King, Jr., and became involved in the Civil Rights movement. Photographs, Chronology, Further Reading, and Index.

2472.   Wolfe, Rinna Evelyn. **Charles Richard Drew, M.D.** New York: Franklin Watts, 1991. 64p. $11.90. ISBN 0-531-20021-3. (First Books). 4-6

Charles Richard Drew (1904-1950) became a noted physician who discovered methods for separating plasma from blood. As an African American, he never received the acclaim that he deserved. Photographs highlight the text. Bibliography, Glossary, and Index.

2473.   Wolfe, Rinna Evelyn. **Mary McLeod Bethune**. New York: Franklin Watts, 1992. 64p. $19.90. ISBN 0-531-20103-1. (First Books). 3-5

Mary McLeod Bethune (1875-1955) attended Miss Wilson's mission school for Black children, where she began to love learning. She was able to go to Concord, North Carolina, and continue her schooling. After graduating, the same Miss Crissman who had funded her high school funded her training at Chicago's Moody Bible Institute. Although Bethune wanted to be a missionary in Africa, she was rejected because she was Black. She decided to go to Florida where she began dreaming about a school for girls. After major fund-raising, her dream came true, and this effort started her own contributions to the community, which she continued throughout her life. Glossary, For Further Reading, and Index.

2474.   Wood, Frances M. **Becoming Rosemary**. New York: Bantam, 1997. 224p. $14.95. ISBN 0-385-32248-8. 5-9

Rosemary Weston expects to continue her daily tasks in North Carolina in 1790. But a cooper and his pregnant wife arrive, and his wife becomes Rosemary's friend. When rumors spread about witchcraft and evil regarding her friend, Rosemary realizes that she must take a stand.

2475.   Wood, Leigh Hope. **The Crow Indians**. New York: Chelsea House, 1993. 79p. $14.95; $6.95pa. ISBN 0-7910-1661-7; 0-7910-1964-0pa. (The Junior Library of American Indians). 3-6

After beginning with the Crow legend of creation, the text gives the history of the Crow, who have lived on the Great Plains for thousands of years in the center of the United States. They were corn farmers more than 1,800 years ago and had long established themselves before others came to take their land in the nineteenth century. The chapters cover their way of life, including their Sun Dance, their battles, and their last traditional leader, Plenty Coups. Photographs enhance the text. Glossary, Chronology, and Index.

2476.   Wood, Leigh Hope. **The Navajo Indians**. New York: Chelsea House, 1992. 79p. $14.95; $6.95pa. ISBN 0-7910-1651-X; 0-7910-2026-6pa. (The Junior Library of American Indians). 3-6

After beginning with the Navajo legend of creation, the text gives the history of the Navajos from approximately 2,000 years ago, when they were living in Canada and Alaska. They migrated south to the American Southwest around 500 years ago and called themselves Diné (the People). The chapters cover their way of life, their exile and return home in the nineteenth century, their crafts, and their dual identity. Photographs enhance the text. Glossary, Chronology, and Index.

2477.   Wood, Marion. **Ancient America**. New York: Facts on File, 1990. 96p. $17.95. ISBN 0-8160-2210-0. (Cultural Atlas for Young People). 6-9

Wood covers the Americas, from the Inuit in the north to the Inca living in the empire that extended as far south as Chile. With as much information as possible, the text gives a picture of conditions in the Americas before the explorers came from Europe to change everything. Chronology, Glossary, Gazetteer, and Index. *New York Public Library's Books for the Teen Age.*

2478.   Woodruff, Elvira. **Dear Levi: Letters from the Overland Trail**. Beth Peck, illustrator. New York: Knopf, 1994. 119p. $14. ISBN 0-679-84641-7. 3-6

In 1851, Austin, 12, follows the Overland Trail on his 3,000-mile journey from Pennsylvania to Oregon, and he writes letters to his younger brother Levi about the trip. Austin's day starts at 4:30 in the morning, when he has to find the family's oxen and attach them to the wagon so the family can have breakfast and begin the day's journey by seven. They travel until noon, let the stock graze, and eat lunch. After an hour, they begin again. The letters let the reader experience this journey, which also has its moments of rest and entertainment.

2479. Woodruff, Elvira. **George Washington's Socks**. New York: Scholastic, 1991. 132p. $3.50pa. ISBN 0-590-44036-5pa. 4-7

In this historical fantasy, a rowboat on Lake Levart entices five children to step inside and head backward in time to the eve of the battle of Trenton, when George Washington is preparing to fight on the icy Delaware River. The children find themselves in the winter of 1776 struggling against Hessians and living the horrors of the war. Although they are immensely relieved when they think themselves into returning to the present, they have learned about the fierceness of battle firsthand.

2480. Woodtor, Dee Parmer. **Big Meeting**. Dolores Johnson, illustrator. New York: Simon & Schuster, Atheneum, 1996. Unpaged. $16. ISBN 0-689-31933-9. K-3

In the 1950s, a girl and her brother look forward to the Homecoming Weekend at the Bethel African Methodist Episcopal church in the southern town of Oakey Streak. They dress up for the Big Meeting, have their aunt tap them with her fan when they think about misbehaving, and enjoy the wonderful food and fellowship after the service. They also enjoy their grandfather's ghost stories.

2481. Woog, Adam. **Duke Ellington**. San Diego, CA: Lucent, 1996. 112p. $16.95. ISBN 1-56006-073-5. (Importance Of). 6 up

Duke Ellington (1899-1974) spent his childhood in Washington, D.C., and wrote his first composition at the age of 14. He taught himself music and received honors throughout the world. He blended popular and African American musical styles with European classical music. He did not like the term "jazz" and thought that it did not apply to his music. He created a big band because he felt that hearing one's music was important. His band could play his compositions on the morning after he finished them. The text presents his life with highlighting photographs. For Further Reading, Additional Works, and Index.

2482. Woog, Adam. **Harry Houdini**. San Diego, CA: Lucent, 1995. 112p. $16.95. ISBN 1-56006-053-0. (Importance Of). 6 up

Harry Houdini (1874-1926) created mystery about himself by telling people that he had been born in Appleton, Wisconsin, when he had actually been born in Pest, Hungary, and immigrated to the United States when he was very young. After he started a career as a magician at 17, he gradually improved his abilities until he could escape from seemingly foolproof restraints. He gave his wife much of the credit for his success, but his personal charisma and knack for using the new media forms, radio and film, for publicity were also major factors. He earned the compliment of being called the "Great Escaper" and of being the best known of all magicians. Notes, For Further Reading, Additional Works Consulted, and Index.

2483. Woog, Adam. **Louis Armstrong**. San Diego, CA: Lucent, 1995. 112p. $16.95. ISBN 1-56006-059-X. (Importance Of). 6 up

The text, with photographs to highlight, tells about Louis Armstrong's life (1900-1971). It also defines jazz and Armstrong's ability to play it. Nine chapters divide his life chronologically and look at his early life, stardom in New Orleans, the beginning of his fame after World War I, his life in Chicago and then on Broadway, his career, and his international fame. For Further Reading and Index.

2484. Wormser, Richard. **Pinkerton: America's First Private Eye**. New York: Walker, 1990. 119p. $17.95. ISBN 0-8027-6964-0. 5-9

The most famous detective in the nineteenth century, Allan Pinkerton grew up in the worst slums of Glasgow, Scotland, and died on his American estate. He believed in upholding the law but broke it without hesitation during his fight against slavery. He fled Scotland because of his pro-labor activities, but in America he despised militant labor. He became a detective by accident, but when he began solving crimes, he changed from barrel making to police work and then opened his own agency. Further Reading and Index.

2485. Wright, Courtni C. **Journey to Freedom: A Story of the Underground Railroad**. Gershom Griffith, illustrator. New York: Holiday House, 1994. Unpaged. $15.95. ISBN 0-8234-1096-X. K-3

From Joshua's first-person point of view, the reader finds that he is an eight-year-old runaway slave with his family and eight others in Harriet Tubman's care while traveling the Underground Railway. They journey by night and rest in safe houses during the day as they walk from Kentucky to Canada during the late fall just as the snows begin.

2486. Wright, Courtni C. **Jumping the Broom**. Gershom Griffith, illustrator. New York: Holiday House, 1994. Unpaged. $15.95. ISBN 0-8234-1042-0. K-3

During slave times, an eight-year-old narrator tells about preparations for her sister's wedding, called "jumping the broom," a ritual symbolizing leaving the past behind. The slaves save food by cooling it in the creek and prepare it for a big feast after the ceremony. The women sew a quilt using pieces of cloth from the mistress's cast-off dresses, and the men build a room for the two. Although no minister is present, the pair are "married" in the eyes of the community.

2487. Wright, Courtni C. **Wagon Train: A Family Goes West in 1865**. Gershom Griffith, illustrator. New York: Holiday House, 1995. Unpaged. $15.95. ISBN 0-8234-1152-4. 2-4

Ginny goes with her African American family on a wagon train from Virginia to California in 1865. They have to cope with hauling water, cooking over open fires, snakes and snake-bite, dust, broken wagon wheels, and hunger on the journey after they leave Independence, Missouri, to travel the Oregon Trail.

2488. Wright, David K. **Arthur Ashe: Breaking the Color Barrier in Tennis**. Springfield, NJ: Enslow, 1996. 128p. $18.95. ISBN 0-89490-689-5. 4-7

Arthur Ashe (1943-1993) rose from a Richmond, Virginia, neighborhood to become one of America's great tennis players, winning at Wimbledon. He always showed courage and discipline while trying to make tennis a color-blind sport. Even when he got heart disease and then AIDS from tainted blood, he kept his strength of character. Photographs, Further Reading, and Index.

2489. Wright, David K. **The Story of the Vietnam Memorial**. Chicago: Childrens Press, 1989. 31p. $8.95. ISBN 0-516-04745-0. (Cornerstones of Freedom). 3-5

The text looks at all aspects of the Vietnam Memorial, from its conceptualization by Jan Scruggs through its design contest to its many visitors. Photographs enhance the text.

2490. Wunderli, Stephen. **The Blue Between the Clouds**. New York: Henry Holt, 1992. 114p. $13.95. ISBN 0-8050-1772-0. 5 up

In Thistle, Utah, Matt, 11, plays with his friend Two Moons during the early 1940s. They help a pilot from World War I rebuild his old Fokker airplane and try to find excitement anywhere they can. When Two Moons has to leave, they have difficulty accepting the changes in their lives.

2491. Wyman, Andrea. **Red Sky at Morning**. New York: Holiday House, 1991. 230p. $13.95. ISBN 0-8234-0903-1. 3-7

In 1909, Callie and her family remain in Indiana while her father travels to Oregon to buy a new farm for their family. While he is gone, her mother dies in childbirth; her sister has to leave home to find work; and she and her German grandfather must run the farm during a diphtheria epidemic. She also finds out things about her father that distress her, but when he returns, she adjusts, and all leave for Oregon.

Y

2492. Yancey, Diane. **Desperadoes and Dynamite: Train Robbery in the United States**. New York: Franklin Watts, 1991. 63p. $18.43. ISBN 0-531-20038-8. (First Books). 4-6

In 1866, train robberies seemed to take over. Among the most famous robbers were Jesse James, an outlaw at 18, with his first train robbery in 1873; Butch Cassidy and the Sundance Kid; and the Dalton Gang. Additional information tells what happened to these people. Photographs, maps, and drawings highlight the text. Further Reading, Glossary, and Index.

2493. Yannuzzi, Della. **Wilma Mankiller: Leader of the Cherokee Nation**. Springfield, NJ: Enslow, 1994. 104p. $17.95. ISBN 0-89490-498-1. (People to Know). 5-8

Wilma Pearl Mankiller (b. 1945) was sworn into office as the first female Principal Chief of the Cherokee Nation in 1985 after overcoming her own severe hardships and intense opposition. She has worked toward a financially independent and self-governing Cherokee Nation by reestablishing a Cherokee tribal judicial system. Chronology, Chapter Notes, Further Reading, and Index.

2494. Yannuzzi, Della A. **Zora Neale Hurston: Southern Storyteller**. Springfield, NJ: Enslow, 1996. 104p. $17.95. ISBN 0-89490-685-2. (African-American Biographies). 6-9

Zora Neale Hurston (1901?-1960) was a complex and well-educated woman who was part of the Harlem Renaissance. The text looks at her life, with its hard work and belief in herself, as she pursued her writing and anthropological research. Photographs, Chronology, Further Reading, Notes, and Index.

2495. Yarbro, Chelsea Quinn. **Floating Illusions**. New York: HarperCollins, 1986. 215p. $12.95. ISBN 0-06-026643-0. 6-8

While Millicent, 14, crosses the Atlantic on an ocean liner in 1910, several people are murdered. Among the friends she makes during her investigation are a magician, a militant feminist, and Anton, a noble. When the magician's life is threatened, he can no longer be a suspect, and Millicent identifies the criminal.

2496. Yates, Elizabeth. **Amos Fortune, Free Man**. Nora S. Unwin, illustrator. New York: Dutton, 1967. 181p. $15. ISBN 0-525-25570-2. 3-6

When an At-mun-shi tribe prince was 15 in 1725, slave traders abducted him. His owners named him Amos Fortune and taught him to read. He was finally able to buy his freedom 45 years later. He continued as an expert tanner and a supportive family member, and he bought freedom for many others until he died in 1801. *Newbery Medal, William Allen White Award, Herald Tribune Award,* and *New Hampshire Governor's Award of Distinction.*

2497. Yep, Laurence. **Dragon's Gate**. New York: HarperCollins, 1993. 275p. $15; $4.95pa. ISBN 0-06-022972-1; 0-06-440489-7pa. 5 up

In this prequel to *Dragonwings*, in 1865, Otter arrives in the Sierra Mountains from Hwangtung Province in China, where he begins helping his adoptive father and uncle build the transcontinental railroad. Otter expects to see goldfields, but he only sees cleared trees and a vast cover of whiteness. His dream is to learn all that he can so that he can return to China and free it from the Manchu invaders. During the difficult work under hostile foremen, his uncle encourages him to have another dream, one in which he will be himself and do what he needs to do rather than what tradition has told him. After a strike for fewer hours and more pay with the other Chinese, and his uncle's death, Otter decides to take his advice. *Newbery Honor, New York Public Library's Books for the Teen Age, American Booksellers Pick of the Lists, Commonwealth Club Silver Medal for Literature, John and Patricia Beatty Award,* and *American Library Association Notable Books for Children.*

2498. Yep, Laurence. **Hiroshima: A Novella**. New York: Scholastic, 1995. 56p. $9.95. ISBN 0-590-20832-2. 3-6

The story begins with details about the *Enola Gay* and its cargo as well as background about why it left its base. It continues with the situation in Hiroshima on August 6, 1945, when *Enola Gay* drops its cargo, an atomic bomb. Sachi, a young girl of 12, survives while her sister dies. Because of her terrible scars, Sachi stays inside for three years, but eventually she comes to the United States for free treatment. The entire situation is carefully documented. Afterword and Sources. *American Library Association Booklist Editors' Choices* and *Notable Children's Trade Books in the Field of Social Studies.*

2499.   Yep, Laurence. **The Star Fisher**. New York: Morrow, 1991. 150p. $12.95. ISBN 0-688-09365-5. 6-9

Jean Lee, 15, has trouble making friends when her family moves from Ohio to West Virginia to open a laundry in 1927. The prejudice that she feels keeps her separate from others, but her younger siblings seem to have no trouble making friends. The landlady helps Jean Lee and her parents become more accepted through a variety of incidents that benefit both the town and the family. *Bulletin Blue Ribbon Book* and *Christopher Award*.

2500.   Yepsen, Roger. **City Trains: Moving Through America's Cities by Rail**. New York: Macmillan, 1993. 96p. $14.95. ISBN 0-02-793675-9. 5-8

This history is illustrated with the various types of public transportation found in cities. They include horsecars, streetcars, trolleys, interurbans, cable cars, subways, light rails, and monorails. Bibliography and Index.

2501.   Yolen, Jane. **All Those Secrets of the World**. Leslie Baker, illustrator. Boston: Little, Brown, 1991. 32p. $14.95. ISBN 0-316-96891-9. K-3

Before Janie, four, sees her father ship out to sea for World War II, he gives her a hundred kisses, she waves a flag, and Grandma takes her for ice cream. The next day, however, she plays on the beach with Michael, and he shows her how much smaller he looks when he runs away in the distance. She becomes frightened and fears that he will drop off the edge of the world like her father's ship. Two years later, Janie greets her father happily, knowing that when he is away, everything is smaller, but when he is back, she is big.

2502.   Yolen, Jane. **Letting Swift River Go**. Barbara Cooney, illustrator. Boston: Little, Brown, 1992. 32p. $15.95. ISBN 0-316-96899-4. K-3

Sally Jane experiences the change of her hometown as it is transformed into a wilderness and then flooded to become the Quabbin Reservoir in Massachusetts during the 1930s. The Swift River flooded the area so that it could collect water for Boston's residents. Before the village is submerged, villagers remove graves, and people move to other places. Sally Jane decides that she will remember the pleasures of the past and look toward the future.

2503.   Young, Ken. **Cy Young Award Winners**. New York: Walker, 1994. 147p. $14.95. ISBN 0-8027-8300-7. 5-8

Named after Denton True "Cy" Young, the Cy Young award goes to the best pitcher in the American and National Baseball Leagues at the end of each baseball season. The text tells the story behind Denny McLain (1968, 1969), Dwight Gooden (1985), Whitey Ford (1961), Sandy Koufax (1963, 1965, 1966), Bob Gibson (1968, 1970), Tom Seaver (1969, 1973, 1975), Steve Carlton (1972, 1977, 1980, 1982), Jim Palmer (1973, 1975), Fernando Valenzuela (1981), and Roger Clemens (1986, 1987, 1991). Appendix and Index.

2504.   Young, Ronder Thomas. **Learning by Heart**. Boston: Houghton Mifflin, 1993. 172p. $3.99pa. ISBN 0-395-65369-X. 5-7

In the 1960s, Rachel, 10, must adjust to her family's move into a new house, a baby brother, and an African American housekeeper, Isabella. Isabella helps Rachel cope while she develops friendships with a Black girl and another girl whom her classmates consider "white trash." Although Rachel wants to accept people for themselves, she has to readjust her whole life when the family store is burned down and her parents can no longer pay for Isabella's help.

2505.   Yount, Lisa. **Black Scientists**. New York: Facts on File, 1991. 111p. $17.95. ISBN 0-8160-2459-5. (American Profiles). 6-12

The Black scientists featured in this text are Daniel Hale Williams, first successful heart surgeon (1856-1931); George Washington Carver (c. 1865-1943), pure scientist who helped poor farmers; Ernest Everett Just (1883-1941), cytologist; Percy Lavon Julian (1899-1975), synthesizer of complex chemicals; Charles Richard Drew (1904-1950) and the first programs to store blood and blood plasma; Jane Cooke Wright (b. 1919), chemotherapy researcher; Bertram O. Fraser-Reid (b. 1934), complex molecule analyzer; and John P. Moon (b. 1938), peripherals engineer working on computer storage and retrieval of data. Chronologies, Bibliographies, and Index.

2506.   Yount, Lisa. **Women Aviators**. New York: Facts on File, 1991. 144p. $17.95. ISBN 0-8160-3062-6. (American Profiles). 6-12

Less than seven years after the Wright brothers flew their first airplane, Blanche Stuart Scott became the first woman to take flying lessons. Other women followed her lead. Among them were Katherine Stinson (1891-1977), Bessie Coleman (1892-1926), Amelia Mary Earhart (1897-1937), Edna Gardner Whyte (1902-1993), Anne Morrow Lindbergh (b. 1906), Jacqueline Cochran (1906?-1980), Geraldine Fredritz Mock (b. 1925), Geraldyn Cobb (b. 1931), Bonnie Linda Tiburzi (b. 1948), Sally Kristin Ride (b. 1951), and Jeana L. Yeager (b. 1952). Chapter Bibliographies and Index.

> Z

2507. Zeinert, Karen. **Elizabeth Van Lew: Southern Belle, Union Spy**. New York: Dillon Press, 1995. 160p. $13.95; $7.95pa. ISBN 0-87518-608-4; 0-382-24960-7pa. (People in Focus). 6-9

Elizabeth Van Lew spied for the North during the Civil War while she lived in Richmond, Virginia, and helped Union prisoners who managed to escape from their guards in Richmond. She had a secret room in her home to hide the soldiers. She also supplied escapees with weapons and directions that led them back to their regiments. Other courageous actions made her work important for the Union. Because of the stigma attached to her after the war by her neighbors, and losses that she incurred in trying to help former slaves, President Grant gave her the job of postmaster. Bibliography, For Further Reading, and Index.

2508. Zeinert, Karen. **The Salem Witchcraft Trials**. New York: Franklin Watts, 1989. 96p. $20.40. ISBN 0-531-10673-X. 5-10

Court records are the basis for this recounting of the Salem witchcraft trials held in Massachusetts. In 1692, a madness swept into Salem town. Many were arrested for witchcraft, and 19 suspected witnesses were hanged. The situation started with the claims of Betty Parris, age nine. The text presents a background of Puritan beliefs and then discusses the trials, beginning with the accusations and ending with the executions. Possible economic and psychological theories may explain these trials, but not until 1957 were the victims absolved of the charges against them. Bibliography and Index.

2509. Zeinert. Karen. **Those Incredible Women of World War II**. Brookfield, CT: Millbrook Press, 1996. 112p. $19.90. ISBN 1-56294-657-9. 5-8

Women struggled to take part in World War II by serving in the army, Navy, or Air Force. They became newspaper reporters and medical personnel. Leading 1,000 women flyers were the Woman's Air Force heads Genia Novak and Delphine Bohn. Olveta Culp Hobby directed the first American military organization for women, Women's Army Auxiliary Corps (WAAC). Jane Kendleigh served as the first Navy flight nurse on a battlefield, and Dr. Emily Barringer fought for women to join the medical corps. A major recorder of the effects of the war was Margaret Bourke-White, a photographer for *Life* magazine. Sigrid Schultz and Dorothy Thompson lived in Germany as journalists. Other correspondents included Ruth Cowan, Sonia Tomara, and Marguerite Higgins. At home, Frances Perkins served as the Secretary of Labor from 1933 until 1945. Afterword, Timeline, Notes, Bibliography, Further Reading, and Index. *New York Public Library's Books for the Teen Age.*

2510. Zeinert, Karen, ed. **The Memoirs of Andrew Sherburne: Patriot and Privateer of the American Revolution**. Seymour Fleishman, illustrator. Hamden, CT: Linnet Books, Shoestring Press, 1993. 96p. $17.50. ISBN 0-208-02354-2. 5-8

At 13 in 1779, Andrew Sherburne went to sea against the British. He was taking a chance because he could come home rich, or he could be maimed, killed, diseased, or hung as a traitor because the British considered George Washington's navy to be no more than a bunch of pirates. Sherburne has many of the bad things happen to him. In his journal, he records his observations, which include colonial naval warfare, press gangs, smallpox, West Indian trade, British laws, and Americans breaking these laws. Glossary and For More Information.

2511. Ziesk, Edra. **Margaret Mead**. New York: Chelsea House, 1990. 109p. $18.95. ISBN 1-55546-667-2. (American Women of Achievement). 5 up

Margaret Mead (1901-1978), an influential social scientist, changed the way many people see themselves and the society in which they live. Her first field trip as an anthropologist was to American Samoa in 1925, where she gathered the data for her book, *Coming of Age in Samoa*. Later she went to New Guinea, left, and returned to study sex roles. With her third husband, also an anthropologist, she made trips to Bali and New Guinea. For the last 40 years of her life, she was a curator at the New York American Museum of Natural History. Photographs enhance the text. Chronology, Further Reading, and Index.

2512. **Air and Space Smithsonian Dreams of Flight**. CD-ROM. System requirements: IBM or compatible PC: 486/25 MHz or higher CPU, 4 MB RAM, 8 MB RAM recommended, Microsoft Windows 3.1 or later, CD-ROM drive, sound card, mouse, SVGA 256 color display, loudspeakers or headphones. Portland, OR: Creative Multimedia, 1995. $29.95. 5 up

The four areas to explore in this CD-ROM are Aviation Pioneers, Flying Machines, Milestones, and Culture. Each section includes multimedia resources, photographs, audio, personal interviews, and aerodynamic demonstrations. The disc includes the history of flight.

2512a. **American History Explorer**. CD-ROM. System requirements: IBM or compatible PC: 386/16 MHz or higher CPU, 4 MB RAM, 8 MB RAM recommended, Microsoft Windows 3.1 or later, hard drive with 2 MB free, CD-ROM drive, sound card, mouse, SVGA 256 color display, loudspeakers or headphones. Hiawatha, IA: Parsons Technology, 1996. $49. 5-9

This multimedia presentation covers Native American settlement to 1875 in eight time periods beginning with Exploration and ending with Restoration. Presidents, election results, biographical facts, slide shows, songs, narrated slides, and captioned photographs are also available. The Map Studio includes 93 maps. Viewers can search media type, title, first words, matching words, or partial words.

2513. **Apollo Interactive: The Complete Insider's Guide**. CD-ROM. System requirements: IBM or compatible PC: 486/33 MHz or higher CPU, 8 MB RAM, Microsoft Windows 3.1 or later, CD-ROM drive, sound card, mouse, SVGA 256 color display, loudspeakers or headphones. Macintosh: 6 MB RAM, System 7.0, 13-inch monitor (256 colors), CD-ROM drive. Los Angeles: WizardWorks Group, 1995. $15. 5 up

The CD-ROM discusses each of the Apollo space voyages from 1967 to 1975. Drawings, animation, and historical video clips of each mission give a sense of its purpose and effect.

2514. **Campaigns, Candidates and the Presidency**. CD-ROM. System requirements: IBM or compatible PC: 386SX or higher CPU, 4 MB RAM, 8 MB RAM recommended, Microsoft Windows 3.1 or later, CD-ROM drive, sound card, mouse, SVGA 256 color display, loudspeakers or headphones. Carlsbad, CA: Compton's NewMedia, 1995. $39.95. 6 up

A biography, personal history, media, and tapes tells about each of the 42 presidents from Washington to Clinton. Signed articles can be sorted by various themes such as policies and issues, historical events, and law and legal cases. Much information is available about the men who have led the United States since its beginning.

2515. **Children's Atlas of the United States**. CD-ROM. System requirements: MS-DOS/MPC: 386/25 MHz or higher CPU, 8 MB RAM, Microsoft Windows 3.1 or later, hard drive with 5 MB free, CD-ROM drive, sound card, mouse, VGA or SVGA 256 colors minimum, loudspeakers or headphones. (Macintosh version available). Skokie, IL: Rand McNally Educational, 1995. $69.95. 3-5

Although the CD-ROM features state maps with all of the expected information, it also gives historical background and development.

2516. **Daring to Fly! From Icarus to the Red Baron**. CD-ROM. System requirements: IBM or compatible PC: 386SX or higher CPU, 4 MB RAM, Microsoft Windows 3.1 or later, CD-ROM drive, sound card, mouse, SVGA 256 color display, loudspeakers or headphones. (Macintosh version available). Sausalito, CA: Arnowitz Studios, 1994. $59.95. 6-12

In the main menu of this CD-ROM, eight topic icons lead to exhibits such as "Science of Flight," "Lighter than Air," "Wings of War," and "Women Aloft" as it presents the history of flight from the dreams in myths through the post–World War I era of aviation.

2517. **Exploring the Titanic**. CD-ROM. System requirements: Macintosh LC or better: 4 MB RAM, System 7.0, color monitor (256 colors minimum), hard drive with 2.5 MB free, CD-ROM drive. New York: Scholastic, 1994. $149. 4-8

This CD-ROM is the interactive version of Robert D. Ballard's book, which details the sinking of the *Titanic* in 1912 and its recovery in 1985 from the submarine *Alvin*. A timeline references the event to other happenings in the world. Other avenues examine the ship, the technology used to locate it, and an exploration of the wreck itself. Twenty-nine synthesized voices give information. Pages from the book are printable as well as text and notes.

2518. **Eyewitness Encyclopedia of Science**. CD-ROM. System requirements: IBM or compatible PC: 386/33 MHz or higher CPU, Windows 3.1 or later, 4 MB RAM, CD-ROM drive, sound card, mouse, SVGA 256 colors, loudspeakers or headphones. (Macintosh version available). New York: Dorling Kindersley, 1994. $79.95. 5-8

Although the CD-ROM covers much more, it includes a "Who's Who" of scientists, their contributions, and information about their lives.

2519. **Her Heritage: A Biographical Encyclopedia of American History**. CD-ROM. System requirements: Macintosh: 8 MB RAM, System 7.0 or higher, color monitor (256 colors minimum), CD-ROM drive. MS-DOS/MPC: 486SX/25 or higher CPU, 4 MB RAM, Windows 3.1 or later, CD-ROM drive, sound card, mouse, SVGA 256 colors minimum, loudspeakers or headphones. Boston: Pilgrim New Media, 1994. $49.95. 4 up

Hundreds of American women listed in this program can be accessed alphabetically, by profession, or by topic. Biographical profiles; pseudonyms and pen names; awards, prizes, and fellowships; excerpts from diaries and memories; slides; and videos present these women. One may place bookmarks on specific women that permits a slide show of only those women who fit a particular topic. One may also make notes that will appear on the computer screen with a person. Video clips include a suffrage march at which Susan B. Anthony appeared.

2520. **History Through Art: 20th Century**. CD-ROM. System requirements: IBM or compatible PC: 386/20 MHz or higher CPU, 4 MB RAM, 8 MB RAM recommended, Microsoft Windows 3.1 or later, CD-ROM drive, sound card, mouse, SVGA 256 color display, loudspeakers or headphones. Macintosh: 8 MB RAM, System 7.0, 13-inch monitor (256 colors), CD-ROM drive. Minneapolis, MN: Gareth Stevens, 1995. $75. 6 up

Urbanization changed artists' views in the twentieth century, and the development of photography reflects these changes. The modes available to study the art of the twentieth century on this CD-ROM are the Feature Presentation, Text, View, Index, Question, and Quiz.

2521. **Inside the White House**. CD-ROM. System requirements: IBM or compatible PC: 386SX or higher CPU, 4 MB RAM, CD-ROM drive, sound card, mouse, SVGA 256 color display, loudspeakers or headphones. New York: Chelsea House, 1995. $59.95. 3-12

Forty-one families have lived in the White House since the time of John Adams. This CD-ROM contains a virtual tour of the White House and of Air Force One in addition to biographies, photographs, and facts about families, pets, and other aspects of the presidency and of the people who lived in it.

2522. **One Tribe**. CD-ROM. System requirements: MS-DOS/MPC: 486/33 MHz or higher CPU, 4 MB RAM, Windows 3.1 or later, CD-ROM drive, sound card, mouse, SVGA 256 colors minimum, loudspeakers or headphones. (Macintosh version available). Los Angeles: Virgin Sound and Vision, 1994. $24. 6-12

The video explores the diversity among humans. Twenty-five themed slide shows cover topics such as faces, rituals, and animals. Included is historical information about the evolution of humans in the areas of North America, Latin America, Europe, Asia, Australia, Africa, and the Arctic/Antarctic.

2523. **Portraits of American Presidents**. CD-ROM. System requirements: MS-DOS/MPC: 486 or higher CPU, 4 MB RAM, Windows 3.1 or later, hard drive with 3 MB free, CD-ROM drive, sound card, mouse, VGA or SVGA 256 colors minimum, loudspeakers or headphones. San Francisco: StarPress, $49.95. 5-12

The presidents are accessed through three chronological lists in categories A New Nation, National Struggle, and World Power. Each presidential entry includes general information about the man; subsequent screens highlight portions of the president's life.

2524. **SkyTrip America**. CD-ROM. System requirements: IBM or compatible PC: 486/33 MHz or higher CPU, 8 MB RAM, Microsoft Windows 3.1 or later, CD-ROM drive, sound card, mouse, SVGA 256 color display, loudspeakers or headphones. New York: Discovery Channel Multimedia, 1996. $39.95. 4-8

This CD-ROM approaches American history as historical fantasy by creating time travel adventures. After choosing a vehicle in which to explore history, the viewer can write in a journal about places "visited" and create connections to video or other features of the program. Tours include Cultural Heritage, Democracy, A History of Immigration, Women in America, and Little Known Facts. Viewers can access information through a timeline and a glossary as well. Games include the Pony Express game, hangman trivia in a ghost town, and a Mining Maze game. Biographical profiles contain facts about such famous people as Jackie Robinson.

2525. **Stowaway! Stephen Biesty's Incredible Cross-Sections**. CD-ROM. System requirements: IBM or compatible PC: 386SX or higher CPU, 4 MB RAM, CD-ROM drive, sound card, mouse, SVGA 256 color display, loudspeakers or headphones. New York: Dorling Kindersley, 1994. $59.95. 6-12

By clicking the mouse on any part of an eighteenth-century warship or one of its crew members, one gets information about the ship. After learning about many details of life on the ship, the viewer eventually finds the stowaway.

2526. **Time Almanac of the 20th Century**. CD-ROM. System requirements: MS-DOS/MPC: 386SX or higher CPU, 4 MB RAM, hard drive with 1.5 MB free, CD-ROM drive, sound card, mouse, SVGA 256 colors minimum, loudspeakers or headphones. Cambridge, MA: Softkey International, 1994. $29.95. 6-12

Users can retrieve information from each decade from the first issue of *Time* magazine in the 1920s through 1993 using four different topics: Elections, Top Stories, Man of the Year, and Portraits. Events that occurred prior to *Time*'s publication are gleaned from other sources. Users can also gain information by keyword searches on medium and topic.

2527. **Total History**. 3 CD-ROMs. System requirements: IBM or compatible PC: 386SX or higher CPU, 4 MB RAM, CD-ROM drive, sound card, mouse, SVGA 256 color display, loudspeakers or headphones. New York: Bureau of Electronic Publishing-Chelsea House, 1995. $99.95. 4-12

Multimedia U.S. History, Multimedia World History (same as *Teach Your Kids World History*), and *Multimedia World Factbook*, all available separately, comprise this package. *World History* provides information about books written throughout history by author or title, time periods, regions, and themes. There is a history of each day of the year as well as in other topics such as wars, technology, exploration, and maps. *U.S. History* presents American People, American Places, the Armed Forces, Exploring the Continent, General History, Science and Technology, Government, and Wars and Conflicts. Both programs provide slides and video clips. *World Factbook* allows access to facts in several ways such as searching topics, timelines, and glossaries. All keep a history of topics consulted during a session.

2528. **Voices of the 30s**. CD-ROM. System requirements: Macintosh: 4 MB RAM, System 7.0 or higher, color monitor, CD-ROM drive. Pleasantville, NY: Sunburst/Wings for Learning, 1994. $199. 5 up

This CD-ROM gives a strong and poignant view of the 1930s. The two categories of themes and resources include images and bibliography. A quotations menu has questions, comments about excerpts, and related topics from books. Six themes to examine are Government, Agriculture, Arts, Economics, History, and Ethics.

2529. **The Way Things Work**. CD-ROM. System requirements: IBM or compatible PC: 386SX or higher CPU, 4 MB RAM, Microsoft Windows 3.1 or later, CD-ROM drive, sound card, mouse, SVGA 256 color display, loudspeakers or headphones. (Macintosh version available). New York: Dorling Kindersley, 1994. $79.95. 6-12

Animations containing a history timeline, brief biographies on inventors, specifications about the inventions, and scientific principles underlying them make this CD-ROM especially informative.

VIDEOTAPES: AN ANNOTATED BIBLIOGRAPHY

A

2530. **Abraham Lincoln**. Videocassette. Color. 10 min. Princeton, NJ: Films for the Humanities and Sciences, 1989. $29.95. (Against the Odds). 4 up

Documentary footage, interviews, and animation help present this profile of Abraham Lincoln, the man who rose from clerking, rail splitting, and managing a mill to President of the United States.

2531. **Across the Plains**. Videocassette. Color. 28 min. Princeton, NJ: Films for the Humanities and Sciences, 1992. $399 series; $109 ea. (The Oregon Trail). 5 up

Featuring oil paintings, black-and-white artwork, diary excerpts, and narration, this program traces the Oregon Trail from Independence, Missouri, to Fort Laramie, Wyoming. It also covers the problems of camping in the wilderness, the perils of accident, and encounters with Native Americans.

2532. **Adventures Behind the Scenes: At the Newspaper**. Videocassette. Color. 20 min. Tallahassee, FL: Dogwood Video, 1995. $29.95. 1-6

A visit behind the scenes to the *Tallahassee Democrat* presents the changes in the newspaper business since computers arrived. Wire service stories and satellite pictures show the technology behind the printed page.

2533. **African American Life**. Videocassette. Color. 25 min. Bala Cynwyd, PA: Library Video, 1995. $29.95. (American History). 2-6

Graphics, still pictures, modern and historical live-action footage, artwork, animation, illustrations, and reenactments present the topic. The video discusses the slave trade, abolitionist movement, and Underground Railroad along with Harriet Tubman, Martin Luther King, Jr., and Malcolm X.

2534. **African Americans**. Videocassette. Color. 30 min. Schlessinger Video. Distr., Bala Cynwyd, PA: Library Video, 1993. $39.95. (Multicultural Peoples of North America). 4-10

Based on the Chelsea House series Peoples of North America, the video highlights the African American culture. It gives reasons for African Americans being in America, explanations of customs and traditions, the history of their transition, and important leaders from the culture. Historians and sociologists discuss these aspects, and an African American family explains its cultural identity and shared memories.

2535. **Alexander Graham Bell: The Voice Heard Round the World** Videocassette. Color. 25 min. Niles, IL: Aims Media, 1984. $49.95. (American Lifestyle). 4-9

The video analyzes Bell's life and his achievements, including the invention of the telephone.

2536. **All Aboard for Philadelphia!** Videocassette. Color and B&W. 35 min. Philadelphia, PA: Historical Society of Pennsylvania, 1995. $21.95. 6 up

The video gives a history of Philadelphia at the turn of the twentieth century by taking viewers on a trolley car with six stops. It shows the industrial area, the center city, industrial neighborhoods, streetcar and railroad suburbs, and the reform efforts to improve the inner city.

2537. **Amelia Earhart**. Videocassette. Color. 13 min. Princeton, NJ: Films for the Humanities and Sciences, 1989. $29.95. (Against the Odds). 4 up

Documentary footage, interviews, and animation help present this profile of Amelia Earhart (1897-1937) who set aviation records and then disappeared during a Pacific Ocean flight.

2538. **America's Westward Expansion**. Videocassette. Color. 30 min. Madison, WI: Knowledge Unlimited, 1996. $59.95. ISBN 1-55933-197-6. 6 up

Contemporary and archival photographs, graphics, and other aspects help to show the development of the West. Among the topics covered in the brief presentation are the Northwest Ordinance, Lewis and Clark, Sacajawea, the Oregon Trail, Manifest Destiny, and the Mexican War. It begins in 1783 and continues to 1861 and the Civil War.

2539. **American Consumerism (1890-1930)**. Videocassette. Color. 30 min. Schlessinger Video. Distr., Bala Cynwyd, PA: Library Video, 1995. $799 series; $39.95 ea. (United States History Video). 5-9

Dramatic readings and performances bring important events and historical figures together in this video that shows how Americans spent their money from 1890 to 1930.

2540. **American Fever**. Videocassette. Color. 15 min. Madison, WI: Her Own Words, 1994. $95. ISBN 1-877933-44-9. 6 up

A female narrator posing as Christie Vold prepares to emigrate from Norway to America in the nineteenth century. The photographs show her at home while packing garments, household items, and food. The video also records the mixed feelings that she has about leaving her home to join her fiancé, who has already left.

2541. **American Impressionists and Realists: In Search of the New**. Videocassette. Color. 22 min. Mayah Productions. Distr., Berkeley, CA: University of California Extension Center, 1995. $175. 6-12

Between the Civil War and World War I, the two groups of artists who influenced the art world were the Impressionists and the Realists. Archival film footage, photographs, and paintings document this period of American history.

2542. **American Independence**. Videocassette. Color. 25 min. Bala Cynwyd, PA: Library Video, 1995. $29.95. (American History). 2-6

Graphics, still pictures, modern and historical live-action footage, artwork, animation, illustrations, and reenactments present the topic. The video includes information on the Boston Tea Party, the Declaration of Independence, the history of the Liberty Bell and Independence Hall, and biographical information on Thomas Jefferson.

2543. **The American Revolution**. Videocassette. Color. 30 min. Schlessinger Video. Distr., Bala Cynwyd, PA: Library Video, 1995. $799 series; $39.95 ea. (United States History Video). 5-9

Dramatic readings and performances bring the important events and historical figures of the eighteenth century together in this video.

2544. **The Amish**. Videocassette. Color. 30 min. Schlessinger Video. Distr., Bala Cynwyd, PA: Library Video, 1993. $39.95. (Multicultural Peoples of North America). 4-10

Based on the Chelsea House series Peoples of North America, this video highlights the Amish culture. It gives reasons for the Amish immigration to America, explanations of customs and traditions, the history of their transition, and important leaders from the culture. Historians and sociologists discuss these aspects, and an Amish family explains its cultural identity, shared memories, and reasons for immigration.

2545. **The Apache**. Videocassette. Color. 30 min. Schlessinger Video. Distr., Bala Cynwyd, PA: Library Video, 1993. $39.95. ISBN 1-879151-52-9. (Indians of North America). 4-10

Based on Chelsea House's Indians of North America series, the video tells the history and culture of the Apaches prior to the arrival of the Europeans and after the Spanish conquest. Interviews with leaders, historians, and teachers along with live-action footage show the real Apache tribe, located in the southwest United States and northern Mexico. *Finalist, Telly.*

2546. **Arab Americans**. Videocassette. Color. 30 min. Schlessinger Video. Distr., Bala Cynwyd, PA: Library Video, 1993. $39.95. (Multicultural Peoples of North America). 4-10

Based on the Chelsea House series Peoples of North America, the video highlights the Arab culture. It gives reasons for Arab immigration to America, explanations of customs and traditions, the history of their transition, and important leaders from the culture. Historians and sociologists discuss these aspects, and an Arab family explains its cultural identity, shared memories, and reasons for immigration.

B

2547. **Balancing the Budget**. Videocassette. Color. 30 min. Toronto: TV Ontario, 1990. $499 series; $99 ea. (Ancient Civilizations). 6 up

Part of a series examining the origins of civilizations, the video investigates the human needs to search for food, to have security, and to be creative. This video looks at the discovery of agriculture and the domestication of animals as well as the rise of economics based on trade in Egypt.

2548. **Beginnings**. Videocassette. Color. 29 min. Princeton, NJ: Films for the Humanities and Sciences, 1993. $399 series; $109 ea. (The Oregon Trail). 5 up

The history of the Oregon Trail shows how propaganda moved people to walk 2,000 miles into the unknown for a political agenda. Letters and notes from travelers enhance this first in a series of four on the Oregon Trail.

2549. **Birth of a Community: Jews and the Gold Rush**. Videocassette. Color. 40 min. Magnes Museum Western Jewish History Center. Distr., Berkeley, CA: University of California Extension Center, 1995. $175. 4-12

Jewish pioneers came to California during the Gold Rush period around 1849. Archival photographs, vocal recreations, old film footage, and historical commentary tell why they came and their way of life after they arrived.

2550. **Black Is My Color: The African American Experience**. Videocassette. Color. 15 min. Raleigh, NC: Rainbow Educational, 1991. $89. 4-8

Both Black and white children discuss the topics of slavery, abolitionism, Civil War, Reconstruction, segregation, and civil rights as they recreate the problems in America during the nineteenth and twentieth centuries.

2551. **The Black West**. Videocassette. Color. 24 min. Grand Rapids, MI: All Media Productions, 1992. $99. 5 up

Artwork and upbeat music provide background for information about the roles of Blacks in the settlement of the West. Among those presented who made a difference are a woman, a lawman, fur traders, explorers, cowboys, outlaws, and swindlers.

2552. **Blind Tom**. Videocassette. Color. 30 min. KCET and BEEM Foundation. Distr., Irwindale, CA: Barr Media, 1991. $75. 4-9

Born into slavery in 1849, Thomas Bethune, known as "Blind Tom," had an extraordinary ability at an early age to memorize music and play the piano. His music saved him from some of the unpleasantness of slave life, but it also unexpectedly bound him to his master after slaves were freed.

2553. **Bright Eyes: Susette La Flesche Tibbles**. Videocassette. Color. 18 min. Fremont, NE: Premier, 1995. $49.95. (Nebraska Native Americans in the 1800's). 3-5

Although educated to be a teacher, Tibbles (1854-1903) toured the country giving lectures to pay for legal action that would give Native Americans their rights. Also in the video is a history of the Omaha and of the Ponca.

C

2554. **Candlemaking**. Videocassette. Color. 11 min. Irwindale, CA: Barr Media, 1992. $60. (American History). 4-9

Live action, reenactments, maps, and graphics explain the pioneer process of candle making.

2555. **Causes of Revolt**. Videocassette. Color. 30 min. Schlessinger Video. Distr., Bala Cynwyd, PA: Library Video, 1995. $799 series; $39.95 ea. (United States History Video). 5-9

Dramatic readings and performances bring important events and historical figures together in this video about the beginnings of the American Revolution.

2556. **Causes of the Civil War**. Videocassette. Color. 30 min. Schlessinger Video. Distr., Bala Cynwyd, PA: Library Video, 1995. $799 series; $39.95 ea. (United States History Video). 5-9

Dramatic readings and performances bring important events and historical figures together in this video discussing the reasons behind the American Civil War.

2557. **Charles Garry: Street Fighter in the Courtroom**. Videocassette. Color. 58 min. San Diego, CA: Media Guild, 1992. $295. 5 up

Charles Garry grew up poor in California during the early 1900s where he faced prejudice as an Armenian immigrant. He became a lawyer, and his notable cases have included his defenses of the Chicago Seven and of Black Panthers Huey Newton and Bobby Seale.

2558. **The Cherokee**. Videocassette. Color. 30 min. Schlessinger Video. Distr., Bala Cynwyd, PA: Library Video, 1993. $39.95. (Indians of North America). 4-10

This video, using photographs and film footage, focuses on the unique history of the Cherokee, who lived in the South and were relocated to Oklahoma during the early half of the nineteenth century. It additionally discusses the government, the spiritual, the mythical, and the role of women in this Native American tribe.

2559. **The Cheyenne**. Videocassette. Color. 30 min. Schlessinger Video. Distr., Bala Cynwyd, PA: Library Video, 1993. $39.95. (Indians of North America). 4-10

The video focuses on the unique history of the Cheyenne using photographs and film footage. It additionally discusses the government, the spiritual, the mythical, and the role of women.

2560. **The Chinook**. Videocassette. Color. 30 min. Schlessinger Video. Distr., Bala Cynwyd, PA: Library Video, 1994. $39.95. (Indians of North America). 4-10

The Chinook inhabited the Columbia River valley, where they traded widely throughout the Pacific Northwest. The video focuses on the unique history of the Chinook using photographs and film footage. It additionally discusses the government, the spiritual, the mythical, and the role of women.

2561. **Choosing a President**. 2 Videocassettes. Color. 17-25 min. ea. Madison, WI: Knowledge Unlimited, 1995. $59.99 ea. 6 up

The two cassettes are *Electing a President* and *The Presidency*. The first shows the process by which a person becomes president, including the electoral college, political parties, the voting process, campaigning, and the general election. The second discusses the roles of the President and the presidential powers granted in the Constitution.

2562. **Christmas**. Videocassette. Color. 30 min. Schlessinger Video. Distr., Bala Cynwyd, PA: Library Video, 1994. ISBN 1-57225-014-3. $395.40 set; $29.95 ea. (Holidays for Children Video). K-4

Children's artwork introduces the history of the holiday along with holiday symbols and customs. Going onsite to Bethlehem to the supposed birthplace of the Christ child shows the Christian basis for this celebration.

2563. **Christopher Columbus**. Videocassette. Color. 17 min. Los Angeles: Churchill, 1991. $205. 4-8

Through illustration and dramatization, the video presents Columbus's attempt to reach the new world—finding the money for the first voyage. Using actors to recreate situations, it also dramatizes the discoveries he made.

2564. **Colonization and Settlement (1585-1763)**. Videocassette. Color. 30 min. Schlessinger Video. Distr., Bala Cynwyd, PA: Library Video, 1995. $799 series; $39.95 ea. (United States History Video). 5-9

Dramatic readings and performances bring important events and historical figures together in this video.

2565. **Columbus Day**. Videocassette. Color. 10 min. Colman Communications. Distr., Niles, IL: United Learning, 1991. $69.95. K-4

An Italian American grandfather tells his four grandchildren about the courage and tenacity Columbus exhibited by trying to sail westward. The video balances Columbus's achievement by commenting that Native Americans do not think celebrating Columbus Day is appropriate because Columbus's men enslaved many of the natives they found.

2566. **The Comanche**. Videocassette. Color. 30 min. Schlessinger Video. Distr., Bala Cynwyd, PA: Library Video, 1993. $39.95. (Indians of North America). 4-10

The Comanche formerly lived on the southern Great Plains and in western Kansas, where they were nomadic buffalo hunters. This video focuses on the unique history of the Comanche using photographs and film footage. It additionally discusses the government, the spiritual, the mythical, and the role of women in the tribe.

2567. **Countdown to Independence: Causes of the American Revolution**. Videocassette. Color. 24 min. Raleigh, NC: Rainbow Educational, 1993. $89. 5-8

Among the causes of the Revolution outlined in the video, which uses full-motion footage, historical stills, and dramatized narration, are taxation without representation, the Boston Tea Party, the Quartering Acts, the Boston Massacre, and the Intolerable Acts. Questions that students answer as they go about their day at school transmit the information in a memorable way.

2568. **The Creek**. Videocassette. Color. 30 min. Schlessinger Video. Distr., Bala Cynwyd, PA: Library Video, 1994. $39.95. (Indians of North America). 4-10

The Creek originally lived in southwest Georgia but were relocated to central Oklahoma and southern Alabama in the nineteenth century. The video focuses on the unique history of the Creek through photographs and film footage. It additionally discusses the government, the spiritual, the mythical, and the role of women.

2569. **The Crow**. Videocassette. Color. 30 min. Schlessinger Video. Distr., Bala Cynwyd, PA: Library Video, 1994. $39.95. (Indians of North America). 4-10

The Crow once lived in the Great Plains, where they were nomadic buffalo hunters, before migrating into North Dakota. The video focuses on the unique history of the Crow using photographs and film footage. It additionally discusses the government, the spiritual, the mythical, and the role of women.

D

2570. **Democracy and Reform**. Videocassette. Color. 30 min. Schlessinger Video. Distr., Bala Cynwyd, PA: Library Video, 1995. $799 series; $39.95 ea. (United States History Video). 5-9

With the election of Andrew Jackson, the first President from the middle class, reform began. Dramatic readings and performances bring important events and historical figures together in this video.

2571. **The Discovery of the Americas**. Videocassette. Color. 16 min. Thursday Prods. Distr., Pinellas, IL: Spoken Arts, 1991. $44.95. 1-6

A migration of peoples across the land bridge from Asia about 20,000 years ago brought people to the Americas from various cultures. They lived without being bothered until the Europeans arrived. Maps and visuals from Betsy and Giulio Maestro's book (Lothrop, 1991) reveal the movements of nomads and ships from archaeological and historical information.

2572. **Dr. Susan La Flesche Picotte: Our Nation's First Woman Indian Doctor**. Videocassette. Color. 18 min. Fremont, NE: Premier, 1995. $49.95. (Nebraska Native Americans in the 1800's). 3-5

Susan La Flesche trained to become a doctor and devoted her life to health education on the reservation in hopes of preventing disease.

E

2573. **The Early Colonists**. 2 Videocassettes. Color. 30 min. Niles, IL: United Learning, 1992. $135. 5-8

The two videos, filmed at living museums in Maryland and Virginia, discuss what brought settlers to the colonies, how slavery was established, and living and survival skills the settlers needed. The two titles are *Forging a New World* and *Home Sweet Home: Daily Life in Early Colonial America*.

2574. **Early Settlers**. Videocassette. Color. 25 min. Bala Cynwyd, PA: Library Video, 1995. $29.95. (American History). 2-6

Graphics, still pictures, modern and historical live-action footage, artwork, animation, illustrations, and reenactments present the topic. The video highlights the Pilgrims and the *Mayflower*, Squanto, the first Thanksgiving, and colonial Williamsburg.

2575. **Elijah Muhammad**. Videocassette. Color. 30 min. Schlessinger Video. Distr., Bala Cynwyd, PA: Library Video, 1994. $39.95. (Black Americans of Achievement). 5 up

A complement to the Chelsea House series Black Americans of Achievement, the video introduces Elijah Muhammad (1897-1975). Historians and other experts comment on his achievements using photos, old film footage, and modern live-action film for illustration.

2576. **Elizabeth Cady Stanton and Susan B. Anthony**. Videocassette. Color. 24 min. Princeton, NJ: Films for the Humanities and Sciences, 1988. $29.95. (Against the Odds). 4 up

Elizabeth Cady Stanton and Susan B. Anthony formed the National Women's Suffrage Association, leading to a national crusade to give the vote to women. Anthony was also among the first to support Black suffrage after the Civil War.

2577. **Equal Rights for All**. Videocassette. Color. 25 min. Bala Cynwyd, PA: Library Video, 1995. $29.95. (American History). 2-6

Graphics, still pictures, modern and historical live-action footage, artwork, animation, illustrations, and reen-actments present the topic. It covers the Bill of Rights, abolitionists, suffragettes, the Gettysburg Address, and the Emancipation Proclamation.

2578. **The Era of Segregation: A Personal Perspective**. Videocassette. Color. 30 min. Madison, WI: Knowledge Unlimited, 1993. $69.95. ISBN 1-5593-3127-5. 6 up

Author Clifton L. Taulbert (*Once Upon a Time When We Were Colored*) looks at the history of segregation through historical footage and photographs. Having endured it himself, Taulbert provides an especially valuable insight into segregation. The video, divided into segments about legal segregation, family and community, the church, schools under segregation, Civil Rights movement, and current issues, shows that problems still exist although much has changed. *1994 Council on Nontheatrical Events, Golden Eagle Award; Silver Medal, New York Festivals; Silver Apple, New England Film & Video Festival; Honorable Mention, Columbus International Film & Video Festival.*

2579. **Estevanico and the Seven Cities of Gold**. Videocassette. Color. 20 min. Jenison, MI: All Media, 1993. $99. 4-6

Estevanico was a slave who went with Andres Dorontes to Florida in the 1500s. He acted as the go-between to the Indians because they liked his flamboyant character and dress. In Texas, he met Indians who told him about cities of gold, and he later led an expedition to the city of Cibola, which he believed was one of the seven cities. Zuni Indians thought he was a spy, and they killed him. But he was the first non-Indian to go into New Mexico and Arizona.

2580. **Expansionism**. Videocassette. Color. 30 min. Schlessinger Video. Distr., Bala Cynwyd, PA: Library Video, 1995. $799 series; $39.95 ea. (United States History Video). 5-9

This video discusses the westward expansion in the early half of the nineteenth century. Dramatic readings and performances bring important events and historical figures together.

F

2581. **Family Life: Multiculturalism**. Videocassette. Color. 18 min. Fremont, NE: Premier, 1995. $49.95. (Nebraska Native Americans in the 1800's). 3-5

The video looks at family life of the Plains Indians during the nineteenth century in Nebraska and shows the similarities between the family values of the Native Americans and the white settlers.

2582. **The Final Steps**. Videocassette. Color. 28 min. Princeton, NJ: Films for the Humanities and Sciences, 1992. $399 series; $109 ea. (The Oregon Trail). 5 up

Featuring oil paintings, black-and-white artwork, diary excerpts, and narration, this program traces the Oregon Trail as it winds to Willamette Valley, Oregon. It discusses the role of the British, the Forty-Niners rushing for gold on the Trail, and the conflict with Native Americans during the later years of the Trail.

2583. **The First Thanksgiving**. Videocassette. Color. 19 min. Video Dialog. Distr., Irwindale, CA: Barr Media, 1991. $75. K-3

This live-action program compares and contrasts the lifestyles of the Pilgrims and the Wampanoag people. It also tells of the difficulties the Pilgrims had on their journey and the helpful attitudes of Samoset and Massasoit.

2584. **Follow the Drinking Gourd**. Videocassette. Color. 30 min. Old Tappan, NJ: Rabbit Ears, 1993. $9.98. ISBN 1-57099-001-8. K-5

Narrated by Morgan Freeman, the video tells the story of one family's escape from slavery on the Underground Railroad. *Gold Apple, New England Film & Video Festival.*

2585. **Fort McHenry: Preserving the Spirit of Liberty**. Videocassette. Color. 35 min. All American Video. Distr., Englewood, CO: SelectVideo, 1993. $19.95. 5 up

Fort McHenry, the national monument known as the "protector of Baltimore," is where the Americans won a battle in the War of 1812 that inspired Francis Scott Key to write "The Star Spangled Banner." This video covers the fort's history.

2586. **Freedom in Diversity**. Videocassette. 12 min. Video Dialog. Distr., San Diego, CA: Media Guild, 1991. $210. (Discovering History). 4-8

When students meet to decide who should be included in a discussion on great Americans, they review the roles of women since the 1700s; Black history from slavery to the present; and what Asians, Hispanics, and other ethnic groups have added to our American heritage.

2587. **From East to West: The Asian-American Experience**. Videocassette. Color. 24 min. Video Dialog. Distr., Raleigh, NC: Rainbow Educational, 1993. $89. 5-8

The migrations to the United States from Asia began in 1850, with the Chinese coming to escape over-population in their own country. The Japanese wanted to avoid high taxes, and the Filipinos followed in an attempt to find homes and money. Their hard work made people fear them and led to the Chinese Exclusion Act of 1882. The second wave of Asian immigration occurred after the Vietnam War, and again, Asians proved to be hard working citizens.

2588. **Frontier Buildings**. Videocassette. Color. 29 min. Irwindale, CA: Barr Media, 1992. $75. (American Frontier). 4-9

This video examines landmark structures on the western frontier.

2589. **Frontier Forts and the American Indian Wars in Texas**. Videocassette. Color. 60 min. Austin, TX: Forest Glen TV, 1993. $29.95. (Texas History Video). 6 up

Research by prominent historians help relate the daily lives of European, African, and Native Americans who battled for the Texas frontier. The video, divided into two segments on Forts and Indians Wars, uses contemporary reenactments to show the realities of frontier life. *Texas Historical Commission Award*.

G

2590. **George Washington Carver: A Man of Vision**. Videocassette. Color. 26 min. Niles, IL: United Learning, 1990. $89. 5 up

George Washington Carver, born a slave in the 1860s, developed an early interest in nature that he used to help him earn a master's degree in agriculture. His humanitarian and spiritual attributes show that one can unite religion and science to help others.

2591. **German Americans**. Videocassette. Color. 30 min. Schlessinger Video. Distr., Bala Cynwyd, PA: Library Video, 1993. $39.95. #6676. (Multicultural Peoples of North America). 4-10

Based on the Chelsea House series Peoples of North America, the video highlights the German culture. It gives reasons for the German immigration to America, explanations of customs and traditions, the history of their transition, and important leaders from the culture. Historians and sociologists discuss these aspects, and a German family explains its cultural identity, shared memories, and reasons for immigration.

2592. **Gettysburg**. Videocassette. Color. 40 min. Regency Home Video. Distr., Worcester, PA: Vision Video, 1994. $29.95. ISBN 1-56364-102-X. 6 up

Filmed on location with Civil War re-enactors, the video is an authentic staging of the Gettysburg battle fought more than 130 years ago. The heavy equipment, the situations of the soldiers, and all other aspects of the battle become clear in this presentation.

2593. **Great Black Innovators**. Videocassette. Color. 35 min. Madison, WI: Knowledge Unlimited, 1995. $55. 4 up

A companion to James Michael Brodie's *Created Equal: The Lives and Ideas of Black American Innovators*, this video highlights various African Americans such as Benjamin Banneker and George Washington Carver as well as other inventors, scientists, and businesspeople. The video uses live footage, historic stills, and interviews.

2594. **The Great Depression and the New Deal**. Videocassette. Color. 30 min. Schlessinger Video. Distr., Bala Cynwyd, PA: Library Video, 1995. $799 series; $39.95 ea. (United States History Video). 5-9

Dramatic readings and performances bring important events and historical figures together in this video.

2595. **Greek Americans**. Videocassette. Color. 30 min. Schlessinger Video. Distr., Bala Cynwyd, PA: Library Video, 1993. $39.95. (Multicultural Peoples of North America). 4-10

Based on the Chelsea House series Peoples of North America, the video highlights the Greek culture. It gives reasons for Greek immigration to America, explanations of customs and traditions, the history of their transition, and important leaders from the culture. Historians and sociologists discuss these aspects, and a Greek family explains its cultural identity, shared memories, and reasons for immigration.

$$\boxed{\text{H}}$$

2596. **Helen Keller**. Videocassette. Color. 10 min. Princeton, NJ: Films for the Humanities and Sciences, 1989. $29.95. (Against the Odds). 4-6

Helen Keller (1880-1968) lost her hearing and her sight at the age of 18 months. With the help of her teacher, Anne Sullivan, she overcame her disabilities to become an author and a lecturer.

2597. **Heritage of the Black West**. Videocassette. Color. 25 min. Washington, DC: National Geographic, 1995. $110. 4-9

The video looks at today's cowboys while giving the history of African Americans in the development of the West. It also discusses the relationship of African Americans of both sexes to the Native Americans who were already in the West when the African Americans arrived.

2598. **Hiroshima Maiden**. Videocassette. Color. 58 min. Arnold Shapiro. Distr., Chicago: Public Media Video, 1990. $29.95. (Wonderworks Family Movie). 5 up

In this professionally acted video, Miyeko, a Japanese girl badly scarred by the bombing of Hiroshima in 1945, comes to Connecticut to live with a family while she has plastic surgery. The son is fearful of her, and neighbors think she can cause radiation sickness in others. She and Johnny have to talk face-to-face before Johnny can understand her needs and respond to the misconceptions of his friends.

2599. **A History of Native Americans**. Videocassette. Color. 30 min. Schlessinger Video. Distr., Bala Cynwyd, PA: Library Video, 1994. $39.95. (Indians of North America). 4-10

This video examines the common histories of the tribes in the series, their relationships with the U.S. government, the role of nature and natural resources, and the roles of women within divergent groups.

2600. **Holiday Facts and Fun: Martin Luther King Day**. Videocassette. Color. 10 min. Colman Communications. Distr., Raleigh, NC: Rainbow Educational, 1992. $69.95. 1-4

This live-action video highlights the life and achievements of Martin Luther King, Jr. The emphasis of the video is that the holiday created in his honor is a time to show respect for everyone.

2601. **Homesteading: 70 Years on the Great Plains, 1862-1932**. Videocassette. Color. 18 min. Delphi. Distr., Niles, IL: United Learning, 1992. $89.95. 5 up

The 1862 Homestead Act offered 160 acres to anyone who would homestead in the Great Plains. The homesteading ended with the Dust Bowl in the 1930s. Those who went and stayed had to work hard to make a life from a piece of land with few trees and almost no water. Mechanical inventions toward the end of the nineteenth century helped, but the natural disaster of drought defeated many.

2602. **The Huron**. Videocassette. Color. 30 min. Schlessinger Video. Distr., Bala Cynwyd, PA: Library Video, 1994. $39.95. (Indians of North America). 4-10

The Huron lived in Ontario until a war with the Iroquois in the mid-seventeenth century destroyed much of the population. Remaining Huron live in northeast Oklahoma and are known as Wyandot. The video focuses on the unique history of the Huron using photographs and film footage. It additionally discusses the government, the spiritual, the mythical, and the role of women.

$$\boxed{\text{I}}$$

2603. **Immigration and Cultural Change**. Videocassette. Color. 30 min. Schlessinger Video. Distr., Bala Cynwyd, PA: Library Video, 1995. $799 series; $39.95 ea. (United States History Video). 5-9

In the second half of the nineteenth century, immigrants arrived to escape persecution and economic distress. Dramatic readings and performances bring important events and historical figures together in this video.

2604. **The Immigration Experience**. Videocassette. 12 min. Video Dialog. Distr., San Diego, CA: Media Guild, 1991. $210. (Discovering History). 4-8

Immigration began around 1850 in the United States, when people from countries such as Ireland, England, and Italy began arriving at Ellis Island. Portrayals of why they came and what they expected humanize this major evolution in America's history.

2605. **Immigration to the United States**. Videocassette. Color. 25 min. Schlessinger Video. Distr., Bala Cynwyd, PA: Library Video, 1995. $359.40 series; $29.95 ea. (American History for Children Video). K-4

This video captures the lives of the foreign-born who have come to America through a collection of major events, documents, individuals, songs, buildings, and statues and monuments in the United States. Graphics, still pictures, modern and historical live-action footage, artwork, animation, illustrations, and reenactments present the topic.

2606. **In Search of the North Pole**. Videocassette. Color. 24 min. Globe Trotter Network. Distr., Irwindale, CA: Barr Media, 1989. $50. 4-6

Using time travel, the program takes two children to the Arctic circle, where they learn the history of those explorers who attempted to reach the North Pole. They join Admiral Robert Peary's expedition where he raised an American flag on April 6, 1909.

2607. **Independence Day**. Videocassette. Color. 30 min. Schlessinger Video. Distr., Bala Cynwyd, PA: Library Video, 1994. ISBN 1-57225-019-4. $359.40 set; $29.95 ea. (Holidays for Children Video). K-4

This video emphasizes the importance of the Revolutionary War, the history of immigration, and drum and fife players in costume. A small July 4th celebration and a visit to Philadelphia are included.

2608. **Indians of California**. Videocassette. Color. 22.5 min. Irwindale, CA: Barr Media, 1991. $125. (Native Americans). 4-8

A brief introduction to the origins of North American Indians comments that more than 100 different tribes lived in the area that is now California. The largest group, the Yokuts, lived in the great central valley. A dramatization shares information about the daily lives of the Yokuts.

2609. **Indians of the Northwest**. Videocassette. Color. 20 min. Irwindale, CA: Barr Media, 1992. $125. (Native Americans). 3-8

The video, with live-action segments, maps, and drawings, focuses on the People of the Potlatch and shows the continuity of Native American culture.

2610. **Indians of the Plains**. Videocassette. Color. 16 min. Irwindale, CA: Barr Media, 1991. $125. (Native Americans). 3-8

The video, with live-action segments, maps, and drawings, focuses on the culture of the Plains Indians and their survival through buffalo hunting.

2611. **Indians of the Southeast**. Videocassette. Color. 20 min. Irwindale, CA: Barr Media, 1991. $125. (Native Americans). 3-8

Although focusing mainly on the Cherokee, the video, with live-action segments, maps, and drawings, includes interaction with the Europeans and how their arrival affected the Native Americans. The viewer sees the dependence of the Indian on the environment for all needs by recreating hunting, farming, and making weapons, baskets, and pottery.

2612. **Indians of the Southwest**. Videocassette. Color. 17 min. Irwindale, CA: Barr Media, 1992. $125. (Native Americans). 3-8

The Indians who have lived in the Southwest include the Navajo, Apache, Uma, and Pima. The video, with live action, maps, and drawings, shows the daily lives of these peoples as well as others.

2613. **Industrialization and Urbanization (1870-1910)**. Videocassette. Color. 30 min. Schlessinger Video. Distr., Bala Cynwyd, PA: Library Video, 1995. $799 series; $39.95 ea. (United States History Video). 5-9

Dramatic readings and performances bring important events and historical figures together in this video.

2614. **Irish Americans**. Videocassette. Color. 30 min. Schlessinger Video. Distr., Bala Cynwyd, PA: Library Video, 1993. $39.95. (Multicultural Peoples of North America). 4-10

Based on the Chelsea House series Peoples of North America, the video highlights the Irish culture. It gives reasons for the Irish immigration to America, explanations of customs and traditions, the history of their transition, and important leaders from the culture. Historians and sociologists discuss these aspects, and an Irish family explains its cultural identity, shared memories, and reasons for immigration.

2615. **The Iroquois**. Videocassette. Color. 30 min. Schlessinger Video. Distr., Bala Cynwyd, PA: Library Video, 1993. $39.95. ISBN 1-879151-57-X. (Indians of North America). 4-10

This video tells the history and culture of the Iroquois prior to the arrival of the Europeans. It focuses on the unique history of the Iroquois confederacy, composed of the Mohawk, Oneida, Onondaga, Cayuga, and Seneca peoples (Five Nations) in the eighteenth century, using photographs and film footage. It additionally discusses the government and its influence on the formation of the U.S. Constitution, the spiritual, the mythical, and the role of women.

2616. **Italian Americans**. Videocassette. Color. 30 min. Schlessinger Video. Distr., Bala Cynwyd, PA: Library Video, 1993. $39.95. (Multicultural Peoples of North America). 4-10

Based on the Chelsea House series Peoples of North America, the video highlights the Italian culture. It gives reasons for the Italian immigration to America, explanations of customs and traditions, the history of their transition, and important leaders from the culture. Historians and sociologists discuss these aspects, and an Italian family explains its cultural identity, shared memories, and reasons for immigration.

J

2617. **Jackie Robinson**. Videocassette. Color. 14 min. Princeton, NJ: Films for the Humanities and Sciences, 1989. $29.95. (Against the Odds). 4 up

Jackie Robinson (1919-1972) was modern major league baseball's first Black player, a skilled ambassador for his people, and a role model. He also was a record-breaker in several sports.

2618. **Jamestown**. Videocassette. Color. 18 min. Irwindale, CA: Barr Media, 1992. $75. (American Frontier). 4-9

This overview of the first major English settlement in America shows on-location footage and comments on the buildings.

2619. **Jamestown: The Beginning**. Videocassette. Color. 17 min. Eugene, OR: New Dimension Media, 1992. $280. ISBN 1-56353-147-X. 5 up

This dramatic reenactment tells of the first English settlement in Virginia in 1607 from the point of view of John Leydon, one of the few settlers who survived the ordeal. *Council on Nontheatrical Events, Golden Eagle.*

2620. **Japanese Americans**. Videocassette. Color. 30 min. Schlessinger Video. Distr., Bala Cynwyd, PA: Library Video, 1993. $39.95. (Multicultural Peoples of North America). 4-10

Based on the Chelsea House series Peoples of North America, the video highlights the Japanese culture. It gives reasons for the Japanese immigration to America, explanations of customs and traditions, the history of their transition, and important leaders from the culture. Historians and sociologists discuss these aspects, and a Japanese family explains its cultural identity, shared memories, and reasons for immigration.

2621. **Jesse Owens**. Videocassette. Color. 30 min. Schlessinger Video. 1994. Distr., Bala Cynwyd, PA: Library Video, 1993. (Black Americans of Achievement). 5 up

A complement to the Chelsea House series Black Americans of Achievement, the video introduces Jesse Owens (1913-1981). Historians and other experts comment on his achievements using photos, old film footage, and modern live-action film for illustration.

2622. **Jewish Americans**. Videocassette. Color. 30 min. Schlessinger Video. Distr., Bala Cynwyd, PA: Library Video, 1993. $39.95. (Multicultural Peoples of North America). 4-10

Based on the Chelsea House series Peoples of North America, the video highlights the Jewish culture. It gives reasons for the Jewish immigration to America, explanations of customs and traditions, the history of their transition, and important leaders from the culture. Historians and sociologists discuss these aspects, and a Jewish family explains its cultural identity, shared memories, and reasons for immigration.

K

2623. **Kentucky Rifle**. Videocassette. Color. 11 min. Irwindale, CA: Barr Media, 1992. $60. (American History). 4-9

Live action, reenactments, maps, and graphics help tell the story of pioneer life. This video explains the care and use of rifles, one of their main tools.

2624. **Korean Americans**. Videocassette. Color. 30 min. Schlessinger Video. Distr., Bala Cynwyd, PA: Library Video, 1993. $39.95. (Multicultural Peoples of North America). 4-10

Based on the Chelsea House series Peoples of North America, the video highlights the Korean culture. It gives reasons for the Korean immigration to America, explanations of customs and traditions, the history of their transition, and important leaders from the culture. Historians and sociologists discuss these aspects, and a Korean family explains its cultural identity, shared memories, and reasons for immigration.

L

2625. Latino Art and Culture in the United States. Videocassette. Color. 28 min. National Museum of American Art/Smithsonian. Distr., Glenview, IL: Crystal Productions, 1995. $85. (America Past and Present). 6 up

This video traces the contributions of the peoples of Latin American heritage to the history and contemporary life of the United States.

2626. The Lenape. Videocassette. Color. 30 min. Schlessinger Video. Distr., Bala Cynwyd, PA: Library Video, 1994. $39.95. (Indians of North America). 4-10

The Lenape lost their land to white settlement in the seventeenth and eighteenth centuries (as the Delaware) and migrated into the Midwest. The video focuses on the unique history of the Lenape using photographs and film footage. It additionally discusses the government, the spiritual, the mythical, and the role of women.

2627. Let Me Tell You All About Trains. Videocassette. Color. 30 min. Grapevine, TX: Traditional Images, 1993. $19.95. K-6

Children accompany their grandfather to a train shop, and he tells them the background of trains and describes what they were like when they were the main form of passenger transportation. He describes the different types of cars, and film footage illustrates his words. The integration of live action and film gives a good overview of trains.

2628. The Lewis and Clark Trail. Videocassette. Color. 20 min. Delphi. Distr., Niles, IL: United Learning, 1992. $89. 5-9

With reenactments, historical photographs, and lines from journals kept by the participants, the video examines the exploration of Lewis and Clark into the West from 1804 to 1806. Covered are the journey's objectives, scientific discoveries, historic importance, and survival methods. Especially striking is the photography of sites along the way and the acknowledgment of contributions that Native Americans like Sacagawea made to the success of the expedition.

2629. The Life and Times of Abraham Lincoln. Videocassette. Color. 14 min. Delphi. Distr., Niles, IL: United Learning, 1992. $79.97. 5-12

Reenactment footage, historical photographs, and illustrations present the places in Lincoln's life in the context of his times. Also included are recitations of excerpts from the Lincoln-Douglas debates, the Emancipation Proclamation, and the Gettysburg Address.

2630. The Life and Times of George Washington. Videocassette. Color. 14 min. Delphi. Distr., Niles, IL: United Learning, 1992. 3-8

Historical art and live-action footage present a brief view of George Washington's life, with much information about Mount Vernon. Lifestyle and social expectations from 1732 to 1799 give a sense of the time.

2631. The Life of George Washington. Videocassette. Color. 30 min. Mt. Vernon Ladies Association. Distr., Whittier, CA: Finley-Holiday, 1989. $29.95. 6 up

In a straightforward manner, almost everything known about George Washington appears in the program. His exact words are featured as the video presents his early life, marriage, French and Indian War incidences, his work in Washington, and his final illness.

2632. Lincoln: A Photobiography. Videocassette. Color. 65 min. Miller-Brody. Distr., Chicago: American School Publishers, 1989. $98. 5-9

In a series of dissolving slides taken from Russell Freedman's Newbery Award–winning book and an actor portraying Lincoln, the program divides into four parts: "Backwoods Boy," "Law and Politics," "Emancipation," and "The Dreadful War."

2633. The Loom. Videocassette. Color. 11 min. Irwindale, CA: Barr Media, 1992. $60. (American History). 4-9

Live action, reenactments, maps, and graphics help tell the story of pioneer weaving and threading a loom.

M

2634. **Making It Happen: Masters of Invention**. Videocassette. Color. 22 min. Bob Oliver Communications. Distr., Van Nuys, CA: Churchill Media, 1995. $99.95. 4 up

This video starts with the days of slavery and moves to the present as it profiles the Black inventors who have made major contributions to the progress of society. They include such men as inventor and astronomer Benjamin Bannecker, Edison's rival Louis Latimer, and Garrett Morgan, the inventor of the traffic signal.

2635. **Malcolm X**. Videocassette. Color. 15 min. Princeton, NJ: Films for the Humanities and Sciences, 1992. $34.95. 4 up

This program explores Malcolm X's philosophical evolution and examines the outside forces that helped him shape his beliefs. His father, a Baptist minister, was murdered; he became a Harlem hustler; and he took a pilgrimage to Mecca. For much of his life he struggled for African American equality.

2636. **Martin Luther King, Jr.** Videocassette. Color. 27 min. Princeton, NJ: Films for the Humanities and Sciences, 1996. $34.95. 4 up

Martin Luther King, Jr., was an ordained minister with a doctor's degree. He fought for freedom, justice, and equality, and his efforts were recognized in 1964 with a Nobel Peace Prize.

2637. **Mary McLeod Bethune**. Videocassette. Color. 30 min. Schlessinger Video. 1994. Distr., Bala Cynwyd, PA: Library Video, 1993. $39.95. (Black Americans of Achievement). 5 up

A complement to the Chelsea House series Black Americans of Achievement, the video introduces Mary McLeod Bethune (1875-1955). Historians and other experts comment on her achievements using photos, old film footage, and modern live action for illustration.

2638. **Matthew Henson**. Videocassette. Color. 30 min. Schlessinger Video. 1994. Distr. Bala Cynwyd, PA: Library Video, 1993. $39.95. (Black Americans of Achievement). 5 up

A complement to the Chelsea House series Black Americans of Achievement, the video introduces Matthew Henson (1866-1955). Historians and other experts comment on his achievements using photos, old film footage, and modern live action for illustration.

2639. **Men of the Frontier**. Videocassette. Color. 27 min. Irwindale, CA: Barr Media, 1992. $75. (American Frontier). 4-9

Some of the men on the frontier were writers. Among them were Mark Twain and Horace Greeley. Still others made contributions to the frontier way of life.

2640. **The Menominee**. Videocassette. Color. 30 min. Schlessinger Video. Distr., Bala Cynwyd, PA: Library Video, 1994. $39.95. (Indians of North America). 4-10

The video focuses on the unique history of the Menominee, who now live in northeast Wisconsin, using photographs and film footage. It additionally discusses the government, the spiritual, the mythical, and the role of women.

2641. **Mining Made the West**. Videocassette. Color. 34 min. Irwindale, CA: Barr Media, 1992. $75. (American Frontier). 4-9

The gold rush, beginning in 1849, brought many people to the West. Silver also had a role in the expansion of the United States.

2642. **Mission Life**. Videocassette. Color. 22 min. Irwindale, CA: Barr Media, 1992. $60. (American History). 4-9

Live action, reenactments, maps, and graphics help tell the story of the missions, based on priests' diaries.

2643. **Missions of California: Mission Santa Barbara**. Videocassette. Color. 10 min. Derry, NH: Chip Taylor Communications, 1989. $150. 4-8

The Franciscans founded Santa Barbara on December 4, 1786, and the mission has survived since its reconstruction in 1815 with six-foot walls. The program presents this mission and its importance during its 200-year history.

2644. **Mississippi Steamboats**. Videocassette. Color. 21 min. Irwindale, CA: Barr Media, 1993. $385. 4 up

Steamboats transported huge quantities of cotton from the plantations to the cities in the nineteenth century, and then they began transporting people. Archival film footage, period art, and photographs present some of the famous characters and events of the time when the steamboats paddled the Mississippi.

2645. **Mountain Men**. Videocassette. Color. 16 min. Irwindale, CA: Barr Media, 1992. $60. (American History). 4-9
Live action, reenactments, maps, and graphics help tell the story of explorers and trappers in the early 1800s.

N

2646. **The Narragansett**. Videocassette. Color. 30 min. Schlessinger Video. Distr., Bala Cynwyd, PA: Library Video, 1993. $39.95. (Indians of North America). 4-10
This video focuses on the unique history of the Narragansett using photographs and film footage. The tribe formerly inhabited Rhode Island, but King Philip's War in 1675-1676 nearly exterminated them. Some descendants remain in the area. The video additionally discusses the government, the spiritual, the mythical, and the role of women in the tribe.

2647. **A Nation in Turmoil**. Videocassette. Color. 30 min. Schlessinger Video. Distr., Bala Cynwyd, PA: Library Video, 1995. $799 series; $39.95 ea. (United States History Video). 5-9
Life began to change for American citizens in the late nineteenth century when people began to move to urban areas and shifted the population balance. Dramatic readings and performances bring important events and historical figures together in this video.

2648. **National Observances**. Videocassette. Color. 25 min. Bala Cynwyd, PA: Library Video, 1995. $29.95. (American History). 2-6
Graphics, still pictures, modern and historical live-action footage, artwork, animation, illustrations, and reenactments present the topic. The video explains the history and significance of Veteran's Day, Labor Day, Memorial Day, Election Day, and Independence Day as well as an overview of the system of government and the voting process.

2649. **Native American Life**. Videocassette. Color. 25 min. Bala Cynwyd, PA: Library Video, 1995. $29.95. (American History). 2-6
Graphics, still pictures, modern and historical live-action footage, artwork, animation, illustrations, and reenactments present the topic. The history, highlighting white colonization, presents Pocahontas and Tecumseh along with U.S. government decisions affecting Native Americans, such as the Indian Removal Act, the Trail of Tears, the Indian Civil Rights Act, and the Indian Self-Determination Act.

2650. **Native American Medicine**. Videocassette. Color. 55 min. Edwardsburg, MI: Meuninck's Media Methods, 1995. $29.95. 6-12
To ward off bad winds and let the healing spirits enter, Native Americans have used smudging, sweeping, dance, music, wild plants, massage, and the sweatlodge. Members of the Ottawa, Mixteca (Mexico), and Shawnee describe the traditional healing secrets of their ancestors.

2651. **Native Americans: People of the Desert**. Videocassette. Color. 24 min. Raleigh, NC: Rainbow Educational, 1992. $99. 4-7
Animated maps and historical reenactments portray the Native Americans who live in the desert. They include the Ute, Pima, Hopi, Navajo, and their ancestors, the Anasazi.

2652. **Native Americans: People of the Forest**. Videocassette. Color. 25 min. Peter Matulavich. Distr., Raleigh, NC: Rainbow Educational, 1994. $99. 4-8
A Chippewa family represents the typical life of an Eastern Woodland Indian. *Council on Nontheatrical Events, Golden Eagle; National Educational Media Gold Apple; Charleston International Film and Video Silver; Columbus International Film and Video Bronze Plaque;* and *Cindy Bronze Award.*

2653. **Native Americans: People of the Northwest Coast**. Videocassette. Color. 23 min. Raleigh, NC: Rainbow Educational, 1994. $99. 5-8
Filmed in 'Ksan, a recreated Gitksan village in British Columbia, the video shows life before the arrival of the Europeans in the seventeenth century, including theories about the migration over the Bering Sea land bridge.

2654. **Native Americans: People of the Plains**. Videocassette. Color. 24 min. Raleigh, NC: Rainbow Educational, 1993. $99. ISBN 1-56701-020-2. 4-8
In showing how the Native Americans hunted buffalo and used all its parts in the community, the video explains how the settlers destroyed the buffalo and, therefore, the livelihood of the Plains Indians. *Council on Nontheatrical Events, Golden Eagle; Gold Apple;* and *New England Film & Video Festival.*

2655. **Native Americans: The History of a People**. Videocassette. Color. 25 min. Madison, WI: Knowledge Unlimited, 1992. $55. 4-12

In part, the video presents two groups of Native Americans who have lived on this continent, hunters and Mound Builders, whose way of life ended more than 600 years ago, probably with the Anasazi. The second part discusses the various ways that European settlers have taken away land privileges and tried to impose Western culture on the Native Americans. Also included are Native Americans' recent attempts to have some of those wrongs righted.

2656. **The Navajo**. Videocassette. Color. 30 min. Schlessinger Video. Distr., Bala Cynwyd, PA: Library Video, 1993. $39.95. (Indians of North America). 4-10

This video focuses on the unique history of the Navajo, or *Diné*, using photographs and film footage. These people have lived in the Southwest and continue to inhabit the area of New Mexico, Arizona, and Utah. The video additionally discusses the government, the spiritual, the mythical, and the role of women in the tribe.

2657. **A New Nation (1776-1815)**. Videocassette. Color. 30 min. Schlessinger Video. Distr., Bala Cynwyd, PA: Library Video, 1995. $799 series; $39.95 ea. (United States History Video). 5-9

Dramatic readings and performances bring important events and historical figures together in this video.

O

2658. **Old Glory**. Videocassette. Color. 10 min. Raleigh, NC: Rainbow Educational, 1994. 2-5

This program provides facts about the American flag, tracing its history from the Revolutionary War to the present and explaining its symbolism.

2659. **Old Sturbridge Village: Growing Up in New England**. Videocassette. Color. 30 min. VideoTours. Distr., Englewood, CO: SelectVideo, 1992. $24.95. 3-8

Set in 1835, this living history museum production tells the story of Sarah, 15, and her brother. The video presents a realistic look at life during that time.

2660. **One World, Many Worlds: Hispanic Diversity in the United States**. Videocassette. Color. 22 min. Raleigh, NC: Rainbow Educational, 1993. 5-8

The program chronicles the history of Hispanic Americans, from the Spanish explorations and exploitations of the New World to the Mexican-American War and the struggles for independence throughout Central and South America. It also looks at the Hispanic influence on American culture.

2661. **The Oregon Trail**. Videocassette. Color. 25 min. Irwindale, CA: Barr Media. 1995. $395. 5-11

Reenactments and contemporary footage present one of the most important components of the westward movement over the United States in honor of its 150th anniversary.

2662. **Our Federal Government: The Legislative Branch**. Videocassette. Color. 28 min. Raleigh, NC: Rainbow Educational, 1993. $99. ISBN 1-56701-023-7. 5-8

Live action, historical prints, graphics, and documentary footage tell about the creation of the legislative branch and its function as part of the federal government. *Bronze Plaque, Columbus International Film & Video Festival*.

2663. **Our Federal Government: The Presidency**. Videocassette. Color. 23 min. Raleigh, NC: Rainbow Educational, 1993. $89. 5-8

This program gives an overview of the presidency, including its history, constitutional powers, and limitations. Documentary footage highlights the presidencies through that of Bill Clinton.

2664. **Our Federal Government: The Supreme Court**. Videocassette. Color. 22 min. Raleigh, NC: Rainbow Educational, 1993. $99. 5-8

The program gives a historical overview of the Supreme Court, beginning with its constitutional origin. The court became influential under John Marshall, and the *Marbury v. Madison* case increased the court's influence on American life. Other cases and information about the court's decisions also appear.

P

2665. **Patrick Henry's Fight for Individual Rights**. Videocassette. Color. 29 min. Chicago: Encyclopaedia Britannica, 1990. $260. 4 up

Reenactments on location at historic sites throughout Virginia, along with historic photographs, show Patrick Henry from his birth in 1736 through his terms as governor of the state and his belief that Americans should have individual rights to protect them from a strong federal government.

2666. **A Picture Book of Martin Luther King, Jr.** Videocassette. Color. 9 min. Pine Plains, NY: Live Oak Media, 1990. $34.95. K-3

Using iconographic stills that Robert Casilla created for David Adler's book of the same title, the video serves both younger children who are not yet capable readers and older children who need an introduction to Martin Luther King, Jr.

2667. **Pilgrim Journey**. Videocassette. Color. 24 min. Princeton, NJ: Films for the Humanities and Sciences, 1989. $34.95. 3-6

A courageous Pilgrim girl tells of the *Mayflower* voyage through her fictional diary. She recounts the hope, despair, and perseverance of the passengers. The replica of the *Mayflower* in Plymouth, Massachusetts, is the setting for the drama.

2668. **The Pilgrims at Plymouth**. Videocassette. Color. 23 min. Video Dialog. Distr., Irwindale, CA: Barr Media, 1991. $125. 4-6

The reenactment of the Pilgrims' voyage to colonial America, their difficulties in choosing a location to settle, the Mayflower Compact, and their suffering during the first winter makes these events come alive. The viewer sees the interaction of the Pilgrims with Chief Samoset and the Wampanoag Indians and with Massasoit at the first Thanksgiving. Faced with too little food for new arrivals, the Pilgrims had a rough time of it. The taking of land from Native Americans is stated plainly, without commentary.

2669. **The Pilgrims' Story**. 2 Videocassettes. Color. 15:40-18:50 min. Huntsville, TX: Educational Video Network, 1995. $79.95 set; $49.95 ea. 6-12

The English Separatists first sought refuge in Holland and then in America, because they wanted freedom of worship. In the New World, they created a new life for themselves as they practiced their chosen religion.

2670. **Placer Gold**. Videocassette. Color. 11 min. Irwindale, CA: Barr Media, 1992. $60. (American History). 4-9

Live action, reenactments, maps, and graphics help tell the story of the life of miners during the California Gold Rush.

2671. **Pocahontas**. Videocassette. Color. 50 min. Golden Films. Distr., New York: Sony Wonder, 1995. $14.98. (Enchanted Tales). K-3

This musical animation tells the story of a young Indian woman, Pocahontas, and the man from England with whom she falls in love.

2672. **Polish Americans**. Videocassette. Color. 30 min. Schlessinger Video. Distr., Bala Cynwyd, PA: Library Video, 1993. $39.95. (Multicultural Peoples of North America). 4-10

Based on the Chelsea House series Peoples of North America, the video highlights the Polish culture. It gives reasons for the Polish immigration to America, explanations of customs and traditions, the history of their transition, and important leaders from the culture. Historians and sociologists discuss these aspects, and a Polish family explains its cultural identity, shared memories, and reasons for immigration.

2673. **Pony Express**. Videocassette. Color. 12 min. Irwindale, CA: Barr Media, 1992. $60. (American History). 4-9

Live action, reenactments, maps, and graphics explain the route of the riders on the Pony Express, the horses, and the equipment.

2674. **Post War U.S.A.** Videocassette. Color. 30 min. Schlessinger Video. Distr., Bala Cynwyd, PA: Library Video, 1995. $799 series; $39.95 ea. (United States History Video). 5-9

Dramatic readings and performances bring important events and historical figures together in this video.

2675. **The Potawatomi**. Videocassette. Color. 30 min. Schlessinger Video. Distr., Bala Cynwyd, PA: Library Video, 1994. $39.95. (Indians of North America). 4-10

The Potawatomi lived in the Midwest in the seventeenth and eighteenth centuries but migrated to Oklahoma, Kansas, Michigan, and Ontario. The video focuses on the unique history of the Potawatomi using photographs and film footage. The video additionally discusses the government, the spiritual, the mythical, and the role of women.

2676. **Prairie Cabin: A Norwegian Pioneer Woman's Story**. Videocassette. 17 min. Madison, WI: Her Own Words, 1991. $95. 4-12

Color slides dissolving one into another enhance this first-person narrative. The video covers the life of a fictitious Norwegian woman who came to the American prairie in the mid-nineteenth century. Views of the cabin, household items, food, and the land, along with Norwegian Christmas customs transported to this new world, create an understanding of the immigrant's condition. The Norwegian singing in the background underscores the memories of home that the protagonist carries.

2677. **Prejudice Monster Within**. Videocassette. Color. 30 min. Madison, WI: Knowledge Unlimited, 1995. $59.99. ISBN 1-55933-194-1. 5-9

The video examines prejudice against African Americans, Native Americans, and Japanese Americans during World War I, the Holocaust, and Bosnia. It uses news clips and insights that will help students to follow the topic.

2678. **Presenting Mr. Frederick Douglass**. Videocassette. Color. 60 min. Princeton, NJ: Films for the Humanities and Sciences, 1990. $149. (Against the Odds). 4 up

This theatrical performance features Fred Morsell as he dramatically recreates Douglass's famous speech on slavery and human rights. It was filmed in Washington, D.C., at the A.M.E. Church where Douglass delivered his last speech, "The Lesson of the Hour."

2679. **President's Day**. Videocassette. 10 min. Colman Communications. Distr., Niles, IL: United Learning, 1992. $69.95. K-4

Actors recreate highlights in the lives of Washington and Lincoln at various stages The biographies are simple overviews because of time limitations, but the facts presented are interesting and informative.

2680. **Progressive Movement**. Videocassette. Color. 30 min. Schlessinger Video. Distr., Bala Cynwyd, PA: Library Video, 1995. $799 series; $39.95 ea. (United States History Video). 5-9

In the second half of the nineteenth century, politics and economics began to change. Dramatic readings and performances bring important events and historical figures together in this video.

2681. **Pueblo**. Videocassette. Color. 30 min. Schlessinger Video. Distr., Bala Cynwyd, PA: Library Video, 1994. $39.95. (Indians of North America). 4-10

The video focuses on the unique history of the Pueblo Indians using photographs and film footage. It additionally discusses the government, the spiritual, the mythical, and the role of women in the tribe.

2682. **Puerto Ricans**. Videocassette. Color. 30 min. Schlessinger Video. Distr., Bala Cynwyd, PA: Library Video, 1993. $39.95. (Multicultural Peoples of North America). 4-10

Based on the Chelsea House series Peoples of North America, the video highlights the Puerto Rican culture. It gives reasons for the Puerto Rican immigration to America, explanations of customs and traditions, the history of their transition, and important leaders from the culture. Historians and sociologists discuss these aspects, and a Puerto Rican family explains its cultural identity, shared memories, and reasons for immigration.

R

2683. **Railroads on the Frontier**. Videocassette. Color. 24 min. Irwindale, CA: Barr Media, 1992. $75. (American Frontier). 4-9

The railroads ran in the East and the West before they crossed the continent. They were important in the development of the frontier.

2684. **Rancho Life**. Videocassette. Color. 21 min. Irwindale, CA: Barr Media, 1992. $60. (American History). 4-9

Live action, reenactments, maps, and graphics help tell the story of pioneer life for Spanish rancheros.

2685. **Reading Terminal Market**. Videocassette. Color. 28 min. Falls Church, VA: Landmark Media, 1993. $225. 6 up

This documentary tribute, with personal narrative, vintage film, and photographs, identifies Philadelphia's Reading Terminal Market and shows how it has contributed to the history of commerce in America.

2686. **The Rebel Slave**. Videocassette. Color. 24 min. Princeton, NJ: Films for the Humanities and Sciences, 1989. $34.95. 3 up

A young slave during the Battle of Gettysburg has to free himself in many ways before he can be truly free. *Silver Award, Houston Film Festival.*

2687. **Reconstruction and Segregation (1870-1910)**. Videocassette. Color. 30 min. Schlessinger Video. Distr., Bala Cynwyd, PA: Library Video, 1995. $799 series; $39.95 ea. (United States History Video). 5-9

Dramatic readings and performances bring important events and historical figures together in this video.

2688. **Rosh Hashanah/Yom Kippur**. Videocassette. Color. 30 min. Schlessinger Video. Distr., Bala Cynwyd, PA: Library Video, 1994. ISBN 1-57225-021-6. $359.40 set; $29.95 ea. (Holidays for Children Video). K-4

Children's artwork introduces the history of the holiday. A boy blowing the ram's horn and information about Moses and the Ten Commandments give a basis for an explanation of the Jewish high holy days.

S

2689. **Sacajawea**. Videocassette. Color. 24 min. Princeton, NJ: Films for the Humanities and Sciences, 1989. $34.95. 3-8

Much of the success of Lewis and Clark's expedition to the Pacific Coast in 1805 rested with Sacajawea, their Indian guide. She translated for them and helped them get safe passage through several stretches of land. From her point of view, she tells of the group's challenges, their struggle to survive, the Missouri River crossing, wild animals, and other discoveries. *Emmy Award; Freedom Foundation Award; Council on Nontheatrical Events, Golden Eagle;* and *Columbus International Film Festival Award.*

2690. **Samuel Adams**. Videocassette. Color. 10 min. Princeton, NJ: Films for the Humanities and Sciences, 1989. $29.95. (Against the Odds). 4-6

Samuel Adams was the instigator of the Boston Tea Party and a patriot who served in the Continental Congress. He always gave his comrades resolve to fight for independence.

2691. **Seeds of Liberty: The Causes of the American Revolution**. Videocassette. Color. 22 min. Video Dialog. Distr., Raleigh, NC: Rainbow Educational, 1993. $89. 5-8

Giving special attention to the period between 1754 and 1767, the video discusses social, economic, and political changes. The topics presented include the French and Indian War, Pontiac, the Proclamation of 1763, the Sugar Act, Parliament, Sam Adams, the Quartering Act, the Stamp Act, Patrick Henry, Virginia Resolves, the Sons of Liberty, Lord North, the Boston Massacre, and Benjamin Franklin.

2692. **The Sellin' of Jamie Thomas**. 2 Videocassettes. Color. 24 min ea. Princeton, NJ: Films for the Humanities and Sciences, 1987. $34.95 ea. 3 up

Jamie Thomas, 11, and his parents are separated when the plantation owner sells all of his slaves. They manage to reunite and begin the flight to freedom. A farmer discovers them, and they struggle to adjust to life in a Quaker town. Jamie attends school for the first time, and his father works until a bounty hunter tries to take them. *Winner, Chicago International Film Festival.*

2693. **The Seminole**. Videocassette. Color. 30 min. Schlessinger Video. Distr., Bala Cynwyd, PA: Library Video, 1993. $39.95. (Indians of North America). 4-10

This video tells the history and culture of the Seminole prior to the arrival of the Europeans and the Spanish conquest. Using photographs and film footage, it focuses on the unique history of the Seminole, who kept the U.S. government from relocating them as they hid in the Florida Everglades. It additionally discusses the government, the spiritual, the mythical, and the role of women.

2694. **Settlers of the West**. Videocassette. Color. 26 min. Irwindale, CA: Barr Media, 1992. $75. (American Frontier). 4-9

Some of those who went west were able to establish a life. Others were not so fortunate. This video discusses Juan Cabrillo, the Spanish discoverer of California in 1542; the Donner Party's difficulties on the Donner Pass; and other settlers.

2695. **Silent Communications: Trail Signs/Sign Language**. Videocassette. Color. 18 min. Fremont, NE: Premier, 1995. $49.95. (Nebraska Native Americans in the 1800's). 3-5

In this video, a tracker shows the signs that Native Americans of the Plains used to give silent messages to those who followed them. A narrator explains the language and a woman gives examples of it. Many thought the reason Indians and settlers could not get along was their inability to communicate successfully.

2696. **The Sky's the Limit**. Videocassette. Color. 13 min. Old Dog Productions. Distr., Niles, IL: United Learning, 1995. $95. 4-10

This program presents highlights of women in aviation, including Harriett Quimby, Bessie Coleman, and Amelia Earhart.

2697. **Slavery and Freedom**. Videocassette. Color. 30 min. Schlessinger Video. Distr., Bala Cynwyd, PA: Library Video, 1995. $799 series; $39.95 ea. (United States History Video). 5-9
Dramatic readings and performances bring important events and historical figures together in this video.

2698. **Song of Sacajawea**. Videocassette. Color. 30 min. Old Tappan, NJ: Rabbit Ears, 1993. $9.95. K-6
This animation tells the story of 17-year-old Sacajawea, a Shoshone woman, who led explorers Lewis and Clark in their expedition to the Pacific Ocean around 1805.

2699. **Spinning Wheel**. Videocassette. Color. 11 min. Irwindale, CA: Barr Media, 1992. $60. (American History). 4-9
Live action, reenactments, maps, and graphics explain the process of spinning from rough wool to smooth thread.

2700. **Squanto and the First Thanksgiving**. Videocassette. Color. 30 min. Old Tappan, NJ: Rabbit Ears, 1993. $9.98. K-4
A Native American, Squanto was captured from his Pawtuxet tribe and taken to Spain, where he was sold into slavery. He eventually regained his freedom and came back to America. There he helped the Pilgrims survive the early years at Plymouth Colony. *Bronze Plaque, Columbus International Film & Video Festival.*

2701. **St. Patrick's Day**. Videocassette. Color. 10 min. Colman Communications. Distr., Niles, IL: United Learning, 1994. $69.95. ISBN 1-56007-495-7. K-4
A brief animated biography introduces St. Patrick, pointing out his role in uniting the Irish nation under one God and spreading Christianity in Ireland. Then the video introduces the holiday associated with him and explains the various traditions that accompany it.

2702. **Stagecoach West**. Videocassette. Color. 13 min. Irwindale, CA: Barr Media, 1992. $60. (American History). 4-9
Live action, reenactments, maps, and graphics explain the life and times of stagecoach drivers and travelers.

2703. **The Steam Engine: G. Stephenson**. Videocassette. Color. 24 min. Irwindale, CA: Barr Media, 1989. $50. 4-6
In this animation, the viewer meets George Stephenson (1781-1848), the inventor of the locomotive.

2704. **The Susan B. Anthony Story: The Women's Suffrage Movement**. Videocassette. Color. 40 min. Richardson, TX: Grace Products, 1994. $89. (In Search of the Heroes). 5-12
Live-action footage of an encounter between a modern girl and Susan B. Anthony helps the girl see that if one dislikes the conditions in which one lives, one can refuse to live by the current rules and try to do something to change them. The historical footage about the suffragettes shows the girl that because someone else struggled in the past, she has rights that she would not otherwise have had. *U.S. International Film & Video Festival Gold Camera, New York Festivals Finalist,* and *Telly Bronze Statuette.*

T

2705. **Thanksgiving**. Videocassette. Color. 30 min. Schlessinger Video. Distr., Bala Cynwyd, PA: Library Video, 1994. ISBN 1-57225-022-4. $359.40 set; $29.95 ea. (Holidays for Children Video). K-4
Children's artwork introduces the history of the holiday. The video also shows a reenactment of the first Thanksgiving at Plimoth Plantation. Native American and traditional Thanksgiving themes broaden the presentation.

2706. **This World Is Not Our Home**. Videocassette. Color. 13 min. Berkeley, CA: University of California Extension Center, 1995. $125. 4-12
A tribal elder of the Pomo tribe in California introduces the history, culture, and traditions of her people.

2707. **Thomas Alva Edison**. Videocassette. Color. 15 min. Princeton, NJ: Films for the Humanities and Sciences, 1988. $29.95. (Against the Odds). 4 up
Thomas Alva Edison (1847-1931) patented more than 1,000 inventions, including the carbon telephone transmitter, the microphone, the phonograph, the incandescent electric lamp, and the forerunner of the motion picture projector.

2708. **Three Worlds Meet (Origins—1620)**. Videocassette. Color. 30 min. Schlessinger Video. Distr., Bala Cynwyd, PA: Library Video, 1995. $799 series; $39.95 ea. (United States History Video). 5-9
Dramatic readings and performances bring important events and historical figures together in this video.

2709. **Through the Rockies**. Videocassette. Color. 28 min. Princeton, NJ: Films for the Humanities and Sciences, 1992. $399 series; $109 ea. (The Oregon Trail). 5 up
Featuring oil paintings, black-and-white artwork, diary excerpts, and narration, this program traces the Oregon Trail from Fort Laramie to Fort Hall, in Idaho. The video explains the problems of trail overcrowding, the dangers of disease such as cholera, various cutoffs and alternate routes, and Mormons on the trail.

2710. **The Times and Dreams of Martin Luther King, Jr.** Videocassette. Color. 30 min. N. Billerica, MA: Curriculum Associates, 1995. $69.95. 4-8
Julian Bond leads a discussion with students. He describes life in the segregated South in the 1950s and what it was like to be a friend of Dr. Martin Luther King, Jr. The discussion leads to how Dr. King's perseverance influenced other nations to promote human rights.

2711. **Totem Poles: The Stories They Tell**. Videocassette. Color. 14 min. Cos Cob, CT: Double Diamond, 1993. $89. 6-9
The colors and designs in totem poles along the Northwest Pacific Coast from Washington State to Alaska tell stories. The video explains some of the messages that the Tlingit, Haida, and Kwakiutl Indians tell in the poles.

2712. **Tragedy to Triumph: An Adventure with Helen Keller**. Videocassette. Color. 40 min. Richardson, TX: Grace Productions, 1995. $89. 5 up
A cast presents a play about Helen Keller and her achievements and tries to show the importance of understanding and accepting people with physical disabilities.

2713. **Tsiolkovski: The Space Age**. Videocassette. Color. 24 min. Irwindale, CA: Barr Media, 1989. $50. 4-9
This animation explains how Tsiolkovski (1857-1935) conducted the crucial research that led him to the invention of the rocket in 1929.

U

2714. **U.S. and the World (1865-1917)**. Videocassette. Color. 30 min. Schlessinger Video. Distr., Bala Cynwyd, PA: Library Video, 1995. $799 series; $39.95 ea. (United States History Video). 5-9
Dramatic readings and performances bring important events and historical figures together in this video.

2715. **U.S. Songs and Poems**. Videocassette. Color. 25 min. Distr., Bala Cynwyd, PA: Library Video, 1995. $29.95. (American History). 2-6
Graphics, still pictures, modern and historical live-action footage, artwork, animation, illustrations, and reenactments present the topic. The video gives the history behind patriotic songs such as "The Star Spangled Banner," "America the Beautiful," "My Country 'Tis of Thee," "Yankee Doodle," "John Henry," and the Pledge of Allegiance.

2716. **United States Constitution**. Videocassette. Color. 25 min. Distr., Bala Cynwyd, PA: Library Video, 1995. $29.95. (American History). 2-6
Graphics, still pictures, modern and historical live-action footage, artwork, animation, illustrations, and reenactments present the topic. The video gives the history of the Constitution along with biographical information on Benjamin Franklin and George Washington.

2717. **United States Expansion**. Videocassette. Color. 25 min. Distr., Bala Cynwyd, PA: Library Video, 1995. $29.95. (American History). 2-6
Graphics, still pictures, modern and historical live-action footage, artwork, animation, illustrations, and reenactments present the topic. The video discusses the Lewis and Clark expedition, information on pioneer life, the relocation of Native Americans, a biography of John Henry, and the story behind Mount Rushmore.

2718. **United States Flag**. Videocassette. Color. 25 min. Distr., Bala Cynwyd, PA: Library Video, 1995. $29.95. (American History). 2-6
Graphics, still pictures, modern and historical live-action footage, artwork, animation, illustrations, and reenactments present the topic. The video discusses the Pledge of Allegiance and "The Star Spangled Banner."

2719. **The Unsinkable Delta Queen**. Videocassette. Color. 43 min. Delaney Communications. Distr., Cincinnati, OH: Sentimental, 1989. $24.95. 6 up

The *Delta Queen*, on the Mississippi River, is a working national historical landmark today. A tour of the boat shows its great paddlewheel, calliope, and elegant Victorian furnishings. During World War II, the boat performed duties for the U.S. government.

2720. **Valentine's Day**. Videocassette. Color. 30 min. Schlessinger Video. Distr., Bala Cynwyd, PA: Library Video, 1994. ISBN 1-57225-023-2. $359.40 set; $29.95 ea. (Holidays for Children Video). K-4

A brief history of St. Valentine and customs of courtship and dating highlight this video.

2721. **Valley Forge: Young Spy**. Videocassette. Color. 24 min. Princeton, NJ: Films for the Humanities and Sciences, 1989. $34.95. 3-6

When he is 12, Josh, a farm boy, goes to George Washington's camp to spy for the British. As he begins to understand the ideals for which the American rebels fight and suffer in the bitter Valley Forge winter, he changes his allegiance and joins the Continental army.

2722. **Washington, D.C.** Videocassette. Color. 25 min. Distr., Bala Cynwyd, PA: Library Video, 1995. $29.95. (American History). 2-6

Graphics, still pictures, modern and historical live-action footage, artwork, animation, illustrations, and reenactments present the history and planning of the capital and Washington, D.C. Information about the Capitol Building, the White House, and the Supreme Court accompanies the significance of the Lincoln, Jefferson, and Vietnam memorials.

2723. **Western Europe: Our Legacy**. Videocassette. Color. 22 min. North Carolina State. Distr., Briarcliff Manor, NY: Benchmark Media, 1994. $395. (World Geography and History). 5-7

Western Europe remains the source for much of the social order and culture in the United States. The ancient Greeks had a democracy, good literature, and philosophy. The Romans had government administration, remnants of our partially Latin-based language, and Catholicism. The Renaissance provided a renewed interest in intellectual, artistic, and economic life. Other legacies were the Industrial Revolution and the influx of immigrants escaping religious and economic difficulties.

2724. **Westward Expansion: The Pioneer Challenge**. Videocassette. Color. 22 min. Raleigh, NC: Rainbow Educational, 1992. $89. 4-8

Live-action photography, maps, and nineteenth-century art enhance this presentation of the geographical influences that both helped and hindered the pioneers attempting to cross the mainland United States. The settlement of Hawaii and Alaska also included concerns about natural resources, natural boundaries, and climate.

2725. **Westward Wagons**. Videocassette. Color. 24 min. Princeton, NJ: Films for the Humanities and Sciences, 1989. $34.95. 3-6

In 1870, a pioneer family travels across the American plains. A man who was a boy of 10 when the journey occurred recalls the adventure, the fear, and the hope for a better life. *Red Ribbon, American Film Festival*; and *Council on Nontheatrical Events, Golden Eagle*.

2726. **What Is an American?** Videocassette. Color. 15 min. Chappaqua, NY: New Castle Communications, 1994. $89. ISBN 1-885285-17-5. (My America: Building a Democracy). K-6

The three major waves of immigration into North America begin with the Native Americans coming over the Bering Strait around 35,000 years ago to the European settlements along the eastern coast. The second wave began in 1820 and continued until 1924. The third wave is now. The reasons for immigration—religious freedom, economic opportunity, and political unrest—most likely undergird all three migrations, although no one can ascertain the reasons for the first. The video shows the importance of all humans regardless of background.

2727. **Who Owns the Sun?** Videocassette. Color. 18 min. Disney Educational. Distr., Deerfield, IL: Coronet/MTI, 1990. $280. 1-6

When Josh, a young boy in the 1800s, asks his parents who owns things like the sun and the stars, they let him know that unlike a horse, no one can own them. When Josh discovers that someone "owns" his father and considers his father his "best slave," Josh is confused. When he asks about owning a man, his parents say that although some men may think they own others, they cannot control their minds. The story ends with the song "Follow the Drinkin' Gourd."

2728. **William Bradford: The First Thanksgiving**. Videocassette. Color. 30 min. Irving, TX: Living History, 1992. $59.95. 1-4

This animated history of the first Thanksgiving presents the desire for religious freedom behind the Puritan voyage, the Mayflower Compact, William Bradford, Miles Standish, and the Native Americans who helped them.

2729. **Women of the West**. Videocassette. Color. 28 min. Irwindale, CA: Barr Media, 1992. $75. (American Frontier). 4-9

Women helped keep the West going once people began to settle it. The video offers insights into the contributions of women in this uncivilized area.

2730. **Women of the West**. Videocassette. Color and B&W. 32 min. Chariot Productions. Distr., Niles, IL: United Learning, 1994. $95. ISBN 56007-244-X. 5-9

Women who went west gained freedom that they did not have if they remained at home. They became homesteaders, entertainers, imported brides, military wives, outlaws, militant feminists, and prostitutes. Old photography, live-action re-creations, and first-person accounts show that the women came from Asian, African American, Native American, and European descent.

2731. **Women with Wings**. Videocassette. Color. 17 min. Oshkosh, WI: Experimental Aircraft, 1995. $12.95. 6 up

Eight women made contributions to aviation during the twentieth century. They include balloonist Sophie Blanchard, barnstormer Margie Hobbs, record-setter Louise Thalen, astronaut trainee Jerrie Cobb, military pilots Hanna Reitsch and Helen Richey, educator Louise Timken, and businesswoman Olive Ann Beech. The video gives a brief biography of each and her achievements.

2732. **Woodland Tribal Arts: Native American Arts**. Videocassette. Color. 23 min. Greenwich, CT: Double Diamond, 1995. $89. 5 up

By focusing on the artifacts of the Woodland Indian tribes such as the Iroquois and the Algonquin, the video tells their story. Among the artifacts are snowshoes, wampum, pottery, canoes, quill boxes, moccasins, longhouses, masks, and willow baskets. In these early settlements, development caused shifts from clay to iron cooking pots and stone to metal tools. The video gives a good sense of early Native American history.

2733. **World War I**. Videocassette. Color. 30 min. Schlessinger Video. Distr., Bala Cynwyd, PA: Library Video, 1995. $799 series; $39.95 ea. (United States History Video). 5-9

Dramatic readings and performances bring important events and historical figures together in this video about World War I.

2734. **The Yankton Sioux**. Videocassette. Color. 30 min. Schlessinger Video. Distr., Bala Cynwyd, PA: Library Video, 1993. $39.95. (Indians of North America). 4-10

The Yankton Sioux occupy a middle position between the Santee and Teton divisions of the Sioux in South Dakota. This video describes the history and culture of the Yankton Sioux prior to the arrival of the settlers. It focuses on the unique history of the tribe using photographs and film footage. It additionally discusses the government, the spiritual, the mythical, and the role of women in the tribe.

2735. **The Year of the Dragon**. Videocassette. Color. 24 min. Princeton, NJ: Films for the Humanities and Sciences, 1992. $34.95. 3-6

Hua Ch'ing, an orphaned Chinese boy, faces prejudice from strangers and the bitterness of a Sierra mountain winter in nineteenth-century America. When the camp's food runs low, he and Jimmy have to hunt for game. They realize during their struggle that they have more in common than they realized.

AUTHOR/ILLUSTRATOR INDEX

Reference is to entry numbers.

Aaseng, Nathan, 1-7
Abbink, Emily, 8
Accorsi, William, author/illus., 9-10
Ace, Katherine, illus., 910, 1404-1405
Acierno, Maria Armengol, 11
Ackerman, Karen, 12-13
Adler, David A., 14-43
Alexander, Lloyd, 44
Aliki, author/illus., 45-47
Allen, John Logan, 48
Allen, Paula Gunn, 49
Allen, Thomas B., illus., 253, 986, 1062, 1945, 2287
Allen, Zita, 50
Almonte, Paul, 51
Alphin, Elaine Marie, 52
Alter, Judith, 53-55
Altman, Linda, 56
Altman, Susan, 57
Alvarez, Mark, 58
Ames, Mildred, 59
Amoss, Berthe, 60
Ancona, George, photographs, 65-68, 430-32
Anderson, Catherine Corley, 61-62
Anderson, Dale, 63-64
Anderson, Joan, 65-68
Anderson, Kelly, 69, 70
Anderson, LaVere, 72
Anderson, Lydia M., illus., 1797, 2363, 2365
Anderson, Peter, 73-78
Anderson, William, 79
Andreasen, Dan, illus., 1266, 2278
Andrews, Elaine, 80
Andronik, Catherine M., 81
Andryszewski, Tricia, 82-83
Angell, Judie, 84
Antle, Nancy, 85-88
Antram, David, illus., 1605
Appel, Marty, 89
Appelbaum, Diana, 90
Applegate, Katherine, 91
Archbold, Rick, 92
Arginteanu, Judy, 93
Armstrong, Jennifer, 94-97
Armstrong, William O., 98
Arnold, Caroline, 99-100
Arrington, Aileen, illus., 2360
Ash, Maureen, 101-102

Ashabranner, Brent, 103-108
Ashabranner, Jennifer, photographs, 106
Asimov, Isaac, 109
Auch, Mary Jane, 110
Avakian, Monique, 111-12
Avi, 113-26
Avishai, Susan, illus., 997
Ayer, Eleanor H., 127
Ayers, Carter M., 128
Ayers, Donna, illus., 1047
Azoturia, Rachel, illus., 2048

Backes, Nick, illus., 2276
Bacon, Paul, illus., 832
Bader, Bonnie, 129-30
Badt, Karin Luisa, 131
Baginskia, Vanda, illus., 1604
Baker, Betty, 132
Baker, Leslie, illus., 2501
Baldwin, Robert F., 133
Balistreri, Francis, illus., 408, 820
Ballard, Robert D., 134
Bandon, Alexandra, 135-42
Banim, Lisa, 143-45
Banks, Sara Harrell, 146
Banta, Melissa, 147
Barboza, Steven, 148
Barnes, Joyce Annette, 149-50
Barnett, Isa, illus., 2142
Barr, Roger, 151-52
Barrett, Katherine, 153
Barrett, Robert, illus., 2283
Barrett, Tracy, 154-55
Barrie, Barbara, 156
Bartoletti, Susan C., 157
Bartone, Elisa, 158-59
Basinger, Jeanine, 160
Bauer, Marian, 161
Baviera, Rocco, illus., 334
Bayley, Dorothy, illus., 394
Bealer, Alex W., 162
Beard, Charles, 163
Beatty, Patricia, 164-90
Beck, Charles, illus., 2140-41
Beckman, Pat Ramsey, 191
Bedard, Michael, 192
Behrens, June, 193-94
Beier, Ellen, illus., 200
Bellairs, John, 195

Beller, Susan Provost, 196
Belton, Sandra, 197
Benchley, Nathaniel, 198
Beneduce, Ann Keay, 199
Benjamin, Anne, 200-202
Bennett, Barbara J., 203
Bennett, Cathereen L., 204
Bennett, Evelyn, 205
Bennett, Russell, 206
Bentley, Bill, 207
Bentley, Judith, 208-10
Bergin, Mark, illus., 1078, 1604, 2130
Berkow, Ira, 211
Berleth, Richard, 212-13
Berliner, Don, 214
Bernotas, Bob, 215-16
Bernstein, Joanne, 217
Berrill, Margaret, 218
Berry, Michael, 219
Berry, S. L., 220-21
Berry, Skip, 222
Bethancourt, T. Ernesto, 223
Beyer, Don E., 224
Bial, Raymond, 225-28
Biegel, Michael David, illus., 1522, 1530
Biel, Timothy L., 229-30, 1569
Birch, Beverley, 231
Bird, E. J., 232, 233
Birling, Paul, illus., 267
Birmingham, Christian, illus., 909
Bishop, Jack, 234
Bisson, Terry, 235
Bittinger, Ned, illus., 345
Black, Shelia, 236
Black, Wallace B., 237-52
Blades, Anne, illus., 1461
Blair, Gwenda, 253
Blake, Arthur, 254
Blake, Robert J., 255
Blakely, Martha, 256
Bland, Celia, 257-60
Blashfield, Jean F., 237-52
Blassingame, Wyatt, 261-62
Blau, Justine, 263
Bleck, Cathie, illus., 1040
Bloom, Lloyd, illus., 18, 355, 1060a
Blos, Joan, 264-68
Blue, Rose, 217, 269-72, 1646-47

Blumberg, Rhoda, 273-74
Bock, William Sauts, illus., 1017-18
Bodkin, Odds, 275
Bodmer, Karl, illus., 748
Bodow, Steven, 276
Bolden, Tonya, 277
Bolick, Nancy O'Keefe, 278-80
Bolognese, Don, 1815-16
Bolognese, Don, illus., 305, 444, 2032
Bolotin, Norman, 281
Bolton, Jonathan, 282
Bond, Barbara Higgins, illus., 1645
Bonvillain, Nancy, 283-85
Bootman, Colin, illus., 812
Borden, Louise, 1260
Bortz, Fred, 286
Borzendowski, Janice, 287
Bosco, Peter I., 288
Boutis, Victoria, 289
Bowen, Andy Russell, 290
Bowen, Gary, author/illus., 291
Bowler, Mike, 292
Bowman, Leslie W., illus., 1226-27, 2389, 2392
Bradby, Marie, 293
Brady, Philip, 294
Braine, Susan, 295
Branch, Muriel Miller, 296
Brandon, David Charles, illus., 1997
Branscum, Robbie, 297
Brashler, William, 298
Bratman, Fred, 299
Brauckmann-Towns, Krista, illus., 96
Bray, Rosemary, 300
Bredeson, Carmen, 301
Brenner, Barbara, 302-305
Brenner, Fred, illus., 1589
Brenner, Martha, 306
Bresnick-Perry, Roslyn, 307
Brighton, Catherine, author/illus., 308
Brill, Marlene Targ, 309-12
Brink, Carol Ryrie, 313
Brodner, Steve, illus., 1282
Bronikowski, Ken, illus., 1620
Brooks, Philip, 314-15
Brower, Pauline, 316
Brown, Bradford, illus., 1778-79
Brown, Charnan, 317
Brown, Don, author/illus., 318
Brown, Drollene P., 319-20
Brown, Fern G., 321-23
Brown, Gene, 324-27
Brown, Jane Clark, author/illus., 328
Brown, Jordan, 329
Brown, Judith Gwyn, illus., 1651
Brown, Kevin, 330
Brown, Maria Magdalena, illus., 1479
Brown, Marion Marsh, 331-32
Brown, Warren, 333

Bruce, T. Taylor, illus., 2087-88
Bruchac, Joseph, 334-35
Bruns, Roger, 336-39
Bryant, Jennifer, 340
Bryant, Michael, illus., 1514, 1524, 1557-58, 1572-73
Bulla, Clyde Robert, 341-43
Bundles, A'Lelia, 344
Bundles, Perry, 344
Bunting, Eve, 345-47
Buranelli, Vincent, 348-49
Burchard, Peter, 342-43, 350
Burford, Betty, 351
Burke, Deirdre, 352
Burke, Kathleen, 353
Burleigh, Robert, 354-55
Burns, Bree, 356
Burns, Ken, 2346-48
Burns, Khephra, 357
Burns, Peggy, 358-59
Butts, Ellen R., 360
Byars, Betsy, 361-63
Bylinsky, Tatyana, author/illus., 364
Byrd, Samuel, illus., 24, 26, 37, 1400-1401, 2290

Cain, Michael, 365-66
Calvert, Patricia, 367
Calvert, Roz, 368
Cameron, Eleanor, 369
Camp, Carole Ann, 370
Canadeo, Anne, 371
Cannon, Marian G., 372
Capek, Michael, 373-74
Caple, Laurie A., illus., 2382
Caras, Roger, 375
Carey, Vicky, illus., 470
Carlson, Jeffrey D., 376
Carlson, Judy, 377
Carlson, Laurie M., 378
Carlson, Susan Johnston, illus., 1599
Carpenter, Nancy, illus., 1002, 1048
Carrick, Carol, 379-82
Carrick, Donald, illus., 379-80, 2302
Carrigan, Mellonee, 383
Carter, Alden R., 384-88
Cary, illus., 71-72, 1307
Casey, Jane Clark, 389-90
Cashman, Greer, 391
Casilla, Robert, illus., 16, 23, 28-29, 32, 36, 41
Castiglia, Julie, 392
Castro, Antonio, illus., 582, 631, 1881, 1992, 2233-34
Catalano, Julie, 393
Catalanotto, Peter, illus., 1425
Caudill, Rebecca, 394
Caulkins, Janet, 395
Cavan, Seamus, 396-98
Cedeno, Maria E., 399
Chabrian, Deborah L., illus., 821

Chadwick, Roxane, 400-401
Chaikin, Miriam, 402
Chambers, Tina, illus., 1763
Chambliss, Maxie, illus., 1776
Chang, Ina, 403
Chantland, Loren, illus., 351
Charleston, Gordon, 404-405
Chessare, Michele, illus., 341
Chilcoat, George W., 2281
Childress, Diana, 406
Chin, Steven A., 407
Chrisman, Abbott, 408
Chrisp, Peter, 409-13
Christian, Mary Blount, 414
Christiansen, Candace, 415
Chu, Daniel, 416
Claflin, Edward Beecher, 417
Clapp, Patricia, 418-19
Clare, John D., 420
Claro, Nicole, 421-22
Clay, Wil, illus., 1706, 1271
Cleaver, Bill, 423
Cleaver, Vera, 423
Clements, Gillian, 424-25
Clifford, Eth, 426-28
Clifford, Mary, 429
Climo, Shirley, 430-33
Clinton, Susan, 434-36
Cobb, Mary, 437
Cochrane, Patricia A., 438
Cocke, William, 439-40
Codye, Corinn, 441-42
Coelho, Tony, 443
Coerr, Eleanor, 444, 444a, 445
Cogancherry, Helen, illus., 998-99, 1373, 1946
Cohen, Daniel, 446-49
Coil, Suzanne M., 450
Cole, Michael D., 451
Cole, Norma, 452
Cole, Robin, illus., 2030
Coleman, Evelyn, 453
Coles, Robert, 454
Collier, Christopher 455-57, 462-63
Collier, James Lincoln, 455-63
Collins, David, 464-74
Collins, Heather, illus., 890
Collins, James L., 475
Collins, Patrick, illus., 1090
Colman, Penny, 476-83
Colver, Anne, 484
Compton, Anita, 485
Conklin, Paul, illus., 105
Conley, Kevin, 486
Conlon-McKenna, Marita, 487
Connell, Kate, 488-90
Connolly, Jay, illus., 577
Conord, Bruce W., 491-92
Conrad, Pam, 493-96
Conway, Celeste, author/illus., 497
Cook, Donald, illus., 306, 2124

Cooney, Barbara, 192, 498-500, 1063a, 2405, 2502
Cooper, Floyd, author/illus., 501, 1064-65, 1077, 1512, 2007
Cooper, Michael L., 502-504
Coote, Roger, 505
Corbin, William, 506
Corbishley, Mike, 507
Corcoran, Barbara, 508-509
Cordoba, Maria, 510
Cormier, Robert, 511-12
Corrick, James A., 513
Cory, Steven, 514
Cosgrave, John O'Hara, II, illus., 1305
Cosner, Shaaron, 515-16
Courtney, Richard, illus., 2454
Cox, Clinton, 517
Crew, Linda, 518
Crews, Donald, author/illus., 519
Crofford, Emily, 520-21
Cross, Gillian, 522
Cross, Robin, 523-26
Cross, Verda, 527
Cuffari, Richard, illus., 1591
Cullen-Clark, Patricia, illus., 1787
Cullen-DuPont, Kathryn, 528
Cuneo, Mary Louise, 529
Currie, Stephen, 530
Curry, Jane Louise, 531-32
Curson, Marjorie N., 533
Curtis, Christopher Paul, 534
Cush, Cathie, 535-37
Cushman, Karen, 538
Cutler, Jane, 539
Cwiklik, Robert, 540-44
Czech, Ken, 545

Daffron, Carolyn, 546
Dailey, Pamela, 254
Daley, William, 547
Dalgliesh, Alice, 548-49
Dallard, Shyrlee, 550
Damon, Duane, 551
Dann, Geoff, illus., 2431
Darby, Jean, 552-54
Dash, Joan, 555
Daugherty, James, illus., 1943
D'Aulaire, Edgar Parin, author/illus., 556-59
D'Aulaire, Ingri, author/illus., 556-59
Davidson, Mary R., 560
Davidson, Sue, 561
Davies, Eryl, 562
Davies, Kath, 563
Davies, Mark, 564
Davis, Allen, illus., 2123
Davis, Frances A., 565
Davis, Lambert, illus., 940
De Angeli, Marguerite, 566-68

de Ruiz, Dana Catharine, 569-70
de Varona, Frank, 571
DeBiasi, Antoinette "Cookie," 1128, 1131, 1133-34, 1139-40, 1142, 1145, 1147-55, 1157
Deem, James M., 572
DeFelice, Cynthia, 573-75
DeFord, Deborah H., 576
Degen, Bruce, illus., 445
Deitch, Kenneth M., 577
Dejohn, Marie, illus., 321
Dellosso, Gabriela, illus., 2390
Demarest, Chris L., author/illus., 578
Denenberg, Barry, 579-81
dePaola, Tomie, illus., 769
DeStefano, Susan, 582
Devaney, John, 583
Dewey, Jennifer Owings, author/illus., 584
Dexter, Catherine, 585
Di Certo, Joseph J., 586
Di Franco, J. Philip, 587
Diamond, Arthur, 588-90
Diamond, Donna, illus., 427, 1277, 1561
Diaz, David, illus., 1272
Dillon, Diane, illus., 943
Dillon, Leo, illus., 943
Dineen, Jacqueline, 2432-33
Dionetti, Michelle, 591
DiSalvo-Ryan, DyAnne, illus., 764, 775
Divito, Anna, illus., 1258
Dixon, Tennessee, illus., 266
Dobson, Steve, illus., 866, 868, 878
Dodson, Bert, illus., 1278, 1323, 2212
Doherty, Craig A., 592-93
Doherty, Katherine M., 592-93
Dolan, Edward F., 594-601
Dolan, Ellen, 602
Dolan, Sean, 603-605
Dominy, Jeannine, 606
Donahue, John, 607
Donahue, Marilyn Cram, 608
Donnelly, Judy, 609-10
Dooling, Michael, illus., 803-804, 1265, 1688
Doremus, Robert, illus., 988
Dorris, Michael, 611
Doss, Michael P., 612
Doubleday, Veronica, 613
Douglass, Frederick, 614
Downing, Julie, illus., 1374
Driemen, J. E., 615-16
Dubowski, Cathy East, 617-19
Ducey, Jean Sparks, 620
Duey, Kathleen, 621-24
Duffy, James, 625
Dugald, Stermer, illus., 220

Duggleby, John, 626-27
Duke, Chris, illus., 1541-43, 1546
Duncan, Dayton, 628-29
Duncan, Lois, 630
Dunlap, Julie, 631-33
Dunn, John, 634
Durrant, Lynda, 635
Durrell, Julie, illus., 201
Durwood, Thomas A., 636
Duvall, Jill, 637-644
Dwyer, Christopher, 645
Dwyer, Frank, 646

Eagle, Ellen, illus., 428
Eagle, Mike, illus., 2111, 2220
Earle, Alice, 647
Edens, John, illus., 1231
Edmonds, Walter, 648
Edwards, Lillie J., 649
Edwards, Pamela Duncan, 649a
Edwards, Pat, 650
Egger-Bovet, Howard, 651, 2087-88
Egielski, Richard, illus., 402, 493
Ehrlich, Elizabeth, 652
Eitzen, Allan, illus., 627, 1601, 1752
Elish, Dan, 653-54
Ellis, Jan Davey, illus., 437, 1089
Ellis, Rafaela, 655-56
Emerson, Kathy Lynn, 657
Emert, Phyllis Raybin, 658
English, June, 659
Erdrich, Heidi Ellen, 660
Erickson, Richard, illus., 133, 514, 1239, 2266
Erlich, Scott, 661
Everett, Gwen, 662-63
Evert, Jodi, ed, 664
Everts, Tammy, 1157-58
Evitts, William J., 665

Faber, Doris, 666-68
Faber, Harold, 668
Falkof, Lucille, 669-72
Farley, Karin Clafford, 673-75
Farley, Rick, illus., 1884
Farnsworth, Bill, illus., 1280, 1883
Farris, John, 676
Fay, Ann, illus., 2059
Feldman, Eve B., 677
Ferrell, Nancy Warren, 678-79
Ferris, Jeri, 680-83
Fichter, George S., 684
Field, James, illus., 2437
Field, Rachel, 685
Finney, Pat, illus., 2273
Fiore, Peter, illus., 1053
Fiorentino, Al, illus., 846
Fireside, Bryna J., 686
Fireside, Harvey, 687
Fisher, Leonard Everett, 688-91

Fitz-Gerald, Christine A., 692
Fitz-Gerald, Christine Maloney, 693-94
Fitzgerald, Gerald, illus., 2259
Flavin, Teresa, illus., 1754
Fleischman, Paul, 695-700
Fleischman, Sid, 701-707
Fleischner, Jennifer, 708
Fleishman, Seymour, illus., 2510
Fleming, Alice, 709
Fleming, Candace, 710
Forberg, Ati, illus., 2303
Forbes, Bart, illus., 1122
Forbes, Esther, 711
Force, Eden, 712
Ford, Barbara, 713-15
Forrester, Sandra, 716
Forsey, Chris, illus., 1624
Foster, Leila Merrell, 717
Fowler, Zinita, 718
Fox, Mary Virginia, 719
Fox, Paula, 720
Fradin, Dennis, 721-34
Fradin, Dennis Brindell, 735-37
Frame, Paul, illus., 469, 840, 1306
Frampton, David, illus., 382
Francisco, Melissa, illus., 279
Frank, Andrew, 738
Frankel, Alona, 391
Frankl, Ron, 739
Franklin, Paula A., 1169
Fraser, Jane, 740
Fraser, Mary Ann, author/illus., 741-43
Frasier, Betty, illus., 1745
Freedman, Russell, 744-51
Freedman, Suzanne, 752-53
Freeman, Suzanne T., 754
Friedrich, Elizabeth, 755
Friese, Kai Jabir, 756
Fritz, Jean, 757-75
Fromm, Peter, 776
Fry, Annette R., 777
Fujiwara, Kim, illus., 1109
Fuleveiler, John, illus., 1256
Fuller, Sarah Betsy, 687

Gaeddert, Louann, 778
Gaines, Anne, 779
Galdone, Paul, illus., 2135-36, 2143-44
Gammell, Stephen, illus., 770, 786b
Gampert, John, illus., 85
Gardner, Robert, 780
Garfunkel, Trudy, 781-82
Garland, Michael, illus., 755
Garland, Sherry, 783-84
Garrett, Michael, 785
Garrick, Jacqueline, illus., 15
Gates, Donald, illus., 1228
Gates, Viola R., 786

Gauch, Patricia L., 786a, 786b
Gaul, Randy, illus., 697
Gehret, Jeanne, 787
Geis, Jacqueline, author/illus., 788
Genet, Donna, 789
Gentry, Tony, 790-92
George, Jean Craighead, 793
Gerber, Alan Jay, 217
Gerrard, Roy, 794-95
Geter, Tyrone, illus., 2077
Gherman, Beverly, 796
Gibbons, Gail, author/illus., 797-98
Giblin, James, 799-804
Gibson, Michael, 805
Giff, Patricia R., 806
Gilleece, David, illus., 1433-36
Gilman, Michael, 807
Ginsburg, Max, illus., 1926, 2243
Gintzler, A. S., 808-10
Gipson, Fred, 811
Girard, Linda Walvoord, 812
Glass, Andrew, illus., 698
Glassman, Bruce, 813
Glassman, Judy, 814
Gleiter, Jan, 815-22
Glenn, Patricia Brown, 823
Glubok, Shirley, 824
Goble, Paul, 825
Goldberg, Jake, 826
Goldin, Barbara Diamond, 827-28
Goldish, Meish, 829-30
Goldman, Martin S., 831
Goldstein, Nathan, illus., 847
Golenbock, Peter, 832
Gonzales, Doreen, 833
Goode, Diane, illus., 1375, 1921
Goor, Nancy, 834
Goor, Ron, 834
Gormley, Beatrice, 835
Gorrell, Gena K., 836
Gorsline, Douglas, illus., 1590, 1598
Gourley, Catherine, 837
Gourse, Leslie, 838-39
Gowing, Toby, illus., 1320-21, 2031, 2414-16, 2419, 2426, 2428
Graff, Polly Anne, 840
Graff, Stewart, 840
Graham, Ian, 841
Graham, Lorenz, 842
Graham, Mark, illus., 1230, 1796, 1919
Granfield, Linda, 843-44
Grater, Lindsay, illus., 1421
Graves, Charles P., 845-47
Gray, James, 848
Green, Carl, 849-50
Green, Carl R., 851-59, 1960-75
Green, Connie Jordan, 860

Green, Rayna, 861
Greenberg, Judith E., 862
Greenberg, Sheldon, illus., 962
Greenblatt, Miriam, 863-64
Greene, Carol, 865-84
Greene, Constance C., 885
Greene, Janice, 886
Greene, Laura Offenhartz, 887
Greene, Richard, 153
Greenfield, Eloise, 888-89
Greenwood, Barbara, 890
Greeson, Janet, 891
Gregory, Kristiana, 892-97
Grey, Edward, 898
Griest, Lisa, 899
Grifalconi, Ann, illus., 1505
Griffin, Peni, 900
Griffith, Gershom, illus., 38, 2485-87
Gross, Ruth Belov, 901
Gross, Virginia T., 902
Guccione, Leslie Davis, 903
Guiberson, Brenda Z., author/illus., 904
Gutierrez, Rudy, illus., 570, 1587
Gutman, Dan, 905
Guttmacher, Peter, 906
Guzzetti, Paula, 907
Guzzi, George, illus., 1827

Haas, Carol, 908
Haddon, Mark, 909
Haeffele, Deborah, illus., 1116
Hagerman, Jennifer, illus., 2202
Hahn, Elizabeth, 910
Hahn, Mary Downing, 911-13
Hakim, Joy, 914-23
Hakim, Rita, 924
Halasa, Malu, 925-26
Hall, Donald, 927-31
Hall, Elizabeth, 1680
Hall, Lynn, 932
Halliburton, Warren, 933
Hamanaka, Shelia, 934-35
Hamilton, Leni, 936
Hamilton, Sue L., 937-38
Hamilton, Virginia, 939-43
Hamlin, Janet, illus., 360, 713, 983, 2401
Hancock, Sibyl, 944
Hanley, Sally, 945
Hanna, Cheryl, illus., 1046
Hansen, Joyce, 946-48
Hanson, Peter E., illus., 682, 1885
Hanson, Rick, illus., 1382, 2221
Harding, Donal, 949
Hargrove, Jim, 950-56
Harlan, Judith, 957
Harness, Cheryl, 958-61
Harrah, Madge, 962
Harris, Edward D., 963

Harris, Jacqueline L., 964
Harrison, Barbara, 965
Hart, Philip S., 966-67
Harvey, Brett, 968-72
Harvey, Miles, 973
Haskins, James, 974-76, 1706-1707
Haskins, Jim, 977
Hass, Shelly O., illus., 1814
Haubrich, Kathy, illus., 1580
Hausman, Gerald, 978
Hawkes, Kevin, illus., 1998
Hawxhurst, Joan C., 979
Haynes, Joyce, illus., 429
Haynes, Richard M., 980
Hays, Michael, illus., 13, 1422
Hayward, Linda, 981
Hazell, Rebecca, author/illus., 982
Heiligman, Deborah, 983
Heiss, Arleen McGrath, 984
Heller, Debbe, illus., 488, 569, 1180
Heller, Linda, illus., 30
Helmer, Diana Star, 985
Henba, Bobbie, illus., 1830
Hendershot, Judith, 986
Henderson, Meryl, illus., 839
Henry, Joanne L., 987-88
Henry, Sondra, 989-91
Herb, Angela, 281
Herda, D. J., 992-96
Herman, Charlotte, 997-1000
Herman, Vestal, illus., 261
Hermes, Patricia, 1001
Herridge, Steve, illus., 292
Hesse, Karen, 1002-1003
Hevly, Nancy, 1005
Hewett, Richard, illus., 99-100
Hewitt, Kathryn, illus., 1269-70
Hicks, Peter, 1006
Hicks, Roger, 1007
Higgens, Paul, illus. 292
High, Linda Oatman, 1008
Highwater, Jamake, 1009
Hildick, E. W., 1010
Hill, Elizabeth Starr, 1011
Hill, Prescott, 1012-14
Hilton, Suzanne, 1015-18
Hilts, Len, 1019-20
Himler, Ronald, illus., 347, 902, 1068, 1070, 1274-75, 1279, 1413, 2094-2101, 2183, 2285-86
Hine, Lewis, photographs, 749
Hintz, Martin, 1021
Hirsch, Charles, 1022
Hite, Sid, 1024
Hoig, Stan, 1025-26
Holder, John, illus., 1826
Holland, Isabelle, 1027-29
Holler, Anne, 1030
Holmes, Burnham, 1031-32

Holmes, Mary Z., 1033-39
Hoobler, Dorothy, 1040-48
Hoobler, Thomas, 1040-48
Hook, Richard, illus., 1080, 2133
Hooks, William H., 1049-52
Hopkins, Lee Bennett, comp., 1053
Hopkinson, Deborah, 1054-56
Horton, Madelyn, 1057
Horvath, Polly, 1058
Hotze, Sollace, 1059-60
Houston, Gloria, 1060a, 1061-63b
Howard, Elizabeth Fitzgerald, 1064-65
Howard, Ellen, 1066-71
Howarth, Sarah, 1072-73
Hoyt-Goldsmith, Diane, 1074
Hull, Mary, 1075
Hull, Robert, sell., 1076
Humble, Richard, 1077-78
Hunt, Irene, 1079
Hunter, Nigel, 1080
Hurmence, Belinda, 1081-82
Hyatt, Patricia Rusch, 1083
Hyman, Trina Schart, illus., 313, 773-74, 1303

IlgenFritz, Elizabeth, 1084
Ingpen, Robert, illus., 2432-35
Ingraham, Erick, illus., 944
Irwin, Hadley, 1085-86
Israel, Fred L., 1087
Italia, Robert, 1088

Jackson, Ellen, 1089
Jacobs, Francine, 1090
Jacobs, William, 1091-97
Jaffe, Steven, 1098
Jakes, John, 1099
Jakoubek, Robert, 1100-1105
James, Betsy, 1106
James, Cary, 1107
James, John, illus., 1604
James, Melissa, illus., 1845
Janovitz, Marilyn, illus., 1499
Jeffers, Susan, illus., 2376
Jeffery, David, 1108
Jeffredo-Warden, Louise V., 1109
Jenkins, Jean, illus., 1409-10
Jenkins, Leonard, illus., 1654
Jenney, Robert, illus., 2188
Jensen, Dorothea, 1110
Jezer, Marty, 1111
Jezierski, Chet, illus., 2122
Johnson, Amy, illus., 464
Johnson, Dolores, author/illus., 1112-13, 2480
Johnson, E. Harper, illus., 1890
Johnson, Jacqueline, 1114
Johnson, James E., 1115
Johnson, Janice, 1116
Johnson, Laurie K., illus., 2374

Johnson, Linda Carlson, 1117
Johnson, Neil, 1118-19
Johnson, Pamela, illus., 2391
Johnson, Steve, illus., 2091
Johnson, William H., illus., 663
Johnston, Julie, 1120
Johnston, Norma, 1121
Johnston, Tony, 1122
Jones, Jan Naimo, illus., 489, 1669
Jones, Rebecca C., 1123
Jones, Richard C., 1342
Jones, Ronald, illus., 1768
Jones, S. D., 1124-25
Joplin, Scott, 1558
Jumper, Moses, 1126
Kalin, Victor, illus., 1877
Kallen, Stuart A., 1127
Kalman, Bobbie, 1128-40, 1141-58
Kaplan, Elizabeth, 109
Karas, G. Brian, illus., 2125
Karl, Jean, 1159
Karr, Kathleen, 1160-65
Kassem, Lou, 1166
Kastner, Jill, illus., 901, 1944
Katz, William Loren, 1167-69
Kaye, Judith, 1170-73
Kaye, Tony, 1174
Keehn, Sally, 1175-76
Kehret, Peg, 1177
Keith, Eros, illus., 720, 942, 1595
Keller, Emily, 1178
Keller, Katie, illus., 1352
Kelley, True, illus., 572
Kellogg, Steven, author/illus., 1179
Kelso, Richard, 1180-82
Kendall, Martha E., 1183
Kendall, Russ, photographs, 2353, 2355-56, 2358
Kent, Deborah, 1184-91
Kent, Zachary, 1192-1213
Kerby, Mona, 1214-17
Kerr, Daisy, 1218
Ketchum, Liza, 1219
Ketteman, Helen, 1220
Kherdian, David, 1221
Kiesler, Kate, illus., 1634
Kilgore, Susi, illus., 442
Kimber, Murray, illus., 1508
Kimmel, Eric, 1222
King, Dave, illus., 2431
King, David C., 1223
King, John, 1224
King, Perry Scott, 1225
Kinsey-Warnock, Natalie, 1226-30
Kirby, Philippa, 1231
Kirkpatrick, Joey, illus., 1233
Kirkpatrick, Katherine, 1232
Kirkpatrick, Patricia, 1233
Kitano, Harry, 1234
Kittleman, Laurence R., 1235
Kittredge, Mary, 1236-38

Kiwak, Barbara, illus., 490
Klausmeier, Robert, 1239
Klausner, Janet, 1240
Kliment, Bud, 1241-43
Klots, Steve, 1244-45
Knight, Amelia Stewart, 1246
Knight, Christopher G.,
    photographs, 1304
Knight, Meribah, 1304
Knight, Theodore, 1247
Kohler, Keith, illus., 609
Koller, Jackie French, 1248-49
Koral, April, 1250
Koslow, Philip, 1251
Kozodoy, Ruth, 1252
Kraft, Betsy Harvey, 1253
Kramer, Sydelle, 2348
Krass, Peter, 1254
Krementz, Jill, author/illus.,
    1255-59
Kressler, Marjory, photographs,
    2354
Kroeger, Mary Kay, 1260
Krohn, Katherine E., 1261
Kroll, Steven, 1262-66
Kronstadt, Janet, 1267
Krovatin, Dan, illus., 1656
Krull, Kathleen, 1268-72
Krupinski, Loretta, author/illus.,
    1273, 2258
Kubinyi, Laszlo, illus., 414
Kudlinski, Kathleen, 1274-80
Kunhardt, Edith, 1281
Kunstler, James Howard, 1282
Kuropas, Myron B., 1283
Kurtz, Henry I., 1284
Kvasnicka, Robert M., 1285
La Farge, Ann, 1286
La Pierre, Yvette, 1287
LaFarelle, Lorenzo G., 1288
Lamb, Susan Condie, illus., 1063
Lambert, Paulette Livers, illus.,
    2326-27
Lampton, Christopher, 1289
Landau, Elaine, 1290-94
Lane, Joyce, 1295
Lang, Susan, 1296
Langley, Myrtle, 1297
Lantz, Paul, illus., 648
Laporte, Michele, illus., 88, 802,
    2359
Larios, Richard, 570
Larsen, Anita, 1298
Larsen, Rebecca, 1299-1300
Lasky, Kathryn, 1301-1304
Latham, Jean Lee, 1305-12
Lattimore, Deborah Nourse, 1313
Lauber, Patricia, 1314
Lavender, David, 1315
Lavender, David Sievert, 1316
Law, Kevin J., 1317

Lawler, Mary, 1318
Lawlor, Laurie, 1319-28
Lawlor, Veronica, selector/illus.,
    1329
Lawrence, Jacob, author/illus.,
    1330-31
Lawson, John, 1332
Lawson, Robert, 1333-34
Lazar, Jerry, 1335
Lazo, Caroline, 1336-37
Leathers, Noel L., 1338
Leavell, J. Perry, Jr., 1339-41
Ledbetter, Cynthia, 1342
Leder, Alan, photographs, 1344
Leder, Jane, 1343
Leder, Jane Mersky, 1344
Lee, Dom, illus., 1584-85
Lee, Ed, illus., 236
Lee, Kathleen, 1345
Lee, Sally, 1346
Lefer, Diane, 1348
Lehrer, Brian, 1349
Lehrman, Robert, 1350
Leighton, Maxinne Rhea, 1351
Leiner, Katherine, 1352
Leland, Dorothy Kupcha, 1353
Lelchuk, Alan, 1354
Lemieux, Margo, 1355
Lemke, Nancy, 1356
Lenski, Lois, 1357-58
Leonard, Laura, 1359-60
Leonard, Richard, illus., 1908
Lepthien, Emilie U., 1361
Leuzzi, Linda, 1362
Levi, Steven C., 1363
Levin, Betty, 1364
Levin, Pamela, 1365
Levine, Ellen, 1366-67
Levinson, Nancy Smiler, 1368-72
Levinson, Rikki, 1373-75
Levitin, Sonia, 1376-79
Lewin, Betsy, illus., 12
Lewin, Ted, illus., 158-59, 1260,
    1504, 1670, 1676-77, 1679
Lewis, Allen, illus., 685
Lewis, T., illus., 543
Lewis-Ferguson, Julinda, 1380
Libreatore, Karen, 1381
Liedahl, Brian, illus., 1548
Liestman, Vicki, 1382
Lillegard, Dee, 1383-86
Lilly, Charles, illus., 1819
Lincoln, Abraham, 1387
Lincoln, Margarette, 1388
Lindbergh, Reeve, 1389
Lindop, Edmund, 1390-94
Lipsyte, Robert, 1395-96
Litowinsky, Olga, 1397
Littlefield, Holly, 1398
Littlesugar, Amy, 1399
Livingston, Myra Cohn, 1400-1401

Lizon, Karen Helene, 1402
Lobel, Arnold, author/illus., 1403
Locker, Thomas, illus., 415, 793
Lodge, Sally, 1404-1405
Loewen, Nancy, 1406
Looby, Chris, 1407
Lorbiecki, Marybeth, 1408
Lord, Athena, 1409-11
Lord, Bette Bao, 1412
LoTurco, Laura, illus., 280
Love, D. Anne, 1413
Low, William, illus., 1510
Lowe, Felix C., 1414
Lowell, Susan, 1415
Lowery, Linda, 1416
Lubetkin, Wendy, 1417
Lucas, Cedric, illus., 1574
Lucas, Eileen, 1418-19
Luce, Celia, 1420
Luce, Willard, 1420
Lunn, Janet, 1421
Lydon, Kerry Raines, 1422
Lynn, Elizabeth A., 1423
Lynn, Patricia, illus., 1016
Lyon, George Ella, 1424-27
Lyons, Mary E., 1428-32
Ma, Wenhai, illus., 828
Maarchesi, Stephen, illus., 1559
MacBride, Roger Lea, 1433-36
Macht, Norman L., 1437-39
MacKinnon, Christy, author/illus.,
    1440
MacLachlan, Patricia, 1441-43
MacMillan, Dianne, 1444-48
Macy, Sue, 1449
Maddox, Kelly, illus., 462
Maestro, Betsy, 1450-55
Maestro, Giulio, illus., 1451-55
Magocsi, Paul R., 1456
Maguire, Kerry, illus., 633, 1408,
    2364
Mahone-Lonesome, Robyn, 1457
Mai, Vo-Dinh, illus., 2215
Malone, Mary, 1458-59
Manley, Joan B., 1460
Manning, Maurie, illus., 676, 1569,
    2119, 2344
Manson, Ainslie, 1461
Marino, Jan, 1462-64
Markham, Lois, 1465-67
Marko, Katherine, 1468
Marlow, Eric, illus., 889
Marrin, Albert, 1469-77
Marschall, Ken, illus., 134, 2237
Marsh, Joan, 1478
Marshall, Felicia, illus., 2204
Marston, Hope Irvin, 1479
Martin, C. L. G., 1480
Martin, Jacqueline Briggs, 1481
Martin, Katherine, 1482
Martindale, Emily, illus., 94

Martinello, Marian L., 1483
Marvin, Isabel R., 1484
Marzollo, Jean, 1485-86
Masheris, Bob, illus., 441, 1869
Mason, Antony, 1487
Mathers, Petra, illus., 1481
Maurer, Richard, 1488
Mayberry, Jodine, 1489-90
Mayo, Edith, ed., 1491
Mays, Victor, illus., 1310
Mazer, Harry, 1492
Mazzio, Joann, 1493
McCall, Edith, 1494-45
McClard, Megan, 1496-97
McClung, Robert, 1498-1500
McCully, Emily Arnold,
      author/illus., 930, 1501-1502
McCurdy, Michael, illus., 90,
      928-29, 1246, 1387, 1753
McDaniel, Melissa, 1503
McDonald, Megan, 1504
McGaw, Laurie, illus., 2110
McGovern, Ann, 1505
McGrath, Patrick, 1506
McGraw, Eloise Jarvis, 1507
McGugan, Jim, 1508
McHale, John E., Jr., 1509
McKeating, Eileen, illus., 1214
McKenzie, Ellen Kindt, 1510-11
McKissack, Frederick, 1513-38
McKissack, Pat, 1512
McKissack, Patricia, 1513-38
McLerran, Alice, 1539
McNeese, Tim, 1540-46
McPhail, David, author/illus., 1547
McPherson, Stephanie
      Sammartino, 1548-52
Meacham, Margaret, 1553
Medearis, Angela Shelf, 1554-58
Meltzer, Milton, 1559-62
Mendez, Adriana, 1563
Merkin, Richard, illus., 1868
Meryman, Richard, 1564
Mettger, Zak, 1565-66
Meyer, Carolyn, 1567
Meyer, Susan E., 1568
Michaels, Steve, illus., 471
Migdale, Lawrence, photographs,
      1769
Migneco, Ronald, 1569
Miles, William, 357
Miller, Brandon Marie, 1570
Miller, Lyle, illus., 14, 43
Miller, Natalie, 1571
Miller, Robert, 1572-73
Miller, William, 1574
Mills, Claudia, 1575
Milton, Joyce, 1576-77

Minahan, John A., 1578
Minor, Wendell, illus., 2288
Minter, Daniel, illus., 453
Mintz, Penny, 1579
Mirocha, Paul, illus., 1415
Mitchell, Barbara, 1580-81
Mitchell, Hetty, illus., 1550, 1581
Mitchell, Margaree King, 1582
Miyake, Yoshi, illus., 612, 815,
      822, 1922, 2190, 2322
Mizell, Linda, 1583
Mochizuki, Ken, 1584-85
Moeri, Louise, 1586
Mohr, Nicholasa, 1587
Molan, Chris, illus., 218, 1920
Monceaux, Morgan, 1588
Monjo, F. N., 1589-98
Monroe, Jean Guard, 1599
Mooney, Martin J., 1600
Moore, Robin, illus., 1833
Moore, Ruth Nulton, 1601
Moores, Ian, illus., 1627
Morgan, Mary, illus., 273
Morin, Isobel V., 1602-1603
Morin, Paul, illus., 1106
Morley, Jacqueline, 1604-1605
Morpurgo, Michael, 1606-1607
Morris, Gilbert, 1608
Morris, Jeffrey, 1609-14
Morris, Juddi, 1615
Morrison, Dorothy Nafus, 1616
Morrow, Barbara, author/illus.,
      1617-18
Morrow, Honoré, 1619
Morrow, Mary Frances, 1620
Moscinski, Sharon, 1621
Moseley, Elizabeth R., 1622
Moser, Barry, 927, 931, 1623
Moss, Miriam, 1624
Muggamin, Howard, 1625
Muhlberger, Richard, 1626
Mulvihill, Patricia Rose, illus.,
      891, 1066
Munro, Bob, 1627
Murdoch, David, 1628-29
Murphy, Claire Rudolf, 1630
Murphy, Jim, 1631-36
Murphy, Virginia Reed, 1637
Myers, Anna, 1638-40
Myers, Walter Dean, 1641-45
Nacht, Merle, illus., 1354
Naden, Corinne, 269-72, 1646-47
Nardo, Don, 1648-49
Nash, Bruce, 1650
Naylor, Phyllis Reynolds, 1651
Negri, Rocco, illus., 1596
Nelson, Sharlene, 1652
Nelson, Ted, 1652

Nelson, Theresa, 1653
Nelson, Vaunda M., 1654
Nesmith, Samuel P., 1483
Neufeld, John, 1655
Newsom, Tom, illus., 1994
Newton, Michael, illus., 1182
Nichols, Joan Kane, 1656
Nicholson, Dorinda
      Makanaonalani Stagner, 1657
Nicholson, Lois, 1658-60
Nirgiotis, Nicholas, 1661
Nixon, Joan L., 1662-66
Nolan, Dennis, illus., 1052, 1351
Nordstrom, Judy, 1667
Norman, Winifred Latimer, 1668
Norrell, Robert J., 1669
O, Ned, illus., 1515-16, 1529
Oberman, Sheldon, 1670
O'Brien, Steven, 1671-72
O'Connor, Barbara, 1673-74
O'Connor, Jim, 1675, 2346
O'Dell, Scott, 1676-80
Oleksy, Walter, 1681
Olsen, Victoria, 1682
Olsen, Violet, 1683
Olson, Arielle, 1684
O'Neal, Michael, 1685-86
Oneal, Zibby, 1687-88
O'Neill, Laurie, 1689-90
O'Rear, Sybil J., 1691
Osborne, Angela, 1692
Osborne, Mary Pope, 1693-94
Osinski, Alice, 1695
Osofsky, Audrey, 1696
Ostendorf, Edward, illus., 1518-19,
      1523, 1525, 1527
Otero, Ben, illus., 212
Ott, Margaret V., 2219
Oughton, Jerrie, 1697-98
Owen, Marna, 1699
Owen, Mary Beth, illus., 426
Owens, Gail, illus., 527, 1319
Owings, Jennifer, illus., 2275
Paananen, Eloise, 1700
Palencar, John, illus., 1823
Palmer, Leslie, 1701
Paparone, Pamela, illus., 1389
Parker, Nancy Winslow,
      author/illus., 1702
Parker, Nancy Winslow, illus.,
      1832, 2412
Parker, Robert Andrew, illus.,
      1220, 1355
Parker, Steve, 1703-1705
Parks, Rosa, 1706-1707
Parlin, John, 1708
Parmenter, Wayne, illus., 1367
Parton, Steven, illus., 2367

Partridge, Elizabeth, 1709
Pasachoff, Naomi, 1710
Pascoe, Elaine, 1711
Patent, Dorothy Hinshaw, 1712
Paterson, Katherine, 1713-15
Patrick, Diane, 1716-18
Patrick, John J., 1719
Patrick-Wexler, Diane, 1720
Patterson, Charles, 1721
Patterson, Lillie, 1722-24
Patterson, Lily, 1668
Paulsen, Gary, 1725-31
Paulsen, Ruth Wright, 1731
Paulson, Timothy J., 1732
Peacock, Judith, 2388
Peck, Beth, illus., 2478
Peck, Richard, 1733
Peduzzi, Kelli, 2267
Peet, Bill, 1734
Peifer, Charles, Jr., 1735
Pellowski, Anne, 1736
Pelta, Kathy, 1737
Pemberton, William E., 1738
Pendergraft, Patricia, 1739-41
Perl, Lila, 1742
Perrin, Gerry, photographs, 824
Pertzoff, Alexander, illus., 1443
Petersen, David, 1743-44
Peterson, Helen Stone, 1745-46
Pfeffer, Susan B., 1747-48
Pfeifer, Kathryn, 1749-50
Pflueger, Lynda, 1751
Phelan, Mary Kay, 1752
Philip, Neil, ed., 1753
Phillips, Ann, 1754
Pile, Robert B., 1755-56
Pinchot, Jane, 1757
Pinkney, Andrea Davis, 1758-60
Pinkney, Brian, illus., 1049,
    1758-60
Pinkney, J. Brian, illus., 1485
Pinkney, Jerry, illus., 888, 941,
    2006, 2246-47
Place, François, illus., 1607
Plain, Nancy, 1761-62
Platt, Richard, 1763-64
Pleasant Company, 1765-67
Plowden, Martha Ward, 1768
Polacco, Patricia, 1769-70
Polikoff, Barbara G., 1771-72
Pollack, Jill S., 1773
Pollard, Michael, 1774-75, 2434-35
Porte, Barbara Ann, 1776
Porter, A. P., 1777
Porter, Connie, 1778-80
Porter, Frederick, illus., 1643
Porter, Janice Lee, illus., 309, 1416
Potter, Robert R., 1781-84
Powers, Christine, illus., 202
Poynter, Margaret, 1785
Pratt, Paula, 1786

Precek, Katharine Wilson, 1787
Prentzas, G. S., 1788
Presnall, Judith Janda, 1789
Press, Skip, 1790
Priceman, Marjorie, illus., 1806
Prichett, Shelley, illus., 1887
Primavera, Elise, illus., 768
Prior, Katherine, 1791-92
Probosz, Kathilyn Solomon, 1793
Provensen, Alice, author/illus.,
    1794-95
Pryor, Bonnie, 1796
Ptacek, Greg, 1797, 2310
Quackenbush, Robert, 1399, 1578,
    1592, 1798-1802
Quiri, Patricia Ryon, 1803-1804
Rabin, Staton, 1805
Rael, Elsa Okon, 1806
Rambeck, Richard, 1807
Ramsey, Marcy Dunn, illus., 1298,
    1553, 2194
Ramstad, Ralph L., illus., 632
Rand, Gloria, 1808
Rand, Jacki Thompson, 1809
Rand, Ted, illus., 1229, 1808
Randall, Marta, 1810
Randolph, Blythe, 1811-12
Randolph, Sallie G., 279-80, 1813
Ransom, Candice F., 1814
Ransome, James, illus., 1051,
    1055, 1582
Raphael, Elaine, 1815-16
Rappaport, Doreen, 1817-25
Rawls, Jim, 1826-27
Ray, Deborah Kogan, author/illus.,
    444a, 968, 970-972, 1828,
    2182
Ray, Delia, 1829
Ray, Mary Lyn, 1830-31
Raymond, Larry, illus., 340, 1841
Read, Thomas Buchanan, 1832
Reason, Sallie, 1007
Redman, Tom, illus., 571, 1108
Reeder, Carolyn, 1833-36
Reef, Catherine, 1837-44
Reese, Joe, 1845
Reisberg, Mira, illus., 307
Reiser, Howard, 1846
Reit, Seymour, 1847
Rennert, Richard, ed., 1848-52
Rennert, Rick, 1853
Reynolds, Lura Shield, 1651
Riccio, Frank, illus., 1497
Rich, Anna, illus., 1555-56
Richards, Kenneth, 1854
Richards, Norman, 1855
Richardson, Joy, 1856
Richman, Daniel A., 1857
Richmond, Merle, 1858
Richter, Conrad, 1859
Ride, Sally, 1860

Riggio, Anita, illus., 591
Riley, Gail Blasser, 1861
Rinaldi, Ann, 1862-63
Ringgold, Faith, author/illus.,
    1864-65
Riskind, Mary, 1866
Ritchie, David, 1867
Ritter, Lawrence S., 1868
Ritz, Karen, illus., 520, 680, 2383
Rivinus, Edward F., 1869
Roach, Marilynne K., 1870
Robbins, Neal E., 1871
Robbins, Phillip, 190
Roberts, Luann, illus., 2277
Roberts, Wills Davis, 1872
Robinet, Harriette Gillem, 1873-75
Robinson, Aminah Brenda Lynn,
    illus., 1892
Robinson, Charles, illus., 767, 987,
    2301
Rochelle, Belinda, 1876
Rockwood, Joyce, 1877
Rodanas, Kristina, illus., 162
Rodowsky, Colby F., 1878
Rodriguez, Consuelo, 1879
Roessel, Monty, 1880
Rogers, Teresa, 1881
Rojankovsky, Feodor, illus., 761
Roman, Joseph, 1882
Roop, Connie, ed., 1884-87
Roop, Peter, 1883-87
Root, Kimberly Bulcken, 618-19,
    1056, 1539
Rorby, Ginny, 1888
Rosales, Melodye, illus., 1780,
    2078
Rose, Deborah Lee, 1889
Rose, Mary Catherine, 1890
Rose, Ted, illus., 275
Rosen, Dorothy Schack, 1891
Rosen, Michael J., 1892
Rosen, Mike, 1893-94
Rosenblum, Richard, author/illus.,
    1895-96
Rosenburg, John M., 1897
Ross, Ramon Royal, 1898-99
Ross, Rhea Beth, 1900-1901
Ross, Stewart, 1902-1903
Rossiter, Phyllis, 1904
Rossne, Meryl, illus., 2104
Rostkowski, Margaret, 1905
Rounds, Glen, 1906
Rowland, Della, 1907-1908
Rowland, Jada, illus., 417
Rowland-Warne, L., 1909
Rubel, David, 1910-12
Ruby, Lois, 1913
Ruff, Donna, illus., 19, 667, 1687
Rushton, Lucy, 1914-15
Russell, Marion, 1916
Russell, Sharman, 1917

Rutberg, Becky, 1918
Ryan, Cary, ed., 1919
Ryan, Peter, 1920
Ryan, Susannah, illus., 1450
Rylant, Cynthia, 1921
Sabin, Francene, 1922
Sadowski, Wiktor, illus., 2438
Salisbury, Graham, 1923-24
Salvini, Donna, illus., 51
San Souci, Robert, 1925-26
Sanchez, Bill, illus., 651
Sandak, Cass R., 1927-41
Sandberg, Peter Lars, 1942
Sandburg, Carl, 1943
Sanders, Scott R., 1944-46
Sandin, Joan, author/illus., 1947-48
Sandin, Joan, illus., 1371, 1825
Sandler, Martin, 1949-50
Sandomir, Larry, 1951
Sandoz, Mari, 1952
Sanford, William, 849-59, 1953-75
Santella, Andrew, 1976
Santoro, Christopher, illus., 1978
Sattler, Helen Roney, 1977-78
Savage, Jeff, 1979-84
Savin, Marcia, 1985
Sawyer, Kem Knapp, 1986
Saxon-Ford, Stephanie, 1987
Say, Allen, author/illus., 1988-89
Scarf, Maggi, 1990
Scheader, Catherine, 1991
Schimpky, David, 1156
Schleichert, Elizabeth, 1992-93
Schlein, Miriam, 1994
Schlissel, Lillian, 1246
Schloredt, Valerie, 231
Schmidt, Gary D., ed., 1995
Schoenherr, Ian, illus., 1159
Schofield, Den, illus., 1496
Schomp, Virginia, 1996
Schott, Jane A., 1997
Schotter, Roni, 1998-99
Schouweiler, Tom, 2000
Schraff, Anne, 2001-2002
Schroeder, Alan, 2003-2007
Schulz, Janet, illus., 1552, 2008
Schulz, Walter A., 2008
Schuman, Michael A., 2009-11
Schwartz, Amy, author/illus., 2012
Schwartz, Joyce R., 360
Schwartzberg, Renée, 2013
Schwarz, Melissa, 2014-16
Scollins, Richard, illus., 1894
Scordato, Ellen, 2017
Scott, Elaine, 2018
Scott, John Anthony, 2019
Scott, Lynn H., 2020
Scott, Richard, 2021
Scott, Robert A., 2019, 2022
Scrace, Carolyn, illus., 1604
Sebestyen, Ouida, 2023

Selfridge, John W., 2024
Selznick, Brian, author/illus., 2025
Sewall, Marcia, author/illus., 704,
   1125, 2026-28
Sewell, Helen, illus., 549
Seymour-Jones, Carole, 2029
Shaffer, Ann, 2030
Shaw, Bill, 416
Shaw, Charles, illus., 818, 2280,
   2323
Shaw, Janet, 2031
Shea, George, 2032
Sheafer, Silvia Anne, 2033
Sheban, Chris, illus., 146
Shed, Greg, illus., 346, 1805, 1889
Sherman, Eileen B., 2034
Sherrow, Victoria, 2035-40
Shine, Andrea, illus., 899, 2375
Shirley, David, 2041-42
Shore, Nancy, 2043
Shortelle, Dennis, 780
Shorto, Russell, 2044-47
Shub, Elizabeth, 2048
Shuker-Haines, Frances, 2049
Shumate, Jane, 2050-51
Shura, Mary Francis, 2052-54
Shuter, Jane, ed., 2055-57
Siegel, Beatrice, 2058
Sills, Leslie, 2059-60
Silverman, Jerry, 2061
Silverstein, Herma, 2062
Simmons, Alex, 2063
Simon, Charnan, 2064-65
Sinnott, Susan, 2066-68
Sipiera, Paul P., 2069
Sis, Peter, illus., 702, 705, 707
Sisco, Tim, illus., 2047
Sita, Lisa, 2070
Skeen, Keith, illus., 2031, 2276
Sklansky, Jeff, 2071
Skurzynski, Gloria, 2072
Slavin, Ed, 2073
Slepian, Jan, 2074
Sloan, Frank, 2075
Sloan, Lois, illus., 1287
Sloate, Susan, 2076
Smalls-Hector, Irene, 2077-78
Smith, Adam, 2079
Smith, Carter, ed., 2079-85
Smith, Cat Bowman, illus., 1377
Smith, Elizabeth Simpson, 2086
Smith, Katherine Snow, 2079
Smith, Patricia Clark, 49
Smith, Robert L., illus., 541
Smith, Tony, illus., 409-10, 505,
   1705
Smith-Baranzini, Marlene, 651,
   2087-88
Smothers, Ethel Footman, 2089-90
Smucker, Anna Egan, 2091
Smucker, Barbara, 2092-93

Sneve, Virginia Driving Hawk,
   2094-101
Snyder, Zilpha Keatley, 2102-2103
Soentpiet, Chris K., illus., 293
Sonder, Ben, 1126, 2104
Sonneborn, Liz, 2105
Soper, Patrick, illus., 1126, 1414
Sorel, Madeline, illus., 1257
Sorensen, Henri, author/illus., 2106
Sorensen, Henri, illus., 1347, 1995
Spackman, Michael 2119
Speaker-Yuan, Margaret, 2107
Speare, Elizabeth George,
   2108-2109
Spedden, Daisy Corning Stone,
   2110
Spencer, Eve, 2111
Spinka, Penina Keen, 2112
Sproule, Anna, 206
St. George, Judith, 2113-17
St. Pierre, Stephanie, 2118
Stacey, Tom, 2119
Stafford, Mark, 2120
Stallones, Jared, 2121
Stamper, Judith Bauer, 2122-23
Standiford, Natalie, 2124
Stanley, Diane, 2125-26
Stanley, Jerry, 2127-29
Steedman, Scott, 2130
Steele, Philip, 2131-33
Steele, William O., 2134-44
Steen, Sandra, 2145-46
Steen, Susan, 2145-46
Stefoff, Rebecca, 2147-57
Stein, R. Conrad, 2158-70
Stein, Wendy, 2171
Steins, Richard, 2172-76
Stepto, Michele, ed., 2177
Stern, Gary M., 2178
Stevens, Bernardine S., 2179
Stevens, Bryna, 2180
Stevens, Carla, 2181-83
Stevens, Rita, 2184-87
Stevenson, Augusta, 2188
Stewart, Elizabeth J., 2189
Stewart, Gail, 2190-92
Stewart, Roger, illus., 841
Stiles, T. L., 2193
Still, Wayne Anthony, illus., 1809
Stine, Megan, 2194-95
Stites, Joe, illus., 823
Stock, Catherine, illus., 268
Stolz, Mary, 2196
Stone, Bruce, 2197
Stout, Harry S., 576
Strauch, Eileen Walsh, 2200
Streissguth, Tom, 2201-2202
Strickland, Brad, 2203
Strigenz, Geri, illus., 1033-35,
   1037, 1039
Stroud, Bettye, 2204

Sufrin, Mark, 2205
Sullivan, Charles, ed., 2206
Sullivan, George, 2207-11
Sullivan, Silky, 2212
Super, Neil, 2213-14
Surat, Michele Maria, 2215
Suter, Joanne, 2216
Swain, Gwenyth, 2217
Swanson, Diane, 2218
Swanson, Gloria M., 2219
Swanson, June, 2220-21
Swertka, Eve, 2222
Taback, Simms, illus., 87
Taitz, Emily, 989-91
Takaki, Ronald, 2223-31
Talbert, Marc, 2232
Talmadge, Katherine, 2233-34
Tames, Richard, 2235
Tamura, David, illus., 407
Tanaka, Shelley, 2236-37
Tanenhaus, Sam, 2238
Taylor, Kimberly Hayes, 2239
Taylor, M. W., 2240
Taylor, Marian W., 2241-42
Taylor, Mildred, 2243-48
Taylor, Richard L., 2249-51
Taylor, Theodore, 2252-55
Tedards, Anne, 2256
Terris, Daniel, 965
Tessendorf, K. C., 2257
Thaxter, Celia, 2258
Thayer, Ernest Lawrence, 2259
Thesman, Jean, 2260-62
Thompson, Ellen, illus., 118
Thompson, John, illus., 1536
Thompson, Kathleen, 815-22
Thompson, Mary, illus., 1326
Thomson, Peggy, 2263
Time-Life, 2264
Tingum, Janice, 2265
Toht, David W., 2266
Tolan, Mary, 2267
Tomes, Margot, illus., 757, 772,
    786a, 1593, 2181
Tomlinson, Michael, 2268
Toor, Rachel, 2269
Topper, Frank, 2270
Towle, Wendy, 2271
Towne, Mary, 2272
Townsend, Tom, 2273
Toynton, Evelyn, 2274
Trimble, Stephen, 2275
Tripp, Valerie, 2276-78
Trivas, Irene, illus., 1486
Truesdell, Sue, illus., 361-63
Trump, Fred, 2279
Tunbo, Frances G., 2280
Tunnell, Michael O., 2281
Turkle, Brinton, illus., 1597

Turner, Ann, 2282-88
Turner, Glennette Tilley, 2289-90
Turner, Robyn Montana, 2291-93
Turvey, Peter, 2294
Twist, Clint, 2295
Uchida, Yoshiko, 2296-303
Unwin, Nora S., illus., 2496
Vagts, Detlev, 163
Vail, John, 2304
Van Der Linde, Laurel, 2305-2306
Van Leeuwen, Jean, 1347,
    2307-2308
Van Steenwyk, Elizabeth, 2309
Vare, Ethlie Ann, 2310
Veglahn, Nancy, 2311
Velasquez, Eric, illus., 756, 1114
Venezia, Mike, author/illus.,
    2312-16
Venti, Anthony Bacon, illus., 758
Ventura, Piero, author/illus.,
    2317-19
Vernon, Roland, 2320
Viola, Herman J., 2321-23
Vogt, Esther Loewen, 2324
Voight, Cynthia, 2325
Von Ahnen, Katherine, 2326-27
Von Schmidt, Eric, illus., 703, 706
Wade, Linda R., 2328-30
Wade, Mary Dodson, 2331
Wadsworth, Elaine, illus., 290
Wadsworth, Ginger, 1916, 2332-34
Walker, Lou Ann, 2335
Walker, Paul Robert, 2336-37,
    2347
Walker, Roger, illus., 507
Wallace, Bill, 2338
Wallner, Alexandra, author/illus.,
    20-22, 25, 27, 35, 39-40,
    2339-40
Wallner, John, illus., 20-22, 25, 27,
    33, 35, 39-40, 42
Walter, Mildred Pitts, 2341
Wangerin, Walter, Jr., 2342
Warburton, Lois, 2343-45
Ward, Geoffrey C., 2346-48
Ward, Helen, 1007
Ward, Lynd, illus., 711, 759, 763
Warner, J. F., 2349-50
Warren, Andrea, 2351
Warren, Scott,
    author/photographer, 2352
Waters, Kate, 2353-58
Watling, James, illus., 86, 213,
    119, 319, 710, 827, 981,
    1259, 1276, 1916, 2308
Weaver, Lydia, 2359-60
Weber, Judith Eichler, 2361
Weber, Michael, 2362
Weidt, Maryann, 2363-65

Weihs, Erika, illus., 381, 1222
Weiner, Eric, 2366-67
Weisberg, Barbara, 2368
Weisbrot, Robert, 2369-70
Weisman, JoAnne B., 577
Weitzman, David, 2371-73
Welch, Catherine A., 2374-75
Wells, Rosemary, 2376
Wentworth, Elaine, illus., 1684
Wesley, Valerie Wilson, 2377
West, Tracey, 2378-80
Westerfeld, Scott, 2381
Wetterer, Charles M., 2384
Wetterer, Margaret K., 2382-84
Wheeler, Jill, 2385-87
Wheeler, Leslie, 2388
Whelan, Gloria, 2389-94
Whipple, Rick, illus., 660, 816-17,
    819, 1036, 1038, 1285
Whitcraft, Melissa, 2395
White, Alana, 2396
White, Deborah Gray, 2397
White, Ruth, 2398-99
White, Tekla, 2400
Whitelaw, Nancy, 2401-2404
Whiteley, Opal, 2405
Whitman, Sylvia, 2406-2409
Whitmore, Arvella, 2410
Whittaker, Dorothy, 2411
Whittier, John Greenleaf, 2412
Wijngaard, Juan, illus., 1378
Wilder, Laura Ingalls, 2413-28
Wilkes, Maria D., 2429
Wilkie, Katherine E., 2430
Wilkinson, Philip, 2431-35
Williams, Brenda, 2437
Williams, Brian, 2436-37
Williams, David, 2438
Williams, Garth, illus., 2413,
    2417-18, 2420-24, 2427
Williams, Neva, 2439
Williams, Richard, illus., 1264
Williams, Victoria M., illus., 1480
Williamson, Ray A., 1599
Williges, Mel, illus., 1181
Willis, Patricia, 2440-41
Wills, Charles, 2270, 2442-50
Wilson, Anthony, 2451
Wilson, Claire, 282, 2452
Wilson, Janet, 844, 2453
Wilson, Kate, 2454
Wilson, Sharon, illus., 2377
Wimmer, Mike, illus., 354, 760
Winnick, Karen, author/illus., 2455
Winslow, Mimi, 2456
Winter, Jeanette, author/illus.,
    1831, 2457-60
Wisler, G. Clifton, 2461-68

Wisniewski, David, author/illus., 2469
Witcover, Paul, 2470
Wolfe, Charles K., 2471
Wolfe, Rinna Evelyn, 2472-73
Wolff, Glenn, illus., 564
Wood, Frances M., 2474
Wood, Gerald, illus., 1604
Wood, Leigh Hope, 2475-76
Wood, Marion, 2477
Woodruff, Elvira, 2478-79
Woodtor, Dee Parmer, 2480
Woodward, Martin, illus., 292
Woog, Adam, 2481-83
Wormser, Richard, 2484

Wray, Kit, illus., 2279
Wright, Courtni C., 2485-87
Wright, David K., 2488-89
Watson, Wendy, illus., 1736
Wunderli, Stephen, 2490
Wyman, Andrea, 2491
Yancey, Diane, 2492
Yannuzzi, Della, 2493-94
Yarbro, Chelsea Quinn, 2495
Yardley, Joanna, illus., 2297
Yates, Elizabeth, 2496
Yep, Laurence, 2497-99
Yepsen, Roger, 2500
Yolen, Jane, 2501-2
Young, Ed, illus., 762

Young, Ken, 2503
Young, Mary O'Keefe, illus., 1398, 2217, 2384
Young, Ronder Thomas, 2504
Yount, Lisa, 2505-6
Ypsilantis, George, 1497
Yuditskaya, Tatyana, illus., 145
Zallinger, Jean Day, illus., 1977
Zeinert, Karen, 2507-10
Zeldis, Malcah, illus., 1281
Ziesk, Edra, 2511
Zudeck, Darryl, illus., 495
Zullo, Allan, 1650

TITLE INDEX

Reference is to entry numbers.

A. Philip Randolph, 945

A. Philip Randolph and the Labor Movement, 540

Abe Lincoln Grows Up, 1943

Abe Lincoln's Hat, 306

The Abenaki, 1290

Abigail Adams: "Dear Partner," 1745

Abigail Adams: Women's Rights Advocate, 1692

Abigail's Drum, 1578

The Abracadabra Kid: A Writer's Life, 701

Abraham Lincoln, 336, 556, 2530

Abraham Lincoln: A Man for All the People: A Ballad, 1400

Abraham Lincoln: For the People, 484

Abraham Lincoln: Healing a Divided Nation, 206

Abraham Lincoln: President of a Divided Country, 865

Abraham Lincoln: 16th President of the United States, 2147

Abraham Lincoln: Sixteenth President of the United States, 950

Across America on an Emigrant Train, 1631

Across Five Aprils, 1079

Across the Lines, 1833

Across the Plains, 2531

Across the Plains in the Donner Party, 1637

Across the Wide Dark Sea: The Mayflower Journey, 2307

Adam and the Golden Cock, 548

Adam Clayton Powell, Jr., 1100

Addie Across the Prairie, 1319

Addie's Dakota Winter, 1320

Addie's Long Summer, 1321

Addy Saves the Day: A Summer Story, Book Five, 1778

Addy's Cook Book, 1765

Addy's Cook Book: A Peek at Dining in the Past with Meals You Can Cook Today, 664

Adventures Behind the Scenes: At the Newspaper, 2532

African-American Inventors, 1513

African American Life, 2533

African Americans, 2534

African Americans: Voices of Triumph: Leadership, 2264

African-Americans in the Thirteen Colonies, 1184

After the Dancing Days, 1905

Aftermath of War, 523

The Age of Discovery: From the Renaissance to American Independence, 2437

An Age of Extremes, 914

Agnes de Mille: Choreographer, 2107

Air and Space Smithsonian Dreams of Flight, 2512

Air Raid—Pearl Harbor: The Story of December 7, 1941, 2252

Airborne: The Search for the Secret of Flight, 1488

Aircraft, 1627

The Airman's War: World War II in the Sky, 1469

The Alamo, 2062

The Alaska Purchase, 446

An Album of War Refugees, 1250

Aldo Leopold: American Ecologist, 73

Aldo Leopold: Living with the Land, 631

Alexander Graham Bell, 1803

Alexander Graham Bell: Making Connections, 1710

Alexander Graham Bell: The Voice Heard Round the World, 2535

Alexander Hamilton, 1671

The Alger Hiss Trial, 1817

All Aboard for Philadelphia!, 2536

All for the Better: A Story of El Barrio, 1587

All the People, 915

All Those Secrets of the World, 2501

Allan Pinkerton, 851

Allen Jay and the Underground Railroad, 309

The Allies Against the Axis: World War II (1940-1950), 2172

Aloha Means Come Back: The Story of a World War II Girl, 1040

Along the Santa Fe Trail: Marion Russell's Own Story, 1916

Alvin Ailey, 1758

Alvin Ailey, Jr.: A Life in Dance, 1380

The Always Prayer Shawl, 1670

Always to Remember: The Story of the Vietnam Veteran's Memorial, 103

The Amazing Impossible Erie Canal, 958

The Amazing Life of Moe Berg: Catcher, Scholar, Spy, 82

Amelia Earhart, 1811, 2537

Amelia Earhart: Aviation Pioneer, 400

Amelia Earhart: Aviator, 2043

Amelia Earhart: Challenging the Skies, 2076

Amelia Earhart: Courage in the Sky, 1214

Amelia Earhart: 1897-1937, 2235

Amelia Earhart: Missing, Declared Dead, 1298

Amelia Earhart: Opposing Viewpoints, 1343

Amelia Earhart Flies Around the World, 563

America Alive: A History, 1159

America in World War I, 594

America in World War II: 1941, 595

America in World War II: 1942, 596

America in World War II: 1943, 597

America in World War II: 1944, 598

America in World War II: 1945, 599

America Prepares for War, 237

An American Army of Two, 891

American Astronomers: Searchers and Wonderers, 370

American Cinema: One Hundred Years of Filmmaking, 160

American Consumerism (1890-1930), 2539

American Dreams, 143

American Fever, 2540

The American Frontier, 151

American Heroes of Exploration and Flight, 2002

American History Explorer, 2512a

American Impressionists and Realists: In Search of the New, 2541
American Independence, 2542
The American Revolution, 2543
American Revolution: "Give Me Liberty, or Give Me Death!," 1185
The American Revolution: How We Fought the War of Independence, 600
American Too, 158
America's Early Canals, 1540
America's First Elephant, 1499
America's First Railroads, 1541
America's War of Independence: A Concise Illustrated History of the American Revolution, 1910
America's Westward Expansion, 2538
The Amish, 2544
Amish Home, 225
Amos Fortune, Free Man, 2496
The Anasazi, 127
Ancient America, 2477
The Ancient Cliff Dwellers of Mesa Verde, 99
An Ancient Heritage: The Arab-American Minority, 104
And Condors Danced, 2102
And Then What Happened, Paul Revere?, 757
Andrew Jackson, 2321
Andrew Jackson: Pioneer and President, 1708
Andrew Jackson: 7th President of the United States, 2148
Andrew Jackson: Seventh President of the United States, 1695
Andrew Johnson: Rebuilding the Union, 617
Andrew Johnson: 17th President of the United States, 2184
Andrew Johnson: Seventeenth President of the United States, 1192
Andrew Wyeth, 1564
Angel Child, Dragon Child, 2215
Angels of the Swamp, 2411
Anisett Lundberg: California, 1851, 621
Anna, Grandpa, and the Big Storm, 2181
Annabelle Swift, Kindergartner, 2012
Anne Hutchinson, 1084
Anne Is Elegant, 529
Anne Morrow Lindbergh: Pilot and Poet, 401
Annie Oakley, 815

Annie Oakley: The Shooting Star, 845
Annie's Promise, 1376
Anthony Burns: The Defeat and Triumph of a Fugitive Slave, 939
The Apache, 2545
The Apache Indians, 421
The Apaches: People of the Southwest, 708
Apollo Interactive: The Complete Insider's Guide, 2513
Apple Is My Sign, 1866
The Apprenticeship of Lucas Whitaker, 573
Arab Americans, 2546
Araminta's Paint Box, 12
Armstrong Lands on the Moon, 404
Around the World in a Hundred Years: From Henry the Navigator to Magellan, 758
Arthur Ashe: Breaking the Color Barrier in Tennis, 2488
Artist in Overalls: The Life of Grant Wood, 626
Artistic Trickery: The Tradition of the Trompe L'Oeil Art, 373
Artists Who Created Great Works, 535
As Far as Mill Springs, 1739
As Long as the Rivers Flow: The Stories of Nine Native Americans, 49
Asian Indian Americans, 135
The Assassination of a Candidate: Robert F. Kennedy, 937
The Assassination of a Leader: Martin Luther King, Jr., 938
The Assassination of Abraham Lincoln, 1103, 1685
The Assassination of John F. Kennedy, 2159
Atomic Dawn: A Biography of Robert Oppenheimer, 615
Aurora Means Dawn, 1944
Autumn of the Royal Tar, 2197
The Aztec Indians, 2035

Babe Didrikson Zaharias, 1423
Babe Ruth, 1437, 1960
Babe Ruth: Sultan of Swat, 1658
The Baby Grand, the Moon in July, and Me, 149
Balancing the Budget, 2547
The Ballad of Belle Dorcas, 1049
The Ballad of Lucy Whipple, 538
The Ballot Box Battle, 1501
Bandits & Outlaws, 1902
The Banjo Player, 1011
The Banshee Train, 275

Bar Mitzvah: A Jewish Boy's Coming of Age, 1222
Barbara Bush, 984
Barbara Frietchie, 2412
Barbara Jordan, 1720
Barbara Jordan: Politician, 269
Barbara McClintock, 1236
Barbara McClintock: Alone in Her Field, 983
Barefoot: Escape on the Underground Railroad, 649a
Barefoot Dancer: The Story of Isadora Duncan, 1673
The Barn, 113
The Baseball Hall of Shame: Young Fans Edition, 1650
Baseball Saved Us, 1584
Bat Masterson, 852
Bataan and Corregidor, 238
The Battle of Chancellorsville, 1193
The Battle of Gettysburg, 384, 513, 1118
The Battle of Lexington and Concord, 1119
The Battle of Little Bighorn, 2442
The Battle of Shiloh, 1194
Battle of the Atlantic, 239
Battle of the Bulge, 240
The Battle of the Little Bighorn in American History, 678
Battles That Changed the Modern World, 63
Be Ever Hopeful, 164
Be Seated: A Book About Chairs, 799
Beacons of Light: Lighthouses, 797
Beautiful Land: A Story of the Oklahoma Land Rush, 85
Becoming a Citizen: Adopting a New Home, 299
Becoming Rosemary, 2474
Before the Wildflowers Bloom, 364
Before the Wright Brothers, 214
The Beginning of Writing, 2343
Beginnings, 2548
Behave Yourself, Bethany Brant, 165
Behind the Lines, 1027
Belle Prater's Boy, 2398
Belle Starr, 853
Belles of the Ballpark, 985
The Bells of Christmas, 940
Belva Lockwood Wins Her Case, 319
Ben and Me, 1333
Ben Carson, 2063
Benedict Arnold, 2331
Benjamin Banneker: Scientist and Mathematician, 486
Benjamin Davis, Jr., 1837
Benjamin Franklin, 557, 1407, 1781, 2191

Benjamin Franklin: A Man with Many Jobs, 866
Benjamin Franklin: Printer, Inventor, Statesman, 14
Benjamin Franklin: Scientist and Inventor, 677
Benjamin Franklin and Electricity, 1703
Benjamin Franklin and His Friends, 1798
Benjamin Harrison: 23rd President of the United States, 2185
Benjamin Harrison: Twenty-Third President of the United States, 434
Benjamin O. Davis, Jr., and Colin L. Powell: The Story of Two American Generals, 91
The Berlin Airlift, 2381
Bernardo de Gálvez, 571
Bernardo de Gálvez: Hero of the American Revolution, 1288
Bess's Log Cabin Quilt, 1413
The Best Bad Thing, 2296
The Bet's On, Lizzie Bingman!, 1900
Betsy Ross, 2339
Better than a Brother, 1494
Betty Friedan: A Voice for Women's Rights, 1559
Betty Friedan: Feminist, 263
Betty Friedan: Fighter for Women's Rights, 989
Beyond the Burning Time, 1301
Beyond the Western Sea, Book Two: Lord Kirkle's Money, 114
Big Annie of Calumet: A True Story of the Industrial Revolution, 2127
The Big Book of America, 1007
The Big Book of U.S. Presidents, 2036
Big Meeting, 2480
Bigger, 367
Bigmama's, 519
Bill Peet: An Autobiography, 1734
Bill Pickett: African-American Rodeo Star, 1961
Bill Pickett: Rodeo-Ridin' Cowboy, 1759
Billie Holiday: Singer, 1241
Billy Bedamned, Long Gone By, 166
Billy the Kid, 849
Birdie's Lighthouse, 1056
Birds in the Bushes: A Story About Margaret Morse Nice, 632
Birth Customs, 1914
Birth of a Community: Jews and the Gold Rush, 2549
The Birth of Black America: The Age of Discovery and the Slave Trade, 738

A Birthday for Blue, 1422
Bismarck!, 2075
The Bittersweet Time, 620
Black Abolitionists and Freedom Fighters, 2239
The Black Americans: A History in Their Own Words, 1560
Black Artists in Photography, 1840-1940, 2207
Black Diamond: The Story of the Negro Baseball Leagues, 1538
Black Eagles: African Americans in Aviation, 977
Black Elk: A Man with a Vision, 867
Black Fighting Men: A Proud History, 1838
Black Hawk: Sac Rebel, 283
Black Is My Color: The African American Experience, 2550
Black Scientists, 2505
Black Stars in Orbit: NASA's African American Astronauts, 357
The Black West, 2551
Black Women Leaders of the Civil Rights Movement, 50
Black Women of the Old West, 1167
Black-Eyed Susan, 94
The Blackfoot, 910
Blind Tom, 2552
The Blizzard of 1896, 232
Bloomers!, 273
The Blue and the Gray, 345
The Blue Between the Clouds, 2490
Blue Skin of the Sea, 1923
Blue Stars Watching, 167
Bluewater Journal: The Voyage of the Sea Tiger, 1273
The Bobbin Girl, 1502
Bonanza Girl, 168
Bonjour, Lonnie, 1864
Book of Firsts: Leaders of America, 1848
Book of the American Indians, 2087
Book of the American Revolution, 651
Booker T. Washington, 816
Booker T. Washington: Educator and Racial Spokesman, 2003
Booker T. Washington: Leader and Educator, 1514
Booker T. Washington: Leader of His People, 1722
The Borning Room, 695
Borrowed Children, 1424
The Boston Coffee Party, 1818
The Boston Tea Party, 1681
Bound for Oregon, 2308
Bound for the Promised Land: The Great Black Migration, 502

A Boy Called Slow: The True Story of Sitting Bull, 334
The Boys' War: Confederate and Union Soldiers Talk About the Civil War, 1632
The Bracelet, 2297
Brady, 759
The Bravest Dog Ever: The True Story of Balto, 2124
The Bread Winner, 2410
Breaking Free: An Anthology of Human Rights Poetry, 1076
Breaking the Chains: African-American Slave Resistance, 1168
A Bride for Anna's Papa, 1484
Brides, Midwives, and Widows, 208
Bridger: The Story of a Mountain Man, 1221
Brigham Young: Pioneer and Mormon Leader, 1962
Bright Eyes: Susette La Flesche Tibbles, 2553
Brooklyn Dodger Days, 1895
Brooklyn Doesn't Rhyme, 267
Brothers of the Heart: A Story of the Old Northwest, 1837-38, 264
Brown v. Board of Education: Equal Schooling for All, 687
Brushy Mountain, 1740
The Buck Stops Here: The Presidents of the United States, 1794
Buckminster Fuller, 1782
Buffalo Bill and the Pony Express, 444
Buffalo Bill Cody: Showman of the Wild West, 1963
Buffalo Gal, 2338
Buffalo Gals: Women of the Old West, 1570
Buffalo Hunt, 744
The Buffalo Jump, 1883
The Buffalo Knife, 2134
Buffalo Soldiers: The Story of Emanuel Stance, 1572
Buffalo Sunrise: The Story of a North American Giant, 2218
Building, 2431
Building a Dream: Mary Bethune's School, 1180
Bull Run, 696
Bull Whackers to Whistle Punks: Logging in the Old West, 1652
Bully for You, Teddy Roosevelt, 760
Business Leaders Who Built Financial Empires, 1489
But No Candy, 1060a
Butch Cassidy, 854
By Crumbs, It's Mine!, 169

By the Dawn's Early Light: The Story of the Star-Spangled Banner, 1262
By the Shores of Silver Lake, 2413

Cabin, 102, 783
The Cabin Faced West, 761
The Cabin Key, 1808
Caddie Woodlawn, 313
Calamity Jane: A Frontier Original, 1964
Calamity Jane: Her Life and Her Legend, 666
Caleb's Choice, 2461
Calico Bush, 685
The California Gold Rush: West with the Forty-Niners, 2309
Call Me Ahnighito, 493
Call Me Francis Tucket, 1725
Calvin Coolidge, 1195
Calvin Coolidge: 30th President of the United States, 2186
The Camel Express, 2030
Campaigns, Candidates and the Presidency, 2514
The Canada Geese Quilt, 1226
Candlemaking, 2554
Canyons Beyond the Sky, 1235
Capital for the Nation, 1025
Captain Grey, 115
The Captive, 946
Capturing Nature: The Writings and Art of John James Audubon, 1884
Carry On, Mr. Bowditch, 1305
Carter G. Woodson: The Father of Black History, 1515
Casey at the Bat, 2259
Casey over There, 1805
Cassie's Journey: Going West in the 1860s, 968
Cat Running, 2103
Catastrophe!: Great Engineering Failure—and Success, 286
Caught in the Act: The Orphan Quartet Two, 1663
Causes of Revolt, 2555
Causes of the Civil War, 2556
The Cave, 1160
Cave Under the City, 1492
The Cay, 2253
The Cayuga, 637
Cecil's Story, 1425
Celia's Island Journey, 2258
The Cellar, 1066
Censorship, 2131
Cesar Chavez, 1879
Cesar Chavez: Farm Worker Activist, 1031
Cesar Chavez: Labor Leader, 399

Cesar Chavez: Leader for Migrant Farm Workers, 833
Cesar Chavez: Union Leader, 491
Cezanne Pinto: A Memoir, 2196
The Challenger, 229
Champion for Children's Health: A Story About Dr. S. Josephine Baker, 1797
Changes for Kirsten, 2031
Changes for Molly, 2276
Changes for Samantha, 2277
Chang's Paper Pony, 444a
Charles Ball and American Slavery, 2055
Charles Eastman: Physician, Reformer, Native American Leader, 74
Charles Eastman: Sioux Physician and Author, 131
Charles Garry: Street Fighter in the Courtroom, 2557
Charles Goodnight: Pioneer Cowman, 1691
Charles Lindbergh, 1812
Charles Lindbergh: Hero Pilot, 465
Charles R. Drew, 1457
Charles Richard Drew, M.D., 2472
Charley Skedaddle, 170
Charlie Parker: Musician, 739
Charlie Young Bear, 2326
Charlotte Forten: A Black Teacher in the Civil War, 350
The Cherokee, 2558
The Cherokee Indians, 422
The Cherokees, 2094
The Cherokees: People of the Southeast, 1418
Chester A. Arthur: 21st President of the United States, 2187
Chester A. Arthur: Twenty-First President of the United States, 317
The Cheyenne, 1404, 2559
The Cheyennes, 2095
The Chicago Fire, 2344
The Chickenhouse House, 1067
Chief Gall: Sioux War Chief, 2050
Chief Joseph: Nez Percé Leader, 2241
Chief Joseph: Nez Percé Warrior, 1953
Chief Joseph and the Nez Percés, 2022
Chief Joseph of the Nez Perce Indians: Champion of Liberty, 719
Chief Sarah: Sarah Winnemucca's Fight for Indian Rights, 1616
Child Labor: Then and Now, 887
Child Star: When Talkies Came to Hollywood, 2359

Children and War, 524
Children of Flight Pedro Pan, 11
Children of Promise: African-American Literature and Art for Young People, 2206
Children of the Dust Bowl: The True Story of the School at Weedpatch Camp, 2128
Children of the Fire, 1873
Children of the Longhouse, 335
Children of the Westward Trail, 2149
The Children of Topaz: The Story of a Japanese-American Internment Camp Based on a Classroom Diary, 2281
Children's Atlas of the United States, 2515
Children's Clothing of the 1800s, 1128
A Child's Day, 1157
Chimney Sweeps: Yesterday and Today, 801
The Chinese American Family Album, 1041
Chinese Americans, 136
The Chinese Americans, 547
Chinese New Year, 1445
Chinese Railroad Workers, 2066
The Chinook, 2560
Chita's Christmas Tree, 1064
Chocolate by Hershey: A Story About Milton S. Hershey, 351
Choosing a President, 2561
Christmas, 2562
Christmas in the Big House, Christmas in the Quarters, 1536
Christmas in the Big Woods, 2414
Christmas on the Prairie, 65
The Christmas Tree Ship, 2457
Christopher Columbus, 817, 2563
Chuck Yeager: Fighter Pilot, 128
Chuck Yeager: The Man Who Broke the Sound Barrier, 1368
The Chumash, 638
Circle of Fire, 1050
Circle of Love, 1664
A Circle Unbroken, 1059
The Circus Comes Home: When the Greatest Show on Earth Rode the Rails, 630
Cities in the Sand: The Ancient Civilizations of the Southwest, 2352
City! New York, 430
City! San Francisco, 431
City Trains: Moving Through America's Cities by Rail, 2500

City! Washington, DC, 432
The Civil War, 230, 2366
Civil Rights: The Long Struggle, 1419
Civil Rights Leaders, 1849
Clara and the Bookwagon, 1369
Clara and the Hoodoo Man, 1709
Clara Barton, 936
Clara Barton: Healing the Wounds, 618
Clara Barton: Soldier of Mercy, 1890
Clarence Darrow, 616
A Clearing in the Forest, 987
Clippers and Whaling Ships, 1542
The Clock, 462
Close Calls: From the Brink of Ruin to Business Success, 1
Close to Home: A Story of the Polio Epidemic, 2360
Clothes: For Work, Play and Display, 1604
Clothing, 2317
Clouds of Terror, 2374
Clyde Tombaugh and the Search for Planet X, 2382
The Coach That Never Came, 171
Coal Mine Peaches, 591
Coast to Coast with Alice, 1083
Cochise, Apache Chief, 2014
Colonial American Craftspeople, 2179
Colonial American Homelife, 2350
Colonial Crafts, 1129
Colonial Holidays and Entertainment, 1402
Colonial Life, 1130
Colonial People, 1072
Colonial Places, 1073
A Colonial Town: Williamsburg, 1131
The Colonial Wars: Clashes in the Wilderness, 385
Colonial Williamsburg, 2145
Colonization and Settlement (1585-1763), 2564
Columbus Day, 1382, 2565
The Comanche, 1405, 2566
The Comanche Indians, 1600
Come Away with Me, 1322
Come Morning, 903
Come Next Spring, 2396
Come This Far to Freedom: A History of African Americans, 1554
Coming-and-Going Men, 697
Coming Home: From the Life of Langston Hughes, 501
Coming Out Right: The Story of Jacqueline Cochran, the First Woman Aviator to Break the Sound Barrier, 2086

Coming to America: The Story of Immigration, 1450
Concord and Lexington, 1667
Conestogas and Stagecoaches, 1543
Conflict in Europe and the Great Depression: World War I (1914-1940), 324
The Congress: America's Lawmakers, 2178
The Connecticut Colony, 722
The Conquest of Everest, 1893
The Conspiracy of the Secret Nine, 257
The Cookcamp, 1726
Coretta Scott King, 1716
Coretta Scott King: Keeper of the Dream, 990
Costume, 1909
Count Basie: Bandleader and Musician, 1242
Countdown to Independence: Causes of the American Revolution, 2567
Courageous Crimefighters, 1088
The Court of the Stone Children, 369
The Covered Wagon and Other Adventures, 2020
Cowboy, 1239, 1629
Cowboy: An Album, 843
Cowboy Charlie: The Story of Charles M. Russell, 2458
Cowboys, 808, 1291
Cowboys and Cow Towns of the Wild West, 1979
Cowboys in the Old West, 2192
Cowboys, Indians and Gunfighters: The Story of the Cattle Kingdom, 1470
Cowboys of the Sky: The Story of Alaska's Bush Pilots, 1363
Cowboys of the Wild West, 745
The Crash of 1929, 1569
Crazy Horse: Sioux War Chief, 906
Crazy Horse: Sioux Warrior, 1954
Crazy Horse: War Chief of the Oglala Sioux, 831
The Creek, 2568
Cross of Gold, 1033
The Crow, 2569
The Crow Indians, 2475
The Crying for a Vision, 2342
Cubans in America, 1563
The Cuckoo's Child, 754
Customs and Traditions, 1158
Cutlass in the Snow, 2048
Cy Young Award Winners, 2503
The Czech Americans, 1987

D-Day, 241
Daisy and the Girl Scouts: The Story of Juliette Gordon Low, 321
Dakota Dugout, 2282
The Dalton Gang, 855
Dame Shirley and the Gold Rush, 1826
Dance at Grandpa's, 2415
The Dancing Tree, 1898
Dandelions, 346
Danger at the Breaker, 2375
A Dangerous Promise, 1665
The Dangerous Voyage, 1608
Daniel Boone, 1323
Daniel Boone: Frontier Hero, 1815
Daniel Boone: Man of the Forests, 868
Daniel Boone: Taming the Wilds, 2430
Daniel Boone: Wilderness Pioneer, 1965
Daniel Boone and the Opening of the Ohio Country, 396
Daniel "Chappie" James, 2213
Dare to Dream: Coretta Scott King and the Civil Rights Movement, 1555
Daring to Fly! From Icarus to the Red Baron, 2516
Dark Harvest: Migrant Farmworkers in America, 105
David Bushnell and His Turtle: The Story of America's First Submarine, 2220
David Farragut, 408
David Farragut and the Great Naval Blockade, 2044
David Glasgow Farragut: Courageous Navy Commander, 717
David Glasgow Farragut: Our First Admiral, 1306
Davy Crockett: Defender of the Alamo, 1966
Davy Crockett: Hero of the Wild Frontier, 1622
Davy Crockett: The Legendary Frontiersman, 1282
The Day It Rained Forever, 902
Day of Darkness, Night of Light, 1480
Day of the Dead: A Mexican-American, 1074
The Day That Elvis Came to Town, 1462
Days of Courage: The Little Rock Story, 1181
Days of Sorrow; Years of Glory: 1831-1850: From the Nat Turner Revolt to the Fugitive Slave Law, 1732

Dear Benjamin Banneker, 1760
Dear Dad, 1034
Dear Dr. Bell . . . Your Friend,
    Helen Keller, 2113
"Dear Friend": Thomas Garrett and
    William Still, Collaborators
    on the Underground
    Railroad, 209
Dear Levi: Letters from the
    Overland Trail, 2478
Dearest Grandmama, 308
Death Customs, 1915
The Declaration of Independence,
    2160
Deep Blues: Bill Traylor,
    Self-Taught Artist, 1428
Deep-Sea Explorer: The Story of
    Robert Ballard, Discoverer
    of the Titanic, 92
The Deer in the Woods, 2416
The Delaware Colony, 723
Democracy and Race: Asian
    Americans and World War
    II, 2223
Democracy and Reform, 2570
Denmark Vesey: Slave Revolt
    Leader, 649
Desert Warfare, 242
Desperadoes and Dynamite: Train
    Robbery in the United
    States, 2492
Devil in Salem Village, 2305
Devil Storm, 1653
DinnieAbbieSister-r-r!, 1373
The Disaster of the Hindenburg:
    The Last Flight of the Greatest
    Airship Ever Built, 2236
Disasters That Shook the World, 536
Discover America's Favorite
    Architects, 823
Discovering Christopher Columbus:
    How History, 1737
Discovery and Settlement: Europe
    Meets the "New World,"
    1490-1700, 325
The Discovery of the Americas,
    1451, 2571
Distant Thunder, 1601
Dive Through the Wave, 2272
Dixie in the Big Pasture, 1081
Dizzy Gillespie: Musician, 790
Dizzy Gillespie and the Birth of
    Bebop, 838
Doc Holliday, 856
A Dog Came, Too, 1461
Dolley Madison, 1804
Dolly Madison: Famous First
    Lady, 560
Dolphin Sky, 1888
Dominican Americans, 137

Door of No Return: The Legend of
    Gorée Island, 148
Dorothea L. Dix: Hospital
    Founder, 1458
Dorothea Lange, 2291
Dorothea Lange: Life Through the
    Camera, 1561
Dorothy Day: Friend to the
    Forgotten, 1186
Dotty's Suitcase, 885
The Double Life of Pocahontas, 762
Douglas MacArthur, 552
Down Home at Miss Dessa's, 2204
Down in the Piney Woods, 2089
Dr. Samuel A. Mudd and the
    Lincoln Assassination, 1509
Dr. Susan La Flesche Picotte: Our
    Nation's First Woman Indian
    Doctor, 2572
Dragon's Gate, 2497
The Dream Jar, 1796
Dreamland, 1998
The Dreams of Mairhe Mehan: A
    Novel of the Civil War, 95
The Dred Scott Case: Slavery and
    Citizenship, 992
The Drinking Gourd, 1589
The Drum, the Doll, and the
    Zombie, 195
Drumbeat . . . Heartbeat: A
    Celebration of the Powwow,
    295
The Drummer of Vicksburg, 2462
Drums at Saratoga, 144
Drylongso, 941
Duke Ellington, 458, 2481
The Dust Bowl, 676
The Dust Bowl: Disaster in the
    Plains, 83
Dust for Dinner, 2283
Dust of the Earth, 423
Dwight D., 553
Dwight D. Eisenhower, 1942
Dwight D. Eisenhower: Man of
    Many Hats, 577
Dwight D. Eisenhower: 34th
    President of the United
    States, 655
Dwight D. Eisenhower:
    Thirty-Fourth President of
    the United States, 951
Dwight D. Eisenhower, John F.
    Kennedy, Lyndon B.
    Johnson, 1390
Dwight David Eisenhower:
    Soldier and Statesman, 1092

E. B. White: Some Writer!, 796
E. B. White: The Elements of a
    Writer, 2265
The Earliest Americans, 1977

Early Artisans, 1132
Early Christmas, 1133
Early City Life, 1134
The Early Colonists, 2573
The Early Family Home, 1135
Early Farm Life, 1136
Early Health and Medicine, 1137
Early Immigration in the United
    States, 665
Early Loggers and the Sawmill, 1138
Early Pleasures and Pastimes, 1139
Early River Travel, 1544
Early Schools, 1140
Early Settler Storybook, 1141
Early Settlers, 2574
Early Stores and Markets, 1142
Early Thunder, 763
Early Travel, 1143
Early Village Life, 1144
Earthquake! A Story of Old San
    Francisco, 1274
Earthquake at Dawn, 892
Earthquake! San Francisco, 1906,
    2454
East Side Story, 129
Eastern Europe, 1490
Eben Tyne, Powdermonkey, 190
Echohawk, 635
Edith Herself, 1068
Edith Wilson: The Woman Who
    Ran the United States, 802
Edward Hopper, 2312
Edward's Portrait, 1617
Eight Mules from Monterey, 172
1812: The War Nobody Won, 1471
18th Century Clothing, 1145
The Eighties, 898
Eighty-Eight Steps to September,
    1463
The Eisenhowers, 1927
El Chino, 1988
Eleanor, 498
Eleanor Roosevelt, 1336, 2269
Eleanor Roosevelt: A Life of
    Discovery, 746
Eleanor Roosevelt: First Lady and
    Humanitarian, 2009
Eleanor Roosevelt: First Lady of
    the World, 667
The Elephant in the Dark, 379
Eli Whitney, 53, 1307
Elie Wiesel: Voice from the
    Holocaust, 2010
Elijah Muhammad, 2575
Elijah Muhammad: Religious
    Leader, 925
Elizabeth Blackwell: Girl Doctor,
    988
Elizabeth Blackwell: Physician, 329
Elizabeth Blackwell: Pioneer
    Woman Doctor, 1308

Elizabeth Cady Stanton and Susan B. Anthony, 2576
Elizabeth Cady Stanton and Women's Liberty, 528
Elizabeth Van Lew: Southern Belle, Union Spy, 2507
Ella Baker: A Leader Behind the Scenes, 550
Ella Fitzgerald: Singer, 1243
Ellis Island, 1839, 2161
Ellis Island: Doorway to Freedom, 1263
Ellis Island: Gateway to the New World, 688
Ellis Island: New Hope in a New Land, 1093
An Ellis Island Christmas, 1351
Elvis, 1406
Elvis Presley: The King, 1261
Emily, 192
Emily Dickinson, 220
Emily Dickinson: American Poet, 869
Emily Dickinson: Poet, 1682
Emily Upham's Revenge, 116
Emma Eileen Grove: Mississippi, 1865, 622
Emma Lazarus, 1348
Empires Lost and Won: The Spanish Heritage in the Southwest, 1472
Encounter at Easton, 117
An Enemy Among Them, 576
Engel v. Vitale: Separation of Church and State, 908
Epidemic, 1289
Equal Rights for All, 2577
The Era of Segregation: A Personal Perspective, 2578
The Erie Canal, 592
Erie Canal: Gateway to the West, 1661
Ernestine and Amanda, 197
Escape from Slavery: Five Journeys to Freedom, 1819
Escape from Slavery: The Boyhood of Frederick Douglass in His Own Words, 614
Estevanico and the Seven Cities of Gold, 2579
Ethnic Islands: The Emergence of Urban Chinese America, 2224
Events That Changed American History, 2388
Everyone Wears His Name: A Biography of Levi Strauss, 991
Expansionism, 2580
Exploration and Conquest: The Americas After Columbus: 1500-1620, 1452

Explorers and Mapmakers, 1920
Explorers, Trappers, and Guides, 210
Explorers Who Found New Worlds, 64
Exploring North America, 1605
Exploring the Titanic, 134, 2517
Extraordinary Asian Pacific Americans, 2067
Extraordinary Black Americans: From Colonial to Contemporary Times, 57
Extremist Groups in America, 1296
Eye on the Wild: A Story About Ansel Adams, 633
Eyes of Darkness, 1009
Eyewitness Encyclopedia of Science, 2518

Facing West: A Story of the Oregon Trail, 1276
A Family Apart, 1662
Family Life: Multiculturalism, 2581
Famous Firsts of Black Women, 1768
Fannie Lou Hamer: From Sharecropping to Politics, 1911
Fannie Lou Hamer and the Fight for the Vote, 476
Farewell, John Barleycorn: Prohibition in the United States, 1021
Farmer Boy, 2417
Farm Boy's Year, 1547
The Farm Summer 1942, 927
The Farmer Through History, 409
Farmers and Ranchers, 969
Farmworker's Friend: The Story of Cesar Chavez, 466
Father Divine: Religious Leader, 2369
Father Junípero Serra: Founder of California Missions, 789
The FDR Way, 1609
Female Writers, 1850
A Fence Away from Freedom: Japanese Americans and World War II, 1366
The Fighting Ground, 118
Filipino Americans, 138
The Final Steps, 2582
The Final Tide, 452
Finding Papa, 1359
Finding Providence: The Story of Roger Williams, 119
Fire at the Triangle Factory, 1398
A Fire in Her Bones: The Story of Mary Lyon, 1891
Fire in the Valley, 2378
Fire in the Wind, 1364

Fire on the Wind, 518
Fire! The Beginnings of the Labor Movement, 827
Firetalking, 1769
The First Air Voyage in the United States: The Story of Jean-Pierre Blanchard, 2340
The First Americans, 916
First Children: Growing Up in the White House, 1352
First Facts About American Heroes, 1223
First Facts About the Presidents, 1711
First Farm in the Valley: Anna's Story, 1736
The First Flight: The Story of the Wright Brothers, 2249
First Flight: The Story of Tom Tate and the Wright Brothers, 2032
The First Flight Across the United States: The Story of Calbraith Perry Rodgers and His Airplane, the Vin Fiz, 2250
The First Four Years, 2418
First Houses: Native American Homes and Sacred Structures, 1599
The First Ride: Blazing the Trail for the Pony Express, 788
The First Solo Flight Around the World: The Story of Wiley Post and His Airplane, the Winnie Mae, 2251
The First Thanksgiving, 793, 981, 2583
The First Thanksgiving Feast, 66
The First Transatlantic Flight, 1894
First World War, 420
Fitchett's Folly, 1878
A Flag for Our Country, 2111
The Flag of the United States, 721
Flaming Arrows, 2135
Flattops at War, 243
Flight: The Journey of Charles Lindbergh, 354
The Flight of the Red Bird, 1820
Floating Illusions, 2495
Florence Sabin: Medical Researcher, 1267
Fly! A Brief History of Flight Illustrated, 1623
Flying Free: America's First Black Aviators, 966
Follow the Drinking Gourd, 2459, 2584
Following My Own Footsteps, 911
Food: Its Evolution Through the Ages, 2318
Food and Fasting, 352
Food for the Settler, 1146

The Foot Warmer and the Crow, 453
For Bread—1893, 1035
For Home and Country: A Civil War Scrapbook, 281
For the Love of Pete, 1464
Forbidden Friendship, 2361
Forest Diplomat: The Story of Hiawatha, 2385
Forest Warrior: The Story of Pontiac, 2386
The Forgotten Players: The Story of Black Baseball in America, 780
Fort Life, 1156
Fort McHenry: Preserving the Spirit of Liberty, 2585
Forts and Castles, 1624, 2436
1492: The Year of the New World, 2319
A Fourth of July on the Plains, 1347
Francis Scott Key, 2395
Francis Scott Key: Poet and Patriot, 1723
Frank Lloyd Wright: Maverick Architect, 565
Frank Thompson: Her Civil War Story, 2180
Franklin D. Roosevelt: 32nd President of the United States, 863
Franklin Delano Roosevelt, 747, 1087
Franklin Delano Roosevelt: President, 583
Franklin Pierce, 2064
Franklin Pierce: 14th President of the United States, 322
The Franklin Roosevelts, 1928
Frederick Douglass, 1215
Frederick Douglass: Abolitionist Editor, 1917
Frederick Douglass: Leader Against Slavery, 1516
Frederick Douglass: The Black Lion, 1517
Frederick Douglass: The Last Day of Slavery, 1574
Frederick Douglass: Voice of Freedom, 1996
Frederick Douglass: Voice of Liberty, 147
Frederick Douglass and the War Against Slavery, 205
Free to Dream: The Making of a Poet, Langston Hughes, 1696
Freedom in Diversity, 2586
The Freedom Riders, 1187
Freedom Rides: Journey for Justice, 974
Freedom's Fruit, 1051

Freedom's Gifts, 2377
Frida María: A Story of the Old Southwest, 1313
Friends Forever, 402
The Friendship, 2243
From Colonies to Country, 917
From East to West: The Asian-American Experience, 2587
From Rags to Riches: People Who Started Businesses from Scratch, 2
From Slave to Civil War Hero: The Life and Times of Robert Smalls, 503
From the Ashes, 191
From the Land of Morning Calm: The Koreans in America, 2225
From Top Hats to Baseball Caps, from Bustles to Blue Jeans: Why We Dress the Way We Do, 1742
From Trails to Turnpikes, 1545
Frontier Buildings, 2588
A Frontier Fort on the Oregon Trail, 2130
Frontier Forts and the American Indian Wars in Texas, 2589
Frontier Home, 226
Frontier Life, 1867
Frontier Surgeons: A Story About the Mayo Brothers, 520
Full Worm Moon, 1355
Funny Papers: Behind the Scenes of the Comics, 2018
Furman v. Georgia: The Death Penalty Case, 993

Games from Long Ago, 1147
Gaps in Stone Walls, 1655
A Gathering of Days: A New England Girl's Journal, 1830-32, 265
Generals Who Changed the World, 2434
Genetics: Unlocking the Secrets of Life, 3
Gentle Annie: The True Story of a Civil War Nurse, 2052
The Gentleman Outlaw and Me—Eli: A Story of the Old West, 912
George Bush, 1738, 2208
George Bush: Forty-First President of the United States, 1196
George Catlin: Painter of the Indian West, 2205
George Catlin: The Man Who Painted Indians, 1761
George Gershwin, 2313

George Goethals: Panama Canal Engineer, 1309
George H. W. Bush: 41st President of the United States, 2150
George Marshall, 1417
George on His Own, 1324
George Washington, 337, 558
George Washington: A Picture Book Biography, 803
George Washington: Father of Our Country, 15
George Washington: Leader of a New Nation, 1693
George Washington Carver, 450, 848, 1659
George Washington Carver: A Man of Vision, 2590
George Washington Carver: Nature's Trailblazer, 1881
George Washington Carver: Scientist and Teacher, 870
George Washington Carver: The Peanut Scientist, 1518
George Washington, First President of the United States, 871
George Washington, Thomas Jefferson, Andrew Jackson, 1391
George Washington's Ghost, 328
George Washington's Mother, 764
George Washington's Socks, 2479
The Georgia Colony, 724
Georgia O'Keeffe, 2292, 2314
Georgia O'Keeffe: An Adventurous Spirit, 314
Georgia O'Keeffe: Painter, 219
Gerald R. Ford: 38th President of the United States, 467
Gerald Ford: Thirty-Eighth President of the United States, 2069
German Americans, 2591
Geronimo, 1108, 1197
Geronimo: Apache Warrior, 1955, 2015
Geronimo and the Struggle for Apache Freedom, 2045
Get Inside Baseball, 51
Get Up and Go: The History of American Road Travel, 2406
Getting the Real Story: Nellie Bly and Ida B. Wells, 561
Gettysburg, 1840, 2592
Gettysburg: Tad Lincoln's Story, 1590
The Gettysburg Address, 1387, 1854
The Ghost Cadet, 52
The Ghost Flyers, 2273
The Ghost in the Noonday Sun, 702
The Ghost of Elvis: And Other Celebrity Spirits, 447

The Ghosts of War, 448
Giants in the Land, 90
Gideon and the Mummy Professor, 1161
Gifford Pinchot: American Forester, 75
A Girl Called Boy, 1082
Glorious Days, Dreadful Days: The Battle of Bunker Hill, 1231
Go Free or Die, 680
Go West, Young Women!, 1162
Going Home to Nicodemus: The Story of an African American Frontier Town and the Pioneers Who Settled It, 416
Going to Town, 2419
Gold: The True Story of Why People Search for It, Mine It, Trade It, Steal It, Mint It, Hoard It, 1562
The Gold Cadillac, 2244
Gold in the Hills, 1325
Gold Miners of the Wild West, 1980
The Gold Rush, 1219
The Gold Rush of 1849: Staking a Claim in California, 254
Gold Star Sister, 1630
Golden Quest, 130
The Golly Sisters Go West, 361
The Golly Sisters Ride Again, 362
Good-Bye, Billy Radish, 2072
Gordon Parks, 222
Grace Hopper: Programming Pioneer, 2401
Grand Papa and Ellen Aroon, 1591
Grandfather's Journey, 1989
Grandma Essie's Covered Wagon, 2438
Grandma Moses: Painter of Rural America, 1687
Grandmother Bryant's Pocket, 1481
Grandpa Jake and the Grand Christmas, 59
Grandpa Was a Cowboy, 2212
Grandpa's Mountain, 1834
Grasshopper Summer, 2284
Graven Images, 698
The Great American Elephant Chase, 522
Great Black Innovators, 2593
The Great Depression, 2158
The Great Depression and the New Deal, 2594
The Great Fire, 1633
Great-Grandma Tells of Threshing Day, 527
The Great Little Madison, 765
Great Lives, 1095
Great Lives: American Government, 668
Great Lives: Human Culture, 2371

Great Lives: Human Rights, 1094
Great Lives: Painting, 824
The Great Migration, 1330
The Great St. Lawrence Seaway, 798
Greek Americans, 2595
The Grist Mill, 1148
Groundhog's Horse, 1877
Grover Cleveland: 22nd and 24th President of the United States, 468
Grover Cleveland: Twenty-Second and Twenty-Fourth President of the United States, 1198
Growing Up in America, 2274
Growing Up in Coal Country, 157
Growing Up in the Old West, 54
Guadalcanal, 244
The Gulf War, 1224
Gunfighters of the Wild West, 1981
Guns for General Washington: A Story of the American Revolution, 1847

The Haidas: People of the Northwest Coast, 284
Hail Columbia, 173
Halsey's Pride, 932
Hand, Heart, and Mind: The Story of the Education of America's Deaf People, 2335
Hand in Hand: An American History Through Poetry, 1053
The Hand of the Necromancer, 2203
Hang Out the Flag, 1468
Hank Greenberg: Hall-of-Fame Slugger, 211
Hannah, 2389
The Happiest Ending, 2298
Happy Birthday Addy! A Springtime Story, Book Four, 1779
Happy Birthday, Martin Luther King, 1485
The Happy Yellow Car, 1058
Hard Times: A Story of the Great Depression, 86
The Harlem Renaissance, 975
Harper & Moon, 1899
Harpers Ferry: The Story of John Brown's Raid, 154
Harriet: The Life and World of Harriet Beecher Stowe, 1121
Harriet and the Promised Land, 1331
Harriet Beecher Stowe, 1104
Harriet Beecher Stowe: Antislavery Author, 258
Harriet Beecher Stowe and the Beecher Preachers, 766
Harriet Tubman, 356

Harriet Tubman: Antislavery Activist, 2240
Harriet Tubman: Call to Freedom, 377
Harriet Tubman: Slavery and the Underground Railroad, 1496
Harris and Me: A Summer Remembered, 1727
Harry Houdini, 2482
Harry S. Truman, 1339
Harry S. Truman: People's President, 469
Harry S. Truman: Thirty-Third President of the United States, 952
The Harvey Girls: The Women Who Civilized the West, 1615
Hattie and the Wild Waves, 499
Hau Kola Hello Friend, 825
A Haunted Year, 1754
Hear the Wind Blow, 1741
Heart of Naosaqua, 2327
Helen Hayes: Actress, 1237
Helen Keller, 1080, 1465, 2596
Helen Keller: A Light for the Blind, 1277
Helen Keller: Humanitarian, 1660
Helen Keller: Toward the Light, 840
Help for Mr. Peale, 1618
Henry Clay: Leader in Congress, 1746
Henry David Thoreau: A Neighbor to Nature, 1841
Henry Hudson: Arctic Explorer and North American Adventurer, 109
Henry O. Flipper, 1750
Her Heritage: A Biographical Encyclopedia of American History, 2519
Her Own Song, 1069
Herbert C. Hoover: 31st President of the United States, 1771
Herbert Hoover: Thirty-First President of the United States, 435
Here and Then, 1426
Here Comes the Mystery Man, 1946
Heritage of the Black West, 2597
Hero of Lesser Causes, 1120
Hero over Here, 1278
Heroes, 1585
The Heroine of the Titanic: A Tale Both True and Otherwise of the Life of Molly Brown, 266
Heroines: Great Women Through the Ages, 982
Hester Bidgood: Investigatrix of Evil Deedes, 1010
Hey You, Sister Rose, 2200

Hiawatha: Founder of the Iroquois Confederacy, 285
Hiawatha: Messenger of Peace, 735
Hiawatha and the Iroquois League, 1497
The High Voyage: The Final Crossing of Christopher Columbus, 1397
Hillbilly Choir, 1901
The Hindenburg Disaster, 2162
Hiroshima: A Novella, 2498
Hiroshima and the Atomic Bomb, 245
Hiroshima Maiden, 2598
A Historical Album of Alabama, 2443
A Historical Album of California, 2444
A Historical Album of Connecticut, 2445
A Historical Album of Florida, 2446
A Historical Album of Illinois, 2447
A Historical Album of Kentucky, 2079
A Historical Album of Massachusetts, 111
A Historical Album of Minnesota, 376
A Historical Album of Nebraska, 2448
A Historical Album of New Jersey, 2270
A Historical Album of New York, 112
A Historical Album of Oregon, 2449
A Historical Album of Texas, 2450
A Historical Album of Virginia, 439
A Historical Album of Washington, 440
The History of Moviemaking, 1023
A History of Native Americans, 2599
History Through Art: 20th Century, 2520
Hole-in-the-Day, 1285
Holiday Facts and Fun: Martin Luther King Day, 2600
Home Crafts, 1149
Home Life in Colonial Days, 647
Homesteaders, 809
Homesteading: 70 Years on the Great Plains, 1862-1932, 2601
Hominids: A Look Back at Our Ancestors, 1978
Honest Abe, 1281
Hooray for the Golly Sisters, 363
The Hopi, 1292
The Hopis, 2096
The Horsecatcher, 1952
The Houdini Box, 2025

The House of Dies Drear, 942
The House on Stink Alley: A Story About the Pilgrims in Holland, 1592
The House on Walenska Street, 997
How Many Miles to Jacksonville?, 1122
How Many Miles to Sundown?, 174
How to Make a Mummy Talk, 572
Howard Carter: Searching for King Tut, 713
Hugh Glass, Mountain Man, 1498
Humbug Mountain, 703
Hunting Neptune's Giants: True Stories of American Whaling, 837
The Huron, 2602

I Am an American: A True Story of Japanese Internment, 2129
I Am Lavinia Cumming, 1415
I Am Regina, 1175
I Am Rosa Parks, 1706
I Be Somebody, 1085
I Lift My Lamp: Emma Lazarus and the Statue of Liberty, 1370
I Pledge Allegiance, 2221
I Sailed with Columbus, 1994
I Speak for the Women: A Story About Lucy Stone, 1548
I Was Dreaming to Come to America: Memories from the Ellis Island Oral History Project, 1329
The Ice Horse, 415
Ida B. Wells: Antilynching Crusader, 980
Ida B. Wells-Barnett: A Voice Against Violence, 1519
Ida B. Wells-Barnett and the Antilynching Crusade, 752
Ida Wells-Barnett: Civil Rights Leader, 1244
If Pigs Could Fly, 1332
If You Were There in 1492, 302
If You Were There in 1776, 303
If Your Name Was Changed at Ellis Island, 1367
An Illustrated History of the World: How We Got to Where We Are, 424
Immigrant Girl: Becky of Eldridge Street, 970
Immigrants, 1949
Immigration, 70
Immigration: How Should It Be Controlled?, 829
Immigration and Cultural Change, 2603
The Immigration Experience, 2604

Immigration to the United States, 2605
Impossible Quests, 627
In Flanders Fields: The Story of the Poem by John McCrae, 844
In Search of the Grand Canyon: Down the Colorado with John Wesley Powell, 741
In Search of the North Pole, 2606
In the Days of the Salem Witchcraft Trials, 1870
In the Kaiser's Clutch, 1163
In the Land of the Big Red Apple, 1433
In the Year of the Boar and Jackie Robinson, 1412
The Incredible Journey of Lewis and Clark, 274
Incredible Jumbo, 2092
Independence Avenue, 2034
Independence Day, 2607
Independence Hall, 2146
India in the West: South Asians in America, 2226
Indian Captive: The Story of Mary Jemison, 1357
The Indian School, 2390
An Indian Winter, 748
Indians of California, 2608
Indians of the Northwest, 2609
Indians of the Plains, 80, 2610
Indians of the Southeast, 2611
Indians of the Southwest, 2612
Indio, 784
Industrialization and Urbanization (1870-1910), 2613
The Ingenious Mr. Peale: Painter, Patriot and Man of Science, 2453
Initiation Customs, 1791
Inside the Metropolitan Museum, 1856
Inside the White House, 2521
Inspirations: Stories About Women Artists, 2059
Into the Deep Forest with Henry David Thoreau, 1634
Introducing Gershwin, 2320
Invasion of Italy, 246
Inventions: Inventors and Ingenious Ideas, 2294
Inventions That Changed Modern Life, 1466
The Invisible Thread, 2299
The Iran Hostage Crisis, 2163
Irene and the Big, Fine Nickel, 2077
Irene Jennie and the Christmas Masquerade, 2078
The Irish-American Experience, 397

The Irish American Family Album, 1042

Irish Americans, 2614

The Irish in America, 1115

The Iron Dragon Never Sleeps, 1256

The Iroquois, 2097, 2615

The Iroquois Indians, 2037

Is There a Woman in the House, 686

Isaac Johnson: From Slave to Stonecutter, 1479

Isadora Duncan: Dancer, 1252

Isadora Duncan: Revolutionary Dancer, 1951

Ishi, 1109

Ishi: The Last of His People, 1743

Island Boy, 500

An Island Far from Home, 607

Island Hopping in the Pacific, 247

Island of the Blue Dolphins, 1676

Issei and Nisei: The Settling of Japanese America, 2227

It Ain't Always Easy, 1164

The Italian American Family Album, 1043

Italian Americans, 2616

The Italian Americans, 587

It's Nothing to a Mountain, 1024

It's the Fourth of July, 1026

I've Got an Idea! The Story of Frederick McKinley Jones, 2219

Iwo Jima and Okinawa, 248

Jack London, 2004

Jackie, 2617

Jackie Kennedy Onassis, 61

Jackie Robinson, 1967, 2021

Jackie Robinson: Baseball Pioneer, 1846

Jackie Robinson: Baseball's First Black Major-Leaguer, 872

Jackie Robinson: He Was the First, 16

Jackie Robinson and the Breaking of the Color Barrier, 2046

Jackie Robinson and the Story of All-Black Baseball, 1675

Jackie Robinson Breaks the Color Line, 1976

Jackson Pollock, 2315

The Jacksons, 1929

Jacob Have I Loved, 1713

Jacques Cousteau: Man of the Oceans, 873

James A. Garfield: 20th President of the United States, 323

James A. Garfield: Twentieth President of the United States, 1383

James Beckwourth: Frontiersman, 603

James Carter: Thirty-Ninth President of the United States, 2328

James E. Carter: 39th President of the United States, 1857

James Farmer: Civil Rights Leader, 2071

James K. Polk: 11th President of the United States, 864

James K. Polk: Eleventh President of the United States, 1384

James K. Polk, Abraham Lincoln, Theodore Roosevelt, 1392

James Madison, 1340

James Madison: 4th President of the United States, 1772

James Madison: Fourth President of the United States, 436

James Madison and Dolley Madison and Their Times, 1799

James Meredith and School Desegregation, 653

James Monroe: 5th President of the United States, 2151

James Monroe: Fifth President of the United States, 693

James Weldon Johnson: "Lift Every Voice and Sing," 1520

Jamestown, 2618

Jamestown: The Beginning, 2619

Jane Addams, 1238

Jane Addams and Hull House, 1188

The Japanese American Family Album, 1044

Japanese Americans, 2620

The Japanese Americans, 1234

The Japanese in America, 1338

A Jar of Dreams, 2300

Jayhawker, 175

Jazz: My Music, My People, 1588

The Jazz Kid, 459

Jazz Stars, 1851

Jedediah Smith and the Mountain Men of the American West, 48

Jefferson Davis, 1199, 1225

Jefferson Davis: Confederate President, 1783

The Jefferson Way, 1610

The Jeffersons, 1930

Jenny of the Tetons, 893

Jericho's Journey, 2463

Jesse James, 857, 2193

Jesse Owens, 1968, 2621

Jesse Owens: Champion Athlete, 791, 1853

Jesse Owens: Olympic Star, 1521

The Jewish American Family Album, 1045

Jewish Americans, 2622

The Jewish Americans, 1625

Jewish Days and Holidays, 391

Jewish Holidays in the Spring, 1446

Jim Beckwourth: Black Trapper and Indian Chief, 261

Jim Bridger: Man of the Mountains, 1420

Jim-Dandy, 1086

Jim Thorpe, 1648, 1869, 1969

Jim Thorpe: Sac and Fox Athlete, 215

Jim Thorpe: Twentieth-Century Jock, 1395

Jim Ugly, 704

Jimmy Carter, 2073

Jimmy Carter: Beyond the Presidency, 383

Jimmy Crack Corn, 1814

Jimmy Spoon and the Pony Express, 894

Jip: His Story, 1714

Jo and the Bandit, 1872

Joe DiMaggio, 89

Joe Louis: A Champ for All America, 1396

Joe Louis: Heavyweight Champion, 1101

John Adams, 310, 646

John Adams: 2nd President of the United States, 2152

The John Adamses, 1931

John Brown: A Cry for Freedom, 842

John Brown: Militant Abolitionist, 1784

John Brown: One Man Against Slavery, 662

John Brown and the Fight Against Slavery, 475

John Brown of Harper's Ferry, 2019

John C. Calhoun and the Roots of the Civil War, 636

John C. Frémont: Soldier and Pathfinder, 1970

John Chapman: The Man Who Was Johnny Appleseed, 874

John Charles Frémont and the Great Western Reconnaissance, 963

John F. Kennedy, 1810

John F. Kennedy: Courage in Crisis, 2024

John F. Kennedy: 35th President of the United States, 669

John F. Kennedy: Thirty-Fifth President of the United States, 1200

John F. Kennedy: Young People's President, 62

John Fitzgerald Kennedy: America's 35th President, 579

John Glenn: Astronaut and Senator, 451

John James Audubon: Wildlife Artist, 76
John Lennon, 492
John Muir, 712, 1342
John Muir: At Home in the Wild, 2234
John Muir: Man of the Wild Places, 875
John Muir: Saving the Wilderness, 1646
John Muir: Wilderness Protector, 2332
John Philip Sousa: The March King, 876
John Quincy Adams, 443
John Ross, 1414
John Russwurm, 287
John Smith, 846
John Tyler: 10th President of the United States, 670
John Tyler: Tenth President of the United States, 1385
John Wesley Powell: Explorer of the Grand Canyon, 338
John Wesley Powell and the Great Surveys of the American West, 779
Johnny Appleseed, 1179
Johnny Tremain, 711
Jonas Salk, 533, 2268
Jonas Salk: Discoverer of the Polio Vaccine, 301
Jonathan Down Under, 176
The Josefina Story Quilt, 445
Joseph Brant: Mohawk Chief, 282
Josepha: A Prairie Boy's Story, 1508
Josephine Baker, 2005
The Journey: Japanese Americans, Racism, and Renewal, 934
Journey Home, 2301
The Journey Home, 1028
Journey to Center Place, 786
Journey to Freedom: A Story of the Underground Railroad, 2485
Journey to Gold Mountain: The Chinese in Nineteenth Century America, 2228
Journey to Nowhere, 110
A Journey to the New World: The Diary of Remember Patience Whipple: Mayflower/Plimoth Colony, 1620, 1302
Journey to Topaz, 2302
Judge Roy Bean, 858
Judith Resnick: Challenger Astronaut, 217
Julia Morgan: Architect, 1107
Julia's Mending, 657
Juliette Low: Founder of the Girl Scouts of America, 193

Jump at de Sun: The Story of Zora Neale Hurston, 1777
Jump Ship to Freedom, 455
Jumping the Broom, 2486
Jungle Warfare, 249
Junípero Serra, 640, 818
Just a Few Words, Mr. Lincoln: The Story of the Gettysburg Address, 767
Just Family, 277
Just Some Weeds from the Wilderness, 177
Justice for Emily, 1747

Kate Shelley: Bound for Legend, 1926
Kate Shelley and the Midnight Express, 2383
Kate's Book, 2053
Kate's House, 2054
Katherine Dunham: Black Dancer, 877
Katherine Dunham: Dancer and Choreographer, 606
Katie Dee and Katie Haw: Letters from a Texas Farm Girl, 1845
Katie Henio: Navajo Sheepherder, 2263
Katie's Trunk, 2285
Keep On Singing: A Ballad of Marian Anderson, 1401
Keep Smiling Through, 1862
Keep the Lights Burning, Abbie, 1885
Keeping Clean, 1218
Keeping Secrets, 1666
Keeping the Good Light, 1232
Kentucky Rifle, 2623
Kidnapping, 2132
Kids at Work: Lewis Hine and the Crusade Against Child Labor, 749
King George's Head Was Made of Lead, 1593
King Philip: Wampanoag Rebel, 1882
King Philip and the War with the Colonists, 541
Kirsten's Cookbook, 1766
Kit Carson, 819
Kit Carson: Frontier Scout, 1971
The Kitchen, 1150
Klara's New World, 2460
Korean Americans, 139, 2624
The Korean Americans, 1349
The Korean War, 2080
The Korean War: "The Forgotten War," 2164

La Causa: The Migrant Farmworkers' Story, 570
Lacy Makes a Match, 178
Langston Hughes, 221
Langston Hughes: Great American Poet, 1522
The Last Innocent Summer, 718
The Last Silk Dress, 1863
Last Stand at the Alamo, 386
Latino Art and Culture in the United States, 2625
Laura Ingalls Wilder, 253
Laura Ingalls Wilder: A Biography, 79
Laura Ingalls Wilder: Author of the Little House Books, 878
Leagues Apart: The Men and Times of the Negro Baseball Leagues, 1868
Leah's Pony, 755
Learning by Heart, 2504
Leaving Eldorado, 1493
Leaving for America, 307
The Leaving Summer, 949
The Legend of Jimmy Spoon, 895
The Legend of the White Doe, 1052
Lena Horne: Entertainer, 1701
The Lenape, 2626
Lester's Dog, 1002
Let Me Tell You All About Trains, 2627
Let My People Go: African Americans 1804-1860, 2397
Let Women Vote!, 311
Letter to the World: The Life and Dances of Martha Graham, 781
Letting Swift River Go, 2502
Lewis and Clark: Explorers of the American West, 1264
Lewis and Clark: Exploring the Northwest, 2295
The Lewis and Clark Expedition, 1506
The Lewis and Clark Trail, 2628
Lewis Howard Latimer, 2289
Lewis Latimer: Scientist, 1668
Liberty for All?, 918
The Life and Times of Abraham Lincoln, 2629
The Life and Times of George Washington, 2630
The Life of Alexander Fleming, 1170
The Life of Benjamin Spock, 1171
The Life of Charles Drew, 2233
The Life of Daniel Hale Williams, 1172
The Life of Dorothea Dix, 1992
The Life of Elizabeth Blackwell, 1993
The Life of Florence Sabin, 1173

The Life of George Washington, 2631

The Light in the Forest, 1859

The Lighthouse Keeper's Daughter, 1684

Lighthouses: Watchers at Sea, 904

Li'l Sis and Uncle Willie: A Story Based on the Life and Paintings of William Johnson, 663

Lily and Miss Liberty, 2182

Lily's Crossing, 806

Lincoln, 1096

Lincoln: A Photobiography, 750, 2632

The Lincoln Memorial, 1189, 1842

The Lincoln Way, 1611

The Lincolns, 1932

Lincoln's Little Girl: A True Story, 2279

Lindbergh, 578

The Lion in the Box, 566

A Lion to Guard Us, 341

Listen for Rachel, 1166

Little Bighorn, 2133

Little Farm in the Ozarks, 1434

Little House in Brookfield, 2429

Little House in the Big Woods, 2420

Little House on Rocky Ridge, 1435

Little House on the Prairie, 2421

Little John and Plutie, 650

Little Louis and the Jazz Band: The Story of Louis "Satchmo" Armstrong, 1556

Little Rock: The Desegregation of Central High, 1689

Little Town in the Ozarks, 1436

Little Town on the Prairie, 2422

Littlejim, 1061

Lives of the Artists: Masterpieces, Messes (and What the Neighbors Thought), 1268

Lives of the Musicians: Good Times, Bad Times (and What the Neighbors Thought), 1269

Lives of the Writers: Comedies, Tragedies (and What the Neighbors Thought), 1270

Living Dangerously: American Women Who Risked Their Lives for Adventure, 1821

The Lizzie Borden Trial, 1822

Locks, Crocs, and Skeeters: The Story of the Panama Canal, 1702

The Log Cabin Quilt, 1070

Loggers and Railroad Workers, 2456

The Lone Hunt, 2136

Lone Star, 156

Lone Star: A Story of the Texas Rangers, 1279

The Long Road to Gettysburg, 1635

The Long Way to a New Land, 1947

A Long Way to Go, 1688

A Long Way to Whiskey Creek, 179

The Long Way Westward, 1948

The Long Winter, 2423

The Look-It-Up Book of Presidents, 262

Looking Out, 289

The Loom, 2633

Lost at the White House:, 899

The Lost Colony of Roanoke: Opposing Viewpoints, 2000

Lost Star: The Story of Amelia Earhart, 1314

Lostman's River, 574

Lou Gehrig, 1438, 1807

Louis Armstrong, 2483

Louis Armstrong: An American Success Story, 460

Louis Armstrong: Jazz Musician, 1523

Louis Armstrong: Musician, 2238

Louis Brandeis: The People's Justice, 753

Louisa May Alcott, 353

Louisa May Alcott: Author, Nurse, Suffragette, 879

Louisa May Alcott: Her Girlhood Diary, 1919

Louise Nevelson: Sculptor, 365

The Luck of Z.A.P. and Zoe, 1409

Lucy's Christmas, 928

Lucy's Summer, 929

Luis W. Alvarez, 441

Lyddie, 1715

Lyndon B. Johnson, 1174

Lyndon B. Johnson: 36th President of the United States, 671

Lyndon B. Johnson: Thirty-Sixth President of the United States, 953

The Lyndon Johnsons, 1933

Ma Dear's Aprons, 1512

Madam C. J. Walker: Building a Business Empire, 477

Madam C. J. Walker: Entrepreneur, 344

Madam C. J. Walker: Pioneer Businesswoman, 2242

Madam C. J. Walker: Self-Made Millionaire, 1524

Maddie in the Middle, 1651

The Madisons, 1934

The Magic Amulet, 2137

Mahalia Jackson: Gospel Singer, 2471

The Mail, 358

Mail Call! The History of the U.S. Postal Service, 278

Make Way for Sam Houston, 768

Making It Happen: Masters of Invention, 2634

Making Thirteen Colonies, 919

Malcolm X, 2635

Malcolm X: Another Side of the Movement, 564

Malcolm X: By Any Means Necessary, 1641

Malcolm X: Racial Spokesman, 2041

Malcolm X and Black Pride, 542

The Man Behind the Magic: The Story of Walt Disney, 153

A Man Named Thoreau, 355

The Man Who Sang in the Dark, 426

The Man Who Was Poe, 120

The Man with the Silver Eyes, 2138

The Mandans, 1361

The Manhattan Project, 2165

The Many Lives of Benjamin Franklin, 45, 1694

Many Thousand Gone: African Americans from Slavery to Freedom, 943

Marching to Freedom: The Story of Martin Luther King, Jr., 1576

Marching Toward Freedom: 1957-1965, 2370

Marcus Garvey: Black Nationalist Leader, 1318

Margaret Bourke-White: A Photographer's Life, 1178

Margaret Bourke-White: Photographer, 546

Margaret Mead, 392, 2511

Maria Martinez: Pueblo Potter, 77

Maria Mitchell: The Soul of an Astronomer, 835

Maria Tallchief, 660

Marian Anderson: A Great Singer, 1525

Marian Anderson: Singer, 2256

Marjory Stoneman Douglas: Guardian of the Everglades, 1986

Marjory Stoneman Douglas: Voice of the Everglades, 340

Mark Twain, 1790

Mark T-W-A-I-N!: A Story About Samuel Clemens, 470

Mark Twain: America's Humorist, Dreamer, Prophet: A Biography, 517

Mark Twain: Author of Tom Sawyer, 880

Mark Twain? What Kind of a Name Is That?, 1800
Marriage Customs, 485
Martha Graham, 1786, 1793
Martha Washington, 1478
Martin Luther King, Jr., 300, 554, 1102, 1717, 2636
Martin Luther King, Jr.: Leader for Civil Rights, 2011
Martin Luther King, Jr.: Leader in the Struggle for Civil Rights, 231
Martin Luther King, Jr.: Man of Peace, 1526
Martin Luther King, Jr.: The Dream of Peaceful Revolution, 1907
Martin Luther King and the Montgomery Bus Boycott, 1724
Martin Luther King, Jr. and the March Toward Freedom, 924
Martin Van Buren: 8th President of the United States, 656
Martin Van Buren: Eighth President of the United States, 954
Mary Alice Peale, 623
Mary Cassatt, 366, 1568, 2293, 2316
Mary Cassatt: An American in Paris, 315
Mary Cassatt: An Artist's Life, 1762
Mary Church Terrell: Leader for Equality, 1527
Mary Lincoln's Dressmaker, 1918
Mary McLean and the St. Patrick's Day Parade, 1265
Mary McLeod Bethune, 888, 1528, 2573, 2637
Mary McLeod Bethune: A Great Teacher, 1529
Mary McLeod Bethune: Educator, 926
Mary Patten's Voyage, 212
Mary Todd Lincoln: President's Wife, 72
The Maryland Colony, 725
Mason and Dixon's Line of Fire, 2114
The Massachusetts Colony, 726
Master of Mahogany: Tom Day, Free Black Cabinetmaker, 1429
The Matchlock Gun, 648
A Matter of Conscience: The Trial of Anne Hutchinson, 1656
Matthew Brady: His Life and Photographs, 2209
Matthew Henson, 2638
Matthew Henson: Arctic Explorer, 605

Matthew Henson: Explorer, 807
May Chinn: The Best Medicine, 360
Mayfield Crossing, 1654
The Mayflower, 2353
Mazemaker, 585
Me and the End of the World, 506
Me and Willie and Pa: The Story of Abraham Lincoln and His Son Tad, 1594
Meet Addy: An American Girl, 1780
Meet Benjamin Franklin, 1990
Meet Felicity: An American Girl, 2278
Melinda Takes a Hand, 180
The Memoirs of Andrew Sherburne: Patriot and Privateer of the American Revolution, 2510
A Memorial for Mr. Lincoln, 106
Men of the Frontier, 2639
The Menominee, 2640
Meriwether Lewis and William Clark, 692
Meriwether Lewis and William Clark: Soldiers, Explorers, and Partners in History, 1744
Message from the Mountains, 1495
Mexican Americans, 140
The Mexican Americans, 393
The Mexican War: Manifest Destiny, 387
The Mexicans in America, 1757
The Midnight Horse, 705
The Military: Defending the Nation, 1700
Milliard Fillmore: 13th President of the United States, 1317
Millard Fillmore: Thirteenth President of the United States, 389
Millie Cooper, Take a Chance, 998
Millie Cooper, 3B, 999
Miners, Merchants, and Maids, 1015
Mining Made the West, 2641
Minty: A Story of Young Harriet Tubman, 2006
Miranda v. Arizona: Rights of the Accused, 1861
A Missing Portrait on Sugar Hill, 1718
Mission Life, 2642
Missions of California: Mission Santa Barbara, 2643
Missions of the Central Coast: Santa Bárbara, Santa Inés, La Purísima Concepción, 194
Missions of the Inland Valleys: San Luis Obispo de Tolosa, San Miguel Arcángel, San Antonio de Padua, and

Nuestra Señora de la Soledad, 316
Missions of the Los Angeles Area: San Gabriel Arcángel, San Fernando Rey de España, San Buenaventura, 1444
Missions of the Monterey Bay Area: San Carlos Borromeo de Carmelo, San Juan Bautista, Santa Cruz, 8
Missions of the San Francisco Bay Area: Santa Clara de Asís, San José de Guadalupe, San Francisco de Asís, San Rafael Arcángel, San Francisco Solano, 2400
Missions of the Southern Coast: San Diego de Alcalà, San Luis de Francia, San Juan Capistrano, 1356
Mississippi Bridge, 2245
Mississippi Chariot, 1874
Mississippi Steamboats, 2644
Moccasin Trail, 1507
The Mockingbird Song, 60
The Mohawk, 639
Molly Donnelly, 2260
Money, 359
Monkey Tag, 776
A Month of Seven Days, 433
Monticello, 1855
The Moon Bridge, 1985
Moon of Two Dark Horses, 1176
Moon Window, 531
Moonshiner's Son, 1835
More than Anything Else, 293
Moriah's Pond, 2090
The Morning Chair, 1125
The Morning Glory War, 814
The Most Wonderful Movie in the World, 714
Mother Jones, 1057
Mother Jones: Labor Crusader, 979
Mother Jones: One Woman's Fight for Labor, 1253
Mother Jones and the March of the Mill Children, 478
Mount Vernon, 1843
The Mountain Man and the President, 2372
Mountain Men, 2645
Mountain Valor, 1062
The Movies of Alfred Hitchcock, 93
Moxie, 1904
Mr. Blue Jeans: A Story About Levi Strauss, 2363
Mr. Civil Rights: The Story of Thurgood Marshall, 2402
Mr. Lincoln's Drummer, 2464
Mr. Lincoln's Whiskers, 2455
Mr. Mysterious & Co, 706

Mr. Peale's Bones, 2379
Mr. Revere and I, 1334
Mr. Tucket, 1728
The Mud Family, 1106
Mummies, Masks, & Mourners, 218
Murals: Cave, Cathedral, to Street, 374
Music from a Place Called Half
    Moon, 1697
Music in the Civil War, 530
Mustang Flats, 2465
My Brother, My Enemy, 962
My Crooked Family, 461
My Daddy Was a Soldier: A World
    War II Story, 1828
My Daniel, 494
My Fellow Americans, 1795
My First Book of Biographies: Great
    Men and Women Every Child
    Should Know, 1486
My Great-Aunt Arizona, 1063
My Name Is Pocahontas, 9
My Prairie Christmas, 971
My Prairie Year, 972
My Wartime Summers, 539
The Mysterious Horseman: An
    Adventure in Prairietown,
    1836, 2354

N. C. Wyeth's Pilgrims, 1925
A Namesake for Nathan, 1595
The Narragansett, 2646
Nat Turner: Slave Revolt Leader, 235
Nat Turner and the Slave Revolt, 155
The Nation Divides: The Civil
    War, 1820-1880, 2173
A Nation in Turmoil, 2647
The Nation in Turmoil: Civil
    Rights and the Vietnam War
    (1960-1973), 326
A Nation Is Born: Rebellion and
    Independence in America,
    1700-1820, 2174
A Nation Torn: The Story of How
    the Civil War Began, 1829
National Observances, 2648
Native American Doctor: The
    Story of Susan La Flesche
    Picotte, 681
Native American Life, 2649
Native American Medicine, 2650
Native American Rock Art:
    Messages from the Past, 1287
Native Americans: People of the
    Desert, 2651
Native Americans: People of the
    Forest, 2652
Native Americans: People of the
    Northwest Coast, 2653
Native Americans: People of the
    Plains, 2654

Native Americans: The History of
    a People, 2655
Native Americans and the U.S.
    Government, 256
The Navajo, 2656
Navajo Code Talkers, 4
The Navajo Indians, 2476
The Navajos, 2098
Nelly Bly: Journalist, 652
Nellie Bly's Monkey: His
    Remarkable Story in His
    Own Words, 268
Nettie's Trip South, 2286
Never Turn Back: Father Serra's
    Mission, 1827
New England Whaler, 133
New Friends in a New Land: A
    Thanksgiving Story, 2122
The New Hampshire Colony, 727
New Hope, 2106
The New Jersey Colony, 728
The New Nation, 920
A New Nation (1776-1815), 2657
The New York Colony, 729
Newcomers to America: Stories of
    Today's Young Immigrants
    (in Their Own Words), 862
Next Spring an Oriole, 2391
Next Stop, Freedom: The Story of
    a Slave Girl, 1046
The Nez Percé, 2099
The Nez Percés: People of the Far
    West, 2038
The Nickel-Plated Beauty, 181
Night Flight, 978
The Night Journey, 1303
Night Journeys, 121
Night of the Full Moon, 2392
Night Riding, 1482
The Night the Bells Rang, 1227
Nine for California, 1377
The Nineteenth Century, 1774
19th Century Clothing, 1151
The Nixons, 1935
No Star Nights, 2091
Nobody Owns the Sky: The Story of
    Brave Bessie Coleman, 1389
Nobody's Daughter, 1748
North American Indian, 1628
The North Carolina Colony, 730
North Star to Freedom: The Story
    of the Underground
    Railroad, 836
Nothing to Fear, 1248
Now Is Your Time: The
    African-American Struggle
    for Freedom, 1642
Now Let Me Fly: The Story of a
    Slave Family, 1112
The Number on My Grandfather's
    Arm, 17

O the Red Rose Tree, 182
Of Things Natural, Wild, and Free,
    1408
Off the Map: The Journals of
    Lewis and Clark, 1886
The Official Baseball Hall of Fame
    Answer Book, 58
Oh, the Places He Went: A Story
    About Dr. Seuss, 2364
Old Blue, 944
Old Blue Tilley, 297
Old Glory, 2658
Old Home Day, 930
Old Sturbridge Village: Growing
    Up in New England, 2659
The Old Synagogue, 1896
Old-Time Toys, 1152
Old Yeller, 811
The Olympic Games, 1247
On Board the Titanic, 2237
On Home Ground, 1354
On the Banks of Plum Creek, 2424
On the Day Peter Stuyvesant
    Sailed into Town, 1403
On the Frontier with Mr. Audubon,
    304
On the Long Trail Home, 2189
On the Way Home, 2425
On the Wings of Peace: Writers
    and Illustrators Speak Out
    for Peace, in Memory of
    Hiroshima and Nagasaki, 935
On to Oregon!, 1619
On Wings of Joy: The Story of
    Ballet from the 16th Century
    to Today, 782
On Winter's Wind, 1001
Once on This Island, 2393
The One Bad Thing About Father,
    1596
One Hundred Shining Candles, 1421
A One-Room School, 1153
One Tribe, 2522
One-Way to Ansonia, 84
One World, Many Worlds:
    Hispanic Diversity in the
    United States, 2660
One Yellow Daffodil, 18
The Oneida, 640
Only Opal: The Diary of a Young
    Girl, 2405
Only the Names Remain: The
    Cherokees and the Trail of
    Tears, 162
The Onondaga, 641
The Oregon Trail, 689, 2661
The Ornament Tree, 2261
The Orphan Train, 777
Orphan Train Rider: One Boy's
    True Story, 2351

Osceola, 2322
Osceola: Patriot and Warrior, 1126
Osceola: Seminole Rebel, 259
Osceola: Seminole Warrior, 1956
Other Bells for Us to Ring, 511
The Ottawa, 1293
Our Century: 1900-1910, 886
Our Century: 1910-1920, 1381
Our Century: 1920-1930, 1012
Our Century: 1930-1940, 1699
Our Century: 1940-1950, 1013
Our Century: 1950-1960, 1124
Our Century: 1960-1970, 1295
Our Century: 1970-1980, 1014
Our Century: 1980-1990, 2216
Our Congress, 2362
Our Elections, 2175
Our Federal Government: The
    Legislative Branch, 2662
Our Federal Government: The
    Presidency, 2663
Our Federal Government: The
    Supreme Court, 2664
Our Golda: The Story of Golda
    Meir, 19
Our National Anthem, 2118
Our National Symbols, 1117
Our People, 1557
Our Song, Our Toil: The Story of
    American Slavery as Told by
    Slaves, 2177
Our Supreme Court, 830
Out from This Place, 947
Out of the Storm, 2440
Outlaws of the American West, 994
Oyster Moon, 1553

P. T. Barnum: The World's
    Greatest Showman, 709
Painting Dreams: Minnie Evans,
    Visionary Artist, 1430
Panama and the United States: Their
    Canal, Their Stormy Years, 601
Panama Canal: Gateway to the
    World, 2115
Papa Tells Chita a Story, 1065
Paperboy, 1260
Parkman and the Plains Indians, 2056
Pass the Quill, I'll Write a Draft: A
    Story of Thomas Jefferson,
    1801
Path of the Pale Horse, 699
Patrick Desjarlait: Conversations
    with a Native American
    Artist, 2439
Patrick Doyle Is Full of Blarney, 96
Patrick Henry's Fight for
    Individual Rights, 2665
Paul Cuffe: Merchant and
    Abolitionist, 588
Paul Laurence Dunbar: Poet, 792

Paul Revere, 820
Paul Revere: Rider for the
    Revolution, 715
Paul Robeson: A Voice of
    Struggle, 1032
Paul Robeson: A Voice to
    Remember, 1530
Paul Robeson: Hero Before His
    Time, 1299
Paul Robeson: Singer and Actor, 661
Peace and Bread: The Story of
    Jane Addams, 1549
Pearl Buck, 1286
Pearl Harbor!, 250, 1054
Pearl Harbor Child: A Child's View
    of Pearl Harbor—From Attack
    to Peace, 1657
Pearl Harbor Is Burning!: A Story
    of World War II, 1275
Peary and Amundsen: Race to the
    Poles, 1487
Peary Reaches the North Pole, 405
The Pennsylvania Colony, 731
Penny in the Road, 1787
The Penobscot, 642
People of Peace, 270
People of the Breaking Day, 2026
People of the West, 628
People Who Changed the World,
    2432
Peppe the Lamplighter, 159
The Perilous Road, 2139
Pets of the Presidents, 395
The Philadelphia Adventure, 44
Phillis Wheatley, 1858
Phillis Wheatley: First African
    American Poet, 881
Phillis Wheatley: Poet, 2039
Phoebe's Folly, 1165
Pianna, 1830
A Picture Book of Abraham
    Lincoln, 20
A Picture Book of Benjamin
    Franklin, 21
A Picture Book of Davy Crockett, 22
A Picture Book of Eleanor
    Roosevelt, 23
A Picture Book of Frederick
    Douglass, 24
A Picture Book of George
    Washington, 25
A Picture Book of Harriet Tubman,
    26
A Picture Book of Helen Keller, 27
A Picture Book of Jackie
    Robinson, 28
A Picture Book of Jesse Owens, 29
A Picture Book of Jewish
    Holidays, 30
A Picture Book of John F.
    Kennedy, 31

A Picture Book of Martin Luther
    King, Jr., 32, 2666
A Picture Book of Patrick Henry, 33
A Picture Book of Paul Revere, 34
A Picture Book of Robert E. Lee, 35
A Picture Book of Rosa Parks, 36
A Picture Book of Sitting Bull, 37
A Picture Book of Sojourner
    Truth, 38
A Picture Book of Thomas Alva
    Edison, 39
A Picture Book of Thomas
    Jefferson, 40
A Picture Book of Thurgood
    Marshall, 41
The Picture History of Great
    Inventors, 425
A Piece of Home, 1378
Pilgrim Journey, 2667
Pilgrim Voices: Our First Year in
    the New World, 1887
Pilgrimages and Journeys, 1792
The Pilgrims at Plymouth, 2668
The Pilgrims of Plimoth, 2027
The Pilgrims' Story, 2669
Pink and Say, 1770
Pinkerton: America's First Private
    Eye, 2484
Pioneer Plowmaker: The Story of
    John Deere, 471
A Pioneer Sampler: The Daily Life
    of a Pioneer Family in 1840,
    890
Pioneering Women of the Wild, 1982
Pioneers of Discovery, 1852
Piper's Ferry, 2466
Pirate, 1763
The Pirate's Handbook: How to
    Become a Rogue of the
    High Seas, 1388
A Place Called Freedom, 1945
A Place Called Heartbreak: A
    Story of Vietnam, 1643
A Place to Belong, 521
A Place to Claim as Home, 2441
Placer Gold, 2670
Plains Warrior: Chief Quanah
    Parker and the Comanches,
    1473
Playing America's Game: The
    Story of Negro League
    Baseball, 504
Plenty Coups, 612
Plowie: A Story from the Prairie,
    1233
Pocahontas, 559, 821, 2671
Pocahontas: Powhatan
    Peacemaker, 1030
Pocahontas: Young Peacemaker, 839
Pocahontas and the Strangers, 342
Polar the Titanic Bear, 2110

Polish Americans, 2672
Pontiac: Ottawa Rebel, 260
The Pony Express: Hoofbeats in the Wilderness, 586
The Pony Express, 2306
Pony Express!, 1266, 2673
Pony Express Riders of the Wild West, 1983
Poor Richard in France, 1597
Portraits of American Presidents, 2523
Post War U.S.A., 2674
The Postwar Years: The Cold War and the Atomic Age (1950-1959), 2176
The Potato Man, 1504
The Potawatomi, 2675
The Powhatan Indians, 1503
Prairie Cabin: A Norwegian Pioneer Woman's Story, 2676
Prairie Songs, 495
Prairie Visions: The Life and Times of Solomon Butcher, 496
Preachers and Teachers, 1005
Pre-Columbian Peoples of North America, 510
Prehistoric People of North America, 406
Prejudice Monster Within, 2677
Presenting Mr. Frederick Douglass, 2678
The President Has Been Shot: True Stories of the Attacks on Ten U.S. Presidents, 1123
President Truman and the Atomic Bomb: Opposing Viewpoints, 1686
Presidents, 1950
President's Day, 2679
Presidents in a Time of Change: A Sourcebook on the U.S. Presidency, 2081
The Presidents in American History, 163
Presidents of a Divided Nation: A Sourcebook on the U.S. Presidency, 2082
Presidents of a Growing Country: A Sourcebook on the U.S. Presidency, 2083
Presidents of a World Power, 2084
Presidents of a Young Republic: A Sourcebook on the U.S. Presidency, 2085
Pride of Puerto Rico: The Life of Roberto Clemente, 2336
The Primrose Way, 1249
Prince Hall: Social Reformer, 589
Prince of Humbugs: A Life of P. T. Barnum, 81
The Printer's Apprentice, 1257

The Private War of Lillian Adams, 508
Progressive Movement, 2680
Promise Me the Moon, 150
The Promised Land, 1029
Prophets of Doom, 449
Prospectors, 810
Proudly Red and Black: Stories of African and Native Americans, 1169
Pueblo, 2681
Pueblo Indian, 514
The Pueblo Indians, 349
Puerto Ricans, 2682
The Pullman Strike of 1894: Turning Point for American Labor, 56
Punch with Judy, 122
Purely Rosie Pearl, 438
The Purple Heart, 2232

Quanah Parker: Comanche Chief, 2452
Quanah Parker: Comanche Warrior, 1957
Quanah Parker: Warrior for Freedom, Ambassador for Peace, 1019
The Quilt-Block History of Pioneer Days: With Projects Kids Can Make, 437

A Race for Land, 2324
Rachel Carson, 10, 826, 1789, 2222
Rachel Carson: Biologist and Author, 1111
Rachel Carson: Friend of Nature, 882
Rachel Carson: Voice for the Earth, 2333
Rachel Carson: Who Loved the Sea, 1310
Rachel Chance, 2262
Radical Red, 625
Railroads: Bridging the Continents, 2345
Railroads on the Frontier, 2683
Rain of Fire, 161
The Rainmakers, 233
Raising Cane: The World of Plantation Hawaii, 2229
Ralph Ellison: Author, 234
Ralph J. Bunche: Peacemaker, 1531
Ralph Nader: Crusader for Safe Consumer Products, 2267
Ramadan and Id Al-Fitr, 1447
Rancho Life, 2684
The Rattle and the Drum: Native American Rituals and Celebrations, 2070
Reading Terminal Market, 2685
The Reagan Way, 1614
The Reagans, 1936

The Real Johnny Appleseed, 1326
The Real McCoy: The Life of an African-American Inventor, 2271
The Rebel Slave, 2686
Rebels Against Slavery: American Slave Revolts, 1537
Reconstruction: America After the Civil War, 1565
Reconstruction and Reform, 921
Reconstruction and Segregation (1870-1910), 2687
Red Cap, 2467
Red Cloud: Sioux War Chief, 1335
Red Cloud: Sioux Warrior, 1958
The Red Cross and the Red Crescent, 1775
Red-Dirt Jessie, 1638
Red Means Good Fortune: A Story of San Francisco's Chinatown, 828
Red Rock over the River, 183
Red Rover, Red Rover, 1427
Red Sky at Morning, 2491
Red-Tail Angels: The Story of the Tuskegee Airmen, 1532
Refugees, 2029
Religion, 1297
The Relocation of the North American Indian, 634
Reluctant Hero: A Snowy Road to Salem in 1802, 294
Remember Betsy Floss: And Other Colonial Riddles, 42
The Remembering Box, 427
Rhoda, Straight and True, 1999
The Rhode Island Colony, 732
Richard Allen: Religious Leader and Social Activist, 1245
Richard King: Texas Cattle Rancher, 1972
Richard M. Nixon: 37th President of the United States, 2153
Richard Nixon, 152
Richard Nixon: Rise and Fall of a President, 1300
Richard Nixon: Thirty-Seventh President of the United States, 1386
Richard M. Nixon, Jimmy Carter, Ronald Reagan, 1393
The Riddle of Penncroft Farm, 1110
The Righteous Revenge of Artemis Bonner, 1644
Rights and Responsibilities: Using Your Freedom, 2049
A Ripple of Hope: The Life of Robert F. Kennedy, 965
Risk n' Roses, 2074

The Road to Seneca Falls: A Story About Elizabeth Cady Stanton, 2217

Roanoke: The Story of the Lost Colony, 288

Robert E. Lee, 333, 372

Robert E. Lee: Hero of the South, 847

Robert E. Lee: Leader in War and Peace, 883

Robert E. Lee: Southern Hero of the Civil War, 1216

Robert E. Lee and the Rise of the South, 619

Robert Frost, 1995

Robert Fulton, 1294

Robert H. Goddard, 673

Robert Peary and the Quest for the North Pole, 645

Rocket Man: The Story of Robert Goddard, 2201

Roe v. Wade: The Abortion Question, 995

Roll of Thunder, Hear My Cry, 2246

Romare Bearden: Artist, 330

Ronald Reagan, 2013, 2210

Ronald Reagan: Fortieth President of the United States, 1201

Ronald W. Reagan: 40th President of the United States, 1871

Rooftop Astronomer: A Story About Maria Mitchell, 1550

Roosevelt and the Americans at War, 525

Rosa Parks, 889

Rosa Parks: Civil Rights Leader, 1075

Rosa Parks: My Story, 1707

Rosa Parks: The Movement Organizes, 756

Rosamund, 1116

The Rose Horse, 1889

Rosh Hashanah/Yom Kippur, 2688

Rosie and the Rustlers, 794

Rosie the Riveter: Women Working on the Home Front in World War II, 479

Rosie's Tiger, 1639

Runaway to Freedom, 2093

Running for Our Lives, 2290

The Russian Americans, 1456

A Russian Jewish Family, 1344

Ruth Law Thrills a Nation, 318

Rutherford B. Hayes: Nineteenth President of the United States, 1202

Sacagawea, 822, 2689

Sacagawea: Indian Interpreter to Lewis and Clark, 331

Sacagawea: Native American Hero, 1973

Sacajawea: The Journey West, 1816

The Sacco-Vanzetti Trial, 1823

The Sailor Through History, 505

Salem, Massachusetts, 1190

The Salem Witchcraft Trials, 2508

Sallie Fox: The Story of a Pioneer Girl, 1353

Salt Lake City, 613

Sam Houston: Hero of Texas, 1311

Sam Houston: Texas Hero, 1974

Sam the Minuteman, 198

Sam's Wild West Show, 87

Samantha's Cookbook, 1767

Samuel Adams, 2690

Samuel Adams: Grandfather of His Country, 674

Samuel Eaton's Day: A Day in the Life of a Pilgrim Boy, 2355

Samuel F. B. Morse: Artist-Inventor, 1312

Samuel Morse, 1217

Samuel's Choice, 213

Samurai of Gold Hill, 2303

San Antonio, 1346

Sanctuary: The Story of Three Arch Rocks, 742

The Santa Fe Trail, 1316

Sarah and Me and the Lady from the Sea, 184

Sarah Anne Hartford: Massachusetts, 1651, 624

Sarah Morton's Day: A Day in the Life of a Pilgrim Girl, 2356

Sarah, Plain and Tall, 1441

Sarah Royce and the American West, 2057

Sarah Winnemucca, 1620

Sarah Winnemucca: Northern Paiute Writer and Diplomat, 2017

Satchel Paige, 2042

Satchmo's Blues, 2007

Save Queen of Sheba, 1586

Save the Everglades, 2123

Saving Damaris, 1360

Saving Sweetness, 2125

Say It with Music: A Story About Irving Berlin, 2202

The Scholastic Encyclopedia of the Presidents and their Times, 1912

A School for Pompey Walker, 1892

Scientists Who Changed the World, 2435

Scouts of the Wild West, 1984

The Sea of Tranquillity, 909

The Sea Rovers: Pirates, Privateers, and Buccaneers, 1474

Searching for Laura Ingalls: A Reader's Journey, 1304

Second Daughter: The Story of a Slave Girl, 2341

The Secret Armies: Spies, Counterspies, and Saboteurs in World War II, 1475

Secret Cities, 507

The Secret Soldier: The Story of Deborah Sampson, 1505

See You in Heaven, 1036

Seeds of Liberty: The Causes of the American Revolution, 2691

Sees Behind Trees, 611

The Sellin' of Jamie Thomas, 2692

The Seminole, 2100, 2693

Seminole Diary: Remembrances of a Slave, 1113

The Seminole Indians, 1251

The Seneca, 643

A Separate Battle: Women and the Civil War, 403

Sequoyah: Inventor of the Cherokee Alphabet, 2051

Sequoyah and the Cherokee Alphabet, 543

Sequoyah's Gift: A Portrait of the Cherokee Leader, 1240

The Serpent Never Sleeps: A Novel of Jamestown and Pocahontas, 1677

Settler Sayings, 1154

Settlers of the West, 2694

The 761st Tank Battalion, 1749

The Seventies, 785

Sewing Quilts, 2287

Shades of Gray, 1836

Shadow Ball: The History of the Negro Leagues, 2346

Shadrach's Crossing, 123

Shaker Boy, 1831

Shaker Hearts, 2288

Shaker Home, 227

Shaker Inventions, 279

Shaker Villages, 280

Shannon: A Chinatown Adventure, San Francisco, 1880, 1280

She Flew No Flags, 1460

Sheridan's Ride, 1832

Shh! We're Writing the Constitution, 769

Ships, 1077

Shirley Chisholm, 1773

Shirley Chisholm: Teacher and Congresswoman, 1991

The Sign of the Beaver, 2108

The Sign Painter's Secret: The Story of a Revolutionary Girl, 1047

Silent Communications: Trail Signs/Sign Language, 2695

Silent Observer, 1440

Silver Days, 1379
Sing Down the Moon, 1678
Singing America: Poems That Define a Nation, 1753
The Sioux, 1006, 2101
Sister, 1071
Sitting Bull, 2323
Sitting Bull: Chief of the Sioux, 216
Sitting Bull: Dakota Boy, 2188
Sitting Bull: Sioux Leader, 276
Sitting Bull: Sioux Warrior, 1959
Sitting Bull and the Battle of the Little Bighorn, 236
Skippack School, 567
The Sky Is Falling, 509
The Sky's the Limit, 2696
Skylark, 1442
SkyTrip America, 2524
The Slave Dancer, 720
Slave Ship: The Story of the Henrietta Marie, 2211
Slavery and Freedom, 2697
Small Steps: The Year I Got Polio, 1177
Smallpox and the American Indian, 590
Smithsonian Book of the First Ladies, 1491
The Smithsonian Visual Timeline of Inventions, 1764
Snapshot: America Discovers the Camera, 545
The Snow Walker, 2384
Snowbound: The Tragic Story of the Donner Party, 1315
Snowshoe Thompson, 1371
Sod Houses on the Great Plains, 1906
Sodbuster, 2266
Sojourner Truth: A Voice for Freedom, 1533
Sojourner Truth: Ain't I a Woman?, 1534
Sojourner Truth: Antislavery Activist, 1254
Sojourner Truth: Crusader for Civil Rights, 1439
Sojourner Truth and the Struggle for Freedom, 417
Soldier of Destiny: A Biography of George Patton, 1735
The Soldier Through History, 410
The Soldier's Voice: The Story of Ernie Pyle, 1674
Something to Shout About, 185
Something's Upstairs: A Tale of Ghosts, 124
Song of Sacajawea, 2698
Song of the Trees, 2247
Songs and Stories from the American Revolution, 2061

Songs from the Loom: A Navajo Girl Learns to Weave, 1880
Soon, Annala, 1374
Sound the Jubilee, 716
Sounder, 98
Sounding the Alarm: A Biography of Rachel Carson, 957
The South Carolina Colony, 733
The Space Shuttle, 684
Spacecraft, 841
Spacious Dreams: The First Wave of Asian Immigration, 2230
The Spanish-American War: Imperial Ambitions, 388
The Spanish Conquests in the New World, 411
Spanish Pioneers of the Southwest, 67
Spies! Women in the Civil War, 480
The Spinner's Daughter, 1399
Spinning Wheel, 2699
Spiritual Leaders, 2337
Spotting the Leopard, 1640
Spray, 255
A Spy in the King's Colony, 145
Squanto and the First Thanksgiving, 2700
Squanto, Friend of the Pilgrims, 343
St. Augustine: America's Oldest City, 2329
St. Patrick's Day, 2701
Stagecoach West, 2702
The Star Fisher, 2499
Stargone John, 1510
Stars and Stripes: Our National Flag, 690
Starting Home: The Story of Horace Pippin, Painter, 1431
Statesmen Who Changed the World, 2433
Stateswoman to the World: A Story About Eleanor Roosevelt, 2365
The Statue of Liberty, 593, 1571
Stay Away from Simon!, 380
Stay Put, Robbie McAmis, 2280
Steal Away, 97
Steal Away Home, 1913
The Steam Engine: G. Stephenson, 2703
Stepping on the Cracks, 913
Stitching Stars: The Story Quilts of Harriet Powers, 1432
Stokely Carmichael: The Story of Black Power, 1114
Stones and Bones: How Archaeologists Trace Human Origins, 2198
Stonewall, 770
Stonewall Jackson: Confederate General, 1751

Stonewall Jackson: Lee's Greatest Lieutenant, 203
Stop the Presses, Nellie's Got a Scoop! A Story of Nellie Bly, 1802
The Store That Mama Built, 1350
Stories in Stone: Rock Art Pictures by Early Americans, 100
Stories on Stone: Rock Art, Images from the Ancient Ones, 584
The Story of Admiral Peary at the North Pole, 1203
The Story of Booker T. Washington, 1535
The Story of Flight, 2199
The Story of Frederick Douglass: Voice of Freedom, 2367
The Story of Harriet Beecher Stowe, 101
The Story of Hillary Rodham Clinton: First Lady of the United States, 1577
The Story of John Brown's Raid on Harpers Ferry, 1204
The Story of Johnny Appleseed, 46
The Story of Jonas Salk and the Discovery of the Polio Vaccine, 955
The Story of Laura Ingalls Wilder, Pioneer Girl, 2194
The Story of Malcolm X: Civil Rights Leader, 2195
The Story of Money, 1453
The Story of Nat Love, 1573
The Story of Ruby Bridges, 454
The Story of Sacajawea: Guide to Lewis and Clark, 1908
The Story of Sequoyah: The Lame One, 2387
The Story of the Battle of Bull Run, 1205
The Story of the Boston Massacre, 1752
The Story of the Negro League Baseball, 298
The Story of the Powers of the Supreme Court, 2166
The Story of the Statue of Liberty, 1454
The Story of the Surrender at Yorktown, 1206
The Story of the Vietnam Memorial, 2489
The Story of the White House, 2357
The Story of the Women's Movement, 102
The Stowaway: A Tale of California Pirates, 896
Stowaway! Stephen Biesty's Incredible Cross-Sections, 2525

Stranded at Plimoth Plantation, 291
A Strange and Distant Shore:
    Indians of the Great Plains in
    Exile, 107
Strangers at the Gates Again:
    Asian American Immigration
    after 1965, 2231
Strawberry Girl, 1358
Strike: The Bitter Struggle of
    American Workers from
    Colonial Times to the
    Present, 481
Striking It Rich: The Story of the
    California Gold Rush, 1258
Struggle for a Continent: The
    French and Indian Wars:
    1690-1760, 1476
The Struggle to Grow:
    Expansionism and
    Industrialization
    (1880-1913), 327
Summer Endings, 1060
The Summer of Stanley, 1228
The Summer of the Great Divide,
    1008
A Summer on Thirteenth Street, 1000
Summertime in the Big Woods, 2426
The Supreme Court, 1844
Susan B. Anthony: And Justice for
    All, 787
Susan B. Anthony: Fighter for
    Women's Rights, 1365
Susan B. Anthony: Voice for
    Women's Voting Rights, 1183
Susan B. Anthony: Woman
    Suffragist, 2368
The Susan B. Anthony Story: The
    Women's Suffrage
    Movement, 2704
Susan Butcher: Sled Dog Racer, 2334
Susan Butcher and the Iditarod
    Trail, 602
Susanna of the Alamo, 1099
Susette La Flesche: Advocate for
    Native American Rights, 332
Sweet Clara and the Freedom
    Quilt, 1055
Sweet Creek Holler, 2399
Switching Well, 900
Sybil Rides for Independence, 320

The Tafts, 1937
The Tainos: The People Who
    Welcomed Columbus, 1090
Take to the Sky, 1327
Tales from the Underground
    Railroad, 488
The Tamarack Tree: A Novel of
    the Siege of Vicksburg, 418

Tapenum's Day: A Wampanoag
    Indian Boy in Pilgrim Times,
    2358
Tar Beach, 1865
Taxation: Paying for Government,
    1022
Teammates, 832
Technology of War, 526
Tecumseh, 1207
Tecumseh: Shawnee Rebel, 544
Tecumseh and the Dream of an
    American Indian Nation, 2047
Ten Mile Day: And the Building of
    the Transcontinental
    Railroad, 743
The Tenement Writer: An
    Immigrant's Story, 2104
Tet: Vietnamese New Year, 1448
Thanksgiving, 2705
The Thanksgiving Story, 549
That Wild Berries Should Grow:
    The Diary of a Summer, 2394
That's One Ornery Orphan, 186
Thee, Hannah!, 568
Theodore Roosevelt, 1467
Theodore Roosevelt: Conservation
    President, 582
Theodore Roosevelt: 26th
    President of the United
    States, 2154
Theodore Roosevelt: Twenty-Sixth
    President of the United
    States, 1208
Theodore Roosevelt Takes Charge,
    2403
The Theodore Roosevelts, 1938
These Happy Golden Years, 2427
These Lands Are Ours:
    Tecumseh's Fight for the
    Old Northwest, 489
They Shall Be Heard: Susan B.
    Anthony & Elizabeth Cady
    Stanton, 490
They Shaped the Game: Ty Cobb,
    Babe Ruth, and Jackie
    Robinson, 1097
They Wrote Their Own Headlines:
    American Women
    Journalists, 2404
They're Off: The Story of the Pony
    Express, 959
Think About Racism, 1583
The 13th Floor: A Ghost Story, 707
This Land Is Your Land: The
    American Conservation
    Movement, 2407
This New Land, 2468
This Time, Tempe Wick?, 786a
This World Is Not Our Home, 2706
Thomas Alva Edison, 348, 2707

Thomas Alva Edison: Bringer of
    Light, 884
Thomas Alva Edison: Great
    Inventor, 43
Thomas Edison, 69
Thomas Edison: Inventing the
    Future, 1579
Thomas Edison and Electricity, 1704
Thomas Jefferson, 339, 1649, 1721
Thomas Jefferson: A Picture Book
    Biography, 804
Thomas Jefferson: 3rd President of
    the United States, 2155
Thomas Jefferson: Third President
    of the United States, 956
Thomas Paine, 2304
Thomas Paine: Revolutionary
    Author, 675
Those Incredible Women of World
    War II, 2509
Thrashin' Time, 2373
Three Names, 1443
Three Worlds Meet
    (Origins—1620), 2708
Through the Rockies, 2709
Thunder at Gettysburg, 786b
Thunder Foot—1730, 1037
Thunder from the Clear Sky, 2028
Thunder Rolling in the Mountains,
    1680
Thurgood Marshall: A Dream of
    Justice for All, 1127
Thurgood Marshall: A Life for
    Justice, 976
Thurgood Marshall: Champion of
    Justice, 1788
Till Victory Is Won: Black Soldiers
    in the Civil War, 1566
Time Almanac of the 20th
    Century, 2526
A Time of Angels, 1003
A Time Too Swift, 1785
The Times and Dreams of Martin
    Luther King, Jr., 2710
The Times of My Life: A Memoir,
    108
Timmy O'Dowd and the Big
    Ditch: A Story of the Glory
    Days on the Old Erie Canal,
    1020
Timothy of the Cay: A
    Prequel-Sequel, 2254
The Tin Heart, 13
Tinker vs. Des Moines: Student
    Rights on Trial, 1824
The Titanic, 1191, 2119
Titanic: Lost and Found, 609
To Fly with the Swallows: A Story
    of Old California, 569
To See with the Heart: The Life of
    Sitting Bull, 2116

To Space and Back, 1860
To the Point: A Story About E. B. White, 464
Today's Special: Z.A.P. and Zoe, 1410
Toilets, Bathtubs, Sinks, and Sewers: A History of the Bathroom, 482
Tomahawk Border, 2140
The Tomorrow Connection, 223
Tools and Gadgets, 1155
Top Entrepreneurs and Their Businesses, 1755
Top Lawyers and Their Famous Cases, 658
Total History, 2527
The Totem Pole Indians of the Northwest, 224
Totem Poles: The Stories They Tell, 2711
Tough Choices: A Story of the Vietnam War, 88
Townsend's Warbler, 700
Tracing Our Irish Roots, 1621
Tracing Our Italian Roots, 1345
Tracks Across America: The Story of the American Railroad, 1825-1900, 691
Tragedy to Triumph: An Adventure with Helen Keller, 2712
The Trail of Tears: The Cherokee Journey from Home, 312
Trail Through Danger, 2141
Train to Somewhere, 347
Trains, 292
Traitor: The Case of Benedict Arnold, 771
The Transcontinental Railroad: Triumph of a Dream, 654
Transport: On Land, Road and Rail, 562
Transportation: Automobiles to Zeppelins, 659
Treasure in the Stream: The Story of a Gold Rush Girl, 1048
Tree by Leaf, 2325
Tree of Freedom, 394
Treemonisha, 1558
The Triangle Factory Fire, 2040
Trouble at the Mines, 1825
Trouble for Lucy, 2183
The True Adventure of Daniel Hall, 2126
The True Adventures of Grizzly Adams, 1500
True Champions: Great Athletes and Their Off-the-Field Heroics, 5

The True Confessions of Charlotte Doyle, 125
True Stories About Abraham Lincoln, 901
The True Story of J. Edgar Hoover and the FBI, 580
The Truman Way, 1612
The Trumans, 1939
Tsiolkovski: The Space Age, 2713
Tucket's Ride, 1729
Tunes for Bears to Dance To, 512
Turn Homeward, Hannalee, 187
The Tuscarora, 644
The Tuskegee Airmen: Black Heroes of World War II, 964
TV's Forgotten Hero: The Story of Philo Farnsworth, 1551
25 Great Moments in Baseball, 2348
Twist of Gold, 1606
Two Chimneys, 1038
Two Very Little Sisters, 381

U.S. Air Force, 271
The U.S. Air Force, 679
U.S. and the World (1865-1917), 2714
U.S. Army, 1284
The U.S. Coast Guard, 1647
The U.S. Marine Corps, 2349
U.S. Songs and Poems, 2715
Ukrainians in America, 1283
Ulysses S. Grant, 207, 1672
Ulysses S. Grant: Eighteenth President of the United States, 1209
Uncle Jed's Barbershop, 1582
Uncle Sam Wants You! Military Men and Women of World War II, 2408
Under the Blood-Red Sun, 1924
Under the Bridge, 1511
Under the Shadow of Wings, 146
The Underground Railroad, 228, 515
The United Nations, 2167
United States Constitution, 2716
United States Expansion, 2717
United States Flag, 2718
United States v. Nixon: Watergate and the President, 996
The Unsinkable Delta Queen, 2719
Up in the Air: The Story of Bessie Coleman, 967
Up the Tracks to Grandma's, 986
Urban Life, 1362
USKids History: Book of the New American Nation, 2088
The USS Arizona, 2168

V Is for Victory: America Remembers World War II, 1271
V Is for Victory: The American Homefront During World War I, 2409
Valentine's Day, 2720
Valley Forge, 2169
Valley Forge: Young Spy, 2721
The Valley in Between, 608
The Vicksburg Veteran, 1598
Victory in Europe, 251
Vietnam War Soldiers, 2214
Vietnamese Americans, 141
The View from the Pighouse Roof, 1683
The Village of Blue Stone, 2275
Vilma Martinez, 442
The Virginia Colony, 734
Virginia's General: Robert E. Lee and the Civil War, 1477
Visions: Stories About Women Artists, 2060
A Visit to Washington, DC, 1255
Visual Timeline of Transportation, 2451
The Voice of the People: American Democracy in Action, 1455
Voices after Midnight, 1733
Voices of the 30s, 2528
Voyage of the Half Moon, 2380
Voyages to the New World, 412

W. E. B. Du Bois: Scholar and Activist, 2120
W. E. B. Du Bois and Racial Relations, 398
Wagon Train: A Family Goes West in 1865, 2487
Wagon Wheels, 305
Wagons West!, 795
Wait for Me, Watch for Me, Eula Bee, 188
Waiting for the Evening Star, 2376
Walk the World's Rim, 132
Walking for Freedom: The Montgomery Bus Boycott, 1182
Walking the Road to Freedom, 682
Walking Up a Rainbow, 2255
A Wall of Names: The Story of the Vietnam Memorial, 610
Walter White: Civil Rights Leader, 740
Walter White and the Power of Organized Protest, 1105
The War at Home, 860
War Behind the Lines, 252
War Comes to Willy Freeman, 456

The War in Georgia, 1698

The War in Vietnam, 805

War Nurses, 516

War, Peace, and All That Jazz, 922

War Terrible War, 923

War with Mexico, 1091

Warren G. Harding: 29th President of the United States, 371

Warren G. Harding: Twenty-Ninth President of the United States, 2330

Washington City Is Burning, 1875

Washington, D.C., 2722

The Washington Way, 1613

The Washingtons, 1940

Washington's Birthday, 736

Watch the Stars Come Out, 1375

The Water Brought Us: The Story of the Gullah-Speaking People, 296

The Watsons Go to Birmingham—1963, 534

The Wave of the Sea-Wolf, 2469

The Way Things Work, 2529

The Way West: Journal of a Pioneer Woman, 1246

Wayah of the Real People, 2142

We Have Conquered Pain: The Discovery of Anesthesia, 737

We Shall Not Be Moved: The Women's Factory Strike of 1909, 555

We Want Jobs! A Story of the Great Depression, 1669

Weasel, 575

A Weed Is a Flower: The Life of George Washington Carver, 47

A Weekend with Winslow Homer, 199

The Well: David's Story, 2248

We'll Race You, Henry, 1580

The West: An Illustrated History for Children, 629

West by Covered Wagon: Retracing the Pioneer Trails, 1712

West by Steamboat, 1546

The West Indian-American Experience, 933

West Indian Americans, 142

Western Europe: Our Legacy, 2723

Westward Expansion: The Pioneer Challenge, 2724

Westward Ho!: An Activity Guide to the Wild West, 378

Westward Wagons, 2725

The Whalers, 413

Whaling Days, 382

What About Annie?, 1575

What I Had Was Singing: The Story of Marian Anderson, 683

What Is an American?, 2726

What Makes a Cassatt a Cassatt?, 1626

What the Dickens!, 532

What Zeesie Saw on Delancey Street, 1806

What's the Big Idea, Ben Franklin?, 772

When Aunt Lucy Rode a Mule & Other Stories, 1776

When I Was Young in the Mountains, 1921

When Justice Failed: The Fred Korematsu Story, 407

When Plague Strikes: The Black Death, Smallpox, AIDS, 800

When the Cruel War Is Over: The Civil War Home Front, 551

When the Great Canoes Came, 429

When Will This Cruel War Be Over? The Diary of Emma Simpson, Gordonsville, Virginia, 1864, 581

When Willard Met Babe Ruth, 931

Where Is Papa Now?, 497

Where Lies Butch Cassidy?, 2190

Where the Broken Heart Still Beats: The Story of Cynthia Ann Parke, 1567

Where Will This Shoe Take You?: A Walk Through the History of Footwear, 1328

Which Way Freedom?, 948

White Hare's Horses, 2112

The White House, 907

The White House: Cornerstone of a Nation, 2117

The White House Kids, 272

Who Comes with Cannons?, 189

Who Invented the Game?, 2347

Who Is Carrie?, 457

Who Owns the Sun?, 2727

"Who Was That Masked Man, Anyway?," 126

Who Were the Founding Fathers?: Two Hundred Years of Reinventing American History, 1098

Who'd Believe John Colter?, 414

A Whole New Ballgame: The Story of the All-American Girls Professional Baseball League, 1449

Why Don't You Get a Horse, Sam Adams?, 773

Wild Bill Hickock, 850

The Wild Horses of Sweetbriar, 1229

Wilderness Cat, 1230

Wilderness Journey, 2143

Wildflower Girl, 487

Will and Orv, 2008

Will Rogers, 1997

Will Rogers: American Humorist, 78

Will Rogers: Cherokee Entertainer, 2105

Will Rogers: Cowboy Philosopher, 1459

Will Rogers: Quotable Cowboy, 204

Will Somebody Please Marry My Sister?, 428

Will You Sign Here, John Hancock?, 774

William Bradford: The First Thanksgiving, 2728

William H. Taft: 27th President of the United States, 672

William H. Taft: Twenty-Seventh President of the United States, 390

William Henry Harrison: 9th President of the United States, 2156

William Henry Harrison: Ninth President of the United States, 694

William McKinley: 25th President of the United States, 472

William McKinley: Twenty-Fifth President of the United States, 1210

William Parker: Rebel Without Rights, 1897

Williamsburg, 1211

Williamsburg: Cradle of the Revolution, 834

A Williamsburg Household, 68

Wilma Mankiller, 1337, 1416, 1809

Wilma Mankiller: Chief of the Cherokee Nation, 813

Wilma Mankiller: Leader of the Cherokee Nation, 2493

Wilma Mankiller: Principal Chief of the Cherokees, 2016

Wilma P. Mankiller: Chief of the Cherokee, 2065

Wilma Unlimited: How Wilma Rudolph Became the World's Fastest Woman, 1272

The Wilsons, 1941

Wings Around the World: The American World Flight of 1924, 2257

Winter Danger, 2144

Winter Days in the Big Woods, 2428

The Winter of Red Snow: The Diary of Abigail Jane Stewart, Valley Forge, Pennsylvania, 1777-1778, 897

The Winter Room, 1730

The Winter Solstice, 1089

Witch Hunt: It Happened in Salem Village, 1259
The Witch of Blackbird Pond, 2109
Witches, 1903
Witches: Opposing Viewpoints, 2171
Witches' Children, 419
With Domingo Leal in San Antonio 1734, 1483
With Every Drop of Blood: A Novel of the Civil War, 463
Witnesses to Freedom: Young People Who Fought for Civil Rights, 1876
The Wizard of Sound: A Story About Thomas Edison, 1581
Woman of Independence: The Life of Abigail Adams, 196
A Woman Unafraid: The Achievements of Frances Perkins, 483
Women Aviators, 2506
Women Business Leaders, 1756
Women in American Indian Society, 861
Women in America's Wars, 2033
Women Inventors and their Discoveries, 2310
Women of Peace: Nobel Peace Prize Winners, 2001
Women of the Lights, 710
Women of the Old West, 55
Women of the U.S. Congress, 1602
Women of the West, 2729, 2730
Women Pioneers, 2157
Women Scientists, 2311
Women Who Achieved Greatness, 537
Women Who Reformed Politics, 1603
Women with Wings, 2731
Women's Voting Rights, 973
Woodland Tribal Arts: Native American Arts, 2732
Woodrow Wilson, 1341
Woodrow Wilson: President, 1813
Woodrow Wilson: 28th President of the United States, 473

Woodrow Wilson, Franklin D. Roosevelt, Harry S. Truman, 1394
Woodsong, 1731
Words by Heart, 2023
The Workers' Detective: A Story About Dr. Alice Hamilton, 1552
A World Full of Animals: The Roger Caras Story, 375
A World of Knowing: A Story About Thomas Hopkins Gallaudet, 290
The World of Young Andrew Jackson, 1016
The World of Young George Washington, 1017
The World of Young Tom Jefferson, 1018
World Series Classics, 905
World War I, 2733
World War I: "The War to End Wars," 1212
World War II in Europe: "America Goes to War," 2170
A World War Two Submarine, 1078
Wounded Knee: The Death of a Dream, 1690
The Wreck of the Zanzibar, 1607
The Wright Brothers: How They Invented the Airplane, 751
The Wright Brothers and Aviation, 1705
Wyatt Earp, 859

The Yankton Sioux, 2734
The Year of No More Corn, 1220
The Year of the Dragon, 2735
The Year of the Perfect Christmas Tree, 1063a
The Year of the Ranch, 1539
Year of the Sevens—1777, 1039
The Year They Walked: Rosa Parks and the Montgomery Bus Boycott, 2058
You Are the General, 6

You Are the General II: 1800-1899, 7
You Want Women to Vote, Lizzie Stanton?, 775
Young Abe Lincoln: The Frontier Days, 1809-1837, 960
Young Abigail Adams, 1922
Young Frederick Douglass: The Slave Who Learned to Read, 812
Young Harriet Tubman: Freedom Fighter, 200
Young Helen Keller: Woman of Courage, 201
Young John Quincy, 961
Young Martin's Promise, 1645
The Young Oxford Companion to the Supreme Court of the United States, 1719
Young Patriot: The American Revolution as Experienced by One Boy, 1636
Young Pocahontas: Indian Princess, 202
Your Friend, Natalie Popper, 1372

Zachary Taylor: 12th President of the United States, 474
Zachary Taylor: Twelfth President of the United States, 1213
Z.A.P., Zoe, & the Musketeers, 1411
Zebulon Pike, 2068
Zebulon Pike: Explorer of the Southwest, 1975
Zebulon Pike and the Explorers of the American Southwest, 2121
Zia, 1679
Zora Neale Hurston, 2470
Zora Neale Hurston: Southern Storyteller, 2494
Zora Neale Hurston: Storyteller of the South, 368

SUBJECT INDEX

Reference is to entry numbers.

Abenaki, 1290
Abolitionists. *See* Brown, John; *and* Stowe, Harriet Beecher
Abolitionists, African American, 2239. *See also* Allen, Richard; Cuffe, Paul; Douglass, Frederick; Terrell, Mary Church; Truth, Sojourner; Tubman, Harriet; *and* Turner, Nat
Abzug, Bella, 686
Activists, Women, 1603
Adams, Abigail, 196, 1692, 1745, 1922
Adams, Ansel, 535, 633
Adams, Grizzly, 1500
Adams, John, 310, 646, 668, 2152
Family, 1931
Adams, John Quincy, 443, 668, 961
Adams, Samuel, 674, 773; Video, 2690
Addams, Jane, 1188, 1238, 1549, 2001
African Americans, 57, 1169, 1554, 1557, 1560, 1642, 1732; Video, 2533, 2534, 2550
Art, 2206
Baseball, 298
Innovators; Video, 2593
Leadership, 2264
Literature, 2206
Soldiers, 1838
Vietnam War, 2214
Women's "Firsts," 1768
In the West, 416; Video, 2551, 2597; Fiction, 305. *See also* Beckwourth, James; *and* Love, Nat
African Americans to Canada; Fiction, 1085
Ailey, Alvin, Jr., 1380, 1758
Aircraft, 1627
Alabama, 2443
Alamo, 386, 1099, 1346, 2062; Fiction, 2463
Alaska, 446

Alaska Bush Pilots, 1363
Alcoholism; Fiction, 461
Alcott, Louisa May, 353, 879, 1270, 1919
Aldrin, Edwin, Jr., 909, 1486
Algonquin, 2732
All-American Girls Professional Baseball League. *See* Baseball
All Soul's Day. *See* Holidays
Allegheny; Fiction, 1175
Alvarez, Luis, 441
American History Explorer; CD-ROM, 2512a
American History Poetry, 1053
American History Survey, 1159
American Indians. *See* Native Americans
American Methodist Episcopal Church. *See* Allen, Richard
American Red Cross. *See* Barton, Clara
American Revolution, 90, 302, 600, 651, 1185, 1223, 1636, 1910; Video, 2542, 2543, 2555; Fiction, 115, 118, 145, 198, 213, 320, 455, 456, 548, 576, 623, 711, 763, 786a, 897, 1047, 1110, 1176, 1818, 1847, 2285
Boston Massacre, 1752
Bunker Hill, 1231
Causes; Video, 2567, 2691. *See also* Adams, Samuel
Concord and Lexington, 1667
Lexington and Concord, Battle of, 1119
Saratoga, 144
Songs and Stories, 2061
Submarine, 2220
Valley Forge, 2169; Video, 2721
Yorktown, 1206
Americans, Deceased, 1795
Americans, Definition of; Video, 2726
Amish, 225; Video, 2544; Fiction, 567

Anasazi, 127, 584, 786, 2275, 2352; Fiction, 233, 1106
Anderson, Marian, 537, 683, 1401, 1768, 2256
Anesthesia, 737
Angelou, Maya, 537, 1850
Annenberg, Walter, 1489
Anthony, Susan B., 102, 490, 787, 1094, 1365, 1486, 2368; Video, 2576, 2704
Anthropologists, 2371. *See also* Mead, Margaret; *and* Hurston, Zora Neale
Antonetty, Evalina Lopez (United Bronx Parents), 1587
Apache, 421, 708, 1108, 1197, 1955, 2014-15, 2045; Video; 2545. *See also* Geronimo
Apollo; CD-ROM, 2513
Appalachia; Fiction, 2399
Appleseed, Johnny, 46, 874, 1179, 1326
Apprentices; Fiction, 698
Arab Americans, 104; Video, 2546
Arawak, 302; Fiction, 783
Archaeologists, 2371
Archaeology, 2198
Architects, 823. *See also* Jefferson, Thomas; Johnson, Philip; Morgan, Julia; Olmsted, Frederick Law; Pei, I. M.; Richardson, Henry Hobson; Rohe, Ludwig Mies van der; Sullivan, Louis Henri; Williams, Paul R.; *and* Wright, Frank Lloyd
Arizona; Fiction, 183
Armed Forces; CD-ROM, 2527
Armenian Americans, Garry, Charles; Video, 2557
Armstrong, Louis, 460, 1523, 1556, 1851, 2007, 2238, 2483
Armstrong, Neil, 486, 909, 1404
Arnold, Benedict, 771, 2331
Art, 20th Century; CD-ROM, 2520

Arthur, Chester A., 317, 2187
Artists, 365, 535; Video, 2541;
  Fiction, 499. *See also*
  Adams, Ansel; Audubon,
  John James; Calder,
  Alexander; Cassatt, Mary;
  Catlin, George; Church,
  Frederick E.; Goble, Paul;
  Homer, Winslow; Hopper,
  Edward; MacKinnon,
  Christy; Moses, Anna
  Mary (Grandma);
  Noguchi, Isamu;
  O'Keeffe, Georgia; Peale,
  Charles Willson; Peet,
  Bill; Pollock, Jackson;
  Russell, Charles M.;
  Warhol, Andy; Whistler,
  James McNeill; Wood,
  Grant; Wyeth, Andrew;
  and Wyeth, N. C.
Artists, African American, 2207.
  See also Bearden, Romare;
  Day, Tom; Evans, Minnie;
  Johnson, William H.;
  Pippin, Horace; Powers,
  Harriet; *and* Traylor, Bill
Artists, Native American. *See*
  Desjarlait, Patrick;
  Martinez, Maria; *and*
  Naranjo, Michael
Ash, Mary Kay, 1756
Ashe, Arthur, 2488
Asian Americans, 2223; Video,
  2587. *See also* Asian
  Pacific Americans;
  Chinese Americans;
  Japanese Americans;
  Korean Americans; *and*
  Vietnamese Americans
Asian Indians, 135
Asian Pacific Americans, 2067.
  See also Asian Americans;
  Chinese Americans;
  Japanese Americans;
  Korean Americans; *and*
  Vietnamese Americans
Assassinations, of Presidents, 1123
Astronauts. *See* Aldrin, Edwin, Jr.;
  Armstrong, Neil; *and*
  Resnick, Judith
Astronauts, African American,
  357. *See also* Jemison, Dr.
  Mae C.
Astronomers, 370
Athletes, Fiction, 1260, 1354. *See
  also* Ruth, Babe
Athletes, African American. *See*
  Ashe, Arthur; Louis, Joe;
  Owens, Jesse; Robinson,

Jackie; *and* Rudolph,
  Wilma
Athletes, Native American. *See*
  Thorpe, Jim
Athletes, Women. *See* Rudolph,
  Wilma; *and* Zaharias,
  Babe Didrikson
Atomic Age, 2176
Atomic Bomb, 1686
Audubon, John James, 76, 304,
  1884
Authors; Fiction, 620. *See also*
  Alcott, Louisa May;
  Ashabranner, Brent; Buck,
  Pearl; Dickinson, Emily;
  Fleischman, Sid; Frost,
  Robert; Lindbergh, Anne
  Morrow; London, Jack;
  Paine, Thomas; Poe, Edgar
  Allan; Polacco, Patricia;
  Sandburg, Carl; Seuss,
  Dr.; Singer, Isaac
  Bashevis; Stowe, Harriet
  Beecher; Thoreau, Henry
  David; Twain, Mark;
  White, E. B.; *and* Wilder,
  Laura Ingalls
Authors, African American. *See*
  Angelou, Maya; Dunbar,
  Paul Laurence; Ellison,
  Ralph; Hughes, Langston;
  Hurston, Zora Neale; *and*
  Wheatley, Phillis
Authors, Native American. *See*
  Erdich, Louise
Automobiles; Fiction, 1083. *See
  also* Ford, Henry
Aviators. *See* Alaska Bush Pilots;
  Lindbergh, Charles; Post,
  Wiley; Rodgers, Calbraith
  Perry; *and* Yeager, Chuck
Aviators, African American. *See*
  Banning, James Herman;
  Bullard, Eugene; Chicago
  Flyers; Coleman, Bessie;
  Julian, Hubert Fauntleroy;
  and Powell, William J.
Aviators, Women; Video, 2731.
  See also Cobb, Geraldyn;
  Cochran, Jacqueline;
  Coleman, Bessie; Earhart,
  Amelia; Law, Ruth;
  Jemison, Dr. Mae C.;
  Lindbergh, Anne Morrow;
  Mock, Geraldine Fredritz;
  Ride, Sally Kristin;
  Tiburzi, Bonnie Linda;
  Whyte, Edna Gardner; *and*
  Yeager, Jeana L.
Aztec, 2035; Fiction, 2112

Back to Africa Movement
  Garvey, Marcus, 1318
Bacon, Henry, 106
Baker, Ella, 550
Baker, George. *See* Father Divine
Baker, Josephine, 2005
Baker, S. Josephine, 1797
Ball, Charles, 2055
Ballard, Robert, 92, 2119
Ballet, 782
Banneker, Benjamin, 486, 1760,
  1852
Banning, James Herman, 966
Bar Mitzvah, 1222
Barnum, P. T., 81, 709
Barton, Clara, 618, 1890
Baseball, 51, 58, 82, 298; Fiction,
  96, 931, 1654. *See also*
  Clemente, Roberto; Cobb,
  Ty; DiMaggio, Joe;
  Gehrig, Lou; Greenberg,
  Hank; Paige, Satchel;
  Robinson, Jackie; *and*
  Ruth, Babe
  All-American Girls Professional
    Baseball League,
    985, 1449
  Beginning, 2347
  Brooklyn Dodgers; Fiction, 1895
  Casey; Fiction, 2259
  Cy Young Award, 2503
  Great Moments, 2348
  Japanese Americans; Fiction,
    1584
  Mistakes, 1650
  Negro Leagues, 504, 780, 1538,
    1868, 2346
  World Series, 905
Basie, Count. *See* Count Basie
Bean, Judge Roy, 858
Bearden, Romare, 330
Beckwourth, James, 261, 603, 1852
Bell, Alexander Graham, 1710,
  1803, 2435; Video, 2535
Berg, Moe, 82
Berlin, Irving, 2202
Berlin Airlift. *See* Marshall,
  George C.
Bethune, Mary McLeod, 888, 926,
  1180, 1528, 1529, 1768,
  2473; Video, 2637
Big Meeting; Fiction, 2480
Bigfoot, 627
Billy the Kid, 849
Bismarck (submarine), 2075
Black Elk, 867
Black Hawk, 283
Black Migration, 502, 1330
Black Power
  Carmichael, Stokely, 1114
Black Seminoles, 57

Blackfoot, 910
Blackwell, Elizabeth, 329, 988, 1308, 1993
Blindness; Fiction, 426, 2389; Video, 2552. *See also* Keller, Helen
Blizzard of 1888, 232; Fiction, 2181, 2384
Bloomers, 273
Blue Jeans
   Strauss, Levi, 991, 2363
Bluford, Guion, 1852
Bly, Nelly (Nellie), 561, 652, 1802; Fiction, 268
Boehm, Helen, 1756
Bond Servants; Fiction, 117, 121
Bonnin, Gertrude, Zitkala-Sa, 1820
Boone, Daniel, 396, 868, 1323, 1815, 1965, 2430
Borden, Lizzie, Trial, 1822
Boston Tea Party, 1681
Bourke-White, Margaret, 537, 546, 1178
Bowditch, Nathaniel, 1305
Boxer, Barbara, 1602
Brady, Matthew, 545, 2209
Brandeis, Louis, 753
Brant, Joseph, 282
Braun, Carol Moseley, 1602
Bridger, Jim, 48, 1221, 1420, 1984
Bridges, Ruby, 454
Brooks, Gwendolyn, 1850
Brotherhood of Sleeping Car Porters, Randolph, A. (Asa) Philip, 945
Brown, John, 154, 475, 662, 842, 1204, 1784, 2019
Brown, Molly, 266
Brown v. Board of Education, 687
Bryan, William Jennings, 668
Buck, Pearl, 1286
Buddhism
   Birth Customs, 1914
   Death Customs, 1915
   Food, 352
   Initiation Rites, 1791
   Marriage Customs, 485
   Pilgrimages, 1792
Budget, United States; Video, 2547
Buffalo, 744, 2218; Fiction, 1883, 2134, 2141, 2338
Buffalo Bill, 444
Buffalo Soldiers, 1572
Buildings, Construction, 2431
Bullard, Eugene, 977
Bunche, Ralph, 1531, 1848
Burns, Anthony, Fugitive Slave Act, 939
Bush, Barbara, 984
Bush, George, 1196, 1738, 2150, 2208

Bushnell, David, 2220
Bushwackers; Fiction, 175
Businessmen and Women. *See* Entrepreneurs
Butcher, Solomon, 496
Butcher, Susan, 602, 2334

Cahokia Mounds, 510
Calamity Jane, 55, 666, 1964
Calder, Alexander, 535
Calhoun, John, 668
California, 2444; Fiction, 130, 172, 178, 538, 569, 608, 1359, 1998, 2012, 2102; Video, 2694
Canals, 798, 1540. *See also* Erie Canal; *and* Panama Canal
Candlemaking; Video, 2554
Cannary, Martha Jane. *See* Calamity Jane
Caras, Roger, 375
Carmichael, Stokely, 1114
Carnegie, Andrew, 1094, 1489
Carson, Ben, 2063
Carson, Kit, 48, 819, 1971, 1984
Carson, Rachel, 10, 537, 826, 882, 957, 1111, 1310, 1486, 1789, 2222, 2333
Carter, Howard, 713
Carter, Jimmy, 383, 1393, 1857, 2073, 2328
Cartoon History, 1098
Carver, George Washington, 47, 450, 848, 870, 1486, 1518, 1659, 1852, 1881, 2505; Video, 2590
Cassatt, Mary, 315, 366, 824, 1268, 1568, 1626, 1762, 2060, 2293, 2316
Cassidy, Butch, 854
Catholicism; Fiction, 714, 776
Catlin, George, 1761, 2205
Cats; Fiction, 1230
Cattle Drives, 1470; Fiction, 944
Cayuga, 637-38
Celebrations. *See* Holidays
Censorship, 2131
Chaco Canyon, 786
Chairs, 799
Challenger, 229, 536
Chapman, John. *See* Appleseed, Johnny
Chavez, Cesar, 399, 491, 570, 833, 1031, 1094, 1486, 1879
Cherokee, 162, 312, 422, 543, 1240, 1337, 1414, 1418, 2051, 2094, 2189; Video, 2558; Fiction, 2142. *See also* Mankiller, Wilma; Ross, John; *and* Sequoyah

Cherry, Fred, 1643
Chesapeake Bay; Fiction, 1713
Chester, Daniel, 106
Cheyenne, 1404, 2095; Video, 2559; Fiction, 1952
Chicago, Great Fire of, 536, 1633, 1871, 1873, 2344
Chicago Flyers, 966
Chief Gall, 2050
Chief Joseph, 719, 1953, 2022, 2241
Chimney Sweeps, 801
Chinese Americans, 136, 547, 1041, 1445, 2224; Fiction, 444a, 828, 1069, 1412. *See also* Wong, Bill
Chinn, May, 360
Chinook; Video, 2560
Chippewa, Hole-in-the-Day, 1285
Chisholm, Shirley, 686, 1602, 1768, 1773, 1848, 1991
Christianity
   Birth Customs, 1914
   Death Customs, 1915
   Food, 352
   Initiation Rites, 1791
   Marriage Customs, 485
   Pilgrimages, 1792
Christmas, 65; Fiction, 566; Video, 2562
Chuckwagon. *See* Goodnight, Charles
Chumash, 638; Fiction, 2112
Church, Frederick E., 824
Cinema, 160, 1023; Fiction, 1163, 2359. *See also* Disney, Walt; Hayes, Helen; *and* Hitchcock, Alfred
Circuit-Riders; Fiction, 165, 297
Circus, 630; Fiction, 381, 1499, 2092. *See also* Barnum, P. T.
Cities, 1362
Citizenship, 2049
Civil Rights Movement, 50, 57, 326, 1181, 1419, 1689, 1876, 1849, 1876, 2370; Fiction, 532. *See also* Baker, Ella; Du Bois, W. E. B.; Farmer, James; Hamer, Fannie Lou; King, Martin Luther, Jr.; Malcolm X; Meredith, James; Montgomery Bus Boycott; Parks, Rosa; Randolph, A. Philip; Terrell, Mary Church; *and* White, Walter

Civil War, 13, 230, 281, 551, 923, 1223, 1632, 1829, 2173, 2366; Fiction, 52, 95, 167, 170, 345, 418, 581, 607, 624, 696, 1062, 1079, 1166, 1425, 1426, 1770, 1780, 1833, 1836, 1863, 2139, 2462, 2464, 2467. *See also* Barton, Clara; Brady, Matthew; Brown, John; Edmonds, Emma; Grant, Ulysses S., Lee; Robert E.; *and* Lincoln, Abraham
Antietam, 63
Before the war, 918
Black Soldiers, 57, 503, 1566
Bull Run, 1205
Causes; Video, 2556
Chancellorsville, 7, 1193
Foods, 664
Forts, 2436
Gettysburg, 63, 384, 513, 1118, 1635, 1840; Video, 2592
Gettysburg Address, 1387, 1854
Music, 530
Navy, 190
Nurses, 2052
Shiloh, 1194
Washington, D.C., 95
Women, 403, 480
Clay, Henry, 668, 1746
Clemens, Samuel Langhorne. *See* Mark Twain
Clemente, Roberto, 2336
Cleveland, Grover, 468, 1198
Clinton, Hillary Rodham, 1577
Clothes, 1128, 1604, 1742, 1909, 2317
Cobb, Ty, 1097
Cochran, Jacqueline, 2002, 2086, 2506
Cody, Buffalo Bill, 1963
Cohen, Ben, 1489
Cold War, 523, 2176
Coleman, Bessie, 966, 967, 977, 1389, 1821, 2506; Video, 2696
Colonial Period, 325, 647, 917, 919, 1072, 1073, 1130, 1223, 2174; Fiction, 341, 648, 685, 707, 1038, 1593, 1787, 2048, 2468; Videos, 2564, 2573-74
African Americans, 1184
Connecticut, 722
Crafts, 1129
Craftspeople, 2179
Delaware, 723
Fort Life, 1156

Home Life, 2350
Humor, 42
Maryland, 725
Massachusetts, 726
New Hampshire, 727
New Jersey, 728
New York, 729
North Carolina, 730; Fiction, 2474
Pamunkey, 429
Pennsylvania, 731
Rhode Island, 732
South Carolina, 733
Virginia, 734
Williamsburg, 834, 1131, 2145
Colonial Wars, 385
Colorado; Fiction, 171, 180, 275
Colter, John, 48, 414
Coltrane, John, 1851
Columbus, Christopher, 64, 302, 817, 1397, 1486, 1737, 1994, 2432; Video, 2563
Columbus Day. *See* Holidays and Celebrations
Comanche, 1405, 1473, 1600, 1957, 2452; Video, 2566; Fiction, 188. *See also* Parker, Cynthia; *and* Parker, Quanah
Comics, 2018
Communists; Fiction, 289
Computers, 2401
Confederacy, Davis, Jefferson, 1199, 1225, 1783
Congress, 2178, 2362
Congressmen. *See* Clay, Henry; *and* Powell, Adam Clayton, Jr.
Congresswomen. *See* Abzug, Bella; Boxer, Barbara; Braun, Carol Moseley; Chisholm, Shirley; Douglas, Helen Gahagan; Feinstein, Dianne; Fenwick, Millicent; Ferraro, Geraldine; Jordan, Barbara; Kassebaum, Nancy Landon; Mikulski, Barbara; Murray, Patty; Perkins, Frances; Rankin, Jeannette; Schroeder, Patricia; *and* Smith, Margaret Chase
Connecticut Colony and State, 722, 2445
Constitution, 769; Video, 2716
Consumerism; Video, 2539
Coolidge, Calvin, 1195, 2186
Cortez, Hernando; Fiction, 132
Cotton Gin, Whitney, Eli, 1307
Count Basie, 1851
Cousteau, Jacques Yves, 873

Cowboys, 745, 808, 843, 1239, 1291, 1470, 1629, 1979, 2192; Fiction, 2212
Crash of 1929, 1569
Crazy Horse, 831, 906, 1954
Creek; Video, 2568
Crick, Francis, 3
Croatan, 1052
Crockett, Davy, 22, 1282, 1622, 1966
Crow, 612, 2475; Video, 2569. *See also* Plenty Coups
Cuba, 11
Cuban Americans, 1563
Cuban Missile Crisis, 326, 2388
Cuffe, Paul, 588; Fiction, 946
Custer, George Armstrong, 2133
Czech Americans, 1987

D-Day, 241
Daguerreotypes; Fiction, 1617
Dalton Gang, 855
Dancers, 782. *See also* de Mille, Agnes; Duncan, Isadora; *and* Graham, Martha
Dancers, African American. *See* Ailey, Alvin, Jr.; *and* Dunham, Katherine
Dancers, Native American. *See* Tallchief, Maria
Danish Americans; Fiction, 1683
Dare, Virginia; Fiction, 1052
Darrow, Clarence, 658. *See also* Scopes Monkey Trial
Davis, Benjamin O., Jr., 91, 1837, 1848
Davis, Jefferson, 668, 1199, 1225, 1783
Day of the Dead. *See* Holidays and Celebrations
Day, Dorothy, 1186
Day, Tom, 1429
de Gálvez, Bernardo, 571, 1288
de Mille, Agnes, 2107
Declaration of Independence, 2160, 2388
Deere, John, 471
Delaware Colony, 723
Delta Queen; Video, 2719
Democracy, 1455; CD-ROM, 2524; Video, 2570
Depression, 324, 1669, 2158, 2388; Fiction, 59, 60, 86, 98, 509, 521, 885, 1058, 1160, 1248, 1424, 1492, 1575, 1582, 1640, 1739, 1834, 2103, 2410
Desert Storm, 6, 63
Desert Tribes; Video, 2651
Desjarlait, Patrick, 2439

Detectives 1088. *See also*
    Pinkerton, Allan
Dickinson, Emily, 220, 869, 1270,
    1682; Fiction, 192
Dickinson, Susanna, 1099
DiMaggio, Joe, 89
Disabled; Fiction, 146
Discovery of the Americas; Video,
    2571
Disney, Walt, 153, 1486, 1489,
    1755
Diversity; Video, 2586
Divorce; Fiction, 1008
Dix, Dorothea, 1458, 1992
Dogs, 2124; Fiction, 367, 704,
    811, 932, 1002, 1461, 1638
Dolls; Fiction, 1233, 1399
Dominican Americans, 137
Donner Party, 1315, 1637
Douglas, Helen Gahagan, 1602
Douglas, Marjory Stoneman, 340,
    1986, 2123
Douglass, Frederick, 24, 147, 205,
    206, 614, 812, 1215, 1486,
    1516, 1517, 1574, 1917,
    1996, 2367; Video, 2678
Dred Scott Decision, 992
Drew, Charles, 1457, 1852, 2233,
    2472, 2505
Du Bois, W. E. B., 398, 2120
Dunbar, Paul Laurence, 792
Duncan, Isadora, 1252, 1673, 1951
Dunham, Katherine, 606, 877
Dust Bowl, 83, 676, 2128; Fiction,
    755, 1904, 2283

Earhart, Amelia, 400, 537, 563,
    982, 1214, 1298, 1314,
    1343, 1811, 2002, 2043,
    2076, 2235, 2506; Video,
    2537, 2696
Early United States, 920, 1223,
    2088, 2174; Video, 2657
Earp, Wyatt, 859
Eastman, Charles, 74, 131
Edison, Thomas Alva, 39, 43, 65,
    348, 884, 1486, 1579,
    1581, 1704; Video, 2707
Educators; Fiction, 1063. *See also*
    Lyon, Mary; *and* Sullivan,
    Annie
Educators, African American. *See*
    Bethune, Mary McLeod;
    Forten, Charlotte; Walker,
    Pompey; Washington,
    Booker T.; *and* Woodson,
    Carter G.
1800s
    Child's Day, 1157
    City Life, 1134
    Clothing, 1151

    Customs and Traditions, 1158
    Games, 1147
    Grist Mills, 1148
    Overview, 1774
    Pleasures and Pastimes, 1139
    Sayings, 1154
    Schools, 1140, 1153
    Stores and Markets, 1142
    Storybooks, 1141
    Toys, 1152
    Travel, 1143
    Village Life, 1144
1830 to 1861, 2274
Eisenhower, Dwight David, 553,
    577, 655, 668, 951, 1092,
    1390, 1942, 2434
    Family, 1927
Elections, Presidential, 2175;
    Video, 2561
Elephants, 379; Fiction, 522
Ellington, Duke, 458, 1486, 1851,
    2481
Ellis Island, 688, 1093, 1263,
    1329, 1367, 1839, 2161;
    Fiction, 84, 1351
Ellison, Ralph, 234
Emancipation Proclamation, 57, 2388
Engineers, 286
Entertainers. *See* Guthrie, Woody;
    Presley, Elvis; *and* Rogers,
    Will
Entertainers, African American,
    1588. *See also* Armstrong,
    Louis; Baker, Josephine;
    Coltrane, John; Ellington,
    Duke; Fitzgerald, Ella;
    Gillespie, Dizzy; Holiday,
    Billie; Horne, Lena;
    Jackson, Mahalia; *and*
    Parker, Charlie
Entrepreneurs, 1, 2, 1755. *See also*
    Annenberg, Walter; Ash,
    Mary Kay; Boehm, Helen;
    Carnegie, Andrew; Chin,
    Leeann; Cohen, Ben;
    Disney, Walt; Fuller,
    Alfred; Giannini, A. P.;
    Greenfield, Jerry; Hearst,
    William Randolph;
    Hershey, Milton; Jobs,
    Steven; Johnson, John;
    Kellogg, W. K.; Knight,
    Phil; Kroc, Ray;
    Rockefeller, John D.;
    Roddick, Anita; Sarnoff,
    David; Sears, Richard;
    Strauss, Levi; Thomson,
    Roy Herbert; Totino,
    Rose; Turner, Ted;
    Walker, Madam C. J.; *and*
    Walton, Sam

Environmentalist Movement, 2407
Environmentalists, 75, 742. *See*
    also Appleseed, Johnny;
    Caras, Roger; Carson,
    Rachel; Douglas, Marjory
    Stoneman; Leopold, Aldo;
    and Muir, John
Epidemics, 1289
    Diphtheria; Fiction, 2491
    Influenza; Fiction, 1003, 1278
    Polio; Fiction, 2360
    Smallpox, 800
Epileptic Seizures; Fiction, 1068
Equal Rights; Video, 2577
Equal Schooling, Brown v. Board
    of Education, 687
Erie Canal, 958, 1020, 1661
Esteban, 132. *See also* Estevanico
Estevanico; Video, 2579. *See also*
    Esteban
Evans, Minnie, 1430
Exploration, North Pole, Historical
    Fantasy; Video, 2606
Explorers, 64, 109, 325, 758, 1451,
    1452, 1605, 1920. *See also*
    Ballard, Robert; Bridger, Jim;
    Columbus, Christopher; de
    Gálvez, Bernardo; Frémont,
    John Charles; Hillary,
    Edmund; Hudson, Henry;
    Lewis and Clark; Peary,
    Robert; Pike, Zebulon;
    Powell, John Wesley; *and*
    Spanish Conquests
Explorers, African American. *See*
    Henson, Matthew
Extremist Groups, 1296

Factories; Fiction, 462, 1398,
    1502, 1715
Families; Fiction, 113, 116, 150,
    166, 519, 657, 1071
Farmer, James, 2071
Farmers and Farming, 409, 969;
    Fiction, 1220, 1547, 1727,
    1730, 2396
Farnsworth, Philo, 1551
Farragut, David, 408, 717, 1306, 2044
Federal Bureau of Investigation.
    See Hoover, J. Edgar
Feinstein, Dianne, 1602
Fenwick, Millicent, 686
Ferraro, Geraldine, 686
Filipino Americans, 138
Fillmore, Millard, 389, 1317
Fires
    Chicago in 1871, 1633, 1873, 2344;
    Menominee, Michigan; Fiction,
    1480
    Triangle Shirtwaist Factory,
    1398, 2040

First Ladies. *See* Presidents' Wives
Fitzgerald, Ella, 1243
Fleischman, Sid, 701
Fleming, Alexander, 1170
Flight, 214, 1488, 1623, 1894,
    2199; Fiction, 2273, 2490;
    CD-ROM, 2512, 2516,
    225. *See also* Blanchard,
    Jean-Pierre; Wright,
    Wilbur; *and* Wright,
    Orville
Flipper, Henry Ossian, 1750
Florida, 2446; Fiction, 1358, 2411
    Everglades; Fiction, 574. *See
    also* Browder, Joe;
    and Douglas,
    Marjory Stoneman
Ford, Gerald, 467, 2069
Ford, Henry, 1580
Forest Tribes; Video, 2652
Fort McHenry, 1262; Video, 2585.
    See also Key, Francis Scott
Forten, Charlotte, 350
Forts, Civil War, 1624
Fortune, Amos, 2496
Foster, Stephen, 1269
1492, 2319
1492 to 1789, 2437
Frank Thompson. *See* Edmonds,
    Emma
Franklin, Benjamin, 14, 21, 557,
    668, 677, 772, 866, 1333,
    1407, 1486, 1694, 1703,
    1781, 1798, 1990, 2191;
    Fiction; 45
Free Blacks. *See* Cuffe, Paul; *and*
    Hall, Prince
Free Speech; Fiction, 1257
Freedom; Fiction, 1945
Freedom Riders, 974, 1187
Frémont, John Charles, 963, 1970
French and Indian Wars, 385, 1476
Friedan, Betty, 263, 989, 1559
Friendship; Fiction, 650
Frontier Life, 226, 251, 1867; Video,
    2588, 2589; Fiction, 1039,
    1872, 2108, 2135, 2136,
    2140, 2143, 2144
Frontiersmen; Video, 2639;
    Fiction, 575, 1728. *See
    also* Adams, Grizzly;
    Boone, Daniel; Carson,
    Kit; Colter, John; *and*
    Crockett, Davy
Frost, Robert, 1995
Fuller, Alfred, 1489
Fuller, Buckminster, 1782
Fulton, Robert, 1294
Furman v. Georgia, 993

Gallatin, Albert 668

Gallaudet, Thomas, 290
Garfield, James A., 323, 1383
Garrett, Thomas, 209
Garvey, Marcus, 1318
Gehrig, Lou, 1438, 1807
Geisel, Theodor. *See* Seuss, Dr.
Genetics, 3
Georgia Colony and State, 724;
    Fiction, 187, 433, 2089
German Americans; Video, 2591
Geronimo, 49, 1108, 1197, 1955,
    2015, 2045
Gershwin, George, 2313, 2320
Gettysburg, 63, 384, 513, 1118,
    1635, 1840; Video, 2592;
    Fiction, 786b, 1590
Gettysburg Address, 1387, 1854
Ghosts
    Elvis, 447
    War, 448
Giannini, A. P., 1489
Gillespie, Dizzy, 790, 838, 1851
Girl Scouts. *See* Low, Juliette
    Gordon
Glass, Hugh, 1498
Glenn, John, 451
Goats; Fiction, 1228
Goble, Paul, 825
Goddard, Robert, 673, 2201
Goethals, George, 1309
Gold, 1562
Gold Rush, 254, 621, 1219, 1258,
    1826, 2309; Video, 2641,
    2670; Fiction, 1048, 1644,
    1826
Goldman, Emma, 1094
Goodnight, Charles, 1691
Government; CD-ROM, 2527
    Executive Branch; Video, 2663
    Legislative Branch; Video, 2662
    Supreme Court; Video, 2664
Graham, Katharine Meyer, 537
Graham, Martha, 781, 1786, 1793
Grant, Ulysses S., 207, 1209, 1672
    Children, 1598
Greek Americans; Video, 2595;
    Fiction, 14091411
Greenberg, Hank, 211
Greenfield, Jerry, 1489
Grief; Fiction, 529
Gulf War. *See* Desert Storm
Gullah, 296
Gunfighters, 1981

Haida, 284
Hale, Nathan, 1595
Hall, Prince, 589
Hamer, Fannie Lou, 476, 1911
Hamilton, Alexander, 668, 1671
Hamilton, Alice, 1552
Hancock, John, 774

Harding, Warren G., 371, 2330
Harlem Renaissance, 975
Harpers Ferry. *See* Brown, John
Harris, Patricia Roberts, 1768
Harrison, Benjamin, 434, 2185
Harrison, William Henry, 694,
    2156
Harvey Girls, 1615
Hawaii; Fiction, 1923
Hayes, Helen, 1237
Hayes, Rutherford, 1202
Hearing Impaired, 2335; Fiction,
    1655, 1866. *See also* Bell,
    Alexander Graham;
    Gallaudet, Thomas; *and*
    Keller, Helen
Hearst, William Randolph, 1489
Henry, Patrick, 33; Video, 2665
Henson, Matthew, 807, 1852,
    2002; Video, 2638
Hershey, Milton, 2, 351
Hiawatha, 285, 735, 1497, 2385
Hickok, Wild Bill, 850
Hillary, Edmund, 1893
Hindenburg Disaster, 2162, 2236
Hinduism
    Birth Customs, 1914
    Death Customs, 1915
    Food, 352
    Initiation Rites, 1791
    Marriage Customs, 485
    Pilgrimages, 1792
Hine, Lewis Wickes, 749, 887
Hispanic Americans; Video, 2660.
    See also Mexican
    Americans; *and* Latin
    American Heritage
Hiss, Alger, 1817
Hitchcock, Alfred, 93
Hohokam, 2352
Hole-in-the-Day, 1285
Holiday, Billie, 1241, 1851
Holidays and Celebrations; Video,
    2648
    All Souls' Day, 1089
    Chinese New Year, 1445
    Christmas, 1133
    Columbus Day, 1382; Video, 2565
    Day of the Dead, 1074
    Halloween, 1089
    Jewish, 1446
    July 4, 1026; Fiction, 1347
    Martin Luther King Day, 1485;
        Video, 2600
    Presidents' Day, 736, 2679
    Ramadan and Id Al-Fitr, 1447
    St. Patrick's Day; Video, 2701
    Tet: Vietnamese New Year,
        1448
    Valentine's Day; Video, 2720
Holliday, John Henry "Doc," 856

Holmes, Oliver Wendell, 668
Homer, Winslow, 199, 824
Homesteaders, Great Plains, 809
Hoover, Herbert C., 435, 1771
Hopi, 1292, 2096
Hopper, Edward, 2312
Hopper, Grace, 2401
Horne, Lena, 1701
Houdini, Harry, 2482; Fiction, 223, 2025
Houston, Sam, 386, 668, 768, 1311, 1974
Hudson, Henry, 109, 2380
Huerta, Dolores, 570
Hughes, Langston, 221, 501, 1270, 1522, 1696
Hull House. *See* Addams, Jane
Human Rights Poetry, 1076
Hunkpapa Sioux, 2116. *See also* Sioux
Huron; Video, 2602
Hurston, Zora Neale, 368, 1270, 1777, 1850, 2470, 2494
Hutchinson, Anne, 1084, 1094, 1095, 1656

Idaho; Fiction, 168, 185
Iditarod Race, Alaska, 602, 1731, 2334
Illinois, 2447
Immigrants, 1093, 1949; Fiction, 997, 1125, 1374-76, 1378
Asian, 222931
Chinese, 2066, 2228; Video, 2735; Fiction, 2361, 2497, 2499
Danish, 2106
Eastern Europeans, 1490
Ellis Island, 1263, 1329, 1367
German Jewish, 1379
Irish, 1621; Fiction, 1606
Italian, 1345
Japanese, 2303
Norwegian; Video, 2540, 2676
Polish, 1769, 2104; Fiction, 1351, 1736
Russian, 1670, 1456
Russian Jewish, 1344; Fiction, 307, 970, 1350, 1378,1796, 2034
Scandinavian; Fiction, 1508
Strauss, Levi, 991
Swedish, 2460; Fiction, 1947, 1948, 2374
Vietnamese, 2215
War Refugees, 1250
Immigration, 70, 665, 829, 862, 1450; Video, 2603-05; CD-ROM, 2524
Independence Day. *See* Holidays and Celebrations
Indian Wars; Fiction, 1086

Industrialization, 327; Video, 2613
Inventors and Inventions, 425, 1764, 2294, 2310; Video, 2634; CD-ROM, 2529. *See also* Bell, Alexander Graham; Bushnell, David; Deere, John; Edison, Thomas Alva; Farnsworth, Philo; Fuller, Buckminster; Goddard, Robert; Morse, Samuel; Shakers; Tsiolkovski; Turing, Alan; *and* Whitney, Eli
Inventors, African American. *See* Jones, Frederick; Latimer, Lewis; Matzeliger, Jan; Rillieux, Norbert; McCoy, Elijah; *and* Woods, Granville T.
Iran Hostage Crisis, 2163
Irish Americans, 397, 1042, 1115, 1621; Video, 2614; Fiction, 487, 511, 1027, 1265
Iroquois, 285, 735, 1497, 2037, 2097, 2385; Video, 2615, 2732. *See also* Hiawatha
Ishi, 1109, 1743
Islam
Birth Customs, 1914
Death Customs, 1915
Food, 352
Initiation Rites, 1791
Marriage Customs, 485
Pilgrimages, 1792
Italian Americans, 587, 1043, 1345; Video, 2616; Fiction, 158, 591

Jackson, Andrew, 668, 1016, 1391, 1695, 1708, 2148, 2321
Family, 1929
Jackson, Jesse, 1849
Jackson, Mahalia, 2471
Jackson, Stonewall, 203, 770, 1751
James, Daniel, 2213
James, Jesse, 857, 2193
Jamestown; Video, 2618, 2619
Japanese Americans, 934, 1044, 1234, 1338, 1366, 1989, 2129, 2227, 2299; Video, 2620; Fiction, 143, 1584, 1585, 1924, 2281, 2296-98, 2300-02
Jayhawker; Fiction, 175
Jazz, 1588, 1851
Jefferson, Thomas, 40, 339, 668, 804, 823, 956, 1018, 1391, 1486, 1610, 1649, 1721, 1801, 2155; Fiction, 1591
Family, 1930

Jemison, Dr. Mae C., 977
Jemison, Mary, 1357
Jewish Americans, 17, 18, 1045, 1222, 1625; Video, 2622; Fiction, 84, 156, 267, 307, 427, 428, 970, 978, 1303, 13721374, 1376, 1379, 1670, 1806, 1889, 1896. *See also* Meir, Golda; *and* Singer, Isaac Bashevis
Gold Rush; Video, 2549
Holidays, 30, 391, 1446; Video, 2688
Jobs, Steven, 1489
Johnson, Andrew, 617, 1192, 2184
Johnson, James Weldon, 1520, 1849
Johnson, John, 1755
Johnson, Lyndon B., 671, 953, 1174, 1390
Family, 1933
Johnson, Philip, 823
Johnson, William H., 663, 1268
Jones, Frederick, 2219
Joplin, Scott. *See* Treemonisha
Jordan, Barbara, 269, 537, 686, 1602, 1720, 1768
Journalists, Women, 2404. *See also* Bly, Nelly (Nellie); *and* Wells-Barnett, Ida B.
Judaism
Birth Customs, 1914
Death Customs, 1915
Food, 352
Initiation Rites, 1791
Marriage Customs, 485
Pilgrimages, 1792
Julian, Hubert Fauntleroy, 966, 977
July 4. *See* Holidays and Celebrations
Just, Ernest Everett, 1852
Justice; Fiction, 949

Kansas; Fiction, 305
Kassebaum, Nancy Landon, 686, 1602
Keckley, Elizabeth, 1918
Keller, Helen, 27, 28, 201 537, 840, 1080, 1277, 1465, 1486, 1660, 2113; Video, 2596, 2712
Kellogg, W. K., 1489
Kennedy, John Fitzgerald, 31, 62, 579, 669, 1200, 1390, 1810, 2024
Assassination, 2159
Kennedy, Robert F., 937, 965
Kentucky, 2079; Fiction, 394, 452
Key, Francis Scott, 1723, 2395
Kidnapping, 2132

King, Coretta Scott, 990, 1555, 1716
King, Martin Luther, Jr., 32, 57,
    231, 300, 554, 924, 938,
    1094, 1095, 1102, 1485,
    1486, 1526, 1576, 1645,
    1717, 1724, 1849, 1907,
    2011, 2432; Video, 2636,
    2666, 2710
King, Richard, 1972
King George's War, 1476
King Philip, 541, 1882, 2028
King William's War, 1476
Knight, Phil, 1489
Korean Americans, 139, 1349,
    2225; Video, 2624
Korean War, 2080, 2164; Fiction,
    1639, 2200
Korematsu, Fred, 407
Kroc, Ray, 1489
Ku Klux Klan; Fiction, 1050

La Flesche, Susan. See Picotte,
    Susan La Flesche; and
    Tibbles, Susette La Flesche
La Follette, Robert, 668
Labor; Fiction, 129, 827, 1825. See
    also Strikes
    Children, 749, 887
    Hamilton, Alice, 1552
    Mother Jones, 478, 979, 1057, 1253
    Nader, Ralph, 2267
Lange, Dorothea, 1561, 2291
Langley, Samuel, 214
Latimer, Lewis, 1513, 1668, 1852,
    2289
Latin American Heritage; Video,
    2625. See also Hispanic
    Americans; and Mexican
    Americans
Law, Ruth, 318
Lawyers, 658. See also Darrow,
    Clarence; and Lockwood,
    Belva
Lazarus, Emma, 1348, 1370
Learning Disabilities; Fiction, 1888
Lee, Robert E., 35, 333, 372, 619,
    847, 1216, 1477, 2434
Legacy, Western Europe; Video, 2723
Lenape; Video, 2626
Lennon, John, 492
Leopold, Aldo, 73, 631, 1408
Leukemia; Fiction, 1463
Lewis and Clark, 64, 274, 692,
    1264, 1506, 1744, 1886,
    2295. See also Sacagawea
Liberia. See Russwurm, John
Lift Every Voice and Sing. See
    Johnson, James Weldon
Lighthouses, 797, 904, 2258;
    Fiction, 1056, 1229, 1232,
    1684, 1885

Female Keepers, 710
Lincoln, Abraham, 20, 206, 306,
    336, 484, 556, 668, 750,
    767, 865, 901, 950, 960,
    1096, 1103, 1281, 1392,
    1400, 1486, 1611, 1685,
    1943, 2147; Video, 2530,
    2629, 2632
    Family, 1594, 1932
    Whiskers; Fiction, 2279, 2455
Lincoln, Mary Todd, 72, 1918
Lincoln Memorial, 106, 1189, 1842
Lindbergh, Anne Morrow, 401,
    2506
Lindbergh, Charles, 354, 465, 578,
    1812
Little Bighorn, 7, 63, 678, 2133,
    2442. See also Sitting Bull
Lockwood, Belva, 319, 658
Loggers, 1138, 1652, 2456;
    Fiction, 518, 1726
London, Jack, 1270, 2004
Lost Colony. See Roanoke
Louis, Joe, 1101, 1396
Louisiana Purchase, 2388. See also
    Lewis and Clark
Love, Nat, 1573
Low, Juliette Gordon, 193, 321
Lyon, Mary, 1891

Madison, Dolley, 560, 1799, 1804
Madison, James, 436, 765, 1340,
    1772, 1799
    Family, 1934
Magicians. See Houdini, Harry
Malcolm X, 542, 564, 1641, 1849,
    2041, 2195; Video, 2635
Mandan, 1361
Manhattan Project, 2165, 2435;
    Fiction, 860
Manifest Destiny, 387
Mankiller, Wilma, 49, 537, 813,
    1337, 1416, 1809, 2016,
    2065, 2493
Mapmakers, 1920
Marshall, George C., 668, 1417, 2381
Marshall, John, 668
Marshall, Thurgood, 41, 668, 976,
    1127, 1788, 1848, 1849,
    2402
Martin Luther King Day. See
    Holidays and Celebrations
Martinez, Vilma, 442
Maryland Colony and State, 725;
    Fiction, 913, 1553
Mason and Dixon Line, 2114
Massachusetts Colony and State,
    111, 726; Fiction, 114,
    294, 891, 2502
Massasoit, 2026. See also Plimoth
Masterson, Bat, 852

Mayflower. See Plimoth
Mayo Brothers, 520
McClintock, Barbara, 537, 983,
    1236
McCoy, Elijah, 2271
McKinley, William, 472, 1210
Mead, Margaret, 392, 537, 2511
Meir, Golda, 19, 537
Memorials. See Lincoln Memorial;
    and Vietnam Memorial
Mennonites; Fiction, 2324
Menominee; Video, 2640
Metacum. See King Philip
Mental Hospitals. See Dix,
    Dorothea
Mentally Disabled; Fiction, 380,
    1364
Meredith, James, 653
Mesa Verde, 99, 507, 510, 514,
    2275. See also Anasazi
Mesquakie; Fiction, 2326-27
Meteorites; Fiction, 493
Metropolitan Museum. See New
    York City
Mexican Americans, 67, 140, 393,
    1074, 1757; Fiction, 1033.
    See also Alvarez, Luis;
    Chavez, Cesar; Martinez,
    Vilma; Hispanic
    Americans; and Latin
    American Heritage
Mexican War, 387, 1091, 1472;
    Fiction, 2466
Michigan; Fiction, 264, 2394
Midwest; Fiction, 1071
Migrant Workers, 105, 438, 2128.
    See also Chavez, Cesar;
    and Huerta, Dolores
Mikulski, Barbara, 686, 1602
Military Defense, 1700
Military Leaders. See Davis,
    Benjamin O., Jr.;
    Eisenhower, Dwight
    David; Grant, Ulysses S.;
    Jackson, Stonewall; James,
    Daniel; Lee, Robert E.;
    MacArthur, Douglas;
    Marshall, George C.;
    Patton, George; Powell,
    Colin L.; and Sheridan,
    Philip H.
Mills. See Factories
Mining, 157
    Coal, 157; Fiction, 1921, 2375
    Colorado; Fiction, 1325
    Gold, 176, 254, 1015, 1325,
        1980; Video, 2641
    Iron; Fiction, 1484
    Pennsylvania Coal; Fiction, 2091
Minnesota, History, 376
Miranda v. Arizona, 1861

Missions, California, 8, 194, 316, 604, 1356, 1444, 1827, 2400; Video, 2642, 2643; Fiction, 1313

Mississippi; Fiction, 510, 941, 1161, 2243, 2248,

Missouri, 703

Mitchell, Maria, 835, 1550

Mogollon, 2352

Mohawk, 282, 335, 639; Fiction, 635. *See also* Brant, Joseph

Money, 359, 1453

Monroe, James, 668, 693, 2151

Montgomery Bus Boycott, 36, 756, 889, 1075, 1182, 1486, 2388. *See also* Parks, Rosa

Monticello, 1855. *See also* Jefferson, Thomas

Moon Walk; Fiction, 149, 909. *See also* Armstrong, Neil

Moravians; Fiction, 1601

Morgan, Julia, 1107

Mormon. *See* Young, Brigham; *and* Salt Lake City

Morrill, Justin, 668

Morrison, Toni, 1850

Morse, Samuel, 1217, 1312

Moses. *See* Tubman, Harriet

Moses, Anna Mary (Grandma), 1687

Mother Jones, 478, 979, 1057, 1253; Fiction, 1825

Mott, Lucretia, 1486

Mount Vernon, 1843

Mountain Men; Video, 2645. *See also* Bridger, Jim; Carson, Kit; Colter, John; Glass, Hugh; *and* Smith, Jedediah

Mudd, Dr. Samuel A., 1509

Muhammad, Elijah, 925; Video, 2575

Muir, John, 712, 875, 1342, 1646, 2234, 2332, 2372

Multiculturalism; Video, 2581

Mummies, 218, 572

Murals, 374

Murray, Patty, 1602

Music; Fiction, 459, 1830, 1901

Musicians. *See* Berlin, Irving; Foster, Stephen; Gershwin, George; Lennon, John; Parker, Charlie; Sousa, John Philip; *and* Entertainers

Musicians, African American. *See* Anderson, Marian; Armstrong, Louis; Ellington, Duke; Gillespie, Dizzy; Robeson, Paul; *and* Entertainers, African American

Muslim Americans, 1447

Nader, Ralph, 2267

Narragansett; Video, 2646

Nation of Islam. *See* Malcolm X; *and* Muhammad, Elijah

National Anthem. *See* United States' Songs and Anthem

Native American Life, 151, 256, 748, 1169, 1404, 1628, 2087; Video, 2599, 2649, 2655; CD-ROM, 2522; Fiction, 611, 893-95, 962, 1037, 1235, 1355, 1676, 1679, 1859, 1877, 2342, 2469

Arts, 2732

Celebrations, 2070

Daily Life, Colonial Times, 2358

Homes, 1599

Medicine; Video, 2650

Powwow, 295

Red River War, 107

Relocation, 634

Rituals, 2070

Rock Art, 1287

Spiritual Leaders, 2337

Tracking; Video, 2695

Woodland Tribal Arts; Video, 2732

Native American Women Leaders, 861. *See also* Mankiller, Wilma; Picotte, Susan La Flesche; Tibbles, Susette La Flesche; *and* Winnemucca, Sarah

Native Americans. *See* Abenaki; Algonquin; Anasazi; Apache; Arawak; Aztec; Blackfoot; Cayuga; Cherokee; Cheyenne; Chinook; Chippewa; Comanche; Creek; Crow; Desert Tribes; Forest Tribes; Haida; Hohokam; Hopi; Hunkpapa Sioux; Huron; Iroquois; Lenape; Mandan; Menominee; Mesquakie; Mogollon; Mohawk; Narragansett; Navajo; Nez Perce (Percé); Northwest Coastal Tribes; Northwest Tribes; Oglala; Omaha; Oneida; Onondaga; Ottawa; Penobscot; Plains Tribes; Pomo; Potawatomi; Powhatan; Pueblo; Sac; Seminole; Seneca; Shawnee; Sioux; Southeast Tribes; Southwest Tribes; Taino; Totem Pole Tribes; Tuscarora; Wampanoag; Yahi; Yankton Sioux; *and* Yokut

Navajo, 4, 1880, 2098, 2263, 2476; Fiction, 1678; Video, 2656

Navigational Charts. *See* Bowditch, Nathaniel

Nebraska, 2448; Fiction, 346, 494

Negro Leagues. *See* Baseball

Nevelson, Louise, 365

New Amsterdam; Fiction, 1403

New Deal; Video, 2594

New England; Fiction, 265, 927-30 Old Sturbridge Village; Video, 2659

New Hampshire Colony and State, 727; Fiction, 531

New Jersey Colony and State, 728, 2270; Fiction, 117, 121

New Mexico; Fiction, 1493

New Nation. *See* Early United States

New York City, 430; Fiction, 457, 1718, 1733, 1899, 2077, 2277

New York State, 112, 729; Fiction, 110, 415

Newspapers; Video, 2532. *See also* Graham, Katharine Meyer

Nez Perce (Percé), 719, 1953, 2022, 2038, 2099, 2241; Fiction, 1680. *See also* Chief Joseph

Nice, Margaret Morse, 632

1900 to 1910, 886, 914, 1223; Fiction, 986, 1064, 1066, 1067, 1512, 1741, 2204, 2378

Recipes, 1767

1910 to 1920, 1381; Fiction, 1651, 1754

1920 to 1930, 922, 1012; Fiction, 1504, 1864

1930 to 1940, 922, 1699; CD-ROM, 2528; Fiction, 1865

1940 to 1950, 1013

1945 and After, 915, 1223; Fiction, 998, 999, 1024, 1060a, 1698, 2074

1950 to 1960, 1124; Fiction, 195, 197, 1482, 1697, 2398

1960 to 1970, 1295; Fiction, 1427, 1462, 2504

1970 to 1980, 785, 1014; Fiction, 1464

1980 to 1990, 898, 2216

Nineteenth Century. *See* 1800s

Nixon, Richard, 152, 668, 1300, 1386, 1393, 2153

Family, 1935

Nobel Prize Winners, 270. *See also* Addams, Jane; Alvarez, Luis; Buck, Pearl; Bunche, Ralph; Crick, James; Fleming,

Alexander; King, Jr., Martin Luther; Marshall, George C.; McClintock, Barbara; Roosevelt, Theodore; Salk, Jonas; Watson, James; Wiesel, Elie; *and* Wilson, Woodrow
Noguchi, Isamu, 1268
Norris, George, 668
North Carolina Colony and State, 730; Fiction, 189, 257
Northwest Coastal Tribes; Video, 2653
Northwest Tribes; Video, 2609

Oakley, Annie, 815, 845
Oglala. *See* Black Elk
Ohio; Fiction, 695, 940
O'Keeffe, Georgia, 219, 314, 535, 824, 1268, 2059, 2292, 2314
Oklahoma; Fiction, 85
Olmsted, Frederick Law, 823
Olympic Games, 1247. *See* Owens, Jesse; Rudolph, Wilma; Thorpe, Jim; *and* Zaharias, Babe Didrikson
Omaha. *See* Picotte, Susan La Flesche; *and* Tibbles, Susette La Flesche
Onassis, Jackie Kennedy, 61
Oneida, 640
Onondaga, 641
Oppenheimer, Robert, 615
Oregon, 2449; Fiction, 177, 184
Oregon Trail, 689, 1712, 2149; Video, 2531, 2548, 2582, 2661, 2709; Fiction, 1116, 1162, 1165, 1276, 1347, 1507, 1619, 1725, 1728, 1729, 2053, 2054, 2183, 2308, 2405
    Fort, 2130
    Knight, Amelia Stewart, 1246
    Parkman, Francis, 2056
Orphan Train, 777, 1011, 2351; Fiction, 347, 1028, 1029, 1164, 1662-66
Orphans, 186; Fiction, 705, 1747, 1748, 2125, 2390, 2441
    Hershey, Milton, 351
Osceola, 259, 1126, 1956, 2322
Ottawa, 1293. *See also* Pontiac
Outlaws, 994. *See also* James, Jesse
Overland Trail; Fiction, 2478
    Donner Party, 1315, 1637
Owens, Jesse, 5, 29, 791, 1486, 1521, 1853, 1968

Paige, Satchel, 2042

Paine, Thomas, 675, 2304
Paiute. *See* Winnemucca, Sarah
Panama Canal, 601, 1702, 2115. *See also* Goethals, George
Parker, Charlie, 739, 1851
Parker, Cynthia, 1567
Parker, Quanah, 1019, 1473, 1567, 1957, 2452
Parker, William, 1897
Parkman, Francis, 2056
Parks, Gordon, 222
Parks, Rosa, 36, 756, 889, 1075, 1486, 1706, 1707, 2058
Patton, George, 1735
Pawtucket; Fiction, 1249
Pawtuxet. *See* Squanto
Peale, Charles Willson, 2379, 2453; Fiction, 1618
Peary, Robert, 64, 405, 645, 1203, 1487, 2002
Peddlars; Fiction, 697, 1946
Peet, Bill, 1734
Pei, I. M., 823
Penicillin, 1170
Pennsylvania, 731; Fiction, 157, 761, 902
Penobscot, 642
Perkins, Frances, 483
Pets; Fiction, 1481. *See also* Dogs; *and* Cats
Philadelphia; Fiction, 44; Video, 2536, 2685
    Independence Hall, 2146
    Liberty Bell, 1117
Philip, King. *See* King Philip
Photography. *See* Adams, Ansel; Bourke-White, Margaret; Brady, Matthew; Butcher, Solomon; Lange, Dorothea; *and* Parks, Gordon
Physicians, 737; Fiction, 573. *See also* Baker, S. Josephine; Blackwell, Elizabeth; Eastman, Charles; Hamilton, Alice; Mayo Brothers; Sabin, Florence; Salk, Jonas; *and* Spock, Benjamin
Physicians, African American. *See* Carson, Ben; Chinn, May; Drew, Charles; *and* Williams, Daniel Hale
Physicians, Native American. *See* Eastman, Charles; *and* Picotte, Susan La Flesche
Pickett, Bill, 1759, 1961
Picotte, Susan La Flesche, 681; Video, 2572
Pierce, Franklin, 322, 2064
Pike, Zebulon, 1975, 2068, 2121
Pilgrims. *See* Plimoth

Pinchot, Gifford, 75
Pinkerton, Allan, 851, 2484
Pinto, Cezanne, 2196
Pioneer Candlemaking; Video, 2554
Pioneer Life, 890; Video, 2623, 2633; Fiction, 987, 1360, 1421, 1422, 1776, 1808, 1944, 24132429
Pioneers, 2020; Video, 2601
    Artisans, 1132
    Families, 1135
    Farms, 1136
    Food, 1146
    Health and Medicine, 1137
    Home Crafts, 1149
    Kitchens, 1150
    Spanish Pioneers, 784
    Tools and Gadgets, 1155
    Women 2157
Pippin, Horace, 1431
Pirates, 1388, 1474, 1763
Plains Tribes, 80; Video, 2610, 2654
Pledge of Allegiance, 2221
Plenty Coups, 612
Plimoth, 291, 549, 1887, 2027, 2307, 2353, 2355-56, 2583; Video, 2667-69, 2705, 2728; Fiction, 1302, 1592, 1608
Plumbing, 482, 1218
Plymouth. *See* Plimoth
Pocahontas, 9, 202, 342, 559, 762, 821, 839, 1030; Video, 2671; Fiction, 1677
Poe, Edgar Allan, 1270; Fiction, 120
Poetry
    American History, 1053
    Human Rights, 1076
    Poems of America, 1753
Polio, 1177; Fiction, 911, 1120, 2272, 2360. *See also* Salk, Jonas
Polish Americans, 2672; Fiction, 1035
Polk, James K., 668, 864, 1384, 1392
Pollock, Jackson, 2315
Pomo; Video, 2706
Pontiac, 260, 2386
Pony Express, 444, 586, 788, 959, 1266, 1983, 2306; Fiction, 2030; Video, 2673
Post, Wiley, 2251
Post War U.S.A.; Video, 2674
Potawatomi; Fiction, 2391, 2392; Video, 2675
Powell, Colin, 1848
Powell, John Wesley, 338, 741, 779

Powell, Adam Clayton, Jr., 1100, 1849
Powell, William J., 966
Powers, Harriet, 1432
Powhatan, 1503. *See also* Pocahontas
Powwow, 295
Prairie Life, 1906, 2266; Fiction, 65, 94, 495, 971, 972, 13191321, 1324, 1441, 1443, 2282, 2354
Prejudice, 1910; Fiction, 2023; Video, 2677
Presidents, 163, 262, 1711, 1794, 1912, 1950, 2036, 2081-85; CD-ROM, 2514, 2523
Presidents' Day. *See* Holidays and Celebrations
Presidents' Homes. *See* Monticello; *and* Mount Vernon
Presidents' Pets, 395
Presidents' Wives, 1491. *See also* Adams, Abigail; Bush, Barbara; Clinton, Hillary Rodham; Lincoln, Mary Todd; Madison, Dolley; Onassis, Jackie Kennedy; Roosevelt, Eleanor; Washington, Martha; *and* Wilson, Edith
Presley, Elvis, 447, 1261, 1406
Progressive Movement; Video, 2680
Prohibition, 1021; Fiction, 123, 1835
Prophets, 449
Prospectors, 810
Pueblo, 349, 514; Video, 2681
Puerto Rican Americans; Video, 2682. *See also* Clemente, Roberto
Puritans; Fiction, 624, 1399, 2109
Pyle, Ernie, 1674

Quakers; Fiction, 189, 568, 2138
Queen Anne's War, 1476
Quilts, 437; Fiction, 182, 445, 1055, 1070, 1226, 1413, 2287. *See also* Powers, Harriet

Racism, 1583
Radiation Sickness; Video, 2598
Railroad Workers, 2066, 2456
Railroads. *See* Transportation
Ramadan. *See* Holidays and Celebrations
Ranchers and Ranch Life, 969; Video, 2684; Fiction, 364, 1483, 1539. *See also* King, Richard
Randolph, A. (Asa) Philip, 540, 945, 1849

Rankin, Jeannette, 668, 686, 1602
Reading, importance of; Fiction, 1061, 1369. *See also* Douglass, Frederick; *and* Washington, Booker T.
Reagan, Ronald, 1201, 1393, 1614, 1871, 2013, 2210
    Family, 1936
Recipes
    Civil War, 664, 1765
    Swedish, 1766
Reconstruction, 921, 1565; Fiction, 164, 179, 1778, 1779, 2465; Video, 2687
Red Cloud, 1335, 1958
Red Cross, 1775. *See also* Barton, Clara
Refugees, 2029
Religions, 1297
Religious Freedom and Tolerance. *See* Hutchinson, Anne
Resnick, Judith, 217
Revere, Paul, 34, 715, 757, 820, 1334
Rhode Island Colony and State, 732; Fiction, 120, 124, 125
Richardson, Henry Hobson, 823
Rickenbacker, Eddie, 679
Riis, Jacob, 1094
Rillieux, Norbert, 1513
Roanoke, 288, 2000
Robeson, Paul, 661, 1032, 1299, 1530
Robinson, Jackie, 5, 16, 832, 872, 1097, 1675, 1846, 1967, 1976, 2021, 2046; Fiction, 1354, 1412; Video, 2617
Rock Art, 100, 1287. *See also* Anasazi
Rockefeller, John D., 1489
Roddick, Anita, 1489
Rodeo Rider. *See* Pickett, Bill
Rodgers, Calbraith Perry, 2250
Roe v. Wade, 995
Rogers, Will, 49, 78, 204, 1459, 1997, 2105
Rohe, Ludwig Mies van der, 823
Roosevelt, Eleanor, 23, 498, 537, 667, 668, 746, 1336, 1486, 2009, 2269, 2365, 2433
Roosevelt, Franklin Delano, 525, 582, 583, 668, 747, 760, 863, 1087, 1208, 1392, 1394, 1467, 1486, 1609, 2154, 2372, 2403
    Family, 1928, 1938
Rosie the Riveter. *See* World War II
Ross, Betsy, 2339
Ross, John, 1414
Royce, Sarah, 2057

Rudolph, Wilma, 1272
Russell, Charles M., 2458
Russian Americans, 1456; Fiction, 129
Russwurm, John, 287
Ruth, Babe, 5, 1097, 1437, 1658, 1960; Fiction, 931

Sabin, Florence, 1173, 1267
Sac. *See* Black Hawk
Sacagawea, 331, 822, 982, 1816, 1908, 1973; Video, 2689, 2698
Sacco-Vanzetti Trial, 1823
Sailors, 505
Salem Witch Trials, 1190, 1259, 1870, 2305, 2508; Fiction, 419, 1010, 1301, 2203
Salk, Jonas, 301, 533, 955, 2268
Salt Lake City, 613
Sampson, Deborah, 1505
San Antonio, 1346. *See also* Alamo
San Francisco, 431; Fiction, 369
San Francisco Earthquake, 536, 892, 1906, 2454; Fiction, 1274, 1415
Sandburg, Carl, 1270
Santa Fe Trail, 1316, 1916; Fiction, 1495
Sarnoff, David, 1489
Schroeder, Patricia, 686
Science and Technology; CD-ROM, 2518, 2527
Scientists, 450; CD-ROM, 2518. *See also* Carson, Rachel; Carter, Howard; McClintock, Barbara; Mead, Margaret; Mitchell, Maria; Nice, Margaret Morse; Peale, Charles Willson; Sabin, Florence; *and* Townsend, John
Scientists, African American. *See* Banneker, Benjamin; Beckwourth, James; Bluford, Guion; Carver, George Washington; Henson, Matthew; Just, Ernest Everett; Latimer, Lewis; *and* Williams, Daniel Hale
Sears, Richard, 1489
Secession, 2388
Segregation; Video, 2578, 2687
Seminole, 1251, 2100; Video, 2693; Fiction, 1113. *See also* Osceola
Seneca, 643
Seneca Falls Convention, 2388
Sequoyah, 543, 1240, 1486, 2051, 2387

Serra, Junípero, 8, 194, 316, 604, 789, 818, 1356, 1444, 1827, 2400
Seuss, Dr., 2364
761st Tank Battalion, 1749
Seventeenth Century. *See* 1620 and Before
Sexual Harrassment; Fiction, 1494
Shakers, 227, 279, 280, 2288; Fiction, 1831
Shawnee; Fiction, 191. *See also* Tecumseh
Shelley, Kate, train rescue, 1926, 2383
Sherburne, Andrew, 2510
Sheridan, Philip H., 1832
Ships and Submarines, 1077-78; CD-ROM, 2525; Fiction, 255, 308, 497, 500, 1273, 2457, 2495, 2501
Shipwrecks; Fiction, 1607, 1878, 2197
Shoes, 1328
Sikhism
  Birth Customs, 1914
  Death Customs, 1915
  Food, 352
  Initiation Rites, 1791
  Marriage Customs, 485
  Pilgrimages, 1792
Singer, Isaac Bashevis, 1270
Sioux, 1006, 1009; Fiction, 1059. *See also* Chief Gall; Crazy Horse; Red Cloud; Sitting Bull; Wounded Knee; *and* Zitkala-Sa
Sitting Bull, 37, 216, 236, 276, 334, 1959, 2116, 2133, 2188, 2323
1620 and Before, 406, 1977-78, 2477; Video, 2708; Fiction, 2137
Slave Auction; Fiction, 2286; Video, 2692
Slave Revolts, 1537
  Turner, Nat, 155, 235
  Vesey, Denmark, 649
Slavery, 738, 943, 1168, 2177, 2211, 2397; Video, 2686, 2697, 2727; Fiction, 68, 97, 453, 463, 716, 720, 779, 947-48, 1036, 1049, 1051, 1082, 1112, 1536, 1714, 2078, 2341, 2377, 2486. *See also* Ball, Charles; Douglass, Frederick; Fortune, Amos; Gorée Island; Johnson, Isaac; Truth, Sojourner; *and* Tubman, Harriet
Smalls, Robert, 503
Smith, John, 846

Smith, Joseph, 1095
Smith, Margaret Chase, 668, 686, 1602
Soldiers, 410
Sound Barrier. *See* Yeager, Chuck
Sousa, John Philip, 876
South Asian Americans, 2226. *See also* Asian Americans; Chinese Americans; Japanese Americans; Korean Americans; *and* Vietnamese Americans
South Carolina Colony and State, 733; Fiction, 296, 277, 947-48
South Dakota; Fiction, 423
Southeast Tribes; Video, 2611
Southwest Tribes; Video, 2612
Space Travel, 1860. *See also* Astronauts; *and* Astronauts, African American
  Challenger, 229, 536
  Shuttle, 229, 536, 684
  Spacecraft, 841
Spanish-American War, 388, 2388; Fiction, 1065
Spies, 1475. *See also* Berg, Moe; Hale, Nathan; *and* Van Lew, Elizabeth
Spinning Wheel; Video, 2699
Spock, Benjamin, 1171
Squanto, 343; Video, 2700
St. Augustine, Florida, 2329
St. Lawrence Seaway, 798
St. Patrick's Day. *See* Holidays and Celebrations
Stagecoachs; Video, 2702
Stance, Emanuel, 1572
Stanton, Elizabeth Cady, 102, 490, 528, 775, 1486, 2217; Video, 2576
Star-Spangled Banner. *See* Key, Francis Scott; *and* United States' Songs
Starr, Belle, 55, 853
Statue of Liberty, 593, 1117, 1454, 1571; Fiction, 2182. *See also* Lazarus, Emma
Steam Engines. *See* Transportation
Steamboats. *See* Transportation; *and* Fulton, Robert
Stone, Lucy, 1548
Stowe, Harriet Beecher, 101, 258, 766, 1104, 1121
Strauss, Levi, 991, 1489, 2363
Strikes, 481
  Big Annie, 2127
  Pullman, of 1894, 56, 2388
  Women's Factory Strike, 555

Submarines. *See* Ships and Submarines
Suffrage Movement, 311
Suffragists; Fiction, 625, 1501, 1688. *See also* Anthony, Susan B.; Mott, Lucretia; Stanton, Elizabeth Cady; *and* Stone, Lucy
Sullivan, Anne, 1486
Sullivan, Louis Henri, 823
Superstitions, 1889; Fiction, 585
Supreme Court, 1719, 1844, 2166; Video, 2664
Supreme Court Cases, 830
  Brown v. Board of Education, 687
  Dred Scott, 992
  Engel v. Vitale, 908
  Furman v. Georgia, 993
  Miranda v. Arizona, 1861
  Roe v. Wade, 995
  Tinker v. Des Moines, 1824
  United States v. Nixon, 996
Supreme Court Justices. *See* Brandeis, Louis; *and* Marshall, Thurgood

Taft, Robert, 668
Taft, William Howard, 390, 672
  Family, 1937
Taino, 1090
Tallchief, Maria, 49, 660, 1486
Taxation, 1022
Taylor, Zachary, 474, 1213
Tecumseh, 489, 544, 1207, 2047
Television. *See* Farnsworth, Philo
Tennessee; Fiction, 754, 1709
Terrell, Mary Church, 1527
Tet. *See* Holidays and Celebrations
Texas, 2450; Fiction, 156, 186, 718, 900, 1653, 1845. *See also* Alamo; Houston, Sam; *and* San Antonio
Texas Rangers; Fiction, 1279
Thanksgiving, 66, 793, 981, 1402; Fiction, 66, 2122. *See also* Plimoth
Thompson, Snowshoe; Fiction, 1371
Thomson, Roy Herbert, 1489
Thoreau, Henry David, 355, 1634, 1841
Thorpe, Jim, 215, 1395, 1648, 1869, 1969
Threshers, 527; Fiction, 2373
Three Arch Rocks, 742
Tibbles, Susette La Flesche; Video, 2553
Titanic, 92, 134, 266, 536, 609, 1191, 2237; CD-ROM, 2517; Fiction, 2110. *See also* Ballard, Robert

Tlingit, Alaska; Fiction, 2469
Tombaugh, Clyde, 2382
Totem Pole Tribes, 224
Totem Poles; Video, 2711
Totino, Rose, 1755
Townsend, John, 700
Trail of Tears, 162. *See also*
    Cherokee; *and* Seminole
Train Robbery, 2492
Trains; Video, 2627; Fiction, 1122.
    See also Transportation
Traitors. *See* Arnold, Benedict
Transcontinental Railroad. *See*
    Transportation
Transportation, 562, 659, 751,
    2451; Fiction, 2255
  Canals, 532, 592
  Cities, 2500
  Delta Queen; Video, 2719
  Railroads and Trains, 292, 691,
      1541, 2345; Video,
      2627, 2683
  River Travel, 1544
  Roads, 1545, 2406
  Stagecoachs; Video, 2702
  Steam Engine; Video, 2703
  Steamboats, 1546; Video, 2644
  Transcontinental Railroad, 654,
      743, 1631, 2388;
      Fiction, 1256
Trapping; Fiction, 2031
Traveling Players, Fiction, 122
Traylor, Bill, 1428
Treemonisha, 1558
Triangle Factory Fire, 1398, 2040
Trompe l'oeil, 373
Truman, Harry S., 469, 668, 952,
    1339, 1394, 1612, 1686
  Family, 1939
Truth, Sojourner, 38, 417, 682,
    1254, 1439, 1533, 1534
Tubman, Harriet, 26, 200, 356, 377,
    680, 982, 1331, 1486, 1496,
    2006, 2240; Fiction, 1046
Turing, Alan, 2435
Turner, Nat, 155, 235
Turner, Ted, 1489
Tuscarora, 644
Tuskegee Institute. *See* Carver,
    George Washington; *and*
    Washington, Booker T.
Tuskegee Airmen, 964, 966, 1532.
    See also Davis, Benjamin
    O., Jr.
Twain, Mark, 470, 517, 880, 1270,
    1790, 1800
Twentieth Century. *See* 1900-1910,
    etc.
20th Century Overview;
    CD-ROM, 2526
Tyler, John, 670, 1385

Ukrainian Americans, 1283;
    Fiction, 2072
Uncle Sam, 1117
Uncle Tom's Cabin. See Stowe,
    Harriet Beecher
Underground Railroad, 57, 228,
    488, 515, 836; Video,
    2584; Fiction, 309, 649a,
    759, 903, 942, 1001, 1046,
    1589, 1913, 2290, 2459,
    2461, 2485. *See also*
    Tubman, Harriet
United Farm Workers. *See* Chavez,
    Cesar
United Nations, 2167
United States, 1007; CD-ROM,
    2515
United States Air Force, 271, 679
United States Army, 1284
United States Coast Guard, 1647
United States Flag, 690, 721, 2111;
    Video, 2658, 2718. *See*
    also Ross, Betsy
United States Marine Corps, 2349
United States Navy. *See* Farragut,
    David
United States Postal Service, 278,
    358
United States v. Nixon, 996
United States' Songs and Anthem,
    1262, 2118; Video, 2715.
    See also Key, Francis Scott
Urbanization; Video, 2613, 2647

Valentine's Day. *See* Holidays and
    Celebrations
Van Buren, Martin, 656, 954
Van Lew, Elizabeth, 2507
Vesey, Denmark, 649
Vietnam, 103, 326; Fiction, 88
Vietnam Memorial, 103, 610, 2489
Vietnam War, 805, 1643, 2388;
    Fiction, 2232
Vietnamese Americans, 141, 1448
Virginia Colony and State, 439, 734

Wagon Trains, 12, 54, 1543, 1712;
    Video, 2725; Fiction, 968,
    1353, 1377, 1586, 2280,
    2284, 2438, 2487
Walker, Alice, 1850
Walker, Madam C. J., 344, 477,
    1489, 1524, 2242
Walker, Pompey, 1892
Walton, Sam, 1489, 1755
Wampanoag, 2026. *See also* King
    Philip
War Nurses, 516
War of 1812, 7; Fiction, 1332,
    1578, 1875, 2393. *See also*

Madison, James; *and*
    Madison, Dolley
Wars, Conflicts, and Technology,
    526; CD-ROM, 2527
Warhol, Andy, 1268
Warships. *See* Ships and
    Submarines
Washington, George, 337
Washington State, 440; Fiction,
    173, 181
Washington, Booker T., 293, 816,
    1514, 1535, 1722, 2003
Washington, D.C., 432, 1025,
    1255; Video, 2722
Washington, George, 15, 337, 558,
    668, 803, 871, 1017, 1391,
    1486, 1613, 1693; Video,
    2630-31; Fiction, 328,
    2479 Family, 1940
Washington, Martha, 71, 1478
Washington, Mary, 764
Watson, James, 3
Webster, Daniel, 668
Wells-Barnett, Ida B., 124, 561,
    752, 980
West Indian Americans, 142, 933
Westward Expansion; Video,
    2538; Fiction, 210
Whalers, 133, 382, 413, 837, 1542;
    Fiction, 702, 2126
Wheatley, Phillis, 881, 1768, 1850,
    1858, 2039
Whistler, James McNeill, 824
White House, 907, 2117, 2357;
    CD-ROM, 2521; Fiction,
    899
  Children, 272, 1352
White, E. B., 464, 796, 1270, 2265
White, Walter, 740, 1105, 1849
Whitney, Eli, 53, 1307
Whyte, Edna Gardner, 2506
Wiesel, Elie, 2010
Wild West, 378, 628, 629, 1223;
    Fiction, 87, 169, 174,
    361-63, 706, 795, 896,
    912. *See also* Bean, Judge
    Roy; Billy the Kid;
    Cassidy, Butch; Cody,
    Buffalo Bill; Cowboys;
    Dalton Gang; Earp, Wyatt;
    Gold Rush; Gunfighters;
    Harvey Girls; Hickok,
    Wild Bill; Holliday, John
    Henry Doc ; James, Jesse;
    Masterson, Bat; Oakley,
    Annie; Outlaws; Pony
    Express; Starr, Belle; *and*
    Sundance Kid
  African American Women, 1167
  Arizona, 183
  Bandits, 1902

Merchants, 1015
Preachers, 1005
Scouts, 1984
Teachers, 1005
Women, 208, 1570, 1982
Wilder, Laura Ingalls, 79, 878, 1304, 2194
Wilder, Rose; Fiction, 143336
Williams, Daniel Hale, 1172, 2505
Williams, Paul R., 823
Williams, Roger, 119, 1094, 1095
Williamsburg, 68, 507, 834, 1131, 1145, 1211, 2145; Fiction, 2278
Wilson, Edith, 802
Wilson, Woodrow, 473, 668, 1341, 1394, 1813
   Family, 1941
Winnemucca, Sarah, 1616, 1620, 2017
Wisconsin, Fiction, 313, 1322, 1327
Witches, 1903, 2171
Women; CD-ROM, 2519
Women at Sea; Fiction, 212
Women in America; CD-ROM, 2524
Women in War, 479, 2033, 2509
Women's Movement, 311, 973; Fiction, 273, 1900. See also Anthony, Susan B.; Friedan, Betty; Mott, Lucretia; Smith, Margaret

Chase; and Stanton, Elizabeth Cady
Wong, Bill, 1988
Wood, Grant, 626
Woodland Tribal Arts; Video, 2732
Woods, Granville T., 1513
Woodson, Carter G., 1515
World Relations from Civil War to World War I, 1865-1917; Video, 2714
World War I, 324, 420, 594, 844, 1212, 1223, 2409; Video, 2733; Fiction, 508, 1063a, 1227, 1805, 1814, 1905, 2261, 2325, 2376
World War II, 4, 6, 237, 244-46, 248-49, 524, 595-99, 922, 935, 1223, 1271, 1475, 2170, 2172, 2408; Fiction, 126, 146, 161, 402, 512, 539, 806, 814, 911, 913, 1000, 1004, 1034, 1040, 1060, 1460, 1468, 1510, 1511, 1519, 1630, 1740, 1785, 1828, 1862, 1898, 1899, 2253, 2254, 2260, 2262, 2276, 2408, 2440, 2498. See also 761st Tank Battalion; D-Day; Manhattan Project; and Tuskegee Airmen

Desert Warfare, 242
Europe, 251, 252
Navajo, 4
Pearl Harbor, 250, 1054, 2252; Fiction, 1275, 1657
Pearl Harbor, USS Arizona, 2168
Rosie the Riveter, 479
Sea Battles, 243, 247
Wounded Knee 1690; Fiction, 1009
Wright, Frank Lloyd, 565, 823
Wright, Orville, 751, 1705, 2008, 2249; Fiction, 2008, 2032
Wright, Wilbur, 751, 1705, 2008, 2249; Fiction, 2008, 2032
Writing, 2343
Wyeth, Andrew, 1564
Wyeth, N. C., 1925

Yahi. See Ishi
Yankton Sioux; Video, 2734. See also Sioux
Yeager, Chuck, 128, 1368
Yeager, Jeana L., 2506
Yellow Fever. See Epidemics
Yokut; Video, 2608
Young, Brigham, 1962

Zaharias, Babe Didrikson, 1423
Zitkala-Sa, 1820